Excellence in Business Communication

SIXTH CANADIAN EDITION

John V. Thill

Communication Specialists of America

Courtland L. Bovée

Professor of Business Communication
C. Allen Paul Distinguished Chair
Grossmont College

Wendy I. Keller

University Lecturer, Trainer and Career Coach

K.M. Moran

Professor of Communications/ESL
Conestoga College

 Pearson

ACQUISITIONS EDITOR: Keriann Mcgoogan
MARKETING MANAGER: Euan White
SENIOR CONTENT MANAGER: John Polanszky
PROJECT MANAGER: Christina Veeren
CONTENT DEVELOPER: Darryl Kamo
MEDIA CONTENT DEVELOPER: Darryl Kamo
MEDIA DEVELOPER: Tiffany Palmer

PRODUCTION SERVICES: Cenveo® Publisher Services
PERMISSIONS PROJECT MANAGEMENT: Integra Publishing Services, Inc.
PHOTO PERMISSIONS RESEARCH: Integra Publishing Services, Inc.
TEXT PERMISSIONS RESEARCH: Integra Publishing Services, Inc.
INTERIOR DESIGNER: Anthony Leung
COVER DESIGNER: Anthony Leung
COVER IMAGE: Peter Bernik/Shutterstock

Pearson Canada Inc., 26 Prince Andrew Place, North York, Ontario M3C 2H4.

978-0-13-431082-4

1 2020

Library and Archives Canada Cataloguing in Publication

Thill, John V., author
    Excellence in business communication / John V. Thill, Communication Specialists of America, Courtland L. Bovée, Professor of Business Communication, C. Allen Paul Distinguished Chair, Grossmont College, Wendy I. Keller. University Lecturer, Trainer and Career Coach. K.M. Moran, Professor of Communications/ESL, Conestoga College. — Sixth Canadian edition.

Includes bibliographical references and indexes.
ISBN 978-0-13-431082-4 (softcover)

    1. Business communication—Case studies. I. Bovée, Courtland L., author II. Keller, Wendy I., 1959-, author III. Moran, Kathleen M., 1955-, author IV. Title.

HF5718.2.C3T45 2017   658.4'5   C2017-903384-0

Brief Contents

Contents

KD 03.05.2020 1730

CHAPTER 9

Writing Negative Messages 245

CHAPTER 10

Writing Persuasive Messages 285

PART IV
PREPARING REPORTS AND ORAL PRESENTATIONS 320

CHAPTER 11
Planning Reports and Proposals 320

CHAPTER 12
Writing Reports and Proposals 367

Preface

Excellence in Business Communication has long provided instructors and students with the most current communication strategies and practices used in today's workplace. This sixth Canadian edition includes up-to-date model documents that reflect the entire spectrum of print and electronic communication media. Students entering today's workforce are expected to use a wide range of tools, from instant messaging to blogging to podcasting, and *Excellence in Business Communication* provides the hands-on experience they need to meet employer expectations.

The text offers a set of tools that simplifies teaching, promotes active learning, and stimulates critical thinking. These components work together at four levels to provide seamless coverage of vital knowledge and skills:

- **Previewing.** Each chapter prepares students with clear learning objectives and a brief, compelling vignette featuring current professional practice.
- **Developing.** Chapter content develops and explains concepts with a concise, carefully organized presentation of textual and visual material. The three-step process of planning, writing, and completing is reinforced throughout the text in examples ranging from email messages to blogs to formal reports.
- **Enhancing.** Contemporary examples, many accompanied by the three-step diagram adapted to each message, show students the specific elements that contribute to successful messages.
- **Reinforcing.** Numerous realistic exercises and activities let students practise vital skills and put their new-found knowledge to immediate use. Communication cases encourage students to think about contemporary business issues as they put their skills to use in a variety of media, including blogging and podcasting.

Why This Edition?

Business communications continue to evolve in response to changes in the global economy, corporate structures, workforce, technology, and management of information. To continue to provide value for readers, textbooks and support materials need to be updated and reflect best practices in these changing environments. The sixth Canadian edition builds on the comprehensive approach of the previous edition and focuses on practices in the following areas:

- Social media questions, activities, and cases using examples from Twitter, Facebook, LinkedIn, and other media outlets;
- Technologies for collaborative writing, including groupware, social networks, and virtual communities;
- Developing cultural competency;
- Diversity in organizations;
- Social media and the impact on networking and job searching;
- Cases featuring email, instant messaging, social networking, blogging, websites, voicemail, and podcasting; and
- Vignettes on innovative companies to highlight their market strategies for success.

Enhancements include the following:

- More discussion about the unique challenges of business communication;
- Delving further into the characteristics of high-performing teams and the role of leadership;
- The role of active listening in effective business communications, including discussions of emotional intelligence and "feeding forward";
- The do's and don'ts of sharing using technology and the protection of information;
- Updates to the effective use of technology and social media across business to consumer (B2C) and business to business (B2B) environments;
- Best practices for giving presentations, including storytelling and the management of questions;
- Discussion of "personal branding" and social media presence as part of a job search or career development strategy;
- How to network with confidence—making a memorable, positive impact; and
- Updates to reflect changes introduced in the new, eighth edition of the *MLA Handbook*.

Key Features of the Text

Each chapter of *Excellence in Business Communication* includes a number of tools designed to guide students through the process of developing their communication skills and preparing them for the business world.

Learning Objectives are listed on the first page of each chapter. This "roadmap" shows what will be covered and what is especially important. Each Learning Objective is repeated in the margin where the material is first covered. The Learning Objectives are summarized at the end of the chapter.

On the Job opens each chapter with a brief story about communications within a real company, such as Royal Bank of Canada, Maple Leaf Foods, and Indigo Books and Music. The chapter itself demonstrates why these communication skills are important to real companies and shows how to apply them. Each chapter ends with the follow-up **On the Job: Performing Communication Tasks** at the featured company. These tasks expand on the chapter's concepts and help students practise real-world decision making.

The **three-step writing process**—planning, writing, and completing—is outlined in Chapters 4 to 6. This process is also highlighted throughout the chapters with selected sample documents and with the end-of-chapter cases.

Sample documents provide models in media, ranging from printed letters to instant messaging. The **annotations** that accompany every model document help students understand how to apply the principles discussed in the chapter.

One of four types of **themed boxes** appears in each chapter, giving valuable tips for the workplace:

- **Sharpening Your Career Skills** gives tips on improving writing and speaking techniques.
- **Business Communication 2.0** provides help with business communications and technological tools.
- **Communicating Across Cultures** offers advice on communicating successfully in the global business world.
- **Promoting Workplace Ethics** examines important ethical issues that face today's employees.

Checklists summarize key points and help students organize their work on communication projects.

Tips for Success give important advice from experts in the field on the chapter's topic. Real people; real experience.

Key Points, highlighted in the margin, emphasize important details from the text and are good tools for reviewing concepts.

Practice is the best way to grasp new business communication techniques and processes. End-of-chapter exercises and cases will help students develop and improve their communication skills.

- **Test Your Knowledge** provides questions that review the chapter topics.
- **Apply Your Knowledge** offers exercises that encourage students to consider the information and apply it to business decisions.
- **Running Cases** present realistic business situations encountered by Noreen and Kwong as they work toward their career goals. Working through these case studies will help students deal with on-the-job tasks.
- **Practise Your Knowledge** provides documents for critique and revision.
- **Exercises** give additional tasks to work through, including teamwork exercises and ethical situations.
- **Cases,** at the end of specific chapters, offer additional opportunities to apply the three-step writing process in work-related situations. Icons highlight cases that use specific media skills—email, blogging, instant messaging, podcasting—as well as "Portfolio Builder" cases, where the projects may be suitable for students' employment portfolios.

Pearson

| MyLab | Business Communication.

MyLab Business Communication is an online homework and tutorial assessment solution designed to help students master concepts, study, and prepare for class. MyLab Business Communication provides students with a better way to practise writing skills and grammar content outside of class, helping them become polished communicators. Log on to www.pearson.com/mylab to access the following interactive tools:

- Relevant video series and exercises
- Study plan
- Interactive flashcards
- Model documents
- Grammar diagnostics

PEARSON eTEXT. The Pearson eText gives students access to their textbook anytime, anywhere. In addition to note taking, highlighting, and bookmarking, the Pearson eText offers interactive and sharing features. Instructors can share their comments or highlights, and students can add their own, creating a tight community of learners within the class.

Instructor Supplements

COMPUTERIZED TEST BANK. Pearson's computerized test banks allow instructors to filter and select questions to create quizzes, tests, or homework. Instructors can revise questions or add their own and may be able to choose print or online options. These questions are also available in Microsoft Word format.

The following additional instructor supplements are available for download from a password-protected section of Pearson Canada's online catalogue (http://catalogue.pearsoned.ca/). Navigate to your book's catalogue page to view a list of supplements that are available. See your local sales representative for details and access.

- The Instructor's Manual provides chapter outlines, suggests solutions to the exercises, and supplies formatted letters for the cases in the letter-writing chapters. Additional resources include diagnostic tests of English skills and supplementary grammar exercises.
- PowerPoint Presentations cover the key concepts in each chapter.

LEARNING SOLUTIONS MANAGERS. Pearson's Learning Solutions Managers work with faculty and campus course designers to ensure that Pearson technology products, assessment tools, and online course materials are tailored to meet your specific needs. This highly qualified team is dedicated to helping schools take full advantage of a wide range of educational resources by assisting in the integration of a variety of instructional materials and media formats. Your local Pearson Canada sales representative can provide you with more details on this service program.

Acknowledgments for the Sixth Canadian Edition

The delivery of an effective textbook requires an understanding of the needs and preferences of instructors and students who will be using the material to facilitate learning. Every aspect must be reviewed for relevance, accuracy, and consistency. This effort would not be possible without the help of a dedicated and thoughtful publishing team.

We are grateful to Jennifer Sutton for presenting us with the opportunity to contribute to the sixth Canadian edition of *Excellence in Business Communication*. We are honoured to work with Pearson Canada staff on this comprehensive text: Acquisition Editor Keriann McGoogan; Senior Content Manager John Polanszky; and Developmental Editors Patti Sayle and Darryl Kamo, who were always patient and available (even at late hours) to share their experience and help us get to production. Thanks also to our Project Managers Colleen Wormald, Christina Veeren, and Revathi Viswanathan; our Copy Editor, Susan Broadhurst; and our Proofreader, Audrey Dorsch, who ensured that all production details of the book were met.

So many others dedicated their time and energy to the production of this edition. We extend sincere thanks for their important contributions.

And, finally, thank you to our families and friends, who have let us put them on hold while we dug in to the world of business communication and hopefully came up with a product that will satisfy our most valued customers, the students and instructors of continued learning.

Wendy Keller

Kathleen Moran

Excellence in Business Communication

1 Achieving Success through Effective Business Communication

LEARNING OBJECTIVES After studying this chapter, you will be able to

1 Explain why effective communication is important to your success in today's business environment

2 Identify eight communication skills that successful employers expect from their employees

3 Describe the five characteristics of effective business communication

4 Discuss six factors that make business communication unique

5 Describe five strategies for communicating more effectively on the job

6 Explain five strategies for using communication technology successfully

7 Discuss the importance of ethics in business communication, and differentiate between an ethical dilemma and an ethical lapse

MyLab Business Communication Visit MyLab Business Communication to access a variety of online resources directly related to this chapter's content.

ON THE JOB: COMMUNICATING AT WAVE

Tetra Images/Alamy Stock Photo

The ability of Wave to harness the power of digital communication is a key ingredient in the company's success.

Enhancing Value with Social Media

www.waveapps.com

Ranked ninth in Deloitte's Technology Fast 50 list (2016) and awarded the title of Best Free Accounting Software for Businesses by Business News Daily (2017), Wave (formerly Wave Accounting) continues to make great strides in the accounting services sector, attracting more than 2.3 million users around the world to date. The company's success is based on filling a market niche, listening to user needs, and harnessing social media to add value to customer relationships.

Started by James Lochrie and Kirk Simpson in 2010, Wave has identified small-business owners, freelancers, and entrepreneurs as needing an alternative to spreadsheets and "shoebox accounting" for managing their finances. Their product is a free, easy-to-use cloud-based accounting software with features that include unlimited invoicing and account tracking, automatic data backup, secure collaboration, and bank and credit card linking. Business and personal dashboards using charts and other graphical displays help users view their income and expenses at a glance. The system can be accessed on any computer: Mac, Windows, or Linux. In late 2016/early 2017 the company released its Android and iPhone apps and added a lending feature, further demonstrating their responsiveness to market needs and customer challenges.

Wave's appeal is not only the free software. Their team of 130+ employees includes a vice president of community, content, and communications, as well as a community manager and customer advocate, whose focus is to develop company–user relationships through social media. The Wave blog describes product enhancements, educates users on software features, and spotlights the success of Wave customers. Guest bloggers such as small-business owners add value to the site through posts titled "5 Things I Wish I Had Known Early in My Business" and "5 Ways to Grow Your Online Community." The online conversation is extended through Facebook and Twitter, where users can find help, get the latest company news, and see Wave's

employees having fun at company events and participating in trade shows.

The rapid growth of social media has merged isolated conversations into a global phenomenon that has permanently changed the nature of business communication. Wave is one of the millions of companies around the world using social media to supplement or even replace traditional forms of customer communication. How would you use social media to help a company enhance its online profile? What technologies would you select to keep the conversation going?[1]

Achieving Career Success through Effective Communication

1 LEARNING OBJECTIVE

Explain why effective communication is important to your success in today's business environment.

Your career success depends on effective communication.

Ambition and great ideas aren't enough; you need to be able to communicate with people in order to succeed in business.

Strong communication skills give you an advantage in the job market.

Improving your communication skills may be the single most important step you can take in your career. You can have the greatest ideas in the world, but they're no good to your company or your career if you can't express them clearly and persuasively. Some jobs, such as sales and customer support, are primarily about communicating. In fields such as engineering or finance, you often need to share complex ideas with executives, customers, and colleagues, and your ability to connect with people outside your field can be as important as your technical expertise. If you have the entrepreneurial urge, you will need to communicate with a wide range of audiences, from investors, bankers, and government regulators to employees, customers, and business partners.

Whether exchanging emails, posting entries on a blog, giving a formal presentation, or chatting with co-workers at lunch, you are engaging in **communication**, the process of transferring information from a sender to a receiver. The essence of communication is sharing—providing data, information, and insights in an exchange that benefits both you and the people with whom you are communicating.[2] However, communication is considered *effective* only when others understand your message correctly and respond to it in the way you want. Effective communication helps you manage your workflow, improves business relationships, enhances your professional image, and provides a variety of other important benefits:

- Closer ties with important communities in the marketplace
- Opportunities to influence conversations, perceptions, and trends
- Increased productivity and faster problem solving
- Better financial results and higher return for investors
- Earlier warning of potential problems, from rising business costs to critical safety issues
- Stronger decision making based on timely, reliable information
- Clearer and more persuasive marketing messages
- Greater employee engagement with their work, leading to higher employee satisfaction and lower employee turnover

Communication is vital to every company's success.

Effective communication is at the centre of virtually every aspect of business because it connects the company with all its **stakeholders**—the groups that your company affects in some way and who themselves have some influence on your company. For example, as a customer or an employee of a particular business, you are a stakeholder. Other stakeholders include government regulators, who create guidelines that businesses must observe, and the media, which report on business and influence public opinion.

If you want to improve efficiency, quality, responsiveness, or innovation, you'll do so with the help of strong communication skills. Conversely, without effective communication, people misunderstand one another and misinterpret information. At every stage of your career, communication is the way you'll succeed, and as you rise in your organization, you'll use more communication channels, such as blogs, videos, and Twitter, to reach your stakeholders.

THE COMMUNICATION PROCESS

Communication doesn't occur haphazardly. Nor does it happen all at once. It is more than a single act. Communication is a dynamic, transactional, or two-way, process that can be broken into eight steps, as shown in Figure 1–1. However, be aware that this is a simplified model; real-life communication is usually more complicated. Both sender and receiver might be talking at the same time, or the receiver might be trying to talk on the phone with one person while instant messaging with another, or the receiver may ignore the sender's request for feedback, and so on.

1. **The sender has an idea.** You conceive an idea and want to share it. The potential success of your communication effort starts here. Its effectiveness depends on the nature of the idea, the composition of the audience and your relationship to these people, and your motivation for wanting to share the idea. For example, if an idea will benefit your department or company and your motivation is to make a contribution, the communication process is off to a strong start. In comparison, if the idea is poorly conceived (perhaps you haven't considered the financial impact of a proposal) or your motivation is suspect (perhaps you're more interested in making an impression on your boss than really contributing), the communication will be more difficult and possibly unsuccessful.

2. **The sender encodes the idea in a message.** When you put your idea into a message (words, images, or a combination of both) that your receiver will understand, you are **encoding** it. Much of the focus of this course is on developing the skills needed to successfully encode your ideas into effective messages. Encoding can fail for a number of reasons, including poor word choices that confuse or anger the audience, imagery that evokes unintended emotional responses, and cultural differences that result in the same words and images meaning different things to different people.

3. **The sender produces the message in a medium.** With the appropriate message to express your idea, you now need some way to send that message to your intended audience. Media for transmitting messages can be

Senders and receivers connect through an eight-step process.

communication process [handwritten margin note]

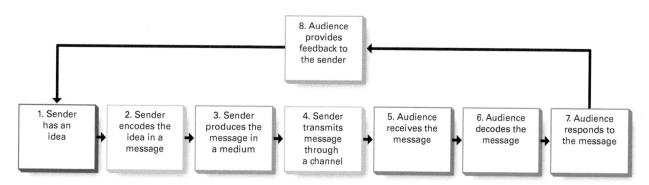

Figure 1–1 The Communication Process

divided into oral, written, and visual, as well as electronic forms of these three. As an experienced user of communication media, you already know that this step requires careful decision making and at least some level of technical skill. Misguided media choices or insufficient technical skill can undermine the best intentions. For instance, a desire to keep everyone informed of every important detail in a project can lead to email overload—and a breakdown in communication as people struggle to keep track of all the messages and the inevitable response threads. In contrast, many companies now find that a blog is a much better way to keep teams informed because this medium can dramatically reduce the number of messages required.

4. **The sender transmits the message through a channel.** Just as technology continues to multiply the number of media options at your disposal, it also continues to provide new **communication channels** you can use to transmit your messages. The distinction between medium and channel can get a bit murky, but think of medium as the *form* a message takes and channel as the system used to *deliver* the message. The channel can be a face-to-face conversation, the Internet, another company—any system capable of delivering messages.

5. **The audience receives the message.** If your message does not meet any obstacles, such as an unintended email deletion, it arrives at your intended audience. However, mere arrival at the destination is not a guarantee that the message will be noticed or understood correctly. For example, if you're giving a speech, your listeners have to be able to hear you, and they have to pay attention. You have no guarantee that your message will actually get through. In fact, one of the biggest challenges you'll face as a communicator in today's crowded business environment is cutting through the clutter and noise in whatever medium you choose.

6. **The audience decodes the message.** If the message is actually received, the audience must then absorb and understand it, a step known as **decoding**. If obstacles do not block the process, the receiver interprets your message correctly; that is, the receiver assigns the same meaning to your words as you intended and responds in the way you desire.

7. **The audience responds to the message.** By crafting messages in ways that show the benefits of responding, senders can increase the chances that recipients will respond in positive ways. However, whether a receiver responds as the sender hopes depends on the receiver (a) *remembering* the message long enough to act on it, (b) being *able* to act on it, and (c) being *motivated* to respond.

8. **The audience provides feedback to the sender.** After decoding your message, the audience has the option of responding in some way. This **feedback** enables you to evaluate the effectiveness of your message: feedback often initiates another cycle through the process, which can continue until both parties are satisfied with the result. Successful communicators place considerable value on feedback, not only as a way to measure effectiveness but also as a way to learn.

Communication process

WHAT EMPLOYERS EXPECT FROM YOU

2 **LEARNING OBJECTIVE**

Identify eight communication skills that successful employers expect from their employees.

No matter how good you are at accounting, law, science, or whatever professional specialty you pursue, most companies expect you to be competent at a wide range of communication tasks. Employers spend millions of dollars on communication training every year, but they expect you to come prepared with basic skills, so you can take full advantage of the learning opportunities they make available to you. Check the Employability Skills 2000+ chart, prepared by the Conference Board of Canada (Figure 1–2), for the skills you need to achieve career success.

To stand out from your competition in the job market, improving your communication skills might be the single most important step you take. In fact, employers start judging your ability to communicate before you even show up for your first interview (e.g., résumés, phone messages, profiles on social media, etc.), and the process of evaluation never really stops. Improving your communication skills helps ensure that others will recognize and reward your talents and contributions. Fortunately, the specific skills that employers expect from you are the very skills that will help you advance in your career:

> Employers are constantly evaluating your communication skills.

1. **Organizing ideas and information logically and completely.** You'll often be required to find, process, and organize substantial amounts of raw data and random information so others can easily grasp its significance. Communications that highlight, clarify, and summarize the most important information are more effective than those that include huge amounts of data without any purpose or focus.

2. **Expressing and presenting ideas and information coherently and persuasively.** Whenever you're asked to offer an opinion or recommendation, you'll be expected to back it up with solid evidence. However, organizing your evidence well is not all you will need to do; you'll also need to convince your audience with compelling arguments that are accurate and ethical.

3. **Listening to others effectively.** Effective listening is not as easy as you might think. Amidst all the distractions on the job, you'll need to use specific skills to detect the real meaning behind the words.

4. **Communicating effectively with people from diverse backgrounds and experiences.** You'll often be called on to communicate with people who differ from you in gender, ethnic background, age, profession, technical ability, and so on.

> **TIPS FOR SUCCESS**
> "Make sure your soft skills (communication, teamwork, problem solving) are on par with your technical abilities, as employers look for well-rounded individuals who will integrate well into their companies."
>
> Paul Hébert, senior advisor, strategic communications, at Acart Communications

5. **Using communication technologies effectively and efficiently.** You're already familiar with email, instant messaging (IM), and online research. Increasingly, employers will also expect you to use web conferencing, electronic presentations, and a variety of other technological tools.

6. **Following accepted standards of grammar, spelling, and other aspects of high-quality writing and speaking.** You and your friends are probably comfortable with informal communication that doesn't put a high value on precision and correctness. However, to be successful in business, you will need to focus on the quality of your communication efforts. Particularly with audiences who don't know you well, careless writing and disregard for accepted standards reflect poorly on both you and your company. Rather than giving you the benefit of the doubt, many people will assume that you either don't know how to communicate or don't care enough to communicate well.

7. **Communicating in a civilized manner that reflects contemporary expectations of business etiquette.** Even when the pressure is on, you'll be expected to communicate with courtesy and respect in a manner that is appropriate to the situation.

communication skills that employers expect

Employability Skills 2000+

The skills you need to enter, stay in, and progress in the world of work—whether you work on your own or as a part of a team.

These skills can also be applied and used beyond the workplace in a range of daily activities.

Fundamental Skills	Personal Management Skills	Teamwork Skills
The skills needed as a base for further development	The personal skills, attitudes and behaviours that drive one's potential for growth	The skills and attributes needed to contribute productively

You will be better prepared to progress in the world of work when you can:

Communicate
- read and understand information presented in a variety of forms (e.g., words, graphs, charts, diagrams)
- write and speak so others pay attention and understand
- listen and ask questions to understand and appreciate the points of view of others
- share information using a range of information and communications technologies (e.g., voice, e-mail, computers)
- use relevant scientific, technological and mathematical knowledge and skills to explain or clarify ideas

Manage Information
- locate, gather and organize information using appropriate technology and information systems
- access, analyze and apply knowledge and skills from various disciplines (e.g., the arts, languages, science, technology, mathematics, social sciences, and the humanities)

Use Numbers
- decide what needs to be measured or calculated
- observe and record data using appropriate methods, tools and technology
- make estimates and verify calculations

Think & Solve Problems
- assess situations and identify problems
- seek different points of view and evaluate them based on facts
- recognize the human, interpersonal, technical, scientific and mathematical dimensions of a problem
- identify the root cause of a problem
- be creative and innovative in exploring possible solutions
- readily use science, technology and mathematics as ways to think, gain and share knowledge, solve problems and make decisions
- evaluate solutions to make recommendations or decisions
- implement solutions
- check to see if a solution works, and act on opportunities for improvement

You will be able to offer yourself greater possibilities for achievement when you can:

Demonstrate Positive Attitudes & Behaviours
- feel good about yourself and be confident
- deal with people, problems and situations with honesty, integrity and personal ethics
- recognize your own and other people's good efforts
- take care of your personal health
- show interest, initiative and effort

Be Responsible
- set goals and priorities balancing work and personal life
- plan and manage time, money and other resources to achieve goals
- assess, weigh and manage risk
- be accountable for your actions and the actions of your group
- be socially responsible and contribute to your community

Be Adaptable
- work independently or as a part of a team
- carry out multiple tasks or projects
- be innovative and resourceful: identify and suggest alternative ways to achieve goals and get the job done
- be open and respond constructively to change
- learn from your mistakes and accept feedback
- cope with uncertainty

Learn Continuously
- be willing to continuously learn and grow
- assess personal strengths and areas for development
- set your own learning goals
- identify and access learning sources and opportunities
- plan for and achieve your learning goals

Work Safely
- be aware of personal and group health and safety practices and procedures, and act in accordance with these

You will be better prepared to add value to the outcomes of a task, project or team when you can:

Work with Others
- understand and work within the dynamics of a group
- ensure that a team's purpose and objectives are clear
- be flexible: respect, be open to and supportive of the thoughts, opinions and contributions of others in a group
- recognize and respect people's diversity, individual differences and perspectives
- accept and provide feedback in a constructive and considerate manner
- contribute to a team by sharing information and expertise
- lead or support when appropriate, motivating a group for high performance
- understand the role of conflict in a group to reach solutions
- manage and resolve conflict when appropriate

Participate in Projects & Tasks
- plan, design or carry out a project or task from start to finish with well-defined objectives and outcomes
- develop a plan, seek feedback, test, revise and implement
- work to agreed quality standards and specifications
- select and use appropriate tools and technology for a task or project
- adapt to changing requirements and information
- continuously monitor the success of a project or task and identify ways to improve

The Conference Board of Canada

255 Smyth Road, Ottawa
ON K1H 8M7 Canada
Tel. (613) 526-3280
Fax (613) 526-4857
Internet: www.conferenceboard.ca/education

Figure 1–2 Employability Skills 2000+ Chart
Download this pamphlet from **www.conferenceboard.ca/topics/education/learning-tools/employability-skills.aspx** and use it as a reference throughout your schooling and career. Where do you stand now in regard to the three skill areas? Where do you need to improve your skills? How do you plan to do this?

Courtesy: The Conference Board of Canada.

8. Communicating ethically, even when choices aren't crystal clear. Whether you're simply reporting on the status of a project or responding to a complicated, large-scale crisis, you're certain to encounter situations that call for you to make sound ethical choices. (See "Promoting Workplace Ethics: Ethical Boundaries—Where Would You Draw the Line?" later on in the chapter.) You'll have the opportunity to practise all these skills throughout this course—but don't stop there. Successful professionals continue to hone communication skills throughout their careers. For example, the Canadian Centre for Ethics and Corporate Policy is a nonprofit organization that provides company leaders who recognize the value of promoting the application of ethical decision making with an opportunity to exchange best practices.[3]

communication skills that employer look for/expect

CHARACTERISTICS OF EFFECTIVE COMMUNICATION

Having the best ideas that will help your company run productively isn't enough; you must express those ideas clearly and persuasively. Employers demand oral and written communication skills from all job candidates, from seasonal and entry-level workers to management employees.

To make your messages effective, make them practical, factual, concise, clear about expectations, and persuasive:[4]

1. **Provide practical information.** Give recipients useful information, whether it's to help them perform a desired action or understand a new company policy.
2. **Give facts rather than impressions.** Use concrete language, specific detail, and information that is clear, convincing, accurate, and ethical. Even when an opinion is called for, present compelling evidence to support your conclusion.
3. **Present information in a concise, efficient manner.** Highlight the most important information, rather than forcing your reader to determine the key points. Most business professionals find themselves wading through a flood of data and information. Messages that clarify and summarize are more effective than those that do not. In today's time-pressured business environment, clear and concise messages are highly valued.
4. **Clarify expectations and responsibilities.** Write messages to generate a specific response from a specific audience. Clearly state what you expect from audience members or what you can do for them. You will see many examples in this book with action requests.
5. **Offer compelling, persuasive arguments and recommendations.** Show your readers precisely how they will benefit from responding to your message the way you want them to. Including reader benefits is the key to persuading employers, colleagues, customers, or clients to adopt a plan of action or purchase a product.

Keep these five important characteristics in mind as you review Figures 1–3 and 1–4. Both emails appear to be well constructed at first glance, but Figure 1–3 is far less effective, as explained in the margin comments. It shows the negative impact that poorly conceived messages can have on an audience. In contrast, Figure 1–4 shows how an effective message can help everyone work more efficiently (in this case, by helping them prepare effectively for an important meeting).

3 LEARNING OBJECTIVE

Describe the five characteristics of effective business communication.

Characteristics of effective communication

SUMMER WILDERNESS CAMP OPPORTUNITIES

Camp Nippising is seeking enthusiastic people with a passion for working with kids and a love of the outdoors. *Applicants will have*

- Camping experience
- Excellent oral and written communication skills
- Standard First Aid with Heartsaver CPR
- Lifeguard certificate

Yellow Dog Productions/The Image Bank/Getty Images

Most companies want employees who can communicate effectively, from entry- to high-level positions. What sorts of jobs have you held that required you to communicate with co-workers and with customers or clients? What were your specific communication tasks, both oral and written?

The vague subject line fails to alert people to the upcoming meeting. →

The greeting is cold → and off-putting.

A negative, accusatory tone here puts readers on the defensive. →

This shows that little thought has been given to creating an agenda and that audience commitments and responsibilities have not been considered. →

The wording here assumes that people who won't attend don't want to, which might not be true. →

The lack of a closing (such as "thank you") contributes to the harsh, abrupt tone. →

Opening paragraph fails to provide necessary background information for anyone who missed the meeting. Referring to the consultant as "This guy" does not provide a proper introduction and minimizes the importance of the meeting. ←

This request for action fails to clarify who needs to do what by when. ←

The meeting information includes the day but not the date, which could lead to confusion. ←

The writer fails to provide alternative contact information or invite questions about the meeting, making it harder for team members to clarify their assignments or raise concerns. ←

Web 2.0 strategy - Message (HTML)

File Edit View Insert Format Tools Actions Help   Type a question for help

Attach as Adobe PDF » | Paragraph ▾ Euphemia ▾ 14 ▾ | A | B I U | ≡ ≡ ≡ ≡ | ⋮≡ ≡ | 律 律 — .

To... | <Customer Service list>

Cc... |

Subject: | Web 2.0 strategy

All,

The consultant we discussed at last week's status meeting is available to meet next Tuesday. This guy has helped a number of customer service organizations, and he'll be available to give us some advice and figure out what our needs are.

Let's not waste this opportunity to learn more about Web 2.0 tools for customer service. I'd like everyone to prepare some intelligent questions ahead of time. We'll forward them to Mr. Johnson so that he can think about them before the meeting. I was rather disappointed last time we brought in an expert like this; I have to beg these people to talk to us, and most of you just sat and stared during the Q&A session.

Details:
Tuesday
10:00 a.m. to whenever
Mt. Shasta room

I consider it very important for everyone on the team to be at this meeting, but if you won't attend, at least try to phone in so you can hear what's going on.

Shari

P.S. This guy is supposedly really sharp, so let's all be on our toes!

Figure 1–3 Ineffective Communication

COMMUNICATION IN ORGANIZATIONAL SETTINGS

No matter what your level in the organization, you have an important communication role.

Internal vs. external communication

In every part of the business organization, communication provides the vital link between people and information. When you join a company, you become a key element in its communication chain. Whether you're a high-level manager or an entry-level employee, you have information that others need to perform their jobs, and others have information that is crucial to you. You exchange information with people inside your organization, called **internal communication**, and you exchange information and ideas with others outside your organization, called **external communication**. This information travels over both *formal* and *informal* channels.

Communicating internally is essential for effective functioning. As an employee, you are in a position to observe first-hand attitudes and behaviours that your supervisors and co-workers cannot see: a customer's reaction to a product display, a supplier's brief hesitation before agreeing to a delivery date, or a slowdown in the flow of customers. Managers and co-workers need such minute information in order to do their jobs. If you don't pass that information along, nobody will—because nobody else knows. Communicating freely helps employees develop a clear sense of the organization's mission and helps managers identify and react quickly to potential problems.

Like internal communication, external communication is essential for conducting business smoothly. Companies constantly exchange messages with customers, vendors, distributors, competitors, investors, journalists, and community representatives. Whether by letter, Web, phone, email, or video, good communication is the first step in creating a favourable impression. Extremely careful planning is required for messages such as statements to the press, letters to investors, advertisements, and price announcements. Therefore, such documents are

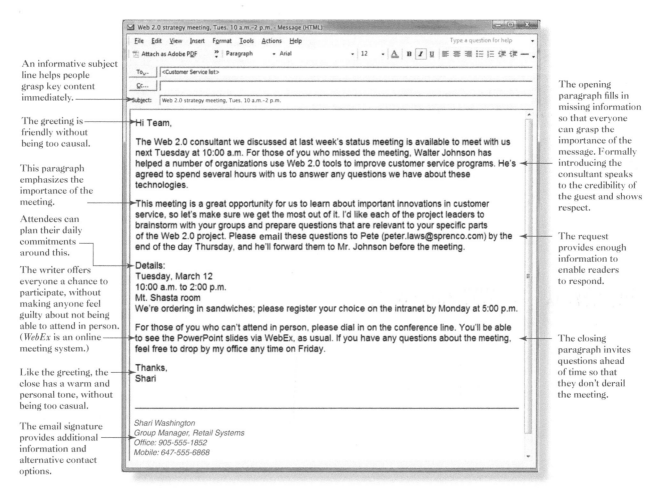

An informative subject line helps people grasp key content immediately.

The greeting is friendly without being too casual.

This paragraph emphasizes the importance of the meeting.

Attendees can plan their daily commitments around this.

The writer offers everyone a chance to participate, without making anyone feel guilty about not being able to attend in person. (*WebEx* is an online meeting system.)

Like the greeting, the close has a warm and personal tone, without being too casual.

The email signature provides additional information and alternative contact options.

The opening paragraph fills in missing information so that everyone can grasp the importance of the message. Formally introducing the consultant speaks to the credibility of the guest and shows respect.

The request provides enough information to enable readers to respond.

The closing paragraph invites questions ahead of time so that they don't derail the meeting.

Figure 1–4 Effective Communication

often drafted by marketing, legal, and/or public relations teams—whose sole job is creating and managing the flow of formal messages to outsiders.

FORMAL COMMUNICATION NETWORK The **formal communication network** is typically shown as an organizational chart, such as the one in Figure 1–5. Such charts summarize the lines of authority; each box represents a link in the chain of command, and each line represents a formal **channel**, or route, for the transmission of official messages. Information may travel down, up, and across an organization's formal hierarchy.

- **Downward flow.** Organizational decisions are often made at the top and then flow down to the people who will carry them out. Most of what filters downward is geared toward helping employees do their jobs and carry out company objectives. From top to bottom, each person must understand each message, apply it, and pass it along.
- **Upward flow.** To solve problems and make intelligent decisions, managers must learn what's going on in the organization. Because they must delegate work to be efficient, executives depend on lower-level employees to furnish them with accurate, timely reports on problems, emerging trends, opportunities for improvement, grievances, and performance. Typically, documents generated for high-level or outside readers or sensitive or complex messages are approved by superiors before being sent out.

formal communication network

Information flows up, down, and across the formal hierarchy.

downward flow

upward flow

Horizontal flow

Courtesy Iron to Iron

The web development firm IRON to IRON (irontoiron.com) helps clients create websites that are easy to navigate and read. Consider the design of this webpage. How does it communicate what the business has to offer?

- **Horizontal flow.** Communication also flows laterally, from one department to another. This horizontal communication helps employees share information and coordinate tasks. Project teams are one example of horizontal communication: in these teams, employees from different departments work together to solve problems and improve the operation of their company.

Formal organizational charts illustrate how information is supposed to flow. In actual practice, however, employees across the organizational hierarchy communicate with one another informally.

INFORMAL COMMUNICATION NETWORK Every organization also has an **informal communication network**, often referred to as the *grapevine* or the *rumour mill*, that encompasses all communication that occurs outside the formal network. Some of this informal communication takes place naturally as a result of employee interaction both on the job and in social settings, and some of it takes place when the formal network doesn't provide information that employees want. In fact, the inherent limitations of formal communication networks helped spur the growth of social media in the business environment.

Some executives are wary of the informal communication network, possibly because

Grapevines flourish when employees don't receive information they want or need.

it threatens their power to control the flow of information. However, smart managers tap into the grapevine. It provides them with a sense of employees' concerns and anxieties, and they can use it to spread and receive informal

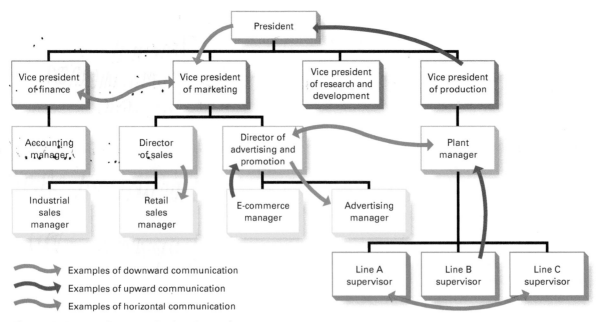

→ Examples of downward communication

→ Examples of upward communication

→ Examples of horizontal communication

Figure 1–5 Formal Communication Network

messages.[5] The grapevine also helps employers determine if their formal means of communication are effective: grapevines tend to be most active when employees believe the formal network is not providing the information they want or need.[6]

INFORMAL OUTSIDE COMMUNICATION Although companies often communicate with outsiders in a formal manner, informal contacts with outsiders are important for learning about customer needs. As a member of an organization, you are an important informal channel for communicating with the outside world. In the course of your daily activities, you unconsciously absorb bits of information that add to the collective knowledge of your company. What's more, every time you speak for or about your company to your friends, potential sales contacts, customers, and so on, you send a message. Many outsiders may form their impression of your organization on the basis of the subtle, unconscious clues you transmit through your tone of voice, facial expression, and general appearance. Although these interactions are informal, they can still be vital to the company's success, so they require the same care and skill as formal communication.

Every employee informally accumulates facts and impressions that contribute to the organization's collective understanding of the outside world.

Informal outside communication

In fact, these informal exchanges are considered so important that a new class of technology has emerged to enable them. Just as Facebook, Twitter, and similar social networking websites help students and other individuals connect, websites such as LinkedIn (www.linkedin.com), XING (www.xing.com), and Ryze (www.ryze.com) help businesspeople connect. These business-oriented solutions typically work by indexing email and IM address books, calendars, and message archives, then looking for connections between names.[7]

Understanding the Unique Challenges of Business Communication

If you have some experience in the business world, you already know that business communication is far more demanding than the communication you typically engage in with family, friends, and school associates. Expectations are higher on the job, and the business environment is so complex that your messages can fail for many reasons, such as human oversight or a technological glitch. Business communication is affected by factors such as the globalization of business and the increase in workforce diversity, the evolution of organizational structures, the growing reliance on teamwork, the increasing value of business information, the pervasiveness of technology, and the need for increased cybersecurity and protection of privacy.

4 LEARNING OBJECTIVE

Discuss six factors that make business communication unique.

Challenges of business comm.

① Globalization

I. THE GLOBALIZATION OF BUSINESS AND THE INCREASE IN WORKFORCE DIVERSITY

Today's businesses increasingly reach across international borders to market their products, partner with other businesses, and employ workers and executives—an effort known as **globalization**. Many North American companies rely on exports for a significant portion of their sales, and managers and employees in these firms need to communicate with many other cultures. Moreover, thousands of companies from all around the world compete for a share of the massive North American market, so chances are you'll do business with or even work for a company based in another country at some point in your career. Increased globalization and workforce diversity mean that employees must understand the laws, customs, and business practices of many countries besides being able to communicate with people who speak different languages. Between 2007 and 2011, 1.6 million people immigrated to Canada. Altogether, Canadians come from more than 200 different ethnic backgrounds.[8] It has been said that Canada's multiculturalism is what "makes us so well liked around the world."[9]

People with different cultural backgrounds and life experiences may have different communication styles.

As we see later in the text, successful companies realize two important facts: (1) the more diverse their workforce, the more attention they need to pay to communication, and (2) a diverse workforce can yield a significant competitive advantage by bringing more ideas and broader perspectives to bear on business challenges.

II. THE EVOLUTION OF ORGANIZATIONAL STRUCTURES

As Figure 1–5 illustrates, every business has a particular structure that defines the relationships between the various people and departments within the organization. These relationships, in turn, affect the nature and quality of communication throughout the organization. Tall structures have many layers of management between the lowest and highest positions, so they can suffer communication breakdowns and delays as messages are passed up and down through multiple layers.

Organizations with tall structures may unintentionally restrict the flow of information.

To overcome such problems, many businesses are now adopting flat structures that reduce the number of layers. With fewer layers, communication generally flows faster and with fewer disruptions and distortions. On the other hand, with fewer formal lines of control and communication in these organizations, individual employees are expected to assume more responsibility for communication. For instance, you may be expected to communicate across department boundaries with colleagues and team members throughout the company.

Flatter organizational structures usually make it easier to communicate effectively.

Specific types of organizational structures present unique communication challenges. In a *matrix structure*, for example, employees report to two managers at the same time, such as a project manager and a department manager. The need to coordinate workloads, schedules, and other matters increases the communication burden on everyone involved. In a *network structure*, sometimes known as a *virtual organization*, a company supplements the talents of its employees with services from one or more external partners, such as a design lab, a manufacturing firm, or a sales and distribution company.

Corporate cultures with an open climate benefit from free-flowing information and employee input.

Regardless of the particular structure a company uses, your communication efforts will also be influenced by the organization's **corporate culture**, the mixture of values, traditions, and habits that give a company its atmosphere and personality. Successful companies encourage employee contributions by ensuring that communication flows freely down, up, and across the organization chart. Open climates encourage candour and honesty, helping employees feel free enough to admit their mistakes, disagree with their boss, and express their opinions.

III. THE GROWING RELIANCE ON TEAMWORK

Working in a team makes you even more responsible for communicating effectively.

Both traditional and innovative company structures can rely heavily on teamwork. Whether the task is to write reports, give oral presentations, produce a video or a product, solve a problem, or investigate an opportunity, companies look for people who can successfully interact in teams and collaborate with others. Why? When teams are successful, they can improve productivity, creativity, employee involvement, and even job security.[10]

In addition to technical skills, companies seek out personnel who can work well in changing environments and communicate complex ideas to a diverse workforce. In an interview with *Fast Company*, career consultant and professor at Arkansas State University, Daniel Alexander Usera points out that while science, technology, engineering, and mathematics (STEM) degrees are in high demand, employees need to be able to function effectively "in a team-based, information-sharing context," which requires strong communication skills.[11] Teams are commonly used in business today, but they're not always successful—and a key reason that teams fail to meet their objectives is poor communication.

IV. THE INCREASING VALUE OF BUSINESS INFORMATION

As competition for jobs, customers, and resources continues to grow, the importance of information continues to escalate as well. Companies in virtually every industry rely heavily on *knowledge workers*, employees at all levels of an organization who specialize in acquiring, processing, and communicating information. Three examples help to illustrate the value of information in today's economy:

Information has become one of the most important resources in business today.

Challenges of business comm. (4), (5), (6)

- **Competitive insights.** Successful companies work hard to understand their competitors' strengths and weaknesses. The more you know about your competitors and their plans, the more able you will be to adjust your own business plans.
- **Customer needs.** Most companies invest significant time and money in an effort to understand their customers' needs. This information is collected from a variety of sources and needs to be analyzed and summarized, so your company can develop goods and services that better satisfy customer needs.
- **Regulations and guidelines.** Today's businesses must understand and follow a wide range of government regulations and guidelines covering such areas as employment, the environment, taxes, and accounting. Your job may include the responsibility of researching and understanding these issues and then communicating them throughout the organization.

V. THE PERVASIVENESS OF TECHNOLOGY

Technology influences virtually every aspect of business communication today. However, even those technological developments intended to enhance communication can actually impede it if not used intelligently. Moreover, keeping current with technology requires time, energy, and constant improvement of skills. If your level of technical expertise doesn't match that of your colleagues and co-workers, the imbalance can put you at a disadvantage and complicate the communication process.

For a concise overview of the technologies you're most likely to encounter, see "Using Technology to Improve Business Communication" later in this chapter.

VI. THE NEED FOR INCREASED CYBERSECURITY AND PROTECTION OF PRIVACY

In 2016 Canadians owned more computer devices per capita than did people in any other country in the world. They also spent more time using the

Less costly than travel, videoconferencing provides many of the same benefits as an in-person meeting. Advanced systems include telepresence and robot surrogates, which use computers to "place" participants in the room virtually, letting them see and hear everyone while being seen and heard themselves. Do you think that such realistic interaction makes meetings more productive? What are the benefits and shortcomings of virtual meetings?

Ethan Hill Photography

Internet than did people in any other country (approximately 40 hours per person, per month) for both business and personal purposes. While providing excellent time efficiencies, socialization opportunities, and communication resources, the ever-evolving cyber environment also presents an increased need for security and protection of privacy. Research shows that "70% of Canadian businesses have been victim to cyber attacks" at an average cost of $15,000 per incident.[12]

Furthermore, less than 33 percent of small to medium-sized Canadian businesses are very familiar with concepts such as "ransomware, social engineering and two-factor authentication," making them very vulnerable to the increasingly sophisticated tactics used by "hactivists."[13]

Cybersecurity is a global issue. Consider, for example, the 2017 WannaCry and Peyta ransomware outbreaks, which affected public and private sectors worldwide.[14] Increased awareness and education is needed at all levels of an organization. In response, the global market projections for cybersecurity products and services are expected to exceed $170 billion by 2020. Job seekers in this industry will also find good opportunities, as the search for "cyber pros" is expected to reach 6 million in the same time frame.[15]

BARRIERS TO EFFECTIVE COMMUNICATION

Throughout your career, you'll find that perfectly prepared messages can fail for a variety of reasons. When interference in the communication process distorts or obscures the sender's meaning, it is called a **communication barrier**. Your attempts to transmit and receive messages can be disrupted, distorted, or even blocked by communication barriers such as these:

Barriers to effective comm.

A number of barriers can block or distort messages before they reach the intended audience.

• **Noise and distractions.** External distractions range from uncomfortable meeting rooms to crowded computer screens with instant messages and reminders popping up all over the place. Internal distractions are thoughts and emotions that prevent audiences from focusing on incoming messages. The common habit of *multitasking*, attempting more than one task at a time, is practically guaranteed to create communication distractions. Moreover, research suggests that "chronic multitasking" can reduce productivity and increase errors.[16]

• **Competing messages.** Having your audience's undivided attention in today's technological world is a distinct challenge. In many cases, you must compete with other messages that are trying to reach your audience at the same time. Too many messages can result in *information overload*, which not only makes it difficult to discriminate between useful and useless information but also amplifies workplace stress.[17]

• **Filters.** Messages can be blocked or distorted by *filters*, any human or technological interventions between the sender and the receiver. Filtering can be both intentional (such as automatically filing incoming messages based on sender or content) or unintentional (such as an overly aggressive spam filter that deletes legitimate emails).

Dmitry Kalinovsky/Shutterstock

Open cultures promote the flow of information. You may work in an open-plan office designed to encourage casual interaction and impromptu meetings. Does a physically flexible environment stimulate the flow of information? Does it encourage creativity?

As you read earlier, the structure and culture of an organization can also inhibit the flow of vital messages. And, in some cases, the people or companies you rely on to deliver your message can distort it or filter it to meet their own needs.

- **Perceptual differences.** Our minds organize incoming sensations into a mental map that represents our individual perception of reality. As a sender, you choose the details that seem important to you. As a receiver, you try to fit new details into your existing pattern; however, if a detail doesn't quite fit, you are inclined to distort the information rather than rearrange your pattern—a process known as **selective perception**.[18] For example, a manager who strongly believes in a particular business strategy might distort or ignore evidence that suggests the strategy is failing. The more your audience members share your experiences—personal, professional, and cultural—the more likely they will be to extract the same meanings that you encode in your messages (see Figure 1–6).

- **Language differences.** The very language we use to communicate can turn into a barrier if two people define a given word or phrase differently. When a boss asks for something "as soon as possible," does that mean within 10 seconds, 10 minutes, or 10 days? When you communicate with non-native speakers of English, you may have to explain such expressions as "he nailed it" and "thinking outside the box."

- **Restrictive environments.** Companies that restrict the flow of information, either intentionally or unintentionally, limit their competitive potential. With their many levels between top and bottom, tall hierarchies often result in significant loss of message quality in both directions.[19] If an organization does not provide an effective means for employees to share their ideas, employees will believe management is not interested in them and will avoid conveying their opinions.[20]

- **Deceptive tactics.** Language itself is made up of words that carry values. So merely by expressing your ideas in a certain way, you influence how others perceive your message and you shape expectations and behaviours.[21] An organization cannot create illegal or unethical messages and remain credible or become successful. Still, some business communicators try to manipulate their receivers by using deceptive tactics: they may exaggerate benefits, quote inaccurate statistics, or hide negative information behind an optimistic attitude. They may state opinions as facts, leave out crucial information, or portray graphic data unfairly. And they may allow personal preferences to influence their own perception and the perception of others.

Barriers to effective comm.

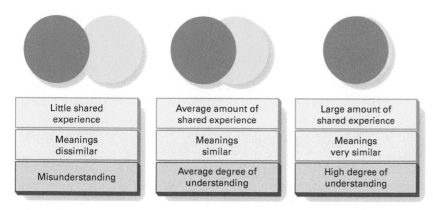

Little shared experience	Average amount of shared experience	Large amount of shared experience
Meanings dissimilar	Meanings similar	Meanings very similar
Misunderstanding	Average degree of understanding	High degree of understanding

Figure 1–6 How Shared Experience Affects Understanding

Communicating More Effectively on the Job

No single solution will overcome all communication barriers. However, a careful combination of strategies can improve your ability to communicate effectively. For example, you can improve your basic communication skills, minimize distractions, adopt an audience-centred approach, make your feedback constructive, and be sensitive to business etiquette.

STRATEGY 1: IMPROVE YOUR BUSINESS COMMUNICATION SKILLS

Work on your communication skills before you start your business career.

Your own skills as a communicator will be as much a factor in your business success as anything else. No matter what your skill level, opportunities to improve are numerous and usually easy to find. As mentioned earlier, many employers provide communication training in both general skills and specific scenarios, but don't wait. Use this course to begin mastering your skills now.

Lack of experience may be the only obstacle between you and effective communication. Perhaps you're worried about a limited vocabulary or uncertain about questions of grammar, punctuation, and style. If you're intimidated by the idea of writing an important document or appearing before a group, you're not alone. Everyone gets nervous about communicating from time to time, even people you might think of as "naturals." People aren't born writing and speaking well; they master these skills through study and practice. Even simple techniques, such as keeping a reading log and writing practice essays, will improve not only your writing skills but also your scholastic performance.[22]

This course lets you practise in an environment that provides honest and constructive feedback. You'll have ample opportunity to plan and produce documents, collaborate in teams, listen effectively, improve nonverbal communication, and communicate across cultures—all skills that will serve your career well.

STRATEGY 2: MINIMIZE DISTRACTIONS

Overcome distraction by
- Using common sense and courtesy
- Sending fewer messages
- Informing receivers of your message's priority

Everyone in the organization can help overcome distractions. Start by reducing as much noise, visual clutter, and interruption as possible. A small dose of common sense and courtesy goes a long way. Turn off your cellphone before you step into a meeting. Don't talk across the tops of cubicles when people inside them are trying to work. Be sensitive to your employer's policies about playing music at work: some people may be able to work with soft music playing, but others can't.

Don't let email, IM, or telephones interrupt you every minute of the day. Set aside time to attend to messages all at once, so you can think and focus the rest of the day. Make sure the messages you send are necessary. Email in particular has made it too easy to send too many messages or send messages to people who don't need them.

In addition, if you must send a message that isn't urgent or crucial, let people know so they can prioritize. If a long report requires no action from recipients, tell them up front, so they don't have to search through it looking for action items. Most email and voicemail systems let you mark messages as urgent; however, use this feature only when it's truly needed. Too many so-called urgent messages that aren't particularly urgent will lead to annoyance and anxiety, not action.

Emotionally charged situations require extra care when communicating.

Try to overcome emotional distractions by recognizing your own feelings and by anticipating emotional reactions from others.[23] When a situation might cause tempers to flare, choose your words carefully. As a receiver, avoid placing blame and reacting subjectively.

STRATEGY 3: ADOPT AN AUDIENCE-CENTRED APPROACH

An **audience-centred approach** means focusing on and caring about the members of your audience, making every effort to get your message across in a way that is meaningful to them. This approach is also known as adopting the "you" attitude. Learn as much as possible about the biases, education, age, status, style, and personal and professional concerns of your receivers. If you're addressing strangers and are unable to find out more about them, project yourself into their position by using your common sense and imagination. Remember that your audience wants to know, "What's in it for me?"

UNDERSTAND HOW AUDIENCES RECEIVE MESSAGES Knowing how audiences receive messages will help you fine-tune an audience-centred approach for each situation. For an audience member to actually receive a message, three events need to occur: the receiver has to *sense* the presence of a message, *select* it from all the other messages competing for attention, and *perceive* it as an actual message (as opposed to random, pointless noise).[24] Today's business audiences are inundated with so many messages and so much noise that they miss or ignore many of the messages intended for them. However, through this course, you will learn a variety of techniques to craft messages that get noticed. In general, follow these five principles to increase your chances of success:

- **Consider audience expectations.** Deliver messages using the media and channels that the audience expects. If colleagues expect meeting notices to be delivered by email, don't suddenly switch gears and start delivering the notices via blog postings without telling anyone. Of course, sometimes going *against* expectations can stimulate audience attention, which is why companies will advertise in unusual ways to get your attention. However, for most business communication efforts, following the expectations of your audience is the most efficient way to get your message across.
- **Ensure ease of use.** Even if audiences are actively looking for your messages, they probably won't see your messages if you make them hard to find. Poorly designed websites with confusing navigation are common culprits in this respect.
- **Emphasize familiarity.** Use words, images, and designs that are familiar to your audience. For example, most visitors to business websites now expect to see information about the company on a page called "About Us."
- **Practise empathy.** Make sure your messages "speak to the audience" by clearly addressing their wants and needs—not yours. People are much more inclined to notice messages that relate to their individual concerns.[25]
- **Design for compatibility.** For the many messages delivered electronically these days, be sure to verify technical compatibility with your audience. For instance, if your website requires visitors to have a particular video capability on their computers, you won't reach audience members who don't have that software installed.

> To improve the odds that your messages will be successfully perceived by your audience, pay close attention to expectations, ease of use, familiarity, empathy, and technical compatibility.

UNDERSTAND HOW AUDIENCES DECODE MESSAGES Even though a message may have been received by the audience, it doesn't "mean" anything until the recipient decodes it and assigns meaning to it. Unfortunately, there is no guarantee that your audience will assign the same meaning that you intended. Even well-crafted, well-intentioned communication efforts can fail because assigning meaning is a highly personal process affected by culture, individual experience, learning and thinking styles, hopes, fears, and even temporary moods. Moreover, audiences tend to extract the meaning they *expect* to get from a message, even if it's the opposite of what the sender intended.[26] In fact, rather than extracting *your* meaning, it's more accurate to state that audience members re-create *their* own meaning—or meanings—from the message.

Culture shapes people's views of the world in profound ways, from determinations of right and wrong to details such as the symbolic meanings attached to specific colours. For example, Canadians tend to admire young professionals who challenge established ways of conducting business. In contrast, in Japan, people generally place a higher value on respect for older colleagues, consensus decision making, and group accomplishment. A younger colleague's bold proposal to radically reshape business strategy could be interpreted more positively in one culture than in the other—quite independent of the proposal's merits alone.

UNDERSTAND HOW AUDIENCES RESPOND TO MESSAGES After your message is delivered, received, and correctly decoded, will audience members respond in the way you'd like them to? Probably—if three events occur.

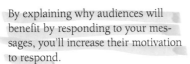

Audiences will likely respond to a message if they remember it, if they're able to respond, and if they're properly motivated to respond.

First, the recipient has to remember the message long enough to act on it. Simplifying greatly, memory works in several stages: *Sensory memory* momentarily captures incoming data from the senses; then, whatever the recipient pays attention to is transferred to *short-term memory*. Information in short-term memory will quickly disappear if it isn't transferred to *long-term memory*, which can be done either actively (such as by memorizing a list of items) or passively (such as when a new piece of information connects with something else the recipient already has stored in long-term memory). Finally, the information needs to be retrieved when the recipient needs to act on it.[27] In general, people find it easier to remember and retrieve information that is important to them personally or professionally. Consequently, by communicating in ways that are sensitive to your audience's wants and needs, you greatly increase the chance that your messages will be remembered and retrieved.

Second, the recipient has to be *able* to respond as you wish. Obviously, if recipients simply cannot do what you want them to do, such as paying for a product you are promoting, they will not respond according to your plan. By understanding your audience you can work to minimize these unsuccessful outcomes.

Third, the recipient has to be *motivated* to respond. You'll encounter many situations in which your audience has the option of responding but isn't required to—the record company may or may not offer your band a contract, the boss may or may not respond to your request for a raise, and so on. Throughout this course, you'll learn the techniques for crafting messages that motivate readers to respond.

By explaining why audiences will benefit by responding to your messages, you'll increase their motivation to respond.

KNOW AS MUCH AS YOU CAN ABOUT YOUR AUDIENCE The more you know about the people you're communicating with, the easier it will be to concentrate on their needs—which, in turn, will make it easier for them to hear your message, understand it, and respond positively. For example, the presentation slide in Figure 1–7 takes an audience-centred approach. Rather than trying to cover all the technical and legal details that are often discussed in insurance plans, this slide addresses the common fears and worries that employees might have as their company moves to a new health insurance plan. Accessible language and clear organization help communicate the message effectively.

If you haven't had the opportunity to communicate with a diverse range of people in your academic career so far, you might be surprised by the different communication styles you will surely encounter on the job. Recognizing and adapting to your audience's style will improve not only the effectiveness of your communication but also the quality of your working relationship.[28]

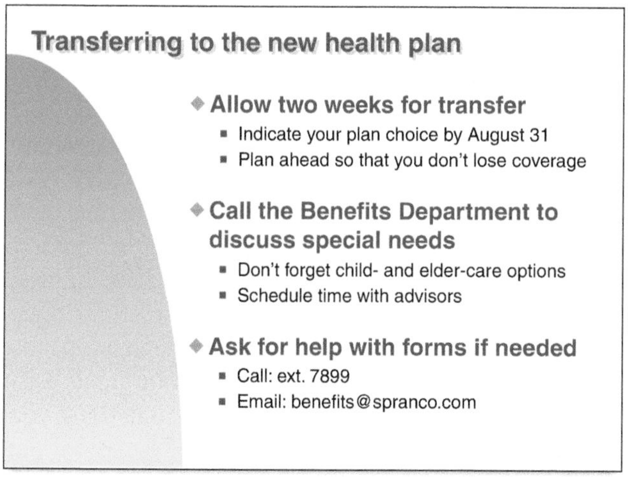

Transferring to the new health plan

◆ **Allow two weeks for transfer**
  ▪ Indicate your plan choice by August 31
  ▪ Plan ahead so that you don't lose coverage

◆ **Call the Benefits Department to discuss special needs**
  ▪ Don't forget child- and elder-care options
  ▪ Schedule time with advisors

◆ **Ask for help with forms if needed**
  ▪ Call: ext. 7899
  ▪ Email: benefits@spranco.com

Figure 1–7 PowerPoint Slide Showing Audience-Centred Communication

The audience-centred approach is emphasized throughout this book, so you'll have plenty of opportunities to practise this approach to communicating more effectively.

STRATEGY 4: MAKE YOUR FEEDBACK CONSTRUCTIVE

You will encounter many situations in which you are expected to give and receive feedback regarding communication efforts. Whether giving or receiving criticism, be sure you do so in a constructive way. **Constructive feedback**, sometimes called *constructive criticism*, focuses on the process and outcomes of communication, not on the people involved (see Table 1–1). In contrast, **destructive feedback** delivers criticism with no effort to stimulate improvement.[29] For example, "This proposal is a confusing mess, and you failed to

Constructive feedback focuses on improvement, not personal criticism.

Table 1–1	Giving Constructive Feedback	
How to Be Constructive	**Explanation**
Evaluate effectiveness.	Does the document accomplish its intended purpose with accurate information and clear language?
Think through your suggested changes carefully.	Isolated or superficial edits can do more harm than good.
Discuss improvements rather than flaws.	Instead of saying, "This illustration is confusing," explain how it can be improved to make it clearer. Use this opportunity to "feed forward."
Focus on controllable behaviour.	Since the writer may not have control over every variable that affected the quality of the message, focus on those elements that the writer can control.
Be specific.	Comments such as "I don't get this" or "Make this clearer" don't identify what the writer needs to fix.
Keep feedback impersonal.	Focus comments on the message, not the person who created it.
Verify understanding.	Ask for confirmation from the recipient to make sure that the person understood your feedback.
Time your feedback carefully.	Make sure the writer will have sufficient time to implement the changes you suggested.
Highlight any limitations your feedback may have.	If you didn't have time to give the document a thorough edit, or if you're not an expert in some aspect of the content, let the writer know so he or she can handle your comments appropriately.

Feeding forward provides input during the development phase of a project or report. The creator is able to benefit from the input in "real time" as opposed to after the fact or shortly before the deadline.

React unemotionally when you receive constructive feedback.

convince me of anything" is destructive feedback. Your goal is to be more constructive: "Your proposal could be more effective with a clearer description of the construction process and a well-organized explanation of why the positives outweigh the negatives." When giving feedback, avoid personal attacks and give clear guidelines for improvement. Is there an opportunity to use a *feed forward* approach in the future? That is, can feedback be provided during the development phase as part of a continuous improvement process?

When you receive constructive feedback, resist the immediate urge to defend your work or deny the validity of the feedback. Remaining open to criticism isn't always easy when you've put long nights and much effort into a project, but feedback is a valuable opportunity to learn and improve. Disconnect your emotions from the work, and view it simply as something you can improve. Many writers also find it helpful to step back, think a while about the feedback, and let their emotions settle down before making corrections. Of course, don't automatically assume that even well-intentioned feedback is necessarily correct. You are responsible for the final quality of the message, so ensure that any suggested changes are valid ones. Once you have had some time to reflect on the feedback, see if you have any questions or need further clarification.

STRATEGY 5: BE SENSITIVE TO BUSINESS ETIQUETTE

Respect, courtesy, and common sense will get you through most etiquette challenges on the job.

In today's hectic, competitive world, the notion of **etiquette** (the expected norms of behaviour in a particular situation) can seem outdated and unimportant. However, the way you conduct yourself can have a profound influence on your company's success and your career. When executives hire and promote you, they expect your behaviour to protect the company's reputation. The more you understand such expectations, the better chance you have of avoiding career-damaging mistakes.

In any setting, long lists of etiquette "rules" can be overwhelming. You'll never memorize all of them or remember to follow them in the heat of the moment. Remember three principles that will get you through almost any situation: respect, courtesy, and common sense. Moreover, these principles will encourage forgiveness if you do happen to make a mistake.

As you encounter new situations, take a few minutes to learn the expectations of the other people involved. You can begin with reading travel guidebooks; they are a valuable source of information about norms and customs in other countries. Don't be afraid to ask questions, either. People will respect your concern and curiosity. You'll gradually accumulate considerable knowledge, which will help you feel comfortable and be effective in a wide range of business situations.

APPLYING WHAT YOU'VE LEARNED TO THE COMMUNICATION PROCESS

With these additional insights into what makes communication succeed, take another look at the communication process model. The communication process presents many opportunities for messages to get lost, distorted, or misinterpreted as they travel from sender to receiver. Fortunately, you can take action at every step in the process to increase your chances of success. Figure 1–8 identifies the key challenges in the process and summarizes the steps you can take along the way to become a more effective communicator.

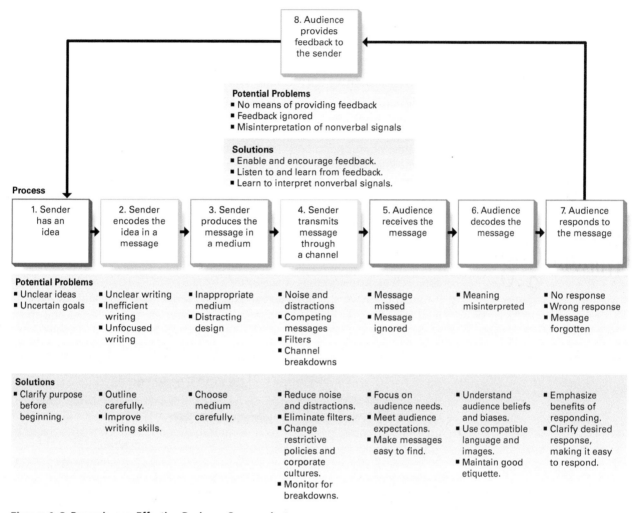

Figure 1–8 Becoming an Effective Business Communicator

Using Technology to Improve Business Communication

Today's businesses rely heavily on technology to improve the communication process. In fact, many of the technologies you might use in your personal life, from microblogs to video games or virtual worlds, are also used in business. You will find that technology is discussed extensively throughout this book, with specific advice on using common tools to meet communication challenges.

Anyone who has used a computer, a smartphone, or other advanced gadget knows that the benefits of technology are not automatic. When poorly designed or inappropriately used, technology can hinder communication more than it helps. Communicate effectively by understanding the social communication model, keeping technology in perspective, guarding against information overload, using technological tools productively, and reconnecting with people frequently.

UNDERSTANDING THE SOCIAL COMMUNICATION MODEL

The basic model presented in Figure 1–1 shows how a single idea moves from one sender to one receiver. In a larger sense, it also helps represent the traditional nature of much business communication, which was primarily defined

6   LEARNING OBJECTIVE

Explain five strategies for using communication technology successfully.

Communicating in today's business environment nearly always requires some level of technical competence.

by a *publishing* or *broadcasting* mindset. Externally, companies issued carefully scripted messages to a mass audience that often had few options for responding to those messages or initiating messages of their own. Customers and other interested parties had few ways to connect with one another to ask questions, share information, or offer support. Internally, communication tended to follow the same "we talk, you listen" model, with upper managers issuing directives to lower-level supervisors and employees.

The social communication model is interactive, conversational, and usually open to all who wish to participate.

called Business Communication 2.0

The conversational and interactive *social communication model* is revolutionizing business communication.

However, a variety of technologies have enabled and inspired a new approach to business communication. In contrast to the publishing mindset, this new **social communication model** is *interactive* and *conversational*. Customers and other groups are now empowered through **social media**, electronic media that transform passive audiences into active participants in the communication process by allowing them to share content, revise content, respond to content, or contribute new content. Just as Web 2.0 signifies this second generation of World Wide Web technologies (that is, social networks, blogs, and other tools that you'll read about), **Business Communication 2.0** is a convenient label for this new approach to business communication.

On the surface, this approach might look like it's just added some new media tools. However, as Figure 1–9 shows, the changes are much deeper and more profound. In a typical 1.0 approach, messages are scripted by designated communicators, approved by someone in authority, distributed through selected channels, and delivered without modification to a passive audience that is not invited or even expected to respond. In the 2.0 approach, the rules change dramatically. Customers and other stakeholders participate in, influence, and often take control of conversations in the marketplace. They rely on one another for information about products, offer technical support, and even participate in group buying using social tools.[30]

The *Business Communication 2.0* approach can increase the speed of communication, lower costs, improve access to expertise, and boost employee satisfaction.

For both internal and external communication, Web 2.0 tools can increase the speed of communication, lower communication costs, improve access to pockets of expertise, and boost employee satisfaction.[31] Of course, no company, no matter how enthusiastically it embraces the 2.0 mindset, is going to be run as a social club in which everyone has a say and a vote. Instead, a hybrid approach is emerging in which some communications follow the traditional approach and others follow the 2.0 approach.[32]

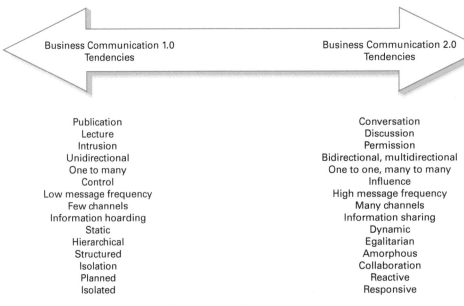

Figure 1–9 Business Communication: 1.0 versus 2.0

If you're an active user of Web 2.0 technologies, you'll fit right in with this new communication environment—and possibly even have a head start on more experienced professionals who are still adapting to the new tools and techniques.

KEEPING TECHNOLOGY IN PERSPECTIVE

Perhaps the single most important point to remember about technology is that it is simply a tool—a means by which you can accomplish certain tasks. Technology is an aid to interpersonal communication, not a replacement for it. Technology can't think for you or communicate for you, and if you lack some essential skills, technology probably can't fill in the gaps.

While this advice might sound obvious, it is easy to get caught up in the "gee whiz" factor, particularly with new technologies. No matter how exotic or entertaining it may be, technology has business value only if it helps deliver the right information to the right people at the right time.

Don't rely too much on technology or let it overwhelm the communication process.

GUARDING AGAINST INFORMATION OVERLOAD

The overuse or misuse of communication technology can lead to **information overload**, in which people receive more information than they can effectively process. Information overload makes it difficult to discriminate between useful and useless information, lowers productivity, and amplifies employee stress both on the job and at home—even to the point of causing health and relationship problems.[33]

As a recipient, you often have some level of control over the number and types of messages you choose to receive. Use the filtering features of your communication systems to isolate high-priority messages that deserve your attention. Also, be wary of subscribing to too many blog feeds, Twitter follows, Facebook updates, and other sources of recurring messages. Focus on the information you truly need to do your job.

As a sender, you can help reduce information overload by making sure you don't send unnecessary messages. In addition, remember to identify important or urgent messages so that the receiver can prioritize any actions that need to be taken.

Information overload results when people receive more information than they can effectively process.

USING TECHNOLOGICAL TOOLS PRODUCTIVELY

Facebook, Twitter, YouTube, IM, and other technologies are key parts of what has been called the "information technology paradox," in which information tools can waste as much time as they save. Concerns over inappropriate use of social networking sites, for example, have led many companies to ban employees from accessing them during work hours.[34]

Inappropriate web use not only distracts employees from work responsibilities but can leave employers open to lawsuits for sexual harassment if inappropriate images are displayed or transmitted around the company.[35] Social media have created another set of managerial challenges, given the risk that employee blogs or social networking pages can expose confidential information or damage a firm's reputation in the marketplace. With all these technologies, the best solution lies in developing clear policies that are enforced evenly for all employees.[36]

In addition to using your tools appropriately, knowing how to use them efficiently can make a big difference in your productivity. You don't have to become an expert in most cases, but you need to be familiar with the basic features and functions of the tools you are expected to use on the job. As a manager, you also need to ensure that your employees have sufficient training to productively use the tools you expect them to use.

Employees who are comfortable using communication technologies have a competitive advantage in today's marketplace.

Radius Images/Alamy Stock Photo

Why should you step out from behind your computer to connect in person? What are the benefits of nondigital face-to-face communication?

RECONNECTING WITH PEOPLE FREQUENTLY

In spite of technology's efficiency and speed, it may not be the best choice for every communication situation. First, even in the best circumstances, technology can't match the rich experience of person-to-person contact. Suppose you email a colleague asking how her sales presentation to an important client went, and she simply replies, "Fine." What does *fine* mean? Is an order expected soon? Did she lose the sale? Was the client rude and she doesn't want to talk about it? If you reconnect with her, perhaps visit her in person, she might provide additional information, or you might be able to offer advice or support during a difficult time.

Second, most people need to connect with other people. You can create impressive documents and presentations without ever leaving your desk or meeting anyone in person. But if you stay hidden behind technology, people won't get to know you nearly as well. You might be funny, bright, and helpful, but you're just a voice on the phone or a name on a document until people can interact with you in person. As technological options increase, people seem to need the human touch even more.

No matter how much technology is involved, communication is still about people connecting with people.

Making Ethical Communication Choices

7 LEARNING OBJECTIVE

Discuss the importance of ethics in business communication, and differentiate between an ethical dilemma and an ethical lapse.

Ethics are the accepted principles of conduct that govern behaviour within a society. Put another way, ethical principles define the boundary between right and wrong. Ethics has been defined as "knowing the difference between what you have a right to do and what is the right thing to do."[37] To make the right choices as a business communicator you have a responsibility to think through not only what you say but also the consequences of saying it.

Any time you try to mislead your audience, the result is unethical communication.

Ethical behaviour is a companywide concern, of course, but because communication efforts are the public face of a company, they are subjected to particularly rigorous scrutiny from regulators, legislators, investors, consumer groups, environmental groups, labour organizations, and anyone else affected by business activities. **Ethical communication** includes all relevant information, is true in every sense, and is not deceptive in any way. In contrast, unethical communication can include falsehoods and misleading information (or can withhold important information). Some examples of unethical communication include the following:[38]

- **Plagiarism.** Plagiarism is presenting someone else's words or other creative product as your own. Note that plagiarism can also be illegal if it violates a **copyright**, which is a form of legal protection for the expression of creative ideas.[39]
- **Omitting essential information.** Information is essential if your audience needs it to make an intelligent, objective decision.
- **Selective misquoting.** Deliberately omitting damaging or unflattering comments to paint a better picture of you or your company is unethical if the picture you create is untruthful.
- **Misrepresenting numbers.** Statistics and other data can be unethically manipulated by increasing or decreasing numbers, exaggerating, altering statistics, or omitting numeric data.
- **Distorting visuals.** Images can also be manipulated in unethical ways, such as making a product seem bigger than it really is or changing the scale of graphs and charts to exaggerate or conceal differences.
- **Failing to respect privacy or information security needs.** Failing to respect the privacy of others or failing to adequately protect information entrusted to your care can also be considered unethical (and is sometimes illegal).

Transparency gives audience members access to all the information they need in order to process messages accurately.

The widespread adoption of social media has increased the attention given to the issue of **transparency**, which in this context refers to a sense of openness—giving all participants in a conversation access to the information they need to accurately process the messages they are receiving. A key aspect of transparency is knowing who is behind the messages one receives. Consider the promotional event that Netflix staged in Toronto to announce the launch of its streaming video service in Canada. The outdoor news conference seemed to attract dozens of curious people who were excited about the availability of Netflix. However, many of these people who "spontaneously" showed up were actually paid actors with instructions to "look really excited, particularly if asked by media to do any interviews about the prospect of Netflix in Canada." The company apologized when the stunt was exposed.[40]

A major issue in business communication transparency is *stealth marketing*, which involves attempting to promote products and services to customers who don't know they're being marketed to. A common stealth marketing technique is rewarding someone to promote products to his or her friends without telling them it's a form of advertising. Critics—including the U.S. Federal Trade Commission (FTC) and the Word of Mouth Marketing Association—assert that such techniques are deceptive because they don't give their targets the opportunity to raise their instinctive defences against the persuasive powers of marketing messages.[41]

> The controversial practice of stealth marketing involves marketing to people without their knowledge.

Aside from ethical concerns, trying to fool the public is simply bad for business. As LaSalle University communication professor Michael Smith puts it, "The public backlash can be long, deep, and damaging to a company's reputation."[42]

DISTINGUISHING AN ETHICAL DILEMMA FROM AN ETHICAL LAPSE

Some ethical questions are easy to recognize and resolve, but others are not. Deciding what is ethical can be a considerable challenge in complex business situations. An **ethical dilemma** involves choosing among alternatives that aren't clear-cut. Perhaps two conflicting alternatives are both ethical and valid, or perhaps the alternatives lie somewhere in the grey area between clearly right and clearly wrong. Every company has responsibilities to multiple groups of people inside and outside the firm, and those various groups often have competing interests. For instance, employees generally want higher wages and more benefits, but investors who have risked their money in the company want management to keep costs low so that profits are strong enough to drive up the stock price. Both sides have a valid ethical position.

> Conflicting priorities and the vast grey areas between right and wrong create ethical dilemmas for an organization's communicators.

In contrast, an **ethical lapse** is making a clearly unethical (and frequently illegal) choice. Suppose you have decided to change jobs and have discreetly landed an interview with your boss's largest competitor. You get along great with the interviewer, who is impressed enough with you to offer you a position on the spot. The new position is a step up from your current job, and the pay is much more than what you're getting now. You accept the job and agree to start next month. Then, as you're shaking hands with the interviewer, she asks you to bring along profiles of your current company's 10 largest customers when you report for work. Do you comply with her request? How do you decide between what's ethical and what is not?

> An ethical lapse is knowing that something is wrong and doing it anyway.

ENSURING ETHICAL COMMUNICATION

Ensuring ethical business communications requires three elements: ethical individuals, ethical company leadership, and the appropriate policies and structures to support employees' efforts to make ethical choices.[43] Moreover, these three elements need to work in harmony. If employees see company executives making unethical decisions and flouting company guidelines, they might conclude that the guidelines are meaningless and emulate their bosses' unethical behaviour.

Employers have a responsibility to establish clear guidelines for ethical behaviour, including business communication. Many companies establish an explicit ethics policy by using a written **code of ethics** to help employees determine what is

> Responsible employers establish clear ethical guidelines for their employees to follow.

Code of Business Conduct

---

2. **POLICY DETAILS**

2.1. **Our Principles of Ethical Conduct**

2.1.1   Personal Integrity

Ethical behaviour is an essential part of our job and is a personal responsibility we all share. It means performing our job fully and competently and it also means being accountable for our behaviour and for supporting the values, principles and standards upon which our reputation rests.

Many aspects of our business are governed by laws and regulations and compliance with such laws is basic to ethical conduct. Bell and its employees are subject to, and are expected to comply with, the laws, rules and regulations of all countries in which we operate, as well as the expectations and requirements of our various regulators. These laws include, but are not limited to, telecommunications laws, securities laws and regulations, laws prohibiting the corruption of foreign officials, as well as lobbying, environmental and employment legislation. Ethical behaviour, however, goes beyond mere compliance with the law. It involves thinking through the possible impact of our decisions on all interested parties – customers, employees, unions, business partners, suppliers, investors, government as well as the communities and environment in which we live and work.

Although the Code lays out the fundamental principles of ethical and legal conduct, it cannot anticipate every ethical dilemma or situation we may encounter as we perform our jobs. This would be impossible given that the communications industry is evolving so rapidly and so unpredictably.

Consequently, we may often find ourselves caught in a situation or facing an ethical problem not explicitly covered in the Code. In this case, we must rely on our internal sense of what is right – our moral compass – to guide us in making the right decision.

When faced with a difficult or unclear situation, it may help to ask the following questions such as:
- how would I feel if, rather than initiating this action, I was on the receiving end?
- how would my customer react if he/she knew I was breaking the rules or distorting the facts to make a sale?
- if I do this, how will I feel afterwards? Would I want my co-workers, friends or family to find out?
- if my actions became public, how would they be reported in the media?

Assuming personal responsibility for our actions means we can't blame someone else for our behaviour. Conversely, no one – not even a manager – can force us to commit an illegal or unethical act that may damage the Company's reputation, or our own.

It also means we have a duty to report illegal acts or violations of Company rules, policies or the Code to management. Turning a blind eye to wrongdoing – in effect condoning such behaviour – is itself unethical.

Any breach of the Code or Company policies or evidence of illegal behaviour will be taken very seriously. Depending on the nature and severity of the case, employees who breach the Code, violate Company policy or commit an illegal act will face immediate discipline, up to and including dismissal, as well as possible civil or criminal prosecution.

2.1.2   Getting Help with Ethical Issues – the Business Conduct Help Line

Individual responsibility does not mean you are on your own when facing an ethical issue. Don't be reluctant to ask any questions you might have on the Code or raise issues.

Like many Canadian corporations, Bell Canada Enterprises (BCE) posts its code of ethical behaviour on its website. Why does an organization do so? Examine several corporate codes of ethics. What similarities do you find among them? What differences do you see?

Courtesy: Bell Canada Enterprises

PROMOTING WORKPLACE ETHICS

Ethical Boundaries: Where Would You Draw the Line?

At the very least, you owe your employer an honest day's work for an honest day's pay: your best efforts, obedience to the rules, a good attitude, respect for your employer's property, and a professional appearance. Such duties and considerations seem clear-cut, but where does your obligation to your employer end? For instance, where would you draw the line in communication situations such as the following?

- Writing your résumé so that an embarrassing two-year lapse won't be obvious
- Telling your best friend about your company's upcoming merger right after mailing the formal announcement to your shareholders
- Hinting to a co-worker (who's a close friend) that it's time for her to look around for something new, when you've already been told confidentially that she's scheduled to be fired at the end of the month
- Saying nothing when you witness one employee taking credit for another's successful idea
- Preserving your position by presenting yourself to supervisors as the only person capable of achieving an objective

- Pirating computer software; that is, using one copy on more than one computer instead of paying for licences to duplicate the product
- Making up an excuse when (for the fourth time this month) you have to pick up your child from school early and miss an important business meeting
- Calling in sick because you're taking a few days off and you want to use up some of the sick leave you've accumulated

The ethics involved in these situations may seem perfectly unambiguous . . . until you think about them. But wherever you are and whatever the circumstances, you owe your employer your best efforts. And time and again, it will be up to you to decide whether those efforts are ethical.

CAREER APPLICATIONS

1. List ethical behaviours you would expect from your employees, and compare your list with those of your classmates.
2. As the supervisor of the office filing clerks, you must deal with several workers who have a tendency to gossip about their colleagues. List five actions you might take to resolve the situation.

acceptable. A code is often part of a larger program of employee training and communication channels that allow employees to ask questions and report instances of questionable ethics. For example, at Bell Canada Enterprises (BCE), employees can seek advice on matters regarding ethical behaviour and report illegal or unethical behaviour using the Business Conduct Help Line, www.clearviewconnects.com, an online confidential and anonymous reporting service.[44] To ensure ongoing compliance with their codes of ethics, many companies also conduct **ethics audits** to monitor ethical progress and to point out any weaknesses that need to be addressed.

However, the law doesn't cover every situation that you'll encounter in your career. In the absence of clear legal boundaries or ethical guidelines, ask yourself the following questions about your business communications:[45]

- Have you defined the situation fairly and accurately?
- What is your intention in communicating this message?
- What impact will this message have on the people who receive it or who might be affected by it?
- Will the message achieve the greatest possible good while doing the least possible harm?
- Will the assumptions you've made change over time? That is, will a decision that seems ethical now seem unethical in the future?
- Are you comfortable with your decision? Would you be embarrassed if it were printed in tomorrow's newspaper or spread across the Internet?

If all else fails, think about a person whom you admire and ask yourself what he or she would think of your decision. If you wouldn't be proud to describe your choice to someone you admire and respect—someone whose opinion of you matters—that's a strong signal that you might be making a poor ethical choice.

If you can't decide whether a choice is ethical, picture yourself explaining it to someone whose opinion you value.

ENSURING LEGAL COMMUNICATION

Business communication is governed by a wide variety of laws designed to ensure accurate, complete messages.

In addition to ethical guidelines, business communication is also bound by a wide variety of laws and regulations, including the following areas:

- **Promotional communication.** Marketing specialists need to be aware of the many laws that govern truth and accuracy in advertising.
- **Contracts.** A *contract* is a legally binding promise between two parties, in which one party makes a specified offer and the other party accepts. Contracts are fundamental to virtually every aspect of business, from product sales to property rental and from credit cards and loans to professional service agreements.[46]
- **Employment communication.** Provincial, territorial, and federal laws govern communication between employers and both potential and current employees. For example, job descriptions must be written in a way that doesn't intentionally or unintentionally discriminate against women, visible minorities, Aboriginal people, persons with disabilities, and persons of any sexual orientation or gender identity.
- **Intellectual property. Intellectual property (IP)** includes patents, copyrighted materials, trade secrets, and even Internet domain names.[47] Bloggers in particular need to be careful about IP protection, given the carefree way that some post the work of others without offering proper credit. For guidelines on this hot topic, get the free *Legal Guide for Bloggers* at www.eff.org/issues/bloggers/legal.
- **Financial reporting.** Finance and accounting professionals who work for publicly traded companies (those that sell stock to the public) must adhere to stringent reporting laws. For example, they must ensure that all investor communications are accurate and transparent.
- **Defamation.** Negative comments about another party raise the possibility of **defamation**, the intentional communication of false statements that damage character or reputation.[48] (Written defamation is called *libel*; spoken defamation is called *slander.*) Someone suing for defamation must prove (1) that the statement is false, (2) that the language is injurious to the person's reputation, and (3) that the statement has been published.
- **Transparency requirements.** Governments around the world are taking steps to help ensure that consumers and other parties know who is behind the information they receive, particularly from online sources. The European Union, for instance, outlaws a number of online marketing tactics, including "flogs," short for "fake blogs," in which an employee or a paid agent posing as an independent consumer posts positive stories about a company's products.[49] In the United States, the FTC recently adopted a requirement that product-review bloggers disclose any relationship—such as receiving payments or free goods—they have with the companies whose products they discuss in their blogs.[50]

If you have any doubts about the legality of a message you intend to distribute, ask for advice from your company's legal department. A small dose of caution can prevent huge legal headaches and protect your company's reputation in the marketplace.

Applying What You've Learned

At the beginning of this chapter, you read about Wave's use of social media to add value to its accounting application product. Every chapter opens with a similar slice-of-life vignette. As you read through each chapter, think about the person and the company highlighted in the vignette. Become familiar with the various concepts presented in the chapter, and imagine how they might apply to the featured scenario.

At the end of each chapter, you'll take part in an innovative simulation called "On the Job: Performing Communication Tasks." You'll play the role of a person working in the highlighted organization, and you'll face a situation you could encounter on the job. You will be presented with communication scenarios, each with several possible courses of action. It's up to you to recommend one course of action from the simulations as homework, as teamwork, as material for in-class discussion, or in a host of other ways. These scenarios let you explore various communication ideas and apply the concepts and techniques from the chapter.

As you tackle each problem, think about the material you covered and consider your own experience as a communicator. You'll probably be surprised to discover how much you already know about business communication.

SUMMARY OF LEARNING OBJECTIVES

1 **Explain why effective communication is important to your success in today's business environment.** Your ability to communicate can help your company become more efficient, innovative, and responsive. As your career advances and you achieve positions of greater responsibility, your communication skills will gain in importance because you will communicate about increasingly important matters to larger and larger audiences. Employers will recognize your communication abilities and value you as an employee.

2 **Identify eight communication skills that successful employers expect from their employees.** Employers expect their employees to organize ideas and information effectively, express and present ideas coherently and persuasively, and listen carefully for the true meaning behind words. They also want employees to communicate well in a diverse workplace, use communication technologies, and follow the standards of correct writing and speaking. Finally, employers expect their workers to practise courtesy and respect and communicate in an ethical manner.

3 **Describe the five characteristics of effective business communication.** Effective business messages supply information that helps others complete tasks, provide factual support for opinions, and clarify and summarize information to help audiences comprehend documents quickly. Good business writing also states the desired action, so the reader knows how to respond, and persuades audiences by showing benefits.

4 **Discuss six factors that make business communication unique.** Business communication is unique because of globalization and diversity, which create opportunities to learn more about markets and to communicate more effectively with various market segments. Another factor is the increasing value placed on business information, which has created the function of knowledge workers, who acquire, process, and communicate information. For its part, technology provides workers with the challenges of using it intelligently and keeping up to date with innovations. Another factor is the evolution toward flatter organizational structures: these structures reduce the number of layers of management, giving employees more

responsibility for communication. In addition, teamwork is a unique feature of business communication: companies increasingly rely on teams and expect each member to communicate effectively in a team. Finally, cybersecurity is a global issue. Increased awareness and education is needed at all levels of an organization in order to protect intellectual property and individual privacy. All of these factors increase the need for effective business communication skills, including the management of barriers, such as information overload or language differences, that can affect the successful transmission and reception of messages.

5 **Describe five strategies for communicating more effectively on the job.** One method is to reduce distractions caused by technology, sounds, and emotional concerns. Successful communicators also focus on the needs of their audience and adapt to their communication styles. Effective communicators also practise their communication skills at every opportunity, provide constructive feedback or feed forward and support continuous improvement, and learn the norms of business etiquette in a variety of situations.

6 **Explain five strategies for using communication technology successfully.** Employees who use communication technology effectively adapt it to their own and their audiences' needs and realize that it does not necessarily supplant traditional communication forms. As well, it's important to understand the social communication model, in which customers and groups have become active, influential participants in communication. Employees should keep technology in perspective, and be familiar with its strengths and its weaknesses in relation to their specific purposes. They should also guard against information overload and use technology productively, remembering that it is only a tool to aid communication. Finally, employees who use communication technology wisely know that face-to-face communication adds the human touch, which is essential for professional relationships.

7 **Discuss the importance of ethics in business communication, and differentiate between an ethical dilemma and an ethical lapse.** Ethics are crucial to effective business communication because they can support or damage a company's reputation in the eyes of its stakeholders. Ethical communicators do not deceive their audiences through language, images, and behaviours that manipulate, discriminate, or exaggerate. They also ensure that they follow the wide variety of laws and regulations that govern business communication. An ethical dilemma involves choosing between two or more alternatives that are neither clearly ethical nor clearly unethical, such as alternatives that are all ethical but conflicting or alternatives that lie somewhere in the grey areas between right and wrong. An ethical lapse involves choosing an alternative that is clearly unethical or illegal, perhaps placing your own desire or ambition above the welfare of others.

ON THE JOB   PERFORMING COMMUNICATION TASKS AT WAVE

You've recently joined the staff of Wave as a summer intern in the community, content, and communications department. In your role, you look for opportunities to help Wave build positive relationships with its customers. Use what you've learned in this chapter to address the following challenges:

1. Your supervisor has given you the job of announcing a free accounting webinar of interest to Wave customers. You need to choose the communication channel that will reach the widest audience to advertise the event. Of the following, which channel do you choose, and why? Be sure to consider the features of each channel.
   a. Wave's blog
   b. Twitter
   c. Facebook
   d. Postal (snail mail) letter

2. Wave has hired another intern to work over the summer. The culture in your office is conscientious and professional but with a generally informal atmosphere. However, as with any company, individual employees vary in how closely their own styles and personalities fit the corporate culture. For example, the new intern tends to communicate in a formal, distant style that some employees find off-putting and impersonal. Your supervisor recognizes that the intern is a good worker but has asked you to speak with him about adapting to the office vibe. How should you initiate the conversation?
   a. Tell your supervisor that the intern is doing his job well, and that's what counts.
   b. In a private conversation with the intern, explain the importance of fitting into the corporate culture and give him a two-week deadline to change his style.
   c. In a private conversation with the intern, explain the reasoning behind the company's informal culture and its contribution to the company's success; suggest that he might find his work here more enjoyable if he modifies his approach somewhat.
   d. Allow the intern to continue communicating in the same style; after all, that's his personal style, and it's not up to the company to change it.

3. One of your jobs at Wave is to respond to comments and questions via Twitter. One follower has been complaining about the software despite frequent requests that she email customer service at Wave. Your supervisor wants you to suggest a solution. Which is the best answer and why?
   a. Using Twitter, invite her to Wave's office for a help session with a customer service specialist.
   b. Complain to Twitter about her posts.
   c. Criticize her tweets on Wave's Twitter account.
   d. Ask her to email customer service at Wave directly to discuss her concerns.

TEST YOUR KNOWLEDGE

1. Define *stakeholders* and explain why they are important.
2. How is globalization changing communication in the workplace?
3. How does effective communication help employees interact with customers and colleagues in this age of technology?
4. How does internal communication differ from external communication?
5. In what directions can information travel within an organization's formal hierarchy?
6. What is the grapevine? Why should managers know how it works?
7. In which of the eight steps of the communication process do messages get encoded and decoded?
8. Why should communicators take an audience-centred approach to communication?
9. How does corporate culture affect the communication climate within an organization?
10. Define *ethics*. Explain the ethical responsibilities of communicators.

APPLY YOUR KNOWLEDGE

1. Why do you think good communication in an organization improves employees' attitudes and performance? Explain.

2. Under what circumstances might you want to limit the feedback you receive from an audience of readers or listeners? Explain.

3. Would written or spoken messages be more susceptible to noise? Why?

4. As a manager, how can you impress on your employees the importance of including both negative and positive information in messages?

5. **Ethical Choices** Because of your excellent communication skills, your supervisor always asks you to write his reports for him. When you overhear the CEO complimenting him on his logical organization and clear writing style, he responds as if he'd written all those reports himself. What kind of ethical choice does this represent? What can you do in this situation? Briefly explain your solution and your reasoning.

6. Search for the Canadian Centre for Ethics and Corporate Policy website and examine its resources section. How can these tools be used to help an organization create an ethical corporate culture? What can an individual employee do to influence a corporate culture that adopts ethical practices?

RUNNING CASES

> CASE 1 Noreen

Noreen is working toward a Bachelor of Business Administration (BBA) and takes her studies via distance education through a Canadian university. She works full time at Petro-Go, an international fuel company, in one of their call centres as a customer service representative (CSR). She is the team leader for a group of CSRs located in the "Go Points" program department. Her future career goal is to complete her BBA and obtain a senior management position within a large international firm.

Noreen is on the social committee, and her manager asks her to organize a potluck lunch for 40 employees in her call centre department.

QUESTIONS

a. Suggest an appropriate type of communication (for example, casual conversation, formal letter, meeting, memo, email, bulletin board notice) and briefly explain your choice.

b. Is this a horizontal flow or a downward flow of communication? Formal or informal?

c. What must Noreen consider when planning this event?

d. What must Noreen consider when communicating the plans?

e. What communication barriers might she encounter, and how should she overcome those barriers?

YOUR TASK

Assume that all the plans are arranged and now Noreen just needs to notify the guests. Write a memo that she will distribute to the 40 employees in her department. Ensure that the necessary details are in the invitation memo. Exchange memos with another student and ask for constructive criticism on how to improve your communication.

> CASE 2 Kwong

Kwong, a new Canadian, is enrolled in a three-year accounting co-op diploma program at a local college. He is currently in his third semester and will be placed in a co-op position next term. There he will apply what he has learned in his studies and at the same time gain valuable work experience. His future career goal is to complete the CGA (Certified General Accountant) requirements and then open his own accounting firm.

Kwong will be interviewed by a prospective co-op employer. He needs to be successful in the interview to obtain the placement.

QUESTIONS

a. What research should Kwong do before the interview?

b. Which employability skills do you think Kwong may currently possess, and which skills may he still need to develop? You can refer to Figure 1–2, or you can print out the Employability Skills 2000+ information from www.conferenceboard.ca/topics/education/learning-tools/employability-skills.aspx.

c. How will he emphasize his strong skills and de-emphasize his weaker skills during the interview?

d. What ethical choices may Kwong have to make?

e. What communication barriers may Kwong be faced with (both oral and written)? Give a specific example.

YOUR TASK

Make a list of the employability skills you believe you possess and employability skills you believe you need to improve. Now compare these to the Employability Skills 2000+ chart in Figure 1–2. What can you do to fill in the gaps? What resources do you have that could help you develop the missing skills?

PRACTISE YOUR KNOWLEDGE

Read the following document and then (1) analyze the strengths and weaknesses of each sentence and (2) revise the document so that it follows this chapter's guidelines.

It has come to my attention that many of you are lying on your time cards. If you come in late, you should not put 8:00 A.M. on your card. If you take a long lunch, you should not put 1:00 P.M. on your time card. I will not stand for this type of cheating. I simply have no choice but to institute a time-clock system. Beginning next Monday, all employees will have to punch in and punch out whenever they come and go from the work area.

The time clock will be right by the entrance to each work area, so you will have no excuse for not punching in. Anyone who is late for work or late coming back from lunch more than three times will have to answer to me. I don't care if you had to take a nap or if you girls had to shop. This is a place of business, and we do not want to be taken advantage of by slackers who are cheaters to boot.

It is too bad that a few bad apples always have to spoil things for everyone.

EXERCISES

1.1 Internal Communication: Planning the Flow

For these tasks, identify the necessary direction of communication (downward, upward, horizontal), suggest an appropriate type of communication (casual conversation, formal interview, meeting, workshop, videoconference, IM, newsletter, memo, bulletin board notice, and so on), and briefly explain your suggestion.

  a. As personnel manager, you want to announce details about this year's company picnic.
  b. As director of internal communication, you want to convince top management of the need for a company newsletter.
  c. As production manager, you want to make sure that both the sales manager and the finance manager receive your scheduling estimates.
  d. As marketing manager, you want to help employees understand the company's goals and its attitudes toward workers.

1.2 Communication Networks: Formal or Informal?

An old school friend suddenly phoned you to say, "I had to call you. You'd better keep this quiet, but when I heard my company was buying you guys out, I was shocked. I had no idea that a company as large as yours could sink so fast. Your group must be in pretty bad shape over there!" Your stomach suddenly turned queasy, and you felt a chill go up your spine. You'd heard nothing about any buyout, and before you could even get your friend off the phone, you were wondering what you should do. Choose one course of action and briefly explain your choice.

  a. Contact your CEO directly and relate what you've heard.
  b. Ask co-workers whether they've heard anything about a buyout.
  c. Discuss the phone call confidentially with your immediate supervisor.
  d. Keep quiet (there's nothing you can do about the situation anyway).

1.3 Ethical Choices: Business Dilemmas

In less than a page, explain why you think each of the following is or is not ethical.

  a. Keeping quiet about a possible environmental hazard you've just discovered in your company's processing plant.
  b. Overselling the benefits of instant messaging to your company's management; they never seem to understand the benefits of technology, so you believe that stretching the truth just a bit is the only way to convince them to make the right choice.
  c. Telling an associate and close friend that she'd better pay more attention to her work responsibilities or management will fire her.
  d. Recommending the purchase of unnecessary equipment to use up your allocated funds before the end of the fiscal year, so your budget won't be cut next year.

1.4 The Changing Workplace: Personal Expression at Work

Blogging has become a popular way for employees to communicate with customers and other parties outside the company. In some cases, employee blogs have been beneficial both for companies and their customers by providing helpful information and "putting a human face" on formal and imposing corporations. However, in some other cases, employees have been fired for posting information that their employers said was inappropriate. One particular area of concern is criticism of the company or individual managers. Should employees be allowed to criticize their employers in a public forum such as a blog? In a brief email message, argue for or against company policies that prohibit any critical information in employee blogs.

1.5 Internet: Codes of Ethics

Industry Canada prepares reports for consumers, researchers, and businesspeople. Visit Industry Canada's website and review its report *Voluntary Codes: A Guide for Their Development and Use* at www.ic.gc.ca/eic/site/oca-bc.nsf/eng/ca00863.html (you can download the PDF version). Read the section titled "Features of Voluntary Codes." Next, find a Canadian corporation (other than BCE) that has a code of ethics posted on the Internet. Does the code of ethics you found follow the features? Write two or three paragraphs describing the extent to which the code you found follows the features, and describe how it can be improved. Submit your essay to your instructor.

1.6 Communication Process: Know Your Audience

Top management has asked you to speak at an upcoming executive meeting to present your arguments for a more open communication climate. Which of the following would be most important for you to know about your audience before giving your presentation? Briefly explain your choice.

a. How many top managers will be attending?
b. What management style members of your audience prefer?
c. How firmly these managers are set in their ways?

1.7 Ethical Choices: The Go-Between

Your boss often uses you as a sounding board for her ideas. Now she seems to want you to act as an unofficial messenger, passing her ideas along to the staff without mentioning her involvement and informing her of what staff members say without telling them you're going to repeat their responses. What questions should you ask yourself as you consider the ethical implications of this situation? Write a short paragraph explaining the ethical choice you will make in this situation.

1.8 Communication Etiquette: Training for All?

Potential customers frequently visit your production facility before making purchase decisions. You and the people who report to you in the sales department have received extensive training in etiquette issues because you deal with high-profile clients so frequently. However, the rest of the workforce has not received such training, and you worry that someone might inadvertently say or do something that would offend a potential customer. In a two-paragraph email, explain to the general manager why you think anyone who might come in contact with customers should receive basic etiquette training.

1.9 Teamwork: Know Your Audience

Your boss has asked your work group to research and report on corporate child-care facilities. Of course, you'll want to know who (besides your boss) will read your report. Working with two team members, list four or five other factors you'll want to know about the situation and about your audience before starting your research. Briefly explain why the items on your list are important.

1.10 Communication Process: Analyzing Miscommunication

Use the eight steps of the communication process to analyze a miscommunication you've recently had with a co-worker, supervisor, classmate, teacher, friend, or family member. What idea were you trying to share? How did you encode and transmit it? Did the receiver get the message? Did the receiver correctly decode the message? How do you know? Based on your analysis, identify and explain the barriers that prevented your successful communication in this instance.

1.11 Ethical Choices: Withholding Information

You've been given the critical assignment of selecting the site for your company's new plant. After months of negotiations with landowners, numerous cost calculations, and investments in ecological, social, and community impact studies, you are about to recommend building the new plant on the Lansing River site. Now, just 15 minutes before your big presentation to top management, you discover a possible mistake in your calculations: site-purchase costs appear to be $50 000 more than you calculated, nearly 10 percent over budget. You don't have time to recheck all your figures, so you're tempted to just go ahead with your recommendation and ignore any discrepancies. You're worried that management won't approve this purchase if you can't present a clean, unqualified solution. You also know that many projects run over their original estimates, so you can probably work the extra cost into the budget later. On your way to the meeting room, you make your final decision. In a few paragraphs, explain the decision you made.

1.12 Communication Etiquette: Different Styles

In group meetings, some of your colleagues have a habit of interrupting and arguing with the speaker, taking credit for ideas that aren't theirs, and criticizing ideas they don't agree with. You're the newest person in the group and not sure if this is accepted behaviour in this company, but it concerns you both personally and professionally. Should you adopt their behaviour or stick with your own communication style, even though your quiet, respectful approach might limit your career potential? In two paragraphs, explain the pros and cons of both approaches.

Communicating in Teams and Mastering Listening and Nonverbal Communication

LEARNING OBJECTIVES   After studying this chapter, you will be able to

1 Explain the advantages and disadvantages of working in teams, including the characteristics of high-performing teams

2 Explain how group dynamics can affect team effectiveness

3 Outline an effective approach to team communication

4 Explain the benefits of collaboration technologies

5 Describe the key steps needed to ensure productive meetings

6 Describe the listening process, and explain how good listeners use active listening to overcome barriers at each stage of the process

7 Clarify the importance of nonverbal communication, and list six categories of nonverbal expression

MyLab Business Communication   Visit MyLab Business Communication to access a variety of online resources directly related to this chapter's content.

ON THE JOB: COMMUNICATING AT ROYAL BANK OF CANADA

Steve Smith/Getty Images

Recognized as one of the best workplaces in Canada, Royal Bank helps its employees succeed in their jobs by encouraging teamwork and free-flowing communication throughout the organization.

Taking Charge of Business through Teamwork

www.rbcroyalbank.com

Guided by the principle of "working together to succeed," Royal Bank of Canada was recognized in 2016 as one of the best workplaces in Canada by the Great Place to Work® Institute and the *Globe and Mail* for the eighth year in a row. With 74 000 employees serving more than 16 million personal, business, and public sector clients, Royal Bank counts on teamwork to keep staff productive and satisfied.

Team skills are essential for a job at Royal Bank. An entry-level sales and service representative position seeks "teamwork, cooperation skills, and listening skills." A business analyst/developer must "effectively communicate and build rapport with team members, stakeholders, and business partners" and "facilitate small- to medium-sized group meetings." A technical systems analyst "facilitates small- to large-group meetings for technical design, decision making, problem solving, and task implementation," among other duties.

Teamwork is an essential component of "flex-time" and "flex-place" arrangements enjoyed by some 30 percent of Royal Bank employees who work in the 1200+ Royal Bank branches across Canada or in one of 30 global offices. Flexible work is characterized by reduced or varied hours, job sharing, a modified workweek, or working off-site from home or a satellite office. For example, four employees at Royal Bank's main Halifax branch coordinated schedules, giving each person a long weekend every two weeks. By learning each other's duties and working the occasional longer day, someone is always available to serve clients. Digital tools play their part, with blogs, intranets, e-newsletters, and online meeting technologies easing the flow of communication. Executives believe teamwork helps employees perform better, have more energy, and maintain a better life outside their jobs when they have more control over their time. A new hiring program for Canadian Forces personnel recognizes the special skills of reservists, including leadership, the ability to handle large projects, and working as a team member.

Teams are an essential part of Royal Bank's culture. If you were a Royal Bank manager, how would you develop effective teams? What would you need to know about getting team members to collaborate? And how could you help your team members improve their listening and meeting skills?[1]

Improving Your Performance in Teams

Your job goal may not be to work at a bank or other financial institution, but chances are quite good that your career will involve working in teams and other group situations that will put your communication skills to the test. A **team** is a unit of two or more people who share a mission and the responsibility for working to achieve their goal.[2] Companies can create *formal teams,* such as human resources or information technology (IT) teams, that are part of the organization's structure, or they can establish *informal teams* that aren't part of the formal organization but are created to solve particular problems, work on specific activities, or encourage employee participation.

Teams are often at the core of **participative management**, the effort to involve employees in the company's decision-making processes.

Team members have a shared mission and are collectively responsible for their work.

TYPES OF TEAMS

The type, structure, and composition of individual teams vary within an organization. Some teams stay together for years; others may meet their goals in just a few days and then disband.

Cross-functional teams bring together people from different areas—IT, sales, and manufacturing, for example—to create a new product or long-term organizational strategy, or to combine their talents on some other assignment. Sometimes as many as eight or more specialties may join a cross-functional team. Cross-functional teams tend to be more innovative when they develop a strong "superordinate identity," meaning that the members identify more with the team and its purpose than with their respective functional areas.[3]

Self-managed or self-directed teams often involve cross-functional teams, with each team member bringing a skill set to be able to make informed decisions, complete certain tasks, or provide services to customers. Companies that implement self-managed teams confirm that their employees experience higher job satisfaction, take ownership of the project or tasks, and are more committed to its outcome. However, self-managed teams don't necessarily work well in every situation or company. Success is very much dependent on whether the culture of the organization supports the decisions made by these teams.

Quality assurance teams ensure that products and services meet prescribed standards. Typically composed of specialists in a single field, these groups may test automobiles to confirm that they run problem-free before leaving the factory floor or test food products to ensure that they meet safety standards.

Task forces are informal teams that assemble to resolve specific issues and disband once their goal has been accomplished. Similar to cross-functional teams,

Some popular types of informal teams are cross-functional teams, quality assurance teams, and task forces. These can operate in face-to-face settings or through virtual platforms.

task forces often include representatives from many departments, so that those who have a stake in the outcome are allowed to provide input. One function of task forces is finding areas where savings can be made. For example, a hospital may bring together people from different departments, such as surgery, nursing, finance, and administration, to find ways to reduce supply costs.[4]

Committees are formal teams that usually have a long lifespan and can become a permanent part of the organizational structure. Committees typically deal with regularly recurring tasks. For example, an executive committee may meet monthly to plan strategy and review results, and a grievance committee may be formed as a permanent resource for handling employee complaints and concerns.

Being a team member often requires taking on additional responsibility for communication: sharing information with team members, listening carefully to their input, and crafting messages that reflect the team's collective ideas and opinions.

Virtual teams allow members to connect from remote locations using a variety of meeting technologies (see "Using Meeting Technologies" later in the chapter). While technology helps make the "space" in which virtual meetings occur easier, the success rate of these teams is very much dependent on the type of membership (including size), leadership, and process.[5]

ADVANTAGES AND DISADVANTAGES OF TEAMS

Teams can play a vital role in helping an organization reach its goals, but they are not appropriate for every situation—and even when they are appropriate, companies need to weigh both the advantages and the disadvantages of a team-based approach. High performing teams can provide a number of advantages:[6]

- **Increased information and knowledge.** By pooling the resources of individuals both internal and external to the team, members have access to more information in the decision-making process.
- **Increased diversity of views.** Team members bring a variety of perspectives, and given equal time and recognition, these differences can generate constructive dialogue and increase opportunities for creativity and innovation.[7]
- **Increased acceptance of a solution.** Those who participate in making a decision are more likely to support it and encourage others to accept it. Because they share in the final product, they are committed to seeing it succeed. This also contributes to job satisfaction when teams achieve their targets.
- **Higher performance levels.** Working in teams can unleash new amounts of creativity and energy in workers who share a sense of purpose and mutual accountability. Effective teams can be better than top-performing individuals at solving complex problems, increasing productivity, and reducing costs. Working in tandem, small task forces can also achieve objectives faster.[8]

Although teamwork has many advantages, it also has a number of potential disadvantages. At their worst, teams are unproductive and frustrating, and they waste everyone's time. Some may actually be counterproductive and arrive at poor decisions due to time pressures, different levels of commitment, or lack of mutual respect among members or lack of shared vision. Teams need to be aware of and work to counter the following disadvantages:

- **Groupthink.** Like all social structures, business teams can generate tremendous pressures to conform to accepted norms of behaviour. **Groupthink** occurs when these peer pressures cause individual team members to withhold contrary or unpopular opinions. Group members may be influenced by a dominant personality who controls the discussion, or the group may be working under a short deadline so that participants cannot explore all

---

Effective communication is essential to every aspect of team performance.

1 LEARNING OBJECTIVE

Explain the advantages and disadvantages of working in teams, including the characteristics of high-performing teams.

Effective teams can pool knowledge, take advantage of diverse viewpoints, and increase acceptance of the solutions the team proposes.

Teams need to address the negative impact of groupthink, hidden agendas, free riders, and excessive costs.

the dimensions of their problem. The result can be decisions that are worse than ones the team members might have made individually.

- **Hidden agendas.** Some team members may have a **hidden agenda—** private, counterproductive motives, such as a desire to take control of the group, to undermine someone else on the team, or to pursue a business goal that runs counter to the team's mission. Others may withdraw or refuse to contribute altogether. Each person's hidden agenda can detract from the team's effectiveness.
- **Free riders.** Free riders, or "social loafers," are team members who don't contribute their fair share to the group's activities. Perhaps these members aren't being held individually accountable for their work. Or perhaps they don't believe they'll receive adequate recognition for their individual efforts. The free-ride attitude can lead to certain tasks remaining unfulfilled and damage team performance and morale.
- **Cost.** Coordinating group activities, aligning schedules, arranging meetings, and coordinating individual parts of a project can consume time, energy, and money. Furthermore, missed objectives can affect the availability of resources for future initiatives and confidence in similar decisions.

In many of Canada's businesses, such as Royal Bank, employees voluntarily band together to raise funds for charitable causes. Are the dynamics of voluntary teams similar to those of management-imposed teams? How are they different?

CHARACTERISTICS OF HIGH PERFORMING TEAMS

Whether team members are physically dispersed or sharing the same office space, the most effective teams have a common purpose with measurable milestones, trust in each other, and support for open dialogue to encourage creativity and reach consensus. They know how to hold members accountable, manage conflict to their advantage, and recover when challenges arise.[9] They act responsibly toward their colleagues, their organization, and society. In addition, group size and makeup (e.g., skill set, background, etc.), the various roles that team members play, their engagement with and commitment to the team, and leadership styles allow a team to focus on their work and not get bogged down in conflict or waste time and resources pursuing unclear goals. Research has shown that two of the most common reasons for underperforming teams are lack of trust and poor communication between members. A lack of trust can result from team members being suspicious of one another's motives or an unwillingness to contribute in a positive way.[10] While the achievement of agreed-upon milestones is important, attention to team members' "socioemotional" needs can contribute significantly to team performance levels. Facilitation of equal participation, recognition of member contributions, and the availability of support and training have been shown to be a significant predictor of a team's potential for success.[11]

GROUP DYNAMICS

The interactions and processes that take place between the members of a team are called **group dynamics**. Some teams are more effective than others simply because the dynamics of the group facilitate member input and the resolution of differences. To keep the process moving forward, productive teams also tend to develop rules that are conducive to business. Some of these rules are formal, such as reporting hierarchies. Others are unstated, informal standards that become group norms or "ways of being." Group dynamics are affected by several factors: the roles that team members assume, the current phase of team development, the team's success in resolving conflict, the team's success in overcoming resistance, and the type of leadership and organizational support the team receives.

ASSUMING TEAM ROLES   Members of a team can play various roles, which fall into three categories (see Table 2–1). Members who assume **self-oriented roles**

2   LEARNING OBJECTIVE

Explain how group dynamics can affect team effectiveness.

Group dynamics are the interactions and processes that take place in a team.

Each member of a group plays a role that affects the outcome of the group's activities.

Table 2–1	**Team Roles People Play**	
Dysfunctional	**Functional**	
Self-Oriented Roles	**Team-Maintenance Roles**	**Task-Facilitating Roles**
Controlling: Dominating others by exhibiting superiority or authority	**Encouraging:** Drawing out other members by showing verbal and nonverbal support, praise, or agreement	**Initiating:** Getting the team started on a line of inquiry
Withdrawing: Retiring from the team either by becoming silent or by refusing to deal with a particular aspect of the team's work	**Harmonizing:** Reconciling differences among team members through mediation or by using humour to relieve tension	**Information giving or seeking:** Offering (or seeking) information relevant to questions facing the team, including from external sources
Attention seeking: Calling attention to oneself and demanding recognition from others	**Compromising:** Offering to yield on a point in the interest of reaching a mutually acceptable decision	**Coordinating:** Showing relationships among ideas, clarifying issues, and summarizing what the team has done
Diverting: Focusing the team's discussion on topics of interest to the individual rather than on those relevant to the task		**Procedure setting:** Suggesting decision-making procedures or ground rules that will move the team toward a goal

Teams composed of multiple superstars may not perform as well as one might expect because high-performing individuals can have trouble putting the team's needs ahead of their own.

are motivated mainly to fulfill personal needs, so they tend to be less productive than other members. The most effective teams encourage their members to address these types of behaviours early on and facilitate an environment in which mutual respect and accountability are given high importance. Surprisingly, "dream teams" composed of multiple superstars often don't perform as well as one might expect because high-performing individuals can have trouble putting the team's needs ahead of their own.[12] In addition, highly skilled and experienced people with difficult personalities might not contribute as they could for the simple reason that other team members may avoid interacting with them.[13] Far more likely to contribute to team goals are those members who assume **team-maintenance roles** to help everyone work well together, and those who assume **task-facilitating roles** to help the team reach its goals.[14]

Roles can also change over time. For instance, in a self-directed team with no formal leader, someone may assume a task-oriented leadership role early in the team's evolution. If this person doesn't prove to be a capable leader, someone else may emerge as a leader as the group searches for more effective direction.[15]

Teams typically evolve through five phases: a common model of this growth includes orientation, conflict, brainstorming, emergence, and reinforcement.

ALLOWING FOR TEAM EVOLUTION Teams typically evolve through a number of phases on their way to becoming productive (see Figure 2–1). A variety of models have been proposed to describe the evolution toward becoming a productive team. The following model identifies the phases a problem-solving team goes through as it evolves:[16]

1. Orientation. Team members socialize, establish their roles, and begin to define their task or purpose. Team-building exercises and activities can help teams

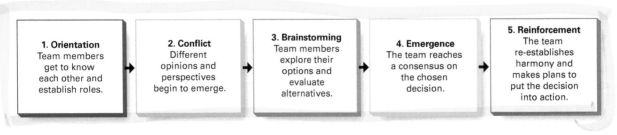

1. Orientation Team members get to know each other and establish roles. → **2. Conflict** Different opinions and perspectives begin to emerge. → **3. Brainstorming** Team members explore their options and evaluate alternatives. → **4. Emergence** The team reaches a consensus on the chosen decision. → **5. Reinforcement** The team re-establishes harmony and makes plans to put the decision into action.

Figure 2–1 Phases of Group Development

Adapted from B. Aubrey Fisher, *Small Group Decision Making: Communication and the Group Process*, 2nd ed. (New York: McGraw-Hill, 1980), 145–149; Robbins and De Cenzo, *Fundamentals of Management*, 334–335; Richard L. Daft, *Management*, 6th ed. (Cincinnati: Thomson South-Western, 2003), 602–603.

break down barriers and help members become acquainted and build trust. Initial ground rules are established.[17] For geographically dispersed virtual teams, creating a "team operating agreement" that sets expectations for online meetings, communication processes, and decision making can help address the disadvantages of distance.[18]

2. **Conflict.** Team members begin to discuss their positions and become more assertive in establishing their roles. If you and the other members have been carefully selected to represent a variety of viewpoints and expertise, disagreements are a natural part of this phase. Conflict, when properly managed, can be a positive force because it helps the group to clarify both the ideas and the processes for reaching their decisions. Conflict also works against the danger of groupthink.[19]

3. **Brainstorming.** Team members air all the options and discuss the pros and cons fully. At the end of this phase, members begin to settle on a single solution to the problem. It's important to avoid judging ideas during brainstorming, so people feel free to contribute all their thoughts, rather than limiting them to ones they believe will win approval. Note that while group brainstorming remains a highly popular activity in today's companies, it may not always be the most productive way to generate new ideas. Some research indicates that having people brainstorm individually and then bring their ideas to a group meeting is more successful.[20]

4. **Emergence.** Consensus is reached when the team finds a solution that is acceptable enough for all members to support (even if they have reservations). Consensus happens only after all members have had an opportunity to communicate their positions and feel that they have been listened to.

5. **Reinforcement.** The team clarifies and summarizes the agreed-upon solution. Members receive their assignments for carrying out the group's decision, and they make arrangements for following up on those assignments. The development of a contingency plan is important to save time and energy, especially when conditions on which the team operates change.

You may also hear the process defined as *forming, storming, norming,* and *performing*, the phases identified by researcher Bruce Tuckman when he proposed one of the earliest models of group development.[21] Additions to the model have been advocated, outlining the importance of a transition or "lessons learned" phase. This is sometimes referred to as *adjourning*. Here, team members are able to capture information on what worked well and what would need to be improved upon in future situations. They also acknowledge and celebrate their accomplishments. Note that these phases are a general framework for team development. Some teams may move forward and backward through several stages before they become productive, and other teams may be productive right away, even while some or all members are in a state of conflict.[22]

RESOLVING CONFLICT Conflict is a natural part of any team experience, and can arise for any number of reasons. Team members may believe that they need to compete for money, information, or other resources. Or members may disagree about who is responsible for a specific task; this disagreement is usually the result of poorly defined responsibilities and job boundaries. Various members can also bring ideas that are equally good but incompatible, such as two different

Christopher Bissell/The Image Bank/Getty Images

Conflict is an inevitable part of working in teams, but an effective team knows how to keep destructive conflict from distracting the team from its objectives. How have you managed team conflict when preparing assignments with other students? In your opinion, what is the most important factor to lessen conflict?

solutions to a given problem. Also, poor communication can lead to misunderstandings about other team members, and intentionally withholding information can undermine trust. Basic differences in values, attitudes, and personalities may lead to arguments. Power struggles may result when one member questions the authority of another or when people or teams with limited authority attempt to increase their power or exert more influence. Conflict can also arise because individuals or teams are pursuing different goals.[23]

Conflict can be both constructive and destructive to a team's effectiveness. Conflict is constructive if it forces important issues into the open, increases the involvement of team members, and generates creative ideas for the solution to a problem. Constructive conflict can prod teams to higher performance, in fact. Teamwork isn't necessarily about happiness and harmony; even teams that have some interpersonal friction can excel with effective leadership and team players committed to strong results. As teamwork experts Andy Boynton and Bill Fischer put it, "Virtuoso teams are not about getting polite results."[24]

In contrast, conflict is destructive if it diverts energy from more important issues, destroys morale, or polarizes or divides the team.[25] Destructive conflict can lead to win–lose or lose–lose outcomes, in which one or both sides lose, to the detriment of the entire team. If you approach conflict with the idea that both sides can satisfy their goals to at least some extent (a *win–win strategy*), no one loses. However, for the win–win strategy to work, everybody must believe that (1) it's possible to find a solution that both parties can accept, (2) cooperation is better for the organization than competition, (3) the other party can be trusted, and (4) greater power or status doesn't entitle one party to impose a solution. Often members will take on a leadership role and help the team navigate the resolution process.

Here are seven measures that can help team members successfully resolve conflict:

1. **Proaction.** Deal with minor conflict before it becomes major conflict.
2. **Communication.** Get those directly involved in the conflict to participate in resolving it. Provide support or training if they are not skilled in effective listening techniques.
3. **Openness.** Get feelings out in the open before dealing with the main issues.
4. **Research.** Seek factual reasons for the problem before seeking solutions.
5. **Flexibility.** Don't let anyone lock into a position before considering other solutions.
6. **Fair play.** Don't let anyone avoid a fair solution by hiding behind the rules.
7. **Alliance.** Get opponents to fight together for a common goal instead of against each other.

OVERCOMING RESISTANCE One particular type of conflict that can affect team progress is resistance to change. Sometimes this resistance is clearly irrational, such as when people resist any kind of change, whether it makes sense or not. Sometimes, however, resistance is perfectly logical. A change may require someone to relinquish authority or give up comfortable ways of doing things. If someone is resisting change, you can be persuasive with calm, reasonable communication:

- **Express understanding.** Most people are ashamed of reacting emotionally in business situations. Show that you sympathize. You might say, "I can understand that this change might be difficult, and if I were in your position, I might be reluctant myself." Help the other person relax and talk about his or her anxiety, so you have a chance to offer reassurance.[26]
- **Make people aware of their resistance.** When people are noncommittal and silent, they may be tuning you out without even knowing why. Continuing with your argument is futile. Deal directly with the resistance without accusing. You might say, "You seem to have reservations about this idea.

Conflict in teams can be either constructive or destructive.

Different leadership styles can escalate or help to effectively manage conflicts within a team.

When you encounter resistance or hostility, maintain your composure and address the other person's emotional needs.

Have I made some faulty assumptions?" Such questions force people to face and define their resistance.[27]

- **Evaluate others' objections fairly.** Use **active listening** to focus on what the other person is expressing, both in words and in feelings. Get the person to open up, so that you can understand the basis for the resistance. The objections of others may raise legitimate points or problems that you'll want to address.[28]

- **Hold your arguments until the other person is ready for them.** Getting your point across depends as much on the other person's frame of mind as it does on your arguments. You can't assume that a strong argument will speak for itself. By becoming more audience centred, you will learn to address the other person's emotional needs first.

Active listening lets the speaker feel that others are interested in what he or she has to say and helps to bring out issues that may otherwise be hidden.

Collaborating on Communication Efforts

You should expect to collaborate on a wide variety of research, writing, design, and presentation projects in your career. When teams collaborate, the collective energy and expertise of the various members can lead to results that transcend what each individual could do otherwise.[29] However, collaborating on team messages requires special effort; the following section offers a number of helpful guidelines.

GUIDELINES FOR COLLABORATIVE WRITING

In any collaborative effort, it's important to recognize that team members coming from different backgrounds may have different work habits or priorities: a technical expert may focus on accuracy and scientific standards; an editor may be more concerned about organization and coherence; and a manager may focus on schedules, cost, and corporate goals. In addition, team members will differ in writing styles, work habits, and personality traits—factors that can complicate the creative nature of communication.

To collaborate effectively, everyone involved must be flexible and open to other opinions, focusing on team objectives rather than on individual priorities.[30] Successful writers know that most ideas can be expressed in many ways, so they avoid the "my way is best" attitude. The following guidelines will help you collaborate more successfully on team messages:[31]

3 LEARNING OBJECTIVE

Outline an effective approach to team communication.

Successful collaboration requires a number of steps, from selecting the right partners and agreeing on project goals to establishing clear processes and avoiding writing as a group.

- **Select collaborators carefully.** Whenever possible, choose a combination of people who have the experience, information, and talent needed for each project. Group size is also important to ensure an efficient turnaround.

- **Agree on project goals before you start.** Starting without a clear idea of where you hope to finish inevitably leads to frustration and wasted time.

- **Give your team time to bond before diving in.** If people haven't had the opportunity to work together before, make sure they can get to know each other before being asked to collaborate. Provide an opportunity for members to build trust through a team-building exercise or social activity.

- **Clarify individual responsibilities.** Because members will depend on each other, make sure individual responsibilities are clear.

- **Establish clear processes.** Make sure everyone knows how the work will be done, including checkpoints and decisions made along the way. Agree to a process for handling conflicts.

- **Avoid writing as a group.** The actual composition is the only part of developing team messages that usually does not benefit from group participation. Group writing is often a slow, painful process that delivers bland results. Plan, research, and outline together, but assign the actual writing to one person. If you must divide and share the writing for scheduling reasons, try to have one person do a final review pass to ensure a consistent style.

- **Make sure tools and techniques are ready and compatible across the team.** Even minor details such as different versions of software can delay projects. If you plan to use technology for sharing or presenting materials, test the system before work begins.
- **Follow up along the way.** Don't assume everything is working just because you don't hear anything negative. Ask team members how they think the project is going and then fix any problems quickly so they don't derail the team's efforts.

TECHNOLOGIES FOR COLLABORATIVE WRITING

4 **LEARNING OBJECTIVE**

Explain the benefits of collaboration technologies.

A variety of collaboration tools exist to help teams write together. Among the simpler tools are group review and commenting features in word processors and the Adobe Acrobat electronic document system (PDF files) and web-based document systems such as Google Docs. More complex solutions include **content management systems** that organize and control the content for many websites (particularly larger corporate sites). A **wiki** (from the Hawaiian word for *quick*) is a website that allows anyone with access to add new material and edit existing material. Figure 2–2 shows ZOHO Projects, a collaborative project management app that helps team members work together in real time, with documents, decisions, messages, and other vital project elements accessible to everyone.

The benefits of wikis include simple operation and the ability to post new or revised material instantly, without a formal review process.

The key benefits of wikis include simple operation—writers don't need to know any of the techniques normally required to create web content—and the freedom to post new or revised material without prior approval. This approach is quite different from a content management system, in which both the organization of the website and the *workflow* (the rules for creating, editing, reviewing, and approving content) are tightly controlled.[32] A content management system is a useful way to maintain consistent presentation on a company's primary public website, whereas wikis allow teams to collaborate with speed and flexibility.

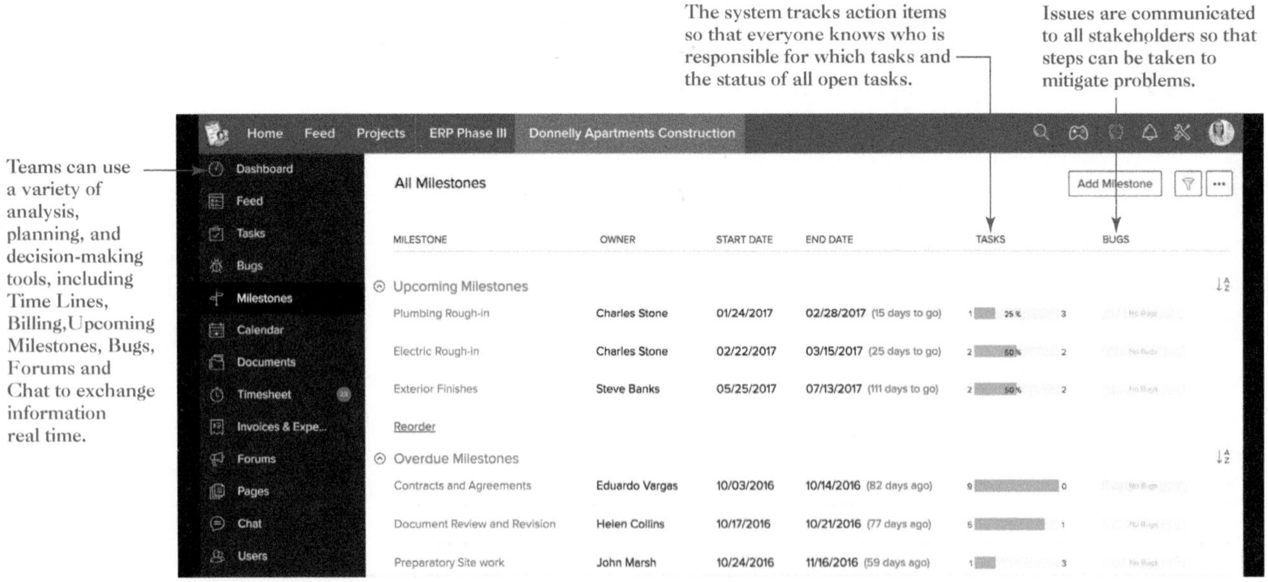

The system tracks action items so that everyone knows who is responsible for which tasks and the status of all open tasks.

Issues are communicated to all stakeholders so that steps can be taken to mitigate problems.

Teams can use a variety of analysis, planning, and decision-making tools, including Time Lines, Billing, Upcoming Milestones, Bugs, Forums and Chat to exchange information real time.

Figure 2–2 ZOHO Projects: An Online Collaborative App

Courtesy of ZOHO.

Team members can exchange information in real time regarding project changes, action items, or any other decisions or questions.

Various aspects of project deliverables can be tracked.

Figure 2–3 An Enterprise Shared Workspace
Use with the permission of Samepage Labs Inc.

Enterprise wiki systems extend the wiki concept with additional features for business use that ensure information quality and confidentiality without losing the speed and flexibility of a wiki. For instance, *access control* lets a team leader identify who is allowed to read and modify the wiki. *Change monitoring* alerts team members when significant changes or additions are made. And *rollback* allows a team to "travel back in time" to see all previous versions of pages.[33]

Groupware is a general term for computer-based systems that let people communicate, share files, review previous message threads, work on documents simultaneously, and connect using social networking tools. These systems help companies capture and share knowledge from multiple experts, bringing greater insights to bear on tough challenges.[34] **Shared workspaces** are online "virtual offices" that give everyone on a team access to the same set of resources and information: databases, calendars, project plans, pertinent instant messaging (IM) and email exchanges, shared reference materials, and team-created documents. Figure 2–3 shows SamePage, an enterprise shared workspace that facilitates collaboration, communication, and knowledge sharing among employees.

Cloud computing has significantly changed the way information can be shared and retrieved. Team members, whether geographically dispersed or in the next cubicle, can collaborate using online software applications and digital storage space.

SOCIAL NETWORKS AND VIRTUAL COMMUNITIES

We have seen that social media and the Web 2.0 approach are revolutionizing business communication. Within that context, **social networking technologies** are redefining teamwork and team communication by helping erase the constraints of geographic and organization boundaries. In addition to enabling and enhancing teamwork, social networks have numerous other business applications and benefits; see Table 7–1 for more information.

Social networking technologies are becoming vital communication links in many companies.

The two fundamental elements of any social networking technology are *profiles* (the information stored about each member of the network) and *connections* (mechanisms for finding and communicating with other members).[35] If you have a Facebook account, you have a basic idea of how social networks function. Thousands of companies now use Facebook, but you may also encounter networks created specifically for business use, the most significant being LinkedIn (www.linkedin.com). Others are Ryze (www.ryze.com) and XING (www.xing.com).

Some companies use social networking technologies to form *virtual communities* or *communities of practice* that link employees with similar professional interests throughout the company and sometimes with customers and suppliers as

A *community of practice* links professionals with similar job interests; a key benefit is accumulating long-term organizational knowledge.

well. The huge advantage that social networking brings to these team efforts is in identifying the best people to collaborate on each problem or project, no matter where they are around the world or what their official roles are in the organization. Such communities are similar to teams in many respects, but one major difference is in the responsibility for accumulating organizational knowledge over the long term. For example, the pharmaceutical company Pfizer has a number of permanent product safety communities that provide specialized advice on drug safety issues to researchers across the company.[36]

Social networking can also help a company maintain a sense of community even as it grows beyond the size that normally permits a lot of daily interaction. At the online retailer Zappos, fostering a supportive work environment is the company's top priority. To encourage the sense of community among its expanding workforce, Zappos uses social networking tools to track employee connections and encourage workers to reach out and build relationships.[37]

Making Your Meetings More Productive

Much of your workplace communication will occur during in-person or online meetings, so to a large degree, your ability to contribute to the company—and to be recognized for your contributions—will depend on your meeting skills. Well-run meetings can help companies solve problems, develop ideas, and identify opportunities. Meetings can also be a great way to promote team building through the experience of social interaction.[38] As useful as meetings can be, though, they can be a waste of time if they aren't planned and managed well. You can help ensure productive meetings by preparing carefully, conducting meetings efficiently, and using meeting technologies wisely. A checklist—Improving Face-to-Face and Virtual Meeting Productivity—is included later in the chapter.

Much of the communication you'll participate in will take place in meetings.

PREPARING FOR MEETINGS

The first step in preparing for a meeting is to make sure the meeting is really necessary. Meetings can consume hundreds or thousands of dollars of productive time while taking people away from other work, so don't hold a meeting if some other form of communication (such as a blog post) can serve the purpose as effectively.[39] If a meeting is truly necessary, proceed with these four planning tasks:

To ensure a successful meeting, decide on your purpose ahead of time, select the right participants, choose the time and facility carefully, and set a clear agenda.

1. **Clarify your purpose.** Although many meetings combine purposes, most focus on one of two types. *Informational meetings* involve sharing information and perhaps coordinating action. *Decision-making meetings* involve persuasion, analysis, and problem solving. Whatever your purpose, make sure it is clear and clearly communicated to all participants.
2. **Select participants for the meeting.** With a clear purpose in mind, it's easier to identify the right participants. If the session is purely informational and one person will do most of the talking, you can invite a large group. For problem-solving and decision-making meetings, invite only those people who are in a direct position to help the meeting reach its objective. The more participants, the more comments and confusion you're likely to get and the longer the meeting will take.
3. **Choose the venue and time.** Online or virtual meetings are often the best way and sometimes the only way to connect people in multiple locations or to reach large audiences. For onsite meetings, review the facility and the seating arrangements. Are rows of chairs suitable, or do you need a conference table or some other arrangement? Pay attention to room temperature, lighting,

ventilation, acoustics, and refreshments; these details can make or break a meeting. If you have control over the timing, morning meetings are often more productive because people are generally more alert and not yet engaged with the work of the day.

4. **Set the agenda.** The success of any meeting depends on the preparation of the participants. People who will be presenting information need to know what is expected of them; nonpresenters need to know what will be presented so they can prepare questions; and everyone needs to know how long the meeting will last. In addition, the agenda helps focus the meeting and is an important tool for guiding the progress of the meeting (see Figure 2–4). A productive agenda answers key questions:

An agenda, committee reports, and debate are all part of Canadian parliamentary procedure. Why is an established order important to both political and business meetings?

- What do we need to do in this meeting to accomplish our goals?
- What additional action should be taken prior to coming to the meeting (e.g., information to be gathered or material to be read)?
- What issues will be of greatest importance to all participants?
- What information must be available in order to discuss these issues?[40]

LEADING AND PARTICIPATING IN MEETINGS

Everyone in a meeting shares the responsibility for making the meeting productive. If you're the designated leader of a meeting, however, you have an extra degree of responsibility and accountability. The following guidelines will help leaders and participants contribute to more effective meetings:

- **Keep the discussion on track.** A good meeting draws out the best ideas and information the group has to offer. Good leaders encourage participants to share. Experience will help you recognize when to push the group forward and when to step back and let people talk. If the meeting lags, ask questions to encourage participation. Conversely, there will be times when you have no choice but to cut off discussion in order to stay on schedule.

Everyone shares the responsibility for successful meetings.

- **Follow agreed-upon rules.** Business meetings run the range from informal to extremely formal, complete with detailed rules for speaking, proposing new items to discuss, voting on proposals, using technology (e.g., phones), and so on. The larger the meeting, the more formal you'll need to be to maintain order. Formal meetings use parliamentary procedure, a time-tested method for planning and running effective meetings. The best-known guide to this procedure is *Robert's Rules of Order.* Check out the online "Survival Tips on Robert's Rules of Order" at www.roberts-rules.com/index.html to help you understand and use this system.
- **Encourage participation.** On occasion, some participants will be too quiet and others too talkative. The quiet participants might be shy; they might be expressing disagreement or resistance; or they might be answering email or texting. Draw them out by asking for their input on issues that particularly pertain to them. For the overly talkative, simply say that time is limited and others need to be heard from.
- **Participate actively.** If you're a meeting participant, contribute to both the subject of the meeting and the smooth interaction of the group. Speak up if you have something useful to say, but don't monopolize the discussion or talk simply to bring attention to yourself.

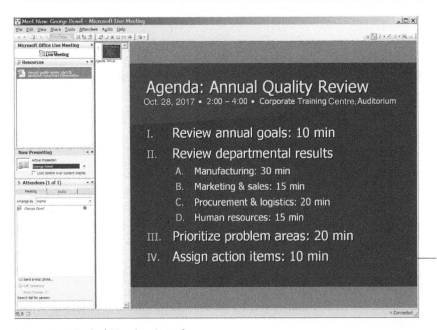

AGENDA

PLANNING COMMITTEE MEETING

Monday, October 28, 2017
10:00 A.M. to 11:00 A.M.

Executive Conference Room

Provides background information on the meeting, such as the main purpose, date, time, and location.

I. Call to Order

II. Roll Call

III. Approval of Agenda

IV. Approval of Minutes from Previous Meeting

V. Chairperson's Report on Site Selection Progress

VI. Subcommittee Reports	Person	Proposed Time
a. New Markets	Alan	5 minutes
b. New Products	Jennifer	5 minutes
c. Finance	Craig	5 minutes
VII. Old Business—Pricing Policy for New Products	Terry	10 minutes
VIII. New Business		
a. Carson and Canfield Data on New Product Sales	Sarah	10 minutes
b. Restructuring of Product Territories Due to New Product Introductions	Edith	10 minutes

IX. Announcements

X. Adjournment

Shows the order in which topics will be covered and allocates time for report-outs.

Agenda: Annual Quality Review
Oct. 28, 2017 • 2:00 – 4:00 • Corporate Training Centre, Auditorium

I. Review annual goals: 10 min

II. Review departmental results
 A. Manufacturing: 30 min
 B. Marketing & sales: 15 min
 C. Procurement & logistics: 20 min
 D. Human resources: 15 min

III. Prioritize problem areas: 20 min

IV. Assign action items: 10 min

Action items are assigned. These may be reviewed for achievement or progress at the next meeting.

Figure 2–4 Typical Meeting Agendas

• **Close effectively.** At the meeting's conclusion, verify that the objectives have been met, and arrange for follow-up work as needed. Summarize either the general conclusion of the discussion or the actions to be taken. Make sure all participants have a chance to clear up any misunderstandings. If appropriate, assign roles and issue an action plan to be reviewed during the next meeting.

To review the tasks that contribute to productive meetings, refer to "Checklist: Improving Face-to-Face and Virtual Meeting Productivity."

For formal meetings, it's good practice to appoint one person to record the *minutes*, a summary of the important information presented and the decisions made during a meeting. In smaller or informal meetings, attendees often make their own notes on their copies of the agenda. In either case, a clear record of the decisions made and the people responsible for follow-up action is essential.

If your company doesn't have a specific format for minutes, follow the generic format shown in Figure 2–5. The specific format of the minutes is less important than making sure you record all the key information, particularly regarding responsibilities that were assigned during the meeting. Key elements include a list of those present and a list of those who were invited but didn't attend, followed by the times the meeting started and ended, all major decisions reached at the meeting, all assignments of tasks to meeting participants, and all subjects that

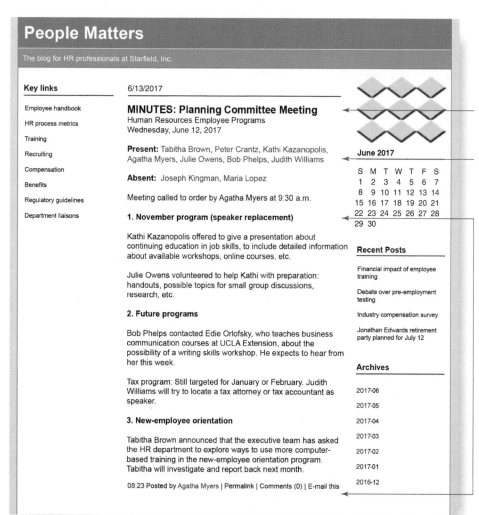

Figure 2–5 Typical Minutes of a Meeting

were deferred to a later meeting. In addition, the minutes objectively summarize important discussions, noting the names of those who contributed major points. Outlines, subheadings, and lists help organize the minutes, and additional documentation (such as tables or charts submitted by meeting participants) are noted in the minutes and attached. Whichever method you use, make sure that responsibilities are clear, so all issues raised at the meeting will be addressed. Many companies today use intranets and blog postings to distribute meeting minutes.

✓ Checklist Improving Face-to-Face and Virtual Meeting Productivity

A. Prepare.

- Determine the meeting's objectives.
- Work out an agenda that will achieve your objectives.
- Select participants.
- Determine the time and location, and reserve a room.
- If you are organizing a virtual meeting, use Coordinated Universal Time (UTC) to avoid confusion, and decide what type of technology you will use. Ensure that all participants have access to and know how to use the software.
- Arrange for light refreshments, if appropriate.
- Determine whether the lighting, ventilation, acoustics, and temperature of the room are adequate.
- Determine seating needs: chairs only or table and chairs.
- For virtual meetings, decide on the language to be used, and communicate ground rules for handling allocation of speaking time, interruptions, and multitasking.

B. Conduct.

- Begin and end the meeting on time. Ask participants to log in early for online meetings, and allow for some "small talk." This helps participants make connections and establish bonds.
- Control the meeting by following the announced agenda.
- Assign someone to capture the minutes, if necessary.
- Encourage full participation, and either confront or ignore those who seem to be working at cross-purposes with the group. Poll participants for agreement or questions.
- Sum up decisions, actions, and recommendations as you move through the agenda, and restate main points at the end. This is especially important for virtual meetings, where participants can lose focus and attention.

C. Follow Up.

- Distribute the meeting's notes or minutes on a timely basis.
- Take the agreed-upon follow-up action.
- If appropriate, schedule the next meeting's date, time and location, and set actions that need to be completed by then.

USING MEETING TECHNOLOGIES

Companies continue to look for innovative ways to promote communication and collaboration while reducing the cost and hassle of meetings.

A growing array of technologies enables professionals to enhance or even replace traditional meetings. Replacing in-person meetings with long-distance, virtual interaction can dramatically reduce costs and resource usage, reduce wear and tear on employees, and give teams access to a wider pool of expertise. Learn how to use these tools effectively and you'll become a more effective contributor and leader in all your meetings.

Meeting technologies have helped spur the emergence of **virtual teams**, whose members work in different locations and interact electronically through **virtual meetings**. IM and teleconferencing are the simplest forms of virtual meetings. Videoconferencing lets participants see and hear each other, demonstrate products, and transmit other visual information. *Telepresence* technologies (see Figure 2–6) enable realistic conferences in which participants thousands of kilometres apart almost seem to be in the same room.[41] The ability to convey nonverbal subtleties such as facial expressions and hand gestures makes these systems particularly good for negotiations, collaborative problem solving, and other complex discussions.[42]

The most sophisticated web-based meeting systems combine the best of real-time communication, shared workspaces, and video-conferencing with other tools, such as *virtual whiteboards*, that let teams collaborate in real time. Such systems are used for everything from spontaneous discussions among small groups to carefully planned, formal events such as customer training seminars or press conferences.[43]

Technology continues to create intriguing opportunities for online interaction. For example, one of the newest virtual tools is online brainstorming, in which a company can conduct "idea campaigns" to generate new ideas from people across the organization. These sessions range from small team meetings to huge events such as IBM's giant InnovationJam, in which 100 000 IBM employees, family members, and customers from 160 countries were invited to brainstorm online for three days.[44]

What are the differences between face-to-face meetings and online meetings? Can online always replace face-to-face?

Companies are also using virtual meetings and other communication activities in virtual worlds that include realistic-looking environments that represent offices and conference rooms. The Team Space system from Sococo (see Figure 2–6) mimics the layout of an office building, allowing users to click into offices, conference rooms, and other spaces to initiate virtual meetings and presentations, participate in phone and IM conferences, and share documents. In the otherworldly environment of Second Life (www.secondlife.com), professionals can create online *avatars* to represent themselves in meetings, training sessions, sales presentations, and even casual conversations with customers they happen to bump into.

The virtual environment is made up of offices, conference rooms, and other spaces where people can interact through IM chat, voice conferencing, and document sharing.

Informal meeting spaces can also be created, such as the "courtyard" shown here.

Colleagues are available at the click of a mouse.

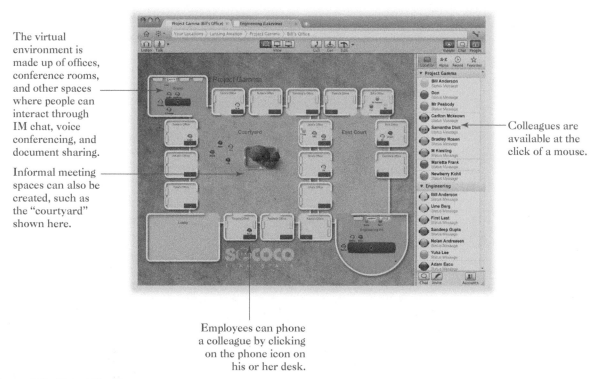

Employees can phone a colleague by clicking on the phone icon on his or her desk.

Figure 2–6 Virtual Meetings

Courtesy Sococo.

Conducting successful telephone or online meetings requires extra planning and more diligence during the meeting.

Conducting successful meetings over the phone or online requires extra planning before the meeting and more diligence during the meeting. Because virtual meetings offer less visual contact and nonverbal communication than in-person meetings, leaders need to make sure everyone stays engaged and has the opportunity to contribute. Paying attention during online meetings takes greater effort as well. Participants need to stay committed to the meeting and resist the temptation to work on unrelated tasks.[45]

Improving Your Listening Skills

Listening is one of the most important skills in the workplace.

Your long-term career prospects are closely tied to your ability and willingness to listen. Effective listening strengthens organizational relationships, alerts an organization to opportunities for innovation, and allows an organization to be aware of problems that can develop into serious image and reputation issues.[46] Some 80 percent of top executives say that listening is the most important skill needed to get things done in the workplace.[47] At Canadian Imperial Bank of Commerce, listening skills are considered a core competency for employees.[48] Throughout your own career, effective listening will give you a competitive edge, enhancing your performance and thus the influence you have within your company.

UNDERSTANDING THE LISTENING PROCESS

6 LEARNING OBJECTIVE

Describe the listening process, and explain how good listeners use active listening to overcome barriers at each stage of the process.

Listening involves five steps: receiving, decoding, remembering, evaluating, and responding.

Listening is a far more complex process than most people think, and most of us aren't very good at it. People listen at or below a 25 percent efficiency rate, remember only about half of what's said during a 10-minute conversation, and forget half of that within 48 hours.[49] Furthermore, when questioned about material we've just heard, we're likely to get the facts mixed up.[50]

Why is such a seemingly simple activity so difficult? The reason is that listening is not a simple process. To listen effectively, you need to successfully complete five separate steps:[51]

1. **Receiving.** You start by physically hearing the message and acknowledging it. Physical reception can be blocked by noise, impaired hearing, or inattention. Some experts also include nonverbal messages as part of this stage, since these factors influence the listening process as well.

2. **Decoding.** Your next step is to assign meaning to sounds, which you do according to your own values, beliefs, ideas, expectations, roles, needs, and personal history.

3. **Remembering.** Before you can act on the information, you need to store it for future processing. Incoming messages must first be captured in short-term memory, and then they are transferred to long-term memory for more permanent storage.

4. **Evaluating.** With the speaker's message captured, your next step is to evaluate it by applying critical thinking skills. Separate fact from opinion and evaluate the quality of the evidence. You should ask, Is the evidence credible? Why is it credible?

5. **Responding.** After you've evaluated the speaker's message, you react. If you're communicating one on one or in a small group, the initial response generally takes the form of verbal feedback. If you're one of many in an audience, your initial response may take the form of applause, laughter, or silence. Later on, you may act on what you have heard.

Good listeners actively overcome the barriers to successful listening.

If any one of these steps breaks down, the listening process becomes less effective or even fails entirely. As both a sender and a receiver, you can reduce the failure rate by recognizing and overcoming a variety of physical and mental barriers to effective listening.

Table 2–2	Recognizing Various Types of Listening[52]		
Type of Listening	**Emphasis Is On...**	**Do's**	**Don'ts**
Content Listening: Primary goal is to understand and retain the speaker's message.	Information gathering and understanding Retention of information	• Ask questions to clarify the material and probe for details. • Focus on the information and look for the main ideas and patterns. • Paraphrase what the speaker says	• Evaluate the speaker's style or presentation at this point. It does not matter whether you agree or disagree, only that you understand.
Critical Listening: Primary goal is to understand and evaluate the meaning of the speaker's message on several levels.	Evaluating the logic of the argument, strength of the evidence, and validity of the conclusion	• Analyze the implications of the message for you and your organization, and the speaker's intentions and motives. • Ask questions to explore different points of view and determine credibility.	• Overlook the reason for omitting certain points or information. • Be misled by bias or the package in which the information is presented. • Confuse opinions for facts.
Empathic Listening: Primary goal is to understand the speaker's feelings, needs, and wants to help the speaker vent the emotions that prevent a calm, clear-headed approach.	Appreciating the speaker's viewpoint, regardless of whether you share that perspective	• Let the speaker know that you appreciate his or her feelings and understand the situation. • Once you establish this connection, help the speaker move on to search for a solution.	• Offer advice unless the person specifically asks for it. • Judge the speaker's feelings or communicate that he or she should not feel a particular emotion.

RECOGNIZING AND UNDERSTANDING ACTIVE LISTENING

Understanding the nature of your listening during a conversation is the first step toward improving your listening skills. People listen in a variety of ways, and although how they listen is often an unconscious choice, it influences both what they hear and the meaning they extract. Refer to the major types of listening shown in Table 2–2, then reflect on your own inclination as a listener and consider how using active listening techniques could make your listening more effective.

To be a good listener, adapt the way you listen to suit the situation.

Active listening involves seeking to understand and interpret the real meaning behind someone's message. This means being nonjudgmental and, if possible, not interrupting the speaker. The idea is to try to consider the communication from the perspective of the speaker without interjecting one's own opinion. The listener has to focus completely on what the speaker is saying and avoid any distractions. Facial expressions, posture, and positioning of the arms should indicate that the listener is interested.

Although the listener may not entirely agree with what the speaker is saying, he or she can ask clarifying questions or paraphrase the message to reduce the possibility of misunderstandings. When it comes time to respond, the listener should avoid attacking the speaker or criticizing him or her. The listener's comments and body language should be open, treating the other person in the same manner he or she would like to be treated. In this way, active listening helps reduce potentially stressful and contentious situations, strengthens rapport and builds stronger relationships, and opens communication between parties.

Steve Gorton/Juice Images/Dorling Kindersley Limited

What type of listening is occurring in this picture? What listening skills must the listener apply in this situation?

OVERCOMING BARRIERS TO EFFECTIVE LISTENING

Your mind can process information much faster than most speakers talk.

Good listeners look for ways to overcome potential barriers throughout the listening process (see Table 2–3). You are unlikely to have control over some barriers to physical reception, such as conference room acoustics, poor cell-phone reception, or background music. However, you can certainly control other barriers, such as interrupting speakers or creating distractions that make it hard for others to pay attention. If you have questions for a speaker, wait until he or she has finished speaking. And don't think that you're not interrupting just because you're not talking. Texting, checking your watch, making eye contact with someone over the speaker's shoulder—these are just a few of the many nonverbal behaviours that can interrupt a speaker and hinder listening for everyone.

Selective listening is one of the most common barriers to effective listening. If your mind wanders, you often stay tuned out until you hear a word or phrase that gets your attention back. But by that time, you're unable to recall what the speaker *actually* said; instead, you remember what you *think* the speaker probably said.[53]

One reason listeners' minds tend to wander is that people think faster than they speak. Most people speak at about 120 to 150 words per minute, but listeners can process audio information at up to 500 words per minute or more.[54] Consequently, your brain has a lot of free time whenever you're listening, and if left unsupervised, it will find a thousand other things to think about. Rather than listening part time, make a conscious effort to focus on the speaker and use the extra time to analyze what you hear, prepare questions you might need to ask, and engage in other relevant thinking.

Overcoming such interpretation barriers can be difficult because you might not even be aware of them. Selective perception leads listeners to mould a message to fit their own conceptual frameworks. Listeners sometimes prejudge; that is, they make up their minds before fully hearing the speaker's message, or they engage in **defensive listening**—protecting their self-image by tuning out anything that doesn't confirm their view of themselves.

Even when your intentions are the best, you can still misinterpret incoming messages if you and the speaker don't share enough language or experience. Lack

Table 2–3	**Distinguishing Good Listeners from Bad Listeners**	
The Bad Listener	**The Good Listener Is an Active Listener**	**To Listen Effectively**
Tunes out dry subjects	Seeks opportunities; asks "What's in it for me?"	1. Find areas of interest.
Tunes out if delivery is poor	Judges content; skips over delivery errors	2. Judge content, not delivery.
Tends to enter into argument	Doesn't judge until comprehension is complete; interrupts only to clarify	3. Reserve judgment until you are sure you completely understand the speaker.
Listens for facts	Listens for central themes	4. Listen for ideas.
Takes extensive notes	Takes fewer notes	5. Take selective notes.
Fakes attention	Demonstrates interest; exhibits active body state	6. Work at listening.
Is distracted easily	Fights or avoids distractions; knows how to concentrate	7. Block out competing thoughts.
Resists difficult material	Uses heavier material as exercise for the mind	8. Paraphrase the speaker's ideas.
Reacts to emotional words	Interprets emotional words; does not get hung up on them	9. Stay open-minded.
Tends to daydream with slow speakers	Listens between the lines; weighs the evidence; mentally summarizes	10. Capitalize on the fact that thought is faster than speech.

of common ground is why misinterpretation is so frequent between speakers of different native languages, even when they're trying to speak the same language. When listening to a speaker whose native language or life experience is different from yours, paraphrase that person's ideas. Give the speaker a chance to confirm what you think you heard or to correct any misinterpretation.

Overcoming memory barriers is a slightly easier problem to solve, but it takes some work. If the information is crucial, record it or write it down. If you do need to memorize something, you can hold the information in short-term memory by repeating it silently to yourself or organizing a long list of items into several shorter lists. To store information in long-term memory, four techniques can help:

> When information is crucial and you can't record it in some way, use memory techniques to make sure you don't forget it.

1. Associate new information with something closely related (such as your favourite restaurant).
2. Categorize the new information into logical groups (such as alphabetizing the names of products you're trying to remember).
3. Visualize words and ideas as pictures.
4. Create mnemonics such as acronyms or rhymes.

For a reminder of the steps you can take to overcome listening barriers, see "Checklist: Overcoming Barriers to Effective Listening."

✓ **Checklist** | **Overcoming Barriers to Effective Listening**

- Lower barriers to physical reception whenever you can (especially interrupting speakers by asking questions or by exhibiting disruptive nonverbal behaviours).
- Avoid selective listening by focusing on the speaker and carefully analyzing what you hear.
- Keep an open mind by avoiding any prejudgment and by not listening defensively.
- Paraphrase the speaker's ideas, giving that person a chance to confirm or correct your interpretation.

- Don't count on your memory; write down or record important information.
- Improve your short-term memory by repeating information or breaking it into shorter lists.
- Improve your long-term memory by association, categorization, visualization, and mnemonics.

Improving Your Nonverbal Communication Skills

Nonverbal communication is the interpersonal process of sending and receiving information, both intentionally and unintentionally, without using written or spoken language. Nonverbal signals play a vital role in communication because they can strengthen a verbal message (when the nonverbal signals match the spoken words), weaken a verbal message (when nonverbal signals don't match the words), or replace words entirely. For example, you might tell a client that a project is coming along nicely, but your forced smile and nervous glances will send an entirely different message.

> Nonverbal communication supplements spoken language.
>
> Nonverbal cues help you ascertain the truth of spoken information.

RECOGNIZING NONVERBAL COMMUNICATION

Paying special attention to nonverbal signals in the workplace will enhance your ability to communicate successfully (see "Sharpening Your Career Skills: Developing Your Business Etiquette"). The range and variety of nonverbal

7 LEARNING OBJECTIVE

Clarify the importance of nonverbal communication, and list six categories of nonverbal expression.

signals are almost endless, but you can grasp the basics by studying six general categories:

1. **Facial expression and eye contact.** Your face is the primary site for expressing your emotions; it reveals both the type and the intensity of your feelings.[55] Your eyes are especially effective for indicating attention and interest, influencing others, regulating interaction, and establishing dominance.[56]

2. **Gesture and posture.** The way you position and move your body expresses both specific and general messages, some voluntary and some involuntary. Many gestures—a wave of the hand, for example—have a specific and intentional meaning. Other types of body movement are unintentional and express a more general message. Slouching, leaning forward, fidgeting, and walking briskly are all unconscious signals that reveal whether you feel confident or nervous, friendly or hostile, assertive or passive, powerful or powerless.

3. **Vocal characteristics.** Your voice also carries both intentional and unintentional messages. A speaker can intentionally control pitch, pace, and stress to convey a specific message. For instance, compare "*What* are you doing?" and "What are *you* doing?" Unintentional vocal characteristics can convey happiness, surprise, fear, and other emotions (for example, fear often increases the pitch and the pace of your speaking voice).

Gary Ombler/Dorling Kindersley Limited

When you speak with friends, colleagues, or teachers, do you consciously analyze their body language? What do the stance, the eye contact, and the gesture suggest about the unspoken messages between the people in this photograph?

4. **Personal appearance.** People often make judgements about status, credibility, and even personality based on our appearance—clothing, grooming, and posture. A professional image sends the message that we are able to work with management, peers, and customers. Not only does our appearance influence people's perception of us, but the way our documents and even our office space are organized tells others about the way we work and our commitment to a particular job and organization.

5. **Touch.** Touch is an important way to convey warmth, comfort, and reassurance—as well as control. Touch is so powerful, in fact, that it is governed by cultural customs that establish who can touch whom and how in various circumstances. In Canada, the United States, and Great Britain, for example, people usually touch less frequently than people in France or Costa Rica. Even within each culture's norms, however, individual attitudes toward touch can vary widely. A manager might be comfortable using hugs to express support or congratulations, but his or her subordinates might interpret those hugs as either a show of dominance or sexual interest.[57] Touch is a complex subject. The best advice: when in doubt, don't touch.

6. **Time and space.** Like touch, time and space can be used to assert authority, imply intimacy, and send other nonverbal messages. For example, some people demonstrate their own importance or disregard for others by making people wait; others show respect by being on time. Similarly, taking care not to invade private space, such as by standing too close when talking, is a way to show respect for others. Keep in mind that expectations regarding both time and space vary by culture.

SHARPENING YOUR CAREER SKILLS: Developing Your Business Etiquette

From business lunches to industry conferences, you may represent your company when you're out in public. Make sure your appearance and actions are appropriate to the situation.

- **Get to know the customs of the culture when you meet new people.** For example, in North America, a firm handshake is expected when two people meet, whereas a respectful bow of the head is more appropriate in Japan. If you are expected to shake hands, be aware that the passive "dead fish" handshake creates an extremely negative impression. If you are physically able, always stand when shaking someone's hand.
- **Use proper introductions.** When introducing yourself, include a brief description of your role in the company. When introducing two other people, speak their first and last names clearly, and then try to offer some information (perhaps a shared professional interest) to help the two people ease into a conversation. Generally speaking, the lower-ranking person is introduced to the senior-ranking person, without regard to gender.
- **Be familiar with dining etiquette.** Business is often conducted over meals, and knowing the basics of dining etiquette will make you more effective in these situations. Start by choosing foods that are easy to eat. Avoid alcoholic beverages in most instances, but if drinking one is appropriate, save it for the end of the meal. Leave business documents in your briefcase until entrée plates have been removed; the business aspect of the meal doesn't usually begin until then.
- **Put your cellphone away.** Just as in the office, when you use your mobile phone around other people in public, you send the message that people around you aren't as important as your call and that you don't respect your caller's privacy. If it's not an emergency, or at least an urgent request from your boss or a customer, wait until you're back in the office.
- **Behave professionally when dining.** Finally, always remember that business meals are a forum for business, not casual socializing. Avoid discussing politics, religion, or any other topic that's likely to stir up emotions. Don't complain about work; don't ask deeply personal questions; avoid profanity; and be careful with humour—a joke that entertains some people could easily offend others.

CAREER APPLICATIONS

1. You are introduced to a new business associate. You extend your hand expecting a handshake, but the person does not extend his. What do you do? Explain your answer.
2. You are at lunch with new clients and you thought you put your cellphone on "silent," but it goes off—and very loudly. What you do? What do you say?

USING NONVERBAL COMMUNICATION EFFECTIVELY

Paying attention to nonverbal cues will make you both a better speaker and a better listener. Are they effective without being manipulative? Consider a situation in which an employee has come to you to talk about a raise. This situation is stressful for the employee, so don't say you're interested in what she has to tell you and then spend your time glancing at your computer or checking your watch. Conversely, if you already know you won't be able to give her the raise, be honest in expressing your emotions. Don't overcompensate for your own stress by smiling too broadly or shaking her hand too vigorously. Both nonverbal signals would raise her hopes without justification. In either case, match your nonverbal cues to the tone of the situation.

Also consider the nonverbal signals you send when you're not talking—the clothes you wear, the way you sit, or the way you walk. Are you talking like a serious business professional but dressing like you belong in a dance club or a frat house? The way you look and act sends signals too; make sure you're sending the right ones.

When you listen, be sure to pay attention to the speaker's nonverbal cues. Do they amplify the spoken words or contradict them? Is the speaker intentionally using nonverbal signals to send you a message that he or she can't put into words? Be observant, but don't assume that you can "read someone like a book."

Work to ensure that your nonverbal signals match the tone and content of your spoken communication

Nonverbal signals are powerful, but they aren't infallible. Just because someone doesn't look you squarely in the eye doesn't mean he or she is lying, contrary to popular belief.[58] Moreover, these and other behaviours may be influenced by culture (in some cultures, sustained eye contact can be interpreted as a sign of disrespect) or might just be ways of coping with stressful situations.[59]

SUMMARY OF LEARNING OBJECTIVES

1 Explain the advantages and disadvantages of working in teams, including the characteristics of high-performing teams. Teams can achieve a higher level of performance than individuals because of the combined intelligence and energy of the group. Individuals tend to perform better in teams because they achieve a sense of purpose by belonging to a group. Teams also bring more input and a greater diversity of views, which tend to result in better decisions. And because team members participate in the decision-making process, they are committed to seeing the results succeed. Teams do have disadvantages, however. If poorly managed, teams can be a waste of everyone's time. If members are pressured to conform, they may develop groupthink, which can lead to poor-quality decisions and ill-advised actions. Some members may let their private motives get in the way. Others may not contribute their fair share, so certain tasks may not be completed.

2 Explain how group dynamics can affect team effectiveness. The roles group members assume result in either the success or the failure of the group's ability to solve problems and make decisions. As teams go through the phases of group formation (orientation, conflict, brainstorming, emergence, and reinforcement) to reach consensus, members who assume team-oriented roles, instead of self-oriented roles, help create team success because they place collective goals above personal ones.

3 Outline an effective approach to team communication. Effective team communication is collaborative. Although team members often come from different backgrounds with different concerns, they must accommodate others' opinions and focus on team objectives instead of individual priorities. Effective team communication includes agreeing on team goals before beginning the project, allowing for early social interaction to create a comfortable work atmosphere, clarifying the work process and schedules, and frequent checking on the group's progress. If team members use technology to share information, they must ensure the system is functional.

4 Explain the benefits of collaboration technologies. Collaboration technologies help professionals plan, prepare, and produce reports, presentations, and other communication efforts anywhere, anytime. Wikis allow online editing from any team member and permit review of previous page versions. Groupware lets people work on documents simultaneously and connect using social net-

working tools. Shared workspaces are online offices that give teams access to the same set of resources, such as databases and project plans.

5 Describe the key steps needed to ensure productive meetings. For a productive meeting, clarify its purpose— is it an informational or decision-making meeting? Then, select the essential participants. Choose the location and time, making sure the environment is suitable. Set the agenda, which is the basis of a productive meeting. As the meeting progresses, be sure to keep it focused, follow a designated procedure, encourage people to talk, and summarize the key points at the end.

6 Describe the listening process, and explain how good listeners use active listening to overcome barriers at each stage of the process. The listening process involves five activities: (a) receiving (physically hearing the message), (b) decoding (assigning meaning to what you hear), (c) remembering (storing the message for future reference), (d) evaluating (thinking critically about the message), and (e) responding (reacting to the message, taking action, or giving feedback). Three barriers can interfere with each stage of the listening process. One is selective listening, which prevents the listener from retaining the real message; this problem can be overcome by listening actively. The second is prejudgment, which involves holding assumptions and sometimes even distorting messages if they don't conform to what you want to hear. Good listeners practise active listening strategies and control prejudgment by listening with an open mind. The third is memory barriers, which good listeners overcome with such techniques as organizing information into patterns and taking notes.

7 Clarify the importance of nonverbal communication, and list six categories of nonverbal expression. Nonverbal communication is important because actions may speak louder than words. Body language is more difficult to control than words and may reveal a person's true feelings, motivation, or character. Consequently, people tend to believe nonverbal signals over the spoken message. In addition, nonverbal communication is more efficient; with a wave of your hand or a wink, you can streamline your thoughts—and do so without much thought. Types of nonverbal expression include facial expression, gesture and posture, vocal characteristics, personal appearance, touching, and use of time and space.

| ON THE JOB | PERFORMING COMMUNICATION TASKS AT ROYAL BANK OF CANADA |

Teamwork permeates all business activities at Royal Bank of Canada. New employees are introduced to the team approach right away, ensuring that everyone contributes to the company's success through effective teamwork. You have recently been promoted to assistant branch manager at your neighbourhood Royal Bank. Your responsibilities include (1) promoting the team concept among all customer service representatives in your branch and (2) serving as a team leader on special projects that involve your staff.

Use what you've learned in this chapter to address the following challenges:

1. Your district manager has asked you and three other employees at your large urban branch to find a solution to the lack of sufficient office space for the growing number of workers at your location. As leader, you schedule team meetings on Thursday afternoons for four weeks to address the problem. After two meetings with your co-workers, you notice that everyone is making vital contributions to the group's efforts—except Jane. During the meetings, she displays very poor listening skills. She often jumps ahead of the topic or interrupts a speaker's train of thought. At other times, she doodles on her notepad instead of taking constructive notes. And she remains silent after team members deliver lengthy reports about possible solutions to the office space problem. What can you do as team leader to help Jane improve her listening skills?
   a. Ask Jane to take extensive notes during each meeting. The process of taking detailed notes will improve her concentration and force her to listen more carefully to team members. After the meeting, she can use her notes as a reference to clarify any questions about team decisions or the nature of assignments to individual team members.
   b. Suggest that Jane mentally summarize the speaker's ideas—or verbally rephrase the ideas in her own words—during the meeting. With some practice, Jane should be able to focus on the topics under discussion and block out distracting thoughts.
   c. Schedule future team meetings for Thursday mornings instead of Thursday afternoons. After devoting most of the workday to her regular duties, Jane may be feeling tired or sluggish by the time of your team meeting.
   d. Prepare a detailed written summary of each meeting. The summary will clarify any points that Jane may have

   missed during the meeting and provide her with a complete reference of team decisions and assignments.

2. As assistant branch manager, you schedule a team meeting to discuss new methods of motivating customer service representatives to achieve their quarterly goals for selling bank products, such as guaranteed investment certificates. During the meeting, one customer service representative disagrees with every suggestion offered by team members, often reacting with a sneer on his face and a belligerent tone of voice. Which of the following strategies is the best way to overcome the rep's resistance?
   a. Ignore his remarks. Keep the meeting on track and avoid destructive confrontations by asking for input from other team members.
   b. Directly confront the sales rep's concerns. Point out the flaws in his arguments, and offer support for the opinions of other team members.
   c. Remain calm and try to understand his point of view. Ask him to clarify his ideas, and solicit his suggestions for motivating sales representatives.
   d. Politely acknowledge his opinions, and then repeat the most valid suggestions offered by other team members in a convincing manner.

3. The district manager realizes his communication skills are important for several reasons: he holds primary responsibility for the region; he needs to communicate with the branch managers who report to him; and his style sets an example for other employees in the region. He asks you to sit in on face-to-face meetings for several days to observe his nonverbal messages. You witness four habits. Which of the following habits do you think is the most negative?
   a. He rarely comes out from behind his massive desk when meeting people; at one point, he offered a congratulatory handshake to a branch manager, and the manager had to lean way over his desk just to reach him.
   b. When a manager hands him a report and then sits down to discuss it, he alternates between making eye contact and making notes on the report.
   c. He is consistently pleasant, even if the person he is meeting is delivering bad news.
   d. He interrupts meetings to answer the phone, rather than letting an assistant get the phone; then he apologizes to visitors for the interruption.

TEST YOUR KNOWLEDGE

1. What are three ways in which an organization's decision making can benefit from teams?

2. What are the main activities that make up the listening process?

3. What questions should an effective agenda answer?

4. How do self-oriented team roles differ from team-maintenance roles and task-facilitating roles?

5. What is groupthink? How can it affect an organization?

6. How can team members successfully resolve conflict?

7. How does content listening differ from critical listening and empathic listening?

8. What are the benefits of wikis and web-based meeting systems as meeting technologies?

9. How is nonverbal communication limited?

10. What is the purpose of using parliamentary procedure?

APPLY YOUR KNOWLEDGE

1. How can nonverbal communication help you run a meeting? How can it help you call a meeting to order, emphasize important topics, show approval, express reservations, regulate the flow of conversation, and invite a colleague to continue with a comment?

2. Your boss frequently asks for feedback from you and her other subordinates, but she blasts anyone who offers criticism, which causes people to agree with everything she says. You want to talk to her about it, but what should you say? List some of the points you want to make when you discuss this issue with her.

3. Is conflict in a team good or bad? Explain your answer.

4. At your last department meeting, three people monopolized the entire discussion. What might you do at the next meeting to encourage other department members to participate voluntarily?

5. You have been invited to a meeting to provide an update on one of your projects. You did not receive an agenda, nor do you know anything about the attendees. What can you do to optimize your time and that of other attendees?

6. **Ethical Choices** Strange instant messages occasionally pop up on your computer screen during your team's virtual meetings, followed quickly by embarrassed apologies from one of your colleagues in another city. You eventually figure out that this person is working from home, even though he says he's in the office; moreover, the messages suggest that he's running a sideline business from his home. Instant messaging is crucial to your team's communication, and you're concerned about the frequent disruptions, not to mention your colleague's potential ethical violations. What should you do? Explain your choice.

RUNNING CASES

> CASE 1 Noreen

Noreen is planning to attend a WebEx online meeting today at 11:00 A.M. Her boss has asked her to participate in the meeting with other Petro-Go "Go Points" team leaders from around the world. The group is to compile statistics regarding the "Go Points" program as well as discuss strategies for expanding the program and improving customer retention. They are to submit a report in one week, detailing their findings and suggestions.

Noreen begins the set-up and login process on her computer at 10:45 A.M. She finds that because she has never participated in a WebEx conference, she is unable to prepare her computer. She calls the technical department, and a technician comes to set it up for her. She finally connects with the group at 12:30 P.M. By this time they are ending the meeting and planning to meet tomorrow at the same time. Noreen apologizes and explains what happened, but she feels rather embarrassed.

The next day Noreen connects on time but is somewhat behind the discussion because she does not know what was discussed the day before. She tries her best to share information but is scrambling to find the data she needs to share with the group. The group divides the workload among them and asks everyone to meet online again at 11:00 A.M. in three days to share and review their work. Noreen types her team's statistics and suggestions for expanding and finishes early. When she meets the group again she discovers that not only did every-

one type their team's statistics and suggestions for expanding the program, but they also compared their team's performance with two other office teams and gave suggestions for improving customer retention. Noreen was not aware they were supposed to include all of this information. One team leader volunteered to compile everything and said he would contact the others tomorrow if he had questions. Noreen knew she would be out of the office for the next three days on training. The report was finished on time, but Noreen's team's section was incomplete. Her boss was not happy.

QUESTIONS

a. Why did Noreen not know what was expected?

b. What could Noreen have done differently to ensure communication would not break down?

c. Should Noreen have alerted the others to the fact that her section was incomplete?

d. Should the group have gone ahead with the report without Noreen's completed section?

e. What could Noreen have done to ensure that she had done the task correctly?

YOUR TASK

Write an email from Noreen to her boss explaining what happened and apologizing for the errors. She should admit fault and offer suggestions for correcting the situation.

> CASE 2 Kwong

Kwong is working on a group project for his business communication class. His group members are Mohamed, Gopan, and Marie. The project is to choose a company and research its channels and methods of communication. The group will submit a formal report and deliver a presentation.

The group divides the tasks for the project: Kwong will create the PowerPoint slides; Marie and Mohamed will gather the information; and Gopan will create the formal report. Mohamed does not attend the next class. The group sends several emails to Mohamed over the course of the next four days, but they get no response. The group emails the professor to make her aware of the situation and to ask for guidance on how to proceed.

The day the project is due, Mohamed meets Gopan outside the classroom door. They have a loud argument that the class overhears. The teacher asks Kwong's group to stay after class to discuss any problems their group may have. The class begins, and Kwong's group does not allow Mohamed to present with them; nor do they accept his work.

After class Gopan complains that Mohamed did his part incorrectly and did not participate. Marie says she came with Mohamed's part done and added it to their project, so they would not lose marks. Mohamed tells the group that he had family problems and apologizes for his absence. Mohamed is willing to accept a zero grade. The professor discusses appropriate behaviour with the team. Gopan apologizes for yelling at Mohamed, and they shake hands.

The next day when each member emailed the professor their peer evaluation forms, both Mohamed and Kwong said they did not wish to work in a group with Gopan again.

The group members each gave Mohamed a low grade because of his lack of participation.

QUESTIONS

a. Do you think having a group contract from the beginning of the group assignment would have helped the situation? Could a contract outlining team member expectations and deliverables have helped ensure that communication would not break down?

b. Was the group being mean by making the professor aware of Mohamed's non-participation? Why did they inform her?

c. Why do you think Mohamed did not wish to work with Gopan again? Why do you think Kwong did not wish to work with Gopan again?

d. What could Gopan have done differently? What could Mohamed have done differently?

e. Should the group have let Mohamed present with them?

YOUR TASK

Create an email to your professor evaluating Gopan's, Mohamed's, Marie's, and Kwong's individual performance on this group assignment. Rate them on

1. Cooperation
2. Participation
3. Contribution
4. Demonstrated interest
5. Communication

Give a brief explanation as to why you rated each member the way you did.

PRACTISE YOUR KNOWLEDGE

A project leader has made notes about covering the following items at the quarterly budget meeting. Prepare a formal agenda by putting these items into a logical order and rewriting, where necessary, to give phrases a more consistent sound.

- Budget Committee Meeting to be held on December 13, 2013, at 9:30 A.M.
- I will call the meeting to order.
- Real estate director's report: A closer look at cost overruns on Greentree site.
- The group will review and approve the minutes from last quarter's meeting.

- I will ask the finance director to report on actual versus projected quarterly revenues and expenses.
- I will distribute copies of the overall divisional budget and announce the date of the next budget meeting.
- Discussion: How can we do a better job of anticipating and preventing cost overruns?
- Meeting will take place in Conference Room 3, with video-conferencing for remote employees.
- What additional budget issues must be considered during this quarter?

EXERCISES

2.1 Teamwork: Meeting Assessment

With a classmate, attend a local community or campus meeting where you can observe a group discussion, vote, or other group action. During the meeting, take notes individually, and afterward, work together to answer the following questions:

a. What is your evaluation of this meeting? In your answer, consider (1) the leader's ability to articulate the meeting's goals clearly, (2) the leader's ability to engage members in a meaningful discussion, (3) the group's dynamics, and (4) the group's listening skills.

b. How did group members make decisions? Did they vote? Did they reach decisions by consensus? Did those with dissenting opinions get an opportunity to voice their objections?

c. How well did the individual participants listen? How could you tell?

d. Did any participants change their expressed views or their votes during the meeting? Why might that have happened?

e. List any barriers to communication that you observed.

f. Compare the notes you took during the meeting with those of your classmate. What differences do you notice? How do you account for these differences?

2.2 Team Communication: Overcoming Barriers

Every month, each employee in your department is expected to give a brief oral presentation on the status of his or her project. However, your department has recently hired an employee with a severe speech impediment that prevents people from understanding most of what he has to say. As department manager, how will you resolve this dilemma? Please explain.

2.3 Team Development: Resolving Conflict

Describe a recent conflict you had with a team member at work or at school, and explain how you resolved it. Did you find a solution that was acceptable to both of you and to the team?

2.4 Ethical Choices: Dealing with a Meeting Controller

During team meetings, one member constantly calls for votes before all the members have voiced their views. As the leader, you asked this member privately about his behaviour. He replied that he was trying to move the team toward its goals, but you are concerned that he is really trying to take control. How can you deal with this situation without removing the member from the group?

2.5 Online Communication: Using Collaboration Technologies

In this project, you will conduct research on your own and then merge your results with those of the rest of your team. Search Twitter for messages on the subject of workplace safety. (You can use Twitter's advanced search page at https://twitter.com/search-advanced or use the "site: twitter.com" qualifier on a regular search engine.) Compile at least five general safety tips that apply to any office setting, and then meet with your team to select the five best tips from all those the team has collected. Collaborate on a blog post that lists the team's top five tips.

2.6 Online Collaboration: Using Collaboration Technologies

In a team assigned by your instructor, use Zoho (www.zoho.com; free for personal use), Google Drive (http://drive.google.com) or a comparable system to collaborate on a set of directions that out-of-town visitors could use to reach a specific point on your campus, such as a stadium or dorm. The team should choose the location and the modes of transportation involved. Be creative—brainstorm the best ways to guide first-time visitors to the selected location using all the media at your disposal.

2.7 Listening Skills: Overcoming Barriers

For the next several days, take notes on your listening performance during at least a half-dozen situations in class, during social activities, and at work, if applicable. Referring to the traits of the good listener in Table 2–3, rate yourself using *always, frequently, occasionally,* or *never* on these positive listening habits. In a report no longer than one page, summarize your analysis and identify specific areas in which you can improve your listening skills.

2.8 Nonverbal Communication: Analyzing Written Messages

Select a business letter and an envelope that you received at work or home. Analyze their appearance. What nonverbal messages do they send? Are these messages consistent with the content of the letter? If not, what could the sender have done to make the nonverbal communication consistent with the verbal communication?

2.9 Nonverbal Communication: Analyzing Body Language

Describe what the following body movements suggest when someone exhibits them during a conversation. How do such movements influence your interpretation of spoken words?

a. Shifting one's body continuously while seated

b. Twirling and playing with one's hair

c. Sitting in a sprawled position

d. Rolling one's eyes

e. Extending a weak handshake

2.10 Collaboration: Working in Teams

In teams of four or five classmates, role play a scenario in which the team is to decide which department at your college will receive a $1 million gift from an anonymous donor. The catch: each member of the team will advocate for a different department (decide among yourselves who represents which departments), which means that all but one member will "lose" in the final decision. Working as a team, decide which department will receive the donation and discuss the results to help everyone on the team support the decision. Be prepared to present your choice and your justification for it to the rest of the class.

2.11 Culturally Diverse Teams

It is quite possible that you have been assigned a team project or exercise as one of the assignments for this course. It is also likely that the group membership is culturally diverse. Use your understanding of the barriers to effective communication to outline strategies you and your project team members could use to promote effective communication and the achievement of your goals.

Communicating Interculturally

LEARNING OBJECTIVES   After studying this chapter, you will be able to

1   Discuss the opportunities and challenges of intercultural communication

2   Define *culture*, and explain how culture is learned

3   Define *ethnocentrism* and *stereotyping*, and then give three suggestions for overcoming these limiting mindsets

4   Explain the importance of recognizing cultural variations, and list six categories of cultural differences

5   List seven recommendations for writing clearly in multilanguage business environments

6   Outline strategies for speaking and listening when communicating with people of other cultures

MyLab Business Communication   Visit MyLab Business Communication to access a variety of online resources directly related to this chapter's content.

ON THE JOB: COMMUNICATING AT IBM

DAI KUROKAWA Feature Photo Service/Newscom

An IBM Corporate Service Corps team has improved health care delivery in Cross River State, Nigeria. For IBM and other multinational companies, international service benefits local communities, develops global leaders, and creates business partnerships.

Building International Advantage through Corporate Service

www.ibm.com

"[IBM's Corporate Service Corps is] not just philanthropy, it's leadership development and business development, and it helps build economic development in the emerging world," says Stanley Litow, IBM's vice president of Corporate Citizenship and Corporate Affairs. With more than 3000 participants so far, IBM's Corporate Service Corps has developed into a highly competitive employee opportunity with up to 500 IBMers a year participating. Ten- to 15-member teams, primarily from mid- to upper management, work on international community-based economic projects to improve how local businesses and governments operate. Communities in Ghana, Nigeria, Romania, the Philippines, Morocco, and Vietnam, among other countries, have benefited from IBM expertise, with IBM employees gaining valuable career experience and IBM itself gaining potential clients.

Launched in 2008, the Corporate Service Corps has so far sent more than 275 teams to more than 37 countries around the world. Participants themselves are drawn from IBM's global workforce, with offices in 200 countries. Teams themselves are multiethnic: a team to Romania, sent to help GreenForest, a manufacturer of office, hotel, and industrial furniture, included experts from the United States, China, Japan, Australia, and India. To qualify, employees must show clear leadership skills, a strong desire to immerse themselves in another culture, knowledge of business and service delivery practices, and evidence of adaptability to challenging global environments.

Members undergo three months of training during which they learn about their host countries, build team relationships through teleconferences and social networking websites, and gain consulting skills suitable for emerging markets. With missions lasting only four weeks, the main goal, according to one participant, is to "be teachers and introduce clients to new ways of thinking about business that they can use on their own." The outcomes may lead to better use of technology to monitor health care, as in Cross River State, Nigeria, or improved management of food quality and safety, as in Ho Chi Minh City, Vietnam.

IBM's Corporate Service Corps builds global citizens, which are essential for successful business. Al Checkra, a software development manager chosen for the project in Romania, remarked, "I felt like I won the lottery when I was accepted." Would you want to work on a corporate service team? What would appeal to you about an international experience?[1]

Understanding the Opportunities and Challenges of Intercultural Communication

1 **LEARNING OBJECTIVE**
Discuss the opportunities and challenges of intercultural communication.

Effective intercultural communication

- Opens up business opportunities around the world
- Improves the contributions of employees in a diverse workforce

You will communicate with people from other cultures throughout your career.

Intercultural communication is the process of sending and receiving messages between people whose cultural backgrounds could lead them to interpret verbal and nonverbal signs differently. Every attempt to send and receive messages is influenced by culture. Your awareness of cultural differences and ability to communicate effectively within different environments will open up business opportunities throughout the world and maximize the contribution of all the employees in a diverse workforce.

THE OPPORTUNITIES IN A GLOBAL MARKETPLACE

Chances are good that you'll be looking across international borders in the course of your career. Thanks to communication and transportation technologies, natural boundaries and national borders are no longer the impassable barriers they once were. Local markets are opening to worldwide competition as businesses of all sizes look for new growth opportunities outside their own countries. Thousands of Canadian businesses depend on exports for significant portions of their revenues. But exports are not the only way in which Canadian companies conduct business abroad. According to Export Development Canada's Foreign Footprints survey results (2016), "foreign affiliate sales eclipsed merchandise goods exports as the largest source of international revenue in 2006 and generated $510 billion in 2013 alone. By comparison, merchandise goods exports created $472 billion in international revenue and services brought in just $93 billion." The survey outlined that while foreign affiliates provide companies with access to a variety of competitive sources and easier entry to new markets, they also often receive support from head office in areas such as marketing, accounting, logistics, and research and development. And while the United States was recognized as continuing to be the most important market for Canadian foreign affiliate investment, substantial growth will be seen in emerging economies such as China, India, and Brazil.[2] If you work in one of these companies, you may well be called on to visit or at least communicate with a wide variety of people who speak languages other than English and who live in cultures quite different from what you're used to.

The diversity of today's workforce brings distinct advantages to businesses:

- A broader range of views and ideas
- A better understanding of diverse markets
- A broader pool of talent from which to recruit

ADVANTAGES OF A MULTICULTURAL WORKFORCE

Even if you never visit another country or transact business on a global scale, you will interact with colleagues from a variety of cultures and with a wide range of life experiences. Over the past few decades, many innovative companies have changed the way they approach diversity, from seeing it as a legal requirement to seeing it as a strategic opportunity to connect with customers and take advantage of the broadest possible pool of talent.[3] Diverse workforces offer a broader spectrum of viewpoints and ideas, help companies understand and identify with diverse markets, and enable companies to tap into the broadest possible talent pool. Says Gordon Nixon, president and chief executive officer of Royal Bank of Canada, "If we succeed at leveraging the diversity of our current and future workforce, we will have unrivalled advantage. But if we fail, we will pay a heavy opportunity cost for our citizens and will face an uphill battle to maintain, let alone enhance, our quality of life."[4]

Diversity is integral to all companies. In November 2010, the Government of Canada announced a plan to help sustain the economic recovery by maintaining high immigration levels.[5] From 2011 to 2015, Canada welcomed an average of 259 000 immigrants per year.[6] Canadian firms have responded to the needs of these employees through training and other supportive measures to improve communication. For example, Toronto's Dalton Pharma Services offers English as a Second Language (ESL) classes to its diverse workforce.[7] Furthermore, for 2016 and 2017, to help offset the aging population and declining labour force, Immigration Canada increased the baseline for permanent resident admissions to 300 000, with more than 50% being economic immigrants.[8]

You and your colleagues don't need to be recent immigrants to constitute a diverse workforce. Differences in everything from age and gender to religion, ethnic heritage, geography, and military experience enrich the workplace. Both immigration and workforce diversity create opportunities—and challenges—for business communicators throughout the world. At RBC, for example, the definition of workplace diversity includes different perspectives, work experience, lifestyles, and cultures and specifically refers to "any dimension that can be used to differentiate groups and people from one another. It means respect for and appreciation of differences in ethnicity, gender, age, national origin, disability, sexual orientation, education, and religion."[9]

See RBC's Diversity 2020 initiatives and progress report at http://www.rbc.com/diversity/diversity-progress-report.html.

This schedule from CHIN Radio (www.chinradio.com), a broadcaster of multicultural programs, reflects the diversity of Canadian society. Besides radio, what other media will help you understand different cultures?

Courtesy: CHIN Radio

THE CHALLENGES OF INTERCULTURAL COMMUNICATION

Cultural diversity affects how business messages are conceived, planned, sent, received, and interpreted in the workplace. Today's diverse workforce encompasses a wide range of skills, traditions, backgrounds, experiences, outlooks, and attitudes toward work—all of which can affect employee behaviour on the job. Supervisors face the challenge of communicating with these diverse employees, motivating them, and fostering cooperation and harmony among

A company's cultural diversity affects how its business messages are conceived, composed, delivered, received, and interpreted.

them. Teams face the challenge of working together closely, and companies are challenged to foster productive relationships with other businesses and with the community as a whole.

Culture influences everything about communication, including
- Language
- Nonverbal signals
- Word meaning
- Time and space issues
- Rules of human relationships

The way you communicate—from the language you speak and the nonverbal signals you send to the way you perceive other people—is influenced by the culture and environment in which you were raised. The meaning of words, the significance of gestures, the importance of time and space, the rules of human relationships—these and many other aspects of communication are defined by culture. To a large degree, your culture influences the way you think, which naturally affects the way you communicate as both a sender and a receiver.[10] So you can see how intercultural communication is much more complicated than simply matching language between sender and receiver. It goes beyond mere words to beliefs, values, attitudes, and emotions.

Throughout this chapter, you'll see examples of how communication styles and habits vary from one culture to another. These examples are intended to illustrate the major themes of intercultural communication, not to give an exhaustive list of styles and habits of any particular culture. Understanding these major themes will help prepare you to explore the nuances and practices of any culture.

Developing Cultural Competency

Cultural competency is an appreciation of cultural differences that affect communication and the ability to adjust one's communication style to ensure that efforts to send and receive messages across cultural boundaries are successful. It requires a combination of attitude, knowledge, and skills.[11]

You are already an expert in culture, at least in the culture you grew up with. You understand how your society works, how people are expected to communicate, what common gestures and facial expressions mean, and so on. However, because you're such an expert in your own culture, your communication is largely automatic; that is, you rarely stop to think about the communication rules you're following. An important step toward successful intercultural communication is becoming more aware of these rules and of the way they influence your communication. A good place to start is to understand what culture is.

UNDERSTANDING THE CONCEPT OF CULTURE

2 LEARNING OBJECTIVE

Define *culture*, and explain how culture is learned.

Culture is a shared system of symbols, beliefs, attitudes, values, expectations, and behavioural norms.

You belong to several cultures, each of which affects the way you communicate.

Culture is a shared system of symbols, beliefs, attitudes, values, expectations, and norms of behaviour. People's cultural background influences the way they prioritize what is important in life, helps define their attitude toward what is appropriate in any given situation, and establishes rules for their behaviour.[12]

Actually, everyone belongs to several cultures. The most obvious is the culture you share with all the people who live in your own country. In addition, you belong to other cultural groups, including an ethnic group, possibly a religious group, and perhaps a profession that has its own special language and customs. For example, with its large population and history of immigration, Canada is home to a vast array of cultures.[13]

Cultures differ widely and, while they are dynamic, the rate at which they change, their degree of complexity, and their acceptance of others may vary. These differences affect the level of trust and openness that you can achieve when communicating with people of other cultures.

People learn culture directly and indirectly from other members of their group. As you grow up in a culture, you are taught who you are and how best to function in that culture by the group's members. Sometimes you are explicitly told which behaviours are acceptable; at other times you learn by observing which values work best in a particular group. In these ways, culture is passed on from person to person and from generation to generation.[14]

In addition to being automatic, established cultures tend to be coherent; that is, they are fairly logical and consistent when viewed from the inside. Certain norms within a culture may not make sense to someone outside the culture, but they probably make sense to those inside. Such coherence generally helps a culture function more smoothly internally, although it can create disharmony between cultures that don't view the world in the same way.

Cultures also tend to be complete; that is, they provide most of their members with most of the answers to life's big questions. This idea of completeness dulls or even suppresses curiosity about life in other cultures. Not surprisingly, such completeness can complicate communication with other cultures.[15]

OVERCOMING ETHNOCENTRISM AND STEREOTYPING

Ethnocentrism is the tendency to judge all other groups according to the standards, behaviours, and customs of one's own group. Given the automatic influence of their own culture, when people compare their culture to others, they often conclude that their own group is superior.[16] An even more extreme reaction is **xenophobia**, a fear of strangers and foreigners. Clearly, businesspeople who take these views will not interpret messages from other cultures correctly; nor are they likely to communicate messages successfully.

Distorted views of other cultures or groups also result from **stereotyping**, assigning a wide range of generalized attributes to an individual on the basis of membership in a particular culture or social group. Whereas ethnocentrism and xenophobia represent negative views of everyone in a particular group, stereotyping is more a matter of oversimplifying and of failing to acknowledge individuality. For example, assuming that an older colleague will be out of touch with the youth market and thinking that a younger colleague can't be an inspiring leader are examples of stereotyping age groups.

Those who want to show respect for other people and to communicate effectively in business need to adopt a more positive viewpoint in the form of **cultural pluralism**—the practice of accepting multiple cultures on their own terms. When crossing cultural boundaries, you'll be even more effective if you move beyond simple acceptance and adapt your own communication style to that of the new cultures you encounter—even integrating aspects of those cultures into your own.[17] Three simple habits can help you avoid both the negativity of ethnocentrism and the oversimplification of stereotyping:

- **Avoid assumptions.** Don't assume that others will act as you do, that they will operate from the same values and beliefs, or that they will use language and symbols the same way you do.
- **Avoid judgments.** When people act differently, don't conclude that they are in error, that their way is invalid, or that their customs are inferior to your own.
- **Acknowledge distinctions.** Don't ignore the differences between another person's culture and your own.

Experts recommend that companies transacting business with people from other nationalities find out as much as possible about their customs and religions. What information about your background would be necessary for your business partners?

Paul Chesley/The Image Bank/Getty Images

Cultures tend to offer views of life that are coherent (internally logical) and complete (answer all of life's big questions).

3   **LEARNING OBJECTIVE**

Define *ethnocentrism* and *stereotyping*, and then give three suggestions for overcoming these limiting mindsets.

Ethnocentrism is the tendency to judge all other groups according to the standards, behaviours, and customs of one's own group.

Stereotyping is assigning generalized attributes to an individual on the basis of membership in a particular group.

Cultural pluralism is the acceptance of multiple cultures on their own terms.

Participation in group activities is an important method of learning about a culture's rules and expectations. What have you learned about other cultures through groups you belong to? Has it influenced how you communicate with others?

Lucky Business/Shutterstock

You can avoid ethnocentrism and stereotyping by avoiding assumptions and judgments and by accepting differences.

Unfortunately, overcoming ethnocentrism and stereotyping is no simple task, even for people who are highly motivated to do so. You may need to change patterns of beliefs that you've had your entire life and even change the way you view yourself and your culture. Moreover, recent research suggests that people often have beliefs and biases that they're not even consciously aware of—and that may even conflict with the beliefs they *think* they have. (To see if you might have some of these *implicit beliefs,* visit the Project Implicit website at https://implicit. harvard.edu/implicit and take some of the simple online tests.)[18]

RECOGNIZING CULTURAL VARIATIONS

4 **LEARNING OBJECTIVE**

Explain the importance of recognizing cultural variations, and list six categories of cultural differences.

Cultural differences can lead to miscommunication in the workplace.

Cultural context is the pattern of physical cues, environmental stimuli, and implicit understanding that conveys meaning between members of the same culture.

High-context cultures rely heavily on nonverbal actions and environmental setting to convey meaning; low-context cultures rely more on explicit verbal communication.

Low-context cultures tend to value written agreements and interpret laws strictly, whereas high-context cultures view adherence to laws as being more flexible.

When you communicate with someone from another culture, your instinct is to encode your message using the assumptions of your own culture. However, members of your audience decode your message according to the assumptions of *their* culture, so your meaning may be misunderstood (see "Communicating across Cultures: Test Your Intercultural Knowledge"). You can begin to learn how people in other cultures want to be treated by recognizing and accommodating six main types of cultural differences: contextual, legal and ethical, social, nonverbal, age, and gender.

1. CONTEXTUAL DIFFERENCES Every attempt at communication occurs within a **cultural context**, the pattern of physical cues, environmental stimuli, and implicit understanding that conveys meaning between two members of the same culture. However, the role that context plays in communication varies widely across different cultures.

In a **high-context culture** such as South Korea or Taiwan, people rely less on verbal communication and more on the context of nonverbal actions and environmental setting to convey meaning. What is left unsaid is often equally important as what is said. For example, a Chinese speaker expects the receiver to discover the essence of a message and uses indirectness and metaphor to provide a web of meaning.[19] The indirect style can be a source of confusion during discussions with people from low-context cultures, who are more accustomed to receiving direct answers. Also, in high-context cultures, the rules of everyday life are rarely explicit; instead, as individuals grow up, they learn how to recognize situational cues such as gestures and tone of voice, or even gender or age and how to respond as expected.[20] The primary role of communication is building relationships, not exchanging information.[21]

In a **low-context culture** such as Canada, the United States, or Germany, people rely more on verbal communication and less on circumstances and cues to convey meaning. In such cultures, rules and expectations are usually spelled out through explicit statements such as "Please wait until I'm finished" or "You're welcome to browse."[22] The primary task of communication in low-context cultures is exchanging information.[23]

Contextual differences are apparent in the way cultures approach situations such as decision making, problem solving, negotiating, interacting among levels in the organizational hierarchy, and socializing outside the workplace.[24] For example, in lower-context cultures, businesspeople tend to first focus on the results of the decisions they face, a reflection of the cultural emphasis on logic and progress. In comparison, higher-context cultures emphasize the means or the method by which the decision will be made. Building or protecting relationships can be as important as the facts and information used in making the decisions.[25] Consequently, negotiators working on business deals in such cultures may spend most of their time together building relationships rather than hammering out contractual details. In low-context cultures, the intention to reduce ambiguity and its potential strain on relationships is part of the incentive for the carefully laid out details of a contract.[26]

Whether you're making a decision, solving a problem, or negotiating a business deal, the communication tactics that work well in a high-context culture may backfire in a low-context culture, and vice versa. The key to success is understanding why the other party is saying and doing particular things and then adapting your approach accordingly.

2. LEGAL AND ETHICAL DIFFERENCES Cultural context also influences legal and ethical behaviour. For example, because low-context cultures value the written word, they consider written agreements binding. But high-context cultures put less emphasis on the written word and consider personal pledges more important than contracts. They also tend to take a more flexible approach regarding adherence to the law, whereas low-context cultures would adhere to the law strictly.[27]

As you conduct business around the world, you'll find that legal systems differ from culture to culture. Making ethical choices across cultures can seem highly complicated, but you can keep your messages ethical by applying the following basic principles:[28]

Yuri Arcurs/Shutterstock

In the low-context cultures of Canada, the United States, and France, for example, employees avoid socializing with fellow workers and value skill as much as position and status. In the high-context cultures of Greece, China, and Japan, for example, business and social relationships mix, and employees value position and status more than skills. Are these assessments of low-context and high-context cultures accurate, based on your experience? What are the dangers of generalizing culture?

- **Actively seek mutual ground.** To allow the clearest possible exchange of information, both parties must be flexible and avoid insisting that an interaction take place strictly in terms of one culture or another.
- **Send and receive messages without judgment.** To allow information to flow freely, both parties must recognize that values vary from culture to culture, and they must trust each other.
- **Send messages that are honest.** To ensure that the information is true, both parties must see things as they are—not as they would like them to be. Both parties must be fully aware of their personal and cultural biases.
- **Show respect for cultural differences.** To protect the basic human rights of both parties, each must understand and acknowledge the other's needs and preserve each other's dignity by communicating without deception.

Honesty and respect are cornerstones of ethical communication, regardless of culture.

3. SOCIAL DIFFERENCES The nature of social behaviour varies among cultures, sometimes dramatically. These behaviours are guided by rules. Some rules are formal and specifically articulated (table manners are a good example), and some are informal and learned over time (such as the comfortable distance to stand from a colleague during a discussion). The combination of both types of rules influences the overall behaviour of everyone in a society most of the time. In addition to the factors already discussed, social norms can vary from culture to culture in the following areas:

Formal rules of etiquette are explicit and well defined, but informal rules are learned through observation and imitation.

- **Roles and status.** Culture influences the roles that people play, including who communicates with whom, what they communicate, and in what way. For example, people in Canada and the United States show respect by addressing top managers as "Mr. Roberts" or "Ms. Tremblay." However, people in China are addressed according to their official titles, such as "President" or "Manager."[29]
- **Use of manners.** What is polite in one culture may be considered rude in another. For example, asking a colleague "How was your weekend?" is a common way of making small talk in Canada and the United States, but the question sounds intrusive to people in cultures where business and private lives are seen as totally separate. Communication consultant Laraine Kaminsky says, "Hospitality matters in a collectivist culture like China. It would be considered impolite to help yourself to food at an event, for example, without also

The rules of polite behaviour vary from country to country.

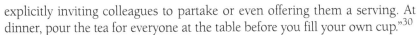

Attitudes toward time, such as strict adherence to meeting schedules, can vary throughout the world.

The meaning of nonverbal signals can vary widely from culture to culture, so you can't rely on assumptions.

explicitly inviting colleagues to partake or even offering them a serving. At dinner, pour the tea for everyone at the table before you fill your own cup."[30]

- **Concepts of time.** Business runs on schedules, deadlines, and appointments, but these matters are regarded differently from culture to culture. People in low-context cultures view time as a limited resource and tend to treat schedules as rigid requirements. However, executives from high-context cultures often see time as more flexible. Meeting a deadline is less important than building a business relationship.[31]

4. NONVERBAL DIFFERENCES Nonverbal communication can be a reliable guide to determining the meaning of a message—but this situation holds true only if the sender and receiver assign the same meaning to nonverbal signals. For example, the simplest hand gestures have different meanings in different cultures. Don't assume that the gestures you grew up with will translate to another culture; doing so could lead to embarrassing mistakes.

When you have the opportunity to interact with people in another culture, the best approach is to study the culture in advance and then observe the way people behave in the following areas:

- **Greetings.** Do people shake hands, bow, or kiss lightly (on one side of the face or both)? Do people shake hands only when first introduced or every time they say hello or goodbye?
- **Personal space.** When people are conversing, do they stand closer together or farther away than you are accustomed to?
- **Touching.** Do people touch each other on the arm to emphasize a point or slap each other on the back to show congratulation? Or do they refrain from touching altogether?
- **Facial expressions.** Do people shake their heads to indicate "no" and nod them to indicate "yes"? This is what people are accustomed to in Canada and the United States, but it is not universal.
- **Eye contact.** Do people make frequent eye contact or avoid it? Frequent eye contact is often taken as a sign of honesty and openness in Canada and the United States, but in other cultures it can be a sign of aggressiveness or lack of respect.
- **Posture.** Do people slouch and relax in the office and in public, or do they sit up straight?
- **Formality.** In general, does the culture seem more or less formal than yours?

Following the lead of people who grew up in the culture is not only a great way to learn, but also a good way to show respect.

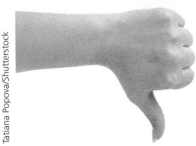

Tatiana Popova/Shutterstock

The "thumbs up" sign means "one" in Germany and "five" in Japan; it is an obscene gesture in Australia and some other countries. The "OK" sign means "zero" or "worthless" in France; indicates money in Japan; and is an obscene gesture in Germany, Brazil, and some other countries. Do you know of other hand signs that are interpreted differently in different countries? Should businesspeople avoid gesturing when interacting with global partners?

A culture's views on youth and aging affect how people communicate with one another.

5. AGE DIFFERENCES Canada celebrates youth in general and successful young businesspeople in particular; for example, newspapers such as the *National Post* publish special supplements highlighting successful entrepreneurs under 40. Youth is associated with strength, energy, possibilities, and freedom, and age is sometimes associated with declining powers and the inability to keep pace. However, older workers can offer broader experience, the benefits of important business relationships nurtured over many years, and high degrees of "practical intelligence"—the ability to solve complex, poorly defined problems.[32]

In contrast, in cultures that value age and seniority, longevity earns respect and increasing power and freedom. For example, in many Asian societies, the oldest employees hold the most powerful jobs, the most impressive titles, and the greatest degree of freedom and decision-making authority. If a younger employee disagrees with one of these senior executives, the discussion is never conducted in public. The notion of "saving face," of avoiding public embarrassment, is too strong. Instead, if a senior person seems to be in error about something, other employees will find a quiet, private way to communicate whatever information they feel is necessary.[33]

COMMUNICATING ACROSS CULTURES — Test Your Intercultural Knowledge

Even well-intentioned businesspeople can make mistakes if they aren't aware of simple but important cultural differences. Can you spot the erroneous assumptions in these scenarios?

1. You are attending a special event at a Chinese hotel with your colleagues. The food is served buffet-style. You are in line with your Chinese associates and select from the choices displayed, expecting your counterparts to follow. Why do they look surprised?

2. You finally made the long trip overseas to meet the new German director of your division. Despite slow traffic, you arrive only four minutes late. His door is shut, so you knock on it and walk in. The chair is too far away from the desk, so you pick it up and move it closer. Then you lean over the desk, stick out your hand and say, "Good morning, Hans, it's nice to meet you." Why is his reaction so chilly?

3. Your meeting went better than you'd ever expected. In fact, you found the Japanese representative for your new advertising agency to be very agreeable; she said yes to just about everything. When you share your enthusiasm with your boss, he doesn't appear very excited. Why?

Here's what went wrong in each situation:

1. In Canada, it is expected that people selecting food from a buffet take it in the order they are in line. In China, it is considered rude to take food before inviting your colleagues to choose before you. In addition, when having tea with Chinese partners, you should pour for everyone at the table before helping yourself.

2. You've just broken four rules of German polite behaviour: punctuality, privacy, personal space, and proper greetings. In time-conscious Germany, you should never arrive even a few minutes late. Also, Germans like their privacy and space, and many adhere to formal greetings of "Frau" and "Herr," even if the business association has lasted for years.

3. The word *yes* may not always mean "yes" in the Western sense. Japanese people may say yes to confirm they have heard or understood something but not necessarily to indicate that they agree with it. You'll seldom get a direct no. Some of the ways that Japanese people say no indirectly include "It will be difficult," "I will ask my supervisor," "I'm not sure," "We will think about it," and "I see."

CAREER APPLICATIONS

1. Have you ever been on the receiving end of an intercultural communication error, such as when someone inadvertently used an inappropriate gesture or figure of speech? How did you respond?

2. If you had arrived late at the office of the German colleague, what would have been a better way to handle the situation?

In addition to cultural values associated with various life stages, the multiple generations within a culture present another dimension of diversity. Today's workplaces can have three or even four generations working side by side. Each of these generations has been shaped by dramatically different world events, social trends, and technological advances, so it is not surprising that they often have different values, expectations, and communication habits. For instance, Generation Y workers have a strong preference for communicating via short electronic messages, but Baby Boomers and Generation Xers sometimes find these brief messages abrupt and impersonal.[34]

6. GENDER DIFFERENCES The perception of the roles of men and women in business also varies from culture to culture, and these differences can affect communication efforts. In some cultures, men hold most or all positions of authority, and women are expected to play a more subservient role. Female executives who visit these cultures may not be taken seriously until they successfully handle challenges to their knowledge, capabilities, and patience.[35]

Improving Intercultural Communication Skills

Communicating successfully from one culture to another requires a variety of skills (see Figure 3–1). You can improve your intercultural skills throughout your entire career. Begin now by studying other cultures and languages,

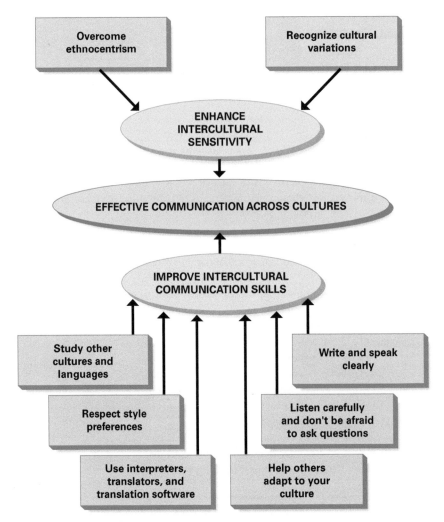

Figure 3–1 Components of Successful Intercultural Communication

respecting preferences for communication styles, learning to write and speak clearly, listening carefully, knowing when to use interpreters and translators, and helping others adapt to your culture.

> **TIPS FOR SUCCESS**
> "Do volunteer work that gives you experience with people from cultures you'll be dealing with. This will help you understand subtleties of social interactions and manners."
>
> Jean-Marc Hachey, international careers consultant

STUDYING OTHER CULTURES

Successful intercultural communication can require the modification of personal communication habits.

Effectively adapting your communication efforts to another culture requires not only knowledge about the culture but also both the ability and the motivation to change your personal habits as needed.[36] Fortunately, you don't need to learn about the whole world all at once. Many companies appoint specialists for specific countries or regions, giving you a chance to focus on fewer cultures at a time. Some firms also provide resources to help employees prepare for interaction with other cultures. On IBM's Global Workforce Diversity intranet site, for instance, employees can click on the GoingGlobal link to learn about customs in specific cultures.[37]

Making an effort to learn about another person's culture is a sign of respect.

Even a small amount of research and practice will help you get through many business situations. In addition, most people respond positively to honest effort and good intentions, and many business associates will help you along if you show an interest in learning more about their cultures. Don't be afraid to ask questions, either. People will respect your concern and curiosity. You will gradually accumulate considerable knowledge, which will help you feel comfortable and be effective in a wide range of business situations. For some of the key issues to research before doing business in another country, refer to Table 3–1.

Table 3–1	**Doing Business in Other Cultures**
Action	**Details to Consider**
Understand social customs	• How do people react to strangers? Are they friendly? Hostile? Reserved? • How do people greet each other? Should you bow? Nod? Shake hands? • How do you express appreciation for an invitation to lunch, dinner, or someone's home? Should you bring a gift? Send flowers? Write a thank-you note? • Are any phrases, facial expressions, or hand gestures considered rude? • How do you attract the attention of a waiter? Do you tip the waiter? • When is it rude to refuse an invitation? How do you refuse politely? • What topics may or may not be discussed in a social setting? In a business setting? • How do social customs dictate interaction between men and women? Between younger people and older people?
Learn about clothing and food preferences	• What occasions require special clothing? • What colours are associated with mourning? Love? Joy? • Are some types of clothing considered taboo for one gender or the other? • How many times a day do people eat? • How are hands or utensils used when eating? • Where is the seat of honour at a table?
Assess political patterns	• How stable is the political situation? • Does the political situation affect businesses in and out of the country? • What are the traditional government institutions? • Is it appropriate to talk politics in social or business situations?
Understand religious and folk beliefs	• To which religious groups do people belong? • Which places, objects, actions, and events are sacred? • Do religious beliefs affect communication between men and women or between any other groups? • Is there a tolerance for minority religions? • How do religious holidays affect business and government activities? • Does religion require or prohibit eating specific foods? At specific times?
Learn about economic and business institutions	• Is the society homogeneous or heterogeneous? • What languages are spoken? • What are the primary resources and principal products? • Are businesses generally large? Family controlled? Government controlled? • What are the generally accepted working hours? • How do people view scheduled appointments? • Are people expected to socialize before conducting business?
Appraise the nature of ethics, values, and laws	• Is money or a gift expected in exchange for arranging business transactions? • Do people value competitiveness or cooperation? • What are the attitudes toward work? Toward money? • Is politeness more important than factual honesty?

Numerous websites and books also offer advice on travelling to and working in specific countries. For example, websites for the World Trade Organization (www.wto.org) and the CIA's World Factbook (www.cia.gov) provide essential information for companies planning to conduct business abroad. Additional information on different customs, tastes, and preferences can be gleaned from newspapers and magazines, and even from the music, movies, and foods of another country. Build your cultural intelligence with a cross-section of sources.

STUDYING OTHER LANGUAGES

English is the most prevalent language in international business, but don't assume that everyone understands it or speaks it in the same way.

Consider what it must be like to work at IBM, where the company's global workforce speaks more than 165 languages. Without the ability to communicate in more than one language, how could this diverse group of people conduct business? As commerce continues to become more globalized, the demand for multilingual communicators continues to grow as well. The ability to communicate in more than one language can make you a more competitive job candidate and open up a wider variety of career opportunities.

If you have a long-term business relationship with people of another culture, it is helpful to learn at least some basic words and phrases of their language.

Even if your colleagues or customers in another country do speak your language, it's worth the time and energy to learn common phrases in theirs. Learning the basics not only helps you get through everyday business and social situations but also demonstrates your commitment to the business relationship. After all, the other person probably spent years learning your language.

Finally, don't assume that two countries speaking the same language speak it in the same way. Canada and the United Kingdom are two countries divided by a common language. For example, *apartment*, *elevator*, and *gasoline* in Canada are *flat*, *lift*, and *petrol* in the United Kingdom.

RESPECTING PREFERENCES FOR COMMUNICATION STYLE

Communication style—including the level of directness, the degree of formality, preferences for written versus spoken communication, and other factors—varies widely from culture to culture. Knowing what your communication partners expect can help you adapt to their particular style. Once again, watching and learning is the best way to improve your skills. However, you can infer some generalities by learning more about the culture. For example, Canadian and U.S. workers typically prefer an open and direct communication style; they find other styles frustrating or suspect. Directness is also valued in Sweden as a sign of efficiency; but, unlike discussions in the United States, heated debates and confrontations are unusual. Italian, German, and French executives don't soften up colleagues with praise before they criticize—doing so seems manipulative to them. However, professionals from high-context cultures, such as Japan or China, tend to be less direct.[38]

Business correspondence is often more formal in other countries than it is in Canada and the United States.

In international correspondence, Canadian and U.S. businesspeople will generally want to be somewhat more formal than they would be when writing to people in their own country. The letter in Figure 3–2 was written by a supplier in Germany to a nearby retailer; you can see how the tone is more formal than would be used in Canada. In Germany, business letters usually open with a reference to the business relationship and close with a compliment to the recipient.

WRITING CLEARLY

5 **LEARNING OBJECTIVE**

List seven recommendations for writing clearly in multilanguage business environments.

In addition to learning the preferred style of your communication partners, you can help ensure successful messages by taking extra care with your writing. When sending written communication to businesspeople from another culture, familiarize yourself with their written communication preferences and

Figure 3–2 Effective German Business Letter (Translated)

The annotations on the letter read:

"Business Leader" is the literal translation of *Geschäftsführer;* a common English translation would be "Managing Director."

The introduction reminds the reader of the ongoing business relationship.

Note how the language is a bit more formal (such as "We provide a five-year guarantee...") than is typical in Canadian and U.S. letters.

The complimentary close is typical of German business letters. (Note the lack of punctuation.)

The date is placed to the right and below the address block (note that some German writers use the format 15 May 2017).

The writer shows respect for the reader and his business needs.

The final paragraph includes a compliment to the recipient.

The signature block does not include a title with the typed name, as Canadian and U.S. letters usually do.

The letter text reads:

Furtwangen Handcrafts
Kussenhofstrasse 150
Furtwangen, Germany

Mister
Karl Wieland
Business Leader
Black Forest Gifts
Friedrichstrasse 98
70174 Stuttgart
GERMANY

15.5.2017

Very honorable Mister Wieland,

The tourist season will soon begin, and we would like to take this opportunity to introduce our new line of hand-carved cuckoo clocks. Last year you were so kind as to purchase two dozen of our clocks. In recognition of our good business relationship we now offer you the opportunity to select from the new models before the line is made available to other purchasers.

As you know, our clocks are of superior quality. Our artisans use only the best wood and carefully carve every detail by hand according to time-honoured practices that have been passed down from generation to generation. We test every clock before it is painted and shipped, and we provide a five-year guarantee on all of our Furtwangen hand-crafted clocks.

Enclosed you will find a copy of our newest brochure and an order form. To express our appreciation, we will take over the shipping costs if you order before 15 May 2017.

We wish you a lot of success in your new Stuttgart location. We are convinced that you will continue to satisfy your regular clientele with your larger exhibition area and expanded stock and that you will also gain many new visitors.

With friendly greetings

Frederick Semper

Frederick Semper

adapt your approach, style, and tone to meet their expectations. Follow these recommendations:[39]

- **Choose words carefully.** Use precise words that don't have the potential to confuse with multiple meanings. For instance, the word *right* has several dozen different meanings and usages, so look for a synonym that conveys the specific meaning you intend, such as *correct, appropriate, desirable, moral, authentic,* or *privilege.*[40]
- **Be brief.** Use simple sentences and short paragraphs, breaking information into smaller chunks that are easier for your reader to process.
- **Use plenty of transitions.** Help readers follow your train of thought by using transitional words and phrases. For example, tie related points together with expressions such as *in addition* and *first, second,* and *third.*
- **Address international correspondence properly.** Refer to the Canada Post instructions for addressing domestic and international mail at

www.canadapost.ca/web/en/kb/details.page?article=addressing_mail_accu&cattype=kb&cat=addressing&subcat=accuracy. You may also want to look at the information on restricted destinations, types of shipments, and observation of custom requirements.

- **Cite dates and numbers carefully.** The Canadian Standards Association has adopted the international standard of year-month-day for dates. Thus, December 5, 2017, is written numerically as 2017–12–05 when following international usage; the arrangement follows the largest element (the year) to the smallest element (the day). However, in practice many Canadian businesses also follow British or U.S. usage and may omit the first two numbers of the year. Consequently, December 5, 2017, may be written 05–12–17, which means 5 December 2017 (British usage) or 12–05–17, which means December 5, 2017 (U.S. usage). Dates in Japan and China typically follow the international standard. You should also be aware of international differences in number formats. For example, 1.000 means one with three decimal places in Canada, the United States, and Great Britain, but it means one thousand in many European countries.

Figure 3–3 Ineffective Intercultural Letter

- **Avoid slang, idiomatic phrases, and business jargon.** Everyday speech and writing is full of slang and **idiomatic phrases**—phrases that mean more than the sum of their literal parts. Examples from Canadian and U.S. English include phrases such as "off the top of my head" and "more bang for the buck." Your audience may have no idea what you're talking about when you use such phrases.
- **Avoid humour and other references to popular culture.** Jokes and references to popular entertainment usually rely on culture-specific information that might be completely unknown to your audience.

Humour does not "travel well" because it usually relies on intimate knowledge of a particular culture.

Compare the letters shown in Figures 3–3 and 3–4, in which a Canadian is writing to a French business partner to explain why his expenses were unusually high for the previous month. Although some of the differences may seem trivial, meeting the expectations of an international audience illustrates both knowledge of and respect for other cultures.

Figure 3–4 Effective Intercultural Letter

Outline strategies for speaking and listening when communicating with people of other cultures

Speaking clearly and getting plenty of feedback are two keys to successful intercultural conversations.

Toronto-based Dalton Pharma Services provides on-site ESL classes, which not only train people in English but also create cohesive teams. Besides language training, what other methods help people of different cultures form effective teams?

SPEAKING AND LISTENING CAREFULLY

Languages vary considerably in the significance of tone, pitch, speed, and volume, which can create challenges for people trying to interpret the explicit meaning of words themselves as well as the overall nuance of a message. The English word *progress* can be a noun or a verb, depending on which syllable you accent. In Chinese, the meaning of the word *mà* changes depending on the speaker's tone; it can mean *mother, pileup, horse,* or *scold.* And routine Arabic speech can sound excited or angry to an English-speaking North American listener.[41]

Whether you're travelling to another country or teaming up with someone who is visiting or immigrating to your country, you're likely to speak with people whose native language is different from yours. Even when you know the vocabulary and grammar of the other person's language, the processing of everyday conversations can be difficult. Immigrants with a working knowledge of English would have difficulty understanding that "Jeat yet?" means "Did you eat yet?" and that "Cannahepya?" means "Can I help you?" Some non-native English speakers don't distinguish between the English sounds *v* and *w*, so they say "wery" for "very." At the same time, Canadians may have trouble pronouncing the German *ch*.

To be more effective in intercultural conversations, follow these practices:

1. Speak slowly and clearly.
2. Don't rephrase until it's obviously necessary (immediately rephrasing something you've just said doubles the translation workload for the listener).
3. Look for and ask for feedback to make sure your message is getting through.
4. Don't talk down to the other person by overenunciating words or oversimplifying sentences.
5. At the end of the conversation, make sure you and the listener agree on what has been said and decided.

To listen more effectively in intercultural situations, accept what you hear without judgment and let people finish what they have to say.

As a listener, you'll need some practice to get a sense of vocal patterns. The key is simply to accept what you hear first, without jumping to conclusions about meaning or motivation. Let other people finish what they have to say. If you interrupt, you may miss something important. You'll also show a lack of respect. If you do not understand a comment, ask the person to repeat it. Any momentary awkwardness you might feel in asking for extra help is less important than the risk of unsuccessful communication.

USING INTERPRETERS, TRANSLATORS, AND TRANSLATION SOFTWARE

You may encounter business situations that require using an *interpreter* (for spoken communication) or a *translator* (for written communication). Interpreters and translators can be expensive, but skilled professionals provide invaluable assistance for communicating in other cultural contexts.[42] Some companies use *back-translation* to ensure accuracy. Once a translator encodes a message into another language, a different translator retranslates the same message into the

Patience and a sense of humour are two helpful assets for overcoming mistakes in intercultural communication. Have you experienced any awkward moments when communicating with someone of another culture? How did you handle them?

original language. This back-translation is then compared with the original message to discover any errors or discrepancies.

A variety of software products and websites offer translation capabilities, from individual words and phrases to documents and entire webpages. Although none of these tools can translate as well as human experts, they can often give you the overall gist of a message.[43] To experience this first hand, try the Translation Software Exercise 3.9 at the end of the chapter.

> For important business communication, use a professional interpreter (for oral communication) or translator (for written communication).

HELPING OTHERS ADAPT TO YOUR CULTURE

Everyone can contribute to successful intercultural communication. Whether a younger person is unaccustomed to the formalities of a large corporation, or a colleague from another country is working on a team with you, look for opportunities to help people fit in and adapt their communication style. For example, if a non-native English speaker is making mistakes that could hurt his or her credibility, you can offer advice on the appropriate words and phrases to use. Most language learners truly appreciate this sort of assistance, as long as it is offered in a respectful manner. Also keep in mind that oral communication in a second language is usually more difficult than written communication; so, instead of asking a foreign colleague to provide detailed information in a conference call, you could ask that colleague to communicate that information in a written response. Moreover, chances are that while you're helping, you'll learn something about the other person's culture and language, too. For a brief summary of ideas on how to improve communication in the workplace, see "Checklist: Improving Intercultural Communication Skills."

> Help others adapt to your culture; doing so will create a more productive workplace and teach you about their cultures as well.

✔ Checklist | Improving Intercultural Communication Skills

- Understand your own culture so that you can recognize its influences on your communication habits.
- Study other cultures so that you can appreciate cultural variations.
- Study the languages of people with whom you communicate, even if you can learn only a few basic words and phrases.
- Help non-native speakers learn English.
- Respect cultural preferences for communication style.

- Write clearly, using brief messages, simple language, generous transitions, and appropriate international conventions.
- Avoid slang, humour, and references to popular culture.
- Speak clearly and slowly, giving listeners time to translate your words.
- Ask for feedback to ensure successful communication.
- Listen carefully and ask speakers to repeat anything you don't understand.
- Use interpreters and translators for important messages.

SUMMARY OF LEARNING OBJECTIVES

1 Discuss the opportunities and challenges of intercultural communication. Effective intercultural communication offers many opportunities in the global marketplace: because of communication and transportation technologies, businesses small and large can enlarge their customer base and sell their products both at home and abroad. The multicultural workplace offers a broad diversity of opinions and ideas, thus creating more creative companies. Cultural diversity also creates challenges to how business messages are planned, prepared, produced, and interpreted: with the broad range of skills and traditions in today's workplaces, businesspeople must be highly sensitive to how the receivers of their messages interpret language and behaviour.

2 Define *culture*, **and explain how culture is learned.** *Culture* is defined as a shared system of beliefs, attitudes, values, expectations, and norms of behaviour. Culture is learned directly, through explicitly taught acceptable behaviours, and implicitly, through observing the values of your group.

3 Define *ethnocentrism* and *stereotyping*, and then give three suggestions for overcoming these limiting mind-sets. *Ethnocentrism* is the tendency to judge all other groups according to one's own standards, behaviours, and customs. *Stereotyping* is predicting individuals' behaviour or character on the basis of their membership in a particular group or class. To overcome ethnocentrism, follow these three suggestions: (a) avoid assumptions, (b) avoid judgments, and (c) acknowledge distinctions.

4 Explain the importance of recognizing cultural variations, and list six categories of cultural differences. It is important to recognize cultural variations to avoid communication breakdown and to demonstrate respect to members of other cultures. The six categories of cultural differences are (1) contextual differences, (2) legal and ethical differences, (3) social differences, (4) nonverbal differences, (5) age differences, and (6) gender differences.

5 List seven recommendations for writing clearly in multilanguage business environments. You can ensure successful messages across cultures by following these recommendations: (a) choose words carefully; (b) be brief; (c) use plenty of transitions; (d) address international correspondence properly; (e) cite dates and numbers carefully; (f) avoid slang, idiomatic phrases, and business jargon; and (g) avoid humour and other references to popular culture.

6 Outline strategies for speaking and listening when communicating with people of other cultures. When speaking with clients and colleagues from other cultures, be sure to speak at a slow pace and enunciate clearly. Don't rephrase until it's obviously necessary. Seek feedback to ensure your audience understands your message. Don't talk down to the other person. Make sure you and your listener agree on the content of the conversation. As a listener, let the speaker finish what he or she has to say before talking. If you do not understand anything, ask the speaker to repeat it.

ON THE JOB   PERFORMING COMMUNICATION TASKS AT IBM

Imagine that you are a member of an IBM Corporate Service Corps team working in the host country with a local business. You decide to help the employees improve their communication abilities. How would you address each of these challenges?

1. The employees want to improve their English-speaking ability. How do you help them?

   a. You ask each employee to prepare a short talk in English on aspects of their work that they will deliver to their colleagues.

   b. You take the group to a café and have them order food in English and speak English while they are there.

   c. You pair off the employees and have them prepare scenarios in English, such as job interviews, to present in front of the group.

   d. From time to time, you invite the group to your temporary apartment where you lead conversations in English.

2. Several of the employees do not make eye contact when delivering speeches because in their culture it is considered rude to make eye contact with other people. How do you persuade them to look at the audience?

   a. You gently encourage them to make eye contact. You explain that in Canada it is common for businesspeople to make eye contact when giving a presentation, and that people who don't are not considered effective speakers.

   b. You don't discuss the issue with the group at all and let them avoid making eye contact. You believe they will understand the importance of eye contact when they give presentations to Canadian businesspeople.

   c. You show videos about making effective presentations, hoping the group will be encouraged to make eye contact after watching them.

   d. You set up team presentations, creating teams with employees who are comfortable making eye contact with an audience and those who are not. You expect that while these teams rehearse their presentations, employees who avoid looking at the audience will be persuaded to make eye contact after working with peers who do.

3. One of the employees is an immigrant from another country. He works well alone, but he resists working with others, even in team settings where collaboration is expected. How do you handle the situation?

   a. Stay out of the way and let the situation resolve itself. The employee has to learn how to get along with the other team members.

   b. Tell the rest of the team to work harder at getting along with him.

   c. Tell the employee he must work with others or he will not progress in the company.

   d. Talk privately with the employee and help him understand the importance of working together as a team. During the conversation, try to uncover why he doesn't participate more in team efforts.

TEST YOUR KNOWLEDGE

1. How have market globalization and cultural diversity contributed to the increased importance of intercultural communication?

2. Why is cultural competency important?

3. How do high-context cultures differ from low-context cultures?

4. In addition to contextual differences, what other categories of cultural differences exist?

5. What is ethnocentrism? How can it be overcome in communication?

6. Why is it a good idea to avoid slang and idioms when addressing a multicultural audience?

7. When should you use interpreters and translators?

8. What are some ways to improve oral and listening skills when communicating with people of other cultures?

9. What are some ways to improve writing skills when communicating with people of other cultures?

10. What is the purpose of back-translation when preparing a message in another language?

APPLY YOUR KNOWLEDGE

1. Does a company that has no business dealings outside Canada need to concern itself with intercultural communication issues? Explain your answer.

2. What are some intercultural communication issues to consider when deciding whether to accept an overseas job with a firm whose headquarters are in your own country? A job in your own country with a local branch of a foreign-owned firm? Explain.

3. How do you think company managers from a country that has a relatively homogeneous culture might react when they do business with the culturally diverse staff of a company based in a less homogeneous country? Explain your answer.

4. Why is it important to understand your own culture when attempting to communicate with people from other cultures?

5. How does making an effort to avoid assumptions contribute to the practice of cultural pluralism?

RUNNING CASES

> CASE 1 Noreen

Noreen is having lunch at the Petro-Go cafeteria. She is sitting with Dan and Karen from her "Go Points" department team. An intern from another country who has been working in Noreen's department arrives and joins the table. After 10 minutes or so, Noreen's teammates get up and move to another table. They start giggling and whispering. The intern feels that they are laughing and talking about her because she heard them mention her name, but she is not sure what they are saying.

The same afternoon Karen comes to Noreen, her team leader, and asks to speak with her in private. They go to a meeting room. Karen explains that since she moved into the cubicle next to the intern, she has not been happy. She says that the intern has an unusual body odour, and others have noticed it as well.

QUESTIONS

a. What should Noreen do?

b. Does Karen have a right to ask to change seats?

c. What misunderstandings may be happening?

d. Could the intern's body odour be caused by a medical condition? Could it be the result of the cultural food she eats?

e. What can be done to prevent the intern from being rejected by her teammates?

f. Review the discussion of stereotyping and the section "Recognizing Cultural Variations." What additional information could help you turn this communication challenge into an opportunity to build a stronger team?

YOUR TASK

If you were Noreen, how would you handle this situation? Would you discuss this matter with the intern or ask your manager to do so? What would you say? Partner with a classmate and role play this situation.

> CASE 2 Kwong

Kwong is on his way to an interview with A1 Accounting, the company he would like to work at during his co-op placement. Kwong arrives 10 minutes late for his interview because he had written the street name incorrectly in his notes, but the receptionist takes him into the interview room right away. There are three managers sitting, waiting at a table. They rise and introduce themselves and shake Kwong's hand. Kwong shakes each interviewer's hand with a soft, two-handed handshake.

During the interview Kwong shows his respect for the managers by avoiding direct eye contact; instead, he gazes at the floor most of the time. Kwong's answers to many of the questions are vague and often ambiguous. When Kwong is asked when he would be available to start, he answers by telling the managers what he would do to get started at his job instead of when he could start work. Kwong answers a few other questions similarly, as if he did not hear the question correctly or did not understand it. Kwong does not get the job.

QUESTIONS

a. Did Kwong communicate well and appear confident during the interview?

b. Why do you think Kwong did not get the job?

c. What do you think the managers were thinking of Kwong?

d. Why did Kwong answer the questions as if he did not hear them correctly?

e. What can Kwong do to improve his skills before the next interview?

YOUR TASK

In pairs, role play an interview and demonstrate an appropriate introduction, handshake, questions and answers, and closing. Assign your actors a role, such as a woman being interviewed by a man, an older person being interviewed by a younger person, a person using a wheelchair being interviewed by a person not in a wheelchair, or a person from a low-context culture being interviewed by a person from a high-context culture. Have others in the class observe and give feedback on potential problems that may occur and how to handle them.

PRACTISE YOUR KNOWLEDGE

Your boss wants to write a brief email message welcoming employees recently transferred to your department from your Hong Kong branch. They all speak English, but your boss asks you to review her message for clarity. What would you do to improve this message, given the intended audience—and why? Would you consider this message to be audience centred? Why or why not?

I wanted to welcome you ASAP to our little family here north of the border. It's high time we shook hands in person and not just across the sea. I'm pleased as punch about getting to know you all, and I for one will do my level best to sell you on Canada.

EXERCISES

3.1 Intercultural Sensitivity: Recognizing Variations

You represent a Canadian toy company that's negotiating to buy miniature truck wheels from a manufacturer in Osaka, Japan. In your first meeting, you explain that your company expects to control the design of the wheels as well as the materials that are used to make them. The manufacturer's representative looks down and says softly, "Perhaps that will be difficult." You press for agreement, and to emphasize your willingness to buy, you show the prepared contract you've brought with you. However, the manufacturer seems increasingly vague and uninterested. What cultural differences may be interfering with effective communication in this situation? Explain.

3.2 Intercultural Communication: Writing for Multiple-Language Audiences

With a team assigned by your instructor, review the Facebook pages of five companies, looking for words and phrases that might be confusing to a non-native speaker of English. If you (or someone on the team) is a non-native speaker, explain to the team why those word choices could be confusing. Choose three sentences, headlines, company slogans, or other pieces of text that contain potentially confusing words and rewrite

them to minimize the chances of misinterpretation. As much as possible, try to retain the tone of the original—although you may find that this is impossible in some instances. Use Google Drive to compile the original selections and your revised versions, then email the documents to your instructor.

3.3 Teamwork: Language and Culture

Working with two other students, prepare a list of 10 examples of slang (in your own language) that might be misinterpreted or misunderstood during a business conversation with someone from another culture. Next to each example, suggest other words you might use to convey the same message. Do the alternatives mean exactly the same as the original slang or idiom?

3.4 Intercultural Communication: Studying Cultures

Choose a specific country, such as India, Portugal, Bolivia, Thailand, or Nigeria, with which you are not familiar. Research the culture and write a brief summary of what a Canadian manager would need to know about concepts of personal space and rules of social behaviour to conduct business successfully in that country.

3.5 Multicultural Workforce: Bridging Differences

Differences in gender, age, and physical abilities contribute to the diversity of today's workforce. Working with a classmate, role play a conversation in which

a. A woman is being interviewed for a job by a male personnel manager

b. An older person is being interviewed for a job by a younger personnel manager

c. An employee who is a native speaker of English is being interviewed for a job by a hiring manager who is a recent immigrant with relatively poor English skills

How did differences between the applicant and the interviewer shape the communication? What can you do to improve communication in such situations?

3.6 Intercultural Sensitivity: Understanding Attitudes

As the director of marketing for a telecommunications firm based in Germany, you're negotiating with an official in Guangzhou, China, who's in charge of selecting a new telephone system for the city. You insist that the specifications be spelled out in the contract. However, your Chinese counterpart seems to have little interest in technical and financial details. What can you do or say to break this intercultural deadlock and obtain the contract so that both parties are comfortable?

3.7 Culture and Time: Dealing with Variations

When a company knows that a scheduled delivery time given by an overseas firm is likely to be flexible, managers may buy in larger quantities or may order more often to avoid running out of product before the next delivery. Identify three other management decisions that may be influenced by differing cultural concepts of time, and make notes for a short (two-minute) presentation to your class.

3.8 Intercultural Communication: Using Interpreters

Imagine that you're the lead negotiator for a company that's trying to buy a factory in Prague, the capital of the Czech Republic. Although you haven't spent much time in the country in the past decade, your parents grew up near Prague, so you understand and speak the language fairly well. However, you wonder about the advantages and disadvantages of using an interpreter anyway. For example, you may have more time to think if you wait for an intermediary to translate the other side's position. Decide whether to hire an interpreter, and then write a brief (two- or three-paragraph) explanation of your decision.

3.9 Internet: Translation Software

Explore the powers and limitations of computer translation at BabelFish, www.babelfish.com. In the box labelled "Enter Text," enter a sentence such as "We are enclosing a purchase order for four dozen computer monitors." Select "English to Spanish" and click on "Translate" to complete the translation. Once you've read the Spanish version, cut and paste it into the "text for translation" box, select "Spanish to English," and click on "Translate." Translate the same English sentence into German, French, or Italian and then back into English. How do the results of each translation differ? What are the implications for the use of automated translation services and back-translation? How could you use this website to sharpen your intercultural communication skills? Summarize your findings in a brief report.

3.10 Intercultural Communication: Improving Skills

You've been assigned to host a group of Swedish college students who are visiting your school for the next two weeks. They've all studied English, but this is their first trip to your area. Make a list of at least eight slang terms and idioms they are likely to hear on campus. How will you explain each phrase? When speaking with the Swedish students, what word or words might you substitute for each slang term or idiom?

3.11 Intercultural Communication: Podcasting

Your company was one of the first to use the Apple iPod and other digital music players as business communication tools. Executives often record messages (such as monthly sales reports) as digital audio files and post them on the company's intranet site as podcasts. Employees from the 14 offices in Europe, Asia, and North America then download the files to their music players and listen to the messages while riding the train to work, eating lunch at their desks, and so on. Your boss asks you to draft the opening statement for a podcast that will announce a revenue drop caused by intensive competitive pressure. She reviews your script and then hands it back with a gentle explanation that it needs to be revised for international listeners. Improve the following statement in as many ways as you can:

> Howdy, guys. Shouldn't surprise anyone that we took a beating this year, given the insane pricing moves our knucklehead competitors have been making. I mean, how those clowns can keep turning a profit is beyond me, what with steel costs still going through the roof and labour costs heating up—even in countries where everybody goes to find cheap labour—and hazardous waste disposal regs adding to operating costs, too.

4 Planning Business Messages

LEARNING OBJECTIVES After studying this chapter, you will be able to

1 Describe the three-step writing process

2 Explain why it's important to define your purpose carefully, and ask four questions that can help you test that purpose

3 Describe the importance of analyzing your audience, and identify the six factors you should consider when developing an audience profile

4 Discuss gathering information for simple messages, and identify three attributes of quality information

5 List factors to consider when choosing the most appropriate medium for your message

6 Explain why good organization is important to both you and your audience

7 Summarize the process for organizing business messages effectively

MyLab Business Communication Visit MyLab Business Communication to access a variety of online resources directly related to this chapter's content.

ON THE JOB: COMMUNICATING AT MaRS DISCOVERY DISTRICT

MaRS is an exciting centre for innovation in the life sciences, health care, and technology. Communications play a major role in promoting the MaRS mission and maintaining connections among all MaRS stakeholders.

Mentoring Canadian Innovators
www.marsdd.com

Called one of the world's largest innovation hubs, the Toronto-based MaRS Discovery District links entrepreneurs with the people and resources to help them become market leaders in their fields. Focused on the areas of life sciences and health care, communications and entertainment, clean technology, and social innovation, MaRS provides mentorship, education, and investment connections to eligible innovators. Established in 2006, MaRS has helped more than 1200 clients grow their businesses with the goal of making positive national and global impacts.

Emerging science and technology firms can apply to work in the MaRS Incubator, where they are given furnished office space and access to equipped labs and can meet other innovators. Businesses such as banks and law firms may choose to maintain a MaRS presence so they can offer on-site advice about financing and legal matters, such as intellectual property concerns. Since 2006, the MaRS Centre has held more than 10 000 meetings, conferences, and events about such topics as global leadership, the future of medicine, and best practices, further benefiting its tenants as well as outside participants. MaRS online offers a wealth of free educational materials, including *Entrepreneurship 101* (a video series about developing a company); educational workbooks on, for example, marketing communications and financing; as well as newsletters and reports.

MaRS is a community of professionals, and promoting the MaRS mission and maintaining relationships among its tenants, clients, and the public requires a variety of professional and personal communication skills. Dealing with both internal and external audiences, MaRS communications managers suggest and write articles for online and print materials, including blogs and the monthly magazine, exploring such topics as innovation, entrepreneurship, science, and technology. The managers collaborate with graphic designers, copy editors, writers, printers, government partners, and internal MaRS stakeholders on communication projects. The job of communications manager also involves research, conducting interviews, and using social media platforms such as Twitter, Facebook, and YouTube to create awareness of the MaRS organization. Attention to detail, project-management skills, and the abilities to multitask and meet tight deadlines are essential to the performance of this job.

If you worked at MaRS, how would you plan messages to different audiences? What essential information would you need? And how would you choose the best channel and medium for communication?[1]

Understanding the Three-Step Writing Process

Like communicators at MaRS, you'll be creating messages for numerous audiences using written, oral, and digital channels. By following the process introduced in this chapter, you can learn to create successful messages that meet audience needs and highlight your skills as a perceptive business professional.

1 **LEARNING OBJECTIVE**

Describe the three-step writing process.

The three-step writing process (see Figure 4–1) helps ensure that your messages are both *effective* (meeting your audience's needs and getting your points across) and *efficient* (making the best use of your time and your audience's time):

1. **Planning business messages.** To plan any message, first *analyze the situation* by defining your purpose and developing a profile of your audience. Once you're sure what you need to accomplish with your message, *gather information* that will meet your audience's needs. Next, *select the right medium* (oral, written, or electronic) to deliver your message. With those three factors in place, you're ready to *organize the information* by defining your main idea, limiting your scope, selecting a direct or an indirect approach, and outlining your content. Planning messages is the focus of this chapter.

The three-step writing process consists of planning, writing, and completing your messages.

1 Planning →	**2** Writing →	**3** Completing
Analyze the Situation Define your purpose, and develop an audience profile. **Gather Information** Determine audience needs, and obtain the information necessary to satisfy those needs. **Select the Right Medium** Choose the best medium for delivering your message. **Organize the Information** Define your main idea, limit your scope, select a direct or an indirect approach, and outline your content.	**Adapt to Your Audience** Be sensitive to audience needs by writing with a "you" attitude, politeness, positive emphasis, and bias-free language. Build a strong relationship with your audience by establishing your credibility and projecting your company's image. Control your style with a conversational tone, plain English, and appropriate voice. **Compose the Message** Choose precise language that will help you create effective sentences and coherent paragraphs.	**Revise the Message** Evaluate content and review readability, then edit and rewrite for conciseness and clarity. **Produce the Message** Use effective design elements and suitable layout for a clean, professional appearance. **Proofread the Message** Review for errors in layout, spelling, and mechanics. **Distribute the Message** Deliver your message using the chosen medium; make sure all documents and all relevant files are distributed successfully.

Figure 4–1 The Three-Step Writing Process

2. **Writing business messages.** Once you've planned your message, *adapt to your audience.* Be sensitive to your audience's needs by adopting the "you" attitude, being polite, emphasizing the positive, and using bias-free language. Build strong relationships with your audience by establishing your credibility and projecting your company's image. Be sure to control your style by using a conversational tone, plain English, and the correct voice. Then, you're ready to *compose your message* by choosing precise language, creating effective sentences, and developing coherent paragraphs. Writing business messages is discussed in Chapter 5.

3. **Completing business messages.** After writing your first draft, *revise your message* by reviewing the content and organization for overall style, structure, and readability. Then edit and rewrite until your message comes across concisely and clearly, with correct grammar, proper punctuation, and effective format. Next *produce your message.* Put it into the form that your audience will receive, and review all design and layout decisions for an attractive, professional appearance. *Proofread* the final draft for typos, spelling errors, and other mechanical problems. Finally, *distribute your message* using the best combination of personal and technological tools. Completing business messages is discussed in Chapter 6.

Throughout this book, you'll learn how to apply these steps to a wide variety of business messages: short messages such as emails and blog postings (Chapters 7 through 10), longer messages such as reports (Chapters 11 through 13), oral presentations (Chapter 14), and the employment messages you can use to build a satisfying career (Chapters 15 and 16).

OPTIMIZING YOUR WRITING TIME

As a starting point, use half your time for planning, one-quarter for writing, and one-quarter for completing your messages.

The more you use the three-step writing process, the more intuitive and automatic it will become. You'll also get better at allotting your time for each task during a writing project. As a general rule, use roughly half your time for planning—defining your purpose, getting to know your audience, immersing yourself in your subject matter, and working out media selection and organization. Use about one-quarter of your time for writing. Reserve the remaining quarter of your time for completing the project so that you don't short-change important completion steps such as revising, producing, proofreading, and distributing.[2]

Of course, these time allotments will change significantly depending on the project; for example, if you know your material intimately, the planning step might take less than half your time. However, if you're including video, photos, and graphical support, the completion step could take far longer than a quarter of your time.

Seasoned professionals understand that there is no right or best way to write all business messages. As you work through the writing process presented in this chapter and Chapters 5 and 6, don't view it as a list of how-to directives but as a way to understand the various tasks involved in effective business writing.[3]

PLANNING EFFECTIVELY

Trying to save time by skimping on planning usually costs you more time in the long run.

When deadlines loom and assignments pile up, it's tempting to rush through the planning phase and jump directly into writing. However, trying to save time up front often costs you more time as you struggle to complete a message that wasn't well thought out. You may also forget important information that leads to more messages being sent out. Even if you have only 20 or 30 minutes to prepare and send a message, work through all three steps quickly to ensure that your time is well used. Analyzing your audience helps you find and assemble the facts they're looking for and deliver that information in a concise and compelling way. Planning your message reduces indecision as you write and helps eliminate work as you review and revise.

Step 1 in the Writing Process: Planning

This chapter discusses the planning phase of writing. While this step may seem long and unnecessary, successful writers spend time thinking about each aspect presented below and do not ignore the need to organize messages for their audience. If you do not spend enough time planning, your messages may not be read, or they will leave a bad impression with your audience. As a communicator, it is your job to get messages across as effectively as possible, so carefully follow the points discussed in the remainder of this chapter.

Is creating an online game similar to planning business messages? How does the three-step process apply to this challenging activity?

Analyzing the Situation

The planning stage of writing is extremely important. When you first start writing in any new situation, it helps to make an outline, even if the outline consists of bullet points. When you begin working on the exercises at the end of the chapter, carefully review step 1 and begin creating an outline. This will help you organize your information for the messages you will write for this course and in the workplace.

Every communication effort takes place in a particular situation, meaning you have a specific message to send to a specific audience under a specific set of circumstances. For example, describing your professional qualifications in an email message to an executive in your own company who understands the company or qualifications jargon differs significantly from describing your qualifications in your LinkedIn profile. The email message is likely to be focused on one specific goal, such as explaining why you would be a good choice to head up a major project, and you have the luxury of focusing on the needs of a single, personally identifiable reader. In contrast, your social networking profile could have multiple goals, such as connecting with your peers in other companies and presenting your qualifications to potential employers, and it might be viewed by hundreds or thousands of readers, each with his or her own needs.

The underlying information for these two messages could be roughly the same, but the level of detail to include, the tone of the writing, the specific word choices—these and other choices you need to make will differ from one situation to another. Making the right choices starts with defining your purpose clearly and understanding your audience's needs.

DEFINING YOUR PURPOSE

All business messages have a **general purpose:** to inform, persuade, or collaborate with an audience. This purpose helps define the overall approach you'll take, from gathering information to organizing your message. Within the scope of its general purpose, each message also has a **specific purpose,** which identifies what you hope to accomplish with your message and what your audience should do or think after receiving your message. For example, is your goal simply to update your audience about an event, or do you want them to take immediate action? State your specific purpose as precisely as possible, even identifying which audience members should respond; how they should respond; and when they should respond, by giving an end date.

After you have defined your specific purpose, you can decide whether that purpose merits the time and effort required for you to prepare and send the message. Test your purpose by asking four questions:

1. Will anything change as a result of your message? Don't contribute to information overload by sending messages that won't change events or actions. For

Your general purpose may be to inform, persuade, or collaborate.

Your specific purpose is what you hope to accomplish with your message and what your audience should do or think after receiving your message.

example, if you don't like your company's latest advertising campaign, but you're not in a position to influence it, sending a critical message to your colleagues won't change anything and won't benefit anyone.

2. Is your purpose realistic? Recognizing whether a goal is realistic is an important part of having good business sense. For example, if you request a raise while the company is struggling, you might send the message that you're not tuned in to the situation around you.

3. Is the time right? People who are busy or distracted when they receive your message are less likely to pay attention to it. Many professions and departments have recurring cycles in their workloads, so messages sent during peak times might be ignored.

4. Is your purpose acceptable to your organization? Your company's business objectives may dictate whether a purpose is acceptable.

When you are satisfied that you have a clear and meaningful purpose and that this is a smart time to proceed, your next step is to understand the members of your audience and their needs.

DEVELOPING AN AUDIENCE PROFILE

The more you know about your audience members, their needs, and their expectations, the more effectively you'll be able to communicate with them. For an example of the kind of information you need to compile in an audience analysis, see the planning sheet in Figure 4–2. Completing a form will help you select the necessary content for your messages, choose the right format, and write using an appropriate tone and style.

To conduct an audience analysis:

Ask yourself key questions about your audience to help achieve your purpose.

1. Identify your primary audience. For some messages, certain audience members might be more important than others. Don't ignore the needs of less influential members, but make sure you address the concerns of the key decision makers.

2. Identify the secondary audience. The secondary audience is composed of people who are given some details of your message—or the entire message itself—by the primary audience. For example, if your message recommends upgrading your department's computers, your manager might copy your message to the company's purchasing director, who would have to approve the decision. Although this director is not the person to whom you addressed your memo, she receives the message because she influences your proposal's outcome.

3. Determine audience composition. Look for both similarities and differences in culture, language, age, education, organizational rank and status, attitudes, experience, motivations, and any other factors that might affect the success of your message. For example, if you're reporting the results of a market research project, the vice president of sales will probably want to know what's happening right now. On the other hand, the vice president of communication might be more interested in how the market will look a year or two from now, when that department's new products will be ready to sell.

If audience members have different levels of understanding of the topic, aim your message at the most influential decision makers.

4. Gauge audience members' level of understanding. If audience members share your general background, they'll probably understand your material without difficulty. If not, your message will need an element of education, and deciding how much information to include can be a challenge. Include only enough information to accomplish the specific purpose of your message. Other material will overwhelm your audience and divert attention from the important points. If the members of your audience have various levels of understanding, gear your coverage to your primary audience (the key decision makers).

Project: A report recommending that we close down the on-site exercise facility and subsidize private memberships at local health clubs.

1	Who is my primary audience?	Nicole Perazzo, vice president of operations
2	Who is my secondary audience?	Nicole's assistants (Sam, Tammy) James Ngomo, vice president of finance Felice Gonzalez, vice president of human resources
3	What is the size of my audience? What is their location?	Five managers total All managers are located in Halifax
4	What is their level of knowledge?	All will have knowledge of the financial situation, but Felice will not have the budget. (Note: summarize budget details in the report to give Felice the financial context.)
5	What are their expectations and preferences?	All are expecting a firm recommendation, supported by a clear financial rationale. They will also want suggestions for communicating the bad news to employees. (I want to send a hard-copy memo to employees; they may prefer email.)
6	What is the probable reaction?	Staff might first resent the change, but they may prefer going to a full-service health club with personal trainers after the change is fully explained.

Figure 4–2 Audience Analysis Worksheet

5. **Understand audience expectations and preferences.** Will members of your audience expect complete details or just a summary of the main points? In general, for internal communication, the higher up the organization your message goes, the fewer details people want to see.

6. **Forecast probable audience reaction.** As you'll read later in the chapter, audience reaction affects message organization. If you expect a favourable response, you can state conclusions and recommendations up front and offer minimal supporting evidence. If you expect skepticism or resistance, introduce conclusions gradually, with more proof.

Gathering Information

When you have a clear picture of your audience and their needs, your next step is to assemble the information that you will include in your message. For simple messages, you may already have all the information at hand, but for more

4   LEARNING OBJECTIVE

Discuss gathering information for simple messages, and identify three attributes of quality information.

complex messages you may need to do considerable research and analysis before you're ready to begin writing. Chapter 11 explores formal techniques for finding, evaluating, and processing information, but you can often use a variety of informal techniques to gather insights and guide your research efforts:

- **Consider other viewpoints.** Putting yourself in someone else's position helps you consider what that person might be thinking, feeling, or planning. What information do people need to move in the direction you would like them to move?
- **Read reports and other company documents.** Annual reports, financial statements, news releases, blogs, marketing reports, and customer surveys provide helpful information. Find out whether your company has a *knowledge management system*, a centralized database that collects the experiences and insights of employees throughout the organization.
- **Talk with supervisors, colleagues, or customers.** Fellow workers and customers may have information you need, or they may know what your audience will be interested in. And one of the huge advantages of social media is the ability to quickly locate experts and sources of vital information.
- **Ask your audience for input.** If you're unsure of what audience members need from your message, ask them. Admitting that you don't know but want to meet their needs will impress an audience more than guessing and getting it wrong.

If you're given a vague request, ask questions to clarify it before you plan a response.

If appropriate, include any additional information that might be helpful, even though the requester didn't specifically ask for it.

Courtesy of the Business Development Bank of Canada (BDC), Aboriginal Banking Unit, photo by Colleen Serban Photography, www.colleenserban.com

BDC ABORIGINAL BANKING | ISSUE 19 | 2012

soar MAGAZINE

CHARITY BUSCH
Both wise and successful beyond her years

JOSH ST. CYR
Soaring with Wasaya Airways

PERSPECTIVE
Ali Fontaine:
Singer rises to the top

BDC
Entrepreneurs first

Canada

Published by the Aboriginal Banking department of the Business Development Bank of Canada (BDC), SOAR magazine includes inspirational stories about Aboriginal youth. How do you think staff develop story ideas for this magazine?

UNCOVERING AUDIENCE NEEDS

In many situations your audience's information needs will be obvious, or readers will be able to tell you what they need. In other situations, though, people may be unable to articulate exactly what is needed. If someone makes a vague or broad request, ask questions to narrow the focus. If your boss says, "Find out everything you can about Interscope Records," ask which aspects of the company and its business are most important. Asking a question or two often forces the person to think through the request and define more precisely what is required.

In addition, try to think of relevant information needs that your audience may not have expressed. Suppose you've been asked to compare two health insurance plans for your firm's employees, but your research has uncovered a third alternative that might be even better. You could then expand your report to include a brief explanation of why the third plan should be considered and compare it with the two original plans. Use judgment; however, in some situations you need to provide only what the audience expects and nothing more.

PROVIDING REQUIRED INFORMATION

Once you've defined your audience's information needs, be ready to satisfy those needs completely (see "Promoting Workplace Ethics: How Much

Information Is Enough?" on page 96). One good way to test the thoroughness of your message is to use the **journalistic approach:** check whether your message answers *who*, *what*, *when*, *where*, *why*, and *how*. Using this test, you can quickly tell whether a message fails to deliver—for example, as does this message requesting information from employees:

> We are exploring ways to reduce our office space leasing costs and would like your input on a proposed plan in which employees who telecommute on alternate days could share offices. Please let me know what you think of this proposal.

The message fails to tell employees everything they need to know in order to provide meaningful responses. The *what* could be improved by identifying the specific information points the writer needs from employees (such as whether individual telecommuting patterns are predictable enough to allow scheduling of shared offices). The writer also doesn't specify *when* the responses are needed or *how* the employees should respond. By failing to address such points, the request is likely to generate a variety of responses, some possibly helpful but some probably not.

> Test the completeness of your document by ensuring it answers all the important questions: *who*, *what*, *when*, *where*, *why*, and *how*.

BE SURE THE INFORMATION IS ACCURATE Inaccurate information communicated in business messages can cause a host of problems, from embarrassment and lost productivity to serious safety and legal issues. Inaccurate information may persist for months or years after you distribute it, or you may commit the organization to promises it isn't able to keep—and the error could harm your reputation as a reliable businessperson.

You can minimize mistakes by double-checking every piece of information you collect. If you consult sources outside the organization, ask yourself whether they are current and reliable. You must be particularly careful when using sources you find online; the simplicity of online publishing and common lack of editorial oversight call for extra care in using online information. Be sure to review any mathematical or financial calculations. Check all dates and schedules, and examine your own assumptions and conclusions to be certain they are valid.

> Be certain that the information you provide is accurate and that the commitments you make can be kept.

BE SURE THE INFORMATION IS ETHICAL By working hard to ensure the accuracy of the information you gather, you'll also avoid many ethical problems in your messages. If you do make an honest mistake, such as delivering information you initially thought to be true but later found to be false, contact the recipients of the message immediately and correct the error. No one can reasonably fault you in such circumstances, and most people will respect your honesty.

Messages can also be unethical if important information is omitted. Of course, as a business professional, you may have legal or other sound business reasons for not including every detail about every matter. Just how much detail should you include? Make sure you include enough detail to avoid misleading your audience. If you're unsure how much information your audience needs, offer as much as you believe best fits your definition of complete, and then offer to provide more upon request.

> Ethics should guide your decisions when determining how much detail to include in your message.

BE SURE THE INFORMATION IS RELEVANT When gathering information for your message, remember that some points will be more important to your audience than others. Audience members will appreciate your efforts to prioritize the information they need and filter out the information they don't. Moreover, by focusing on the information that concerns your audience the most, you increase your chances of accomplishing your own communication goals.

> Figure out what points will especially interest your audience, then give those points the most attention.

TIPS FOR SUCCESS

"The most effective writers are those who view what they compose from the reader's vantage point. Ask yourself, Does the intended reader have your background, your education, and your experience with the subject at hand? If not, adjust your text accordingly."

Ray Dreyfack, systems executive, Fabergé Perfumes, business writer and consultant

Corporate Responsibility 101:
A Resource for Students

The document uses a graphic to draw the reader's attention. Note that the colour scheme is the same for the graphic and the visual, so there is a sense of continuity for the reader.

This document answers most of the questions students ask about corporate responsibility and sustainability at RBC®.

For additional information, visit rbc.com/community-sustainability and click on "Our Approach."

What's in a word?

For years, there has been lots of debate over the meaning of the term "corporate responsibility". Some people use the term to mean 'a charitable donations program'. When others use it, they mean 'employee volunteerism". Still others mean 'community relations." And things get even more complicated with the use of terms such as corporate social responsibility, corporate accountability, sustainability, the triple bottom line, corporate citizenship and shared value. We believe that words matter, and that each of the terms listed here has a meaning distinctly different from the others.

At RBC, use the term "corporate responsibility" to mean:

"conducting ourselves with integrity every day, sustaining our company's long-term viability, being transparent and accountable, and helping build a better future for our clients, employees, communities and shareholders."

The phrase 'conducting ourselves with integrity" is the critical piece here. Corporate responsibility is about our behaviour and our actions. It's not a single program, managed by a single department.

We consider corporate responsibility to be like a multi-textured fabric, woven strong with many threads and strands. The central thread is our long-standing commitment to conducting ourselves with integrity for our clients, and with concern for people and the planet. This commitment twines through and strengthens our economic impact, as well as our performance in the marketplace, the workplace, the environment, the community. Woven together with our commitment to diversity, all these strands create a durable fabric that we call 'corporate responsibility'. We need them all. In isolation, none of the strands will last. Here's an illustration of how the components of corporate responsibility fit together at RBC:

Brief to medium-length paragraphs keep the information accessible and engage the reader.

The document incorporates visual support to represent the concepts in an easy-to-understand manner.

Figure 4–3 Audience-Focused Document (selected pages)

If you don't know your audience, or if you're communicating with a large group of people with diverse interests, use common sense to identify points of particular interest. Audience factors such as age, job, location, income, and education can give you a clue. If you're trying to sell memberships in a health club, you might adjust your message for athletes, busy professionals, families, and people in different locations or in different income brackets. The comprehensive facilities and professional trainers would appeal to athletes, whereas the low monthly rates would appeal to students on tight budgets. As Figure 4–3 shows, your main goal is to tell audience members what they need to know in an accessible format and style. This corporate responsibility document from Royal Bank Financial Group uses formatting features and a question/answer approach for its student audience.

Some messages necessarily reach audiences with a diverse mix of educational levels, subject awareness, and other variables. In these cases, your only choice is to try to accommodate the likely range of audience members.

Selecting the Right Medium

A **medium** is the form through which you choose to communicate your message. You may choose to talk with someone face to face, leave a voicemail message, post to a blog, send an email, or create a webcast—and there are many other media to choose from. The range of media possibilities is wide and growing wider all the time. In fact, with so many options now available, selecting the best medium for a given message is itself an important communication skill.

A numbered list draws attention to specific information.

The FAQ format is used to focus on specific topics.

The RBC Six

Here are RBC's six pledges to help us build a better future for our clients, employees, communities and shareholders.

1. **Integrity:** We will conduct ourselves with integrity in everything we do, guided by our comprehensive Code of Conduct. We will demonstrate sound corporate governance principles, provide full and plain disclosure of financial results and disclose reliable performance data on key nonfinancial items that may represent risks or opportunities.

2. **Economic Impact:** We will have a positive impact on the economy, creating good jobs, paying our fair share of taxes and purchasing goods and services responsibly from suppliers of all sizes. We will provide credit to households, businesses and investors so they can prosper.

3. **Marketplace:** We will earn the right to be our clients' first choice by serving them responsibly. We will strive to ensure that our clients have access to the right products, services and advice so that they can make the best financial decisions possible.

4. **Workplace:** We will be a workplace of choice by creating strong partnerships with our employees and respecting diversity. In an era when financial "products" are seen as commodities, our success depends on the skills, knowledge and commitment of our employees.

5. **Environment:** We will take responsibility for our indirect and direct environmental impact. The RBC Environmental Blueprint™ contains 44 commitments to help us reduce our environmental footprint, lend responsibly and provide "green" products and services to our clients.

6. **Community:** We will build on our generations-long history of support for communities where we live and work, addressing today's needs and seeding tomorrow's success. We will provide focused, significant support to key causes and activities that are important to our company, clients and communities. We will also maintain a broad base of support for a wide range of social, cultural and environmental organizations that help maintain the fabric of communities.

Who or what department is responsible for corporate responsibility at RBC? At RBC, our whole company, every employee, is responsible for behaving responsibly, and it's built right into our Code of Conduct, which reads:

"It is our duty as a corporate citizen to add value to society while earning a profit for our shareholders. RBC companies take responsibility for the effects of their actions, both social and economic."

You could say that at RBC, corporate responsibility is functionally decentralized, because it is integrated right into our businesses.

At the Board level, a number of committees share responsibility for the integrity of our conduct as well as our programs and performance in the workplace, marketplace, community and for the environment.

That being said, some of our stakeholders, such as the responsible investment community, are interested in a high-level, holistic picture of how all the elements of corporate responsibility fit together at RBC. In fact, we are actually required to provide detailed reporting about our corporate responsibility efforts by Canadian banking regulations. As such we have assigned formal responsibility for these duties within Corporate Citizenship, a group that includes Corporate Responsibility, Corporate Environmental Affairs and Donations. Our 2011 Corporate Responsibility Report outlines the various board committees and departments that have responsibility for 'responsibility.'

How do I get a job in "corporate responsibility" at RBC? We always advise potential job seekers that jobs in "corporate responsibility"

at RBC may not always bear that title. Remember, we consider corporate responsibility to be about conducting ourselves with integrity every day—and we don't have a single "behaviour" department. A wide range of departments are responsible for activities that fall under our definition of "corporate responsibility", including Corporate Citizenship (comprising Donations, Corporate Environmental Affairs and Corporate Responsibility Strategy & Reporting), Human Resources, Procurement, Risk Management, Community and Brand Sponsorships, Donations, Real Estate Operations, Government and Regulatory Affairs, Finance, Compliance and Corporate Communications.

We encourage job seekers to be as specific as possible when inquiring about the actual discipline or area that interests them. Most often, when

Figure 4–3 Audience-Focused Document (selected pages) (*continued*)

Courtesy: RBC

Although media categories have become increasingly blurred in recent years, for the sake of discussion, you can think of media as being *oral*, *written*, *visual*, or *electronic* (which often combines several media types).

ORAL MEDIA

Oral media include face-to-face conversations, interviews, speeches, and in-person presentations and meetings. By giving communicators the ability to see, hear, and react to one another, traditional oral media are useful for encouraging people to ask questions, make comments, and work together to reach a consensus or decision. For example, experts recommend that managers engage in frequent "walk-arounds," chatting with employees to get input, answer their questions, and interpret important business events and trends.[4]

Of course, if you don't want a lot of questions or interaction, oral media can be an unwise choice. However, consider your audience carefully before deciding to limit interaction by choosing a different medium. As a manager, you will encounter unpleasant situations (declining an employee's request for a raise, for example) in which sending an email message or otherwise avoiding personal contact will seem appealing. Avoiding personal interaction in difficult circumstances demonstrates weakness; in many such cases, you owe the other party the

Oral communication is best when you need to encourage interaction, express emotions, or monitor emotional responses.

sirtravelalot/Shutterstock

The higher you rise in an organization, the more time you spend talking and listening. Your ability to communicate with people from virtually any background will be key to your success. How can you be a sensitive communicator when you need to communicate bad news orally?

Nonelectronic written messages have been replaced in many instances by electronic media, although printed messages still have a place in business today.

In some situations, a message that is predominantly visual, with text used to support the illustration, can be more effective than a message that relies primarily on text.

opportunity to ask questions or express concerns. Moreover, facing the tough situations in person will earn you a reputation as an honest, caring manager.

WRITTEN MEDIA

Written messages take many forms, from traditional memos to glossy reports that rival magazines in production quality. **Memos** are brief, printed documents, generally no more than a page long, traditionally used for the routine, day-to-day exchange of information within an organization. In many organizations, social networking, instant messaging (IM), email, blogs, and other electronic media have largely replaced paper memos.

Letters are brief, written messages one to two pages long and generally sent to recipients outside the organization, so in addition to conveying a particular message, they perform an important public relations function in fostering good working relationships with customers, suppliers, and others. Letters can be sent in hard copy or as email attachments. Many organizations save time and money on routine communication with *form letters*, in which a standard message is personalized as needed for each recipient. Form letters are particularly handy for such one-time mass mailings as sales messages about products, information about organizational activities, and goodwill messages such as seasonal greetings. Chapters 8 through 10 discuss memos, letters, IM, and other short-message forms, and Appendix A explains how to format these business documents.

Reports and proposals are usually longer than letters and memos, although both can be created in memo or letter format. These documents come in a variety of lengths, ranging from a few pages to several hundred, and are usually fairly formal in tone. Chapters 11 through 13 discuss reports and proposals in detail.

VISUAL MEDIA

Although you probably won't work with many messages that are purely visual (with no text), the importance of visual elements in business communication continues to grow. Traditional business messages rely primarily on text, with occasional support from graphical elements such as charts, graphs, or diagrams to help illustrate points discussed in the text. However, many business communicators are discovering the power of messages in which the visual element is dominant and supported by small amounts of text. For the purposes of this discussion, you can think of visual media as any format in which one or more visual elements play a central role in conveying the message content. Figure 4–4 shows how the message about CRM, customer relationship management (a category of software that helps companies manage their interactions with customers), can be presented more effectively by basing the message on a dominant visual and using text to support that image.

Why should I care about CRM?

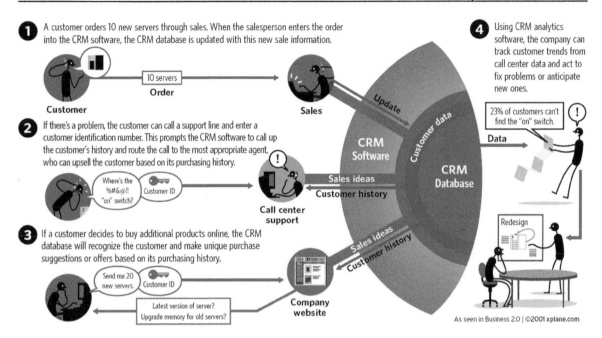

Figure 4–4 Visual Media

Courtesy: XPlane

Messages that combine powerful visuals with supporting text, sometimes known as *infographics*, can be effective for a number of reasons. Audiences are bombarded with messages, so anything that communicates quickly is welcome. Visuals are also effective at describing complex ideas and processes because they can reduce the work required for an audience to identify the parts and relationships that make up the whole. Also, in a multilingual business world, diagrams, symbols, and other images can lower communication barriers by requiring less language processing. Finally, visual images can be easier to remember than purely textual descriptions or explanations. Chapter 12 offers more information on visual design.

ELECTRONIC MEDIA

The range of electronic media is broad and continues to grow, from phone calls and podcasts to blogs and wikis to email and text messaging. When you want to make a powerful impression, using electronic media can increase the excitement and visual appeal with interactivity, animation, audio, and video.

The growth of electronic communication options is both a blessing and a curse for business communicators. On the one hand, you have more tools than ever before to choose from, with more ways to deliver rational and emotional content. On the other hand, the sheer range of choices can complicate your job because you often need to choose among multiple media, and you need to know how to use each medium successfully.

From the audience's perspective, a common frustration with electronic media is lack of integration, with people being forced to use to an ever-growing arsenal of separate but overlapping media options to stay informed.[5] As the options multiply, the struggle to monitor multiple sources of information can consume considerable time and energy. To minimize frustration and maximize productivity, company managers should establish clear expectations for the use of electronic media and carefully integrate—or officially choose *not* to use—each new media innovation.

> In general, use electronic media to deliver messages quickly, to reach widely dispersed audiences, and to take advantage of rich multimedia formats.

> Audiences can get frustrated with the sheer number of electronic media in the workplace.

You'll learn more about using electronic media throughout this book (in Chapter 7, in particular), but for now, here is a quick overview of the major electronic media being used in business:

- **Electronic versions of oral media.** These include telephone calls, teleconferencing, voicemail messages, audio recordings such as compact discs and podcasts, *voice synthesis* (creating audio signals from computer data), *voice recognition* (converting audio signals to computer data), and even animated online characters.

  Internet telephony services, such as Skype, that use VoIP (which stands for *voice over IP*, the Internet protocol) continue to grow in popularity. Although audio-only telephone calls can't convey all the nonverbal signals of an in-person conversation, they can convey quite a few, including tone of voice, pace, laughter, pauses, and so on. Of course, video phone calls can replace much of the nonverbal content missing from audio calls; 40 percent of Skype's call volume is video calls.[6]

- **Electronic versions of written media.** These options range from email and IM to blogs, websites, social networks, and wikis. These media are in a state of constant change, in terms of both what is available and who tends to use which media. For example, email has been a primary business medium for the past decade or two, but it is being replaced in many cases by IM, blogs, text messaging, and communication via social networks.[7] Chapter 7 takes a closer look at email, IM, blogs, and social networks; Chapter 12 discusses wikis in more detail.

- **Electronic versions of visual media.** These choices can include electronic presentations (using Microsoft PowerPoint, Google Drive, Apple Keynote, and other software), computer animation (using software such as Adobe Flash to create many of the animated sequences you see on websites, for example), and video (YouTube quickly became a major business communication channel). **Multimedia** refers to the use of two or more media to craft a single message, typically some combination of audio, video, text, and visual graphics. Multimedia advances continue to create intriguing communication possibilities, such as *augmented reality*, in which computer-generated text, graphics, and sounds are superimposed onto a user's physical reality, either on a device display or directly onto the physical world itself.

FACTORS TO CONSIDER WHEN CHOOSING MEDIA

5 **LEARNING OBJECTIVE**

List factors to consider when choosing the most appropriate medium for your message.

Media range from *rich* (many cues, simple feedback, personalization) to *lean* (few information cues, few feedback mechanisms, no personalization).

In some situations, you have little or no choice of which medium to use. For instance, your department might use IM for all short internal messages and a wiki for longer status reports, and you'll be expected to use those media as well. In other situations, you'll have the opportunity to choose the medium (or media) for a particular message. Table 4–1 lists the general advantages and disadvantages of each medium. In addition, be sure to consider how your message is affected by these important factors:

- **Media richness.** *Richness* is a medium's ability to (1) convey a message through more than one *informational cue* (visual, verbal, vocal), (2) facilitate feedback, and (3) establish personal focus. The richest medium is face-to-face communication: it's personal, it provides immediate feedback (verbal and nonverbal), and it conveys the emotion behind a message.[8] Multimedia presentations and multimedia webpages are also rich, with the ability to present images, animation, text, music, and sound effects. Many electronic media are also *interactive*, in that they enable audiences to participate in the communication process. For example, a website can allow visitors to select

Table 4–1	Media Advantages and Disadvantages	
Media Type	**Advantages**	**Disadvantages**
Oral	• Provide opportunity for immediate feedback • Promote interaction • Involve rich nonverbal cues (both physical gestures and vocal inflection) • Allow you to express the emotions behind the message	• Restrict participation to those physically present • Unless recorded, provide no permanent, verifiable record of the communication • In most cases, reduce communicator's control over the message • Other than for messages that are prewritten and rehearsed, offer no opportunity to revise or edit spoken words
Written	• Allow you to plan and control your message • Reach geographically dispersed audiences • Offer a permanent, verifiable record • Minimize the distortion that can result with oral and some forms of electronic messages • Can be used to avoid immediate interactions • Can help you control the emotional aspects of an interchange by eliminating interpersonal communication	• Offer limited opportunities for timely feedback • Lack the rich nonverbal cues provided by oral media • Can require more time and more resources to create and distribute, relative to oral media • Elaborate documents can require special skills in preparation and production
Visual	• Can convey complex ideas and relationships quickly • Often less intimidating than long blocks of text, particularly for non-native readers • Can reduce the burden on the audience to figure out how the pieces of a message or concept fit together	• Can require artistic skills to design • Require some technical skills to create • Can require more time to create than an equivalent amount of text • Are more difficult to transmit and store than simple textual messages
Electronic	• Deliver messages quickly • Reach geographically dispersed audiences • Can offer the persuasive power of multimedia formats • Enable audience interaction through social media features • Can increase accessibility and openness within an organization and between an organization and its external stakeholders	• Are easy to overuse (sending too many messages to too many recipients) • Present privacy risks and concerns (exposing confidential data, employer monitoring, accidental forwarding) • Present security risks (viruses and spyware, network breaches) • Create productivity concerns (frequent interruptions, lack of integration among multiple electronic media in use at the same time, and time wasted on nonbusiness uses)

the types of information they want to see, to provide feedback, or to use a variety of online calculators or other tools. At the other extreme are the leanest media—those that communicate in the simplest ways and provide no opportunity for audience feedback (see Figure 4–5). In general, use richer media to send nonroutine or complex messages, to humanize your presence

Leaner: fewer cues, no interactivity, no personal focus

Standard reports **Static webpages** **Mass media** **Posters & signs**

Custom reports **Letters & memos** **Email & IM** **Wikis** **Blogs** **Podcasts**

Telephone calls **Teleconferencing** **Video**

Face-to-face conversations **Multimedia presentations** **Multimedia webpages** **Virtual reality**

Richer: multiple cues, interactive, personalized

Figure 4–5 Media Richness

Welcome to World Voyager Vacations

Courtesy: World Voyager Vacations

Many websites now feature talking animated figures, such as avatars, giving website visitors a more enhanced online experience. Do these figures serve a meaningful purpose? Do they engage potential customers or detract from the text and other visuals?

Some media deliver messages faster than others, but instantaneous delivery shouldn't be used to create a false sense of urgency.

When choosing the appropriate medium, don't forget to consider your audience's expectations.

throughout the organization, to communicate caring to employees, and to gain employee commitment to company goals. Use leaner media to send routine messages or to transfer information that doesn't require significant explanation.[9]

- **Message formality.** Your media choice is a nonverbal signal that affects the style and tone of your message. For example, a printed memo or letter is likely to be perceived as a more formal gesture than an email message.
- **Media limitations.** Every medium has limitations. For example, IM is ideal for communicating simple, straightforward messages, but it is less effective for sending complex ones.
- **Urgency.** Some media establish a connection with the audience faster than others, so choose wisely if your message is urgent. However, be sure to respect audience members' time and workloads. If a message isn't urgent and doesn't require immediate feedback, choose a medium such as email that allows people to respond at their convenience.
- **Cost.** Cost is both a real financial factor and a perceived nonverbal signal. For example, depending on the context, extravagant (and expensive) video or multimedia presentations can send a nonverbal signal of sophistication and professionalism—or careless disregard for company budgets.
- **Audience preferences.** Be sure to consider which medium or media your audience expects or prefers.[10] For example, businesspeople in Canada, the United States, and Germany emphasize written messages, whereas in Japan professionals emphasize oral messages—perhaps because Japan's high-context culture carries so much of the message in nonverbal cues and "between the lines" interpretation.[11]

PROMOTING WORKPLACE ETHICS — How Much Information Is Enough?

Imagine that your company creates a variety of home furniture products, with extensive use of fine woods. To preserve the look and feel of the wood, your craftspeople use an oil-based finish that you purchase from a local building products wholesaler. The workers apply the finish with rags, which are thrown away after each project. After a news report about spontaneous combustion of waste rags in other furniture shops, you grow concerned enough to contact the wholesaler and ask for verification of the product's safety. The wholesaler knows that you've been considering a nonflammable, water-based alternative from another source but tries to reassure you with the following email message:

> Seal the rags in an approved container and dispose of it according to local regulations. As you probably already know, municipal regulations require all commercial users of solvent-based materials to dispose of leftover finishes at the municipality's hazardous waste facility.

You're still not satisfied. You visit the website of the oil's manufacturer and find the following cautionary statement about the product you're currently using:

Improper disposal of oil-soaked rags and other materials can lead to serious fire hazards. As certain oil-based finishes cure, the chemical reactions that take place can generate enough heat to cause spontaneous combustion of vapors and oil-soaked material. To temporarily store oil-soaked rags and other waste safely, immerse them fully in water in a metal container and close the container with an airtight seal. Dispose of the container in accordance with local regulations.

CAREER APPLICATIONS

1. Was the wholesaler guilty of an ethical lapse in this case? If yes, explain what you think the lapse is and why you believe it is unethical. If no, explain why you think the statement qualifies as ethical.
2. Would the manufacturer's warning be as effective without the second sentence, which explains spontaneous combustion? Why or why not?

- **Accessibility concerns.** Many provinces have or are in the process of enacting legislation that must be followed when creating messages so that people with disabilities have equal access to information. For example, if you create a video to send your message, you may need to include subtitles so that people with hearing issues can read your message as well. Make sure you follow the legislation in your province or territory.

Organizing Your Information

For anything beyond the simplest messages, organization can make the difference between success and failure. Compare the draft and revision versions of the message in Figure 4–6, in which the writer is requesting the replacement of a faulty DVD drive. The draft version exhibits four of the most common organization mistakes:

Most disorganized communication suffers from problems with clarity, relevance, grouping, and completeness.

1. **Taking too long to get to the point.** The writer, Jill Saunders, didn't introduce her topic, the faulty DVD drive, until the second paragraph. Then she waited until the final paragraph to state her purpose: requesting a replacement. *Solution:* Make the subject and purpose clear, and get to the point without wasting the reader's time.
2. **Including irrelevant material.** The first draft is full of irrelevant information: that Nutri-Veg has 3000 stores, that its online presence is growing, and so on. *Solution:* Include only information that is related to the subject and purpose.
3. **Getting ideas mixed up.** Saunders tries to make several points: (a) Her company has been a customer for a long time; (b) her company has purchased numerous items at ComputerTime; (c) the DVD drive doesn't work; and (d) Saunders wants a replacement. However, the ideas are mixed up and located in the wrong places. *Solution:* Group similar ideas and present them in a logical way, where one idea leads to the next.
4. **Leaving out necessary information.** ComputerTime may want to know the make, model, and price of the DVD drive; the date of purchase; and the specific problems the device has had. Saunders also failed to say what she wants the store to do: send her a new DVD drive of the same type, send her a different model, or simply refund her money. *Solution:* Include all the information necessary for the audience to respond as the writer wishes.

The revised version corrects all four mistakes, and the result is a much stronger letter.

As you'll see in the following chapters, various types of messages may require different organizational schemes. Nevertheless, in every case you can organize your message in a logical and compelling way by recognizing the importance of good organization, defining your main idea, limiting your scope, choosing either a direct or an indirect approach, and outlining your content.

To organize a message, define your main idea, limit the scope, choose the direct or indirect approach, and group your points.

RECOGNIZING THE IMPORTANCE OF GOOD ORGANIZATION

In addition to helping you, good organization helps the members of your audience in three key ways. First, it helps your audience understand your message. In a well-organized message, you make the main point clear at the outset, present additional points to support that main idea, and satisfy all the information needs of the audience. But if your message is poorly organized, your meaning can be obscured and your audiences may form inaccurate conclusions about what you've written or said.

Second, good organization helps receivers accept your message. If your writing appears confused and disorganized, people will likely conclude that the *thinking* behind the writing is also confused and disorganized. Moreover,

6 **LEARNING OBJECTIVE**

Explain why good organization is important to both you and your audience.

Poor organization can waste time, reduce efficiency, and damage relationships.

Good organization helps audience members understand your message, accept your message, and save time.

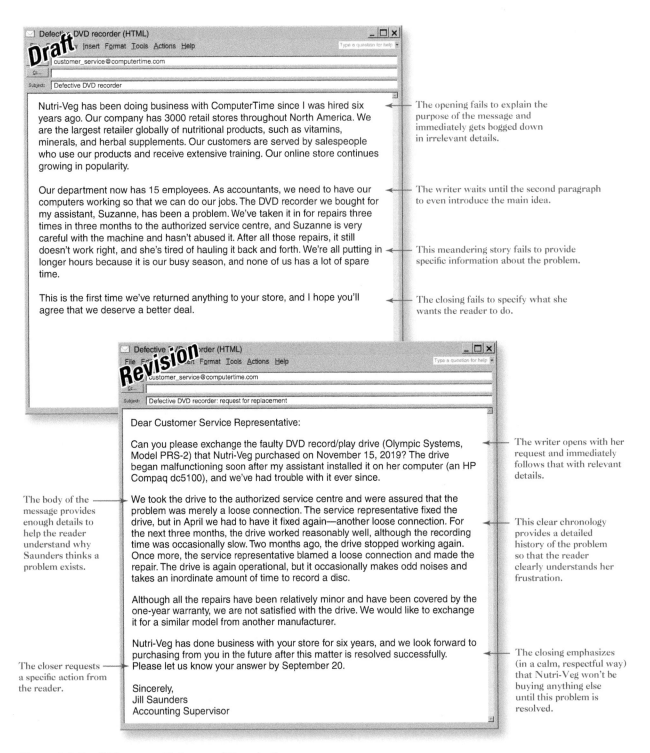

Figure 4–6 Email Message with Improved Organization

effective messages often require a bit more than simple, clear logic. A diplomatic approach helps receivers accept your message, even if it's not exactly what they want to hear. In the case of ComputerTime's response to Jill Saunders's request for a replacement product from a different manufacturer, ComputerTime isn't able to do exactly what Saunders requested (they've arranged a replacement from the same manufacturer instead). Consequently, the response letter from Linda Davis has a negative aspect to it, but the style of the letter is tactful and positive (see Figure 4–7).

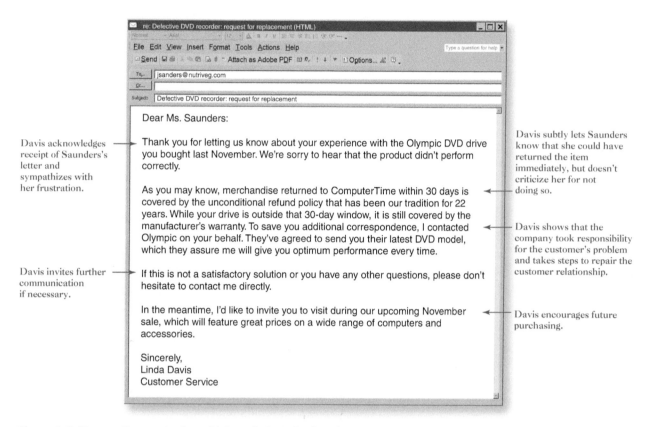

Davis acknowledges receipt of Saunders's letter and sympathizes with her frustration.

Davis invites further communication if necessary.

Davis subtly lets Saunders know that she could have returned the item immediately, but doesn't criticize her for not doing so.

Davis shows that the company took responsibility for the customer's problem and takes steps to repair the customer relationship.

Davis encourages future purchasing.

Figure 4–7 Message Demonstrating a Diplomatic Organization Plan

Third, good organization saves your audience time. Well-organized messages are efficient. They contain only relevant ideas, and they are brief. Moreover, each piece of information is located in a logical place in the overall flow; each section builds on the one before to create a coherent whole, without forcing people to look for missing pieces.

In addition to saving time and energy for your readers, good organization saves *you* time and consumes less of your creative energy. Writing moves more quickly because you don't waste time putting ideas in the wrong places or composing material that you don't need. You spend far less time rewriting, trying to extract sensible meaning from disorganized rambling. Finally, organizational skills are good for your career because they help you develop a reputation as a clear thinker who cares about your readers.

DEFINING YOUR MAIN IDEA

The **topic** of your message is the overall subject, and your **main idea** is a specific statement about that topic (see Table 4–2). For example, if you believe that the current system of using paper forms for filing employee insurance claims is expensive and slow, you might craft a message in which the topic is employee insurance claims and the main idea is that a new web-based claim-filing system would reduce costs for the company and reduce reimbursement delays for employees.

In longer documents and presentations, you often need to unify a mass of material, so you'll need to define a main idea that encompasses all the individual points you want to make. Finding a common thread through all these points can be a challenge. Sometimes you won't even be sure what your main idea is until

7 LEARNING OBJECTIVE

Summarize the process for organizing business messages effectively.

The topic is the overall subject; the main idea is a specific statement about the topic.

Table 4–2	Defining the Topic and Main Idea		
General Purpose	**Specific Purpose**	**Topic**	**Main Idea**
To inform	Teach customer service representatives how to file insurance claims.	Insurance claims	Proper filing saves the company time and money.
To persuade	Convince top managers to increase spending on research and development.	Funding for research and development	Competitors spend more than we do on research and development.
To collaborate	Acquire technology and sales figures to devise a computer program that tracks sales by geographical region.	Sales	Using a computer program that tracks sales by region will easily highlight geographical areas that need improved representation of products.

you sort through the information. For especially challenging assignments like these, consider a variety of techniques to generate creative ideas:

- **Brainstorming.** Working alone or with others, generate as many ideas and questions as you can, without stopping to criticize or organize. After you capture all these pieces, look for patterns and connections to help identify the main idea and the groups of supporting ideas. If your assignment is to find a way to increase sales, for example, you might find a cluster of ideas relating to new products, another relating to advertising strategies, and another related to pricing. Identifying such clusters helps you see the major issues and determine the most important idea.
- **Journalistic approach.** Introduced earlier in the chapter, the journalistic approach asks *who, what, when, where, why,* and *how* questions to distill major ideas from piles of unorganized information.
- **Question-and-answer chain.** Start with a key question, from the audience's perspective, and work back toward your message. Ask yourself: "What is the audience's main question? What do audience members need to know?" Write down and examine your answers. As additional questions emerge, write down and examine those answers. Follow the chain of questions and answers until you have replied to every conceivable question that might occur to your audience. By thinking about your material from your audience's perspective, you are likely to define your main idea.
- **Storyteller's tour.** Some writers find it best to talk through a communication challenge before they write. Pretend you're giving a colleague a guided tour of your message and record what you say. Then listen to your talk, identify ways to tighten and clarify the message, and repeat the process. Working through this recording several times will help you distill the main idea down to a single, concise message.
- **Mind mapping.** You can generate and organize ideas using a graphic method called *mind mapping*. It is a helpful technique for identifying and organizing the many ideas and pieces of information that a complex writing task usually entails. Software (MindJet's MindManager in Figure 4–8) makes it easy to create graphical output, which shows the writer's own concerns about a report, her insights into the audience's concerns, and several issues related to writing and distributing the report. You can find a number of free mind mapping tools online, including https://bubbl.us/.

LIMITING YOUR SCOPE

The **scope** of your message is the range of information you present, the overall length, and the level of detail—all of which need to correspond to your main

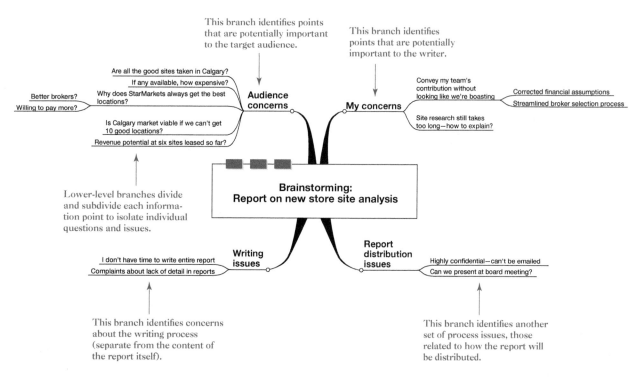

This branch identifies points that are potentially important to the target audience.

This branch identifies points that are potentially important to the writer.

Lower-level branches divide and subdivide each information point to isolate individual questions and issues.

This branch identifies concerns about the writing process (separate from the content of the report itself).

This branch identifies another set of process issues, those related to how the report will be distributed.

Figure 4–8 Using the Mind-Mapping Technique to Plan a Writing Project

idea. For a report outlining your advice on whether to open a new restaurant in Calgary, your message, including all supporting evidence, needs to focus on that question alone. Your plan for new menu selections and your idea for a new source of financing both would be outside the scope of your message.

Whatever the length of your message, limit the number of major support points to half a dozen or so—and if you can get your idea across with fewer points, all the better. Listing 20 or 30 support points might feel as if you're being thorough, but your audience will view such detail as rambling and mind numbing. Instead, look for ways to group supporting points under major headings, such as finance, customers, competitors, employees, or whatever is appropriate for your subject. Just as you might need to refine your main idea, you may also need to refine your major support points so that you have a smaller number with greater impact.

The number of words, pages, or minutes you need to communicate and support your main idea depends on your topic, your audience members' familiarity with the material, their receptivity to your conclusions, and your credibility. You'll need fewer words to present routine information to a knowledgeable audience that already knows and respects you. You'll need more words to build a consensus about a complex and controversial subject, especially if the members of your audience are skeptical or hostile strangers.

> Limit the number of support points; having fewer strong points is a better approach than using many weak points.

CHOOSING BETWEEN DIRECT AND INDIRECT APPROACHES

After you've defined your ideas, you're ready to decide on the sequence you will use to present your points. You have two basic options:

- **Direct approach.** When you know your audience will be receptive to your message, use a direct approach: start with the main idea (such as a recommendation, a conclusion, or a request) and follow that with your supporting evidence.
- **Indirect approach.** When your audience will be skeptical about or even resistant to your message, use an **indirect approach:** start with the evidence first and build your case before presenting the main idea.

> Use a direct approach if the audience's reaction is likely to be positive and the indirect approach if it is likely to be negative.

To choose between these two alternatives, analyze your audience's likely reaction to your purpose and message. Bear in mind, however, that each message is unique. No simple formula will solve all your communication problems. For example, although an indirect approach may be best when you're sending bad news to outsiders, if you're writing a memo to an associate you may want to get directly to the point, even if your message is unpleasant. The direct approach might also be a good choice for long messages, regardless of your audience's attitude—because delaying the main idea could cause confusion and frustration. Figure 4–9 summarizes how your approach may differ depending on the likely audience reaction. The type of message also influences the choice of a direct or indirect approach.

ROUTINE AND POSITIVE MESSAGES The most straightforward business messages are *routine* and *positive* ones. If you're inquiring about products or placing an order, your audience will usually want to comply. If you're announcing a price cut, granting an adjustment, accepting an invitation, or congratulating a colleague, your audience will most likely be pleased to hear from you. If you're providing routine information as part of your regular business, your audience will probably be neutral, neither pleased nor displeased.

Aside from being easy to understand, routine messages are easy to prepare. In most cases you use the direct approach. In the opening, you state your main idea directly, without searching for some creative introduction. By starting off with your positive idea, you emphasize the pleasing aspect of your message. You put your audience in a good frame of mind and encourage them to be receptive to whatever else you have to say. The body of your message can then provide all necessary details. The close should be cordial and emphasize your good news or make a statement about the specific action desired. Routine and positive messages are discussed in greater detail in Chapter 8.

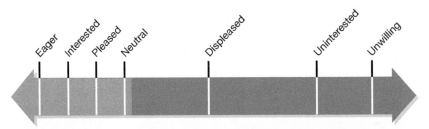

	Direct Approach	**Indirect Approach**	
Audience Reaction	Eager/interested/ pleased/neutral	Displeased	Uninterested/unwilling
Message Opening	Start with the main idea, the request, or the good news.	Start with a neutral statement that acts as a transition to the reasons for the bad news.	Start with a statement or question that captures attention.
Message Body	Provide necessary details.	Give reasons to justify a negative answer. State or imply the bad news, and make a positive suggestion.	Arouse the audience's interest in the subject. Build the audience's desire to comply.
Message Close	Close with a cordial comment, a reference to the good news, or a statement about the specific action desired.	Close cordially.	Request action.

Figure 4–9 Choosing between the Direct and Indirect Approaches

NEGATIVE MESSAGES Unfortunately, being a business communicator also means you'll face situations in which you need to deliver bad news. Because your audience will be disappointed, these messages usually benefit from the indirect approach—putting the evidence first and building up to the main idea. This approach strengthens your case as you go along, not only making the receiver more receptive to the eventual conclusion but also treating the receiver in a more sensitive manner, which helps you retain as much goodwill as possible. Astute businesspeople know that every person they encounter could be a potential customer, supplier, or contributor or could influence someone who is a customer, supplier, or contributor.

Successful communicators take extra care with their negative messages. They often open with a neutral statement that is related to the main idea and that acts as a transition to the reasons for the bad news. In the body, they give the reasons that justify the negative answer, announcement, or information before they state or imply the bad news. And they are always careful to close cordially.

If you have bad news, try to put it somewhere in the middle, cushioned by other more positive ideas.

The challenge of negative messages lies in being honest but kind. You don't want to sacrifice ethics and mislead your audience, nor do you want to be overly blunt. To achieve a good mix of candour and kindness, focus on some aspect of the situation that makes the negative news a little easier to take.

Using the indirect approach allows you to get your message across to an uninterested or skeptical audience.

Keep in mind that the indirect approach is neither manipulative nor unethical. As long as you can be honest and reasonably brief, you're often better off opening a bad-news message with a neutral point and putting the negative information after the explanation. Then, if you can close with something fairly positive, your audience may feel able to tolerate the situation—they may not like it, but they may not be hostile either (which is often all you can hope for when you must deliver bad news). Negative messages are discussed further in Chapter 9.

PERSUASIVE MESSAGES Persuasive messages present a special communication challenge because you're asking your audience to give, do, or change something, whether it's contributing to a charity, buying a product, or changing a belief or an attitude. Professionals who specialize in persuasive messages such as sales letters and other advertising spend years perfecting their craft, and the best practitioners command salaries on a par with some high-ranking executives. You might not have the opportunity to take your skills to that level, but you can learn some basic techniques to improve your own persuasive messages.

Persuasive messages can be challenging because you're generally asking your audience to give up something, such as time, money, power, and so on.

Before you try to persuade people to do something, capture their attention and get them to consider your message with an open mind. Make an interesting point and provide supporting facts that encourage your audience to continue paying attention. In most persuasive messages, the opening mentions a reader benefit, refers to a problem that the recipient might have, poses a question, or mentions an interesting statistic. Then the body builds interest in the subject and arouses audience members' desire to comply. Once you have them thinking, you can introduce your main idea. The close is cordial and requests the desired action. Persuasive messages are discussed at greater length in Chapter 10.

OUTLINING YOUR CONTENT

After you have chosen the right approach, it's time to figure out the most logical and effective way to present your major points and supporting details. Get into the habit of creating outlines when you're preparing business messages. You'll save time, get better results, and do a better job of navigating through complicated business situations. Even if you're just jotting down three or four key points, making an outline will help you organize your thoughts for faster writing. When you're preparing a longer, more complex message, an outline is indispensable because it helps you visualize the relationships among the various parts.

A good way to visualize how all the points will fit together is to construct an outline.

ALPHANUMERIC OUTLINE	DECIMAL OUTLINE
I. First Major Point	I.0 First Major Point
A. First subpoint	1.1 First subpoint
B. Second subpoint	1.2 Second subpoint
1. Evidence	1.2.1 Evidence
2. Evidence	1.2.2 Evidence
a. Detail	1.2.2.1 Detail
b. Detail	1.2.2.2 Detail
3. Evidence	1.2.3 Evidence
C. Third subpoint	1.3 Third subpoint
II. Second Major Point	2.0 Second Major Point
A. First subpoint	2.1 First subpoint
1. Evidence	2.1.1 Evidence
2. Evidence	2.1.2 Evidence
B. Second subpoint	2.2 Second subpoint

Figure 4–10 Two Common Outline Forms

The basic outline formats shown in Figure 4–10 (1) use numbers or numbers and letters to identify each point and (2) indent points to show which ideas are of equal status. An effective outline divides a topic into at least two parts, restricts each subdivision to one category, and ensures that each group is separate and distinct (see Figure 4–11). These outlines are especially useful for longer documents, such as reports.

You may want to experiment with other organizational schemes in addition to traditional outlines.

Another way to visualize the outline of your message is to create an "organization chart" similar to the charts used to show a company's management structure (see Figure 4–12). The main idea is shown in the highest-level box and, like a top executive, establishes the big picture. The lower-level ideas, like lower-level employees, provide the details. All the ideas are logically organized into divisions of thought, just as a company is organized into divisions and departments.[12] Using a visual chart instead of a traditional outline has many benefits. Charts help you (1) see the various levels of ideas and how the parts fit together, (2) develop new ideas, and (3) restructure your information flow. The mind-mapping technique used to generate ideas works in a similar way.

RIGHT:

I. Alternatives for Improving Profits
  A. Increasing sales
    1. Internet advertising
    2. Radio advertising
  B. Reducing production costs
    1. Modernizing plants
    2. Using more off-shore labour

WRONG:

I. Alternatives for Improving Profits
  A. Increasing sales
    1. Internet advertising
  B. Reducing production costs
    1. Modernizing plants
    2. Using more off-shore labour

When dividing a topic in an outline, be sure to divide it into at least two parts. A topic cannot be divided into only one part.

In the second (wrong) example, subtopic A is divided only once. Either the writer hasn't developed her ideas sufficiently or has only one idea (Internet advertising) for increasing sales. If she has only one idea for increasing sales, then that idea should be subtopic A (A. Increasing Internet sales).

Figure 4–11 Topic Division in Outlines

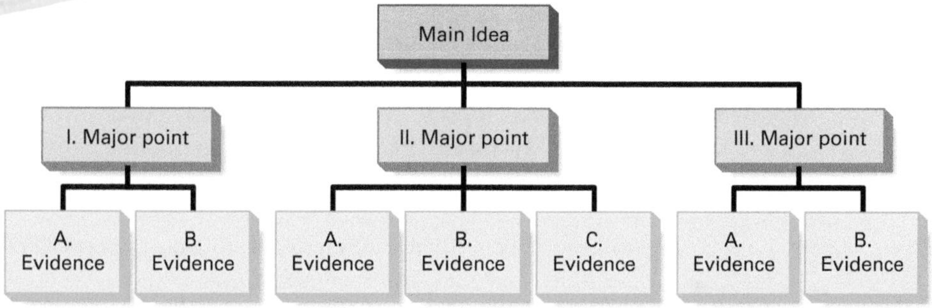

Figure 4–12 Organization Chart Method for Outlining

Whichever outlining or organizing scheme you use, start your message with the main idea, follow that with major supporting points, and then illustrate these points with evidence.

START WITH THE MAIN IDEA The main idea helps you establish the goals and general strategy of the message, and it summarizes two vital considerations: (1) *what* you want your audience to do or think and (2) *why* they should do so. Everything in your message either supports the main idea or explains its implications. As discussed earlier in this chapter, some messages state the main idea quickly and directly, whereas other messages delay the main idea until after the evidence is presented.

STATE THE MAJOR POINTS You need to support your main idea with the major points that clarify and explain your ideas in more concrete terms. If your purpose is to inform and the material is factual, your major points might be based on something physical or financial—something you can visualize or measure, such as activities to be performed, functional units, spatial or chronological relationships, or parts of a whole. When you're describing a process, the major points are almost inevitably steps in the process. When you're describing an object, the major points correspond to the parts of the object. When you're giving a historical account, major points represent events in the chronological chain. If your purpose is to persuade or to collaborate, select major points that develop a line of reasoning or a logical argument that proves your central message and motivates your audience to act.

Major supporting points clarify your main idea.

You can divide major points according to physical relationships, the description of a process, the components of an object, or a historical chronology.

PROVIDE EXAMPLES AND EVIDENCE After you've defined the main idea and identified major supporting points, think about examples and evidence that can confirm, illuminate, or expand on your supporting points. Choose examples and evidence carefully so that these elements support your overall message without distracting or overwhelming your audience. For example, if you're advocating that your company increase its advertising budget, you can support your major point by providing evidence that your most successful competitors spend more on advertising than you do. You can also describe a case in which a particular competitor increased its ad budget and achieved an impressive sales gain. Then you can show that over the past five years, your firm's sales have gone up and down in response to the amount spent on advertising.

Back up your supporting points with carefully selected examples and evidence.

If you're developing a long, complex message, you may need to carry the outline down several levels. Remember that every level is a step along the chain from the abstract to the concrete, from the general to the specific. The lowest level contains the evidence, the individual facts and figures that tie the generalizations to the observable, measurable world. The higher levels are the concepts that reveal why those facts are significant.

Each major point must be supported with enough specific evidence to be convincing, but not so much that your message becomes long and boring.

Up to a point, the more evidence you provide, the more conclusive your case will be. If your subject is complex and unfamiliar, or if your audience is skeptical, you'll need a lot of facts and figures to demonstrate your points. On the other hand, if your subject is routine and your audience is positively inclined, you can be more sparing with the evidence. You want to provide enough support to be convincing but not so much that your message becomes boring or inefficient.

Another way to keep your audience interested is to vary the type of detail you include. As you draft your message, incorporate the methods described in Table 4–3. Employ both facts and figures in narrative sections, add relevant description, and include some examples or a reference to authority. Where appropriate, reinforce details with visual aids. A variety of approaches adds richness and meaning to the whole.

If your schedule permits, put aside your outline for a day or two before you begin composing your first draft. Then review it with a fresh eye, looking for opportunities to improve the flow of ideas. For a summary of the planning tasks involved in preparing your messages, see "Checklist: Planning Business Messages."

Table 4–3	**Six Types of Detail**	
Type of Detail	**Example**	**Comment**
Facts and figures	Sales are strong this month. We have two new contracts worth $5 million and a good chance of winning another worth $2.5 million.	Adds more credibility than any other type. Can become boring if used excessively. Most common type used in business.
Example or illustration	We've spent four months trying to hire recent accounting graduates, but so far only one person has joined our firm. One candidate told me that she would love to work for us, but she can get $5000 more a year elsewhere.	Adds life to a message, but one example does not prove a point. Idea must be supported by other evidence as well.
Description	Upscale hamburger restaurants target burger lovers who want more than the convenience and low prices of McDonald's. These places feature wine and beer, half-pound burgers, and generous side dishes (nachos, potato skins). "Atmosphere" is key.	Helps audience visualize the subject by creating a sensory impression. Does not prove a point but clarifies it and makes it memorable. Begins with overview of function; defines its purpose, lists major parts, and explains how it operates.
Narration	Under former management, executives worked in blue jeans, meetings rarely started on time, and lunches ran long. When Jim Wilson became CEO, he completely overhauled the operation. A Queen's MBA who favours custom-tailored suits, Wilson has cut the product line in half and chopped $12 million off expenses.	Works well for attracting attention and explaining ideas but lacks statistical validity.
Reference to authority	I discussed this idea with Jackie Loman in the Sudbury plant, and she was very supportive. As you know, Jackie has been in charge of that plant for the past six years. She is confident that we can speed up the number 2 line by 150 units an hour if we add another worker.	Bolsters a case while adding variety and credibility. Works only if "authority" is recognized and respected by the audience.
Visual aids	Graphs, charts, tables	Helps audience grasp specific data. Used more in memos and reports than in letters.

✓ Checklist   Planning Business Messages

A. Analyze your situation.
- Determine whether the purpose of your message is to inform, persuade, or collaborate.
- Identify what you want your audience to think or do.
- Make sure your purpose is worthwhile and realistic.
- Make sure the time is right for your message.
- Make sure the right person is delivering your message.
- Make sure your purpose is acceptable to your organization.
- Identify the primary audience.
- Identify the secondary audience.
- Determine audience size and composition.
- Estimate your audience's level of understanding and probable reaction to your message.

B. Gather information.
- Decide whether to use formal or informal techniques for gathering information.
- Find out what your audience wants to know.
- Provide all required information and make sure it's accurate, ethical, and pertinent.

C. Select the best medium for your message.
- Understand the advantages and disadvantages of oral, written, and electronic media.
- Consider media richness, message formality, media limitations, urgency, cost, and audience preferences.

D. Organize your information.
- Define your main idea.
- Limit your scope.
- Choose a direct or indirect approach.
- Outline content by starting with the main idea, adding major points, and illustrating with evidence.

SUMMARY OF LEARNING OBJECTIVES

1 Describe the three-step writing process. First, planning consists of analyzing your purpose and developing a profile of your audience, gathering information (whether formally or informally), selecting the right medium, and organizing the information. Second, writing consists of adapting your message to your audience and composing the words, sentences, and paragraphs that form your message. Third, completing your message consists of revising your message by evaluating content and then rewriting and editing for clarity; producing your message by using effective design elements; proofreading your message for typos, spelling errors, and mechanics; and distributing your message.

2 Explain why it's important to define your purpose carefully, and ask four questions that can help you test that purpose. You must know enough about the purpose of your message to shape that message in a way that will achieve your goal. To decide whether you should proceed with your message, ask four questions: (a) Will anything change as a result of my message? (b) Is my purpose realistic? (c) Is the time right? (d) Is my purpose acceptable to my organization?

3 Describe the importance of analyzing your audience, and identify the six factors you should consider when developing an audience profile. Analyzing your audience helps you predict how your audience will react to your message. It also helps you know what to include in your message and how to include it. To develop an audience profile, determine your primary audience (key decision makers), your secondary audience, audience composition, your audience's level of understanding, audience expectations and preferences, and the audience's probable reaction.

4 Discuss gathering information for simple messages, and identify three attributes of quality information. You can collect relevant information informally by considering others' viewpoints, browsing through company files, chatting with supervisors or colleagues, or asking your audience for input. You can test the quality of your information by checking whether it is accurate, ethical, and pertinent.

5 List factors to consider when choosing the most appropriate medium for your message. Media richness, the value of a medium for communicating a message, is a factor to consider for message transmission. Richness is determined by the medium's ability to (a) convey a message using more than one informational cue (visual, verbal, vocal), (b) facilitate feedback, and (c) establish personal focus. Other factors to consider when selecting a medium (or media) include the message's formality, media limitations, urgency, cost, and audience preferences.

6 Explain why good organization is important to both you and your audience. Audiences benefit from good organization in several ways. A well-organized message saves your audience time, because they don't have to reread a message to make sense of it. They are also better able to understand the content, so they can accept the message more easily and can make better decisions based on its information. Communicators also benefit from good organization: well-organized messages consume less creative energy and speed the drafting stage.

7 **Summarize the process for organizing business messages effectively.** The process for organizing messages

effectively has four parts. First, define the main idea of the message by making a specific statement about the topic. Second, limit the scope of the message by adjusting the space and detail you allocate to major points. Third, choose either a direct or an indirect approach by anticipating the audience's reaction to the message and by matching the approach to message length and message type. Fourth, group the points by constructing an outline to visualize the relationship between the ideas and the supporting material.

ON THE JOB PERFORMING COMMUNICATION TASKS AT MARS

You have been hired as a summer intern in the MaRS communication department. Use what you've learned in this chapter to solve the following situations, and be prepared to explain why your choice is best:

1. You have been asked to contribute content to the MaRS Facebook page. Your supervisor has not given you any specific direction, but has left it up to you to decide on the content itself. Of the following, select the best choice for dealing with this task:

   a. You approach the task by reviewing the activities of all MaRS tenants within the past five days.

   b. You approach the task by reviewing the activities of MaRS tenants operating within a specific field, such as health care, within the past five days.

   c. You decide to focus only on reviewing upcoming conferences that will be held at MaRS.

   d. You decide to focus only on providing related links of interest through the MaRS Facebook page.

2. Assume that you decided to profile one of MaRS Incubator's tenants on the Facebook page. How do you approach creating this post?

   a. You decide only to interview the tenant. That will give you enough information.

   b. You decide to interview the tenant and do research on the tenant's area of interest. This will give you informa-

tion about the tenant and provide a context for the tenant's field.

   c. You decide only to take photographs of the tenant's offices and labs and post them with a short comment about the tenant. This will be appealing because it is visual.

   d. You decide to take photographs and include a medium-length piece about the tenant. This will be effective because it is both visual and descriptive.

3. When creating your piece about a MaRS tenant, you need to determine your audience. Who is it and how does it affect the writing style of your posting?

   a. You determine that the audience will be only people who work in the MaRS Incubator. Thus your posting will be written in a style that includes a lot of technical terms.

   b. Your audience will mainly be people connecting to the MaRS Facebook page through links. Thus your posting will be written in both a technical and an explanatory style.

   c. The sole audience will be people working in all areas of MaRS. Thus your writing style will be technical, as you believe all people who work at MaRS have a technical background.

   d. Your audience will be all of MaRS stakeholders and people who connect to the MaRS Facebook page through the MaRS website. Thus your posting will be written in completely accessible language.

TEST YOUR KNOWLEDGE

1. What are the three steps in the writing process?

2. What types of purposes do all business messages have?

3. What do you need to know to develop an audience profile?

4. How can you test the thoroughness of the information you include in a message?

5. What are the main advantages of oral media? Of written media? Of visual media? Of electronic media?

6. How do you choose the medium for your message?

7. How does the audience benefit from a well-organized message?

8. What are the steps in the process for organizing messages?

9. What elements do you consider when choosing between a direct and an indirect approach?

APPLY YOUR KNOWLEDGE

1. Some writers argue that planning messages wastes time because they inevitably change their plans as they go along. How would you respond to this argument? Explain your answer.

2. As a member of the public relations department, what medium would you recommend using to inform the local community that your toxic-waste cleanup program has been successful? Why?

3. Would you use a direct or an indirect approach to ask employees to work overtime to meet an important deadline? Explain your answer.

4. Which approach would you use to let your boss know that you'll be out half a day this week to attend your uncle's funeral—direct or indirect? Why?

5. **Ethical Choices** The company president has asked you to draft a memo to the board of directors informing them that sales in a line of gourmet fruit jams the company recently acquired have far exceeded anyone's expectations. However, you happen to know that this increase reflects a trend across the industry, with many consumers switching from moderately priced jams to gourmet products. In fact, sales of your company's traditional products have slipped in recent months. You were not asked to add this information, but you think it's important for the board to be able to put the new sales data in proper context. What should you do?

RUNNING CASES

> CASE 1 Noreen

Noreen's manager informs her of a new Petro-Go company promotion for Canadian customers owning a "Go Points" card. The first step is to prepare the service stations.

The promotion details are as follows: (1) cardholders will now receive double points when they purchase more than $30 of gasoline in one visit (regular points up to $30 and then double points over $30); (2) cardholders will earn a new reward redemption—Petro-Go gift certificates ($20 certificate for a 250-point redemption); and (3) cardholders will win a free 6-litre container of windshield washer fluid when their accumulated points reach each 1000-point interval.

Noreen is asked to create a letter to inform the service station owners/operators when the promotion begins, how it will be advertised, what the promotion offers, and how they will use their equipment to offer and track this promotion. An instruction booklet on where and how to place signs, how to update equipment, and how to manage card points will be attached to the letter. Noreen needs to prepare this booklet by gathering information from past promotional materials and then choosing only what she needs for this task. This letter needs to be distributed as soon as possible. There is much to be done.

QUESTIONS

a. What information must Noreen gather?
b. Why is it so important that Noreen's letter be concise and accurate?
c. What would be the best way to distribute this information to the service stations?
d. What will the audience's general attitude be toward the message?
e. How many key ideas are in this letter? How will Noreen emphasize them?

YOUR TASK

The station owners/operators need to know how and where to put up promotional signs and how to update point-of-sale machines and registers using key codes and sequences. Write two sets of instructions for the service stations—the first set will be for a reader who has never used that type of machine or provided a promotion before, and the second set will be for a reader who is familiar with that type of machine and has provided promotions in the past. Use your imagination. Briefly explain how your two audiences affect your instructions.

> CASE 2 Kwong

Kwong has done some research into Canadian business culture. He has also attended several college workshops to improve his English and speaking skills. Thanks to his efforts and improved

understanding, he has now obtained a co-op placement with Accountants For All accounting firm. With the tax season quickly approaching, Kwong's manager knows that their previous customers will once again look for an accounting firm to help them file their tax returns. Kwong's manager asks him to produce a promotional letter that will help bring back previous customers.

QUESTIONS

a. What does Kwong need to plan?
b. How should he get started?
c. What information should Kwong put in this promotional letter?
d. How should Kwong organize his letter?
e. How much detail does he need to provide?

YOUR TASK

List five messages you have received lately, such as direct-mail promotions, letters, email messages, phone solicitations, and lectures. For each, determine the general and the specific purpose; then, answer the following questions:

1. Was the message well timed?
2. Did the sender choose an appropriate medium for the message?
3. Did the appropriate person deliver the message?
4. Was the sender's purpose realistic?

PRACTISE YOUR KNOWLEDGE

A writer is working on an insurance information brochure and is having trouble grouping ideas logically into an outline. Prepare the outline, paying attention to appropriate subordination of the ideas. If necessary, rewrite phrases to give them a more consistent sound.

Accident Protection Insurance Plan

- Coverage is only pennies a day
- Benefit is $100 000 for accidental death on common carriers
- Benefit is $100 a day for hospitalization as a result of motor vehicle or common carrier accident
- Benefit is $20 000 for accidental death in a motor vehicle accident

- Individual coverage is only $17.85 per quarter; family coverage is just $26.85 per quarter
- No physical exam or health questions
- Convenient payment—billed quarterly
- Guaranteed acceptance for all applicants
- No individual rate increases
- Free, no-obligation examination period
- Cash paid in addition to any other insurance carried
- Covers accidental death when riding as fare-paying passenger on public transportation, including buses, trains, jets, ships, trolleys, subways, or any other common carrier
- Covers accidental death in motor vehicle accidents occurring while driving or riding in or on an automobile, truck, camper, motor home, or non-motorized bicycle

EXERCISES

4.1 Message Planning Skills: Self-Assessment

How good are you at planning business messages? Use the chart below to rate yourself on each element of planning an audience-centred business message. Then examine your ratings to identify where you are strongest and where you can improve, using the tips in this chapter.

4.2 Planning Messages: General and Specific Purpose

Make a list of communication tasks you'll need to accomplish in the next week or so (for example, a job application, a letter of complaint, a speech to a class, an order for a product). For each, determine a general and a specific purpose.

Element of Planning	Always	Frequently	Occasionally	Never
1. I start by defining my purpose.	_____	_____	_____	_____
2. I analyze my audience before writing a message.	_____	_____	_____	_____
3. I investigate what my audience wants to know.	_____	_____	_____	_____
4. I check that my information is accurate, ethical, and pertinent.	_____	_____	_____	_____
5. I consider my audience and purpose when selecting media.	_____	_____	_____	_____

4.3 Planning Messages: Specific Purpose

For each of the following communication tasks, state a specific purpose (if you have trouble, begin with "I want to . . .").

  a. A report to your boss, the store manager, about the outdated items in the warehouse
  b. A memo to clients about your booth at the upcoming trade show
  c. A letter to a customer who hasn't made a payment for three months
  d. A memo to employees about the department's high cellphone bills
  e. A phone call to a supplier checking on an overdue parts shipment
  f. A report to future users of the computer program you have chosen to handle the company's mailing list

4.4 Planning Messages: Audience Profile

For each communication task below, write brief answers to three questions: Who is my audience? What is my audience's general attitude toward my subject? What does my audience need to know?

  a. A final-notice collection letter from an appliance manufacturer to an appliance dealer, sent 10 days before initiating legal collection procedures
  b. An unsolicited sales letter asking readers to purchase 8-gigabyte thumb drives at near-wholesale prices
  c. An advertisement for peanut butter
  d. Fliers to be attached to doorknobs in the neighbourhood, announcing reduced rates for chimney lining or repairs
  e. A cover letter sent along with your résumé to a potential employer
  f. A request (to the seller) for a price adjustment on a piano that incurred $150 in damage during delivery to a banquet room in the hotel you manage

4.5 Meeting Audience Needs: Necessary Information

Choose a product (such as an in-car touch screen display, a tablet, or a smartphone) that you know how to operate well. Write two sets of instructions for operating the device: one set for a reader who has never used that type of device, and one set for someone who is generally familiar with that type of device but has never operated the specific model. Briefly explain how your two audiences affect your instructions. (Limit your instructions to the basic functions, such as placing and receiving calls on a smartphone.)

4.6 Selecting Media: Identifying an Audience

Barbara Lin is in charge of public relations for a cruise line that operates out of Vancouver. She is shocked to read a letter in a local newspaper from a disgruntled passenger, complaining about the service and entertainment on a recent cruise. Lin will have to respond to these publicized criticisms in some way. What audiences will she need to consider in her response?

What medium should she choose? If the letter had been published in a travel publication widely read by travel agents and cruise travellers, how might her course of action differ?

4.7 Teamwork: Audience Analysis

With a team assigned by your instructor, compare the Facebook pages of three companies in the same industry. Analyze the content on all the available tabs. What can you surmise about the intended audience for each company? Which of the three does the best job of presenting the information its target audience is likely to need? Prepare a brief presentation, including slides that show samples of the Facebook content from each company.

4.8 Internet: Planning Your Message

Go to the TELUS website at http://about.telus.com/community/english and follow the link to the latest annual report (look under Investor Relations). Locate and read the CEO's letter to investors in the report. Who is the primary audience for this message? Who is the secondary audience? What is the general purpose of the message? What do you think this audience wants to know from the CEO of TELUS? Summarize your answers in a brief (one-page) memo or oral presentation.

4.9 Message Organization: Outlining Your Content

Using the Nutri-Veg email in this chapter (Figure 4–6), draw an organizational chart similar to the one shown in Figure 4–12. Fill in the main idea, the major points, and the evidence provided in this letter. (Note: Your diagram may be smaller than the one provided in Figure 4–12.)

4.10 Message Organization: Limiting Scope

Suppose you are preparing to recommend that top management install a new heating system that uses a process called cogeneration, in which production waste is used to generate heat. The following information is in your files. Eliminate topics that aren't essential; then arrange the other topics so your report will give top managers a clear understanding of the heating system and a balanced, concise justification for installing it.

- History of the development of the cogeneration heating process
- Scientific credentials of the developers of the process
- Risks assumed in using this process
- Your plan for installing the equipment in your building
- Stories about its successful use in comparable facilities
- Specifications of the equipment that would be installed
- Plans for disposing of the old heating equipment
- Costs of installing and running the new equipment
- Advantages and disadvantages of using the new process
- Detailed 10-year cost projections
- Estimates of the time needed to phase in the new system
- Alternative systems that management might wish to consider

4.11 Message Organization: Choosing an Approach

Indicate whether a direct or an indirect approach would be best in each situation, then briefly explain why. Would any of these messages be inappropriate for email? Explain.

a. A message to the owner of an automobile dealership, complaining about poor service work
b. A message from a recent graduate requesting a letter of recommendation from a former instructor
c. A message turning down a job applicant
d. An announcement that, because of high air-conditioning costs, the plant temperature will be held at 24°C during the summer
e. A final request to settle a delinquent debt

4.12 Message Organization: Audience Focus

If you were trying to persuade people to take the following actions, how would you organize your argument?

a. You want your boss to approve your plan for hiring two additional people.
b. You want to be hired for a job.
c. You want to be granted a business loan.

d. You want to collect a small amount from a regular customer whose account is slightly past due.
e. You want to collect a large amount from a customer whose account is seriously past due.

4.13 Ethical Choices: Providing Information

Your supervisor, whom you respect, has asked you to withhold important information that you think should be included in a report you are preparing. Disobeying him could be disastrous for your relationship with him and possibly your career. Obeying him could violate your personal code of ethics. What should you do? On the basis of the discussion in Chapter 1, would you consider this situation to be an ethical dilemma or an ethical lapse? Please explain.

4.14 Three-Step Process: Other Applications

In an email message to your instructor, explain how the material discussed in this chapter can also apply to meetings, as discussed in Chapter 2. (Hint: Review the section headings in this chapter and think about making your meetings more productive.)

Writing Business Messages

LEARNING OBJECTIVES After studying this chapter, you will be able to

1 Explain the importance of adapting your messages to the needs and expectations of your audience

2 Explain why establishing credibility is vital to the success of your communication efforts

3 Discuss how to achieve a businesslike tone with a style that is clear and concise

4 Describe how to select words that are not only correct but also effective

5 Explain how sentence style affects emphasis within your message

6 Cite five ways to develop coherent paragraphs

MyLab Business Communication Visit MyLab Business Communication to access a variety of online resources directly related to this chapter's content..

ON THE JOB: COMMUNICATING AT **CREATIVE COMMONS**

Koichi Mitsui/AFLO/Newscom

Creative Commons, chaired by Joi Ito, uses a variety of communication vehicles to convince copyright owners to explore new ways of sharing and protecting their creative works.

Redefining Two Centuries of Copyright Law for the Digital Age

http://creativecommons.org

Have you ever noticed that tiny © symbol on books, DVDs, music CDs, and other media products? This symbol means that the person or organization that created the item is granted *copyright* protection—the exclusive legal right to produce, distribute, and sell that creation. Anyone who wants to resell, redistribute, or adapt such works usually needs to secure permission from the current copyright holder.

However, what if you *want* people to remix the song you just recorded or use your graphic designs in whatever artistic compositions they might want to create? Or if you want to give away some of your creative works to get your name out there, without giving up all your legal rights to them? Alternatively, suppose you need a few photos or a video clip for a website. In all of these cases, permission would normally have to be sought and granted for use of the material. Other than for limited personal and educational use, a conventional copyright requires every person to negotiate a contract for every application or adaptation of every piece of work he or she wants to use.

The search for some middle ground between "all rights reserved" and simply giving your work away led to the founding of Creative Commons. This nonprofit organization's goal is to provide a simple, free, and legal way for musicians, artists, writers, teachers, scientists, and others to collaborate and benefit through the sharing of art and ideas. Instead of the everything-or-nothing approach of traditional copyright, Creative Commons offers a more flexible range of "some rights reserved" options.

Through a variety of media, Creative Commons continues to promote the benefits of simplifying the legal constraints on sharing and reusing intellectual property, whether for creative expression or scientific research. Millions of Creative Commons licences have been initiated for musical works, short films, educational materials, novels, and more. This approach can't solve the entire dilemma of copyrights in the digital age, but it has already created a better way for creative people to communicate and collaborate.

If you worked at Creative Commons, how would you write messages about the purpose and process of this organization? How would you adapt your message for your audience? What media would you use?[1]

Adapting to Your Audience: Being Sensitive to Audience Needs

1 **LEARNING OBJECTIVE**

Explain the importance of adapting your messages to the needs and expectations of your audience.

Readers and listeners want to know how your messages will benefit them.

As they work to persuade their audiences to consider new forms of copyright protection, Joi Ito and his colleagues at Creative Commons realize that it takes more than just a great idea to change the way people think. Expressing ideas clearly and persuasively starts with adapting to one's audience.

With a solid plan in place (see Chapter 4), you're ready to choose the words and craft the sentences and paragraphs that will carry your ideas to their intended audiences. The second step in the three-step writing process (Figure 5–1) includes two vital tasks: adapting to your audience and composing your message. With many organizations reaching international clients, word choice is very important for addressing audiences. Make sure you avoid slang, business speak, and clichés.

Whether consciously or not, audiences greet most incoming messages with a question: "What's in this for me?" If your intended audience thinks a message does not apply to them or doesn't meet their needs, they won't be inclined to pay attention to it. Look at the Creative Commons website, which uses video interviews with Creative Commons employees, newsletters, and case studies, among other communication media, to engage people and educate them about Creative Commons's goals. For example, through a case study about an African sleeping sickness test, scientists can learn how to license their findings to provide free access to their research. Artists who want to provide music online can download a booklet titled "New Ways of Doing Music Business" for licensing

3-Step writing process ✓

1 Planning →	**2** Writing →	**3** Completing
	Adapt to Your Audience Be sensitive to audience needs by writing with a "you" attitude, politeness, positive emphasis, and bias-free language. Build a strong relationship with your audience by establishing your credibility and projecting your company's image. Control your style with a conversational tone, plain English, and appropriate voice. **Compose the Message** Choose precise language that will help you create effective sentences and coherent paragraphs.	

Figure 5–1 Step 2 in the Three-Step Writing Process: Write Your Messages

guidance. By adapting your communication to your readers' particular needs and expectations, you'll provide a more compelling answer to "What's in this for me?" and improve the chances of your message being successful.

Adapting your message is not always a simple task. Some situations will require you to balance competing or conflicting needs—for example, when you're trying to convince people to change their minds or when you're delivering bad news. To adapt your message to your audience, be sensitive to their needs, build a strong relationship with them, and control your style to maintain a professional tone.

Even in simple messages intended merely to share information, it's possible to use all the right words and still not be sensitive to your audience and their needs. You can improve your audience sensitivity by adopting the "you" attitude, maintaining good standards of etiquette, emphasizing the positive, and using bias-free language.

USING THE "YOU" ATTITUDE

Chapter 1 introduced the notion of the audience-centred approach, trying to see a subject through your audience's eyes. Now you want to project this approach in your messages by adopting a "you" attitude—speaking and writing in terms of your audience's wishes, interests, hopes, and preferences.

The "you" attitude is best implemented by expressing your message in terms of the audience's interests and needs.

On the simplest level, you can adopt the "you" attitude by replacing terms that refer to yourself and your company with terms that refer to your audience. In other words, use *you* and *yours* instead of *I*, *me*, *mine*, *we*, *us*, and *ours*:

Instead of This	Use This
To help us process this order, we must ask for another copy of the requisition.	So that your order can be filled promptly, please send another copy of the requisition.
We are pleased to announce our new flight schedule from Toronto to Montreal, which is any hour on the hour.	Now you can fly from Toronto to Montreal any hour on the hour.
We offer MP3 players with 16, 32, or 64 gigabytes of storage capacity.	Select your MP3 player from three models, with 16, 32, or 64 gigabytes of storage capacity.

When business messages use an "I" or "we" attitude, the writer risks sounding selfish and uninterested in the audience. The message tells what the sender wants, and the audience is expected to go along with it. Even so, using *you* and *yours* requires finesse. If you overdo it, you're likely to create awkward sentences and run the risk of sounding overly enthusiastic and artificial.[2]

The "you" attitude is not intended to be manipulative or insincere. It's an extension of the audience-centred approach. In fact, the best way to implement the "you" attitude is to think sincerely about your audience when composing your message.

Nor is the "you" attitude simply a matter of using one pronoun rather than another; it's a matter of genuine empathy. You can use *you* 25 times in a single page and still ignore your audience's true concerns. In other words, it's the thought and sincerity that count, not the pronoun *you*. If you're talking to a retailer, try to think like a retailer; if you're dealing with a production supervisor, put yourself in that position; if you're writing to a dissatisfied customer, imagine how you would feel at the other end of the transaction. The important thing is your attitude toward audience members and your appreciation of their position.

Be aware that on some occasions it's better to avoid using *you*, particularly if doing so will sound overly authoritative or accusing. For instance, instead of saying, "You failed to deliver the customer's order on time," you could minimize ill will by saying, "The customer didn't receive the order on time," or "Let's figure out a system that will ensure on-time deliveries."

Avoid using *you* and *yours* when doing so
- Makes you sound dictatorial
- Makes someone else feel guilty
- Goes against your organization's style

Instead of This	Use This
You should never use that type of paper in the copy machine.	That type of paper doesn't work very well in the copy machine.
You must correct all five copies by noon.	All five copies must be corrected by noon.

As you practise using the "you" attitude, be sure to consider the attitudes of other cultures and the policies of your organization. In some cultures, it is improper to single out one person's achievements because the whole team is responsible for the outcome; in that case, using the pronoun *we* or *our* (when you and your audience are part of the same team) would be more appropriate. Similarly, some companies have a tradition of avoiding references to *you* and *I* in their memos and formal reports.

MAINTAINING STANDARDS OF ETIQUETTE

Another good way to demonstrate interest in your audience and to earn their respect is to demonstrate etiquette in your messages. You know how it feels to be treated inconsiderately; when that happens, you probably react emotionally and then pay less attention to the offending message. By being courteous to members of your audience, you show consideration for them and foster a more successful environment for communication.

Although you may be tempted now and then to be brutally frank, express the facts in a kind and thoughtful manner.

On those occasions when you experience frustration with co-workers, customers, or others you deal with, you might be tempted to respond in blunt terms. However, venting your emotions rarely improves the situation and can damage your reputation. Demonstrate your diplomatic skills by controlling your emotions and communicating calmly and politely:

Instead of This	Use This
Once again, you've managed to bring down the website through your incompetent programming.	Let's go over what went wrong with the last site update so that we can improve the process.
You've been sitting on our order for two weeks, and we need it now!	Our production schedules depend on timely delivery of parts and supplies, but we have not yet received the order you promised to deliver two weeks ago. Please respond today with a firm delivery commitment.

Use extra tact when communicating with people higher up the organization chart or outside the company.

Of course, some situations require more diplomacy than others. If you know your audience well, a less formal approach might be more appropriate. However, when you are communicating with people who outrank you or with people outside your organization, an added measure of courtesy is usually needed.

Written communication and most forms of electronic media generally require more tact than oral communication. In the "ineffective" example in Figure 5–2, notice how the customer service agent's unfortunate word choices immediately derail this instant messaging exchange. In the "effective" example, a more sensitive approach allows both people to focus on solving the problem.

Unlike writing, when you're speaking, your words are softened by your tone of voice and facial expression. In addition, you can adjust your approach according to the feedback you get. If you inadvertently offend someone in writing, you usually won't get the immediate feedback to resolve the situation. In fact, you may never know that you offended your audience.

EMPHASIZING THE POSITIVE

You can communicate negative news without being negative.

You will encounter situations throughout your career in which you need to convey unwanted news. However, there is a big difference between delivering negative news and being negative. When the tone of your message is negative,

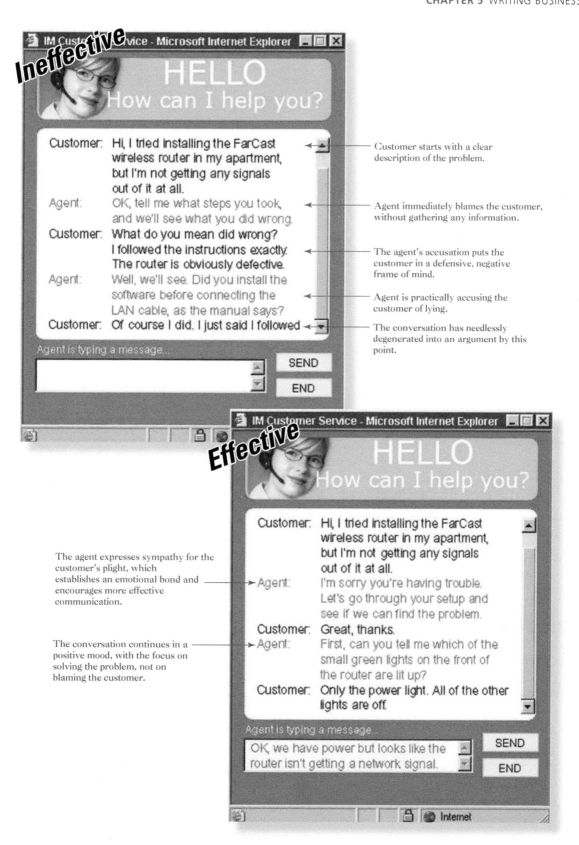

Figure 5–2 Fostering a Positive Relationship with an Audience

Courtesy: Pearson Education, Inc.

you put unnecessary strain on business relationships, which can cause people to distance themselves from you and your ideas. If you're facing a potentially negative situation, seek ways to soften the blow or emphasize positive aspects of a situation. Never hide the negative news, but always try to find positive points that will foster a good relationship with your audience:[3]

Instead of This	Use This
It is impossible to repair your car today.	Your car can be ready by Tuesday. Would you like a loaner until then?
We apologize for inconveniencing you during our remodelling.	The renovations now under way will help us serve you better.
We wasted $300 000 advertising in that magazine.	Our $300 000 advertising investment did not pay off; let's analyze the experience and apply the insights to future campaigns.

When you are offering criticism or advice, focus on what the person can do to improve.

When you find it necessary to criticize or correct, don't dwell on the other person's mistakes. Avoid referring to failures, problems, or shortcomings. Focus instead on what the person can do to improve:

Instead of This	Use This
The problem with this department is a failure to control costs.	The performance of this department can be improved by tightening cost controls.
You filled out the order form wrong.	Please check your colour preferences on the enclosed card so we can process your order.

Show your audience how they will benefit from complying with your message.

If you're trying to persuade the audience to buy a product, pay a bill, or perform a service for you, emphasize what's in it for them. Don't focus on why *you* want them to do something. An individual who sees the possibility for personal benefit is more likely to respond positively to your appeal:

Instead of This	Use This
We will notify all three credit reporting agencies if you do not pay your overdue bill within 10 days.	Paying your overdue bill within 10 days will prevent a negative entry on your credit record.
I am tired of seeing so many errors in the customer service blog.	Proofreading your blog postings will help you avoid embarrassing mistakes that generate more customer service complaints.

Avoid words with negative connotations; use meaningful euphemisms instead.

In general, state your message without using words that might hurt or offend your audience. Substitute *euphemisms* (mild terms) for those that have unpleasant meanings. You can be honest without being harsh. Gentle language won't change the facts, but it will make them more acceptable:

Instead of This	Use This
cheap merchandise	economy merchandise
used cars	preowned cars
failing	underperforming
elderly	senior citizen
fake	imitation or faux

On the other hand, don't carry euphemisms to extremes, or your audience will view your efforts as insincere or miss your meaning. It would be unethical to speak to your community about "manufacturing byproducts" when you're really talking about plans for disposing of toxic waste. Even if it is unpleasant, people respond better to an honest message delivered with integrity than they do to a sugar-coated message filled with empty talk.

USING BIAS-FREE LANGUAGE

Chapter 3 points out that you are often unaware of the influence of your own culture on your behaviour, and this circumstance extends to the language you use. Any bias present in your culture is likely to show up in your language, often in subtle ways that you might not even recognize. However, chances are that your audience will. **Bias-free language** avoids words and phrases that unfairly and even unethically categorize or stigmatize people in ways related to gender, race, ethnicity, age, or disability. Contrary to what some might think, biased language is not simply about "labels." To a significant degree, language reflects the way people think and what they believe, and biased language may well perpetuate the underlying stereotypes and prejudices that it represents.[4] Moreover, since perception is a large part of communication, being fair and objective isn't enough; to establish a good relationship with your audience, you must also *appear* to be fair.[5] Good communicators make every effort to change biased language (see Table 5–1). Bias can come in a variety of forms:

Avoid biased language that might offend your audience.

Table 5–1	**Overcoming Bias in Language**	
Examples	**Unacceptable**	**Preferable**
Gender Bias		
Using words containing "man"	Mankind	Humanity, human beings, human race, people
	Man-made	Artificial, synthetic, manufactured, constructed
	Manpower	Human power, human energy, workers, workforce
	Businessman	Executive, business manager, businessperson
	Salesman	Sales representative, salesperson, clerk, sales agent
	Foreman	Supervisor
Using female-gender words	Authoress, actress, stewardess	Author, actor, flight attendant
Using special designations	Woman doctor, male nurse	Doctor, nurse
Using *he* to refer to *everyone*	The average worker, he	The average worker, he or she
Identifying roles with gender	The typical executive spends four hours of his day in meetings.	Most executives spend four hours each day in meetings.
	Consumer, she	Consumers, they
	The nurse/teacher, she	Nurses/teachers, they
Identifying women by marital status	Don Harron and Catherine	Don Harron and Catherine McKinnon
	Don Harron and Ms. McKinnon	Mr. Harron and Ms. McKinnon
Racial/Ethnic Bias		
Assigning stereotypes	My black assistant speaks more articulately than I do.	My assistant speaks more articulately than I do.
	Not surprisingly, Shing Tung-Yau excels in mathematics.	Shing Tung-Yau excels in mathematics.
Identifying people by race or ethnicity	Frank Clementi, Italian-Canadian CEO	Frank Clementi, CEO
Age Bias		
Including age when irrelevant	Mary Kirazy, 58, has just joined our trust department.	Mary Kirazy has just joined our trust department.
Disability Bias		
Putting the disability before the person	Disabled workers face many barriers on the job.	Workers with physical challenges face many barriers on the job.
	An epileptic, Tracy has no trouble doing her job.	Tracy's epilepsy has no effect on her job performance.

- **Gender bias.** Avoid sexist language by using the same label for everyone (don't call a woman *chairperson* and then call a man *chairman*). Reword sentences to use *they* or no pronoun at all. Vary traditional patterns by sometimes putting women first (*women and men*, *she and he*, *her and his*). Note that the preferred title for women in business is *Ms.*, unless the individual asks to be addressed as *Miss* or *Mrs.* or has some other title, such as *Dr.*

- **Racial and ethnic bias.** Avoid language suggesting that members of a racial or ethnic group have stereotypical characteristics. The best solution is to avoid identifying people by race or ethnic origin unless such a label is relevant to the matter at hand—and it rarely is.

- **References to Canada's Aboriginal peoples.** The Canadian Constitution recognizes three groups of Aboriginal peoples: Indians, Métis, and Inuit. They each have their own heritage, languages, cultural practices, and spiritual beliefs. The term *Indian* describes all the Aboriginal peoples in Canada who are not Inuit or Métis. Many Aboriginal peoples today are offended by the term *Indian* and prefer *First Nations*. Many First Nations peoples have adopted the term *First Nation* to replace the term *band* to designate their community. As an accurate and ethical communicator, be sure to use the terms that Canada's Aboriginal peoples prefer.

- **Age bias.** As with gender, race, and ethnic background, mention the age of a person only when it is relevant. Moreover, be careful of the context in which you use words that refer to age. Such words carry a variety of positive and negative connotations—and not only when referring to people beyond a certain age. For example, *young* can imply youthfulness, inexperience, or even immaturity, depending on how it's used.

- **Disability bias.** Physical, mental, sensory, or emotional impairments should never be mentioned in business messages unless those conditions are directly relevant to the subject. If you must refer to someone's disability, put the person first and the disability second.[6] For example, by saying "employees with physical challenges," not "handicapped employees," you focus on the whole person, not the disability. The Canadian Human Rights Commission guarantees equal opportunities for people who have or have had a condition that might handicap them. The goal of bias-free communication is to abandon stereotyped assumptions about what a person can do or will do and to focus on an individual's unique characteristics.

Adapting to Your Audience: Building Strong Relationships with Your Audience

2 LEARNING OBJECTIVE

Explain why establishing credibility is vital to the success of your communication efforts

Focusing on your audience's needs is vital to effective communication, but you also have your own priorities as a communicator. Sometimes these needs are obvious and direct, such as when you're appealing for a budget increase for your department. At other times, the need may be more subtle. For example, you may want to explain your company's environmental practices when dealing with customers concerned about environmental issues. Two key efforts help you address your own needs while building positive relationships with your audience: establishing your credibility and projecting your company's image.

ESTABLISHING YOUR CREDIBILITY

People are more likely to react positively to your message when they have confidence in you.

Your audience's response to every message you send depends heavily on their perception of your **credibility,** a measure of your believability based on how reliable you are and how much trust you evoke in others. With colleagues and long-term customers, you've already established some degree of credibility based on past communication efforts. As long as you haven't let people down in the past, they are inclined to accept each new message from you. However, with audiences who don't know you, you need to establish credibility before they accept—or perhaps even pay attention to—your messages. Whether you're working to build credibility with a new audience, to maintain credibility with an existing audience, or even to restore credibility after a mistake, consider emphasizing the following characteristics:

- **Honesty.** Honesty is the cornerstone of credibility. No matter how famous, important, charming, or attractive you are, if you don't tell the truth, most people will eventually lose faith in you. On the other hand, demonstrating honesty and integrity will earn you the respect of your colleagues and the trust of everyone you communicate with, even if they don't always agree with or welcome the messages you have to deliver.

- **Objectivity.** Audiences appreciate the ability to distance yourself from emotional situations and to look at all sides of an issue. They want to believe that you have their interests in mind, not just your own.

- **Awareness of audience needs.** Let your audience know that you understand what's important to them. If you've done a thorough audience analysis, you'll know what your audience cares about and their specific issues and concerns in a particular situation.

- **Credentials, knowledge, and expertise.** Every audience wants to be assured that the messages they receive come from people who know what they're talking about—that's why public speakers, for example, often arrange to be introduced with brief summaries of their experience and qualifications. When you need to establish credibility with a new audience, put yourself in their position and try to identify the credentials that would be most important to them. Is it your education, a professional certification, special training, or success on the job? Express these qualifications clearly and objectively, without overshadowing the message. Sometimes it's as simple as using the correct technical terms or mentioning your role in a successful project.

- **Endorsements.** An endorsement is a statement on your behalf by someone who is accepted by your audience as an expert. If your audience doesn't know anything about you, you might be able to get assistance from someone they do know and trust. For example, when delivering a presentation, you could quote a recognized authority on your subject, even if you don't know the authority personally. Once the audience learns that you've done your research, they'll be more receptive to your messages.

- **Performance.** Who impresses you more, the person who always says, "If you ever need me, all you have to do is call," or the one who actually shows up when you need to move or when you need a ride to the airport? It's easy to say you can do something, but following through can be much harder. That's why demonstrating impressive communication skills is not enough; people need to know they can count on you to get the job done.

- **Sincerity.** When you offer praise, don't use hyperbole, such as "you are the most fantastic employee I could ever imagine." Instead, point out specific qualities that warrant praise.

To enhance your credibility, emphasize such factors as honesty, objectivity, and awareness of audience needs.

Show you are aware of a person's contributions and are not making generic thanks:

Instead of This	Use This
My deepest, heartfelt thanks for the excellent job you did. It's hard these days to find workers like you. You are just fantastic! I can't stress enough how happy you have made us with your outstanding performance.	Thanks for the great job you did filling in for Sean at the convention on such short notice. Despite the difficult circumstances, you managed to attract several new orders with your demonstration of the new line of coffeemakers. Your dedication and sales ability are truly appreciated.

Even though arrogance turns listeners off, displaying too much modesty or too little confidence can hurt your credibility. If you lack faith in yourself, you're likely to communicate an uncertain attitude that undermines your credibility; audiences need to know that you believe in yourself and your message. The key to being believable is to believe in yourself. If you are convinced that your message is sound, you can state your case with authority so that your audience has no doubts. Avoid vague sentiments and confidence-draining words such as *if*, *hope*, and *trust*:

Instead of This	Use This
We hope this recommendation will be helpful.	We're glad to make this recommendation.
If you'd like to order, mail us the reply card.	To order, mail the reply card.
We trust that you'll extend your service contract.	By extending your service contract, you can continue to enjoy top-notch performance from your equipment.

In addition, credibility is established by awareness of the language the audience knows and expects. It has become common practice to "speak to an issue," or "dig deeper," or even examine a "paradigm shift." The problem with language like this is that it is essentially meaningless. What does it really mean to "think outside the box"? How would someone from another culture interpret this? By using slang, clichés, and "business speak," you can negatively affect your credibility because your readers could misunderstand or misinterpret what you are trying to say. If you are not sure whether your language is too informal, try putting words or phrases into a search engine to see what the results are. Credibility is built by communicating clearly and concisely to your audience.

Finally, keep in mind that credibility can take days, months, or even years to establish—and it can be wiped out in an instant. An occasional mistake or letdown is usually forgiven, but major lapses in honesty or integrity can destroy your reputation. On the other hand, when you do establish credibility, communication becomes much easier because you no longer have to spend time and energy convincing people that you are a trustworthy source of information and ideas.

PROJECTING THE COMPANY'S IMAGE

Your company's interests and reputation take precedence over your personal communication style.

When you communicate with anyone outside your organization, it is more than a conversation between two individuals. You represent your company and therefore play a vital role in helping the company build and maintain positive relationships with all its stakeholders. Most successful companies work hard to foster a specific public image, and your external communication efforts need to project that image. As part of this responsibility, the interests and preferred communication style of your company must take precedence over your own views and personal communication style.

Many organizations have specific communication guidelines that show everything from the correct use of the company name to preferred abbreviations and other grammatical details. Specifying a desired style of communication is more difficult, however. Observe more experienced colleagues to see how they communicate, and never hesitate to ask for editorial help to make sure you're conveying the appropriate tone. For example, with clients entrusting thousands or millions of dollars to it, an investment firm communicates in a style quite different from that of a clothing retailer. And a clothing retailer specializing in high-quality business attire communicates in a style different from that of a store catering to the latest trends in casual wear.

Adapting to Your Audience: Controlling Your Style and Tone

Your communication **style** involves the choices you make to express yourself: the words you select, the manner in which you use those words in sentences, and the way you build paragraphs from individual sentences. Your style creates a certain **tone,** or overall impression, in your messages. You can vary your style to sound forceful or objective, personal or formal, colourful or dry. The right choice depends on the nature of your message and your relationship with the reader.

3 **LEARNING OBJECTIVE**

Discuss how to achieve a businesslike tone with a style that is clear and concise.

USING A CONVERSATIONAL TONE

The tone of your business messages can range from informal to conversational to formal. If you're in a large organization and you're communicating with your superiors or with customers, your tone would tend to be more formal and respectful.[7] However, that formal tone might sound distant and cold if used with close colleagues.

Compare the three versions of the message in Table 5–2. The first is too formal and stuffy for today's audiences, whereas the third is too casual for any audience other than close associates or friends. The second message demonstrates the **conversational tone** used in most business communication—plain language that sounds businesslike without being stuffy or full of jargon.

Most business messages aim for a conversational style that is warm but still businesslike.

Table 5–2	Three Levels of Tone: Formal, Conversational, and Informal	
Formal Tone	**Conversational Tone**	**Informal Tone**
Reserved for the most formal occasions	**Preferred for most business communication**	**Reserved for communication with friends and close associates**
Dear Ms. Navarro:	Dear Ms. Navarro:	Hi Gabriella,
Enclosed is the information that was requested during our telephone conversation on May 14.	Here's the information you requested during our phone conversation on Friday. As I mentioned, Lefebvre Financial Services has excellent financial advisors.	Hope all is well. Just sending along the information you asked for.
As I mentioned at that time, Lefebvre Financial Services has personal financial advisors of exceptional quality.	In addition, our experienced pension and benefits team will help you with your retirement plans. They can give information to a Lefebvre advisor with your permission; please let us know.	As I said on Friday, Lefebvre Financial Services has great financial advisors with a lot of experience.
As you were also informed, our organization has a highly trained team of pension and benefits specialists who will also assist you with your retirement planning concerns. If you want one of them to provide information to a Lefebvre advisor, please inform us with your permission.	If you would like more information, please call any time between 9:00 and 5:00, Monday through Friday.	Also, our pension and benefits team will help with your retirement plans. They'll be happy to speak with you and contact a Lefebvre rep with your permission.
If you have questions or would like additional information, you may certainly contact me during regular business hours.	Sincerely,	Just call me if you want to know more—any time from 9:00 to 5:00 is fine.
Sincerely yours,	Samuel G. Berenz	Take care,
Samuel G. Berenz		Sam

Before writing a letter or an email message on behalf of your company, think about how you project the company image. What image does this photo of Lowe's employees project? Why is image so important? In what ways do employees project their company's image to the public?

You can achieve a conversational tone in your messages by following these guidelines:

- **Avoid obsolete and pompous language.** Business language used to be much more formal than it is today, but some out-of-date phrases still appear. You can avoid using such language if you ask yourself, "Would I say this if I were talking with someone face to face?" Similarly, avoid using big words, trite expressions, and overly complicated sentences to impress others. Such pompous language sounds self-important (see Table 5–3).

- **Avoid preaching and bragging.** People who think that they know everything and that others know nothing can be very irritating. If you need to remind your audience of something obvious, insert the information casually, into the middle of a paragraph, where it will sound like a secondary comment rather than a major revelation. When speaking, you can preface the obvious with a comment like, "As you know." To maintain a favourable image, avoid bragging about your accomplishments or those of your organization (unless your audience is a part of your organization).

- **Be careful with intimacy.** Most business messages should avoid intimacy, such as sharing personal details or adopting a casual, unprofessional tone. However, when you do have a close relationship with your audience, such as among the members of a close-knit team, a more intimate tone is sometimes appropriate and even expected.

- **Be careful with humour.** Humour can be an effective tool to inject interest into dry subjects or take the sting out of negative news, but it can easily backfire and divert attention from your message. The humour must be connected to the point you're trying to make. Business messages are not a forum

| Table 5–3 | Staying Up to Date and Accessible with Business Language |

Obsolete	Accessible
in due course	today, tomorrow (or a specific time)
permit me to say that	(permission is not necessary)
we are in receipt of	we received
pursuant to	(omit)
in closing, I'd like to say	(omit)
the undersigned	I; we
kindly advise	please let me/us know
attached please find	enclosed is or I/we have enclosed
it has come to my attention	I have just learned; Ms. Garza has just told me
In closing, I'd like to say	(Omit; just say whatever you need to say.)
we wish to inform you that	(Omit; just say whatever you need to say.)
please be advised that	(Omit; just say whatever you need to say.)

Pompous	Accessible
Upon procurement of additional supplies, I will initiate fulfillment of your order.	I will fill your order when I receive more supplies.
Perusal of the records indicates a substantial deficit for the preceding accounting period due to the continued utilization of obsolete equipment.	The records show a company loss last year due to the use of old equipment.

for sharing jokes. Never use humour in formal messages or when you're communicating across cultural boundaries: your international audience may not appreciate your humour or even realize that you're trying to be funny.[8] If you don't know your audience well or you're not skilled at using humour in a business setting, don't use it at all. When in doubt, leave it out.

USING PLAIN LANGUAGE

What do you think this sentence is trying to say?

> We continually exist to synergistically supply value-added deliverables such that we may continue to proactively maintain enterprise-wide data to stay competitive in tomorrow's world.[9]

If you don't have any idea what it means, you're not alone. However, this is a real sentence from a real company, written in an attempt to explain what the company does and why. This sort of incomprehensible, buzzword-filled writing is driving a widespread call to use *plain language* (or *plain English,* specifically, when English is involved).

Plain language presents information in a simple, unadorned style that allows your audience to easily grasp your meaning, without struggling through specialized, technical, or convoluted language. The Plain English Campaign (a nonprofit group in England campaigning for clear language) defines plain English as language "that the intended audience can read, understand and act upon the first time they read it."[10] You can see how this definition supports using the "you" attitude and shows respect for your audience. In addition, plain language can make companies more productive and more profitable simply because people spend less time trying to figure out messages that are confusing or aren't written to meet their needs.[11]

On the Creative Commons website, for example, licensing terms are available in three versions: a complete "legal code" document that spells out contractual details in specific legal terms that meet the needs of legal professionals, a "human-readable" version that explains the licensing terms in nontechnical language that anyone can understand, and a "machine readable" version fine-tuned for search engines and other systems (see Figure 5–3).[12]

For all its advantages, plain language does have some limitations. It sometimes lacks the precision or subtlety necessary for scientific research, engineering documents, intense feeling, and personal insight. Moreover, it doesn't embrace all cultures and dialects equally. But even though it's intended for audiences who speak English as their primary language, plain language can also help you simplify the messages you prepare for audiences who speak English only as a second or even third language. For example, by choosing words that have only one interpretation, you will surely communicate more clearly with your intercultural audience.[13]

Plain language also refers to the use of concrete terms and the elimination of slang, jargon, and clichés, as well as business speak and doubling up of words. Phrases like "new and improved," "a terrible tragedy," "refer back," or "a large majority" are examples of these unnecessary word pairings. You also want to avoid words like *huge, large,* or *small,* as these are difficult to imagine and can mean a variety of things based on your perception. A "huge" house could be 10 000 square feet in North America, but 2000 square feet in countries where land for building is not available. Where possible, use numbers to quantify your meaning.

Audiences can understand and act on plain language without reading it over and over.

SELECTING ACTIVE OR PASSIVE VOICE

Your choice of active or passive voice also affects the tone of your message. You are using **active voice** when the subject performs the action and the object receives it: "John rented the office." You're using **passive voice** when the subject

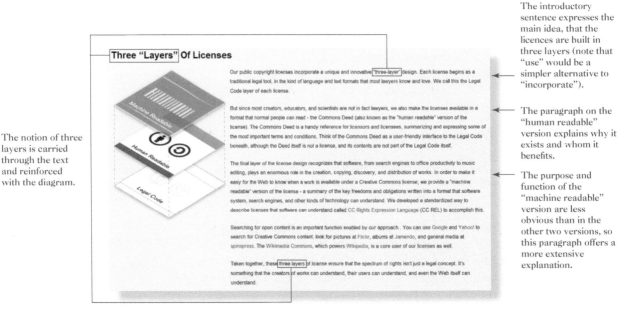

The notion of three layers is carried through the text and reinforced with the diagram.

The introductory sentence expresses the main idea, that the licences are built in three layers (note that "use" would be a simpler alternative to "incorporate").

The paragraph on the "human readable" version explains why it exists and whom it benefits.

The purpose and function of the "machine readable" version are less obvious than in the other two versions, so this paragraph offers a more extensive explanation.

Figure 5–3 Plain Language at Creative Commons

Courtesy: Creative Commons

receives the action: "The office was rented by John." As you can see, the passive voice combines the helping verb *to be* with a form of the verb that is usually similar to the past tense. When you use active sentences, your messages generally sound less formal and make it easier for readers to determine who performed the action (see Table 5–4). In contrast, using passive voice de-emphasizes the subject and implies that the action was done by something or someone.

Active sentences are usually stronger than passive ones.

Use passive sentences to soften bad news, to put yourself in the background, or to create an impersonal tone.

When to use { passive voice

Using the active voice makes your writing more direct, livelier, and easier to read. In contrast, the passive voice is not wrong grammatically, but it is often cumbersome, can be unnecessarily vague, and can make sentences longer. In most cases, the active voice is your best choice.[14] Nevertheless, using the passive voice can help you demonstrate the "you" attitude in some situations:

- When you want to be diplomatic about pointing out a problem or error (the passive version seems less like an accusation)
- When you want to point out what's being done without taking or attributing either the credit or the blame (the passive version leaves the actor completely out of the sentence)

Table 5–4	Choosing Active or Passive Voice

Avoid passive voice to make your writing lively and direct.

Dull and Indirect in Passive Voice	*Lively and Direct in Active Voice*
The new procedure was developed by the operations team.	The operations team developed the new procedure.
Legal problems are created by this contract.	This contract creates legal problems.
Reception preparations have been undertaken by our public relations people for the new CEO's arrival.	Our public relations people have begun planning a reception for the new CEO.

Passive voice is helpful when you need to be diplomatic or want to focus attention on problems or solutions rather than on people.

Accusatory or Self-Congratulatory in Active Voice	*More Diplomatic in Passive Voice*
You lost the shipment.	The shipment was lost.
I recruited seven engineers last month.	Seven engineers were recruited last month.
We are investigating the high rate of failures on the final assembly line.	The high rate of failures on the final assembly line is being investigated.

• When you want to avoid personal pronouns to create an objective tone (the passive version may be used in a formal report, for example)

The second half of Table 5–4 illustrates several situations in which the passive voice helps you focus your message on your audience.

Composing Your Message

After you've decided how you can adapt to your audience, you're ready to begin composing your message. As you write your first draft, let your creativity flow. Don't draft and edit at the same time or worry about getting everything perfect. Make up words if you can't think of the correct word; draw pictures, talk out loud—do whatever it takes to get the ideas out of your head and captured on screen or paper. If you've scheduled carefully, you'll have time to revise and refine the material later, before showing it to anyone. In fact, many writers find it helpful to establish a personal rule of *never* showing a first draft to anyone. By working in this "safe zone," away from the critical eyes of others, your mind will stay free to think clearly and creatively. See "Sharpening Your Career Skills: Beating Writer's Block—Ten Workable Ideas to Get Words Flowing."

4 LEARNING OBJECTIVE

Describe how to select words that are not only correct but also effective.

> **TIPS FOR SUCCESS**
> "Use strong verbs and active voice. When you feel the need to toss in an adjective or adverb, consider it a red flag that your nouns and verbs may lack precision, or you wouldn't be seeking a modifier. Make every word contribute to the information. Eliminate such redundancies as *important essentials, serious crisis, past history, previous experience, completely inaudible.*"
>
> Dianna Booher, CEO, Booher Consultants

CHOOSING PRECISE WORDS

You may find it helpful to hone your craft by viewing your writing at three levels: strong words, effective sentences, and coherent paragraphs. Starting at the word level, successful writers pay close attention to the correct use of words.[15] If you make errors of grammar or usage, you lose credibility with your audience—even if your message is otherwise correct. Poor grammar suggests to readers that you're uninformed, and they may choose not to trust an uninformed source. Moreover, poor grammar can imply that you don't respect your audience enough to get things right.

The "rules" of grammar and usage can be a source of worry for writers because some of these rules are complex and some evolve over time. Even professional editors and grammarians occasionally have questions about correct usage, and they sometimes disagree about the answers. For example, the word *data* is the plural form of *datum*, yet some experts now prefer to treat *data* as a singular noun when it's used in nonscientific material to refer to a collection of facts or figures.

With practice, you'll become more skilled in making correct choices. If you have doubts about what is correct, you have many ways to find the answer. Consult the many special reference books and resources available in libraries, in bookstores, and on the Internet.

In addition to using words correctly, successful writers and speakers take care to find the most effective words and phrases to convey their meaning. Selecting and using words effectively is often more challenging than using words correctly because it's a matter of judgment and experience. Careful writers continue to work at their craft to find words that communicate with power.

Hone your craft by viewing your writing at three levels: strong words, effective sentences, and coherent paragraphs.

If you're not sure of correct grammar or usage, look it up; you'll avoid embarrassing mistakes and learn at the same time.

Effectiveness is the second consideration when choosing words.

USING FUNCTIONAL AND CONTENT WORDS CORRECTLY

Functional words (conjunctions, prepositions, articles, and pronouns) express the relationships among content words (nouns, verbs, adjectives, and adverbs).

Words can be divided into two main categories: **Functional words** express relationships and have only one unchanging meaning in any given context. They include conjunctions, prepositions, articles, and pronouns. Your main concern with functional words is to use them correctly. **Content words** are multidimensional and therefore subject to various interpretations. They include nouns, verbs, adjectives, and adverbs. These words carry the meaning of a sentence. In your sentences, content words are the building blocks, and functional words are the mortar that holds them together. In the following sentence, all the content words are underlined:

> <u>Some objective observers</u> of the <u>cookie market give Christie's</u> the <u>edge</u> in <u>quality</u>, but <u>President's Choice is lauded</u> for <u>superior distribution</u>.

Both functional words and content words are necessary, but your effectiveness as a communicator depends largely on your ability to choose the right content words for your message.

SHARPENING YOUR CAREER SKILLS

Beating Writer's Block: Ten Workable Ideas to Get Words Flowing

Putting words on a page or on screen can be a real struggle. Some people get stuck so often that they develop a mental block. If you get writer's block, here are some ways to get words flowing:

- **Use positive self-talk.** Stop worrying about how well or easily you write, and stop thinking of writing as difficult, time consuming, or complicated. Tell yourself that you're capable and that you can do the job. Also, recall past examples of your writing that were successful.
- **Know your purpose.** Be specific about what you want to accomplish with this particular assignment. Without a clear purpose, writing can indeed be impossible.
- **Visualize your audience.** Picture audience backgrounds, interests, subject knowledge, and vocabulary (including the technical jargon they use). Such visualization can help you choose an appropriate style and tone for your writing.
- **Create a productive environment.** Write in a location that's meant for writing only, and make that setting pleasant. Set up "writing appointments." Scheduling a session from 9:30 A.M. to noon is less intimidating than an indefinite session. Also, keep your mind fresh with scheduled breaks.
- **Make an outline or a list.** Even if you don't create a formal outline, jot down a few notes about how your ideas fit together. As you go along, you can revise your notes so that you end up with a plan that gives direction and coherence.
- **Just start.** Put aside all worries, fears, and distractions—anything that gives you an excuse to postpone writing. Then put down any thoughts you have about your topic. Don't worry about whether these ideas can actually be used; just let your mind range freely.

- **Write the middle first.** Start wherever your interest is greatest and your ideas are most developed. You can follow new directions, but note ideas to revisit later. When you finish one section, choose another without worrying about sequence. Just get your thoughts down.
- **Push obstacles aside.** If you get stuck at some point, don't worry. Move past the thought, sentence, or paragraph, and come back to it later. Get started simply by writing or talking about why you're stuck: "I'm stuck because …" Also brainstorm. Before you know it, you'll be writing about your topic.
- **Read a newspaper or magazine.** Read an article that uses a style similar to yours. Choose one you'll enjoy so that you'll read it more closely.
- **Exercise!** Simply getting out of your chair, stretching your arms, taking deep breaths, and getting outside for half an hour or so will refresh your mind and give a new perspective on your task.

When deadlines loom, don't panic. Concentrate on the major ideas first, and save the details for later, after you have something on the page. If you keep the process in perspective, you'll succeed.

CAREER APPLICATIONS

1. List the ways you procrastinate, and discuss what you can do to break these habits.
2. Analyze your own writing experiences. What negative self-talk do you use? What might you do to overcome this tendency?

UNDERSTANDING DENOTATION AND CONNOTATION

Content words have both a denotative and a connotative meaning. The **denotative meaning** is the literal, or dictionary, meaning. The **connotative meaning** includes all the associations and feelings evoked by the word.

The denotative meaning of *desk* is "a table used for writing." Some desks may have drawers or compartments, and others may have a flat top or a sloping top, but the literal meaning is generally well understood. The connotative meaning of *desk* may include thoughts associated with work or study, but the word *desk* has fairly neutral connotations—neither strong nor emotional. However, some words have much stronger connotations than others. For example, the connotations of the word *fail* are negative and can carry strong emotional meaning. If you say that the sales department *failed* to meet its annual quota, the connotative meaning suggests that the group is inferior, incompetent, or below some standard of performance. However, the reason for not achieving 100 percent might be an inferior product, incorrect pricing, or some other factor outside the control of the sales department. In contrast, by saying that the sales department achieved 70 percent of its quota, you clearly communicate that the results were less than expected—without triggering all the negative emotions associated with *failure*.

Content words have both a denotative (explicit, specific) meaning and a connotative (implicit, associative) meaning.

BALANCING ABSTRACT AND CONCRETE WORDS

Words vary dramatically in the degree of abstraction or concreteness they convey. An **abstract word** expresses a concept, quality, or characteristic. Abstractions are usually broad, encompassing a category of ideas, and they are often intellectual, academic, or philosophical. *Love, honour, progress, tradition,* and *beauty* are abstractions. In contrast, a **concrete word** stands for something you can touch or see. Concrete terms are anchored in the tangible, material world. *Chair, table, horse, rose, kick, kiss, red, green,* and *two* are concrete words; they are direct, clear, and exact. Incidentally, technology continues to generate new words and new meanings that describe things that don't have a physical presence but are nonetheless concrete: *software, database, signal,* and *code* are all concrete terms as well.

You might assume that concrete words are better than abstract words because they are more precise, but this isn't always the case. Imagine talking about business without referring to such concepts as *morale, productivity, profits, quality, motivation,* and *guarantees.* Abstractions permit us to rise above the common and tangible.

As you can imagine, abstractions tend to cause more trouble for writers and readers than concrete words. Abstractions tend to be "fuzzy" and can be interpreted differently, depending on the audience and the circumstances. The best way to minimize such problems is to blend abstract terms with concrete ones, the general with the specific. State the concept, then pin it down with details expressed in more concrete terms. Save the abstractions for ideas that cannot be expressed any other way. In addition, abstract words such as *small, numerous, sizable, near, soon, good,* and *fine* are imprecise, so try to replace them with terms that are more accurate. Instead of referring to a *sizable loss,* give an exact number.

The more abstract a word is, the more it is removed from the tangible, objective world of things that can be perceived with the senses.

In business communication, use concrete, specific terms whenever possible; use abstractions only when necessary.

FINDING WORDS THAT COMMUNICATE WELL

By practising your writing, learning from experienced writers and editors, and reading extensively, you'll find it easier to choose words that communicate your thoughts exactly. When you compose business messages, think carefully to find the most precise and powerful words for each situation (see Table 5–5).

- **Choose precise words.** Choose words that express your thoughts clearly, specifically, and dynamically. Nouns and verbs are the most concrete and should do most of the communication work in your messages. Verbs are

Try to use words that are precise and familiar.

Table 5–5	Finding Words That Communicate with Power

Avoid Unfamiliar Words	Use Familiar Words
ascertain	find out, learn
consummate	close, bring about
peruse	read, study
circumvent	avoid
increment	growth, increase
unequivocal	certain

Avoid Clichés and Buzzwords	Use Plain Language
an uphill battle	a challenge
writing on the wall	prediction
call the shots	be in charge
take by storm	attack
cost an arm and a leg	expensive
a new ball game	fresh start
fall through the cracks	be overlooked
think outside the box	be creative

especially powerful because they tell what's happening in the sentence, so make them dynamic and specific. For instance, you could replace *fall* with *slide*, *slip*, *plummet*, *drop*, or *decline* to suggest the magnitude of the decrease. Here's another helpful clue: if you find yourself using a lot of adjectives and adverbs, you're probably trying to compensate for weak nouns and verbs. Saying that *sales plummeted* is stronger and more efficient than saying *sales dropped dramatically* or *sales experienced a dramatic drop*.

- **Choose familiar words.** You'll communicate best with words that are familiar to both you and your readers. Efforts to improve a situation can be *ameliorative*, but saying they are *helpful* is a lot more effective. Moreover, using an unfamiliar word for the first time in an important document can lead to embarrassing mistakes.

Avoid clichés and trendy buzzwords in your writing, and use jargon only when your audience is completely familiar with it.

- **Avoid clichés and buzzwords.** Although familiar words are generally the best choice, beware of terms and phrases so common or so trendy that they have lost some of their power to communicate. Most people use these phrases not because they think it makes their message more vivid and inviting but because they don't know how to express themselves otherwise and don't invest the energy required for original writing.[16]

- **Use jargon carefully. Jargon** is the specialized language of a particular profession or industry. Handle jargon with care. It is usually an efficient way to communicate within specific groups that understand their own special terms, but it will confuse people who are not members of those groups. For example, when a recording engineer wants to communicate that a particular piece of music is devoid of reverberation and other sound effects, it's a lot easier to describe the track as "dry." Of course, to people who aren't familiar with such insider terms, jargon is meaningless and intimidating—one more reason it's so important to understand your audience before you start writing.

Remember, your business writing skills will improve through imitation and practice. As you read business journals, newspapers, and even novels, make a note of the words you think are effective and keep them in a file. Doing so will expand your vocabulary and make it easier to find a precise word when you are writing.

Composing Your Message: Creating Effective Sentences

In English, words don't make much sense until they're combined in a sentence to express a complete thought. Thus the words *Jill*, *receptionist*, *the*, *smiles*, and *at* can be organized into "Jill smiles at the receptionist." Now that you've constructed the sentence, you can begin exploring the possibilities for improvement, looking at how well each word performs its particular function. Nouns and noun equivalents are the topics (or subjects) you're communicating about, and verbs and related words (or predicates) make statements about those subjects. In a complicated sentence, adjectives and adverbs modify the subject and predicate, and various connectors hold the words together.

5 LEARNING OBJECTIVE

Explain how sentence style affects emphasis within your message.

CHOOSING FROM THE FOUR TYPES OF SENTENCES

Sentences come in four basic varieties: simple, compound, complex, and compound–complex. A **simple sentence** has one main clause (a single subject and a single predicate), although it may be expanded by nouns and pronouns serving as objects of the action and by modifying phrases. Here's a typical example (with the subject underlined once and the predicate verb underlined twice):

> Profits increased in the past year.

A simple sentence has one main clause.

A **compound sentence** has two main clauses that express two or more independent but related thoughts of equal importance, usually joined by *and*, *but*, or *or*. In effect, a compound sentence is a merger of two or more simple sentences (independent clauses) that are related. For example,

> Wage rates have declined by 5 percent, and employee turnover has been high.

A compound sentence has two main clauses.

The independent clauses in a compound sentence are always separated by a comma or by a semicolon (in which case the conjunction—*and*, *but*, or—is dropped).

A **complex sentence** expresses one main thought (the independent clause) and one or more subordinate thoughts (dependent clauses) related to it, often separated by a comma. The subordinate thought, which comes first in the following sentence, could not stand alone:

> Although you may question Gerald's conclusions, you must admit that his research is thorough.

A complex sentence has one main clause and one subordinate clause.

A **compound–complex sentence** has two main clauses, at least one of which contains a subordinate clause:

> Profits have increased in the past year, and although you may question Gerald's conclusions, you must admit that his research is thorough.

A compound–complex sentence has two main clauses and at least one dependent clause.

When constructing a sentence, choose the form that matches the relationship of the ideas you want to express. If you have two ideas of equal importance, express them as two simple sentences or as one compound sentence. However, if one idea is less important than the other, place it in a dependent clause to form a complex sentence. For example, although the following compound sentence uses a conjunction to join two ideas, they aren't truly equal:

> The chemical products division is the strongest in the company, and its management techniques should be adopted by the other divisions.

By making the first thought subordinate to the second, you establish a cause-and-effect relationship. The following complex sentence is much more effective because it clearly explains why the other divisions should adopt the chemical division's management techniques:

> Because the chemical products division is the strongest in the company, its management techniques should be adopted by the other divisions.

To make your writing as effective as possible, strive for variety and balance using all four sentence types. If you use too many simple sentences, you won't be able to express the relationships among your ideas properly, and your writing will sound choppy and abrupt. If you use too many long, compound sentences, your writing will sound monotonous. On the other hand, an uninterrupted series of complex or compound–complex sentences is hard to follow.

USING SENTENCE STYLE TO EMPHASIZE KEY THOUGHTS

Emphasize parts of a sentence by
- Devoting more words to them
- Putting them at the beginning or at the end of the sentence
- Making them the subject of the sentence

In every message, some ideas are more important than others. You can emphasize these key ideas through your sentence style. One obvious technique is to give important points the most space. When you want to call attention to a thought, use extra words to describe it. Consider this sentence:

> The chairperson of the board called for a vote of the shareholders.

To emphasize the importance of the chairperson, you might describe her more fully:

> Having considerable experience in corporate takeover battles, the chairperson of the board called for a vote of the shareholders.

You can increase the emphasis even more by adding a separate, short sentence to augment the first:

> The chairperson of the board called for a vote of the shareholders. She has considerable experience in corporate takeover battles.

You can also call attention to a thought by making it the subject of the sentence. In the following example, the emphasis is on the person:

> *I* can write letters much more quickly using a computer.

However, by changing the subject, the computer takes centre stage:

> The *computer* enables me to write letters much more quickly.

You can adjust the emphasis given to a subordinate idea by placing the dependent clause at the beginning, middle, or end of the sentence.

Another way to emphasize an idea is to place it either at the beginning or at the end of a sentence:

Less Emphatic: We are cutting the *price* to stimulate demand.

More Emphatic: To stimulate demand, we are cutting the *price*.

In complex sentences, the placement of the dependent clause hinges on the relationship between the ideas expressed. If you want to emphasize the idea, put the dependent clause at the end of the sentence (the most emphatic position) or at the beginning (the second most emphatic position). If you want to downplay the idea, bury the dependent clause within the sentence.

Most Emphatic: The electronic parts are manufactured in Mexico, *which has lower wage rates than Canada.*

Emphatic: *Because wage rates are lower there,* the electronic parts are manufactured in Mexico.

Least Emphatic: Mexico, *which has lower wage rates,* was selected as the production point for the electronic parts.

Techniques such as these give you a great deal of control over the way your audience interprets what you have to say.

Composing Your Message: Crafting Unified, Coherent Paragraphs

After arranging precise words in effective sentences, your next step is to arrange those sentences into coherent paragraphs. Paragraphs organize sentences related to the same general topic. Readers expect every paragraph to be *unified*—focusing on a single topic—and *coherent*—presenting ideas in a logically connected way. By carefully arranging the elements of each paragraph, you help your readers grasp the main idea of your document and understand how the specific pieces of support material back up that idea.

CREATING THE ELEMENTS OF THE PARAGRAPH

Paragraphs vary widely in length and form, but a typical paragraph contains three basic elements: a topic sentence, support sentences that develop the topic, and transitional words and phrases.

TOPIC SENTENCE An effective paragraph deals with a single topic and the sentence that introduces that topic is called the **topic sentence.** In informal and creative writing, the topic sentence may be implied rather than stated. In business writing, the topic sentence is generally explicit and is often the first sentence in the paragraph. The topic sentence gives readers a summary of the general idea that will be covered in the rest of the paragraph. The following examples show how a topic sentence can introduce the subject and suggest the way that subject will be developed:

> The medical products division has been troubled for many years by public relations problems. [In the rest of the paragraph, readers will learn the details of the problems.]
>
> Relocating the plant to St. John's has two main disadvantages. [The disadvantages will be explained in subsequent sentences.]
>
> To get a refund, you must supply us with some additional information. [The details of the necessary information will be described in the rest of the paragraph.]

In addition to helping your readers, topic sentences help you as a writer because they remind you of the purpose of each paragraph and thereby help you stay focused.

SUPPORT SENTENCES In most paragraphs, the topic sentence needs to be explained, justified, or extended with one or more support sentences. These related sentences must all have a bearing on the general subject and must provide enough specific details to make the topic clear:

> The medical products division has been troubled for many years by public relations problems. Since 2008 the local newspaper has published 15 articles that portray the division in a negative light. We have been accused of everything from mistreating laboratory animals to polluting the local groundwater. Our facility has been described as a health hazard. Our scientists are referred to as "Frankensteins," and our profits are considered "obscene."

Most paragraphs consist of
- A topic sentence that reveals the subject of the paragraph
- Related sentences that support and expand the topic
- Transitional elements that help readers move between sentences and paragraphs

nyul/Fotolia

Even when reading online, your audience expects each paragraph to address one main idea and all the paragraphs in a document to link together logically. Besides devoting one idea to each paragraph, what other methods can you use to help readers comprehend your online documents?

The support sentences are all more specific than the topic sentence. Each one provides another piece of evidence to demonstrate the general truth of the main thought. Also, each sentence is clearly related to the general idea being developed, which gives the paragraph its unity. A paragraph is well developed if it contains enough information to make the topic sentence convincing and interesting, and if it doesn't contain any extraneous, unrelated sentences.

Transitional elements include
- Connecting words (conjunctions)
- Repeated words or phrases
- Pronouns
- Words that are frequently paired

TRANSITIONS Transitions connect ideas by showing how one thought is related to another. They also help alert the reader to what lies ahead so that shifts and changes don't cause confusion. In addition to helping readers understand the connections you're trying to make, transitions give your writing a smooth, even flow.

Depending on the specific need within a document, transitional elements can range in length from a single word to an entire paragraph or more. You can establish transitions in a variety of ways:

- **Use connecting words:** Use conjunctions such as *and, but, or, nevertheless, however, in addition,* and so on.
- **Echo a word or phrase from a previous paragraph or sentence:** "A system should be established for monitoring inventory levels. *This system* will provide ..."
- **Use a pronoun that refers to a noun used previously:** "Ms. Kim is the leading candidate for the president's position. *She* has excellent qualifications."
- **Use words that are frequently paired:** "The machine has a *minimum* output of ... Its *maximum* output is ..."

Some transitional elements alert the reader to a change in mood from the previous material. Some announce a total contrast with what's gone on before, some announce a causal relationship, and some signal a change in time. Here is a list of transitions frequently used to move readers smoothly between clauses, sentences, and paragraphs:

Additional detail: moreover, furthermore, in addition, besides, first, second, third, finally

Causal relationship: therefore, because, accordingly, thus, consequently, hence, as a result, so

Comparison: similarly, here again, likewise, in comparison, still

Contrast: yet, conversely, whereas, nevertheless, on the other hand, however, but, nonetheless

Condition: although, if

Illustration: for example, in particular, in this case, for instance

Time sequence: formerly, after, when, meanwhile, sometimes

Intensification: indeed, in fact, in any event

Summary: in brief, in short, to sum up

Repetition: that is, in other words, as I mentioned earlier

Consider using a transition whenever it might help the reader understand your ideas and follow you from point to point. You can use transitions inside paragraphs to tie related points together and between paragraphs to ease the shift from one distinct thought to another. In longer reports, a transition that links major sections or chapters is often a complete paragraph that serves as a mini-introduction to the next section or as a summary of the ideas presented in the section just ending. Here's an example:

> Given the nature of this product, the alternatives are limited. As the previous section indicates, we can stop making it altogether, improve it, or continue with the current model. Each alternative has advantages and disadvantages, which are discussed in the following section.

This paragraph makes it clear to the reader that the analysis of the problem (offered in the previous section) is now over and that the document is making a transition to an analysis of alternatives (to be offered in the next section).

Keep in mind that transitions are not a substitute for effective organization. Put your ideas into a strong framework first, and then use transitions to link them together even more strongly.

CHOOSING THE BEST WAY TO DEVELOP EACH PARAGRAPH

Unification and coherence strongly depend on how you develop your paragraphs. Five of the most common development techniques are illustration, comparison or contrast, cause and effect, classification, and problem and solution (see Table 5–6).

6 LEARNING OBJECTIVE

Cite five ways to develop coherent paragraphs.

Table 5–6	**Five Techniques for Developing Paragraphs**	
Technique	**Description**	**Example**
Illustration	Giving examples that demonstrate the general idea	Some of our most popular products are available through local distributors. For example, Everett & Lemmings carries our frozen soups and entrées. The J. B. Green Company carries our complete line of seasonings, as well as the frozen soups. Wilmont Foods, also a major distributor, now carries our new line of frozen desserts.
Comparison or contrast	Using similarities or differences to develop the topic	When the company was small, the recruiting function could be handled informally. The need for new employees was limited, and each manager could comfortably screen and hire her or his own staff. However, our successful bid on the Owens contract means that we will be doubling our labour force over the next six months. To hire that many people without disrupting our ongoing activities, we will create a separate recruiting group within the human resources department.
Cause and effect	Focusing on the reasons for something	The heavy-duty fabric of your Wanderer tent probably broke down for one of two reasons: 1. A sharp object punctured the fabric, and without reinforcement, the hole was enlarged by the stress of pitching the tent daily for a week, or 2. The fibres gradually rotted because the tent was folded and stored while still wet.
Classification	Showing how a general idea is broken into specific categories	Successful candidates for our supervisor trainee program generally come from one of several groups. The largest group, by far, consists of recent graduates of accredited business management programs. The next largest group comes from within our own company, as we try to promote promising workers to positions of greater responsibility. Finally, we do occasionally accept candidates with outstanding supervisory experience in related industries.
Problem and solution	Presenting a problem and then discussing the solution	Selling handmade toys online is a challenge because consumers are accustomed to buying heavily advertised toys from major chain stores or well-known websites such as Amazon.ca. However, if we develop an appealing website, we can compete on the basis of product novelty and quality. In addition, we can provide unusual crafts at a competitive price: a rocking horse of birch with a hand-knit tail and mane; a music box with the child's name painted on the top.

In practice, you'll occasionally combine two or more methods of development in a single paragraph. Before settling for the first approach that comes to mind, consider the alternatives so that your message is communicated with clarity and meaning.

Using Technology to Compose and Shape Your Messages

Take full advantage of your software's capabilities to help you produce effective, professional messages in less time.

Careful and informed use of technology can help you compose and shape better messages in less time. Software (including word processors and online publishing systems for websites and blogs) provides a wide range of tools to help writers compose documents:

- **Style sheets, style sets, templates, and themes.** *Style sheets*, *style sets*, *templates*, and *themes* are various ways of ensuring consistency throughout a document and from document to document. These tools also make it easy to redesign an entire document or screen simply by redefining the various styles or selecting a different design theme. Style sheets or sets are collections of formatting choices for words, paragraphs, and other elements. Rather than manually formatting every element, you simply select one of the available styles. Templates usually set overall document parameters such as page size and provide a specific set of styles to use. Templates can be particularly handy if you create a variety of document types, such as letters, calendars, agendas, and so on. Themes tend to address the overall look and feel of the page or screen, including colour palettes and background images.
- **Boilerplate and document components.** *Boilerplate* refers to a standard block of saved text that is reused in multiple documents. Moving beyond simple text blocks, some systems can store fully formatted document components such as cover pages and sidebars.
- **Autocorrection or autocompletion.** Some programs can automate text entry and correction using a feature called autocompletion, autocorrection, or something similar. In Microsoft Word, for example, the AutoCorrect feature lets you build a library of actions that automatically fill in longer entries based on the first few characters you type (such as entering a full description of the company after you type the word *boilerplate*) or correct common typing errors (such as typing *teh* instead of *the*). Use these features carefully, though. First, they can make changes you might not want in every instance. Second, you may grow to rely on them to clean up your typing, but they won't be there to help when you're using other systems.
- **File merge and mail merge.** Most word-processing software makes it easy to combine files, which is an especially handy feature when several members of a team write different sections of a report. Mail merge lets you personalize form letters by automatically inserting names and addresses from a database.
- **Endnotes, footnotes, indexes, and tables of contents.** Your computer can help you track footnotes and endnotes, renumbering them every time you add or delete references. For a report's indexes and table of contents, you can simply flag the items you want to include and the software assembles the lists for you.

As with other forms of communication technology, using these tools efficiently and effectively requires some balance. You need to learn enough about the features to be handy with them, without spending so much time that the tools distract you from the writing process. For a reminder of the tasks involved in writing your messages, see "Checklist: Writing Business Messages."

✓ Checklist   Writing Business Messages

A. Adapt to your audience.
- Use the "you" attitude.
- Maintain good etiquette through polite communication.
- Emphasize the positive whenever possible.
- Use bias-free language.
- Establish your credibility in the eyes of your audience.
- Project your company's preferred image.
- Use a conversational but still professional and respectful tone.
- Use plain language for clarity.

B. Compose your message.
- Choose precise words that communicate efficiently.
- Make sure you use functional and content words correctly.

- Pay attention to the connotative meaning of your words.
- Balance abstract and concrete terms to convey your meaning accurately.
- Avoid clichés and trendy buzzwords.
- Use jargon only when your audience understands it and prefers it.
- Vary your sentence structure for impact and interest.
- Develop coherent, unified paragraphs.
- Use transitional elements generously to help your audience follow your message.

SUMMARY OF LEARNING OBJECTIVES

1 Explain the importance of adapting your messages to the needs and expectations of your audience. Your audience wants to know why you are communicating with them and how your message will benefit them. By showing awareness of their needs and expectations, you are answering their question "What's in it for me?" and establishing a good relationship. Practising the "you" attitude, emphasizing the positive, and using bias-free language will also demonstrate your sensitivity to your audience.

2 Explain why establishing credibility is vital to the success of your communication efforts. Your audiences will more likely accept your messages if you establish your credibility with them. Behaving honestly, objectively, reliably, and sincerely, and showing your awareness of your audiences' needs, demonstrate your credibility and will make your audiences more likely to respond positively to you. Establishing your credentials and expertise will communicate your credibility to audiences that don't know you, thus making them more receptive to your messages.

3 Discuss how to achieve a businesslike tone with a style that is clear and concise. You can achieve a businesslike tone by using plain language, which is language that is easily understood. Plain language avoids pompous and out-of-date phrases; in their place, it uses accessible and current vocabulary that audiences with a grade 8 or grade 9 education can easily understand. Using the active voice instead of the passive voice is another way to achieve a businesslike tone. Where the passive voice tends to create a dull and indirect style, the active voice is lively and direct. However, the passive voice is useful when you

must be diplomatic with your audience, because its indirect nature can create an objective tone.

4 Describe how to select words that are not only correct but also effective. To select the best words, first make sure they are correct by checking grammar and usage guides. Next, make sure the words you select are effective by knowing how to use functional and content words. Choose words that have fewer connotations and no negative connotations. Blend abstract words with concrete ones, narrowing from the general to the specific, and select words that communicate clearly and specifically. Avoid clichés, and use jargon only if your audience will understand it.

5 Explain how sentence style affects emphasis within your message. The emphasis of key ideas in your message is influenced by sentence style. For example, using more words to describe ideas will give them greater stress. You can also make your ideas the subject of sentences or place them at the beginning or end of sentences; these techniques will highlight your ideas. Being familiar with the four types of sentences (simple, compound, complex, and compound–complex) will assist you in giving emphasis to your information and thoughts.

6 Cite five ways to develop coherent paragraphs. Each paragraph should have a topic sentence that expresses the main idea and uses transitional elements for unity. Paragraphs can be developed by illustration (giving examples), by comparison and contrast (pointing out similarities or differences), by focusing on cause and effect (giving reasons), by classification (discussing categories), and by focusing on the solution to a problem (stating a problem and showing how to solve it).

ON THE JOB | PERFORMING COMMUNICATION TASKS AT CREATIVE COMMONS

To achieve their mission of popularizing a new approach to copyrighting songs, artwork, literature, and other creative works, the staff at Creative Commons need to convince people that the traditional approach to copyright doesn't meet the needs of today's digital society. This is no small challenge: not only do they need to persuade people to reconsider more than 200 years of legal precedent and habit, they also need to communicate with an extremely diverse audience—everyone from lawyers and business managers to artists, writers, musicians, and scientists. In the third year of your business program, you've joined Creative Commons as a communication intern. Apply your knowledge of effective writing to the following three scenarios:[17]

1. A key part of the communication challenge for Creative Commons is translating legal documents into language that musicians, artists, and others with no legal training can easily understand. Which of the following does the best job of adapting the following legal phrase (which is part of the licensing contracts) into language for a general audience?

   The above rights may be exercised in all media and formats whether now known or hereafter devised. The above rights include the right to make such modifications as are technically necessary to exercise the rights in other media and formats.

   a. The rights granted by this licensing contract extend to any current or future media, and you also have the right to modify the material as needed to meet the technical needs of any media.
   b. You may use this material in any present or future media and modify it as needed to work with any media.
   c. Be advised that your rights within the scope of this contract include the right to use this material in any media that either exists now or might be devised in the future. Moreover, you are also granted the right to modify the material as any current or future media might technically demand.
   d. You are hereby granted the right to use this material in any media, including modifications required by that media.

2. The single most important concept in the Creative Commons approach is the idea of a spectrum of possibilities between *all rights reserved* (a conventional copyright) and *no rights reserved* (being in the public domain, where anybody is free to use material in any way they please). Review the structure of the following four sentences and choose the one that does the best job of emphasizing the importance of the "spectrum of possibilities."

   a. Conventional copyright, in which the creator reserves all rights to a work, and the public domain, in which the creator gives up all rights, represent two black-and-white extremes.
   b. Between the all-or-nothing extremes of a conventional copyright and being in the public domain, Creative Commons sees a need for other possibilities.
   c. The primary contribution of Creative Commons is developing a range of possibilities between the extremes of *all rights reserved* (conventional copyright) and *no rights reserved* (public domain).
   d. The black-and-white choice of *all rights reserved* (conventional copyright) and *no rights reserved* (public domain) does not meet everyone's needs, so Creative Commons is developing a range of possibilities between these two extremes.

3. Like many other organizations these days, Creative Commons must occasionally deal with online rumours spread by bloggers who aren't always sure of their facts. You've been asked to reply to an email query from a *National Post* reporter who read a blog rumour that Creative Commons's real objective is to destroy ownership of all copyrights. Which of the following has the right style and tone for your response?

   a. That blog posting is an absolute crock. The person who wrote it is either a liar or a fool.
   b. As our website and other materials strive to make clear, the objective of Creative Commons is to work within the framework of existing copyright law but to establish a range of possibilities for people whose needs aren't met by conventional copyright choices.
   c. You wouldn't believe how much time and energy we have to spend defending ourselves against idiotic rumours like this.
   d. Creative Commons has never expressed, in print or in online materials, nor in any speeches or presentations given by any of our current or former staff or board members, any plans or strategies that would allow anyone to reach a valid conclusion that our intent is to weaken existing copyright protections.

TEST YOUR KNOWLEDGE

1. How is your audience likely to respond to a message that doesn't seem to be about their concerns or is written in language they don't understand?

2. What is the "you" attitude, and why is it important?

3. What contributes to a communicator's credibility?

4. What is plain language, and why is it important?

5. What are the characteristics of bias-free language?

6. How can you avoid a pompous and preachy tone in your messages?

7. What is the difference between denotative language and connotative language?

8. What is the difference between abstract words and concrete words?

9. How can different sentence types emphasize key thoughts?

10. How can word-processing tools help you create your messages more efficiently?

APPLY YOUR KNOWLEDGE

1. How can you apply the "you" approach when you don't know your audience personally?

2. When composing business messages, how can you be yourself and project your company's image at the same time?

3. What steps can you take to make abstract concepts such as *opportunity* feel more concrete in your messages?

4. Considering how fast and easy it is, should instant messaging completely replace meetings and other face-to-face communication in your company? Why or why not?

5. **Ethical Choices** In Canada it is estimated that 6 percent of children and 4 percent of adults have food allergies. Every year at least 30 000 of these people end up in the emergency room after suffering an allergic reaction, and every year approximately 200 of them die. Many of these tragic events are tied to poorly written food labels that either fail to identify dangerous allergens or use scientific terms that most consumers don't recognize.[18] Do food manufacturers have a responsibility to ensure that consumers read, understand, and follow warnings on food products? Explain your answer.

RUNNING CASES

> CASE 1 Noreen

Now that the letter has gone to the service station owners/operators informing them of the upcoming promotion (see the case in Chapter 4), Noreen's manager at Petro-Go has asked her to send an informative promotional letter to all existing Canadian "Go Points" customers.

The promotion details are as follows:

1. Canadian cardholders will now receive double points when they purchase more than $30 of gasoline in one visit (regular points up to $30 then double points over $30).

2. There is a new reward redemption available—Petro-Go gift certificates ($20 certificate for a 250-point redemption).

3. A gift of a 6-litre container of windshield washer fluid is available when accumulated points reach each 1000-point interval.

Of course, the letter must be approved by the manager before it will be distributed.

QUESTIONS

a. Is the direct or indirect approach best for this message? Why?

b. How will Noreen use the "you" attitude in the letter?

c. Why is it so important that Noreen's letter use bias-free language?

d. How will this letter differ in tone from the one sent to the employees?

e. What considerations will Noreen think of when developing the paragraphs of the letter?

YOUR TASK

Create the letter. Apply the skills you have learned in Chapters 4 and 5. (Remember to create a company logo.)

Now, consider how Noreen would put this information into a webpage. Write a list of factors she would have to consider when adding this information to the existing company website.

> CASE 2 Kwong

Kwong is working on producing a promotional letter for Accountants For All accounting firm that will entice past customers to return this upcoming tax season. He has checked the database and discovered addresses and email accounts for past customers. He informs his manager of his plan to email all past customers with the promotional news as well as deliver the letter through postal mail. The main promotional points Kwong wishes to convey are these:

1. 20% discount for repeat customers

2. 10% discount for families of four or more, students, or seniors

3. Only one promotional discount may be applied

QUESTIONS

a. How should Kwong begin the letter?

b. How will Kwong emphasize the promotional discounts?

c. How will he make the message easier to read?

d. How should the subject line read in the email message?

e. Why send email and postal mail?

YOUR TASK

Create the letter. Apply the skills you have learned in Chapters 4 and 5. (Remember to create a company logo.) Once the letter is complete, create the email message. Apply the skills you have learned in Chapters 4 and 5.

PRACTISE YOUR KNOWLEDGE

Read the following document, then (1) analyze the strengths and weaknesses of each sentence and (2) revise the document so that it follows this chapter's guidelines.

I am a new publisher with some really great books to sell. I saw your announcement in *Publishers Weekly* about the bookseller's show you're having this summer, and I think it's a great idea. Count me in, folks! I would like to get some space to show my books. I thought it would be a neat thing if I could do some airbrushing on T-shirts live to help promote my hot new title, *T-Shirt Art*. Before I got into publishing, I was an airbrush artist, and I could demonstrate my techniques. I've done hundreds of advertising illustrations and have been

a sign painter all my life, so I'll also be promoting my other book, hot off the presses, *How to Make Money in the Sign Painting Business*.

I will be starting my PR campaign about May with ads in *PW* and some art trade papers, so my books should be well known by the time the show comes around in August. In case you would like to use my appearance there as part of your publicity, I have enclosed a biography and photo of myself.

P.S. Please let me know what it costs for booth space as soon as possible so that I can figure out whether I can afford to attend. Being a new publisher is pretty expensive!

EXERCISES

5.1 Audience Relationship: Courteous Communication

Substitute a better phrase for each of the following:

a. You claim that

b. It is not our policy to

c. You neglected to

d. In which you assert

e. We are sorry you are dissatisfied

f. You failed to enclose

g. We request that you send us

h. Apparently you overlooked our terms

i. We have been very patient

j. We are at a loss to understand

5.2 Audience Relationship: The "You" Attitude

Rewrite these sentences to reflect your audience's viewpoint:

a. Your email order cannot be processed; we request that you use the order form on our website instead.

b. We insist that you always bring your credit card to the store.

c. We want to get rid of all our 15-inch LCD screens to make room in our warehouse for the new 19-, 23-, and 35-inch monitors. Thus, we are offering a 25 percent discount on all sales of 15-inch models this week.

d. I am applying for the position of bookkeeper in your office. I feel my grades prove that I am bright and capable, and I think I can do a good job for you.

e. As requested, we are sending the refund for $25.

f. If you cared about doing a good job, you would've made the extra effort required to learn how to use the machinery properly.

g. Your strategy presentation this morning absolutely blew me away; there's no way we can fail with all the brilliant ideas you've pulled together—I'm so glad you're running the company now!

h. Regarding your email message from September 28 regarding the slow payment of your invoice, it's important for you to realize that we've just undergone a massive upgrade of our accounts payable system and payments have been delayed for everybody, not just you.

i. I know I'm late with the asset valuation report, but I haven't been feeling well and I just haven't had the energy needed to work through the numbers yet.

5.3 Audience Relationship: Emphasize the Positive

Revise these sentences to be positive rather than negative:

a. To avoid damage to your credit rating, please remit payment within 10 days.

b. We don't make refunds on returned merchandise that is soiled.

c. Because we are temporarily out of Baby Cry dolls, we won't be able to ship your order for 10 days.

d. You failed to specify the colour of the blouse that you ordered.

e. You should have realized that waterbeds will freeze in unheated houses during winter. Therefore, our guarantee does not cover the valve damage. You must pay the $22.50 valve-replacement fee (plus postage).

5.4 Audience Relationship: Emphasize the Positive

Provide euphemisms for the following words and phrases:
a. stubborn
b. wrong
c. stupid
d. incompetent
e. loudmouth

5.5 Audience Relationship: Bias-Free Language

Rewrite each of the following to eliminate bias:
a. A skilled artisan, the Indian Alice Beaver is especially known for her beadwork.
b. He needs a wheelchair, but he doesn't let his handicap affect his job performance.
c. A pilot must have the ability to stay calm under pressure and then he must be trained to cope with any problem that arises.
d. Candidate Renata Parsons, married and the mother of a teenager, will attend the debate.
e. Senior citizen Sam Nugent is still an active salesperson.

5.6 Ethical Choices

Your company has been a major employer in the local community for years, but shifts in the global marketplace have forced some changes in the company's long-term direction. In fact, the company plans to reduce local staffing by as much as 50 percent over the next 5 to 10 years, starting with a small layoff next month. The size and timing of future layoffs has not been decided, although there is little doubt more layoffs will happen at some point. In the first draft of a letter aimed at community leaders, you write that "this first layoff is part of a continuing series of staff reductions anticipated over the next several years." However, your boss is concerned about the vagueness and negative tone of the language and asks you to rewrite that sentence to read, "This layoff is part of the company's ongoing efforts to continually align its resources with global market conditions." Do you think this suggested wording is ethical, given the company's economic influence in the community? Please explain your answer.

5.7 Message Composition: Controlling Style

Rewrite the following letter to Mrs. Betty Crandall (RR #1 New Norway, AB T0B 3L0) so that it conveys a helpful, personal, and interested tone:

We have your letter of recent date to our Ms. Dobson. Owing to the fact that you neglected to include the size of the dress you ordered, please be advised that no shipment of your order was made, but the aforementioned shipment will occur at such time as we are in receipt of the aforementioned information.

5.8 Message Composition: Selecting Powerful Words

Write a concrete phrase for each of these vague phrases (make up any information you need):
a. sometime this spring
b. a substantial saving
c. a large number attended
d. increased efficiency
e. expanded the work area
f. flatten the website structure
g. an incredible computer

5.9 Message Composition: Selecting Powerful Words

List terms that are stronger than the following:
a. ran after
b. seasonal ups and downs
c. bright
d. suddenly rises
e. moves forward

5.10 Message Composition: Selecting Powerful Words

As you rewrite these sentences, replace the clichés with fresh, personal expressions:
a. Being a jack-of-all-trades, Dave worked well in his new general manager job.
b. Moving Truc into the accounting department, where she was literally a fish out of water, was like putting a square peg into a round hole, if you get my drift.
c. I knew she was at death's door, but I thought the doctor would pull her through.
d. Movies aren't really my cup of tea; as far as I am concerned, they can't hold a candle to a good book.
e. It's a dog-eat-dog world out there in the rat race of the asphalt jungle.

5.11 Message Composition: Selecting Powerful Words

Suggest short, simple words to replace each of the following:
a. inaugurate
b. terminate
c. utilize
d. anticipate
e. assistance
f. endeavour
g. ascertain
h. procure
i. consummate
j. advise
k. alteration
l. forwarded
m. fabricate
n. nevertheless
o. substantial

5.12 Message Composition: Selecting Powerful Words

Write up-to-date, less-stuffy versions of these phrases; write none if you think there is no appropriate substitute:

a. As per your instructions
b. Attached herewith
c. In lieu of
d. In reply I wish to state
e. Please be advised that

5.13 Message Composition: Creating Effective Sentences

Suppose that end-of-term frustrations have produced this email message to Professor Anne Brewer from a student who believes he should have received a B in his accounting class. If this message were recast into three or four clear sentences, the teacher might be more receptive to the student's argument. Rewrite the message to show how you would improve it:

I think that I was unfairly awarded a C in your accounting class this term, and I am asking you to change the grade to a B. It was a difficult term. I don't get any money from home, and I have to work mornings at the Pancake House (as a cook), so I had to rush to make your class, and those two times that I missed class were because they wouldn't let me off work because of special events at the Pancake House (unlike some other students who just take off when they choose). On the midterm examination, I originally got a 75 percent, but you said in class that there were two different ways to answer the third question and that you would change the grades of students who used the "optimal cost" method and had been counted off 6 points for doing this. I don't think that you took this into account, because I got 80 percent on the final, which is clearly a B. Anyway, whatever you decide, I just want to tell you that I really enjoyed this class, and I thank you for making accounting so interesting.

5.14 Message Composition: Creating Effective Sentences

Rewrite each sentence so that it is active rather than passive:

a. The raw data are entered into the customer relationship management system by the sales representative each Friday.
b. High profits are publicized by management.
c. The policies announced in the directive were implemented by the staff.
d. Our computers are serviced by the Santee Company.
e. The employees were represented by Janet Hogan.

5.15 Message Composition: Writing Effective Paragraphs

In the following paragraph, identify the topic sentence and the related sentences (those that support the idea of the topic sentence):

Sync in a snap with Auto-Sync. By default, iTunes automatically copies your entire music library to your iPod and deletes songs on your iPod that are not listed in iTunes. Or you can use Playlist Sync and select the playlists you want to sync with your iPod. If you have more songs in your iTunes library than you can fit on your iPod, let iTunes create a playlist to fill your iPod, or just update your iPod by dragging over individual songs.[19]

Now add a topic sentence to this paragraph:

Our analysis of the customer experience should start before golfers even drive through the front gate here at Glencoe Meadows; it should start when they phone in or log on to our website to reserve tee times. When they do arrive, the first few stages in the process are also vital: the condition of the grounds leading up to the club house, the reception they receive when they drop off their clubs, and the ease of parking. From that point, how well are we doing with check-in at the pro shop, openings at the driving range, and timely scheduling at the first tee? Then there's everything associated with playing the course itself and returning to the clubhouse at the end of the round.

5.16 Teamwork: Paragraph Techniques

Working with four other students, divide the following five topics among yourselves and each write one paragraph on his or her selected topic. Be sure each student uses a different technique when writing his or her paragraph: one student should use the illustration technique, one the comparison or contrast technique, one a discussion of cause and effect, one the classification technique, and one a discussion of problem and solution. Then exchange paragraphs within the team and pick out the main idea and general purpose of the paragraph one of your teammates wrote. Was everyone able to correctly identify the main idea and purpose? If not, suggest how the paragraph might be rewritten for clarity.

a. Types of digital cameras (or dogs or automobiles) available for sale
b. Advantages and disadvantages of eating at fast-food restaurants
c. Finding that first full-time job
d. Good qualities of my car (or house, or apartment, or neighbourhood)
e. How to make a dessert recipe (or barbecue a steak or make coffee)

5.17 Internet: Plain Language

Visit the Investor Education Fund website (www.getsmarteraboutmoney.ca) and review the information under the Planning tab. Does the information follow the plain-language guidelines described in this chapter? Can you suggest any improvements to organization, words, sentences, or paragraphs?

5.18 Message Organization: Transitional Elements

Add transitional elements to the following sentences to improve the flow of ideas. (Note: You may need to eliminate or add some words to smooth out your sentences.)

a. Steve Case saw infinite possibilities in online business. Steve Case was determined to turn his vision into reality. The techies scoffed at his strategy of building a simple Internet service for ordinary people. Case doggedly pursued his dream. He analyzed other online services. He assessed the needs of his customers. He responded to their desires for an easier way to access information over the Internet. In 1992, Steve Case named his company America Online (AOL). Critics predicted the company's demise. By the end of the century, AOL was a profitable powerhouse. An ill-fated merger with Time Warner was a financial disaster and led to Case's ousting from the company.

b. Facing some of the toughest competitors in the world, Harley-Davidson had to make some changes. The company introduced new products. Harley's management team set out to rebuild the company's production process. New products were coming to market, and the company was turning a profit. Harley's quality standards were not on par with those of its foreign competitors. Harley's costs were still among the highest in the industry. Harley made a U-turn and restructured the company's organizational structure. Harley's efforts have paid off.

c. Whether you're indulging in a doughnut in Charlottetown or Vancouver, Tim Hortons wants you to enjoy the same delicious taste with every bite. The company maintains consistent product quality by carefully controlling every step of the production process. Tim Hortons tests all raw ingredients against established quality standards. Every delivery of wheat flour is sampled and measured for its moisture content and protein levels. Tim Hortons blends the ingredients. Tim Hortons tests the doughnut mix for quality. Tim Hortons delivers the mix to its stores. Financial critics have recognized Tim Hortons's success. Product innovations have shown that the company has a bright future.

5.19 Ethical Choices: Connotative Language

Under what circumstances would you consider the use of terms that are high in connotative meaning to be ethical? When would you consider it to be unethical? Explain your reasoning.

5.20 Plain Language

Go through this chapter and find examples of slang, clichés, jargon, and business speak. Try to replace these words with plain language.

Completing Business Messages

LEARNING OBJECTIVES   After studying this chapter, you will be able to

1. Discuss the value of careful revision, and list the main tasks involved in completing a business message

2. Explain four writing techniques you can use to improve the readability of your messages

3. Describe the steps you can take to improve the clarity of your writing

4. Discuss why it's important to make your message more concise, and give four tips on how to do so

5. Explain how design elements help determine the effectiveness of your documents

6. Highlight the types of errors to look for when proofreading

7. Discuss the most important issues to consider when distributing your messages

MyLab Business Communication   Visit MyLab Business Communication to access a variety of online resources directly related to this chapter's content..

ON THE JOB: COMMUNICATING AT FREE THE CHILDREN

Photo Courtesy of Free The Children

Founder of WE, Craig Kielburger has received numerous awards for his work, including the Nelson Mandela Human Rights Award. His organization shows young people that they are able to help children around the world by getting involved in Free The Children's educational programs.

Engaging Young Audiences for Social Change

www.WE.org

How does an organization communicate its mission, particularly if it is a charity? How can an organization inspire young people to join that mission and help change the world?

Since its founding in 1995 by 12-year-old Craig Kielburger, Toronto-based Free The Children (now known as WE) has motivated youth to raise funds or work on projects fulfilling the organization's vision of improving the lives of impoverished children around the world. Its achievements include building more than 650 schools and school rooms, distributing over 207 000 school and health kits, and helping more than 500 000 people get access to health care. Overall, more than 1 million children and young adults have become involved in programs in over 45 countries.

Kielburger was himself inspired to start the organization when reading about a young Pakistani boy who escaped from working 12 hours a day, 6 days a week in a carpet factory and began speaking out about the rights of children. To focus international attention on child labour abuses, Kielburger soon went on a fact-finding mission to Southeast Asia, drawing media attention and raising the issue of child labour to worldwide prominence. From that time, WE has grown to become a major force in improving lives through "children helping children through education."

The challenge faced by WE is to continue engaging young people, as well as expand its extensive network of corporate and nonprofit partners. A key part of this effort is the WE interactive website, where visitors can learn about WE by reading blogs and viewing videos showcasing international projects. Directed toward a young web-savvy audience, the website is an educational portal that not only explains WE's mission but also inspires visitors to join in improving the global community.

Maintaining WE's online appeal requires attention to detail. Layout, photos, video, and interactive features all contribute to its continuing strength. If you volunteered to help WE maintain its website, what details would you pinpoint for revision? What process would you follow to keep it fresh and inviting to its young audience?[1]

Revising Your Message: Evaluating the First Draft

Professional communicators recognize that the first draft is rarely as tight, clear, and compelling as it needs to be. Careful revision can mean the difference between a rambling, unfocused message and a lively, direct message that gets results. Figure 6–1 lists the tasks in the third step of the three-step writing process: revising your message to achieve optimum quality, then producing, proofreading, and distributing it.

The revision process varies somewhat, depending on the medium and the nature of your message. For informal messages to internal audiences, particularly when using instant messaging (IM), text messaging, email, or blogging, the revision process is often as simple as quickly looking over your message to correct any mistakes before sending or posting it. However, don't fall into the common trap of thinking that these electronic media are so new and different and informal that you don't need to worry about grammar, spelling, clarity, and other fundamentals of good writing. These qualities can be even *more* important in electronic media, not less, particularly if these messages are the only contact your audience has with you. Audiences are likely to equate the quality of your writing with the quality of your thinking, decision making, and other business skills. Moreover, even minor errors can cause confusion, frustration, and costly delays.

The time required for revision can vary from just a moment or two for a simple message to many hours or even days for a complex report or multimedia document.

In any medium, readers tend to equate the quality of your writing with the quality of your thinking.

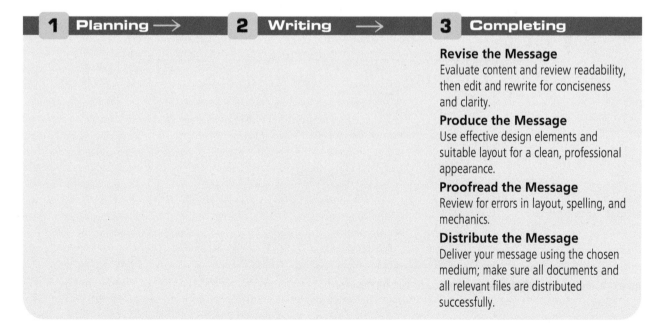

1 Planning →	**2** Writing →	**3** Completing
		Revise the Message Evaluate content and review readability, then edit and rewrite for conciseness and clarity. **Produce the Message** Use effective design elements and suitable layout for a clean, professional appearance. **Proofread the Message** Review for errors in layout, spelling, and mechanics. **Distribute the Message** Deliver your message using the chosen medium; make sure all documents and all relevant files are distributed successfully.

Figure 6–1 Step 3 in the Three-Step Writing Process: Complete Your Message

The two circled sentences say essentially the same thing, so this edit combines them into one sentence.

Changing *adjusting* to *adjustment* makes it parallel with *evaluation*.

Replacing *its* with *your piano's* avoids any confusion about which noun that *it* is supposed to replace.

The simple complimentary close replaces a close that was stylistically over the top.

Delauny Music
56 Spring Gardens Road • Halifax, NS B2J 3R1
(902) 555-5555 • delaunymusic.net

June 21, 2018

Need 7 blank lines here

Ms. Claudia Banks
112 Barrington Street
Halifax, NS B9J 1Q8

Dear Ms. Banks:

On behalf of everyone at Delauny Music, it is my pleasure to thank you for your recent purchase of a Yamaha CG1 grand piano. The Cg1 carries more than a century of Yamaha's heritage in design and production of world-class musical instruments and ~~you can bet it~~ will give you many years of playing and listening pleasure. Our commitment to your satisfaction doesn't stop with your purchase, however. ~~Much to the contrary, it continues for as long as you own your piano, which we hope, of course, is for as long as you live.~~ As a vital first step, please remember to call us ~~your local Yamaha dealer,~~ sometime within three to eight months after your piano was delivered to take advantage of the ~~free~~ Yamaha Servicebond[SM] Assurance Program. This free service program includes a thorough evaluation and ~~adjusting~~ *adjustment* of the instrument after you've had some time to play your piano and your piano has had time to adapt to its environment.

In addition to this ~~vital~~ *important* service appointment, a regular program of tuning is ~~absolutely~~ essential to ensure ~~its~~ *your piano's* impeccable performance. Our piano specialists recommend four tunings during the first year and two tunings every year thereafter ~~that.~~ As your local Yamaha *dealer* we are ideally positioned to provide you with optimum service for both regular tuning and any maintenance or repair needs you may have ~~over the years.~~

~~All of us at Delauny Music~~ thank you for your recent purchase ~~and~~ wish you ~~many~~ many years of satisfaction with your new Yamaha CG1 grand piano. *We*

Sincerely,
~~Respectfully yours in beautiful music~~

Madeline Delauny
Owner

tjr

The phrase *you can bet* is too informal for this message.

The sentence beginning with "Much to the contrary . . ." is awkward and unnecessary.

This edit inserts a missing word (*dealer*).

This group of edits removes unnecessary words in several places.

	Common Proofreading Symbols
~~strikethrough~~	Delete text
ℓ	Delete individual character or a circled block of text
∧	Insert text (text to insert is written above)
⊙	Insert period
⋏	Insert comma
⌐	Start new line
⌗	Start new paragraph
≡	Capitalize

Figure 6–2 Improving a Customer Letter through Careful Revision

Delauny Music
56 Spring Gardens Road • Halifax, NS B2J 3R1
(902) 555-5555 • delaunymusic.net

June 21, 2018

Ms. Claudia Banks
112 Barrington Street
Halifax, NS B9J 1Q8

Dear Ms. Banks:

Thank you for your recent purchase. We wish you many years of satisfaction with your new Yamaha CG1 grand piano. The CG1 carries more than a century of Yamaha's heritage in design and production of world-class musical instruments and will give you many years of playing and listening pleasure.

Our commitment to your satisfaction doesn't stop with your purchase, however. As a vital first step, please remember to call us sometime within three to eight months after your piano was delivered to take advantage of the Yamaha Servicebond^{SM} Assurance Program. This free service program includes a thorough evaluation and adjustment of the instrument after you've had some time to play your piano and your piano has had time to adapt to its environment.

In addition to this important service appointment, a regular program of tuning is essential to ensure your piano's impeccable performance. Our piano specialists recommend four tunings during the first year and two tunings every year thereafter. As your local Yamaha dealer, we are ideally positioned to provide you with optimum service for both regular tuning and any maintenance or repair needs you may have.

Sincerely,

Madeline Delauny

Madeline Delauny
Owner

tjr

Figure 6–3 Revised Customer Letter

Fortunately, revising simple messages doesn't take much time or effort. With IM, for example, you need only a second or two to skim each message to make sure you haven't said something clumsy or incorrect. With more complex messages, try to put your draft aside for a day or two before you begin the revision process so that you can approach the material with a fresh eye. Then start with the "big picture," making sure that the document accomplishes your overall goals before moving to finer points, such as readability, clarity, and conciseness. If you are unsure about the clarity of your message, it is helpful to have a colleague read your draft. Ask for concrete comments, such as where wording or tone can be improved. Compare the messages in Figures 6–2 and 6–3 for an example of how careful revision can improve a letter: the revised version provides the requested information more clearly, in an organized way, with a friendlier style, and with precise mechanics. The *proofreading symbols* are still widely used when printed documents are edited and revised. However, in many instances, you'll use the electronic markup features in your word processor or other software, as shown in Figure 6–5 on page 159.

For longer documents, try to put aside your draft for a day or two before you begin the revision process.

EVALUATING YOUR CONTENT, ORGANIZATION, STYLE, AND TONE

1 LEARNING OBJECTIVE

Discuss the value of careful revision, and list the main tasks involved in completing a business message.

When you begin the revision process, focus your attention on content, organization, style, and tone. To evaluate the content of your message, ask yourself these questions:

- Is the information accurate?
- Is the information relevant to your audience?
- Is there enough information to satisfy your reader's needs?
- Is there a good balance between general information (giving readers enough background information to appreciate the message) and specific information (giving readers the details they need to understand the message)?

When you are satisfied with the content of your message, review its organization. Ask yourself another set of questions:

- Are all your points covered in the most logical order?
- Do the most important ideas receive the most space, and are they placed in the most prominent positions?
- Would the message be more convincing if it were arranged in another sequence?
- Are any points repeated unnecessarily?
- Are details grouped together logically, or are some still scattered through the document?
- If you need further information, have you provided an end date and contact information?

Next consider whether you have achieved the right style and tone for your audience. Is your writing formal enough to meet the audience's expectations without being too formal or academic? Is it too casual for a serious subject? Does your message emphasize the audience's needs over your own?

The beginning and end of a message have the greatest impact on your readers.

Spend a few extra moments on the beginning and end of your message; these sections have the greatest impact on the audience. Be sure the opening of your document is relevant and geared to the reader's probable reaction. In longer documents, check that the first few paragraphs establish the subject, purpose, and organization of the material. Review the conclusion to ensure that it summarizes the main idea and leaves the audience with a positive impression.

EVALUATING, EDITING, AND REVISING THE WORK OF OTHERS

At many points in your career, you will be asked to evaluate, edit, or revise the work of others. Whether you're suggesting improvements or actually making the improvements yourself (as you might on a wiki site, for example), you can make a contribution by using all the skills you have learned in Chapters 4 and 5 and in this chapter.

Before you evaluate and revise someone else's writing, make sure you understand the writer's intent with the message.

Before you dive into someone else's work, recognize the dual responsibility that doing so entails. First, unless you've been specifically asked to rewrite something in your own style or to change the emphasis of the message, remember that your job is to help the other writer succeed at his or her task, not to impose your writing style or pursue your own agenda. In other words, make sure your input focuses on making the piece more effective, not on making it more like something you would have written. Second, make sure you understand the writer's intent before you begin suggesting or making changes. If you try to edit or revise without knowing what the writer hoped to accomplish, you run the risk of making the piece less effective, not more. With those thoughts in mind, answer the following questions as you evaluate someone else's writing:

- What is the purpose of this document or message?
- Who is the target audience?

- What information does the audience need?
- Does the document provide this information in a well-organized way?
- Does the writing demonstrate the "you" attitude toward the audience?
- Is the tone of the writing appropriate for the audience?
- Can the readability be improved?
- Is the writing clear? If not, how can it be improved?
- Is the writing as concise as it could be?
- Does the design support the intended message?

You can read more about using these skills in the context of wiki writing in Chapter 12.

Revising to Improve Readability

After checking the content, organization, style, and tone of your message, make a second pass to improve *readability*. Most professionals are inundated with more reading material than they can ever hope to consume, and they'll appreciate your efforts to make your documents easier to read. You'll benefit from this effort, too: if you earn a reputation for well-crafted documents that respect the audience's time, people will pay more attention to your work.

You may be familiar with one of the many indexes that have been developed over the years in an attempt to measure readability. For example, the Flesch-Kincaid Grade Level score computes reading difficulty relative to grade-level achievement. Thus, a score of 10 suggests that a document can be read and understood by the average grade 10 student. Most business documents score in the 8–11 range. Technical documents often score in the 12–14 range. A similar scoring system, the Flesch Reading Ease score, ranks documents on a 100-point scale: the higher the score, the easier the document is to read.

Readability indexes offer a useful reference point, but they are all limited by what they are able to measure: word length, number of syllables, sentence length, and paragraph length. They can't measure any other factors that affect readability, such as audience analysis, writing clarity, and document design. Compare these two paragraphs:

> Readability indexes offer a useful reference point, but they are all limited by what they are able to measure: word length, number of syllables, sentence length, and paragraph length. They can't measure any of the other factors that affect readability, from "you" orientation to writing clarity to document design.
>
> Readability indexes can help. But they don't measure everything. They don't measure whether your writing clarity is good. They don't measure whether your document design is good or not. Reading indexes are based on word length, syllables, sentences, and paragraphs.

The first paragraph scores 12.0 on grade level and 27.4 on reading ease, meaning it is supposedly rather difficult to read. The second paragraph scores much better on both grade level (8.9) and reading ease (45.8). However, the second example is choppy, unsophisticated, and poorly organized, and much less satisfying to read. As a general rule, then, don't assume that a piece of text is readable if it scores well on a readability index—or that it is difficult to read if it doesn't score well.

Beyond shortening words and sentences for readability measurements, you can improve the readability of a message by making the document easy to skim. Most business audiences—particularly influential senior managers—skim longer documents looking for key ideas, conclusions, and recommendations. If they determine that the document contains valuable information or requires a

2 LEARNING OBJECTIVE

Explain four writing techniques you can use to improve the readability of your messages.

Readability formulas can give you a helpful indication, but they can't measure everything that affects readability.

The effort to make your documents more readable will pay for itself in greater career success.

response, they will read it more carefully when time permits. You can adopt a number of techniques to make your message easier to skim: varying sentence length, using shorter paragraphs, using lists and bullets instead of narrative, and adding effective headings and subheadings.

VARYING YOUR SENTENCE LENGTH

To keep readers' interest, use both long and short sentences.

Variety is a creative way to make your messages interesting and readable. By choosing words and sentence structures with care, you can create a rhythm that emphasizes important points, enlivens your writing style, and makes your information appealing to your reader. For example, a short sentence that highlights a conclusion at the end of a substantial paragraph of evidence makes your key message stand out. Effective documents, therefore, usually use a mixture of sentences that are short (up to 15 words), medium (15–25 words), and long (more than 25 words). Make sure you write in full sentences, though. Sentence fragments are very jarring for readers.

Each sentence length has its advantages. Short sentences can be processed quickly and are easier for non-native speakers and translators to interpret. Medium-length sentences are useful for showing the relationships among ideas. Long sentences are often the best way to convey complex ideas, list multiple related points, or summarize or preview information.

Of course, each sentence length also has disadvantages. Too many short sentences in a row can make your writing choppy. Medium-length sentences lack the punch of short sentences and the informative power of longer sentences. Long sentences are usually harder to understand than short sentences because they are packed with information that must all be absorbed at once. Because readers can absorb only a few words per glance, longer sentences are also more difficult to skim. Thus, the longer your sentence, the greater the possibility that the reader who skims it will not read enough words to process its full meaning. By choosing the best sentence length for each communication need and remembering to mix sentence lengths for variety, you'll get your message across while keeping your documents lively and interesting.

KEEPING YOUR PARAGRAPHS SHORT

Short paragraphs are easier to read than long ones.

Large blocks of text can be visually daunting, so the optimum paragraph length is short to medium in most cases. Unless you break up your thoughts somehow, you'll end up with a three-page paragraph that's guaranteed to intimidate even the most dedicated reader. Short paragraphs (of 100 words or fewer; this paragraph has 90 words) are easier to read than long ones, and they make your writing look inviting. They also help audiences read more carefully. You can also emphasize an idea by isolating it in a short, forceful paragraph.

However, don't overuse short paragraphs. Be careful to use one-sentence paragraphs only occasionally and only for emphasis. Also, if you need to divide a subject into several pieces to keep paragraphs short, help your readers keep the ideas connected by guiding them with plenty of transitional elements.

USING LISTS AND BULLETS TO CLARIFY AND EMPHASIZE

Lists are effective tools for highlighting and simplifying material.

An effective alternative to using conventional sentences is to set off important ideas in a list—a series of words, names, or other items. Lists can show the sequence of your ideas, heighten their impact visually, and increase the likelihood that a reader will find the key points. In addition, lists provide readers with clues, simplify complex subjects, highlight the main point, break up the page visually, ease the skimming process for busy readers, and give the reader a breather. Consider the difference between the following two approaches to the same information:

Narrative

Owning your own business has many advantages. One is the easy opportunity to pursue your own personal passion. Another advantage is the satisfaction of working for yourself. As a sole proprietor, you also have the advantage of privacy because you do not have to reveal your information or plans to anyone.

List

Owning your own business has three advantages:

- opportunity to pursue personal passion
- satisfaction of working for yourself
- privacy of information

When creating a list, you can separate items with numbers, letters, or bullets (a general term for any kind of graphical element that precedes each item). Bullets are generally preferred over numbers, unless the list is in some logical sequence or ranking, or specific list items will be referred to later on. When creating bullets or lists, do not use a colon before them unless a full sentence leads to the list of items. The following three steps need to be performed in the order indicated, and the numbers make that clear:

1. Find out how many employees would like on-site daycare facilities.
2. Determine how much space the daycare centre would require.
3. Estimate the cost of converting a conference room for the on-site facility.

Lists are easier to locate and read if the entire numbered or bulleted section is set off by a blank line before and after, as the preceding examples demonstrate. Furthermore, when using lists, make sure to introduce them clearly so that people know what they're about to read. One way to introduce lists is to make them a part of the introductory sentence:

The board of directors met to discuss the revised annual budget. To keep expenses in line with declining sales, the directors voted to

- Cut everyone's salary by 10 percent
- Close the employee cafeteria
- Reduce travel expenses

Another way to introduce a list is to precede it with a complete introductory sentence, followed by a colon:

The decline in company profit is attributable to four factors:

- Slower holiday sales
- Higher employee wages
- Increased transportation and fuel costs
- Slower inventory turnover

Regardless of the format you choose, the items in a list should be parallel; that is, they should all use the same grammatical pattern. For example, if one list item begins with a verb, all list items should begin with a verb. If one item is a noun phrase, all should be noun phrases.

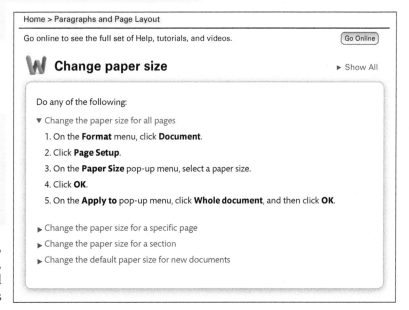

Home > Paragraphs and Page Layout

Go online to see the full set of Help, tutorials, and videos.   Go Online

W Change paper size   ▶ Show All

Do any of the following:

▼ Change the paper size for all pages
1. On the **Format** menu, click **Document**.
2. Click **Page Setup**.
3. On the **Paper Size** pop-up menu, select a paper size.
4. Click **OK**.
5. On the **Apply to** pop-up menu, click **Whole document**, and then click **OK**.

▶ Change the paper size for a specific page
▶ Change the paper size for a section
▶ Change the default paper size for new documents

This Microsoft Word help screen uses a numbered list to explain a formatting process. Why are numbers used instead of bullets? Would the instructions be as clear in narrative form?

Nonparallel List Items	Parallel List Items
• improve our bottom line	• improve our bottom line
• identification of new foreign markets for our products	• identify new foreign markets for our products
• global market strategies	• develop our global market strategies
• issues regarding pricing and packaging size	• resolve pricing and packaging issues

Parallel forms are easier to read and skim. You can create parallelism by repeating the pattern in words, phrases, clauses, or entire sentences (see Table 6–1).

ADDING HEADINGS AND SUBHEADINGS

Use headings and subheadings to show the organization of your material, draw the reader's attention to key points, and show connections between ideas.

A **heading** is a brief title that tells readers about the content of the section that follows. **Subheadings** are subordinate to headings, indicating subsections within a major section. Headings and subheadings serve these important functions:

- **Organization.** Headings show your reader at a glance how the document is organized. They act as labels to group related paragraphs together and effectively organize your material into short sections.
- **Attention.** Informative, inviting, and in some cases intriguing headings grab the reader's attention, make the text easier to read, and help the reader find the parts he or she needs to read—or skip.
- **Connection.** Using headings and subheadings together helps readers see the relationship between main ideas and subordinate ones so that they can understand your message more easily. Moreover, headings and subheadings visually indicate shifts from one idea to the next.

Informative headings are generally more helpful than descriptive ones.

Use the same grammatical form for each heading.

Headings fall into two categories. **Descriptive headings**, such as "Cost Considerations," identify a topic but do little more. **Informative headings**, such as "A New Way to Cut Costs," put your reader right into the context of your message.

Informative headings guide readers to think in a certain way about the topic. They are also helpful in guiding your work as a writer, especially if written in terms of questions you plan to address in your document. Well-written informative headings are self-contained, which means that readers can read just the headings and subheadings and understand them without reading the rest of the document. For example, "Introduction" conveys little information,

Table 6–1	**Achieving Parallelism**
Method	**Example**
Parallel words	The letter was approved by Nguyen, Gitlen, Merlin, and Carlucci.
Parallel phrases	We are gaining market share in supermarkets, in department stores, and in specialty stores.
Parallel clauses	I'd like to discuss the issue after Vicki gives her presentation but before Marvin shows his slides.
Parallel sentences	In 2014 we exported 30 percent of our production. In 2013 we exported 50 percent.

whereas the heading "Staffing Shortages in Finance and Accounting Cost the Company $150 000 Last Year" provides a key piece of information and captures the reader's attention. Whatever types of headings you choose, keep them brief, and use parallel construction as you would for an outline, list, or series of words.

Editing for Clarity and Conciseness

After you've reviewed and revised your message for readability, your next step is to ensure that your message is as clear and as concise as possible.

EDITING FOR CLARITY

To ensure clarity, look closely at your paragraph organization, sentence structure, and word choices. Do your paragraphs have clear topic sentences? Are the transitions between ideas obvious? Then ask yourself whether your sentences are easy to decipher. Are your statements simple and direct? Perhaps a sentence is so complicated that readers can't unravel it. Next, review your word choices. You might have chosen a word that is so vague that readers can interpret it in several ways. Perhaps pronouns or tenses switch midsentence so that readers lose track of who is talking or when an event took place.[2]

See Table 6–2 for examples of the following tips:

- **Break up overly long sentences.** Don't connect too many clauses with *and* or *or.* If you find yourself stuck in a long sentence, you're probably making the sentence do more than it can reasonably do, such as expressing two dissimilar thoughts or peppering the reader with too many pieces of supporting evidence at once (did you notice how difficult this long sentence was to read?). You can often clarify your writing style by separating a string of items into individual sentences.
- **Rewrite hedging sentences.** Sometimes you have to write *may* or *seems* to avoid stating a judgment as a fact. However, when you have too many such hedges, you risk coming across as unsure of what you're saying.
- **Impose parallelism.** When you have two or more similar ideas to express, make them parallel. Repeating the same grammatical construction shows that the ideas are related, of similar importance, and on the same level of generality. Parallelism is discussed earlier in this chapter in the section on lists and bullets.
- **Correct dangling modifiers.** Sometimes a modifier is not just an adjective or an adverb but an entire phrase modifying a noun or a verb. Be careful not to leave this type of modifier dangling, with no connection to the subject of the sentence. The first unacceptable example under "Dangling Modifiers" in Table 6–2 implies that the red sports car has both an office and the legs to walk there. The second example shows one frequent cause of dangling modifiers: passive construction.
- **Reword long noun sequences.** When multiple nouns are strung together as modifiers, the resulting sentence can be hard to read. You might be trying too hard to create the desired effect. See if a single well-chosen word will do the job. If the nouns are all necessary, consider moving one or more to a modifying phrase, as shown in Table 6–2. Although you may add a few more words, your audience won't have to work as hard to understand the sentence.

3 LEARNING OBJECTIVE

Describe the steps you can take to improve the clarity of your writing.

Clarity is essential to getting your message across accurately and efficiently.

Don't be afraid to present your opinions without qualification.

When you use the same grammatical pattern to express two or more ideas, you show that they are comparable thoughts.

Table 6–2	**Revising for Clarity**	
Issues to Review	Unacceptable	Preferable
Overly Long Sentences		
Taking compound sentences too far	The magazine will be published January 1, and I'd better meet the deadline if I want my article included.	The magazine will be published January 1. I'd better meet the deadline if I want my article included.
Hedging Sentences		
Overqualifying sentences	I believe that Mr. Johnson's employment record seems to show that he may be capable of handling the position.	Mr. Johnson's employment record shows that he is capable of handling the position.
Unparallel Sentences		
Using dissimilar construction for similar ideas	Mr. Simms had been drenched with rain, bombarded with telephone calls, and his boss shouted at him.	Mr. Sims had been drenched with rain, bombarded with telephone calls, and shouted at by his boss.
	Ms. Reynolds dictated the letter, and next she signed it and left the office.	Ms. Reynolds dictated the letter, signed it, and left the office.
	To waste time and missing deadlines are bad habits.	Wasting time and missing deadlines are bad habits.
Dangling Modifiers		
Placing modifiers close to the wrong nouns and verbs	Walking to the office, a red sports car passed her.	A red sports car passed her while she was walking to the office.
	After a three-week slump, we increased sales.	After a three-week slump, sales increased.
Long Noun Sequences		
Stringing too many nouns together	The window sash installation company will give us an estimate on Friday.	The company that installs window sashes will give us an estimate on Friday.
Camouflaged Verbs		
Changing verbs and nouns into adjectives	The manager undertook implementation of the rules.	The manager implemented the rules.
	Verification of the shipments occurs weekly.	Shipments are verified weekly.
Changing verbs into nouns	reach a conclusion about	conclude
	make a discovery of	discover
	give consideration to	consider
Sentence Structure		
Separating subject and predicate	A 10% decline in market share, which resulted from quality problems and an aggressive sales campaign by Armitage, the market leader in the Maritimes, was the major problem in 2013.	The major problem in 2013 was a 10% loss of market share, which resulted from both quality problems and an aggressive sales campaign by Armitage, the market leader in the Maritimes.
Separating adjectives, adverbs, or prepositional phrases from the words they modify	Our antique desk lends an air of strength and substance with thick legs and large drawers.	With its thick legs and large drawers, our antique desk lends an air of strength and substance.
Awkward References	The Law Office and the Accounting Office distribute computer supplies for legal secretaries and beginning accountants, respectively.	The Law Office distributes computer supplies for legal secretaries; the Accounting Office distributes those for beginning accountants.
Too Much Enthusiasm	We are extremely pleased to offer you a position on our staff of exceptionally skilled and highly educated employees. The work offers extraordinary challenges and a very large salary.	We are pleased to offer you a position on our staff of skilled and well-educated employees. The work offers challenges and an attractive salary.

- **Replace camouflaged verbs.** Watch for words that end in *-ion*, *-tion*, *-ing*, *-ment*, *-ant*, *-ent*, *-ence*, *-ance*, and *-ency*. These endings often change verbs into nouns and adjectives, requiring you to add a verb just to get your point across. To prune and enliven your messages, use verbs instead of noun phrases.
- **Clarify sentence structure.** Keep the subject and predicate of a sentence as close together as possible. When the subject and predicate are far apart, readers may need to read the sentence twice to figure out who did what. Similarly, adjectives, adverbs, and prepositional phrases usually make the most sense when they're placed as close as possible to the words they modify.
- **Clarify awkward references.** In an effort to save words, business writers sometimes use expressions such as *the above-mentioned*, *as mentioned above*, *the aforementioned*, *the former*, *the latter*, and *respectively*. These words cause readers to jump from point to point, which hinders effective communication. You'll often be more successful using specific references (such as "as described in the second paragraph on page 22"), even if that means adding a few more words.
- **Moderate your enthusiasm.** An occasional adjective or adverb intensifies and emphasizes your meaning, but too many can degrade your writing and damage your credibility. When using an adjective or adverb to enhance your meaning, be accurate and concrete. The word *incredible* (which means "not to be believed") is often used to describe a quality. The sentence "Your product is incredible" would be better phrased as "Your product's ease-of-use will please consumers."

Subject and predicate should be placed as close together as possible, as should modifiers and the words they modify.

Showing enthusiasm for ideas is fine, but be careful not to go so far that you sound unprofessional.

EDITING FOR CONCISENESS

In addition to clarity, readers appreciate conciseness in business messages. The good news is that most first drafts can be cut by as much as 50 percent.[3] By reorganizing your content, improving the readability of your document, and correcting your sentence structure for clarity, you will have already eliminated most of the excess. Now it is time to examine every word. As you begin editing, simplify, prune, and strive for order. See Table 6–3 for examples of the following tips:

- **Delete unnecessary words and phrases.** To test whether a word or phrase is essential, write the sentence without it. If the meaning doesn't change, leave it out. For example, *very* can be a useful word to achieve emphasis, but more often it's simply clutter. There's no need to call someone "very methodical." The person is either methodical or not. In addition, avoid the clutter of too many or poorly placed relative pronouns (*who*, *that*, *which*). Even articles can be excessive (mostly too many *thes*). However, well-placed relative pronouns and articles prevent confusion, so make sure you don't obscure the meaning of the sentence by removing them.
- **Shorten long words and phrases.** Short words are generally more vivid and easier to read than long ones. Shorter phrases are easier to process and understand quickly. Remember, though, the idea is to use short, simple words, *not* simple concepts.[4]
- **Eliminate redundancies.** In some word combinations, the words tend to say the same thing. For example, "visible to the eye" is redundant because *visible* is enough without further clarification; "to the eye" adds nothing.

Make your documents tighter by removing unnecessary words.

What parallels can you draw between post-game analysis and editing business messages? What do coaches look for when reviewing a game that their team either won or lost? Can you adapt the process that coaches use to editing your own work?

- **Recast "It is/There are" starters.** If you start a sentence with an indefinite pronoun such as *it* or *there*, you can probably rephrase the sentence to make it shorter. For example, "We believe ..." is a stronger opening than "It is believed that ..."

Sometimes you'll find that the most difficult problem in a sentence can be solved by simply removing the problem itself. When you come upon a troublesome element, ask yourself, "Do I need it at all?" Possibly not. In fact, you may find that it was giving you so much grief precisely because it was trying to do an unnecessary job.[5] Once you remove the troublesome element, the afflicted sentence will read correctly and smoothly. Of course, before you delete anything, you'll probably want to keep copies of your current version. Take advantage of the "undo" and "redo" functions in your software to experiment with adding and removing various elements.

Table 6–3	**Revising for Conciseness**	
Issues to Review	**Unacceptable**	**Preferable**
Unnecessary Words and Phrases		
Using wordy phrases	for the sum of	for
	in the event that	if
	prior to the start of	before
	in the near future	soon
	at this point in time	now
	due to the fact that	because
	in view of the fact that	because
	until such time as	when
	with reference to	about
Using too many relative pronouns	Cars that are sold after January will not have a six-month warranty.	Cars sold after January will not have a six-month warranty.
	Employees who are driving to work should park in the underground garage.	Employees driving to work should park in the underground garage.
Using too few relative pronouns	The project manager told the engineers last week the specifications were changed.	The project manager told the engineers last week that the specifications were changed.
		The project manager told the engineers that last week the specifications were changed.
Long Words and Phrases		
Using overly long words	During the preceding year, the company accelerated productive operations.	Last year the company sped up operations.
	The action was predicated on the assumption that the company was operating at a financial deficit.	The action was based on the belief that the company was losing money.
Using wordy phrases rather than infinitives	If you want success as a writer, you must work hard.	To be a successful writer, you must work hard.
	He went to the library for the purpose of studying.	He went to the library to study.
	The employer increased salaries so she could improve morale.	The employer increased salaries to improve morale.

Table 6–3	**Revising for Conciseness** *(continued)*	
Issues to Review	**Unacceptable**	**Preferable**
Redundancies		
Repeating meanings	absolutely complete	complete
	basic fundamentals	fundamentals
	follows after	follows
	free and clear	free
	refer back	refer
	repeat again	repeat
	collect together	collect
	future plans	plans
	return back	return
	important essentials	essentials
	end result	result
	actual truth	truth
	final outcome	outcome
	uniquely unusual	unique
	surrounded on all sides	surrounded
Using double modifiers	modern, up-to-date equipment new or improved	modern equipment new or improved
"It Is/There Are" Starters		
Starting sentences with *it* or *there*	It would be appreciated if you would sign the lease today.	Please sign the lease today.
	There are five employees in this division who were late to work today.	Five employees in this division were late to work today.

For a reminder of the tasks involved in revision, see "Checklist: Revising Business Messages."

USING TECHNOLOGY TO REVISE YOUR MESSAGE

When it's time to revise and polish your message, your word processor can help you add, delete, and move text with functions such as *cut* and *paste* (taking a block of text out of one section of a document and pasting it in somewhere else) and *find* and *replace* (tracking down words or phrases and changing them if necessary). Be careful using the "Replace all" option; it can result in some unintended errors. For example, finding *power* and replacing all occurrences with *strength* will also change the word *powerful* to *strengthful.*

To assist with revision, software tools such as *revision marks* and *commenting* keep track of proposed editing changes electronically and provide a history of a document's revisions. Microsoft Word, the most commonly used word-processing software in business offices, offers handy tools for reviewing draft documents. As shown in Figure 6–4, text to be added is underlined, and text to be deleted is moved to bubbles off to the side. The writer can then choose to accept or reject each suggested change. Adobe Acrobat lets you attach comments to PDF files (see Figure 6–5). (Note that Adobe Acrobat is not the same product as the free Adobe Reader.) Using revision marks and commenting features is also a practical way to keep track of editing changes made by team members. Both Word and Acrobat let you use different colours for each reviewer, as well, so you can keep everyone's comments separate.

Revision marks and commenting features are great ways to track the revision process when multiple reviewers are involved.

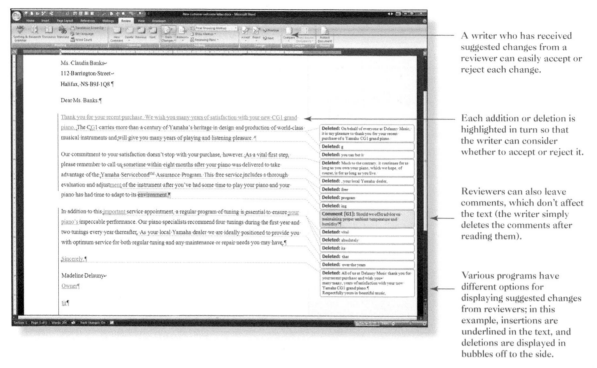

A writer who has received suggested changes from a reviewer can easily accept or reject each change.

Each addition or deletion is highlighted in turn so that the writer can consider whether to accept or reject it.

Reviewers can also leave comments, which don't affect the text (the writer simply deletes the comments after reading them).

Various programs have different options for displaying suggested changes from reviewers; in this example, insertions are underlined in the text, and deletions are displayed in bubbles off to the side.

Figure 6–4 Revision Marks in Microsoft Word

© Microsoft Word

✓ Checklist   Revising Business Messages

A. Evaluate content, organization, style, and tone.
- Ensure that the information is accurate, relevant, and sufficient.
- Check that all necessary points appear in logical order.
- Verify that you present enough support to make the main idea convincing and interesting.
- Ensure the beginning and end are effective.
- Ensure you've achieved the right style and tone.

B. Review for readability.
- Consider using a readability index, being sure to interpret the answer carefully.
- Use a mix of short and long sentences.
- Keep paragraphs short.
- Use bulleted and numbered lists to emphasize key points.
- Make the document easy to skim with headings and subheadings.

C. Edit for clarity.
- Break up overly long sentences and rewrite hedging sentences.
- Use parallelism to simplify reading.
- Correct dangling modifiers.
- Reword long noun sequences and replace camouflaged verbs.
- Clarify sentence structure and awkward references.
- Moderate your enthusiasm to maintain a professional tone.

D. Edit for conciseness.
- Delete unnecessary words and phrases.
- Shorten long words and phrases.
- Eliminate redundancies.
- Rewrite sentences that start with "It is" or "There are."

Spell-checkers, grammar-checkers, and computerized thesauruses can all help with the revision process, but they can't take the place of good writing and editing skills.

In addition to the many revision tools, four software functions can help bring out the best in your documents. First, a *spell-checker* compares your document with an electronic dictionary, highlights unrecognized words, and suggests correct spellings. Spell-checkers are wonderful for finding typos, but they are no substitute for good spelling skills. For example, if you use *their* when you mean

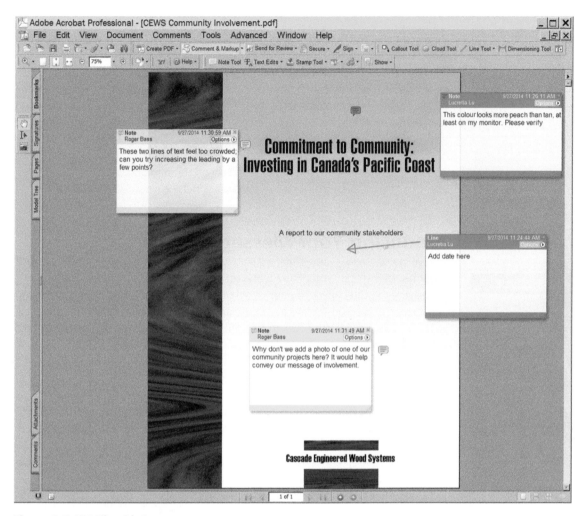

Figure 6–5 PDF File with Comments

Adobe product screenshot(s) reprinted with permission from Adobe Systems Incorporated.

to use *there*, your spell-checker won't notice, because *their* is spelled correctly. If you're in a hurry and accidentally omit the *p* at the end of *top,* the spell-checker will read *to* as correct. Plus, some "errors" that the spell-checker indicates may actually be proper names, technical words, words that you misspelled on purpose, web addresses, or simply words that weren't included in the spell-checker's dictionary. It's up to you to decide whether each flagged word should be corrected or left alone, to find the errors that the spell-checker has overlooked, and to catch problems that the spell-checker itself might introduce (such as inserting unwanted hyphens or suggesting incorrect word replacements).

You can set the default language to Canadian English in the most recent version of Microsoft Word through the Tools menu. Macintosh users can do the same through the International menu in System Preferences.

Second, a computer *thesaurus* (either within your software or on a website such as http://thesaurus.com) offers alternatives to a particular word. The best uses of a thesaurus are to find fresh, interesting words when you've been using the same word too many times and to find words that most accurately convey your intended meaning. Don't use a thesaurus simply to find impressive-sounding words, however, and don't assume that all the alternatives suggested are correct for each situation.

Third, a *grammar-checker* tries to do for your grammar what a spell-checker does for your spelling. Because the program doesn't have a clue about what you're trying to say, it can't tell whether you've said it clearly or correctly. However, grammar-checkers can highlight items you should consider changing, such as passive voice, long sentences, and words that tend to be misused.

Fourth, a *style-checker* can monitor your word and sentence choices and suggest alternatives that might produce more effective writing. For example, the style-checking options can range from basic issues, such as spelling out numbers and using contractions, to more subjective matters, such as sentence structure and the use of technical terminology.

By all means, use any software that you find helpful when revising your documents. Just remember that it's unwise to rely on them to do all your revision work and that you are responsible for the final product.

Producing Your Message

5 LEARNING OBJECTIVE

Explain how design elements help determine the effectiveness of your documents.

Production quality affects both readability and audience perceptions of you and your message.

Document design sends strong nonverbal signals—make sure the signals you send are positive and appropriate.

Now it's time to put your hard work on display. The *production quality* of your message—the total effect of page or screen design, graphical elements, typography, paper, and so on—plays an important role in the effectiveness of your message. A polished, inviting design not only makes your document easier to read but also conveys a sense of professionalism and importance.[6]

DESIGNING FOR READABILITY

Design affects readability in two important ways. First, if used carefully, design elements can improve the effectiveness of your message. If done poorly, design elements can act as barriers, blocking your communication. Second, the visual design itself sends a nonverbal message to the audience, influencing their perceptions of the communication before they read a single word. View any business website on the Internet and ask yourself what nonverbal message it sends and how you are influenced by it.

Effective design helps you establish the tone of your document and helps guide your readers through your message. As the blog in Figure 6–6 shows, the clean and restrained design is more than adequate for its purpose, which is

Figure 6–6 Designing for Readability.

Used with the Permission of Bruce McGraw.

to share ideas on project management strategies and techniques. To achieve an effective design, pay careful attention to the following design elements:

- **Consistency.** Throughout each message, be consistent in your use of margins, typeface, type size, and spacing (paragraph indents, between columns, and around photographs). Also be consistent when using recurring design elements, such as vertical lines, columns, and borders. In many cases, you'll want to be consistent not only within a message but also across multiple messages; that way, audiences who receive messages from you recognize your documents and know what to expect.
- **Balance.** Balance is a subjective issue. One document may have a formal, rigid design in which the various elements are placed in a grid pattern, while another has a less formal design in which elements flow more freely across the page—and both could be in balance. Like the tone of your language, visual balance can be too formal, just right, or too informal for a given message.
- **Restraint.** Strive for simplicity in design. Don't clutter your message with too many design elements, too much highlighting, too many colours, or too many decorative touches. Let "simpler" and "fewer" be your guiding concepts.
- **Detail.** Pay attention to details that affect your design and thus your message. For example, headings and subheadings that appear at the bottom of a column or a page can annoy readers when the promised information doesn't appear until the next column or page. Also, narrow columns with too much space between words can be distracting.

For effective design, pay attention to
- Consistency
- Balance
- Restraint
- Detail

Even without special training, you can make your printed and electronic messages more effective by understanding the use of white space, margins and line justification, typefaces, and type styles.

WHITE SPACE Any space free of text or artwork, whether in print or online, is considered **white space** (note that "white space" isn't necessarily white; it is simply blank). These unused areas provide visual contrast and important resting points for your readers. White space includes the open area surrounding headings, margins, vertical space between columns, paragraph indents or extra space between unindented paragraphs, and horizontal space between lines of text. To increase the chance that readers will read your documents, be generous with white space, which makes pages feel less intimidating and easier to read.[7]

White space separates elements in a document and helps guide the reader's eye.

MARGINS AND JUSTIFICATION Margins define the space around your text and between text columns. They're influenced by the way you place lines of type, which can be set (1) justified (flush on the left and flush on the right), (2) flush left with a ragged right margin, (3) flush right with a ragged left margin, or (4) centred. This paragraph is justified, whereas the paragraphs in Figure 6–3 are flush left with a ragged-right margin.

Most business documents use a flush-left margin and a ragged-right margin.

Magazines, newspapers, and books often use justified type because it can accommodate more text in a given space. However, justified type needs to be used with care. First, it creates a denser look because the uniform line lengths decrease the amount of white space along the right margin. Second, it produces a more formal and less personalized look. Third, unless it is used with some skill and attention, justified type can be more difficult to read because it can produce large gaps between words and excessive hyphenation at the ends of lines. The publishing specialists who create magazines, newspapers, and books have the time and skill needed to carefully adjust character and word spacing to eliminate these problems. (In some cases, sentences are even rewritten in order to improve the appearance of the printed page.) Because most business communicators don't have that time or skill, it's best to avoid justified type in most business documents.

Flush-left, ragged-right type "lightens" your message's appearance. It gives a document an informal, contemporary feeling of openness. Spacing between words is the same, and only long words that fall at the ends of lines are hyphenated.

Centred type is rarely used for text paragraphs but is commonly used for headings and subheadings. Flush-right, ragged-left type is rarely used in business documents.

TYPEFACES **Typeface**, or font, refers to the physical design of letters, numbers, and other text characters. (*Font* and *typeface* are often used interchangeably, although strictly speaking, a font is a set of characters in a given typeface.) Typeface influences the tone of your message, making it look authoritative or friendly, businesslike or casual, classic or modern, and so on (see Table 6–4). Choose fonts that are appropriate for your message. Most computers offer dozens of font choices, but most of these are inappropriate for general business usage.

Serif typefaces have small crosslines (called *serifs*) at the ends of each letter stroke. Serif faces such as Times New Roman are commonly used for regular paragraph text (as in this book), but they can look busy and cluttered when set in large sizes for headings or other display treatments. Typefaces with rounded serifs can look friendly; those with squared serifs can look official.

Sans serif typefaces have no serifs (*sans* is French for "without"). The visual simplicity of sans serif typefaces such as Helvetica and Arial makes them ideal for the larger sizes used in headlines. Sans serif faces can be difficult to read in long blocks of text, however, unless they are formatted with generous amounts of *leading* (pronounced *ledding*), or spacing between lines.

The classic style of document design uses a sans serif typeface for headings and a serif typeface for regular paragraph text. However, many contemporary documents and websites now use a sans serif face for both. Whichever combination you use, make sure that the result is reader friendly and that it conveys the right personality for the situation.

TYPE STYLES **Type style** refers to any modification that lends contrast or emphasis to type, including boldface, italic, underlining, and other highlighting and decorative styles. Using boldface type for subheads breaks up long expanses of text. You can also boldface isolated words in the middle of a text block to draw more attention to them. For example, the key terms in each chapter in this book are set in bold. Italic type also creates emphasis, although not as pronounced as boldface. Italic type has specific uses as well, such as highlighting quotations and indicating foreign words, irony, humour, book and movie titles, and unconventional usage.

Avoid using any type style in ways that might interfere with reading.

As a general rule, avoid using any style in a way that slows your audience's progress through the message. For example, underlining or using all uppercase letters can interfere with your reader's ability to recognize the shapes of words; improperly placed boldface or italicized type can slow down your reader; and shadowed or outlined type can seriously hinder legibility.

Table 6–4	**Typeface Personalities: Serious to Casual to Playful**	
Serif Typefaces (best for text)	**Sans Serif Typefaces (best for headlines; some work well for text)**	**Specialty Typefaces (for decorative purposes only)**
Bookman Old Style	Arial	ᴀɴɴᴀ
Century Schoolbook	**Eras Bold**	Bauhaus
Courier	Franklin Gothic Book	Edwardian
Garamond	Frutiger	*Lucida Handwriting*
Rockwell	Gill Sans	𝕰𝖚𝖈𝖑𝖎𝖉 𝕱𝖗𝖆𝖐𝖙𝖚𝖗
Times New Roman	Verdana	**STENCIL**

Type size is an important consideration as well. For most printed business messages, use a type size of 10 to 12 points for regular text and 12 to 18 points for headings and subheadings (a point is approximately 1/72 of an inch). Resist the temptation to reduce type size to squeeze in text or to enlarge it to fill up space. Type that is too small is hard to read, whereas extra-large type looks unprofessional. Be particularly careful with small type online. Small type that looks fine on a medium-resolution screen can be hard to read on both low-resolution screens (because these displays can make letters look jagged or fuzzy) and high-resolution screens (because these monitors reduce the apparent size of the type even further).

In Ontario, the government is phasing in new requirements for documents that help those with physical challenges to read and manipulate information. The *Accessibility for Ontarians with Disabilties Act* (AODA) has specific guidelines for formatting, including font type and size. You should familiarize yourself with the requirements as soon as possible; visit the website at http://www.aoda.ca.

DESIGNING MULTIMEDIA DOCUMENTS

A **multimedia document** contains a combination of text, graphics, photographs, audio, animation, video, and interactivity (such as hyperlinks that access webpages or software programs). As rich media, multimedia documents can convey large amounts of information quickly, engage people in multiple ways, express emotions, and allow recipients to personalize the communication process to their own needs. However, these documents are more difficult to create than documents that contain only text and static images. To design and create multimedia documents, you need to consider the following factors:

- **Creative and technical skills.** Depending on what you need to accomplish, creating and integrating multimedia elements can require some creative and technical skills. Fortunately, many basic tasks, such as adding photographs or video clips to a webpage, have gotten much easier in recent years. And even if you don't have the advantage of formal training in design, by studying successful examples you can start to get a feel for what works and what doesn't.

  > Multimedia documents can be powerful communication vehicles, but they require more time, tools, and skills to create.

- **Tools.** The hardware and software tools needed to create and integrate media elements are now widely available and generally affordable. For example, with simpler and less expensive consumer versions of professional photo and video editing software, you can often perform all the tasks you need for business multimedia (see Figure 6–7).

- **Time and cost.** The time and cost of creating multimedia documents has dropped dramatically in recent years. However, you still need to consider these elements—and exercise good judgment when deciding whether to include multimedia and how much to include. Make sure the time and money you plan to spend will be paid back in communication effectiveness.

- **Content.** To include various media elements in a document, you need to create them if you have the time, tools, and skills, or you need to acquire them if you don't. Millions of graphics, photos, video clips, and other elements are available online, but you need to make sure you can legally use each item. One good option is to search Creative Commons (http://creativecommons.org) for multimedia elements available for use at no charge but with various restrictions (such as giving the creator credit).

  > Make sure you have the legal right to use any media elements that you include in your documents.

- **Message structure.** Multimedia documents often lack a rigid linear structure from beginning to end, which means you need to plan for readers to take multiple, individualized paths through the material. Chapter 11 discusses the challenge of information architecture, the structure and navigational flow of websites and other multimedia documents.

Figure 6–7 Multimedia Tools

Source: Photo by Ryan Lackey. Adobe product screenshot(s) reprinted with permission from Adobe Systems Incorporated.

- **Compatibility.** Some multimedia elements require specific software to be installed on the recipient's viewing device. Another challenge is the variety of screen sizes and resolutions, from large, high-resolution computer monitors to tiny mobile phone displays. Make sure you understand the demands your message will place on the audience.

USING TECHNOLOGY TO PRODUCE YOUR MESSAGE

Production tools vary widely, depending on the software and systems you're using. Some IM and email systems offer limited formatting and production capabilities, whereas most word processors now offer some capabilities that rival professional publishing software for many day-to-day business needs. *Desktop publishing* software such as Adobe InDesign goes beyond word processing, with more advanced layout capabilities designed to accommodate photos, technical drawings, and other elements. (Such programs are used mainly by design professionals.) For online content, web publishing and blogging systems make it easy to produce great-looking pages quickly.

Learning to use the basic features of your communication tools will help you produce better messages in less time.

No matter what system you're using, become familiar with the basic formatting capabilities. A few hours of exploration on your own or an introductory training course can dramatically improve the production quality of your documents. Depending on the types of messages you're creating, you'll benefit from being proficient with the following features:

- **Templates, themes, style sheets, and style sets.** As Chapter 5 notes, you can save a significant amount of time during production by using templates, themes, style sheets, and style sets. Many companies provide these to their employees to ensure a consistent look and feel for all print and online company documents.

- **Page setup.** Use page setup to control margins, orientation (*portrait* is vertical; *landscape* is horizontal), and the location of *headers* and *footers* (text and graphics that repeat at the top and bottom of every page).
- **Column formatting.** Most business documents use a single column of text per page, but multiple columns can be an attractive format for documents such as newsletters. Columns are also handy to format long lists.
- **Paragraph formatting.** Take advantage of the various paragraph-formatting controls to enhance the look of your documents. You can offset quotations by increasing margin width around a single paragraph, subtly compress line spacing to fit a document on a single page, or use hanging indents to offset the first line of a paragraph.
- **Numbered and bulleted lists.** Let your word processor do the busywork of formatting numbered and bulleted lists. It can also automatically renumber lists when you add or remove items.

> **TIPS FOR SUCCESS**
> "The way you present your information will increase the clarity of your message. Using bold subheadings and indents helps to highlight your points."
>
> Gina Cuciniello, communication trainer

- **Tables.** Tables are an effective way to display any information that lends itself to rows and columns: calendars, numerical data, comparisons, and so on. Use paragraph and font formatting thoughtfully within tables.
- **Pictures, text boxes, and objects.** Print and online publishing software lets you insert a wide variety of elements. *Text boxes* are small blocks of text that stand apart from the main text and can be placed anywhere on the page; they are great for captions, callouts, margin notes, and so on. *Objects* can be anything from a spreadsheet to a sound clip to an engineering drawing.

FORMATTING FORMAL LETTERS AND MEMOS

Formal business letters usually follow certain design conventions, as the letter in Figure 6–3 illustrates. Most business letters are printed on *letterhead stationery*, which includes the company's name, address, and other contact information. The first thing to appear after the letterhead is the date (spell out the month instead of using numbers, as many cultures use the day/month/year numbers differently), followed by the inside address, which identifies the person receiving the letter. Next is the salutation, usually in the form of *Dear Mr.* or *Ms. Last Name*. The message comes next, followed by the complimentary close, usually *Sincerely* or *Cordially*. And last comes the signature block: space for the signature, followed by the sender's printed name and title. For in-depth information on letter formats, see Appendix A, "Format and Layout of Business Documents."

Business letters typically have the following elements:
- Preprinted letterhead stationery
- Date
- Inside address
- Salutation
- Complimentary close
- Signature block

Like letters, business memos usually follow a preset design, as shown in Figure 6–8, which shows the typical elements. Memos have largely been replaced by electronic media in many companies, but if they are still in use at the firm you join, the company may have a standard format or template for you to use. Most memos begin with a title such as *Memo*, *Memorandum*, or *Interoffice Correspondence*. Following that are usually four headings: *Date*, *To*, *From*, and *Subject*. (*Re:*, short for *Regarding*, is sometimes used instead of *Subject*.) Memos usually don't use a salutation, complimentary close, or signature, although signing your initials next to your name on the *From* line is standard practice in most companies. Bear in mind that memos are often distributed without sealed envelopes, so they are less private than most other message formats.

Memos are usually identified by a title such as Memo or Memorandum.

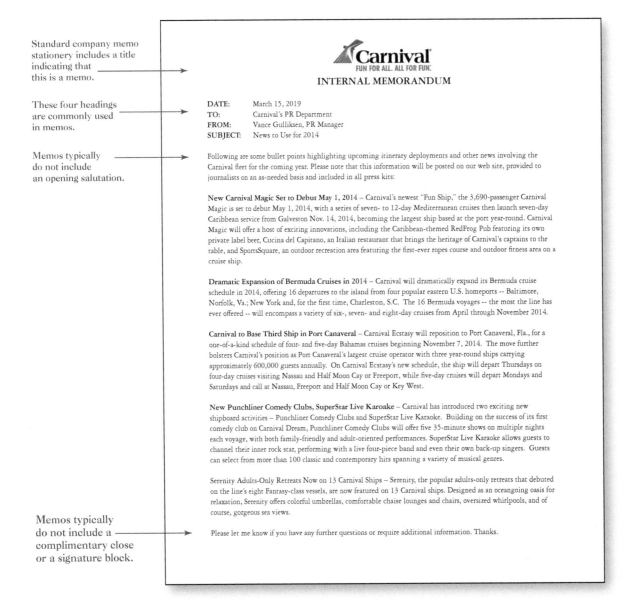

Standard company memo stationery includes a title indicating that this is a memo.

These four headings are commonly used in memos.

Memos typically do not include an opening salutation.

Memos typically do not include a complimentary close or a signature block.

Figure 6–8 A Typical Business Memo

Courtesy: Carnival Corporation

Proofreading Your Message

Highlight the types of errors to look for when proofreading.

Your credibility is affected by your attention to the details of mechanics and form.

Proofreading is the quality inspection stage for your documents, as your last chance to ensure that your document is ready to carry your message—and your reputation—to the intended audience. Even a small mistake can doom your efforts, so take proofreading seriously.

Look for two types of problems: (1) undetected mistakes from the writing, design, and layout stages and (2) mistakes that crept in during production. For the first category, you can review format and layout guidelines in Appendix A. The second category can include anything from computer glitches, such as missing fonts, to problems with the ink used in printing. Be particularly vigilant with complex documents and complex production processes that involve teams of people and multiple computers. Strange things can happen as files move from computer to computer, especially when a lot of graphics and different fonts are

✓ Checklist   Proofing Business Messages

A. Look for writing errors.
- Typographical mistakes
- Misspelled words
- Grammatical errors
- Punctuation mistakes

B. Look for missing elements.
- Missing text sections
- Missing exhibits (drawings, tables, photographs, charts, graphs, online images, and so on)
- Missing source notes, copyright notices, or other reference items

C. Look for design and formatting mistakes.
- Incorrect or inconsistent font selections
- Column sizing, spacing, and alignment

- Margins
- Special characters
- Clumsy line and page breaks
- Page numbers
- Page headers and footers
- Adherence to company standards
- Links (make sure they're active and link to the correct pages)
- Downloadable files (make sure they're stored in the appropriate folder so audiences can access them)

---

involved. See "Checklist: Proofing Business Messages" for a list of items to review during proofing.

Resist the temptation to treat proofreading as a casual scan up and down the page or screen. Instead, approach it as a methodical procedure in which you look for specific problems that may occur. Start by reviewing the advice in "Sharpening Your Career Skills: Proofread Like a Pro to Create Perfect Documents." You might also find it helpful to create a checklist of items to review; this can be a handy tool when you need to review one of your own documents or you're asked to review someone else's work. To ensure that your message is error-free, print a copy of it and read it from the last sentence to the first. This helps trick your brain into thinking it is seeing something new and breaks the logic pattern. We see so many errors every day that we tend to ignore them, but reading a document from the bottom to the top forces the brain to pay close attention to each sentence.

A methodical approach to proofreading will help you find the problems that need to be fixed.

The amount of time you need to spend on proofing depends on both the length and complexity of the document and the situation. A typo in a memo to your team might be forgiven, but a typo in a financial report, a contract, or a medical file certainly could be serious. As with every task in the writing process, practice helps—you become not only more familiar with what errors to look for but also more skilled in identifying those errors.

Distributing Your Message

With the production finished, you're ready to distribute the message. You often have several options for distribution; consider the following factors when making your choice:

Discuss the most important issues to consider when distributing your messages.

- **Cost.** Cost isn't a major concern for most messages, but for lengthy reports or multimedia production, it may well be. Printing, binding, and delivering reports can be an expensive proposition, so weigh the cost versus the benefits before you decide. Be sure to consider the nonverbal message you send regarding cost as well. Overnight delivery of a printed report could look responsive in one situation but wasteful in another, for example.

- **Convenience.** How much work is involved for you and your audience? For instance, if you use a file-compression utility to shrink the size of email

Make sure your delivery method is convenient for your audience members.

SHARPENING YOUR CAREER SKILLS

Proofread Like a Pro to Create Perfect Documents

Before you click on "Send" or tote that stack of reports off to the shipping department, make sure your document represents the best possible work you can do. Your colleagues will usually overlook errors in everyday emails, but higher-profile mistakes in messages to outside audiences can damage your company and hinder your career.

Use these techniques from professional proofreaders to help ensure high-quality output:

- **Make multiple passes.** Go through the document several times, focusing on a different aspect each time. The first pass might be to look for omissions and errors in content; the second pass might be to check for typographical, grammatical, and spelling errors; and a final pass could be for layout, spacing, alignment, colours, page numbers, margins, and other design features.
- **Use perceptual tricks.** It's common to disregard transposed letters, improper capitalization, and misplaced punctuation when rereading your own material. Change the way you process the visual information by

1. Reading each page from the bottom to the top (starting at the last word in each line)
2. Placing your finger under each word and reading it silently
3. Making a slit in a sheet of paper that reveals only one line of type at a time
4. Reading the document aloud and pronouncing each word carefully
5. Temporarily reformatting the document so that it looks fresh to your eyes

- **Double-check high-priority items.** Double-check the spelling of names and the accuracy of dates, addresses, and any number that could cause grief if incorrect (such as telling a potential employer that you'd be happy to work for $5000 a year when you meant to say $50 000).
- **Give yourself some distance.** If you have time, set the document aside and proofread it the next day. You will be able to catch your errors with a fresh review.
- **Be vigilant.** Avoid reading large amounts of material in one sitting and don't proofread when you're tired.
- **Stay focused.** Concentrate on what you're doing. Block out distractions and focus as completely as possible on your proofreading task.
- **Review complex electronic documents on paper.** Some people have trouble proofreading webpages, online reports, and other electronic documents onscreen. If you have trouble, try to print the materials so you can review them on paper.
- **Take your time.** Quick proofreading is not careful proofreading.

CAREER APPLICATIONS

1. Why is it valuable to have other people proofread your documents?
2. Proofread the following sentence:

   aplication of thse methods in stores in Vancouver nd Winnipeg have resultted in a 30 drop in roberies an a 50 percent decling in violnce there, acording ot the develpers if the securty sytem, Hanover brothrs, Inc.

attachments, make sure your recipients have the means to expand the files on arrival. For extremely large files, consider recordable media such as DVDs or a file-hosting site such as MediaFire (www.mediafire.com).

- **Time.** How soon does the message need to reach the audience? Don't waste money on overnight delivery if the recipient won't read the report for a week. Remember not to mark any messages, printed or electronic, as "urgent" if they aren't truly urgent.
- **Security and privacy.** The convenience offered by electronic communication needs to be weighed against security and privacy concerns. For the most sensitive messages, your company will probably restrict both the people who can receive the documents and the means you can use to distribute them. In addition, most computer users are wary of opening attachments these days, particularly word processor files. Instead of sending Word files, which might be vulnerable to macro viruses and other risks, convert your Word documents to PDF files that can be viewed using Adobe Reader.

Chapter 7 offers more advice on distributing podcasts, blogs, and other messages in electronic formats.

SUMMARY OF LEARNING OBJECTIVES

1 **Discuss the value of careful revision, and list the main tasks involved in completing a business message.** Careful revision will produce a correctly written and professional document that will impress your readers and help them in their own tasks. Revision consists of (1) evaluating content, organization, style, and tone; (2) reviewing readability; (3) editing for clarity and conciseness; and (4) proofreading the final version after it has been produced.

2 **Explain four writing techniques you can use to improve the readability of your messages.** You can help your reader easily comprehend your messages by (1) varying sentence length, which will make your message compelling by adding variety and highlighting specific ideas; (2) keeping paragraphs short to medium length to create an inviting document; (3) using bullets and lists, which will clarify information through highlighting it and create a visually appealing document for complex subjects; and (4) using headings and subheadings to guide the reader through your message and attract attention.

3 **Describe the steps you can take to improve the clarity of your writing.** Clear writing comes with careful and methodical revision. As you clarify your message, you should divide overly long sentences to tighten your writing and rewrite hedging sentences to sound confident. Use parallelism to highlight related ideas and correct dangling modifiers so that your meaning is accurate. Reword long noun sequences and replace camouflaged verbs to be concise. Clarify sentence structure and awkward references to enhance readability and avoid confusion. Moderate your enthusiasm to maintain your credibility.

4 **Discuss why it's important to make your message more concise, and give four tips on how to do so.** Businesspeople are more likely to read documents that give information efficiently. To make business messages more concise, include only necessary material and write clean sentences by (1) deleting unnecessary words and phrases, (2) shortening overly long words and phrases,

(3) eliminating redundancies, and (4) recasting It is and There are starters.

5 **Explain how design elements help determine the effectiveness of your documents.** When selecting and applying design elements, ensure their effectiveness by being consistent throughout your document; balancing space between text, art, and white space; showing restraint in the number of elements you use; and paying attention to every detail. White space provides contrast and gives readers a resting point. Margins and justification define the space around the text and contribute to the amount of white space. Typefaces, or fonts, influence the tone of the message. Type styles provide contrast or emphasis.

6 **Highlight the types of errors to look for when proofreading.** When proofreading the final version of your document, always look for errors in grammar, usage, and punctuation and watch for spelling mistakes and typos. Ensure that nothing is missing, such as a source note, figure, text, or exhibit. Check for design errors, such as elements that appear in the wrong font, misaligned elements (for example, columns in a table or figures on a page), and formatting mistakes (including uneven spacing between lines and words and incorrect line breaks). Finally, ensure that your layout conforms to company guidelines.

7 **Discuss the most important issues to consider when distributing your messages.** Keep in mind cost, convenience, time, security, and privacy when distributing your message. Balance cost versus benefits when selecting your distribution method for long documents, because printing, binding, and delivering long reports can be expensive. Furthermore, ensure that your reader needs your document immediately to justify an expensive delivery method (for example, overnight express). Finally, use secure transmission methods for sensitive documents, follow company guidelines for recipients, and use Adobe PDF instead of Word files to avoid viruses.

ON THE JOB | PERFORMING COMMUNICATION TASKS AT FREE THE CHILDREN

The WE website is a key communication medium for promoting the organization's programs to improve the lives of children around the world. As a recently hired volunteer in the Toronto office, you think that WE should introduce audio podcasts to its site so visitors can download information and listen to it whenever they wish. You are now editing a draft of your report and need to resolve these communication situations:

1. Podcasts are an established communication medium. You believe that if WE posted podcasts created by volunteers who describe their experiences, more young people

would be attracted to volunteering at the organization. Which of the following sentences is the best way to suggest this opportunity?

a. In just a few short years, podcasts have developed into an extremely popular communication medium, allowing anyone to create web content for downloading on computers and MP3 players.

b. Podcasting can be audio and video, and people can find podcasts by visiting a specific organization or company or a site such as http://podcastalley.com.

c. Podcasting has grown as a way for nonprofit organizations to generate interest in their activities.

d. We're going to be extremely sorry if we don't get into podcasting.

2. Like all staff at WE, the communications director is extremely busy, with limited time to devote to reading reports and other business documents. You've learned that headings and subheadings are an effective way to get your points across, even if your reader does nothing more than skim through one of your reports. Which is the most effective subheading to head the section about the benefits of podcasting?

a. The Importance of Podcasting as a Communication Tool

b. The Podcasting Appeal: Attracting Volunteers through Education and Fun

c. Podcasting Appeals to Many Young Internet Surfers

d. The Great Opportunity in Podcasting on the WE Website

3. You want the communications coordinator to get a real feel for podcasting, so you decide to enhance the electronic version of your report with multimedia. Which is the best way to go beyond your text to show the reader the potential of podcasting?

a. Add a sound clip with you talking about WE so that the reader understands the immediacy of a podcast.

b. Include a link to the Center for Creative Leadership on iTunes U to help the reader understand how podcasts can transmit a wide variety of content about WE.

c. Include a link to the podcast section in Wikipedia to give the reader a good understanding of how podcasts work.

d. Include a PowerPoint presentation that you've created about podcasting.

TEST YOUR KNOWLEDGE

1. Why should you take care to revise messages before sending them?

2. What are the pros and cons of readability indexes?

3. How can you improve the readability of your messages?

4. How do readers benefit from white space and headings?

5. What is parallel construction? Why is it important?

6. When should you use numbered lists? Bulleted lists?

7. What are some ways you can make a document more concise?

8. What are the benefits and shortcomings of using technology to revise your messages?

9. When should you use email to distribute your messages?

10. Why are typeface and type styles important considerations when producing your messages?

APPLY YOUR KNOWLEDGE

1. Why is it helpful to let a first draft "age" for a while before you begin the editing process?

2. Given the choice of only one, would you prefer to use a grammar-checker or a spell-checker? Why?

3. When you design a formal business letter, which design elements do you have to consider? Which are optional?

4. Which distribution method would you choose for a highly confidential strategic planning report that needs to be sent to top executives at six locations in North America, Asia, and Europe? Explain your choice.

5. **Ethical Choices** What are the ethical implications of murky, complex writing in a document explaining how customers can appeal the result of a decision made in the company's favour during a dispute?

RUNNING CASES

> CASE 1 Noreen

Petro-Go has just merged with Best Gas and has consequently nearly doubled in size. Many staff positions have changed and will continue to change. New staff positions will become available, and others will be reassigned. Noreen has applied for and received a promotion and is now the manager of the "Go

Points" team. Until a manager is assigned to the "Collections" team, Noreen has been asked to take on the acting manager role until further notice.

Noreen is asked to create a memo that will be sent to all employees of both companies informing them of the merger.

There will be changes in procedures and job assignments once upper-level management determines the most effective way to handle business in this larger form. In the meantime, there is a temporary management hierarchy in place for reporting purposes.

QUESTIONS
a. What decisions will have to be made?
b. What information will have to be gathered before Noreen begins?

c. If the memo is not proofread carefully and there are errors in it, could it affect the company image? How?
d. What is the best way to distribute the memo?
e. What design elements will need to be considered?

YOUR TASK
Create the memo to all employees. Apply the skills you have learned in Chapters 4, 5, and 6.

> CASE 2 Kwong

Kwong's manager at Accountants For All accounting firm was very impressed with the promotional letter Kwong sent to all past customers. He has asked Kwong to revise the letter for a promotional flyer that will reach new customers. The plan is to deliver the flyer to local businesses as well as several hundred homes in the area. Kwong's manager hopes to increase new business by building credibility, emphasizing competitive prices, and mentioning promotions for repeat customers, seniors, students, and families of four or more.

QUESTIONS
a. What must Kwong consider with regard to the layout or format of the flyer, graphics, typefaces, sentence length, and language?

b. What company contact information should Kwong include?
c. What type of company image is Kwong trying to portray?
d. How should Kwong have the flyer distributed?
e. What should Kwong look for when proofreading the flyer? Should Kwong request that another colleague also proofread the flyer?

YOUR TASK
Create the flyer from Accountants For All. Apply the skills you have learned in Chapters 4, 5, and 6.

PRACTISE YOUR KNOWLEDGE

Read the following documents, and then (1) analyze the strengths and weaknesses of each sentence and (2) revise each document so that it follows the guidelines in Chapters 4, 5, and 6.

DOCUMENT 6.A

The move to our new offices will takes place over this coming weekend. For everything to run smooth, everyone will have to clean out thier own desk and pack up the contents in boxes that will be provided. You will need to take everything off of the walls to, and please pack it along with the boxes.

If you have a lot of personal belongings, you should bring it home with you. Likewise with anything valuable. I do not mean to infer that items will be stolen, irregardless it is better to be safe than sorry.

On Monday, we will be unpacking, putting things away, and than get back to work. The least amount of disruption is anticipated by us, if everyone does their part. Hopefully, there will be no negative affects on production schedules, and current deadlines will be met.

DOCUMENT 6.B

For delicious, air-popped popcorn, please read the following instructions: The popper is designed to pop ½ cup of popcorn kernels at one time. Never add more than ½ cup. A half cup of corn will produce three to four quarts of popcorn. More batchs may be made separately after completion of the first batch. Popcorn is popped by hot air. Oil or shortening are not needed for popping corn. Add only popcorn kernels to the poping chamber. Standard grades of popcorn are recommended for use. Premium- or gourmet-type popping corns may be used. Ingredients such as oil, shortening, butter, margarine, or salt should never be added to the popping chamber. The popper, with popping chute in position, may be preheted for two minutes before adding the corn. Turn the popper off before adding the corn. Use electricity safely and wisely. Observe safty precautions when using the popper. Do not touch the popper when it is hot. The popper should not be left unattended when it is plugged into an outlet. Do not use the popper if it or it's cord has been damaged. Do not use the popper if it is not working properly. Before using the first time, wash the chute and butter/measuring cup in hot soapy water. Use a dishcloth or sponge. Wipe the outside of the popper base. Use a damp cloth. Dry the base. Do not immerse the popper base in water or other liquid. Replace the chute and butter/measuring cup. The popper is ready to use.

EXERCISES

6.1 Message Readability: Writing Paragraphs

Rewrite the following paragraph to vary sentence length and to shorten the paragraph so it looks more inviting to readers.

Although major league hockey remains popular, more people are attending women's league hockey games because they can spend less on admission, snacks, and parking and still enjoy the excitement of Canada's pastime. British Columbia has the Vancouver Griffins, the Richmond Steelers, and the North Island Eagles; Quebec has Laval Mistral and Montreal Wingstar; southern Ontario has the Toronto Sting, the Beatrice Aeros, and the Brampton Thunder. These teams play in relatively small arenas, so fans are close enough to see and hear everything, from the smack of the stick hitting the puck to the crash of a body check. Best of all, the cost of a family outing to see rising stars play in a local women's league game is just a fraction of what the family would spend to attend a major league game in a much larger, more crowded arena.

6.2 Message Readability: Using Bullets

Rewrite the following paragraph using a bulleted list:

Our forensic accounting services provide the insights needed to resolve disputes, recover losses, and manage risk intelligently. One of our areas of practice is insurance claims accounting and preparation services, designed to help you maximize recovery of insured value. Another practice area is dispute advisory, in which we can assist with discovery, expert witness testimony, and economic analysis. A third practice: construction consulting. This service helps our clients understand why large-scale construction projects fail to meet schedule or budget requirements. Fourth, we offer general investigative and forensic accounting services, including fraud detection and proof of loss analysis.[8]

6.3 Revising Messages: Clarity

Divide these sentences into shorter ones by adding more periods:

 a. The next time you write something, check your average sentence length in a 100-word passage, and if your sentences average more than 16 to 20 words, see whether you can break up some of the sentences.
 b. Don't do what the village blacksmith did when he instructed his apprentice as follows: "When I take the shoe out of the fire, I'll lay it on the anvil, and when I nod my head, you hit it with the hammer." The apprentice did just as he was told, and now he's the village blacksmith.
 c. Unfortunately, no gadget will produce excellent writing, but using a readability index gives us some guideposts to follow for making writing easier to read because it reminds us to use short sentences and simple words.
 d. Know the flexibility of the written word and its power to convey an idea, and know how to make your words behave so that your readers will understand.

 e. Words mean different things to different people, and a word such as *block* may mean city block, butcher block, engine block, auction block, or several other things.

6.4 Revising Messages: Conciseness

Cross out unnecessary words in the following phrases:
 a. consensus of opinion
 b. new innovations
 c. long period of time
 d. at a price of $50
 e. still remains

6.5 Revising Messages: Conciseness

Revise the following sentences, using shorter, simpler words:
 a. The antiquated calculator is ineffectual for solving sophisticated problems.
 b. It is imperative that the pay increments be terminated before an inordinate deficit is accumulated.
 c. There was unanimity among the executives that Ms. Hassan's idiosyncrasies were cause for a mandatory meeting with the company's personnel director.
 d. The impending liquidation of the company's assets was cause for jubilation among the company's competitors.
 e. The expectations of the president for a stock dividend were accentuated by the preponderance of evidence that the company was in good financial condition.

6.6 Revising Messages: Conciseness

Use infinitives as substitutes for the overly long phrases in these sentences:
 a. For living, I require money.
 b. They did not find sufficient evidence for believing in the future.
 c. Bringing about the destruction of a dream is tragic.

6.7 Revising Messages: Conciseness

Rephrase the following in fewer words:
 a. in the near future
 b. in the event that
 c. in order that
 d. for the purpose of
 e. with regard to
 f. it may be that
 g. in very few cases
 h. with reference to
 i. at the present time
 j. there is no doubt that

6.8 Revising Messages: Conciseness

Condense these sentences to as few words as possible:
 a. We are of the conviction that writing is important.
 b. In all probability, we're likely to have a price increase.
 c. Our goals include making a determination about that in the near future.

d. When all is said and done at the conclusion of this experiment, I'd like to summarize the final windup.

e. After a trial period of three weeks, during which time she worked for a total of 15 full working days, we found her work was sufficiently satisfactory, so we offered her full-time work.

6.9 Revising Messages: Modifiers

Remove all the unnecessary modifiers from these sentences:

a. Tremendously high pay increases were given to the extraordinarily skilled and extremely conscientious employees.

b. The union's proposals were highly inflationary, extremely demanding, and exceptionally bold.

6.10 Revising Messages: Hedging

Rewrite these sentences so that they no longer contain any hedging:

a. It would appear that someone apparently entered illegally.

b. It may be possible that sometime in the near future the situation is likely to improve.

c. Your report seems to suggest that we might be losing money.

6.11 Revising Messages: Indefinite Starters

Rewrite these sentences to eliminate the indefinite starters:

a. There are several examples here to show that Elaine can't hold a position very long.

b. It would be greatly appreciated if every employee would make a generous contribution to Mildred Cook's retirement party.

c. It has been learned in Ottawa today from generally reliable sources that an important announcement will be made shortly by the Prime Minister's Office.

d. There is a rule that states that we cannot work overtime without permission.

e. It would be great if you could work late for the next three Saturdays.

6.12 Revising Messages: Parallelism

Present the ideas in these sentences in parallel form:

a. Mr. Luzon is expected to lecture three days a week, to counsel two days a week, and must write for publication in his spare time.

b. She knows not only accounting, but she also reads Latin.

c. Both applicants had families, university degrees, and were in their thirties, with considerable accounting experience but few social connections.

d. This book was exciting, well written, and held my interest.

e. Don is both a hard worker and he knows bookkeeping.

6.13 Revising Messages: Awkward References

Revise the following sentences to delete the awkward references:

a. The vice president in charge of sales and the production manager are responsible for the keys to 34A and 35A, respectively.

b. The keys to 34A and 35A are in executive hands, with the former belonging to the vice president in charge of sales and the latter belonging to the production manager.

c. The keys to 34A and 35A have been given to the production manager, with the aforementioned keys being gold embossed.

d. A laser printer and an inkjet printer were delivered to John and Megan, respectively.

e. The walnut desk is more expensive than the oak desk, the former costing $300 more than the latter.

6.14 Revising Messages: Dangling Modifiers

Rewrite these sentences to clarify the dangling modifiers:

a. Running down the railroad tracks in a cloud of smoke, we watched the countryside glide by.

b. Lying on the shelf, Ruby saw the seashell.

c. Based on the information, I think we should buy the property.

d. Being cluttered and filthy, Sandy took the whole afternoon to clean up her desk.

e. After proofreading every word, the memo was ready to be signed.

6.15 Revising Messages: Noun Sequences

Rewrite the following sentences to eliminate the long strings of nouns:

a. The focus of the meeting was a discussion of the mortgage rate issue.

b. Following the government report recommendations, we are revising our job applicant evaluation procedures.

c. The production department quality assurance program components include employee training, supplier cooperation, and computerized detection equipment.

d. The supermarket warehouse inventory reduction plan will be implemented next month.

e. The MacDonald McKenzie University business school graduate placement program is one of the best in the country.

6.16 Revising Messages: Sentence Structure

Rearrange the following sentences to bring the subjects closer to their verbs:

a. Trudy, when she first saw the bull pawing the ground, ran.

b. It was Terri who, according to Ted, who is probably the worst gossip in the office (Tom excepted), mailed the wrong order.

c. William Oberstreet, in his book *Investment Capital Reconsidered*, writes of the mistakes that bankers through the decades have made.

d. Anya Federov, after passing up several sensible investment opportunities, despite the warnings of her friends and family, invested her inheritance in a jojoba plantation.

e. The president of U-Stor-It, which was on the brink of bankruptcy after the warehouse fire, the worst tragedy in the history of the company, prepared a press announcement.

6.17 Revising Messages: Camouflaged Verbs

Rewrite each sentence so that the verbs are no longer camouflaged:

a. Adaptation to the new rules was performed easily by the employees.

b. The assessor will make a determination of the tax due.

c. Verification of the identity of the employees must be made daily.

d. The board of directors made a recommendation that Mr. Rossini be assigned to a new division.

e. The auditing procedure on the books was performed by the vice president.

f. I believe Caitlyn apparently has somewhat greater influence over employees in the accounting department.

g. It seems as if this letter of resignation means you might be leaving us.

6.18 Producing Messages: Design Elements

Review a copy of the syllabus your instructor provided for this course. Which design elements were used to improve readability? Can you identify ways to make the document easier to read or more user-friendly in general? Create your own version, experimenting with different design elements and design choices. How do your changes affect readability? Exchange documents with another student and critique each other's work.

6.19 Web Design: Readability

Visit the Wildlands League website at www.wildlandsleague. org and evaluate the use of design in presenting the network's programs and features. What design improvements can you suggest to enhance readability of the information posted on this page?

6.20 Teamwork: Peer Review

Team up with another student and exchange your revised versions of Document 6.A or 6.B (see exercises under "Practise Your Knowledge"). Review the assignment to ensure that the instructions are clear. Then read and critique your teammate's revision to see whether it can be improved. After you have critiqued each other's work, take a moment to examine the way you expressed your comments and how you felt listening to the other student's comments. Can you identify ways to improve the critiquing process in situations such as this?

6.21 Proofreading Messages: Email

Proofread the following email message and revise it to correct any problems you find:

Our final company orrientation of the year will be held on Dec. 20. In preparation for this sesssion, please order 20 copies of the Policy handbook, the confindentiality agreenemt, the employee benefits Manual, please let me know if you anticipate any delays in obtaining these materials.

6.22 Ethical Choices: Message Distribution

Three of your company's five plants exceeded their expense budgets last month. You want all the plants to operate within their budgets from now on. You want to use email to let all five managers see the memo you're sending to the managers of the three over-budget plants. Is this a good idea? Why or why not?

7 Crafting Messages for Electronic Media

LEARNING OBJECTIVES   After studying this chapter, you will be able to

1 Identify the electronic media available for short messages, and discuss the challenges of communicating through social media

2 Describe the use of social networks, user-generated content sites, community Q&A sites, and community participation sites in business communication

3 Describe the evolving role of email in business communication, and explain how to adapt the three-step writing process to email messages

4 Describe the business benefits of instant messaging (IM), and identify guidelines for effective IM in the workplace

5 Describe the role of blogging and microblogging in business communication today, and explain how to adapt the three-step writing process to blogging

6 Explain how to adapt the three-step writing process to podcasting

MyLab Business Communication   Visit MyLab Business Communication to access a variety of online resources directly related to this chapter's content.

ON THE JOB: COMMUNICATING AT PETRO-CANADA

Lisa F. Young/Shutterstock

Petro-Canada's multiauthor blog, PumpTalk, features articles by employees who write about gas pricing and fuel efficiency in a friendly and clear manner.

Answering Consumer Concerns through Blogging

www.pumptalk.ca

Starting in 2006 with YouTube videos that responded in plain talk to questions about the varying price of gas, Petro-Canada's social media venture has grown into a full online presence best represented by their PumpTalk blog. A Suncor Energy business, with more than 1500 gas stations across Canada, the Petro-Canada brand is familiar to millions of Canadians, who can connect with the company through its YouTube channel, Flickr photostream, Twitter feed, and LinkedIn and Facebook pages. Online subjects include fuel efficiency, driver safety and driving tips, vehicle maintenance and oil industry news, and corporate topics such as Petro-Canada's community support. The PumpTalk blog (available separately as *Blogue Pleins gaz* for French-speaking readers) is an online forum that discusses topics of daily concern to Canadians who want explanations about their gas dollars.

The contributors to PumpTalk are Julie Siabanis, Petro-Canada's social media advisor in the refining and marketing division, who came to the company with a background in automotive marketing and research, and Corinn Smith, senior advisor for communications and stakeholder relations, who sees the blog's goal as to be "a place where questions can be asked and conversations can be facilitated. You might not always like our answers or explanations, but we strive to provide a place where we can share." Rounding out the contributing team are Rosemary Row of LinkBucket Media (one of Suncor's partner agencies), who writes and edits web content for Suncor eCommunications, and guest bloggers from partners of the Petro-Points loyalty program. Blog entries are written in a familiar, accessible style, with headings such as "Out of the Ground and into the Pump—Getting Fuel to You" and "Trunk or Treats and Spooky Cars: When Hallowe'en Hits the Road." The light tone engages the reader, but the content—such as how crude oil is processed into gasoline or a reminder to drive safely on a favourite holiday—is communicated in a clear and straightforward way. Visitors can access archives, which contain blogs on such topics as long weekend gas pricing and links of interest, such as gas price influencers. Participation is encouraged, with the advice to "stay on topic" and "refrain from strong language."

If you wrote for the PumpTalk blog, how would you analyze its audience? How would you prepare and write your entries?[1]

Electronic Media for Business Communication

1 **LEARNING OBJECTIVE**

Identify the electronic media available for short messages, and discuss the challenges of communicating through social media.

Petro-Canada could have used any number of media to communicate with its customers about the price of gas and other fuel-related issues. However, the choice of a blog post is significant because it represents a fundamental change in business communication and the relationships between companies and their stakeholders, a change enabled by the rapid growth of social media. Figure 7–1 shows the rapid rise and wide reach of four major social media platforms: Facebook, Twitter, LinkedIn, and YouTube, all of which you probably access on a daily basis.

The considerable range of electronic media available for brief business messages continues to grow as communication technologies evolve:

- **Social networking and community participation sites.** Social networking sites such as Facebook and LinkedIn, user-generated content (UGC) sites such as YouTube and Instagram, community Q&A sites, and a variety of social bookmarking and tagging sites provide an enormous range of communication tools.
- **Email.** Although it is replaced in many instances by other tools that provide support for instant communication and real-time collaboration, email continues to be an effective medium for reaching customers, colleagues, and partners. Statistics show that there were 2.6 billion email users around the world in 2016, with predictions for 2020 topping 3 billion users sending 257.7 billion emails (many of these from mobile devices).[2]
- **Instant messaging (IM).** IM usage rivals email in many companies. IM offers greater speed than email, as well as simple operation and fewer problems with unwanted messages or security and privacy problems.
- **Text messaging.** Phone-based text messaging has a number of applications in business communication, including order and status updates, marketing and sales messages, electronic coupons, and customer service.[3]
- **Blogging and microblogging.** The ability to update content quickly and easily makes blogs and microblogs (such as Twitter) a natural medium when communicators want to get messages out quickly.
- **Podcasting.** You may be familiar with podcasts as the online equivalent of recorded radio or video broadcasts (video podcasts are often called *vidcasts* or *vodcasts*). Businesses are now using podcasts to replace or supplement some conference calls, newsletters, training courses, and other communication activities.
- **Online video.** Now that YouTube and similar websites have made online video available to hundreds of millions of web users, video has been

Even with the widespread use of electronic media, printed memos, and letters still play an important role in business communication.

transformed from a fairly specialized tool to a mainstream business communication medium. More than half of the world's largest companies now have their own *branded channels* on YouTube, for example.[4]

The lines between these media often get blurry as systems expand their capabilities or people use them in new ways. For example, Facebook Messages integrates IM, text messages, and email capabilities, in addition to being a social networking system.[5] Similarly, some people consider Twitter to be a social network, and it certainly offers some of that capability. However, because blog-like messaging is Twitter's core function, this chapter classifies it as a microblogging system.

Most of your business communication is likely to be via electronic means, but don't overlook the benefits of printed messages such as letters and memos. Here are several situations in which you should consider using a printed message rather than electronic alternatives:

- **When you want to make a formal impression.** For special messages, such as sending congratulations or condolences, the formality of printed documents usually makes them a much better choice than electronic messages.
- **When you are legally required to provide information in printed form.** Business contracts and government regulations sometimes require that information be provided on paper. The laws that cover such disclosures continue to evolve, so make sure you consult with your firm's legal staff if you're not sure.
- **When you want to stand out from the flood of electronic messages.** Ironically, the growth of electronic messages creates an opportunity for printed memos and letters. If your audience's computers are overflowing with Twitter updates, email, and IM, sometimes a printed message can stand out enough to get noticed.
- **When you need a permanent, unchangeable, or secure record.** Letters and memos are reliable. Once printed, they can't be erased with a single keystroke or surreptitiously modified the way some electronic messages can be. Printed documents are also more difficult to copy and forward.

Again, most of your on-the-job communication is going to be through electronic media. This chapter focuses on electronic media for brief business messages.

COMPOSITIONAL MODES FOR ELECTRONIC MEDIA

As you use electronic media in this course, it's best to focus on the principles of social media communication and the fundamentals of planning, writing, and completing messages, rather than on the specific details of any one medium or system.[6] Fortunately, the basic communication skills required usually transfer from one system to another. You can succeed with written communication in virtually all electronic media by using one of nine *compositional modes*:

- **Conversations.** IM is a great example of a written medium that mimics spoken conversation. With IM, the ability to think, compose, and type relatively quickly is important to maintaining the flow of an electronic conversation.
- **Comments and critiques.** One of the most powerful aspects of social media is the opportunity for interested parties to express opinions and provide feedback. Sharing helpful tips and insightful commentary is also a great way to build your personal brand. To be an effective commenter, focus on short chunks of information that a broad spectrum of other site visitors will find helpful.

Courtesy: Tracx, https://www.tracx.com/resources/blog/social-media-demographics-2017-marketers

Figure 7–1 Social Media Stats Infographic 2017

Communicating successfully with electronic media requires a wide range of writing approaches.

- **Orientations.** The ability to help people find their way through an unfamiliar system or new subject is a valuable writing skill and a talent that readers greatly appreciate. Unlike summaries (see next item), orientations don't give away the key points in the collection of information but rather tell readers where to find those points and how to navigate through the collection.
- **Summaries.** At the beginning of an article or webpage, a summary functions as a miniature version of the document, giving readers all the key points while skipping over details. For example, Figure 7–2 shows "Pearson Canada at a Glance," outlining the company's mission and the services it provides. In some instances, a summary is all a reader needs. At the end of an article or webpage, it functions as a review, reminding readers of the key points they've just read.
- **Reference material.** One of the challenges of planning and writing reference material is that people typically don't read such material in a linear sense but rather search through to find particular data points, trends, or other specific elements. Making the information accessible via search engines is an important step. However, readers don't always know which search terms will yield the best results, so include an orientation, and organize the material in logical ways with clear headings that promote skimming.
- **Narratives.** Narratives work best when they have an intriguing beginning that ignites readers' curiosity, a middle section that moves quickly through the challenges that an individual or company faced, and an inspiring or

The heading "Pearson Canada at a Glance" signals the presence of a summary.

The video provides a brief overview of the Mission of and Services provided by Pearson Canada. Text follows the video and offers more in-depth information.

Figure 7–2 Writing Summaries for Electronic Media

Courtesy: Pearson Canada

instructive ending that gives readers information they can apply in their own lives and jobs.

- **Teasers.** Teasers intentionally withhold key pieces of information as a way to pull readers or listeners into a story or other document. In electronic media, the space limitations and URL linking capabilities of Twitter and other microblogging systems make them a natural tool for the teaser approach. Be sure that the *payoff*, the information a teaser links to, is valuable and legitimate.

- **Status updates and announcements.** If you use social media frequently, much of your writing will involve status updates and announcements. Be sure to post only those updates that readers will find useful, and include only the information they need.

- **Tutorials.** Given the community nature of social media, the purpose of many messages is to share how-to advice. Becoming known as a reliable expert is a great way to build customer loyalty for your company while enhancing your own personal value.

With Twitter and other super-short messaging systems, the ability to write a compelling *teaser* is an important skill.

As you approach a new communication task using electronic media, ask yourself what kind of information audience members are likely to need and then choose the appropriate compositional mode. Of course, many of these modes are also used in written media, but over time you may find yourself using all of them in various electronic and social media contexts. Whichever mode you decide to use, be sure your message is consistent with your brand and other media postings.

CREATING CONTENT FOR SOCIAL MEDIA

No matter what media or compositional mode you are using for a particular message, writing for social media requires a different approach from traditional media. Social media have changed the relationship between the sender and the receiver, so the nature of the message needs to change as well. Whether you're writing a blog or posting a product demonstration video to YouTube, consider these tips for creating successful content for social media:[7]

- **Remember that it's a conversation, not a lecture or a sales pitch.** One of the great appeals of social media is the feeling of conversation, of people talking *with* one another instead of one person talking *at* everyone else. For all its technological sophistication, in an important sense social media provide a new spin on the age-old practice of *word-of-mouth* communication. Companies often encourage employees to act as brand ambassadors, but there is an associated risk of sharing confidential information and compromising trade secrets. Effective social media policies are designed to provide guidelines on acceptable practices.

- **Write informally but not carelessly.** Write as a human being, not as a cog in a faceless corporate machine. At the same time, don't get sloppy; no one wants to slog through misspelled words and poorly constructed sentences to find the message.

- **Create concise, specific, and informative headlines.** Avoid the temptation to engage in clever wordplay with headlines. This advice applies to all forms of business communication, of course, but it is essential for social media. Readers don't want to spend time and energy figuring out what your witty headlines mean. Search engines won't know what they mean, either, so fewer people will find your content.

- **Get involved and stay involved.** Social media understandably make some businesspeople nervous because they don't permit a high level of control over messages. However, don't hide from criticism. Take the opportunity to correct misinformation or explain how mistakes will be fixed.

- **If you need to promote something, do so indirectly.** Just as you wouldn't hit people with a company sales pitch during an informal social gathering, refrain from blatant promotional efforts in social media.
- **Be transparent and honest.** Honesty is always essential, of course, but a particular issue that has affected the reputations of a few companies in recent years is hiding behind an online blogging persona—either a fictitious character whose writing is actually done by a corporate marketing specialist or a real person who fails to disclose an affiliation with a corporate sponsor.
- **Think before you post!** Because of careless messages, individuals and companies have been sued for Twitter updates, employees have been fired for Facebook wall postings, vital company secrets have been leaked, and business and personal relationships have been strained. Unless you are sending messages through a private channel, assume that every message will be read by people far beyond your original audience.

A momentary lapse of concentration while using social media can cause tremendous career or company damage.

Social Networking and Community Participation Sites

2 **LEARNING OBJECTIVE**

Describe the use of social networks, user-generated content sites, community Q&A sites, and community participation sites in business communication.

Social networks, online services that enable individual and organizational members to form connections and share information, have become a major force in business communication. For example, Facebook is now the most-visited website on the Internet, and a number of companies, such as Adidas, Red Bull, and Starbucks, have millions of fans on their Facebook pages.[8] This section takes a look at the business communication uses of social networks and a range of related technologies, including *user-generated content (UGC) sites*, *community Q&A sites*, and *community participation sites*.

SOCIAL NETWORKS

Businesses now use several types of social networks, including public, general-purpose networks such as Facebook and Google+; public, business-oriented networks (LinkedIn is the largest of these); and a variety of specialized networks. This last group includes networks that help small-business owners get support and advice, those that connect entrepreneurs with investors, and those, such as Segway Social and Specialized, created by individual companies to enhance the sense of community among their customer bases. Some companies have built private social networks for internal use only. For example, Lockheed Martin created its Unity network, complete with a variety of social media applications, to meet the expectations of younger employees accustomed to social media and to capture the expert knowledge of older employees nearing retirement.[9]

Business communicators make use of a wide range of social networks.

BUSINESS COMMUNICATION USES OF SOCIAL NETWORKS With their ability to reach virtually unlimited numbers of people through a variety of electronic formats, social networks are a great fit for many business communication needs (see Table 7–1). In fact, a significant majority of consumers now want the businesses they patronize to use social networking for distributing information and interacting with customers—and companies that aren't active in social networking risk getting left behind.[10]

In addition to the collaboration uses discussed earlier in the text, here are some of the key business applications of social networks:

Social networks are vital tools for distributing information as well as gathering information about the business environment.

- **Gathering market intelligence.** With hundreds of millions of people expressing themselves via social media, you can be sure that smart companies are listening. For example, *sentiment analysis* is an intriguing research

Table 7–1	**Business Uses of Social Networking Technology**
Business Challenge	**Example of Social Networking in Action**
Supporting customers	Allowing customers to develop close relationships with product experts within the company
Integrating new employees	Helping new employees navigate their way through the organization, finding experts, mentors, and other important contacts
Easing the transition after reorganizations and mergers	Helping employees connect and bond after internal staff reorganizations or mergers with other organizations
Overcoming structural barriers in communication channels	Bypassing the formal communication system in order to deliver information where it is needed in a timely fashion
Assembling teams	Identifying the best people, both inside the company and in other companies, to collaborate on projects
Fostering the growth of communities	Helping people with similar—or complementary—interests and skills find each other in order to provide mutual assistance and development
Solving problems	Finding "pockets of knowledge" within the organization—the expertise and experience of individual employees
Preparing for major meetings and events	Giving participants a way to meet before an event takes place, helping to ensure that the meeting or event becomes more productive more quickly
Accelerating the evolution of teams	Accelerating the sometimes slow process of getting to know one another and identifying individual areas of expertise
Maintaining business relationships	Giving people an easy way to stay in contact after meetings and conferences
Sharing and distributing information	Making it easy for employees to share information with people who may need it and for people who need information to find employees who might have it
Finding potential customers, business partners, and employees	Identifying strong candidates by matching user profiles with current business needs and linking from existing member profiles

technique in which companies track social networks and other media with automated language-analysis software that tries to take the pulse of public opinion and identify influential opinion makers. Social media can be "an incredibly rich vein of market intelligence," says Margaret Francis, an expert in online business strategies.[11]

- **Recruiting new employees and finding business partners.** Companies use social networks to find potential employees, short-term contractors, subject-matter experts, product and service suppliers, and business partners. On LinkedIn, for example, members can recommend each other based on current or past business relationships, which helps remove the uncertainty of initiating business relationships with complete strangers.

- **Sharing product information.** Businesses don't invest time and money in social networking simply to gain fans. The ultimate goal is profitable, sustainable relationships with customers, and attracting new customers is one of the primary reasons businesses use networks and other social media.[12] However, the traditional notions of marketing and selling need to be adapted to the social networking environment because customers and potential customers don't join a network merely to be passive recipients of advertising messages. They want to participate, to connect with fellow enthusiasts, to share knowledge about products, to communicate with company insiders, and to influence the decisions that affect the products they value. This notion of interactive participation is the driving force behind **conversation marketing**, in which companies *initiate* and *facilitate* conversations in a networked community of customers and other interested parties.

Product promotion can be done on social networks, but it needs to be done in a low-key, indirect way.

• **Fostering brand communities.** Social networking is playing an important role in the rapid spread of **brand communities**, groups of people united by their interest in and ownership or use of particular products. As Figure 7–3 shows, SunRype has a substantial fan base on Facebook, giving the company the opportunity to connect with thousands of enthusiastic customers. These communities can be formal membership organizations, such as the Certified Management Accountants Group, or informal networks of people with similar interests. They can be fairly independent from the company behind the brand or can have the active support and involvement of company management.[13] A strong majority of consumers now trust their peers more than any other source of product information—including conventional advertising techniques—so formal and informal brand communities are becoming an essential information source in consumer buying decisions.[14] Continuing innovations such as Google+'s Sparks feature, which helps people connect with others with common interests, will make social networks even more important in developing brand communities.

STRATEGIES FOR BUSINESS COMMUNICATION ON SOCIAL NETWORKS
Social networks offer many communication options, but with those opportunities comes a certain degree of complexity. Moreover, the norms and practices of business social networking continue to evolve. Follow these guidelines to make the most of social networks for both personal branding and company communication:[15]

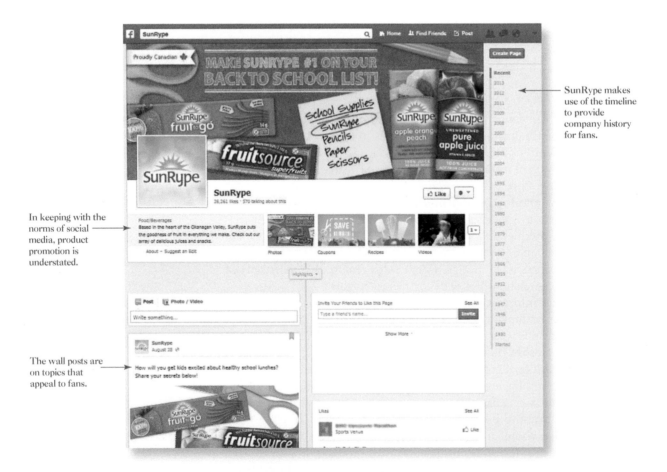

SunRype makes use of the timeline to provide company history for fans.

In keeping with the norms of social media, product promotion is understated.

The wall posts are on topics that appeal to fans.

Figure 7–3 Business Communication on Social Networks: SunRype

Courtesy Facebook

- **Choose the best compositional mode for each message, purpose, and network.** As you visit various social networks, take some time to observe the variety of message types you see in different parts of each website. For example, the informal status update mode works well for Facebook wall posts but would be less effective for company overviews and mission statements.
- **Join existing conversations, in addition to starting your own.** Search for online conversations that are already taking place. Answer questions, solve problems, and respond to rumours and misinformation.
- **Anchor your online presence in your hub.** Although it's important to join conversations and be visible where your stakeholders are active, it's equally important to anchor your presence at your own central *hub*—a web presence that you own and control. This can be a conventional website or a combination of a website, a blog, and a company-sponsored online community, for example.[16] Use the hub to connect the various "spokes" of your online presence (as an individual or a company) to better coordinate outgoing messages and to provide a clear inbound path for people who want to engage with you. As part of this, take advantage of the many automated links that are available on social media platforms. For example, you can link to your blog from your LinkedIn profile or automatically feed your blog entries onto your Facebook page.
- **Facilitate community building.** Make it easy for customers and other audiences to connect with the company and with each other. For example, you can use the group feature on Facebook, LinkedIn, and other social networks to create and foster special-interest groups within your networks. Groups are a great way to connect people who are interested in specific topics, such as owners of a particular product. Provide a "sweet spot" where your audience can land with frequent updates on topics of interest.[17]
- **Restrict conventional promotional efforts to the right time and right place.** Persuasive communication efforts are still valid for specific communication tasks, such as regular advertising and the product information pages on a website, but efforts to inject blatant "salespeak" into social networking conversations will usually be rejected by the audience.
- **Maintain a consistent personality.** Each social network is a unique environment with particular norms of communication.[18] For instance, as a business-oriented network, LinkedIn has a more formal "vibe" than Facebook. However, while adapting to the expectations of each network, be sure to maintain a consistent personality.[19] The computer giant HP uses the same (fairly formal-sounding) company overview on LinkedIn and Facebook, while its wall updates on Facebook are "chattier" and more in keeping with the tone expected by Facebook visitors.[20]
- **Manage conversational threads.** Conversations with customers and other important parties often carry over to multiple messages, involve multiple employees, and sometimes cross over multiple media as well (such as when a Twitter conversation is moved to direct messaging for privacy). With so many channels in place, companies often use systems to track these *conversational threads* so that messages aren't dropped and all parties can communicate productively.

Communicating via social networks is complicated and requires a thoughtful, well-integrated strategy.

TIPS FOR SUCCESS

"While your social network can identify potential opportunities, help you build trust in your area of expertise, and position you to stay top of mind with future clients, you can't forget that business is still done face-to-face. This means that turning your efforts into revenue for your firm will require you to move your online relationship offline."

Sarah Johnson, certified financial planner

USER-GENERATED CONTENT SITES

User-generated content (UGC) sites, where users rather than website owners contribute most or all of the content, have also become serious business tools. In fact, research suggests that video company profiles on YouTube have more measurable impact than company profiles on Facebook, LinkedIn, and other prominent sites.[21]

YouTube, now a major channel for business communicators, hosts everything from product demonstration videos to TV commercials.

Video (including *screencasts*, recordings of onscreen activity on a computer with audio narration) is a powerful medium for product demonstrations, interviews, industry news, training, facility tours, and other uses. Moreover, the business communication value of sites such as YouTube goes beyond the mere ability to deliver content. The social aspects of these sites, including the ability to vote for, comment on, and share material, encourage enthusiasts to spread the word about the companies and products they endorse.[22]

As with other social media, the keys to effective user-generated content are making it valuable and making it easy. First, provide content that people want to see and to share with colleagues. A video clip that explains how to use a product more effectively will be more popular than a clip that talks about how amazing the company behind the product is.

Creating compelling and useful content is the key to leveraging the reach of social networks.

Second, make material easy to find, consume, and share. Short (no more than 3 to 5 minutes), personalized, and interactive videos tend to grab attention and promote more frequent sharing on social media sites.[23] For example, a *branded channel* on YouTube lets a company organize all its videos in one place, making it easy for visitors to browse the selection or subscribe to get automatic updates of future videos. Sharing features let fans share videos through email or their accounts on Twitter, Facebook, and other platforms. Figure 7–4 shows how the software company Autodesk hosts its community participation site for customers who work in the fields of digital entertainment and visualization. Users can ask questions and share quick tips, advice, and ideas on how to best work with the software in video games, animations, product designs, and other creative projects. They can also read blogs written by Autodesk employees or contribute

Users can exchange best practices, seek solutions to problems, and exchange ideas.

In addition to tutorials, company employees share their expertise via blogs.

Information sharing is further encouraged by asking users to write about their real-world project experiences.

Figure 7–4 Community Participation Sites

Courtesy: Autodesk, Inc.

articles about their real-world experiences. Tutorials are available and can be sorted using an advanced search option.

COMMUNITY Q&A SITES

Community Q&A sites, where visitors answer questions posted by other visitors or by representatives of companies, are useful for routine communication such as customer support questions. Examples include dedicated customer support communities such as those hosted on Get Satisfaction (http://getsatisfaction.com), public sites such as Yahoo! Answers (http://answers.yahoo.com) and Quora (www.quora.com), and member-only sites such as LinkedIn Help Center (http://help.linkedin.com). Responding to questions on Q&A sites can be an effective way to build your personal brand, to demonstrate your company's commitment to customer service, and to counter misinformation about your company and its products.

Community Q&A sites offer great opportunities for building your personal brand.

COMMUNITY PARTICIPATION SITES

Community participation sites are designed to pool the inputs of multiple users in order to benefit the community as a whole (see Figure 7–4). These include *social bookmarking* or *content recommendation sites* such as Delicious (http://del.icio.us), Digg (www.digg.com), and StumbleUpon (www.stumbleupon.com); *group buying sites* such as Groupon (www.groupon.com); *crowdsourcing sites* such as InnoCentive (www.innocentive.com) that invite people to submit or collaborate on research challenges and product designs; and *product and service review* websites that compile reviews from people who have purchased products or patronized particular businesses.

Community participation sites pool the input of multiple users in order to benefit the community as a whole.

As one example of the way these sites are changing business communication, Yelp (www.yelp.ca) has become a major influence on consumer behaviour at a local level by aggregating millions of reviews of stores, restaurants, and other businesses in large cities across Canada and the United States.[24] With the voice of the crowd affecting consumer behaviour, businesses need to (1) focus on performing at a high level so that customers reward them with positive reviews and (2) get involved on Yelp. (The site encourages business owners to tell potential customers about themselves as well.) These efforts could pay off much more handsomely than advertising and other conventional communication efforts.

Email

Email has been a primary business communication medium for many years, although newer tools such as instant messaging (IM), blogs, microblogs, social networks, and shared workspaces are taking over specialized tasks for which they are better suited.[25] In fact, email can seem out of step in a world of instantaneous and open communication, where many users are accustomed to rapid-fire updates from Twitter, public forums on social networks, and never-ending streams of incoming information.[26]

3 **LEARNING OBJECTIVE**

Describe the evolving role of email in business communication, and explain how to adapt the three-step writing process to email messages.

However, email still has compelling advantages that will keep it in steady use in many companies, even as it evolves and becomes integrated with other electronic media. First, email is universal. Anybody with an email address can reach anybody else with an email address, no matter which systems the senders and receivers are on. You don't need to join a special group or be friended by anyone in order to correspond. Second, email is still the best medium for many private, short- to medium-length messages. Unlike with microblogs

Email can seem a bit "old school" in comparison to social networks and other technologies, but it is still one of the more important business communication media.

and IM, for instance, mid-size messages are easy to compose and easy to read on email. Third, email's noninstantaneous nature is an advantage when used properly. Many business messages don't need the rapid update rates of IM or Twitter, and the implied urgency of those systems can be a productivity-sapping interruption. Email allows senders to compose substantial messages in private and on their own schedule, and it allows recipients to read those messages at their leisure.

PLANNING EMAIL MESSAGES

The biggest complaints about email are that there is just too much of it and that too many messages are of little or no value. You can help with this problem during the planning step by making sure every message has a useful, business-related purpose.

Be aware that many companies now have formal email policies that specify how employees can use email, including restrictions against using company email service for personal messages and sending material that might be deemed objectionable. In addition, many employers now monitor email, either automatically with software programmed to look for sensitive content or manually via security staff actually reading selected email messages. Regardless of formal policies, though, every email user has a responsibility to avoid actions that could cause trouble, from downloading virus-infected software to sending inappropriate photographs. *Email hygiene* refers to all the efforts that companies are making to keep email clean and safe—from spam blocking and virus protection to content filtering.[27]

Finally, be sure to respect the chain of command. In many companies, any employee can email anyone else, including the president and CEO. However, take care that you don't abuse this freedom. For instance, don't send a complaint straight to the top just because it's easy to do so. Your efforts will be more effective if you follow the organizational hierarchy and give each person a chance to address the situation in turn.

WRITING EMAIL MESSAGES

Business email is a more formal medium than you are probably accustomed to with email for personal communication (see Figure 7–5, which shows an efficient email). The expectations of writing quality for business email are higher than for personal email, and the consequences of bad writing or poor judgment can be much more serious. For example, email messages and other electronic documents have the same legal weight as printed documents, and they are often used as evidence in lawsuits and criminal investigations.[28]

Follow these tips for effective email messages:

- **Give your messages a single purpose.** Effective emails avoid confusing readers with several purposes. Don't ask your reader to attend a meeting and also congratulate her on surpassing her sales quota in the same email; develop each purpose in separate messages.[29]
- **Make your subject line informative.** The email subject line is one of the most important parts of an email message because it helps recipients decide which messages to read and when to read them. To capture your audience's attention, make your subject lines informative and compelling. Go beyond simply describing or classifying your message; use the opportunity to build interest with keywords, quotations, directions, or questions.[30] For example, "July sales results" accurately describes the content of the message, but "July sales results: good news and bad news"

Avoid sending unnecessary messages or "cc"-ing people who don't really need to see particular messages.

Email presents considerable legal hazards, and many companies have formal email policies.

Respect the chain of command in your company when sending email messages.

Business email messages are more formal than the email messages you send to family and friends.

A poorly written subject line could lead to a message being deleted or ignored.

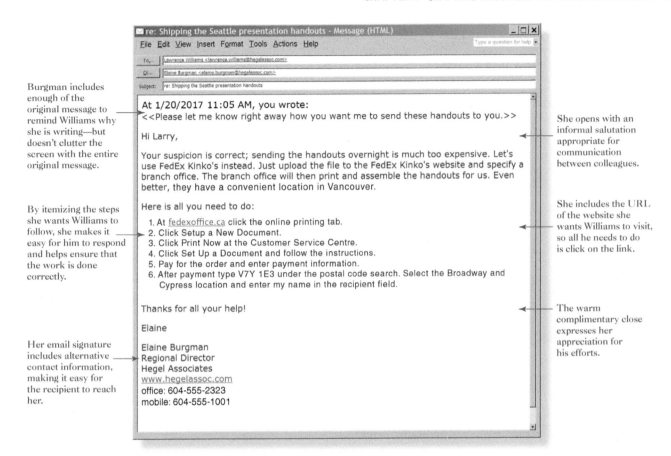

Burgman includes enough of the original message to remind Williams why she is writing—but doesn't clutter the screen with the entire original message.

By itemizing the steps she wants Williams to follow, she makes it easy for him to respond and helps ensure that the work is done correctly.

Her email signature includes alternative contact information, making it easy for the recipient to reach her.

She opens with an informal salutation appropriate for communication between colleagues.

She includes the URL of the website she wants Williams to visit, so all he needs to do is click on the link.

The warm complimentary close expresses her appreciation for his efforts.

Figure 7–5 Email for Business Communication

is more intriguing. Readers will want to know why some news is good and some is bad.

Also, if you and someone else are replying back and forth based on the same original message, periodically modify the subject line of your message to reflect the revised message content. When numerous messages have identical subject lines, trying to find a particular one can be confusing and frustrating. For instance, if you come up with a solution to the scheduling problem on the website redesign project, modify the subject line to read something like "Website redesign: staffing solution" so that people can find that specific message when they need to.

- **Phrase the introduction carefully.** Many email programs display the first few words or lines of incoming messages, even before the recipient opens them. As noted by social media public relations expert Steve Rubel, you can "tweetify" the opening lines of your email messages to make them stand out. In other words, choose the first few words carefully to grab your reader's attention.[31]

- **Make your email easy to follow.** Paragraph length, topic sentences, headings and lists, and white space will ensure your message is read. Write short, focused, logically organized paragraphs, and use topic sentences at the beginning of each paragraph to make your email easy to follow. Skip two lines between paragraphs so that each paragraph stands out. By using bulleted or numbered lists (use a hyphen if your reader's email system will not accept graphic bullets), you will also improve the readability of your message. Insert headings for lengthy emails (use capital letters so that headings are distinct) at the top of main sections to make your text easy to review.[32]

COMPLETING EMAIL MESSAGES

Particularly for important messages, taking a few moments to revise and proofread might save you hours of headaches and damage control. The more important the message, the more carefully you need to proof. Also, favour simplicity when it comes to producing your email messages. A clean, easily readable font, in black on a white background, is sufficient for nearly all email messages. Take advantage of your email system's ability to include an **email signature**, a small file that automatically includes such items as your full name, title, company, and contact information at the end of your messages.

When you're ready to distribute your message, pause to verify what you're doing before you click "Send." Make sure you've included everyone necessary—and no one else. Don't click "Reply All" when you mean to click only "Reply." The difference could be embarrassing or even career threatening. Don't include people in the "cc" (courtesy copy) or "bcc" (blind courtesy copy) fields unless you know how these features work. (Everyone who receives the message can see who is on the cc line but not who is on the bcc line.) Also, don't set the message priority to "high" or "urgent" unless your message is truly urgent. And if you intend to include an attachment, be sure that it is indeed attached.

To review the tips and techniques for successful email, see Table 7–2 and "Checklist: Creating Effective Email Messages."

Think twice before hitting "Send." A simple mistake in your content or distribution can cause major headaches.

Table 7–2	**Tips for Effective Email Messages**
Tip	**Why It's Important**
When you request information or action, make it clear what you're asking for, why it's important, and how soon you need it; don't make your reader write back for details.	People will be tempted to ignore your messages if they're not clear about what you want or how soon you want it.
When responding to a request, either paraphrase the request or include enough of the original message to remind the reader what you're replying to.	Some businesspeople get hundreds of email messages a day and may need to be reminded what your specific response is about.
If possible, avoid sending long, complex messages via email.	Long messages are easier to read as printed reports or web content.
Adjust the level of formality to the message and the audience.	Overly formal messages to colleagues are perceived as stuffy and distant; overly informal messages to customers or top executives are perceived as disrespectful.
Activate a signature file, which automatically pastes your contact information into every message you create.	You save the trouble of retyping vital information and ensure that recipients know how to reach you through other means.
Don't let unread messages pile up in your in-basket.	You'll miss important information and create the impression that you're ignoring other people.
Never type in all caps.	ALL CAPS ARE INTERPRETED AS SHOUTING.
Don't overformat your messages with background colours, coloured type, unusual fonts, and so on.	Such messages can be difficult and annoying to read onscreen, or they might appear as a scrambled message on the screen of the receiver.
Remember that messages can be forwarded anywhere and saved forever.	Don't let a moment of anger or poor judgment haunt you for the rest of your career.
Use the "return receipt requested" feature only for the most critical messages.	This feature triggers a message back to you whenever someone receives or opens your message; many consider this an invasion of privacy.
Make sure your computer has up-to-date virus protection.	One of the worst breaches of "netiquette" is unknowingly infecting other computers because you haven't bothered to protect your own system.
Pay attention to grammar, spelling, and capitalization.	Some people don't think email needs formal rules, but careless messages make you look unprofessional and can annoy readers.
Use acronyms sparingly.	Shorthand such as IMHO (in my humble opinion) and LOL (laughing out loud) can be useful in informal correspondence with colleagues, but don't use them in formal messages.

✓ Checklist   Creating Effective Email Messages

A. Plan email messages.
- Make sure every email message you send is necessary.
- Follow company email policy; understand the restrictions your company places on email usage.
- Practise good email hygiene by not opening suspicious messages, keeping virus protection up to date, and following other company guidelines.
- Follow the chain of command.

B. Write email messages.
- Remember that business email is more formal than personal email.
- Recognize that email messages carry the same legal weight as other business documents.
- Pay attention to the quality of your writing, and use correct grammar, spelling, and punctuation.
- Make your subject lines informative by clearly identifying the purpose of your message.
- Give messages a single purpose, and make your subject lines compelling by wording them in a way that intrigues your audiences.

- Use the first few words of the email body to catch the reader's attention (e.g., keywords, quotations, directions, questions).
- Use effective formatting, including headings to break up lengthy content, to make your email easy to follow.

C. Complete email messages.
- Revise and proofread carefully to avoid embarrassing mistakes.
- Keep the layout of your messages simple and clean.
- Use an email signature file to give recipients your contact information.
- Double-check your recipient list before sending.
- Don't cc or bcc anyone who doesn't really need to see the message.
- Don't mark messages as "urgent" unless they truly are urgent.
- When sending messages back and forth, periodically modify the subject line to reflect revised message content.

Instant Messaging and Text Messaging

Computer-based **instant messaging (IM)**, in which users' messages appear on each other's screens instantly, is used extensively for internal and external communication. IM is available in both stand-alone systems and as a function embedded in groupware, collaboration systems, social networks, and other platforms.

Phone-based **text messaging** (sometimes known as *short messaging service* or *SMS*) has many applications in business, including marketing (alerting customers about new sale prices, for example), customer service (such as airline flight status, order status, package tracking, and appointment reminders), security (for example, authenticating mobile banking transactions), crisis management (such as updating all employees working at a disaster scene), and process monitoring (alerting computer technicians to system failures, for example).[33] As it becomes more tightly integrated with other communication media, text messaging is likely to find even more widespread use in business communication. For example, texting is now integrated into systems such as Facebook Messages and Gmail, and branded "StarStar numbers" can deliver web-based content such as videos, software apps, and electronic coupons to mobile phones.[34]

The advice offered in this section applies primarily to IM but is relevant to text messaging as well.

4   LEARNING OBJECTIVE

Describe the business benefits of instant messaging (IM), and identify guidelines for effective IM in the workplace.

UNDERSTANDING THE BENEFITS AND RISKS OF IM

The benefits of IM include rapid response to urgent messages, lower cost than phone calls, ability to mimic conversation more closely than email, and availability on a wide range of devices and systems.[35] In addition, because it more closely resembles one-on-one conversation, IM doesn't get misused as a one-to-many broadcast method as often as email does.[36]

IM offers many benefits:
- Rapid response
- Low cost
- Ability to mimic conversation
- Wide availability

The potential drawbacks of IM include security problems (computer viruses, network infiltration, and the possibility that sensitive messages might be intercepted by outsiders), the need for *user authentication* (making sure that online correspondents are really who they appear to be), the challenge of logging messages for later review and archiving (a legal requirement in some industries), incompatibility between competing IM systems, and *spim* (unsolicited commercial messages, similar to email spam). Fortunately, with the growth of *enterprise instant messaging* (*EIM*), or IM systems designed for large-scale corporate use, many of these problems are being overcome.

ADAPTING THE THREE-STEP PROCESS FOR SUCCESSFUL IM

Although instant messages are often conceived, written, and sent within a matter of seconds, the principles of the three-step process still apply:

View every IM exchange as a conversation with a specific goal in mind.

- **Planning instant messages.** View every IM exchange as a conversation; while you may not deliberately plan every individual statement you make or question you pose, take a moment to plan the overall exchange. If you're requesting something, think through exactly what you need and the most effective way to ask for it. If someone is asking you for something, consider his or her needs and your ability to meet them before you respond. And although you rarely need to organize instant messages in the sense of creating an outline, try to deliver information in a coherent, complete way that minimizes the number of individual messages required.
- **Writing instant messages.** As with email, the appropriate writing style for business IM is more formal than the style you may be accustomed to with personal IM or text messaging. You should generally avoid IM acronyms (such as *FWIW* for "for what it's worth" or *HTH* for "hope that helps") except when communicating with close colleagues. In the IM exchange in Figure 7–6,

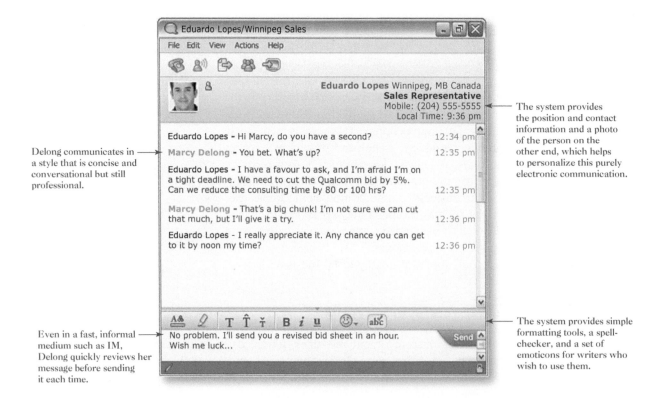

Delong communicates in a style that is concise and conversational but still professional.

Even in a fast, informal medium such as IM, Delong quickly reviews her message before sending it each time.

The system provides the position and contact information and a photo of the person on the other end, which helps to personalize this purely electronic communication.

The system provides simple formatting tools, a spell-checker, and a set of emoticons for writers who wish to use them.

Figure 7–6 Instant Messaging for Business Communication

notice how the participants communicate quickly and rather informally but still maintain good etiquette and a professional tone. This style is even more important if you or your staff use IM to communicate with customers and other outside audiences.

- **Completing instant messages.** One of the biggest attractions of IM is that the completing step is so easy. You don't have to produce the message in the usual sense, and distribution is as simple as hitting "Enter" or clicking a "Send" button. However, don't skip over the revising and proofreading tasks. Quickly scan each message before you send it, to make sure you don't have any missing or misspelled words and that your message is clear and complete.

Regardless of the system you're using, you can make IM more efficient and effective by following these tips:[37]

- Unless an IM conversation or meeting is scheduled, make yourself unavailable when you need to focus on other work.

Understand the guidelines for successful business IM before you begin to use it.

- If you're not on a secure system, don't send confidential information.
- Be extremely careful about sending personal messages—they have a tendency to pop up on other people's computers at embarrassing moments.
- Don't use IM for important but impromptu meetings if you can't verify that everyone concerned will be available.
- Unless your system is set up for it, don't use IM for lengthy, complex messages; email is better for those.
- Try to avoid carrying on multiple IM conversations at once, to minimize the chance of sending messages to the wrong people or making one person wait while you tend to another conversation.
- Follow all security guidelines designed to keep your company's information and systems safe from attack.

To review the advice for effective IM in the workplace, see "Checklist: Using IM Productively."

✓ Checklist   Using IM Productively

- Pay attention to security and privacy issues, and be sure to follow all company guidelines.
- Treat IM as a professional communication medium, not an informal, personal tool; avoid using IM slang with all but close colleagues.
- Maintain good etiquette, even during simple exchanges.

- Protect your own productivity by making yourself unavailable when you need to focus.
- In most instances, don't use IM for confidential messages, complex messages, or personal messages.
- Review messages before sending them.
- Avoid multiple IM conversations in order to minimize sending messages to the wrong person or causing unnecessary delays in response.

Blogging and Microblogging

A **blog** (short for *weblog*) is an easily updatable online journal that can combine the global reach and reference value of a conventional website with the conversational exchanges of email or IM. Blogging first began to catch on in business communication because blogs provided a much easier way for senders to update and distribute fresh content and for receivers to get new information automatically (through *feeds* or *newsfeeds*, of which *RSS* is the best known). Blogging also began to take on a more personal and informal tone than regular business websites, helping to "put a human face" on companies

5 **LEARNING OBJECTIVE**

Describe the role of blogging and microblogging in business communication today, and explain how to adapt the three-step writing process to blogging.

Blogs combine the global reach and value of a website with the conversational exchanges of email or IM.

and increase the lines of communication between experts and executives on the inside and customers and other stakeholders on the outside. Another important role that blogging has acquired is making individuals and companies easier to find through search engines.[38] With all these benefits, blogs are now a common tool in business communication, and many companies have multiple bloggers, writing either as a team on an individual blog (as with Petro-Canada) or on their own blogs.

Good business bloggers pay close attention to several important elements:

- **Communicating with personal style and an authentic voice.** Traditional business messages designed for large audiences tend to be carefully scripted and written in a "corporate voice" that is impersonal and objective. In contrast, successful business blogs such as Petro-Canada's are written by individuals

Table 7–3	Tips for Effective Business Blogging
Tip	**Why It's Important**
Don't blog without a clear plan.	Without a clear plan, your blog is likely to wander from topic to topic and fail to build a sense of community with your audience.
Post frequently; the whole point of a blog is fresh material.	If you won't have a constant supply of new information or new links, create a traditional website instead.
Make it about your audience and the issues that are important to them.	Readers want to know how your blog will help them, entertain them, or give them a chance to communicate with others who have similar interests.
Write in an authentic voice; never create an artificial character who supposedly writes a blog.	*Flogs*, or fake blogs, violate the spirit of blogging, show disrespect for your audience, and will turn audiences against you as soon as they uncover the truth. Fake blogs used to promote products are now illegal in some countries.
Link generously—but carefully.	Providing interesting links to other blogs and websites is a fundamental aspect of blogging, but make sure the links will be of value to your readers and don't point to inappropriate material.
Keep it brief.	Most online readers don't have the patience to read lengthy reports. Rather than writing long, report-style posts, write brief posts that link to in-depth reports on your website.
Don't post anything you wouldn't want the entire world to see.	Future employers, government regulators, competitors, journalists, and community critics are just a few of the people who might eventually see what you've written.
Don't engage in blatant product promotion.	Readers who think they're being advertised to will stop reading.
Take time to write compelling, specific headlines for your postings.	Readers usually decide within a couple of seconds whether to read your postings; boring or vague headlines will turn them away instantly.
Pay attention to spelling, grammar, and mechanics.	No matter how smart or experienced you are, poor-quality writing undermines your credibility with intelligent audiences.
Respond to criticism openly and honestly.	Hiding sends the message that you don't have a valid response to the criticism. If your critics are wrong, patiently explain why you think they're wrong. If they are right, explain how you'll fix the situation.
Listen and learn.	If you don't take the time to analyze the comments people leave on your blog or the comments other bloggers make about you, you're missing out on one of the most valuable aspects of blogging.
Respect intellectual property.	Improperly using material you don't own is not only unethical but can be illegal as well.
Be scrupulously honest and careful with facts.	Honesty is an absolute requirement for every ethical business communicator, of course, but you need to be extra careful online because inaccuracies (both intentional and unintentional) are likely to be discovered quickly and shared widely.
If you review products on your blog, disclose any beneficial relationships you have with the companies that make those products.	Bloggers who receive free products or other compensation from companies whose products they write about are now required to disclose the nature of these relationships.

and exhibit their personal style. Audiences relate to this fresh approach and often build closer emotional bonds with the blogger's organization as a result.

- **Delivering new information quickly.** The ability to post new material as soon as you create it helps you to respond quickly when needed (such as during a crisis), and it lets your audiences know that an active conversation is taking place.
- **Choosing topics of peak interest to audiences.** Successful blogs cover topics that readers care about, and they emphasize useful information while downplaying product promotion.[39] These topics don't need to be earth shaking or cutting edge—they just need to be things that matter to target readers. For instance, a pair of researchers at Clorox blog for the company under the name "Dr. Laundry," dispensing helpful advice on removing stains and tackling other household chores.[40]
- **Encouraging audiences to join the conversation.** Not all blogs invite comments, although most do. These comments can be a valuable source of news, information, and insights. In addition, the relatively informal nature of blogging seems to make it easier for company representatives to let their guards down and converse with their audiences. Of course, not all comments are helpful or appropriate, which is why many bloggers *moderate* comments, previewing them before allowing them to be displayed.

Most business blogs invite readers to leave comments as a way to encourage participation among stakeholders.

Table 7–3 offers a number of specific suggestions for successful business blogging.

UNDERSTANDING THE BUSINESS APPLICATIONS OF BLOGGING

Blogs are a potential solution whenever you have a continuing stream of information to share with an online audience—and particularly when you want the audience to have the opportunity to respond. Here are some of the many ways businesses are using blogs:[41]

- **Anchoring the social media presence.** The multiple threads of any social media program should be anchored in a central hub that the company or individual owns and controls. Blogs make an ideal social media hub.
- **Project management and team communication.** Using blogs is a good way to keep project teams up to date, particularly when team members are geographically dispersed. For instance, the trip reports that employees file after visiting customers or other external parties can be enhanced vividly with *mobile blogs*, or *moblogs*.
- **Internal company news.** Companies can use blogs to keep employees informed about general business matters, from facility news to benefit updates. By reducing the need for grapevines to spring up, blogs can enhance communication across all levels of a company.
- **Customer support.** Customer support blogs answer questions, offer tips and advice, and inform customers about new products.
- **Public relations and media relations.** Many company employees and executives now share company news with both the general public and journalists via their blogs.
- **Recruiting.** Using a blog is a very effective way to let potential employees know more about your company, the people who work there, and the nature of the company culture, as shown in GE's Twitter recruiting feed (see Figure 7–7). Conversely, companies can scan blogs and microblogs to find promising candidates.
- **Policy and issue discussions.** Executive blogs in particular provide a public forum for discussing legislation, regulations, and other broad issues of interest to an organization.

The business applications of blogs include a wide range of internal and external communication tasks.

GE uses the background image on its Twitter page to provide a small amount of customized information (in this case, the list of GE divisions whose job openings are posted via this Twitter account).

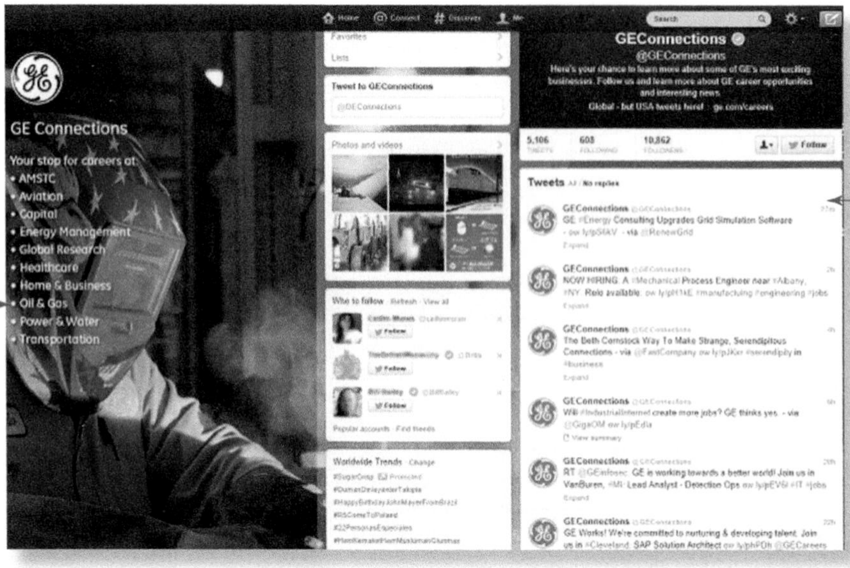

Note that this Twitter account allows visitors to find information by searching for or monitoring hashtag terms.

Figure 7–7 Recruiting on Twitter

Courtesy General Electric, Inc.

- **Crisis communication.** Using blogs is an efficient way to provide up-to-the-minute information during emergencies, correct misinformation, or respond to rumours.
- **Market research.** Blogs can be a clever mechanism for soliciting feedback from customers and experts in the marketplace. In addition to using its own blogs for research, every company needs to monitor blogs that are likely to discuss its operations, executives, and products. Negative product reviews, rumours, and other information can spread across the globe in a matter of hours, and managers need to know what the online community is saying—whether it's positive or negative. *Reputation analysts* such as Evolve24 (www .evolve24.com) have developed ways to automatically monitor blogs and other online sources to see what people are saying about their corporate clients and evaluate risks and opportunities in the global online conversation.[42]
- **Brainstorming.** Online brainstorming via blogs offers a way for people to toss around ideas and build on one another's contributions.
- **Word-of-mouth marketing.** Bloggers and microbloggers often make a point of providing links to other blogs and websites that interest them, giving marketers a great opportunity to have their messages spread by enthusiasts. (Word-of-mouth marketing is often called *viral marketing* in reference to the transmission of messages in much the same way that biological viruses are transmitted from person to person. However, viral marketing is not really an accurate metaphor. As industry analyst and blogger Brian Solis puts it, "There is no such thing as viral marketing."[43] Real viruses spread from host to host on their own, whereas word-of-mouth marketing spreads *voluntarily* from person to person. The distinction is critical, because you need to give people a good reason—good content, in other words—to pass along your message.)
- **Influencing traditional media news coverage.** According to social media consultant Tamar Weinberg, "the more prolific bloggers who provide valuable and consistent content are often considered experts in their subject matter" and are often called upon when journalists need insights into various topics.[44]
- **Community building.** Blogging is a great way to connect people with similar interests, and popular bloggers often attract a community of readers who connect with one another through the commenting function.

BUSINESS COMMUNICATION 2.0 — Let Social Media Work for You

Social media tools continue to evolve and offer more than ways to post family reunion photos, keep current with friends, or follow your favourite celebrity or cause. They have become an integral part of doing business (business to business [B2B] and business to consumer [B2C]) and opened alternate and potentially efficient channels to network, connect with customers and colleagues, and stay up to date with global events.

However, if we don't pay attention, the time spent perusing and communicating on social networks and the information that we share or like can actually become a source of stress and anxiety and detract us from achieving our goals.

Here are a few ideas for getting social media to work for you as a business professional:

- **Inform yourself about your company's social media policies.** Many businesses have guidelines on how they would like their employees to engage with social media. These guidelines explain business and legal implications.
- **Keep business and personal communications separate.** Don't send personal messages via company email or IM systems. Don't store any personal data (photos or other files) on company electronic devices. Watch what you post on your social media networks. Keep current on privacy tools. Privacy settings are not always "private"; by being aware of this you can avoid potentially embarrassing situations or liability issues.

- **Don't download or share questionable content, (e.g., videos or photos).** The content you download and share reflects on you as a professional. Perceptions of you are influenced by what you share. Furthermore, companies are liable for any digital content that is saved and transmitted. As well, you risk inviting viruses and phishing schemes.
- **Look for popular blogs within your industry to identify best practices, and contribute to the content there.** Check your company guidelines regarding sharing and web contributions. Be respectful when providing your viewpoint. Contribute regularly, but keep your message current and consistent across networks.
- **Manage the information that is coming to you via social media updates.** Determine the type of information you will need in order to achieve your goals, whether they relate to a project or to moving along your career path. Don't be distracted by "edu-tainment." Review your sources regularly to see if they are still relevant. To avoid information overload, eliminate those sources that are no longer useful.

CAREER APPLICATIONS

1. Is sending personal messages via company email a good idea? Explain.
2. How can you determine whether a social media source is worth paying attention to?

Emily Bennington, "Social Media in the Workplace: Setting Standards," Monster, https://hiring.monster.com/hr/hr-best-practices/small-business/social-media-trends/employee-social-media-policy.aspx; Government of Canada, "Official Use of Social Media, Guideline On," March 4, 2014, https://www.tbs-sct.gc.ca/pol/doc-eng.aspx?id=27517; Jennifer Bond and George Waggott, "Social Media Policies in the Workplace: What Works Best?", The Canadian Bar Association, September 24, 2014, http://www.cba.org/Publications-Resources/CBA-Practice-Link/2015/2014/Social-media-policies-in-the-workplace-What-works; Travis Balinas, "Social Media Etiquette for Business: 25 Do's and Don'ts, OutboundEngine, February 1, 2017, https://www.outboundengine.com/blog/social-media-etiquette-for-business-25-dos-donts/; and Your Workplace Staff, "The Do's and Don'ts of Social Media," Your Workplace, September 15, 2003, http://www.yourworkplace.ca/the-dos-and-donts-of-social-media/3/.

The possibilities of blogs are almost unlimited, so be on the lookout for new ways to use them to foster positive relationships with colleagues, customers, and other important audiences.

ADAPTING THE THREE-STEP PROCESS FOR SUCCESSFUL BLOGGING

The three-step writing process is easy to adapt to blogging tasks. The planning step is particularly important if you're considering starting a blog, because you're planning an entire communication channel, not just a single message. Pay close attention to your audience, your purpose, and your scope:

- **Audience.** Defining the target audience for a blog can be challenging. You want an audience large enough to justify the time you'll be investing but narrow enough that you can meet readers' needs and not try to be all things to all people.
- **Purpose.** A business blog needs to have a business-related purpose that is important to your company and to your chosen audience. Tammy Beltrami, owner of Aria Boutique clothing store, uses her blog and a variety of other

Before you launch a blog, have a clear understanding of your target audience, the purpose of your blog, and the scope of subjects you plan to cover.

social media tools to build a sense of community among her customers and to promote the store in a way that is compelling without being obtrusive (see Figure 7–8). Moreover, the purpose has to "have legs"—that is, it needs to be something that can drive the blog's content for months or years. For instance, if you're a technical expert, you might create a blog to give the audience tips and techniques for using your company's products more effectively—a never-ending subject that's important to both you and your audience. This would be the general purpose of your blog; each posting would have a specific purpose within the context of that general purpose. Including links to relevant business and industry blogs is another way to provide information that is important to your audience. Finally, whether you are writing on a company blog or your own personal blog, make sure you understand your employer's blogging guidelines.[45]

- **Scope.** Defining the scope of your blog can be a bit tricky. You want to cover a subject area that is broad enough to offer discussion possibilities for months or years but narrow enough to have an identifiable focus.

Write blog postings in a comfortable—but not careless—style.

Use a comfortable, personal writing style in your blog. Blog audiences don't want to hear from your company; they want to hear from *you*. Bear in mind, though, that comfortable does not mean careless. Sloppy writing damages your credibility. Successful blog content also needs to be interesting, valuable to readers, and as brief as possible.[46] In addition, although audiences expect you to be knowledgeable in the subject area your blog covers, you don't need to know everything about a topic. If you don't have all the information yourself, provide

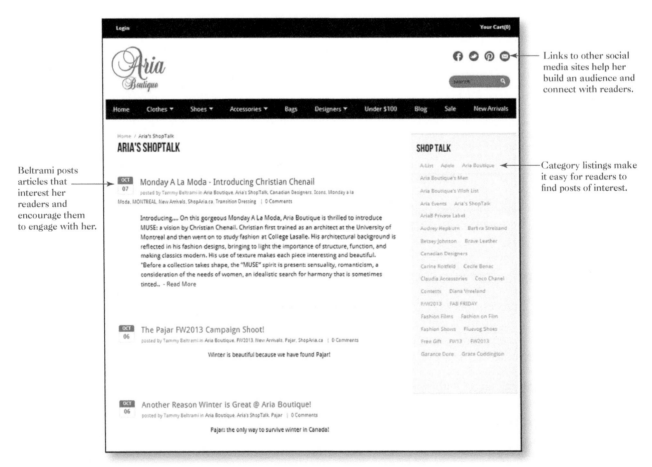

Figure 7–8 Elements of an Effective Business Blog

Courtesy: Aria Boutique

links to other blogs and websites that supply relevant information. In fact, *media curation*, selecting content that will be useful and interesting to your target audience, in much the same way that museum curators decide which pieces of art to display, is one of the most valuable aspects of blogging.

As with email subject lines, compelling headlines for blog posts are an essential tool to draw in readers. A headline needs to grab the reader's attention in a split second by promising something useful, surprising, challenging, or otherwise different from what the reader already knows. Headlines should be as short as possible and suggest that the information in the post will be easy to read and use. "List" headlines that cut right to the heart of something readers care about, such as "10 Reasons You Didn't Get that Promotion" or "Seven Ways to Save Money with Your Smartphone," are particularly popular among bloggers.

Completing messages for your blog is usually quite easy. Evaluate the content and readability of your message, proofread to correct any errors, and post using your blogging system's tools. Be sure to include one or more *newsfeed options* (often called *RSS newsfeeds*) so that your audience can automatically receive headlines and summaries of new blog posts. Whatever blogging system you are using can provide guidance on setting up newsfeeds. Make your material easier to find by **tagging** it with descriptive words. Visitors to your blog who want to read everything you've written about recruiting just click on that word to see all your posts on that subject. Tagging can also help audiences locate your posts on social bookmarking sites. Monitor traffic to your blog and use tools such as Google Analytics to identify which sources generate conversations.[47]

MICROBLOGGING

A **microblog** is a variation on blogging in which messages are restricted to specific character counts. Twitter (http://twitter.com) is the best known of these systems, but many others exist. Some companies have private microblogging systems for internal use only; these systems are sometimes referred to as *enterprise microblogging* or *internal micromessaging*.[48]

Many of the concepts of regular blogging apply to microblogging as well, although the severe length limitations call for a different approach to composition. The current limit on Twitter, for instance, is 140 characters, including spaces, and if you include a URL, the limit for the rest of the message is 120 characters.

Microblog messages often involve short summaries or teasers that provide links to more information. In fact, Twitter updates are frequently used to announce or promote new posts on regular blogs. In addition, microblogs tend to have a stronger social networking aspect that makes it easier for writers and readers to forward messages and for communities to form around individual writers.[49]

Like regular blogging, microblogging quickly caught on with business users and is now a mainstream business medium. Microblogs are used for virtually all of the blog applications mentioned earlier. In addition, microblogs are frequently used for providing company updates, offering coupons and notice of sales, presenting tips on product usage, sharing relevant and interesting information from experts, serving as the backchannel in meetings and presentations, and interacting with customers individually. For example, outdoor clothing and equipment supplier Patagonia uses Twitter both as a general communication tool and as a way to interact with their customers one-to-one. Like many companies they respond to customer queries and complaints posted on Twitter. They also retweet topics important to their customers which provides value and builds a community based on shared interests.

As microblogging evolves, the technology is gaining features that continue to enhance its value as a business communication medium. On Twitter, for instance, users have adopted the *hashtag* (the # symbol followed by a unique term) to help readers track topics of interest. For example, to establish a backchannel for a conference, you can create a unique hashtag (such as #WBSDCC, the hashtag used by Warner Brothers during a recent San Diego Comic-Con[50]) to help people follow messages on a particular subject. *Retweeting*, the practice of forwarding messages from other Twitter users, is the microblogging equivalent of sharing content from other bloggers via media curation.

Finally, keep in mind that Twitter is a publishing platform. Unless you set your account to private, anyone can see and search for your tweets—and every public tweet from every Twitter user is being archived by the U.S. Library of Congress.[51]

"Checklist: Blogging for Business" summarizes some of the key points to remember when creating and writing a business blog.

✔ Checklist | **Blogging for Business**

- Consider creating a blog or microblog account whenever you have a continuing stream of information to share with an online audience.
- Identify an audience that is broad enough to justify the effort but narrow enough to have common interests.
- Identify a purpose that is comprehensive enough to provide ideas for a continuing stream of posts.
- Consider the scope of your blog carefully; make it broad enough to attract an audience but narrow enough to keep you focused.
- Include links to relevant business and industry blogs.

- Communicate with a personal style and an authentic voice but don't write carelessly.
- Deliver new information quickly and regularly.
- Choose topics of peak interest to your audience.
- Encourage audiences to join the conversation.
- Consider using Twitter or other microblog updates to alert readers to new posts on your regular blog.
- Make your material easier to find by tagging it with descriptive words.
- Monitor traffic to your blog regularly and analyze reader behaviour and preferences.

Podcasting

6 LEARNING OBJECTIVE

Explain how to adapt the three-step writing process to podcasting.

Podcasting is the process of recording audio or video files and distributing them online. Although podcasting is not used as widely as blogging and some other electronic media, it does offer a number of interesting possibilities for business communication.

UNDERSTANDING THE BUSINESS APPLICATIONS OF PODCASTING

Podcasting can be used to deliver a wide range of audio and video messages.

The most obvious use of podcasting is to replace existing audio and video messages, such as one-way teleconferences in which a speaker provides information without expecting to engage in conversation with the listeners. Training is another good use of podcasting; you may have already taken a course via podcasts. Marketing departments can replace expensive printed brochures with video podcasts that demonstrate new products in action. Sales representatives who travel to meet with potential customers can listen to audio podcasts or view video podcasts to get the latest information on their companies' products. Human resources departments can offer video tours of their companies to entice new recruits. Podcasts are also an increasingly common feature on blogs, letting audiences listen to or watch recordings of their favourite bloggers. Some services can even transcribe blogs into podcasts and vice versa.[52]

ADAPTING THE THREE-STEP PROCESS
FOR SUCCESSFUL PODCASTING

Although it might not seem obvious at first, the three-step writing process adapts quite nicely to podcasting. First, focus the planning step on analyzing the situation, gathering the information you'll need, and organizing your material. One vital planning step depends on whether you intend to create podcasts for limited use and distribution (such as a weekly audio update to your virtual team) or a **podcasting channel** with regular recordings on a consistent theme designed for a wider public audience. As with planning a blog, if you intend to create a podcasting channel, be sure to think through the range of topics you want to address over time to verify that you have a sustainable purpose.[53]

The three-step process adapts quite well to podcasting.

As you organize the content for a podcast, pay close attention to previews, transitions, and reviews. These steering devices are especially vital in audio recordings because audio lacks the headings and other elements that audiences rely on in print media. Moreover, scanning back and forth to find specific parts of an audio or video message is much more difficult than with textual messages, so you need to do everything possible to make sure your audience successfully receives and interprets your message on the first try.

Steering devices such as transitions, previews, and reviews are vital in podcasts.

One of the attractions of podcasting is the conversational, person-to-person feel of the recordings, so unless you need to capture exact wording, speaking from an outline and notes rather than a prepared script is often the best choice. However, no one wants to listen to rambling podcasts that take several minutes to get to the topic or struggle to make a point, so don't try to make up your content on the fly. Effective podcasts, like effective stories, have a clear beginning, middle, and end.

Plan your podcast content carefully; editing is more difficult with podcasts than with textual messages.

The completing step is where podcasting differs most dramatically from written communication, for the obvious reason that you are recording and distributing audio or video files. Particularly for more formal podcasts, start by revising your script or thinking through your speaking notes before you begin to record. Also, think about the language and images of your content. The closer you can get to recording your podcasts in one take, the more productive you'll be, because editing audio is more time consuming than editing text.

Figure 7–9 illustrates the basic process of recording and distributing podcasts, but the process can vary depending on such factors as the production quality you need to achieve and whether you plan to record in a studio setting or on the go (using a mobile phone or digital recorder to capture your voice).

Most personal computers, smartphones, and other devices now have basic audio recording capability, including built-in microphones, and free editing software is available online (at http://audacity.sourceforge.net, for example). If you need higher production quality or greater flexibility, you'll need additional pieces of hardware and software, such as an audio processor (to filter out extraneous noise and otherwise improve the audio signal), a mixer (to combine multiple audio or video signals), a better microphone, more sophisticated recording and editing software, and perhaps some physical improvements in your recording

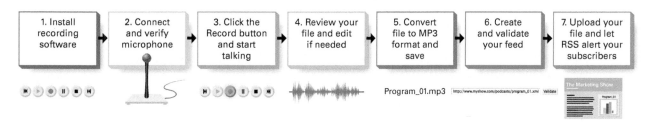

Figure 7–9 The Podcasting Process

location to improve the acoustics. You can find more information at Podcast Alley (www.podcastalley.com/forum).

Podcasts can be distributed in several ways, including through media stores such as iTunes, by dedicated podcast hosting services, or on a blog with content that supports the podcast channel. If you distribute your podcast on a blog, you can provide additional information and use the commenting feature of the blog to encourage feedback from your audience.[54]

For a quick review of the key points of business podcasting, see "Checklist: Planning and Producing Business Podcasts."

✓ Checklist   Planning and Producing Business Podcasts

- Consider podcasting whenever you have the opportunity to replace existing audio or video messages.
- If you plan a podcast channel with a regular stream of new content, make sure you've identified a theme or purpose that is rich enough to sustain your effort.
- Pay close attention to previews, transitions, and reviews to help prevent your audience from getting lost.

- Decide whether you want to improvise or speak from a written script.
- If you improvise, do enough planning and organization to avoid floundering and rambling in search of a point.
- Remember that editing is much more difficult to do with audio or video than with textual media and plan your content and recording carefully.

SUMMARY OF LEARNING OBJECTIVES

1 Identify the electronic media available for short messages, and discuss the challenges of communicating through social media. Electronic media available for short messages are social networking and community participation sites, email, instant messaging, text messaging, blogging and microblogging, podcasting, and online video. Communication challenges when using social media include the fact that it may not suit certain kinds of messages, such as sending congratulations or condolences. Social media may prevent your message from reaching your audiences, because your audience may be overwhelmed with electronic messages. Finally, social media is characterized by its impermanence and lack of security: it does not provide a lasting, unchangeable, or secure record of information, characteristics essential to many types of business communication.

2 Describe the use of social networks, user-generated content sites, community Q&A sites, and community participation sites in business communication. Social networks (such as Facebook and LinkedIn) are important for recruiting employees, obtaining business partners and business advice, and developing customer relationships. They are also important means for gathering market intelligence, sharing product information, and fostering brand communities. For successful use of social networks, be sure to select the right message type for each topic, purpose, and network; join conversations in addition to starting your own; base your presence in a central location, such as your website; use ready-made connections for

audience participation; limit promotional efforts to avoid audience rejection; suit your online personality for each digital medium; and manage threads effectively.

3 Describe the evolving role of email in business communication, and explain how to adapt the three-step writing process to email messages. Email has been partially replaced by new tools such as instant messaging, blogs, microblogs, social networks, and shared workspaces, some of which are more instantaneous methods of sending and responding to messages. However, email still has its place in business communication: it is universally available; it is the best medium for private messages; and its mid-size messages are easy to compose and read, unlike microblogs and IM. Because of its nature, email allows senders to compose substantial messages at their leisure. When planning email messages, be sure to follow company policies about sensitive content and general email use. When writing emails, make both subject lines and the first few words of the message informative and compelling and apply high writing standards and good judgment, as messages have the same legal weight as printed documents. When completing emails, revise and proofread carefully, include a professional email signature, and don't click "Send" until you've clearly determined your recipients.

4 Describe the business benefits of instant messaging (IM), and identify guidelines for effective IM in the workplace. Instant messaging has the ability to mimic conversation, offers a rapid response (for example, it can provide emergency alerts during crisis management), is inexpensive, and has wide availability. When planning instant messages, view them as conversations with specific purposes and objectives. When preparing these messages, maintain a more formal style, avoiding IM acronyms, because you are writing for business audiences. When completing your message, be sure to revise and proofread, to avoid mistakes that may affect your professional image.

5 **Describe the role of blogging and microblogging in business communication today, and explain how to adapt the three-step writing process to blogging.** In business, blogging can be used to anchor an organization's social media presence, communicate company news both internally and externally, streamline team communication, provide customer support, recruit employees, serve as public forums for policy discussions, and market products. When planning blogs, be sure to understand your blog's purpose, target audience, and topic's scope. When writing blogs, use a personal style that shows your per-

sonality, but be sure it follows correct writing practices. Your blog content should be useful and interesting to your reader, and headlines should grab attention. Completing blogs requires careful proofreading and editing, as for any message, and inclusion of a newsfeed option so audiences can automatically receive new posts.

6 **Explain how to adapt the three-step writing process to podcasting.** First, plan your podcast by analyzing the situation, gathering the necessary information, and organizing it. Also determine the frequency of distribution and the topics to be addressed over time. Second, prepare the podcast by thinking about the language and images of your content and guiding devices such as previews, transitions, and reviews. Prepare a speaking outline and notes, rather than a script, so that the podcast sounds conversational and personal. Third, because editing podcasts is more difficult than editing videocasts or written text, review your outline carefully before recording.

ON THE JOB   PERFORMING COMMUNICATION TASKS AT PETRO-CANADA

You recently joined the corporate communications staff at Petro-Canada, and one of your responsibilities is editing the PumpTalk blog. Study the scenarios that follow and apply what you learned about blogging in this chapter to choose the best course of action.

1. Pressure is building to stop the practice of moderating the blog by reviewing reader comments and selecting which ones will appear online. You've received a number of adamant messages saying that PumpTalk won't be a "real" blog until anyone is allowed to write any sort of comment without being "censored" by the company. However, you know that every blog is vulnerable to inappropriate and irrelevant comments, and you don't want PumpTalk to turn into a free-for-all shouting match. Which of the following messages should you post on the blog to explain that the current policy of reviewing and filtering comments will continue?

   a. There are plenty of free-for-all blogs and websites on the Internet; if you want to rant and rave, I suggest you try one of those.

   b. Please bear in mind that this blog is a Petro-Canada company commercial communication endeavour and, as such, it must adhere to company standards for communication style. I therefore regret to inform you that we cannot allow a free-form, unmonitored exchange as part of this blog.

   c. Our blog; our rules. Seriously, though, this is a professional communication channel designed primarily to give Petro-Canada staff the opportunity to share their thoughts with customers and vice versa. As such, we need to make sure that the primary messaging effort doesn't get lost in the noise that can flare up in unregulated online forums.

   d. Every web surfer knows that online discussions can get a little out of hand at times, degenerating into shouting matches, name calling, and off-topic rants. In order to continue providing the congenial, information-driven blog that readers have come to expect, we believe it is necessary to exercise a minimal amount of control over the content.

2. The multiauthor concept generally works well for PumpTalk. It divides the writing workload, and it gives readers the opportunity to hear from several voices discussing different topics. One member of the team is moving to another position in the company, so you need to recruit a new blogger to replace her. Your plan is to send an email message to everyone in the company, providing a brief reminder of the blog's purpose, describing the writing style you're looking for, and inviting interested writers to submit sample blog entries for evaluation. Which of the following paragraphs is the best way to describe the preferred writing style for the blog? (This message is for employees only; it won't be seen by the public.)

   a. PumpTalk has connected with thousands of readers because the writing is *engaging* (people want to read and respond), *personal* (readers want to get to know real, live human beings, not a faceless corporation), *honest* (we don't sugar-coat anything or hide from criticism), and *friendly* (our readers want to enjoy the experience).

   b. What kind of writing are we looking for? Well, let me tell you exactly what we need. We need writing that is above all (1) engaging—it makes people *want* to read and become involved in the conversation. Plus, (2), the writing must be *personal*; we don't need anybody to repeat "the company line" here; we want *your unique* thoughts and opinions. However, (3), we, of course

(!), need writing that is consistent with PumpTalk's approach that combines honesty with friendliness.

c. You should be able to produce copy that meets the following criteria: Your writing must be engaging, personal, honest, and friendly. Writing that does not meet these criteria, no matter how well written in other respects, will not be accepted for online publication.

d. I'll be short and to the point: the writing we want for this blog must be engaging, personal, honest, and friendly.

3. For the sample blog entries you solicited in your email message, you asked candidates to start their entries with a brief paragraph introducing themselves. Which of the following seems like the most compatible style for PumpTalk?

a. Hi everyone! I'm Janice McNathan, and I couldn't be more excited to be joining PumpTalk! I've worked at some great companies before, but nobody seems to have as much fun as the PumpTalk blog guys, so I know I'm going to have a great time writing for this blog!

b. Charlie Parker here. I'm just a lowly auditor. Pretty much, I keep tabs on accounts and I make sure all the paperwork stays in order. I can't promise any exciting stories of adventure in the oil fields, but maybe something interesting will come up. Maybe you'd like some discussion of the financial side of the oil industry?

c. I'm Rick Munoz, and I've always wanted to be a professional writer. My career sort of took a detour, though, and I wound up as a programmer who works behind the scenes at the Petro-Canada website. I really appreciate this opportunity to hone my craft, and who knows—maybe this will be the break I need to make it as a "real" writer. You'll be able to say "I knew that guy before he became famous!"

d. Excuse me while I wipe the oil off my hands; I don't want to mess up this shiny new keyboard! Hi, I'm Kristal Yan, a field mechanic at Petro-Canada's facility in Lewis, Alberta. I've been an avid reader of PumpTalk since it started, and I really look forward to participating in this wonderful conversation. I hope to provide some interesting observations from the field. Feel free to ask any questions you may have about drilling and how things work in the oil fields.

TEST YOUR KNOWLEDGE

1. What are the compositional modes for electronic media?

2. What should you avoid when using social media for business purposes?

3. What are the marketing uses of social networks?

4. What are effective practices for user-generated content sites?

5. How do you capture your reader's attention in email?

6. When should the "cc" and "bcc" features be used in email?

7. Why is instant messaging usage overtaking email in many companies?

8. Who is the optimum audience for a blog?

9. How does one write for a blog?

10. How is microblogging relevant to business communication?

11. When should you use podcasts?

APPLY YOUR KNOWLEDGE

1. Given the strict limits on length, should all your microblogging messages function as teasers that link to more detailed information on a blog or website? Why or why not?

2. Is leveraging your connections on social networks for business purposes ethical? Why or why not?

3. Communication on a major project is suffering because several team members are in the habit of writing cryptic or careless instant messages that often force recipients to engage in several rounds of follow-up messaging to figure out what the sender had in mind. As project leader, you've spoken with these team members about the need to write clearer messages, but they respond that careful planning and writing defeats the whole purpose of *instant* messaging. How should you handle the situation?

4. If one of the benefits of blogging and microblogging is the personal, intimate style of writing, is it a good idea to limit your creativity by adhering to conventional rules of grammar, spelling, and mechanics? Why or why not?

5. In your work as a video game designer, you know that eager players search the Web for any scrap of information they can find about upcoming releases. In fact, to build interest, your company's public relations department carefully doles out small bits of information in the months before a new title hits the market. However, you and others in the company are also concerned about competitors getting their hands on all this "prerelease" information. If they learn too much too soon, they can use the information to improve their own products more quickly. You and several other designers and programmers maintain blogs that give players insights into game design techniques and that occasionally share tips and tricks. You have thousands of readers, and you believe that your blog helps build customer loyalty. The company president wants to ban blogging entirely so that bloggers don't accidentally share too much prerelease information about upcoming games. Would this be a wise move? Why or why not?

RUNNING CASES

> CASE 1 Noreen

Noreen has been asked to create an entry for the new blog at the Petro-Go website. All visitors to the website can read the blog, which is edited by Petro-Go's director of corporate communications. Management at all levels will post messages that focus on Petro-Go's environmental awareness, community relations, and community investment. The blog catchphrase is "We care about the communities we live and work in." Management wants to promote goodwill with current and potential customers. They want to be viewed as "the good gas company." Posts will discuss new and continuing initiatives, future goals, donations, and sponsorships.

QUESTIONS

a. Should all website visitors be allowed to add content to the blog and not just management? Why or why not?

b. Will this blog help attract new customers and retain existing customers? Explain your answer.

c. How often should new postings be uploaded? Why?

d. Give two other blog topics that might help attract visitors to the site and that would be appropriate for this company.

e. Who would be most interested in reading the blog? Why?

YOUR TASK

As Noreen, write a posting for the blog about how your team's office is going green. Include an interesting heading for your post. Do an online search to discover ways in which business offices are becoming more eco-friendly. Incorporate some of those eco-friendly practices in your post. Email your proposed posting to your instructor for approval. Remember to format the email message in a professional manner.

> CASE 2 Kwong

Kwong's manager asks him to work with the IT specialist and put together the first of a series of 52 video podcasts (also known as *vidcasts* or *vodcasts*). One podcast will be uploaded to the company website each week. The podcasts will give website visitors tips on personal and business tax planning and reporting. This first podcast will show Kwong discussing personal tax planning. Kwong's manager hopes that existing and potential customers will find value in the videos.

QUESTIONS

a. Before creating the first podcast for the series, what questions will Kwong need to ask his manager?

b. How can Kwong make the podcast interesting?

c. Why are previews, transitions, and reviews more important in video and audio recordings than they are in print media?

d. Is Kwong the right employee to represent the company on this podcast? For the podcast series? Explain your answer.

e. Could this company benefit from including a blog on its website? Why or why not?

YOUR TASK

The podcast's purpose is to offer tax planning tips to existing and potential customers. Narrow the scope of the topic for this first podcast to three personal tax tips. You will need to review government taxation guidelines before offering suggestions to your audience. You may wish to include some helpful website URLs for your audience. Prepare a document for your instructor that details the information to be conveyed in the podcast and the order in which it will be presented. Use the following document headings: Plan (the podcast's setting, length, and main points), Introduction (including a preview of topics), Body (the three tips you will discuss and the information you will share), and Conclusion (how you will conclude). Apply the three-step writing process and remember to use previews, transitions, and reviews in your dialogue. Email your proposed plan for the podcast to your instructor for approval. Remember to format the email message in a professional manner.

PRACTISE YOUR KNOWLEDGE

MESSAGE 7.A: IMPROVING IM SKILLS

Review this IM exchange and explain how the customer-service agent could have handled the situation more effectively.

AGENT:	Thanks for contacting Home Exercise Equipment. What's up?
CUSTOMER:	I'm having trouble assembling my home gym.
AGENT:	I hear that a lot! LOL
CUSTOMER:	So is it me or the gym?
AGENT:	Well, let's see. Where are you stuck?
CUSTOMER:	The crossbar that connects the vertical pillars doesn't fit.
AGENT:	What do you mean doesn't fit?
CUSTOMER:	It doesn't fit. It's not long enough to reach across the pillars.
AGENT:	Maybe you assembled the pillars in the wrong place. Or maybe we sent the wrong crossbar.
CUSTOMER:	How do I tell?
AGENT:	The parts aren't labelled so could be tough. Do you have a measuring tape? Tell me how long your crossbar is.

MESSAGE 7.B: DRAFTING EFFECTIVE BLOG POSTS

Revise the following blog post based on what you've learned in this chapter.

[headline]

We're DOOMED!!!!!

[post]

I was at the Sikorsky plant in Stratford yesterday, just checking to see how things were going with the assembly line retrofit we did for them last year. I think I saw the future, and it ain't pretty. They were demo'ing a prototype robot from Motoman that absolutely blows our stuff out of the water. They wouldn't let me really see it, but based on the 10-second glimpse I got, it's smaller, faster, and more manoeuvrable than any of our units. And when I asked about the price, the guy just grinned. And it wasn't the sort of grin designed to make me feel good.

I've been saying for years that we need to pay more attention to size, speed, and manoeuvrability instead of just relying on our historical strengths of accuracy and payload capacity, and you'd have to be blind not to agree that this experience proves me right. If we can't at least show a design for a better unit within two or three months, Motoman is going to lock up the market and leave us utterly in the dust.

Believe me, being able to say "I told you so" right now is not nearly as satisfying as you might think!!

EXERCISES

7.1 Media: Selecting the Right Medium for Your Message

For each of these message needs, choose a medium that you think would work effectively and explain your choice. (More than one medium could work in some cases; just be prepared to support your particular choice.)

  a. A technical support service for people trying to use their digital music players
  b. A message of condolence to the family of an employee who passed away recently
  c. A message from the CEO of a small company to the employees of the firm, explaining that she is leaving the company to join a competitor
  d. A series of observations on the state of the industry, intended mostly for professionals within the industry
  e. A series of messages, questions, and answers surrounding the work of a team assigned to a confidential company project

7.2 Social Networking: Creating a Blog Post

Pick a company in any industry that interests you. Imagine you are doing strategic planning for this firm and need to identify one of your company's key competitors. (Hint: You can use the free listings on www.hoovers.com to find several top competitors for most medium and large companies in Canada and the United States; search for a company, then on that company's profile page click on a company in the Top 3 Competitors area.) Now search through the competitor's website to find three strategically relevant pieces of information, such as the hiring of a new executive or the launch of a major new product. In a post on your class blog, share the information you found and the sources you used. (If you can't find useful information at the company's site, pick another company or try another industry.)

7.3 Email: Writing Informative Subject Lines

Using your imagination to make up whatever details you need, revise the following email subject lines to make them more informative:

  a. New budget figures
  b. Marketing brochure—your opinion
  c. Production schedule

7.4 Email: Writing Correctly

The following email message contains numerous errors related to what you've learned about planning and writing business messages. Using the information it contains, write a more effective version.

FROM: Felicia August
SUBJECT: Those are the breaks, folks

Some of you may not like the rules about break times; however, we determined that keeping track of employees while they took breaks at times they determined rather than regular breaks at prescribed times was not working as well as we would have liked it to work. The new rules are not going to be an option. If you do not follow the new rules, you could be docked from your pay for hours when you turned up missing, since your direct supervisor will not be able to tell whether you were on a "break" or not and will assume that you have walked away from your job. We cannot be responsible for any errors that result from your inattentiveness to the new rules. I have already heard complaints from some of you and I hope this memo will end this issue once and for all. The decision has already been made.

Starting Monday, January 1, you will all be required to take a regular 15-minute break in the morning and again in the afternoon, and a regular 30-minute lunch at the times specified by your supervisor, NOT when you think you need a break or when you "get around to it."

There will be no exceptions to this new rule!

Felicia August
Manager
Billing and Accounting

7.5 IM: Creating a Businesslike Tone

Your firm, which makes professional paint sprayers, uses IM extensively for internal communication and frequently for external communication with customers and suppliers. Several customers have recently forwarded copies of messages they've received from your staff, asking if you know how casually some employees are treating this important medium. You decide to revise parts of several messages to show your staff a more appropriate writing style. Rewrite these sentences, making up any information you need, to convey a more businesslike style and tone. (Look up the acronyms online if you need to.)

  a. IMHO, our quad turbo sprayer is best model 4U.
  b. No prob; happy2help!
  c. FWIW, I use the L400 myself & it rocks.
  d. Most cust see 20–30% reduct in fumes w/this sprayer—of course, YMMV.

7.6 Blogging: Keeping Emotions under Control

The members of the project team of which you are the leader have enthusiastically embraced blogging as a communication medium. Unfortunately, as emotions heat up during the project, some of the blog posts are getting too casual, too personal, and even sloppy. Because your boss and other managers around the company also read this project blog, you don't want the team to look unprofessional in anyone's eyes. Revise the following blog post so that it communicates in a more businesslike manner while retaining the informal, conversational tone of a blog. (Be sure to correct any spelling and punctuation mistakes you find as well.)

Well, to the profound surprise of absolutely nobody, we are not going to be able meet the June 1 commitment to ship 100 operating tables to MedHelp Surgical Supply. (For those of you who have been living in a cave the past six month, we have been fighting to get our hands on enough high-grade chromium steel to meet our production schedule.) Sure enough, we got news, this morning that we will only get enough for 30 tables. Yes, we look like fools for not being able to follow through on promises we made to the customer, but no, this didn't have to happpen. Six month's ago, purchasing warned us about shrinking supplies and suggested we advance-buy as much as we would need for the next 12 months, or so. We naturally tried to followed their advice, but just as naturally were shot down by the bean counters at corporate who trotted out the policy about never buying more than three months worth of materials in advance. Of course, it'll be us—not the bean counters who'll take the flak when everybody starts asking why revenues are down next quarter and why MedHelp is talking to our friends at Crighton Manuf!!! Maybe, some day this company will get its head out of the sand and realize that we need to have some financial flexibility in order to compete.

7.7 Microblogging: Tweeting to Customers

Busy knitters can go through a lot of yarn in a hurry, so most keep a sharp eye out for sales. You're on the marketing staff of Knitting-Warehouse, and you like to keep your loyal shoppers up to date with the latest deals. Visit the Knitting-Warehouse website at www.knitting-warehouse.com, select any on-sale product that catches your eye, and write a Twitter update that describes the product and the sale. Be sure to include a link back to the website so your Twitter followers can learn more. (Unless you are working on a private Twitter account that is accessible only by your instructor and your classmates, don't actually send this Twitter update. Email it to your instructor instead.)

7.8 Podcasting: Streamlining Your Content

You began recording a weekly podcast to share information with your large and far-flung staff. After a month, you ask for feedback from several of your subordinates, and you're disappointed to learn that some people stopped listening to the podcast after the first couple weeks. Someone eventually admits that many staffers feel the recordings are too long and rambling, and the information they contain isn't valuable enough to justify the time it takes to listen. You aren't pleased, but you want to improve. An assistant transcribes the introduction to last week's podcast so you can review it. You immediately see two problems. Revise the introduction based on what you've learned in this chapter.

So there I am, having lunch with Anju Gill, who just joined and took over the Central sales region from Jackson Stroud. In walks our beloved CEO with Selma's old boss at Uni-Plex; turns out they were finalizing a deal to co-brand our products and theirs and to set up a joint distribution program in all four domestic regions. Pretty funny, huh? Selma left Uni-Plex because she wanted to sell our products instead, and now she's back selling her old stuff, too. Anyway, try to chat with her when you can; she knows the biz inside and out and probably can offer insight into just about any sales challenge you might be running up against. We'll post more info on the co-brand deal next week; should be a boost for all of us. Other than those two news items, the other big news this week is the change in commission reporting. I'll go into the details in a minute, but when you log onto the intranet, you'll now see your sales results split out by product line and industry sector. Hope this helps you see where you're doing well and where you might beef things up a bit. Oh yeah, I almost forgot the most important bit. Speaking of our beloved CEO, Thomas is going to be our guest of honour, so to speak, at the quarterly sales meeting next week and wants an update on how petroleum prices are affecting customer behaviour. Each district manager should be ready with a brief report. After I go through the commission reporting scheme, I'll outline what you need to prepare.

CASES | APPLYING THE THREE-STEP WRITING PROCESS TO CASES

Apply each step to the following cases, as assigned by your instructor.

1 Planning →

Analyze the Situation
Identify both your general purpose and your specific purpose. Clarify exactly what you want your audience to think, feel, or believe after receiving your message. Profile your primary audience, including their backgrounds, differences, similarities, and likely reactions to your message.

Gather Information
Identify the information your audience will need to receive, as well as other information you may need in order to craft an effective message.

Select the Right Medium
The medium is identified for each case here, but when on the job, make sure your medium is both acceptable to the audience and appropriate for the message.

Organize the Information
Define your main idea, limit your scope, choose a direct or indirect approach, and outline necessary support points and other evidence.

2 Writing →

Adapt to Your Audience
Show sensitivity to audience needs by using a "you" attitude, politeness, positive emphasis, and bias-free language. Understand how much credibility you already have—and how much you may need to establish. Project your company's image by maintaining an appropriate style and tone. Consider cultural variations and the differing needs of internal and external audiences.

Compose the Message
For written messages, draft your message using clear but sensitive words, effective sentences, and coherent paragraphs. For podcasts, outline your message and draft speaking notes to ensure smooth recording; use plenty of previews, transitions, and reviews to help audiences follow along.

3 Completing

Revise the Message
Evaluate content and review readability, then edit and rewrite for conciseness and clarity.

Produce the Message
For written messages, use effective design elements and suitable layout for a clean, professional appearance. For podcasts, record your messages using whatever equipment you have available (professional podcasts may require upgraded equipment).

Proofread the Message
Review for errors in layout, spelling, and mechanics. Listen to podcasts to check for recording problems.

Distribute the Message
Deliver your message using the chosen medium; make sure all documents and all relevant files are distributed successfully.

Social Networking SKILLS

1. Online Etiquette: Controlling Negative Blogging

Employees who take pride in their work are a practically price-less resource for any business. However, pride can sometimes manifest itself in negative ways when employees come under criticism—and public criticism is a fact of life in social media. Imagine that your company has recently experienced a rash of product quality problems, and these problems have generated some unpleasant and occasionally unfair criticism on a variety of social media sites. Someone even set up a Facebook page specifically to give customers a place to vent their frustrations.

You and your public relations team jump into action, responding to complaints with offers to provide replacement products and help customers who have been affected by the quality problems. Everything seemed to be going as well as could

be expected, when you were checking a few industry blogs one evening and discovered that a couple of engineers in your company's product design lab have been responding to complaints on their own. They identified themselves as company employees and defended their product design, blaming the company's production department and even criticizing several customers for lacking the skills needed to use such a sophisticated product. Within a matter of minutes, you see their harsh comments being retweeted and reposted on multiple sites, only fuelling the fire of negative feedback against your firm. Needless to say, you are horrified.

Your task: You manage to reach the engineers by private message and tell them to stop posting messages, but you realize you have a serious training issue on your hands. Write a post for the internal company blog that advises employees on how to respond appropriately when they are representing the company online. Use your imagination to make up any details you need.

| Social Networking SKILLS |

2. Based on My Experience: Analyzing Your Online Image

Social media can be a great way to socialize during your student years, but employers are increasingly checking up on the online activities of potential hires to avoid bringing in employees who may reflect poorly on the company.

Your task: Team up with another student and review each other's public presence on Facebook, LinkedIn, Instagram, YouTube, Twitter, Flickr, blogs, and any other website that an employer might check during the interview and recruiting process. Identify any photos, videos, messages, or other material that could raise a red flag when an employee is evaluating a job candidate. Write your teammate an email message that lists any risky material.

| Email SKILLS |

3. Based on My Experience: Personal Branding

You've been labouring all summer at an internship, learning how business is conducted. You've done work nobody else wanted to do, but that's okay. Even the smallest tasks can make a good impression on your future résumé.

This morning, your supervisor asks you to write a description of the job you've been doing. "Include everything, even the filing," she suggests, "and address it to me in an email message." She says a future boss might assign such a task prior to a performance review. "You can practise describing your work without exaggeration—or too much modesty," she says, smiling.

Your task: Using good techniques for short messages and relying on your real-life work experience, write an email that will impress your supervisor. Make up any details you need.

| Email SKILLS | | Portfolio BUILDER |

4. Marketing and Sales Messages: Product Promotion

One-quarter of all motor vehicle accidents that involve children under age 12 are side-impact crashes—and these crashes result in higher rates of injuries and fatalities than those with front or rear impacts.[55]

Your task: You work in the consumer information department at Britax, a leading manufacturer of car seats. Your manager has asked you to prepare an email message that can be sent out whenever parents request information about side-impact crashes and the safety features of Britax seats. Start by researching side-impact crashes at http://www.consumerreports.org/cro/carseats/child-seat-side-impact-protection. Then review Britax product safety standards at https://us.britax.com/why-britax/safety-standards/. Using these sources, write a three-paragraph message that explains the seriousness of side-impact crashes, describes how injuries and fatalities can be minimized in these crashes, and describes how Britax's car seats are designed to help protect children in side-impact crashes.

| Email SKILLS |

5. Sensitive Email: Dealing with a Difficult Customer

Many companies operate on the principle that the customer is always right, even when the customer *isn't* right. They take any steps necessary to ensure happy customers, a lot of repeat sales, and a positive reputation among potential buyers. Overall, this is a smart and successful approach to business. However, most companies eventually encounter a nightmare customer who drains so much time, energy, and profits that the only sensible option is to refuse the custom's business. For example, the nightmare customer might be someone who constantly berates you and your employees, repeatedly makes outlandish demands for refunds and discounts, or simply requires so much help that you not only lose money on this person but also no longer have enough time to help your other customers. "Firing" a customer is an unpleasant step that should be taken only in the most extreme cases and only after other remedies have been attempted (such as talking with the customer about the problem), but it is sometimes necessary for the well-being of your employees and your company.

Your task: If you are currently working or have held a job in the recent past, imagine that you've encountered just such a customer. If you don't have job experience to call on, imagine that you work in a retail location somewhere around campus or in your neighbourhood. Identify the type of behaviour this imaginary customer exhibits and the reasons the behaviour can no longer be accepted. Write a brief email message to the customer to explain that you will no longer be able to accommodate him or her as a customer. Calmly explain why you have had to reach this difficult decision. Maintain a professional tone and keep your emotions in check.

| Email SKILLS |

6. Environmental Planning: Email Announcing a Committee Meeting

You've probably worked as a volunteer on a committee or with team members for class assignments. You know how hard it is to get a diverse group of individuals together for a productive meeting. Maybe you've tried different locations—one member's home or a table at the library. This time you're going to suggest a local restaurant.

The committee you're leading is a volunteer group planning a trash-clearing project at an area park. Your meeting goal is to brainstorm ways to encourage public participation in this environmental event, to be held next Earth Day.

Your task: Develop a short email message telling committee members about the meeting. Include the time, date, duration, and location (choose a place you know). Mention the meeting goal to encourage attendance.

| Email SKILLS |

7. Sales Email: Promoting a New Lifestyle Magazine

Consumers looking for beauty, health, and lifestyle magazines have an almost endless array of choices, but even in this crowded field, Logan Olson found her own niche. Olson, who was born with congenital heart disease, suffered a heart attack at age 16 that left her in a coma and caused serious brain damage. The active and outgoing teen had to relearn everything from sitting up to feeding herself. As she recovered, she looked for help and advice in conquering such daily challenges as finding fashionable clothes that were easier to put on and makeup that was easier to apply. Mainstream beauty magazines didn't seem to offer any information for young women with disabilities, so she started her own magazine targeted at young adults living with disabilities. Olson had to overcome many challenges, but she never quit. In 2006, she launched her magazine to "offer readers reassurance that they are not alone, a feeling she longed for when she was recovering from surgery."[56]

Your task: Logan Olson's story is one of many inspirational testimonials featured in *ABILITY Magazine* (abilitymagazine. com), a bimonthly publication featuring health, disability, and human potential. Write a promotional email message to be sent to young adults with disabilities as well as families and friends who might like to give gift subscriptions, promoting the benefits of subscribing to *ABILITY*. You can learn more about *ABILITY* at https://abilitymagazine.com/home/about-us/.[57]

| IM SKILLS |

8. Developing Chat Service Templates: Educating Consumers about TV

High-definition television can be a joy to watch—but, oh, what a pain to buy. The field is littered with competing technologies and arcane terminology that is meaningless to most consumers. Moreover, it's nearly impossible to define one technical term without invoking two or three others, leaving consumers swimming in an alphanumeric soup of confusion. The manufacturers themselves can't even agree on which of the *18* different digital TV formats truly qualify as "high definition." As a sales support manager for Crutchfield, www.crutchfield.com, a leading U.S. online retailer of audio and video systems, you understand the frustration buyers feel; your staff is deluged daily by their questions.

Your task: To help your staff respond quickly to consumers who ask questions via Crutchfield's online IM chat service, you are developing a set of "canned" responses to common questions. When a consumer asks one of these questions, a sales advisor can simply click on the ready-made answer. Start by writing concise, consumer-friendly definitions of the following terms: *resolution, HDTV, 1080p,* and *HDMI.* Explore the Learning Center on the Crutchfield website to learn more about these terms. Answers.com (www.answers.com) and CNET (www.cnet.com) are two other handy sources.[58]

| IM SKILLS |

9. Based on My Experience: Instant Messaging for Customer Support

Instant messaging is frequently used in customer support situations where a customer needs help selecting, using, or troubleshooting a problem. In this activity, two two-person teams will use IM to simulate problem solving by helping classmates discuss important academic or life decisions. One team will be the "clients," who are struggling with the decisions, and the other will be the "advisors," who coach them toward solutions.

Your task: First choose a free IM/chat system such as Google Talk, Facebook Chat, or any other system on which you can communicate privately in real time. Now choose two decision-making scenarios from your school or personal lives, such as deciding on a major, choosing whether to work during the upcoming summer or attend class, figuring out where to live next year, or any other decision that you're willing to have your group discuss later in front of the whole class. Choose decisions that are complicated enough to support an IM conversation lasting at least five minutes.

Decide which team will be the advisors and which will be the clients and move the teams to separate locations (make sure you have Internet access). In each team, one person will be the communicator first, and the other will be the observer, monitoring how well the IM conversation progresses and making note of any confusion, inefficiencies, or other issues.

When you're set up in your separate locations, begin the IM exchange with the communicator from the client team asking the advisor for help with a decision. The advisor should ask probing questions to find out what the client really wants to gain from the decision and help him or her work through the various alternatives. Discuss the decision scenario for at least five minutes. The observers should take notes but should not be involved in the IM exchange in any way.

After working through one of the decision scenarios, swap roles inside each team so that the observer becomes the communicator and vice versa. Now work through the second decision scenario.

Afterward, meet as a full team after the role playing and compare notes about how well each conversation went, how well the technology supported the communicators' needs, and what you might do differently in a business context to ensure smooth communication and customer satisfaction. Be prepared to discuss your observations and conclusions with the rest of the class.

| Blogging SKILLS |

10. Based on My Experience: Blogging about Study Abroad

Studying abroad for a semester or a year can be a rewarding experience in many ways—improving your language skills, experiencing another culture, making contacts in the international business arena, and building your self-confidence.

Your task: Write a post for your class blog that describes your school's study-abroad program and summarizes the steps involved in applying for international study. If your school doesn't offer study-abroad opportunities, base your post on the program offered at another institution in your province.

| Blogging SKILLS | | Portfolio BUILDER |

11. Blogging for GM: Promoting the Volt

U.S. automakers haven't had much good news to share lately. GM, in particular, has been going through a rough time, entering bankruptcy, shedding assets, and relying on bailouts from the U.S. and Canadian governments to stay in business. The news isn't entirely bleak, however. Chevrolet, one of the brands in the GM automotive stable, has recently introduced the Volt, a gas/electric hybrid that might finally give drivers a viable alternative to the wildly popular Toyota Prius.

Your task: Working with a team assigned by your instructor, write a post for GM's dealer-only blog that describes the new Volt and the benefits it offers car owners. Include at least one photo and one link to the Volt section of GM's website. You can learn more about the Volt at GM's website, www.gm.ca.

Blogging SKILLS

12. Blogging for Comic-Con: Pop Culture Rules!

Comic-Con International is an annual convention that highlights a wide variety of pop culture and entertainment media, from comic books and collectibles to video games and movies. From its early start as a comic book convention that attracted several hundred fans and publishing industry insiders, Comic-Con has become a major international event with more than 125 000 attendees.

Your task: Several readers of your pop culture blog have been asking for your recommendation about visiting Comic-Con in San Diego next summer. Write a two- or three-paragraph posting for your blog that explains what Comic-Con is and what attendees can expect to experience at the convention. Be sure to address your posting to fans, not industry insiders. You can learn more at www.comic-con.org.[59]

Microblogging SKILLS

13. Twitter Teaser: Promoting a Career Resource

Twitter updates are a great way to alert people to helpful articles, videos, and other online resources.

Your task: Find an online resource (it can be a website quiz, a YouTube video, a PowerPoint presentation, a newspaper article, or anything else appropriate) that offers some great tips to help university and college students prepare for job interviews. Write a teaser of no more than 120 characters that hints at the benefits other students can get from this resource. If your class is set up with private Twitter accounts, use your private account to send your message. Otherwise, email it to your instructor. Be sure to include the URL; if you're using a Twitter account, the system should shorten it to 20 characters to keep you within the 140-character limit.

Microblogging SKILLS

14. Updates and Announcements: Flight Sale!

JetBlue is known for its innovations in customer service and customer communication, including its pioneering use of the Twitter microblogging system. Nearly 2 million JetBlue fans and customers follow the company on Twitter to get updates on flight status during weather disruptions, facility upgrades, and other news.[60]

Your task: Write a message of no more than 120 characters that announces the limited-time availability of flights and travel packages—flights plus hotel rooms, for example—at JetBlue's store on eBay. (Limiting your message to 120 characters allows room for a 20-character URL, which you don't need to include in your message.) The key selling point is that travellers may be able to purchase flights they want at steep discounts. If your class is set up with private Twitter accounts, use your private account to send your message. Otherwise, email it to your instructor.

Podcasting SKILLS

15. Personal Branding: Introducing Yourself to a Potential Employer

While writing the many letters and email messages that are part of the job search process, you find yourself wishing that you could just talk to some of these companies so your personality could shine through. Well, you've just gotten that opportunity. One of the companies that you've applied to has emailed you back, asking you to submit a two-minute podcast introducing yourself and explaining why you would be a good person to hire.

Your task: Identify a company that you'd like to work for after graduation and select a job that would be a good match for your skills and interests. Write a script for a two-minute podcast (roughly 250 words). Introduce yourself and the position you're applying for, describe your background, and explain why you think you're a good candidate for the job. Make up any details you need. If your instructor asks you to do so, record the podcast and submit the file.

Podcasting SKILLS   Portfolio BUILDER

16. Based on My Experience: Suggestions for Improving Your College or University

With any purchase decision, from a restaurant meal to a college or university education, recommendations from satisfied customers are often the strongest promotional messages.

Your task: Write a script for a one- to two-minute podcast (roughly 150 to 250 words) explaining why your university or college is a good place to get an education. Your audience is grade 11 and grade 12 (CEGEP in Quebec) students. You can choose to craft a general message, something that would be useful to all prospective students, or you can focus on a specific academic discipline, the athletic program, or some other important aspect of your college or university experience. Either way, make sure your introductory comments make it clear whether you are offering a general recommendation or a specific recommendation. If your instructor asks you to do so, record the podcast and submit the file electronically.

Podcasting SKILLS

17. Podcasting Pitch: Training People to Sell Your Favourite Product

What product do you own (or use regularly) that you can't live without? It could be something as seemingly minor as a favourite pen or something as significant as a medical device that you literally can't live without. Now imagine you're a salesperson for this product; think about how you would sell it to potential buyers. How would you describe it and how would you explain the benefits of owning it? After you've thought about how you would present the product to others, imagine that you've been promoted to sales manager, and it is your job to train other people to sell the product.

Your task: Write the script for a brief podcast (200 to 300 words) that summarizes for your sales staff the most important points to convey about the product. Imagine that they'll listen to your podcast while driving to a customer's location or preparing for the day's activity in a retail store (depending on the nature of the product). Be sure to give your staffers a concise overview message about the product and several key support points.

8 Writing Routine and Positive Messages

LEARNING OBJECTIVES After studying this chapter, you will be able to

1 Outline an effective strategy for writing routine requests

2 Describe an effective strategy for writing routine replies and positive messages

3 Discuss the importance of knowing who is responsible when granting claims and requests for adjustment

4 Explain how creating informative messages differs from responding to information requests

5 Describe the importance of goodwill messages and explain how to make them effective

MyLab Business Communication   Visit MyLab Business Communication to access a variety of online resources directly related to this chapter's content.

ON THE JOB: COMMUNICATING AT INDIGO BOOKS AND MUSIC

As Indigo's founder and CEO (chief executive officer), Heather Reisman is the primary decision maker for her firm's image and activities. Her goal is to create an environment where book lovers can enjoy "the best of a proprietor-run shop combined with the selection of a true emporium." Indigo's position in the Canadian book market is testimony to Reisman's ability to communicate her vision clearly to Indigo executives, front-line staff, and customers.

Becoming Canada's Bookseller

www.chapters.indigo.ca

Heather Reisman's business is her passion. The CEO of Indigo Books and Music, Reisman created Indigo in 1996 as "the world's first cultural department store," where consumers can buy books, e-readers, DVDs, CDs, gift items, and fine stationery. At that time, her chief competitor was Chapters, Inc another superstore chain, which merged with Indigo in 2001, with Reisman becoming the controlling shareholder. Today, Indigo is Canada's largest retail bookstore, with 89 large-format stores under the Indigo and Chapters banners and 123 small-format stores, including Coles, Indigospirit, Smith-Books, and The Book Company.

Reisman's challenge is to nurture Canadian interest in books. A book lover herself, she highlights her "personal picks" on the website and in-store. Yet Indigo is intended to be more than retail outlets: Reisman envisions them as "cultural havens for book lovers to meet local, national, and international artists." Online, customers can participate in a community of readers by posting and reading book reviews, viewing members' book lists, and joining book clubs. They can also contribute to the Indigo Ideas platform on Facebook, as well as vote on suggestions for improving the business.

Reisman's company raises money for the Indigo Love of Reading Foundation, which supplies new books and learning materials to high-needs elementary schools. Reisman sees literacy as a way to raise the self-esteem of young Canadians and involves customers in this mission by encouraging donations through the website or stores. Through another program, FUNdraisers, schools and groups can hold in-store student programs, with Indigo donating a portion of purchases made by invited guests.

As you read this chapter, put yourself in Heather Reisman's position. To maintain your business and social goals, you must send clear messages to customers and store managers, requesting both information and action. How can you obtain the facts you need to make your decisions? How will you communicate your goals so Indigo can maintain its stature in consumers' eyes?[1]

Strategy for Routine Requests

Much of the vital communication between a company and its customers is about routine matters, from product operation hints and technical support to refunds and ordering glitches. These messages fall into two groups: requests for information or action from another party, and a variety of routine and positive messages. This chapter addresses these types of messages; Chapter 9 covers messages in which you convey negative information, and Chapter 10 addresses persuasive messages.

Making requests is a routine part of business. In most cases, your audience will be prepared to comply, as long as you're not being unreasonable or asking people to do something they would expect you to do yourself. By applying a clear strategy and tailoring your approach to each situation, you'll be able to generate effective requests quickly.

Like all business messages, routine requests have three parts: an opening, a body, and a close. Using the direct approach, open with your main idea, which is a clear statement of your request. Use the body to give details and justify your request. Then close by requesting specific action (see Figure 8–1).

Keep your paragraphs short, and in each paragraph address only one issue. This helps your reader focus on what is important to you. Also, use no more than one bulleted or numbered list per message. An email or letter with too many bullets or numbers makes it unclear to the reader what is most important in the message.

STATING YOUR REQUEST UP FRONT

Begin routine requests by placing your request first—up front is where it stands out and gets the most attention. Of course, getting right to the point should not be interpreted as a licence to be abrupt or tactless.

- **Pay attention to tone.** Even though you expect a favourable response, the tone of your initial request is important. Instead of demanding action ("Send me your latest catalogue"), soften your request with words such as *please* and *I would appreciate.*
- **Assume that your audience will comply.** An impatient demand for rapid service isn't necessary. You can generally make the assumption that your audience will comply with your request once the reason for it is clearly understood.
- **Be specific.** State precisely what you want. For example, if you request the latest market data from your research department, ensure that you say whether you want a one-page summary or a hundred pages of raw data.

EXPLAINING AND JUSTIFYING YOUR REQUEST

Use the body of your message to explain your initial request. Make the explanation a smooth and logical outgrowth of your opening remarks. If possible, point out how complying with the request could benefit the reader. For example, if you would like some assistance interpreting complex quality-control data, point

Online product ordering is simple, be it from large retailers or artisans who sell their products through commercial marketplaces such as etsy.com. You merely click the item and quantity, and your purchase is added to your electronic shopping cart, with shipping and taxes automatically calculated. But how do you phrase order messages to small businesses that don't use online ordering? What medium do you select? How do you organize your message?

1 LEARNING OBJECTIVE

Outline an effective strategy for writing routine requests.

For routine requests and positive messages

- State the request or main idea
- Give necessary details
- Close with a cordial request for specific action

Take care that your direct approach doesn't come across as abrupt or tactless.

Forestpath/Shutterstock

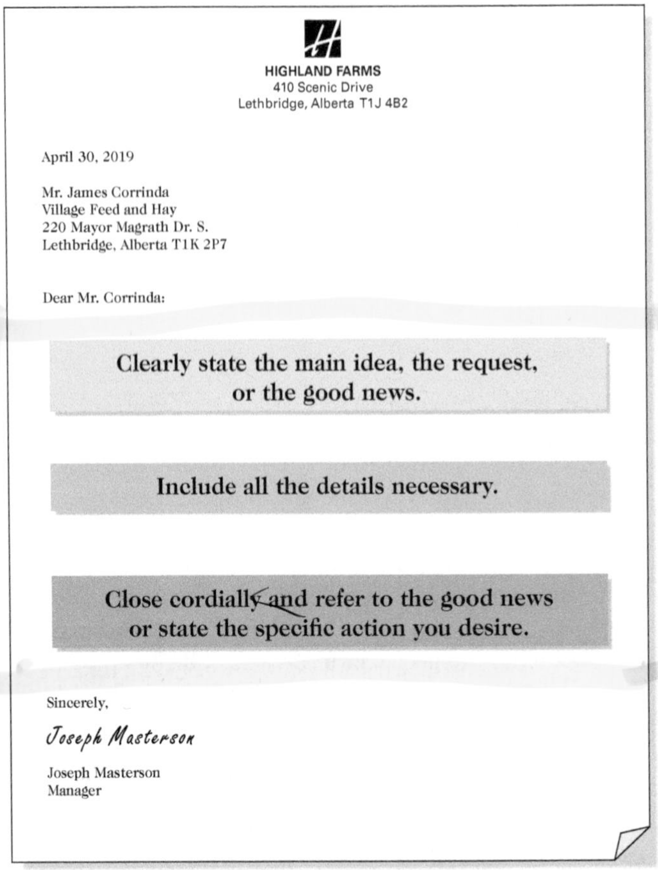

HIGHLAND FARMS
410 Scenic Drive
Lethbridge, Alberta T1J 4B2

April 30, 2019

Mr. James Corrinda
Village Feed and Hay
220 Mayor Magrath Dr. S.
Lethbridge, Alberta T1K 2P7

Dear Mr. Corrinda:

**Clearly state the main idea, the request,
or the good news.**

Include all the details necessary.

**Close cordially and refer to the good news
or state the specific action you desire.**

Sincerely,

Joseph Masterson

Joseph Masterson
Manager

Figure 8–1 Organizing Routine and Positive Messages

out how a better understanding of quality-control issues would improve customer satisfaction and ultimately lead to higher profits for the entire company.

Whether you're writing a formal letter or a simple instant message, you can use the body of your request to list a series of questions. This list of questions helps organize your message and helps your audience identify the information you need. Just keep in mind a few basics:

- **Ask the most important questions first.** If cost is your main concern, you might begin with a question such as "What is the cost for shipping the merchandise by air versus truck?" Then ask more specific but related questions about, say, discounts for paying early.
- **Ask only relevant questions.** To help expedite the response to your request, ask only those questions that are central to your main request. Doing so will generate an answer sooner and make better use of the other person's time.
- **Deal with only one topic per question.** If you have an unusual or complex request, break it down into specific, individual questions so the reader can address each one separately. Don't put the burden of untangling a complicated request on your reader. This consideration not only shows respect for your audience's time but also gets you a more accurate answer in less time.

> Using lists helps readers sort through multiple related items or multiple requests.

REQUESTING SPECIFIC ACTION IN A COURTEOUS CLOSE

> Close request messages with
>
> - A request for some specific action
> - Information about how you can be reached
> - An expression of appreciation

Close your message with three important elements: (1) a specific request, (2) information about how you can be reached (if it isn't obvious), and (3) an expression of appreciation or goodwill. When you ask readers to perform a specific action, ask that they respond by a specific time, if appropriate (for example, "Please send the figures by May 5 so I can return first-quarter results to you before the May 20 conference."). Plus, by including your phone number, email address, office hours, and other contact information, you help your readers respond easily.

Conclude your message by sincerely expressing your goodwill and appreciation. However, don't thank the reader "in advance" for cooperating. If the reader's reply warrants a word of thanks, send it after you've received the reply. To review, see "Checklist: Writing Routine Requests."

✓ Checklist Writing Routine Requests

A. State your request upfront.
- Write in a polite, undemanding, personal tone.
- Use the direct approach, since your audience will probably respond favourably.
- Be specific and precise.

B. Explain and justify your request.
- Justify the request or explain its importance.
- Explain any potential benefits of responding.

- Break complex requests into individual questions that are limited to only one topic each.

C. Request specific action in a courteous close.
- Make it easy to comply by including appropriate contact information.
- Express your gratitude.
- State clearly any important deadlines.

COMMUNICATING ACROSS CULTURES   How Direct Is Too Direct?

Being direct is civil, considerate, and honest—or so say people in Canada and the United States. Others view that same directness as being abrupt, rude, and intrusive—even dishonest and offensive. Countries such as Mexico, Japan, Saudi Arabia, Italy, and the Philippines all tend to have high-context cultures (see discussion in Chapter 3). That is, the people in these countries depend on shared knowledge and inferred messages to communicate; they gather meaning more from context and less from direct statement.

Offering a little constructive criticism may actually hurt your Japanese assistant's dignity. In fact, in high-context cultures, avoid saying outright, "You are wrong." You could cause the other person to lose face. When making requests, determine whether to use a direct or an implied message by considering audience attitudes toward destiny, time, authority, and logic:

- **Destiny.** Do audience members believe they can control events themselves or do they see events as predetermined and uncontrollable? If you're supervising employees who believe that fate controls a construction deadline, your crisp email message requesting them to stay on schedule may be hard for them to understand. It may even be insulting.
- **Time.** Do audience members view time as exact, precise, and not to be wasted, or do they see time as relative, relaxed, and necessary for developing interpersonal relationships? If you see time as money and you get straight to business in your memo to your Mexican manager, your message may be overlooked in the confusion over your disregard for social propriety.

- **Authority.** Do audience members conduct business more autocratically or more democratically? In Japan, rank and status are highly valued, so when communicating downward, you may need to be even more direct than you're used to being in Canada. And when communicating upward, you may need to be much less direct than usual.
- **Logic.** Do audience members pursue logic in a straight line, from point *a* to point *b*, or do they communicate in circular or spiral patterns of logic? If you organize a speech or letter in a straightforward and direct manner, your message may be considered illogical, unclear, and disorganized.

You may want to decide not only how direct to be in written messages but also whether to write at all. Perhaps a phone call or a visit would be more appropriate. By finding out how much or how little a culture tends toward high-context communication, you'll know whether to be direct or to rely on nuance when communicating with the people there.

CAREER APPLICATIONS

1. Research a high-context culture such as Japan, Korea, or China, and write a one- or two-paragraph summary of how someone in that culture would go about requesting information.
2. When you write to someone in a high-context culture, would it be better to (a) make the request directly in the interest of clarity or (b) match your audience's unfamiliar logic and make your request indirectly? Explain your answer.

Common Examples of Routine Requests

The types of routine requests are innumerable and range from asking favours to requesting credit. However, many of the routine messages that you'll write will likely fall into a few main categories: asking for information and action, asking for recommendations, and making claims and requesting adjustments.

ASKING FOR INFORMATION AND ACTION

When you need to know about something, to elicit an opinion from someone, or to request a simple action, you usually need only ask. In essence, simple requests say

- What you want to know or what you want readers to do
- Why you're making the request
- Why it may be in your readers' interest to help you

Routine requests can be handled with simple, straightforward messages, but more complicated requests can require additional justification and explanation.

If your reader is able to do what you want, such a straightforward request gets the job done quickly. Use the direct approach by opening with a clear statement of your reason for writing. However, do not waste the reader's time by starting the request with "I am writing to you to…" This is obvious, and does not need to be stated. Keep the opening clear and concise. In the body, provide whatever explanation is needed to justify your request. Make sure you use more than one paragraph and order your thoughts around one central idea per paragraph. In some situations, readers might be unwilling to respond unless they understand how the request benefits them, so be sure to include this information in your explanation. You can assume some shared background when communicating about a routine matter to someone in the same company. Then close with a specific description of what you expect and include a deadline, if appropriate.

Figure 8–2, an email request, asks district managers to fill out an attached information collection form. Although the request is not unusual and responding to it is part of the managers' responsibility, Helene Clausen asks for their help in a courteous manner and points out the benefits of responding.

In contrast to requests sent internally, those sent to people outside the organization usually adopt a more formal tone, such as the following example:

Dear Bioverse:

Please provide additional information on distribution opportunities for your Healthy Ponds product line, as mentioned on your website.

Enviro Domestic is a 20-year-old firm with a well-established design, retail, and service presence in the Ottawa area, and we believe your bioremediation products would make a compelling addition to our offerings.

In particular, we would appreciate answers to the following questions:

1. Do you offer exclusive regional distribution contracts?
2. Do you offer factory training for sales and service specialists?
3. Do you plan to expand beyond water bioremediation solutions into other landscaping products?

Please let us hear from you by February 15.

The opening makes an overall request in polite question form (no question mark).

The writer identifies an affiliation and reason for writing.

The body specifies exactly what the writer wishes to know to assist the recipient in responding.

The close makes a polite request and gives a specific answer deadline.

A more complex request might require not only greater detail but also information on how responding will benefit the reader.

ASKING FOR RECOMMENDATIONS

Always ask for permission before using someone as a reference.

The need to inquire about people arises often in business. For example, before awarding credit, contracts, jobs, promotions, or scholarships, some companies ask applicants to supply references: a list of people who can vouch for their

1 Planning →

Analyze the Situation
Verify that the purpose is to request information from company managers.

Gather Information
Gather accurate, complete information about local competitive threats.

Select the Right Medium
Choose email for this internal message, which also allows the attachment of a Word document to collect the information.

Organize the Information
Clarify that the main idea is collecting information that will lead to a better competitive strategy, which will in turn help the various district managers.

2 Writing →

Adapt to Your Audience
Show sensitivity to audience needs with a "you" attitude, politeness, positive emphasis, and bias-free language. The writer already has credibility, as manager of the department.

Compose the Message
Maintain a style that is conversational but still businesslike, using plain English and appropriate voice.

3 Completing

Revise the Message
Evaluate content and review readability; avoid unnecessary details.

Produce the Message
Simple email format is all the design this message needs.

Proofread the Message
Review for errors in layout, spelling, and mechanics.

Distribute the Message
Deliver the message via the company's email system.

The informative subject line alerts the audience to an important request.

The attachment is, in fact, included, as stated in the email.

The body acknowledges that responding to the request will require some work, but the result will benefit everyone.

The opening explains the context of the message, then gets to the point. Clausen acknowledges the request.

The body explains the benefit of responding to the request.

The close provides a clear deadline, then concludes in a courteous manner.

Eudora - [All District Mgrs, Competitive Threat Analysis]

File   Edit   Mailbox   Message   Transfer   Special   Tools   Window   Help

To: <All District Mgrs>
From: hh_clausen@early-ed.ca
Subject: Competitive Threat Analysis
Cc:
Bcc:
Attached: C:\Strategic planning\Competitive Analysis template.doc;

Hello everyone,

At last week's off-site meeting, Charles asked me to coordinate our companywide competitive threat analysis project. In order to devise a comprehensive strategic response that is sensitive to local market variations, we need your individual insights and advice.

To minimize the effort for you and to ensure consistent data collection across all regions, I've attached a template that identifies all the key questions we'd like to have answered.

Questions include 1) what companies provide similar services in your area? 2) How are the prices similar for our products and theirs? 3) How does their customer service compare to ours?

I realize this will require several hours of work on your part, but the result will be a truly nationwide look at our competitive situation. From this information, we can create a plan for next fiscal year that makes the best use of finite resources while adapting to your local district needs.

To allow sufficient time to compile your inputs before the November 12 board meeting, please email your responses to me by November 8. Thanks for your help and timely attention to this important project.

Helene

Helene H. Clausen
Director, Strategic Initiatives
Early Education Solutions, Inc.
101 Student Union Blvd, Suite 455
Vancouver, BC V6T 1A8
tel: 604-555-1200
fax: 604-555-1210
www.early-ed.ca

Figure 8–2 Effective Message Requesting Action

Courtesy: Mozilla Foundation

ability, skills, integrity, character, and fitness for the job. Before you volunteer someone's name as a reference, ask permission to do so. Some people won't let you use their names, perhaps because they don't know enough about you to feel comfortable writing a letter or because they have a policy of not providing recommendations.

Refresh the memory of any potential references you haven't been in touch with for a while.

Because requests for recommendations and references are routine, you can organize your inquiry using the direct approach. Open your message by clearly stating why the recommendation is required (if it's not for a job, be sure to explain what it is for) and that you would like your reader to write the letter. If you haven't had contact with the person for some time, use the opening to recall the nature of the relationship you had, the dates of association, and any special events that might bring a clear, favourable picture of you to mind. Consider including an updated résumé if you've had significant career advancement since your last contact.

Close your message with an expression of appreciation and the full name and address of the person to whom the letter should be sent. When asking for an immediate recommendation, you should also mention the deadline. Always be sure to enclose a stamped, preaddressed envelope, as a convenience to the other party. The letter in Figure 8–3 covers all these points and adds important information about some qualifications that might be of special interest to her potential employer.

When making a claim

- Explain the problem and give details
- Provide backup information
- Request specific action

MAKING CLAIMS AND REQUESTING ADJUSTMENTS

If you're dissatisfied with a company's product or service, you can opt to make a **claim** (a formal complaint) or request an **adjustment** (a settlement of a claim).

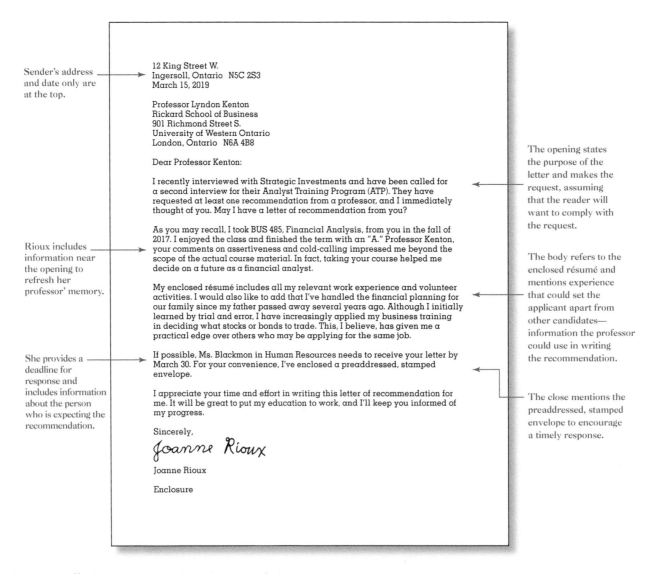

Sender's address and date only are at the top.

12 King Street W.
Ingersoll, Ontario N5C 2S3
March 15, 2019

Professor Lyndon Kenton
Rickard School of Business
901 Richmond Street S.
University of Western Ontario
London, Ontario N6A 4B8

Dear Professor Kenton:

I recently interviewed with Strategic Investments and have been called for a second interview for their Analyst Training Program (ATP). They have requested at least one recommendation from a professor, and I immediately thought of you. May I have a letter of recommendation from you?

The opening states the purpose of the letter and makes the request, assuming that the reader will want to comply with the request.

Rioux includes information near the opening to refresh her professor' memory.

As you may recall, I took BUS 485, Financial Analysis, from you in the fall of 2017. I enjoyed the class and finished the term with an "A." Professor Kenton, your comments on assertiveness and cold-calling impressed me beyond the scope of the actual course material. In fact, taking your course helped me decide on a future as a financial analyst.

My enclosed résumé includes all my relevant work experience and volunteer activities. I would also like to add that I've handled the financial planning for our family since my father passed away several years ago. Although I initially learned by trial and error, I have increasingly applied my business training in deciding what stocks or bonds to trade. This, I believe, has given me a practical edge over others who may be applying for the same job.

The body refers to the enclosed résumé and mentions experience that could set the applicant apart from other candidates—information the professor could use in writing the recommendation.

She provides a deadline for response and includes information about the person who is expecting the recommendation.

If possible, Ms. Blackmon in Human Resources needs to receive your letter by March 30. For your convenience, I've enclosed a preaddressed, stamped envelope.

I appreciate your time and effort in writing this letter of recommendation for me. It will be great to put my education to work, and I'll keep you informed of my progress.

The close mentions the preaddressed, stamped envelope to encourage a timely response.

Sincerely,

Joanne Rioux

Joanne Rioux

Enclosure

Figure 8–3 Effective Letter Requesting a Recommendation

In either case, it's important to maintain a professional tone in all your communication, no matter how angry or frustrated you might be. Keeping your cool will help you get the situation resolved sooner.

In most cases, and especially in your first letter, assume that a fair adjustment will be made, and follow the plan for direct requests. Open with a straightforward statement of the problem. In the body, give a complete, specific explanation of the detail; provide any information an adjuster would need to verify your complaint. In your close, politely request specific action or convey a sincere desire to find a solution. If appropriate, suggest that the business relationship will continue if the problem is solved satisfactorily. Be prepared to back up your claim with invoices, sales receipts, cancelled cheques, dated correspondence, and any other relevant documents. Send copies and keep the originals for your files.

If the remedy is obvious, tell your reader exactly what you expect from the company, such as exchanging incorrectly shipped merchandise for the right item or issuing a refund if the item is out of stock. In some cases you might ask the reader to resolve a problem. However, if you're uncertain about the precise nature of the trouble, you could ask the company to make an assessment, then advise you on how the situation could be fixed. Supply your contact information so the company can discuss the situation with you if necessary. Compare the tone of the draft version in Figure 8–4 with the revised version. If you were the person receiving the complaint, which version would you respond to more favourably?

A rational, clear, and courteous approach is best for any routine request. To review the tasks involved in making claims and requesting adjustments, see "Checklist: Making Claims and Requesting Adjustments."

> Be prepared to document any claim you make with a company. Send copies and keep the original documents.

✓ Checklist | Making Claims and Requesting Adjustments

- Maintain a professional tone, even if you're extremely frustrated.
- Open with a straightforward statement of the problem.
- Provide specific details in the body.
- Present facts honestly and clearly.

- Politely summarize desired action in the closing.
- Clearly state what you expect as a fair settlement, or ask the reader to propose a fair adjustment.
- Explain the benefits of complying with the request, such as your continued patronage.

Strategy for Routine Replies and Positive Messages

Just as you'll make numerous requests for information and action throughout your career, you'll also respond to similar requests from other people. You'll have several goals for such messages: to communicate the information or the good news, to answer all questions, to provide all required details, and to leave your reader with a good impression of you and your firm.

Because readers receiving these messages will generally be interested in what you have to say, you can usually use the direct approach. Place your main idea (the positive reply or the good news) in the opening, use the body to explain all the relevant details, and close cordially—perhaps highlighting a benefit to your reader.

> **2 LEARNING OBJECTIVE**
>
> Describe an effective strategy for writing routine replies and positive messages.
>
> Use a direct approach for positive messages.

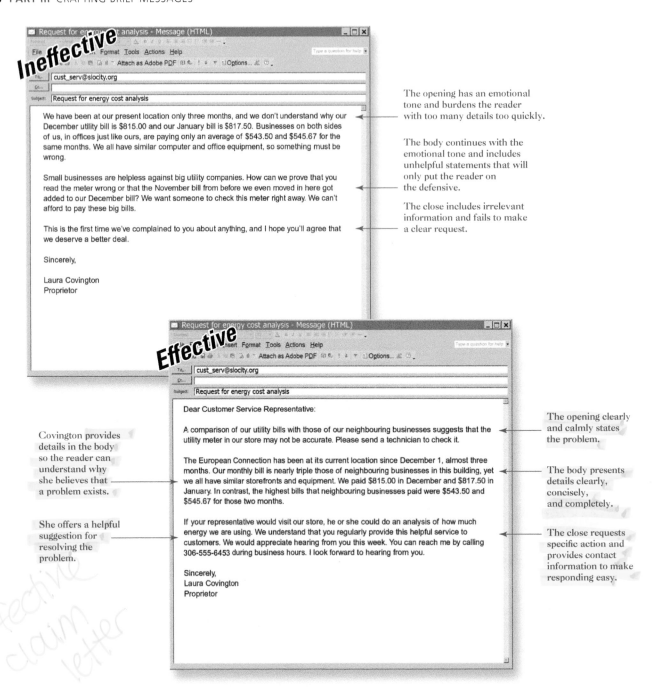

Figure 8–4 Effective and Ineffective Versions of a Claim Letter

STARTING WITH THE MAIN IDEA

By opening your routine and positive messages with the main idea or good news, you're preparing your audience for the detail that follows. Make your opening clear and concise. Although the following introductory statements make the same point, one is cluttered with unnecessary information that buries the purpose and fails to focus on the reader, whereas the other is brief and to the point:

Instead of This	Use This
I am pleased to inform you that after careful consideration of a diverse and talented pool of applicants, each of whom did a thorough job of analyzing Bild Pharmaceuticals' training needs, we have selected your bid.	Your bid to provide public speaking and presentation training to the sales staff has been accepted by Bild Pharmaceuticals.

The best way to write a clear opening is to have a clear idea of what you want to say. Before you put one word on paper, ask yourself, "What is the single most important message I have for the audience?"

PROVIDING NECESSARY DETAILS AND EXPLANATION

Use the body to explain your point completely so that your audience won't be confused or doubtful about your meaning. As you provide the details, maintain the supportive tone established in the opening. This tone is easy to continue when your message is entirely positive, as in this example:

Customer relationship management (CRM) software stores a variety of customer information—addresses and phone numbers, previous orders, personal facts such as birthdates, hobbies, and interests. This information helps companies generate routine, good-news, and goodwill messages such as new product announcements to selected customers. While CRM software helps businesses retain customers and raise profits, does it also pose the danger of violating one of our most prized possessions, our privacy?

Redsnapper/Alamy Stock Photo

> Your educational background and internship have impressed us, and we believe you would be a valuable addition to Green Valley Properties. As discussed during your interview, your salary will be $4600 per month plus benefits. Please plan to meet with our benefits manager, Paula Sanchez, at 9:30 A.M. on Monday, March 23. She will assist you with all the paperwork necessary to tailor our benefit package to your family situation. She will also arrange various orientation activities to help you fit in with our company.

However, if your routine message is mixed and must convey mildly disappointing information, put the negative portion of your message into as favourable a context as possible:

Try to embed any negative information in a positive context.

Instead of This	Use This
No, we no longer carry the Sportsgirl line of sweaters.	The new Olympic line has replaced the Sportsgirl sweaters that you asked about. Olympic features a wider range of colours and sizes and more contemporary styling.

In this example, the more complete description is less negative and emphasizes how the audience can benefit from the change. Be careful, though: you can use negative information in this type of message *only* if you're reasonably sure the audience will respond positively. Otherwise, use the indirect approach (discussed in Chapter 9).

If you are communicating to customers, you might also want to use the body of your message to assure the customer of the wisdom of his or her purchase selection (without being condescending or self-congratulatory). Using such favourable comments, often know as *resale*, is a good way to build customer relationships. These comments are commonly included in acknowledgments of orders and other routine announcements to customers, and they are most effective when they are relatively short and specific:

> The zipper on the carrying case you purchased is double-stitched and guaranteed for the life of the product.
> The KitchenAid mixer you ordered is our best-selling model. It should meet your cooking needs for many years.

ENDING WITH A COURTEOUS CLOSE

Your message is most likely to succeed if your readers are left feeling that you have their best interests in mind. You can accomplish this task either by highlighting

Make sure that the audience understands what to do next and how that action will benefit them.

a benefit to the audience or by expressing appreciation or goodwill. If follow-up action is required, clearly state who will do what next. See "Checklist: Writing Routine Replies and Positive Messages" to review the primary tasks involved in this type of business message.

✓ **Checklist**   **Writing Routine Replies and Positive Messages**

A. Start with the main idea.
- Be clear and concise.
- Identify the single most important message before you start writing.

B. Provide necessary details and explanation.
- Explain your point completely to eliminate any confusion or lingering doubts.
- Maintain a supportive tone throughout.

- Embed negative statements in positive contexts or balance them with positive alternatives.
- Talk favourably about the choices the customer has made.

C. End with a courteous close.
- Let your readers know that you have their personal well-being in mind.
- Tell readers how to proceed, if further action is required, and encourage them to act promptly.

Common Examples of Routine Replies and Positive Messages

As with routine requests, you'll encounter the need for a wide variety of routine replies and positive messages. Most routine and positive messages fall into six main categories: answers to requests for information and action, grants of claims and requests for adjustment, recommendations, informative messages, good-news announcements, and goodwill messages.

ANSWERING REQUESTS FOR INFORMATION AND ACTION

Every professional answers requests for information and action from time to time. If the response to a request is a simple yes or some other straightforward information, the direct approach is appropriate. A prompt, gracious, and thorough response will positively influence how people think about you and the organization you represent. Figure 8–5 shows a quick and courteous exchange typical of instant messaging (IM) communication in such areas as customer service and technical support. The agent (Janice) solves the problem quickly and presents a positive image of the company.

When you're answering requests and a potential sale is involved, you have three main goals: (1) to respond to the inquiry and answer all questions, (2) to leave your reader with a good impression of you and your firm, and (3) to encourage the future sale. The following message meets all three objectives:

> Here is the brochure "Entertainment Unlimited" that you requested. This booklet describes the vast array of entertainment options available to you with an Ocean Satellite Device (OSD).
>
> On page 12 you'll find a list of the 338 channels that the OSD brings into your home. You'll have access to movies, sports, and music channels; 24-hour news channels; local channels; and all the major television networks. OSD gives you a clearer picture and more precise sound than those old-fashioned dishes that took up most of your yard—and OSD uses only a small dish that mounts easily on your roof.
>
> More music, more cartoons, more experts, more news, and more sports are available to you with OSD than with any other cable or satellite connection in this region. It's all there, right at your fingertips.

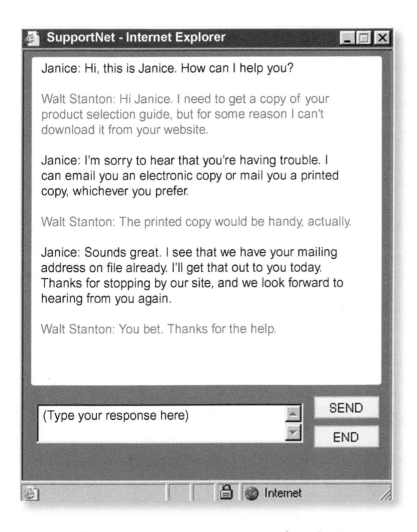

Figure 8–5 Effective Instant Messaging Response to Information Request

Just call us at 1-800-555-4331, and an OSD representative will come to your home to answer your questions. You'll love the programming and the low monthly cost. Call us today!

GRANTING CLAIMS AND REQUESTS FOR ADJUSTMENT

Even the best-run companies make mistakes, from shipping the wrong order to billing a customer's credit card inaccurately. In other cases, the customer or a third party might be responsible for the mistake, such as misusing a product or damaging it in shipment. Each of these events represents a turning point in your relationship with your customer. If you handle the situation well, your customer will likely be even more loyal than before because you've proven that you're serious about customer satisfaction. However, if a customer believes that you mishandled a complaint, you'll make the situation even worse. Dissatisfied customers often take their business elsewhere without notice and tell numerous friends and colleagues about the negative experience. A transaction that might be worth only a few dollars by itself could cost you many times that amount in lost business. In other words, every mistake is an opportunity to improve a relationship.

Few people go to the trouble of requesting an adjustment unless they actually have a problem, so most businesses start from the assumption that the customer is correct. From there, your response to the complaint depends on both your

3 **LEARNING OBJECTIVE**

Discuss the importance of knowing who is responsible when granting claims and requests for adjustment.

company's policies for resolving such issues and your assessment of whether the company, the customer, or some third party is at fault.

RESPONDING TO A CLAIM WHEN YOUR COMPANY IS AT FAULT Whenever you communicate about a mistake your company has made, do so carefully. Before you respond, ensure that you know your company's policies, which might even dictate specific legal and financial steps to be taken. For serious problems that go beyond routine errors, your company should have a *crisis management plan* that outlines communication steps both inside and outside the organization (see Chapter 9).

Most routine responses should take your company's specific policies into account and address the following points:

- **Acknowledge receipt of the customer's claim or complaint.** Even if you can't solve the problem immediately, at least let the other party know that somebody is listening.
- **Take (or assign) personal responsibility for setting matters straight.** Customers want to know that someone is listening and responding.
- **Sympathize with the customer's inconvenience or frustration.** Letting the customer see that you're on his or her side helps defuse the emotional element of the situation.
- **Explain precisely how you have resolved, or plan to resolve, the situation.** If you can respond exactly as the customer requested, be sure to communicate that. If you can't, explain why.
- **Take steps to repair the relationship.** Keeping your existing customers is almost always less expensive than acquiring new customers, so look for ways to mend the relationship and encourage future business.
- **Follow up to verify that your response was correct.** Follow-up not only helps improve customer service but also gives you another opportunity to show how much you care about your customer.

Maintain a sincere, professional tone when responding to a complaint.

In addition to these positive steps, maintain a professional demeanour. Don't blame anyone in your organization by name; don't make exaggerated, insincere apologies; don't imply that the customer is at fault; and don't promise more than you can deliver.

As with requests for information or action, companies often create customizable templates for granting claims and requests for adjustment. In the following example, a large mail-order clothing company created a form letter to respond to customers who complain that they haven't received exactly what was ordered:

Your letter concerning your recent Ross River order has been forwarded to our director of order fulfillment. Your complete satisfaction is our goal, and a customer service representative will contact you within 48 hours to assist with the issues raised in your letter.

In the meantime, please accept the enclosed $10 gift certificate as a token of our appreciation for your business. Whether you're skiing or driving a snowmobile, Ross River Gear offers you the best protection available from wind, snow, and cold—and Ross River has been taking care of customers' outdoor needs for over 27 years.

We appreciate the time you took to write to us. Your input helps us better serve you and all our customers.

The opening acknowledges receipt of the customer's communication.

The body explains what will happen next and when, without making promises the writer can't keep.

The body takes steps to repair the relationship and ensure continued business.

The close states the company's concern for all its customers.

In contrast, a response letter written as a personal answer to a unique claim would open with a clear statement of the good news: the settling of the claim according to the customer's request. The following is a more personal response from Ross River Gear:

> Here is your heather-blue wool-and-mohair sweater (size large) to replace the one returned to us with a defect in the knitting. Thanks for giving us the opportunity to correct this situation. Customers' needs have come first at Ross River Gear for 27 years.
>
> I've enclosed our newest catalogue and a $10 gift certificate that's good toward any purchase from it. Whether you are skiing or driving a snowmobile, Ross River Gear offers you the best protection available from wind, snow, and cold. Please let us know how we may continue to serve you and your sporting needs.

RESPONDING TO A CLAIM WHEN THE CUSTOMER IS AT FAULT Communication about a claim is a delicate matter when the customer is clearly at fault. If you refuse the claim, you may lose your customer—as well as many of the customer's friends and colleagues, who will hear only one side of the dispute. You must weigh the cost of making the adjustment against the cost of losing future business from one or more customers. Some companies have strict guidelines for responding to such claims, whereas others give individual employees and managers some leeway in making case-by-case decisions.

If you choose to grant the claim, you can open with the good news, being sure to specify exactly what you're agreeing to do, such as replacing the merchandise or refunding the purchase price. The body of the message is tricky because you want to discourage such claims in the future by steering the customer in the right direction. For example, customers sometimes misuse products or fail to follow the terms of service agreements, such as forgetting to cancel hotel reservations at least 24 hours in advance and thereby incurring the cost of one night's stay. Even if you do grant a particular claim, you don't want to imply that you will grant similar claims in the future. The challenge is to diplomatically remind the customer of proper usage or procedures without being condescending ("Perhaps you failed to read the instructions carefully") or preachy ("You should know that wool shrinks in hot water"). Close in a courteous manner that expresses your appreciation for the customer's business (Figure 8–6 educates a customer about how to treat his in-line skates).

To grant a claim when the customer is at fault, try to discourage future mistakes without insulting the customer.

RESPONDING TO A CLAIM WHEN A THIRD PARTY IS AT FAULT Sometimes neither your firm nor your customer is at fault. For example, ordering a DVD from Chapters.Indigo.ca involves not only the company but also a delivery service such as a private courier or Canada Post, the manufacturer of the DVD, a credit card issuer, and a company that processes credit card transactions. Any one of these other partners might be at fault, but the customer is likely to blame Chapters.Indigo.ca, since that is the entity primarily responsible for the transaction.

No general scheme applies to every case involving a third party, so evaluate the situation carefully and know your company's policies before responding. For instance, an online retailer and the companies that manufacture its merchandise might have an agreement which specifies that the manufacturers automatically handle all complaints about product quality. However,

When a third party is at fault, your response depends on your company's agreements with that organization.

1 Planning →

Analyze the Situation
The purpose is to grant the customer's claim, tactfully educate him, and encourage further business.

Gather Information
Gather information on product care, warranties, and resale information.

Select the Right Medium
An email message is appropriate in this case because the customer contacted the company via email.

Organize the Information
You're responding with a positive answer, so a direct approach is fine.

2 Writing →

Adapt to Your Audience
Show sensitivity to audience needs with a "you" attitude, politeness, positive emphasis, and bias-free language.

Compose the Message
Style is respectful while still managing to educate the customer on product usage and maintenance.

3 Completing

Revise the Message
Evaluate content and review readability; avoid unnecessary details.

Produce the Message
Emphasize a clean, professional appearance.

Proofread the Message
Review for errors in layout, spelling, and mechanics.

Distribute the Message
Email the reply.

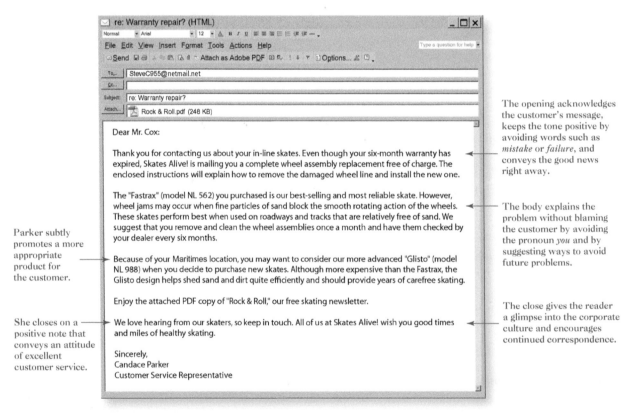

Parker subtly promotes a more appropriate product for the customer.

She closes on a positive note that conveys an attitude of excellent customer service.

The opening acknowledges the customer's message, keeps the tone positive by avoiding words such as *mistake* or *failure*, and conveys the good news right away.

The body explains the problem without blaming the customer by avoiding the pronoun *you* and by suggesting ways to avoid future problems.

The close gives the reader a glimpse into the corporate culture and encourages continued correspondence.

Figure 8–6 Responding to a Claim When the Buyer Is at Fault

regardless of who eventually resolves the problem, if customers contact you, you need to respond with messages that explain how the problem will be solved. Pointing fingers is unproductive and unprofessional; resolving the situation is the only issue customers care about. See "Checklist: Granting Claims and Adjustment Requests" to review the tasks involved in these kinds of business messages.

✓ Checklist   Granting Claims and Adjustment Requests

A. Responding when your company is at fault
- Be aware of your company's policies in such cases before you respond.
- Refer to the company's crisis management plan for serious situations.
- Start by acknowledging receipt of the claim or complaint.
- Take or assign personal responsibility for resolving the situation.
- Sympathize with the customer's frustration.
- Explain how you have resolved the situation (or plan to).
- Take steps to repair the customer relationship.
- Verify your response with the customer and keep the lines of communication open.

B. Responding when the customer is at fault
- Weigh the cost of complying with or refusing the request.
- Open with the good news if you choose to comply.
- Use the body of the message respectfully to educate the customer about steps needed to avoid a similar outcome in the future.
- Close with an appreciation for the customer's business.

C. Responding when a third party is at fault
- Evaluate the situation and review your company's policies before responding.
- Avoid placing blame; focus on the solution.
- Regardless of who is responsible for resolving the situation, let the customer know what will happen to resolve the problem.

TIPS FOR SUCCESS

"Most professors have contact with hundreds of students a year....

Thus it is difficult to remember the specific accomplishments of each individual. Provide a résumé with each request, plus any other information that would be helpful."

Julie K. Henderson, APR, accredited public relations professional

PROVIDING RECOMMENDATIONS

When writing a letter of recommendation, your goal is to convince readers that the person being recommended has the characteristics necessary for the job, project assignment, or other objective the person is seeking. A successful recommendation letter contains a number of relevant details (see Figure 8–7):

- The candidate's full name
- The position or other objective the candidate is seeking
- The nature of your relationship with the candidate
- An indication of whether you're answering a request from the person or taking the initiative to write
- Facts and evidence relevant to the candidate and the opportunity
- A comparison of this candidate's potential with that of peers, if available (for example, "Ms. Jonasson consistently ranked in the top 10 percent of her class.")
- Your overall evaluation of the candidate's suitability for the opportunity

As surprising as this might sound, the most difficult recommendation letters to write are often those for truly outstanding candidates. Your audience will have trouble believing uninterrupted praise for someone's talents and accomplishments. To enhance your credibility—and the candidate's—illustrate your general points with specific examples that point out the candidate's abilities and fitness for the job opening.

Writing a recommendation letter can be a complex legal matter, so be sure to check your company's policies and human resources department before writing a recommendation.[2] Also, keep in mind that every time you write a recommendation, you're putting your own reputation on the line. If the person's shortcomings are so pronounced that you don't think he or she is a good fit for the job,

Recommendation letters are vulnerable to legal complications, so consult with your company's legal department before writing one.

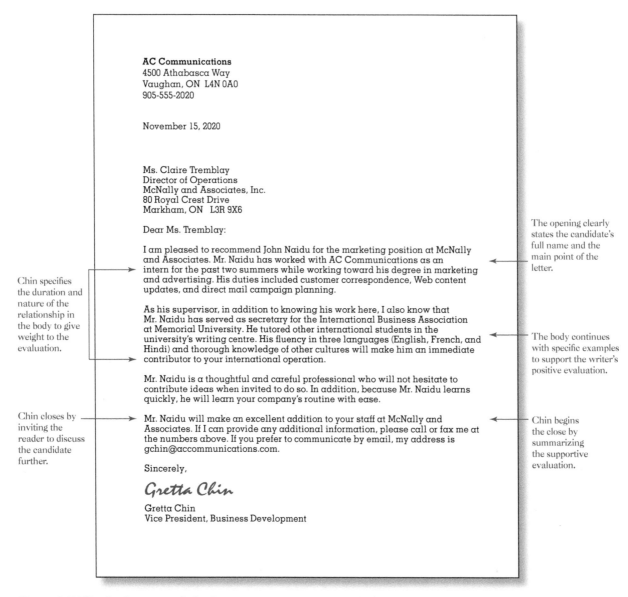

Figure 8–7 Effective Recommendation Letter

[Marginal annotations, left side:]

Chin specifies the duration and nature of the relationship in the body to give weight to the evaluation.

Chin closes by inviting the reader to discuss the candidate further.

[Letter content:]

AC Communications
4500 Athabasca Way
Vaughan, ON L4N 0A0
905-555-2020

November 15, 2020

Ms. Claire Tremblay
Director of Operations
McNally and Associates, Inc.
80 Royal Crest Drive
Markham, ON L3R 9X6

Dear Ms. Tremblay:

I am pleased to recommend John Naidu for the marketing position at McNally and Associates. Mr. Naidu has worked with AC Communications as an intern for the past two summers while working toward his degree in marketing and advertising. His duties included customer correspondence, Web content updates, and direct mail campaign planning.

As his supervisor, in addition to knowing his work here, I also know that Mr. Naidu has served as secretary for the International Business Association at Memorial University. He tutored other international students in the university's writing centre. His fluency in three languages (English, French, and Hindi) and thorough knowledge of other cultures will make him an immediate contributor to your international operation.

Mr. Naidu is a thoughtful and careful professional who will not hesitate to contribute ideas when invited to do so. In addition, because Mr. Naidu learns quickly, he will learn your company's routine with ease.

Mr. Naidu will make an excellent addition to your staff at McNally and Associates. If I can provide any additional information, please call or fax me at the numbers above. If you prefer to communicate by email, my address is gchin@accommunications.com.

Sincerely,

Gretta Chin

Gretta Chin
Vice President, Business Development

[Marginal annotations, right side:]

The opening clearly states the candidate's full name and the main point of the letter.

The body continues with specific examples to support the writer's positive evaluation.

Chin begins the close by summarizing the supportive evaluation.

---

the only choice is to not write the letter at all. Unless your relationship with the person warrants an explanation, simply suggest that someone else might be in a better position to provide a recommendation.

SHARING ROUTINE INFORMATION

All companies send routine informative messages, such as project updates and policy statements. For example, you may need to inform employees of organizational changes or tell customers about new shipping and return policies. Use the opening of informative messages to state the purpose (to inform) and briefly mention the nature of the information you are providing. Unlike the replies discussed earlier, such routine messages are not solicited by your reader, so make it clear up front why the reader is receiving this particular message. In the body, provide the necessary details and end your message with a courteous close.

Most routine communications are neutral. That is, they stimulate neither a positive nor a negative response from readers. For example, when you send departmental meeting announcements and reminder notices, you'll generally receive a neutral response from your readers (unless the purpose of the meeting is unwelcome). Simply present the factual information in the body of the message, and don't worry about the reader's attitude toward the information.

Some informative messages may require additional care. For example, policy statements or procedural changes may be good news for a company, perhaps by saving money. However, it may not be obvious to employees that such savings may make available additional employee resources or even pay raises. In instances where the reader may not initially view the information positively, use the body of the message to highlight the potential benefits from the reader's perspective. (For situations in which negative news will have a profound effect on the recipients, consider the indirect techniques discussed in Chapter 9.)

ANNOUNCING GOOD NEWS

To develop and maintain good relationships, smart companies recognize that it's good business to advertise positive developments. These can include opening new facilities, appointing a new executive, introducing new products or services, or sponsoring community events. Because good news is always welcome, use the direct approach.

Writing to a successful job applicant is one of the most pleasant good-news messages you might have the opportunity to write. The following example uses the direct approach and provides information that the recipient needs:

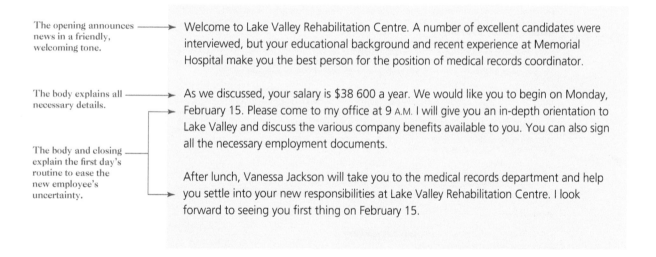

The opening announces news in a friendly, welcoming tone. → Welcome to Lake Valley Rehabilitation Centre. A number of excellent candidates were interviewed, but your educational background and recent experience at Memorial Hospital make you the best person for the position of medical records coordinator.

The body explains all necessary details. → As we discussed, your salary is $38 600 a year. We would like you to begin on Monday, February 15. Please come to my office at 9 A.M. I will give you an in-depth orientation to Lake Valley and discuss the various company benefits available to you. You can also sign all the necessary employment documents.

The body and closing explain the first day's routine to ease the new employee's uncertainty. → After lunch, Vanessa Jackson will take you to the medical records department and help you settle into your new responsibilities at Lake Valley Rehabilitation Centre. I look forward to seeing you first thing on February 15.

Although messages such as these are pleasant to write, they require careful planning and evaluation to avoid legal troubles. For example, messages that imply lifetime employment or otherwise make promises about the length or conditions of employment can be interpreted as legally binding contracts, even if you never intended to make such promises. Similarly, downplaying potentially negative news (such as rumours of a takeover) that turns out to affect the hired person in a negative way can be judged as fraud. Consequently, experts advise that a company's legal staff either scrutinize each offer letter or create standardized content to use in such letters.[3]

Job-offer letters should be reviewed by legal experts familiar with employment law because they can be viewed as legally binding contracts.

Good-news announcements are usually communicated via a letter or a **news release**, also known as a *press release*, a specialized document used to share relevant information with the local or national news media. (News releases are also used to announce negative news, such as plant closings.) In most companies, news releases are usually prepared (or at least supervised) by specially trained writers in the public relations department (see Figure 8–8). The content follows

BCE

News releases

Bell's $500,000 donation improves access to mental health therapy

A news release may include a sub-headline to add detail to the main headline.

Concordia's Applied Psychology Centre and Centre for Clinical Research in Health receive major gift from Bell Let's Talk mental health initiative to enhance treatment services

The first paragraph focuses on one subject only and avoids unrelated news.

MONTREAL, Feb. 6, 2013 /CNW Telbec/ - Treatment for anxiety, depression and mood disorders — mental health problems that affect one in five Canadians — is now more accessible to Montreal-area residents, thanks to the Bell Let's Talk mental health initiative. As part of this multi-year charitable program, Bell has generously given $500,000 to Concordia University's Department of Psychology to subsidize therapy and assessment at the university's Applied Psychology Centre and Centre for Clinical Research in Health.

"Bell's gift will have an immediate beneficial impact on Concordia's psychology program and its capacity to serve our community," says Concordia President Alan Shepard. "With Bell's support, our researchers can progress further in the study and treatment of mental health problems, and this reinforces our everyday connection to the local community."

A quotation adds information and adds variety to the writing style of the news release.

Bell's donation will subsidize therapeutic services for those individuals who need help to pay for treatment. Clients can either be referred by doctors and clinics throughout the Montreal area or refer themselves. The psychological services they receive at the Applied Psychology Centre benefit from advances in Concordia-based clinical and health research.

Paragraphs are short.

Martine Turcotte, Bell's Vice Chair of Québec, says the Bell Let's Talk mental health initiative — anchored by Bell Let's Talk Day on February 12 — is helping make a real difference in people's lives. "With the $50-million Bell Let's Talk initiative, Bell and its 17,000 Québec employees are firmly engaged in our commitment to de-stigmatize mental illness and improve access to mental health care," she says. "Supporting Concordia's Applied Psychology Centre and Centre for Clinical Research in Health is a concrete action the Bell team has taken to help people recover from mental illness, while at the same time contributing to research and education that advances treatment."

"This donation from Bell helps people in the community through work conducted at Concordia," says Adam Radomsky, director of the Centre for Clinical Research in Health and a professor in Concordia's Department of Psychology. "Support from Bell allows our PhD students to gain clinical experience and enhances our ability to provide much needed evidence-based psychological services that improve people's mental health."

Bell Let's Talk Day is February 12:
For every text message sent and every long distance call made by Bell and Bell Aliant customers on February 12, every tweet using #BellLetsTalk, and every Facebook share of our Bell Let's Talk message, Bell will donate 5 cents more to programs dedicated to mental health (regular long distance and text charges apply). Last year's Bell Let's Talk Day raised $3,926,014.20 in additional funding for mental health initiatives across the country.

About Bell:
Bell is Canada's largest communications company, providing consumers and business with solutions to all their communications needs: Bell Mobility wireless, high-speed Bell Internet, Bell Satellite TV and Bell Fibe TV, Bell Home Phone local and long distance, and Bell Business Markets IP-broadband and information and communications technology (ICT) services. Bell Media is Canada's premier multimedia company with leading assets in television, radio and digital media. Bell is wholly owned by BCE Inc. (TSX, NYSE: BCE). For Bell products and services, please visit Bell.ca. For BCE corporate information, please visit BCE.ca.

- On April18, John Molson School of Business Dean Steve Harvey tackles the subject of mental health and the workplace with Mary Deacon,chair of the Bell Let's Talk mental health initiative. Read more at **www.concordia.ca/now/what-we-do/research/20130122/living-well-aging-well.php**.

Related links:

- Bell Let's Talk mental health Initiative: www.bell.ca/letstalk
- Concordia Applied Psychology Centre: **http://psychology.concordia.ca/appliedpsychologycentre.php**
- Concordia Centre for Clinical Research in Health: **http://psychology.concordia.ca/ccrh**

SOURCE: Bell Canada

Scott McCulloch
Senior Advisor, Communications, Advancement and Alumni Relations
Concordia University
Tel: 514-848-2424, ext. 3825
Mobile: 514-513-8535
Email: scott.mcculloch@concordia.ca
Website: concordia.ca/alumni-giving
Twitter: twitter.com/ConcordiaAlumni

Véronique Arsenault
Bell Media Relations
Tel.: 1-855-391-5263
Email: veronique.arsenault@bell.ca
Twitter: @Bell_News

Figure 8–8 Online News Release

Courtesy: Bell Canada Enterprises

the customary pattern for a positive message: good news followed by details and a positive close. However, news releases have a critical difference: you're not writing directly to the ultimate audience (such as the readers of a newspaper); you're trying to interest an editor or a reporter in a story, and that person will then write the material that is eventually read by the larger audience. To write a successful news release, keep the following points in mind:[4]

- Ensure that your information is newsworthy and relevant to the specific publications or websites to which you are sending it. Editors are overwhelmed with news releases, so those without real news content are disposed of—and can damage the writer's credibility, too.
- Focus on one subject; don't try to pack a single news release with multiple, unrelated news items.
- Put your most important idea first. Don't force editors to hunt for the news.
- Be brief: break up long sentences and keep paragraphs short.
- Eliminate clutter such as redundancy and extraneous facts.
- Be as specific as possible.
- Minimize self-congratulatory adjectives and adverbs; if the content of your message is newsworthy, the media professionals will be interested in the news on its own merits.
- Follow established industry conventions for style, punctuation, and format.

Online distribution systems such as CNW (www.newswire.ca) and PR Newswire (www.prnewswire.com) make it easy for even the smallest companies to reach editors and reporters at the most prominent publications around the world. Many companies also create special media pages on their websites that contain their latest news releases, background information on the company, and archives of past news releases.

Until recently, news releases were crafted in a way to provide information to reporters, who would then write their own articles if the subject matter was interesting to their readers. Thanks to the Internet and social media, however, the nature of the news release is changing. Many companies now view it as a general-purpose tool for communicating directly with customers and other audiences, creating *direct-to-consumer news releases*. As media expert David Meerman Scott puts it, "Millions of people read press releases directly, unfiltered by the media. You need to be speaking directly to them."[5]

Many companies now release news directly to the public rather than relying on the news media to share it.

The newest twist on news releases is the *social media release*, which has several advantages over the traditional release. First, the social media release emphasizes bullet-point content over narrative paragraphs so that bloggers, editors, and others can assemble their own stories, rather than being forced to rewrite the material in a traditional release. Second, as an electronic-only document (a specialized webpage, essentially), the social media release offers the ability to include videos and other multimedia elements. Third, social bookmarking buttons make it easy for people to help publicize the content.[6]

FOSTERING GOODWILL

All business messages should be written with an eye toward fostering goodwill among business contacts, but some messages are written primarily and specifically to build goodwill. You can use these messages to enhance your relationships with customers, colleagues, and other businesspeople by sending friendly or even unexpected notes with no direct business purpose.

Effective goodwill messages must be sincere and honest. Otherwise, you'll appear to be interested in personal gain rather than in benefiting customers, co-workers, or your organization. To come across as sincere, avoid exaggerating,

5 **LEARNING OBJECTIVE**

Describe the importance of goodwill messages and explain how to make them effective.

Goodwill is the positive feeling that encourages people to maintain a business relationship.

Ensure that your compliments are both sincere and honest.

and back up any compliments with specific points. In addition, readers often regard more restrained praise as being more sincere:

Instead of This	Use This
Words cannot express my appreciation for the great job you did. Thanks. No one could have done it better. You're terrific! You've made the whole firm sit up and take notice, and we are ecstatic to have you working here.	Thanks again for taking charge of the meeting in my absence and doing such an excellent job. With just an hour's notice, you managed to pull the legal and public relations departments together so we could present a united front in the negotiations. Your dedication and communication abilities have been noted and are truly appreciated.

Even though the second version is longer, it is a more effective message because it is specific and sincere.

Taking note of significant events in someone's personal life helps cement the business relationship.

SENDING CONGRATULATIONS One prime opportunity for sending goodwill messages is to congratulate someone for a significant business achievement—perhaps for being promoted or for attaining an important civic position. Compare the congratulatory notes in Figure 8–9, in which a manager at Office Supply corporate headquarters congratulates an advertising agency that was awarded a prestigious national contract. The draft version sounds vague and insincere, and it doesn't bother to actually offer congratulations until the final sentence. In contrast, the revised version moves swiftly to the subject: the good news. It gives reasons for expecting success and avoids extravagant and essentially meaningless praise such as "Only you can do the job!"

The highlights in people's personal lives—weddings, births, and graduations—are also occasions for such goodwill messages. You may congratulate business acquaintances on their own achievements or on the accomplishments of a spouse or child. You may also take note of personal events, even if you don't know the reader well. If you're already friendly with the reader, a more personal tone is appropriate.

An effective message of appreciation documents a person's contributions.

SENDING MESSAGES OF APPRECIATION An important business quality is the ability to recognize the contributions of employees, colleagues, suppliers, and other associates. Your praise does more than just make the person feel good; it encourages further excellence. Moreover, a message of appreciation may become an important part of someone's personnel file. So, when you write a message of appreciation, specifically mention the person or people you want to praise. The brief message that follows expresses gratitude and reveals the happy result:

Clive Chilvers/Alamy Stock Photo

Employee volunteer activities not only contribute to the community but also can bring employees together. How should management acknowledge employee volunteerism? Are notes of appreciation sufficient? What are other methods for showing recognition?

Thank you and everyone on your team for the heroic efforts you took to bring our servers back up after last Friday's flood. We were able to restore business right on schedule first thing Monday morning. You went far beyond the level of contractual service in restoring our data centre within 16 hours. I would especially like to highlight the contribution of networking specialist Julienne Marks, who worked for 12 straight hours to reconnect our Internet service. If I can serve as a reference in your future sales activities, please do not hesitate to ask.

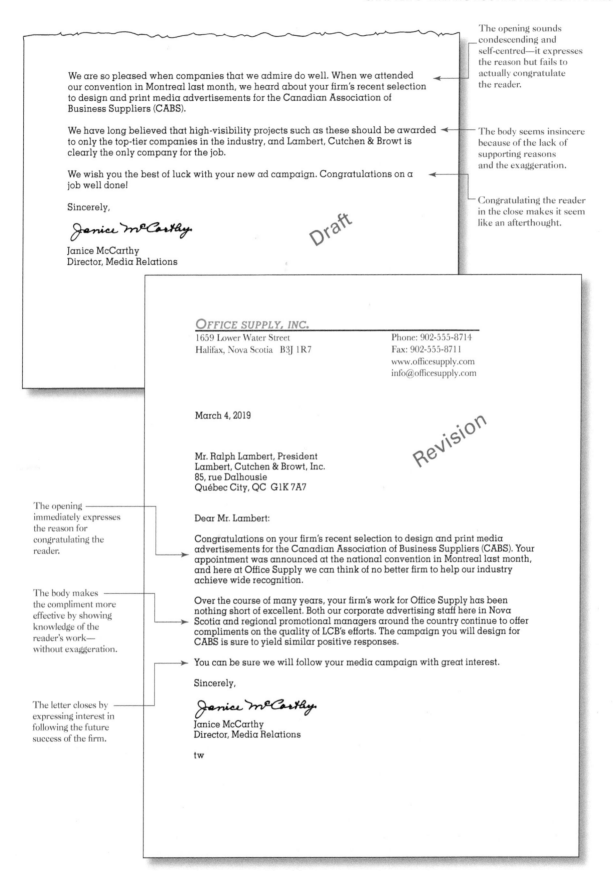

The opening sounds condescending and self-centred—it expresses the reason but fails to actually congratulate the reader.

We are so pleased when companies that we admire do well. When we attended our convention in Montreal last month, we heard about your firm's recent selection to design and print media advertisements for the Canadian Association of Business Suppliers (CABS).

We have long believed that high-visibility projects such as these should be awarded to only the top-tier companies in the industry, and Lambert, Cutchen & Browt is clearly the only company for the job.

The body seems insincere because of the lack of supporting reasons and the exaggeration.

We wish you the best of luck with your new ad campaign. Congratulations on a job well done!

Sincerely,

Janice McCarthy

Janice McCarthy
Director, Media Relations

Congratulating the reader in the close makes it seem like an afterthought.

Draft

OFFICE SUPPLY, INC.

1659 Lower Water Street
Halifax, Nova Scotia B3J 1R7

Phone: 902-555-8714
Fax: 902-555-8711
www.officesupply.com
info@officesupply.com

March 4, 2019

Revision

Mr. Ralph Lambert, President
Lambert, Cutchen & Browt, Inc.
85, rue Dalhousie
Québec City, QC G1K 7A7

The opening immediately expresses the reason for congratulating the reader.

Dear Mr. Lambert:

Congratulations on your firm's recent selection to design and print media advertisements for the Canadian Association of Business Suppliers (CABS). Your appointment was announced at the national convention in Montreal last month, and here at Office Supply we can think of no better firm to help our industry achieve wide recognition.

The body makes the compliment more effective by showing knowledge of the reader's work— without exaggeration.

Over the course of many years, your firm's work for Office Supply has been nothing short of excellent. Both our corporate advertising staff here in Nova Scotia and regional promotional managers around the country continue to offer compliments on the quality of LCB's efforts. The campaign you will design for CABS is sure to yield similar positive responses.

You can be sure we will follow your media campaign with great interest.

The letter closes by expressing interest in following the future success of the firm.

Sincerely,

Janice McCarthy

Janice McCarthy
Director, Media Relations

tw

Figure 8–9 Poor and Improved Versions of a Letter Congratulating a Business Acquaintance

OFFERING CONDOLENCES In times of serious trouble and deep sadness, well-written condolences and expressions of sympathy can mean a great deal to people who've experienced loss. This type of message is difficult to write, but don't let the difficulty of the task keep you from responding promptly. Those who have experienced a health problem, the death of a loved one, or a business misfortune appreciate knowing that others care.

The primary purpose of condolence messages is to let the audience know that you and the organization you represent care about the person's loss.

Open a message of condolence with a brief statement of sympathy, such as "I was deeply sorry to hear of your loss." In the body, mention the good qualities or the positive contributions made by the person or business. State what the person or business meant to you or to your colleagues. In closing, offer your condolences and best wishes. Here are a few general suggestions for writing condolence messages:

- **Keep reminiscences brief.** Recount a memory or an anecdote (even a humorous one), but don't dwell on the details of the loss lest you add to the reader's anguish.
- **Write in your own words.** Write as if you were speaking privately to the person. Don't quote "poetic" passages or use stilted or formal phrases.
- **Be tactful.** Mention your shock and dismay, but remember that bereaved and distressed loved ones take little comfort in lines such as "Richard was too young to die" or "Starting all over again will be so difficult." Try to strike a balance between superficial expressions of sympathy and painful references to a happier past or the likelihood of a bleak future.
- **Take special care.** Ensure that you spell names correctly and are accurate in your review of facts. Be prompt.
- **Write about special qualities of the deceased.** You may have to rely on reputation to do this, but let the grieving person know you valued his or her loved one.
- **Consider mentioning special attributes or resources of the bereaved person.** If you know that the bereaved person has attributes or resources that will be a comfort in the time of loss, such as personal resilience, religious faith, or a circle of close friends, mentioning these can make the reader feel more confident about handling the challenges he or she faces.

The following example, a message by a manager to his administrative assistant after learning of her husband's death, shows sensitivity and sincerity:

> My sympathy to you and your children. All your friends at Carter Electric were so very sorry to learn of John's death. Although I never had the opportunity to meet him, I do know how very special he was to you. Your tales of your family's camping trips and his rafting expeditions were always memorable.

To review the tasks involved in writing goodwill messages, see "Checklist: Sending Goodwill Messages."

✓ Checklist | Sending Goodwill Messages

- Be sincere and honest.
- Don't exaggerate or use vague, grandiose language. Support positive statements with specific evidence.
- Use congratulatory messages to build goodwill with clients and colleagues.
- Send messages of appreciation to emphasize how much you value the work of others.

- When sending condolence messages, open with a brief statement of sympathy, followed by an expression of how much the deceased person meant to you or your firm (as appropriate), and then close by offering your best wishes for the future.

SUMMARY OF LEARNING OBJECTIVES

1 **Outline an effective strategy for writing routine requests.** When writing a routine request, open by stating your specific request. At the same time, avoid being abrupt or tactless: pay attention to tone; assume that your audience will comply; and be specific. Use the body of a routine request to justify your request and explain its importance. Close routine requests with a request for some specific action (including a deadline when possible), information about how you can be reached, and an expression of goodwill.

2 **Describe an effective strategy for writing routine replies and positive messages.** When writing routine and positive replies, open concisely and clearly with your main idea. Follow the opening with the necessary details and explanation, ensuring that you maintain a courteous, supportive tone. End with a courteous close, incorporating an audience benefit or expressing goodwill. If reader follow-up is required, make the action detailed.

3 **Discuss the importance of knowing who is responsible when granting claims and requests for adjustment.** In messages granting a claim, the explanatory section differs depending on who is at fault. If your company is at fault, avoid reacting defensively, and be careful when referring to company errors. Rather than placing blame, explain your company's efforts to do a good job. Remember not to make any unrealistic promises or guarantees. If your customer is at fault, you must help your reader realize what

went wrong so it won't happen repeatedly. However, you don't want to sound condescending, preachy, or insulting. If a third party is at fault, you can honour the claim with no explanation, or you can honour the claim and explain that the problem was not your fault.

4 **Explain how creating informative messages differs from responding to information requests.** When writing informative messages and responses to information requests, open with the main idea. However, because informative messages are not solicited by your audience, you must clarify early in your message why the reader is receiving it. Furthermore, most informative messages are neutral, unlike responses to information requests, which motivate either a positive or negative reader response. In situations where readers may not view the information positively, stress potential reader benefits in the message body to encourage a positive reaction.

5 **Describe the importance of goodwill messages and explain how to make them effective.** Goodwill messages are important for building relationships with customers, co-workers, and other businesspeople. These friendly, unexpected notes have no direct business purpose, but they make people feel good about doing business with the sender. To make goodwill messages effective, be honest and sincere. Avoid exaggerating, back up compliments with specific points, and give restrained praise.

ON THE JOB   PERFORMING COMMUNICATION TASKS AT INDIGO BOOKS AND MUSIC

Heather Reisman wants to offer Canada's book lovers "the best of a small proprietor-run shop combined with the selection of a true emporium." The impact she has made demonstrates her ability to communicate with customers and employees. You have recently taken a job at Indigo Books and Music's head office as an administrative assistant on the management team. One of your jobs entails drafting emails to Indigo store managers. Using the principles outlined in this chapter for writing direct requests, handle each situation to the best of your ability. Be prepared to explain your choices.

1. You are asked to contact the store managers to find out how the company's website has affected sales in retail outlets over the past six months. Which is the best opening for this email?

   a. I have recently joined Heather Reisman's staff as an administrative assistant. She has asked me to write to you to obtain your feedback on the impact on store sales

of the company's website over the last six months. Please reply to the following questions within five working days. [List of questions follows.]

   b. Please tell us what you think of www.chapters.indigo.ca. Ms. Reisman wants to evaluate its impact on our business. Within the next few days, can you take a few moments to jot down your thoughts on its impact? Specifically, Ms. Reisman would like to know . . . [List of questions follows.]

   c. By April 14, please submit written answers to the following questions on the Indigo website. [List of questions follows.]

   d. Has the website affected sales in your store over the past six months? We're polling all store managers for the impact of online retailing. Is it thumbs up or thumbs down on the Web?

2. Which is the best choice for the middle section of the email?

   a. Specifically, has store business decreased because of the website? If so, what is the percentage decrease in sales over the past six months? Over the comparable period past year? Have customers mentioned the website? If so, have their comments been positive or negative? Has employee morale been affected by the site? How?

   b. By replying to the following questions, you will help us decide whether to continue with the website as is or change it:

      1. Has business decreased in your store since Indigo has had the website? If it has, what is the percentage decrease in sales over the past six months? Over the comparable period last year?

      2. Have customers mentioned the website? If so, have their comments been positive or negative? Give some typical examples.

      3. Has employee morale been affected by the website? How?

   c. By circling the response that most accurately reflects your store's experience, please answer the following questions regarding the company's new website:

      1. Over the last six months, sales have
         a. increased
         b. decreased
         c. remained about the same

      2. Customers (have/have not) mentioned the website. Their comments have been primarily (positive/negative).

      3. Employee morale (has/has not) been affected by the website.

   d. Ms. Reisman needs to know the following:

      1. How have overall store sales changed over the past six months because of the company's website?

      2. What do customers think of the site? Attach complimentary customer comments.

      3. What do employees think of the site? Attach complimentary employee comments.

3. For a courteous close with a request for specific action, which paragraph is the best?

   a. Thank you for your cooperation. Please submit your reply in writing by April 14.

   b. Ms. Reisman is meeting with her senior staff on April 16 to discuss the website. She would like to have your reaction in writing by April 14 so that she can present your views during that meeting. If you have any questions, please contact me at (416) 555-2886.

   c. You may contact me at (416) 555-2886 if you have any questions or need additional information about this survey. Ms. Reisman requires your written response by April 14 so she can discuss your views with her senior staff on April 16.

   d. Thank you for your input. As the front-line troops in the battle for sales, you are in a good position to evaluate the impact of the website. We here at corporate headquarters want to increase overall company sales, but we need your feedback. Please submit your written evaluation by April 14 so Ms. Reisman can use the results as ammunition in her meeting with senior staff on April 16.

TEST YOUR KNOWLEDGE

1. What is an effective strategy for writing a routine request?

2. When is a request routine?

3. Why is tone important in routine messages?

4. How do you ask for specific action in a courteous manner?

5. How does the question of fault affect what you say in a message granting a claim?

6. How does a claim differ from an adjustment?

7. How can you avoid sounding insincere when writing a goodwill message?

8. What are some guidelines for writing condolence messages?

APPLY YOUR KNOWLEDGE

1. When organizing request messages, why is it important to know whether any cultural differences exist between you and your audience? Explain.

2. Your company's error cost an important business customer a new client; you know it and your customer knows it. Do you apologize, or do you refer to the incident in a positive light without admitting any responsibility? Explain.

3. Why is it good practice to explain why replying to a request could benefit the reader?

4. Every time you send a direct-request memo to Ted Erasmus, who works in another department in your company, he delays or refuses to comply. You're beginning to get impatient. Should you send Erasmus a memo to ask what's wrong? Complain to your supervisor about Erasmus's uncooperative attitude? Arrange a face-to-face meeting with Erasmus? Bring up the problem at the next staff meeting? Explain.

5. **Ethical Choices** You have a complaint against one of your suppliers, but you have no documentation to back it up. Should you request an adjustment anyway? Why or why not?

RUNNING CASES

> CASE 1 Noreen

Now that Petro-Go is a larger company (see Chapter 6 for details on the merger with Best Gas), upper management has established a new procedure: regular semi-annual bonuses will be distributed to all employees who meet performance targets. The letter announcing this development will include a list of performance expectations and bonus goals.

Noreen is asked to write the letter on her manager's behalf informing the "Go Points" and "Collections" teams of this new bonus opportunity. Petro-Go will mail the letter, once approved, to each of the team members, letting them know that, because of their hard work over the past six months, they will each receive a bonus cheque. The cheques will be enclosed with the letters. Each member will receive a bonus amount based on their individual performance and achievements captured in the Petro-Go semi-annual statistics and progress reports.

QUESTIONS

a. Is this a routine or good-news letter or both?

b. What information should Noreen begin the letter with? Why?

c. How should Noreen end the letter? Why?

d. Does Noreen need to include an announcement about the merger in this letter?

e. What tone will Noreen use in this letter?

YOUR TASK

Write the letter. Remember to use company letterhead (create it yourself) and include an enclosure notation for the two enclosures. Also thank the team for their hard work and dedication to the company over the past six months. Let the employees know they can contact Noreen if they have questions or comments.

This letter contains confidential information and should state so on the envelope and on the letter itself. Prepare the envelope. (See Appendix A for letter and envelope formats.)

> CASE 2 Kwong

Kwong's boss at Accountants For All asks him to write a letter replying to a corporate customer's request for information. Kwong needs to write to Albridge and Scranton Ltd. to give them the details of the past five years' tax summaries. John Albridge would like to know the total expenses claimed, primarily the vehicle expense deduction, and the total amount of refund/amount owed each year. Kwong needs to attach copies of each year's summary statement as well.

This is a good opportunity for Kwong to thank Albridge and Scranton Ltd. for their past business and let them know that Accountants For All looks forward to their future business.

QUESTIONS

a. Should Kwong list the information requested in the letter or simply attach the summary statements and refer the reader to those statements?

b. Is this a routine or goodwill letter or both?

c. Is the direct or indirect approach best for this letter? Why?

d. Is it best to thank the customer for their past business in the introductory part of the letter? Why or why not?

e. Where in the letter should Kwong include the information about looking forward to doing future business with Albridge and Scranton Ltd.?

YOUR TASK

Write the letter. Remember to use company letterhead (create it yourself) and include an enclosure notation. Also thank the customer for their past and anticipated future business. Leave the customer with a contact name at Accountants For All for further inquiries.

This letter contains confidential information; the envelope and the letter itself should state this. Prepare the envelope. (See Appendix A for letter and envelope formats.)

PRACTISE YOUR KNOWLEDGE

Read the following documents, then (1) analyze the strengths and weaknesses of each sentence and (2) revise each document so that it follows this chapter's guidelines.

DOCUMENT 8.A: REQUESTING ROUTINE INFORMATION FROM A BUSINESS

Our university is closing its dining hall for financial reasons, so we want to do something to help the students prepare their own food in their residence rooms if they so choose. Your colourful ad in *University Management Magazine* caught our eye. We need the following information before we make our decision:

- Would you be able to ship the microwaves by August 15? We realize this is short notice, but our board of trustees just made the decision to close the dining hall last week, and we're scrambling around trying to figure out what to do.

- Do they have any kind of a warranty? Students can be pretty hard on things, as you know, so we will need a good warranty.
- How much does it cost? Do you give a discount for a big order?
- Do we have to provide a special electrical outlet?
- Will students know how to use them, or will we need to provide instructions?

As I said before, we're on a tight time frame and need good information from you as soon as possible to help us make our decision about ordering. You never know what the board might come up with next. I'm looking at several other companies, also, so please let us know ASAP.

DOCUMENT 8.B: MAKING CLAIMS AND REQUESTS FOR ADJUSTMENT

At a local business-supply store, I recently purchased your Negotiator Pro for my computer. I bought the CD because I saw your ad for it in *MacWorld* magazine, and it looked as if it might be an effective tool for use in my corporate seminar on negotiation.

Unfortunately, when I inserted it in my office computer, it wouldn't work. I returned it to the store, but since I had already opened it, they refused to exchange it for a CD that would work or give me a refund. They told me to contact you and that you might be able to send me a version that would work with my computer.

You can send the information to me at the letterhead address. If you cannot send me the correct disc, please refund my $79.95. Thanks in advance for any help you can give me in this matter.

DOCUMENT 8.C: RESPONDING TO CLAIMS AND ADJUSTMENT REQUESTS WHEN THE CUSTOMER IS AT FAULT

We read your letter requesting your deposit refund. We couldn't figure out why you hadn't received it, so we talked to our maintenance engineer as you suggested. He said you had left one of the doors off the hinges in your apartment to get a large sofa through the door. He also confirmed that you had

paid him $35.00 to replace the door, since you had to turn in the U-Haul trailer and were in a big hurry.

This entire situation really was caused by a lack of communication between our housekeeping inspector and the maintenance engineer. All we knew was that the door was off the hinges when it was inspected by Sally Tarnley. You know that our policy states that if anything is wrong with the apartment, we keep the deposit. We had no way of knowing that George just hadn't gotten around to replacing the door.

But we have good news. We approved the deposit refund, which will be mailed to you from our home office in Halifax, NS. I'm not sure how long that will take, however. If you don't receive the cheque by the end of next month, give me a call.

Next time, it's really a good idea to stay with your apartment until it's inspected as stipulated in your lease agreement. That way, you'll be sure to receive your refund when you expect it. Hope you have a good summer.

DOCUMENT 8.D: WRITING A LETTER OF RECOMMENDATION

Your letter to Michael McKay, president of SoundWave Electronics, was forwarded to me because I am the human resources director. In my job as head of HR, I have access to performance reviews for all of the SoundWave employees in Canada. This means, of course, that I would be the person best qualified to answer your request for information on Nick Oshinski.

In your letter of the 15th, you asked about Nick Oshinski's employment record with us because he has applied to work for your company. Mr. Oshinski was employed with us from January 3, 2008, until February 27, 2009. During that time, Mr. Oshinski received ratings ranging from 2.5 up to 9.6, with 10 being the top score. As you can see, he must have done better reporting to some managers than to others. In addition, he took all vacation days, which is a bit unusual. Although I did not know Mr. Oshinski personally, I know that our best workers seldom use all the vacation time they earn. I do not know if that applies in this case.

In summary, Nick Oshinski performed his tasks well depending on who managed him.

EXERCISES

8.1 Revising Messages: Directness and Conciseness

Revise the following short email messages so they are more direct and concise; develop a subject line for each revised message:

a. I'm contacting you about your recent email request for technical support on your cable Internet service. Part of the problem we have in tech support is trying to figure out exactly what each customer's specific problem is so that

we can troubleshoot quickly and get you back in business as quickly as possible. You may have noticed that in the online support request form, there are a number of fields to enter your type of computer, operating system, memory, and so on. While you did tell us you were experiencing slow download speeds during certain times of the day, you didn't tell us which times specifically, nor did you complete all the fields telling us about your computer. Please return to our support website and resubmit your request, being sure to provide all the necessary information; then we'll be able to help you.

b. Thank you for contacting us about the difficulty you had collecting your luggage at Fort Simpson Airport. We are very sorry for the inconvenience this has caused you. As you know, travelling can create problems of this sort regardless of how careful the airline personnel might be. To receive compensation, please send us a detailed list of the items that you lost and complete the following questionnaire. You can email it back to us.

c. Sorry it took us so long to get back to you. We were flooded with résumés. Anyway, your résumé made the final 10, and after meeting three hours yesterday, we've decided we'd like to meet with you. What is your schedule like for next week? Can you come in for an interview on June 15 at 3:00 P.M.? Please get back to us by the end of this workweek and let us know if you will be able to attend. As you can imagine, this is our busy season.

d. We're letting you know that because we use over a tonne of paper a year and because so much of that paper goes into the wastebasket to become so much more environmental waste, starting Monday, we're placing green plastic bins outside the elevators on every floor to recycle that paper and in the process, minimize pollution.

8.2 Revising Messages: Directness and Conciseness

Rewrite the following sentences so that they are direct and concise. If necessary, divide your answer into two sentences.

a. We wanted to invite you to our special 40 percent off by-invitation-only sale. The sale is taking place on November 9.

b. We wanted to let you know that we are giving a tote bag and a voucher for five iTunes downloads with every $50 donation you make to our radio station.

c. The director planned to go to the meeting that will be held on Monday at a little before 11 A.M.

d. In today's meeting, we were happy to have the opportunity to welcome Paul Eccleson. He reviewed some of the newest types of order forms. If you have any questions about these new forms, feel free to call him at his office.

8.3 Internet: Analyzing an E-card

Analyze the following message:

Dear Bill,

I would like to take the tome to congradulate you on your new promotion. I know I spent lots of time with you to help you improve your skills so that you can now launch yourself in this new carrer. I hope you do me proud!

Would you send this message? Why? Is it personal enough? Is it appropriate? How would you improve it?

8.4 Teamwork: Choosing Format and Approach

With another student, identify the purpose and select the most appropriate format for communicating these written messages. Next, consider how the audience is likely to respond to each message. Based on this audience analysis, determine whether the direct or indirect approach would be effective for each message. Explain your reasoning.

a. A notice to all employees about the placement of recycling bins by the elevator doors

b. The first late-payment notice to a good customer who usually pays his bills on time

8.5 Revising Messages: Conciseness, Courteousness, and Specificity

Critique the following closing paragraphs. How would you rewrite each to be concise, courteous, and specific?

a. I need your response sometime soon so I can order the parts in time for your service appointment. Otherwise your air-conditioning system may not be in tip-top condition for the start of the summer season.

b. Thank you in advance for sending me as much information as you can about your products. I look forward to receiving your package in the very near future.

c. To schedule an appointment with one of our knowledgeable mortgage specialists in your area, you can always call our hotline at 1-800-555-8765. This is also the number to call if you have more questions about mortgage rates, closing procedures, or any other aspect of the mortgage process. Remember, we're here to make the home-buying experience as painless as possible.

8.6 Ethical Choice: Customer Service

Your company markets a line of automotive accessories for people who like to "tune" their cars for maximum performance. A customer has just written a furious email, claiming that a supercharger he purchased from your website didn't deliver the extra engine power he expected. Your company has a standard refund process to handle situations such as this, and you have the information you need to inform the customer about that. You also have information that could help the customer find a more compatible supercharger from one of your competitors, but the customer's email message is so abusive that you don't feel obligated to help. Is this an appropriate response? Why or why not?

CASES   APPLYING THE THREE-STEP WRITING PROCESS TO CASES

Apply each step to the following cases, as assigned by your instructor.

1 Planning →   **2** Writing →   **3** Completing

Analyze the Situation
Identify both your general purpose and your specific purpose. Clarify exactly what you want your audience to think, feel, or believe after receiving your message. Profile your primary audience, including their backgrounds, differences, similarities, and likely reactions to your message.

Gather Information
Identify the information your audience will need to receive, as well as other information you may need in order to craft an effective message.

Select the Right Medium
Make sure your medium is both acceptable to the audience and appropriate for the message.

Organize the Information
Choose a direct or indirect approach based on the audience and the message; most routine requests and routine and positive messages should employ a direct approach. Identify your main idea, limit your scope, then outline necessary support points and other evidence.

Adapt to Your Audience
Show sensitivity to audience needs with a "you" attitude, politeness, positive emphasis, and bias-free language. Understand how much credibility you already have—and how much you may need to establish. Project your company's image by maintaining an appropriate style and tone.

Compose the Message
Draft your message using precise language, effective sentences, and coherent paragraphs.

Revise the Message
Evaluate content and review readability, then edit and rewrite for conciseness and clarity.

Produce the Message
Use effective design elements and suitable layout for a clean, professional appearance.

Proofread the Message
Review for errors in layout, spelling, and mechanics; verify overall document quality.

Distribute the Message
Deliver your message using the chosen medium; make sure all documents and all relevant files are distributed successfully.

Routine Requests

❙Letter Writing SKILLS❙

1. Step on It: Letter to Floorgraphics Requesting Information about Underfoot Advertising

You work for Mary Utanpitak, owner of Better Bike and Ski Shop. Yesterday, Mary met with Schwinn sales representative Tom Beeker, who urged her to sign a contract with Floorgraphics. That company leases floor space from retail stores and then creates and sells floor ads to manufacturers such as Schwinn. Floorgraphics will pay Mary a fee for leasing the floor space, as well as a percentage for every ad it

sells. Mary was definitely interested and turned to you after Beeker left.

"Tom says that advertising decals on the floor in front of the product reach consumers right where they're standing when making a decision," explained Mary. "He says the ads increase sales from 25 to 75 percent."

You both look down at the dusty floor, and Mary laughs. "It seems funny that manufacturers will pay hard cash to put their names where customers are going to track dirt all over them! But if Tom's telling the truth, we could profit in three ways: from the leasing fee, the increased sales of products being advertised, and the share in ad revenues. That's not so funny."

Your task: Mary Utanpitak asks you to write a letter for her signature to CEO Richard Rebh at Floorgraphics, Inc. (1725 E. 3rd Avenue, Vancouver, BC, V5M 5R6) asking for financial details and practical information about the ads. For example, how will you clean your floors? Who installs and removes the ads? Can you terminate the lease if you don't like the ads?[7]

▌Email SKILLS ▌

2. Breathing Life Back into Your Biotech Career: Email Requesting a Recommendation

After five years of work in the human resources department at Cell Genesys (a company that is developing cancer treatment drugs), you were laid off in a round of cost-cutting moves that rippled through the biotech industry in recent years. The good news is that you found stable employment in the grocery distribution industry. The bad news is that in the three years since you left Cell Genesys, you truly miss working in the exciting biotechnology field and having the opportunity to be a part of something as important as helping people recover from life-threatening diseases. You know that careers in biotech are uncertain, but you have a few dollars in the bank now, and you're willing to ride that roller coaster again.

Your task: Draft an email to Calvin Morris, your old boss at Cell Genesys, reminding him of the time you worked together and asking him to write a letter of recommendation for you.[8]

▌Email SKILLS ▌

3. Please Tell Me: Email Requesting Routine Information about a Product

As a consumer, you've probably seen hundreds of products that you'd like to buy (if you haven't, look at the advertisements in your favourite magazine for ideas). Choose a big-ticket item that is rather complicated, such as a stereo system or a vacation in the Caribbean.

Your task: You surely have some questions about the features of your chosen product or about its price, guarantees, local availability, and so on. Write an email to the company or organization that's offering it, and ask four questions that are important to you. Ensure that you include enough background information for the reader to answer your questions satisfactorily.

▌Text-Messaging SKILLS ▌

4. Tracking the New Product Buzz: Text Message to Colleagues at a Trade Show

The vast Consumer Electronics Show (CES) is the premier promotional event in the industry. More than 130 000 industry insiders from all over the world come to see the exciting new products on display from nearly 1500 companies—everything from video game gadgets to Internet-enabled refrigerators with built-in computer screens. You've just stumbled on a video game controller that has a built-in webcam to allow networked gamers to see and hear each other while they play. Your company also makes game controllers, and you're worried that your customers will flock to this new controller-cam. You need to know how much "buzz" is circulating around the show: Have people seen it? What are they saying about it? Are they excited about it?

Your task: Compose a text message to your colleagues at the show, alerting them to the new controller-cam and asking them to listen for any "buzz" that it might be generating among the attendees at the Las Vegas Convention Center and the several surrounding hotels where the show takes place. Here's the catch: your text messaging service limits messages to 160 characters, including spaces and punctuation, so your message can't be any longer than this.[9]

▌Letter Writing SKILLS ▌

5. Couch Potato: Letter Requesting Refund from House of Couches Furniture Store

You finally saw the couch you need: the colour is perfect (royal blue), the length is just right (it could seat you, your husband, and the kids), and the style is ideal for your furnishings (modern but classic). With the scratch-and-save card, you bought it at a 40 percent discount, bringing the price to a mere $600 plus delivery and taxes.

The salesperson who served you said that for an extra $10 you can have "deluxe delivery": the new couch will be taken out of its box and put into place, and the cardboard and your old couch removed. You wouldn't have to arrange removal on your own. "Deluxe delivery" sounded great, and the price was right. You decided to pay for it.

The day of delivery, your couch arrived wrapped in plastic. The deliverymen dropped it in the middle of your living room and started to leave, with their hands out for a tip. You reminded them about "deluxe delivery." They removed the plastic covering, took your old, sagging couch to the garage after you asked them twice, saying they didn't remove couches from the owner's property. They left grumbling. You could have done everything with the help of your spouse and saved the $10.

That afternoon you called customer service at House of Couches seeking a refund of the $10 you paid for "deluxe delivery." The representative refused to honour your request, saying that the deliverers fulfilled the "deluxe delivery" conditions.

Your task: You feel that the salesperson lied to you and that the customer service representative was rude. You decide to write to the owner of House of Couches, Fritz Wegman, to seek satisfaction. His address is House of Couches, 2 Broad Street, Regina, SK, S1P 1Y2.

6. Website: Email Message from Knitsmart Yarn and Needles Requesting Additional Information

Knitting, an enjoyable hobby that whiled away cold winter evenings in Corner Brook, Newfoundland, has given cousins Lee O'Reilly and Siobhan Gavin a local following and fame throughout the hand-knitting community in the Atlantic provinces as well as in fashionable shops in Canada's large cities. First teaching their young relatives and neighbours the art of knitting, they soon branched into selling yarn out of Lee's basement and then running small classes for different skill levels. After opening a small yarn shop in Corner Brook's shopping district, they began creating their own knitwear designs and selling them as kits, supplied with yarn and knitting needles, through their shop and catalogue. After their designs caught the eye of a Holt Renfrew buyer, their business took off beyond what the cousins ever imagined. Their colourful sweater and hat designs are worn by not only socialites but also film and stage performers attracted to their uniqueness. Little did the cousins think that their hobby would become a cottage industry and then a major business.

You've been working at Knitsmart Yarn and Needles during your summer break from university, and you think it's time that Lee and Siobhan branched into new territory: the World Wide Web. You think that the cousins should build a website where they can gain new customers, interest other people in their craft, and inspire knitters around the world with their patterns. You find an advertisement in the local newspaper for a company that creates websites (Webtech), but the classified ad gives little information beyond a phone number and an email address.

Your task: You will set aside time next week to discuss the opportunities a Knitsmart website offers to Lee and Siobhan. Write an email message requesting more information from Webtech about what the company can do for Knitsmart Yarn and Needles.

7. Transglobal Exchange: Instant Message Request for Information from a Chinese Manufacturer

Fortunately, your company, Diagonal Imports, chose the Sametime enterprise instant messaging software produced by IBM Lotus. Other products also allow you to carry on real-time exchanges with colleagues on the other side of the planet, but Sametime supports bidirectional machine translation, and you're going to need it.

The problem is that production on a popular line of decorative lighting appliances produced at your Chinese manufacturing plant inexplicably came to a halt last month. As the product manager in Canada, you have many resources you could call on to help, such as new sources for faulty parts. But you can't do anything if you don't know the details. You've tried telephoning top managers in China, but they're not giving you the responses you need.

Finally, your friend Kuei-chen Tsao has returned from a business trip. You met her during your trip to China last year. She doesn't speak English, but she's the line engineer responsible for this particular product: a fibre-optic lighting display that features a plastic base with a rotating colour wheel. As the wheel turns, light emitted from the spray of fibre-optic threads changes colour in soothing patterns. Product #3347XM is one of Diagonal's most popular items, and you've got orders from novelty stores around Canada waiting to be filled. Kuei-chen should be able to explain the problem, determine whether you can help, and tell you how long before regular shipping resumes.

Your task: Write the first of what you hope will be a productive instant message exchange with Kuei-chen. Remember that your words will be machine translated.[10]

Routine Messages

8. Listening to Business: Using the iPod to Train Employees

As a training specialist in Winnebago Industry's human resources department, you're always on the lookout for new ways to help employees learn vital job skills. While watching a production worker page through a training manual while learning how to assemble a new recreational vehicle, you get what seems to be a great idea: record the assembly instructions as audio files that workers can listen to while performing the necessary steps. With audio instructions, they wouldn't need to keep shifting their eyes between the product and the manual—and constantly losing their place. They could focus on the product and listen for each instruction. Also, the new system wouldn't cost much at all; any computer can record the audio files, and you'd simply make them available on an intranet site for download onto iPods or other digital music players.

Your task: You immediately run your new idea past your boss, who has heard about podcasting but doesn't think it has any place in business. He asks you to prove the practicality of the idea. You need to send him an email listing various podcasts that you think are beneficial to the public. Research podcasts that give instructions, and then write a message to your boss with a list of these. Remember that this is a routine message and that you are providing information to someone who has limited knowledge of this genre. Reader focus is extremely important.

9. Got It Covered? Letter from American Express about SUV Rentals

You can always tell when fall arrives at American Express— you are deluged with complaints from customers who've just received their summer vacation bills. Often these angry calls are about a shock-inducing damage repair bill from a car rental agency. Vacation car rentals can be a lot more complicated than most people think. Here's what happens.

Your credit card customers are standing at the Hertz or Avis counter, ready to drive away, when the agent suggests an upgrade to, say, a Ford Expedition or another large SUV. Feeling happy-go-lucky while on vacation, your customers say, "Why not?" and hand over their American Express card.

As they drive off in large vehicles that many are unaccustomed to handling, 9 out of 10 are unaware that the most common accidents among rental cars take place at low speeds in parking lots. Also, the upgraded vehicle they're driving is no longer fully covered either by their regular auto insurance or by the secondary car rental insurance they expect from American Express. If they've agreed to pay the additional $10 to $25 a day for the car rental agency's "collision and liability damage waiver fee," they will be able to walk away from any accident with no liability. Otherwise, they're running a costly risk.

Soon they pull into a shopping mall with the kids to pick up the forgotten sunscreen and sodas, where they discover that the luxury road-warrior-mobile is not so easy to park in stalls designed in the 1970s and 1980s when compact cars were all the rage. *Thwack*—there goes the door panel. *Crunch*—a rear bumper into a light post. *Wham!* There goes the family bank account, but they don't realize it yet—not until they receive the bill from the rental agency, the one that comes *after* their auto insurance and credit card companies have already paid as much as they're going to pay for damages.

Auto insurers typically provide the same coverage for rentals as you carry on your own car. When customers use their credit card to pay for car rentals, American Express offers secondary protection that generally covers any remaining unpaid damages. But there are important exceptions.

Neither insurance nor credit card companies will pay the "loss of vehicle use fees" that car rental agencies always tack on. These fees can run into thousands of dollars, based on the agency's revenue losses while their car is in the repair shop. When your customers are billed for this fee, they invariably call you, angrily demanding to know why American Express won't pay it. And if they've rented an SUV, they're even angrier.

American Express Green and Gold cards provide secondary coverage up to $55 000, and the Platinum card extends that to $75 000. But large SUVs such as the Ford Expedition, GMC Yukon, and Chevrolet Suburban are not covered at all. Such exclusions are common. For example, Diners Club specifically excludes "high-value, special interest or exotic cars"—such as the Ferraris, Maseratis, and even Rolls-Royces that are urged on customers by rental agencies.

Your task: As assistant vice president of customer service, you'd like to keep the phone lines cooler this summer and fall. It's April, so there's still time. Write a form letter to be sent to all American Express customers, urging them to check their rental car coverages, advising them against renting vehicles that are larger than they really require, and encouraging them to consider paying the rental agency's daily loss waiver fees.[11]

Blogging SKILLS

10. Here's How It Will Work: Explaining the Brainstorming Process

Austin, Texas, advertising agency GSD&M Advertising brainstorms new advertising ideas using a process it calls *dynamic collaboration*. A hand-picked team of insiders and outsiders is briefed on the project and given a key question or two to answer. The team members then sit down at computers and anonymously submit as many responses as they can within five minutes. The project moderators then pore over these responses, looking for any sparks that can ignite new ways of understanding and reaching out to consumers.

Your task: For these brainstorming sessions, GSD&M recruits an eclectic mix of participants from inside and outside the agency—figures as diverse as economists and professional video gamers. To make sure everyone understands the brainstorming guidelines, prepare a message to be posted on the project blog. In your own words, convey the following four points as clearly and succinctly as you can:

- **Be yourself.** We want input from as many perspectives as possible, which is why we recruit such a diverse array of participants. Don't try to get into what you believe is the mindset of an advertising specialist; we want you to approach the given challenge using whatever analytical and creative skills you normally employ in your daily work.
- **Create, don't edit.** Don't edit, refine, or self-censor while you're typing during the initial five-minute session. We don't care if your ideas are formatted beautifully, phrased poetically, or even spelled correctly. Just crank 'em out as quickly as you can.
- **It's about the ideas, not the participants.** Just so you know up front, all ideas are collected anonymously. We can't tell who submitted the brilliant ideas, the boring ideas, or the already-tried-that ideas. So while you won't get personal credit, you can also be crazy and fearless. Go for it!
- **The winning ideas will be subjected to the toughest of tests.** Just in case you're worried about submitting ideas that could be risky, expensive, or difficult to implement—don't fret. As we narrow down the possibilities, the few that remain will be judged, poked, prodded, and assessed from every angle. In other words, let us worry about containing the fire; you come up with the sparks.[12]

Routine Replies

Email SKILLS

11. Auto-Talk: Email Messages for Highway Bytes Computers to Send Automatically

You are the director of customer service at Highway Bytes, which markets a series of small, handlebar-mounted computers for bicyclists. These Cycle Computers do everything, from computing speed and distance travelled to displaying street maps. Serious cyclists love them, but your company is growing so fast that you can't keep up with all the customer service requests you receive every day. Your boss wants not only to speed up response time but also to reduce staffing costs and allow your technical experts the time they need to focus on the most difficult and important questions.

You've just been reading about automated response systems, and you quickly review a few articles before discussing the options with your boss. Artificial intelligence researchers have been working for decades to design systems that can actually converse with customers, ask questions, and respond to requests. Some of today's systems have vocabularies of thousands of words and the ability to understand simple sentences. For example, *chatterbots* are automated bots that can actually mimic human conversation. (You can see what it's like to carry on a conversation with a bot by visiting www.jabberwacky.com.)

Unfortunately, even though chatterbots hold a lot of promise, human communication is so complex that a truly automated customer service agent could take years to perfect (and may even prove to be impossible). However, the simplest automated systems are called *autoresponders* or *email-on-demand*. They are fast and extremely inexpensive. They have no built-in intelligence, so they do nothing more than send back the same reply to every message they receive.

You explain to your boss that although some messages you receive require the attention of your product specialists, many are simply requests for straightforward information. In fact, the customer service staff already answer some 70 percent of email queries with three ready-made attachments:

- **Installing Your Cycle Computer.** Gives customers advice on installing the Cycle Computer the first time or reinstalling it on a new bike. In most cases, the computer and wheel sensor bolt directly to the bike without modification, but certain bikes do require extra work.
- **Troubleshooting Your Cycle Computer.** Provides a step-by-step guide to figure out what might be wrong with a malfunctioning Cycle Computer. Most problems are simple, such as dead batteries or loose wires, but others are beyond the capabilities of your typical customer.
- **Upgrading the Software in Your Cycle Computer.** Tells customers how to attach the Cycle Computer to their home or office PC and download new software from Highway Bytes.

Your boss is enthusiastic when you explain that you can program your current email system to look for specific words in incoming messages and then respond based on what it finds. For example, if a customer message contains the word "installation," you can program the system to reply with the "Installing Your Cycle Computer" attachment. This reconfigured system should be able to handle a sizable portion of the hundreds of emails your customer service group gets every week.

Your task: First, draft a list of keywords that you'll want your email system to look for. You'll need to be creative and spend some time with a thesaurus. Identify all the words and word combinations that could identify a message as pertaining to one of the three subject areas. For example, the word *attach* would probably indicate a need for the installation material, whereas new software would most likely suggest a need for the upgrade attachment.

Second, draft three short email messages to accompany each ready-made attachment, explaining that the attached document answers the most common questions on a particular subject (for example, installation, troubleshooting, or upgrading). Your messages should invite recipients to write back if the attached document doesn't solve the problem, and don't forget to provide the email address: support2@highwaybytes.com.

Third, draft a fourth message to be sent out whenever your new system is unable to figure out what the customer is asking for. Simply thank the customer for writing and explain that the query will be passed on to a customer service specialist who will respond shortly.

▌Email SKILLS▐

12. Error Correction: Granting a Claim for a Wrong Product

Your company sells flower arrangements and gift baskets. Holidays are always a rush, and the overworked staff makes the occasional mistake. Last week, somebody made a big one. As a furious email message from a customer named Anders Ellison explains, he ordered a Valentine's Day bouquet for his wife, but the company sent a bereavement arrangement instead.

Your task: Respond to Ellison's email message, apologizing for the error, promising to refund all costs that Ellison incurred, informing him that the correct arrangement will arrive tomorrow (and he won't be charged anything for it), and offering Ellison his choice of any floral arrangement or gift basket for free on his wife's birthday.

▌Email SKILLS▐

13. Shopping for Talent: Memo at Clovine's Recommending a Promotion

You enjoy your duties as manager of women's sportswear at Clovine's—a growing chain of moderate to upscale department stores in British Columbia. You especially enjoy being able to recommend someone for a promotion. Today, you received a memo from Rachel Cohen, head buyer for women's apparel. She is looking for a smart, aggressive employee to become assistant buyer for Clovine's women's sportswear division. Clovine's likes to promote from within, and Rachel is asking all managers and supervisors for likely candidates. You have just the person she's looking for.

Jennifer Ramirez is a salesclerk in the designer sportswear boutique of your main store in Vancouver, and she has caught your attention. She's quick, friendly, and good at sizing up a customer's preferences. Moreover, at recent department meetings, she's made some intelligent remarks about new trends in fashion.

Your task: Write a memo to Rachel Cohen, head buyer, women's sportswear, recommending Jennifer Ramirez and evaluating her qualifications for the promotion. Rachel can check with the human resources department about Jennifer's educational and employment history; you're mainly interested in conveying your positive impression of Jennifer's potential for advancement.

Email SKILLS

14. Cable Hiccups: Email Reply to an Unhappy Cable Internet Customer

As a customer service agent working for your local cable company, you've received the occasional complaint such as the one you're looking at on your computer monitor. The writer says:

I'm fed up with your cable Internet service. I've had my new computer for about a year and used the slow dial-up ISP service only because the manufacturer included it for free. I got your high-speed cable Internet service because your advertising promised it was 30 times faster than dial-up. I've used it since March, and I'm very disappointed. I'm paying $39.95 a month, plus taxes, but twice in the last month I've been unable to connect and service is a lot slower than advertised. What a rip-off!

I'm a student and I work part-time. I do a lot of my research for essays and reports over the Internet. Not to mention email. I have deadlines to meet. I want you to cancel my service and refund me my last two months' payments.

You know that many people complain that the cable line is shared with neighbours, which might slow down service. But slowdowns are rare with cable and happen with high-speed phone lines too. Cable Internet service has a lot of capacity and can provide rapid access to the Internet, even though lines are shared. You think the writer is exaggerating and just wants to get his money back because the message is dated April 6, near the end of the school term.

Your task: You'll send a positive email to the writer indicating that your company will refund the amount he requests. Write to TopGuy@ihome.com. You've been trained to educate consumers about cable Internet service.

Positive Messages

Blogging SKILLS | Portfolio BUILDER

15. Leveraging the Good News: Blog Announcement of a Prestigious Professional Award

You and your staff in the public relations department at Epson were delighted when the communication campaign you created for wearable technology (www.epson.ca/For-Home/Wearables/h/h4) received the prestigious Silver Anvil award by the Canadian Public Relations Society. Now you'd like to give your team a pat on the back by sharing the news with the rest of the company.

Your task: Write a one-paragraph message for the PR department blog (which is read by people throughout the company but is not accessible outside the company) announcing the award. Take care not to "toot your own horn" as the manager of the PR department, and use the opportunity to compliment the rest of the company for designing and producing such an innovative product.[13]

Letter Writing SKILLS

16. ABCs: Form Letter Thanking Volunteers

Working together with government, educators, labour, and business, ABC Canada, a national literacy organization, promotes awareness of literacy and works to involve the private sector in supporting literacy. Its aim is "to promote a fully literate Canadian population." People in your firm, Fine Paper Company, participated in the annual PGI Golf Tournament for Literacy, which was founded by Peter Gzowski, one of Canada's great broadcasters and writers, and best known for his morning show on the CBC. The PGI is a very successful fundraising event, having generated $5 million over more than a decade. PGI tournaments are held in every province and territory.

Statistics Canada's report *Literary Skills for the Knowledge Society* notes that "22 percent of adult Canadians have serious problems with printed materials" and that "24 to 26 percent of Canadians can only deal with simple reading tasks."

Not only does your firm support the PGI Golf Tournament with monetary donations—and golf lovers—but the CEO, Laurent DesLauriers, established a volunteer program for employees to donate their time at local community centres to help adults learn to read. This program has become a success at Fine Paper Company.

Your task: As a human resources specialist at Fine Paper Company, you are sometimes asked to write goodwill letters to employees, a job you enjoy doing. Mr. DesLauriers has directed the office to send a thank-you letter to all the volunteers—those who participated in the golf tournament and those who volunteer their time at the community centres. You will compose a form letter, which will be merged with individual employees' names and addresses.[14]

Memo Writing SKILLS

17. Learn While You Earn: Memo Announcing Burger House's Educational Benefits

Your boss, Mike Andrade, owner of three Burger House restaurants in downtown Montreal, is worried about employee turnover. He needs to keep 50 people on his payroll to operate the outlets, but recruiting and retaining those people is tough. The average employee leaves after about seven months, so Andrade has to hire and train 90 people a year just to maintain a 50-person crew. At a cost of $1500 per hire, the price tag for all that turnover is approximately $62 000 a year.

Andrade knows that a lot of his best employees quit because they think that flipping burgers is a dead-end job. But what if it weren't a dead end? What if a person could really get someplace flipping burgers? What if Andrade offered to pay his employees' way through school if they remained with the store? Would that keep them behind the counter?

He's decided to give educational incentives a try. Employees who choose to participate will continue to earn their usual wages, but they will also get free books and tuition, keyed to the number of hours they work each week. Those who work 10 to 15 hours a week can take one free course at any local college or university; those who work 16 to 25 hours can take two courses; and those who work 26 to 40 hours can take three courses. The program is open to all employees, regardless of how long they have worked for Burger House, but no one is obligated to participate.

Your task: Draft a memo for Mr. Andrade to send out announcing the new educational incentives.[15]

Letter Writing SKILLS

18. Our Sympathy: Condolence Letter to a Mackie Insurance Underwriter

As chief administrator for the underwriting department of Mackie Health Plans in Montreal, Quebec, you're facing a difficult task. One of your best underwriters, Jean Dary, recently lost his wife in an automobile accident (he and his teenage daughter weren't with her at the time). Because you're the boss, everyone in the close-knit department is looking to you to communicate the group's sympathy and concern.

Someone suggested a simple greeting card that everyone could sign, but that seems so impersonal for someone you've worked with every day for nearly five years. So you decided to write a personal note on behalf of the whole department. Although you met Jean's wife, Rosalia, at a few company functions, you knew her mostly through Jean's frequent references to her. You didn't know her well, but you do know important things about her life, which you can celebrate in the letter.

You plan to suggest that when he returns to work, he might like to move his schedule up an hour so that he'll have more time to spend with his daughter, Lisa, after school. It's your way of helping make their lives a little easier for them during this period of adjustment.

Your task: Write the letter to Jean Dary, who lives at 4141 rue Peel #10, Montreal, QC, H3B 1B3. (Feel free to make up any details you need.)[16]

9 Writing Negative Messages

ON THE JOB: COMMUNICATING AT MAPLE LEAF FOODS

Michael McCain, president and CEO of Maple Leaf Foods, was praised by crisis management experts for his leadership during the Listeria crisis in summer and fall 2008, when 22 people died from food-borne bacteria. His prompt action, empathy, and transparency helped the company regain the confidence of consumers and maintain its prominence in the food industry.

REUTERS/Mike Cassese

Leading in a Crisis
www.mapleleaf.ca

In the summer and fall of 2008, Michael McCain, president and CEO of Maple Leaf Foods, faced the severest challenge of his career: dealing with fatal food-borne bacteria in several products made by the company that were linked to the deaths of 22 people.

Communication was the key to McCain's success in restoring public confidence in Maple Leaf Foods, a firm with more than 24 000 employees and $5.2 billion in sales in 2008. The first announcement dealing with the crisis appeared on August 17, 2008, when the company issued a health hazard alert warning the public about two meat products possibly contaminated with *Listeria monocytogenes* bacteria, especially dangerous to pregnant women, the elderly, and people with weakened immune systems. Another news release followed three days later, on August 20, announcing an expanded withdrawal of Maple Leaf products and the closure of the company's Toronto plant. On August 23, McCain taped a television statement responding to findings by government health agencies that linked the deaths of several people to the same *Listeria* strain found in some Maple Leaf products. In addition to the shutdown of the company's Toronto plant, McCain apologized and expressed his sympathy to the people and families affected by the crisis.

In the weeks that followed, Maple Leaf Foods published open letters in newspapers across Canada. The company described precautionary measures: recalling 191 products in addition to the three that were contaminated, contacting more than 15 000 retail and food service customers nationwide to ensure the products were removed from shelves, and engaging an outside technical expert panel to conduct a comprehensive investigation to identify the likely source of the contamination. Furthermore, McCain recorded additional television advertisements and videos explaining Maple Leaf's plans that were made available on the company's website and YouTube. In each announcement McCain showed the human face of the company.

McCain's prompt actions and sensitivity to the victims and their families earned him the 2008 Business Newsmaker of the Year Award. Experts praised him for applying effective crisis management strategy: being proactive, speaking honestly and transparently, and maintaining constant communication with employees and the public. But McCain commented, "This is not about some contrived strategy. It's just about a tragic situation and an organization's desire to make it right."[1]

If you had to handle a business crisis, how would you plan your communications? How would you deliver your messages? How would you demonstrate sensitivity to your audiences?

Using the Three-Step Writing Process for Negative Messages

1 LEARNING OBJECTIVE

Apply the three-step writing process to negative messages.

Negative messages can have as many as five goals:

- Give the bad news.
- Ensure acceptance of the bad news.
- Maintain reader's goodwill.
- Maintain organization's good image.
- Reduce future correspondence on the matter.

Analysis, investigation, and adaptation help you avoid alienating your readers.

Chances are slim that you'll be in a position like Michael McCain's, but communicating negative news is a fact of life for all business professionals, whether it's saying no to a request, sharing unpleasant or unwelcome information, or issuing a public apology. With the techniques you'll learn in this chapter, however, you can communicate unwelcome news successfully while minimizing unnecessary stress for everyone involved.

When you need to send a negative message, you have five goals: (1) to convey the bad news; (2) to gain acceptance for the bad news; (3) to maintain as much goodwill as possible with your audience; (4) to maintain a good image for your organization; and (5) if appropriate, to reduce or eliminate the need for future correspondence on the matter (however, in a few cases, you want to encourage discussion). Five goals are clearly a lot to accomplish in one message, so careful planning and execution are critical with negative messages.

STEP 1: PLANNING A NEGATIVE MESSAGE

When planning negative messages, you can't avoid the fact that your audience does not want to hear what you have to say. To minimize the damage to business relationships and to encourage the acceptance of your message, analyze the situation carefully to better understand the context in which the recipient will process your message.

Be sure to consider your purpose thoroughly—whether it's straightforward (such as rejecting a job application) or more complicated (such as drafting a negative performance review, in which you not only give the employee feedback on past performance but also help the person develop a plan to improve future performance). With a clear purpose and your audience's needs in mind, identify and gather the information your audience will need to understand and accept your message. Negative messages can be intensely personal to the recipient, and in many cases recipients have a right to expect a thorough explanation of your answer.

Adam Gregor/Fotolia

Higher fees or loan refusals are two examples of bad-news messages that banks send to customers. Is it more difficult for banks to communicate bad news than for other types of businesses? Are there special image or ethical concerns that banks face?

Selecting the right medium is critical. For example, bad news for employees should be delivered in person whenever possible, to guard their privacy, demonstrate respect, and give them an opportunity to ask questions. Doing so isn't always possible or feasible, though, so you will have times when you need to share important negative information through written or electronic media.

When preparing negative messages, choose the medium with care.

Defining your main idea in a negative message is often more complicated than simply saying no. For example, if you need to respond to a hardworking employee who requested a raise, your message would go beyond saying no to explain how he or she can improve performance by working smarter, not just harder.

Finally, the organization of a negative message requires particular care. One of the most critical planning decisions is choosing whether to use the direct or indirect approach (see Figure 9–1). A negative message using the direct approach opens with the bad news, proceeds to the reasons for the situation or the decision, and ends with a positive statement aimed at maintaining a good relationship with the audience. In contrast, the indirect approach opens with the reasons behind the bad news before presenting the bad news itself.

Appropriate organization helps readers accept your negative news.

To help decide which approach to take in any situation you encounter, ask yourself the following questions:

You need to consider a variety of factors when choosing between direct and indirect approaches for negative messages.

- **Will bad news come as a shock?** The direct approach is fine for business situations in which people readily acknowledge the possibility of receiving bad news. However, if bad news might come as a shock to readers, use the indirect approach to help them prepare for it.
- **Does the reader prefer short messages that get right to the point?** For example, if you know that your boss always wants brief messages that get right to the point, even when they deliver bad news, use the direct approach.
- **How important is this news to the reader?** For minor or routine scenarios, the direct approach is nearly always best. However, if the reader has an emotional investment in the situation or the consequences to the reader are considerable, the indirect approach is often best because it gives you a chance to prepare that reader to accept your news.
- **Do you need to maintain a close working relationship with the reader?** Pay attention to the relationship as you deliver bad news. The indirect approach makes it easier to soften the blow of bad news and can therefore be the better choice when you need to preserve a good relationship.

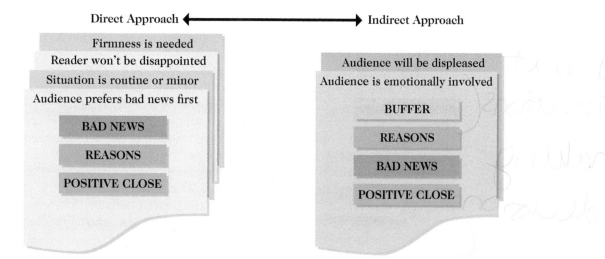

Figure 9–1 Choosing the Indirect or Direct Approach for Negative Messages

- **Do you need to get the reader's attention?** If someone hasn't responded to repeated messages, the direct approach can help you get his or her attention.
- **What is your organization's preferred style?** Some companies have a distinct communication style, ranging from blunt and direct to gentle and indirect.
- **How much follow-up communication do you want?** If you want to discourage a response from your reader, the direct approach signals the finality of your message more effectively. However, if you use the indirect approach to list your reasons before announcing a decision, you allow a follow-up response from your reader—which might actually be the best strategy at times. For example, if you're rejecting a project team's request for funding based on the information you currently have, you might be wise to invite the team to provide any new information that could encourage you to reconsider your decision.

STEP 2: WRITING A NEGATIVE MESSAGE

When you are adapting a negative message to your audience, pay close attention to effectiveness and diplomacy. After all, your audience does not want to hear bad news or something they will disagree with, so messages perceived to be unclear or unkind will amplify the audience's stress. The section "Continuing with a Clear Statement of the Bad News" later in this chapter has advice on conveying unpleasant news with care and tact. Cultural expectations also play a role, from the organizational culture within a company to regional variations around the world.

Compared with external audiences, internal audiences often expect more detail in negative messages.

The disappointing nature of negative messages requires that you maintain your audience focus and be as sensitive as possible to audience needs. For example, internal audiences often have expectations regarding negative messages that differ from those of external audiences. In some cases, the two groups can interpret the news in different or even opposite ways. Employees will react negatively to news of an impending layoff, for instance, but company shareholders might welcome the news as evidence that management is trying to control costs. In addition, if a negative message such as news of a layoff is being sent to internal and external audiences, employees will expect not only more detail but also to be informed before the public is told.

You may need to adjust the content of negative messages for various external audiences.

Negative messages to outside audiences require attention to the diverse nature of the audience and the concern for confidentiality of internal information. A single message might have a half-dozen audiences, all with differing opinions and agendas. You may not be able to explain things to the level of detail that some of these people want if doing so would release proprietary information such as future product plans.

If your credibility hasn't already been established with an audience, lay out your qualifications for making the decision in question. Recipients of negative messages who don't think you are credible are more likely to challenge your decision. And as always, projecting and protecting your company's image is a prime concern; if you're not careful, a negative answer could spin out of control into negative feelings about your company.

When you use language that conveys respect and avoids an accusing tone, you protect your audience's pride. This kind of communication etiquette is always important, but it demands special care with negative messages. Moreover, you can ease the sense of disappointment by using positive words rather than negative, counterproductive ones (see Table 9–1).

You'll likely spend more time on word, sentence, and paragraph choices for negative messages than for any other type of business writing. People who receive

Table 9–1	Choosing Positive Words	
Examples of Negative Phrasings	**Positive Alternatives**	
Your request *doesn't make any sense*.	Please clarify your request.	
The *damage* won't be fixed for a week.	The item will be repaired next week.	
Although it wasn't our *fault*, there will be an *unavoidable delay* in your order.	Your order will be processed as soon as we receive an aluminum shipment from our supplier, which we expect to happen within 10 days.	
You are clearly *dissatisfied*.	We are doing what we can to correct the situation.	
I was *shocked* to learn that you're unhappy.	Thank you for sharing your concerns about the service you received while shopping with us.	
Unfortunately, we haven't received it.	It hasn't arrived yet.	
The enclosed statement is *wrong*.	Please recheck the enclosed statement.	

negative messages often look for subtle shades of meaning, seeking flaws in your reasoning or other ways to challenge the decision. By writing clearly and sensitively, you can take some of the sting out of bad news and help your reader accept the decision and move on.

STEP 3: COMPLETING A NEGATIVE MESSAGE

The need for careful attention to detail continues as you complete your message. Revise your content to ensure that everything is clear, complete, and concise—bearing in mind that even small flaws are magnified as readers react to your negative news. Produce clean, professional documents, and proofread carefully to eliminate mistakes. Finally, be especially sure that your negative messages are delivered promptly and successfully. Delaying when you need to convey negative news can be a serious breach of etiquette.

Using the Direct Approach for Negative Messages

As you apply the three-step writing process to develop negative messages, keep three points in mind. First, before you organize the main points of a message, it is vital to choose a direct or an indirect approach. Second, before actually composing your message, be sensitive to variations across cultures or between internal and external audiences. And third, to fulfill the spirit of audience focus, ensure that you maintain high ethical standards.

A negative message using the direct approach opens with the bad news, proceeds to the reasons for the situation or the decision, and ends with a positive statement aimed at maintaining a good relationship with the audience. Depending on the circumstances, the message may also offer alternatives or a plan of action to fix the situation under discussion. Stating bad news at the beginning can have two advantages: (1) it makes a shorter message possible, and (2) it allows the audience to reach the main idea of the message in less time.

OPENING WITH A CLEAR STATEMENT OF THE BAD NEWS

Whether it's something relatively minor, such as telling a supplier that you're planning to reduce the size of your orders in the future, or something major, such as telling employees that revenues dropped the previous quarter, come right out and say it. However, if the news is likely to be devastating, maintain

2   LEARNING OBJECTIVE

Explain how to use the direct approach effectively when conveying negative news.

Use the direct approach when your negative answer or information will have minimal personal impact.

a calm, professional tone that keeps the focus on the news and not on individual failures or other possible factors. Also, if necessary, remind the reader why you're writing.

Reminds the reader that your company has a standing order and announces the change immediately → Please modify our standing order for the FL-205 shipping cases from 3000 per month to 2500 per month.

Reminds the reader that he or she applied for life insurance with your firm and announces your decision → Transnation Life is unable to grant your application for SafetyNet term life insurance.

Eases into the bad news with a personal acknowledgment to the staff, even though it delivers the news directly and immediately → In spite of everyone's best efforts to close more sales this past quarter, revenue fell 14 percent compared to the third quarter last year.

Notice how the third example still manages to ease into the bad news, even though it delivers the news directly and quickly. In all three instances, the recipient gets the news immediately, without reading the reasons why the news is bad.

PROVIDING REASONS AND ADDITIONAL INFORMATION

In most cases, you'll follow the direct opening with an explanation of why the news is negative:

Reassures the reader that the product in question is still satisfactory but is no longer needed in the same quantity → Please modify our standing order for the FL-205 shipping cases from 3000 per month to 2500 per month. **The FL-205 continues to meet our needs for medical packaging, but our sales of that product line have levelled off.**

Offers a general explanation as the reason the application was denied and discourages further communication on the matter → Transnation Life is unable to grant your application for SafetyNet term life insurance. **The SafetyNet program has specific health history requirements that your application does not meet.**

Lets readers know why the news is negative and reassures them that job performance is not the reason → In spite of everyone's best efforts to close more sales this past quarter, revenue fell 14 percent compared to the third quarter last year. **Reports from the field offices indicate that the economic downturn in Asia has reduced demand for our products.**

The amount of detail you provide depends on your relationship with the audience.

The extent of your explanation depends on the nature of your news and your relationship with the reader. In the first example, a company wants to assure its long-time supplier that the product is still satisfactory. It's in the best interest of both parties to maintain a positive relationship even when circumstances between them are sometimes negative.

In the second example, the insurance company provides a general reason for the denial because listing a specific health issue might encourage additional communication from the applicant, and the company's decision is final. In the third example, the explanation points out why the news is bad and also reassures employees that no one in the firm is personally responsible for the failure.

In some situations, it's a good idea to follow the explanation with a statement of how you plan to correct or respond to the negative news. For example, in the case of the sales decline, follow up by telling the staff you plan to increase advertising to help stimulate sales. Alternatively, invite ideas from the staff. In any event, your readers will want to know how they should respond to the news, so additional information would be helpful.

Sometimes detailed reasons should not be provided.

You will encounter some situations in which explaining negative news is neither appropriate nor helpful, for example, when the reasons are confidential, excessively complicated, or irrelevant to the reader. To maintain a cordial work-ing relationship with the reader, explain why you can't provide the information.

Should you apologize when delivering bad news? The answer isn't quite as simple as one might think, partly because the notion of *apology* is hard to pin down. To some people, it simply means an expression of sympathy that some-thing negative has happened to another person. At the other extreme, it means admitting fault and taking responsibility for specific compensations or correc-tions to atone for the mistake.

Some experts have advised that a company should never apologize, even when it knows it has made a mistake, as the apology might be taken as a con-fession of guilt that could be used against the company in a lawsuit.[2] The best general advice in the event of a serious mistake or accident is to immediately and sincerely express sympathy and offer help, if appropriate, without admit-ting guilt; then seek the advice of your company's lawyers before elaborating. As one recent survey concluded, "The risks of making an apology are low, and the potential reward is high."[3]

The decision about whether to apolo-gize depends on a number of factors.

CLOSING ON A POSITIVE NOTE

After you've explained the negative news, close the message in a positive, but still honest and respectful, manner.

Close your message in a positive but respectful tone.

Please modify our standing order for the FL-205 shipping cases from 3000 per month to 2500 per month. The FL-205 continues to meet our needs for medical packaging, but our sales of that product line have levelled off. **We appreciate the great service you continue to provide and look forward to doing business with you.**

Reinforces the relationship you have with the reader and provides a positive view toward the future without unduly promising a return to the old level of business

Transnation Life is unable to grant your application for SafetyNet term life insurance. The SafetyNet program has specific health history requirements that your application does not meet. **We wish you success in finding coverage through another provider.**

Ends on a respectful note, know-ing that life insurance is an impor-tant subject for the reader, but also makes it clear that the company's decision is final

In spite of everyone's best efforts to close more sales this past quarter, revenue fell 14 percent compared to the third quarter last year. Reports from the field offices indicate that the economic downturn in Asia has reduced demand for our products. **However, I continue to believe that we have the best product for these customers, and we'll continue to explore ways to boost sales in these key markets.**

Helps readers respond to the news by letting them know that the company plans to fix the situation, even if the plan for doing so isn't clear yet

Notice how all three examples deliver bad news quickly and efficiently, without being unduly disrespectful or overly apologetic. Consider offering your readers an alternative solution, if you can. For example, if you know that another insur-ance company has a program for higher-risk policies, you can alert your reader to that opportunity.

Using the Indirect Approach for Negative Messages

The indirect approach helps readers prepare for the bad news by presenting the reasons for it first. However, the indirect approach is *not* meant to obscure bad news, delay it, or limit your responsibility. Rather, the purpose of this approach is to ease the blow and help readers accept the situation. When done poorly, the indirect approach can be disrespectful and even unethical. But when done well,

3 LEARNING OBJECTIVE

Explain how to use the indirect approach effectively when conveying negative news.

Use the indirect approach when some preparation will help your audience accept your bad news.

A well-written buffer establishes common ground with the reader.

Poorly written buffers mislead or insult the reader.

it is a good example of audience-oriented communication crafted with attention to both ethics and etiquette.

OPENING WITH A BUFFER

Messages using the indirect approach open with a **buffer**, a neutral, noncontroversial statement that establishes common ground with your reader (refer to Figure 9–1). Some critics believe that using a buffer is manipulative and unethical—and even dishonest. However, buffers are unethical only if they're insincere or deceptive. Showing consideration for the feelings of others is never dishonest.

A poorly written buffer might trivialize the reader's concerns, divert attention from the problem with insincere flattery or irrelevant material, or mislead the reader into thinking your message actually contains good news. A good buffer, on the other hand, can express your appreciation for being considered (if you're responding to a request), assure your reader of your attention to the request, or indicate your understanding of the reader's needs. A good buffer also needs to be relevant and sincere.

Consider these possible responses to a manager of the order fulfillment department, who requested some temporary staffing help from your department (a request you won't be able to fulfill):

Establishes common ground with the reader and validates the concerns that prompted the original request without promising a positive answer →

Our department shares your goal of processing orders quickly and efficiently.

Establishes common ground, but in a negative way that downplays the recipient's concerns →

As a result of the last downsizing, every department in the company is running shorthanded.

Potentially misleads the reader into concluding that you will comply with the request →

You folks are doing a great job over there, and I'd love to be able to help out.

Trivializes the reader's concerns by opening with an irrelevant issue →

Those new provincial labour regulations are driving me crazy over here; how about in your department?

Only the first of these buffers can be considered effective; the other three are likely to damage your relationship with the other manager—and to lower his or her opinion of you. Table 9–2 shows several types of effective buffers you could use to open a negative message tactfully.

Given the damage that a poorly composed buffer can do, consider every buffer carefully before you send it. Is it respectful? Is it relevant? Is it neutral, implying neither yes nor no? Does it provide a smooth transition to the reasons that follow? If you can answer yes to every question, you can proceed confidently to the next section of your message. However, if a little voice inside your head tells you that your buffer sounds insincere or misleading, it probably is, in which case you'll need to rewrite it.

PROVIDING REASONS AND ADDITIONAL INFORMATION

An effective buffer serves as a stepping stone to the next part of your message, in which you build up the explanations and information that will culminate in your negative news. The nature of the information you provide is similar to that of the direct approach—it depends on the audience and the situation—but the way you portray this information differs because your reader doesn't know your conclusion yet.

Phrase your reasons to signal the negative news ahead.

An ideal explanation section leads readers to your conclusion before you actually say it. That is, before you actually say "no," the reader has followed your line

Table 9–2	**Types of Buffers**	
Buffer Type	**Strategy**	**Example**
Agreement	Find a point on which you and the reader share similar views.	We both know how hard it is to make a profit in this industry.
Appreciation	Express sincere thanks for receiving something.	Your cheque for $127.17 arrived yesterday. Thank you.
Cooperation	Convey your willingness to help in any way you realistically can.	Employee Services is here to smooth the way for all associates with their health insurance, retirement planning, and continuing education needs.
Fairness	Assure the reader that you've closely examined and carefully considered the problem, or mention an appropriate action that has already been taken.	For the past week, we have carefully monitored those using the photocopying machine to see whether we can detect any pattern of use that might explain its frequent breakdowns.
Good news	Start with the part of your message that is favourable.	A replacement knob for your range is on its way, shipped February 10 via Canada Post.
Praise	Find an attribute or an achievement to compliment.	The Stratford Group clearly has an impressive record of accomplishment in helping clients resolve financial reporting problems.
Resale	Favourably discuss the product or company related to the subject of the letter.	With their heavy-duty, full-suspension hardware and fine veneers, the desks and file cabinets in our Montclair line have become a hit with value-conscious professionals.
Understanding	Demonstrate that you understand the reader's goals and needs.	So you can more easily find the printer with the features you need, we are enclosing a brochure that describes all the Panasonic printers currently available.

of reasoning and is ready for the answer. By giving your reasons effectively, you help maintain focus on the issues at hand and defuse the emotions that always accompany significantly bad news.

As you lay out your reasons, guide your readers' responses by starting with the most positive points first and moving forward to increasingly negative ones. Provide enough detail for the audience to understand your reasons, but be concise; a long, roundabout explanation will just make your audience impatient. Your reasons need to convince your audience that your decision is justified, fair, and logical.

If appropriate, use the explanation section to suggest how the negative news might in fact benefit your reader. Suppose you work for a multinational company that wants to hire an advertising agency to support your offices in a dozen different countries, and you receive a proposal from an agency that has offices in only one of those countries. In your list of reasons, indicate that you don't want to impose undue hardship on the agency by requiring significant amounts of international travel. However, use this technique with care; it's easy to insult readers by implying that they shouldn't ask for the benefits or opportunities they sought originally.

Avoid hiding behind company policy to cushion bad news. If you say, "Company policy forbids our hiring anyone who does not have two years' supervisory experience," you imply that you won't consider anyone on his or her individual merits. Skilled and sympathetic communicators explain company policy (without referring to it as "policy") so that the audience can try to meet the requirements at a later time. Consider this response to an employee:

Because these management positions are quite challenging, the human relations department has researched the qualifications needed to succeed in them. The findings show that the two most important qualifications are a bachelor's degree in business administration and two years' supervisory experience.

Shows the reader that the decision is based on a methodical analysis of the company's needs and not on some arbitrary guideline

Establishes the criteria behind the decision and lets the reader know what to expect

Well-written reasons are

- Detailed
- Tactful
- Individualized
- Unapologetic
- Positive

The paragraph does a good job of stating reasons for the refusal:

- It provides enough detail to logically support the refusal.
- It implies that the applicant is better off avoiding a program in which he or she might fail.
- It shows the company's policy as logical rather than arbitrary.
- It offers no apology for the decision because no one is at fault.
- It avoids negative personal expressions (for example, "You do not meet our requirements").

Even valid, well-thought-out reasons won't convince every reader in every situation. However, if you've done a good job of laying out your reasoning, then you've done everything you can to prepare the reader for the main idea, which is the negative news itself.

CONTINUING WITH A CLEAR STATEMENT OF THE BAD NEWS

To handle bad news carefully

- De-emphasize the bad news visually and grammatically.
- Use a conditional statement if appropriate.
- Tell what you did do, not what you didn't do.

After you've prepared the audience to receive the bad news, the next task is to present the news as clearly and as kindly as possible. Three techniques are especially useful for saying no. First, de-emphasize the bad news:

- Minimize the space or time devoted to the bad news—without trivializing it or withholding any important information.
- Subordinate bad news in a complex or compound sentence ("My department is already shorthanded, so I'll need all my staff for at least the next two months"). This construction pushes the bad news into the middle of the sentence, the point of least emphasis.
- Embed bad news in the middle of a paragraph or use parenthetical expressions ("Our profits, which are down, are only part of the picture").

However, keep in mind that it's possible to abuse de-emphasis. For example, if the primary point of your message is that profits are down, it would be inappropriate to marginalize that news by burying it in the middle of a sentence. State the negative news clearly and then make a smooth transition to any positive news that might balance the story.

Second, use a conditional (*if* or *when*) statement to imply that the audience could have received, or might someday receive, a favourable answer ("When you have more managerial experience, you are welcome to apply for any openings that we may have in the future"). Such a statement could motivate applicants to improve their qualifications. However, you must avoid any suggestion that you might reverse the decision you've just made or any phrasing that could give a rejected applicant false hope.

Third, emphasize what you can do or have done, rather than what you cannot do. Say, "We sell exclusively through retailers, and the one nearest you that carries our merchandise is … " rather than "We are unable to serve you, so please call your nearest dealer." Also, by implying the bad news, you may not need to actually state it ("The five positions currently open have been filled with people whose qualifications match those uncovered in our research"). By focusing on the positive and implying the bad news, you make the impact less personal.

Don't disguise bad news when you emphasize the positive.

When implying bad news, ensure that your audience understands the entire message—including the bad news. Withholding negative information or over-emphasizing positive information is unethical and unfair to your reader. If an implied message might lead to uncertainty, state your decision in direct terms. Just be sure that you avoid overly blunt statements that are likely to cause pain and anger:

Instead of This	Use This
I *must refuse* your request.	I will be out of town on the day you need me.
We *must deny* your application.	The position has been filled.
I *am unable* to grant your request.	Contact us again when you have established …
We *cannot afford to* continue the program.	The program will conclude on May 1.
Much as I would like to attend …	Our budget meeting ends too late for me to attend.
We *must turn down* your extension request.	Please send in your payment by June 14.

CLOSING ON A RESPECTFUL NOTE

As with the direct approach, the conclusion of the indirect approach is your opportunity to emphasize your respect for your audience, even though you've just delivered unpleasant news. Express best wishes without ending on a falsely upbeat note. If you can find a positive angle that's meaningful to your audience, by all means consider adding it to your conclusion. However, don't pretend that the negative news didn't happen or that it won't affect the reader. Suggest alternative solutions if such information is available. In a message to a customer or potential customer, an ending that includes resale information or sales promotions may also be appropriate. If you've asked readers to decide between alternatives or to take some action, make sure that they know what to do, when to do it, and how to do it. Whatever type of conclusion you use, follow these guidelines:

- **Avoid a negative or uncertain conclusion.** Don't refer to, repeat, or apologize for the bad news, and refrain from expressing any doubt that your reasons will be accepted (avoid statements such as "I trust our decision is satisfactory").
- **Limit future correspondence.** Encourage additional communication *only* if you're willing to discuss your decision further (if you're not, avoid wording such as "If you have further questions, please write").
- **Be optimistic about the future, as appropriate.** Don't anticipate problems that haven't occurred yet. (Avoid statements such as "Should you have further problems, please let us know").
- **Be sincere.** Steer clear of clichés that are insincere in view of the bad news (if you can't help, don't say, "If we can be of any help, please contact us").

A positive close
- Builds goodwill
- Offers a suggestion for action
- Provides a look toward the future

Finally, keep in mind that the closing is the last thing the audience has to remember you by. Even though they're disappointed, leave them with the impression that they were treated with respect.

Maintaining High Standards of Ethics and Etiquette

All business messages demand attention to ethics and etiquette, of course, but these considerations take on special importance when you are delivering bad news—for several reasons. First, a variety of laws and regulations dictate the content and delivery of many business messages with potentially negative content, such as the release of financial information by a public company.

4   LEARNING OBJECTIVE

Explain the importance of maintaining high standards of ethics and etiquette when delivering negative messages.

Second, negative messages can have a significant negative impact on the lives of those receiving them. Even if the news is conveyed legally and conscientiously, good ethical practice demands that these situations be approached with care and sensitivity. Third, emotions often run high when negative messages are involved, for both the sender and the receiver. Senders need to not only manage their own emotions but also consider the emotional state of their audiences.

For example, in a message announcing or discussing workforce cutbacks, you have the emotional needs of several stakeholder groups to consider. The employees who lost their jobs are likely to experience fear about their futures and possibly a sense of betrayal. The employees who kept their jobs are likely to feel anxiety about the long-term security of their jobs, the ability of company management to turn things around, and the level of care and respect the company has for its employees. These "survivors" may also feel guilty about keeping their jobs while some colleagues lost theirs. Outside the company, investors, suppliers, and segments of the community affected by the layoffs (such as retailers and homebuilders) will have varying degrees of financial interest in the outcome of the decision. Writing such messages requires careful attention to all these needs while balancing respect for the departing employees with a positive outlook on the future.

The challenge of sending—and receiving—negative messages fosters a tendency to delay, downplay, or distort the bad news.[4] However, doing so may be unethical, if not illegal. In recent years, numerous companies have been sued by shareholders, consumers, employees, and government regulators for allegedly withholding or delaying negative information in such areas as company finances, environmental hazards, and product safety. In many of these cases, the problem was slow, incomplete, or inaccurate communication between the company and external stakeholders. In others, problems stemmed from a reluctance to send or receive negative news within the organization.

Effectively sharing bad news within an organization requires commitment from everyone involved. Employees must commit to sending negative messages when necessary and to doing so in a timely fashion, even when that is unpleasant or difficult. Conversely, managers must commit to maintaining open communication channels, truly listening when employees have negative information to share, and not punishing employees who deliver bad news.

Employees who observe unethical or illegal behaviour within their companies and are unable to resolve the problems through normal channels may have no choice but to resort to **whistleblowing**, expressing their concerns internally through company ethics hotlines—or externally through social media or the news media if they perceive no other options. The decision to "blow the whistle" on one's own employer is rarely easy or without consequences; more than 80 percent of whistleblowers in one U.S. survey said they were punished in some way for coming forward with their concerns.[5] Although whistleblowing is sometimes characterized as "ratting on" colleagues or managers, it has an essential function. According to international business expert Alex MacBeath, "Whistleblowing can be an invaluable way to alert management to poor business practices within the workplace. Often whistleblowing can be the only way that information about issues such as rule breaking, criminal activity, cover-ups, and fraud can be brought to management's attention before serious damage is suffered."[6] Recognizing the value of this feedback, many companies have formal reporting mechanisms that give employees a way to voice ethical and legal concerns to management. Various government bodies have also instituted protections for whistleblowers, partly in recognition of the role that workers play in food safety and other vital areas.[7]

Sharing bad news effectively requires commitment from everyone in the organization.

Finally, recognize that some negative news scenarios will also test your self-control and sense of etiquette and tempt you to respond with a personal attack. Customer service employees often undergo training specifically to help them keep their own emotions on an even keel when they are on the receiving end of anger or criticism from upset customers.[8] However, keep in mind that negative messages can have a lasting impact on both the people who receive them and the people who send them. As a communicator, you have a responsibility to minimize the negative impact of your negative messages through careful planning and sensitive, objective writing. As much as possible, focus on the actions or conditions that led to the negative news, not on personal shortcomings or character issues. Develop a reputation as a professional who can handle the toughest situations with dignity.

For a reminder of successful strategies for creating negative messages, see "Checklist: Creating Negative Messages."

Negative situations can put your sense of self-control and business etiquette to the test.

✓ Checklist   Creating Negative Messages

A. Choose the best approach.
- Consider using the direct approach when the audience is aware of the possibility of negative news, when the reader is not emotionally involved in the message, when you know that the reader would prefer the bad news first, when you know that firmness is necessary, or when you want to discourage a response.
- Consider using the indirect approach when the news is likely to come as a shock or surprise, when your audience has a high emotional investment in the outcome, or when you want to maintain a good relationship with the audience.

B. For the indirect approach, open with an effective buffer.
- Establish common ground with the audience.
- Validate the request, if you are responding to a request.
- Don't trivialize the reader's concerns.
- Don't mislead the reader into thinking the coming news might be positive.

C. Provide reasons and additional information.
- Explain why the news is negative.
- Adjust the amount of detail to fit the situation and the audience.

- Avoid explanations when the reasons are confidential, excessively complicated, or irrelevant to the reader.
- If appropriate, state how you plan to correct or respond to the negative news.
- Seek the advice of company lawyers if you're unsure what to say.

D. State the bad news clearly.
- State the bad news as positively as possible, using tactful wording.
- De-emphasize bad news by minimizing the space devoted to it, subordinating it, or embedding it.
- If your response might change in the future if circumstances change, explain the conditions to the reader.
- Emphasize what you can do or have done, rather than what you can't or won't do.

E. Close on a positive note.
- Express best wishes without being falsely positive.
- Suggest actions that readers might take, if appropriate, and provide them with necessary information.
- Encourage further communication only if you're willing to discuss the situation further.
- Keep a positive outlook on the future.

Sending Negative Messages on Routine Business Matters

Professionals and companies receive a wide variety of requests and proposals and cannot respond positively to every single one. In addition, mistakes and unforeseen circumstances can lead to delays and other minor problems that occur in the course of business. Occasionally, companies must send negative messages to suppliers and other parties. Whatever the purpose, crafting routine negative responses and messages quickly and graciously is an important skill for every businessperson.

MAKING NEGATIVE ANNOUNCEMENTS ON ROUTINE BUSINESS MATTERS

Many negative messages are written in response to requests from an internal or external correspondent, but on occasion managers need to make unexpected announcements of a negative nature. For example, a company might decide to consolidate its materials purchasing with fewer suppliers and thereby need to tell several firms it will no longer be buying from them. Internally, management may need to announce the elimination of an employee benefit or other changes that employees will view negatively.

Although such announcements happen in the normal course of business, they are generally unexpected. Accordingly, except in the case of minor changes, the indirect approach is usually the better choice. Follow the steps outlined for indirect messages: open with a buffer that establishes some mutual ground between you and the reader; advance your reasoning; announce the change; and close with as much positive information and sentiment as appropriate under the circumstances.

Negative announcements on routine business matters usually should be handled with the indirect approach because the news is unexpected.

REJECTING SUGGESTIONS AND PROPOSALS

Managers receive a variety of suggestions and proposals, both solicited and unsolicited, from internal and external sources. For an unsolicited proposal from an external source, you may not even need to respond if you don't already have a working relationship with the sender. However, if you need to reject a proposal that you solicited, you owe the sender an explanation, and because the news will be unexpected, the indirect approach is better. In general, the closer your working relationship, the more thoughtful and complete you need to be in your response. For example, if you are rejecting a proposal from an employee, explain your reasons fully and carefully so that the employee can understand why the proposal was not accepted and so that you don't damage an important working relationship.

REFUSING ROUTINE REQUESTS

When you are unable to meet the request, your primary communication challenge is to give a clear negative response without generating negative feelings or damaging either your personal reputation or the company's. As simple as these messages may appear to be, they can test your skills as a communicator because you often need to deliver negative information while maintaining a positive relationship with the other party.

The direct approach will work best for most routine negative responses. It not only helps your audience get your answer quickly and move on to other possibilities but also helps you save time, since the direct approach is often easier to write. Figure 9–2 shows how Mohammed Mansour used this approach to refuse a favour from an acquaintance.

The indirect approach is preferable when the stakes are high for you or for the receiver, when you or your company has an established relationship with the person making the request, or when you're forced to decline a request that you might have said yes to in the past. Lisa McKinnon used the indirect approach in her letter to Phillippe DiCastro, a financial analyst (see Figure 9–3). The tone of the letter is intended to maintain a good relationship with the reader although the favour is refused.

Saying no is a routine part of business and shouldn't reflect negatively on you.

When turning down an invitation or a request for a favour, consider your relationship with the reader.

The bad news is stated in the opening.

The writer buffers the bad news by presenting the reason.

The writer suggests an alternative— showing that he cares about the tour and has given the matter some thought.

The close seeks action and expresses goodwill. The use of the recipient's first name enhances the personal tone.

Figure 9–2 Letter Declining a Favour Using the Direct Strategy

Consider the following points as you develop your routine negative messages:

- **Manage your time carefully.** Focus your time on the most important relationships and requests, and then get in the habit of crafting quick standard responses for less important situations.
- **If the matter is closed, don't imply that it's still open.** If your answer is truly no, don't use phrases such as "Let me think about it and get back to you" as a way to delay saying no. Such delays waste time for you and the other party and project a weak image.
- **Offer alternative ideas if you can.** The letters in Figures 9–2 and 9–3 include options that might help the reader. However, remember to use your time wisely in such matters. Unless the relationship is important to your company, you probably shouldn't spend time researching alternatives for the other person.

Figure 9–3 Letter Declining a Favour Using the Indirect Strategy

If you aren't in a position to offer additional information or assistance, don't imply that you are.

- **Don't imply that other assistance or information might be available if it isn't.** Don't close your negative message with a cheery but insincere "Please contact us if we can offer any additional assistance." An empty attempt to mollify hostile feelings could simply lead to another request you'll have to refuse.

HANDLING BAD NEWS ABOUT TRANSACTIONS

Bad news about transactions, the sale and delivery of products and services, is always unwelcome and usually unexpected. These messages have three goals: (1) to modify the customer's expectations regarding the transaction; (2) to explain how you plan to resolve the situation; and (3) to repair whatever damage might have been done to the business relationship.

The specific content and tone of each message can vary widely, depending on the nature of the transaction and your relationship with the customer. Telling an individual consumer that his new sweater will arrive a week later than you promised is a much simpler task than telling General Motors that 30 000 transmission parts will be a week late, especially since you know the company will be forced to idle a multimillion-dollar production facility as a result.

If you haven't done anything specific to set the customer's expectations—such as promising delivery within 24 hours—the message simply needs to inform the customer, with little or no emphasis on apologies (see Figure 9–4). (Bear in mind, though, in this age of online ordering and overnight delivery, customers have been conditioned to expect instantaneous fulfillment of nearly every transaction, even if you haven't promised anything.) Notice how the email message in Figure 9–4, which is a combination of good and bad news, uses the indirect approach to turn the good news into a buffer for the bad news. In this case, the customer wasn't promised delivery by a certain date, so the writer simply informs the customer when to expect the rest of the order. The writer also took steps to repair the relationship and encourage future business with her firm.

If you did set the customer's expectations and now find you can't meet them, your task is more complicated. In addition to resetting the customer's expectations and explaining how you'll resolve the problem, you may need to include an element of apology. The scope of the apology depends on the magnitude of the mistake. For the customer who ordered the sweater, a simple apology, followed by a clear statement of when the sweater will arrive, would probably be sufficient. For larger business-to-business transactions, the customer may want an explanation of what went wrong to determine whether you'll be able to perform as you promise in the future.

> Some negative messages regarding transactions carry significant business ramifications.

> Your approach to bad news about business transactions depends on what you've done previously to set the customer's expectations.

> If you've failed to meet expectations that you set for the customer, an element of apology should be considered.

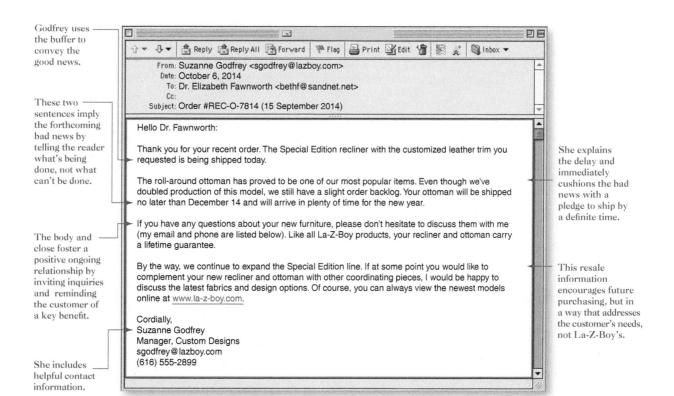

Godfrey uses the buffer to convey the good news.

These two sentences imply the forthcoming bad news by telling the reader what's being done, not what can't be done.

The body and close foster a positive ongoing relationship by inviting inquiries and reminding the customer of a key benefit.

She includes helpful contact information.

She explains the delay and immediately cushions the bad news with a pledge to ship by a definite time.

This resale information encourages future purchasing, but in a way that addresses the customer's needs, not La-Z-Boy's.

From: Suzanne Godfrey <sgodfrey@lazboy.com>
Date: October 6, 2014
To: Dr. Elizabeth Fawnworth <bethf@sandnet.net>
Cc:
Subject: Order #REC-O-7814 (15 September 2014)

Hello Dr. Fawnworth:

Thank you for your recent order. The Special Edition recliner with the customized leather trim you requested is being shipped today.

The roll-around ottoman has proved to be one of our most popular items. Even though we've doubled production of this model, we still have a slight order backlog. Your ottoman will be shipped no later than December 14 and will arrive in plenty of time for the new year.

If you have any questions about your new furniture, please don't hesitate to discuss them with me (my email and phone are listed below). Like all La-Z-Boy products, your recliner and ottoman carry a lifetime guarantee.

By the way, we continue to expand the Special Edition line. If at some point you would like to complement your new recliner and ottoman with other coordinating pieces, I would be happy to discuss the latest fabrics and design options. Of course, you can always view the newest models online at www.la-z-boy.com.

Cordially,
Suzanne Godfrey
Manager, Custom Designs
sgodfrey@lazboy.com
(616) 555-2899

Figure 9–4 Effective Email Advising of a Back Order

To help repair the damage to the relationship and encourage repeat business, many companies offer discounts on future purchases, free merchandise, or other considerations. Even modest efforts can go a long way to rebuilding the customer's confidence in your company. However, you don't always have a choice. Business-to-business purchasing contracts often include performance clauses that legally entitle the customer to discounts or other restitution in the event of late delivery. To review the concepts covered in this section, see "Checklist: Handling Bad News about Transactions."

✓ **Checklist   Handling Bad News about Transactions**

- Reset the customer's expectations regarding the transaction.
- Explain what happened and why, if appropriate.
- Explain how you'll resolve the situation.
- Repair any damage done to the business relationship, perhaps offering future discounts, free merchandise, or other considerations.

- Offer a professional, businesslike expression of apology if your organization made a mistake.

REFUSING CLAIMS AND REQUESTS FOR ADJUSTMENT

Use the indirect approach in most cases of refusing a claim.

Customers who make a claim or request an adjustment tend to be emotionally involved, so the indirect approach is usually the better choice. To avoid accepting responsibility for the unfortunate situation and avoid blaming or accusing the customer, pay special attention to the tone of your letter.

A tactful and courteous letter can build goodwill even while denying the claim, as shown in Figure 9–5. Here, Village Electronics recently received a letter from Daniel Lindmeier, who purchased a digital video camera a year ago. He wrote to say that the unit doesn't work correctly and to inquire about the warranty. Lindmeier incorrectly believes that the warranty covers one year, when it actually covers only three months. Walter Brodie uses an indirect approach to convey the bad news and to offer additional helpful information.

1 Planning →

Analyze the Situation
Verify that the purpose is to decline a request and offer alternatives; audience is likely to be surprised by the refusal.

Gather Information
Determine audience needs and obtain the necessary information.

Select the Right Medium
For formal messages, printed letters on company letterhead are best.

Organize the Information
The main idea is to refuse the request, so limit your scope to that; select an indirect approach based on the audience and the situation.

2 Writing →

Adapt to Your Audience
Adjust the level of formality based on degree of familiarity with the audience; maintain a positive relationship by using the "you" attitude, politeness, positive emphasis, and bias-free language.

Compose the Message
Use a conversational but professional style and keep the message brief, clear, and as helpful as possible.

3 Completing

Revise the Message
Evaluate content and review readability to make sure the negative information won't be misinterpreted; make sure your tone stays positive without being artificial.

Produce the Message
Emphasize a clean, professional appearance on company letterhead.

Proofread the Message
Review for errors in layout, spelling, and mechanics.

Distribute the Message
Deliver your message using the chosen medium.

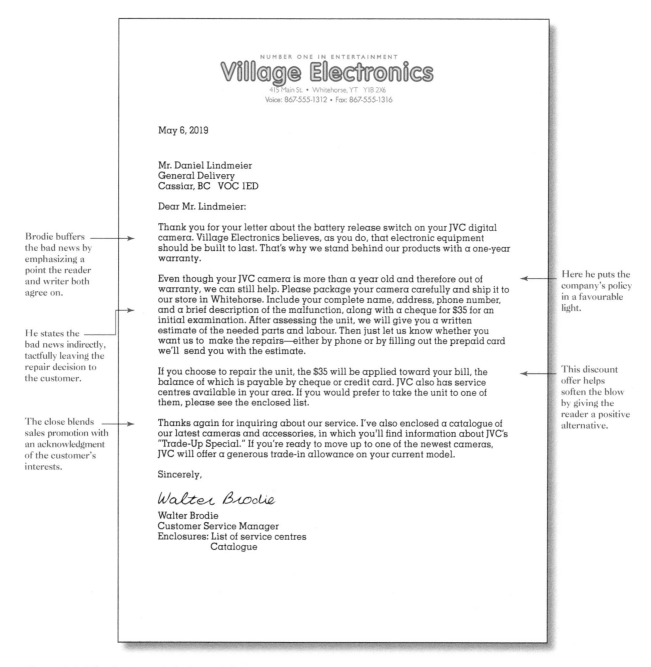

Brodie buffers the bad news by emphasizing a point the reader and writer both agree on.

He states the bad news indirectly, tactfully leaving the repair decision to the customer.

The close blends sales promotion with an acknowledgment of the customer's interests.

Here he puts the company's policy in a favourable light.

This discount offer helps soften the blow by giving the reader a positive alternative.

NUMBER ONE IN ENTERTAINMENT

Village Electronics

415 Main St. • Whitehorse, YT Y1B 2X6
Voice: 867-555-1312 • Fax: 867-555-1316

May 6, 2019

Mr. Daniel Lindmeier
General Delivery
Cassiar, BC V0C 1E0

Dear Mr. Lindmeier:

Thank you for your letter about the battery release switch on your JVC digital camera. Village Electronics believes, as you do, that electronic equipment should be built to last. That's why we stand behind our products with a one-year warranty.

Even though your JVC camera is more than a year old and therefore out of warranty, we can still help. Please package your camera carefully and ship it to our store in Whitehorse. Include your complete name, address, phone number, and a brief description of the malfunction, along with a cheque for $35 for an initial examination. After assessing the unit, we will give you a written estimate of the needed parts and labour. Then just let us know whether you want us to make the repairs—either by phone or by filling out the prepaid card we'll send you with the estimate.

If you choose to repair the unit, the $35 will be applied toward your bill, the balance of which is payable by cheque or credit card. JVC also has service centres available in your area. If you would prefer to take the unit to one of them, please see the enclosed list.

Thanks again for inquiring about our service. I've also enclosed a catalogue of our latest cameras and accessories, in which you'll find information about JVC's "Trade-Up Special." If you're ready to move up to one of the newest cameras, JVC will offer a generous trade-in allowance on your current model.

Sincerely,

Walter Brodie

Walter Brodie
Customer Service Manager
Enclosures: List of service centres
            Catalogue

Figure 9–5 Effective Letter Refusing a Claim

When refusing a claim, avoid language that might have a negative impact on the reader. Instead, demonstrate that you understand and have considered the complaint carefully. Then, even if the claim is unreasonable, rationally explain why you are refusing the request. Remember, don't apologize and don't hide behind "company policy." End the letter on a respectful and action-oriented note.

If you deal with enough customers over a long enough period, chances are you'll get a request that is particularly outrageous. However, you need to control your emotions and approach the situation as calmly as possible to avoid saying or writing anything that the recipient might interpret as defamation (see "Maintaining High Standards of Ethics, Legal Compliance, and Etiquette" in Chapter 10). To avoid being accused of defamation, follow these guidelines:

- Refrain from using any kind of abusive language or terms that could be considered defamatory.

When refusing a claim
- Demonstrate your understanding of the complaint
- Explain your refusal
- Suggest alternative action

You can help avoid defamation by not responding emotionally or abusively.

- Provide accurate information and stick to the facts.
- Never let anger or malice motivate your messages.
- Consult your company's legal advisors whenever you think a message might have legal consequences.
- Communicate honestly and ensure that what you're saying is what you believe to be true.
- Emphasize a desire for a good relationship in the future.

Most important, remember that nothing positive can come out of antagonizing a customer, even a customer who has verbally abused you or your colleagues. Reject the claim or request for adjustment and move on to the next challenge. For a brief review of the tasks involved when refusing claims, see "Checklist: Refusing Claims."

✓ Checklist   Refusing Claims

- Use an indirect approach since the reader is expecting or hoping for a positive response.
- Indicate your full understanding of the nature of the complaint.
- Explain why you are refusing the request, without hiding behind company policy.
- Provide an accurate, factual account of the transaction.

- Emphasize ways processes and procedures should have been handled, rather than dwelling on a reader's negligence.
- Avoid any appearance of defamation.
- Avoid expressing personal opinions.
- End with a positive, friendly, helpful close.
- Make any suggested action easy for readers to comply with.

Sending Negative Organizational News

5   LEARNING OBJECTIVE

List the important points to consider when conveying negative organizational news.

The messages described in the previous section deal with internal matters or individual interactions with external parties. From time to time, managers must also share negative information with the public at large, and sometimes respond to negative information as well. Most of these scenarios have unique challenges that must be addressed on a case-by-case basis, but the general advice offered here applies to all of them. One key difference among all these messages is whether you have time to plan the announcement. The following section addresses negative messages that you do have time to plan for, and the section after that, "Communicating in a Crisis," offers advice on communication during emergencies.

COMMUNICATING UNDER NORMAL CIRCUMSTANCES

Negative organizational messages to external audiences often require extensive planning.

Businesses must convey a range of negative messages regarding their ongoing operations. A company may need to make decisions that are unpopular with customers (such as price increases, product cancellations, product recalls), with employees (such as layoffs, benefit reductions, plant closings), or with other groups (such as relocating to a new community, replacing a board member, cancelling a contract with a supplier). Because you're using a single announcement to reach a variety of people, each of whom may react differently, these messages need to be planned with great care. The letter in Figure 9–6 is a mass mailing to trade customers, such as interior designers and owners of home decor stores, from a wallpaper manufacturer. It announces a change in practice that might inconvenience some readers but provides overriding benefits.

A more significant event, such as a plant closing, can affect hundreds or thousands of people in many organizations. Employees need to find new jobs,

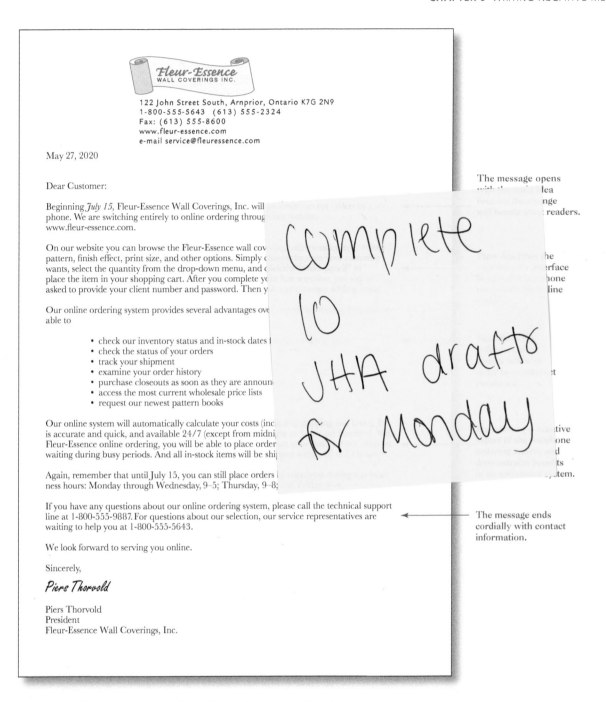

Figure 9–6 Effective Letter Describing Change in Company Practice

get training in new skills, or perhaps get emergency financial help—issues that need to be addressed. School districts may have to adjust budgets and staffing levels if many of your employees plan to move in search of new jobs. Your customers need to find new suppliers. Your suppliers may need to find other customers of their own. Government agencies may need to react to everything from a decrease in tax revenues to an influx of people seeking unemployment benefits.

When making negative announcements, follow these guidelines:

- **Match your approach to the situation.** A modest price increase won't shock most customers, so the direct approach is fine. However, cancelling a product that people count on is another matter, so building up to the news through the indirect approach might be better.

- **Consider the unique needs of each group.** As the plant-closing example illustrates, various people have different information needs.
- **Give each audience enough time to react as needed.** For example, employees, particularly higher-level executives, may need as much as six months or more to find new jobs.
- **Give yourself enough time to plan and manage a response.** You will receive numerous complaints, questions, or product returns after you make your announcement, so ensure that you're ready with answers and additional follow-up information.
- **Look for positive angles but don't give false optimism.** If eliminating a seldom-used employee benefit means employees will save money, you can promote that positive angle. On the other hand, laying off 10 000 people does not give them "an opportunity to explore new horizons." It's a traumatic event that can affect employees, their families, and their communities for years. The best you may be able to do is to thank people for their past support and wish them well in the future.

> ## TIPS FOR SUCCESS
> "A clearly written media policy can help minimize your firm's media liabilities and promote a public perception of your firm—it's all in what you say and how you say it."
>
> David M. Freedman and Janice E. Purtell, communication consultants

- **Minimize the element of surprise whenever possible.** This step can require considerable judgment on your part, but if you recognize that current trends are pointing toward negative results sometime in the near future, it's often better to let your audience know ahead of time. For example, a common complaint in many shareholder lawsuits is a claim that the company didn't let investors know business was deteriorating until it was too late.
- **Seek expert advice if you're not sure.** Many significant negative announcements have important technical, financial, or legal elements that require the expertise of lawyers, accountants, or other specialists. If you're not sure how to handle every aspect of the announcement, ask.

Negative situations will test your skills as a communicator and leader. People may turn to you and say, "Okay, so things are bad; now what do we do?" Inspirational leaders try to seize such opportunities as a chance to reshape or reinvigorate the organization, and they offer encouragement to those around them. In Figure 9–7, a message to employees at Sybervantage, Frank Leslie shares the unpleasant news that a hoped-for licensing agreement with Warner Brothers has been rejected. Rather than dwell on the bad news, he focuses on options for the future. The upbeat close diminishes the effect of the bad news without hiding or downplaying the news itself.

COMMUNICATING IN A CRISIS

As the example with Maple Leaf Foods (profiled in the chapter opener) shows, some of the most critical instances of business communication occur during internal or external crises. These can include industrial accidents, crimes or scandals involving company employees, on-site hostage situations, terrorist

Give people as much time as possible to react to negative news.

Ask for legal help and other assistance if you're not sure how to handle a significant negative announcement.

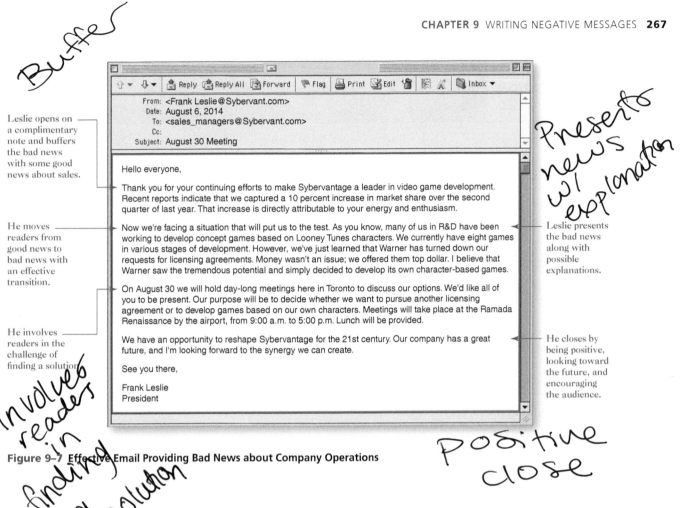

Buffer (handwritten)

Presents news w/ explanation (handwritten)

Involves readers in finding a solution (handwritten)

Positive close (handwritten)

Leslie opens on a complimentary note and buffers the bad news with some good news about sales.

He moves readers from good news to bad news with an effective transition.

He involves readers in the challenge of finding a solution.

Leslie presents the bad news along with possible explanations.

He closes by being positive, looking toward the future, and encouraging the audience.

From: <Frank Leslie@Sybervant.com>
Date: August 6, 2014
To: <sales_managers@Sybervant.com>
Cc:
Subject: August 30 Meeting

Hello everyone,

Thank you for your continuing efforts to make Sybervantage a leader in video game development. Recent reports indicate that we captured a 10 percent increase in market share over the second quarter of last year. That increase is directly attributable to your energy and enthusiasm.

Now we're facing a situation that will put us to the test. As you know, many of us in R&D have been working to develop concept games based on Looney Tunes characters. We currently have eight games in various stages of development. However, we've just learned that Warner has turned down our requests for licensing agreements. Money wasn't an issue; we offered them top dollar. I believe that Warner saw the tremendous potential and simply decided to develop its own character-based games.

On August 30 we will hold day-long meetings here in Toronto to discuss our options. We'd like all of you to be present. Our purpose will be to decide whether we want to pursue another licensing agreement or to develop games based on our own characters. Meetings will take place at the Ramada Renaissance by the airport, from 9:00 a.m. to 5:00 p.m. Lunch will be provided.

We have an opportunity to reshape Sybervantage for the 21st century. Our company has a great future, and I'm looking forward to the synergy we can create.

See you there,

Frank Leslie
President

Figure 9-7 Effective Email Providing Bad News about Company Operations

attacks, information theft, product tampering incidents, and financial calamities. During a crisis, employees, their families, the surrounding community, and others will demand information, and rumours can spread unpredictably and uncontrollably (see "Business Communication 2.0: We're under Attack! Responding to Rumours and Criticism in a Social Media Environment"). You can also expect the news media to descend quickly, asking questions of anyone they can find.

Although you can't predict these events, you can prepare for them. Companies that respond quickly with the information people need tend to fare much better in these circumstances than those that go into hiding or release bits and pieces of uncoordinated or inconsistent information. Companies such as Johnson & Johnson (in a Tylenol-tampering incident) and Maple Leaf Foods emerged from crisis with renewed respect for their decisive action and responsive communication. In contrast, Exxon continues to be cited as a classic example of how not to communicate in a crisis—more than a quarter century after one of its tankers spilled 250 000 barrels of oil into Alaska's Prince William Sound. The company frustrated the media and the public with sketchy, inconsistent information and an adamant refusal to accept responsibility for the full extent of the environmental disaster. The company's CEO didn't talk to the media for nearly a week; other executives made contradictory statements, which further undermined public trust. The mistakes had a lasting impact on the company's reputation and consumers' willingness to buy its products.[9]

The key to successful communication efforts during a crisis is having a **crisis management plan**. In addition to defining operational procedures to deal with

Dick Hemingway

Should you use the indirect or direct strategy when communicating all bad news? Many people in finance believe that, when communicating the falling fortunes of one's investments, the direct strategy is best. Why?

Anticipation and planning are key to successful communication in a crisis.

We're under Attack! Responding to Rumours and Criticism in a Social Media Environment

For all the benefits they bring to business, social media and other communication technologies have created a major new challenge: responding to online rumours and attacks on a company's reputation. Consumers and other stakeholders can now communicate through blogs, Twitter, YouTube, Facebook, advocacy sites such as http://makingchangeatwalmart.org, community participation websites such as www.epinions.com and www.planetfeedback.com, company-specific sites such as www.verizonpathetic.com, community Q&A sites such as http://getsatisfaction.com, and numerous e-commerce shopping sites that encourage product reviews.

Customers who feel they have been treated unfairly like these sites because they can use the public exposure as leverage. Many companies appreciate the feedback from these sites, too, and many actively seek out complaints to improve their products and operations. However, false rumours and unfair criticisms can spread around the world in a matter of minutes and endanger company reputations. Responding to rumours and countering negative information requires an ongoing effort and case-by-case decisions about which messages require a response. Follow these four steps:

- **Engage early, engage often.** Perhaps the most important step in responding to negative information has to be done *before* the negative information appears, and that is to engage with communities of stakeholders as a long-term strategy. Companies that have active, mutually beneficial relationships with customers and other interested parties are less likely to be attacked unfairly online and more likely to survive such attacks if they do occur. In contrast, companies that ignore constituents or jump into "spin doctoring" mode when a negative situation occurs don't have the same credibility as companies that have done the long, hard work of fostering relationships within their physical and online communities.
- **Monitor the conversation.** If people are interested in what your company does, chances are they are blogging, tweeting, podcasting, posting videos, writing on Facebook walls, and otherwise sharing their opinions. Use the available technologies to listen to what people are saying.
- **Evaluate negative messages.** When you encounter negative messages, resist the urge to fire back immediately. Instead, evaluate the source, the tone, and the content of the message and then choose a response that fits the situation. For example, the Public Affairs Agency of the U.S. Air Force groups senders of negative messages into four categories: "trolls" (those whose only intent is to stir up conflict), "ragers" (those who are just ranting or telling jokes), "the misguided" (those who are spreading incorrect information), and "unhappy customers" (those who have had a negative experience with the Air Force).
- **Respond appropriately.** After you have assessed a negative message, take the appropriate response based on an overall public relations plan. The Air Force, for instance, doesn't respond to trolls or ragers, responds to misguided messages with correct information, and responds to unhappy customers with efforts to rectify the situation and reach a reasonable solution.

Whatever you do, don't assume that a positive reputation doesn't need to be diligently guarded and defended. Everybody has a voice now, and some of those voices don't care to play by the rules of ethical communication.

CAREER APPLICATIONS

1. A legitimate complaint about your restaurant on Yelp also contains a statement that your company "doesn't care about its customers." How should you respond?
2. A few bloggers are circulating false information about your company, but the problem is not widespread—yet. Should you jump on the problem now and tell the world the rumour is false, even though most people haven't heard it yet? Explain your answer.

the crisis itself, the plan also outlines communication tasks and responsibilities, which can include everything from media contacts to news release templates (see Table 9–3). The plan should clearly specify which people are authorized to speak for the company, contact information for all key executives, and a list of the media outlets and technologies that will be used to disseminate information. Experts attribute the success of Michael McCain's handling of the *Listeria* contamination crisis at Maple Leaf Foods to an effective crisis plan. In fact, many companies today regularly test crisis communications in realistic practice drills lasting a full day or more.[10]

Table 9–3	How to Communicate in a Crisis	

(handwritten annotation: Preparing for by Planning ahead)

When a Crisis Hits:

Do	Don't
Prepare for trouble ahead of time by identifying potential problems, appointing and training a response team, and preparing and testing a crisis management plan.	Don't blame anyone for anything.
Get top management involved as soon as the crisis hits. *(handwritten: Get top management involved)*	Don't speculate in public.
Set up a news centre for company representatives and the media, equipped with phones, computers, and other electronic tools for preparing news releases and online updates. At the news centre, take the following steps:	Don't refuse to answer questions.
• Issue frequent news updates, and have trained personnel available to respond to questions around the clock.	Don't release information that will violate anyone's right to privacy.
• Provide complete information packets to the media as soon as possible.	Don't use the crisis to pitch products or services.
• Prevent conflicting statements and provide continuity, appointing a single person, trained in advance, to speak for the company.	Don't play favourites with media representatives.
• Tell receptionists and other employers to direct all media calls to the news centre.	
Tell the whole story—openly, completely, and honestly. If you are at fault, apologize.	
Demonstrate the company's concern by your statements and your actions.	

(handwritten annotation: Don't blame anyone)

Sending Negative Employment Messages

Most managers must convey bad news about individual employees from time to time. Recipients have an emotional stake in your message, so taking the indirect approach is usually advised. In addition, choose the media you use for these messages with care. For example, email and other written forms let you control the message and avoid personal confrontation, but one-on-one conversations are more sensitive and facilitate questions and answers. Companies often have policies on reference letters and other negative employment messages that managers are required to follow.[11]

6 LEARNING OBJECTIVE

Describe successful strategies for sending negative employment-related messages.

REFUSING REQUESTS FOR EMPLOYEE REFERENCES AND RECOMMENDATION LETTERS

Negative employment messages have legal implications; that's why many former employers refuse to write recommendation letters—especially for people whose job performance has been unsatisfactory.[12] When sending refusals to prospective employers, your message may be brief and direct:

Our human resources department has authorized me to confirm that Yolanda Johnson worked for Tandy, Inc., for three years, from June 2010 to July 2012. Best of luck as you interview administrative applicants.

Implies that company policy prohibits the release of any more information but does provide what information is available

Ends on a positive note

This message doesn't need to say, "We cannot comply with your request." It simply gets down to the business of giving readers the information that is allowable.

Refusing an applicant's direct request for a recommendation letter is another matter. Any refusal to cooperate may seem a personal slight and a threat to the applicant's future. Diplomacy and preparation help readers accept your refusal:

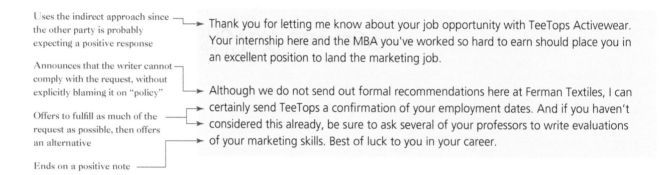

Uses the indirect approach since the other party is probably expecting a positive response →

Thank you for letting me know about your job opportunity with TeeTops Activewear. Your internship here and the MBA you've worked so hard to earn should place you in an excellent position to land the marketing job.

Announces that the writer cannot comply with the request, without explicitly blaming it on "policy" →

Offers to fulfill as much of the request as possible, then offers an alternative →

Ends on a positive note →

Although we do not send out formal recommendations here at Ferman Textiles, I can certainly send TeeTops a confirmation of your employment dates. And if you haven't considered this already, be sure to ask several of your professors to write evaluations of your marketing skills. Best of luck to you in your career.

This letter deftly and tactfully avoids hurting the reader's feelings, because it makes positive comments about the reader's recent activities, implies the refusal, suggests an alternative, and uses a polite close.

REFUSING SOCIAL NETWORKING RECOMMENDATION REQUESTS

One of the greatest values offered by business social networks is the opportunity for members to make introductions and recommendations. However, the situation with recommendations in a social networking environment is more complicated than with a traditional recommendation letter because the recommendations you make become part of your online profile. With a traditional letter, only a few hiring managers might read your recommendations, but on a network such as LinkedIn, other network members (or even the general public, in some instances) can see whom you've recommended and what you've written about these people. Much more so than with traditional letters, then, the recommendations you make in a social network become part of your brand.[13] Moreover, networks make it easy to find people and request recommendations, so chances are you will get more requests than you would have otherwise—and sometimes from people you don't know well.

Social networks have created new challenges in recommendation requests, but they also offer more flexibility in responding to these requests.

Fortunately, social networks give you a bit more flexibility when it comes to responding to these requests. One option is to simply ignore or delete the request. Some people make it personal policy to ignore requests from networkers they don't know. Of course, if you do know a person, ignoring a request could create an uncomfortable situation, so you will need to decide each case based on your relationship with the requester. Another option is to refrain from making recommendations at all, and just letting people know this policy when they ask. Whatever you decide, remember that it is your choice.[14]

If you choose to make recommendations and want to respond to a request, you can write as much or as little information about the person as you are comfortable sharing. Unlike an offline recommendation, you don't need to write a complete letter. You can write a briefer statement, even just a single sentence that focuses on one positive aspect.[15] This flexibility allows you to respond positively in those situations in which you have mixed feelings about a person's overall abilities.

REJECTING JOB APPLICATIONS

Application rejection messages are routine communications, but saying no is never easy, and recipients are emotionally invested in the decision. Expert opinions differ on the level of information to include in a rejection message, but the safest strategy is to avoid sharing any explanations for the company's decision and to avoid making or implying any promises of future consideration:[16]

- **Personalize the email message or letter by using the recipient's name.** For example, mail merge makes it easy to insert each recipient's name into a form letter.
- **Open with a courteous expression of appreciation for having applied.** In a sense, this is like the buffer in an indirect message because it gives you an opportunity to begin the conversation without immediately and bluntly telling the reader that his or her application has been rejected.
- **Convey the negative news politely and concisely.** The passive voice is helpful in this situation because it shifts focus away from the people involved and thereby depersonalizes the response. For example, "Your application was not among those selected for an interview" is less blunt than the active phrase "We have rejected your application."
- **Avoid explaining why an applicant was rejected or why other applicants were chosen instead.** Although it was once more common to offer such explanations, and some experts still advocate this approach, the simplest strategy from a legal standpoint is to avoid offering reasons for the decision. Avoiding explanations lowers the possibility that an applicant will perceive discrimination in the hiring decision or be tempted to challenge the reasons given.
- **Don't state or imply that the application will be reviewed at a later date.** Saying that "we will keep your résumé on file for future consideration" can create false hopes for the recipient and leave the company vulnerable to legal complaints if a future hiring decision is made without actually reviewing this candidate's application again. If the candidate might be a good fit for another position in the company in the future, you can suggest he or she reapply if a new job opening is posted.
- **Close with positive wishes for the applicant's career success.** A brief statement such as "We wish you success in your career" is sufficient.

Naturally, you should adjust your tactics to the circumstances. A simple and direct message is fine when someone has only submitted a job application, but rejecting a candidate who has made it at least partway through the interview process requires greater care. Personal contact has already been established through the interview process, so a phone call may be more appropriate.

The email response in Figure 9–8 rejecting a job applicant takes care to avoid making or implying any promises about future opportunities, beyond inviting the person to apply for positions that may appear in the future. Note that this encouragement would not be appropriate if the company did not believe the applicant was a good fit for the company in general.

GIVING NEGATIVE PERFORMANCE REVIEWS

The main purpose of a **performance review** is to improve employee performance by (1) emphasizing and clarifying job requirements, (2) giving employees feedback on their efforts toward fulfilling those requirements, and (3) guiding continued efforts by developing a plan of action, which includes rewards and opportunities. Performance reviews help companies set organizational standards and communicate organizational values.[17] Documentation of performance problems can also protect a company from being sued for unlawful termination.[18]

An important goal of any performance evaluation is giving the employee a plan of action for improving his or her performance.

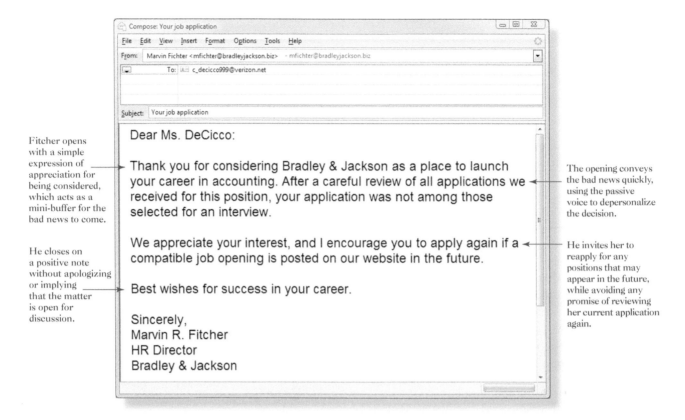

Fitcher opens with a simple expression of appreciation for being considered, which acts as a mini-buffer for the bad news to come.

He closes on a positive note without apologizing or implying that the matter is open for discussion.

The opening conveys the bad news quickly, using the passive voice to depersonalize the decision.

He invites her to reapply for any positions that may appear in the future, while avoiding any promise of reviewing her current application again.

Figure 9–8 Effective Message Rejecting a Job Applicant

With pay raises and promotion opportunities often depending on how employees are rated in this process, annual reviews often are a stressful occurrence for managers and workers alike. The worst possible outcome in an annual review is a negative surprise, such as when an employee has been working toward different goals than the manager expects or has been underperforming throughout the year but didn't receive any feedback or improvement coaching along the way.[19] In some instances, failing to confront performance problems in a timely fashion can make a company vulnerable to lawsuits.[20]

By giving employees clear goals and regular feedback, you can help avoid unpleasant surprises in a performance review.

To avoid negative surprises, managers should meet with employees to agree on clear goals for the upcoming year and then provide regular feedback and coaching as needed throughout the year if employee performance falls below expectations. Ideally, the annual review is more of a confirmation of the past year's performance and a planning session for the next year.

Some companies have gone so far as to abandon the traditional employee review altogether. The online retailer Zappos, for example, has replaced annual performance reviews with frequent status reports that give employees feedback on routine job tasks and an annual assessment of how well each employee embodies the company's core values.[21]

Even when goals have been agreed on and employees have received feedback and coaching, managers will encounter situations in which an employee's performance has not met expectations. These situations require objective, written appraisals of the performance shortcomings. Such appraisals can help the manager and employee work on an improvement plan. They also establish documentary evidence of the employee's performance in the event that disciplinary action is needed, or the employee later disputes management decisions regarding pay or promotions.[22]

When you need to write a negative review, keep the following points in mind:[23]

- **Document performance problems.** As you provide feedback throughout the year, keep a written record of performance issues. You will need this information in order to write an effective appraisal and to support any decisions that need to be made about pay, promotions, or termination.
- **Evaluate all employees consistently.** Consistency not only is fair but also helps protect the company from claims of discriminatory practices.
- **Write in a calm, objective voice.** The employee is not likely to welcome your negative assessment, but you can manage the emotions of the situation by maintaining professional reserve in your writing.
- **Focus on opportunities for improvement.** As you document performance problems, identify specific steps the employee can take to correct them. This information can serve as the foundation for an improvement plan for the coming year.
- **Keep job descriptions up to date.** Performance evaluations should be based on the criteria listed in an employee's job description. However, if a job evolves over time in response to changes in the business, the employees' current activities may no longer match an outdated job description.

Negative evaluations should provide careful documentation of performance concerns.

TERMINATING EMPLOYMENT

If an employee's performance cannot be brought up to company standards or if other factors such as declining sales cause a reduction in the workforce, a company often has no choice but to terminate employment. As with other negative employment messages, termination is fraught with emotions and legal ramifications, so careful planning, complete documentation, and sensitive writing are essential.

Termination messages should always be written with input from the company's legal staff, but here are general writing guidelines to bear in mind:[24]

Carefully word a termination letter to avoid creating undue ill will and grounds for legal action.

- Clearly present the reasons for this difficult action, whether it is the employee's performance or a business decision unrelated to specific employees.
- Make sure the reasons are presented in a way that cannot be construed as unfair or discriminatory.
- Follow company policy and any relevant legal guidelines (such as employment contracts) to the letter.
- Avoid personal attacks or insults of any kind.
- Ask another manager to review the letter before issuing it. An objective reviewer who isn't directly involved might spot troublesome wording or faulty reasoning.
- Deliver the termination letter in person if at all possible. Arrange a meeting that will ensure privacy and freedom from interruptions.

Any termination is clearly a negative outcome for both employer and employee, but careful attention to content and tone in the termination message can help the employee move on gracefully and minimize the misunderstandings and anger that can lead to expensive lawsuits. To review the tasks involved in this type of message, see "Checklist: Writing Negative Employment Messages."

Checklist | Writing Negative Employment Messages

A. Refusing requests for employee references and recommendation letters
- Don't feel obligated to write a recommendation letter if you don't feel comfortable doing so.
- Take a diplomatic approach to minimize hurt feelings.
- Compliment the reader's accomplishments.
- Suggest alternatives if available.
- Use the options available to you on social networks, such as ignoring a request from someone you don't know or writing a recommendation on a single positive attribute.

B. Rejecting job applications
- If possible, respond to all applications, even if you use only a form message to acknowledge receipt.
- If you use the direct approach, take care to avoid being blunt or cold.
- If you use the indirect approach, don't mislead the reader in your buffer or delay the bad news for more than a sentence or two.
- Avoid explaining why the applicant was rejected.
- Suggest alternatives if possible.

C. Giving negative performance reviews
- Document performance problems throughout the year.
- Evaluate all employees consistently.
- Keep job descriptions up to date as employee responsibilities change.
- Maintain an objective and unbiased tone.
- Use nonjudgmental language.
- Focus on problem resolution.
- Make sure negative feedback is documented and shared with the employee.
- Don't avoid confrontations by withholding negative feedback.
- Ask the employee for a commitment to improve.

D. Terminating employment
- State your reasons accurately and make sure they are objectively verifiable.
- Avoid statements that might expose your company to a wrongful termination lawsuit.
- Consult company lawyers to clarify all terms of the separation.
- Deliver the letter in person if at all possible.
- End the relationship on terms as positive as possible.

SUMMARY OF LEARNING OBJECTIVES

1 Apply the three-step writing process to negative messages. Because the way you say "no" can be far more damaging than the fact that you're saying it, planning your bad-news messages is crucial. Ensure that your purpose is specific, necessary, and appropriate for your chosen medium. Determine how your audience prefers to receive bad news. Collect all the facts necessary to support your negative decision, and adapt your tone to the situation as well as to your audience. Bad-news messages may be organized according to the direct or the indirect approach, and your choice depends on audience preference as well as the situation. In addition, carefully choose positive words to construct diplomatic sentences. Finally, revision, design, and proofreading are necessary to ensure that you are saying exactly what you want to say in the best possible way.

2 Explain how to use the direct approach effectively when conveying negative news. The direct approach to bad-news messages puts the bad news up front, follows with the reasons (and perhaps offers an alternative), and closes with a positive statement. Use the direct approach when you know your audience prefers receiving bad news up front or if the bad news will cause readers little pain or disappointment. An advantage to the direct approach for negative messages is that it saves readers time by helping them reach the main idea more quickly.

3 Explain how to use the indirect approach effectively when conveying negative news. The indirect approach to bad-news messages begins with a buffer (a neutral or positive statement), explains the reasons, clearly states the bad news (de-emphasizing it as much as possible), and closes with a positive statement. If used ineffectively, the indirect approach may be disrespectful and may mislead the reader. To avoid these problems, ensure that the buffer does not trivialize the reader's concerns but establishes common ground in a neutral manner. The body of the message should build up the explanation for the decision, preparing the reader through facts and logical reasoning. Give the most positive points first and, if possible, demonstrate how the negative decision might benefit the reader. End by clearly expressing the bad news, but de-emphasize the news without trivializing it. Focus on what could be done instead of what cannot be accomplished.

4 Explain the importance of maintaining high standards of ethics and etiquette when delivering negative messages. Sending negative news is an unpleasant task, but this news must be delivered in a timely and sensitive manner. Ignoring bad news can violate laws and regulations, such as those governing financial communications; thus, an ethical communicator faces bad news head-on. Negative news can have a life-changing effect on the receiver; consequently, an ethical communicator sends this news with sensitivity to the receiver's situation and emotions. Furthermore, ethical communicators deliver bad news accurately, overcoming any reluctance to avoid the circumstances and mislead the receiver. By facing difficult situations honestly and considerately, communicators ultimately help others and are viewed with respect.

5 **List the important points to consider when conveying negative organizational news.** Although you can't anticipate the nature and circumstance of every possible adverse situation, you can prepare by deciding how to handle such issues as communication with employees and the public. Determine whether the direct or indirect approach is suitable for the situation. Understand your audience and their needs, and allocate enough time to plan the response. Consider positive sides of the situation, but don't mislead your audience. Obtain expert help for assistance outside of your own knowledge. Furthermore, when communicating in a crisis, ensure that your organization has a crisis communication plan that clarifies all communication tasks and responsibilities.

6 **Describe successful strategies for sending negative employment-related messages.** When refusing requests for employee references, your message can be brief and direct, giving only the information permitted by your company. When refusing social networking recommendations, you can ignore or delete the request, or inform the sender of your organization's policy. When rejecting job applicants, personalize the message and convey the negative news briefly and politely. When giving negative performance reviews, clarify job requirements; provide feedback on the employee's progress, being sure to document shortcomings; and develop a plan of action to guide development.

ON THE JOB PERFORMING COMMUNICATION TASKS AT MAPLE LEAF FOODS

Effective communication was one of the key skills demonstrated by Michael McCain and his team at Maple Leaf Foods during the food contamination crisis in 2008. As an administrative assistant in communications at Maple Leaf Foods, you need to send effective messages in negative situations. Your current task is to respond to proposals from graphic designers who want to produce Maple Leaf Foods' annual report. Although a company's proposal may be rejected, Maple Leaf Foods still wants to maintain the firm's goodwill and keep opportunities open for the future. Use this chapter's strategies to face the challenge of saying "no" with tact and understanding.

1. You have received a proposal from a graphic design company that, you believe, would create an effective and engaging annual report. But the applicant has not effectively discussed his company's previous work, one of the key questions in the proposal package. You'd like the applicant to resubmit the proposal, but he will have to wait an additional six weeks for a response. Which paragraph does the best job of presenting the bad news?

   a. It's too bad you neglected to answer fully the key question about the previous work your company did. If you want us to consider your firm as a candidate for producing our annual report, you'd better fill out the questionnaire completely.

   b. We know completing the proposal is a demanding and time-consuming process. As the instructions indicate, all key questions must be fully answered if the proposal is to receive consideration. We are returning your proposal package so you can review your answer to Question 4, dealing with previous design work.

   c. We appreciate the work you put into completing your supplier proposal. You did a thorough job, but please expand on Question 4.

2. Continuing with the case of the incomplete proposal, which closing paragraph would you choose? Why?

   a. We do appreciate that you took a lot of time to work on the proposal, but we can't read it until you complete it. And you won't hear from us for another six weeks.

   b. If you need further assistance in completing your proposal, please consult the Internet bookmarks listed in the guidebook. We look forward to receiving your revised supplier proposal.

   c. Thank you for your attention to this matter.

3. Personal contacts are an important source of new business opportunities in many industries. In some cases, businesspeople develop these contacts through active participation in industry or professional groups and visits to trade shows, alumni societies, and other groups. You've recently received a request from a former classmate (Marcia DeLancey) who owns her own graphic design firm. She wants to visit your office to present her portfolio. However, your supervisor is already familiar with her work when she was an employee at another firm and knows her style would not fit Maple Leaf Foods' requirements. You didn't know DeLancey all that well; in fact, you had to think for a minute to remember who she was (this is the first contact you've had with her since you both graduated five years ago). Which opening would be most appropriate, keeping in mind she can't make the grade?

   a. Congratulations on owning your own company! I hope you enjoy your work as much as I enjoy mine. Thank you for your recent inquiry—evaluating such requests is one of my key responsibilities.

   b. Great to hear from you. I'd love to catch up on old times with you and find out how you're doing in your new job. I bounced around a bit after university, but I really feel that I've found my niche here at Maple Leaf Foods.

   c. I'm sorry to say that Maple Leaf Foods has already evaluated your work through submissions by your previous firm and found it did not fit our style. However, I do appreciate your getting in touch, and I hope all is well with you.

TEST YOUR KNOWLEDGE

1. Why is it particularly important to adapt your medium and tone to your audience's needs and preferences when writing a bad-news message?

2. What are the main goals in delivering bad news?

3. What are the advantages of using the direct approach to deliver bad news at the beginning of a message?

4. What is the sequence of elements in a bad-news message organized using the indirect approach?

5. What is a buffer? Why do some critics consider it unethical?

6. When using an indirect approach to announce a negative decision, what is the purpose of presenting your reasons before explaining the decision itself?

7. What are the techniques for de-emphasizing bad news?

8. What are the ethical considerations for delivering bad news?

9. What are the characteristics of effective crisis communication?

10. When giving a negative review to an employee, what guidelines should you follow?

APPLY YOUR KNOWLEDGE

1. Why is it important to end negative messages on a positive note, whenever possible?

2. If company policy changes, should you explain those changes to employees and customers at about the same time? Why or why not?

3. If your purpose is to convey bad news, such as refusing a request, should you take the time to suggest alternatives to your reader? Why or why not?

4. How do social networks make the practices of requesting and granting or denying recommendations both easier and more difficult?

5. Why is choice of medium important when delivering performance reviews?

6. **Ethical Choices** Is intentionally de-emphasizing bad news the same as distorting graphs and charts to de-emphasize unfavourable data? Why or why not?

RUNNING CASES

> CASE 1 Noreen

In her role as collections manager, Noreen has to write a letter informing customers with overdue accounts that the interest rate has risen by 1 percent, effective 30 days from the date on the letter. This policy means Petro-Go's current interest rate is 14 percent and in 30 days will increase to 15 percent. Overdue accounts are charged with compounding interest (that is, interest on both the previous month's balance and the interest already charged on that month's balance).

QUESTIONS

a. What does it mean to use the "you" attitude in this type of message?

b. Is the direct or indirect approach best for this bad-news message? Why?

c. What must be considered to avoid defamation of the customer's character or reputation?

d. How will Noreen end this message on a positive note?

e. Should Noreen suggest ways for the customer to avoid paying late payment charges in this letter?

YOUR TASK

Write the letter. Remember to use company letterhead (create it yourself) and include an enclosure notation. Include a 1-800 number customers can call for further information.

Both the letter and the envelope should indicate the information is confidential. Prepare the envelope. (See Appendix A for letter and envelope formats.)

> CASE 2 Kwong

Kwong has returned to Accountants For All to complete his third co-op work term required by his college diploma. The owner, being very impressed with Kwong's past work performance and knowing that he has completed the required courses, promotes Kwong to corporate accountant status. He asks Kwong to write a letter to an important corporate client, Trisix, informing Marion Beattie, chief financial officer, that the quote Accountants For All gave them for this year's tax services was incorrect. The actual charge will be $500 more than discussed previously in an office meeting with Accountants For All's owner. The increased fee is due to the fact that Trisix's ledger was not accurate and Accountants For All's staff had to review receipts and adjust ledger entries manually. The initial price quote did not include manual handling of receipts. The letter should attempt to maintain a good customer relationship.

QUESTIONS

a. What facts must Kwong gather before writing the letter?

b. How will he choose positive words for this bad news?

c. Kwong has chosen the indirect approach for this letter. Suggest a reasonable buffer.

d. Should Kwong apologize?

e. How will Kwong end this message on a positive note? Why is this important?

YOUR TASK

Write the letter. Apply the guidelines for writing bad-news messages that this chapter discusses.

PRACTISE YOUR KNOWLEDGE

Read the following documents, then (1) analyze the strengths and weaknesses of each sentence and (2) revise each document so that it follows this chapter's guidelines.

DOCUMENT 9.A: PROVIDING NEGATIVE NEWS ABOUT TRANSACTIONS

Your' spring fraternity party sounds like fun. We're glad you've again chosen us as your caterer. Unfortunately, we have changed a few of our policies, and I wanted you to know about these changes in advance so we won't have any misunderstandings on the day of the party.

We will arrange the delivery of tables and chairs as usual the evening before the party. However, if you want us to set up, there is now a $100 charge for that service. Of course, you might want to get some of the brothers and pledges to do it, which would save you money. We've also added a small change for cleanup. This is only $3 per person (you can estimate because I know a lot of people come and go later in the evening).

Other than that, all the arrangements will be the same. We'll provide the skirting for the band stage, tablecloths, bar set-up, and, of course, the barbecue. Will you have the tubs of ice with soft drinks again? We can do that for you as well, but there will be a fee.

Please let me know if you have any problems with these changes, and we'll try to work them out. I know its going to be a great party.

DOCUMENT 9.B: REFUSING REQUESTS FOR CLAIMS AND ADJUSTMENTS

I am responding to your letter of about six weeks ago asking for an adjustment on your wireless hub, model WM39Z. We test all our products before it leaves the factory; therefore, it could not have been our fault that your hub didn't work.

If you or someone in your office dropped the unit, it might have caused the damage. Or the damage could have been caused by the shipper if he dropped it. If so, you should file a claim with the shipper. At any rate, it wasn't our fault. The parts are already covered by warranty. However, we will provide labour for the repairs for $55, which is less than our cost, since you are a valued customer.

We will have a booth at the upcoming trade show there and hope to see you or someone from your office. We have many new models of office machines that we're sure you'll want to see. I've inclosed our latest catalogue. Hope to see you there.

DOCUMENT 9.C: REJECTING JOB APPLICATIONS

I regret to inform you that you were not selected for our summer intern program at Equifax. We had over a thousand résumés and cover letters to go threw and simply could not get to them all. We have been asked to notify everyone that we have already selected students for the 25 positions based on those who applied early and were qualified.

We're sure you will be able to find a suitable position for summer work in your feild and wish you the best of luck. We deeply regret any inconvenience associated with our reply.

EXERCISES

9.1 Selecting the Approach: Various Scenarios

Select the approach you would use (direct or indirect) for these negative messages:

a. An email message to your boss informing her that one of your key clients is taking its business to a different accounting firm

b. An email message to a customer informing her that one of the books she ordered over the Internet is temporarily out of stock

c. An instant message to a customer explaining that the high-resolution monitor he ordered for his computer is on back order and that, as a consequence, the shipping of the entire order will be delayed

d. A blog post to all employees notifying them that the company parking lot will be repaved during the first week of June and that the company will provide a shuttle service from a remote parking lot during that period

e. A letter from a travel agent to a customer stating that the airline will not refund her money for the flight she missed but that her tickets are valid for one year

f. A form letter from a Canadian airline to a customer explaining that they cannot extend the expiration date of the customer's frequent flyer miles even though the customer was living overseas for the past three years and unable to use the miles during that time

g. A letter from an insurance company to a policyholder denying a claim for reimbursement for a special dental procedure that is not covered under the terms of the customer's policy

h. A letter from an electronics store stating that the customer will not be reimbursed for a malfunctioning cellphone still under warranty (the terms of the warranty do not cover damages to phones that were accidentally dropped from a moving car)

i. An announcement to the repairs department listing parts that are on back order and will be three weeks late

9.2 Teamwork: Communicating Bad News

Working alone, revise the following statements to de-emphasize the bad news. (Hint: Minimize the space devoted to the bad news, subordinate it, embed it, or use the passive voice.) Then team up with a classmate and read each other's revisions. Did you both use the same approach in every case? Which approach seems to be more effective for each revised statement?

a. The airline can't refund your money. The "Conditions" segment on the back of your ticket states that there are no refunds for missed flights. Sometimes the airline makes exceptions, but only when life and death are involved. Of course, your ticket is still valid and can be used on a flight to the same destination.

b. I'm sorry to tell you, we can't supply the custom decorations you requested. We called every supplier and none of them can do what you want on such short notice. You can, however, get a standard decorative package on the same theme in time. I found a supplier that stocks these. Of course, it won't have quite the flair you originally requested.

c. We can't refund your money for the malfunctioning MP3 player. You shouldn't have immersed the unit in water while swimming; the user's manual clearly states the unit is not designed to be used in adverse environments.

9.3 Using Buffers: Practice

Answer the following questions pertaining to buffers:

a. You have to tell a local restaurant owner that your plans have changed and you have to cancel the 90-person banquet scheduled for next month. Do you need to use a buffer? Why or why not?

b. Write a buffer for a letter declining an invitation to speak at an association's annual fundraising event. Show your appreciation for being asked.

c. Write a buffer declining a high-school group visit to your factory because it does not provide access to the two students who are in wheelchairs.

d. Write a memo cancelling the office end-of-year party because the company does not have enough money to hold it this year. Do you need to use a buffer? Why or why not?

e. Write a buffer for a letter cancelling a school group's reservation to attend a theatre's musical show in two months. It's been cancelled because box office sales have been generally poor.

9.4 Internet: Bad News Strategy

Public companies occasionally need to issue news releases announcing or explaining downturns in sales, profits, demand, or other business factors. Search the Web to locate a company that has issued a press release that recently reported lower earnings or other bad news, and access the news release on that firm's website. Alternatively, find the type of press release you're seeking by reviewing press releases at www.newswire.ca (CNW) or www.prnewswire.com. How does the headline relate to the main message of the release? Is the release organized according to the direct or the indirect approach? What does the company do to present the bad news in a favourable light—and does this effort seem sincere and ethical to you?

9.5 Ethical Choices: Communicating Escalating Rates

The insurance company where you work is planning to raise all premiums for health care coverage. Your boss has asked you to read a draft of her letter to customers announcing the new higher rates. The first two paragraphs discuss some exciting medical advances and the expanded coverage offered by your company. Only in the final paragraph do customers learn that they will have to pay more for coverage starting next year. What are the ethical implications of this draft? What changes would you suggest?

9.6 Social Media: Responding to Online Messages

Your company uses social media to announce various changes and advances. Most of the time, the responses from the public are positive; however, sometimes people post negative comments. How would you respond to the following:

a. Your new commercial stinks. You show happy people using your products, but I have only been annoyed with what I have purchased. False advertising!

b. Your company sucks.

c. Don't believe what you hear. I bought clothing from them and everything fell apart in the first washing. They don't give refunds for defective products.

d. Used the service. People are rude. Hate it.

e. Only dealt with the company once. Never again.

CASES	APPLYING THE THREE-STEP WRITING PROCESS TO CASES

Apply each step to the following cases, as assigned by your instructor.

1 Planning →

Analyze the Situation
Identify both your general purpose and your specific purpose. Clarify exactly what you want your audience to think, feel, or believe after receiving your message. Profile your primary audience, including their backgrounds, differences, similarities, and likely reactions to your message.

Gather Information
Identify the information your audience will need to receive, as well as other information you may need in order to craft an effective message.

Select the Right Medium
Make sure your medium is both acceptable to the audience and appropriate for the message. Realize that written media are inappropriate for some negative messages.

Organize the Information
Choose a direct or indirect approach based on the audience and the message; many negative messages are best delivered with an indirect approach. If you use the indirect approach, carefully consider which type of buffer is best for the situation. Identify your main idea, limit your scope, and then outline necessary support points and other evidence.

2 Writing →

Adapt to Your Audience
Show sensitivity to audience needs by using a "you" attitude, politeness, positive emphasis, and bias-free language. Understand how much credibility you already have—and how much you may need to establish. Project your company's image by maintaining an appropriate style and tone. Consider cultural variations and the differing needs of internal and external audiences.

Compose the Message
Draft your message using clear but sensitive words, effective sentences, and coherent paragraphs.

3 Completing

Revise the Message
Evaluate content and review readability, then edit and rewrite for conciseness and clarity.

Produce the Message
Use effective design elements and suitable layout for a clean, professional appearance.

Proofread the Message
Review for errors in layout, spelling, and mechanics.

Distribute the Message
Deliver your message using the chosen medium; make sure all documents and all relevant files are distributed successfully.

Negative Replies to Routine Requests

|IM SKILLS|

1. No Deal: Refusing a Refund by Instant Message

Your company has learned that selling instructional videos presents a difficult business dilemma. For its first five years of operation, the company had a generous return policy in which customers could return any DVD after 10 days, even if it had been opened. However, as return rates began to climb, management began to suspect that some customers were abusing the policy by watching DVDs long enough to learn whatever they wanted to learn and then returning them and asking for refunds. The company disliked penalizing the majority of its customer base by changing the policy, but returns cost money, and the company's profits were taking a bigger and bigger hit every year. Starting last year, the company now accepts returns only if the product packaging has not been opened.

Your task: Team up with two other students. One of you will play the role of a customer who purchased the "Kickboxing Fundamentals" DVD two weeks ago. One of you will play the role of a service agent who assists customers with orders and returns.

Using Facebook's chat function or any other free instant messaging (IM) service, role play an exchange in which the customer initiates the conversation and asks for a refund, saying that the program doesn't meet his or her needs. The reason offered is that the techniques shown in the video are quite basic, and he or she is already past that skill level.

Early in the exchange, the service agent needs to ask whether the DVD package has been unsealed. The customer replies that it has, after which the agent will respond that the company can accept only unopened DVDs for refund or exchange. The customer can continue to argue that there is no way to truly evaluate a DVD without watching the entire program, because every person might have a different understanding of what "fundamentals" means. However, the company's policy is firm.

Make up whatever details you need to complete the exchange, keeping in mind the following points:

- The video title and the product description on the website clearly indicate that this kickboxing program is intended for beginners.
- The website clearly states that DVDs can be returned only if they are unopened.
- In addition, the online shopping cart requires customers to check a box to indicate that they have read the return policy.
- The agent might suggest to the customer that he or she could offer it for sale on Craigslist, sell it to a store that buys used movies, or donate it to a library.

The third member of the team should sit beside either the customer or the agent and evaluate the IM exchange, without participating. If possible, capture the IM stream for offline analysis. The evaluator will then give both participants written feedback on the content and tone of their messages, offering suggestions for improvement. Be prepared to discuss the experience and the analysis with your class.

▌Memo Writing SKILLS▌

2. Suffering Artists: Memo Declining High-Tech Shoes at Centennial Ballet Theatre

Here at the Centennial Ballet Theatre (CBT), where you're serving as assistant to Artistic Director Kenneth MacLachlan, the notion of suffering for the art form has been ingrained since the early 1800s, when the first ballerina rose up en pointe. Many entrepreneurs are viewing this painful situation with hopeful enthusiasm, especially when they discover that dancers worldwide spend about $150 million annually on their shoes—those "tiny torture chambers" of cardboard and satin (with glued linen or burlap to stiffen the toes). The pink monstrosities (about $75 a pair) rarely last beyond a single hard performance.

A company the size of CBT spends about $500 000 a year on ballet slippers—plus the cost of its staff physical therapist and all those trips to chiropractors, podiatrists, and surgeons to relieve bad necks, backs, knees, and feet. Entrepreneurs believe there must be room for improvement, given the current advantages of orthopedics, space-age materials, and high-tech

solutions for contemporary athletes. There's no denying that ballerinas are among the hardest-working athletes in the world.

The latest entrepreneur to approach CBT is Melinda Ellis of Grey Ellis, Inc. No one in the ballet company blames her for wanting to provide a solution to the shoe problem. She buttonholed Marvin King, executive director and a member of CBT's board of governing trustees, with a proposal for providing new, high-performance pointe shoes in exchange for an endorsement. It truly is a good idea. It's just a hard sell among the tradition-oriented dancers.

Ellis's alternative pointe shoes offer high-impact support and toe cushions. They're only $70 a pair, and supposedly they can be blow-dried back into shape after a performance. When the cost-conscious board member urged the company to give them a try, you were assigned to collect feedback from dancers.

So far, not good. For example, principal ballerina Grace Durham: She'd rather numb her feet in icy water, dance through "zingers" of toe pain, and make frequent visits to the physical therapist than wear Ellis's shoes, she insisted after a brief trial. The others agree. Apparently, they like breaking in the traditional satin models with hammers and door slams and throwing them away after a single performance of *Swan Lake*. Too stiff, they say of the new shoes. Adds Durham, "I'm totally settled into what I'm doing."

You've seen those sinewy, wedge-shaped feet bleeding backstage. You feel sorry for Ellis; it was a good idea. Maybe she should try younger dancers.

Your task: MacLachlan has asked you to write an internal memo in his name to Marvin King, executive director of the CBT, explaining the dancers' refusal to use the new high-tech Grey Ellis pointe shoes. In your memo ensure that you include the dancers' reasons as well as your own opinion regarding the matter. You'll need to decide whether to use the direct or indirect approach; include a separate short note to your instructor justifying your selection.[25]

▌Letter Writing SKILLS▌

3. Message Strategies: Negative Announcements on Routine Matters

Your company, PolicyPlan Insurance Services, is a 120-employee insurance claims processor based in Vancouver. PolicyPlan has engaged Sparkleen Services for interior and exterior cleaning for the past five years. Sparkleen did exemplary work for the first four years, but after a change of ownership last year, the level of service has plummeted. Offices are no longer cleaned thoroughly, you've had to call the company at least six times to remind them to take care of spills and other messes that they're supposed to address routinely, and they've left toxic cleaning chemicals in a public hallway on several occasions. You have spoken with the owner about your concerns twice in the past three months, but his assurances that service would improve have not resulted in any noticeable improvements. When the evening cleaning crew forgot to lock the lobby door last Thursday—leaving your entire facility vulnerable to theft from midnight until 8 A.M. Friday morning—you decided it was time for a change.

Your task: Write a letter to Jason Allred, owner of Sparkleen Services, 4000 Broughton Street, Vancouver, BC, V7F 2R3, telling him that PolicyPlan will not be renewing its annual cleaning contract with Sparkleen Services when the current contract expires at the end of this month. Cite the examples identified above, and keep the tone of your letter professional.

Letter Writing SKILLS

4. Photo Finish: No Credit to Todd Rooker, Photographer

You've dealt with Todd Rooker, a photographer of weddings and family events, for the past 13 years with no problem. He's sent numerous jobs to you for developing and has always paid on time. But for the last two jobs he has asked your company, Best Photo Labs, to extend credit. He says the wedding and special events market is drying up in his neighbourhood, and he's getting few referrals from old customers. He has to work as an industrial photographer during the day for a friend's firm and can only work evenings at his own business. He isn't making the money he used to, but he hopes to get enough cash flowing from his day job to pay Best Photo Labs for developing his photos. He sure can't ask for money from his customers until they see the finished pictures.

But Best Photo Labs has a business to run, and they can't rely on goodwill to pay their technicians, rent, and utilities, as well as for developing chemicals and photographic paper.

Your task: As the office manager for Best Photo Labs, you've dealt with Todd Rooker's account for several years. You know he's a nice guy and a good photographer. Write Todd a tactful letter refusing credit. Todd's address is Todd Rooker, Professional Photographer, 195 Argyle St., Fredericton, NB, E3B 1T6.

Email SKILLS | **Portfolio** BUILDER

5. Message to the Boss: Refusing a Project on Ethical Grounds

A not-so-secret secret is getting more attention than you'd really like after an article in *BusinessWeek* gave the world an inside look at how much money you and other electronics retailers make from extended warranties (sometimes called service contracts). The article explained that typically half of the warranty price goes to the salesperson as a commission and that only 20 percent of the total amount customers pay for warranties eventually goes to product repair.

You also know why extended warranties are such a profitable business. Many electronics products follow a predictable pattern of failure: a high failure rate early in their lives, then a "midlife" period during which failures go way down, and concluding with an "old age" period when failure rates ramp back up again (engineers refer to the phenomenon as the bathtub curve because it looks like a bathtub from the side—high at both ends and low in the middle). Those early failures are usually covered by manufacturers' warranties, and the extended warranties you sell are designed to cover that middle part of the lifespan. In other words, many extended warranties cover the period of time during which consumers are least likely to need them and offer no coverage when consumers need them most. (Consumers can actually benefit from extended warranties in a few product categories, including laptop computers and plasma TVs. Of course, the more sense the warranty makes for the consumer, the less financial sense it makes for your company.)

Your task: Worried that consumers will start buying fewer extended warranties, your boss has directed you to put together a sales training program that will help cashiers sell the extended warranties even more aggressively. The more you ponder this challenge, though, the more you're convinced that your company should change its strategy so that it doesn't rely on profits from these warranties so much. In addition to offering questionable value to the consumer, they risk creating a consumer backlash that could lead to lower sales of all your products. You would prefer to voice your concerns to your boss in person, but both of you are travelling on hectic schedules for the next week. You'll have to write an email instead. Draft a brief message explaining why you think the sales training specifically and the warranties in general are both bad ideas.[26]

Letter Writing SKILLS

6. Pay or Sell: Last Chance to Settle Condo Management Fees

You don't like writing such letters, but during your five years as a property manager for Provide Corporation, you've had to tell condo owners that if they don't pay their monthly maintenance fees, Provide will attach a lien to their bank accounts as they are permitted to do by provincial law. The problem you're having now is with Mrs. Edith Bookman, a recent widow who has fallen behind two months in her maintenance fees. The money she—and all the other apartment owners—pay each month goes toward maintaining the building and grounds to keep the property healthy and attractive. Without the monthly maintenance fee from each owner, the condo would fall into disrepair, and everyone would have to pay a special assessment to bring it back to standard. No one wants that to happen.

You know that things are difficult for Mrs. Bookman right now. You've consulted with the condo's board of directors, made up of owners who give direction to the property manager when needed. They've told you not to attach a lien to Mrs. Bookman's account now, although provincial law says you could. Instead, they want to give her another month to pay the arrears.

Your task: Write a letter to Mrs. Bookman following the board's direction. Explain that she must pay her two months' arrears with her third payment, and why doing so is important. If she doesn't, Provide will attach a lien to her bank account for the balance owed as well as a $500 administrative lien fee, which it is legally allowed to do. Mrs. Bookman lives at 1335 St. Albert Trail NW, Suite 3E, Edmonton, AB, T5L 4R3.

|Letter Writing SKILLS|

7. More to Come: Letter Explaining Delay of Anne of Green Gables T-shirt

Each year thousands of people attend the Charlottetown Festival to see plays featuring Lucy Maud Montgomery's fictional characters. Montgomery's stories have been loved by Canadians and by millions around the world since the publication of her first novel, *Anne of Green Gables*, in 1908. Prince Edward Island has benefited immensely from tourists who travel there during the festival season to enjoy not only the theatre but also the sea, beaches, and Montgomery's birthplace. Souvenirs are popular among both Canadian and foreign visitors, who buy them for friends and relatives back home.

This summer's festival was so successful that your local store, Little Things, has sold out its stock of child- and youth-sized T-shirts featuring Anne's image. You've received a letter from a German tourist explaining that when his nieces and nephews saw his daughter's T-shirt, they each wanted one, too. He's included his credit card number and expiry date, and wants two green T-shirts in size 6X, three white shirts in size 10–12, and two in size 14–16. His letter is dated October 6, 2018, and he is hoping to get the shirts in time for Christmas. Your problem is that you have only two blue shirts, size 6X— no green—in stock, and one white shirt, size 10–12. You do have many white shirts in size 14–16. More T-shirts won't be available until March 2019, as the product is seasonal. You also have some other items in stock, such as stickers, always popular with kids, and buttons.

Your task: Write to Josef Mandelheim, Sonnenstrasse 4, 86669 Erlingshofen, Germany. Explain what you can do. Child-sized shirts are $8.95 each, youth-sized $10.95, duty is 12 percent of the total, there is no GST, and shipping is $32.00.

Negative Organizational News

|Email SKILLS| |Portfolio BUILDER|

8. Sorry, but We Don't Have a Choice: Email about Monitoring Employee Blogs

You can certainly sympathize with employees when they complain about having their email and instant messages monitored when using company equipment or when employees publicly state an active connection with the company on their social media accounts, but you're only implementing a company policy that all employees agree to abide by when they join the company. Your firm, Nebcor Builders of Ottawa, Ontario, is one of the growing number of Canadian companies with such monitoring systems in place. More and more companies use these systems (which typically operate by scanning messages for keywords that suggest confidential, illegal, or otherwise inappropriate content) in an attempt to avoid instances of sexual harassment and other problems.

As the chief information officer, the manager in charge of computer systems in the company, you're often the target when employees complain about being monitored. Consequently, you know you're really going to hear it when employees learn that the monitoring program will be expanded to personal blogs as well.

Your task: Write an email to be distributed to the entire workforce, explaining that the automated monitoring program is about to be expanded to include employees' personal blogs. Explain that while you sympathize with employee concerns regarding privacy and freedom of speech, the management team's responsibility is to protect the company's intellectual property and the value of the company name. Therefore, employees' personal blogs will be added to the monitoring system to ensure that employees don't intentionally or accidentally expose company secrets or criticize management in a way that could harm the company.[27]

|Blogging SKILLS| |Portfolio BUILDER|

9. Product Recall: Blog Post for Negative Organizational Announcement

XtremityPlus is known for its outlandish extreme-sports products, and the Looney Launch is no exception. Fulfilling the dream of every childhood daredevil, the Looney Launch is an aluminum and fibreglass contraption that quickly unfolds to create the ultimate bicycle jump. The product has been selling as fast as you can make it, even though it comes plastered with warning labels proclaiming that its use is inherently dangerous.

As XtremityPlus's CEO, you were nervous about introducing this product, and your fears were just confirmed: you've been notified of the first lawsuit by a parent whose child broke several bones after crash-landing off a Looney Launch.

Your task: Write a post for your internal blog, explaining that the Looney Launch is being removed from the market immediately. Tell your employees to expect some negative reactions from enthusiastic customers and retailers, but explain that (a) the company can't afford the risk of additional lawsuits and (b) even for XtremityPlus, the Looney Launch pushes the envelope a bit too far. The product is simply too dangerous to sell in good conscience.

|Email SKILLS|

10. Product Recall: Email to Retailers

Now it's time to follow up the internal employee message about the Looney Launch (see Case 9) with a message to the retailers that carry the product.

Your task: Write an email message to retailers explaining that the Looney Launch is being removed from the market and explaining why you've reached this decision. Apologize for the temporary disruption this will cause to their businesses but emphasize that it's the right decision from both legal and social perspectives. Thank them for their continuing efforts to sell XtremityPlus products and assure them that your company will continue to offer exciting and innovative products for extreme-sports enthusiasts.

11. Listen to the Music, Partner: Delivering an Ultimatum to a Business Associate

You're a marketing manager for Stanton, one of the premier suppliers of DJ equipment (turntables, amplifiers, speakers, mixers, and related accessories). Your company's latest creation, the FinalScratch system, has been flying off retailers' shelves. Both professional and amateur DJs love the way that FinalScratch gives them the feel of working with vinyl records by letting them control digital music files from any analogue turntable or CD player, while giving them access to the endless possibilities of digital music technology. (For more information about the product, go to www.stantondj.com.) Sales are strong everywhere except in Music99 stores, a retail chain in the Ontario–Quebec region. You suspect the cause: the owners of this chain refused to let their salespeople attend the free product training you offered when FinalScratch was introduced, claiming their people were smart enough to train themselves.

To explore the situation, you head out from Stanton headquarters in Markham, Ontario, on an undercover shopping mission. After visiting a few Music99 locations, you're appalled by what you see. The salespeople in these stores clearly don't understand the FinalScratch concept, so they either give potential customers bad information about it or steer them to products from your competitors. No wonder sales are so bad at this chain.

Your task: You're tempted to pull your products out of this chain immediately, but based on your experience in this market, you know how difficult and expensive it is to recruit new retailers. However, this situation can't go on; you're losing thousands of dollars of potential business every week. Write a letter to Gil Atami, the CEO of Music99 (1108 Sherbrooke St. East, Montreal, QC, H2L 1M2), expressing your disappointment in what you observed and explaining that the Music99 sales staff will need to agree to attend product training or else your company's management team will consider terminating the business relationship. You've met Mr. Atami in person once and talked on the phone several times, and you know him well enough to know that he will not be pleased by this ultimatum. Music99 does a good job selling other Stanton products—and he'll probably be furious to learn that you were "spying" on his sales staff.[28]

12. Cellphone Violations: Email Message to Associates at Smith Rooney Law Firm

"Company policy states that personnel are not to conduct business using cellphones while driving," David Finch reminds you. He's a partner at the law firm of Smith Rooney in St. John's, Newfoundland, where you work as his administrative assistant.

You nod, waiting for him to explain. He already issued a memo about this rule last year, after that 15-year-old girl was hit and killed by an attorney from another firm. Driving back from a client meeting, the attorney was distracted while talking on her cellphone. The girl's family sued the firm and won $10 million, but that's not the point. The point is that cellphones can cause people to be hurt, even killed.

Finch explains, "Yesterday one of our associates called his secretary while driving his car. We can't allow this. Recently in Windsor a driver caused a fatal accident when reaching for his cellphone; his van turned over, and the accident killed his nephew and two friends. The van caught fire because they were transporting a canister of gasoline to a farm. From now on, any violation of our cellphone policy will result in suspension without pay, unless the call is a genuine health or traffic emergency."

Your task: Finch asks you to write an email message to all employees, announcing the new penalty for violating company policy.[29]

13. Responding to Rumours and Public Criticism: Using Yelp to Protect Your Business

The consumer reviews on Yelp (www.yelp.ca) can be a promotional boon to any local business—provided the reviews are positive, of course. Negative reviews, fair or not, can affect a company's reputation and drive away potential customers. Fortunately for business owners, sites like Yelp give them the means to respond to reviews, whether they want to apologize for poor service, offer some form of compensation, or correct misinformation in a review.

Your task: Search Yelp for a negative review (one or two stars) on any business in any city. Find a review that has some substance to it, not just a simple, angry rant. Now imagine that you are the owner of that business, and write a reply that could be posted via the "Add Owner Comment" feature. Use information you can find on Yelp about the company and fill in any details by using your imagination. Remember that your comment will be visible to everyone who visits Yelp. (Be sure to review "Business Communication 2.0: We're under Attack! Responding to Rumours and Criticism in a Social Media Environment" for tips.)

14. Helping a Friend: Using Email and LinkedIn to Write a Recommendation

You're delighted to get a message from an old friend and colleague, Heather Lang. You're delighted right up to the moment you read her request that you write a recommendation about her web design and programming skills for your LinkedIn profile. You would do just about anything for Lang—anything except recommend her web design skills. She is a master programmer whose technical wizardry saved more client projects than you can count, but when it comes to artistic design, Lang simply doesn't have "it." From gaudy colour schemes to unreadable type treatment and confusing layouts, her design sense is as weak as her technical acumen is strong.

Your task: First, write a brief email to Lang, explaining that you would be most comfortable highlighting her technical skills because that is where you believe her true strengths lie. Second, write a two-sentence recommendation that you could include in your LinkedIn profile, recommending Lang's technical skills. Make up or research any details you need.

IM SKILLS

15. Midair Let-Down: Tweet about Flight Cancellations at Premier Airlines

Premier Airlines was one of the first companies to incorporate the Twitter microblogging service into its customer communications, and many flyers now follow the airline's tweets. Messages include announcements about fare sales (such as limited-time auctions on eBay or special on-site sales at shopping malls), schedule updates, and even personalized responses to people who tweet questions or complaints about the company.[30]

Your task: Write a tweet alerting Premier Airlines customers to the possibility that Hurricane Isaac might disrupt flight schedules from August 13 through August 15. Tell them that decisions about delays and cancellations will be made on a city-by-city basis and will be announced on Twitter and the company's website. The URL will take 20 characters, so you have 120 characters (including spaces) for your message.

Podcasting SKILLS

16. No Perks: Podcast about Employee Concierge

An employee concierge seemed like a great idea when you added it as an employee benefit last year. The concierge handles a wide variety of personal chores for employees, everything from dropping off dry cleaning to ordering event tickets or sending flowers. Employees love the service, and you know that the time they save can be devoted to work or family activities. Unfortunately, profits are way down, and concierge usage is up—up so far that you'll need to add a second concierge to keep up with the demand. As painful as it will be for everyone, you decide that the company needs to stop offering the service.

Your task: Script a brief podcast, announcing the decision and explaining why it was necessary. Make up any details you need. If your instructor asks you to do so, record your podcast and submit the file.

IM SKILLS

17. Quick Answer: Instant Message Turning Down Employee Request at Hewlett-Packard

If she'd asked you a week ago, Branka Bilic might have been granted her request to attend a conference on the use of blogging for business, which is being held in Boston next month. Instead, Bilic waited until you were stuck in this meeting, and she needs your response within the hour. She'll have to take no for an answer: with travel budgets under tight restrictions, you would need at least three days to send her request up the chain of command. Furthermore, Bilic hasn't given you sufficient justification for her attendance, since she's already familiar with blogging.

Your task: Write a 60- to 75-word instant message to Branka Bilic, declining her request. Decide whether the direct or indirect approach is appropriate.[31]

Memo Writing SKILLS

18. Employee Development: Negative Performance Review

Elaine Bridgewater, the former professional golfer you hired to oversee your golf equipment company's relationship with retailers, knows the business inside and out. As a former touring pro, she has unmatched credibility. She also has seemingly boundless energy, solid technical knowledge, and an engaging personal style. Unfortunately, she hasn't been quite as attentive as she needs to be when it comes to communicating with retailers. You've been getting complaints about voicemail messages gone unanswered for days, confusing emails that require two or three rounds of clarification, and reports that are haphazardly thrown together. As valuable as Bridgewater's other skills are, she's going to cost the company sales if this goes on much longer. The retail channel is vital to your company's survival, and she's the employee most involved in this channel.

Your task: Draft a brief (one page maximum) informal performance appraisal and improvement plan for Bridgewater. Be sure to compliment her on the areas in which she excels but don't shy away from highlighting the areas in which she needs to improve, too: punctual response to customer messages; clear writing; and careful revision, production, and proofreading. Use what you've learned in this course so far to supply any additional advice about the importance of these skills.

Memo Writing SKILLS

19. Performance Review

Team up with someone in your class and interview each other about a job you currently have or one you had in the past. Get details about the organization that employed your partner, the organization's objectives and goals, and your partner's responsibilities and duties. Ask your partner about the strengths and weaknesses of his or her performance in that job (be sure to get concrete details). Using the guidelines in this chapter, write a performance review for your partner in memo format.

10 Writing Persuasive Messages

LEARNING OBJECTIVES After studying this chapter, you will be able to

1. Apply the three-step writing process to persuasive messages

2. Identify seven ways to establish credibility in persuasive messages

3. Describe the AIDA model for persuasive messages

4. Distinguish between emotional and logical appeals, and discuss how to balance them

5. Explain why it is important to identify potential objections before you start writing persuasive messages

6. Explain how to modify your approach when writing promotional messages for social media

7. Identify steps you can take to avoid ethical lapses in marketing and sales messages

MyLab Business Communication Visit MyLab Business Communication to access a variety of online resources directly related to this chapter's content.

ON THE JOB: COMMUNICATING AT FUTURPRENEUR CANADA

Monkey Business Images/Shutterstock

A good idea must be matched with a sound and persuasive business plan to obtain mentorship and financial support from Futurpreneur. Since 1996 Futurpreneur has been helping young entrepreneurs launch and sustain their unique businesses.

Gearing up for Business

www.futurpreneur.ca

VanHack, a job-search site for technology professionals; Fireside Analytics, a data analysis firm; and DigiLearn, a technology coaching firm for seniors, are just three innovative business ventures nourished with support and funding from Futurpreneur.

A nationwide charity, Futurpreneur offers potential entrepreneurs between ages 18 and 39 personal guidance, online resources, and start-up financing to help them transform their ideas into reality. Futurpreneur assists young people unable to get advice and funding through customary sources. Since its founding in 1996, Futurpreneur has aided more than 8600 promising entrepreneurs, whose businesses have created more than 34 000 new jobs and generated more than $244 million in tax revenue.

To benefit from Futurpreneur, people with a great business idea first visit the website, where they can view videos, read real-life success stories, and take a self-assessment quiz to determine whether starting their own business is right for them. They can learn about the Futurpreneur program, which includes pre-launch coaching, loan programs, and a close mentoring relationship with volunteer business leaders. At this point, they can register as a Futurpreneur entrepreneur and access services such as the online interactive business planner. With a solid business plan in place, references, and experience or training in their business idea, they can apply for a start-up

Futurpreneur loan of up to $15 000. Eligible applicants attend a face-to-face interview before their business plan is approved and they are matched with a mentor, a successful businessperson in their region. Over the course of two years, they work closely together to market and expand the venture.

With a lot of effort and good advice, a budding entrepreneur can become one of Futurpreneur's success stories. If you had an idea for a new business, how would you persuade Futurpreneur of its value? What strategies would you use to gain its interest and support?[1]

Using the Three-Step Writing Process for Persuasive Messages

1 LEARNING OBJECTIVE

Apply the three-step writing process to persuasive messages.

Persuasion is the attempt to change someone's attitudes, beliefs, or actions.

Successful businesses rely on persuasive messages in both internal and external communication. Whether you're convincing your boss to open a new office in Europe or encouraging potential customers to try your products, you need to call on your abilities of **persuasion**—the attempt to change an audience's attitudes, beliefs, or actions.[2] As with every type of business message, the three-step writing process improves persuasive messages.

STEP 1: PLANNING A PERSUASIVE MESSAGE

Having a great idea or a great product is not enough; you need to be able to convince others of its merits.

In the current information-saturated business environment, having a great idea or a great product is no longer enough. Every day, untold numbers of good ideas go unnoticed (or get misunderstood) and good products go unsold simply because the messages meant to promote them aren't compelling enough to rise above the competitive noise. Creating successful persuasive messages demands careful attention to all four tasks in the planning step, starting with an insightful analysis of your purpose and your audience.

ANALYZING THE SITUATION A clear purpose is doubly important in persuasive messages because you are asking the audience to do something—to take action, make decisions, and so on. Let's say you want to persuade members of top management to support a particular research project. But what does "support" mean? Do you want them to pat you on the back and wish you well? Or do you want them to give you a staff of five researchers and a $1 million annual budget? With a clear, specific goal in mind, you'll find it much easier to craft effective persuasive messages.

In addition to having a clear purpose, the best persuasive messages are closely connected to your audience's desires and interests.[3] Consider these important questions: Who is my audience? What are my audience members' needs? What do I want them to do? How might they resist? Are there alternative positions I need to examine? What does the decision maker consider to be the most important issue? How might the organization's culture influence my strategy?

Demographics include characteristics such as age, gender, occupation, income, and education.

Psychographics include characteristics such as personality, attitudes, and lifestyle.

To understand and categorize audience needs, you can refer to specific information such as **demographics** (the age, gender, occupation, income, education, and other quantifiable characteristics of the people you're trying to persuade) and **psychographics** (personality, attitudes, lifestyle, and other psychological characteristics). When analyzing your audience members, take into account their cultural expectations and practices so that you don't undermine your persuasive message by using an inappropriate appeal or by organizing your message in a way that seems unfamiliar or uncomfortable to your audience.

If you aim to change someone's attitudes, beliefs, or actions through a persuasive message, it is vital to understand his or her **motivation**—the combination of forces that drive people to satisfy their needs. Table 10–1 identifies some of the needs that psychologists have identified or suggested as being important in influencing human motivation. Obviously, the more closely a persuasive message aligns with a recipient's existing motivation, the more effective the message is likely to be. For example, if you try to persuade consumers to purchase a product on the basis of its fashion appeal, that message will connect with consumers who are motivated by a desire to be in fashion but probably won't connect with consumers driven more by practical function or financial concerns.

Effective persuasive messages are closely aligned with audience motivations, those forces that drive people to satisfy their needs.

Table 10–1	Human Needs That Influence Motivation
Need	**Implications for Communication**
Basic physiological requirements: The needs for food, water, sleep, oxygen, etc.	Everyone has these needs, but the degree of attention an individual gives to them often depends on whether the needs are being met; for instance, an advertisement for sleeping pills will have greater appeal to someone suffering from insomnia than to someone who has no problem sleeping.
Safety and security: The need for protection from bodily harm; the need to know that loved ones are safe; needs for financial security, protection of personal identity, career security, and other assurances	These needs influence both consumer and business decisions in a wide variety of ways; for instance, advertisements for life insurance often encourage parents to think about the financial security of their children and other loved ones.
Affiliation and belonging: The needs for companionship, acceptance, love, and popularity	The need to feel loved, accepted, or popular drives a great deal of human behaviour, from the desire to be attractive to potential mates to wearing the clothing style that a particular social group is likely to approve of.
Power and control: The need to feel in control of situations or to exert authority over others	You can see many examples appealing to this need in advertisements: take control of your life, your finances, your future, your career, and so on. Many people who lack power want to know how to get it, and people who have power often want others to know they have it.
Achievement: The need to feel a sense of accomplishment—or to be admired by others for accomplishments	This need can involve both knowing (when people experience a feeling of accomplishment) and showing (when people are able to show others that they've achieved success); advertising for luxury consumer products frequently appeals to this need.
Adventure and distraction: The need for excitement or relief from daily routine	People vary widely in their need for adventure; some crave excitement— even danger—while others value calmness and predictability. Some needs for adventure and distraction are met virtually, such as through horror movies, thriller novels, and violent video games.
Knowledge, exploration, and understanding: The need to keep learning	For some people, learning is usually a means to an end, a way to fulfill some other need; for others, acquiring new knowledge is the goal.
Aesthetic appreciation: The desire to experience beauty, order, and symmetry.	Although this need may seem "noncommercial" at first glance, advertisers appeal to it frequently, from the pleasing shape of a package to the quality of the gemstones in a piece of jewellery.
Self-actualization: The need "to be all that one can be," to reach one's full potential as a human being	Psychologists Kurt Goldstein and Abraham Maslow popularized self-actualization as the desire to make the most of one's potential, and Maslow identified it as one of the higher-level needs in his classic hierarchy; even if people met most or all of their other needs, they would still feel the need to self-actualize. A frequently heard phrase that summarizes this feeling is "be all that you can be."
Helping others: The need to believe that one is making a difference in the lives of other people	This need is the central motivation in fundraising messages and other appeals to charity.

Businesses continue to find creative new ways to reach target audiences with persuasive messages. If you're a video gamer, you've probably noticed the brand-name products that appear in many of today's games. Is it ethical to include these products when young children play video games?

GATHERING INFORMATION Once your situation analysis is complete, gather the information necessary to close the gap between what your audience knows, believes, or feels right now and what you want them to know, believe, or feel as a result of receiving your message. Most persuasive messages are a combination of logical and emotional factors, but the ratio varies dramatically from message to message. You can get a sense of this variation by comparing the websites of Motorola (telecommunication products, www.motorola.ca), Chrysler (automobiles, www.chrysler.ca), and Lancôme (beauty products, www.lancome.ca). Motorola relies primarily on straightforward product information to convince buyers, whereas Lancôme tries to evoke a more emotional response through its visual and verbal imagery. Chrysler is somewhere in the middle, providing plenty of facts and figures about its cars but also including strong emotional messages about the joy of driving. By identifying the mix of factors that will most likely persuade your audience, you'll know what sort of information you need to gather.

You'll learn more about the types of information to offer when you read "Developing Persuasive Business Messages" later in the chapter. Chapter 11 presents advice on how to find the information you need.

SELECTING THE RIGHT MEDIUM Persuasive messages can be found in virtually every communication medium, from instant messages and podcasts to radio advertisements and skywriting. For persuasive business messages, your choice of medium will closely follow the guidelines that Chapter 4 presents. However, for marketing and sales messages, your options are far more numerous. In fact, advertising agencies employ media specialists whose only job is to analyze the media options available and select the most cost-effective combination for each client and each ad campaign.

You may need to use multiple media to reach your entire audience.

In some situations, various members of your audience might prefer different media for the same message. Some consumers like to do all their car shopping in person, whereas others do most of their car-shopping research online. Some people don't mind promotional emails for products they're interested in; others resent every piece of commercial email they receive. If you can't be sure you can reach most or all of your audience with a single medium, you need to use two or more, such as following up an email campaign with printed letters.

ORGANIZING YOUR INFORMATION Successful persuasion requires close attention to all four aspects of organizing your information—defining your main idea, limiting your scope, choosing a direct or indirect approach, and grouping your points in a meaningful way. The most effective main ideas for persuasive messages have one element in common: they are about the receiver, not the sender. For example, if you're trying to convince others to join you in a business venture, explain how it will help them, not how it will help you.

Limit your scope to include only the information needed to help your audience take the next step toward making a favourable decision.

Limiting your scope is vital. To limit the scope of each message effectively, include only the information needed to help your audience take the next step toward making the ultimate decision or taking the ultimate action you want. In simple scenarios such as persuading teammates to attend a special meeting, you might put everything you have to say into a single, short message. But if you want your company to invest several million dollars in your latest product idea, the scope of your first message might be limited to securing 10 minutes at the next executive committee meeting so you can introduce your idea and get permission to explore it.

As with routine and negative messages, the best organizational approach is based on your audience's likely reaction to your message. However, because the nature of persuasion is to convince your audience to change their attitudes, beliefs, or actions, most persuasive messages use an indirect approach. That means you'll want to explain your reasons and build interest before asking for a decision or for action—or perhaps even before revealing your purpose. You'll see examples of the indirect approach in action later in this chapter. Remember that the best messages are clear, concise, and to the point. Do not waste your reader's time with long, drawn-out messages, as you risk losing the reader's attention or creating the impression that you are wasting his or her time.

Consider using the direct approach whenever you know your audience is ready to hear your proposal. If your boss wants to change shipping companies and asks for your recommendation, you'll probably want to open with your choice and then provide your reasons as backup. Similarly, if there's a good chance your audience will agree with your message, don't force them to wade through pages of reasoning before seeing your main idea. If they happen not to agree with your pitch, they can move into your reasoning to see why you're promoting that particular idea. The direct approach is also called for if you've been building your case through several indirect messages, and it's now time to make your request.

In the email message in Figure 10–1, Bette McGiboney, an administrative assistant to the athletic director of Central Alberta Institute of Technology,

Use the direct approach if your audience is ready to hear your proposal.

The direct subject line engages the reader by announcing the nature of the message (a proposal) and a compelling benefit to the reader (saving money).

The writer describes the solution in enough detail to help the reader imagine how it will work.

The opening statement is followed by a summary of the problem she proposes to solve.

The body of the message builds interest in the solution by highlighting key benefits in a bulleted list, and then provides additional details.

Here the writer motivates the reader with implied endorsement from other people, then she asks for an answer by a specific time to motivate action.

Figure 10–1 Proposal Email Using a Direct Approach

presented a solution to the problem of high phone bills during the month of August. She already has a close relationship with her boss, who is likely to welcome the money-saving idea, so the direct approach is a fast, efficient way to communicate her proposal.

If you use the direct approach keep in mind that even though your audience may be easy to convince, you'll still want to include at least a brief justification or explanation. Don't expect your reader to accept your idea on blind faith. For example, consider the following two openers:

Less Effective	More Effective
I recommend building our new retail outlet on the West Main Street site.	After comparing the four possible sites for our new retail outlet, I recommend West Main Street as the only site that fulfills our criteria for visibility, proximity to mass transportation, and square footage.

For persuasive business messages, the choice of approach is influenced by your authority, expertise, or power within the organization.

Your choice between the direct and indirect approaches is also influenced by the extent of your authority, expertise, or power in an organization. Generally, the more of these qualities you have in a given situation, the more likely that the direct approach will work for you because audience members are more apt to accept whatever you have to say. Conversely, if you're writing on a subject outside your recognized expertise, or if you're trying to persuade higher-level managers, the indirect approach is usually better because it allows you to build credibility as you present your reasoning.

STEP 2: WRITING A PERSUASIVE MESSAGE

2 LEARNING OBJECTIVE

Identify seven ways to establish credibility in persuasive messages.

Persuasive messages are often unexpected or even unwelcome, so the "you" attitude is crucial.

Cultural differences influence your persuasion attempts.

Persuasive messages are often uninvited and occasionally even unwelcome, so adopting the "you" attitude is particularly critical when you write them. Most people won't even pay attention to your message, much less respond to it, if it isn't about them. You can encourage a more welcome reception by (1) using positive and polite language, (2) understanding and respecting cultural differences, (3) being sensitive to organizational cultures, and (4) taking steps to establish your credibility.

Positive language usually happens naturally with persuasive messages, since you're promoting an idea or product you believe in. However, take care not to inadvertently insult your readers by implying that they've made poor choices in the past.

Demonstrating an understanding and respect for cultural differences is crucial to persuasion. For example, a message that seems forthright and direct in a low-context culture might seem brash and intrusive in a high-context culture.

Just as social culture affects the success of persuasive messages, so too does the culture within various organizations. Some organizations handle disagreement and conflict in an indirect, behind-the-scenes way, whereas others accept and even encourage open discussion and sharing of viewpoints.

Finally, when trying to persuade a skeptical or hostile audience, credibility is essential. You must convince people that you know what you're talking about and that you're not trying to mislead them. Your credibility is even more important in persuasive messages than it is in other business messages (see Chapter 5). Without it, your efforts to persuade will seem ineffective at best and manipulative at worst. Establishing your credibility in persuasive messages takes time. Chapter 5 lists characteristics essential to building and maintaining your credibility, including honesty, objectivity, awareness of audience needs, knowledge and expertise, endorsements, performance, and communication style.

In addition to those elements, you can improve your credibility in persuasive messages with these techniques:

- **Use simple language.** In most persuasive situations, your audience will be cautious, watching for fantastic claims, insupportable descriptions, and emotional manipulation. Express yourself plainly and simply.
- **Support your message with facts.** Documents, statistics, and research results all provide objective evidence for what you have to say, which adds to your credibility. The more specific and relevant your proof, the better.
- **Identify your sources.** Telling your audience where your information comes from improves your credibility, especially if your audience already respects these sources.
- **Establish common ground.** Those beliefs, attitudes, and background experiences that you have in common with your audience members will help them identify with you.
- **Be objective.** Your ability to understand and acknowledge all sides of an issue helps you present fair and logical arguments in your persuasive message. Top executives often ask if their employees have considered all the possibilities before committing to a single choice.
- **Display your good intentions.** Show your audience your genuine concern, good faith, and truthfulness. Let them see how you are focusing on their needs. Your willingness to keep your audience's best interests at heart helps you create persuasive messages that are not only more effective but also more ethical.
- **Avoid the "hard sell."** You've no doubt experienced a "hard sell," an aggressive approach that uses strong, emotional language and high-pressure tactics to convince people to make a firm decision in a hurry. Audiences tend to instinctively resist this approach. No one likes being pressured into making a decision, and communicators who take this approach can come across as being more concerned with meeting their own goals than with satisfying the needs of their audiences. In contrast, a "soft sell" is more like a comfortable conversation in which the sender uses calm, rational persuasion to help the recipient make a smart choice.

Audiences often respond unfavourably to over-the-top language, so keep your writing simple and straightforward.

STEP 3: COMPLETING A PERSUASIVE MESSAGE

Professionals know from experience that the details determine the success of a persuasive message, so they're careful when crafting this part of the writing process. Advertisers may have a dozen or more people review a message before it's released to the public. Ads and commercial websites are often tested extensively with representative recipients to ensure that the intended audience gets the information the sender intends.

When you evaluate your content, judge your argument objectively and don't overestimate your credibility. When revising for clarity and conciseness, carefully match the purpose and organization to audience needs. If possible, ask an experienced colleague who knows your audience well to review your draft. Make sure your design elements complement, rather than detract from, your persuasive argument. In addition, meticulous proofreading will identify any mechanical or spelling errors that would weaken your persuasive potential. Finally, ensure that your distribution methods fit your audience's expectations and preferences. Don't start your persuasive efforts on the wrong foot by annoying your audience with an unwelcome delivery method.

With the three-step model in mind, you're ready to begin composing persuasive messages, starting with *persuasive business messages* (such as those that try to convince readers to approve new projects or enter into business partnerships), followed by *marketing and sales messages* (such as those that try to convince readers to consider and then purchase products and services).

Developing Persuasive Business Messages

3 **LEARNING OBJECTIVE**

Describe the AIDA model for persuasive messages.

Persuasive business messages comprise a broad and diverse category, with audiences that range from a single person in your own department to government agencies, investors, business partners, community leaders, and other external groups.

Your success as a businessperson is closely tied to your ability to convince others to accept new ideas, change old habits, or act on your recommendations. As you move into positions of greater responsibility, your persuasive messages could start to influence multimillion-dollar investments and the careers of hundreds or thousands of employees. Obviously, the increase in your persuasive skills needs to be matched by the care and thoroughness of your analysis and planning so that the ideas you convince others to adopt are sound.

No matter where your career leads, your success will depend on your ability to craft effective persuasive messages.

STRATEGIES FOR PERSUASIVE BUSINESS MESSAGES

The goal of your persuasive business message is to convince your reader that your request or idea is reasonable and that it will benefit him or her in some way. Within the context of the three-step process, effective persuasion involves four essential strategies: framing your arguments, balancing emotional and logical appeals, reinforcing your position, and anticipating objections. (Note that all these concepts in this section apply as well to marketing and sales messages, covered later in the chapter.)

FRAMING YOUR ARGUMENTS As noted earlier, most persuasive messages use the indirect approach. Experts in persuasive communication have developed a number of indirect models for such messages. One of the best known is the **AIDA model**, which organizes messages into these four phases:

Organize persuasive messages using the AIDA model:

- Attention
- Interest
- Desire
- Action

- **Attention.** Your first objective is to engage your readers or listeners in a way that encourages them to want to hear about your main idea. Write a brief and engaging opening sentence, without making extravagant claims or irrelevant points. Look for some common ground on which to build your case. And, while you want to be positive and confident, make sure you don't start out with a *hard sell*—a pushy, aggressive opening. Doing so often puts audiences on guard and on the defensive. In the memo in Figure 10–2, Randy Thumwolt uses the AIDA model in a persuasive memo about his program that would try to reduce Host Marriott's annual plastics costs and try to curtail consumer complaints about the company's recycling record. Note how Thumwolt "sells the problem" before attempting to sell the solution. Few people are interested in hearing about solutions to problems they don't know about or don't believe exist.
- **Interest.** Explain the relevance of your message to your audience. Continuing the theme you started with, paint a more detailed picture of the problem you propose to solve with the solution you're offering (whether it's a new idea, a new process, a new product, or whatever). In Figure 10–2, Thumwolt's interest section introduces an additional, unforeseen problem with plastic product containers. Also, Thumwolt breaks out his suggestions into an easy-to-read list, a format that engages the reader's notice.
- **Desire.** Help audience members embrace your idea by explaining how the change will benefit them, either personally or professionally. Reduce resistance by identifying and answering in advance any questions the audience

1 Planning →

Analyze the Situation
The purpose is to solve an ongoing problem, so the audience will be receptive.

Gather Information
Determine audience needs, and obtain the necessary information on recycling problem areas.

Select the Right Medium
A printed memo is appropriate for this formal communication.

Organize the Information
Your main idea is to propose a recycling solution, so limit the scope to the problem at hand; use an indirect approach to lay out the extent of the problem.

2 Writing →

Adapt to Your Audience
Adjust the level of formality based on degree of familiarity with the audience; maintain a positive relationship by using the "you" attitude, politeness, positive emphasis, and bias-free language.

Compose the Message
Use a conversational but professional style, and keep the message brief, clear, and as helpful as possible.

3 Completing

Revise the Message
Evaluate content and review readability to make sure the information is clear and complete without being overwhelming.

Produce the Message
Emphasize a clean, professional appearance on company letterhead.

Proofread the Message
Review for errors in layout, spelling, and mechanics.

Distribute the Message
Deliver your message using the chosen medium.

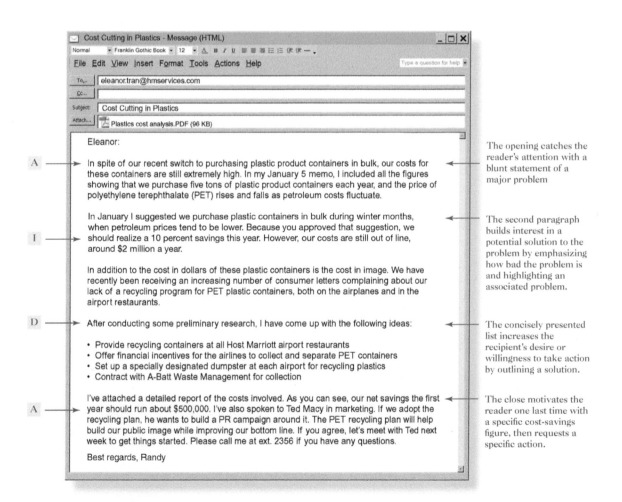

Figure 10–2 Persuasive Memo Using the AIDA Model

might have. If your idea is complex, you may need to explain how you would implement it. Back up your claims to increase audience willingness to take the action that you suggest in the next section.

- **Action.** Suggest the action you want readers to take, and phrase it in a way that emphasizes the benefits to them or to the organization they represent. Make the action as easy as possible to take, including offering to assist, if appropriate. Be sure to provide all the information the audience needs to take the action, including deadlines and contact details.

The AIDA model and similar plans are ideal for the indirect approach.

The AIDA plan is tailor-made for using the indirect approach, allowing you to save your main idea for the action phase. However, you can also use AIDA for the direct approach, in which case you use your main idea as an attention-getter, build interest with your argument, create desire with your evidence, and re-emphasize your main idea in the action phase with the specific action you want your audience to take.

When your AIDA message uses an indirect approach and is delivered by memo or email, keep in mind that your subject line usually catches your reader's eye first. Your challenge is to make it interesting and relevant enough to capture reader attention without revealing your main idea. If you put your request in the subject line, you're likely to get a quick "no" before you've had a chance to present your arguments.

Instead of This	Use This
Request for development budget to add automated IM response system	Reducing the cost of customer support inquiries

The AIDA approach has limitations:
- *It essentially talks at audiences, not with them*
- *It focuses on one-time events, not long-term relationships*

With either the direct or the indirect approach, AIDA and similar models do have limitations. First, AIDA is a unidirectional method that essentially talks *at* audiences, not *with* them. Second, AIDA is built around a single event, such as asking an audience for a decision, rather than on building a mutually beneficial, long-term relationship.[4] AIDA is still a valuable tool for the right purposes, but as you'll read later in the chapter, a conversational approach is more compatible with today's social media.

4 LEARNING OBJECTIVE

Distinguish between emotional and logical appeals, and discuss how to balance them.

BALANCING EMOTIONAL AND LOGICAL APPEALS Imagine you're sitting at a control panel, with one knob labelled "logic" and another labelled "emotion." As you prepare your persuasive message, you carefully adjust each knob, tuning the message for maximum impact. Too little emotion, and your audience might not care enough to respond. Too much emotion, and your audience might think you haven't thought through the tough business questions.

Generally speaking, persuasive business messages rely more heavily on logical appeals than on emotional appeals because the main idea is usually to save money, increase quality, or improve some other practical, measurable aspect of business. To find the optimum balance, consider four factors: (1) the actions you hope to motivate, (2) your reader's expectations, (3) the degree of resistance you need to overcome, and (4) how far you feel empowered to go to sell your point of view.[5]

Emotional appeals attempt to connect with the reader's feelings or sympathies.

Emotional Appeals As its name implies, an **emotional appeal** calls on feelings, basing the argument on audience needs or sympathies. For example, you can make use of the emotion surrounding certain words. The word *freedom* evokes strong feelings, as do words such as *success, prestige, compassion, free, value,* and *comfort.* Such words put your audience in a certain frame of mind and help them accept your message. However, emotional appeals aren't necessarily effective by themselves because the audience wants proof that you can solve a business problem. Even if your audience reaches a conclusion primarily based on emotions, they'll look to you to provide logical support as well.

Logical Appeals A **logical appeal** calls on reasoning and evidence. The basic approach with a logical appeal is to make a claim based on a rational argument supported by solid evidence. When appealing to your audience's logic, use three types of reasoning:

- **Analogy.** With analogy, you reason from specific evidence to specific evidence, in effect "borrowing" from something familiar to explain something unfamiliar. For example, to convince management to add chat room capability to the company's groupware system, you could explain that it is like a neighbourhood community centre, only online.

- **Induction.** With inductive reasoning, work from specific evidence to a general conclusion. To convince your team to change a certain production process, you could point out that every company that adopted it showed an increase in profits, so it must be a smart idea.

Companies work hard to persuade consumers to buy their products. What appeals do manufacturers of cosmetics make? Are these appeals successful?

- **Deduction.** With deductive reasoning, you work from a generalization to a specific conclusion. To persuade your boss to hire additional customer support staff, point to industry surveys that show how crucial customer satisfaction is to corporate profits.

Logical appeals are based on the reader's notions of reason; these appeals can use analogy, induction, or deduction.

Every method of reasoning is vulnerable to misuse, both intentional and unintentional, so verify your rational arguments carefully. For example, in the case of the production process, are there any other factors that affect the integrity of your reasoning? What if that process works well only for small companies with few products, and your firm is a multinational giant with 10 000 products? To avoid faulty logic, follow these guidelines:[6]

- **Avoid hasty generalizations.** Make sure you have plenty of evidence before drawing conclusions.

- **Avoid circular reasoning.** *Circular reasoning* is a logical fallacy in which you try to support your claim by restating it in different words. The statement "We know temporary workers cannot handle this task because temps are unqualified for it" doesn't prove anything because the claim and the supporting evidence are essentially identical. It doesn't prove *why* the temps are unqualified.

- **Avoid attacking an opponent.** If your persuasive appeal involves countering a competitive appeal made by someone else, make sure you attack the argument your opponent is making, not his or her character or qualifications.

- **Avoid oversimplifying a complex issue.** Make sure you present all the factors and don't reduce a wide range of choices to a simple "either/or" scenario if that isn't the case.

- **Avoid mistaken assumptions of cause and effect.** If you can't isolate the impact of a specific factor, you can't assume it's the cause of whatever effect you're discussing. The weather improves in spring, and people start playing baseball in spring. Does good weather cause baseball? No. There is a *correlation* between the two—meaning the data associated with them tend to rise and fall at the same time, but there is no *causation*—no proof that one causes the other. The complexity of many business situations makes cause and effect a particular challenge. You lowered prices and sales went up. Were

Logical flaws include hasty generalizations, circular reasoning, attacks on opponents, oversimplifications, false assumptions of cause and effect, faulty analogies, and illogical support.

lower prices the cause? Maybe, but it might have been caused by a better advertising campaign, a competitor's delivery problems, or some other factor.

- **Avoid faulty analogies.** Be sure that the two objects or situations being compared are similar enough for the analogy to hold. For example, explaining that an Internet firewall is like a prison wall is a poor analogy, because a firewall keeps things out, whereas a prison wall keeps things in.
- **Avoid illogical support.** Make sure the connection between your claim and your support is truly logical and not based on a leap of faith, a missing premise, or irrelevant evidence.

Choose your words carefully and use abstractions to enhance emotional content.

REINFORCING YOUR POSITION After you've worked out the basic elements of your argument, step back and look for ways to bolster the strength of your position. Are all your claims supported by believable evidence? Would a quotation from a recognized expert help make your case?

Next, examine your language. Can you find more powerful words to convey your message? For example, if your company is in serious financial trouble, talking about *survival* is more powerful than talking about *continued operations*. Using vivid abstractions such as this along with basic facts and figures can bring your argument to life. As with any powerful tool, though, use vivid language and abstractions carefully and honestly.

In addition to individual word choices, consider using *metaphors* and other figures of speech. If you want to describe a quality-control system as being designed to catch every possible product flaw, you might call it a "spider web" to imply that it catches everything that comes its way. Similarly, anecdotes (brief stories) can help your audience grasp the meaning and importance of your arguments. Instead of just listing the number of times the old laptop computers your department uses have failed, you could describe what happened when your computer broke down during a critical presentation.

Beyond specific words and phrases, look for other factors that can reinforce your position. When you're asking for something, your audience will find it easier to grant your request if they stand to benefit from it as well.

5 LEARNING OBJECTIVE

Explain why it is important to identify potential objections before you start writing persuasive messages.

ANTICIPATING OBJECTIONS Even the most powerful persuasive messages can expect to encounter some initial resistance. The best way to deal with audience resistance is to anticipate as many objections as you can and address them in your initial message before your audience can even bring them up. By doing so you not only address such issues right away, but also demonstrate a broad appreciation of the issue and imply confidence in your message.[7] This anticipation is particularly important in written messages, when you don't have the opportunity to detect and respond to objections on the spot.

Even powerful persuasive messages can encounter resistance from the audience.

For example, if you know that your proposal to switch to lower-cost materials will raise concerns about product quality, address these issues head-on in your message. If you wait until people raise the concern after reading your message, chances are they will already have gravitated toward a firm no before you have a chance to address their concerns. At the very least, waiting until people object will introduce additional rounds of communication that will delay the response you want to receive.

Present all sides of an issue when you expect to encounter strong resistance.

To uncover potential audience objections, try to poke holes in your own theories and ideas before your audience does. Then find solutions to the problems you've uncovered. If possible, ask your audience members for their thoughts on the subject before you put together your argument; people are more likely to support solutions they help create.

Keep three things in mind when anticipating objections. First, you don't always have to explicitly discuss a potential objection. You could simply mention that the lower-cost materials have been tested and approved by the quality-control department. Second, if you expect a hostile audience, one biased against your plan from the beginning, present all sides of the story. As you cover each option, explain the pros and cons. You'll gain additional credibility if you present these options before presenting your recommendation or decision.[8] Third, successful persuasion is often a process of give-and-take, particularly in the case of persuasive business messages, where you don't always get everything you asked for in terms of budgets, investments, and other commitments. Be open to compromise.

To review the steps involved in developing persuasive messages, refer to "Checklist: Developing Persuasive Messages."

✓ Checklist   Developing Persuasive Messages

A. Get your reader's attention.
- Open with a reader benefit, a stimulating question, a problem, or an unexpected statement.
- Establish common ground by mentioning a point your audience can agree with.
- Show that you understand the audience's concerns.

B. Build your reader's interest.
- Expand and support your opening claim or promise.
- Emphasize the relevance of your message to your audience.

C. Increase your reader's desire.
- Make audience members want to change by explaining how the change will benefit them.
- Back up your claims with relevant evidence.

D. Motivate your reader to take action.
- Suggest the action you want readers to take.
- Stress the positive results of the action.
- Make the desired action clear and easy.

E. Balance emotional and logical appeals.
- Use emotional appeals to help the audience accept your message.
- Use logical appeals when presenting facts and evidence for complex ideas or recommendations.
- Avoid faulty logic.

F. Reinforce your position.
- Provide additional evidence of the benefits of your proposal and your own credibility in offering it.
- Use abstractions, metaphors, and other figures of speech to bring facts and figures to life.

G. Anticipate objections.
- Anticipate and answer potential objections.
- Present the pros and cons of all options if you anticipate a hostile reaction.

COMMON EXAMPLES OF PERSUASIVE BUSINESS MESSAGES

Throughout your career, you'll have numerous opportunities to write persuasive messages within your organization, such as reports suggesting more efficient operating procedures or messages requesting money for new equipment. Similarly, you may produce a variety of persuasive messages to people outside the organization, such as websites shaping public opinions, proposals soliciting investment funds, or letters requesting adjustments that go beyond a supplier's contractual obligations. In addition, many of the routine requests you studied in Chapter 8 can become persuasive messages if you want a nonroutine result or believe that you haven't received fair treatment. Most messages can be divided into persuasive requests for action, persuasive presentation of ideas, and persuasive claims and requests for adjustment.

PERSUASIVE REQUESTS FOR ACTION The bulk of your persuasive business messages will involve requests for action. In some cases, your request will be anticipated or will require minimal effort on the recipient's part, so the direct approach is fine. In others, you'll need to introduce your intention indirectly. Open with an attention-getting device and show readers that you know something about their concerns, such as maintaining customer satisfaction. Use the interest and desire sections of your message to demonstrate that you have good reason for

Most persuasive business messages involve a request for action.

making such a request and to cover what you know about the situation: the facts and figures, the benefits of helping, and any history or experience that will enhance your appeal. Your goals are (1) to gain credibility and (2) to make your readers believe that helping you will indeed help solve a significant problem. When you've demonstrated that your message is relevant to your reader, you can close with a request for some specific action or decision.

Leslie Jorgensen applies the AIDA strategy in the memo in Figure 10–3. She believes the new Airbus A380 could help Oceana Pacific Airways meet its growth needs while lowering its operating costs. She now needs her boss's approval for a study of the plane's market potential. Note that because she also wants to provide some printed materials to support her argument, she opted for a printed memo rather than an email message.

When requesting a favour that is routine (for example, asking someone to attend a meeting in your absence), use the direct approach and the format for routine messages (see Chapter 8). However, when asking for a special favour (for example, asking someone to chair an event or to serve as the team leader because you can no longer fill that role), use persuasive techniques to convince your reader of the value of the project. Include all necessary information about

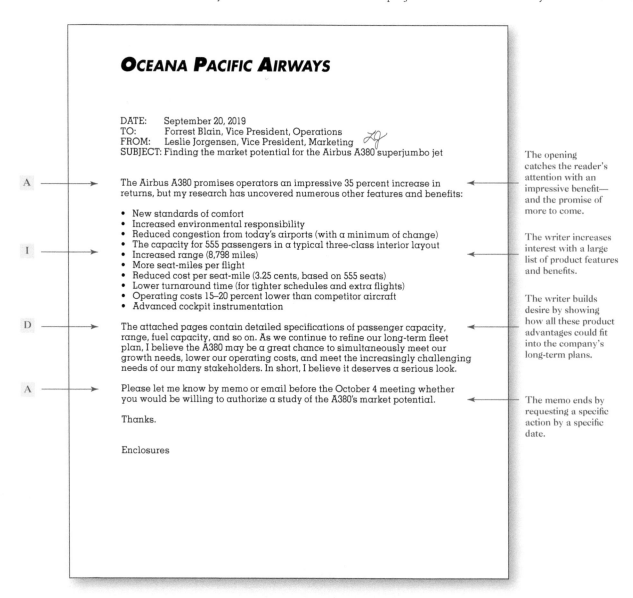

Figure 10–3 Persuasive Memo Using the AIDA Model to Request Action

the project and any facts and figures that will convince your reader that his or her contribution will be enjoyable, easy, important, and of personal benefit.

PERSUASIVE PRESENTATION OF IDEAS You may encounter situations in which you simply want to change attitudes or beliefs about a particular topic, without asking the audience to decide or do anything—at least not yet. The goal of your first message might be nothing more than convincing your audience to re-examine long-held opinions or admit the possibility of new ways of thinking.

For example, the World Wide Web Consortium (a global association that defines many of the guidelines and technologies behind the World Wide Web) has launched a campaign called the Web Accessibility Ini-

Why is the ability to persuade others to accept and support your ideas an essential career skill?

tiative. Although the consortium's ultimate goal is making websites more accessible to people who have disabilities or age-related limitations, a key interim goal is simply making website developers more aware of the need. As part of this effort, the Consortium has developed a variety of presentations and documents that highlight the problems many web visitors face.[9]

Sometimes the objective of persuasive messages is simply to encourage people to consider a new idea.

PERSUASIVE CLAIMS AND REQUESTS FOR ADJUSTMENT Most claim letters and requests for adjustment are routine messages and use the direct approach discussed in Chapter 8. However, consumers and business professionals sometimes encounter situations in which they believe they haven't received a fair deal by following normal procedures. For example, suppose you purchase something and, after the warranty expires, discover that the item was defective. You write the company a routine request asking for a replacement, but your request is denied. You're not satisfied, and you still believe you have a strong case. Perhaps you just didn't communicate it well enough the first time. Persuasion is necessary in such cases.

If a routine claim or request did not meet your needs, you may need to craft a more persuasive message to explain why you deserve a more satisfactory response.

Because you've already paid for the product, you can't threaten to withhold payment. Instead, try to convey the essentially negative information in a way that will get positive results. Fortunately, most people in business are open to settling your claim fairly. It's to their advantage to maintain your goodwill and to resolve your problem quickly.

The key ingredients of a good persuasive claim are a complete and specific review of the facts and a confident and positive tone. Do not threaten to take your business elsewhere. This creates a negative tone and does not help your case. Keep in mind that you have the right to be satisfied with every transaction. Begin persuasive claims by stating the basic problem or reviewing what has been done about the problem so far, if anything. The recipient might be juggling numerous claims and other demands on his or her attention, so be clear, calm, and complete when presenting your case. Be specific about how you would like to see the situation resolved.

Next, give your reader a good reason for granting your claim. Show how the individual or organization is responsible for the problem and appeal to your reader's sense of fair play, goodwill, or moral responsibility. Explain how you feel about the problem, but don't get carried away; don't complain too much; and don't make threats. People generally respond most favourably to requests that are both calm and reasonable. Close on a positive note that reflects how a successful resolution of the situation will repair or maintain a mutually beneficial working relationship.

Developing Marketing and Sales Messages

Marketing and sales messages use many of the same techniques as persuasive business messages.

Marketing and sales messages use the same basic techniques as other persuasive messages, with the added emphasis of encouraging someone to participate in a commercial transaction. Although the terms *marketing message* and *sales message* are often used interchangeably, they are slightly different. **Marketing messages** usher potential buyers through the purchasing process without asking them to make an immediate decision. **Sales messages** take over at that point, encouraging potential buyers to make a purchase decision then and there. Marketing messages focus on such tasks as introducing new brands to the public, providing competitive comparison information, encouraging customers to visit websites for more information, and reminding buyers that a particular product or service is available (see Figure 10–4). In contrast, a sales message makes a specific request for people to place an order for a particular product or service.

Most marketing and sales messages, particularly in larger companies, are created and delivered by professionals with specific training in marketing, advertising, sales, or public relations. However, as a manager, you may be called on to review the work of these specialists or even to write such messages in smaller companies, and having a good understanding of how these messages work will help you be a more effective manager. The essential steps to address include assessing customer needs; analyzing your competition; determining key selling points and benefits; anticipating purchase objections; applying the AIDA model or a similar organizational plan; adapting your writing to social media, as needed; and maintaining high standards of ethics, legal compliance, and etiquette.

The site offers handy links to earlier and later blog posts, making it easy for readers to browse.

Embedded links provide additional information about wedding dress designers, content that many readers will find helpful as well.

The page margin promotes a sale on wedding gowns but does so in a subtle way that doesn't hinder a reader's appreciation of the information offered in the article.

The list of recent posts helps readers find other marketing messages that may address their needs.

Also provided are links to product selections (organized by designer name).

Figure 10–4 Marketing versus Sales Messages

Courtesy: RLT Enterprises.

ASSESSING AUDIENCE NEEDS

Successful marketing and sales messages start with an understanding of audience needs. For some products and services, this assessment is a simple matter. For example, customers compare only a few basic attributes when purchasing paper, including its size, weight, brightness, colour, and finish. In contrast, they might consider dozens of features when shopping for real estate, cars, professional services, and other complex purchases. In addition, customer needs often extend beyond the basic product or service. Clothes do far more than simply keep you warm. What you wear makes a statement about who you are, which social groups you want to be associated with (or not), and how you view your relationship with the people around you.

Begin by assessing audience needs, interests, and emotional concerns—just as you would for any business message. Form a mental image of the typical buyer for the product you wish to sell. Ask yourself what audience members might want to know about this product. How can your product help them? Are they driven by price, or is quality more important to them?

> Understanding the purchase decision from the buyer's perspective is a vital step in framing an effective marketing or sales message.

ANALYZING YOUR COMPETITION

Marketing and sales messages nearly always compete with messages from other companies trying to reach the same audience. When Nike plans a marketing campaign to introduce a new shoe model to current customers, the company knows that its audience has also been exposed to messages from New Balance, Reebok, and numerous other shoe companies. In crowded markets, writers sometimes have to search for words and phrases that other companies aren't already using. They might also want to avoid themes, writing styles, or creative approaches that are too similar to those of competitors' messages.

> Most marketing and sales messages have to compete for the audience's attention.

DETERMINING KEY SELLING POINTS AND BENEFITS

With some insight into audience needs and existing messages from the competition, you're ready to decide which aspects of your product or service to highlight. For all but the simplest products, you'll want to prioritize the items you plan to discuss. You'll also want to distinguish between the features of the product and the benefits that those features offer the customers. As Table 10–2 shows, **selling points** are the most attractive features of an idea or product, whereas **benefits** are the particular advantages that readers will realize from those features. Selling points focus on the product. Benefits focus on the user. For example, if you say that your snow shovel has "an ergonomically designed handle," you've described a good feature. But to persuade someone to buy that shovel, say "The ergonomically designed handle will reduce your risk of back injury." That's a benefit.

> Selling points focus on the product; benefits focus on the user.

Table 10–2	**Features versus Benefits**
Product or Service Feature	**Customer Benefit**
AirFlow's turbo dual-fuel system combines our Everwarm 7 fuel pump with our Everwarm 95 furnace.	AirFlow's turbo dual-fuel system provides the optimum balance of comfort and energy efficiency.
Our marketing communication audit accurately measures the impact of your advertising and public relations efforts.	Find out whether your message is reaching the target audience and whether you're spending your marketing budget in the best possible manner.
The spools in our fly-fishing reels are machined from solid blocks of aircraft-grade aluminum.	Go fishing with confidence: these lightweight reels will stand up to the toughest conditions.

1 Planning →	2 Writing →	3 Completing
Analyze the Situation The purpose is to sell a product, so the audience will be neutral, uninterested, or perhaps unwilling.	**Adapt to Your Audience** Adjust the level of formality based on degree of familiarity with the audience; maintain a positive relationship by using the "you" attitude, politeness, positive emphasis, and bias-free language.	**Revise the Message** Evaluate content and review readability to make sure the information is clear and complete without being overwhelming.
Gather Information Determine audience needs, and obtain the necessary information to present a persuasive message.		**Produce the Message** Emphasize a clean, professional appearance on company letterhead.
Select the Right Medium A printed letter is appropriate for this formal communication.	**Compose the Message** Use a conversational but professional style, and keep the message brief, clear, and as helpful as possible.	**Proofread the Message** Review for errors in layout, spelling, and mechanics.
Organize the Information Your main idea is to offer a product for sale, so limit your scope to that issue; use the AIDA approach to propose the solution.		**Distribute the Message** Deliver your message using the chosen medium.

For your message to be successful, your product's distinguishing benefit must correspond to your readers' primary needs or emotional concerns.

Consider how SecureAbel Alarms uses the AIDA model to persuade students to buy its residence-room alarm system (see Figure 10–5). The features of the system include its portability, piercing alarm, and programmable control units. The benefits include simple installation, simple operation, and a sense of security.

ANTICIPATING PURCHASE OBJECTIONS

Anticipating objections is crucial to effective marketing and sales messages.

As with persuasive business messages, marketing and sales messages often encounter objections, and once again, the best way to handle them is to identify them up front and address as many as you can. Objections can include perceptions of high price, low quality, incompatibility, or unacceptable risk. Consumers might worry that a car won't be safe enough for a family, that a jacket will make them look unattractive, or that a hair salon will botch a haircut. Business buyers might worry about disrupting operations or failing to realize the financial returns on a purchase.

Price can be a particularly tricky issue in any message. Whether you highlight or downplay the price of your product, prepare your readers for it. Words such as *luxurious* and *economical* provide unmistakable clues about how your price compares with that of competitors. Such words will help your readers accept your price when you finally state it.

If price is a major selling point, give it a position of prominence, such as in the headline or as the last item in a paragraph. If price is not a major selling point, you could leave the price out altogether or de-emphasize it by putting the figure in the middle of a paragraph that comes well after you've presented the benefits and selling points. Here's an example:

Emphasizes the rarity of the edition to signal value and thus prepare the reader for the big-ticket price that follows →

Places the actual price in the middle of a sentence and ties it in with another reminder of the exclusivity of the offer →

Only 100 prints of this exclusive, limited-edition lithograph will be created. On June 15, they will be made available to the general public, but you can reserve one now for only $350, the special advance reservation price. Simply rush the enclosed reservation card back today so that your order is in before the June 15 publication date.

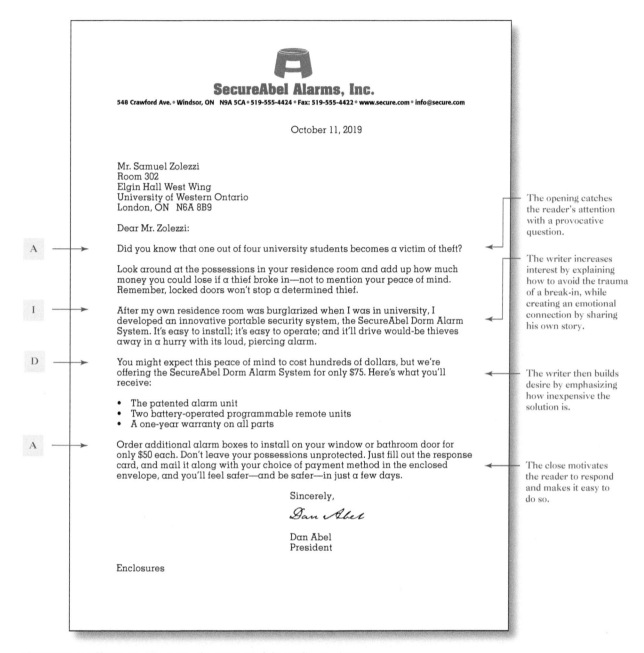

SecureAbel Alarms, Inc.
548 Crawford Ave. • Windsor, ON   N9A 5CA • 519-555-4424 • Fax: 519-555-4422 • www.secure.com • info@secure.com

October 11, 2019

Mr. Samuel Zolezzi
Room 302
Elgin Hall West Wing
University of Western Ontario
London, ON   N6A 8B9

Dear Mr. Zolezzi:

A → Did you know that one out of four university students becomes a victim of theft?

The opening catches the reader's attention with a provocative question.

Look around at the possessions in your residence room and add up how much money you could lose if a thief broke in—not to mention your peace of mind. Remember, locked doors won't stop a determined thief.

I → After my own residence room was burglarized when I was in university, I developed an innovative portable security system, the SecureAbel Dorm Alarm System. It's easy to install; it's easy to operate; and it'll drive would-be thieves away in a hurry with its loud, piercing alarm.

The writer increases interest by explaining how to avoid the trauma of a break-in, while creating an emotional connection by sharing his own story.

D → You might expect this peace of mind to cost hundreds of dollars, but we're offering the SecureAbel Dorm Alarm System for only $75. Here's what you'll receive:

- The patented alarm unit
- Two battery-operated programmable remote units
- A one-year warranty on all parts

The writer then builds desire by emphasizing how inexpensive the solution is.

A → Order additional alarm boxes to install on your window or bathroom door for only $50 each. Don't leave your possessions unprotected. Just fill out the response card, and mail it along with your choice of payment method in the enclosed envelope, and you'll feel safer—and be safer—in just a few days.

The close motivates the reader to respond and makes it easy to do so.

Sincerely,

Dan Abel

Dan Abel
President

Enclosures

Figure 10–5 Effective Letter Using the AIDA Model to Sell a Product

Whenever price is likely to cause an objection, look for ways to increase the perceived value of the purchase and decrease the perceived cost. For example, to help blunt the impact of the price of a home gym, you might say that it costs less than a year's worth of health club dues—plus, customers save on transportation costs by exercising at home. Of course, any attempts to minimize perceptions of price or other potential negatives must be ethical.

APPLYING AIDA OR A SIMILAR MODEL

Most marketing and sales messages are prepared according to the AIDA plan or some variation of it. A typical AIDA-organized message begins with an attention-getting device, generates interest by describing some of the product's or service's unique features, increases desire by highlighting the benefits that are most appealing to your audience, and closes by suggesting the action you want the audience to take.

You can use a variety of attention-getting devices in marketing and sales messages.

GETTING ATTENTION You can use a wide range of techniques to attract the audience's attention:

- **Your product's strongest benefit.** "iPod touch. Engineered for Maximum Funness" (emphasizing the photography and entertainment features of Apple's iPod touch).[10]
- **A piece of genuine news.** "Bundle Prices that Can't Be Beat" (promoting a Bell Canada plan where customers save money by combining selected telecommunication services).[11]
- **A point of common ground with the audience.** "Tough on Dirt, Gentle on the Earth" (promoting the environmentally friendly aspects of Biokleen cleaning products).[12]
- **A personal appeal to the reader's emotions and values.** "The only thing worse than paying taxes is paying taxes when you don't have to."
- **The promise of savings.** "From the big screen to your flat screen for free."[13]
- **A sample or demonstration of the product.** "These videos can provide more detail on Mint's unique and award-winning approach to personal financial management."[14]
- **A solution to a problem.** "Fees to check a bag can add $50 to the cost of a round trip. So the FlightWise Carry-On Backpack is designed to fit in all carry-on storage spaces, even underseat, saving you money with every flight."[15]

Of course, words aren't the only attention-getting device at your disposal. Strong, evocative images are common attention-getters. With online messages, you have even more options, including audio, animation, and video. Even more so than in persuasive business messages, it's important to carefully balance emotion and logic in marketing and sales messages. As shown in Figure 10–6, Bigelow Tea uses an effective combination of visual and textual messages in this emotional appeal.

BUILDING INTEREST Use the interest section of your message to build on the intrigue you created with your opening. This section should also offer support for whatever claims or promises you might have made in the opening. Apple's description of the iPod touch provides one example. After the headline "iPod Touch—Engineered for Maximum Funness," the webpage continues with information on one of the key features of the iPod Touch—its camera:[16]

> **iPod Touch—Engineered for Maximum Funness**
>
> Picture your life and all its big, small, and everything-in-between moments with a 5-megapixel iSight camera that also shoots 1080p HD video. The new panorama feature lets you capture your whole wide world. Advanced optics, tap to focus, and LED flash and face detection give iPod touch serious point-and-shoot skills. And the iPod touch loop keeps it all close at hand.

Notice how this paragraph highlights the key photographic functions that support the iPod touch as an innovative digital camera: high-resolution images, wide-angle photography, easy focusing, and face recognition technology. These are combined with personal advantages, such as the ability to "capture your whole wide world."

INCREASING DESIRE To build desire for a product, a service, or an idea, continue to expand on and explain how accepting it will benefit the recipient. Think carefully about the sequence of support points and use plenty of subheadings, hyperlinks, and other devices to help people quickly find the information they need. For example, after reading this much about the iPod, some users might want to know more about other entertainment features, such as shared photostreams and photo editing. Apple makes it easy to find the information each individual wants. This ability to provide flexible access to information is just one of the reasons the Web is such a powerful medium for marketing and sales.

The red-orange colour of the tea, enhanced with the glow of backlighting through the translucent liquid, speaks of warmth and comfort.

Complementary colours suggest freshness and elegance, adding to the emotional appeal.

The text uses the storytelling technique to explain the creation of Bigelow's signature Constant Comment tea flavour and does so in a way that highlights the emotional appeal of drinking tea.

Without using any images of people, the solitary teacup (left), the multiple glasses of iced tea (centre), and the brunch setting suggested by the tea and food (right) convey both the pleasures of a quiet time alone as well as the pleasures of sharing tea with friends and family.

Figure 10–6 Emotional and Logical Appeals

Courtesy: RC Bigelow

Throughout the body of your message, remember to keep the focus on the audience, not on your company or your product. When you talk about product features, remember to stress the benefits and talk in terms that make sense to users. Stating that the iPod touch, when fully charged, has up to 40 hours of audio playback time and 8 hours of video playback time is a lot more meaningful to most readers than saying that it has 32 or 64 gigabytes of memory, depending on the model. Action words give strength to any business message, but they are especially important in sales letters. Compare the following:

To build interest, expand on and support the promises in your attention-getting opening.

Less Effective	More Effective
The NuForm desk chair is designed to support your lower back and relieve pressure on your legs.	The NuForm desk chair supports your lower back and relieves pressure on your legs.

The second version expresses the idea in fewer words and emphasizes what the chair does for the user ("supports") rather than the intentions of the design team ("is designed to support").

To keep readers interested, use colourful verbs and adjectives that convey a dynamic image. Be careful, however, not to overdo it: If you say "Your factory floors will sparkle like diamonds," your audience will find it hard to believe, which may prevent them from believing the rest of your message.

To keep readers interested, use strong, colourful language without overdoing it.

To increase desire, as well as boost your credibility, provide support for your claims. You can't assume that your audience will believe what you say just because you've said it in writing. You'll have to give them proof. Support is especially important if your product is complicated, costs a lot, or represents some unusual approach.

Creative marketers find many ways to provide support: testimonials from satisfied users, articles written by industry experts, competitive comparisons, product samples and free demonstrations, independent test results, and movies or computer animations that show a product in action. YouTube and other video hosting sites in particular have been a boon to marketers because they offer an easy, inexpensive way to demonstrate products. You can also highlight guarantees that demonstrate your faith in your product and your willingness to back it up.

After you've generated sufficient interest and desire, you're ready to persuade readers to take the preferred action.

MOTIVATING ACTION After you have raised enough interest and built up the reader's desire for your offering, you're ready to ask your audience to take action. Whether you want people to pick up the phone to place an order or visit your website to download a free demo version of your software, persuade them to do it right away with an effective *call to action*. You might offer a discount to the first 1000 people who order, put a deadline on the offer, or simply remind them that the sooner they order, the sooner they'll be able to enjoy the product's benefits. Even potential buyers who want the product can get distracted or forget to respond, so encouraging immediate action is important. Make the response action as simple and as risk-free as possible. If the process is confusing or time-consuming, you'll lose potential customers.

Notice how many calls to action are built into the home page of ParticipACTION's website, shown in Figure 10–7. ParticipACTION is a nonprofit organization committed to encouraging physical fitness through safe and effective exercise.

The general public is encouraged to register to tailor the site to their interests and needs.

The primary visual encourages readers to become active.

The call to action asks readers to share their physical fitness stories at the website.

The site uses a number of simple active phrases to entice readers to navigate deeper into the site.

Figure 10–7 The Call to Action in a Persuasive Message

Courtesy: ParticipACTION

WRITING PROMOTIONAL MESSAGES FOR SOCIAL MEDIA

The AIDA model and similar approaches have been successful with marketing and sales messages for decades, but communicating with customers in the social media landscape requires a different approach. As earlier chapters emphasize, potential buyers in a social media environment are no longer willing to be passive recipients in a structured, one-way information delivery process or to rely solely on promotional messages from marketers. In addition, they tend to trust one another more than they trust advertisers, and many shoppers rely on social media to learn about products before making purchase decisions.[17]

This notion of interactive participation is the driving force behind **conversation marketing**, in which companies initiate and facilitate conversations in a networked community of customers, journalists, bloggers, and other interested parties. The term **social commerce** encompasses any aspect of buying and selling products and services or supporting customers through the use of social media.

Given this shift from unidirectional talks to multidirectional conversations, marketing and sales professionals must adapt their approach to planning, writing, and completing persuasive messages. Follow these guidelines:[18]

- **Facilitate community building.** Make sure customers and other audiences can connect with your company and one another. Accomplishing this goal can be as simple as activating the commenting feature on a blog, or it may involve having a more elaborate social commerce system.
- **Listen at least as much as you talk.** Listening is just as essential for online conversations as it is for in-person conversations. Of course, trying to stay on top of a social media universe composed of millions of potential voices is no easy task. A variety of automated tools can help, from free alerts on search engines to sophisticated linguistic monitoring systems.
- **Initiate and respond to conversations within the community.** Through content on your website, blog postings, social network profiles and messages, newsletters, and other tools, make sure you provide the information customers need in order to evaluate your products and services. Use an objective, conversational style; people in social networks want useful information, not "advertising speak."
- **Provide information that people want.** Whether through industry-insider news, in-depth technical guides to using your products, video tutorials, or brief answers to questions posted on community Q&A sites, fill the information gaps about your company and its products. This strategy of *content marketing* helps you build trusted relationships with potential buyers by repeatedly demonstrating that you understand and care about meeting their needs.[19]
- **Identify and support your champions.** In marketing, *champions* are enthusiastic fans of your company and its products. Champions are so enthusiastic that they help spread your message (through their blogs, for instance), defend you against detractors, and help other customers use your products. As Michael Zeisser of Liberty Interactive put it, "We concluded that we could succeed only by being genuinely useful to the individuals who initiate or sustain virtual word-of-mouth conversations."[20]

> ## TIPS FOR SUCCESS
> "Newsletters can be great relationship builders, but the content should be varied. Otherwise, they become tedious and lose their customer value."
>
> Edmund O. Lawler, professor of journalism and writer on advertising

- **Be authentic; be transparent; be real.** Trying to fool the public through fake blogs and other tactics is not only unethical (and possibly illegal) but

6 **LEARNING OBJECTIVE**

Explain how to modify your approach when writing promotional messages for social media.

Social commerce involves the use of social media in buying, selling, and customer support.

Promoting products and services through social media requires a more conversational approach.

also almost guaranteed to eventually backfire in a world where people have unprecedented access to information. Similarly, trying to tack social media onto a consumer-hostile business is likely to fail as soon as stakeholders see through the superficial attempt to "be social." In contrast, social media audiences respond positively to companies that are open and conversational about themselves, their products, and subjects of shared interest.

- **Don't rely on the news media to distribute your message.** In traditional public relations efforts, marketers have to persuade the news media to distribute their messages to consumers and other audiences by producing news stories. These media are still important, but you can also speak directly to these audiences through blogs and other electronic tools.

- **Integrate conventional marketing and sales strategies at the right time and in the right places.** AIDA and similar approaches are still valid for specific communication tasks, such as conventional advertising and the product promotion pages on your website.

MAINTAINING HIGH STANDARDS OF ETHICS, LEGAL COMPLIANCE, AND ETIQUETTE

7 **LEARNING OBJECTIVE**

Identify steps you can take to avoid ethical lapses in marketing and sales messages.

The word *persuasion* has negative connotations for some people, especially in a marketing or sales context. They associate persuasion with dishonest and unethical practices that lead unsuspecting audiences into accepting unworthy ideas or buying unneeded products. However, effective businesspeople view persuasion as a positive force, aligning their own interests with what is best for their audiences. They influence audience members by providing information and aiding understanding, which allows audiences the freedom to choose.[21] To maintain the highest standards of business ethics, always demonstrate the "you" attitude by showing honest concern for your audience's needs and interests.

Marketing and sales messages are covered by a wide range of laws and regulations.

As marketing and selling grow increasingly complex, so do the legal ramifications of marketing and sales messages. In Canada, the Competition Bureau has the authority to administer and enforce the *Competition Act* and the *Consumer Packaging and Labelling Act* (as well as other consumer-related legislation). The legal aspects of promotional communication can be complex, and most companies require marketing and sales people to obtain clearance from company lawyers before sending messages. In any event, pay close attention to the following legal aspects of marketing and sales communication:[22]

- **Marketing and sales messages must be truthful and nondeceptive.** The *Competition Act* considers messages to be deceptive if they include statements that are likely to mislead reasonable customers and the statement is an important part of the purchasing decision. Failing to include important information is also considered deceptive. The *Competition Act* also looks at *implied claims*, those you don't explicitly make but that can be inferred from what you do or don't say.

- **You must back up your claims with evidence.** According to the *Competition Act*, offering a money-back guarantee or providing letters from satisfied customers is not enough; you must still be able to support your claims with objective evidence such as a survey or scientific study. According to the *Consumer Packaging and Labelling Act*, if you claim that your food product lowers cholesterol, you must have scientific evidence to support that claim.

- **Complaints about misleading marketing and sales messages may lead to prosecution.** If you imply or make an offer and can't fulfill it, the practices may be reviewed by the federal court or a provincial superior court.

- **In most cases, you can't use a person's name, photograph, or other identity without permission.** Doing so is considered an invasion of privacy. You can use images of people considered to be public figures, as long as you don't unfairly imply that they endorse your message.

Before you launch a marketing or sales campaign, ensure that you're up to date on the latest regulations affecting spam (or *unsolicited bulk email*, as it's officially known), customer privacy, and data security. The electronic marketplace is of special concern to the government.[23]

Meeting your ethical and legal obligations will go a long way toward maintaining good communication etiquette as well. However, you may still face etiquette decisions within ethical and legal boundaries. For example, you can produce a marketing campaign that complies with all applicable laws and yet is still offensive or insulting to your audience. An audience-centred approach, involving respect for your readers and their values, should help you avoid any such etiquette missteps.

Technology also gives communicators new ways to demonstrate sensitivity to user needs. For, example automated RSS newsfeeds from blogs and updates sent from company pages on Facebook can alert customers to information in which they've expressed an interest. *Opt-in* email newsletters, sent only to those people who have specifically requested information, are another technology that shows the "you" attitude at work.

Maintaining high ethical standards is a key aspect of good communication etiquette.

Communication technologies such as RSS, opt-in email newsletters, and Facebook page updates can help you be sensitive to audience needs.

PROMOTING WORKPLACE ETHICS | Selling Ethically Online

Before you sell products online, become familiar with the *Canadian Code of Practice for Consumer Protection in Electronic Commerce*. Developed by professional associations such as the Retail Council of Canada, federal and provincial government agencies, and corporations, its intent is to protect consumers during any online transaction. By subscribing to the following guidelines, you will conduct your business ethically and avoid complaints and lawsuits:

- **Provide complete and current contact and policy information.** Customers often need to contact companies to ask questions, learn about their warranties, change orders, and complain. Your website should include all contact information (postal address, email address, phone and fax numbers) and details regarding payment methods, return policies, warranties, and the complaint process. You should also state your policies on privacy and unsolicited email. As the *Code of Practice* states, all information should be "clearly presented in plain language, truthful, conspicuous and easily accessible . . . at appropriate stages of consumers' decision making, particularly before consumers confirm transactions or provide any personal information."
- **Describe products fully.** Customers want to know what they are buying. You should describe your products accurately and in detail, and include any information that customers would see if they bought the product in a store, such as health and safety warnings or suggestions for parental supervision. If you neglect to disclose product information fully or deliver a product materially different from that described, you must honour any refund request, including charges the buyer incurred for returning the product.

- **Respect consumers' right to privacy.** As an online vendor, you must make your privacy policy easily accessible on your website. Tell your customers the kind of information you collect, its purpose, how it will be used, and to whom it may be disclosed. Consumers must know how they can review their personal information and, when necessary, how they can correct or remove it. You cannot require your customers to disclose personal data as a condition of sale beyond that needed to complete the transaction. Your customers' right to privacy also extends to unsolicited email. The *Code of Practice* notes that online vendors should not send email to customers without their consent, and that marketing messages should include a provision, in plain language, for removal from electronic marketing messages, with a return email address for that purpose.

You can learn more about the *Canadian Code of Practice for Consumer Protection in Electronic Commerce* at http://cmcweb.ca/eic/site/cmc-cmc.nsf/eng/fe00064.html.

CAREER APPLICATIONS

1. Review two websites that sell products online, such as www.canadiantire.ca or www.mec.ca (Mountain Equipment Co-op). In what areas do they follow the guidelines set in the *Canadian Code of Practice for Consumer Protection in Electronic Commerce*? How can these websites be improved in terms of consumer protection?
2. Do you think that following the guidelines in the *Canadian Code of Practice for Consumer Protection in Electronic Commerce* improves the potential of commercial websites to sell products? Justify your answer.

SUMMARY OF LEARNING OBJECTIVES

1 Apply the three-step writing process to persuasive messages. Because persuasive messages can be complicated and sensitive, several planning tasks need extra attention. You'll be persuading people to take action that they probably wouldn't have taken without your message, so analyzing your purpose is crucial. In addition, audience analysis may be more detailed for persuasive messages, so gauge psychological and social needs in addition to cultural differences. Also, when persuading a skeptical audience, your credibility must be unquestionable, so spend some extra effort to establish it. Since your attempts to persuade could be viewed by some as manipulative, strive for the highest ethical standards. Finally, keep your message clear and concise.

2 Identify seven ways to establish credibility in persuasive messages. When persuading your audience, ensure that you speak simply and avoid exaggeration. Support your message with objective evidence and name your sources. Understand your audience's beliefs and attitudes so that you can establish common ground. Present all sides of the argument, show honest interest in your audience's concerns, and avoid pressuring your audience.

3 Describe the AIDA model for persuasive messages. When using the AIDA plan, open your message by getting *attention* with a reader benefit, a problem, a stimulating question, a piece of news, or an unexpected statement. You build *interest* with facts, details, and additional reader benefits. You increase *desire* by providing more evidence and reader benefits and by anticipating and answering possible objections. You conclude by motivating a specific *action*, emphasizing the positive results of that action, and making it easy for the reader to respond.

4 Distinguish between emotional and logical appeals, and discuss how to balance them. Emotional appeals call on human feelings, using arguments based on audience needs or sympathies. However, these appeals aren't effective by themselves. Logical appeals call on human reason (whether using analogy, induction, or deduction). Use logic together with emotion, thereby supplying rational support for an idea that readers have already embraced emotionally. In general, logic will be your strongest appeal, with only subtle emotion. However, when persuading someone to purchase a product, join a cause, or make a donation, you can heighten emotional appeals.

5 Explain why it is important to identify potential objections before you start writing persuasive messages. Being aware of specific audience objections to your persuasive purpose will help you gain the support of audience members. You can address your audience's opposition, thus demonstrating your understanding of their particular concerns. You heighten your credibility because you show you are not biased, so you may influence your audience to agree with your viewpoint.

6 Explain how to modify your approach when writing promotional messages for social media. When writing promotional messages for social media use digital tools, such as search engine alerts, to keep you updated on the virtual conversation for your message. Fill in the gaps in audience knowledge through videos or other online means. Write in a simple, friendly style, avoiding hype. Use the AIDA and similar strategies when appropriate, such as for product promotion.

7 Identify steps you can take to avoid ethical lapses in marketing and sales messages. Avoid ethical lapses in marketing and sales messages by ensuring they are honest and accurate. Use language precisely, and support your claims with objective facts. Do not use any identifying features of an individual without permission. Being familiar with legislation such as the *Competition Act* and the *Consumer Packaging and Labelling Act* (as well as other consumer-related legislation) is an important part of preparing marketing and sales messages.

ON THE JOB   PERFORMING COMMUNICATION TASKS AT FUTURPRENEUR

As an aspiring entrepreneur, you believe there are others like you who want to launch their own business but need the advice of local business leaders. Indeed, you have consulted with students in your new venture start-up class, and you all agree that a monthly networking group, where you can meet with Futurpreneur coaches in your area, would provide you all with valuable guidance. Your first step is getting a central meeting place. You decide to contact the chairperson of your school's business program, seeking her support. Use your knowledge of persuasive messages to choose the best alternative in each of the following situations. Be prepared to explain why your choice is the most effective one.

1. You are drafting an email to be sent to the chairperson. She is not familiar with Futurpreneur's programs. Which version is the best attention-getter for this email?

   a. No, this isn't a letter asking for a higher grade. We know that you have a valuable resource you may be able to share with us: meeting room space.

   b. Don't let that unused meeting room time go to waste! Let enterprising students use that time! We're looking for a meeting room in the Business department. If you let us have any unscheduled time, you'll be giving your students a chance to network with coaches who can help us start our own business.

c. If you could put available meeting room time to productive use by helping your students, wouldn't you be interested? Donate some of our department's unscheduled meeting room time to students in the entrepreneurial classes who want to meet with Futurpreneur coaches. You'll gain the satisfaction of helping your students by giving them a central place to meet and to learn from the success of other businesspeople.

2. Which version is the most effective interest and desire section for your letter?

a. You may have unused meeting room time after 4:00 P.M. Just two hours a month would be enough time for students to meet with Futurpreneur coaches and gain valuable knowledge about starting up a business. We would bring our own computers to access the school's wireless network. By giving us regular meeting room time, you will enhance your students' studies and careers by providing a location where they can share ideas and information with business leaders in a relaxed and quiet atmosphere. You will see them take into the classroom the enthusiasm they've developed from seeing how entrepreneurs started their own businesses and became successful.

b. All we need is two hours a month. So please check the meeting room schedule. Just two hours a month, ideally in the late afternoon or early evening, is all we need. You will be proud of your department's donation, which will help serve your students. Help the next generation of entrepreneurs by donating unscheduled meeting time today!

c. Your entrepreneurial students need your help. Any unused meeting time—just two hours a month—will help us meet with local business leaders and get real-life knowledge about starting up a small business. Please take a moment to check the schedule.

If you give us the meeting room once a month, the Business department will benefit by further educating its students with real-world advice. But the people who will really benefit will be your students, because they will be enhancing what they learn in the classroom with real-world advice and become more successful when they graduate.

3. Newspapers managed and written by students are common on many university and college campuses. Imagine that you have created an advertisement seeking students who would like to meet with Futurpreneur coaches. Because of limited funds, you would like the advertising space to be donated. Which appeal to your audience would be most effective in a letter seeking free advertising space?

a. An entirely emotional appeal stressing the needs of the students and the satisfaction of helping a worthy cause

b. An entirely logical appeal stressing that the advertisements can be inserted whenever the newspapers have unused space, thus saving editors the trouble of rearranging articles and other advertisements to make the page look good, or using meaningless filler

c. A combination of emotional and logical appeals, stressing both the satisfaction of helping a worthy cause and the rationale behind printing the advertisement wherever the editors have available space

TEST YOUR KNOWLEDGE

1. How can you build credibility with an audience when planning a persuasive message?

2. What is the AIDA plan? How does it apply to persuasive messages?

3. What mistakes should you avoid when developing a persuasive message to overcome resistance?

4. How do benefits differ from key selling points?

5. How do emotional appeals differ from logical appeals?

6. What types of reasoning can you use in logical appeals?

7. How can semantics affect a persuasive message?

8. What are some questions to ask when gauging the audience's needs during the planning of a persuasive message?

9. What are some similarities between sales messages and bad-news messages?

10. What ethical and legal responsibilities influence sales and marketing messages?

APPLY YOUR KNOWLEDGE

1. Why is it important to present both sides of an argument when writing a persuasive message to a potentially hostile audience?

2. Why do the AIDA model and similar approaches need to be modified when writing persuasive messages in social media?

3. When is it appropriate to use the direct organizational approach in persuasive messages?

4. What is likely to happen if your persuasive message starts immediately with a call to action? Why?

5. As an employee, how many of your daily tasks require persuasion? List as many as you can think of. Who are your audiences? How do their needs and characteristics affect the way you develop your persuasive messages at work?

6. **Ethical Choices** Are emotional appeals ethical? Why or why not?

RUNNING CASES

> CASE 1 Noreen

Noreen is reviewing overdue accounts. At 30-days (first notice) and again at 60-days (second notice) past due, a reminder letter is sent to customers. At 90-days (third and final notice) past due, a letter is sent to customers informing them of the fact that at 120-days past due legal action will be taken. At 120-days past due, an account is sent out for legal proceedings.

Petro-Go also asks the customers to contact the company to discuss payment arrangements and offers to help them devise an affordable and manageable payment plan before legal action takes place. Petro-Go has many strategies for helping customers manage their debts efficiently. The letter is an attempt to persuade the customer to make at least the minimum payments to avoid legal action. Legal action will hurt the customer's credit score and future ability to obtain credit.

QUESTIONS

a. How will Noreen apply the "you" attitude?
b. How will she balance emotional and logical appeals? Give examples.
c. What must Noreen avoid doing in the letter?
d. What are some persuasive tools Noreen will use?
e. Is it ethical for Noreen to threaten legal action?

YOUR TASK

Write the letter. Apply the guidelines for writing persuasive messages that this chapter discusses.

> CASE 2 Kwong

Kwong sees the announcement below on his college's website offering scholarships. He decides to apply. He needs to write a persuasive letter to the college's Financial Aid office convincing the selection committee that he should be one of the two students chosen to receive this scholarship money. Kwong wants to put the $5000 toward starting his own accounting firm once he graduates. Kwong will graduate at the end of this semester, thereby gaining advanced standing in the CGA program. The CGA program should take Kwong only one year to complete.

ASSOCIATION OF ENTREPRENEURS SCHOLARSHIPS 2 × $5000.00—Awarded to two final-year business students who demonstrate community service and entrepreneurial experience or goals and show successful academic progression of study.

QUESTIONS

a. What tone and approach should Kwong use for this persuasive letter?
b. What are some questions Kwong needs to ask himself about his audience?
c. How will Kwong establish his credibility?
d. What supporting facts or evidence should Kwong include with his application letter?
e. How will Kwong get his audience's attention?

YOUR TASK

Write the letter. Apply the guidelines for writing persuasive messages that this chapter discusses.

PRACTISE YOUR KNOWLEDGE

Read the following documents, and then (1) analyze the strengths and weaknesses of each sentence and (2) revise each document so that it follows this chapter's guidelines.

DOCUMENT 10.A: WRITING PERSUASIVE REQUESTS FOR ACTION

At Tolson Auto Repair, we have been in bussiness for over 25 years. We stay in business by always taking in to account what the customer wants. That's why we are writing. We want to know your opinions to be able to better conduct our business.

Take a moment right now and fill out the enclosed questionnaire. We know everyone is busy, but this is just one way we have of ensuring that our people do their jobs correctly. Use the enclosed envelope to return the questionnaire.

And again, we're happy you chose Tolson Auto Repair. We want to take care of all your auto needs.

DOCUMENT 10.B: WRITING PERSUASIVE CLAIMS AND REQUESTS FOR ADJUSTMENT

Dear TechStar Computing:

I'm writing to you because of my disappointment with my new 22-inch PC monitor with built-in audio. The display part works all right, but the audio volume is set too high and the volume button doesn't turn it down. It's driving us crazy. The volume buton doesn't seem to be connected to anything and simply doesn't work. I can't believe you would put out a product like this without testing it first.

I depend on my computer to run my small business and wanna know what you are going to do about it. This reminds me of every time I buy electronic equipment from what seems like any company. Something is always wrong. I thought quality was supposed to be important, but I guess not.

Anyway, I need this fixed right away. Please tell me what you want me too do.

DOCUMENT 10.C: WRITING SALES LETTERS

We know how awful dinning hall food can be, and that's why we've developed the "Mealaweek Club." Once a week, we'll deliver food to your dormitory or apartment. Our meals taste great. We have pizza, buffalo wings, hamburgers, curly fries, vegie wraps, and more!

When you sign up for just six months, we will ask what day you want your delivery. We'll ask you to fill out your'e selection of meals. And the rest is up to us. At Mealaweek, we deliver! And payment is easy. We accept MasterCard and Visa or a personel cheque. It will save money, especially when compared to eating out.

Simply fill out the enclosed card and indicate your method of payment. As soon as we approve your credit or cheque, we'll begin delivery. Tell all your friends about Mealaweek. We're the best idea since sliced bread!

EXERCISES

10.1 Teamwork: Analyzing the Persuasive Strategy

With another student, analyze the persuasive message to Eleanor Tran (Figure 10–2) by answering the following questions:
- **a.** What techniques are used to capture the reader's attention?
- **b.** Does the writer use the direct or the indirect organizational approach? Why?
- **c.** Is the subject line effective? Why or why not?
- **d.** Does the writer use an emotional or a logical appeal? Why?
- **e.** What reader benefits are included?
- **f.** How does the writer establish credibility?
- **g.** What tools does the writer use to reinforce his position?

10.2 Composing Subject Lines: Capturing Attention

Compose effective subject lines for the following persuasive messages:
- **a.** An email request to your supervisor to purchase a new high-speed colour laser printer for your office. You've outsourced quite a bit of your printing to AlphaGraphics, and you're certain this printer will pay for itself in six months.
- **b.** A letter to area residents soliciting customers for your new business, "Meals à la Car," a carryout dining service that delivers from most local restaurants. All local restaurant menus are on the Internet. Mom and Dad can dine on egg rolls and chow mein while the kids munch on pepperoni pizza.
- **c.** A memo to the company president requesting that managers be allowed to carry over their unused vacation days to the following year. Apparently, many managers cancelled their fourth-quarter vacation plans to work on the installation of a new company computer system. Under their current contract, vacation days not used by December 31 can't be carried over to the following year.

10.3 Ethical Choices: Persuasion or Manipulation?

Your boss has asked you to post a message on the company's internal blog urging everyone in your department to donate money to the company's favourite charity, an organization that operates a special summer camp for physically challenged children. You wind up writing a lengthy posting packed with facts and heartwarming anecdotes about the camp and the children's experiences. When you must work that hard to persuade your audience to take an action such as donating money to a charity, aren't you being manipulative and unethical? Explain.

10.4 Focusing on Benefits: Features versus Benefits

Determine whether the following sentences focus on features or benefits; rewrite as necessary to focus all the sentences on benefits.
- **a.** All-Cook skillets are coated with a durable, patented non-stick surface.
- **b.** You can call anyone and talk as long as you like on Saturdays and Sundays with our new FamilyTalk wireless plan.
- **c.** With 8-millisecond response time, the Samsung LN-S4095D 47-inch LCD TV delivers fast video action that is smooth and crisp.[24]

10.5 Message Analysis: Marketing and Sales Messages

The daily mail often brings a selection of sales messages. Find a direct-mail package from your mailbox that includes a sales letter. Then answer the following questions to help analyze and learn from the approach used by the communication professionals who prepare these glossy sales messages. Your instructor might also ask you to share the package and your observations in a class discussion.
- **a.** Who is the intended audience?
- **b.** What are some of the demographic and psychographic characteristics of the intended audience?
- **c.** What is the purpose of the direct-mail package? Has it been designed to solicit a phone-call response, make a mail-order sale, obtain a charitable contribution, or do something else?
- **d.** What technique was used to encourage you to open the envelope?
- **e.** Did the letter writer follow the AIDA model or something similar? If not, explain the letter's organization.
- **f.** What emotional appeals and logical arguments does the letter use?
- **g.** What selling points and consumer benefits does the letter offer?
- **h.** Did the letter and the rest of the package provide convincing support for the claims made in the letter? If not, what is lacking?

CASES	APPLYING THE THREE-STEP WRITING PROCESS TO CASES

Apply each step to the following cases, as assigned by your instructor.

1 Planning →

Analyze the Situation
Identify both your general purpose and your specific purpose. Clarify exactly what you want your audience to think, feel, or believe after receiving your message. Profile your primary audience, including their backgrounds, differences, similarities, and likely reactions to your message.

Gather Information
Identify the information your audience will need to receive, as well as other information you may need in order to craft an effective message.

Select the Right Medium
Make sure your medium is both acceptable to the audience and appropriate for the message.

Organize the Information
Choose a direct or indirect approach based on the audience and the message; most persuasive messages employ an indirect approach (often following the AIDA model). Identify your main idea, limit your scope, then outline necessary support points and other evidence.

2 Writing →

Adapt to Your Audience
Show sensitivity to audience needs with a "you" attitude, politeness, positive emphasis, and bias-free language. Understand how much credibility you already have—and how much you may need to establish with any particular audience. Project your company's image by maintaining an appropriate style and tone.

Compose the Message
Draft your message using precise language, effective sentences, and coherent paragraphs. Support your claims with objective evidence; balance emotional and logical arguments.

3 Completing

Revise the Message
Evaluate content and review readability, then edit and rewrite for conciseness and clarity.

Produce the Message
Use effective design elements and suitable layout for a clean, professional appearance.

Proofread the Message
Review for errors in layout, spelling, and mechanics.

Distribute the Message
Deliver your message using the chosen medium; make sure all documents and all relevant files are distributed successfully.

Persuasive Requests for Action

Blogging SKILLS | **Portfolio** BUILDER

1. That's the Point: Encouraging Your Boss to Tweet

You've been trying for months to convince your boss, company CEO Will Florence, to start using Twitter. You've told him that top executives in numerous industries now use Twitter as a way to connect with customers and other stakeholders without going through the filters and barriers of formal corporate communications, but he doesn't see the value.

Your task: You come up with the brilliant plan to demonstrate Twitter's usefulness using Twitter itself. First, find three executives from three companies who are on Twitter (choose any companies and executives you find interesting). Second, study their tweets to get a feel for the type of information they share. Third, if you don't already have a Twitter account set up for this class, set one up for the purposes of this exercise (you can deactivate later). Fourth, write four tweets to demonstrate the value of executive microblogging: one that summarizes the value of having a company CEO use Twitter and three support tweets, each one summarizing how your three real-life executive role models use Twitter.

Letter Writing SKILLS

2. Give a Little to Get a Lot: Suggesting a Printing Service

The coffee shop across the street from your tiny apartment is your haven-away-from-home—great beverages, healthy snacks, an atmosphere that is convivial but not so lively that you can't focus on your homework, and free wireless. It lacks only one thing: some way to print out your homework and other files when you need hardcopy. Your school's libraries and computer labs provide printers, but you live five kilometres from campus, and it's a long walk or an inconvenient bus ride.

Your task: Write a letter to the owner of the coffee shop, encouraging her to set up a printing service to complement the free wireless access. Propose that the service run at break-even prices, just enough to pay for paper, ink cartridges, and the cost of the printer itself. The benefit to the shop would be enticing patrons to spend more time—and therefore more of their coffee and tea money—in the shop. You might also mention that you had to take the bus to campus in order to print this letter, so you bought your afternoon latte somewhere else.

| Memo Writing SKILLS |

3. Always Urgent: Memo Pleading Case for Hosting a Canadian Blood Services Mobile Clinic

This morning as you drove to your job as desk clerk at the Midwood Community Centre in Saint John, New Brunswick, you were concerned to hear on the radio that the local Canadian Blood Services chapter put out a call for blood because national supplies have fallen dangerously low. During highly publicized disasters, people are emotional and eager to help out by donating blood. But in calmer times, only 5 percent of eligible donors think of giving blood. You're one of those few.

Not many people realize that donated blood lasts for only 72 hours. Consequently, the mainstay of emergency blood supplies must be replenished in an ongoing effort.

Donated blood helps victims of accidents and disease, as well as surgery patients. Just yesterday you were reading about a girl named Melissa, who was diagnosed with multiple congenital heart defects and underwent her first open-heart surgery at one week old. Now 5, she's used well over 50 units of donated blood, and she wouldn't be alive without them. In a thank-you letter, her mother lauded the many strangers who had "given a piece of themselves" to save her precious daughter—and countless others. You also learned that a donor's pint of blood can benefit up to four other people.

Today, you're going to do more than just roll up your own sleeve. You know the local CBS chapter sets up a mobile clinic at fire stations, schools, and community centres. What if you could convince Midwood's board of directors to support a blood clinic? The meeting rooms and fitness centre are usually full, and people who've never visited before might come out to donate blood. With materials from CBS, you're confident you can organize the centre's hosting effort and handle the promotion. (Last year you headed Midwood's successful Toys for Tots drive.)

To give blood, one must be healthy, at least 17 years old (with an age limit of 71), and weigh at least 50 kilograms. Donors can give every 56 days. You will distribute information about donating, urging potential donors to make an appointment and to eat well, drink water, and be rested before the clinic is set up.

The CBS's mission statement says that "Canadian Blood Services operates Canada's blood supply in a manner that gains the trust, commitment, and confidence of all Canadians by providing a safe, secure, cost-effective, affordable, and accessible supply of quality blood, blood products, and their alternatives."

Your task: Write a memo persuading the Midwood Community Centre's board of directors to host a public Canadian Blood Services blood drive. You can learn more about what's involved in hosting a blood drive at www.bloodservices.ca (click "Get Involved"). Ask the board to provide bottled water, orange juice, and snacks for donors. You'll organize food service workers to handle the distribution, but you'll need the board's approval to let your team volunteer during work hours. Use a combination of logical and emotional appeals.[25]

| Email SKILLS |

4. Caribbean Recognition: Email to City Council

The request seems simple enough: members of the Caribbean Business Association of your city have asked the city council to erect two signs designating the neighbourhood where many Caribbean businesses are located as the Caribbean Business District. The area has been home to your family's restaurant, Island Tastes, for many years.

But some members of the community complained when the issue was brought up during a city council session. "We should be focusing on unifying the community as a whole and its general diversity," they argued, "not dividing the city up into small ethnic districts." Some council members had been intrigued, however, by the prospect of creating a new tourist destination by marking the Caribbean Business District officially—that's what it actually is and has been for as long as you can remember. However, the issue was tabled for later consideration.

As the manager of your family's restaurant, you agree with those council members who think the designation would attract visitors. Moreover, the Caribbean Business Association has returned to the city council with an offer to pay for the cement structures that will designate the neighbourhood as the Caribbean Business District. The association is willing to spend up to $30 000 for the design and installation of the signs.

Your task: As a member of the Caribbean Business Association, you've been asked to support the request with an email message to Cathy Stanford, your city's deputy mayor, at cstandford@council.yc.[26]

| Memo Writing SKILLS |

5. No More Driving: Memo about Telecommuting to Bachman, Trinity, and Smith

Sitting in your Toronto office at the accounting firm of Bachman, Trinity, and Smith, clacking away on your computer, it seems as though you could be doing this work from your home. You haven't spoken to any co-workers in more than two hours. As long as you complete your work on time, does your location matter?

As an entry-level accountant, you've participated in on-location audits at major companies for nearly a year now. If your bosses trust you to work while staying at a hotel, why not let you work from home, where you already have an office with a computer, phone, and fax machine? You'd love to regain those two hours you lose commuting to and from work every day.

Your task: To support this idea, visit the website of Tel-Coa–The Telework Coalition at www.telcoa.org (check out the blog). You'll find support for a memo persuading your boss, senior partner Marjorie Bachman, to grant you a six-month trial as a telecommuter.[27]

6. Helping Out: Persuasive Memo to Good Eats Store Managers

Good Eats is a chain of organic food stores with locations in Ottawa. The stores are big and well lit, like their more traditional grocery store counterparts. They are also teeming with a wide variety of attractively displayed foods and related products.

However, Good Eats is different from the average supermarket. Its products include everything from granola sold in bulk to environmentally sensitive household products. The meats sold come from animals that were never fed antibiotics, and the cheese is from cows said to be raised on small farms and treated humanely.

Along with selling these products to upscale shoppers, the company has been giving food to homeless shelters. Every third weekend, Good Eats donates nonperishable food to three soup kitchens downtown. Company executives believe they are in a unique position to help others.

You work for the chief operating officer of Good Eats. You've been asked to find ways to expand the donation program by involving the company's eight branches, most of which are in the suburbs. Ideally, the company would be able to increase the number of people it helps and to get more of its employees involved.

You don't have a great deal of extra money for the program, so the emphasis has to be on using resources already available to the stores. One idea is to use trucks from suburban branches to make the program mobile. Another idea is to join forces with a retail chain to give food and clothing to individuals. The key is to be original and not exclude any idea, no matter how absurd it might seem. The only stipulation is to keep ideas politically neutral. Good Eats executives do not want to be seen as supporting any party or candidate. They just want to be good corporate citizens.

Your task: Send persuasive memos to all managers at Good Eats requesting ideas to expand the program. Invite employees to contribute ideas, for this or any other charitable project for the company.[28]

Persuasive Claims and Requests for Adjustment

7. Mobile Woes: Email Requesting Adjustment

You thought it was strange that no one called you on your new cellphone, even though you had given your family members, friends, and boss your new number. Two weeks after getting the new phone and agreeing to a $49 monthly fee, you called the service provider, InstantCall, just to see if everything was working. Sure enough, the technician discovered that your incoming calls were being routed to an inactive number. You're glad she found the problem, but then it took the company nearly two more weeks to fix it. When you called to complain about paying for service you didn't receive, the customer service agent suggests you send an email to Judy Hinkley at the company's regional business office to request an adjustment.

Your task: Decide how much of an adjustment you think you deserve under the circumstances and then send an email message to Hinkley to request the adjustment to your account. Write a summary of events in chronological order, supplying exact dates for maximum effectiveness. Make up any information you need, such as problems that the malfunctioning service caused at home or at work.

8. Endless Trouble: Claim Letter to Abe's Pool Installation

As chief administrator, you worked hard to convince the board of directors of Westlake Therapy and Rehabilitation Centre that a small 2.5-by-4.5–metre Endless Pool would be a wonderful addition to the facility.

Because the pool produces an adjustable current flow, a swimmer can swim "endlessly" against it, never reaching the pool's edge. With this new invention by a Philadelphia manufacturer, your patients could experience a complete range of water therapy in a year-round indoor pool small enough to fit in a standard living room! The board agreed, choosing the optional two-metre depth, which would allow for additional therapeutic uses but would require a special platform and installation in a room with a high ceiling.

The old gymnasium would become your new Water Therapy Pavilion. Total cost with custom features: $20 080, plus $8000 budgeted for installation.

According to the manufacturer, "The Endless Pool has been designed as a kit for bolt-together assembly. It can be assembled by two reasonably handy people with no prior installation experience following detailed procedural videos." You can do it yourself, they proclaim, or hire a local contractor.

You've hired Abe's Pool Installation, which will build the special access platform and install the pool. You passed along the instructional videos, along with the manufacturer's hotline numbers. They've offered a pre-installation engineering consultation for your customized pool, without additional charge, as you told Abe. They'll also be glad to help determine whether the planned site can handle the pool's 10-tonne filled weight. Abe nodded and told you not to worry.

Finally, Abe's crew completed the platform and amid much excitement from your staff, assembled the galvanized steel pool. At a grand ribbon-cutting dedication ceremony, you personally flipped the switch.

Immediately the hydraulic motor began moving 140 000 litres of water per minute through a grille at the front, which smoothes and straightens the current. Everyone's excitement grew as the first wave of water washed down the centre of the pool. But instead of entering the turning vane arrays (which were supposed to recirculate the water through hidden channels back to the front of the pool), the water kept going, splashing out the back of the pool onto the platform and the gathered onlookers . . . at 140 000 litres per minute. Panic and shouts erupted as you fumbled quickly to turn the thing off.

Final damage included a collapsed platform, a ruined floor, an incorrectly installed pool, and numerous dry-cleaning bills from onlookers. Fortunately, no one was hurt. Estimated cost, including floor repair: $10 000. Abe is not returning your phone calls. But local reporters are coming to film the damage tomorrow, and it's your job to conduct their tour.

Your task: Write a claim letter to Abe Hanson, Owner, Abe's Pool Installation, 7650 Fort Sheppard Dr., Nelson, British Columbia, V1L 6A5.[29]

|Letter Writing SKILLS|

9. Jump In! Promoting Water Polo for Youth

Water polo is an active sport that provides great opportunities for exercise and for learning the collaborative skills involved in teamwork. You can learn more at www.waterpolo.ca.

Your task: Write a one-page letter to parents of 10- to 14-year-old boys and girls, promoting the health and socialization benefits of water polo and encouraging them to introduce their children to the sport through a local club. Tell them they can learn more about the sport and find a club in their area by visiting the Canadian Water Polo website.

Marketing and Sales Messages

|Podcasting SKILLS|

10. Listen Up: Podcast Promoting a Podcast Station

Your new podcast channel, School2Biz, offers advice to business students making the transition from university to career. You provide information on everything from preparing résumés to interviewing to finding a place in the business world and building a successful career. As you expand your audience, you'd eventually like to turn School2Biz into a profitable operation (perhaps by selling advertising time during your podcasts). For now, you're simply offering free advice.

Your task: You've chosen Juice (http://juicereceiver .sourceforge.net) the first website on which to promote School2Biz. This site lets podcasters promote their feeds with brief text listings, such as this description of Toolmonger Tool Talk: "Chuck and Sean from the web's first tool blog, Toolmonger.com, keep you up-to-date on the newest hand and power tools, and answer your home improvement, automotive, and tool-related questions."

As your instructor directs, either write a 50-word description of your new podcast that can be posted on Juice or record a 30-second podcast describing the new service. Make up any information you need to describe School2Biz. Be sure to mention who you are and why the information you present is worth listening to.[30]

|Letter Writing SKILLS|

11. Letter Promoting Your Province for Business

Your provincial government works hard to attract businesses that are considering expanding or relocating entirely from another province. Your office has services and resources that reach out to these companies and oversee the incentive programs the province offers to both new and established businesses.

Your task: As an assistant in the communication office of your provincial government, you play an important role in reaching out to companies that want to expand or relocate to your area. Research the business pages on your provincial government's website and review the reasons why a business would find it desirable to relocate to your province. Summarize these reasons in a form letter that will be sent to business executives throughout the country. Ensure that you introduce yourself and your purpose in the letter, and close with a compelling call to action (have them reach you by telephone at 1-800-555-2930 or by email at your office, for example, yourname@yourprovince.ca). As you plan your letter, imagine yourself as the CEO of a company and consider what a complex choice it would be to move to another province.

|Social Networking SKILLS| |Teamwork SKILLS| |Portfolio BUILDER|

12. Selling Your Program: Creating an Online Marketing Message

You chose your university or college based on certain expectations, and you've been enrolled long enough now to have some idea about whether those expectations have been met. In other words, you are something of an expert about the "consumer benefits" your school can offer prospective students.

Your task: In a team of four students, interview six other students who are not taking this business communication course. Try to get a broad demographic and psychographic sample, including students in a variety of majors and programs. Ask these students (1) why they chose this college or university and (2) whether the experience has met their expectations so far. To ensure the privacy of your respondents, do not record their names with their answers. Each member of the team should then answer these same two questions, so that you have responses from a total of 10 students.

After compiling the responses (you might use Google Drive or a similar collaboration tool so that everyone on the team has easy access to the information), analyze them as a team to look for any recurring "benefit themes." Is it the quality of the education? Research opportunities? Location? The camaraderie of school sporting events? The chance to meet and study with fascinating students from a variety of backgrounds? Identify two or three strong benefits that your college or university can promise—and deliver—to prospective students.

Now nominate one member of the team to draft a short marketing message that could be posted on the Notes tab of your school's Facebook page. The message should include a catchy title that makes it clear the message is a student's perspective on why this is a great place to get a college education. When the draft is ready, the other members of the team should review it individually. Finally, meet as a team to complete the message.

▌Letter Writing SKILLS▐ ▌Portfolio BUILDER▐

13. Greener Cleaners: Letter Promoting "Environmentally Sound" Franchise

When you told everyone you aspired to work for an environmentally responsible business, you didn't imagine you'd be in dry cleaning. But now that you are director of franchise development for Hangers Cleaners, you go home every night with a "clean conscience" (your favourite new pun).

Co-founders Joseph DeSimone, James McClain, and Timothy Romack established Micell Technologies, Inc. in 1995 after research resulted in the first breakthrough in dry-cleaning technology in nearly 50 years. They developed a cleaning process, called Micare, which uses liquid carbon dioxide (CO_2) and specially developed detergents to clean clothes. There's no heat required and no further need for the toxic perchloroethylene (perc) or petroleum traditionally used in dry cleaning.

In 2001 Micell sold all licensing, all intellectual property, and all interest in Hangers Cleaners to Cool Clean Technologies, which now manufactures the "CO_2OL Clean" dry-cleaning machine that your franchise relies on. Hangers franchise owners don't have to deal with regulatory paperwork, zoning restrictions, or expensive insurance and taxes for hazardous waste disposal. And unlike petroleum-based solvents, the CO_2 used in the CO_2OL Clean machine is noncombustible. It's the same substance that carbonates beverages, and it's captured from the waste stream of industries that produce it as a byproduct. Moreover, 98 percent of the CO_2 used in a Hangers outlet is recycled and used again, which helps keep prices competitive. A leading consumer

products group recently rated the CO_2OL Clean machine the best dry-cleaning alternative.

You've already sold franchises in three provinces and 23 states. Customers love the fact that their clothes don't carry toxic fumes after cleaning, and employees are happy to be working in a safe and cool environment. The process is actually gentler on clothes (no strong solvents or heat), reducing fading and shrinking and helping them last longer. You aren't dry cleaners, you're "garment care specialists."

And beyond the progressive corporate atmosphere, you simply love the design of Hangers stores. When Micell originally established the chain, it hired dry-cleaning experts and architects alike to come up with a sleek, modern, high-end retail "look" that features a cool, clean, light-filled interior and distinctive signage out front. It's more akin to a Starbucks than the overheated, toxic-smelling storefront most customers associate with dry cleaning. This high-end look is making it easier to establish Hangers as a national brand, attracting investors and franchisees rapidly as word spreads about the new "greener cleaner."

Your task: Develop a sales letter that can be mailed in response to preliminary inquiries from potential franchise owners. You'll include brochures covering franchise agreements and CO_2OL Clean specifics, so focus instead on introducing and promoting the unique benefits of Hangers Cleaners. Your contact information is Hangers Cleaners, 3505 County Road 42 West, Burnsville, MN, 55306-3803; phone 952-882-5000; toll-free 866-262-9274.[31]

▌IM SKILLS▐

14. Tweet Promotion: Using Tweet Sequences for Product Interest

Effective microblogging messages emphasize clarity and conciseness—and so do effective sales messages.

Your task: Find the website of any product that can be ordered online (any product you find interesting and that is appropriate to use for a class assignment). Adapt the information on the website, using your own words, and write four tweets to promote the product. The first should get your audience's attention (with an intriguing benefit claim, for example); the second should build audience interest by providing some support for the claim you made in the first message; the third should increase readers' desire to have the product by layering on one or two more buyer benefits; and the fourth should motivate readers to take action to place an order. Your first three tweets can be up to 140 characters, but the fourth should be limited to 120 to accommodate a URL (you don't need to include the URL in your message, however).

If your class is set up with private Twitter accounts, use your private account to send your messages. Otherwise, email your four messages to your instructor or post them on your class blog, as your instructor directs.

| IM SKILLS |

15. Helping Children: Instant Message Holiday Fund Drive at IBM

At IBM, you're one of the coordinators for the annual Employee Charitable Contributions Campaign. Since 1978, the company has helped employees contribute to more than 2000 health and human service agencies. These groups may offer child care, treat substance abuse, provide health services, or fight illiteracy, homelessness, and hunger. Some offer disaster relief or care for the elderly. All deserve support. They're carefully screened by IBM, one of the largest corporate contributors of cash, equipment, and people to nonprofit organizations and educational institutions in Canada, the United States, and around the world. As your literature states, the program "has engaged our employees more fully in the important mission of corporate citizenship."

During the winter holidays, you target agencies that cater to the needs of displaced families, women, and children. It's not difficult to raise enthusiasm. The prospect of helping children enjoy the holidays—children who otherwise might have nothing—usually awakens the spirit of your most distracted workers. But some of them wait until the last minute and then forget.

They have until Wednesday, December 16, to come forth with cash contributions. To make it in time for holiday deliveries, they can also bring in toys, food, and blankets through Monday, December 21. They shouldn't have any trouble finding the collection bins; they're everywhere, marked with bright red banners. But some will want to call you with questions or (hopefully) to make credit card contributions; they can reach you at 1-800-555-3899, ext. 3342.

Your task: It's December 14. Write a 75- to 100-word instant message encouraging last-minute gifts.[32]

| Blogging SKILLS |

16. Encouraging Accessibility: Blog Post

Like most other companies today, your firm makes extensive use of the Web for internal and external communication. However, after reading about the Web Accessibility Initiative (WAI), you've become concerned that your company's various websites haven't been designed to accommodate people with disabilities or age-related limitations. Fortunately, as one of the company's top managers, you have a perfect forum for letting everyone in the company know how important accessible web design is: your internal blog is read by the vast majority of employees and managers throughout the company.

Your task: Visit the WAI website, at www.w3.org/WAI, and read the two articles "Introduction to Web Accessibility" (in the "Getting Started" section, click on "Introduction to Accessibility") and "Developing a Web Accessibility Business Case for Your Organization" (in the "Getting Started" section, click on "Business Case"). Using the information you learn in these articles, write a post for your blog that emphasizes how important it is for your company's websites to be made more accessible. You don't have direct authority over the company's web developers, so it would be inappropriate for you to request them to take any specific action. Your goal is simply to raise awareness and encourage everyone to consider the needs of the company's online audiences. Don't worry about the technical aspects of web accessibility; focus instead on the benefits of improving accessibility.[33]

LEARNING OBJECTIVES   After studying this chapter, you will be able to

1   Distinguish between informational reports, analytical reports, and proposals

2   Describe an effective process for conducting business research, and explain how to evaluate the credibility of an information source

3   Explain the role of secondary research, and describe the two basic categories of online research tools

4   Explain the role of primary research, and identify the two most common forms of primary research for business communication purposes

5   Explain how to plan informational reports and website content

6   Describe the three most common ways to organize analytical reports

7   Explain how to plan proposals

MyLab Business Communication   Visit MyLab Business Communication to access a variety of online resources directly related to this chapter's content.

ON THE JOB: COMMUNICATING AT DELL INC.

Dell Inc. designs, manufactures, and customizes products and services to customer requirements, offering an extensive selection of hardware, software, and peripherals. In the fast-paced world of computer technology, the company uses reports to communicate its strategies, activities, and financial results.

Maintaining Position in a Changing Industry

www.dell.ca

Faced with consumer demand for tablets and smartphones over PCs, Dell Inc. is challenged to maintain its market share in the $3 trillion computer industry. Founded by Michael Dell in 1984, the company won renown as the fastest growing computer firm in history, serving the public sector, large enterprise, small business, and individual consumers. But constantly changing developments in technology have changed the way people communicate and work, and Dell must continually look for innovations to maintain its presence.

Flexibility was one reason for Dell's early prominence among PC manufacturers. For example, in the early 1990s, the company briefly experimented with selling consumer computers in retail outlets. But after studying retail sales reports that were based on careful data analysis, Michael Dell determined that selling directly to consumers online and by phone were the most profitable approaches for his business and, in 1994, abandoned the in-store venture. However, in 2007, Dell re-established retail partnerships with Walmart, Staples, Best Buy, and other major chains, such as Gome in China. New reports examining market trends indicated that the "walk model," as Michael Dell calls traditional shopping, was now a profitable complement to the click and talk methods. Back in 2009, Dell consumer products were available in more than 40 000 retail outlets worldwide, contributing to the company's financial success.

Dell is seeking new areas for growth, such as cloud computing and training services for its customers, and joining with other companies to improve service and offerings to individuals and businesses. Reports are an important way Dell communicates its strategies to investors, customers, and competitors. These reports must do more than simply summarize and present carefully researched data. They must analyze data to identify and discuss such pertinent issues as customer preferences, market trends, and industry developments. The company's 2016 interactive online annual report to shareholders is one example. In the annual report, Michael Dell discusses such matters as strategic acquisitions, new services for consumers and business, and the company's sustainability and social responsibility practices. Through the interactive shareholder letter, the reader can click on key terms that lead to information about financial performance, innovations, collaborations with clients, and charitable donations, among numerous other areas.

If you wrote reports for Dell, you would need to decide your reporting medium, focus your problem, plan your overall strategy, and conduct research. How would you break down your tasks and approach writing reports for Dell Inc.?[1]

Applying the Three-Step Writing Process to Reports and Proposals

Reports play a significant role in Dell Inc.'s success, as they do in all businesses. Whether you prepare or receive them, reports are the foundation of sound decisions and solutions. Reports fall into three basic categories (see Figure 11–1):

Distinguish between informational reports, analytical reports, and proposals.

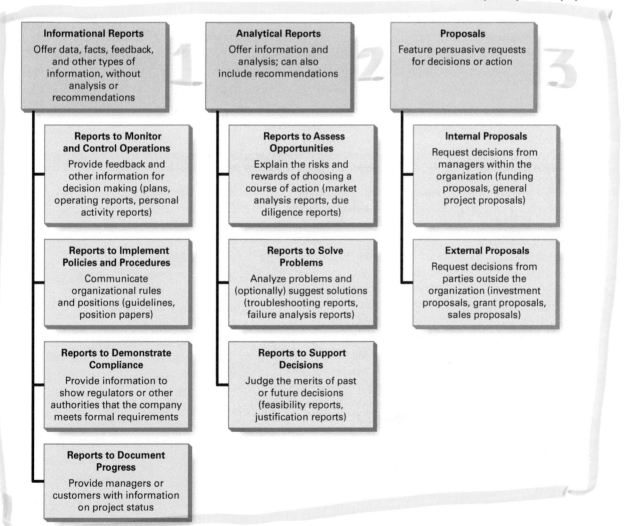

Figure 11–1 Common Types of Business Reports and Proposals

1. **Informational reports** offer data, facts, feedback, and other types of information, without analysis or recommendations.
2. **Analytical reports** provide both information and analysis, and they can also include recommendations.
3. **Proposals** offer structured persuasion for internal or external audiences.

The nature of reports varies widely, from one-page trip reports that follow a standard format to detailed business plans and proposals that can run hundreds of pages. Try to view every business report as an opportunity to demonstrate your understanding of your audience's challenges and your ability to contribute to your organization's success.

The three-step process you studied in Chapters 4 through 6 and applied to short messages in Chapters 7 through 10 is even more beneficial with reports and proposals because a methodical, efficient approach to planning, writing, and completing is even more valuable with these larger projects (see Figure 11–2). This chapter addresses the planning step, focusing on two major areas that require special attention in long documents: gathering and organizing information. Chapter 12 covers the writing step and also includes advice on creating effective visuals for your reports and proposals. Chapter 13 describes the tasks involved in completing reports and proposals.

> The purpose and content of business reports vary widely; in some cases, you'll follow strict guidelines, but in others the organization and format will be up to you.

ANALYZING THE SITUATION

> Given the length and complexity of many reports, it's crucial to define your purpose clearly, so you don't waste time with unnecessary rework.

The complexity of many reports and the amount of work involved put a premium on carefully analyzing the situation before you begin to write. Pay special attention to your **statement of purpose,** which explains *why* you are preparing the report and *what* you plan to deliver in the report (see Table 11–1).

1 Planning →	**2** Writing →	**3** Completing
Analyze the Situation Clarify the problem or opportunity at hand; define your purpose; develop an audience profile; and develop a work plan.	**Adapt to Your Audience** Be sensitive to audience needs by using a "you" attitude, being polite, and using bias-free language. Build a strong relationship with your audience by establishing your credibility and projecting your company's image. Control your style with a tone and voice appropriate to the situation.	**Revise the Message** Evaluate content and review readability; edit and rewrite for conciseness and clarity.
Gather Information Determine audience needs and obtain the information necessary to satisfy those needs; conduct a research project if necessary.		**Produce the Message** Use effective design elements and suitable layout for a clean, professional appearance; seamlessly combine textual and graphical elements.
Select the Right Medium Choose the best medium for delivering your message; consider delivery through multiple media.	**Compose the Message** Choose precise language that will help you create effective sentences and coherent paragraphs throughout the introduction, body, and close of your report or proposal.	**Proofread the Message** Review for errors in layout, spelling, and mechanics.
Organize the Information Define your main idea; limit your scope; select a direct or an indirect approach; and outline your content using an appropriate structure for an informational report, analytical report, or proposal.		**Distribute the Message** Deliver your report using the chosen medium; make sure all documents and all relevant files are distributed successfully.

Figure 11–2 Three-Step Writing Process for Reports and Proposals

Table 11–1	**Problem Statements versus Purpose Statements**

Problem Statement	Statement of Purpose
Our company's market share is steadily declining.	To explore new ways of promoting and selling our products and to recommend the approaches most likely to stabilize our market share
Our current computer network lacks sufficient bandwidth and cannot be upgraded to meet our future needs.	To analyze various networking options and to recommend the system that will best meet our company's current and future needs
We need $2 million to launch our new product.	To convince investors that our new business would be a sound investment, so we can obtain desired financing
Our current operations are too decentralized and expensive.	To justify the closing of the Sudbury plant and the transfer of Ontario operations to a single eastern location to save the company money

The most useful way to phrase a purpose statement is to begin with an infinitive phrase (*to* plus a verb), which helps pin down your general goal (*to inform, to identify, to analyze,* and so on). For instance, in an informational report, your statement of purpose can be as simple as one of these:

> To identify potential markets for our new smartphone apps
>
> To update the board of directors about the progress of our research into carbon-fibre composites
>
> To submit required information to the Ontario Securities Commission

Your statement of purpose for an analytical report often needs to be more comprehensive. When Linda Moreno, the cost accounting manager for an electronics company, was asked to find ways of reducing employee travel and entertainment costs, she phrased her statement of purpose accordingly:

> . . . to analyze the T&E [travel and entertainment] budget, evaluate the impact of recent changes in airfares and hotel costs, and suggest ways to tighten management's control over T&E expenses.

Because Moreno was assigned an analytical report rather than an informational report, she had to go beyond merely collecting data; she had to draw conclusions and make recommendations. You'll see her complete report in Chapter 13.

When writing a proposal, you must also be guided by a clear statement of purpose to help focus on crafting a persuasive message. Here are several examples:

> To secure funding in next year's budget for new conveyor systems in the warehouse
>
> To get management approval to reorganize the North American sales force
>
> To secure $2 million from outside investors to start production of the new titanium mountain bike

Remember, the more specific your purpose statement, the more useful it will be as a guide to planning your report. Furthermore, if you've been assigned the report by someone else, always double-check your statement of purpose with that person to ensure that you've interpreted the assignment correctly.

In addition to considering your purpose carefully, you will also want to prepare a *work plan* for most reports and proposals in order to make the best use of your time. For simpler reports, the work plan can be an informal list of tasks and a simple schedule. However, if you're preparing a lengthy report, particularly when you're collaborating with others, you'll want to develop a more detailed work plan.

The statement of purpose for a proposal should help guide you in developing a persuasive message.

A detailed work plan saves time and often produces more effective reports.

This plan might include the following elements:

- **Statement of the problem or opportunity (for analytical reports and proposals):** The problem statement clarifies the challenge you face and helps you and anyone working with you stay focused on the core problem.
- **Statement of the purpose and scope of your investigation:** The purpose statement describes what you plan to accomplish with this report and, thus, the boundaries of your work. Stating which issues you'll cover and which issues you won't cover is especially important with complex, lengthy investigations.
- **Discussion of the tasks that need to be accomplished to complete the report:** Ensure that you indicate your sources of information, the research necessary, and any constraints (for example, on time, money, personnel, or data). This section helps establish your credibility as a researcher and the validity of your information.
- **Review of project assignments, schedules, and resource requirements:** Indicate who will be responsible for specific tasks, when tasks will be completed, any special needs, such as equipment and technical advice, and how much the investigation will cost. (Collaborative writing is discussed in detail in Chapter 2.)
- **Plans for following up after delivering the report:** Follow-up can be as simple as ensuring that people received the information they needed or as complex as conducting additional research to evaluate the outcome of the recommendations you made. Follow-up signals that you care about your work's effectiveness and its impact on the organization.

Some work plans also include a tentative outline, if the author has had the opportunity to think through the organization of the report. The work plan in Figure 11–3 includes such an outline. A formal work plan such as this is a vital tool for planning and managing complex writing projects. The preliminary outline here helps guide the research; the report writers may modify the outline when they begin writing the report.

In addition, project management charts are useful tools for scheduling and tracking tasks from start to finish. With graphical representation of project time-lines and workflow, these charts are strong visual aids that can keep you and your collaborators organized. You can find many examples online, from simple to complex, by entering "project management software" in a search engine. Figure 11–4 is a simple example that can be adapted to your needs.

GATHERING INFORMATION

Some reports require formal research projects in order to gather all the necessary information.

Obtaining the information needed for many reports and proposals requires careful planning, and you may even need to do a separate research project just to acquire the data and information you need (see "Supporting Your Messages with Reliable Information"). To stay on schedule and on budget, be sure to review both your statement of purpose and your audience's needs so that you collect all the information you need—and only the information you need. In some cases, you won't be able to collect every piece of information you'd like, so prioritize your needs up front and focus on the most important questions.

SELECTING THE RIGHT MEDIUM

The best medium for any given report might be anything from a professionally printed and bound document to an online executive dashboard that displays only report highlights.

Just as you would for other business messages, select the medium for your report based on the needs of your audience and the practical advantages and disadvantages of the choices available to you. In addition to the general media

The problem statement clearly and succinctly defines the problem the writers intend to address. →

STATEMENT OF THE PROBLEM
The rapid growth of our company over the past five years has reduced the sense of community among our staff. People no longer feel like part of an intimate organization that values teamwork.

PURPOSE AND SCOPE OF WORK
The purpose of this study is to determine whether social networking technology such as Facebook at Work and HipChat would help rebuild a sense of community within the workforce and whether encouraging the use of such tools in the workplace will have any negative consequences. The study will attempt to assess the impact of social networks in other companies in terms of community-building, morale, project communication, and overall productivity.

← This paragraph identifies exactly what will be covered by the research and addressed in the final report.

This section explains how the researchers will find the data and information they need. →

SOURCES AND METHODS OF DATA COLLECTION
Data collection will start with secondary research, including a review of recently published articles and studies of the use of social networking in business and a review of product information published by technology vendors. Primary research will focus on an employee and management survey to uncover attitudes about social networking tools. We will also collect anecdotal evidence from bloggers and others with experience using networks in the workplace.

PRELIMINARY OUTLINE
The preliminary outline for this study is as follows:
  I. What experiences have other companies had with social networks in the workplace?
      A. Do social networks have a demonstrable business benefit?
      B. How do employees benefit from using these tools?
      C. Has network security and information confidentiality been an issue?
 II. Is social networking an appropriate solution for our community-building needs?
      A. Is social networking better than other tools and methods for community building?
      B. Are employees already using social networking tools on the job?
      C. Will a company-endorsed system distract employees from essential duties?
      D. Will a company system add to managerial workloads in any way?
III. If we move ahead, should we use a "business-class" network such as HipChat or a consumer tool such as Facebook?
      A. How do the initial and ongoing costs compare?
      B. Do the additional capabilities of a business-class network justify the higher costs?
 IV. How should we implement a social network?
      A. Should we let it grow "organically," with employees choosing their own tools and groups?
      B. Should we make a variety of tools available and let employees improvise on their own?
      C. Should we designate one system as the official company social network and make it a permanent, supported element of the information technology infrastructure?
  V. How can we evaluate the success of a new social network?
      A. What are the criteria of success or failure?
      B. What is the best way to measure these criteria?

← The preliminary outline has enough detail to guide the research and set reader expectations.

The assignments and schedule section clearly lists responsibilities and due dates. →

TASK ASSIGNMENTS AND SCHEDULE
Each phase of this study will be completed by the following dates:

Primary research: Hank Waters	September 15, 2018
Employee and management survey: Julienne Cho	September 22, 2018
Analysis and synthesis of research: Hank Waters	October 6, 2018
Comparison of business and consumer solutions: Julienne Cho	October 13, 2018
Comparison of implementation strategies: Hank Waters	October 13, 2018
Final report: Hank Waters	October 20, 2018

Figure 11–3 Work Plan for a Report

PROJECT: SOCIAL NETWORKS IN THE WORKPLACE STUDY						
Primary research	Hank Waters					
Employee and management survey	Julienne Cho					
Analysis and synthesis of research			Hank Waters			
Comparison of business and consumer solutions				Julienne Cho		
Comparison of implementation strategies				Hank Waters		
Final report						Hank Waters
	Sept. 1–15	Sept. 16–22	Sept. 23–29	Sept. 30–Oct. 6	Oct. 7–13	Oct. 14–20

Figure 11–4 Project Management Chart

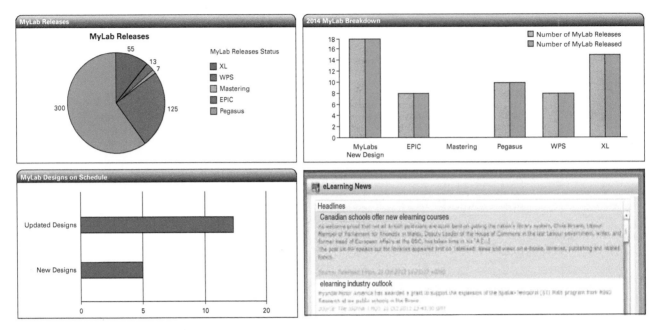

Figure 11–5 Executive Dashboards

selection criteria discussed in Chapter 4, consider several points for reports and proposals:

- **Audiences have specific media requirements.** You will have to follow company culture for distributing your report. Executives in many corporations now expect to review reports via their in-house intranets, sometimes in conjunction with an *executive dashboard* (see Figure 11–5), a customized online presentation of key operating variables such as revenue, profits, quality, customer satisfaction, and project progress. Dashboards are essentially super-summarized, live reports. The latest generation of software makes it easy to customize screens to show each manager the specific summaries he or she needs to see.

- **Audiences may want to provide written feedback on your report or proposal.** You will have to determine if your readers prefer to write comments on a printed document or to use the commenting and markup features in a word-processing program or Adobe Acrobat.

- **Will multiple people need to update the document over time?** A wiki could be an ideal choice because it is easy to use.

- **Audiences will assess your professional image according to your choice of media.** Technology provides a wide array of products and features for enhancing reports; however, any special effects you choose must suit the message. For example, a routine sales report dressed up in expensive multimedia will look like a waste of valuable company resources—and will affect how your readers view your abilities as an employee.

ORGANIZING YOUR INFORMATION

The direct approach is used often for reports because it is efficient and easy to follow. When an audience is likely to be receptive or at least open minded, use the direct approach: lead with a summary of your key findings, conclusions, recommendations, or proposal, whichever is relevant. This "up-front" arrangement is by far the most popular and convenient for business reports. It saves time and makes the rest of the report easier to follow. For those who have questions or want more information, later parts of the report provide complete findings and supporting details.

However, if the audience is unsure about your credibility or is not ready to accept your main idea without first seeing some reasoning or evidence, the indirect approach is a better choice because it gives you a chance to prove your points and gradually overcome audience reservations. To enable the use of AIDA-style persuasion (Attention, Interest, Desire, Action), unsolicited proposals in particular often use the indirect approach. Bear in mind, though, that the longer the document, the less effective the indirect approach is likely to be.

Both approaches have merit, so businesspeople often combine them, revealing their conclusions and recommendations in stages as they go along rather than putting them all first or last. As the direct version of the introduction in Figure 11–6 shows, the writer quickly presents the report's recommendation, followed by the conclusions that led to that recommendation. In the indirect version, the same topics are introduced in the same order, but no conclusions are drawn about them; the conclusions and the ultimate recommendation appear later, in the body of the report.

When you outline your content, use informative ("talking") headings rather than simple descriptive ("topical") headings (see Table 11–2). When in question

Use the direct approach for most reports; consider the indirect approach if you haven't established credibility with your readers, or if your main idea will be met with resistance.

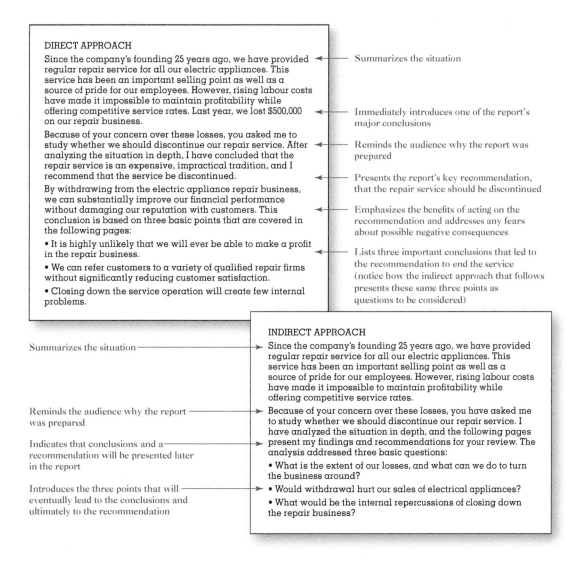

Figure 11–6 Direct Approach versus Indirect Approach in an Introduction

Table 11–2	Types of Outline Headings		
DESCRIPTIVE (TOPICAL)	**INFORMATIVE (TALKING) OUTLINE**		
OUTLINE	**Question Form**	**Summary Form**	

I. Industry Characteristics
    A. Annual sales
    B. Profitability
    C. Growth rate
        1. Sales
        2. Profit
	I. What is the nature of the industry?
	    A. What are the annual sales?
	    B. Is the industry profitable?
	    C. What is the pattern of growth?
	        1. Sales growth?
	        2. Profit growth?
		I. Flour milling is a mature industry.
		    A. Market is large.
		    B. Profit margins are narrow.
		    C. Growth is modest.
		        1. Sales growth averages less than 3 percent a year.
		        2. Profits are flat.	

or summary form, informative headings force you to really think through the content rather than simply identify the general topic area. Using informative headings will not only help you plan more effectively but also facilitate collaborative writing. A heading such as "Industry Characteristics" could mean five different things to the five people on your writing team, so use a heading that conveys a single, unambiguous meaning, such as "Flour milling is a mature industry."

For a quick review of adapting the three-step process to long reports, refer to "Checklist: Adapting the Three-Step Writing Process to Informational and Analytical Reports." Sections later in this chapter provide specific advice on how to plan informational reports, analytical reports, and proposals.

✔ **Checklist** | **Adapting the Three-Step Writing Process to Informational and Analytical Reports**

A. Analyze the situation.
- Clearly define your purpose before you start writing.
- If you need to accomplish several goals in the report, identify all of them in advance.
- Prepare a work plan to guide your efforts.

B. Gather information.
- Determine whether you need to launch a separate research project to collect the necessary information.
- Reuse or adapt existing information whenever possible.

C. Select the right medium.
- Base your decision on audience expectations (or requirements, as the case may be).

- Consider the need for commenting, revising, distributing, and storing.
- Remember that the medium you choose also sends a message.

D. Organize your information.
- Use the direct approach if your audience is receptive.
- Use the indirect approach if your audience is skeptical.
- Use the indirect approach when you don't want to risk coming across as arrogant.
- Combine approaches if doing so will help build support for your primary message.

Supporting Your Messages with Reliable Information

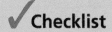

Describe an effective process for conducting business research, and explain how to evaluate the credibility of an information source.

Audiences expect you to support your message with solid research. As you've probably discovered while doing school projects, effective research involves a lot more than simply typing a few terms into a search engine. Save time and get better results by using a clear process:

1. **Plan your research.** Planning is the most important step of any research project; a solid plan yields better results in less time.

2. **Locate the data and information you need.** The research plan tells you *what* to look for; your next step is to figure out *where* the data and information are and *how* to access them.

3. **Process the data and information you've located.** The data and information you find probably won't be in a form you can use immediately and will require some processing, which might involve anything from statistical analysis to resolving the differences between two or more expert opinions.

4. **Apply your findings.** You can apply your research findings in three ways: summarizing information for someone else's benefit, drawing conclusions based on what you've learned, or developing recommendations.

5. **Manage information efficiently.** Many companies today are trying to maximize the return on the time and money they invest in business research by collecting and sharing research results in a variety of computer-based systems, known generally as **knowledge management (KM)** systems. At the very least, be sure to share your results with any colleagues who may be able to benefit from them.

Rob Bartee/Alamy Stock Photo

You don't have to become an expert on every subject you undertake, but you must learn enough about the subject you're exploring to pose intelligent questions. How is research like exploration or detective work?

You can see the sequence of these steps in Figure 11–7. The sections that follow offer more details on the research process, starting with planning your research.

PLANNING YOUR RESEARCH

With so much information online these days, it's tempting just to punch some keywords into a search engine and then grab something from the first screen or two of results. However, this haphazard approach limits your effectiveness and can lead to expensive and embarrassing mistakes.

To maximize your chances of finding useful information and minimize the time you spend looking for it, start by familiarizing yourself with the subject so that you can frame insightful questions. As you explore the general subject area, try to identify basic terminology, significant trends, important conflicts, influential people, and potential sources of information. Next, develop a **problem statement** that will define the purpose of your research. This statement should explicitly define the decision you need to make or the conclusion you need to reach at the end of the process. For example, a retailer might want to know whether consumers are starting to turn away from bottled water because of concerns about cost and the environmental impact of plastic packaging and transportation. The problem statement could be "We need to determine whether we should reduce the number or variety of bottled water brands carried in our stores."

Researching without a plan wastes time and usually produces unsatisfactory results.

The problem statement guides your research by focusing on the decision you need to make or the conclusion you need to reach.

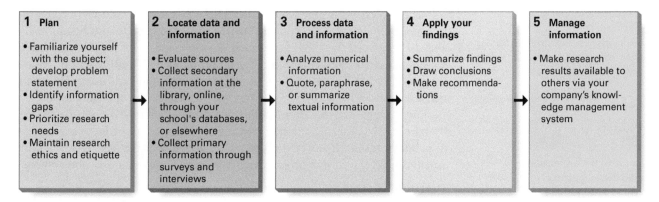

1 Plan	2 Locate data and information	3 Process data and information	4 Apply your findings	5 Manage information
• Familiarize yourself with the subject; develop problem statement • Identify information gaps • Prioritize research needs • Maintain research ethics and etiquette	• Evaluate sources • Collect secondary information at the library, online, through your school's databases, or elsewhere • Collect primary information through surveys and interviews	• Analyze numerical information • Quote, paraphrase, or summarize textual information	• Summarize findings • Draw conclusions • Make recommendations	• Make research results available to others via your company's knowledge management system

Figure 11–7 The Research Process

BEING AN ETHICAL RESEARCHER

With a prioritized list of questions, you're almost ready to start your research. Before taking that step, however, it's important to be aware that research carries some significant ethical responsibilities. Your research tactics affect the people from whom you gather data and information, the people who read your results, and the people who are affected by the way you present those results. To avoid ethical lapses, keep the following points in mind:

- **Don't force a specific outcome by skewing your research.** If you go in with strong biases or opinions, you're more likely to favour information that supports your position and gloss over information that doesn't. If you go in with an open mind and are willing to accept whatever you find, your research will be more valuable.

- **Respect the privacy of your research participants.** For example, don't observe or record people without their consent or publicly disclose personal information that you promised to keep private.[2]

- **Document sources and give appropriate credit.** Whether you use published documents, personal interviews, or company records, citing your sources is not only fair to the people who created and provided the information, but doing so also builds your credibility as a writer.

- **Respect the intellectual property and digital rights of your sources.** *Intellectual property* refers to the ownership of unique ideas that have commercial value in the marketplace.[3] Intellectual property laws cover everything from artists' works to industrial processes, so ensure that you can legally use the information you uncover.

- **Don't distort information from your sources.** For example, if an industry expert says that a sales increase is *possible*, don't quote her as saying that a sales increase is *probable*.

- **Don't misrepresent who you are or what you intend to do with the research results.** One prominent example of misrepresentation in recent years is known as *pretexting*, which is essentially lying about who you are (such as posing as a journalist) in order to gain access to information that you couldn't get otherwise. Pretexting is not only unethical but also illegal in many instances.[4]

In addition to ethics, research etiquette deserves careful attention. For example, respect the time of anyone who agrees to be interviewed or to be a research participant, and maintain courtesy throughout the interview or research process.

LOCATING DATA AND INFORMATION

The range of sources available to business researchers today can be overwhelming. The good news is that if you have a question about an industry, a company, a market, a new technology, or a financial topic, somebody else has probably already researched the subject. Research done previously for another purpose is considered **secondary research** (covered on pages 335–340) when the results are reused in a new project. This secondary information can be anything from magazine articles to survey results. Start with secondary research for your project because it might save you considerable time and money for the overall assignment. If you can't find existing research that meets your needs, you'll have to engage in **primary research** (covered on pages 340–345), which is new research done specifically for the current project, such as surveys, interviews, and observations.

EVALUATING SOURCES No matter where you're searching, it is your responsibility to separate quality information from unreliable junk so you don't taint

Privacy is one of the most important issues in the research field today.

Primary research involves collecting information for the first time, specifically for a new project; secondary research involves finding and reusing information that others have gathered in previous projects.

You have the responsibility to evaluate your sources carefully to avoid embarrassing and potentially damaging mistakes.

your results or damage your reputation. Web 2.0 tools have complicated this challenge by making many new sources of information available. On the positive side, independent sources communicating through blogs, Twitter and other microblogging sites, wikis, user-generated content sites, and podcasting channels can provide valuable and unique insights, often from experts whose voices might never be heard otherwise. On the negative side, these nontraditional information sources often lack the editorial boards and fact checkers commonly used in traditional publishing. You cannot assume that the information you find in blogs and other sources is accurate, objective, and current. Answer the following questions about each piece of material:

- **Does the source have a reputation for honesty and reliability?** Generally speaking, you can feel more comfortable using information from an established source that has a reputation for accuracy. For sources that are new or obscure, your safest bet is to corroborate anything you learn with information from several other sources.
- **Is the source potentially biased?** To interpret an organization's information, you need to know its point of view. For example, information about a particular company can be presented quite differently by a competitor, a union trying to organize the company's workforce, an investment research firm, and an environmental advocacy group. Information from a source with a particular point of view isn't necessarily bad, of course, but knowing this context is always helpful and sometimes essential for interpreting the information correctly.
- **What is the purpose of the material?** For example, was the material designed to inform others of new research or advance a political position? Was it designed to promote or sell a product? Be sure to distinguish among advertising, advocating, and informing. And don't lower your guard just because an organization has a reassuring name like the American Institute for the Advancement of All Things Good and Wonderful; many innocuously labelled groups advocate a particular line of political, social, or economic thinking.
- **Is the author credible?** Is the author a professional journalist? An industry insider? An informed amateur? Merely someone with an opinion?
- **Where did the source get *its* information?** Try to find out who collected the data, the methods they used, their qualifications, and their professional reputation.
- **Can you verify the material independently?** Verification can uncover biases or mistakes, which is particularly important when the information goes beyond simple facts to include projections, interpretations, and estimates. The more independent sources you can find that verify a piece of information, the more confidence you can have in it—as long as they're not all quoting the same source, naturally.
- **Is the material current?** Make sure you are using the most current information available by checking the publication date of a source. Look for a "posted on" or "updated on" date with online material. If you can't find a date, don't assume that the information is current without verifying it through some other channel.
- **Is the material complete?** Have you accessed the entire document or only a selection from it? If it's a selection, which parts were excluded? Do you need more detail?

You probably won't have time to conduct a thorough background check on all your sources, so focus your efforts on the most important or most suspicious pieces of information. And if you can't verify critical facts or figures, be sure to let your readers know that.

KEEPING TRACK OF YOUR RESEARCH Before doing research, you should think about how you will keep track of the information you gather. The following strategies will streamline the research stage:

- **Bookmark, download, or print out pages from library databases**. Most library databases give you the option to set up a folder of "marked" articles that you can review later. You can email the list to yourself, either as citations, citations with abstracts, or full articles.
- **Write down the complete bibliographic information when recording information manually**. Spending an extra minute or two double-checking your handwritten or keyboarded citation against your source will prevent backtracking later on as you near your deadline.
- **Mark up printouts or photocopies.** Highlight key phrases, facts, or sections, and write comments in the margins. You can then record your notes on cards or enter them directly into a computer.
- **Take notes by computer.** By recording notes in electronic format you can easily search for words (using the "find" function), sort the notes by column headings, and copy information directly into the document draft. Keep copies in a number of locations, such as in the cloud or on a thumb drive, to ensure you don't lose your work.
- **Read topic sentences first.** The topic sentence, generally the first sentence of a paragraph) will help you decide whether the source may contain useful information. If it does, then read the entire paragraph.

USING YOUR RESEARCH RESULTS

After you've collected all the necessary information, the next step is to transform it into the specific content you need. For simple projects, you may be able to drop your material, such as statistics from secondary sources and brief quotations from experts in the field, directly into your report, presentation, or other application. However, when you have gathered a significant amount of information or raw data from surveys, you need to process the material before you can use it. This step can involve analyzing numeric data; quoting, paraphrasing, or summarizing textual material; drawing conclusions; and making recommendations.

Mean, *median*, and *mode* provide specific insights into sets of numerical data.

ANALYZING DATA Business research often yields numeric data, such as sales figures, and survey responses, but these numbers, by themselves, might not provide the insights you or your audience require. Are sales going up or going down? What percentage of employees surveyed are so dissatisfied that they're ready to look for new jobs?

Fortunately, even without advanced statistical techniques, you can use simple arithmetic to help extract meaning from sets of research data. Table 11–3

Table 11–3	Three Types of Data Measures: Mean, Median, and Mode
Salesperson	**Sales ($)**
Simpson	3 000
Chu	5 000
Carrick	6 000
Sharma	7 000 ——————— Mean
Kuszaj	7 500 ——————— Median
Kemble	8 500 ┐
O'Toole	8 500 │ Mode
Caruso	8 500 ┘
Harari	9 000
Total	$63 000

shows several answers you can gain about a collection of numbers, for instance. The **mean** (which is what people are usually referring to when they use the term *average*) is the sum of all the items in the group divided by the number of items in that group. The **median** is the "middle of the road," or the midpoint of a series, with an equal number of items above and below it. The **mode** is the number that occurs more often than any other in the sample; it's the best answer to a question such as "What is the usual amount?" Each of the three measures can tell you different things about a set of data.

It's also helpful to look for **trends,** which are any repeatable patterns taking place over time, including growth, decline, and cyclical trends that vary between growth and decline. Trend analysis is common in business. By looking at data over a period of time, you can detect patterns and relationships that help you answer important questions. In addition, researchers frequently explore the relationships between subsets of data using a technique called *cross-tabulation*. For instance, if you're trying to figure out why total sales rose or fell, you might look separately at sales data by customer age, gender, location, and product type.

Trends suggest directions or patterns in a series of data points.

Whenever you process numeric data, make sure to double-check all your calculations and document the operation of any spreadsheets you plan to share with colleagues. Also, step back and look at your entire set of data before proceeding with any analysis. Do the numbers make sense based on what you know about the subject? Are there any individual data points that stand out as suspect? Business audiences like the clarity of numbers; it's your responsibility to deliver numbers they can count on.

QUOTING, PARAPHRASING, AND SUMMARIZING INFORMATION You can use textual information from sources in three ways. *Quoting* a source means you reproduce it exactly as you found it, and you either set it off with quotation marks (for shorter passages) or extract it in an indented paragraph (for longer passages). Use direct quotations when the original language will enhance your argument or when rewording the passage would lessen its impact. However, try not to quote sources at great length. Too much quoting creates a choppy patchwork of varying styles and gives the impression that all you've done is piece together the work of other people.

Quoting a source means reproducing the content exactly and indicating who created the information originally.

You can often maximize the impact of secondary material in your own writing by *paraphrasing* it, or restating it in your own words and with your own sentence structures.[5] Paraphrasing helps you maintain a consistent tone while using vocabulary familiar to your audience. Of course, you still need to credit the originator of the information, but not with quotation marks or indented paragraphs.

Paraphrasing is expressing someone else's ideas in your own words and documenting the source of the idea.

To paraphrase effectively, follow these tips:[6]

- Reread the original passage until you fully understand its meaning and are able to express it in your own words.
- Use language that matches the flow and tone of the rest of your report and that your audience is familiar with.
- Check your version with the original source to verify that you have not altered the meaning.
- Use quotation marks to identify any unique terms or phrases you have borrowed exactly from the source.
- Record the source so that you can give proper credit if you use this material in your report.

Summarizing is similar to paraphrasing, as a summary is in your own words and sentences, but it presents the gist of the material in fewer words than the original. An effective summary identifies the main ideas and major support

Summarizing is similar to paraphrasing but distills the content into fewer words and still provides information about the original source.

Table 11–4	**Summarizing Effectively**		
Original Material (114 Words)		**36-Word Summary**	**19-Word Summary**
Our facilities costs spiralled out of control last year. The 23% jump **was far ahead of every other cost category in the company and many times higher than the 4% average rise for commercial real estate in the Winnipeg metropolitan area. The rise can be attributed to many factors, but the major factors include repairs** (mostly electrical and structural problems at the downtown office), **energy** (most of our offices are heated by electricity, the price of which has been increasing much faster than for oil or gas), and last but not least, **the loss of two sublease tenants** whose rent payments made a substantial dent in our cost profile for the past five years.		Compared to other areas in the company, "facilities" outpaced all by rising 23% last year. **This increase was more than four times higher than the average for Winnipeg. Costs were due to refurbishment, power, and rental loss.**	Facilities outpaced others in cost by 23% last year **because of rising refurbishment and power costs and rental loss.**
Main idea			
Key support points			
Details			

All universities and colleges penalize students for committing plagiarism—claiming the words, ideas, artistic works, and research data of others as your own. Penalties may range from zero on the assignment to expulsion. What are your school's penalties for plagiarism? To prevent plagiarism, document your sources using one of the systems explained in Appendix B, "Documentation of Report Sources."

A conclusion is a logical interpretation of the information at hand.

A recommendation is a suggested course of action based on what you have concluded about a particular situation.

points from your source material but leaves out most details, examples, and other information that is less critical to your audience. Summarizing is not always a simple task, and your audience will judge your ability to separate significant issues from less significant details. Identify the main idea and the key support points, and separate these from details, examples, and other supporting evidence (see Table 11–4).

Of course, all three approaches require careful attention to ethics. When quoting directly, take care not to distort the original intent of the material by quoting selectively or out of context. And never resort to plagiarism, presenting someone else's ideas as your own.

DRAWING CONCLUSIONS A **conclusion** is a logical interpretation of the facts and other information in a report. A sound conclusion is not only logical but flows from the information included in a report, meaning that it should be based on the information included in the report and shouldn't rely on information that isn't in the report. Moreover, if you or the organization you represent has certain biases that influence your conclusion, ethics obligate you to inform the audience accordingly.

Reaching good conclusions based on the evidence at hand is one of the most important skills you can develop in your business career. In fact, the ability to see patterns and possibilities that others can't see is one of the hallmarks of innovative business leaders. Consequently, take your time with this part of the process. Play "devil's advocate," attacking your conclusion as an audience might to make sure it stands up to rigorous scrutiny.

MAKING RECOMMENDATIONS Whereas a conclusion interprets information, a **recommendation** suggests action—what to do in response to the information. The following example illustrates the difference between a conclusion and a recommendation:

Conclusion	Recommendation
On the basis of its track record and current price, I believe that this company is an attractive buy.	I recommend that we offer to buy the company at a 10 percent premium over the current market value of its stock.

To be credible, recommendations must be based on logical analysis and sound conclusions. They must also be practical and acceptable to the people who have to make your recommendations work. Finally, when making a recommendation, be certain that you have adequately described the steps needed to implement your recommendation.

Conducting Secondary Research

Even if you intend to eventually conduct primary research, start with a review of any available secondary research. Inside your company, you might be able to find a variety of reports and other documents that could help. Outside the company, business researchers can choose from a wide range of print and online resources, both in libraries and online. Table 11–5 provides a small sample of the many secondary resources available.

FINDING INFORMATION AT A LIBRARY

Public, corporate, and university and college libraries offer printed sources with information that is not available online and online sources that are available only by subscription. Libraries are also where you'll find one of your most important resources: librarians. Reference librarians are trained in research techniques and can often help you find obscure information you can't find on your own. They can also direct you to the typical library's many sources of business information:

- **Newspapers and periodicals.** Libraries offer access to a wide variety of popular magazines, general business magazines, *trade journals* (which provide information about specific professions and industries), and *academic journals* (which provide research-oriented articles from researchers and educators).
- **Business books.** Although less timely than newspapers, periodicals, and online sources, business books provide comprehensive coverage, in-depth analysis, and broad perspective that often can't be found anywhere else.
- **Directories.** Thousands of directories are published in electronic and print formats, and many include membership information for all kinds of professions, industries, and special-interest groups.
- **Almanacs and statistical resources.** Almanacs are useful guides to factual and statistical information about countries, politics, the labour force, and so on. See the Statistics Canada, Human Resources and Skills Development Canada, and Industry Canada websites. These resources contain statistics about life, work, government, population patterns, business, and the environment.
- **Government publications.** Information on laws, court decisions, tax questions, regulatory issues, and other governmental concerns can often be found in collections of government documents.
- **Electronic databases.** Databases offer vast collections of computer-searchable information, often in specific areas such as business, law, science, technology, and education. Some of these are available only by institutional subscription, so the library can be your only way to gain access to them. Some libraries offer remote online access to some or all databases; for others, you'll need to visit in person.

FINDING INFORMATION ONLINE

The Internet is a tremendous source of business information, provided that you know where to look and how to use the tools available. Roughly speaking, the tools fall into two categories: those you can use to actively *search* for existing

3 **LEARNING OBJECTIVE**

Explain the role of secondary research, and describe the two basic categories of online research tools.

You'll want to start most projects by conducting secondary research first.

Libraries offer information and resources you can't find anywhere else—including experienced research librarians.

Local, provincial, territorial, and federal government agencies publish a huge array of information that is helpful to business researchers.

Internet research tools fall into two basic categories: search tools and monitoring tools.

Table 11–5	**Important Resources for Business Research**

COMPANY, INDUSTRY, AND PRODUCT RESOURCES (URLs are provided for online resources)

AnnualReports.com (www.annualreports.com). Free access to annual reports from thousands of public companies.

Brands and Their Companies/Companies and Their Brands. Contains data on more than 430 000 consumer products and 100 000 manufacturers, importers, marketers, and distributors. Also available as an online database; ask at your library.

Canadian Business Resource (www.cbr.ca). Corporate and executive profiles from over 6000 Canadian companies, including stock ranking; website updated several times a week; subscription-based.

Fraser's Canadian Trade Directory (www.frasers.com). Directory of Canadian companies, products, and brands; free.

Hoover's Business Directory (www.hoovers.com). In-depth coverage of 85 million companies and 900 industry segments.

Innovation, Science and Economic Development Canada (www.ic.gc.ca). Click on the "Just for businesses" tab for information on Canadian companies and industry statistics.

***Report on Business* Magazine Top 1000 (www.theglobeandmail.com/report-on-business/rob-magazine/top-1000).** Contact, financial, and product information on Canada's largest corporations.

U.S. Securities and Exchange Commission (SEC) Filings (www.sec.gov/edgar.shtml). SEC filings including annual reports and prospectuses for 35 000 U.S. public firms.

TMX Company Spotlights (www.companyspotlight.com). Video, webcasts, presentations, and annual reports for more than 30 000 Canadian and international companies.

RESEARCH DIRECTORIES AND INDEXES

Books in Print. Database indexes nearly 20 million books, audio books, and video titles from around the world. Available in print and professional online versions.

Canadian Books in Print. Contains more than 52 000 titles; author and title index is extensively cross-referenced; subject index lists titles under 800 different subject categories.

Encyclopedia of Associations. Index of thousands of associations, listed by broad subject category, specific subject, association, and location. Available as an online database as well.

Reader's Guide to Periodical Literature. Classic index of general-interest magazines, categorized by subject and author; also available in electronic format, including a version with the full text of thousands of articles.

TRADEMARKS AND PATENTS

Canadian Patents Database (www.ic.gc.ca/opic-cipo/cpd/eng/introduction.html). Access to over 93 years of patent descriptions and images in over 200 000 patent documents.

Canadian Trade marks Database (www.cipo.ic.gc.ca/eic/site/cipoInternet-Internetopic.nsf/eng/h_wr03082.html). Trademark information, including designs, wares, and services.

Official Gazette of the United States Patent and Trademark Office (www.uspto.gov/news/og/index.jsp). Weekly publication (one for trademarks and one for patents) providing official record of newly assigned trademarks and patents, product descriptions, and product names.

United States Patent and Trademark Office (www.uspto.gov). Trademark and patent information records.

STATISTICS AND OTHER BUSINESS DATA

Bureau of Economic Analysis (www.bea.gov). Large collection of American economic and government data.

Canadian Human Rights Commission (www.chrc-ccdp.ca). Legislation and policies regarding employment equity and other human rights legislation.

Canadian Legislature (www.parl.gc.ca). Information about bills, committees, and the Canadian Parliament.

Department of Finance Canada (www.fin.gc.ca). Comprehensive directory to resources about Canada's financial institutions and markets.

Europa—The European Union (www.europa.eu). A portal that provides up-to-date coverage of current affairs, legislation, policies, and EU statistics.

Employment and Social Development Canada (www.canada.ca/en/employment-social-development.html). Comprehensive labour and employment information.

Innovation, Science and Economic Development Canada (www.ic.gc.ca). Wide-ranging information about the Canadian economy, business, and employment; includes company directories and consumer information.

Statistics Canada (www.statcan.gc.ca). Comprehensive collection of business, census, and other data.

U.S. Bureau of Labor Statistics (www.bls.gov). Extensive national and regional information on labour and business, including employment, industry growth, productivity, Consumer Price Index (CPI), and overall U.S. economy.

COMMERCIAL DATABASES (Require subscriptions; check with your school library)

ABI/INFORM Trade & Industry. Access to more than 750 periodicals and newsletters that focus on specific trades or industries.

CBCA Complete—Canadian Business & Current Affairs. Database of over 700 Canadian industry and professional periodicals and newsletters; covers business, science, and technology.

CPI.Q—Canadian Periodical Index. Citations, abstracts, and full-text articles from periodicals published in or providing major coverage of Canadian business, technology, arts, and other areas.

Gale Business & Company Resource Center. A comprehensive research tool designed for undergraduate and graduate students, job searchers, and investors; offers a wide variety of information on companies and industries.

LexisNexis. Several thousand databases covering legal, corporate, government, and academic subjects.

ProQuest. Thousands of periodicals and newspapers with extensive archives.

information and those you can use to *monitor* selected sources for new information. (Some tools can perform both functions.)

ONLINE SEARCH TOOLS The most familiar search tools are general-purpose **search engines,** such as Google and Bing, which scan millions of websites to identify individual webpages that contain a specific word or phrase and then attempt to rank the results from most useful to least useful. Website owners use *search engine optimization* techniques to help boost their rankings in the results, but the ranking algorithms are kept secret to prevent unfair manipulation of the results.

For all their ease and power, conventional search engines have four primary shortcomings: (1) no human editors are involved to evaluate the quality or ranking of the search results; (2) various engines use different search techniques, so they often find different material; (3) search engines can't reach all the content on some websites (this part of the Internet is sometimes called the *hidden Internet* or the *deep Internet*); and (4) unless you clear your browser regularly, cookies can affect your search by narrowing the focus based on previous activity.

A variety of tools are available to overcome the main weaknesses of general-purpose search engines, and you should consider one or more of them in your business research. First, "human-powered search engines" such as [inside] (www.inside.com) offer manually compiled results for popular search queries that aim to provide more accurate and more meaningful information, although for a much narrower range of topics than a regular search engine.[7] Similarly, **web directories,** such as weblocal at www.weblocal.ca, use human editors to categorize and evaluate websites. A variety of other directories focus on specific media types, such as blogs or podcasts.

Second, *metacrawlers* or *metasearch engines* help overcome the differences among search engines by formatting your search request for multiple search engines, making it easy to find a broader range of results. With a few clicks, you can compare results from multiple search engines to make sure you are getting a broad view of the material. Table 11–6 lists some of the most popular search engines, metacrawlers, and directories.

Third, **online databases** help address the challenge of the hidden Internet by offering access to newspapers, magazines, journals, electronic copies of books, and other resources often not available with standard search engines. Some of these databases offer free access to the public, but others require a subscription (check with your library). Also, a variety of specialized search engines now exist to reach various parts of the hidden Internet. Online databases also offer peer-reviewed information, which means there is an outside body monitoring the publication for accuracy. This can add credibility to facts and figures you cite in reports.

ONLINE MONITORING TOOLS One of the most powerful aspects of online research is the ability to automatically monitor selected sources for new

Courtesy: Google, Inc.

Specialized search capabilities such as Google Books can help you locate texts that might be of value in your research efforts. Is consulting Google Books enough to qualify as good research?

General-purpose search engines are tremendously powerful tools, but they do have several shortcomings that you need to consider.

"Human-powered search engines" and web directories rely on human editors to evaluate and select content.

Online databases and specialty search engines can help you access parts of the hidden Internet.

The tools available for monitoring online sources for new information can help you track industry trends, consumer sentiment, and other information.

Table 11–6   The Broad Spectrum of Online Search Tools

GENERAL-PURPOSE SEARCH ENGINES

AOL Search	http://search.aol.com
Ask.com	www.ask.com
Bing	www.bing.com
Google	www.google.ca
Yahoo! Search	http://ca.search.yahoo.com

METACRAWLERS, CLUSTERING ENGINES, AND HYBRID SITES

Bovée & Thill's Web Search	http://businesscommunicationblog.com/websearch
Dogpile	www.dogpile.com
ixquick	www.ixquick.com
MetaCrawler	www.metacrawler.com
Search.com	www.search.com
SurfWax	www.surfwax.com
TheBrain	www.thebrain.com
WebCrawler	www.webcrawler.com
ZapMeta	www.zapmeta.com

WEB DIRECTORIES AND ONLINE LIBRARIES

.dash	www.dotdash.com
Answers.com	www.answers.com
CEOExpress	http://ceoexpress.com
Internet Public Library	www.ipl.org
Library and Archives Canada	www.collectionscanada.gc.ca
Library of Congress	www.loc.gov
Library Spot	www.libraryspot.com
Online libraries	http://www.librarydir.org
Questia (requires subscription)	www.questia.com
USA.gov (U.S. government portal)	www.usa.gov

NEWS SEARCH ENGINES AND SOCIAL TAGGING SITES

10 × 10	https://10x10photographyproject.com
BoardReader	www.boardreader.com
Digg	www.digg.com
Google News	http://news.google.ca
NewsNow	www.newsnow.co.uk
Newseum	www.newseum.org
WorldNews	www.wn.com
Yahoo! News	http://ca.news.yahoo.com

BLOG, VIDEO, AND PODCAST SEARCH ENGINES AND DIRECTORIES

Alltop	www.alltop.com
American Rhetoric (speeches)	www.americanrhetoric.com
Bing videos	www.bing.com/videos
blinkx	www.blinkx.com
Google Video search	www.google.com/videohp
Podcast Alley	www.podcastalley.com
Technorati	www.technorati.com
Shop Small Biz	http://shopsmallbiz.ca
Yahoo! Video search	http://ca.video.search.yahoo.com
YouTube	www.youtube.com

PERIODICAL AND BOOK SEARCH ENGINES

Google Book search	http://books.google.com
Google Scholar search	http://scholar.google.com

information. The possibilities include subscribing to newsfeeds from blogs and websites, following people on Twitter and other microblogs, setting up alerts on search engines and online databases, and using specialized monitors such as TweetBeep (https://twitter.com/tweetbeep?lang=en) and TweetDeck (www.tweetdeck.com) to track tweets that mention specific companies or other terms.

Exercise some care when setting up monitoring tools, however, because it's easy to get overwhelmed by the flood of information. Remember that you can always go back and search your information sources if you need to gather additional information.

SEARCH TIPS Search engines, web directories, and databases work in different ways, so make sure you understand how to optimize your search and interpret the results. With a *keyword search*, the engine or database attempts to find items that include all the words you enter. A *Boolean search* lets you define a query with greater precision, using such operators as AND (the search must include two terms linked by AND), OR (it can include either or both words), or NOT (the search ignores items with whatever word comes after NOT). *Natural language searches* let you ask questions in everyday English. *Forms-based searches* help you create powerful queries by simply filling out an online form.[8]

> Search tools work in different ways, and you can get unpredictable results if you don't know how each one operates.

To make the best use of any search tool, keep the following points in mind:

- **Think before you search.** The results you get from a search engine can create the illusion that the Internet is a neatly organized warehouse of all the information in the universe, but the reality is far different. The Internet is an incomplete, unorganized hodgepodge of millions of independent websites with information that ranges in value from priceless to utter rubbish. After you have identified what you need to know, spend a few moments thinking about where that information might be found, how it might be structured, and what terms various websites might use to describe it.
- **Read the instructions and pay attention to the details.** A few minutes of learning can save hours of inefficient search time.
- **Review the search and display options carefully.** You must avoid misinterpreting the results; some kinds of settings can make a large difference in the results you see.
- **Vary your terms.** Variations of your terms, such as *adolescent* and *teenager* or *management* and *managerial*, will help you find the results you need. Also, use fewer search terms to find more results; use more search terms to find fewer results.
- **Look beyond the first page of results.** Don't assume that the highest-ranking results are the best sources for you. For example, materials that haven't been optimized for search engines won't rank as highly (meaning they won't show up in the first few pages of results), but they may be far better for your purposes.

> Before you begin searching, think about where the information you need might be located, how it might be structured, and what terms might be used to describe it.

Search technologies continue to evolve rapidly, so look for new ways to find the information you need. Some new tools search specific areas of information (such as Twitter) in better ways, whereas others approach searches in new ways. For instance, Yolink (www.yolink.com) finds webpages like a regular search engine does but then also searches through documents and webpages that are linked to those first-level results.[9]

Other powerful search tools include *desktop search engines* that search all the files on your personal computer, *enterprise search engines* that search all the computers on a company's network, *research and content managers* such as the free Zotero browser extension (www.zotero.com), and *social tagging* or *bookmarking sites* such as Digg (http://digg.com) and Delicious (http://del.icio.us).

DOCUMENTING YOUR SOURCES

Proper documentation of the sources you use is both ethical and an important resource for your readers.

Documenting your sources serves three important functions: (1) it properly and ethically credits the person who created the original material; (2) it shows your audience that you have sufficient support for your message; and (3) it helps readers explore your topic in more detail, if desired. Be sure to take advantage of the source documentation tools in your software, such as automatic endnote or footnote tracking.

Appendix B discusses the common methods of documenting sources. Whatever method you choose, documentation is necessary for books, articles, tables, charts, diagrams, song lyrics, scripted dialogue, letters, speeches—anything that you take from someone else, including ideas and information that you've presented through paraphrasing or summarizing. However, you do not have to cite a source for knowledge that's generally known among your readers, such as the fact that Facebook is a large social network or that computers are pervasive in business today.

Copyright law covers the expression of creative ideas, and copyrights can cover a wide range of materials, including reports and other documents, web content, movies, sound recordings, lectures, computer programs, and even choreographed dance routines. Copyright protection is initiated the moment the expression is put into fixed form. Copyright law does not protect such elements as titles, names, short phrases, slogans, familiar symbols, or lists of ingredients or contents. It also doesn't protect ideas, procedures, methods, systems, processes, concepts, principles, discoveries, or devices, although it does cover their description, explanation, or illustration.[10] However, many of the entities not covered under copyright law are covered under other legal protections, such as patents for devices and processes and trademarks for slogans.

Merely crediting the source is not always enough. According to the fair dealing doctrine, you can use other people's work only as long as you don't unfairly prevent them from benefiting as a result. For example, if you reproduce someone else's copyrighted questionnaire in a report you're writing, even if you identify the source thoroughly, you may be preventing the author from selling a copy of that questionnaire to your readers.

In an age when instant global connectivity makes it effortless to copy and retransmit electronic files, the protection of intellectual property has become a widespread concern. **Intellectual property (IP)** includes patents, copyrighted materials, trade secrets, and Internet domain names.[11] Bloggers need to be particularly careful about IP protection, given the carefree way that some post the work of others without offering proper credit.[12] Copyright law can be a complicated issue, so consult your company's legal department if you have any questions about material you plan to use. For general information, explore the Canadian Intellectual Property Office website (www.cipo.ic.gc.ca) and the Government of Canada publication on the topic (http://publications.gc.ca/site/eng/ccl/aboutCopyright.html).

Conducting Primary Research

4 **LEARNING OBJECTIVE**

Explain the role of primary research, and identify the two most common forms of primary research for business communication purposes.

If secondary research can't provide the information and insights you need, you may need to gather the information yourself with primary research. The two most common primary research methods are surveys and interviews. Other primary techniques are observations (including tracking the behaviour of website visitors) and experiments in special situations such as test marketing, but they're less commonly used for day-to-day business research.

CONDUCTING SURVEYS

A carefully prepared and conducted survey can provide invaluable insights but only if it is *reliable* (would produce identical results if repeated under similar conditions) and *valid* (measures what it's supposed to measure). To conduct a survey that generates reliable and valid results, you need to choose research participants carefully and develop an effective set of questions. A good research handbook can guide you through the process of selecting a sufficient number of representative participants. For important surveys on strategically important topics with a lot at stake, you're usually better off hiring a research specialist who knows how to avoid errors during planning, execution, and analysis.

When selecting people to participate in a survey, the most critical task is getting a representative *sample* of the entire population in question. For instance, if you want to know how Canadian consumers feel about something, you can't just survey a few hundred people in a shopping mall. Different types of consumers shop at different times of the day and different days of the week, and many consumers do not shop at malls. The online surveys you see on many websites today potentially suffer from the same *sampling bias*: they capture only the opinions of people who visit the sites and want to participate, which might not be a representative sample of the population. A good handbook on survey research will help you select the right people for your survey, including selecting enough people to have a statistically valid survey.[13]

To develop an effective survey questionnaire, start with the information needs you identified at the beginning of the research process. Then break these points into specific questions, choosing an appropriate type of question for each point (see Figure 11–8). The following guidelines will help you produce results that are valid and reliable:[14]

- **Provide clear instructions.** Respondents need to know exactly how to fill out your questionnaire. Entry mistakes will distort your results.

- **Don't ask for information that people can't be expected to remember.** For example, a question such as "How many times did you go grocery shopping last year" will generate unreliable answers.
- **Keep the questionnaire short and easy to answer.** Don't make any individual questions difficult to answer, and don't expect people to give you more than 10 or 15 minutes of their time.
- **Whenever possible, formulate questions to provide answers that are easy to analyze.** Numbers and facts are easier to summarize than opinions, for example.
- **Avoid leading questions that could bias your survey.** If you ask, "Do you prefer that we stay open in the evenings for customer convenience?" you'll no doubt get a "yes." Instead, ask, "What time of day do you normally do your shopping?"
- **Avoid ambiguous questions.** If you ask "Do you shop at the mall often?" some people might interpret *often* to mean "every day," whereas others might think it means "once a week" or "once a month."
- **Ask only one question at a time.** A compound question such as "Do you read books and magazines?" doesn't allow for the respondent who reads one but not the other.

Marketing surveys are a common way to gather data directly from customers. What ethical guidelines should marketers follow when interviewing subjects?

QUESTION TYPE	EXAMPLE
Open-ended	How would you describe the flavour of this ice cream?
Either-or	Do you think this ice cream is too rich? _____ Yes _____ No
Multiple-choice	Which description best fits the taste of this ice cream? (Choose only one.) a. Delicious b. Too fruity c. Too sweet d. Too intensely flavoured e. Bland f. Stale
Scale	Please mark an X on the scale to indicate how you perceive the texture of this ice cream. Too light Light Creamy Too creamy
Checklist	Which of the following ice cream brands do you recognize? (Check all that apply.) _____ Ben & Jerry's _____ Breyers _____ President's Choice _____ Chapman's _____ Häagen-Dazs
Ranking	Rank these flavours in order of your preference, from 1 (most preferred) to 5 (least preferred): _____ Vanilla _____ Cherry _____ Strawberry _____ Chocolate _____ Coconut
Short-answer	In the past two weeks, how many times did you buy ice cream in a grocery store? _____ In the past two weeks, how many times did you buy ice cream in an ice cream shop? _____

Figure 11–8 Types of Survey Questions

- **Provide respondents with even-number choices in a scale.** If you ask people to choose from 1 to 5, unless they have strong opinions, they will choose the middle number, which can skew your results or even produce results that do not provide useful information.
- **Make the survey adaptive.** With an online survey, you can program the software to branch automatically based on audience inputs. Not only does this sort of real-time adaptation deliver better answers, but it reduces frustration for survey respondents as well.[15]

You have probably noticed simple polls and surveys on many websites. Online surveys, such as the one offered by Object Planet (see Figure 11–9),

Online surveys are fast and convenient, but in order to produce meaningful data, they must be designed with the same care as offline surveys.

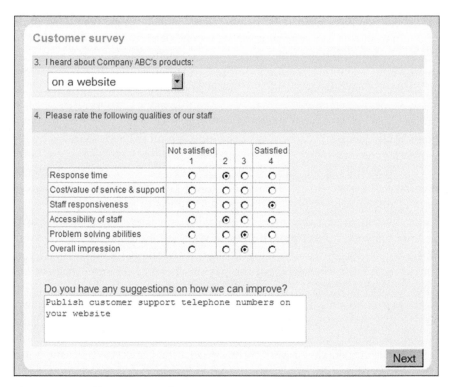

Figure 11–9 Online Survey Tools

offer a number of advantages, including speed, cost, and the ability to adapt the question set along the way based on a respondent's answers. However, to deliver reliable and valid results, they must be designed and administered as carefully as offline surveys. For example, you can't assume that the results from a survey on your company's website reflect the attitudes, beliefs, or behaviours of the population as a whole, because the visitors to your website are almost guaranteed not to be an accurate cross-section of the entire population.

CONDUCTING INTERVIEWS

Getting in-depth information straight from an expert or an individual concerned about an issue can be a valuable method for collecting primary information. Interviews can dig deeper than the "hands-off" approach of surveys, and skilled interviewers can also watch for nonverbal signals that provide additional insights. Interviews can take a variety of formats, from email exchanges to group discussions. Although interviews are relatively easy to conduct, they require careful planning to get the best results and make the best use of the other person's time. Planning an interview is similar to planning any other form of communication. You begin by analyzing your purpose, learning about the other person, and formulating your main idea. Then you decide on the length, style, and organization of the interview.

Be aware that the answers you receive in an interview are influenced by the types of questions you ask, by the way you ask them, and by each subject's cultural and language background. Potentially significant factors include the person's race, gender, age, educational level, and social status.[16]

Ask **open-ended questions** to invite the expert to offer opinions, insights, and information, such as "Why do you believe that South America represents a better opportunity than Europe for this product line?" Bear in mind that, although open-ended questions can extract significant amounts of information,

Interviews can take place online, over the phone, or in person, and they can involve individuals or groups.

Open-ended questions, which can't be answered with a simple yes or no, can provide deeper insights, opinions, and information.

they do give you less control over the interview. Someone might take 10 seconds or 10 minutes to answer a question, so plan to be flexible.

Ask **closed-ended questions** to elicit a specific answer, such as yes or no. However, including too many closed-ended questions in an interview will make the experience feel more like a simple survey and won't take full advantage of the interview setting. When you do ask a question that implies a straightforward answer, such as "Do you think we should expand distribution in South America?" explore the reasoning behind the expert's answer with follow-up questions.

Think carefully about the sequence of your questions and the subject's potential answers so you can arrange questions in an order that helps uncover layers of information. Also consider providing the other person with a list of questions at least a day or two before the interview, especially if you'd like to quote your subject in writing or if your questions might require your subject to conduct research or think extensively about the answers. If you want to record the interview, ask the person ahead of time and respect his or her wishes.

As soon as possible after the interview, take a few moments to write down your thoughts, go over your notes, and organize your material. Look for important themes, helpful facts or statistics, and direct quotes. If you made a recording, *transcribe* it (take down word for word what the person said) or take notes from the recording just as you would while listening to someone in person. Before recording, make sure you have the interviewee's permission. Some companies may require a special document with dates, times, and signatures. Others may be more informal. Check with your organization first. Protect your recording so that it is not used by someone else, and make sure it is used only for the purpose you stated to the interviewee. Software is available to help with the job of transcription. However, review the transcription for accuracy before you use it for analysis.

> *Arrange the sequence of questions to help uncover layers of information.*

TIPS FOR SUCCESS

"Good notes are invaluable. ... Don't assume you can remember everything. You'll forget 80 percent of what you hear. Have good notes to refresh your memory. They will be a lifesaver."

Linda M. Cummins, former senior vice president, Communications, ArvinMeritor, Inc.

Face-to-face interviews give you the opportunity to gauge the reaction to your questions and observe the nonverbal signals that accompany the answers, but interviews don't necessarily have to take place in person. Email interviews have become common, partly because they give subjects a chance to think through their responses thoroughly rather than rushing to fit the time constraints of a face-to-face interview.[17] Also, email interviews might be the only way you will be able to access some experts.

In addition to individual interviews, business researchers can use a form of group interview known as the **focus group**. In this format, a moderator guides a group through a series of discussion questions while the rest of the research team observes through a one-way mirror. The key advantage of focus groups is the opportunity to learn from group dynamics as the various participants bounce ideas and questions off each other. By allowing a group to discuss topics and problems in this manner, the focus group technique can uncover much richer information than a series of individual interviews.[18]

As a reminder of the tasks involved in interviews, see "Checklist: Conducting Effective Information Interviews."

Image Source/Getty Images

A successful interview requires careful planning and organization to ensure that you get the information you really need. How have you planned interviews? How can you improve your approach?

✓ Checklist	Conducting Effective Information Interviews

- Learn about the person you are going to interview.
- Formulate your main idea to ensure effective focus.
- Choose the length, style, and organization of the interview.
- Select question types to elicit the specific information you want.

- Design each question carefully to collect useful answers.
- Limit the number of questions you ask.
- Consider recording the interview if the subject permits.
- Review your notes as soon as the interview ends.

Planning Informational Reports

Informational reports provide the material that employees, managers, and others need in order to make decisions, take action, and respond to dynamic conditions inside and outside the organization. Although these reports come in dozens of particular formats, they can be grouped into four general categories:

5 **LEARNING OBJECTIVE**

Explain how to plan informational reports and website content.

Informational reports are used to monitor and control operations, to implement policies and procedures, to demonstrate compliance, and to document progress.

- **Reports to monitor and control operations.** Managers rely on a wide range of reports to see how well their companies are functioning. *Plans* establish expectations and guidelines to direct future action. Some of the most significant of these are *business plans* (see "Sharpening Your Career Skills: Creating an Effective Business Plan"). Many business plans are actually a combination of an informational report (describing conditions in the marketplace), an analytical report (analyzing threats and opportunities and recommending specific courses of action), and a proposal (persuading investors to put money into the firm in exchange for a share of ownership). *Operating reports* provide feedback on a wide variety of an organization's functions, including sales, inventories, expenses, shipments, and so on. *Personal activity reports* provide information regarding an individual's experiences during sales calls, industry conferences, market research trips, and so on.
- **Reports to implement policies and procedures.** Reports are the most common vehicle for conveying guidelines, approved procedures, and other organizational decisions. *Policy reports* range from brief descriptions of business procedures to manuals that run dozens or hundreds of pages. *Position papers*, sometimes called *white papers* or *backgrounders*, outline an organization's official position on issues that affect the company's success. Figure 11–10 explains a building access policy for a firm where many scientists work irregular hours, especially when a deadline approaches or when experiments need constant monitoring.
- **Reports to demonstrate compliance.** Businesses are required to submit a variety of *compliance reports*, from tax returns to reports that describe the proper handling of hazardous materials.
- **Reports to document progress.** Supervisors, investors, and customers frequently expect to be informed of the status of projects and other activities. *Progress reports* range from simple updates in memo form to comprehensive status reports.

ORGANIZING INFORMATIONAL REPORTS

In most cases, the direct approach is the best choice for informational reports. However, if the information is both surprising and disappointing, such as a project that is behind schedule or over budget, you might consider using the

The messages conveyed by informational reports can range from extremely positive to extremely negative, so the approach you take warrants careful consideration.

The report begins with ample introductory and background information, since this is a special policy report.

Headings establish topics and emphasize major points.

DIGI-OPTIC
RESEARCH

BUILDING ACCESS PROCEDURES

PURPOSE

The nature of our business demands a balance between free access to lab facilities and security for both equipment and information. One of the implications of our success in recent years is a dramatic increase in the number of employees, so much so that we can no longer rely on an informal approach to security. We've designed this new program to minimize the burden on employees while maximizing security. The program involves four elements:

- Photo ID badges for all employees
- A building access checkpoint
- A procedure for reporting unauthorized or suspicious entry
- Policies regarding personal guests and professional visitors

Employee ID Badges

To make personnel identification both easy and accurate, each employee will be issued a photo ID badge that must be worn at all times while in the building. The Human Resources department will arrange photo sessions for all current employees. Badges for future new hires will be made during the new employee orientation session.

Access Checkpoint

During normal working hours, 8:00 a.m. to 5:00 p.m. Monday through Friday, all employees will enter the building through the front door. Employees must show their photo ID badge to the receptionist before entering the lab.

For access after hours, all department heads will identify which employees need to enter the building outside normal working hours. A list of these employees will be kept at the receptionist's desk. After hours and on weekends the desk will be manned by a security guard. Each employee wanting to enter the building must show the guard a valid company ID card and must be included on the authorization list. If the employee is not on the list, the security guard will deny access.

Reporting Unauthorized or Suspicious Entry

We all stand to benefit from improved security, so the company considers it everyone's responsibility to watch for and report unauthorized or suspicious entry to the building.

The report follows the format used in the company's policy and procedures manual.

The list emphasizes the important elements of the policy, as well as the steps in the procedure.

Figure 11–10 Building an Access Policy (excerpt)

indirect approach to build up to the bad news. Most informational reports use a **topical organization**, arranging material in one of the following ways:

- **Comparison.** If you need to show similarities and differences (or advantages and disadvantages) between two or more entities, organize your report in a way that helps your readers see those similarities and differences clearly.
- **Importance.** Build up from the least important item to most important if you expect that the audience will read the entire report, or start with the most important item and progress to the least important if you suspect the readers are interested in only the more important items.
- **Sequence.** Any information that concerns a process or procedure is a good candidate for organizing by sequence. Discuss the steps or stages in the order in which they occur.
- **Chronology.** Describe a development or an event by the order in which incidents occurred. For example, when discussing a sales trend over time,

you can organize the study according to what happened in January, what happened in February, and so on.

- **Geography.** If location is important, organize your study according to geography, perhaps by region of the world or by area of a city.
- **Category.** If you're asked to review several distinct aspects of a subject, look at one category at a time, such as sales, profit, cost, or investment.

Whichever pattern you choose, use it consistently so that readers can easily follow your discussion from start to finish. Bear in mind, however, that in many instances, you might be expected to follow a particular type of organization.

SHARPENING YOUR CAREER SKILLS | Creating an Effective Business Plan

The most important report you may ever get the chance to write is a business plan for a new or growing young company. A comprehensive business plan forces you to think about personnel, marketing, facilities, suppliers, distribution, and a host of other issues that are vital to your success. If you are starting out on a small scale and using your own money, your business plan may be relatively informal. But at a minimum, you should describe the basic concept of the business and outline its specific goals, objectives, and resource requirements. A formal plan, suitable for use with banks or investors, should cover these points:

- **Summary.** In one or two paragraphs, summarize your business concept, particularly the *business model*, which defines how the company will generate revenue and produce a profit. The summary must be compelling, catching the investor's attention and giving him or her reasons to keep reading. Describe your product or service and its market potential. Highlight some things about your company and its leaders that will distinguish your firm from the competition. Summarize your financial projections, and indicate how much money you will need from investors or lenders and where it will be spent.
- **Mission and objectives.** Explain the purpose of your business and what you hope to accomplish.
- **Company and industry.** Give full background information on the origins and structure of your venture and the characteristics of its industry.
- **Products or services.** Give a complete but concise description of your products or services, focusing on their unique attributes.
- **Market and competition.** Provide data that will persuade investors that you understand your target market and can achieve your sales goals. Be sure to identify the strengths and weaknesses of your competitors.
- **Management.** Summarize the background and qualifications of the key management personnel in your company. Include résumés in an appendix.

- **Marketing strategy.** Provide projections of sales and market share and outline a strategy for identifying and contacting customers, setting prices, providing customer services, advertising, and so forth. Whenever possible, include evidence of customer acceptance, such as advance product orders.
- **Design and development plans.** If your product requires design or development, describe the nature and extent of what needs to be done, including costs and possible problems.
- **Operations plan.** Provide information on facilities, equipment, and personnel requirements.
- **Overall schedule.** Forecast important milestones in the company's growth and development, including when you need to be fully staffed and when your products will be ready for the market.
- **Critical risks and problems.** Identify all negative factors and discuss them honestly.
- **Financial projections and requirements.** Include a detailed budget of start-up and operating costs, as well as projections for income, expenses, and cash flow for the first three years of business. Identify the company's financing needs and potential sources, if appropriate.
- **Exit strategy.** Explain how investors will be able to cash out or sell their investment, such as through a public stock offering, sale of the company, or a buyback of the investors' interest.

A complete business plan obviously requires a considerable amount of work. However, by thinking your way through all these issues, you'll enjoy a smoother launch and a greater chance of success in your new adventure.

CAREER APPLICATIONS

1. Why is it important to identify critical risks and problems in a business plan?
2. Many experts suggest that you write a business plan yourself rather than hire a consultant to write it for you. Why is this a good idea?

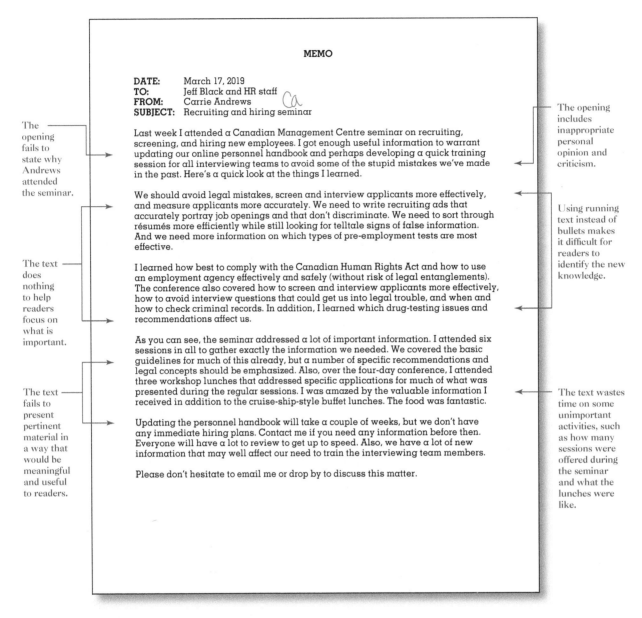

The opening fails to state why Andrews attended the seminar.

The text does nothing to help readers focus on what is important.

The text fails to present pertinent material in a way that would be meaningful and useful to readers.

The opening includes inappropriate personal opinion and criticism.

Using running text instead of bullets makes it difficult for readers to identify the new knowledge.

The text wastes time on some unimportant activities, such as how many sessions were offered during the seminar and what the lunches were like.

MEMO

DATE: March 17, 2019
TO: Jeff Black and HR staff
FROM: Carrie Andrews
SUBJECT: Recruiting and hiring seminar

Last week I attended a Canadian Management Centre seminar on recruiting, screening, and hiring new employees. I got enough useful information to warrant updating our online personnel handbook and perhaps developing a quick training session for all interviewing teams to avoid some of the stupid mistakes we've made in the past. Here's a quick look at the things I learned.

We should avoid legal mistakes, screen and interview applicants more effectively, and measure applicants more accurately. We need to write recruiting ads that accurately portray job openings and that don't discriminate. We need to sort through résumés more efficiently while still looking for telltale signs of false information. And we need more information on which types of pre-employment tests are most effective.

I learned how best to comply with the Canadian Human Rights Act and how to use an employment agency effectively and safely (without risk of legal entanglements). The conference also covered how to screen and interview applicants more effectively, how to avoid interview questions that could get us into legal trouble, and when and how to check criminal records. In addition, I learned which drug-testing issues and recommendations affect us.

As you can see, the seminar addressed a lot of important information. I attended six sessions in all to gather exactly the information we needed. We covered the basic guidelines for much of this already, but a number of specific recommendations and legal concepts should be emphasized. Also, over the four-day conference, I attended three workshop lunches that addressed specific applications for much of what was presented during the regular sessions. I was amazed by the valuable information I received in addition to the cruise-ship-style buffet lunches. The food was fantastic.

Updating the personnel handbook will take a couple of weeks, but we don't have any immediate hiring plans. Contact me if you need any information before then. Everyone will have a lot to review to get up to speed. Also, we have a lot of new information that may well affect our need to train the interviewing team members.

Please don't hesitate to email me or drop by to discuss this matter.

Figure 11–11 Ineffective Informational Report

Of course, effective informational reports must also be audience centred, logical, focused, and easy to follow, with generous use of previews and summaries. Your audience expects you to sort out the details and separate major points from minor points. In other words, readers expect you to put in all the thought and effort it takes to make the best use of their time.

Compare the two versions of the personal activity report in Figure 11–11 and Figure 11–12. At a quick glance, Figure 11–11 may seem to do a good job of meeting audience needs, but this report has a number of weaknesses that distract from the writer's intent and make readers struggle to extract the main points. The version of the report in Figure 11–12 is much easier to read and presents pertinent information in a clear, concise way.

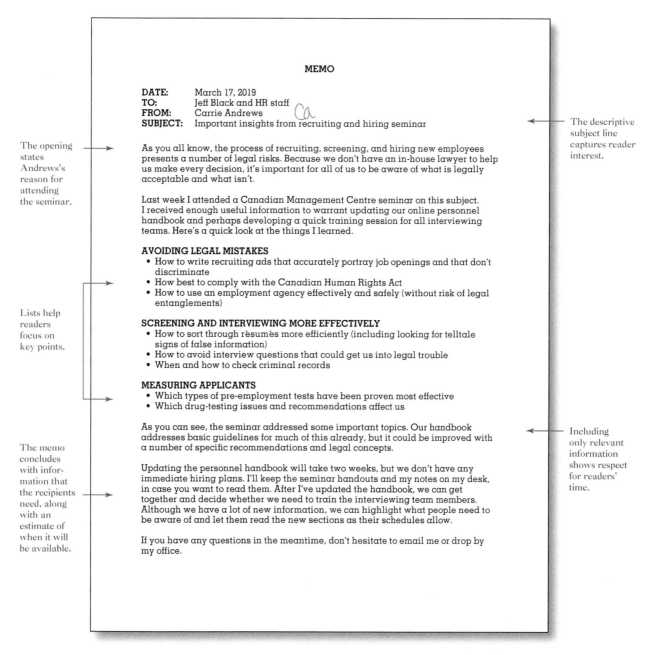

The opening states Andrews's reason for attending the seminar.

The descriptive subject line captures reader interest.

Lists help readers focus on key points.

The memo concludes with information that the recipients need, along with an estimate of when it will be available.

Including only relevant information shows respect for readers' time.

Figure 11–12 Effective Informational Report

ORGANIZING WEBSITE CONTENT

Many websites, particularly company websites, function as informational reports, offering sections with information about the company, its history, its products and services, its executive team, and so on. While most of what you've already learned about informational reports applies to website writing, the online experience requires some special considerations and practices.

As you begin to plan a website, start by recognizing the unique nature of online communication:

- **Web readers are demanding.** If site visitors can't find what they're looking for in a matter of minutes, they'll leave and look elsewhere.[19]

When planning online reports or other website content, remember that the online reading experience differs from offline reading in several important ways.

Like many corporate websites, the site of Canadian National Railway (CNR) has to accommodate the needs of a wide variety of visitors looking for different types of data. Has CNR grouped information to minimize the number of clicks required to access desired pages? How is this goal achieved?

- **Reading online can be difficult.** Studies show that reading speeds are about 25 percent slower on a monitor than on paper.[20] Reading from computer screens can also be tiring on the eyes, even to the point of causing headaches, double vision, blurred vision, and other physical problems.[21]
- **The Web is a nonlinear, multidimensional medium.** Readers of online material move around in any order they please; there often is no beginning, middle, or end. As a web writer, you need to anticipate the various paths your readers will want to follow and to make sure you provide the right hyperlinks in the right places to help readers explore successfully.

The *information architecture* of a website is the equivalent of the outline for a paper report, but it tends to be much more complicated than a simple linear outline.

Many websites have multiple audiences and multiple communication functions, so planning websites is more challenging than planning printed reports. Professional website designers often use the term **information architecture** to describe the structure and navigational flow of all the parts of a website. In a sense, the information architecture is a three-dimensional outline of the site, showing (1) the vertical hierarchy of pages from the home page down to the lower level, (2) the horizontal division of pages across the various sections of the site, and (3) the links that tie all these pages together, both internally (between various pages on the site) and externally (between your site and other websites).

To organize your site effectively, keep the following advice in mind:

- **Plan your site structure and navigation before you write.** Don't make the mistake of writing a traditional printed report and then adding links to make it a website. Most likely, you will need a different structure for the information, so plan your site structure and navigation before you write.[22]
- **Let your readers be in control.** Most readers want to navigate using paths they establish themselves, so create links and pathways that let them explore on their own. Help your readers by starting with a home page that clearly points the way to various sections of the site, and then offer plenty of descriptive labels, subheads, and previews that let readers figure out where to go next.
- **Break your information into chunks.** Help online readers scan and absorb information by breaking it into self-contained, easily readable chunks that are linked together logically.

Courtesy: CN Rail

Planning Analytical Reports

The purpose of analytical reports is to analyze, to understand, to explain—to think through a problem or an opportunity and figure out how it affects the company and how the company should respond. In many cases, you'll also be expected to make a recommendation based on your analysis. As you saw in Figure 11–1, analytical reports fall into three basic categories:

6 **LEARNING OBJECTIVE**

Describe the three most common ways to organize analytical reports.

- **Reports to assess opportunities.** Every business opportunity carries some degree of risk and also requires a variety of decisions and actions in order to capitalize on the opportunity. You can use analytical reports to assess risk and required decisions and actions. For instance, *market analysis reports* are used to judge the likelihood of success for new products or sales. *Due diligence reports* examine the financial aspects of a proposed decision, such as acquiring another company.
- **Reports to solve problems.** Managers often ask for *troubleshooting reports* when they need to understand why something isn't working properly and what needs to be done to fix it. A variation, the *failure analysis report*, studies events that happened in the past, with the hope of learning how to avoid similar failures in the future.
- **Reports to support decisions.** *Feasibility reports* are called for when managers need to explore the ramifications of a decision they're about to make, such as switching materials used in a manufacturing process. *Justification reports* explain a decision that has already been made.

Analytical reports are used to assess opportunities, to solve problems, and to support decisions.

Writing analytical reports presents a greater challenge than writing informational reports because you need to use your reasoning abilities and persuasive skills in addition to your writing skills. With analytical reports, you're doing more than simply delivering information: you're also thinking through a problem or an opportunity and presenting your conclusions in a compelling and persuasive manner. Finally, because analytical reports often convince other people to make significant financial and personnel decisions, your reports carry the added responsibility of the consequences of these decisions.

To help define the problem that your analytical report will address, answer these questions:

- What needs to be determined?
- Why is this issue important?
- Who is involved in the situation?
- Where is the trouble located?
- How did the situation originate?
- When did it start?

Not all of these questions apply in every situation, but asking them helps you define the problem being addressed and limits the scope of your discussion.

Break down the perceived problem into a series of logical, connected questions that identify cause and effect. This process is sometimes called **problem factoring**. You probably subconsciously approach most problems this way, identifying cause-and-effect relationships that might pinpoint the source of the problem. When you speculate on the cause of a problem, you're forming a **hypothesis**, a potential explanation that needs to be tested. By subdividing a problem and forming hypotheses based on available evidence, you can tackle even the most complex situations.

Problem factoring is the process of breaking a problem down into smaller questions to help identify causes and effects.

As with all other business messages, the best organizational structure for each analytical report depends largely on your audience's likely reaction. The

Before you choose an approach, determine whether your audience is receptive or skeptical.

three basic structures involve focusing on conclusions, focusing on recommendations, and focusing on logic.

FOCUSING ON CONCLUSIONS

Focusing on conclusions is often the best approach when you're addressing a receptive audience.

When writing for audiences that are likely to accept your conclusions—either because they've asked you to perform an analysis or they trust your judgment—consider using a direct approach that focuses immediately on your conclusions. This structure communicates the main idea quickly, but it presents some risks. Even if audiences trust your judgment, they may have questions about your data or the methods you used. Moreover, starting with the conclusion may create the impression that you have oversimplified the situation. To give readers the opportunity to explore the thinking behind your conclusion, support that conclusion with solid reasoning and evidence. Figure 11–13 presents an outline of a report analyzing the success of an outsourced training program. The writer opened with the conclusion but supported it with clear evidence, not personal opinion. Readers who accept the conclusion can stop reading, and those who desire more information can continue.

FOCUSING ON RECOMMENDATIONS

When readers want to know what you think they should do, organize your report to focus on recommendations.

A slightly different approach is useful when your readers want to know what they ought to do in a given situation (as opposed to what they ought to conclude). You'll often be asked to solve a problem or assess an opportunity, rather than just study it. The actions you want your readers to take become the main subdivisions of your report.

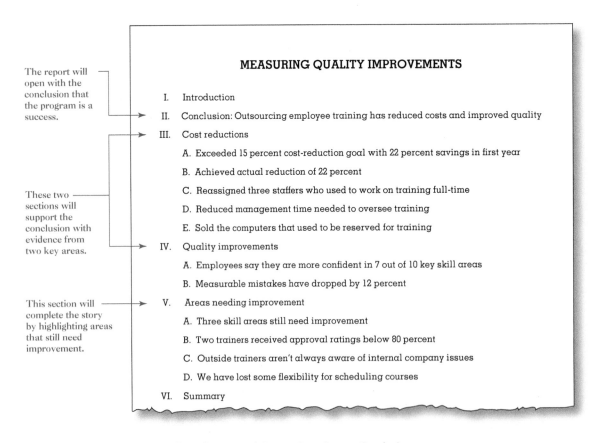

The report will open with the conclusion that the program is a success.

These two sections will support the conclusion with evidence from two key areas.

This section will complete the story by highlighting areas that still need improvement.

MEASURING QUALITY IMPROVEMENTS

I.   Introduction

II. Conclusion: Outsourcing employee training has reduced costs and improved quality

III. Cost reductions

    A. Exceeded 15 percent cost-reduction goal with 22 percent savings in first year

    B. Achieved actual reduction of 22 percent

    C. Reassigned three staffers who used to work on training full-time

    D. Reduced management time needed to oversee training

    E. Sold the computers that used to be reserved for training

IV. Quality improvements

    A. Employees say they are more confident in 7 out of 10 key skill areas

    B. Measurable mistakes have dropped by 12 percent

V.   Areas needing improvement

    A. Three skill areas still need improvement

    B. Two trainers received approval ratings below 80 percent

    C. Outside trainers aren't always aware of internal company issues

    D. We have lost some flexibility for scheduling courses

VI. Summary

Figure 11–13 Preliminary Outline of a Research Report Focusing on Conclusions

When structuring a report around recommendations, use the direct approach as you would for a report that focuses on conclusions. Then, unfold your recommendations using a series of five steps:

1. Establish the need for action in the introduction by briefly describing the problem or opportunity.
2. Introduce the benefit(s) that can be achieved if the recommendation is adopted, along with any potential risks.
3. List the steps (recommendations) required to achieve the benefit, using action verbs for emphasis.
4. Explain each step more fully, giving details on procedures, costs, and benefits; if necessary, also explain how risks can be minimized.
5. Summarize your recommendations.

FOCUSING ON LOGICAL ARGUMENTS

When readers are skeptical or hostile to the conclusion or recommendation you plan to make, use an indirect approach that logically builds toward your conclusion or recommendation. If you guide the audience along a rational path toward the answer, they are more likely to accept it when they encounter it. The two most common logical approaches are known as the *2 + 2 = 4 approach* and the *yardstick approach* (see Table 11–7).

THE 2 + 2 = 4 APPROACH The **2 + 2 = 4 approach** is so named because it convinces readers of your point of view by demonstrating that everything adds up. The main points in your outline are the main reasons behind your conclusions and recommendations. You support each reason with the evidence you collected during your analysis. With its natural feel and versatility, the $2 + 2 = 4$ approach is generally the most persuasive and efficient way to develop an analytical report for skeptical readers, so try this structure first. You'll find that most of your arguments fall naturally into this pattern.

As national sales manager of a sporting goods company, Binh Phan was concerned about his firm's ability to sell to its largest customers. His boss, the vice president of marketing, shared these concerns and instructed Phan to analyze the situation and recommend a solution.

Phan's troubleshooting report appears in Figure 11–14. The main idea is that the company should establish separate sales teams for these major accounts,

Logical arguments can follow two basic approaches: 2 + 2 = 4 (adding everything up) and the yardstick method (comparing ideas against a predetermined set of standards).

Table 11–7	**Common Ways to Structure Analytical Reports**		
	Focus on Conclusions or Recommendations	**FOCUS ON LOGICAL ARGUMENT**	
Element		**Use 2 + 2 = 4 Model**	**Use Yardstick Model**
Readers	Are likely to accept	Hostile or skeptical	Hostile or skeptical
Approach	Direct	Indirect	Indirect
Writer credibility	High	Low	Low
Advantages	Readers quickly grasp conclusions or recommendations	Works well when you need to show readers how you built toward an answer by following clear, logical steps	Works well when you have a list of criteria (standards) that must be considered in a decision; alternatives are all measured against same criteria
Drawbacks	Structure can make topic seem too simple	Can make report longer	Readers must agree on criteria; can be lengthy because of the need to address each criterion for every alternative

rather than continuing to service them through the company's four regional divisions. However, Phan knew his plan would be controversial because it required a big change in the company's organization and in the way sales reps are paid. His thinking had to be clear and easy to follow, so he used the $2 + 2 = 4$ approach to focus on his reasons.

THE YARDSTICK APPROACH The **yardstick approach** is useful when you need to use a number of criteria to decide which option to select from two or more possibilities. With this approach, you begin by discussing the problem or opportunity, and then you list the criteria that will guide the decision. The body of the report then evaluates the alternatives against those criteria.

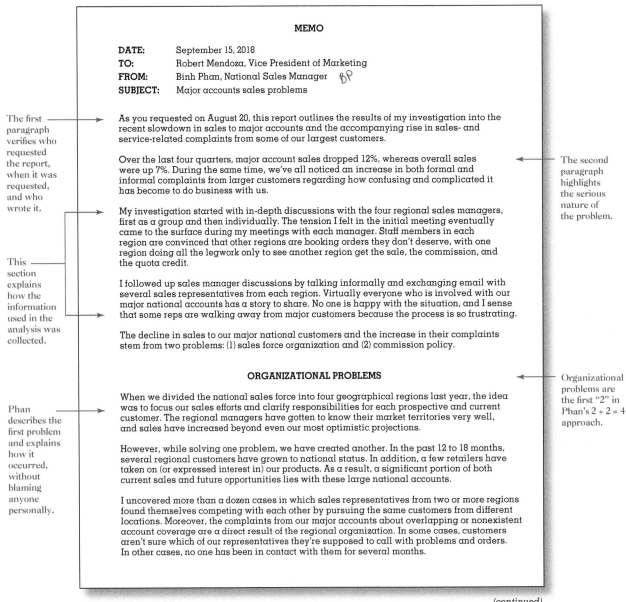

The first paragraph verifies who requested the report, when it was requested, and who wrote it.

This section explains how the information used in the analysis was collected.

Phan describes the first problem and explains how it occurred, without blaming anyone personally.

The second paragraph highlights the serious nature of the problem.

Organizational problems are the first "2" in Phan's $2 + 2 = 4$ approach.

MEMO

DATE: September 15, 2018
TO: Robert Mendoza, Vice President of Marketing
FROM: Binh Phan, National Sales Manager   BP
SUBJECT: Major accounts sales problems

As you requested on August 20, this report outlines the results of my investigation into the recent slowdown in sales to major accounts and the accompanying rise in sales- and service-related complaints from some of our largest customers.

Over the last four quarters, major account sales dropped 12%, whereas overall sales were up 7%. During the same time, we've all noticed an increase in both formal and informal complaints from larger customers regarding how confusing and complicated it has become to do business with us.

My investigation started with in-depth discussions with the four regional sales managers, first as a group and then individually. The tension I felt in the initial meeting eventually came to the surface during my meetings with each manager. Staff members in each region are convinced that other regions are booking orders they don't deserve, with one region doing all the legwork only to see another region get the sale, the commission, and the quota credit.

I followed up sales manager discussions by talking informally and exchanging email with several sales representatives from each region. Virtually everyone who is involved with our major national accounts has a story to share. No one is happy with the situation, and I sense that some reps are walking away from major customers because the process is so frustrating.

The decline in sales to our major national customers and the increase in their complaints stem from two problems: (1) sales force organization and (2) commission policy.

ORGANIZATIONAL PROBLEMS

When we divided the national sales force into four geographical regions last year, the idea was to focus our sales efforts and clarify responsibilities for each prospective and current customer. The regional managers have gotten to know their market territories very well, and sales have increased beyond even our most optimistic projections.

However, while solving one problem, we have created another. In the past 12 to 18 months, several regional customers have grown to national status. In addition, a few retailers have taken on (or expressed interest in) our products. As a result, a significant portion of both current sales and future opportunities lies with these large national accounts.

I uncovered more than a dozen cases in which sales representatives from two or more regions found themselves competing with each other by pursuing the same customers from different locations. Moreover, the complaints from our major accounts about overlapping or nonexistent account coverage are a direct result of the regional organization. In some cases, customers aren't sure which of our representatives they're supposed to call with problems and orders. In other cases, no one has been in contact with them for several months.

(continued)

Figure 11–14 Analytical Report Using the $2 + 2 = 4$ Approach

2

Phan brings the first problem to life by complementing the general description with a specific example.

An example should help illustrate the problem. CanSport, with retail outlets in the Maritimes and on the west coast, was being pitched by reps from our West, Central, and East regions. Because we give our regional offices a lot of negotiating freedom, the three reps were offering the client different prices. But all of CanSport's buying decisions are made at their headquarters in Montreal, so all we did was confuse the customer. A critical problem with the current organization is that we're often giving our weakest selling and support efforts to the largest customers in the country.

COMMISSION PROBLEMS

Commission problems are the second "2" in Phan's 2 + 2 = 4 approach.

He simplifies the reader's task by maintaining a parallel structure for the discussion of the second problem: a general description followed by a specific example.

The regional organization problems are compounded by the way we assign commissions and quota credit. Salespeople in one region can invest a lot of time in pursuing a sale, only to have the customer place the order in another region. So some sales rep in the second region ends up with the commission on a sale that was partly or even entirely earned by someone in the first region. Therefore, sales reps sometimes don't pursue leads in their regions, thinking that a rep in another region will get the commission.

For example, Athletic Express, with outlets in four provinces spread across all four regions, finally got so frustrated with us that the company president called our headquarters. Athletic Express has been trying to place a large order for tennis and golf accessories, but none of our local reps seem interested in paying attention. I spoke with the rep responsible for Winnipeg, where the company is headquartered, and asked her why she wasn't working the account more actively. Her explanation was that last time she got involved with Athletic Express, the order was actually placed from their Vancouver regional office, and she didn't get any commission after more than two weeks of selling time.

RECOMMENDATIONS

Phan concludes the 2 + 2 = 4 approach: organizational problems + commission problems = the need for a new sales structure.

He explains how the new organizational structure will solve both problems.

Our sales organization should reflect the nature of our customer base. To accomplish that goal, we need a group of reps who are free to pursue accounts across regional borders—and who are compensated fairly for their work. The most sensible answer is to establish a national account group. Any customers whose operations place them in more than one region would automatically be assigned to the national group.

He acknowledges that the recommended solution does create a temporary compensation problem, but expresses confidence that a solution to that can be worked out.

In addition to solving the problem of competing sales efforts, the new structure will also largely eliminate the commission-splitting problem because regional reps will no longer invest time in prospects assigned to the national accounts team. However, we will need to find a fair way to compensate regional reps who are losing long-term customers to the national team. Some of these reps have invested years in developing customer relationships that will continue to yield sales well into the future, and everyone I talked to agrees that reps in these cases should receive some sort of compensation. Such a "transition commission" would also motivate the regional reps to help ensure a smooth transition from one sales group to the other. The exact nature of this compensation would need to be worked out with the various sales managers.

3

SUMMARY

The summary concisely restates both the problem and the recommended solution.

The regional sales organization is effective at the regional and local levels but not at the national level. We should establish a national accounts group to handle sales that cross regional boundaries. Then we'll have one set of reps who are focused on the local and regional levels and another set who are pursuing national accounts.

To compensate regional reps who lose accounts to the national team, we will need to devise some sort of payment to reward them for the years of work invested in such accounts. This can be discussed with the sales managers once the new structure is in place.

Figure 11–14 Analytical Report Using the 2 + 2 = 4 Approach *(continued)*

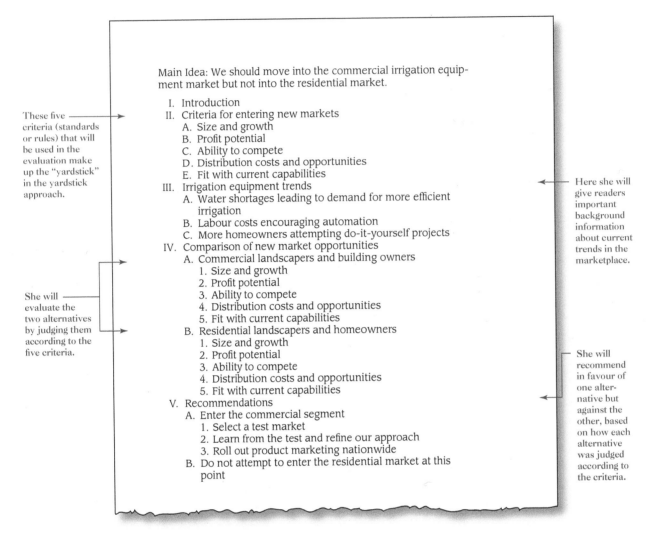

These five criteria (standards or rules) that will be used in the evaluation make up the "yardstick" in the yardstick approach.

She will evaluate the two alternatives by judging them according to the five criteria.

Main Idea: We should move into the commercial irrigation equipment market but not into the residential market.

I. Introduction
II. Criteria for entering new markets
   A. Size and growth
   B. Profit potential
   C. Ability to compete
   D. Distribution costs and opportunities
   E. Fit with current capabilities
III. Irrigation equipment trends
   A. Water shortages leading to demand for more efficient irrigation
   B. Labour costs encouraging automation
   C. More homeowners attempting do-it-yourself projects
IV. Comparison of new market opportunities
   A. Commercial landscapers and building owners
      1. Size and growth
      2. Profit potential
      3. Ability to compete
      4. Distribution costs and opportunities
      5. Fit with current capabilities
   B. Residential landscapers and homeowners
      1. Size and growth
      2. Profit potential
      3. Ability to compete
      4. Distribution costs and opportunities
      5. Fit with current capabilities
V. Recommendations
   A. Enter the commercial segment
      1. Select a test market
      2. Learn from the test and refine our approach
      3. Roll out product marketing nationwide
   B. Do not attempt to enter the residential market at this point

Here she will give readers important background information about current trends in the marketplace.

She will recommend in favour of one alternative but against the other, based on how each alternative was judged according to the criteria.

Figure 11–15 Outline of an Analytical Report Using the Yardstick Approach

Figure 11–15 is an outline of a feasibility report that uses the yardstick approach, using five criteria to evaluate two alternative courses of action. The report was provided by a market analyst for a large company that makes irrigation equipment for farms and ranches. Because the company was successful in the agricultural market, it started to run out of customers. To keep the company growing, the firm needed to find another market. Two alternatives considered were commercial buildings and residences. The author of the report was determined to make careful recommendations because, even though she didn't make the final decision, the information and the professional opinions that she provided weighed heavily on the decision process.

The yardstick approach has two potential drawbacks. First, your audience needs to agree with the criteria you're using in your analysis. If they don't, they won't agree with the results of the evaluation. If you have any doubt about their agreement, build consensus before you start your report, if possible, or take extra care to explain why the criteria you're using are the best ones in this particular case. Second, the yardstick approach can get a little boring when you have many options to consider or many criteria to compare them against. One way to minimize the repetition is to compare the options in tables and then highlight the most unusual or important aspects of each alternative in the text so that you get the best of both worlds. This approach allows you to compare all the alternatives against the same yardstick while calling attention to the most significant differences among them.

Planning Proposals

The specific formats for proposals are innumerable, but they can be grouped into two general categories. *Internal proposals* request decisions from managers within the organization, such as proposals to buy new equipment or launch new research projects. *External proposals* request decisions from parties outside the organization. Examples of external proposals include *investment proposals*, which request funding from external investors; *grant proposals*, which request funds from government agencies and other sponsoring organizations; and *sales proposals*, which suggest individualized solutions for potential customers and request purchase decisions.

7 **LEARNING OBJECTIVE**

Explain how to plan proposals.

The most significant factor in planning a proposal is whether the recipient has asked you to submit a proposal. *Solicited proposals* are generally prepared at the request of external parties that require a product or a service, but they may also be requested by such internal sources as management or the board of directors. To solicit proposals from potential suppliers, an organization might prepare a formal invitation to bid, called a **request for proposal (RFP)**, which includes instructions that specify exactly the type of work to be performed or products to be delivered, along with budgets, deadlines, and other requirements. Suppose that a municipal transit commission wants to purchase new, accessible buses to improve service for their elderly and physically challenged customers. Companies then respond by preparing proposals that show how they would meet the requirements spelled out in the RFP. In most cases, organizations that issue RFPs also provide strict guidelines on what the proposals should include, and you need to follow these guidelines carefully in order to be considered.

The best strategy for a proposal depends on whether it is unsolicited or solicited.

Unsolicited proposals offer more flexibility but a completely different sort of challenge than solicited proposals because recipients aren't expecting to receive them. In fact, your audience may not be aware of the problem or opportunity you are addressing, so before you can propose a solution, you might first need to convince your readers that a problem or an opportunity exists. Consequently, using an indirect approach is often a wise choice for unsolicited proposals.

Regardless of its format and structure, a good proposal explains what a project or course of action will involve, how much it will cost, and how the recipient and his or her organization will benefit. You can see all these elements in Figure 11–16, Shandel Cohen's internal proposal for an automatic email response system that would replace a labour-intensive process of mailing out printed brochures every time a potential customer requests information.

Cohen manages the customer-response section of the marketing department at a personal computer manufacturer. Her section sends out product information requested by customers and the field sales force. Cohen has observed that the demand for information increases when a new product is released and that it diminishes as a product matures. This fluctuating demand causes drastic changes in her section's workload. Employees either have more work than they can handle, or they don't have enough to keep consistently busy. A cycle of layoffs and hiring was not a desired option. Cohen is also concerned about the amount of printed material that's discarded when products are upgraded or replaced.

MEMO

DATE: July 8, 2019
TO: Jamie Engle
FROM: Shandel Cohen
SUBJECT: Saving $145k/year with an automated email response system

A subject line with a compelling promise catches the reader's attention.

THE PROBLEM:
Expensive and Slow Response to Customer Information Requests

Our new product line has been well received, and orders have surpassed our projections. This very success, however, has created a shortage of printed brochures, as well as considerable overtime for people in the customer response centre. As we introduce upgrades and new options, our printed materials quickly become outdated. If we continue to rely on printed materials for customer information, we have two choices: Distribute existing materials (even though they are incomplete or inaccurate), or discard existing materials and print new ones.

"The Problem" describes the current situation and explains why it should be fixed.

THE SOLUTION:
Automated Email Response System

With minor additions and modifications to our current email system, we can set up an automated system to respond to customer requests for information. This system can save us time and money and can keep our distributed information current.

Automated email response systems have been tested and proven effective. Many companies already use this method to respond to customer information requests, so we will be relying on established technology. Using the system is easy, too: Customers simply send a blank email message to a specific address, and the system responds by sending an electronic copy of the requested brochure.

"The Solution" explains the proposed solution in enough detail to make it convincing, without burdening the reader with excessive detail.

Benefit #1: Always-Current Information

Rather than discard and print new materials, we would need to keep only the electronic files up to date on the server. We could be able to provide customers and our field sales organization with up-to-date, correct information as soon as the upgrades or options are available.

Listing a number of compelling benefits as subheadings builds reader interest in the proposed solution.

Benefit #2: Instantaneous Delivery

Almost immediately after requesting information, customers would have that information in hand. Electronic delivery would be especially advantageous for our international customers. Regular mail to remote locations sometimes takes weeks to arrive, by which time the information may already be out of date. Both customers and field salespeople will appreciate the automatic mail-response system.

Benefit #3: Minimized Waste

With our current method of printing every marketing piece in large quantities, we discard thousands of pages of obsolete catalogues, data sheets, and other materials every year. By maintaining and distributing the information electronically, we would eliminate this waste. We would also free up a considerable amount of expensive floor space and shelving that is required for storing printed materials.

(continued)

Figure 11–16 An Internal Proposal

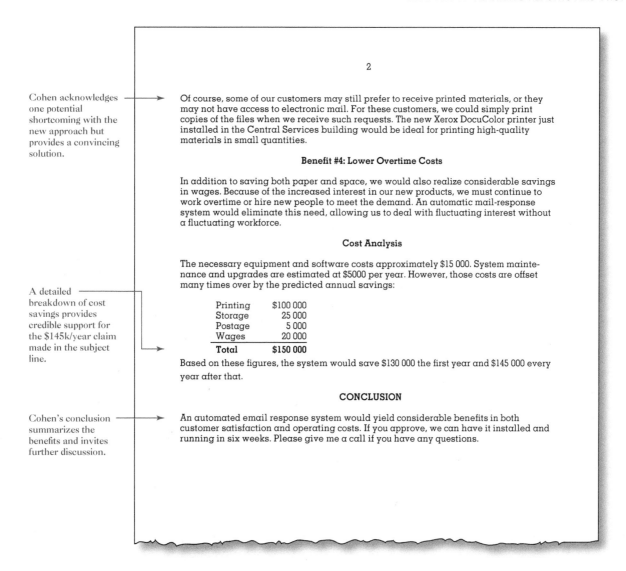

Cohen acknowledges one potential shortcoming with the new approach but provides a convincing solution.

2

Of course, some of our customers may still prefer to receive printed materials, or they may not have access to electronic mail. For these customers, we could simply print copies of the files when we receive such requests. The new Xerox DocuColor printer just installed in the Central Services building would be ideal for printing high-quality materials in small quantities.

Benefit #4: Lower Overtime Costs

In addition to saving both paper and space, we would also realize considerable savings in wages. Because of the increased interest in our new products, we must continue to work overtime or hire new people to meet the demand. An automatic mail-response system would eliminate this need, allowing us to deal with fluctuating interest without a fluctuating workforce.

Cost Analysis

The necessary equipment and software costs approximately $15 000. System mainte-nance and upgrades are estimated at $5000 per year. However, those costs are offset many times over by the predicted annual savings:

A detailed breakdown of cost savings provides credible support for the $145k/year claim made in the subject line.

Printing	$100 000
Storage	25 000
Postage	5 000
Wages	20 000
Total	**$150 000**

Based on these figures, the system would save $130 000 the first year and $145 000 every year after that.

CONCLUSION

Cohen's conclusion summarizes the benefits and invites further discussion.

An automated email response system would yield considerable benefits in both customer satisfaction and operating costs. If you approve, we can have it installed and running in six weeks. Please give me a call if you have any questions.

Figure 11–16 An Internal Proposal *(continued)*

SUMMARY OF LEARNING OBJECTIVES

1 Distinguish between informational reports, analytical reports, and proposals. Informational reports focus on facts and are intended mainly to inform and educate readers, not to persuade them. Informational reports include those for monitoring and controlling operations (plans, operating reports, and personal activity reports), implementing policies and procedures (guidelines or position papers), demonstrating compliance (reports to regulators), and documenting progress. Analytical reports analyze and interpret data and may make recommendations based on the data. Many analytical reports are intended to persuade readers to accept a decision, action, or recommendation. Troubleshooting, failure analysis, feasibility, and justification reports are examples of analytical reports. Propos-als persuade readers to make decisions and take action;

proposals may be internal (funding and project proposals) or external (investment, grant, and sales proposals).

2 Describe an effective process for conducting business research, and explain how to evaluate the credibility of an information source. To plan your research effec-tively, develop a problem statement that defines the pur-pose of the research. Identify gaps in your information to help you use your time well. Locate data and information, and evaluate your sources by determining such qualities as honesty and reliability, potential bias, author credibility, currency, and completeness.

3 Explain the role of secondary research, and describe the two basic categories of online research tools. Use secondary research to fill in the gaps in your knowledge and to enhance the credibility of your report. The two main categories of online research tools are search tools and monitoring tools. The most common online search tools are search engines, which identify and rank the results from millions of webpages by most to least useful. Search engines provide access to periodicals, scholarly and trade journals, and other targeted search results. However, the quality of the results may be poor. Online monitoring tools, such as TweetBeep and newsfeeds, give users the ability to automatically monitor selected sources for new information.

4 Explain the role of primary research, and identify the two most common forms of primary research for business communication purposes. Primary research is new research; it is undertaken specifically for your study and complements secondary research by filling in areas lacking in periodicals and journals. The two most common forms are surveys and interviews. Surveys must be valid and representative to be useful, and interviews must be conducted with a clear purpose and careful preparation.

5 Explain how to plan informational reports and website content. Plan informational reports and website content by determining their purpose, audience needs, and organization. Most informational reports describe operations, policy or procedure implementation, compliance, and progress on a project. They typically use a topical organization (such as comparison, importance, or chronology). To organize website content, the creator must be aware of

the multidimensional nature of the online experience and consider chunking information for reader ease and creating a reader-controlled structure.

6 Describe the three most common ways to organize analytical reports. Focusing on conclusions is one way to organize analytical reports. In this approach, you present the main idea quickly, but you risk the audience questioning your data or methodology. To overcome such problems, ensure that you support your conclusions with logical reasoning and firm evidence. Focusing on recommendations, another report structure, also requires the direct approach: begin by describing the problem and follow with benefits if your audience accepts your recommendations. The report then describes the steps needed to attain the benefits. A third way to structure reports is by focusing on logical arguments. A useful method for dealing with skeptical readers, it uses an indirect approach and logically builds to your conclusions and recommendations.

7 Explain how to plan proposals. Planning proposals is dependent on whether they are solicited (requested by an outside organization) or unsolicited (self-generated based on a perceived need). Solicited proposals must respond to all the requirements in the request for proposal (RFP), which typically demands information about the type of work needed, budgets, deadlines, and other information. Authors of unsolicited proposals must convince their readers that there is a problem to be addressed; consequently, the indirect approach would be a better strategy in such instances.

ON THE JOB   PERFORMING COMMUNICATION TASKS AT DELL INC.

To keep its position in the computer industry, Dell Inc. must continue to improve customer service. You are a manager in customer relations, and your supervisor has asked you to plan a report that will outline ways to increase customer satisfaction. You'll need to conduct the necessary research, analyze the findings, and present your recommendations. From the following, choose the best responses, and be prepared to explain why your choices are best.

1. Which represents the most appropriate statement of purpose for this study?

   a. The purpose of this study is to identify any customer service problems at Dell.

   b. This study answers the following question: What improvements in customer service can Dell make to increase overall customer satisfaction?

   c. This study identifies the Dell customer service representatives who are most responsible for poor customer satisfaction.

   d. This study identifies steps that Dell's customer service representatives should undertake to change customer service practices at Dell.

2. You have tentatively identified the following factors for analysis:

   I. To improve customer service, we need to hire more customer service representatives.
      a. Compute competitors' employee-to-sales ratios.
      b. Compute our employee-to-sales ratio.

   II. To improve customer service, we need to hire better customer service representatives.
      a. Assess skill level of competitors' customer service representatives.
      b. Assess skill level of our customer service representatives.

   III. To improve customer service, we need to retrain our customer service representatives.
      a. Review competitors' training programs.
      b. Review our training programs.

   IV. To improve customer service, we need to compensate and motivate our people differently.
      a. Assess competitors' compensation levels and motivational techniques.
      b. Assess our compensation levels and motivational techniques.

Should you proceed with the investigation on the basis of this preliminary outline, or should you consider other approaches to factoring the problem?

a. Proceed with this outline.

b. Do not proceed. Factor the problem by asking customers how they perceive current customer service efforts at Dell. In addition, ask customer service representatives what they think should be done differently.

c. Do not proceed. Factor the problem by surveying nonbuyers to find out if current customer service efforts influenced their decision not to buy from Dell. In addition, ask nonbuyers what they think should be done differently.

d. Do not proceed. Factor the problem by asking customer service representatives for suggestions on how to improve customer service. In addition, ask nonbuyers and current customers what they think should be done differently.

3. Which work plan is the best option for guiding your study of ways to improve customer service?

a. Version 1

Statement of problem: As part of Dell Inc.'s continuing efforts to offer the most attractive computers in the world, management wants to improve customer service. The challenge here is to identify service improvements that are meaningful and valuable to the customer without being too expensive or time consuming.

Purpose and scope of work: The purpose of this study is to identify ways to increase customer satisfaction by improving customer service at Dell. A four-member study team, composed of the vice president of customer relations and three customer service representatives, has been appointed to prepare a written service-improvement plan. To accomplish this objective, this study will survey customers to learn what changes they'd like to see in terms of customer service. The team will analyze these potential improvements in terms of cost and time requirements and then will design new service procedures that customer service representatives can use to better satisfy customers.

Sources and methods of data collection and analysis: The study team will assess current customer service efforts by

1. Querying customer service representatives regarding their customer service

2. Observing representatives in action dealing with customers through email responses and telephone calls

3. Surveying current Dell owners regarding their purchase experiences

4. Surveying visitors to the Dell website who decide not to purchase from Dell (by intercepting a sample of these people as they leave the website)

The team will also view competitive websites to determine first-hand how they treat customers, and the team will submit online questionnaires to a sample of computer owners and classify the results by brand name. Once all these data have been collected, the team will analyze them to determine where buyers and

potential buyers consider customer service to be lacking. Finally, the team will design procedures to meet their expectations.

Schedule:

Jan. 11–Jan. 31:	Query customer service representatives.
	Observe representatives in action.
	Survey current Dell owners.
	Survey nonbuyers at the Dell website.
Feb. 1–Feb. 15:	Visit competitive websites.
	Conduct online survey of computer owners.
Feb. 16–Mar. 15:	Analyze data.
	Draft new procedures.
Mar. 16–Mar. 25:	Prepare final report.
Mar. 29:	Present to management/customer service committee.

b. Version 2

Statement of problem: Dell's customer service representatives need to get on the ball in terms of customer service, and we need to tell them what to do to fix their customer service shortcomings.

Purpose and scope of work: This report will address how we plan to solve the problem. We'll design new customer service procedures and prepare a written report from which customer service representatives can learn.

Sources and methods of data collection: We plan to employ the usual methods of collecting data, including direct observation and surveys.

Schedule:

Collect data.	Jan. 11–Feb. 15
Analyze data.	Feb. 16–Mar. 1
Draft new procedures.	Mar. 2–Mar. 15
Prepare final report.	Mar. 16–Mar. 25
Present to management/ customer service committee.	Mar. 29

c. Version 3

Task 1—Query customer service representatives: We will interview a sampling of customer service representatives to find out what steps they take to ensure customer satisfaction. Dates: Jan. 11–Jan. 20

Task 2—Observe representatives in action: We will observe a sampling of customer service representatives as they work with potential buyers and current owners to learn first-hand what steps employees typically take. Dates: Jan. 21–Jan. 29

Task 3—Survey current Dell owners: Using a sample of names from Dell's database of current owners, we'll ask owners how they felt about the purchase process when they bought their computer and how they feel they've been treated since then. We'll also ask them to suggest steps we could take to improve service. Dates: Jan. 15–Feb. 15

Task 4—Survey nonbuyers at Dell: While we are observing customer service representatives, we will also approach visitors to the Dell website who leave the site without making a purchase. As visitors exit the site, we'll present a quick online survey, asking them what they think about Dell's customer service policies and practices and whether these had any bearing on their decision not to buy a Dell product. Dates: Jan. 21–Jan. 31

Task 5—Visit competitive websites: Under the guise of shoppers looking for new computers, we will visit a selection of competitive websites to discover how they treat customers and whether they offer any special service that Dell doesn't. Dates: Feb. 1–Feb. 15

Task 6—Conduct online survey of computer owners: Using Internet-based technology, we will survey a sampling of computer owners (of all brands). We will then sort the answers by brand of computer owned to see which dealers are offering which services. Dates: Jan. 15–Feb. 15

Task 7—Analyze data: Once we've collected all these data, we'll analyze them to identify (1) services that customers would like to see Dell offer, (2) services offered by competitors that aren't offered by Dell, and (3) services currently offered by Dell that may not be all that important to customers. Dates: Feb. 16–Mar. 1

Task 8—Draft new procedures: From the data we've analyzed, we'll select new services that should be considered by Dell. We'll also assess the time and money burdens that these services are likely to present, so management can see whether each new service will yield a positive return on investment. Dates: Mar. 2– Mar. 15

Task 9—Prepare final report: This is essentially a documentation task, during which we'll describe our work, make our recommendations, and prepare a formal report. Dates: Mar. 16–Mar. 25

Task 10—Present to management/customer relations committee: We'll summarize our findings and recommendations and make the full report available to dealers at the quarterly meeting. Date: Mar. 29

d. **Version 4**

Problem: To identify meaningful customer service improvements that can be implemented by Dell.

Data collection: Use direct observation and online surveys to gather details about customer service at the Dell website and at competing websites. Have the study team survey current Dell owners and people who visited dell.ca but did not buy, and send an online questionnaire to computer owners.

Schedule:

Step 1: Data collection. Work will begin on January 11 and end on February 15.

Step 2: Data analysis. Work will begin on February 16 and end on March 1.

Step 3: Drafting new procedures. Work will begin on March 2 and end on March 15.

Step 4: Preparation of the final report. Work will begin on March 16 and end on March 25.

Step 5: Presentation of the final report. The report will be presented to management and the customer service committee on March 29.

TEST YOUR KNOWLEDGE

1. How do informational reports differ from analytical reports?
2. What is included in a work plan for a report, and why is it important?
3. What is the difference between the mean, the median, and the mode?
4. What is paraphrasing, and what is its purpose?
5. How does primary information differ from secondary information?
6. What are the disadvantages of using search engines?
7. What are the guidelines for conducting effective surveys?
8. What types of questions can be posed during an interview?
9. What principles are important when creating website content?
10. How does a conclusion differ from a recommendation?

APPLY YOUR KNOWLEDGE

1. Why must you be careful when using information from the Internet in a business report?
2. Why are unsolicited proposals more challenging to write than solicited proposals?
3. Can you use the same approach for planning website content as you use for planning printed reports? Why or why not?
4. If you were writing a recommendation report for an audience that doesn't know you, would you use the direct approach, focusing on the recommendation, or the indirect approach, focusing on logic? Why?
5. **Ethical Choices** Companies occasionally make mistakes that expose confidential information, such as when employees lose laptop computers containing sensitive data files or webmasters forget to protect confidential webpages from search engine indexes. If you conducted an online search that turned up competitive information on webpages that were clearly intended to be private, what would you do? Explain your answer.

RUNNING CASES

> CASE 1 Noreen

Noreen would like to propose a new project to upper-level management: reorganizing two departments into one.

Currently, the "Go Points" department is on the fourth floor and is staffed by 20 sales/service reps. They (1) make sales calls to existing Petro-Go credit card holders to offer the points program, (2) receive calls from existing points program customers who have enquiries, and (3) call existing points customers to announce promotions, offers, and so on.

The Petro-Go credit card department is on the third floor and is staffed by 30 sales/service reps. They (1) make sales calls to recruit new credit card customers, (2) receive calls from existing credit card holders who have enquiries, and (3) call existing credit card customers to announce promotions, offers, and so on.

Noreen thinks that by joining the credit card sales/service department with the "Go Points" department, customers will be better served by one-stop shopping. She also feels that the credit card sales/service staff could easily modify their call routines to include information about the "Go Points" program,

and the "Go Points" staff could easily be trained on the credit card policies and procedures.

QUESTIONS

a. Is this a solicited proposal?
b. How will Noreen use the "you" attitude in this proposal?
c. What costs might be involved?
d. What supporting facts or evidence do you think might help Noreen justify this proposal?
e. What are some concerns or problems that may arise during this project?

YOUR TASK

Create a work plan for Noreen to use as a guide (see Figures 11–2 and 11–3) in writing her proposal. Include the following elements:

- Statement of the problem
- Statement of the purpose and scope
- Discussion of the tasks to be accomplished
- Review of timelines and resources required

> CASE 2 Kwong

Kwong applies to and gets hired by a large national telephone service provider, ET Canada, in the accounting department. He plans to complete his CGA studies part time because he finds his expenses increasing and he needs to have more income. His goal of opening his own accounting firm is still alive but will take a little longer to achieve.

One of his first tasks is to work on the company's annual report with a team from the finance department. The annual report will be posted on the Internet and distributed to all shareholders.

QUESTIONS

a. Which type of report best describes an annual report—an analytical report, an operating report, or a progress report?
b. What information is included in a company annual report?
c. Where will Kwong find the information he needs for the annual report?

d. What teamwork skills will Kwong need to be an effective team member?
e. How will Kwong format the headings in the report so the reader knows where each new section begins and which subtopics relate to which heading?

YOUR TASK

Research a public Canadian utility company. Public companies usually have more information available than private companies. Use the SEDAR (System for Electronic Document Analysis and Retrieval) website to find a list of Canadian public companies and their annual reports. Review several company annual reports for utility service providers. Make a list of the common headings and sections within the annual reports. Create a table of contents that Kwong might use in ET Canada's annual report.

PRACTISE YOUR KNOWLEDGE

Message for Analysis: Evaluating a Report

Public companies file comprehensive financial annual reports electronically. Many companies post links to these reports on their websites along with links to other company reports. Visit the website of the Montreal sport shirt manufacturer Gildan Activewear at www.gildan.com and find the company's most recent annual financial reports. (Click "Corporate" on the

home page and then click the "Investors" link. Then click "Financials & Filings") Analyze the style and format of the annual report. For which audience(s) is the annual report targeted? Who besides members of the Canadian Security Regulatory Authority might be interested in the annual report? Do you find this report easy to read? Interesting? Detailed? Explain your answer.

EXERCISES

11.1 Planning: Analyzing the Situation

South by Southwest (SXSW) is a family of conferences and festivals in Austin, Texas, that showcase some of the world's most creative talents in music, interactive media, and film. In addition to being a major entertainment venue for a week every March, SXSW is also an increasingly important *trade show*, an opportunity for companies to present products and services to potential customers and business partners. You work for a company that makes music training equipment, such as an electronic keyboard with an integrated computer screen that guides learners through every step of learning to play the keyboard. Your manager has asked you to look into whether the company should rent an exhibition booth at SXSW next year. Prepare a work plan for an analytical report that will assess the promotional opportunities at SXSW and make a recommendation on exhibiting. Include the statement of purpose, a problem statement for any research you will conduct, a description of what will result from your investigation, the sources and methods of data collection, and a preliminary outline. Visit the SXSW website at http://sxsw.com for more information.[23]

11.2 Planning: Analyzing the Situation

Sales at The Style Shop, a clothing store for men, have declined for the third month in a row. Your boss is not sure if this decline is due to a weak economy or if it's due to another unknown reason. She has asked you to investigate the situation and to submit a report to her highlighting some possible reasons for the decline. Develop a statement of purpose for your report.

11.3 Research: Documenting Sources

Select five business articles from a combination of print and online sources. Develop a resource list, using Appendix B as a guideline.

11.4 Teamwork: Evaluating Sources

Break into small groups and find four websites that provide business information such as company or industry news, trends, analysis, facts, or performance data. Using the criteria discussed under "Evaluating Sources," evaluate the credibility of the information presented on these websites.

11.5 Research: Using Research Results

Select an article from a reputable business magazine such as *Canadian Business*, *Report on Business* magazine, or *Fortune* (blog or website). Read the article and highlight its key points. Summarize the article in fewer than 100 words, paraphrasing the key points.

11.6 Research: Conducting Secondary Research

Using online, database, or printed sources, find the following information. Be sure to properly cite your source, using the formats discussed in Appendix B.
a. Contact information for the Chartered Accountants of Canada
b. Median weekly earnings of men and women by occupation
c. Current market share for Perrier water
d. Performance ratios for office supply retailers
e. Annual stock performance for Canadian National Railway
f. Number of franchise outlets in Canada
g. Composition of the Canadian workforce by profession

11.7 Understanding Business Reports and Proposals: Report Classification

Using the information presented in this chapter, identify the report type represented by each example. In addition, write a brief paragraph about each, explaining who the audience is likely to be, what type of data would be used, and whether conclusions and recommendations would be appropriate.
a. A statistical study of the pattern of violent crime in a large city during the last five years
b. A report prepared by a seed company demonstrating the benefits of its seed corn for farmers
c. A report prepared by an independent testing agency evaluating various types of nonprescription cold remedies
d. A trip report submitted at the end of a week by a travelling salesperson
e. A report indicating how 20 hectares of undeveloped land could be converted into an industrial park
f. An annual report to be sent to the shareholders of a large corporation
g. A written report by a police officer who has just completed an arrest

11.8 Analyzing Data: Calculating the Mean

Your boss has asked you to analyze and report on your division's sales for the first nine months of this year. Use the following data from company invoices to calculate the mean for each quarter and all averages for the year to date. Then, identify and discuss the quarterly sales trends.

January	$24 600	April	$21 200	July	$29 900
February	25 900	May	24 600	August	30 500
March	23 000	June	26 800	September	26 600

11.9 Research: Conducting Primary Research (Surveys)

You work for a movie studio that is producing a young director's first motion picture—the story of a group of unknown musicians finding work and making a reputation in a competitive industry. Unfortunately, some of your friends say that the 182-minute movie is simply too long. Others say they couldn't imagine any sequences to cut out. Your boss wants to test the movie on a regular audience and ask viewers to complete a questionnaire that will help the director decide whether edits are needed and, if so, where. Design a questionnaire that you can use to solicit valid answers for a report to the director about how to handle the audience's reaction to the movie.

11.10 Research: Conducting Primary Research (Interviews)

You're conducting an information interview with a manager in another division of your company. Partway through the interview, the manager shows clear signs of impatience. How should you respond? What might you do differently to prevent this from happening in the future? Explain your answers.

11.11 Message Strategies: Informational Reports

Imagine you're the manager of campus recruiting for Manulife Financial, a major Canadian financial services company. Each of your four recruiters interviews up to 11 fourth-year students every day. What kind of personal activity report can you design to track the results of these interviews? List the areas you would want each recruiter to report on and explain how each would help you manage the recruiting process (and the recruiters) more effectively.

11.12 Message Strategies: Informational Reports

Assume that your university or college president has received many student complaints about campus parking problems. You are appointed to chair a student committee organized to investigate the problems and recommend solutions. The president gives you a file labelled "Parking: Complaints from Students," and you jot down the essence of the complaints as you inspect the contents. Your notes look like this:

- Inadequate student spaces at critical hours
- Poor night lighting near the computer centre
- Inadequate attempts to keep resident neighbours from occupying spaces
- Dim marking lines
- Motorcycles taking up full spaces
- Discourteous security officers
- Spaces (usually empty) reserved for campus officials
- Relatively high parking fees
- Full fees charged to night students even though they use the lots only during low demand periods
- Vandalism to cars and a sense of personal danger
- Inadequate total space
- Harassment of students parking on the street in front of neighbouring houses

Now prepare an outline for an informational report to be submitted to committee members. Use a topical organization for your report that categorizes this information.

11.13 Message Strategies: Informational Reports

From your school library, company websites, or an online service such as www.annualreportservice.com, find the annual reports recently released by two corporations in the same industry. Analyze each report and be prepared to discuss the following questions in class:

  a. What organizational differences, if any, do you see in the way each corporation discusses its annual performance? Are the data presented clearly so that shareholders can draw conclusions about how well the company performed?

  b. What goals, challenges, and plans do top managers emphasize in their discussion of results?

  c. How do the format and organization of each report enhance or detract from the information being presented?

11.14 Message Strategies: Analytical Reports

Three years ago, your company (a carpet manufacturer) modernized its Ontario plant in anticipation of increasing demand for carpets. Because of the depressed housing market, the increase in demand for new carpets has been slow to materialize. As a result, the company has excess capacity at its Ontario and New Brunswick plants. On the basis of your research, you have recommended that the company close the New Brunswick plant. The company president has asked you to prepare a justification report to support your recommendation. Here are the facts you gathered by interviewing the respective plant managers:

Operational Statistics

- *Ontario plant:* This plant has newer equipment; productivity is higher; it employs 100 nonunion production workers; and it ships $12 million in carpets a year. The hourly base wage is $16.
- *New Brunswick plant:* New Brunswick plant employs 80 union production workers and ships $8 million in carpets a year. The hourly base wage is $20.

Financial Implications

- *Savings by closing New Brunswick plant:* (1) Increase productivity by 17 percent; (2) reduce labour costs by 20 percent (total labour savings would be $1 million per year; see "Assumptions," below); (3) achieve annual local tax savings of $120 000 (Ontario has a more favourable tax climate).
- *Sale of Moncton, New Brunswick, land:* Purchased in 1952 for $200 000. Current market value $2.5 million. Net profit (after capital gains tax) over $1 million.
- *Sale of plant and equipment:* Fully depreciated. Any proceeds are a windfall.
- *Costs of closing New Brunswick plant:* One-time deductible charge of $250 000 (relocation costs of $100 000 and severance payments totalling $150 000).

Assumptions

- Transfer 5 workers from New Brunswick to Ontario.
- Hire 45 new workers in Ontario.
- Lay off 75 workers in New Brunswick.
- Ontario plant would require a total of 150 workers to produce the combined volume of both plants.

a. Which approach (focus on conclusions, recommendations, or logical arguments) will you use to structure your report to the president? Why?

b. Suppose this report were to be circulated to plant managers and supervisors instead. What changes, if any, might you make in your approach?

c. List some conclusions that you might draw from the above information to use in your report.

d. Using the structure you selected for your report to the president, draft a final report outline with first- and second-level informative headings.

11.15 Teamwork: Proposals

Break into small groups and identify an operational problem occurring at your campus that involves either registration, university housing, food services, parking, or library services. Then develop a workable solution to that problem. Finally, develop a list of pertinent facts that your team will need to gather to convince the reader that the problem exists and that your solution will work.

11.16 Message Strategies: Proposals

Read the step-by-step hints and examples for writing a funding proposal at www.learnerassociates.net/proposal. Review the entire sample proposal online. What details did the writer decide to include in the appendices? Why was this material placed in the appendices and not the main body of the report? According to the writer's tips, when is the best time to prepare a project overview?

11.17 Ethical Choices

Your company operates a website featuring children's games and puzzles. The vice president of marketing needs to know more about the children who visit the site so she can plan new products. She has asked you to develop an online survey questionnaire to collect the data. What ethical issues do you see in this situation? What should you do?

LEARNING OBJECTIVES After studying this chapter, you will be able to

1 Explain how to adapt to your audiences when writing reports and proposals

2 Describe five characteristics of effective report content

3 Explain six strategies to strengthen your proposal argument

4 Determine the topics commonly covered in a proposal introduction, body, and closing

5 Identify six characteristics of effective writing in online reports

6 Discuss six principles of graphic design that can improve the quality of your visuals

7 Explain how to choose which points in your message to illustrate

MyLab Business Communication Visit MyLab Business Communication to access a variety of online resources directly related to this chapter's content.

ON THE JOB: COMMUNICATING AT FEDEX

At FedEx, many kinds of reports are used to track both system and employee performance, as well as to assemble information needed for making managerial decisions. Not only does CEO Frederick Smith read innumerable reports now, but as a university student he wrote a very famous one that detailed the idea of his air express delivery service and persuaded investors to fund him.

Mark Richards/PhotoEdit, Inc

Delivering on Time, Every Time

www.FedEx.com

Imagine collecting, transporting, and delivering more than 9 million letters and packages every day. Now imagine that every one of these parcels must arrive at its destination when expected. That's the standard against which Federal Express managers—and customers—measure performance. Living up to this exacting standard day in and day out presents founder and chief executive officer Frederick W. Smith and his entire management team with a variety of communication challenges.

When FedEx began operations in 1973, its services covered 22 U.S. cities. Today it delivers throughout the United States and Canada, and to 220 countries around the world. FedEx operates more than 658 airplanes, maintains a fleet of 150 000 motorized vehicles, and employs more than 400 000 people worldwide.

FedEx must battle a host of rivals, including United Parcel Service (UPS), Purolator (owned by Canada Post), and DHL. Competition is fierce, so FedEx must constantly introduce new methods or ideas to maintain its industry position and serve its customers better. The firm offers a host of online business tools, including address books, an address checker, complete international shipping documents, text alerts, and customizable portals where FedEx customers can track shipments and access signature proofs of delivery. Businesses can also add common FedEx functions to their retail websites and link directly to their own order management systems.

With competitors offering more and customers expecting more, Smith and his management team have their work cut out for them. Monitoring and controlling company operations, training new employees, tracking competitor service and performance, making a host of decisions about how to serve customers better—all these activities require the communication of timely, accurate information, and much of that information comes in the form of reports. To keep the business running smoothly, maintain satisfied customers, and hold competitors at bay, FedEx managers receive and prepare reports of all kinds. So how do Smith and his managers use reports for internal communication? How can FedEx writers make their reports readable and convenient to use? What makes one report better than another?[1]

Composing Reports and Proposals

Report writers, including FedEx managers, will be the first to tell you how important the writing stage is in the development of successful reports and proposals. This chapter builds on the writing techniques and ideas you learned in Chapter 5 and examines issues that are particularly important when preparing longer message formats (see Figure 12–1). In addition, you'll get an introduction to creating effective visuals, which are a vital aspect of many reports and proposals.

As with shorter messages, take time before you start writing to ensure that you're ready to adapt your approach to your audience.

ADAPTING TO YOUR AUDIENCE

1 LEARNING OBJECTIVE

Explain how to adapt to your audiences when writing reports and proposals.

Long or complex reports demand a lot from readers, making the "you" attitude even more important.

Like all successful business messages, effective reports and proposals are adapted to the intended audience as much as possible. To ensure your success with reports, be sensitive to audience needs, build strong relationships with your audience, and control your style and tone.

Chapter 5 introduced four aspects of audience sensitivity, and all four apply to reports and proposals: adopting the "you" attitude, maintaining good standards of etiquette, emphasizing the positive, and using bias-free language. Reports and proposals that are highly technical, complex, or lengthy can put heavy demands on your readers, so the "you" attitude takes on even greater

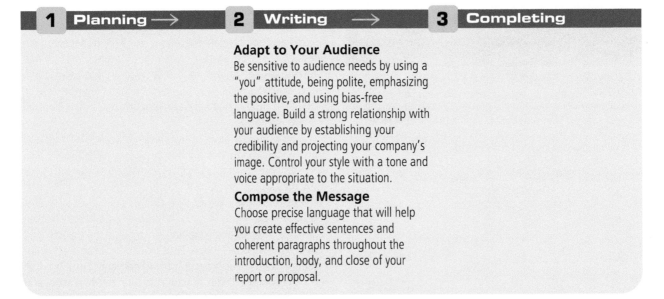

Figure 12–1 Step 2 in the Three-Step Writing Process for Reports and Proposals

importance with these long messages. As you'll see later in this chapter, part of that attitude includes helping your readers find their way through your material, so they can understand critical information.

Whether your report is intended for people inside or outside the company, plan how you will adapt your style and your language to reflect the image of your organization. Many organizations have specific guidelines for communicating with public audiences; be sure you're aware of these preferences before you start writing.

If you know your readers reasonably well and your report is likely to meet with their approval, you can generally adopt a fairly informal tone (as long as this is appropriate in your organization, of course). To make your tone less formal, speak to readers in the first person, refer to them as *you*, and refer to yourself as *I* (or *we* if there are multiple report authors).

To make your tone more formal, use the impersonal style: emphasize objectivity, ensure that content is free from personal opinion, and build your argument on provable facts. When creating a formal tone, eliminate all references to *you* and *I* (including *we*, *us*, and *our*). Your tone should also be businesslike and unemotional. Be careful to avoid jokes, similes, and metaphors, and minimize the use of colourful adjectives or adverbs.

A more formal tone is appropriate for longer reports, especially those dealing with controversial or complex information. You'll also need a more formal tone when your report will be sent to other parts of the organization or to outsiders, such as customers, suppliers, or members of the community. The excerpt from *Healthy Eating After School*, published by Health Canada, uses a number techniques to create a formal tone, as shown in Figure 12–2.

Many companies have specific guidelines for reports, particularly those intended for external audiences.

Reports destined for audiences outside Canada and the United States often require a more formal tone to match the expectations of audiences in many other countries.

Corporate reports to the community require a writing style and tone appropriate to the audience. What audiences read community reports? Should the writing style be formal or informal? What level of language should be used? Why are images important for these reports?

Communicating with people in other cultures often calls for more formality for two reasons. First, the business environment outside Canada and the United States tends to be more formal in general, and that formality must be reflected in your communication. Second, the techniques you use to make a document informal (for example, employing humour and idiomatic language) tend to translate poorly or not at all from one culture to another. Using a less formal tone in cross-cultural reports and proposals increases the risk of offending people and the chance of miscommunicating information.

DRAFTING REPORT CONTENT

With a clear picture of how you need to adapt to your audience, you're ready to begin composing your first draft. This section offers advice on drafting content for both reports and proposals, along with several strategies for making your content more readable. When you compose reports and proposals, follow the advice Chapter 5 offered: use the most precise vocabulary, create the most effective sentences, and develop the most coherent paragraphs.

As with other written business communications, the text of reports and proposals has three main sections: an introduction (or *opening*), a body, and a close. The content and length of each section varies with the type and purpose of the

Summary

There is global and national concern about rising rates of obesity, as well as patterns of healthy eating, food skills, and levels of physical activity, among children and youth. Many view the after-school time period as an opportunity to enhance physical activity. Some after-school programs seek to contribute to broad health outcomes for Canadian children by blending objectives related to recreation and physical activity, education and learning, and nutrition, health and wellness.

This report is a synthesis of published and unpublished literature from Canada and abroad, along with insights collected from key informants whose initiatives, including programs, are already underway. Its purpose is to share with governments and other stakeholders working at all levels, the key learnings from a literature review and key informant interviews on how to integrate healthy eating and food skills into after-school physical activity initiatives. Both the evidence and lessons learned could be considered when integrating healthy eating into other after-school initiatives.

The challenge

Evidence supports a relationship between healthy eating patterns during childhood and:

- optimal health, growth and cognitive development;
- academic performance; and
- prevention of chronic diseases later in life, including overweight and obesity.

Growing evidence suggests that children and youth in Canada may be making unhealthy food choices that are inconsistent with national dietary guidance, thus increasing risks to their nutritional health. This includes eating energy-dense, nutrient-poor foods. A growing body of evidence supports a link between sedentary behaviour, such as watching television, and the consumption of these foods. The combination of these behaviours increases the risk that more energy is being consumed than expended. This in turn contributes to overweight and obesity. The after-school time period is a high-risk time for these behaviours.

The evidence

Incorporating healthy eating and physical activity into after-school programs is often cited as a way to contribute to broader obesity prevention efforts. Taking action that is multifaceted and comprehensive is key. This includes engaging parents and building community capacity to enhance programs and policies that support healthy eating and physical activity for children and youth.

Healthy Eating After School   3

The sidebar annotations:

> Words such as "synthesis," "informants," "initiatives," and "learnings" help give the report a formal tone.

> The sentences in this paragraph are precise and use language appropriate for the purpose of this report. In contrast, a document aimed primarily at consumers might say "junk food" instead of "energy-dense, nutrient-poor foods" and "sitting in front of the TV" instead of "sedentary behaviour, such as watching television."

> The writers avoid using personal pronouns such as "I" and "we" in order to maintain the report's objective tone and purpose, which is to provide evidence that shows the benefits of incorporating nutritious food into school settings.

Figure 12–2 Choosing the Right Tone for Business Reports (excerpt)

document, the document's organizational structure, and the length and depth of the material. The document's degree of formality and your relationship with your audience will also influence the document's subject matter and extent.

The *introduction* (or *opening*) is the first section in the text of any report or proposal. An effective introduction fulfills at least four aims:

- Puts the report or proposal in a broader context by tying it to a problem or an assignment

> Your introduction needs to put the report in context for the reader, introduce the subject, preview main ideas, and establish the tone of the document.

- Introduces the subject or purpose of the report or proposal and indicates why the subject is important
- Previews the main ideas and the order in which they'll be covered
- Establishes the tone of the document and the writer's relationship with the audience

The *body*, or main section, usually consists of the major divisions or sections with various levels of headings. These divisions present, analyze, and interpret the information gathered during your investigation, and they support the recommendations or conclusions discussed in your document. The body contains the proof, the detailed information necessary to support your conclusions and recommendations. Note how the recommendation report in Figure 12–3 uses the report body to articulate a recommendation—a move to a fully interactive

The body of your report presents, analyzes, and interprets the information you gathered during your investigation.

DATE: July 7, 2018
TO: Board of Directors, Executive Committee members
FROM: Alycia Jenn, Business Development Manager
SUBJECT: Website expansion

The opening reminds readers of the origin and purpose of the report.

In response to your request, my staff and I investigated the potential for expanding our website from its current "brochureware" status (in which we promote our company and its products but don't provide any way to place orders online) to full e-commerce capability (including placing orders and checking on order delivery status). After analyzing the behaviour of our customers and major competitors and studying the overall development of electronic retailing, we have three recommendations:

1. We should expand our online presence from "brochureware" to e-commerce capability within the next six months.

2. We should engage a firm that specializes in online retailing to design and develop the new e-commerce capabilities.

3. We must take care to integrate online retailing with our store-based and mail-order operations.

The report uses the direct approach, and the writer's recommendations are listed immediately after the opening.

1. WE SHOULD EXPAND THE WEBSITE TO FULL E-COMMERCE CAPABILITY

The body presents logical reasons for recommending that the firm expand its website to include e-commerce.

First, does e-commerce capability make sense today for a small company that sells luxury housewares? Even though books and many other products are now commonly sold online, in most cases this enterprise involves simple, low-cost products that don't require a lot of hands-on inspection before purchasing. As we've observed in our stores, shoppers like to interact with our products before purchasing them. However, a small but growing number of websites do sell specialty products, using such tactics as "virtual product tours" (in which shoppers can interactively view a product in three dimensions, rather than simply looking at a static photograph) and generous return policies (to reduce the perceived risk of buying products online).

Second, do we need to establish a presence now in order to remain competitive in the future? The answer is an overwhelming "yes." The initial steps taken by our competitors are already placing us at a disadvantage among those shoppers who are already comfortable buying online, and every trend indicates our minor competitive weakness today will turn into a major weakness in the next few years:

- Several of our top competitors are beginning to implement full e-commerce, including virtual product tours. Our research suggests that these companies aren't yet generating significant financial returns from these online investments, but their online sales are growing.

- Younger consumers who grew up with the World Wide Web will soon be reaching their peak earning years (ages 35-54). This demographic segment expects e-commerce in nearly every product category, and we'll lose them to the competition if we don't offer it.

The writer supports her reasoning with evidence.

- The Web is erasing geographical shopping limits, presenting both a threat and an opportunity. Even though our customers can now shop websites from anywhere in the world (so that we have thousands of competitors instead of a dozen), we can now target customers anywhere in the world.

(continued)

Figure 12–3 Effective Problem-Solving Report Focusing on Recommendations

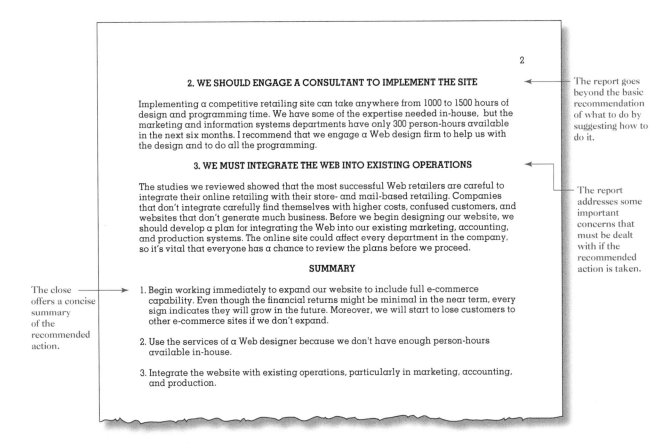

2

2. WE SHOULD ENGAGE A CONSULTANT TO IMPLEMENT THE SITE

Implementing a competitive retailing site can take anywhere from 1000 to 1500 hours of design and programming time. We have some of the expertise needed in-house, but the marketing and information systems departments have only 300 person-hours available in the next six months. I recommend that we engage a Web design firm to help us with the design and to do all the programming.

3. WE MUST INTEGRATE THE WEB INTO EXISTING OPERATIONS

The studies we reviewed showed that the most successful Web retailers are careful to integrate their online retailing with their store- and mail-based retailing. Companies that don't integrate carefully find themselves with higher costs, confused customers, and websites that don't generate much business. Before we begin designing our website, we should develop a plan for integrating the Web into our existing marketing, accounting, and production systems. The online site could affect every department in the company, so it's vital that everyone has a chance to review the plans before we proceed.

SUMMARY

1. Begin working immediately to expand our website to include full e-commerce capability. Even though the financial returns might be minimal in the near term, every sign indicates they will grow in the future. Moreover, we will start to lose customers to other e-commerce sites if we don't expand.

2. Use the services of a Web designer because we don't have enough person-hours available in-house.

3. Integrate the website with existing operations, particularly in marketing, accounting, and production.

The report goes beyond the basic recommendation of what to do by suggesting how to do it.

The report addresses some important concerns that must be dealt with if the recommended action is taken.

The close offers a concise summary of the recommended action.

Figure 12–3 Effective Problem-Solving Report Focusing on Recommendations (continued)

e-commerce website—to a company's board of directors. This report section provides enough information to support the argument, without burdening the high-level readership with a lot of tactical details.

The *close* is the final section in the text of your report or proposal. It has three important functions:

- Emphasizes the main points of the message
- Summarizes the benefits to the reader if the document suggests a change or some other course of action
- Brings all the action items together in one place and gives the details about who should do what, when, where, and how

The close might be the only part of your report some readers have time for, so ensure that it conveys the full weight of your message.

Research shows that the final section of a report or proposal leaves a lasting impression. The close gives you one last chance to ensure that your report says what you intended.[2] In fact, readers who are in a hurry might skip the body of the report and read only the summary, so ensure that it carries a strong, clear message.

CREATING REPORT EFFECTIVENESS

2 LEARNING OBJECTIVE

Describe five characteristics of effective report content.

Your credibility and career advancement potential are underscored with every business report you write, so ensure that your content is

- **Accurate.** Double-check your facts and references in addition to checking for typographical errors. If an audience even senses that your information is shaky, they'll start to view all your work with a skeptical eye.

- **Complete.** To help colleagues or supervisors make an informed decision, include everything necessary for readers to understand the situation, problem, or proposal. Support all key assertions using an appropriate combination of illustrations, explanations, and facts.[3] In a recent FedEx annual report, for example, Frederick Smith and his team provided a concise and easily understandable overview of the company's global operations. The subject matter is presented in a way that any investor interested in the company's stock can comprehend.[4]
- **Balanced.** Present all sides of the issue fairly and equitably, and include all the essential information, even if some information doesn't support your line of reasoning. Omitting relevant information or facts creates an incomplete and partial argument. Your audience will believe your report is one-sided, and your credibility will suffer.
- **Clear and logical.** Clear sentence structure and good transitions are essential.[5] Save your readers time by ensuring that your sentences are uncluttered, contain well-chosen words, and proceed logically. To help your readers move from one point to the next, make your transitions clear and logical. For a successful report, identify the ideas that belong together, and organize them in a way that's easy to understand.[6]
- **Documented properly.** If you use primary and secondary sources for your report or proposal, ensure that you properly document and give credit to your sources, as Chapter 11 explains.

Keeping these points in mind will help you draft the most effective introduction, body, and close for your report. Note how the report excerpt in Figure 12–4 offers the client a complete but concise update of the company's landscaping services. In addition to providing routine information, the writer also informs the client of progress on two problem areas, one that the firm has been able to resolve and one that was just discovered. In the case of the problem with the soil, you might be tempted not to share any information with the client until you've resolved the problem, but doing so could affect the client's budgets and other plans. The writer behaves in an ethical manner by telling the client about the problem at an early stage.

REPORT INTRODUCTION The specific elements you should include in an introduction depend on the nature and length of the report, the circumstances under which you're writing it, and your relationship with the audience. An introduction could contain all of the following topics, although you'll want to choose the most relevant ones for each report you write:

Carefully select the elements to include in your introduction; strive for a balance between necessary, expected information and brevity.

- **Authorization.** The person who assigned the report and the date he or she assigned it; in long reports, this material appears in a *letter of transmittal* for external audiences and a transmittal memo for internal audiences (see Chapter 13) to accompany the report.
- **Problem/opportunity/purpose.** The reason the report was written and its practical outcomes and accomplishments.
- **Scope.** What is and what isn't covered in the report. The scope also helps with the critical job of setting the audience's expectations.
- **Background.** The historical conditions or factors that led up to the report; this section enables readers to understand how the problem, situation, or opportunity developed and what has been done about it so far.
- **Sources and methods**. The primary and secondary sources of information used; as appropriate, this section explains how samples were selected, how questionnaires were constructed (which should be included in an appendix with any cover letters), what follow-up was done, and other matters related to methodology. This section builds reader confidence in the work and in the sources and methods used.

Johnson Landscaping

2430 Grafton Street, Halifax, NS B3S 2W1 (902) 555-1961 / Fax (902) 555-0742
E-mail: info@ johnscape.com

May 31, 2019
Mr. Steve Gamvrellis, Facilities Manager
United Food Processing
255 Sackville Street
Halifax, NS B2M SV1

Dear Mr. Gamvrellis:

This report will bring you up to date on the work done for your company by
Johnson Landscaping during the month of May 2019.

GROUND PREPARATION AND SPRINKLER INSTALLATION

Initial ground preparation and sprinkler system installation is complete. We
cleared, tilled, levelled, and raked 25 000 square metres for lawn and beds.
Installation of the sprinkler system for 15 000 square metres of lawn and beds
was completed on May 19.

BED PLANTING

From May 22 to May 30, shrubs and ornamental perennials were planted in
7000 square metres of beds. Beds were prepared for 3000 square metres of
annuals.

SPECIAL ISSUES AND SOLUTIONS

We've resolved the flooding discovered last month near the south end of the
shipping and receiving dock. It appears that an old plumbing repair had failed
under the employee cafeteria, causing water to flow under the building and
occasionally flood a small portion of the new lawn area.

In several of the perennial borders we've created along the east side of the
main building, a series of soil samples indicates an extremely high level of
acidity, much higher than would occur under natural conditions. We suspect
that the problem may have been caused by a small chemical spill at some
point in the past. We'll try to resolve this issue next month with soil
amendments. I'll contact you if this solution is likely to affect your budget
planning.

PLANS FOR JUNE

1. Distribute beauty bark and plant remaining annuals.
2. Resolve the soil quality issue in the perennial bed and make soil
   amendments as needed.
3. Monitor and adjust the automated sprinkling system to ensure adequate
   watering.

Letter format is appropriate for a simple interim progress report.

The opening introduces the purpose of the report.

The body uses clear headings to help the reader find items of interest.

The writer doesn't hesitate to bring up problems that need to be solved, but he offers possible solutions for further investigation.

He outlines plans for the next reporting period (the month of June).

Figure 12–4 Effective Progress Report Offering Complete Content (Excerpt)

- **Definitions.** A list of terms that might be unfamiliar to your audience, along with brief definitions; this section is unnecessary if readers are familiar with the terms you've used in your report—and they all agree on what the terms mean, which isn't always the case. If you have any question about reader knowledge, define any terms that might be misinterpreted; terms may also be defined in the body, explanatory notes, or glossary.
- **Limitations.** Factors beyond your control that affect report quality, such as budgets, schedule constraints, or limited access to information or people; if appropriate, this section can also express any doubts you have about any aspect of your report. Such candour may be uncomfortable to you, but it helps your readers assess your information accurately, and it helps establish your report's integrity.
- **Report organization.** The organization of the report (what topics are covered and in what order), along with a rationale for following this plan; this section is a road map that guides the reader through the report.

In a relatively brief report, these topics may be discussed in only a paragraph or two. Here's an example of a brief indirect opening, taken from the introduction of a memo on why a new line of luggage has failed to sell well. The writer's ultimate goal is to recommend a shift in marketing strategy.

> The performance of the Venturer line can be improved. In the two years since its introduction, this product line has achieved a sales volume lower than we expected, resulting in a drain on the company's overall earnings. The purpose of this report is to review the luggage-buying habits of consumers in all markets where the Venturer line is sold so that we can determine where to focus our marketing campaign.

This paragraph quickly introduces the subject (disappointing sales), tells why the problem is important (drain on earnings), and indicates the main points to be addressed in the body of the report (review of markets where the Venturer line is sold), without revealing what the conclusions and recommendations will be.

In a longer formal report, the discussion of these topics may span several pages and constitute a significant section within the report.

REPORT BODY As with the introduction, the body of your report can require some tough decisions about which elements to include and how much detail to offer. Here again, your decisions depend on many variables, including the needs of your audience. Some situations require detailed coverage; others can be handled with more concise treatment. Provide only enough detail in the body to support your conclusions and recommendations; you can put additional detail in tables, charts, and appendices. If you were writing a report that would be read by both high-level executives (who need only summaries and "big picture" information) and functional staff (who need specific details), you could address major points in the body and refer readers to specific places in an appendix for more details.

As with the introduction, the report body should contain only enough information to convey your message in a convincing fashion; don't overload the body with interesting but unnecessary material.

The topics commonly covered in a report body include

- Explanations of a problem or opportunity
- Facts, statistical evidence, and trends
- Results of studies or investigations
- Discussion and analysis of potential courses of action
- Advantages, disadvantages, costs, and benefits of a particular course of action
- Procedures or steps in a process
- Methods and approaches
- Criteria for evaluating alternatives and options
- Conclusions and recommendations
- Supporting reasons for conclusions or recommendations

For analytical reports using the direct organizational approach, you'll generally state your conclusions or recommendations in the introduction and use the body of your report to provide your evidence and support (as illustrated in Figures 12–3 and 12–4). If you're using an indirect approach, you'll likely use the body to discuss your logic and reserve your conclusions or recommendations until the very end.

REPORT CLOSE The content and length of your report close depend on your choice of direct or indirect order, among other variables. If you're using a direct approach, you can end with a summary of key points (usually not necessary in short memo-style reports) listed in the order they appear in the report body. If you're using an indirect approach, you can use the close to present your conclusions or recommendations if you didn't end the body with them. Keep in mind

The nature of your close depends on the type of report (informational or analytical) and the approach (direct or indirect).

that a conclusion or recommendation isn't the place to introduce new facts; your audience should have all the information they need by the time they reach this point in your report.

If your report is intended to prompt others to action, use the ending to spell out exactly what should happen next. Readers may agree with everything you say in your report but still fail to take any action if you're vague about the outcomes. Providing a schedule and specific task assignments is helpful because concrete plans tend to motivate action. If you'll take all the actions yourself, ensure that your readers understand this fact so that they'll know what to expect from you. The personal activity report in Figure 12–5 is a good example of efficiently conveying key information points, including a clear plan of action in the close. Note the use of hyperlinks to maps, photos, and a related report, all of which are stored on the same secure intranet site.

For long reports, you may need to divide your close into separate sections for conclusions, recommendations, and actions.

In a short report, the close may be only a paragraph or two. However, the close of a long report may have separate sections for conclusions, recommendations, and actions. Using separate sections helps your reader locate this material

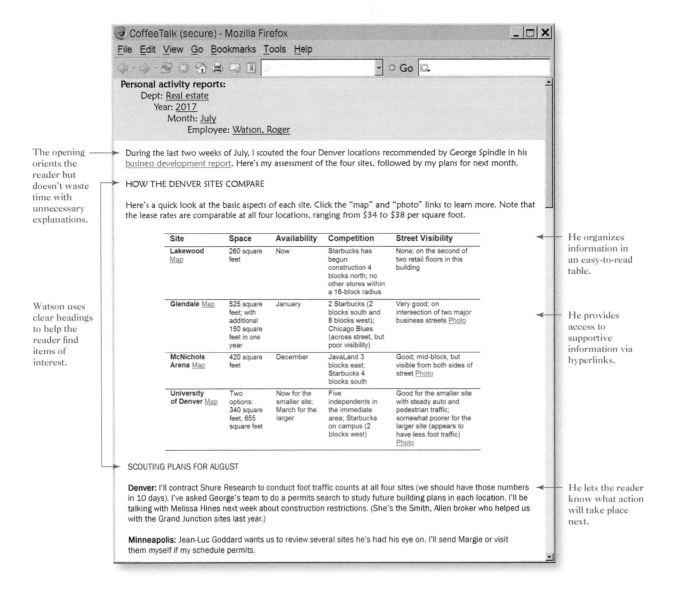

Figure 12–5 Effective Report Expressing Action Plan in the Close

Courtesy: Mozilla Foundation

and focus on each element. Such an arrangement also gives you a final opportunity to emphasize this important content.

If you have multiple conclusions, recommendations, or actions, you may want to number and list them. An appropriate lead-in to such a list might be, "The findings of this study lead to the following conclusions." A statement that could be used for a list of recommendations might be, "Based on the conclusions of this study, we make the following recommendations." A statement that could be used for actions might be, "To accomplish our goals on time, we must complete the following actions before the end of the year." Remember that when you use numbers, the reader expects the first item to be the most important. If you feel all items are of equal importance, use a bulleted list instead.

DRAFTING PROPOSAL CONTENT

With proposals, the content for each section is governed by many variables—the most important being the source of your proposal. If your proposal is unsolicited, you have some latitude in the scope and organization of content. However, if you are responding to a request for proposal (RFP), you need to follow the instructions in the RFP in every detail. Most RFPs spell out precisely what you should cover and in what order, so all bids will be similar in form and therefore easier to compare.

3 LEARNING OBJECTIVE

Explain six strategies to strengthen your proposal argument.

The general purpose of any proposal is to persuade readers to take an action, such as purchase goods or services, fund a project, or implement a program. Thus, your approach to writing a proposal is similar to that used for persuasive sales messages (see Chapter 10). As with other persuasive messages, the AIDA method of gaining attention, building interest, creating desire, and motivating action is an effective structure. Here are some additional strategies to strengthen your argument:[7]

Approach proposals the same way you approach persuasive messages.

- **Demonstrate your knowledge and credibility.** Show your reader that you have the knowledge and experience to solve the problem or address the opportunity outlined in your proposal.
- **Provide concrete information and examples.** Avoid vague, unsupported generalizations such as "We are losing money on this program." Instead, provide quantifiable details such as the amount of money being lost, how, and why. Explain how much money your proposed solution will save. Spell out your plan and give details on how the job will be done. Such concrete information persuades readers; unsupported generalizations do not.
- **Research the competition.** If you're competing against other companies for a potential customer's business, use trade publications, newspaper articles, industry directories, and the Internet to become familiar with the products, services, and prices of these other companies.
- **Prove that your proposal is workable.** Your proposal must be appropriate and feasible for your audience. It should be consistent with your audience's capabilities.

Business proposals need to provide more than just attractive ideas—readers look for evidence of practical, achievable solutions.

- **Adopt a "you" attitude.** Relate your product, service, or personnel to the reader's exact needs, either as stated in the RFP for a solicited proposal or as discovered through your own investigation for an unsolicited proposal.
- **Package your proposal attractively.** Ensure that your proposal is letter perfect, inviting, and readable. Readers will prejudge the quality of your products, services, and capabilities by the quality of the proposal you submit. Errors, omissions, or inconsistencies will work against you—and maybe even cost you important career and business opportunities.

In an unsolicited proposal, your introduction needs to convince readers that a problem or opportunity exists.

PROPOSAL INTRODUCTION The introduction presents and summarizes the problem you want to solve (or the opportunity you want to exploit), along with your proposed solution. It orients readers to the remainder of the text. If your proposal is solicited, its introduction should refer to the RFP, so readers know which RFP you're responding to. If your proposal is unsolicited, your introduction should mention any factors that led you to submit your proposal, such as previous conversations you've had with readers. The following topics are commonly covered in a proposal introduction:

- **Background or statement of the problem.** This is a brief review of the reader's situation and establishes a need for action. Readers may not perceive a problem or opportunity the same way you do. In unsolicited proposals, you need to convince them that a problem or opportunity exists before you can convince them to accept your solution. In a way that is meaningful to your reader, discuss the current situation and explain how the reader's circumstances can be improved.
- **Solution.** This is a brief description of the change you propose; it highlights your key selling points and their benefits, showing how your proposal will help readers meet their business objectives. In a sales proposal, the solution would be the products or services you offer, along with any accessories, warranties, professional services such as installation, and other enhancements. In other types of proposals, the solution would be defined by the nature of the proposal.
- **Scope.** This is a statement of the boundaries of the proposal—what you will and will not do.
- **Organization.** This orients the reader to the structure of the proposal and calls attention to the major divisions of information.

In short proposals, your discussion of these topics will be brief—perhaps only a sentence or two for each one. For long, formal proposals, each topic may warrant separate subheadings and several paragraphs of discussion.

Readers understand that a proposal is a persuasive message, so they're willing to accommodate a degree of promotional emphasis in your writing—as long as it is professional and focused on their needs.

PROPOSAL BODY The proposal's body has the same purpose as the body of other reports: it gives complete details on the proposed solution and specifies what the anticipated results will be. Because a proposal is by definition a persuasive message, your audience expects you to promote your plan in a confident but professional manner. Even when you're expressing an idea that you believe in passionately, maintain an objective tone so that you don't risk overselling your message.

In addition to providing facts and evidence to support your conclusions, an effective body covers this information:

- **Proposed solution.** Describe what you have to offer: your concept, product, or service. Stress the benefits of your product, service, or investment opportunity that are relevant to your readers' needs and point out any advantages that you have over your competitors.

The work plan indicates exactly how you will accomplish the solution presented in the proposal.

- **Work plan.** Describe how you'll accomplish what must be done. Explain the steps you'll take, their timing, the methods or resources you'll use, and the person(s) responsible. Specifically include when the work will begin, how it will be divided into stages, when you will finish, and whether any follow-up is involved. For solicited proposals, ensure that your dates match those specified in the RFP. Keep in mind that if your proposal is accepted, the work plan is contractually binding, so don't promise more than you can deliver.
- **Statement of qualifications.** Describe your organization's experience, personnel, and facilities—all in relation to reader needs. The qualifications

section can be an important selling point, and it deserves to be handled carefully. You can supplement your qualifications by including a list of client references, but get permission ahead of time to use these references.

* **Costs.** Cover pricing, reimbursable expenses, discounts, and so on. Coverage can vary widely, from a single price amount to detailed breakdowns by part number, service category, and so on. If you're responding to an RFP, follow the instructions it contains. In other cases, your firm probably has a set policy for discussing costs.

In an informal, short proposal, discussion of some or all of these elements may be grouped together. If the proposal is directed toward an audience outside your organization, use a letter format, as the proposal in Figure 12–6 does.

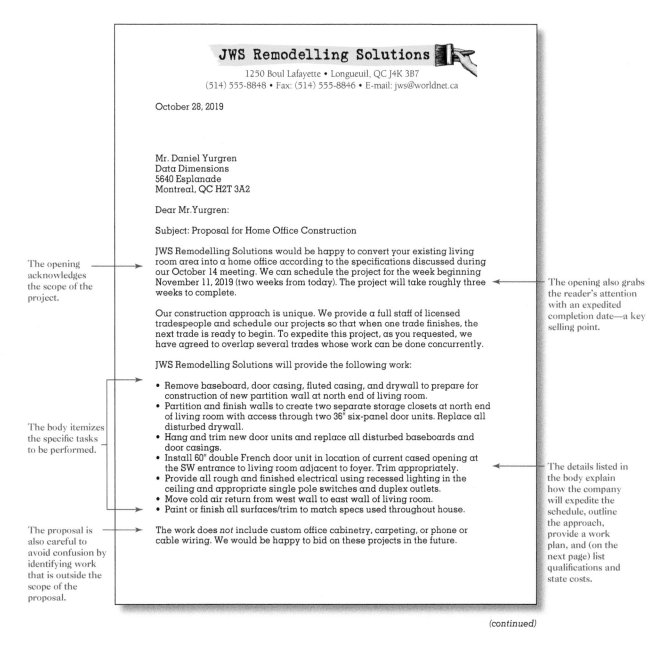

The opening acknowledges the scope of the project.

The body itemizes the specific tasks to be performed.

The proposal is also careful to avoid confusion by identifying work that is outside the scope of the proposal.

The opening also grabs the reader's attention with an expedited completion date—a key selling point.

The details listed in the body explain how the company will expedite the schedule, outline the approach, provide a work plan, and (on the next page) list qualifications and state costs.

(continued)

Figure 12–6 Effective Solicited Proposal in Letter Form

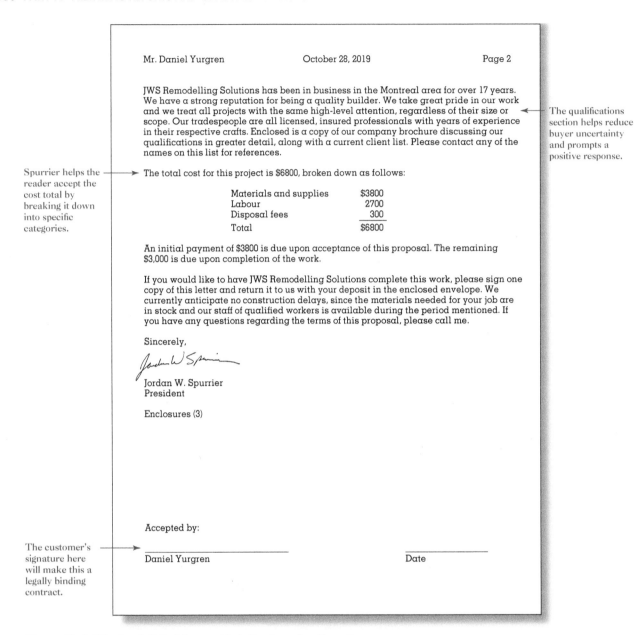

Mr. Daniel Yurgren   October 28, 2019   Page 2

JWS Remodelling Solutions has been in business in the Montreal area for over 17 years. We have a strong reputation for being a quality builder. We take great pride in our work and we treat all projects with the same high-level attention, regardless of their size or scope. Our tradespeople are all licensed, insured professionals with years of experience in their respective crafts. Enclosed is a copy of our company brochure discussing our qualifications in greater detail, along with a current client list. Please contact any of the names on this list for references.

> *The qualifications section helps reduce buyer uncertainty and prompts a positive response.*

> *Spurrier helps the reader accept the cost total by breaking it down into specific categories.*

The total cost for this project is $6800, broken down as follows:

Materials and supplies	$3800
Labour	2700
Disposal fees	300
Total	$6800

An initial payment of $3800 is due upon acceptance of this proposal. The remaining $3,000 is due upon completion of the work.

If you would like to have JWS Remodelling Solutions complete this work, please sign one copy of this letter and return it to us with your deposit in the enclosed envelope. We currently anticipate no construction delays, since the materials needed for your job are in stock and our staff of qualified workers is available during the period mentioned. If you have any questions regarding the terms of this proposal, please call me.

Sincerely,

Jordan W. Spurrier
President

Enclosures (3)

Accepted by:

_____   _____
Daniel Yurgren   Date

> *The customer's signature here will make this a legally binding contract.*

Figure 12–6 Effective Solicited Proposal in Letter Form *(continued)*

In a long, formal proposal, the discussion of these elements will be extensive and thorough. In this case, the proposal will be presented as a long report with multiple parts, accompanied by a memo or letter of transmittal as Chapter 13 discusses.

> *The close is your last chance to convince the reader of the merits of your proposal, so make doubly sure it's clear, compelling, and audience-oriented.*

PROPOSAL CLOSE The final section of a proposal generally summarizes the key points, emphasizes the benefits that readers will realize from your solution, summarizes the merits of your approach, restates why you and your firm are a good choice, and asks for a decision from the client. The close is your last opportunity to persuade readers to accept your proposal. In both formal and informal proposals, make this section relatively brief, assertive (but not brash or abrupt), and confident.

ESTABLISHING A TIME PERSPECTIVE

In what time frame will your report exist? Will you write in the past or present tense? The person who wrote this paragraph never decided:

> Of those interviewed, 25 percent *report* that they *are* dissatisfied with their present brand. The wealthiest participants *complained* most frequently, but all income categories *are* interested in trying a new brand. Only 5 percent of the interviewees *say* they *had* no interest in alternative products.

By switching from tense to tense when describing the same research results, you can confuse your readers. They wonder whether the shift is significant or whether you are just being careless. Eliminate the potential for such confusion by using tense consistently.

Also ensure that you observe the chronological sequence of events in your report. If you describe the history or development of something, start at the beginning and cover each event in the order of its occurrence. If you explain the steps in a process, take each step in proper sequence.

Unexplained shifts in time perspective can both confuse readers and lead them to question the thinking behind your report or proposal.

HELPING READERS FIND THEIR WAY

Time-pressed readers want to browse reports and quickly find information of interest. To help them find what they're looking for and stay on track as they navigate through your documents, learn to make good use of headings and links, smooth transitions, and previews and reviews:

Help your audiences navigate your reports by providing clear directions to key pieces of content.

- **Headings and links.** Readers should be able to follow the structure of your document and pick up the key points of your message from the headings and subheadings (see Chapter 6 for a review of what makes an effective heading). Follow a simple, consistent arrangement that clearly distinguishes levels, as shown in Figure 12–7.
- **Transitions.** Chapter 5 defines transitions as words or phrases that tie ideas together and show how one thought is related to another. In a long report, an entire paragraph might be used to highlight transitions from one section to the next, such as in this example:

Transitions connect ideas by helping readers move from one thought to the next.

> . . . *As you can see*, our profits have decreased by 12 percent over the past eight months.
>
> To counteract *this decline in profits*, we have three alternatives. *First*, we can raise our selling prices of existing products. *Second*, we can increase our offering by adding new products. *Third*, we can reduce our manufacturing costs. *However*, each alternative has both advantages and disadvantages.

The phrase *As you can see* alerts readers to the fact that they are reading a summary of the information just presented. The phrase *this decline in profits* lets readers know that the text will include something else about that previous topic. The words *first*, *second*, and *third* help readers stay on track as the three alternatives are introduced, and the word *however* alerts readers to the fact that evaluating the three alternatives requires some additional discussion. Effective transitions such as these can help readers grasp what they've learned so far while preparing to receive new information.

- **Previews and reviews.** *Preview sections* introduce important topics by helping readers get ready for new information. Previews are particularly helpful

Previews help readers prepare for upcoming information, and reviews help them verify and clarify what they've just read.

TITLE

The title is centred at the top of the page in all-capital letters, usually boldfaced, often in a large font, and often using a sans serif typeface. When the title runs to more than one line, the lines are usually double-spaced and arranged as an inverted pyramid (longer line on the top).

FIRST-LEVEL HEADING

A first-level heading indicates what the following section is about, perhaps by describing the subdivisions. All first-level headings are grammatically parallel, with the possible exception of such headings as "Introduction," "Conclusions," and "Recommendations." Some text appears between every two headings, regardless of their levels. Still boldfaced and serif, the font may be smaller than that used in the title but still larger than the typeface used in the text and still in all capital letters.

Second-Level Heading

Like first-level headings, second-level headings indicate what the following material is about. All second-level headings within a section are grammatically parallel. Still boldfaced and serif, the font may either remain the same or shrink to the size used in the text, and the style is now initial capitals with lower case. Never use only one second-level heading under a first-level heading. (The same is true for every other level of heading.)

Third-Level Heading
A third-level heading is worded to reflect the content of the material that follows. All third-level headings beneath a second-level heading should be grammatically parallel.

Fourth-Level Heading. Like all the other levels of heading, fourth-level headings reflect the subject that will be developed. All fourth-level headings within a subsection are parallel. Fourth-level headings are generally the lowest level of heading used. However, you can indicate further breakdowns in your ideas by using a list:

1. *The first item in a list*. You may indent the entire item in block format to set it off visually. Numbers are optional.

2. *The second item in a list*. All lists have at least two items. An introductory phrase or sentence may be italicized for emphasis, as shown here.

Figure 12–7 Heading Format for Reports

when the information is complex, unexpected, or unfamiliar. In contrast, *review sections* come after a body of material and summarize the information for your readers. Reviews help readers absorb details while keeping track of the big picture. Previews and reviews can be written in sentence format, bulleted lists (see Chapter 6), or a combination of the two. Both are effective, but bullets can increase your document's readability by adding white space to the document design:

Sentence Format	Bulleted List
The next section discusses the advantages of advertising on the Internet. Among them are currency, global reach, affordability, and interactivity.	As the next section shows, advertising on the Internet has four advantages: • Currency • Global reach • Affordability • Interactivity

To review the tasks discussed in this section, see "Checklist: Composing Business Reports and Proposals."

✔ **Checklist** | **Composing Business Reports and Proposals**

A. Review and fine-tune your outline.
- Match your parallel headings to the tone of your report.
- Understand how the introduction, body, and close work together to convey your message.

B. Draft report content.
- Use the introduction to establish the purpose, scope, and organization of your report.
- Use the body to present and interpret the information you gathered.
- Use the close to summarize major points, discuss conclusions, or make recommendations.

C. Draft proposal content.
- Use the introduction to discuss the background or problem, your solution, the scope, and organization.
- Use the body to explain persuasively the benefits of your proposed approach.

- Use the close to emphasize reader benefits and summarize the merits of your approach.

D. Establish a consistent time frame.
- Avoid switching from tense to tense.
- Observe the chronological sequence of events.

E. Help readers find their way.
- Provide headings to improve readability and clarify the framework of your ideas.
- Use hyperlinks online to allow readers to jump from section to section.
- Create transitions that tie ideas together and show how one thought relates to another.
- Preview important topics to help readers get ready for new information.
- Review key information to help readers absorb details and keep the big picture in mind.

USING TECHNOLOGY TO CRAFT REPORTS AND PROPOSALS

Creating lengthy reports and proposals can be a huge task, so take advantage of technological tools to help throughout the process. You've read about some of these tools in earlier chapters; here are some of the most important ones for developing reports and proposals:

Look for ways to use technology to reduce the mechanical work involved in writing long reports.

- **Templates.** Beyond simply formatting documents, report templates can identify the specific sections required for each type of report. For example, a marketing plan could include such sections as a competitive analysis, market analysis, launch plans, financial analysis, and promotional and customer support plans. The template could automatically insert headings for each section, with reminders of the content to include.
- **Linked and embedded documents.** In many reports and proposals, you need to include graphics, spreadsheets, databases, and other elements produced in other software programs. Make sure you know how the software handles the files, or you may receive some unpleasant surprises. For example, in Microsoft Office you can choose to either *link* or *embed* an incoming element, such as a table from a spreadsheet. If you link, the element will be updated whenever you or someone else updates the spreadsheet. In contrast, if you embed it, the files are no longer connected; changes in the spreadsheet will not show up in the report document.
- **Electronic forms.** For recurring forms such as sales reports and compliance reports, consider creating a word-processing file that combines *boilerplate* text for material that doesn't change from report to report. To accommodate information that does change (such as last week's sales results), use *form tools* such as text boxes (in which users can type new text) and check boxes (which can be used to select from a set of predetermined choices). The completed file can then be printed, emailed, or posted to a website.

- **Electronic documents.** Portable document format (PDF) files have become a universal replacement for printed reports and proposals. Using Adobe Acrobat or similar products, you can quickly convert reports and proposals to PDF files that are easy to share electronically. Note that PDFs have long been considered safer than word processor files, but recent discoveries indicate that PDFs could also be used to transmit computer viruses.[8] For information on protecting yourself when using Adobe Reader for PDFs, visit www.adobe.com/security.html.
- **Multimedia documents.** To enhance the communication and persuasion powers of the written word, combine your report with video clips, animation, presentation software slides, screen-casts (recordings of onscreen activity), and other elements.
- **Proposal-writing software.** Proposal-writing software can automatically personalize proposals, ensure proper structure (making sure you don't forget any sections, for example), organize storage of all your boilerplate text, and scan RFPs to identify questions and requirements and fill in potential answers from a centralized knowledge base.[9]

Writing for Websites and Wikis

5 LEARNING OBJECTIVE

Identify six characteristics of effective writing in online reports.

In addition to standalone reports and proposals, you may be asked to write in-depth content for websites or to collaborate on a wiki. The basic principles of report writing apply to both formats, but each has some unique considerations as well.

DRAFTING WEBSITE CONTENT

Major sections on websites, particularly those that are fairly static (unlike, say, a blog) function in much the same way as reports. The skills you've developed for report writing adapt easily to this environment, as long as you keep a few points in mind:

- **Take special care to build trust with your intended audiences.** Careful readers can be skeptical of online content. Make sure your content is accurate, current, complete, and authoritative.
- **As much as possible, adapt your content for a global audience.** Translating content is expensive, so some companies compromise by *localizing* the home page while keeping the deeper, more detailed content in its original language.
- **Keep your language clear and concise, with few idioms and slang.** If a potential client is using a tool like Google Translate, complex language does not translate well (or even accurately).
- **Create compelling content.** In an environment that presents many reading challenges, compelling, reader-oriented content is key to success.[10] Wherever you can, use the *inverted pyramid* style, in which you cover the most important information briefly at first and then gradually reveal successive layers of detail—letting readers choose to see those additional layers if they want to.
- **Present your information in a concise, skimmable format.** Effective websites use a variety of means to help readers skim pages quickly, including lists, careful use of colour and boldface, informative headings, and helpful summaries that give readers a choice of learning more if they want to.
- **Write effective links that serve for both site navigation and content skimming.** Above all else, clearly identify where a link will take readers. Don't rely on cute wordplay that obscures the content, and don't force readers to click through and try to figure out where they're going.

COLLABORATING ON WIKIS

As Chapter 2 points out, using wikis is a great way for teams and other groups to collaborate on writing projects, from brief articles to long reports and reference works; Figure 12–8 shows a wiki IBM created to facilitate cooperation with its external business partners. The benefits of wikis are compelling, but they do require a unique approach to writing. To be a valuable wiki contributor, keep these points in mind:[11]

Being an effective wiki collaborator requires a different writing mindset.

- Let go of traditional expectations of authorship, including individual recognition and control.
- Encourage all team members to improve one another's work.
- Use page templates and other formatting options to make sure your content matches the rest of the wiki.
- Use the separate editing and discussion capabilities appropriately.
- Take advantage of the *sandbox*, if available; this is a "safe," nonpublished section of the wiki where team members can practise editing and writing.

Wikis usually have guidelines to help new contributors integrate their work into the group's ongoing effort. Be sure to read and understand these guidelines, and don't be afraid to ask for help.

If you are creating a new wiki, think through your long-term purpose carefully, just as you would with a new blog or podcast channel. Doing so will help you craft appropriate guidelines, editorial oversight, and security policies. For instance, the PlayStation development team at Sony uses a wiki to keep top managers up to date on new products, and because this information is highly confidential, access to the wiki is tightly controlled.[12]

If you are adding a page or an article to an existing wiki, figure out how this new material fits in with the existing organization. Also, learn the wiki's preferred style for handling incomplete articles. For example, on the wiki that contains the user documentation for the popular WordPress blogging software, contributors are discouraged from adding new pages until the content is "fairly complete and accurate."[13]

Make sure you understand how a new wiki page will fit in with the existing content.

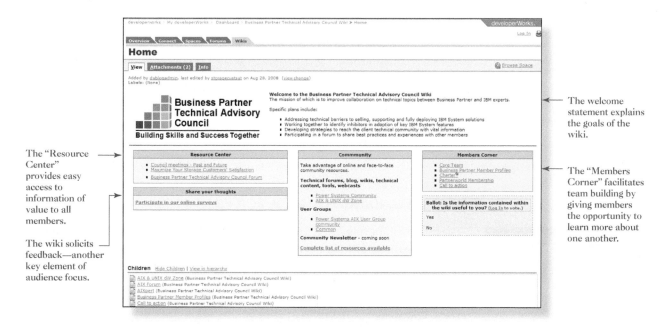

Figure 12–8 IBM Business Partner Wiki

Courtesy: Reprint Courtesy of International Business Machines Corporation, © International Business Machines Corporation. First published on the IBM developerWorks community at http://www.ibm.com/developerworks/community.

If you are revising or updating an existing wiki article, use the list of questions in Chapter 6 (on pages 148–149) to evaluate the content before you make changes. If you don't agree with published content and plan to revise it, you can use the wiki's discussion facility to share your concerns with other contributors. The wiki environment should encourage discussions and even robust disagreements, as long as everyone remains civil and respectful.

Illustrating Your Reports with Effective Visuals

Carefully crafted visuals enhance the power of your words.

Well-designed visual elements can enhance the communication power of textual messages and, in some instances, even replace textual messages. Visuals can often convey some message points (such as spatial relationships, correlations, procedures, and emotions) more effectively and more efficiently than words. Generally speaking, in a given amount of time, well-designed images can convey much more information than text.[14] Visuals attract and hold people's attention, helping your audience understand and remember your message. Busy readers often jump to visuals to try to get the gist of a message, and attractive visuals can draw readers more deeply into your reports and presentations. Using pictures is also an effective way to communicate with the diverse audiences that are common in today's business environment.

Like words, visuals often carry connotative or symbolic meanings.

In addition to their direct information value, visuals often have connotative meaning as well. As you read in Chapter 5, many words and phrases carry connotative meanings, which are all the mental images, emotions, and other impressions that the word or phrase evokes in audience members. A significant part of the power—and risk—of visual elements derives from their connotative meanings as well. Even something as simple as a watermark symbol embedded in letterhead stationery can boost reader confidence in whatever message is printed on the paper.[15]

Many colours, shapes, and other design elements have visual symbolism; and their symbolic, connotative meaning can evolve over time and have different meanings to different cultures. For example, a red cross on a white background stands for emergency medical care in many countries. But the cross is also a Christian symbol, so the International Federation of Red Cross and Red Crescent Movement uses a red crescent in Islamic countries—even though the original Red Cross symbol is based on the flag of Switzerland and not on any religious icons. In 2007, the red crystal was adopted as a third emblem intended to avoid specific religious associations. Being aware of these symbolic meanings and using them to your advantage are important aspects of being an effective business communicator.

UNDERSTANDING VISUAL DESIGN PRINCIPLES

6 LEARNING OBJECTIVE

Discuss six principles of graphic design that can improve the quality of your visuals.

Visual literacy is the ability to create and interpret visual messages.

Given the importance of visuals in today's business environment, **visual literacy**—the ability (as a sender) to create effective images and (as a receiver) to correctly interpret visual messages—has become a key business skill.[16] Just as creating effective sentences, paragraphs, and documents requires working knowledge of the principles of good writing, creating effective visuals requires some knowledge of the principles of good design. For example, Figure 12–9a violates numerous principles of effective design, as you can see in the annotations. Figure 12–9b will never win any awards for exciting or innovative design, but it does its job efficiently and effectively.

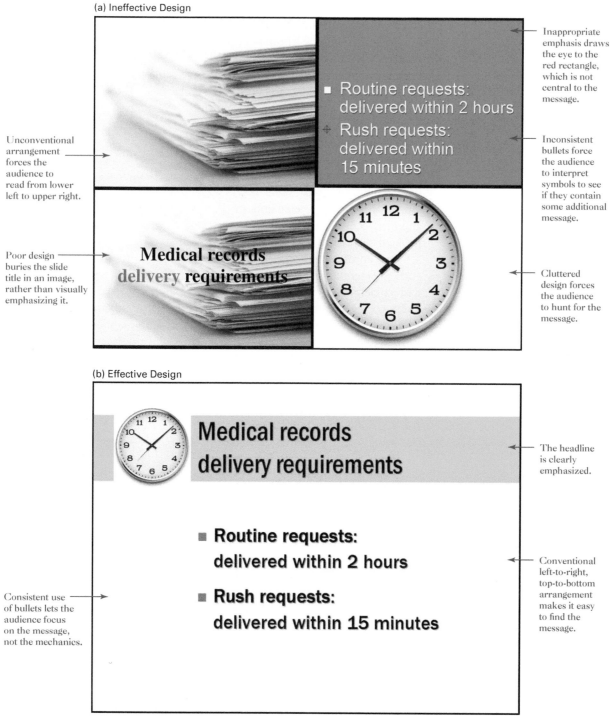

Figure 12–9 Ineffective and Effective Visual Designs

Sergiy Tryapitsyn/123RF and Yanas/Shutterstock

Even if you have no formal training in design, being aware of the following six principles will help you be a more effective visual communicator:

- **Consistency.** Readers view a series of visuals as a whole, assuming that design elements will be consistent from one page to the next. Think of continuity as *visual parallelism*, in the same way that textual parallelism helps audiences understand and compare a series of ideas.[17] You can achieve visual parallelism in a variety of ways, through the consistent use of colour,

When designing visuals, observe the principles of consistency, contrast, balance, emphasis, convention, and simplicity.

shape, size, texture, position, scale, or typeface. For example, if your first chart shows results for Division A in blue, the audience will expect Division A to be shown in blue throughout the report or presentation.

• **Contrast.** Readers expect visual distinctions to match verbal ones. To emphasize differences, depict items in contrasting colours, such as red and blue or black and white. To emphasize similarities, make colour differences more subtle. In a pie chart, you might show two similar items in two shades of blue and a dissimilar item in yellow. Keep in mind that accent colours draw attention to key elements, but they lose their effect if you overdo them.

• **Balance.** The human eye tends to compare visual images with physical structures, and images that appear to be out of balance can be as unsettling as a building that looks like it's about to tip over. Balance can be either *formal*, in which the elements in the images are arranged symmetrically around a central point or axis, or *informal*, in which elements are not distributed evenly but stronger and weaker elements are arranged in a way that achieves an overall effect of balance. A common approach to informal balance is weighing one visually dominant element against several smaller or weaker elements.[18] Generally speaking, formal balance is calming and serious, whereas informal balance tends to feel dynamic and engaging (which is why most advertising uses this approach, for example).

• **Emphasis.** Audiences usually assume that the dominant element in a design is the most important, so make sure that the visually dominant element really does represent the most important information. You can do this through colour, position, size, or placement, for example. Conversely, be sure to downplay visually less important items. For example, avoid using strong colours for minor support points, and de-emphasize background features such as the grid lines on a chart.

• **Convention.** Just as written communication is guided by an array of spelling, grammar, punctuation, and usage conventions, visual communication is guided by a variety of generally accepted rules or conventions that dictate virtually every aspect of design.[19] Moreover, many conventions are so ingrained that people don't even realize they are following conventions. For example, if English is your native language, you assume that ideas progress across the page from left to right because that's the direction in which English text is written. Whether it's the sequence of steps in a process diagram or elapsed time along the bottom of a graph, you automatically expect this left-to-right flow. However, if you are a native Arabic or Hebrew speaker, you might automatically assume that flow on a page or screen is from right to left because that is the direction in which those languages are written. Flouting conventions often causes breakdowns in communication, but in some cases, it can be done to great effect.[20] For example, flipping an organization chart upside down—putting the customers at the top, with frontline employees directly beneath them and on down to the chief executive at the bottom—can be an effective way to emphasize that customers come first and the responsibility of managers is supporting employees in their efforts to satisfy customers.

• **Simplicity.** As Figure 12–9 indicates, simpler is usually better when using visuals for business communication. When you're designing graphics for your documents, remember that you're conveying information, not creating artwork. Limit the number of colours and design elements you use and take care to avoid *chartjunk*, a term coined by visual communication specialist Edward R. Tufte for decorative elements that clutter documents and potentially confuse readers without adding any relevant information.[21] Computers make it far too easy to add chartjunk, from clip art illustrations to three-dimensional bar charts that display only two dimensions of data. When you need to show distinctions between visual elements, follow Tufte's strategy of the smallest effective difference. In his words, "Make all visual distinctions as subtle as possible, but still clear and effective."[22] For example, the slices in a pie chart don't need to be distinguished by both colour and texture; one or the other will do the job more efficiently.

UNDERSTANDING THE ETHICS OF VISUAL COMMUNICATION

The potential power of visuals places an ethical burden on every business communicator. This responsibility involves not only the obvious requirement of avoiding intentional ethical lapses but the more complicated and often more subtle requirement of avoiding unintentional lapses as well. Ethical problems can range from photos that play on racial or gender stereotypes to images that imply cause-and-effect relationships that may not exist to graphs that distort data.

Visuals are powerful, and you have the responsibility to use them ethically.

For example, photographs can influence perceptions of physical size (and perhaps of quality, value, danger, or other associated variables), depending on the way the various elements are arranged in the picture. To increase the perceived size of a product, an advertiser might show a close-up of it being held by someone with smaller-than-average hands. Conversely, a large hand would make the product seem smaller.

You can work to avoid ethical lapses in your visuals by following these guidelines:[23]

- Consider all possible interpretations—and misinterpretations; will audience biases, beliefs, or backgrounds lead them to different conclusions than you intend?
- Provide enough background information to help audiences interpret the visual information correctly.
- Don't hide or minimize visual information that runs counter to your argument—and don't exaggerate visual information that supports your argument.
- Don't oversimplify complex situations by hiding complications that are important to the audience's understanding of the situation.
- Don't imply cause-and-effect relationships without providing proof that they exist.
- Avoid emotional manipulation or other forms of coercion.
- Be careful with the way you aggregate, or group, data. For example, aggregating daily sales data by weeks or months can obscure daily fluctuations that could be meaningful to your audience.
- Use visuals only if you have permission from the original artist or if you are using free images or those you have created yourself from your data.

You can take many steps to emphasize or de-emphasize specific elements in your visuals, but make sure you don't inadvertently commit an ethical lapse while doing so.

Visuals can't always speak for themselves; make sure your audience has enough context to interpret your visuals correctly.

IDENTIFYING POINTS TO ILLUSTRATE

To help identify which parts of your message can benefit from visuals, step back and consider the flow of the entire message from the audience's point of view. Which parts might seem complex, open to misinterpretation, or even just a little bit dull? Are there any connections between ideas or data sets that might not be obvious if they are addressed only in text? Is there a lot of numerical data or other discrete factual content that would be difficult to read if presented in paragraph form? Is there a chance the main idea won't "jump off the page" if it's covered only in text? Will readers greet the message with skepticism and therefore look for plenty of supporting evidence? If you answer yes to any of these questions, you probably need one or more visuals.

7 LEARNING OBJECTIVE

Explain how to choose which points in your message to illustrate.

When you're deciding which points to present visually, think of the five Cs:

- **Clear.** The human mind is extremely adept at processing visual information, whether it's something simple, such as the shape of a stop sign, or complicated, such as the floor plan for a new factory. If you're having difficulty conveying an idea in words, take a minute to brainstorm some visual possibilities.
- **Complete.** Visuals, particularly tables, often serve to provide the supporting details for your main idea or recommendation. Moreover, the process of summarizing, concluding, or recommending often requires you to narrow down your material or exclude details; a table or another visual can provide such details without getting in the way of your main message.
- **Concise.** You've probably heard the phrase "A picture is worth a thousand words." If a particular section of your message seems to require extensive description or explanation, see whether there's a way to convey that information visually in order to reduce your word count.
- **Connected.** A key purpose of many business messages is to show connections of some sort—similarities or differences, correlations, cause-and-effect relationships, and so on. Whenever you want readers to see such a connection, consider whether a chart, diagram, or another illustration can help.
- **Compelling.** Your readers live in a highly visual world. Will one or more illustrations make your message more persuasive, more interesting, more likely to get read? You never want to insert visuals simply for decorative purposes, but even if a particular point can be expressed equally well via text or visuals, consider adding the visual to make your report or presentation more compelling.

As you identify which points in your document would benefit from visuals, make sure that each visual you decide on has a clear purpose (see Table 12–1).

SELECTING THE RIGHT TYPE OF VISUAL

Once you've identified which points would benefit most from visual presentation, your next decision is to choose which type of visual to use for each message point. As you see in Figure 12–10, you have many choices for business graphics. For certain types of information, the decision is usually obvious. If you want to present a large set of numerical values or detailed textual information, a table is the obvious choice in most cases. However, if you're presenting data broken down geographically, a colour-coded map might be

Table 12–1	**When to Use Visuals**

Purpose	Example Applications
To clarify	Support text descriptions of quantitative or numerical information, trends, spatial relationships, or physical constructions.
To simplify	Break complicated descriptions into components that can be depicted with conceptual models, flowcharts, organization charts, or diagrams.
To emphasize	Call attention to particularly important points by illustrating them with line, bar, pie, and other types of charts.
To summarize	Review major points in the narrative by providing a chart or table that summarizes key items.
To reinforce	Present information in both visual and written forms to increase readers' retention.
To attract	Engage readers visually and emotionally; provide visual relief from long blocks of text.
To impress	Build credibility by putting ideas into visual form to convey the impression of authenticity and precision.
To unify	Depict the relationship among points, such as visually integrating the steps in a process by presenting them in a flowchart.

more effective to show overall patterns rather than individual data points. Also, certain visuals are used more commonly for certain applications; for example, your audience is likely to expect line charts to show trends and bar charts to show comparisons. Line charts usually show data variations relative to a time axis (such as sales month by month), whereas bar charts more often compare discrete groups (such as sales by demographic segment). Similarly, although a bar chart can show the percentages that make up a whole, this job is usually reserved for pie charts.

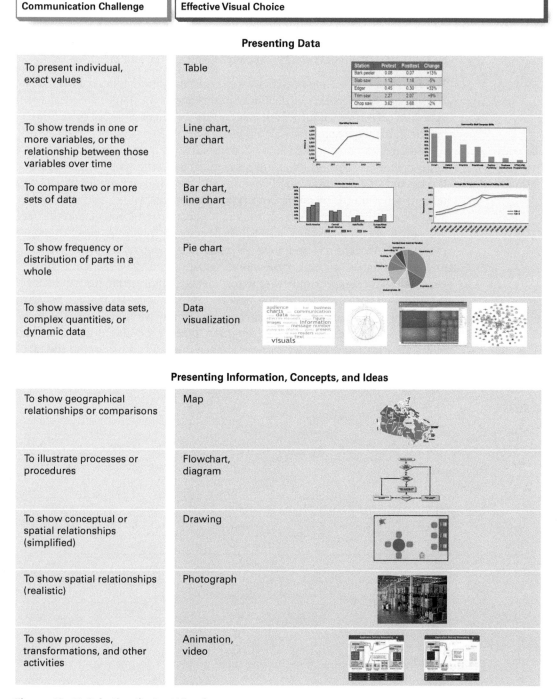

Figure 12–10 Selecting the Best Visual

Champiofoto/Shutterstock

The following sections explore the most common types of visuals in more detail, starting with visuals designed to present data.

VISUALS FOR PRESENTING DATA Business professionals have a large number of choices for presenting data, from general-purpose line, bar, and pie charts to specialized charts for product portfolios, financial analysis, and other professional functions. The visuals most commonly used to present data include tables, line and surface charts, bar charts, pictograms, Gantt charts, and pie charts.

Tables When you need to present detailed, specific information, choose a table, a systematic arrangement of data in columns and rows. Tables are ideal when your audience needs information that would be either difficult or tedious to handle in the main text.

Most tables contain the standard parts illustrated in Figure 12–11. Every table includes vertical columns and horizontal rows, with useful headings along the top and side. The number of columns and rows you can comfortably fit in a table depends on the medium. For printed documents, you can adjust font size and column/row spacing to fit a considerable amount of information on the page and still maintain readability. For online documents, you often need to reduce the number of columns and rows to ensure that your tables are easily readable online. Tables for oral presentations usually need to be the simplest of all because you can't expect audiences to read detailed information from the screen.

Although complex information may require formal tables that are set apart from the text, you can present some data more simply within the text. You make the table, in essence, a part of the paragraph, typed in tabular format. Such text tables are usually introduced with a sentence that leads directly into the tabulated information. Here's an example from the Scotiabank 2011 Corporate Social Responsibility report:

Printed tables can display extensive amounts of data, but tables for online display and electronic presentations need to be simpler.

Overview of Scotiabank's microfinance services

	Total loans (CDN)	Average loan size (CDN)	# of customers
Chile (Banco del Desarrollo)	$60 million	$2,960	20,294
Dominican Republic	$31 million	$2,150	14,400
Guatemala	$41 million	$3,090	13,090
Jamaica	$0.4 million	$300	1,400
Peru	$458 million	$3,700	124,000
Total	**$590 million**		**173,184**

* We define microfinance clients as self-employed or micro-business owners with annual revenues below US$100,000.

Courtesy of The Bank of Nova Scotia.

When you prepare tables, follow these guidelines to make your tables easy to read:

• Use common, understandable units, and clearly identify the units you use, whether dollars, percentages, price per tonne, and so on.

	Multicolumn Heading			Single-Column Heading
	Column Subheading	Column Subheading	Column Subheading	
Row Heading	xxx	xxx	xxx	xxx
Row Heading	xxx	xxx	xxx	xxx
Row Subheading	xxx	xxx	xxx	xxx
Row Subheading	xxx	xxx	xxx	xxx
Row Heading	xxx	xxx	xxx	xxx
Row Heading	xxx	xxx	xxx	xxx
TOTALS	xxx	xxx	xxx	xxx

Figure 12–11 Parts of a Table

- Express all items in a column in the same unit and round off for simplicity.
- Label column headings clearly and use a subhead if necessary.
- Separate columns or rows with lines or extra space to make the table easy to follow; in complex tables, consider highlighting every other row or column in a pale, contrasting colour.
- Provide totals or averages of columns or rows when relevant.
- Document the source of the data using the same format as a text footnote (see Appendix B).

Although numerical tables are more common, tables can also contain words, symbols, or other facts and figures. Word tables are particularly appropriate for presenting survey findings or for comparing various items against a specific standard.

Line Charts and Surface Charts A **line chart**, or *line graph*, illustrates trends over time or plots the relationship of two variables. In line charts showing trends, the vertical axis (or *y*-axis) shows the amount, and the horizontal axis (or *x*-axis) shows the time or other quantity against which the amount is measured. Moreover, you can plot just a single line or overlay multiple lines to compare different entities. The line chart in Figure 12–12 shows the fluctuations in average kiln temperatures for two kilns during the day shift.

A **surface chart**, also called an **area chart**, is a form of line chart with a cumulative effect; all the lines add up to the top line, which represents the total

Line charts are commonly used to show trends over time or the relationship between two variables.

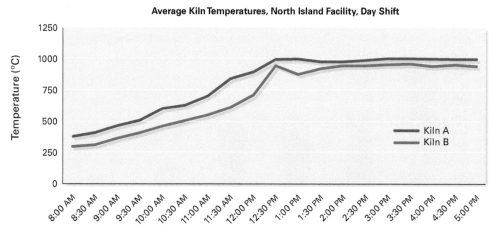

Figure 12–12 Line Chart

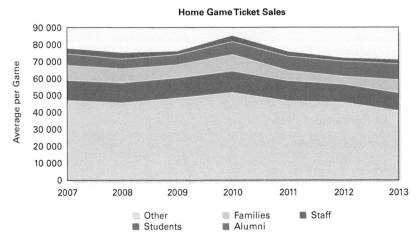

Figure 12–13 Surface Chart

(see Figure 12–13). This form of chart helps you illustrate changes in the composition of something over time. When preparing a surface chart, put the most important segment against the baseline, and restrict the number of strata to four or five.

Bar Charts and Pie Charts A **bar chart**, or *bar graph*, portrays numbers by the height or length of its rectangular bars, making a series of numbers easy to read or understand. Bar charts are particularly valuable when you want to (1) compare the size of several items at one time; (2) show changes in one item over time; (3) indicate the composition of several items over time; and (4) show the relative size of components of a whole.

As the charts in Figure 12–14 suggest, bar charts can appear in various forms. *Singular* bar charts (Figure 12–14a) compare one set of data, using the same colour or pattern for each set. *Grouped* bar charts (Figure 12–14b) compare more than one set of data, using a different colour or pattern for each set. *Deviation* bar charts (Figure 12–14c) identify positive and negative values, or winners and losers. *Segmented* bar charts (Figure 12–14d), also known as stacked bar charts, show how individual components contribute to a total number, using a different colour or pattern for each component. *Combination* bar and line charts (Figure 12–14e) compare quantities that require different intervals. *Paired* bar charts (Figure 12–14f) show the correlations between two items.

Most readers expect pie charts to show the distribution of parts within a whole.

Like segmented bar charts and area charts, a **pie chart** shows how the parts of a whole are distributed. However, pie charts have the advantage of familiarity; most people expect parts-of-a-whole to be displayed via a pie

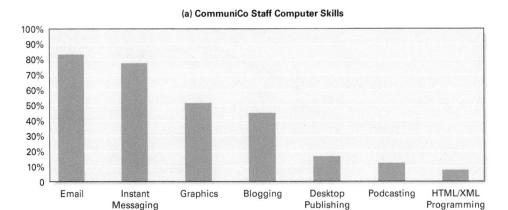

Figure 12–14 The Versatile Bar Chart

(b) Worldwide Market Share

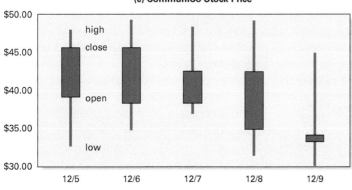

(c) CommuniCo Stock Price

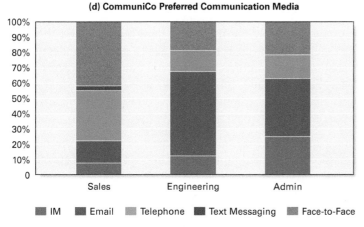

(d) CommuniCo Preferred Communication Media

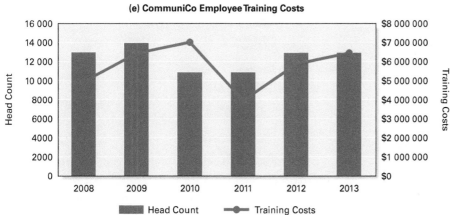

(e) CommuniCo Employee Training Costs

Figure 12–14 The Versatile Bar Chart *(continued)*

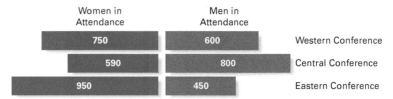

(f) Conference Attendance by Gender

Figure 12–14 **The Versatile Bar Chart** *(continued)*

chart. Each segment represents a slice of a complete circle, or *pie*. As you can see in Figure 12–15, pie charts are an effective way to show percentages or to compare one segment with another.

When creating pie charts, restrict the number of slices in the pie to eight or fewer. Otherwise, the chart looks cluttered and is difficult to label. If necessary, combine the smallest pieces together in a "miscellaneous" category. Ideally, the largest or most important slice of the pie, the segment you want to emphasize, is placed at the twelve o'clock position; the rest are arranged clockwise either in order of size or in some other logical progression.

Use different colours or patterns to distinguish the various pieces. Patterns are often a better choice if you are printing in black and white, or if you have a colour-blind audience. If you want to draw attention to the segment that is of the greatest interest to your readers, use a brighter colour for that segment, draw an arrow to the segment, or explode it; that is, pull the segment away from the rest of the pie. In any case, label all the segments and indicate their values in either percentages or units of measure so your readers will be able to judge the value of the wedges. Remember, the segments must add up to 100 percent if percentages are used or to the total number if numbers are used.

Pie charts are used frequently, but they aren't necessarily the best choice for many data presentations. The pie chart in Figure 12–15 does make it easy to see that assemblers are the largest employee category, but other comparisons of slice sizes (such as Sales, Engineers, and Admin) are not as easy to make and require a numerical rather than a visual comparison. In contrast, the bar chart gives a quick visual comparison of every data point.

Data visualization tools let you display vast data sets, dynamic data, and textual information graphically.

Data Visualization Conventional charts and graphs are limited in several ways. Most types can show only a limited number of data points before becoming too cluttered to interpret; they often can't show complex relationships among data

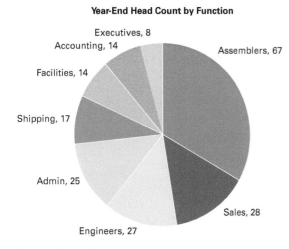

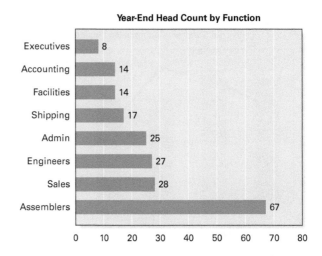

Figure 12–15 **Pie Charts versus Bar Charts**

(a) Website Linkage Map. This interactive network diagram shows the most active links to and from Apple's homepage (**www.apple.com**). *Website linkage map by TouchGraph.com*

(b) Facebook Friend Wheel. This network diagram shows how the connections of Barry Graubart (an executive with an e-commerce company) are connected with one another.

(c) Tag Cloud. This "word chart" shows the relative frequency of the 50 most-used words in this chapter (other than common words such as *and, or,* and *the*).

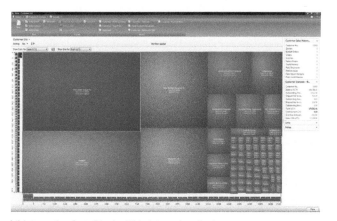

(d) Interactive Data Display. This interactive display conveys two company performance variables at once (sales and profits) for a large data set by using the size and colour of the individual blocks.

Figure 12–16 Data Visualization

Courtesy: (a) TouchGraph LLC, (b) ContentMatters LLC, (d) © Microsoft Office 2013.

points; and they can represent only numerical data. As computer technologies continue to generate massive amounts of data that can be combined and connected in endless ways, a diverse class of display capabilities known as **data visualization** works to overcome all these drawbacks.

Unlike charts and graphs, data visualization is less about clarifying individual data points and more about extracting broad meaning from giant masses of data or putting the data in context.[24] The range of data visualization displays is virtually endless; Figure 12–16 shows a few of the many different ways to display complex sets of data. For instance, the Facebook "friend wheel" in Figure 12–16b offers a visual sense of this particular Facebook user's network by showing which of his friends are friends of each other and thereby indicating "clustering" within the network (work friends, social friends, and so on). The diagram doesn't attempt to show quantities but rather the overall nature of the network.

Visuals for Presenting Information, Concepts, and Ideas In addition to facts and figures, you can present other types of information visually, from spatial relationships (such as the floor plan for a new office building) to abstract ideas (such as progress or competition). The most common types of visuals for these applications include flowcharts, organization charts, maps, drawings, diagrams, photographs, animation, and video.

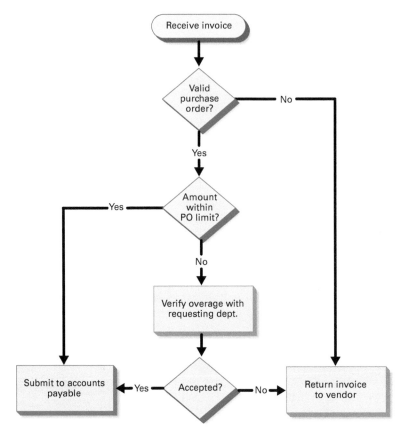

Figure 12–17 Flowchart

Flowcharts and Organization Charts A **flowchart** (see Figure 12–17) illustrates a sequence of events from start to finish; it is an indispensable tool for illustrating processes, procedures, and sequential relationships. For general business purposes, you don't need to be too concerned about the specific shapes in a flowchart, but use them consistently. However, you should be aware of the formal flowchart "language," in which each shape has a specific meaning (diamonds are decision points and rectangles are process steps). If you're communicating with computer programmers and others accustomed to formal flowcharting, ensure that you use the correct symbols in each case to avoid confusion.

As the name implies, an **organization chart** illustrates the positions, units, or functions of an organization and the way they interrelate. An organization's normal communication channels are almost impossible to describe without the benefit of a chart like the one in Figure 12–18. These charts aren't limited to organizational structures, of course; as you saw in Chapter 4, they can also be used to outline messages.

Use maps to represent statistics by geographical area and to show spatial relationships.

Maps and Geographic Information Systems Maps can show location, distance, points of interest (such as competitive retail outlets), and geographical distribution of data, such as sales by region or population by province. In addition to presenting facts and figures, maps are useful for showing market territories, distribution routes, and facilities locations.

When combined with databases and aerial or satellite photography in *geographic information systems (GISs)*, maps become extremely powerful visual reporting tools. As one example, retailing specialists can explore the demographic and psychographic makeup of neighbourhoods within various driving distances from a particular store location. Using such information, managers can plan everything from new building sites to delivery routes to marketing campaigns.

Figure 1 Administration of
Atlantic University

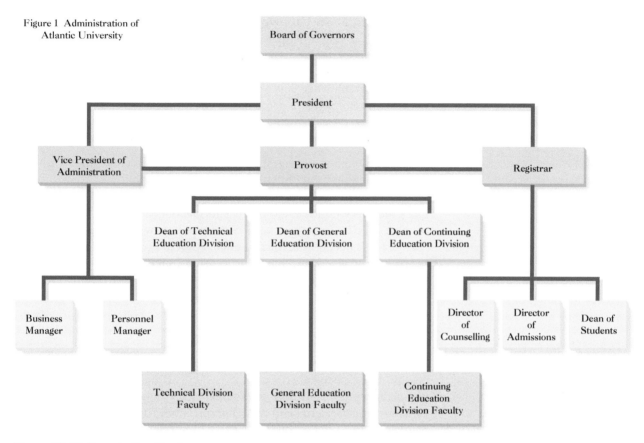

Figure 12–18 Organization Chart

Drawings, Diagrams, Infographics, and Photographs The opportunities to use drawings, diagrams, and photographs are virtually endless. Drawings can show everything from building sites to product concepts. Simple diagrams can show the network of suppliers in an industry, the flow of funds through a company, or the process for completing the payroll each week. More complex diagrams can convey technical topics such as the operation of a machine or repair procedures. Drawings or diagrams that contain enough visual and textual information to function as independent, stand-alone documents are sometimes called **infographics**. Figure 4–4 and Figure 7–1 are good examples. (Note that infographics are not the same as the often dysfunctional "slideuments," which are a mixture of slides and documents and are ineffective as either.)

Word processors and presentation software now offer fairly advanced drawing capabilities, but for more precise and professional illustrations, you may need a specialized package, such

Infographics are diagrams that contain enough textual information to function as stand-alone documents.

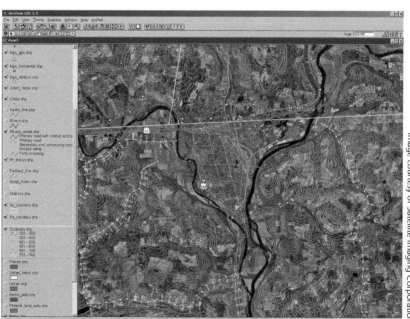

Image courtesy of Satellite Imaging Corporation

This map is a simple version of a geographic information system (GIS), in this case showing hotels and motels in a neighbourhood near New York's LaGuardia Airport. How can a real estate company use this type of map? How can a GIS map help a chain of restaurants find locations in new areas?

as Microsoft Visio, Adobe Illustrator, or Google SketchUp. Moving a level beyond those programs, *computer-aided design* (CAD) systems such as Autodesk's AutoCAD can produce extremely detailed architectural and engineering drawings.

Photographs offer both functional and decorative value, and nothing can replace a photograph when you need to show exact appearances. Because audiences expect photographs to show literal visual truths, you must take care to avoid misleading results when using image processing tools such as Adobe Photoshop. To use photographs successfully, consider these guidelines:

Use photographs for visual appeal and to show exact appearances.

- **Consider whether a diagram would be more effective than a photograph.** Photographs are often unmatched in their ability to communicate spatial relationships, sizes, shapes, and other physical parameters, but sometimes they communicate too much information. A simplified diagram can be more effective for some purposes because it allows you to emphasize the specific elements of the scene that are relevant to the problem at hand.
- **Learn how to use basic image-processing functions.** For most business reports, websites, and presentations, you won't need to worry about more advanced image-processing functions and special effects. However, you need to know such basic operations as the difference between resizing (changing the size of an image without removing any parts of it) and cropping (cutting away parts of the image).
- **Make sure the photographs have communication value.** Except for covers, title slides, and other special uses, it's usually best to avoid including photographs simply for decorative value.
- **Be aware of copyrights and model permissions.** Just as with textual information you find online, you can't simply insert online photographs into your documents. Unless they are specifically offered for free, you have to assume that someone owns the photos and is entitled to payment or at least a photo credit. When you find a photo you'd like to use, see whether the owner has posted licensing terms. In addition, professional photographers are careful to have any person who poses in photos sign a model release form, which gives the photographer permission to use the person's image.

Make sure you have the right to use photographs you find online.

Rendering is artist's concept, courtesy of Empire Communities

To show investors what a new building would look like in its environment, an artist combined a photograph of a scale model of the building with a photograph of the actual streetscape. Because the target audience clearly understands that the building doesn't exist, this sort of image manipulation is not unethical. Why is it important to alert your audience to photographic manipulation?

Animation and Video Computer animation and video are among the most specialized forms of business visuals. When they are appropriate and done well, they offer unparalleled visual impact. An interactive diagram lets website visitors choose the information most relevant to their individual needs. At a simple level, you can animate shapes and text within electronic presentations (see Chapter 14). At a more sophisticated level, software such as Adobe Flash enables the creation of multimedia files that include computer animation, digital video, and other elements.

The combination of low-cost digital video cameras and video-sharing websites such as YouTube has spurred a revolution in business video applications in recent years. Product demonstrations, company overviews, promotional presentations, and training seminars are among the most popular applications of business video. *Branded channels* on YouTube allow companies to present their videos as an integrated collection in a customized user interface.

Branded channels on YouTube have become an important business communication outlet.

Producing and Integrating Visuals

Now that you understand the communication power of visuals and have chosen the best visuals to illustrate key points in your report, website, or presentation, it's time to get creative. This section offers advice on creating visuals, integrating them with your text, and verifying the quality of your visual elements.

CREATING VISUALS

Computers make it easy to create visuals, but they also make it easy to create ineffective, distracting, and even downright ugly visuals. However, by following the basic design principles discussed on pages 386 to 389, you can create all the basic visuals you need—visuals that are attractive and effective. If possible, have a professional designer set up a *template* for the various types of visuals you and your colleagues need to create. In addition to helping ensure an effective design, using templates saves you the time of making numerous design decisions every time you create a chart or graphic.

Computer software offers a variety of tools but doesn't automatically give you the design sensibility that is needed for effective visuals.

Remember that the style and quality of your visuals communicates a subtle message about your relationship with the audience. A simple sketch might be fine for a working meeting but inappropriate for a formal presentation or report. On the other hand, elaborate, full-colour visuals may be viewed as extravagant for an informal report but may be entirely appropriate for a message to top management or influential outsiders.

Charlie Schuck/Photodisc/Getty Images

The use of colour in visuals accelerates learning, retention, and recall by 55 to 78 percent, and it increases motivation and audience participation by up to 80 percent. Is colour suitable for all visuals? On what occasions is it appropriate to use black and white instead of colour?

INTEGRATING VISUALS WITH TEXT

For maximum effectiveness and minimum disruption for the reader, visual elements need to be carefully integrated with the text of your message so that readers can move back and forth between text and visuals with as little disruption as possible. In some instances, visual elements are somewhat independent from the text, as in the *sidebars* that occasionally accompany magazine articles. Such images are related to the content of the main story, but they aren't referred to by a specific title or figure number. For reports and most other business documents, however, visuals are tightly integrated with the text so that readers can move back and forth between text and visuals with as little disruption as possible. Successful integration involves four decisions: maintaining a balance between visuals and text, referring to visuals in the text, placing the visuals in the document, and writing titles and other descriptions.

Maintain a balance between text and visuals and pace your visuals in a way that emphasizes your key points.

BALANCING ILLUSTRATIONS AND WORDS Strong visuals enhance the descriptive and persuasive power of your writing, but putting too many visuals into a report can distract your readers. If you're constantly referring to tables, drawings, and other visual elements, the effort to switch back and forth from words to visuals can make it difficult for readers to maintain focus on the thread of your message. The space occupied by visuals can also disrupt the flow of text on the page or screen.

As always, take your readers' specific needs into account. If you're addressing an audience with multiple language backgrounds or widely varying reading skills, you can shift the balance toward more visual elements to help overcome any language barriers. The professional experience, education, and training of your audience should influence your approach as well. For example, detailed statistical plots and mathematical formulas are everyday reading material for quality-control engineers but not for most salespeople or top executives.

To tie visuals to the text, introduce them in the text and place them near the points they illustrate.

REFERENCING VISUALS Unless a visual element clearly stands on its own, visuals should be referred to by number in the text of your report. Some report writers refer to all visuals as "exhibits" and number them consecutively throughout the report; many others number tables and figures separately (everything that isn't a table is regarded as a figure). In a long report with numbered sections, illustrations may have a double number (separated by a period or a hyphen) representing the section number and the individual illustration number within that section. Whichever scheme you use, make sure it's clear and consistent.

Help your readers understand the significance of visuals by referring to them before readers encounter them in the document or onscreen. The following examples show how you can make this connection in the text:

Figure 1 summarizes the financial history of the motorcycle division over the past five years, with sales broken into four categories.

Total sales were steady over this period, but the mix of sales by category changed dramatically (see Figure 2).

The underlying reason for the remarkable growth in our sales of youth golf apparel is suggested by Table 4, which shows the growing interest in junior golf around the world.

When describing the data shown in your visuals, be sure to emphasize the main point you want to make. Don't make the mistake of simply repeating the data to be shown. Paragraphs that do are guaranteed to put the reader to sleep:

> Among women who replied to the survey, 17.4 percent earn less than $9 per hour; 26.4 percent earn $9 to $11; 25.7 percent, $12 to $14; 18.0 percent, $15 to $24; 9.6 percent, $25 to $49; and 2.9 percent, $50 and over.

The visual will provide all these details; there is no need to repeat them in the text. Instead, use round numbers that summarize the core message:

> Over two-thirds of the women who replied earn less than $12 per hour.

PLACING VISUALS Position your visuals so that your audience won't have to flip back and forth (in printed documents) or scroll (onscreen) between the visuals and the text. Ideally, it's best to place each visual within, beside, or immediately after the paragraph it illustrates so that readers can consult the explanation and the visual at the same time. If possible, try to avoid bunching several visuals in one section of the document. (Bunching is unavoidable in some cases, such as when multiple visuals accompany a single section of text—as in this chapter, for instance.)

WRITING TITLES, CAPTIONS, AND LEGENDS Titles, captions, and legends provide more opportunities to connect your visual and textual messages. A **title** is similar to a subheading: it provides a short description that identifies the content and purpose of the visual, along with whatever label and number you're using to refer to the visual. A **caption** usually offers additional discussion of the visual's content and can be several sentences long, if appropriate. Captions can also alert readers that additional discussion is available in the accompanying text. Titles usually appear above visuals, and captions appear below, but effective designs can place these two elements in other positions. Sometimes titles and captions are combined in a single block of text as well. As with all other design decisions, be consistent throughout your report or website. A **legend** helps readers decode the visual by explaining what various colours, symbols, or other design choices mean. Legends aren't necessary for simple graphs, such as a line chart or bar chart with only one series of data, but they are invaluable with more complex graphics.

> Use titles, captions, and legends to help audiences interpret visuals quickly and successfully.

> The title of a visual functions in the same way as a subheading, whereas the caption provides additional detail if needed.

Readers should be able to grasp the point of a visual without digging into the surrounding text. For instance, a title that says simply "Refineries" doesn't say much at all. A **descriptive title** that identifies the topic of the illustration provides a better idea of what the chart is all about. An **informative title** tells even more by calling attention to the conclusion that ought to be drawn from the data. Here's an example of the difference:

Descriptive Title	Informative Title
Relationship between Petroleum Demand and Refinery Capacity in Canada	Shrinking Refinery Capacity Results from Stagnant Petroleum Demand

Don't assume that titles, captions, and legends are minor details. They are often the first elements that people read in a document—and sometimes the only elements that people read—so use them effectively to communicate your key points. For a review of the important points to remember when creating visuals, see "Checklist: Creating Effective Visuals."

✓ Checklist   Creating Effective Visuals

- Emphasize visual consistency to connect parts of a whole and minimize audience confusion.
- Avoid arbitrary changes of colour, texture, typeface, position, or scale.
- Highlight contrasting points through colour, position, and other design choices.
- Decide whether you want to achieve formal or informal balance.
- Emphasize dominant elements and de-emphasize less important pieces in a design.
- Understand and follow (at least most of the time) the visual conventions your audience expects.
- Strive for simplicity and clarity; don't clutter your documents with meaningless decoration.
- Follow the guidelines for avoiding ethical lapses.
- Carefully consider your message, the nature of your information, and your audience to choose which points to illustrate.

- Select the proper types of graphics for the information at hand and for the objective of the message.
- Be sure the visual contributes to overall understanding of the subject.
- Understand how to use your software tools to maximize effectiveness and efficiency.
- Integrate visuals and text by maintaining a balance between illustrations and words, clearly referring to visuals within the text, and placing visuals carefully.
- Use titles, captions, and legends to help readers understand the meaning and importance of your visuals.
- Verify the quality of your visuals by checking for accuracy, proper documentation, and honesty.

VERIFYING THE QUALITY AND INTEGRITY OF YOUR VISUALS

Proof visuals as carefully as you proof text.

Visuals have a particularly strong impact on your readers and on their perceptions of you and your work. Ensure that you check visuals for mistakes such as typographical errors, inconsistent colour treatment, confusing or undocumented symbols, and misaligned elements. Be sure your computer hasn't done something unexpected, such as arranging pie chart slices in an order you don't want or plotting line charts in unusual colours. Also take a few extra minutes to ensure that your visuals are absolutely accurate, properly documented, and honest.

- **Is the visual accurate?** Check visuals for mistakes such as typographical errors, inconsistent colour treatment, confusing or undocumented symbols, and misaligned elements. Does each visual deliver your message accurately? Have you inserted the right visuals in the right places? Also verify that information in visuals and accompanying text matches. For data presentations, particularly if you're producing charts with a spreadsheet, verify any formulas used to generate the numbers, and make sure you've selected the right numbers for each chart.
- **Is the visual properly documented?** As with the textual elements in your reports and presentations, visuals based on other people's research, information, and ideas require full citation. (Note that in many books, including this one, source notes for visuals are collected in one place at the end of the book.) Also, anticipate any questions or concerns your audience may have and address them with additional information as needed. For example, if you're presenting the results of survey research, many readers will want to know who participated in the survey, how many people responded, and when the questions were asked. You could answer these questions with a note in the caption along the lines of "652 accountants,

PROMOTING WORKPLACE ETHICS
Ethical Communication and Distorting the Data

Take a quick look at these three line charts, which display the level of impurities found in a particular source of drinking water. Chart A suggests that the source has a consistently high level of impurities throughout the year, chart B indicates that the level of impurities jumps up and down throughout the year, and chart C shows an impurity level that is fairly consistent throughout the year—and fairly low.

Here's the problem: All three charts are displaying the *exact same data.*

Look again at chart A. The vertical scale is set from 0 to 120, sufficient to cover the range of variations in the data. However, what if you wanted to persuade an audience that the variations from month to month were quite severe? In chart B, the scale is "zoomed in" on 60 to 110, making the variations look much more dramatic. The result could be a stronger emotional impact on the reader, creating the impression that these impurities are out of control.

On the other hand, what if you wanted to create the impression that the situation was fine, with low levels of impurities and no wild swings from month to month. You would follow the example in chart C, where the scale is expanded from 0 to 200, which appears to minimize the variations in the data. This graph is visually "calmer," potentially creating the opposite impression—that there's really nothing to worry about.

If all three graphs show the same data, is any one of them more honest than the others? The answer to this question depends on your intent and your audience's information needs. For example, if dramatic swings in the measurement from month to month suggest a problem with the quality of your product or the safety of a process that affects the public, then visually minimizing the swings might well be considered dishonest.

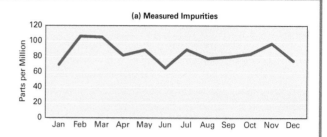

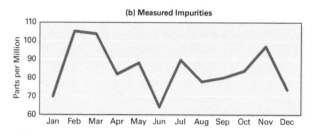

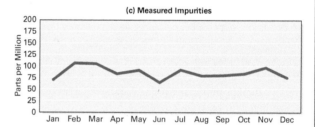

CAREER APPLICATIONS

1. What sort of quick visual impression would such a chart give if the vertical scale were set to 0 to 500? Why?
2. If the acceptable range of impurities in this case is from 60 to 120 parts per million, which chart is the fairest way to present the data? Why?

surveyed the week of January 17." Similarly, if you found a visual in a secondary source, list that source on or near the graphic to help readers assess the information. To avoid cluttering your graphic, use a shortened citation or note on the graphic itself and include a complete citation elsewhere in the report.

• **Is the visual honest?** As a final precaution, step back and make sure your visuals communicate truthful messages (see "Promoting Workplace Ethics: Ethical Communication and Distorting the Data"). Make sure they don't hide information the audience needs, imply conclusions that your information doesn't support, or play on audience emotions in manipulative or coercive ways.

Review each visual to ensure that it doesn't intentionally or unintentionally distort the meaning of the underlying information.

SUMMARY OF LEARNING OBJECTIVES

1 Explain how to adapt to your audiences when writing reports and proposals. Successful reports and proposals require careful use of language and tone. You may use personal pronouns if you are familiar with your audience, but use an impersonal style if you are not. A more formal tone is appropriate when reports are sent to outsiders or when they contain controversial or complex information. When writing for people of other cultures, avoid humour and idiomatic language, because these techniques do not translate effectively from one culture to the next.

2 Describe five characteristics of effective report content. Effective reports represent your credibility to both internal and external readers. To ensure that your credibility is maintained, your reports must (1) be factually accurate, (2) contain all necessary information that is well supported with evidence, (3) present the issues fairly, representing all sides of your argument, (4) flow logically and clearly, and (5) be properly documented.

3 Explain six strategies to strengthen your proposal argument. Write compelling proposals by showcasing your knowledge and experience, which demonstrate your ability to tackle the problem or opportunity. Additionally, support the proposal with concrete and specific examples. Supply information about the competition if relevant, and prove that the proposal is realistic and workable. You must also highlight how the product or service will benefit the reader. Finally, check your proposal for correctness, and format it in an inviting way.

4 Determine the topics commonly covered in a proposal introduction, body, and closing. The proposal introduction summarizes the problem, provides the recommended solution, states the document's scope, and previews its organization. The proposal body develops the solution, describes a work plan, states the qualifications of the writer and his or her organization, and covers the solution's implementation costs. The proposal close provides a general summary and reinforces reader benefits and the writer's capabilities.

5 Identify six characteristics of effective writing in online reports. Online reports require special features in addition to those of hard-copy reports. First, because readers may mistrust online content, build trust through accurate and current information and include the date material was posted. Second, make sure your information is complete. Do not select information that only supports your viewpoint. Third, adapt your content for a global audience; one way is through localizing the home page for cultural practices while keeping more detailed content in the original language. Fourth, be sure content is structured to attract and maintain interest by using the inverted pyramid style. Fifth, write concisely so readers can skim pages easily. Sixth, identify where links will take readers, so they understand they can access information easily. Finally, include documentation.

6 Discuss six principles of graphic design that can improve the quality of your visuals. To design the most effective visuals for business reports, keep the following principles in mind. First, to avoid confusing readers, be consistent in your use of design elements such as colour, shape, size, position, scale, and typeface. Second, use strong contrasting colours to show difference and subtle colours to show similarity. Third, ensure that your document is balanced to avoid a jarring appearance. Fourth, give visual emphasis to the most important points, as your reader expects. Fifth, take into account your audience's culture, education, and other background experiences, because your readers may have specific associations with certain symbols and images. Sixth, avoid clutter and chartjunk to maintain clarity and project professionalism.

7 Explain how to choose which points in your message to illustrate. Ideas and information that are too complicated to describe in words are prime candidates for visual illustration; so is information that is connected in some way (such as cause-and-effect relationships). In addition, points that should have an impact on readers can be shown visually to heighten their importance.

ON THE JOB | PERFORMING COMMUNICATION TASKS AT FEDEX

Reports are essential to maintaining FedEx's prominence in the courier industry. They are written by internal auditors, for example, to justify expenditures for equipment intended to improve procedures and practices, by human resources managers to recommend training programs, by technical staff to explain potential innovations, and by many others to ensure that FedEx continues to run smoothly and provide value to its customers.

You have recently been hired as an administrative assistant at FedEx Canada's head office to help with a variety of special projects. In each situation, choose the best communication alternative from among those listed. Be prepared to explain your choice.

1. To keep track of the industry, you have been instructed to research two online services offered by FedEx's top competitors: online pickup requests and online package tracking. How should you introduce your report? Choose the best opening from the four shown below.

   a. Begin by introducing the purpose of the study (to review what online services competitors are offering) and making recommendations about how FedEx can better compete with these offerings.

   b. Begin by introducing the purpose of the study (to review what online services competitors are offering) and outlining how you will present your data.

   c. Begin by giving a brief history of the rivalry between FedEx and its top three competitors.

   d. Begin by summarizing FedEx efforts to stay on top of the technology wave and how important such technology will be to the company's future.

2. As you work on your report about competitors' online services, you want to include a visual that compares FedEx Canada's online statistics with those of its major rivals. For example, in your research you learn how many people visit the FedEx.ca website each month and how many online tracking requests FedEx.ca receives each day. You also locate the same information for all major competitors. What is the best way to present this information?

   a. Use a table to present the numbers for each company.

   b. Use a line chart to present the numbers for each company.

   c. Use a bar chart to present the numbers for each company.

   d. Use a pie chart to present the numbers for each company.

3. CEO Frederick W. Smith wants to celebrate the company's achievements by creating a special advertising insert on FedEx's history. He wants to distribute this insert inside the April issue of a national business magazine. The magazine's publisher is excited about the concept and has asked Smith to send her "something in writing." You are asked to draft the proposal, which should be no more than 10 pages long. Which outline should you use?

   a. Version 1

       I. An overview of FedEx's history

         a. How company was founded

         b. Overview of company services

         c. Overview of markets served

         d. Overview of transportation operations

       II. The FedEx magazine insert

         a. Historic events to be included

         b. Employees to be interviewed

         c. Customers to be discussed

         d. Production schedule

       III. Pros and cons of FedEx magazine insert

         a. Pros: Make money for magazine, draw new customers for FedEx

         b. Cons: Costs, questionable audience interest

   b. Version 2

       I. Introduction: Overview of the FedEx special insert

         a. Purpose

         b. Content

         c. Timing

       II. Description of the insert

         a. Text

           1. Message from CEO

           2. History of FedEx

           3. Interviews with employees

           4. Customer testimonials

         b. Advertising

           1. Inside front and back covers

           2. Colour spreads

           3. Congratulatory ads placed by customers

       III. Next steps

       IV. Summary

   c. Version 3

       Who: FedEx

       What: Special magazine insert

       When: Inserted in April issue

       Where: Coordinated by magazine's editors

       Why: To celebrate FedEx's anniversary

       How: Overview of content, production responsibilities, and schedule

   d. Version 4

       I. Introduction: The rationale for producing a magazine insert promoting FedEx

         a. Insert would make money for magazine.

         b. Insert would boost morale of FedEx employees.

         c. Insert would attract new customers.

       II. Insert description

         a. Interview with founder Frederick Smith

         b. Interviews with employees

         c. Description of historic moments

         d. Interviews with customers

         e. Advertisements

       III. Production plan

         a. Project organization

         b. Timing and sequence of steps

         c. FedEx's responsibilities

         d. Magazine's responsibilities

       IV. Detailed schedule

       V. Summary of benefits and responsibilities

TEST YOUR KNOWLEDGE

1. Why is the "you" attitude particularly important with long or complex reports and proposals?
2. What is key advice for wiki collaborators?
3. How are audiences likely to react if they spot several errors in your reports?
4. What strategies strengthen your proposal arguments?
5. How do online reports differ from hard-copy reports?
6. How do visuals enhance the communication impact of your writing?
7. How do you select report content for visual representation?
8. How do you verify the accuracy of the visuals in your report?
9. What tools can you use to help readers follow the structure and flow of information in a long report?
10. What ethical issue is raised by the use of technology to alter photographs in reports?

APPLY YOUR KNOWLEDGE

1. Should a report always explain the writer's method of gathering evidence or solving a problem? Why or why not?
2. Besides telling readers why an illustration is important, why refer to it in the text of your document?
3. When you read a graph, how can you ensure that the visual impression you receive is an accurate reflection of reality? Please explain.
4. If you want your audience to agree to a specific course of action, should you exclude any references to alternatives that you don't want the audience to consider? Why or why not?
5. **Ethical Choices** If a company receives a solicited formal proposal outlining the solution to a particular problem, is it ethical for the company to adopt the proposal's recommendations without hiring the firm that submitted the proposal? Why or why not?

RUNNING CASES

> CASE 1 Noreen

Noreen's boss likes the idea Noreen proposed to merge the "Go Points" department with the Petro-Go credit card sales/service department. The boss would like Noreen to write an analysis and justification report to support the idea and plan to merge the two departments into one.

Currently, the "Go Points" department is on the fourth floor and staffed by 20 sales/service reps. They (1) make sales calls to existing Petro-Go credit card holders to offer the points program, (2) receive calls from existing points program customers who have enquiries, and (3) call existing points customers to announce promotions and offers.

The Petro-Go credit card department is on the third floor and staffed by 30 sales/service reps. They (1) make sales calls to recruit new credit card customers, (2) receive calls from existing credit card holders who have enquiries, and (3) call existing credit card customers to announce promotions and offers.

Noreen thinks that by joining the credit card sales/service department with the "Go Points" department, customers will be better served by one-stop shopping. She also feels that the credit card sales/service staff could easily modify their

call routines to include information about the "Go Points" program, and the "Go Points" staff could easily be trained on the credit card policies and procedures.

QUESTIONS

a. What information must Noreen gather?
b. What logical arguments can Noreen use?
c. What are the five steps Noreen should follow to focus her report around recommendations?
d. What type of visuals might Noreen include in the report?
e. How will Noreen leave a strong and lasting impression on the reader at the end of her report?

YOUR TASK

With a partner, use your imagination to write an analytical memo report from Noreen to her managers (use your names) that gives an analysis of the situation and justifies the merger. When structuring a report around recommendations, follow the five steps listed on pages 352 to 353. Include at least one visual in your report (you will need to use your imagination).

> CASE 2 Kwong

Kwong is working with the annual report project team to gather, summarize, and compile the annual report for ET Canada. The annual report will be posted on the Internet and distributed to all shareholders. The report will include several charts and tables. Revenue will be reported in the annual report, and Kwong will use a table to show product lines offered by ET Canada and the revenue for each over the past few years.

QUESTIONS

a. Why will placing the information in a table help the reader?

b. Would this annual report best be organized in chronological, geographical, or category order?

c. Should the company's annual report use the direct approach or the indirect approach?

d. Would the 2 + 2 = 4 approach help with this annual report?

e. List three factors Kwong should consider when he is deciding how many and what type of visuals to include in the annual report.

YOUR TASK

Create an internal memo to Kwong showing ET Canada's product line analysis for this year and last year. The memo is from the chief information officer. The memo contains a table showing revenues for each product line for this year and last year. Product lines are Local and Access, Long Distance, Wireless, Data, Video, Terminal Sales, and Other. The table also includes a column for percentage of change between this year and last year as well as column totals. The memo also contains a bar/column chart that displays the revenues for each product line for the two years. Kwong plans to add this information to the company annual report.

PRACTISE YOUR KNOWLEDGE

Documents for Analysis

DOCUMENT 12.A:

Examine the pie charts in Figure 12–19 below and point out any problems or errors you notice.

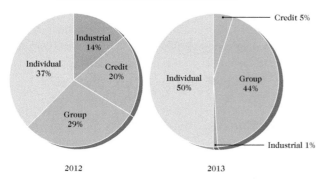

Figure 12–19 Pie Chart for Analysis (Document 12.A)

DOCUMENT 12.B

Examine the line chart in Figure 12–20 below and point out any problems or errors you notice.

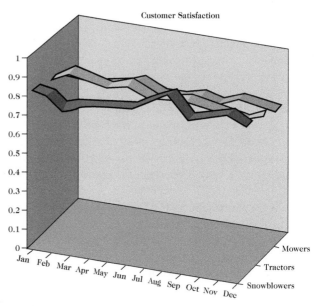

Figure 12–20 Line Chart for Analysis (Document 12.B)

EXERCISES

12.1 Business Reports: Building Audience Rapport

Review the reports shown in Figures 12–3 and 12–4. Give specific examples of how each report establishes a good relationship with the audience. Consider such things as using the "you" attitude, emphasizing the positive, establishing credibility, being polite, using bias-free language, and projecting a good company image.

12.2 Composing Reports: Report Content

You are writing an analytical report on the Canadian sales of your newest product. Of the following topics, identify those that should be covered in the report introduction, body, and close. Briefly explain your decisions:

a. Regional breakdowns of sales across the country
b. Date the product was released in the marketplace
c. Sales figures from competitors selling similar products worldwide
d. Predictions of how the Canadian economy will affect sales over the next six months
e. Method used for obtaining the above predictions
f. The impact of similar products being sold in Canada by Chinese competitors
g. Your recommendation as to whether the company should sell this product internationally
h. Actions that must be completed by year end if the company decides to sell this product internationally

12.3 Teamwork: Graphic Design

Team up with a classmate to design graphics based on a comparison of the use of smartphones by Canadians. One teammate should sketch a horizontal bar chart and the other should sketch a vertical one from the estimates that follow. Then, exchange visual aids and analyze how well each conveys the use of smartphones by age group. Would the bar chart look best with vertical or horizontal bars? Why? What scale is best? How does the direction used in the bar chart enhance or obscure the meaning or impact of the data? What suggestions can you make for improving your teammate's visual aid?

Estimates show that 92 percent of teens use their smartphones for apps like Snapchat. Among the 20 to 35 age group, 82 percent use their phones for checking social media sites. Those 36 to 49 years old use theirs for game apps 68 percent of the time. Those 50 to 65 years old use smartphones for checking news and weather 74 percent of the time. Finally, those 66 years and older use theirs for phone calls 95 percent of the time.

12.4 Composing Reports: Supporting a Solution

Find an article in a business newspaper or journal (in print or online) that recommends a solution to a problem. Identify the problem, the recommended solution(s), and the supporting evidence provided by the author to justify his or her recommendation(s). Did the author cite any formal or informal studies as evidence? What facts or statistics did the author include? Did the author cite any criteria for evaluating possible options? If so, what were they?

12.5 Composing Reports: Navigational Clues

Review a long business article in a journal or newspaper. Highlight examples of how the article uses headings, transitions, previews, and reviews to help the readers find their way.

12.6 Ethical Choices: Survey Questions

Your boss has asked you to prepare a feasibility report to determine whether the company should advertise its custom-crafted cabinetry in the weekly neighbourhood newspaper. Based on your primary research, you think they should. As you draft the introduction to your report, however, you discover that the survey administered to the neighbourhood newspaper subscribers was flawed. Several questions were poorly written and misleading. You used the survey results, among other findings, to justify your recommendation. The report is due in three days. What actions should you take, if any, before you complete your report?

12.7 Improving Visuals: Applying the Six Principles of Graphic Design

From online sources, find three visual presentations of data, information, or concepts. Which of the three presents its data or information most clearly? What design choices promote this level of clarity? What improvements would you make to the other visuals to make them clearer?

12.8 Writing Reports: Pie Charts

As director of new business development for a growing advertising agency, you're interested in how companies spend their advertising dollars. Create a pie chart based on the information that shows national advertising spending by media category. Summarize these findings (in two or three sentences) for publication in a report to top management.[25]

Media type	Expenditure (in $ billions)
Television	42.5
Newspaper	38.4
Direct mail	38.4
Miscellaneous	22.6
Radio	12.3
Yellow Pages	10.8
Magazines	9.0
Business papers	3.8
Outdoor	1.3
Total	$179.1

12.9 Annual Report: Selecting the Right Visual

You're preparing the annual report for FretCo Guitar Corporation. For each type of information, select the right chart or visual to illustrate the text. Explain your choices.

a. Data on annual sales for the past 20 years
b. Comparison of FretCo sales, product by product (electric guitars, bass guitars, amplifiers, acoustic guitars), for this year and last year
c. Explanation of how a FretCo acoustic guitar is manufactured
d. Explanation of how the FretCo Guitar Corporation markets its guitars
e. Data on sales of FretCo products in each of 12 countries
f. Comparison of FretCo sales figures with sales figures for three competing guitar makers over the past 10 years

12.10 Sales Trends: Selecting the Right Chart

Here are last year's sales figures for the appliance and electronics megastore where you work. Construct charts based on these figures that will help you explain to the store's general manager seasonal variations in each department.

Store Sales in 2016 (in $ thousands)

Month	Home Electronics	Computers	Appliances
January	$68	$39	$36
February	72	34	34
March	75	41	30
April	54	41	28
May	56	42	44
June	49	33	48
July	54	31	43
August	66	58	39
September	62	58	36
October	66	44	33
November	83	48	29
December	91	62	24

12.11 Company Expansion: Creating Maps

You work for C & S Holdings, a company that operates coin-activated, self-service car washes. Research shows that the farther customers live from a car wash, the less likely they are to visit. You know that 50 percent of customers at each of your car washes live within a 4-kilometre radius of the location, 65 percent live within 6 kilometres, 80 percent live within 8 kilometres, and 90 percent live within 10 kilometres. C & S's owner wants to open two new car washes in your city and has asked you to prepare a report recommending locations. Using a map of your city (try www.mapquest.ca), choose two possible locations for car washes and create a visual depicting the customer base surrounding each location (make up whatever population data you need).

12.12 Presenting Information, Concepts, and Ideas: Photographs

As directed by your instructor, team up with other students, making sure that at least one of you has a digital camera or smartphone capable of downloading images to your word-processing software. Find a busy location on campus or in the surrounding neighbourhood, someplace with lots of signs, storefronts, pedestrians, and traffic. Scout out two different photo opportunities, one that maximizes the visual impression of crowding and clutter and one that minimizes this impression. For the first, assume that you are someone who advocates reducing the crowding and clutter, so you want to show how bad it is. For the second, assume that you are a real estate agent or someone else who is motivated to show people that even though the location offers lots of shopping, entertainment, and other attractions, it's actually a rather calm and quiet neighbourhood. Insert the two images in a word-processing document and write a caption for each that emphasizes the two opposite messages just described. Finally, write a brief paragraph discussing the ethical implications of what you've just done. Have you distorted reality or just presented it in ways that work to your advantage? Have you prevented audiences from gaining the information they would need to make informed decisions?

CASES — APPLYING THE THREE-STEP WRITING PROCESS TO CASES

Apply each step to the following cases, as assigned by your instructor.

1 Planning →

Analyze the Situation
Clarify the problem or opportunity at hand, define your purpose, develop an audience profile, and develop a work plan.

Gather Information
Determine audience needs, and obtain the information necessary to satisfy those needs; conduct a research project if necessary.

Select the Right Medium
Choose the best medium for delivering your message; consider delivery through multiple media.

Organize the Information
Define your main idea, limit your scope, select a direct or an indirect approach, and outline your content using an appropriate structure for an informational report, analytical report, or proposal.

2 Writing →

Adapt to Your Audience
Be sensitive to audience needs by using a "you" attitude, politeness, positive emphasis, and bias-free language. Build a strong relationship with your audience by establishing your credibility and projecting your company's image. Control your style with a tone and voice appropriate to the situation.

Compose the Message
Choose precise language that will help you create effective sentences and coherent paragraphs throughout the introduction, body, and close of your report or proposal.

3 Completing

Revise the Report
Evaluate content and review readability; edit and rewrite for conciseness and clarity.

Produce the Report
Use effective design elements and suitable layout for a clean, professional appearance; seamlessly combine textual and graphical elements.

Proofread the Report
Review for errors in layout, spelling, and mechanics.

Distribute the Report
Deliver your report using the chosen medium; make sure all documents and all relevant files are distributed successfully.

Informational Reports

1. My Progress to Date: Interim Progress Report on Your Academic Career

As you know, the bureaucratic process involved in getting a degree or certificate is nearly as challenging as any course you could take.

Your task: Prepare an interim progress report detailing the steps you've taken toward completing your graduation or certification requirements. After examining the requirements listed in your school catalogue, indicate a realistic schedule for completing those that remain. In addition to course requirements, include steps such as completing the residency requirement, filing necessary papers, and paying necessary fees. Use memo format for your report and address it to anyone who is helping or encouraging you through school.

2. Gavel to Gavel: Personal Activity Report of a Meeting

Meetings, conferences, and conventions abound in the academic world. You've probably attended meetings to complete group projects for your classes, and you may have attended trade conventions or academic conferences.

Your task: Prepare a personal activity report on a meeting, convention, or conference that you recently attended. Use memo format and direct the report to other students in your field who were not able to attend.

3. Check That Price Tag: Informational Report on Trends in Costs

Your university's administration has asked you to compare your school's tuition costs with those of one nearby and determine which has risen more quickly. Research the trend by checking your university's annual tuition costs for each of the most recent four years. Then, research the four-year tuition trends for neighbouring universities. For both universities, calculate the percentage change in tuition costs from year to year and between the first and fourth year.

Your task: Prepare an informal report (using the letter format) presenting your findings and conclusions to the president of your school. Include graphics to explain and support your conclusions.

4. Social Media and the Workplace: Writing a Team Wiki Report

The use of social networks by employees during work hours remains a controversial topic, with some companies encouraging networking, some at least allowing it, and others prohibiting it.

Your task: Using the free wiki service offered by Zoho (www.zoho.com/wiki) or a comparable system, in a group of three students collaborate on a report that summarizes the potential advantages and disadvantages of allowing social network usage in the workplace.

5. Helping the Incoming Class: Writing a Team Report

If you're like many other university or college students, your first year was more than you expected: more difficult, more fun, more frustrating, more expensive, more exhausting, more rewarding—more of everything, positive and negative.

Your task: With several other students, identify five or six things you wish you would've realized or understood better before you started your first year. These can relate to your school life (such as "I didn't realize how much work I would have for my classes" or "I should've asked for help as soon as I got stuck") and to your personal and social life ("I wish I would've been more open to meeting people"). Use these items as the foundation of a brief informational report that you could post on a blog that is read by high school students and their families. Your goal with this report is to help the next generation of students make a successful and rewarding transition to university or college.

Analytical Reports

6. My Next Career Move: Feasibility Report Organized around Recommendations

If you've ever analyzed your career objectives, you'll be quite comfortable with this project.

Your task: Write a memo report directed to yourself and signed with a fictitious name. Indicate a possible job that your education will qualify you for, mention the advantages of the position in terms of your long-range goals, and then outline the actions you must take to get the job.

7. Staying the Course: Unsolicited Proposal Using the 2 + 2 = 4 Approach

Think of a course you believe will add value to the core curriculum at your school. Conversely, if you would like to see a course offered as an elective rather than being required, write your email report accordingly.

Your task: Write a short email proposal using the 2 + 2 = 4 approach (refresh your memory by reviewing Chapter 11, if necessary). Prepare your proposal to be submitted to the academic dean by email. Ensure that you include all the reasons supporting your idea.

8. Planning My Program: Problem-Solving Report Using the Yardstick Approach

Assume that you will have time for only one course next term.

Your task: List the pros and cons of four or five courses that interest you, and use the yardstick approach to settle on the course that is best for you to take at this time. Write your report in memo format, addressing it to your academic advisor.

9. Restaurant Review: Troubleshooting Report on a Restaurant's Food and Operations

Visit any restaurant, possibly your school cafeteria. The workers and fellow customers will assume that you are an ordinary customer, but you are really a spy for the owner.

Your task: After your visit, write a short report to the owner, explaining (a) what you did and what you observed, (b) any violations of policy that you observed, and (c) your recommendations for improvement. The first part of your report (what you did and what you observed) will be the longest. Include a description of the premises, inside and out. Tell how long it took for each step of ordering and receiving your meal. Describe the service and food thoroughly. You are interested in both the good and the bad aspects of the establishment's décor, service, and food. For the second section (violations of policy), use some common sense. If all the servers but one have their hair covered, you may assume that policy requires hair to be covered; a dirty window or restroom obviously violates policy. The last section (recommendations for improvement) involves professional judgment. What management actions will improve the restaurant?

10. On the Books: Troubleshooting Report on Improving the Campus Bookstore

Imagine that you are a consultant hired to improve the profits of your campus bookstore.

Your task: Visit the bookstore and look critically at its operations. Then draft a letter to the bookstore manager offering recommendations that would make the store more profitable, perhaps suggesting products it should carry, hours that it should remain open, or added services that it should make available to students. Ensure that you support your recommendations.

11. Day and Night: Problem-Solving Report on Stocking a 24-Hour Convenience Store

When a store is open all day, every day, when's the best time to restock the shelves? That's the challenge at Store 24, a retail chain that never closes. Imagine you're the assistant manager of a Store 24 branch that just opened near your campus. You want to set up a restocking schedule that won't conflict with prime shopping hours. Think about the number of customers you're likely to serve in the morning, afternoon, evening, and overnight hours. Consider, too, how many employees you might have during these four periods.

Your task: Using the scientific approach, write a problem-solving report in letter form to the store manager (Isabel Chu) and the regional manager (Eric Angstrom), who must agree on a solution to this problem. Discuss the pros and cons of each period and include your recommendation for restocking the shelves.

Proposals

12. "Would You Carry It?" Unsolicited Sales Proposal Recommending a Product to a Retail Outlet

Select a product you are familiar with and imagine that you are the manufacturer trying to get a local retail outlet to carry it. Use the Internet and other resources (see the sources in Table 11–5) to gather information about the product.

Your task: Write an unsolicited sales proposal in letter format to the owner (or manager) of the store, proposing that the item be stocked. Use the information you gathered to describe some product features and benefits to the store. Then, make up some reasonable figures, highlighting what the item costs, what it can be sold for, and what services your company provides (for example, return of unsold items, free replacement of unsatisfactory items, or necessary repairs).

13. Where Is Everybody? Proposal to Sell GPS Fleet Tracking System

As a sales manager for Air-Trak, one of your responsibilities is writing sales proposals for potential buyers of your company's Air-Trak tracking system. The Air-Trak uses the Global Positioning System (GPS) to track the location of vehicles and other assets. For example, the dispatcher for a trucking company can simply click a map display on a computer screen to find out where all the company's trucks are at that instant. Air-Trak lists the following as benefits of the system:

- Making sure vehicles follow prescribed routes with minimal loitering time
- "Geofencing," in which dispatchers are alerted if vehicles leave
- Route optimization, in which fleet managers can analyze routes and destinations to find the most time- and fuel-efficient path for each vehicle
- Comparisons between scheduled and actual travel
- Enhanced security to protect both drivers and cargo

Your task: Write a brief proposal to Doneta Zachs, fleet manager for First Place Van Lines Inc. (Head Office) 2014 Miners Avenue, Saskatoon, SK S7K 4Z7. Introduce your company, explain the benefits of the Air-Trak system, and propose a trial deployment in which you would equip five Saskatchewan division trucks. For the purposes of this assignment, you don't need to worry about the technical details of the system; focus on promoting the benefits and asking for a decision regarding the test project. (You can learn more about Air-Trak at https://www.air-trak.com.)[26]

13 Completing Reports and Proposals

LEARNING OBJECTIVES   After studying this chapter, you will be able to

1   Characterize the four tasks involved in completing business reports and proposals

2   Explain the functions of the letter of transmittal

3   Explain the difference between a synopsis and an executive summary

4   Describe the three supplementary parts of a formal report

5   Explain how prefatory parts of a proposal differ, depending on whether the proposal is solicited or unsolicited

MyLab Business Communication   Visit MyLab Business Communication to access a variety of online resources directly related to this chapter's content.

ON THE JOB: COMMUNICATING AT THE BILL & MELINDA GATES FOUNDATION

Charlie Schuck/Photodisc/Getty Images

Much of the communication effort of Jeff Raikes, CEO of the Bill & Melinda Gates Foundation, involves one-on-one conversations with both the people the foundation helps and the researchers who create solutions to health and education challenges. However, written reports and proposals play an equally important role in his work.

Creating Effective Partnerships to Tackle Some of the World's Most Challenging Problems

www.gatesfoundation.org

Microsoft co-founder Bill Gates is accustomed to creating change on a global scale, and he now applies the same energy and strategic thinking to charitable causes. Backed by billions of dollars in endowments, the Bill & Melinda Gates Foundation acts as a catalyst, bringing resources together in a way that "increases the momentum, scale, and sustainability of change." The strategy is applied to such important social challenges as containing the AIDS epidemic, eradicating malaria, improving high schools, and making sure people everywhere have access to the digital revolution made possible by the Internet.

Meeting challenges of such staggering complexity and coordinating the resources of organizations all over the world is obviously no small task, and communication plays a vital role in this effort. In particular, reports and proposals link the various groups involved in the foundation's activities and inform the public about ongoing challenges and progress.

The foundation is staffed with people who have demonstrated effective leadership and communication skills, including Jeff Raikes, a former Microsoft executive, who serves as chief executive officer. Raikes is deeply involved in reports and proposals, as both a writer and a reader. In addition to co-authoring the foundation's annual report, he reads numerous proposals from organizations asking for part of the more than $1.5 billion the foundation provides every year. The foundation receives some 3000 formal grant requests every month, and the review process is thorough.

Raikes examines proposals from various angles, listening to his colleagues' perspectives and asking all sorts of questions: Is this really the best approach? What's going to make the biggest difference? Could this proposal be a catalyst that attracts other organizations to participate?

Raikes and his colleagues recognize that they are tackling problems of almost unimaginable complexity, but with systematic thinking, unstoppable optimism, unmatched financial resources, and effective communication skills they remain committed to improving life for people the world over. If you worked at the Gates Foundation, how would you assess proposals? What elements would you look for to select groups for funding?[1]

Revising Reports and Proposals

1 **LEARNING OBJECTIVE**

Characterize the four tasks involved in completing business reports and proposals.

Experienced business communicators recognize that the process of writing a report or proposal doesn't end with a first draft. This chapter addresses all four tasks involved in completing longer messages: revising, producing, proofreading, and distributing (see Figure 13–1). Although the tasks covered in this chapter are similar in concept to those you studied for short messages in Chapter 6, completing reports and proposals can require considerably more work. And as you've probably experienced with school reports already, computers, printers, network connections, and other resources break down at the last minute, when you're frantic to finish and have no time to spare. When completing an important report on the job, try to leave yourself double or even triple the amount of time you think you'll need so that last-minute glitches don't compromise the quality of all your hard work.

Formal reports have a higher degree of polish and production quality, and they often contain elements not found in informal reports.

Most of the discussion in this chapter applies to *formal* reports and proposals, those documents that require an extra measure of polish and professionalism. Few reports and proposals require every component described in this chapter, but be sure that you carefully select the elements you want to include in each of your documents.

1 Planning → **2** Writing → **3** Completing

Revise the Message
Evaluate content and review readability, then edit and rewrite for conciseness and clarity.

Produce the Message
Use effective design elements and suitable layout for a clean, professional appearance; seamlessly combine text and graphical elements.

Proofread the Message
Review for errors in layout, spelling, and mechanics.

Distribute the Message
Deliver your report using the chosen medium; make sure all documents and all relevant files are distributed successfully.

Figure 13–1 Step 3 in the Three-Step Writing Process for Reports

The revision process is essentially the same for reports as for any business message, although it may take considerably longer, depending on the length of your document. Evaluate your organization, style, and tone, ensuring that you've said what you want to say in the most logical order and in a way that responds to your audience's needs. Then work to improve the report's readability by varying sentence length, keeping paragraphs short, using lists and bullets, adding headings and subheadings, and using transitions. Keep revising the content until it is clear, concise, and compelling.

Tight, efficient writing that is easy to skim is always a plus, but it's especially important for impatient online audiences.[2] Review online report content carefully; strip out all information that doesn't meet audience needs, and condense everything else as much as possible. Audiences will gladly return to sites that deliver quality information quickly—and they'll avoid sites that don't.

Revising for clarity and conciseness is especially important for online reports because reading online can be difficult.

Producing Formal Reports

When you are satisfied with your text, you're ready to produce your report by incorporating the design elements discussed in Chapter 6. At this point you also start to add in charts, graphs, and other visuals, as well as any missing textual elements, such as previews and reviews.

In some organizations, you'll be able to rely on the help of specialists in design and production, particularly when you are working on important, high-visibility reports. You may also have clerical help available to assist with the mechanical assembly and distribution. However, for most reports in many of today's lean-staffed companies, you should count on doing most or all of the production work yourself.

In today's leanly staffed companies, you should be prepared to produce formal reports with little or no assistance from design specialists or other professionals.

The parts you include in a report depend on the type of report you are writing, how long it is, what your audience expects and requires, and what your organization dictates. The components listed in Figure 13–2 fall into three

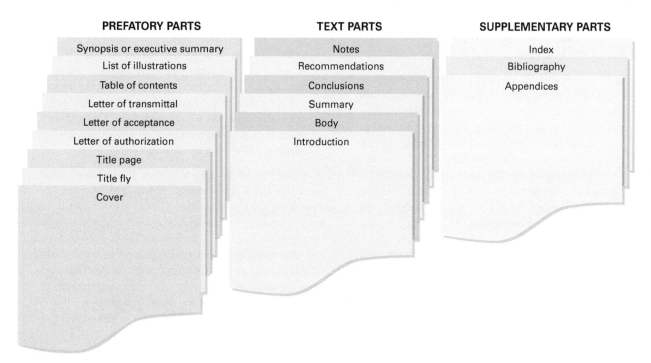

Figure 13–2 Parts of a Formal Report

PREFATORY PARTS	TEXT PARTS	SUPPLEMENTARY PARTS
Synopsis or executive summary	Notes	Index
List of illustrations	Recommendations	Bibliography
Table of contents	Conclusions	Appendices
Letter of transmittal	Summary	
Letter of acceptance	Body	
Letter of authorization	Introduction	
Title page		
Title fly		
Cover		

categories, depending on where they are found in a report: *prefatory parts* (pieces belonging at the front of the report), *text* of the report, and *supplementary parts*. Depending on the level of formality you need to achieve, you can select from these elements to complete your formal report. For an illustration of how the various parts fit together, see Linda Moreno's Electrovision report in "Report Writer's Notebook: Analyzing a Formal Report."

If you want a section to stand out, start it on a new page.

Many of the components in a formal report start on a new page, but not always. Inserting page breaks consumes more paper and adds to the bulk of your report. On the other hand, starting a section on a new page helps your readers navigate the report and recognize transitions between major sections or features.

When you want a particular section to stand apart, you'll generally start it and the material after it on new pages (in the same way that each chapter in this book starts on a new page). Most prefatory parts, such as the table of contents, should also be placed on their own pages. However, the various parts in the report text are often run together. If your introduction is only a paragraph long, don't bother with a page break before moving into the body of your report. If the introduction runs longer than a page, however, a page break can signal to the reader that a major shift is about to occur in the flow of the report.

REPORT WRITER'S NOTEBOOK — Analyzing a Formal Report

The report presented in the following pages was prepared by Linda Moreno, manager of the cost accounting department at Electrovision, a high-tech company. Electrovision's main product is optical character recognition equipment, which is used by postal services throughout the world for sorting mail. Moreno's job is to help analyze the company's costs. She has this to say about the background of the report:

For the past three or four years, Electrovision has been on a roll. Our A-12 optical character reader was a real breakthrough, and postal services grabbed up as many as we could make. Our sales and profits kept climbing, and morale was fantastic. Everybody seemed to think that the good times would last forever. Unfortunately, everybody was wrong. When one of our major clients announced that it was postponing all new equipment purchases because of cuts in its budget, we woke up to the fact that we are essentially a one-product company with one customer. At that point, management started scrambling around looking for ways to cut costs until we could diversify our business a bit.

The vice president of operations, Dennis McWilliams, asked me to help identify cost-cutting opportunities in travel and entertainment. On the basis of his personal observations, he felt that Electrovision was overly generous in its travel policies and that we might be able to save a significant amount by controlling these costs more carefully. My investigation confirmed his suspicion.

I was reasonably confident that my report would be well received. I've worked with Dennis for several years and know what he likes: plenty of facts, clearly stated conclusions, and specific recommendations for what should be done next. I also knew that my report would be passed on to other Electrovision executives, so I wanted to create a good impression. I wanted the report to be accurate and thorough, visually appealing, readable, and appropriate in tone.

When writing the analytical report that follows, Moreno based the organization on conclusions and recommendations presented in direct order. The first two sections of the report correspond to Moreno's two main conclusions: that Electrovision's travel and entertainment costs are too high and that cuts are essential. The third section presents recommendations for achieving better control over travel and entertainment expenses. As you review the report, analyze both the mechanical aspects and the way Moreno presents her ideas. Be prepared to discuss the way the various components convey and reinforce the main message.

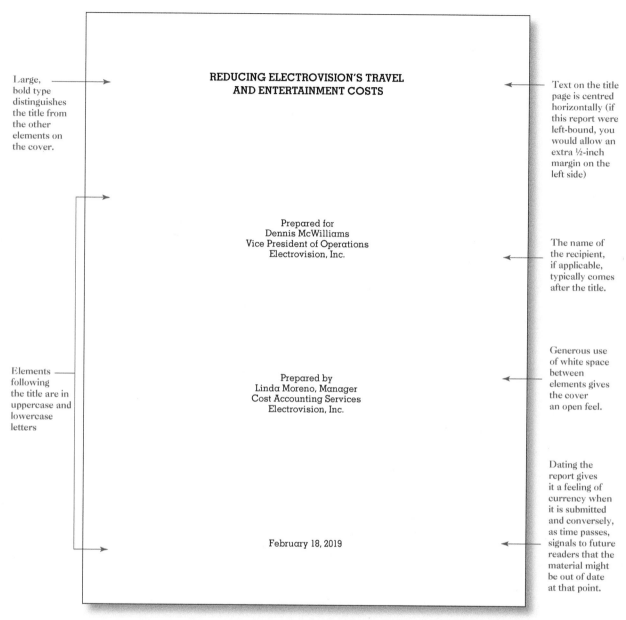

Large, bold type distinguishes the title from the other elements on the cover.

REDUCING ELECTROVISION'S TRAVEL AND ENTERTAINMENT COSTS

Text on the title page is centred horizontally (if this report were left-bound, you would allow an extra ½-inch margin on the left side)

Prepared for
Dennis McWilliams
Vice President of Operations
Electrovision, Inc.

The name of the recipient, if applicable, typically comes after the title.

Elements following the title are in uppercase and lowercase letters

Prepared by
Linda Moreno, Manager
Cost Accounting Services
Electrovision, Inc.

Generous use of white space between elements gives the cover an open feel.

Dating the report gives it a feeling of currency when it is submitted and conversely, as time passes, signals to future readers that the material might be out of date at that point.

February 18, 2019

The "how to" tone of Moreno's title is appropriate for an action-oriented report that emphasizes recommendations. A neutral title, such as "An Analysis of Electrovision's Travel and Entertainment Costs," would be more suitable for an informational report.

The memo format is appropriate for this internal report; the letter format would be used for transmitting an external report.

MEMORANDUM

DATE: February 18, 2019
TO: Dennis McWilliams, Vice President of Operations
FROM: Linda Moreno, Manager of Cost Accounting Services *LM*
SUBJECT: Reducing Electrovision's Travel and Entertainment Costs

Here is the report you requested February 1 on Electrovision's travel and entertainment costs.

Your suspicions were right. We are spending far too much on business travel. Our unwritten policy has been very open, leaving us with no real control over T&E expenses. Although this hands-off approach may have been understandable when Electrovision's profits were high, we can no longer afford the luxury of going first class.

Moreno expects a positive response, so she presents her main conclusion right away.

The tone is conversational, yet still businesslike and respectful.

The solutions to the problem seem rather clear. We need to have someone with centralized responsibility for travel and entertainment costs, a clear statement of policy, an effective control system, and a business-oriented travel service that can optimize our travel arrangements. We should also investigate alternatives to travel, such as videoconferencing. Perhaps more important, we need to change our attitude. Instead of viewing travel funds as a bottomless supply of money, all travelling employees need to act as if they were paying the bills themselves.

Getting people to economize is not going to be easy. In the course of researching this issue, I've found that our employees are deeply attached to their generous travel privileges. I think some would almost prefer a cut in pay to a loss in travel status. We'll need a lot of top management involvement to sell people on the need for moderation. But we must keep this in mind: People will be very bitter if we create a two-class system in which top executives get special privileges while the rest of the employees make the sacrifices.

Acknowledging help given by others is good etiquette and a way to foster positive working relationships.

I'm grateful to Mary Lehman and Connie McIllvain for their help in rounding up and sorting through five years' worth of expense reports. I cannot praise them enough for the effort put into this time-consuming task.

Thanks for giving me the opportunity to work on this; I appreciate gaining insight into Electrovision's T&E issues. If you have any questions about the report, please call or email me.

She closes graciously, with thanks and an offer to discuss the results.

In this report, Moreno decided to write a brief memo of transmittal and include a separate executive summary. Short reports (fewer than 10 pages) often combine the synopsis or executive summary with the memo or letter of transmittal.

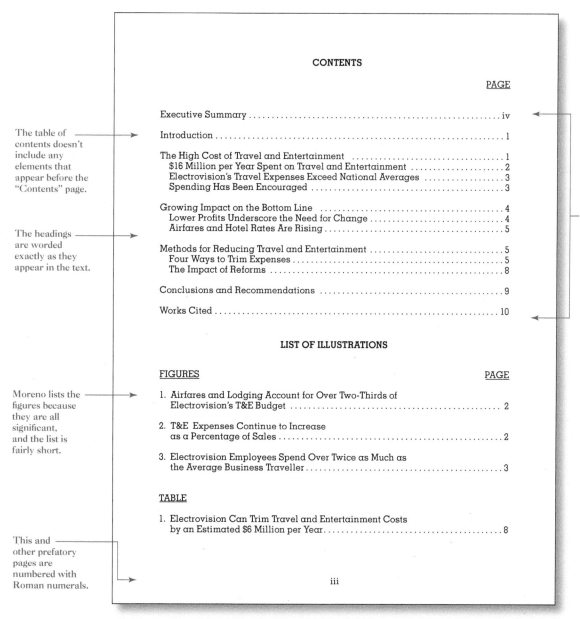

The table of contents doesn't include any elements that appear before the "Contents" page.

The headings are worded exactly as they appear in the text.

Moreno lists the figures because they are all significant, and the list is fairly short.

This and other prefatory pages are numbered with Roman numerals.

The table lists only the page number on which a section begins, not the entire range of numbers.

CONTENTS

LIST OF ILLUSTRATIONS

iii

Moreno included only first- and second-level headings in her table of contents, even though the report contains third-level headings. She prefers a shorter table of contents that focuses attention on the main divisions of thought. She used informative titles, which are appropriate for a report to a receptive audience.

The executive summary begins by stating the purpose of the report.

Moreno presents the points in the executive summary in the same order as they appear in the report, using subheadings that summarize the content of the main sections of the report.

The page numbering in the executive summary continues with Roman numerals.

EXECUTIVE SUMMARY

This report analyzes Electrovision's travel and entertainment (T&E) costs and presents recommendations for reducing those costs.

Travel and Entertainment Costs Are Too High

Travel and entertainment is a large and growing expense category for Electrovision. The company spends over $16 million per year on business travel, and these costs have been increasing by 12 percent annually. Company employees make roughly 1880 trips each year at an average cost per trip of $8500. Airfares are the biggest expense, followed by hotels, meals, and rental cars.

The nature of Electrovision's business does require extensive travel, but the company's costs are excessive: Our employees spend almost three times more than the average business traveller. Although the location of the company's facilities may partly explain this discrepancy, the main reason for our high costs is a management style that gives employees little incentive to economize.

Cuts Are Essential

Electrovision management now recognizes the need to gain more control over this element of costs. The company is currently entering a period of declining profits, prompting management to look for every opportunity to reduce spending. At the same time, rising airfares and hotel rates are making T&E expenses more significant.

Electrovision Can Save $6 Million per Year

Fortunately, Electrovision has a number of excellent opportunities for reducing T&E costs. Savings of up to $6 million per year should be achievable, judging by the experience of other companies. A sensible travel management program can save companies 9 to 18 percent a year simply on accommodation, food, and car rental (Baker, "SLA Use Spreading" 14; Baker, "Study Eyes Expense Tactics"; *Expense Management Strategies*, 6). Given that we purchase many more business-class tickets than the average, we should be able to achieve these, or greater, savings— at least 25 percent to 35 percent (McDougall 45; "Replicon Productivity Index"). Four steps will help us cut costs:

1. Hire a director of travel and entertainment to assume overall responsibility for T&E spending, policies, and technologies, including the hiring and management of a national travel agency.
2. Educate employees on the need for cost containment, both in avoiding unnecessary travel and reducing costs when travel is necessary.
3. Negotiate preferential rates with travel providers.
4. Implement technological alternatives to travel, such as virtual meetings.

As necessary as these changes are, they will likely hurt morale, at least in the short term. Management will need to make a determined effort to explain the rationale for reduced spending. By exercising moderation in their own travel arrangements, Electrovision executives can set a good example and help other employees accept the changes. On the plus side, using travel alternatives such as web conferencing will reduce the travel burden on many employees and help them balance their business and personal lives.

iv

Her audience is receptive, so the tone in the executive summary is forceful; a more neutral approach would be better for hostile or skeptical readers.

The executive summary uses the same font and paragraph treatment as the text of the report.

Moreno decided to include an executive summary because her report is aimed at a mixed audience, some of whom are interested in the details of her report and others who just want the "big picture." The executive summary is aimed at the second group, giving them enough information to make a decision without burdening them with the task of reading the entire report.

Her writing style matches the serious nature of the content without sounding distant or stiff. Moreno chose the formal approach because several members of her audience are considerably higher up in the organization, and she did not want to sound too familiar. In addition, her company prefers the impersonal style for formal reports.

The report title appears on the first page of the text, centred and two inches from the top of the page.

REDUCING ELECTROVISION'S TRAVEL AND ENTERTAINMENT COSTS

INTRODUCTION

Electrovision has always encouraged a significant amount of business travel. To compensate employees for the stress and inconvenience of frequent trips, management has authorized generous travel and entertainment (T&E) allowances. This philosophy has been good for morale, but last year Electrovision spent $16 million on travel and entertainment—$7 million more than it spent on research and development.

This year's T&E costs will affect profits even more, because of increases in airline fares and hotel rates. Also, the company anticipates that profits will be relatively weak for a variety of other reasons. Therefore, Dennis McWilliams, Vice President of Operations, has asked the accounting department to explore ways to reduce the T&E budget.

The purpose of this report is to analyze T&E expenses, evaluate the effect of recent hotel and airfare increases, and suggest ways to tighten control over T&E costs. The report outlines several steps that could reduce Electrovision's expenses, but the precise financial impact of these measures is difficult to project. The estimates presented here provide a "best guess" view of what Electrovision can expect to save.

In preparing this report, the accounting department analyzed internal expense reports for the past five years to determine how much Electrovision spends on travel and entertainment. These figures were then compared with average travel business costs reported in the *Business Travel News Corporate Travel Index 2012* and by investigating fee structures of air carriers, hotels, and car rental agencies. We also analyzed trends and suggestions published in a variety of business journal articles to see how other companies are coping with the high cost of business travel.

THE HIGH COST OF TRAVEL AND ENTERTAINMENT

Although many companies view travel and entertainment as an incidental cost of doing business, the dollars add up. At Electrovision the bill for airfares, hotels, rental cars, meals, and entertainment totalled $16 million last year. Our T&E budget has increased by 12 percent per year for the past five years. Compared to the average Canadian business traveller, Electrovision's expenditures are high, largely because of management's generous policy on travel benefits.

The introduction opens by establishing the need for action.

Moreno mentions her sources and methods to increase credibility and to give readers a complete picture of the study's background.

The Arabic numeral 1 is used for the first page, centred about 1 inch from the bottom of the page.

1

In her brief introduction, Moreno counts on topic sentences and transitions to indicate that she is discussing the purpose, scope, and limitations of the study.

2

Arabic numerals are used to number the second and succeeding pages of the text in the upper right-hand corner, where the top and right-hand margins meet

$16 Million per Year Spent on Travel and Entertainment

Electrovision's annual budget for travel and entertainment is only 8 percent of sales. Because this is a relatively small expense category compared with such items as salaries and commissions, it is tempting to dismiss T&E costs as insignificant. However, T&E is Electrovision's third-largest controllable expense, directly behind salaries and information systems.

Last year Electrovision personnel made about 1880 trips at an average cost per trip of $8500. The typical trip involved a round-trip flight of 8000 km, meals, hotel accommodations for four or five days, and a rental car. Roughly 80 percent of trips were made by 20 percent of the staff—top management and sales personnel travelled most, averaging 17 trips per year.

Figure 1 illustrates how the T&E budget is spent. The largest categories are airfares and lodging, which together account for $7 out of $10 that employees spend on travel and entertainment. This spending breakdown has been relatively steady for the past five years and is consistent with the distribution of expenses experienced by other companies.

Figure 1
Airfares and Lodging Account for Over
Two-Thirds of Electrovision's T&E Budget

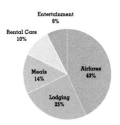

Although the composition of the T&E budget has been consistent, its size has not. As mentioned earlier, these expenditures have increased by about 12 percent per year for the past five years, roughly twice the rate of the company's sales growth (see Figure 2). This rate of growth makes T&E Electrovision's fastest-growing expense item.

Figure 2
T&E Expenses Continue to Increase as a
Percentage of Sales

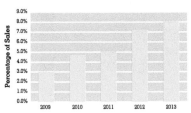

Moreno opens the first main section of the body with a topic sentence that introduces an important fact about the subject of the section. Then she orients the reader to the three major points developed in the section.

The visual is placed as close as possible to the point it illustrates.

Each visual has a title that clearly indicates what it's about; titles are consistently placed to the left of each visual.

3

Electrovision's Travel Expenses Exceed National Averages

Much of our travel budget is justified. Two major factors contribute to Electrovision's high T&E budget:

- With our headquarters in Kanata, Ontario, and our major customers in the U.S., Central and South America, and Western Europe, we naturally spend a lot of money on cross-country and international flights.

- A great deal of travel takes place between our headquarters here in Kanata and the manufacturing operations in Salt Lake City, Utah; Seattle, Washington; and Dublin, Ireland. Corporate managers and division personnel make frequent trips to coordinate these disparate operations.

However, even though a good portion of Electrovision's travel budget is justifiable, the company spends considerably more on T&E than the average business traveller (see Figure 3).

Figure 3
Electrovision Employees Spend
Three Times More than the Average
Business Traveller

Source: *Business Travel News Corporate Travel Index 2012* and company records.

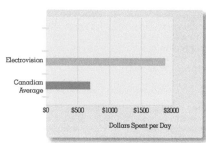

Basing my calculations on the *Business Travel News Corporate Travel Index 2012* and my own research into airfares, Canadian companies spend an average of $2900 for each traveller, based on airfare, hotel rates, meals, and rental car rates. For a 4.5 day trip, the daily rate is about $644 per day. In contrast, Electrovision's average daily expense over the past year has been about $1888 per day, or about three times higher than average. This figure is based on the average trip cost of $8500 listed earlier and an average trip length of 4.5 days.

Spending Has Been Encouraged

Although a variety of factors may contribute to this differential, Electrovision's relatively high T&E costs are at least partially attributable to the company's philosophy and management style. Since many employees do not enjoy business travel, management has tried to make the trips more pleasant by authorizing business-class airfare, luxury hotel accommodations, and full-size rental cars. The sales staff is encouraged to entertain clients at top restaurants and to invite them to cultural and sporting events.

The visuals are numbered consecutively and referred to by their numbers in the text.

Moreno introduces visuals before they appear and indicates what readers should notice about the data.

The chart in Figure 3 is simple but effective; Moreno includes just enough data to make her point. Notice that she is as careful about the appearance of her report as she is about the quality of its content.

4

The cost of these privileges is easy to overlook, given the weakness of Electrovision's system for keeping track of T&E expenses:

Notice that the sentence before the colon is complete.

A bulleted list makes it easy for readers to identify and distinguish related points.

- The monthly financial records do not contain a separate category for travel and entertainment; the information is buried under Cost of Goods Sold and under Selling, General, and Administrative Expenses.

- Each department head is given authority to approve any expense report, regardless of how large it may be.

- Receipts are not required for expenditures of less than $100.

- Individuals are allowed to make their own travel arrangements.

- No one is charged with the responsibility for controlling the company's total spending on travel and entertainment.

GROWING IMPACT ON THE BOTTOM LINE

During the past three years, the company's healthy profits have resulted in relatively little pressure to push for tighter controls over all aspects of the business. However, as we all know, the situation is changing. We're projecting flat to declining profits for the next two years, a situation that has prompted all of us to search for ways to cut costs. At the same time, rising airfares and hotel rates have increased the impact of T&E expenses on the company's financial results.

Informative headings focus reader attention on the main points. Such headings are appropriate when a report uses the direct approach and is intended for a receptive audience. However, descriptive headings are more effective when a report uses the indirect approach and readers are less receptive.

Lower Profits Underscore the Need for Change

The report is formatted with an extra line of white space above headings to help readers associate each heading with the text it describes.

The next two years promise to be difficult for Electrovision. After several years of steady increases in spending, many of our clients are tightening procurement policies for automated mail-handling equipment. Funding for the A-12 optical character reader has been cancelled. As a consequence, the marketing department expects sales to drop by 15 percent. Although Electrovision is negotiating several other promising R&D contracts, the marketing department does not foresee any major procurements for the next two to three years.

At the same time, Electrovision is facing cost increases on several fronts. As we have known for several months, the new production facility now under construction in Montreal is behind schedule and over budget. Labour contracts in Salt Lake City and Seattle will expire within the next six months, and plant managers there anticipate that significant salary and benefits concessions may be necessary to avoid strikes.

Moreover, marketing and advertising costs are expected to increase as we attempt to strengthen these activities to better cope with competitive pressures. Given the expected decline in revenues and increase in costs, the Executive Committee's prediction that profits will fall by 12 percent in the coming fiscal year does not seem overly pessimistic.

Moreno designed her report to include plenty of white space, so even those pages that lack visuals are still attractive and easy to read.

5

Airfares and Hotel Rates Are Rising

Business travellers have grown accustomed to frequent fare wars and discounting in the travel industry in recent years. Excess capacity and aggressive price competition, particularly in the airline business, made travel a relative bargain.

Moreno supports her argument with objective facts and sound reasoning.

However, that situation has changed as weaker competitors have been forced out and the remaining players have grown stronger and smarter. Airlines and hotels are better at managing inventory and keeping occupancy rates high, which translates into higher costs for Electrovision. Last year saw some of the steepest rate hikes in years. Business airfares (tickets most likely to be purchased by business travellers) jumped more than 40 percent in many markets. The trend is expected to continue, with rates increasing at least another 10 percent overall (Koenig, B2).

Given the fact that air and hotel costs account for 70 percent of our T&E budget, the trend toward higher prices in these two categories will have serious consequences, unless management takes action to control these costs.

METHODS FOR REDUCING T&E COSTS

By implementing a number of reforms, management can expect to reduce Electrovision's T&E budget by as much as 35 percent. This estimate is based on the general assessment made by *Business Travel News* and the Get There Corporate Travel Survey (Business Travel News; "Travel Expenses") and on the fact that we have an opportunity to significantly reduce air travel costs by eliminating business-class travel. However, these measures are likely to be unpopular with employees. To gain acceptance for such changes, management will need to sell employees on the need for moderation in T&E allowances.

The recommendations are realistic, noting both the benefits and the risks of taking action.

Four Ways to Trim Expenses

By researching what other companies are doing to curb T&E expenses, the accounting department has identified four prominent opportunities that should enable Electrovision to save about $6 million annually in travel-related costs.

Institute Tighter Spending Controls

A single individual should be appointed director of travel and entertainment to spearhead the effort to gain control of the T&E budget. More than 30 percent of North American companies employ travel managers (Boehmer 11). The director should be familiar with the travel industry and should be well versed in both accounting and information technology. The director should report to the vice president of operations. The director's first priorities should be to establish a written T&E policy and a cost-control system.

Electrovision currently has no written policy on travel and entertainment, a step that is widely recommended by air travel experts; in fact, more than 75 percent of respondents to an American Express study of Canadian corporations said that they have established travel policies (Craig-Bourdin). Creating a policy

Moreno creates a forceful tone by using action verbs in the third-level subheadings of this section. This approach is appropriate to the nature of the study and the attitude of the audience. However, in a status-conscious organization, the imperative verbs might sound presumptuous coming from a junior member of the staff.

6

would clarify management's position and serve as a vehicle for communicating the need for moderation. At a minimum, the policy should include the following:

- All travel and entertainment should be strictly related to business and should be approved in advance.

- Except under special circumstances to be approved on a case-by-case basis, employees should travel by coach and stay in mid-range business hotels.

- The T&E policy should apply equally to employees at all levels.

In addition to making key points easy to find, bulleted lists help break up the text to relieve the reader's eye.

To implement the new policy, Electrovision will need to create a system for controlling T&E expenses. Each department should prepare an annual T&E budget as part of its operating plan. These budgets should be presented in detail so that management can evaluate how T&E dollars will be spent and can recommend appropriate cuts. To help management monitor performance relative to these budgets, the director of travel should prepare monthly financial statements showing actual T&E expenditures by department.

The director of travel should also be responsible for retaining a business-oriented travel service that will schedule all employee business trips and look for the best travel deals, particularly in airfares. In addition to centralizing Electrovision's reservation and ticketing activities, the agency will negotiate reduced group rates with hotels and rental car firms. The agency selected should have offices nationwide so that all Electrovision facilities can channel their reservations through the same company. This is particularly important in light of the dizzying array of often wildly different airfares available between some cities. It's not uncommon to find dozens of fares along commonly travelled routes ("BTN Quantifies" 1; Wan, Zou, and Dressner 629). In addition, the director can help coordinate travel across the company to secure group discounts whenever possible (McDougall 45).

Moreno lists the steps needed to implement her recommendations.

Reduce Unnecessary Travel and Entertainment

One of the easiest ways to reduce expenses is to reduce the amount of travelling and entertaining that occurs. An analysis of last year's expenditures suggests that as much as 30 percent of Electrovision's travel and entertainment is discretionary. The professional staff spent $2.8 million attending seminars and conferences last year. Although these gatherings are undoubtedly beneficial, the company could save money by sending fewer representatives to each function and perhaps by eliminating some of the less valuable seminars.

Similarly, Electrovision could economize on trips between headquarters and divisions by reducing the frequency of such visits and by sending fewer people on each trip. Although there is often no substitute for face-to-face meetings, management could try to resolve more internal issues through telephone, electronic, and written communication.

Electrovision can also reduce spending by urging employees to economize. Instead of flying business class, employees can fly coach class or take advantage

Moreno takes care not to overstep the boundaries of her analysis. For instance, she doesn't analyze the value of the seminars that employees attend every year, so she avoids any absolute statements about reducing travel to seminars.

7

of discount fares. Rather than ordering a $75 bottle of wine, employees can select a less expensive bottle or dispense with alcohol entirely. People can book rooms at moderately priced hotels and drive smaller rental cars.

Obtain Lowest Rates from Travel Providers

Apart from urging employees to economize, Electrovision can also save money by searching for the lowest available airfares, hotel rates, and rental car fees. Currently, few employees have the time or knowledge to seek out travel bargains. When they need to travel, they make the most convenient and comfortable arrangements. A professional travel service will be able to obtain lower rates from travel providers.

Judging by the experience of other companies, Electrovision may be able to trim as much as 35% from the travel budget simply by looking for bargains in airfares and negotiating group rates with hotels and rental car companies. Electrovision should be able to achieve these economies by analyzing its travel patterns, identifying frequently visited locations, and selecting a few hotels that are willing to reduce rates in exchange for guaranteed business. At the same time, the company should be able to save up to 40 percent on rental car charges by negotiating a corporate rate.

The possibilities for economizing are promising; however, making the best travel arrangements often requires trade-offs such as the following:

By pointing out possible difficulties and showing that she has considered all angles, Moreno builds reader confidence in her judgment.

- The best fares might not always be the lowest. Indirect flights are usually cheaper, but they take longer and may end up costing more in lost work time.

- The cheapest tickets often require booking 14 or even 30 days in advance, which is often impossible for us.

- Discount tickets are usually nonrefundable, which is a serious drawback when a trip needs to be cancelled at the last minute.

Replace Travel with Technological Alternatives

Less-expensive travel options promise significant savings, but the biggest cost reductions over the long term might come from replacing travel with virtual meeting technology. Both analysts and corporate users say that the early kinks that hampered online meetings have largely been worked out, and the latest systems are fast, easy to learn, and easy to use (Prigg 52). For example, Webex (a leading provider of webconferencing services) offers everything from simple, impromptu team meetings to major online events with up to 300 participants (*Cisco Webex Meeting Centre* Product Overview).

One of the first responsibilities of the new travel director should be an evaluation of these technologies and a recommendation for integrating them throughout Electrovision's operations.

Note how Moreno makes the transition from section to section. The first sentence under the second heading on this page refers to the subject of the previous paragraph and signals a shift in thought.

8

The Impact of Reforms

By implementing tighter controls, reducing unnecessary expenses, negotiating more favourable rates, and exploring alternatives to travel, Electrovision should be able to reduce its T&E budget significantly. As Table 1 illustrates, the combined savings should be in the neighbourhood of $6 million, although the precise figures are somewhat difficult to project.

Table 1
Electrovision Can Trim Travel and Entertainment Costs
by an Estimated $6 Million per Year

SOURCE OF SAVINGS	ESTIMATED SAVINGS
Switching from business-class to coach airfare	$2 300 000
Negotiating preferred hotel rates	940 000
Negotiating preferred rental car rates	460 000
Systematically searching for lower airfares	375 000
Reducing interdivisional travel	675 000
Reducing seminar and conference attendance	1 250 000
TOTAL POTENTIAL SAVINGS	**$6 000 000**

To achieve the economies outlined in the table, Electrovision will incur expenses for hiring a director of travel and for implementing a T&E cost-control system. These costs are projected at $115 000: $105 000 per year in salary and benefits for the new employee and a one-time expense of $10 000 for the cost-control system. The cost of retaining a full-service travel agency is negligible, even with the service fees that many are now passing along from airlines and other service providers.

The measures required to achieve these savings are likely to be unpopular with employees. Electrovision personnel are accustomed to generous T&E allowances, and they are likely to resent having these privileges curtailed. To alleviate their disappointment

- Management should make a determined effort to explain why the changes are necessary.

- The director of corporate communication should be asked to develop a multifaceted campaign that will communicate the importance of curtailing T&E costs.

- Management should set a positive example by adhering strictly to the new policies.

- The limitations should apply equally to employees at all levels in the organization.

An informative title in the table is consistent with the way headings are handled throughout this report, and it is appropriate for a report to a receptive audience.

The in-text reference to the table highlights the key point the reader should get from the table.

Including financial estimates helps management envision the impact of the suggestions, even though the estimated savings are difficult to project accurately.

Note how Moreno calls attention in the first paragraph to items in the following table, without repeating the information in the table.

9

She uses a descriptive heading for the last section of the text. In informational reports, this section is often called "Summary"; in analytical reports, it is called "Conclusions" or "Conclusions and Recommendations."

Presenting the recommendations in a list gives each one emphasis.

Moreno summarizes her conclusions in the first two paragraphs—a good approach because she organized her report around conclusions and recommendations, so readers have already been introduced to them.

CONCLUSIONS AND RECOMMENDATIONS

Electrovision is currently spending $16 million per year on travel and entertainment. Although much of this spending is justified, the company's costs are high relative to competitors' costs, mainly because Electrovision has been generous with its travel benefits.

Electrovision's liberal approach to travel and entertainment was understandable during years of high profitability; however, the company is facing the prospect of declining profits for the next several years. Management is therefore motivated to cut costs in all areas of the business. Reducing T&E spending is particularly important because the bottom-line impact of these costs will increase as airline fares increase.

Electrovision should be able to reduce T&E costs by as much as 40 percent by taking four important steps:

1. *Institute tighter spending controls.* Management should hire a director of travel and entertainment who will assume overall responsibility for T&E activities. Within the next six months, this director should develop a written travel policy, institute a T&E budget and a cost-control system, and retain a professional, business-oriented travel agency that will optimize arrangements with travel providers.

2. *Reduce unnecessary travel and entertainment.* Electrovision should encourage employees to economize on T&E spending. Management can accomplish this by authorizing fewer trips and by urging employees to be more conservative in their spending.

3. *Obtain lowest rates from travel providers.* Electrovision should also focus on obtaining the best rates on airline tickets, hotel rooms, and rental cars. By channelling all arrangements through a professional travel agency, the company can optimize its choices and gain clout in negotiating preferred rates.

4. *Replace travel with technological alternatives.* With the number of computers already installed in our facilities, it seems likely that we could take advantage of desktop videoconferencing and other distance-meeting tools. Technological alternatives won't be quite as feasible with customer sites, since these systems require compatible equipment at both ends of a connection, but such systems are certainly a possibility for communication with Electrovision's own sites.

Because these measures may be unpopular with employees, management should make a concerted effort to explain the importance of reducing travel costs. The director of corporate communication should be given responsibility for developing a plan to communicate the need for employee cooperation.

Moreno doesn't introduce any new facts in this section. In a longer report she might have divided this section into subsections, labelled "Conclusions" and "Recommendations," to distinguish between the two.

10

WORKS CITED

Baker, Michael B. "SLA Use Spreading, Especially for TMC Services." *Business Travel News* 17 May 2007: 14. Print.

Baker, Michael B. "Study Eyes Expense Tactics." *Business Travel News* (BTNOnline). 20 Jan. 2009. Web. 2 June 2009.

Boehmer, Jay. "Procurement Gains Corporate Ground Service Appreciation." *Business Travel News* 21 May 2007: 11. Print.

"BTN Quantifies '07 Road Warrior Norms in 100 Cities." *The Controller's Report* May 2007: 1. Print.

Business Travel News. Business Travel News Corporate Index 2012. Web. 18 Feb. 2013.

Craig-Bourdin, Margaret. "Business Travel Survey Roundup." *CA Magazine* Jan.–Feb. 2007. Web. 17 Oct. 2007. <http://www.camagazine.com/3/7/8/5/7/index1.shtml>.

Koenig, David. "Airlines Eye Bright Future." *Telegraph-Herald* (Dubuque, Iowa) 30 Jan. 2011: B2.

McDougall, Diane. "Travel - Managing the Cost Crunch." *CMA Management* 80.5 (2006): 44. Print.

Prigg, Mark. "Face to Interface." Businesstraveller.com. Apr. 2011. Web. 15 Aug. 2012.

"Replicon Productivity Index Shows Business Travel Expenses are on the Rise." Entertainment Close-Up. 1 Sept. 2011. Web. 10 Apr. 2012.

"Travel Expenses: Survey: 61 Percent Expect Travel Budgets to Jump 10 Percent This Year." *The Controller's Report* 8 (Aug. 2011): 12-13. Web.

"Travel Trends: Marshal Your Buying Power." *Canadian Business* 79.20 (2006): 33. Print.

Wan, Xiang, Li Zou, and Martin Dresner, "Assessing the Price Effects of Airline Alliances on Parallel Routes," *Transportation Research Part E* 45 (2009): 619–620. Print.

WebEx. *Cisco Webex Meeting Center*. Product Overview. 2013. Web. 20 Feb. 2013.

MLA style lists references alphabetically by the author's last name, and when the author is unknown, by the title of the reference. (See Appendix B for additional details on preparing reference lists.)

Moreno's list of references follows the style recommended in the *MLA Style Manual*. The box below shows how these sources would be cited following APA style.

10

REFERENCES

Baker, M. B. (2007, May 21). SLA use spreading, especially for TMC services. *Business Travel News*, 14.

Baker, M. B. (2009, January 20). Study eyes expense tactics. *Business Travel News* (BTNOnline). Retrieved from http://www.btnonline.com

Boehmer, J. (2007, May 21). Procurement gains corporate ground service appreciation, *Business Travel News*, 11.

BTN quantifies '07 road warrior norms in 100 cities. (2007, May). *The Controller's Report*, 1.

Business Travel News. (2012). Business Travel News corporate travel index 2012. Retrieved from http://businesstravelnews.texterity.com/businesstravelnews/20120319#pg1

Craig-Bourdin, M. (2007, October 17). Business travel survey roundup [Electronic version]. *CA Magazine*.

Koenig, D. (2011, January 30). Airlines eye bright future. *Telegraph-Herald* (Dubuque, Iowa), p. B2.

McDougall, D. (2006). Travel—managing the cost crunch. *CMA Management*, *80*(5), 44.

Prigg, M. (2011 April). Face to interface. Businesstraveller.com.

Replicon productivity index shows business travel expenses are on the rise (2011, September 1). Entertainment Close-Up.

Travel expenses: Survey: 61 percent expect travel budgets to jump 10 percent this year. (2011, August). *The Controller's Report*, 8, 12–13.

Travel Trends: Marshal your buying power. (2006). *Canadian Business*, *79*(20), 33.

Wan, X., Zou, L., & Dresner, M. (2009). Assessing the price effects of airline alliances on parallel routes. *Transportation Research Part E 45*, 619–620.

Webex. (2013). Cisco Webex Meeting Center. Product Overview. Retrieved from http://www.webex.com/product-overview/meeting-center.html

PREFATORY PARTS

Prefatory parts are front-end materials that provide key preliminary information so readers can decide whether and how to read the report.[3] Many of these parts—such as the table of contents, list of illustrations, and executive summary—are easier to prepare after the text has been completed, because they are based on the main text of the report. When your text is complete, you can also use your word processor to compile the table of contents and the list of illustrations.

COVER Many companies have standard covers for reports, made of heavy paper and imprinted with the company's name and logo. If your company has no standard covers, you can usually find something suitable in a good stationery store. Look for a cover that is attractive, convenient, and appropriate to the subject matter.

Covers are typically labelled with the report title, the writer's name (optional), and the submission date (also optional). Think carefully about the title. You want it to be concise and compelling while still communicating the essence of the subject matter. For example, you can reduce the length of your title by eliminating phrases such as *A Report of*, *A Study of*, or *A Survey of*.

TITLE FLY AND TITLE PAGE The **title fly** is a single sheet of paper with only the title of the report on it. It's not essential, but it adds a touch of formality.

The **title page** includes four blocks of information: (1) the title of the report; (2) the name, title, and address of the person, group, or organization that authorized the report (if anyone); (3) the name, title, and address of the person, group, or organization that prepared the report; and (4) the date on which the report was submitted. On some title pages the second block of information is preceded by the words *Prepared for* or *Submitted to*, and the third block of information is preceded by *Prepared by* or *Submitted by*. In some cases the title page serves as the cover of the report, especially if the report is relatively short and is intended solely for internal use.

Formal reports can contain a variety of prefatory parts, from a cover page to a synopsis or executive summary.

DutchScenery/Fotolia

Years ago, report writers commonly prepared their reports on manual or electric typewriters. What are the differences between using old-fashioned typewriters to prepare reports and using computers with word-processing software? Are there any advantages to typewriters? Any disadvantages to using computers? What are they?

LETTER OF AUTHORIZATION AND LETTER OF ACCEPTANCE If you received written authorization to prepare the report, you may want to include that letter or memo in your report. This **letter of authorization** (or *memo of authorization*) is a document you received, asking or directing you to prepare the report. If you wrote a **letter of acceptance** (or *memo of acceptance*) in response to that communication, accepting the assignment and clarifying any conditions or limitations, you might also include that letter here in the report's prefatory parts.

In general, the letters of authorization and acceptance are included in only the most formal reports. However, in any case where a significant amount of time has passed since you received the letter of authorization, or you do not have a close working relationship with the audience, consider including both letters to ensure that everyone is clear about the report's intent and the approach you took to create it. You don't want your weeks or months of work to be diminished by any misunderstandings.

A letter of authorization is the document that instructed you to produce a report; a letter of acceptance is your written agreement to produce the report.

LETTER OF TRANSMITTAL The **letter of transmittal** (or *memo of transmittal*), a specialized form of a cover letter, introduces your report to your audience. The letter of transmittal says what you'd say if you were handing the report

2 **LEARNING OBJECTIVE**

Explain the functions of the letter of transmittal.

directly to the person who authorized it, so the style is less formal than the rest of the report. For example, the letter would use personal pronouns (*you*, *I*, and *we*) and conversational language. Moreno's Electrovision report includes a one-page transmittal memo from Moreno to her boss (the person who requested the report).

The transmittal letter usually appears right before the table of contents. If your report will be widely distributed, however, you may decide to include the letter of transmittal only in selected copies, so you can make certain comments to a specific audience. If your report discusses layoffs or other issues that affect people in the organization, you may want to discuss your recommendations privately in a letter of transmittal to top management. If your audience is likely to be skeptical of or even hostile to something in your report, the transmittal letter is a good opportunity to acknowledge their concerns and explain how the report addresses the issues they care about.

Depending on the nature of your report, your letter of transmittal can follow either the direct approach for routine or positive messages described in Chapter 8 or the indirect approach for negative messages described in Chapter 9. Open by officially conveying the report to your readers and summarizing its purpose. Such a letter typically begins with a statement such as "Here is the report you asked me to prepare on . . ." The rest of the introduction includes information about the scope of the report, the methods used to complete the study, limitations, and any special messages you need to convey.

In the body of the transmittal letter, you may also highlight important points or sections of the report, give suggestions for follow-up studies, and offer any details that will help readers understand and use the report. You may also wish to acknowledge help given by others—if your report is extensive, you probably received assistance from many people, and this letter is a high-visibility way to show your appreciation. The conclusion of the transmittal letter is a note of thanks for having been given the report assignment, an expression of willingness to discuss the report, and an offer to assist with future projects.

> If you don't include a synopsis, you can summarize the report's contents in your letter of transmittal.

If the report does not have a synopsis, the letter of transmittal may summarize the major findings, conclusions, and recommendations. This material would be placed after the opening of the letter.

TABLE OF CONTENTS The table of contents (often titled simply *Contents*) indicates in outline form the coverage, sequence, and relative importance of the information in the report. The headings used in the text of the report are the basis for the table of contents. Depending on the length and complexity of the report, you may need to decide how many levels of headings to show in the contents; you want to strike a balance between simplicity and completeness. Contents that show only first-level heads are easy to scan but could frustrate people looking for specific subsections in the report. Conversely, contents that show every level of heading—down to fourth or fifth level in detailed reports—identify all the sections but can intimidate readers and blur the focus by detracting from your most important message points. Where the detailed table of contents could have dozens or even hundreds of entries, consider including two tables: a high-level table that shows only major headings, followed by a detailed table that includes everything (as this and many other textbooks do). No matter how many levels you include, ensure that readers can easily distinguish between them.

> To save time and reduce errors, use the table of contents generator in your word processor.

Also, take extra care to verify that your table of contents is accurate, consistent, and complete. Even minor errors could damage your credibility if readers turn to a given page expecting to find something that isn't there, or if they find headings that seem similar to the table of contents but aren't worded quite the same. To ensure accuracy, construct the table of contents after your report is

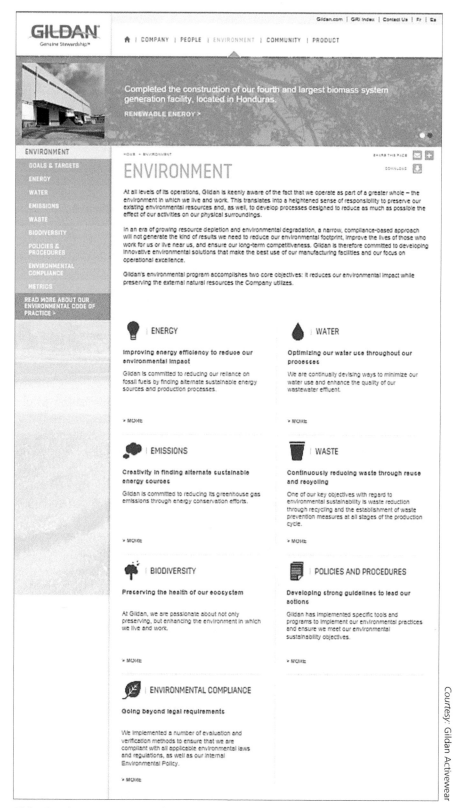

Gildan, best known as a supplier of sport shirts for the screen print market, promotes its corporate social responsibility through online reports. What do you notice about the organization of the Gildan environmental report? Who are its audiences? How are images selected and used?

complete, thoroughly edited, and proofread. This way, the headings and sub-headings aren't likely to change or move from page to page. If possible, use the automatic features in your word processor to generate the table of contents. Doing so helps improve accuracy by eliminating typing mistakes, and it keeps your table current in the event you do have to repaginate or revise headings late in the process.

LIST OF ILLUSTRATIONS If you have more than a handful of illustrations in your report, or you want to call attention to your illustrations, include a list of illustrations after the table of contents. For simplicity's sake, some reports refer to all visuals as *illustrations* or *exhibits*. In other reports, as in Moreno's Electrovision report, tables are labelled separately from other types of visuals, which are called *figures*. Regardless of the system you use, ensure that you include titles and page numbers.

If you have enough space on a single page, include the list of illustrations directly beneath the table of contents. Otherwise, put the list on the page after the contents page. When tables and figures are numbered separately, they should also be listed separately. The two lists can appear on the same page if they fit; otherwise, start each list on a separate page.

Explain the difference between a synopsis and an executive summary.

Take time writing your synopsis or executive summary; it's one of the most important parts of your report.

SYNOPSIS OR EXECUTIVE SUMMARY A **synopsis** is a brief overview (one page or less) of a report's most important points, designed to give readers a quick preview of the contents. It's often included in long informational reports dealing with technical, professional, or academic subjects and can also be called an **abstract.** Because it's a concise representation of the whole report, it may be distributed separately to a wide audience; then, interested readers can request a copy of the entire report. The synopsis or abstract can also be indexed as a separate entry in electronic databases, so think carefully about the best way to preview the report's contents.

The phrasing of a synopsis can be either informative or descriptive. An informative synopsis presents the main points of the report in the order in which they appear in the text. A descriptive synopsis, on the other hand, simply tells what the report is about, using only moderately greater detail than the table of contents; the actual findings of the report are omitted. Here are examples of statements from each type:

Informative Synopsis	Descriptive Synopsis
Sales of super-premium ice cream make up 11 percent of the total ice cream market.	This report contains information about super-premium ice cream and its share of the market.

A synopsis and an executive summary both summarize a report's content, but an executive summary is more comprehensive.

The way you handle a synopsis reflects the approach you use in the text. If you're using an indirect approach in your report, you're better off with a descriptive synopsis. An informative synopsis, with its focus on conclusions and key points, may be too confrontational if your audience is skeptical. You don't want to disrupt the communication process by providing a controversial beginning. No matter which type of synopsis you use, be sure to present an accurate picture of the report's contents.[4]

Many report writers prefer to include an **executive summary** instead of a synopsis or an abstract. Whereas a synopsis is a prose table of contents that outlines the main points of the report, an executive summary is a fully developed "mini" version of the report itself. An executive summary is more comprehensive than a synopsis; it can contain headings, well-developed transitions, and even visual elements. It is often organized in the same way as the report, using a direct or an indirect approach, depending on the audience's receptivity.

Executive summaries are intended for readers who lack the time or motivation to study the complete text. As a general rule, keep the length of an executive summary proportionate to the length of the report. A brief business report may have only a one-page or shorter executive summary. Longer business reports may have a two- or three-page summary. Anything longer, however, might cease to be a summary.[5]

Linda Moreno's Electrovision report provides one example of an executive summary. After reading the summary, audience members know the essentials of the report and are in a position to make a decision. Later, when time permits, they may read certain parts of the report to obtain additional detail. However, from daily newspapers to websites, businesspeople are getting swamped with more and more data and information. They are looking for ways to cut through all the clutter, and reading executive summaries is a popular shortcut. Because you can usually assume that many of your readers will not read the main text of your report, ensure that you cover all your important points (along with significant supporting information) in the executive summary.

Many reports require neither a synopsis nor an executive summary. Length is usually the determining factor. Most reports of fewer than 10 pages either omit such a preview or combine it with the letter of transmittal. However, if your report is more than 20 pages long, include either a synopsis or an executive summary as a convenience for readers. Which one you provide depends on the traditions of your organization.

TEXT OF THE REPORT

Although reports may contain a variety of components, the heart of a report is always composed of three main parts: an introduction, a body, and a close (which may consist of a summary, conclusions, or recommendations, or some combination of the three). As Chapter 12 points out, the length and content of each part varies with the length and type of report, the organizational structure, and the reader's familiarity with the topic. Following is a brief review of the three major parts of the report text.

- **Introduction.** A good introduction prepares your readers to follow and comprehend the information in the report body. It invites the audience to continue reading by telling them what the report is about, why they should be concerned, and how the report is organized. If your report has a synopsis or an executive summary, minimize redundancy by balancing the introduction with the material in your summary—as Linda Moreno does in her Electrovision report. For example, Moreno's executive summary is fairly detailed, so she keeps her introduction brief. If you believe that your introduction needs to repeat information that has already been covered in one of the prefatory parts, vary the wording to minimize the feeling of repetition.
- **Body.** This section contains the information that supports your conclusions and recommendations as well as your analysis, logic, and interpretation of the information. See the body of Linda Moreno's Electrovision report for an example of the types of supporting detail commonly included in this section. Pay close attention to her effective use of visuals. Most inexperienced writers have a tendency to include too much data in their reports or place too much data in paragraph format instead of using tables and charts. Such treatment increases the chance of boring or losing an audience. If you find yourself with too much information, include only the essential supporting data in the body, use visuals, and place any additional information in an appendix.

- **Close.** The close of your report should summarize your main ideas, highlight your conclusions or recommendations (if any), and list any courses of action that you expect readers to take or that you will be taking yourself. This section may be labelled "Summary" or "Conclusions and Recommendations." If you have organized your report in a direct pattern, your close should be relatively brief, such as Linda Moreno's. With an indirect organization, you may be using this section to present your conclusions and recommendations for the first time, in which case this section might be fairly extensive.

SUPPLEMENTARY PARTS

4 LEARNING OBJECTIVE

Describe the three supplementary parts of a formal report.

The supplementary parts provide additional detail and reference materials.

Use an appendix for materials that are too lengthy for the body or not directly relevant to all audience members.

Supplementary parts follow the text of the report and provide information for readers who seek more detailed discussion. For online reports, put supplements on separate webpages and allow readers to link to them from the main report pages. Supplements are more common in long reports than in short ones, and they typically include appendices, a bibliography, and an index.

APPENDICES An **appendix** contains materials related to the report but not included in the text because they are too long or not relevant to everyone in the audience. If your company has an intranet, shared workspaces, or other means of storing and accessing information online, consider putting your detailed supporting evidence there and referring readers to those sources for more detail.

The content of report appendices varies widely, including any sample questionnaires and cover letters, sample forms, computer printouts, statistical formulas, financial statements and spreadsheets, copies of important documents, and multipage illustrations that would break up the flow of text. You might also include a glossary as an appendix or as a separate supplementary part.

If you have multiple categories of supporting material, give each type a separate appendix. Appendices are usually identified with a letter and a short, descriptive title—for example, "Appendix A: Questionnaire," "Appendix B: Computer Printout of Raw Data." All appendices should be mentioned in the text and listed in the table of contents.

A bibliography fulfills your ethical obligation to credit your sources, and it allows readers to consult those sources for more information.

BIBLIOGRAPHY To fulfill your ethical and legal obligation to credit other people for their work, and to assist readers who may wish to research your topic further, include a **bibliography**, a list of the secondary sources you consulted when preparing your report. In her Electrovision report, Linda Moreno labelled her bibliography "Works Cited" because she listed only the works that were mentioned in the report. Call this section "Sources" or "References" if it includes works consulted but not mentioned in your report. Moreno uses the author–date system to format her bibliographic sources. An alternative is to use numbered footnotes (bottom of the page) or endnotes (end of the report). For more information on citing sources, see Appendix B.

In addition to providing a bibliography, some authors prefer to cite references in the report text. Acknowledging your sources in the body of your report demonstrates that you have thoroughly researched your topic. Furthermore, mentioning the names of well-known or important authorities on the subject helps build credibility for your message. The source references should be handled as conveniently and inconspicuously as possible. One approach, especially for internal reports, is simply to mention a source in the text:

> According to Dr. Lewis Morgan of Northwestern Hospital, hip replacement operations account for 7 percent of all surgery performed on women age 65 and over.

However, if your report will be distributed to outsiders, include additional information on where you obtained the data. Most students are familiar with citation methods suggested by the Modern Language Association (MLA) or the American Psychological Association (APA). *The Chicago Manual of Style* is a reference often used by typesetters and publishers. All of these sources encourage the use of in-text citations (inserting the author's last name and a year of publication or a page number directly into the text).

INDEX An **index** is an alphabetical list of names, places, and subjects mentioned in your report, along with the pages on which they occur (see the indexes in this book for examples). If you think your readers will need to access specific points of information in a lengthy report, consider including an index that lists all key topics, product names, markets, important persons—whatever is relevant to your subject matter. As with your table of contents, accuracy is critical. The good news is that you can also use your word processor to compile the index. Just ensure that you update the index (and any automatically generated elements, for that matter) right before you distribute your report. In addition, have another person spot-check the index to ensure that your entries are correct and easy to follow.

If your report is lengthy, an index can help readers locate specific topics quickly.

Producing Formal Proposals

The goal of a proposal is to impress readers with your professionalism and to make your offering and your company stand out from the competition. Consequently, proposals addressed to external audiences, including potential customers and investors, are nearly always formal. For smaller projects and situations where you already have a working relationship with the audience, the proposal can be less formal and omit some components described in this section.

Formal proposals must be produced with a high degree of polish and professionalism.

Formal proposals contain many of the same components as other formal reports (see Figure 13–3). The difference lies mostly in the text, although a few of the prefatory parts are also different. With the exception of an occasional

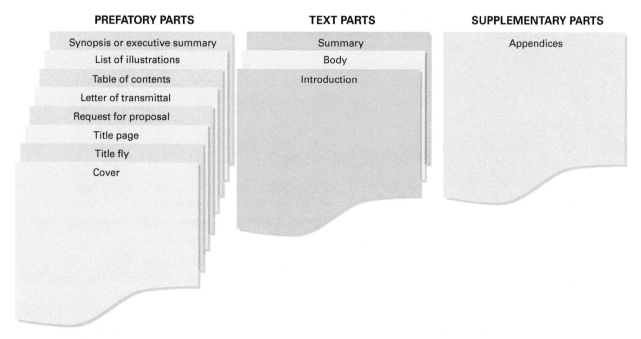

Figure 13–3 Parts of a Formal Proposal

appendix, most proposals have few supplementary parts. As always, if you're responding to a request for proposal (RFP) follow its specifications to the letter, ensuring that you include everything it asks for and nothing it doesn't ask for.

PREFATORY PARTS

The cover, title fly, title page, table of contents, and list of illustrations are handled the same as in other formal reports. However, you'll want to handle other prefatory parts a bit differently, such as the copy of the RFP, the synopsis or executive summary, and the letter of transmittal.

COPY OF THE RFP RFPs usually have specific instructions for referring to the RFP itself in the proposal, because the organizations that issue RFPs need a methodical way to track all their active RFPs and the incoming responses. Some organizations require that you include a copy of the entire RFP in your proposal; others simply want you to refer to the RFP by name or number or perhaps include just the introductory section of the RFP. Make sure you follow the instructions in every detail. If there are no specific instructions, use your best judgment based on the length of the RFP and whether you received a printed copy or accessed it online. In any event, make sure your proposal refers to the RFP in some way so that the audience can associate your proposal with the correct RFP.

SYNOPSIS OR EXECUTIVE SUMMARY Although you may include a synopsis or an executive summary for your reader's convenience when your proposal is long, these components are often less useful in a formal proposal than they are in a formal report. If your proposal is unsolicited, your transmittal letter will already have caught the reader's interest, making a synopsis or an executive summary redundant. It may also be less important if your proposal is solicited, because the reader is already committed to studying your proposal to find out how you intend to satisfy the terms of a contract. The introduction of a solicited proposal would provide an adequate preview of the contents.

LETTER OF TRANSMITTAL The way you handle the letter of transmittal depends on whether the proposal is solicited or unsolicited. If the proposal is solicited, the transmittal letter follows the pattern for positive messages, highlighting those aspects of your proposal that may give you a competitive advantage. If the proposal is unsolicited, approach the transmittal letter as a persuasive message. The letter must persuade the reader that you have something worthwhile to offer, something that justifies the time required to read the entire proposal.

TEXT OF THE PROPOSAL

As with reports, the text of a proposal is composed of three main parts: an introduction, a body, and a close. As Chapter 12 notes, the content and depth of each part depend on whether the proposal is solicited or unsolicited, formal or informal. Here's a brief review:[6]

- **Introduction.** This section presents and summarizes the problem you intend to solve and your solution to that problem, including any benefits the reader will receive from your solution.
- **Body.** This section explains the complete details of the solution: how the job will be done, how it will be divided into tasks, what method will be used to do it (including the required equipment, material, and personnel),

when the work will begin and end, how much the entire job will cost (including a detailed breakdown, if required or requested), and why your company is qualified.

- **Close.** This section emphasizes the benefits that readers will realize from your solution, and it urges readers to act.

Figure 13–4 is an informal proposal submitted by Dixon O'Donnell, vice president of O'Donnell & Associates, a geotechnical engineering firm that conducts a variety of environmental testing services. The company is bidding on the mass grading and utility work specified by AGI Builders. As you review this document, pay close attention to the specific items addressed in the proposal's introduction, body, and close.

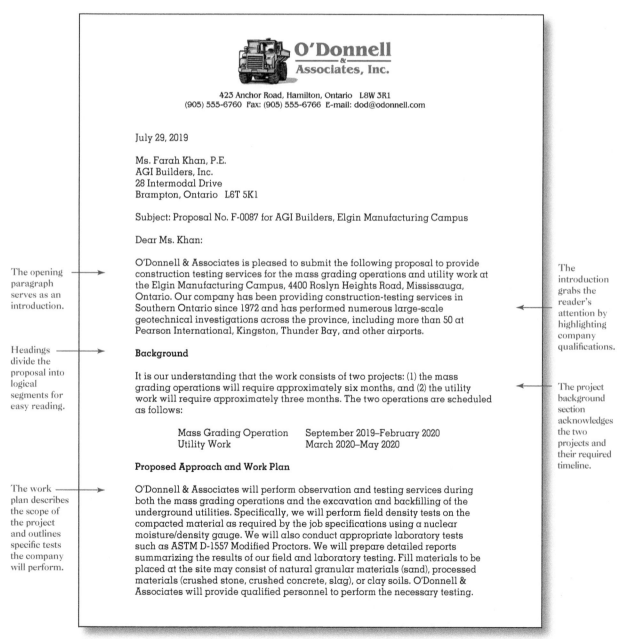

O'Donnell & Associates, Inc.

423 Anchor Road, Hamilton, Ontario L8W 3R1
(905) 555-6760 Fax: (905) 555-6766 E-mail: dod@odonnell.com

July 29, 2019

Ms. Farah Khan, P.E.
AGI Builders, Inc.
28 Intermodal Drive
Brampton, Ontario L6T 5K1

Subject: Proposal No. F-0087 for AGI Builders, Elgin Manufacturing Campus

Dear Ms. Khan:

The opening paragraph serves as an introduction. → O'Donnell & Associates is pleased to submit the following proposal to provide construction testing services for the mass grading operations and utility work at the Elgin Manufacturing Campus, 4400 Roslyn Heights Road, Mississauga, Ontario. Our company has been providing construction-testing services in Southern Ontario since 1972 and has performed numerous large-scale geotechnical investigations across the province, including more than 50 at Pearson International, Kingston, Thunder Bay, and other airports. ← *The introduction grabs the reader's attention by highlighting company qualifications.*

Headings divide the proposal into logical segments for easy reading. → **Background**

It is our understanding that the work consists of two projects: (1) the mass grading operations will require approximately six months, and (2) the utility work will require approximately three months. The two operations are scheduled as follows: ← *The project background section acknowledges the two projects and their required timeline.*

Mass Grading Operation	September 2019–February 2020
Utility Work	March 2020–May 2020

Proposed Approach and Work Plan

The work plan describes the scope of the project and outlines specific tests the company will perform. → O'Donnell & Associates will perform observation and testing services during both the mass grading operations and the excavation and backfilling of the underground utilities. Specifically, we will perform field density tests on the compacted material as required by the job specifications using a nuclear moisture/density gauge. We will also conduct appropriate laboratory tests such as ASTM D-1557 Modified Proctors. We will prepare detailed reports summarizing the results of our field and laboratory testing. Fill materials to be placed at the site may consist of natural granular materials (sand), processed materials (crushed stone, crushed concrete, slag), or clay soils. O'Donnell & Associates will provide qualified personnel to perform the necessary testing.

(continued)

Figure 13–4 Dixon O'Donnell's Informal Solicited Proposal

Ms. Farah Khan, P.E., AGI Builders, Inc.   July 29, 2019   Page 2

The work plan also explains who will be responsible for the various tasks.

Sandeep Patel will be the lead field technician responsible for the project. A copy of Mr. Patel's résumé is included with this proposal for your review. Sandeep will coordinate field activities with your job site superintendent and make sure that appropriate personnel are assigned to the job site. Overall project management will be the responsibility of Joseph Proesel. Project engineering services will be performed under the direction of Dixon O'Donnell, P.E. All field personnel assigned to the site will be familiar with and abide by the Project Site Health and Safety Plan prepared by Carlson Environmental, Inc., dated April 2014.

The project leader's résumé is attached to the proposal, providing additional detail without cluttering up the body of the proposal.

Qualifications

O'Donnell & Associates has been providing quality professional services since 1972 in the areas of

The qualifications section grabs attention by mentioning compelling qualifications.

- Geotechnical engineering
- Materials testing and inspection
- Pavement evaluation
- Environmental services
- Engineering and technical support (CADD) services

The company provides Phase I and Phase II environmental site assessments, preparation of LUST site closure reports, installation of groundwater monitoring wells, and testing of soil/groundwater samples for environmental contaminants. Geotechnical services include all phases of soil mechanics and foundation engineering, including foundation and lateral load analysis, slope stability analysis, site preparation recommendations, seepage analysis, pavement design, and settlement analysis.

O'Donnell & Associates' materials testing laboratory is certified by AASHTO Accreditation Program for the testing of Soils, Aggregate, Hot Mix Asphalt and Portland Cement Concrete. A copy of our laboratory certification is included with this proposal. In addition to in-house training, field and laboratory technicians participate in a variety of certification programs, including those sponsored by the American Concrete Institute (ACI).

Describing certifications (approvals by recognized industry associations or government agencies) helps build the company's credibility.

Costs

On the basis of our understanding of the scope of the work, we estimate the total cost of the two projects to be $100 260.00, as follows:

(continued)

Figure 13–4 Dixon O'Donnell's Informal Solicited Proposal *(continued)*

Ms. Farah Khan, P.E., AGI Builders, Inc.   July 29, 2019   Page 3

Cost Estimates

A clear and complete itemization of estimated costs builds confidence in dependability of the project's financial projections.

Cost Estimate: Mass Grading	Units	Rate ($)	Total Cost ($)
Field Inspection			
Labour	1320 hours	$38.50	$ 50 820.00
Nuclear Moisture Density Metre	132 days	35.00	4 620.00
Vehicle Expense	132 days	45.00	5 940.00
Laboratory Testing			
Proctor Density Tests (ASTM D-1557)	4 tests	130.00	520.00
Engineering/Project Management			
Principal Engineer	16 hours	110.00	1 760.00
Project Manager	20 hours	80.00	1 600.00
Administrative Assistant	12 hours	50.00	600.00
Subtotal			$ 65 860.00

Cost Estimate: Utility Work	Units	Rate ($)	Total Cost ($)
Field Inspection			
Labour	660 hours	$ 38.50	$ 25 410.00
Nuclear Moisture Density Meter	66 days	5.00	2 310.00
Vehicle Expense	66 days	45.00	2 970.00
Laboratory Testing			
Proctor Density Tests (ASTM D-1557)	2 tests	130.00	260.00
Engineering/Project Management			
Principal Engineer	10 hours	110.00	1 100.00
Project Manager	20 hours	80.00	1 600.00
Administrative Assistant	15 hours	50.00	750.00
Subtotal			$ 34 400.00
Total Project Costs			**$100 260.00**

This estimate assumes full-time inspection services. However, our services may also be performed on an as-requested basis, and actual charges will reflect time associated with the project. We have attached our standard fee schedule for your review. Overtime rates are for hours in excess of 8.0 hours per day, before 7:00 a.m., after 5:00 p.m., and on holidays and weekends.

To give the client some budgetary flexibility, the proposal offers an alternative to the fixed-fee approach—which may lower any resistance to accepting the bid.

(continued)

Figure 13–4 Dixon O'Donnell's Informal Solicited Proposal *(continued)*

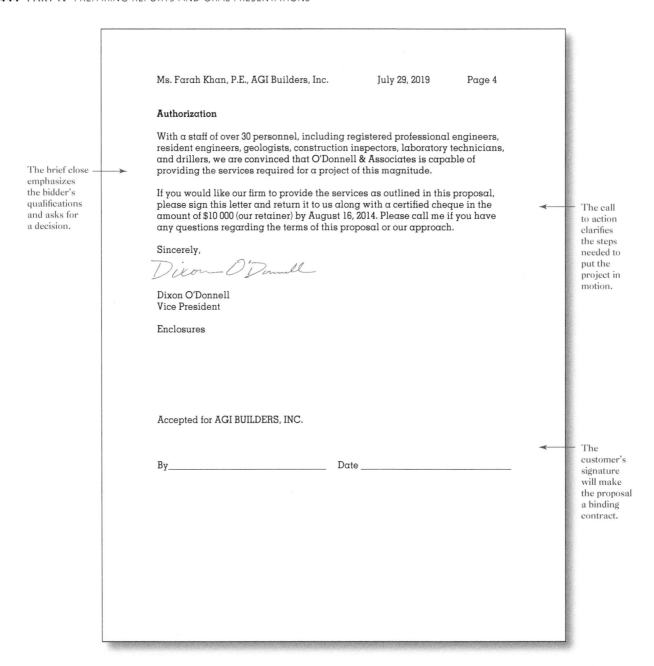

The brief close emphasizes the bidder's qualifications and asks for a decision.

Ms. Farah Khan, P.E., AGI Builders, Inc.   July 29, 2019   Page 4

Authorization

With a staff of over 30 personnel, including registered professional engineers, resident engineers, geologists, construction inspectors, laboratory technicians, and drillers, we are convinced that O'Donnell & Associates is capable of providing the services required for a project of this magnitude.

If you would like our firm to provide the services as outlined in this proposal, please sign this letter and return it to us along with a certified cheque in the amount of $10 000 (our retainer) by August 16, 2014. Please call me if you have any questions regarding the terms of this proposal or our approach.

The call to action clarifies the steps needed to put the project in motion.

Sincerely,

Dixon O'Donnell
Vice President

Enclosures

Accepted for AGI BUILDERS, INC.

By_____   Date _____

The customer's signature will make the proposal a binding contract.

Figure 13–4 Dixon O'Donnell's Informal Solicited Proposal *(continued)*

Proofreading Reports and Proposals

After you have assembled all the various components of your report or proposal, revised the entire document's content for clarity and conciseness, and designed the document to ensure readability and a positive impression on your readers, you have essentially produced your document in its final form. Now you need to review it thoroughly one last time, looking for inconsistencies, errors, and missing components. For example, if you changed a heading in the report's text part, ensure that you also changed the corresponding heading in the table of contents and in all references to that heading in your report. Proofing can catch minor flaws that might diminish your credibility—and major flaws that might damage your career.

Proofreading the text portions of your report is essentially the same as proofreading any business message—you check for typos, spelling errors, and mistakes in punctuation. Proof your visuals thoroughly, as Chapter 12 points out, and ensure that they are positioned correctly. If you need specific tips on proofreading documents, look back at Chapter 6 for some reminders on what to look for when proofreading text and how to proofread like a pro.

Whenever possible, arrange for someone with "fresh eyes" to proofread the report, somebody who hasn't been involved with the text so far. At this point in the process, you are so familiar with the content that your mind is likely to fill in missing words, fix misspelled words, and subconsciously compensate for other flaws without you even being aware of it. Someone with fresh eyes might see mistakes that you've passed over a dozen times without noticing. An ideal approach is to have two people review it, one who is an expert in the subject matter and one who isn't. The first person can ensure its technical accuracy, and the second can ensure that a wide range of readers will understand it.[7]

> Ask for proofreading assistance from someone who hasn't been involved in the development of your proposal; he or she might see errors that you've overlooked.

Distributing Reports and Proposals

All of the distribution issues you explored in Chapter 6 apply to reports and proposals, as long as you take into account the length and complexity of your documents. For physical distribution, consider spending the few extra dollars for a professional courier or package delivery service, if that will help your document stand apart from the crowd. The online tracking offered by Canada Post, FedEx, UPS, and other services can verify that your document arrived safely. On the other hand, if you've prepared the document for a single person or small group, delivering it in person can be a nice touch. Not only can you answer any immediate questions about it, but you can also promote the results in person—reminding the recipient of the benefits contained in your report or proposal.

For electronic distribution, unless your audience specifically requests a word processor file, provide documents as PDF files. Many people are reluctant to open word processor files these days, particularly from outsiders, given the vulnerability of such files to macro viruses and other contaminations. Moreover, using PDF files lets you control how your document is displayed on your audience's computers, ensuring that your readers see your document as you intended.

If your company or client expects you to distribute your reports via a web-based content management system, intranet, or extranet, ensure that you upload the correct file(s) to the correct online location. Verify the onscreen display of your report after you've posted it, too; ensure that graphics, charts, links, and other elements are in place and operational.

When you've completed your formal report and sent it off to your audience, your next task is to wait for a response. If you don't hear from your readers within a week or two, you might want to ask politely whether the report arrived. (Some RFPs specify a response time frame. In such a case, *don't* pester the recipient ahead of schedule, or you'll hurt your chances.) In hope of stimulating a response, you might ask a question about the report, such as "How do you think accounting will react to the proposed budget increase?" You might also offer to answer any questions or provide additional information. To review the ideas presented in this chapter, see "Checklist: Completing Formal Reports and Proposals."

✓ Checklist | Completing Formal Reports and Proposals

A. Prefatory parts
- Use your company's standard report covers, if available.
- Include a concise, descriptive title on the cover.
- Include a title fly only if you want an extra-formal touch.
- On the title page, list (1) report title; (2) name, title, and address of the group or person who authorized the report; (3) name, title, and address of the group or person who prepared the report; and (4) date of submission.
- Include a copy of the letter of authorization, if appropriate.
- If responding to an RFP, follow its instructions for including a copy or referring to the RFP by name or tracking number.
- Include a letter of transmittal that introduces the report.
- Provide a table of contents in outline form, with headings worded exactly as they appear in the body of the report.
- Include a list of illustrations if the report contains a large number of them.

- Include a synopsis (brief summary of the report) or executive summary (a condensed "mini" version of the report) for longer reports.

B. Text of the report
- Draft an introduction that prepares the reader for the content that follows.
- Provide the information that supports your conclusions, recommendations, or proposals in the body of the report.
- Don't overload the body with unnecessary detail.
- Close with a summary of your main idea.

C. Supplementary parts
- Use appendices to provide supplementary information or supporting evidence.
- List any secondary sources you used in a bibliography.
- Provide an index if your report contains a large number of terms or ideas and is likely to be consulted over time.

SUMMARY OF LEARNING OBJECTIVES

1 Characterize the four tasks involved in completing business reports and proposals. To complete business reports and proposals, revise, produce, proofread, and distribute the document as you would any other business message. Revising reports and proposals involves evaluating content and organization, reviewing style and readability, and editing for conciseness and clarity. After revision, produce your report by designing it with appropriate graphical features and white space and adding visual support and any missing transitional elements. Proofread your report for correct spelling, grammar, and punctuation, and, if distributing it electronically, use PDFs for reader convenience and document security.

2 Explain the functions of the letter of transmittal. The letter of transmittal (or memo of transmittal) serves as a cover letter for a proposal. Written in a personal style, it typically presents the reader with the proposal's key ideas, explains how the proposal addresses the audience's concerns, highlights important issues, and advises readers on how to understand and apply the proposal's contents. The letter of transmittal also provides an opportunity for the proposal's author to acknowledge the help of others and establish goodwill with the audience.

3 Explain the difference between a synopsis and an executive summary. A synopsis is a brief outline of a report's contents; it is usually no longer than a page. A

synopsis can be either informative (presenting the main points in the order in which they appear in the report body) or descriptive (telling generally what the report is about). Typically, if the report follows the indirect approach, a descriptive synopsis is the better, more tactful choice. If the report follows the direct approach, an informative synopsis that focuses on conclusions and key points is better. The executive summary is a capsule version of the entire report, listing key details and benefits and using headings, transitions, and even visual support to communicate the full contents of the report text.

4 Describe the three supplementary parts of a formal report. Three supplementary parts of the formal report are the appendix, bibliography, and index. The appendix contains materials related to the report but too lengthy to include or lacking direct relevance. These materials may include sample questionnaires, financial statements, and complex illustrations. The bibliography lists the secondary sources you consulted to prepare the report and fulfills your ethical and legal obligation to acknowledge the work of others. The index lists alphabetically the names, places, and subjects mentioned in the report, with corresponding page numbers. To help the reader access specific information, the index must be accurate and contain all key topics.

5 **Explain how prefatory parts of a proposal differ, depending on whether the proposal is solicited or unsolicited.** First, a proposal solicited through an RFP should refer to it so the soliciting organization can manage the responses systematically. Because an unsolicited proposal does not respond to an RFP, this element does not appear in the proposal. Second, in an unsolicited proposal the transmittal letter may eliminate the need for a synopsis, because the letter has piqued the reader's interest in the proposal itself. Similarly, in a solicited proposal, the synopsis may play a minor role, because readers are already interested in how you want to help them. Finally, in an unsolicited proposal, the transmittal letter should follow the persuasive strategy, because you are approaching the organization through your own incentive. In a solicited proposal, the transmittal letter should follow the strategy for positive messages, by emphasizing the proposal contents that differentiate you from the competition.

ON THE JOB | PERFORMING COMMUNICATION TASKS AT THE BILL & MELINDA GATES FOUNDATION

A decade into your business career, you've decided to put your communication skills to use in an effort to improve global health. You recently joined the Bill & Melinda Gates Foundation as a program officer in global health strategies.

Malaria is one of the foundation's primary health concerns. This mosquito-borne disease has been largely eradicated in many parts of the world, but it remains an active and growing menace in other areas (particularly sub-Saharan Africa). Worldwide, malaria kills more than 1 million people every year, most of whom are children.

You are writing an informational report that will be made available on the foundation's website, summarizing the current crisis and progress being made toward the eventual control and eradication of malaria. How will you handle the following challenges?[8]

1. A wide variety of people visit the foundation's website, from researchers who are interested in applying for grants to reporters writing about health and education issues to members of the general public. Consequently, you can't pin down a specific audience for your report. In addition, because people will simply download a PDF file of the report from the website, you don't have the opportunity to write a traditional letter or memo of transmittal. How should you introduce your report to website visitors?

   a. Write a brief description of the report, explaining its purpose and content; post this information on the website, above the link to the PDF file so that people can read it before they decide whether to download the file.
   b. Provide an email link that people can use to send you an email message if they'd like to know more about the report before reading it.
   c. Write a news release describing the report and post this document on the website's "Press Room" section.
   d. Count on the title of the report to introduce its purpose and content; don't bother writing an introduction.

2. Which of the following report titles would do the best job of catching readers' attention with an emotional "hook" that balances the urgency of the crisis with the reasons for hope?

   a. Children Who Don't Need to Die: The Urgent Global Malaria Crisis
   b. Preventing 1 Million Malaria Deaths Every Year: The Urgent Global Challenge—And Reasons for Hope
   c. Malaria: It Killed 2000 More Children Today
   d. Malaria: Progress Toward Eradicating This Global Disease

3. The Gates Foundation is known around the world for the quality of its work, and that includes the quality of its communication efforts. Which of the following proofreading strategies should you use to make sure your report is free of errors?

   a. Take advantage of technology. Double-check the settings in your word processor to make sure every checking tool is activated as you type, including the spell-checker, grammar-checker, and style-checker. When you're finished with the first draft, run each of these tools again, just to make sure the computer didn't miss anything.
   b. Recognize that no report, particularly a complex 48-page document with multiple visuals and more than 60 sources, is going to be free of errors. Include a statement on the title page apologizing for any errors that may still exist in the report. Provide your email address and invite people to send you a message when they find errors.
   c. As soon as you finish typing the first draft, immediately review it for accuracy while the content is still fresh in your mind. After you have done this, you can be reasonably sure that the document is free from errors. If you wait a day or two, you'll start to forget what you've written, thereby lowering your chances of catching errors.
   d. Put the report aside for at least a day and then proofread it carefully. Also, recruit two colleagues to review it for you—one who can review the technical accuracy of the material and one who has a good eye for language and clarity.

TEST YOUR KNOWLEDGE

1. What are the major components of formal reports?

2. In what circumstances should you include letters of authorization and letters of acceptance in your reports?

3. What are the features of an executive summary?

4. What are the major components of a formal proposal?

5. How should you handle the RFP for a solicited proposal?

6. How should you handle the letter of transmittal for an unsolicited proposal?

APPLY YOUR KNOWLEDGE

1. Is an executive summary a persuasive message? Explain your answer.

2. Under what circumstances would you include more than one index in a lengthy report?

3. If you were submitting a solicited proposal to build an indoor pool, would you include as references the names and addresses of other clients for whom you recently built similar pools? Would you include these references in an unsolicited proposal? Where in either proposal would you include these references? Why?

4. If you included a bibliography in your report, would you also need to include in-text citations? Explain.

5. **Ethical Choices** How would you report on a confidential survey in which employees rated their managers' capabilities? Both employees and managers expect to see the results. Would you give the same report to employees and managers? What components would you include or exclude for each audience? Explain your choices.

RUNNING CASES

> CASE 1 Noreen

Noreen has an assignment to complete for her Business Communications class: to research the social and business customs of a foreign country and then submit a report on her findings.

Noreen is excited about this assignment because her employer, Petro-Go, is considering new gas stations and offices in another country. She plans to do a thorough investigation and hopes to share her findings and report with her manager. She feels that having an understanding of the social and business customs of the country where Petro-Go intends to do business will help the company prosper.

QUESTIONS

a. List three sources of information Noreen can use to research foreign business and social customs.

b. Does Noreen have to acknowledge the sources of information she uses even if she does not quote the authors?

c. How will Noreen know that the sources are trustworthy?

d. What correlation will Noreen need to make between the headings in her report and the table of contents?

e. Should the report include an executive summary?

YOUR TASK

Choose a non-English-speaking country and write a long formal report summarizing the country's social and business customs. Include at least one visual. Review Chapter 3 and use Table 3–1 as a guide for the types of information you should include in your report.

> CASE 2 Kwong

Kwong needs to prepare a business plan so he can apply for a business grant and licence to open his accounting firm, which he has named CG Accounting.

QUESTIONS

a. Is this business plan a formal or informal report?

b. List three sources where Kwong can find sample business plans or information on how to prepare a business plan.

c. The business plan, like any report, must appear professionally formatted. What formats will Kwong need to apply throughout the report?

d. Where can Kwong find information about competitors in the industry?

e. Which prefatory and supplementary report parts may be required in this business plan?

YOUR TASK

Team up with a partner in your class. Conduct some research and review several business plans. Create a business plan for Kwong's company, CG Accounting.

Include the following sections:

> Executive Summary, Table of Contents, References, and other prefatory and supplementary sections as required. Include at least one visual.

> Business Overview
  • Description of business
  • Major demographic, economic, social, and cultural factors
  • Major players (for example, suppliers, distributors, and clients)

- Nature of the industry, trends in the industry
- Government regulations
- Market segment, market trends
- Products and services
- Pricing and distribution
- Implications of risk factors
- Competitors and type of competition
- Competitors' strengths and weaknesses
- Competitive advantage

> Sales and Marketing Plan
> Operating Plan
- Business location and requirements, advantages, lease details, equipment, technology, research and development, and environmental aspects
> Human Resources Plan
> Action Plan and Timetable
> Financial Plan
- Projected profit and loss

PRACTISE YOUR KNOWLEDGE

DOCUMENT 13.A

Visit the Environment and Climate Change Canada webpage at www.ec.gc.ca/dd-sd/default.asp?lang=En&n=917F8B09-1. Download the PDF of the Progress Report of the Federal Sustainable Development Strategy 2010–2013. Use the information in this chapter on the executive summary to analyze and explain the role of this section in the report.

DOCUMENT 13.B

Go to the Government of Canada website (www.canada.ca) and find a report that has been published recently. Considering what you have learned in this chapter, how closely does the government report follow the information you now have? Is there any area for improvement? Is there any area lacking? How would you notify the government about this?

EXERCISES

13.1 Teamwork: Creating an Informational Report

You and a classmate are helping Linda Moreno prepare her report on Electrovision's travel and entertainment costs (see "Report Writer's Notebook: Analyzing a Formal Report"). This time, however, the report is to be informational rather than analytical, so it will not include recommendations. Review the existing report and determine what changes would be needed to make it an informational report. Be as specific as possible. For example, if your team decides the report needs a new title, what title would you use? Now draft a transmittal memo for Moreno to use in conveying this informational report to Dennis McWilliams, Electrovision's vice president of operations.

13.2 Producing Reports: Letter of Transmittal

You are president of the Friends of the Library, a nonprofit group that raises funds and provides volunteers to support your local library. Every February you send a report of the previous year's activities and accomplishments to the County Arts Council, which provides an annual grant of $1000 toward your group's summer reading festival. Now it's February 6, and you've completed your formal report. Here are the highlights:

- Back-to-school book sale raised $2000.
- Holiday craft fair raised $1100.
- Promotion and prizes for summer reading festival cost $1450.
- Materials for children's program featuring local author cost $125.
- New reference databases for library's career centre cost $850.
- Bookmarks promoting library's website cost $200.

Write a letter of transmittal to Erica Maki, the council's director. Because she is expecting this report, use the direct approach.

Ensure that you express gratitude for the council's ongoing financial support.

13.3 Internet: Analyzing a Proposal

Follow the step-by-step hints and examples for writing a funding proposal at www.learnerassociates.net/proposal. Review the writing hints and the entire sample proposal online. What details did the author decide to include in the appendices? Why was this material placed in the appendices and not the main body of the report?

13.4 Ethical Choices: Team Challenge

You submitted what you thought was a masterful report to your boss more than three weeks ago. The report analyzes current department productivity and recommends several steps that you think will improve employee output without increasing individual workloads. Brilliant, you thought. But you haven't heard a word from your boss. Did you overstep your boundaries by making recommendations that might imply that she has not been doing a good job? Did you overwhelm her with your ideas? You'd like some feedback. In your last email to her, you asked if she had read your report. So far you've received no reply. Then yesterday, you overheard the company vice president talk about some productivity changes in your department. The changes were ones that you had recommended in your report. Now you're worried that your boss submitted your report to senior management and will take full credit for your terrific ideas. What, if anything, should you do? Should you confront your boss about this? Should you ask to meet with the company vice president? Discuss this situation among your teammates and develop a solution to this sticky situation. Present your solution to the class, explaining the rationale behind your decision.

APPLYING THE THREE-STEP WRITING PROCESS TO CASES

Apply each step to the following cases, as assigned by your instructor.

Short Formal Reports Requiring No Additional Research

▌Portfolio BUILDER▌

1. Giving It the Online Try: Report Analyzing the Advantages and Disadvantages of Corporate Online Learning

As the newest member of the corporate training division of Paper Products, Inc., you have been asked to investigate and analyze the merits of creating online courses for the company's employees. The president of your company thinks e-learning might be a good employee benefit and a terrific way for employees to learn new skills that they can use on the job. You've done your research; here's a copy of your notes:

Online courses open up new horizons for working adults, who often find it difficult to juggle conventional classes with jobs and families.

Adults over 25 now represent nearly half of higher-ed students; most are employed and want more education to advance their careers.

Some experts believe that online learning will never be as good as face-to-face instruction.

Online learning requires no commute and is appealing for employees who travel regularly.

Enrollment in postsecondary online courses is expected to grow from 2 million students in 2013 to 5 million students in 2018.

E-learning is a cost-effective way to get better-educated employees.

More than one-third of the $50 billion spent on employee training every year is spent on e-learning.

At IBM, 200 000 employees received training online last year, and 75 percent of the company's Basic Blue course for new managers is online. E-learning cut IBM's training bill by $350 million last year—mostly because online courses don't require travel.

There are no national statistics, but a recent report from the *Chronicle of Higher Education* found that the dropout rates for online learners range from 20 to 50 percent. The research does not explain why the dropout rates for e-learners are higher.

A recent study of corporate online learners reported that employees want the following from their online courses: university credit or a certificate; active correspondence with an online facilitator who has frequent virtual office hours; access to 24-hour, seven-day-a-week technical support; and the ability to start a course anytime.

Corporate e-learners said that their top reason for dropping a course was lack of time. Many had trouble completing courses from their desktops because of frequent distractions caused by co-workers. Some said they could only access courses through the company's intranet, so they couldn't finish their assignments from home.

Besides lack of time, corporate e-learners cited the following as e-learning disadvantages: lack of management oversight, lack of motivation, problems with technology, lack of student support, individual learning preferences, poorly designed courses, and substandard/inexperienced instructors.

A recent study by GE Capital found that finishing a corporate online course was dependent on whether managers gave reinforcement on attendance, how important employees were made to feel, and whether employee progress in the course was tracked.

Sun Microsystems found that interactivity can be a critical success factor for online courses. Company studies showed that only 25 percent of employees finish classes that are strictly self-paced. But 75 percent finish when given similar assignments and access to tutors through email, phone, or online discussion.

Company managers must supervise e-learning just as they would any other important initiative.

For online learning to work, companies must develop a culture that takes online learning just as seriously as classroom training.

For many e-learners, studying at home is optimal. Whenever possible, companies should offer courses through the Internet or provide intranet access at home. Having employees studying on their own time will more than cover any added costs.

Corporate e-learning has grown into a $2.3 billion market, making it one of the fastest-growing segments of the education industry.

Fast and cheap, e-training can shave companies' training costs while it saves employees travel time.

Pharmaceutical companies such as Merck are conducting live, interactive classes over the web, allowing sales reps to learn about the latest product information at home rather than flying them to a conference centre.

McDonald's trainers can log on to Hamburger University to learn such skills as how to assemble a made-to-order burger.

One obstacle to the spread of online corporate training is the mismatch between what employees really need—customized courses that are tailored to a firm's products and its unique corporate culture—and what employers can afford.

Eighty percent of companies prefer developing their own online training courses. But creating even one customized e-course can take months, involve armies of experts, and cost from $25 000 to $50 000. Thus, most companies either stick with classroom training or buy generic courses on such topics as how to give performance appraisals and understanding basic business ethics. Employers can choose from a wide selection of noncustomized electronic courses.

For online learning to be effective, content must be broken into short "chunks" with lots of pop quizzes, online discussion groups, and other interactive features that let students demonstrate what they've learned. For example, The Sales Activator (www.salesactivator.com) has eLearning courses for both sales and service, with reports of progress generated for each individual as he or she works through the modules.

Dell expects 90 percent of its learning solutions to be totally or partially technology enabled.

The Home Depot has used e-training to cut a full day from the time required to train new cashiers.

Online training has freed up an average of 17 days every year for Black & Decker's sales representatives.

Your task: Write a short (3- to 5-page) memo report to the director of human resources, Kerry Simmons, presenting the advantages and disadvantages of e-learning and making a recommendation as to whether Paper Products, Inc. should invest time and money in training its employees this way. Ensure that you organize your information so that it is clear, concise, and logically presented. Simmons likes to read "the bottom line" first, so be direct: present your recommendation up front and support your recommendation with your findings.[9]

Portfolio BUILDER

2. Building a New Magazine: Finding Opportunity in the Remodelling Craze

Spurred on in part by the success of such hit shows as *Colour Confidential*, *Sarah 101*, and *Designer Superstar Challenge*, homeowners across the country are redecorating, remodelling, and rebuilding. Many people are content with superficial changes, such as new paint or new accessories, but some are more ambitious. These homeowners want to move walls, add rooms, redesign kitchens, and convert garages to home theatres—the big stuff.

As with many consumer trends, publishers try to create magazines that appeal to carefully identified groups of potential readers and the advertisers who'd like to reach them. The do-it-yourself (DIY) market is already served by numerous magazines, but you see an opportunity in those homeowners who tackle the heavy-duty projects. Tables 13–1 through 13–3 summarize the results of some preliminary research you asked your company's research staff to conduct.

Your task: You think the data show a real opportunity for a "big projects" DIY magazine, although you'll need more extensive research to confirm the size of the market and refine the editorial direction of the magazine. Prepare a brief analytical report that presents the data you have, identifies the opportunity or opportunities you've found (suggest your own ideas based on Tables 13–1 through 13–3), and requests funding from the editorial board to pursue further research.

Table 13–1	Rooms Most Frequently Remodelled by DIYers

Room	Percentage of Homeowners Surveyed Who Have Tackled or Plan to Tackle at Least a Partial Remodel
Kitchen	60
Bathroom	48
Home office/study	44
Bedroom	38
Media room/home theatre	31
Den/recreation room	28
Living room	27
Dining room	12
Sun room/solarium	8

Table 13–2	Average Amount Spent on Remodelling Projects

Estimated Amount	Percentage of Surveyed Homeowners
Under $5k	5
$5–10k	21
$10–20k	39
$20–50k	22
More than $50k	13

Table 13–3	Tasks Performed by Homeowner on a Typical Remodelling Project

Task	Percentage of Surveyed Homeowners Who Perform or Plan to Perform Most or All of This Task Themselves
Conceptual design	90
Technical design/architecture	34
Demolition	98
Foundation work	62
Framing	88
Plumbing	91
Electrical	55
Heating/cooling	22
Finish carpentry	85
Tile work	90
Painting	100
Interior design	52

Short Formal Reports Requiring Additional Research

Portfolio BUILDER

3. Selling Overseas: Research Report on the Prospects for Marketing a Product in Another Country

Select a fairly inexpensive product that you currently own and a country with which you're not familiar. The product could be a moderately priced watch, radio, or other device. Now imagine that you are with the international sales department of the company that manufactures and sells the item and that you are proposing to make it available in the country you have selected.

First, learn as much as possible about the country where you plan to market the product. Check almanacs, encyclopedias, the Internet, and library databases for the most recent information, paying particular attention to descriptions of the social life of the inhabitants, their economic conditions, and cultural traditions that would encourage or discourage use of the product.

Your task: Write a short report that describes the product you plan to market abroad, briefly describes the country you have selected, indicates the types of people in this country who would find the product attractive, explains how the product would be transported into the country (or possibly manufactured there if materials and labour are available), recommends a location for a regional sales centre, and suggests how the product should be sold. Your report is to be submitted to the chief operating officer of the company, whose name you can either make up or find in a corporate directory. The report should include your conclusions (how the product will do in this new environment) and your recommendations for marketing (steps the company should take immediately and those it should develop later).

|Portfolio BUILDER|

4. A Ready-Made Business: Finding the Right Franchise Opportunity

After 15 years in the corporate world, you're ready to strike out on your own. Rather than building a business from the ground up, however, you think that buying a franchise is a better idea. Unfortunately, some of the most lucrative franchise opportunities, such as the major fast-food chains, require significant start-up costs—some more than a half million dollars. Fortunately, you've met several potential investors who seem willing to help you get started in exchange for a share of ownership. Between your own savings and these investors, you estimate that you can raise from $350 000 to $600 000, depending on how much ownership share you want to concede to the investors.

You've worked in several functional areas already, including sales and manufacturing, so you have a fairly well-rounded business résumé. You're open to just about any type of business, too, as long as it provides the opportunity to grow; you don't want to be so tied down to the first operation that you can't turn it over to a hired manager and expand into another market.

Your task: To convene a formal meeting with the investor group, you need to first draft a report outlining the types of franchise opportunities you'd like to pursue. Write a brief report identifying five franchises that you would like to explore further (choose five based on your own personal interests and the criteria identified above). For each possibility, identify the nature of the business, the financial requirements, the level of support the company provides, and a brief statement of why you could run such a business successfully (based on your own experience, education, and personal qualities). Ensure that you carefully review the information you find about each franchise company to ensure that you can qualify for it. For example, McDonald's doesn't allow investment partnerships to buy franchises, so you won't be able to start up a McDonald's outlet until you have enough money to do it on your own.

For a quick introduction to franchising, see How Stuff Works (http://money.howstuffworks.com/franchising.htm). You can learn more about the business of franchising from the Canadian Franchise Association (www.cfa.ca) and search for specific franchise opportunities at Canada Franchise Opportunities. com (http://canadafranchiseopportunities.com). In addition, many companies that sell franchises, such as Subway, offer additional information on their websites.

5. Picking the Better Path: Research Report Assisting a Client in a Career Choice

You are employed by Open Options, a career-counselling firm, where your main function is to help clients make career choices. Today a client with the same name as yours (a truly curious coincidence!) came to your office and asked for help deciding between two careers, careers that you yourself had been interested in (an even greater coincidence!).

Your task: Do some research on the two careers and then prepare a short report that your client can study. Your report should compare at least five major areas, such as salary, working conditions, and education required. Interview the client to understand his or her personal preferences regarding each of the five areas. For example, what is the minimum salary the client will accept? By comparing the client's preferences with the research material you collect, such as salary data, you will have a basis for concluding which of the two careers is better. The report should end with a career recommendation. (Note: One good place for career-related information is the Training and Careers page on the Service Canada website at www .canada.ca/en/services/jobs/opportunities.html).

Long Formal Reports Requiring No Additional Research

6. Customer Service Crisis: Report Summarizing and Explaining Customer Service Problems

You are the operations manager for Continental Security Systems (CSS), a mail-order supplier of home-security systems and components. Your customers are do-it-yourself homeowners who buy a wide range of motion sensors, automatic telephone diallers, glass breakage detectors, video cameras, and other devices.

The company's aggressive pricing has yielded spectacular growth in the past year, and everyone is scrambling to keep up with the orders arriving every day. Unfortunately, customer service has often taken a back seat to filling those orders. Your boss, the company's founder and president, knows that service is slipping, and she wants you to solve the problem. You started with some internal and external surveys to assess the situation. Some of the most significant findings from the research are presented in Tables 13–4 through 13–6.

Your task: Use the information in Tables 13–4 to 13–6 to write a report recommending ways to improve customer service at CSS.

Table 13–4	**Customer Complaints over the Last 12 Months**	
Type of Complaint	**Number of Occurrences**	**Percentage of Total**
Delays in responding	67	30%
Product malfunction	56	25
Missing parts	45	20
No answer when calling for help	32	14
Rude treatment	18	8
Overcharge	5	2

Note: Percentages don't add to 100 because of rounding.

Table 13–5 — Customer Perceptions and Opinions

Statement	Agree	Disagree
CSS offers a competitive level of customer service.	12%	88%
I recommended CSS to friends and colleagues.	4	96
I plan to continue buying from CSS.	15	85
I enjoy doing business with CSS.	9	91

Table 13–6 — How Complaints Were Resolved

Resolution	Percentage
Employee receiving the phone call	20% solved the problem
Employee referred customer to manager	30
Customer eventually solved the problem by himself or herself	12
Unable to solve problem	23
Resolution unknown	15

Portfolio BUILDER

7. Moving the Workforce: Understanding Commute Patterns

Your company is the largest private employer in your metropolitan area, and the 43 500 employees in your workforce have a tremendous impact on local traffic. A group of city and district transportation officials recently approached your CEO with a request to explore ways to reduce this impact. The CEO has assigned you the task of analyzing the workforce's transportation habits and attitudes as a first step toward identifying potential solutions. He's willing to consider anything from subsidized bus passes to company-owned shuttle buses to telecommuting, but the decision requires a thorough understanding of employee transportation needs. Tables 13–7 through 13–11 summarize data you collected in an employee survey.

Your task: Present the results of your survey in an informational report using the data provided in Tables 13–7 through 13–11.

Table 13–7 — Employee Carpool Habits

Frequency of Use: Carpooling	Portion of Workforce
Every day, every week	10 138 (23%)
Certain days, every week	4 361 (10%)
Randomly	983 (2%)
Never	28 018 (64%)

Table 13–8 — Use of Public Transportation

Frequency of Use: Public	Portion of Workforce
Every day, every week	23 556 (54%)
Certain days, every week	2 029 (5%)
Randomly	5 862 (13%)
Never	12 053 (28%)

Table 13–9 — Effect of Potential Improvements to Public Transportation

Which of the Following Would Encourage You to Use Public Transportation More Frequently (check all that apply)	Portion of Respondents
Increased perceptions of safety	4 932 (28%)
Improved cleanliness	852 (5%)
Reduced commute times	7 285 (41%)
Greater convenience: fewer transfers	3 278 (18%)
Greater convenience: more stops	1 155 (6%)
Lower (or subsidized) fares	5 634 (31%)
Nothing could encourage me to take public transportation	8 294 (46%)

Note: This question was asked of those respondents who use public transportation randomly or never, a subgroup that represents 17 915 employees or 41 percent of the workforce.

Table 13–10 — Distance Travelled to/from Work

Distance You Travel to Work (one way)	Portion of Workforce
Less than 2 km	531 (1%)
2 to 5 km	6 874 (16%)
6 to 15 km	22 951 (53%)
16 to 30 km	10 605 (24%)
More than 30 km	2 539 (6%)

Table 13–11 — Is Telecommuting an Option?

Does the Nature of Your Work Make Telecommuting a Realistic Option?	Portion of Workforce
Yes, every day	3 460 (8%)
Yes, several days a week	8 521 (20%)
Yes, random days	12 918 (30%)
No	18 601 (43%)

Long Formal Reports Requiring Additional Research

8. Travel Opportunities: Report Comparing Two Destinations

You plan to take a two-week trip abroad sometime within the next year. Because a couple of destinations appeal to you, you will have to do some research before you can make a decision.

Your task: Prepare a lengthy comparative study of two countries that you would like to visit. Begin by making a list of important questions you will need to answer. Do you want a relaxing vacation or an educational experience? What types of services will you require? What will your transportation needs be? Where will you have the least difficulty with the language? Using resources in your library, the Internet, and perhaps travel agencies, analyze the suitability of these two destinations with respect to your own travel criteria. At the end of the report, recommend the better country to visit this year.

▌Portfolio BUILDER ▌

9. Secondary Sources: Report Based on Library and Online Research

As a student and active consumer, you may have considered one or more of the following questions at some point in the past few years:

a. What criteria distinguish the top-rated MBA programs in the country? How well do these criteria correspond to the needs and expectations of business? Are the criteria fair for students, employers, or business schools?

b. Which of three companies you might like to work for has the strongest corporate ethics policies?

c. What will the music industry look like in the future? What's next after online stores such as Apple iTunes and digital players such as the iPod?

d. Which industries and job categories are forecast to experience the greatest growth—and therefore the greatest demands for workers—in the next 10 years?

e. What has been the impact of Starbucks's aggressive growth on small, independent coffee shops? On mid-sized chains or franchises? In Canada or in another country?

f. How large is the "industry" of university sports? How much do football or basketball programs contribute—directly or indirectly—to other parts of a typical university?

g. How much have minor league sports—soccer, hockey, and arena football—grown in small- and medium-market cities? What is the local economic impact when these municipalities build stadiums and arenas?

Your task: Answer one of those questions using secondary research sources for information. Ensure that you document your sources in the correct form. Give conclusions and offer recommendations where appropriate.

Formal Proposals

▌Portfolio BUILDER ▌

10. Polishing the Presenters: Offering Your Services as a Presentation Trainer

Presentations can make—or break—both careers and businesses. A good presentation can bring in millions of dollars in new sales or fresh investment capital. A bad presentation might cause any number of troubles, from turning away potential customers to upsetting fellow employees to derailing key projects. To help business professionals plan, create, and deliver more effective presentations, you offer a three-day workshop that covers the essentials of good presentations:

- Understanding your audience's needs and expectations
- Formulating your presentation objectives
- Choosing an organizational approach
- Writing openings that catch your audience's attention
- Creating effective graphics and slides
- Practising and delivering your presentation
- Leaving a positive impression on your audience
- Avoiding common mistakes with Microsoft PowerPoint
- Making presentations online using web-casting tools
- Handling questions and arguments from the audience
- Overcoming the top 10 worries of public speaking (including How can I overcome stage fright? and I'm not the performing type; can I still give an effective presentation?)

Here is some additional information about the workshop:

- **Workshop benefits:** Students will learn how to prepare better presentations in less time and deliver them more effectively.
- **Who should attend:** Top executives, project managers, employment recruiters, sales professionals, and anyone else who gives important presentations to internal or external audiences.
- **Your qualifications:** 12 years of business experience, including 8 years in sales and 6 years in public speaking; experience speaking to audiences as large as 300 people; 6 speech-related articles published in professional journals; experience conducting successful workshops for 75 companies.
- **Workshop details:** Three-day workshop (9 A.M. to 3:30 P.M.) that combines lectures, practice presentations, and both individual and group feedback. Minimum number of students per workshop: 6. Maximum number of students: 12.
- **Pricing:** The cost is $3500, plus $100 per student; 10 percent discount for additional workshops.
- **Other information:** Each attendee will have the opportunity to give three practice presentations that will last from three to five minutes. Everyone is encouraged to bring PowerPoint files containing slides from actual business presentations. Each attendee will also receive

a workbook and a digital video recording of his or her final class presentation on DVD. You'll also be available for phone or email coaching for six months after the workshop.

Your task: Identify a company in your local area that might be a good candidate for your services. Learn more about them by visiting their website so you can personalize your proposal. Using the information listed above, prepare a sales proposal that explains the benefits of your training and what students can expect during the workshop.

▍Portfolio BUILDER▍

11. Healthy Alternatives: Proposal to Sell Snacks and Beverages at Local High Schools

For years, a controversy has been brewing over the amount of junk food and soft drinks being sold through vending machines in local schools. Schools benefit from revenue-sharing arrangements, but many parents and health experts are concerned about the negative effects of these snacks and beverages. You and your brother have almost a decade of experience running juice stands in malls, and you'd love to find some way to expand your business into schools. After a quick brainstorming session, the two of you craft a plan that makes good business sense while meeting the financial concerns of school administrators and the nutritional concerns of parents and dieticians. Here are the notes from your brainstorming session:

- Set up portable juice bars in local schools offering healthy fruit and vegetable drinks along with simple, healthy snacks.
- Offer schools 30 percent of profits in exchange for free space and long-term contracts.
- Provide job training opportunities for students (for example, during athletic events).
- Provide detailed dietary analysis of all products sold.
- Establish a nutritional advisory board composed of parents, students, and at least one certified health professional.
- Assure schools and parents that all products are safe (for example, no stimulant drinks, no dietary supplements).
- Support local farmers and specialty food preparers by buying locally and giving these vendors the opportunity to test market new products at your stands.

Your task: Based on the ideas listed, draft a formal proposal to the local school board outlining your plan to offer high schools healthier alternatives to soft drinks and pre-packaged snack foods. Invent any details you need to complete your proposal.

▍Portfolio BUILDER▍

12. Career Connections: Helping Employees Get the Advice They Need to Move Ahead

It seems like everybody in your firm is frustrated. On the one hand, top executives complain about the number of lower-level employees who want promotions but just don't seem to "get it" when it comes to dealing with customers and the public, recognizing when to speak out and when to be quiet, knowing how to push new ideas through the appropriate channels, and performing other essential but difficult-to-teach tasks. On the other hand, ambitious employees who'd like to learn more feel that they have nowhere to turn for career advice from people who've been there. In between, a variety of managers and mid-level executives are overwhelmed by the growing number of mentoring requests they're getting, sometimes from employees they don't even know.

You've been assigned the challenge of proposing a formal mentoring program—and a considerable challenge it is:

- The number of employees who want mentoring relationships far exceeds the number of managers and executives willing and able to be mentors; how will you select people for the program?
- The people most in demand for mentoring also tend to be some of the busiest people in the organization.
- After several years of belt tightening and staff reductions, the entire company feels overworked; few people can imagine adding another recurring task to their seemingly endless to-do lists.
- What's in it for the mentors? Why would they be motivated to help lower-level employees?
- How will you measure the success or failure of the mentoring effort?

Your task: Identify potential solutions to the issues (make up any information you need) and draft a proposal to the executive committee for a formal, companywide mentoring program that would match selected employees with successful managers and executives.

LEARNING OBJECTIVES   After studying this chapter, you will be able to

1   Explain the importance of oral presentations in your career success

2   Explain how to adapt the planning step of the three-step process to oral presentations

3   Discuss the three functions of an effective introduction, and identify different ways to get your audience's attention

4   Identify six ways to keep your audience's attention during your presentation

5   Describe the six major design and writing tasks required to enhance your presentation with effective visuals

6   Identify six methods that effective speakers use to handle questions responsively

7   Describe the important aspects of delivering a presentation in today's online environment

MyLab Business Communication   Visit MyLab Business Communication to access a variety of online resources directly related to this chapter's content.

ON THE JOB: COMMUNICATING AT TELEFILM CANADA

Sarah Hadley/Alamy Stock Photo

As Telefilm's executive director, Carolle Brabant speaks to a variety of audiences to raise the profile of the Canadian film industry and ensure its growth. Oral communication is an essential part of Brabant's job.

Promoting Canada's Film Industry
www.telefilm.ca

Carolle Brabant promotes the Canadian film and multimedia industry at home and around the world. As executive director of Telefilm Canada, a Crown corporation reporting to the Minister of Canadian Heritage, Brabant manages an agency of 200 employees and a multimillion-dollar budget. In 2014–2015, total Canadian film and TV production was worth $7.1 billion— a 20 percent increase over the previous year and an all-time high. This sector continues to make a significant contribution to GDP ($9 billion in 2015) and generated 148 500 full-time equivalent (FTE) jobs for Canadians. The Quebec film *Incendies* is one example that shows Telefilm's success: it earned eight Genie and nine Jutra awards and was nominated for the Academy Award for Best Foreign Language Film.

Raising the profile of the Canadian film industry is a challenging task. In addition to overseeing the planning of numerous reports and industry conferences, Brabant communicates directly with Telefilm's many stakeholders through press conferences, keynote addresses at professional forums and film festivals, and speeches to a variety of government and industry audiences. For example, a speech to the Academy of Canadian Cinema and Television highlights the need for new media business models for the industry to "survive and indeed thrive." Another speech, to the Quebec MBA association, stresses the importance of a private donation fund to allow both Canadian and private donors to support film production.

Explaining Telefilm's mission and activities clearly and convincingly is a large part of Brabant's job. Analyzing her audiences and understanding how to appeal to them are essential to her success as Telefilm's executive director— and the growth of Canada's film and media industry. If you worked with Brabant, how would you approach planning and developing speeches and presentations for Telefilm Canada? How would you prepare your text and visual support? And how would you polish your delivery style and platform manner?[1]

Building Your Career with Presentations

Carolle Brabant's experience shows that presentation skills are vital in today's business environment. Oral presentations offer important opportunities to put all your communication skills on display—not just in research, planning, writing, and visual design but also in interpersonal and nonverbal communication. Presentations can also let you demonstrate your ability to think on your feet, grasp complex issues, and handle challenging situations—all attributes that managers and executives look for when searching for talented employees to promote. You might even have an opportunity to give a short presentation as part of a job interview.

If the thought of giving a speech or presentation makes you nervous, keep three points in mind. First, everybody gets nervous when speaking in front of a group. Even professional speakers and entertainers get nervous after years of experience. Second, being nervous is actually good; it means you care about the topic, your audience, and your career success. With practice, you can convert those nervous feelings into positive energy. Third, you don't have to be a victim of your own emotions when it comes to oral presentations. You can take control of the situation by using the planning and development techniques that you'll learn in this chapter—starting with how to adapt the three-step writing process to the unique challenges of oral presentations.

1 LEARNING OBJECTIVE

Explain the importance of oral presentations in your career success.

Oral presentations involve all of your communication skills, from research to nonverbal communication.

Feeling nervous is perfectly normal when you're faced with an oral presentation; the good news is there are positive steps you can take to reduce your anxiety.

Planning a Presentation

Although you don't often write out presentations word for word, nearly every task in the three-step writing process applies to oral presentations, with some modifications (see Figure 14–1). Gathering information for oral presentations is essentially the same as it is for written communication projects. The other three planning tasks have some special applications when it comes to oral presentations; they are covered in the following sections.

On the subject of planning, be aware that preparing a professional-quality business presentation can take a considerable amount of time. Nancy Duarte, whose design firm has years of experience creating presentations for corporations, offers this rule of thumb: for a one-hour presentation that uses 30 slides, allow 36 to 90 hours to research, conceive, create, and practise.[2] Not every one-hour presentation justifies a week or two of preparation, of course, but the important presentations that can make your career or your company certainly can.

2 LEARNING OBJECTIVE

Explain how to adapt the planning step of the three-step process to oral presentations.

While you don't usually write your oral presentations word for word, the three-step writing process is easily adaptable to oral presentations.

Creating a high-quality presentation for an important event can take many days, so be sure to allow enough time.

ANALYZING THE SITUATION

As with written communications, analyzing the situation involves defining your purpose and developing an audience profile (see Table 14–1). The purpose of most of your presentations will be to inform or to persuade, although you may

Knowing your audience's state of mind will help you adjust both your message and your delivery.

1 Planning →	**2 Writing** →	**3 Completing**
Analyze the Situation Define your purpose, and develop a profile of your audience, including their likely emotional states and language preferences. **Gather Information** Determine audience needs, and obtain the information necessary to satisfy those needs. **Select the Right Medium** Choose the best medium or combination of media for delivering your presentation, including handouts and other support materials. **Organize the Information** Define your main idea, limit your scope and verify timing, select the direct or indirect approach, and create an outline of your content.	**Adapt to Your Audience** Adapt your content, presentation style, and room setup to the audience and the specific situation. Be sensitive to audience needs and expectations with a "you" attitude, politeness, positive emphasis, and bias-free language. Plan to establish your credibility as required. **Compose Your Presentation** Choose an attention-getting introduction; structure the body with supporting and transition points; and select a memorable close. Prepare supporting visuals and speaking notes. Anticipate the types of questions the audience may ask, and prepare your answers.	**Revise the Message** Evaluate your content and speaking notes. **Master Your Delivery** Choose your delivery mode, and practise your presentation. Create effective handouts that support your visuals. Decide whether you will use "backchannel" or electronic media techniques to communicate with your audience. **Prepare to Speak** Verify facilities and equipment, including online connections and software setups. Hire an interpreter if necessary. **Overcome Anxiety** Take steps to feel more confident and appear more confident on stage.

Figure 14–1 The Three-Step Oral Presentation Process

Table 14–1	**Analyzing Audiences for Oral Presentations**

Task	Actions
To determine audience size and composition	**1.** Estimate how many people will attend. What roles do they play? Are there any key decision makers? **2.** Consider whether they share professional interests or other affiliations that can help you establish common ground with them. **3.** Analyze the mix of men and women, age ranges, socioeconomic and ethnic groups, occupations, and geographic regions represented. Meeting norms and expectations vary across cultures.
To predict the audience's probable reaction	**1.** Analyze why audience members are attending the presentation. **2.** Determine the audience's general attitude toward the topic: interested, moderately interested, unconcerned, open-minded, or hostile. **3.** Analyze the mood that people will be in when you speak to them. **4.** Find out what kind of backup information will be most important or relevant for the audience: technical data, historical information, financial data, demonstrations, samples, and so on. **5.** Consider whether the audience has any biases that might work against you. **6.** Anticipate possible objections or questions.
To gauge the audience's experience	**1.** Analyze whether everybody has the same background and level of understanding. **2.** Determine what the audience already knows about the subject. **3.** Decide what background information the audience will need to better understand the subject. **4.** Consider whether the audience is familiar with the vocabulary you intend to use. **5.** Analyze what the audience expects from you. What might be their attitude toward the topic? **6.** Think about the mix of general concepts and specific details you will need to present.

occasionally need to make a collaborative presentation, such as when you're leading a problem-solving, brainstorming session or providing a summary report of a group project.

When you develop your audience profile, start by identifying your primary and secondary audience, and learn as much as possible about their background,

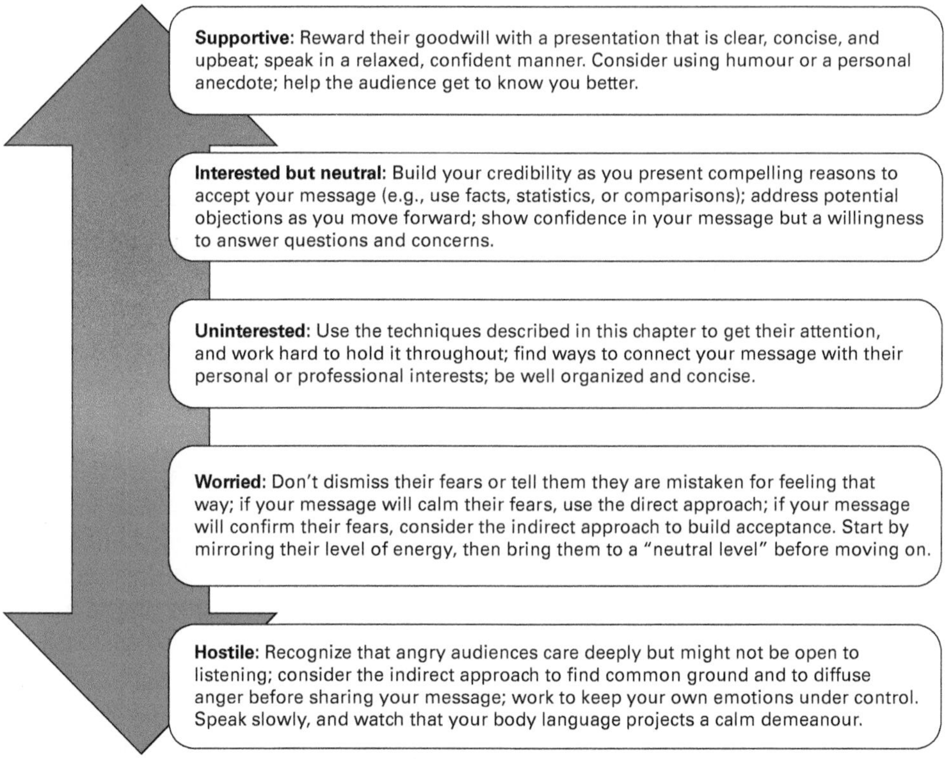

Supportive: Reward their goodwill with a presentation that is clear, concise, and upbeat; speak in a relaxed, confident manner. Consider using humour or a personal anecdote; help the audience get to know you better.

Interested but neutral: Build your credibility as you present compelling reasons to accept your message (e.g., use facts, statistics, or comparisons); address potential objections as you move forward; show confidence in your message but a willingness to answer questions and concerns.

Uninterested: Use the techniques described in this chapter to get their attention, and work hard to hold it throughout; find ways to connect your message with their personal or professional interests; be well organized and concise.

Worried: Don't dismiss their fears or tell them they are mistaken for feeling that way; if your message will calm their fears, use the direct approach; if your message will confirm their fears, consider the indirect approach to build acceptance. Start by mirroring their level of energy, then bring them to a "neutral level" before moving on.

Hostile: Recognize that angry audiences care deeply but might not be open to listening; consider the indirect approach to find common ground and to diffuse anger before sharing your message; work to keep your own emotions under control. Speak slowly, and watch that your body language projects a calm demeanour.

Figure 14–2 Planning for Various Audience Mindsets

level of knowledge and experience, attitude, expectations, and preferences. Try to anticipate their emotional state and probable reaction to the topic so you can plan your presentation approach accordingly. Will your listeners be supportive, hostile, or somewhere in-between? Figure 14–2 offers tips for dealing with a variety of audience mindsets.

As you analyze the situation, also consider the circumstances. Is the audience in the room or online? How many people will be present, and how will they be seated? Can you control the environment to minimize distractions? What equipment will you need? Such variables can influence not only the style of your presentation but also the content itself.

SELECTING THE RIGHT MEDIUM

The task of selecting the right medium might seem obvious. After all, you are speaking, so it's an oral medium. However, you have an array of choices from live, in-person presentations to *webcasts* (online presentations that people either view live or download later from your website), *screencasts* (recordings of activity on computer displays with audio voiceover), or *twebinars* (the use of Twitter as a *backchannel* for real-time conversation during a web-based seminar [3]). Some of these media allow for more immediate feedback than others. Decisions about the level of interactivity and audience participation will be important to the scope and flow of your presentation.

Learn as much as you can about the setting and circumstances of your presentation, from the size of the audience to seating arrangements, level of seniority, background, and attitudes toward the topic being presented.

TIPS FOR SUCCESS

"Learn about the executives you'll be addressing. Who are they exactly? What are their challenges? What will they expect from you? Once you find out, create your presentation around what they want to know."

Jim Gray, media and presentation coach, Media Strategy

ORGANIZING YOUR PRESENTATION

Organizing a presentation involves the same tasks as organizing a written message: define your main idea, limit your scope, select a direct or an indirect approach, and outline your content. Keep in mind that when reading written reports, audiences can skip back and forth, backing up if they miss a point or become confused and jumping ahead if they aren't interested in a particular part or are already familiar with the content. However, in an oral presentation, audiences are more or less trapped in your time frame and sequence. For some presentations, you should plan to be flexible and respond to audience feedback, such as skipping over sections the audience doesn't need to hear and going into more detail in other sections.

For example, say that your presentation is a proposal and that you believe your audience will be hostile to the idea. You plan to structure your proposal using an indirect approach. Simple enough, until you suddenly realize that the members of your audience have already heard of your idea through other channels, and they like it. Now they have to sit through an extended presentation of your reasons so that you can convince them to accept an idea they already accept. With a printed report, your audience would simply skip ahead, but they can't do that with an oral presentation. Fortunately, you can use hyperlinks to build flexibility into your presentation, but only if you plan ahead.

Numerous organizations use webcasts to announce financial news, new products, and management changes. Webcasts can be viewed and listened to long after the speaker has left the podium. How should speakers prepare presentations for this technology? Is preparation different for live audiences?

Courtesy: The Bank of Nova Scotia

If you can't express your main idea in a single sentence, you probably haven't defined it clearly enough.

DEFINING YOUR MAIN IDEA If you've ever heard a speaker struggle to get his or her main point across ("What I really mean to say is . . ."), you know how frustrating such an experience can be for an audience. To avoid that struggle, figure out the one message you want audience members to walk away with. Then compose a one-sentence summary that links your subject and purpose to your audience's frame of reference. Here are some examples:

> Convince management that reorganizing the technical support department will improve customer service and reduce employee turnover.
>
> Convince the board of directors that they should build a new plant in New Brunswick to eliminate manufacturing bottlenecks and improve production quality.
>
> Address employee concerns regarding a new health care plan by showing how the plan will reduce costs and improve the quality of their care.

Each statement puts a particular slant on the subject, one that directly relates to the audience's interests. By focusing on your audience's needs and using the "you" attitude, you help keep their attention and convince them that your points are relevant. For example, a group of new employees will be much more responsive to your discussion of plant safety procedures if you focus on how the procedures can save lives and prevent injuries, rather than focusing on company rules, saving the company money, or conforming to government guidelines.

LIMITING YOUR SCOPE Limiting your scope is important with any message, but it's particularly vital with presentations, for two reasons. First, for most presentations, you must work within strict time limits. Often, multiple presenters are scheduled to speak one right after the other, so time allotments are rigid, permitting little or no flexibility. If you overestimate the amount of material you can cover within your allotted time, you're left with only unpleasant alternatives: rushing through your presentation, skipping some information you've so carefully prepared, or trying to steal a few minutes from the next presenter. Or if you don't have enough material prepared to fill your time slot, you might be left standing in front of the audience trying to ad lib information you haven't prepared.

Second, the longer you speak, the more difficult it is to hold the audience's attention level, and the more difficult it is for your listeners to retain your key points.[4] Even if you are not given a time limit, keep your presentation as short as possible, taking only as much of the audience's time as you need to accomplish your purpose.

The only sure way to know how much material you can cover in a given time is to practise your presentation after you complete it. As an alternative, if you're using conventional structured slides, you can figure on three or four minutes per slide as a rough guide.[5] Of course, be sure to factor in time for introductions, coffee breaks, demonstrations, question-and-answer sessions, and anything else that takes away from your speaking time.

Viewing time constraints as a creative challenge can actually help you develop more effective presentations. Limitations can force you to focus on the most essential message points that are important to your audience.[6]

CHOOSING YOUR APPROACH With a well-defined main idea to guide you and a clear idea about the scope of your presentation, you can begin to arrange your message. If you have 10 minutes or less, organize your presentation much as you would a letter or a brief memo: use the direct approach if the subject involves routine information or good news, and use the indirect approach if the subject involves bad news or persuasion. Plan your introduction to arouse interest and to give a preview of what's to come. For the body of the presentation, be prepared to explain the who, what, when, where, why, and how of your subject. In the final section, review the points you've made, and close with a statement that will help your audience remember the subject of your speech. Figure 14–3 presents an outline of a short presentation that updates management on the status of a key project; the presenter has some bad news to deliver, so she opted for an indirect approach to lay out the reasons for the delay before sharing the news of the schedule slip.

Longer presentations are organized like reports. If the purpose is to motivate or inform, use a direct approach and a structure imposed naturally by the subject: importance, sequence, chronology, spatial orientation, geography, or category. If your purpose is to analyze, persuade, or collaborate, organize your material around conclusions and recommendations or around a logical argument. Use a direct order if the audience is receptive and an indirect order if you expect resistance.

Regardless of the length of your presentation, remember that simplicity of organization is especially valuable in oral communication. If listeners lose the thread of your presentation, they'll have a hard time catching up and following your message in the remainder of your speech. Look for the most obvious

Limiting your scope is important for two reasons: to ensure that your presentation fits the allotted time and to ensure that your content meets audience needs and expectations.

The only sure way to measure the length of your presentation is to complete a practice run.

Organize short presentations the same way you would a letter or brief memo; organize long presentations as you would a report or proposal.

Simplicity is critical in the organization of oral presentations.

Progress Report: August 2017

Purpose: To update the Executive Committee on our product development schedule.

I.   Review goals and progress
    A. Mechanical design:
       1. Goal: 100%
       2. Actual: 80%
       3. Reason for delay: Unanticipated problems with case durability
    B. Software development:
       1. Goal: 50%
       2. Actual: 60%
    C. Material sourcing:
       1. Goal: 100%
       2. Actual: 45% (and materials identified are at 140% of anticipated costs)
       3. Reason for delay: Purchasing is understaffed and hasn't been able to research sources adequately

II. Discuss schedule options
    A. Option 1: Reschedule product launch date
    B. Option 2: Launch on schedule with more expensive materials

III. Suggest goals for next month

IV. Q&A

Figure 14–3 Effective Outline for a 10-Minute Presentation

and natural way to organize your ideas, using a direct approach whenever possible. Explain at the beginning how you've organized your material, and limit the number of main points to three or four—even when the speech or presentation is lengthy.

Finally, remind yourself that just like every other good business message, an effective presentation has a clear introduction, body, and close. In fact, one noted presentation expert even advises a three-act storytelling structure (the approach used in many novels, movies, and TV shows). Act I introduces the "story" you're about to tell and grabs the audience's attention. Act II explores the complications, evidence, support points, and other information needed to understand the story and its conclusion. Act III resolves all the complications and presents a solution that addresses the problem introduced in Act I and that is strongly supported by all the evidence introduced in Act II.[7] More techniques on how to compose the actual content of your presentation follow.

In addition to planning your speech, a presentation outline helps you plan your speaking notes.

PREPARING YOUR OUTLINE A presentation outline performs the same all-important function as an outline for a written report: helping you organize the message in a way that maximizes its impact on your audience. To ensure effective organization, prepare your outline in several stages:[8]

- State your purpose and main idea, and then use these to guide the rest of your planning.
- Organize your major points and subpoints in logical order, expressing each major point as a single, complete sentence.
- Identify major points in the body first, and then outline the introduction and close.

- Identify transitions between major points or sections, and then write these transitions in full-sentence form.
- Prepare your bibliography or source notes; highlight the sources you want to identify by name during your talk.
- Choose a compelling title; even if the title won't be published, it will help you focus your thoughts around your main idea.[9]

Figure 14–4 is an outline for a 30-minute analytical presentation. It is organized around conclusions and presented in direct order. The outline clearly identifies the purpose and the distinct points to be made in the introduction, body, and close. Notice also how the speaker wrote her major transitions in full-sentence form to be sure she can clearly phrase these critical passages when it's time to speak.

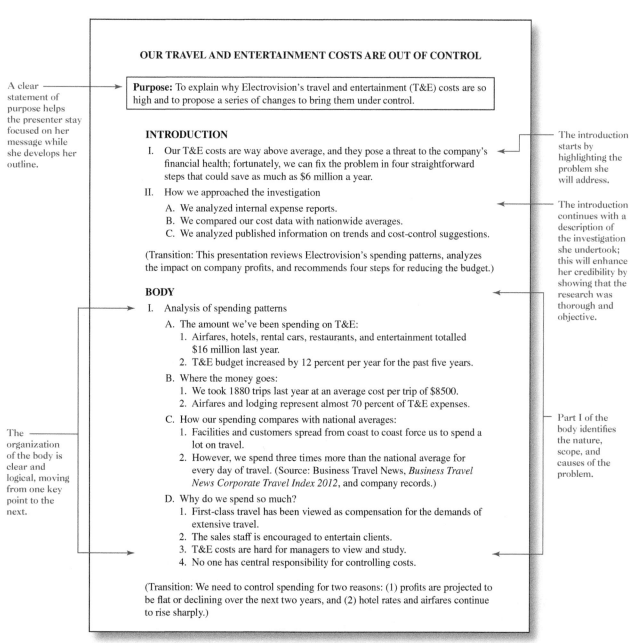

A clear statement of purpose helps the presenter stay focused on her message while she develops her outline.

The organization of the body is clear and logical, moving from one key point to the next.

OUR TRAVEL AND ENTERTAINMENT COSTS ARE OUT OF CONTROL

Purpose: To explain why Electrovision's travel and entertainment (T&E) costs are so high and to propose a series of changes to bring them under control.

INTRODUCTION

I. Our T&E costs are way above average, and they pose a threat to the company's financial health; fortunately, we can fix the problem in four straightforward steps that could save as much as $6 million a year.

II. How we approached the investigation

    A. We analyzed internal expense reports.
    B. We compared our cost data with nationwide averages.
    C. We analyzed published information on trends and cost-control suggestions.

(Transition: This presentation reviews Electrovision's spending patterns, analyzes the impact on company profits, and recommends four steps for reducing the budget.)

BODY

I. Analysis of spending patterns

    A. The amount we've been spending on T&E:
        1. Airfares, hotels, rental cars, restaurants, and entertainment totaled $16 million last year.
        2. T&E budget increased by 12 percent per year for the past five years.

    B. Where the money goes:
        1. We took 1880 trips last year at an average cost per trip of $8500.
        2. Airfares and lodging represent almost 70 percent of T&E expenses.

    C. How our spending compares with national averages:
        1. Facilities and customers spread from coast to coast force us to spend a lot on travel.
        2. However, we spend three times more than the national average for every day of travel. (Source: Business Travel News, *Business Travel News Corporate Travel Index 2012*, and company records.)

    D. Why do we spend so much?
        1. First-class travel has been viewed as compensation for the demands of extensive travel.
        2. The sales staff is encouraged to entertain clients.
        3. T&E costs are hard for managers to view and study.
        4. No one has central responsibility for controlling costs.

(Transition: We need to control spending for two reasons: (1) profits are projected to be flat or declining over the next two years, and (2) hotel rates and airfares continue to rise sharply.)

The introduction starts by highlighting the problem she will address.

The introduction continues with a description of the investigation she undertook; this will enhance her credibility by showing that the research was thorough and objective.

Part I of the body identifies the nature, scope, and causes of the problem.

(continued)

Figure 14–4 Effective Outline for a 30-Minute Presentation

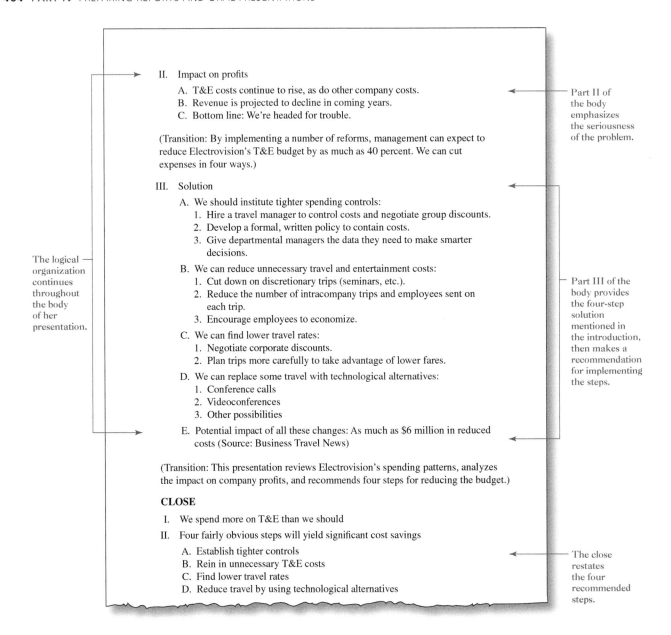

The logical organization continues throughout the body of her presentation.

II. Impact on profits
  A. T&E costs continue to rise, as do other company costs.
  B. Revenue is projected to decline in coming years.
  C. Bottom line: We're headed for trouble.

(Transition: By implementing a number of reforms, management can expect to reduce Electrovision's T&E budget by as much as 40 percent. We can cut expenses in four ways.)

III. Solution
  A. We should institute tighter spending controls:
    1. Hire a travel manager to control costs and negotiate group discounts.
    2. Develop a formal, written policy to contain costs.
    3. Give departmental managers the data they need to make smarter decisions.
  B. We can reduce unnecessary travel and entertainment costs:
    1. Cut down on discretionary trips (seminars, etc.).
    2. Reduce the number of intracompany trips and employees sent on each trip.
    3. Encourage employees to economize.
  C. We can find lower travel rates:
    1. Negotiate corporate discounts.
    2. Plan trips more carefully to take advantage of lower fares.
  D. We can replace some travel with technological alternatives:
    1. Conference calls
    2. Videoconferences
    3. Other possibilities
  E. Potential impact of all these changes: As much as $6 million in reduced costs (Source: Business Travel News)

(Transition: This presentation reviews Electrovision's spending patterns, analyzes the impact on company profits, and recommends four steps for reducing the budget.)

CLOSE
  I. We spend more on T&E than we should
  II. Four fairly obvious steps will yield significant cost savings
    A. Establish tighter controls
    B. Rein in unnecessary T&E costs
    C. Find lower travel rates
    D. Reduce travel by using technological alternatives

Part II of the body emphasizes the seriousness of the problem.

Part III of the body provides the four-step solution mentioned in the introduction, then makes a recommendation for implementing the steps.

The close restates the four recommended steps.

Figure 14–4 Effective Outline for a 30-Minute Presentation *(continued)*

You may find it helpful to create a simpler speaking outline from your planning outline.

Many speakers like to prepare both a detailed *planning outline* and a simpler *speaking outline* that provides all the cues and reminders they need to present their material. To prepare an effective speaking outline, follow these steps:[10]

- Start with the planning outline, and then strip away anything you don't plan to say to your audience (statement of general purpose, main idea, bibliography, and so on).
- Condense points and transitions to key words or phrases, choosing words that will prompt you to remember what each point is about. However, write out statistics, quotations, and other specifics so that you don't stumble over them.
- Add delivery cues, such as places in your outline where you plan to pause for emphasis or use a visual. Consider using coloured font (or ink for handwritten notes) to highlight them.
- Arrange your notes on numbered cards, or use the notes capability in your presentation software.

Developing and Writing a Presentation

Although you usually don't write out a presentation word for word, you still engage in the writing process (see step 2 in Figure 14–1)—developing your ideas, structuring support points, phrasing your transitions, and so on. Depending on the situation and your personal style, the eventual presentation might follow your initial words closely, or you might express your thoughts in fresh, spontaneous language.

ADAPTING TO YOUR AUDIENCE

Your audience's size, cultural norms, and expectations; the venue (in person or online); your subject; your purpose; your budget; and the time available for preparation and delivery—all influence the style of your presentation. If you're speaking to a small group, particularly people you already know, you can use a casual style that encourages audience participation. Deliver your remarks in a conversational tone, using notes to jog your memory if necessary.

> Adapting to your audience involves a number of issues, from speaking style to technology choices.

If you're addressing a large audience and the event is an important one, establish a more formal atmosphere. During formal presentations, speakers are often located on a stage or platform, standing behind a lectern and using a microphone so their remarks can be heard throughout the room.

Whether your presentation is formal or informal, always choose your words carefully. If you try to impress your audience with obscure or unfamiliar vocabulary, your message will be lost. Make sure you can define all the words you use, and be sure you can pronounce them. If you repeatedly stumble over a word as you rehearse, use a different one.[11]

COMPOSING YOUR PRESENTATION

Like written documents, oral presentations—whether they are 10 or 60 minutes long—are composed of distinct elements: the introduction, body, and close.

> **3 LEARNING OBJECTIVE**
>
> Discuss the three functions of an effective introduction, and identify different ways to get your audience's attention.

PRESENTATION INTRODUCTION A good introduction arouses the audience's interest in your topic, establishes your credibility, and prepares the audience for what will follow. That's a lot to pack into the first few minutes of your presentation, so give yourself plenty of time to develop the words and visuals you'll use to get your presentation off to a great start.

> An effective introduction arouses interest in your topic, establishes your credibility, and prepares the audience for the body of your presentation.

Getting Your Audience's Attention Some subjects are naturally more interesting to some audiences than others. If you will be discussing a matter of profound significance that will personally affect the members of your audience, the title of your presentation itself will have enough emotional appeal to grab their attention. Other subjects call for further clarification or triggers. Here are six ways to arouse audience interest.[12]

> Spend some time thinking about the best way to capture the audience's attention and interest with your opening remarks.

- **Unite the audience around a common goal.** Invite them to help solve a problem, capitalize on an opportunity, or otherwise engage in the topic of your presentation.
- **Tell a story.** Slice-of-life stories are naturally interesting and can be compelling. Be sure your story is one to which your audience can relate and illustrates an important point. Keep the story concise but memorable.
- **Pass around a sample or otherwise appeal to listeners' senses.** Psychologists say that you can get people to remember your points by appealing to their senses. The best way to do so is to pass around a sample. If your company is in the textile business, let the audience handle some of your fabrics.

If you sell chocolates, give everybody a taste. Samples or demonstrations can also be used to compare products or services and reinforce key points.

- **Ask a question.** Asking questions will get the audience actively involved in your presentation and, at the same time, will give you information about them and their needs. Just as with storytelling, it is important that the question relates to the topic in a meaningful way.
- **State a startling statistic.** People respond to details. If you can interject an interesting statistic, you can often wake up your audience. Try to connect the statistic to the audience. Sometimes this can be combined with an initial question and then a response that provides the data.
- **Use humour.** Open with an amusing observation about yourself, the subject matter of the presentation, or the circumstances surrounding the presentation—but make sure any humorous remarks are relevant, appropriate, and not offensive to anyone in the audience. In general, avoid humour when you and the audience don't share the same native language or culture; it's too easy for humour to fall flat or backfire.

Regardless of which technique you choose, make sure you can give audience members a reason to care and to believe that the time they're about to spend listening to you will be worth their while.[13]

Building Your Credibility Audiences tend to decide within a few minutes whether you're worth listening to, so establishing your credibility quickly is vital.[14] If you're a well-known expert in the subject matter or have earned your audience's trust in other situations, you'll need to build credibility in your introduction. If someone else will introduce you, he or she can present your credentials. If you will be introducing yourself, keep your comments brief, but don't be afraid to mention your accomplishments. Your listeners will be curious about your qualifications, so tell them briefly who you are, why you're there, and how they'll benefit from listening to you. You might say something like this:

> I'm Petra Maly, a market research analyst with Information Resources Corporation. For the past five years, I've specialized in studying high-technology markets. Your director of engineering, John LaBarre, has asked me to talk to you about recent trends in computer-aided design to help you direct your research efforts.

If you will be introduced by a master of ceremonies or another speaker, that person should be able to briefly itemize your qualifications as a way to build your credibility with the audience. Should the speaker use humour when introducing you? Why? Why not?

This speaker establishes credibility by tying her credentials to the purpose of her presentation. By mentioning her company's name, her specialization and position, and the name of the audience's boss, she lets her listeners know immediately that she is qualified to tell them something they need to know. She puts them at ease by connecting her background and experience to their concerns.

Previewing Your Message In addition to arousing audience interest and building your credibility, a good introduction gives your audience a preview of what's ahead, helping them understand the structure and content of your message. A reader can get an idea of the structure and content of a report by looking at the table of contents and scanning the headings, but in a presentation you need to provide that framework with a preview.

Your preview should summarize the main idea of your presentation, identify major supporting points, and indicate the order in which you'll develop those points. Tell your listeners in so many words, "This is the subject, and these are the points I will cover." Provide an agenda or visual "map" to help the audience understand how the individual facts and figures are related to your main idea as you move into the body of your presentation. If you are using an indirect approach, your preview can discuss the nature of your main idea without disclosing it.

Offer a preview to help your audience understand the importance, the structure, and the content of your message.

PRESENTATION BODY The bulk of your speech or presentation is devoted to a discussion of the main points in your outline. No matter what organizational pattern you're using, your goals are to ensure that (1) the organization of your presentation is clear, (2) your presentation holds the audience's attention, and (3) your presentation provides the audience with accurate and relevant information.

Connecting Your Ideas In written documents, you can show how ideas are related on the page or screen by employing a variety of design clues: headings, paragraph indentions, white space, and lists. However, with oral communication—particularly when you aren't using visuals for support—you have to rely primarily on words to link various parts and ideas.

For the small links between sentences and paragraphs, use one or two transitional words: *therefore, because, in addition, in contrast, moreover, for example, consequently, nevertheless,* or *finally.* To link major sections of a presentation, use complete sentences or paragraphs, such as "Now that we've reviewed the problem, let's take a look at some solutions." Every time you shift topics, ensure that you stress the connection between ideas. Summarize what's been said, and then preview what's to come.

Use transitions generously to help the audience follow and process your messages, particularly in longer presentations.

The longer your presentation, the more important your transitions become. If you will be presenting many ideas, audience members may have trouble absorbing them and seeing the relationships among them. Your listeners need clear transitions to guide them to the most important points. Carmine Gallo, author of *Talk Like TED,* recommends building in "soft breaks" such as videos or demonstrations every 10 minutes. The longer the presentation, the more the listener has to organize, comprehend, and remember. The opportunity to ask questions or interact helps with the processing of new information.[15] Furthermore, by repeating key ideas in your transitions, you can compensate for lapses in your audience's attention. Visual maps are also useful.

Holding Your Audience's Attention A successful introduction will have grabbed your audience's attention; now the body of your presentation needs to hold that attention. Here are six helpful tips for keeping the audience tuned to your message:

4 LEARNING OBJECTIVE

Identify six ways to keep your audience's attention during your presentation.

The most important way to hold an audience's attention is to show how your message relates to their individual needs and concerns.

1. **Relate your subject to your audience's needs.** People are interested in topics and issues that affect them personally. As much as possible, present every point in light of your audience's needs and values. Build on these needs with new and relevant information that they can use.
2. **Use clear, vivid language.** People become bored quickly when they don't understand the speaker. If your presentation involves abstract ideas, show how those abstractions connect with everyday life. Speak in a conversational tone. Use familiar words, short sentences, and concrete examples. Vary vocabulary as well to keep the presentation fresh for your audience. Pause at key points to help the audience absorb the information and continue to follow your presentation.
3. **Explain the relationship between your subject and familiar ideas.** Show how your subject is related to ideas that audience members already understand, and give people a way to categorize and remember your points.[16]

Stress the key aspects of your presentation by providing the audience with keywords or memorable anecdotes. Reinforce these with examples or data. Use these keywords or signposts again when you summarize or switch directions during your presentation.

4. **Limit the number of points.** Your outline will have helped you identify the key points of your presentation, the order in which you will present them, and the amount of time to be spent on each one. Overcrowding the presentation with too much information can cause you to lose the audience or influence their opinion in an undesirable direction. In deciding on what to include, focus on ideas that the audience may not have considered (but things they should know), that generate emotion (how should they feel?), and that ensure the audience will talk about the concepts (what do you want them to do?) after they have left the room. Use examples that are tangible and linked to the human experience. These tend to "stick" better than information that is presented in a more abstract context.[17]

5. **Illustrate your ideas with visuals.** Visuals—whether in digital form, as props, or as handouts—enliven your message, help you connect with audience members, and help them remember your message more effectively. Balance the use of visuals with the content of your message.

6. **Ask for opinions or pause occasionally for questions or comments.** Even though you have anticipated the types of questions that may arise and have addressed these in the body of the presentation, audience feedback will help determine whether your listeners understand the key points. Feedback also gives your audience a chance to switch from listening to participating for a time, which helps them engage with your message and develop a sense of shared ownership. Depending on how you have structured your presentation, allowing for questions during your delivery can also help you immediately adapt the message. (See also "Handling Questions Responsively" later in this chapter.)

Plan your close carefully so that your audience leaves with a clear summary of your main idea and in an emotional state that is appropriate to your purpose.

PRESENTATION CLOSE The close of a speech or presentation is critical for two reasons: audiences tend to focus more carefully as they wait for you to wrap up, and they will leave with your final words ringing in their ears. Before closing your presentation, tell listeners that you're about to finish, so they'll make one final effort to listen intently. Don't be afraid to sound obvious. Consider saying something such as "In conclusion" or "To sum it all up." You want people to know that this is the final segment of your presentation.

When you repeat your main idea in the close, emphasize what you want your audience to do or to think.

Restating Your Main Points After you announce your close, repeat your main idea and reinforce it with your key supporting points. Emphasize what you want your audience to do or to think, and stress the key motivating factor that will encourage them to respond that way. For example, to conclude a presentation on your company's executive compensation program, you can repeat the recommendations and finish with a memorable statement to motivate your audience to take action:

We can all be proud of the way our company has grown. However, if we want to continue that growth, we need to take four steps to ensure that our best people don't start looking for opportunities elsewhere:

- First, increase the overall level of compensation
- Second, establish a cash bonus program
- Third, offer a variety of stock-based incentives
- Fourth, improve our health insurance and pension benefits

By taking these steps, we can ensure that our company retains the management talent it needs to face our industry's largest competitors.

Repetition of key ideas greatly improves the chance that your audience will hear your message in the way you intended.

Ending with Clarity and Confidence If you've been successful with the introduction and body of your presentation, your listeners now have the information they need, and they're in the right frame of mind to put that information to good use. Now you're ready to end on a strong note that confirms expectations about any actions or decisions that will follow the presentation—and to bolster the audience's confidence in you and your message one final time.

Some presentations require the audience to reach a decision or agree to take specific action, in which case the close provides a clear wrap-up. If the audience agrees on an issue covered in the presentation, briefly review the consensus. If they don't agree, make the lack of consensus clear by saying something like, "We seem to have some fundamental disagreement on this question." Then be ready to suggest a method of resolving the differences.

If you expect any action to occur as a result of your speech, be sure to explain who is responsible for doing what. List the action items and, if possible within the time available, establish due dates and assign responsibility for each task.

Make sure your final remarks are memorable and expressed in a tone that is appropriate to the situation. For example, if your presentation is a persuasive request for project funding, you might emphasize the importance of this project and your team's ability to complete it on schedule and within budget. Expressing confident optimism will send the message that you believe in your ability to perform. Conversely, if your purpose was to alert the audience to a problem or risk, false optimism will undermine your message.

At the completion of your presentation, your audience should feel satisfied. The close is not the place to introduce new ideas or to alter the mood of the presentation. Even if parts of your presentation are downbeat, close on a positive note. As with everything else in your oral presentation, compose your closing remarks carefully. You don't want to wind up on stage with nothing to say but "Well, I guess that's it."

> Plan your final statement carefully, so you can end on a strong, positive note.

> Make sure your final remarks are memorable and have the right emotional tone.

Enhancing Your Presentation with Effective Visuals

Slides and other visuals can improve the quality and impact of your oral presentation by creating interest, illustrating points that are difficult to explain in words alone, adding variety, and increasing the audience's ability to absorb and remember information.

You can select from an assortment of visuals to enhance oral presentations. Don't overlook "old-school" technologies such as overhead transparencies, chalkboards, whiteboards, and flipcharts—they can all have value in the right circumstances. However, the medium of choice for most business presentations is an electronic slide presentation using Microsoft PowerPoint, Apple Keynote, Google Drive, or similar software. Electronic presentations are easy to edit and update; you can add sound, photos, video, and animation; they can be incorporated into online meetings, webcasts, and *webinars* (a common term for web-based seminars); and you can record self-running presentations for trade shows, websites, and other uses.

Electronic presentations are practically universal in business today, but their widespread use is not always welcome. You may have already heard the expression "death by PowerPoint," which refers to the agonizing experience of sitting through too many poorly conceived and poorly delivered slide shows.

> **5 LEARNING OBJECTIVE**
>
> Describe the six major design and writing tasks required to enhance your presentation with effective visuals.
>
> Thoughtfully designed visuals create interest, illustrate complex points in your message, add variety, and help the audience absorb and remember information.

In the words of presentation expert and author Garr Reynolds, "most presentations remain mind-numbingly dull, something to be endured by presenter and audience alike."[18]

Focus on making your presentations simple and authentic.

That's the bad news. The good news is that presentations can be an effective communication medium and an experience that is satisfying, and sometimes even enjoyable, for presenter and audience alike. Follow Reynolds's advice and start with the mindset of *simplicity* (clear ideas presented clearly) and *authenticity* (talking *with* your audience about things they care about, rather than talking at them or trying to be a "performer"). Plan the story you are going to tell before building the slides. You may even want to create a storyboard. By using these strategies, you'll be well on your way to becoming an effective presenter.

CHOOSING STRUCTURED OR FREE-FORM SLIDES

Structured slides are usually based on templates that give all the slides in a presentation the same general look (which usually involves a lot of bullet points); free-form slides are much less rigid and emphasize visual appeal.

Perhaps the most important design choice you face when creating slides is whether to use conventional **structured slides** or the looser, **free-form slides** that many presentation specialists now advocate. Consider the two rows of slides in Figure 14–5. Compare the rigid, predictable design of the two slides in the top row with the more dynamic free-form designs in the bottom row. Although the two free-form slides don't follow the same design structure, they are visually linked by colour and font choices. (Note that Figure 14–5d is a humorous way of conveying the first bullet point in Figure 14–5b.) The structured slides in

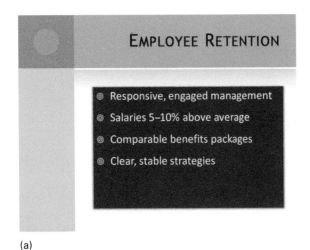

(a)

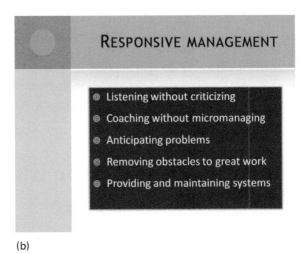

(b)

ESB Basic/Shutterstock

(c)

Jirasuda Saenkhamthum/123RF and spaxia/123RF

(d)

Figure 14–5 Structured versus Free-Form Slide Design

the top row follow the same basic format throughout the presentation; in fact, they're based directly on the templates built in to PowerPoint. The free-form slides in the bottom row don't follow a rigid structure.

However, choosing a free-form design strategy does not mean you can just randomly change the design from one slide to the next. Effectively designed slides should still be unified by design elements such as colour and typeface selections, as Figures 14–5c and 14–5d show. Also, note how Figure 14–5d combines visual and textual messages to convey the point about listening without criticizing. This complementary approach of pictures and words is a highlight of free-form design. Table 14–2 shows some of the advantages and challenges of these two design strategies.

DESIGNING EFFECTIVE SLIDES

Lack of design awareness, inadequate training, schedule pressures, and the instinctive response of doing things the way they've always been done can lead to ineffective slides and lost opportunities to really connect with audiences. Another reason for ineffective slides is the practice of treating slide sets as stand-alone documents that can be read on their own, without a presenter.

Use presentation software wisely to avoid the "death by PowerPoint" stigma that presentations have in the mind of many professionals.

The ideal solution is to create an effective slide set and a separate handout document that provides additional details and supporting information. This way, you can optimize each piece to do the job it is really meant to do. An alternative is to use the notes field in your presentation software to include your speaking notes for each slide. Anyone who gets a copy of your slides can at least follow along by reading your notes, although you will probably need to edit and embellish them to make them understandable by others.

Rather than packing your slides with enough information to make them readable as standalone documents, complement well-designed slides with printed handouts.

DESIGNING SLIDES AROUND A KEY VISUAL With both structured and free-form design strategies, it is often helpful to structure specific slides around a key visual that helps organize and explain the points you are trying to make. For

Organizing a slide around a key visual can help the audience quickly grasp how ideas are related.

Table 14–2	**Which Type of Slides Will Help You Best Convey Your Message?**		
Type	**Advantages**		**Challenges**
Structured Slides (e.g., Pre-built templates available through software or company-approved templates)	• Fast, easy to develop, offer consistency; no need to recreate the theme or colours (i.e., professional appearance). • Provide a blueprint that the audience can follow. Good for project updates, monthly status reports, or canned sales presentations. • Speakers have more information on the slide to help cue what they will say next. • Useful to question-and-answer (Q&A) sessions.		• Can be text heavy and and limit creativity because of background designs. • May cause the audience to become overwhelmed ("death by PowerPoint") by the amount of information if not properly orchestrated. • Inclusion of videos, animation, etc., needs to be balanced with the template style so as to not overwhelm the content.
Free-Form Slides (e.g., Often used for educational or motivational speeches.)	• Allow for a more dynamic presentation with the use of text and complementary visual cues. • Facilitate the processing of information in smaller chunks and help the audience make connections between topics and concepts. • Match a "storytelling" approach to presentations.		• Involve more expertise and time to develop the slides (e.g., select the appropriate images and balance content). • Information presented in smaller chunks must be connected and presented in context. • Consistency in terms of style and colour is still important. • Presenters are responsible for filling in the "white space" and providing more of the content.

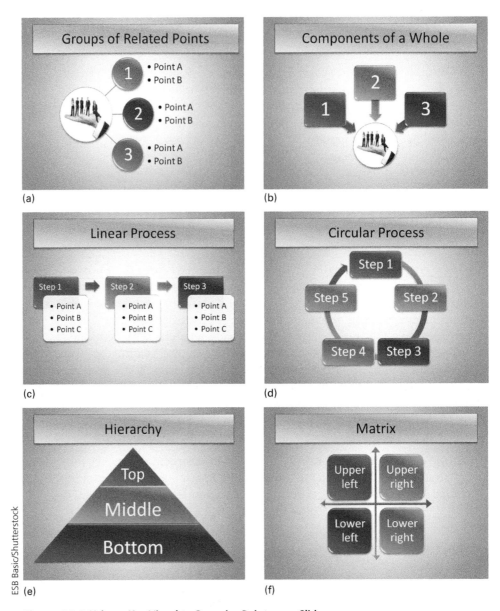

ESB Basic/Shutterstock

Figure 14–6 Using a Key Visual to Organize Points on a Slide

example, a pyramid suggests a hierarchical relationship, and a circular flow diagram emphasizes that the final stage in a process loops back to the beginning of the process. Figure 14–6 shows six of the many types of visual designs you can use to organize information on a slide. Simple graphical elements such as the "SmartArt" images in Microsoft PowerPoint make it easy to organize slide content using a key visual. Whether you're trying to convey the relationship of ideas in a hierarchy, a linear process, a circular process, or just about any other configuration, a key visual can work in tandem with your written and spoken messages to help audiences get your message.

Use slide text sparingly and only to emphasize key points, not to convey your entire message.

WRITING READABLE CONTENT One of the most common mistakes beginners make—and one of the chief criticisms levelled at structured slide designs in general—is stuffing slides with too much text. Doing so overloads the audience with too much information too fast, takes attention away from the speaker by forcing people to read more, and requires the presenter to use smaller type.

Effective text slides are clear, simple guides that help the audience understand and remember the speaker's message. Use text to highlight key points,

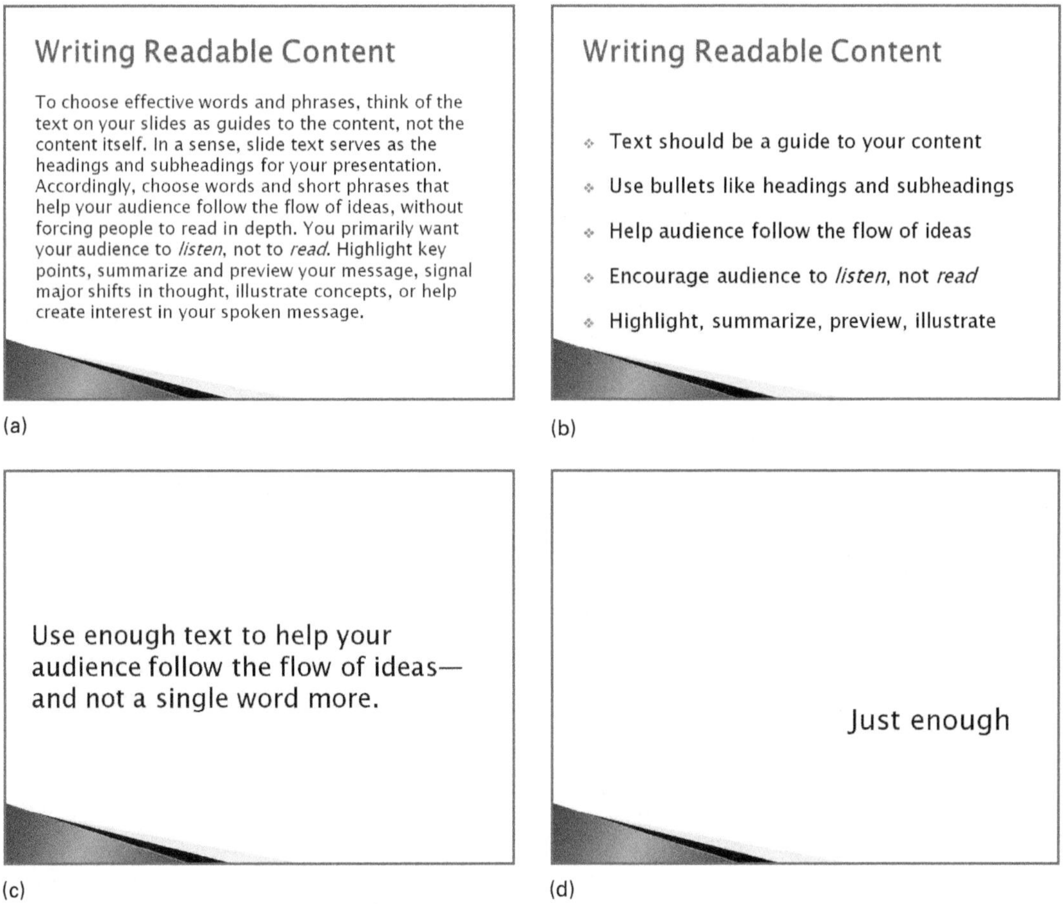

Writing Readable Content

To choose effective words and phrases, think of the text on your slides as guides to the content, not the content itself. In a sense, slide text serves as the headings and subheadings for your presentation. Accordingly, choose words and short phrases that help your audience follow the flow of ideas, without forcing people to read in depth. You primarily want your audience to *listen*, not to *read*. Highlight key points, summarize and preview your message, signal major shifts in thought, illustrate concepts, or help create interest in your spoken message.

(a)

Writing Readable Content

❖ Text should be a guide to your content

❖ Use bullets like headings and subheadings

❖ Help audience follow the flow of ideas

❖ Encourage audience to *listen*, not *read*

❖ Highlight, summarize, preview, illustrate

(b)

Use enough text to help your audience follow the flow of ideas— and not a single word more.

(c)

Just enough

(d)

Figure 14–7 Writing Text for Slides

summarize and preview your message, signal major shifts in thought, illustrate concepts, or help create interest in your spoken message.

Notice the progression toward simplicity in the slides in Figure 14–7. Figure 14–7a is a paragraph that would distract the audience for an extended period of time. Figure 14–7b offers concise, readable bullets, although too many slides in a row in this structured design would become tedious. Figure 14–7c distills the message down to a single thought that is complete on its own but doesn't convey all the information from the original and would need embellishment from the speaker. Figure 14–7d pushes this to the extreme, with only the core piece of the message to serve as an "exclamation point" for the spoken message. Figure 14–7c, and especially Figure 14–7d, could be made even more powerful with a well-chosen visual that illustrates the idea of following the flow. In short, effective text slides supplement your words and help the audience follow the flow of ideas.

CREATING CHARTS AND TABLES FOR SLIDES Charts and tables for presentations need to be simpler than visuals for printed documents. Detailed images that look fine on the printed page can be too dense and too complicated for presentations. Remember that your audience will view your slides from across the room—not from a foot or two away, as you do while you create them. Keep the level of detail to a minimum, eliminating anything that is not absolutely essential. If necessary, break information into more than one chart or table. If necessary, provide detailed versions of charts and tables in a handout.

Charts and tables for presentations need to be simpler than visuals for printed documents. When possible, use images or charts to convey a point, show a comparison, or present an idea. These are more memorable for the audience.

For example, if you're adapting visuals originally created for a written report, eliminate anything that is not absolutely essential to the message. If necessary, break information into more than one graphic illustration. Whenever you can do so without confusing the audience, look for shorter variations of numerical values. For example, round off a number such as $12,507 to $12 or $12.5 and then label the axis to indicate thousands.

With the basic design in place, use graphical elements to highlight key points. Leave plenty of white space; use colours that stand out from the slide's background; and choose a font that's clear and easy to read. Use arrows, boldface type, and colour to direct your audience's eyes to the main point of a visual.

SELECTING DESIGN ELEMENTS As you create slides, pay close attention to the interaction of colour, background and foreground designs and artwork, typefaces, and type styles.

Colour is more than just decoration; colours have meanings themselves, based on both cultural experience and the relationships that you established between the colours in your designs.

- **Colour.** Colour is a critical design element that can grab attention, emphasize important ideas, and create contrast. Colour can increase willingness to read by up to 80 percent, and it can enhance learning and improve retention by more than 75 percent.[19] Your colour choices can also stimulate various emotions, as Table 14–3 suggests. For example, if you wish to excite your audience, add some warm colours such as red and orange to your slides. If you wish to achieve a more relaxed and receptive environment, blue would be a better choice.[20] When selecting colour, limit your choices to a few complementary ones, and keep in mind that some colours work better together than others. Contrasting colours, for example, increase readability. So, when selecting colour for backgrounds, titles, and text, avoid choosing colours that are close in hue, such as brown on green or blue on purple.[21] Room lighting will also affect legibility.

Make sure the background of your slides stays in the background; it should never get in the way of the informational elements in the foreground.

- **Background designs and artwork.** All visuals have two layers or levels of graphic design: the *background* and the *foreground*. The background is the equivalent of paper in a printed report. Keep the background simple; cluttered or flashy backgrounds tend to distract from your message. As part of the background, you may want to add a company logo, the date, the presentation title, and a slide number. Just be sure to keep all these elements small and unobtrusive.

Table 14–3	Colour and Emotion	
Colour	**Emotional Associations**	**Best Uses**
Blue	Peaceful, soothing, tranquil, cool, trusting	Background for business presentations (usually dark blue); safe and conservative
White	Neutral, innocent, pure, wise	Font colour of choice for most business presentations with a dark background
Yellow	Warm, bright, cheerful, enthusiastic	Text bullets and subheadings with a dark background
Red	Passionate, dangerous, active, painful	To promote action or stimulate the audience; seldom used as a background ("in the red" specifically refers to financial losses)
Green	Assertive, prosperous, envious, relaxed	Highlight and accent colour (green symbolizes money in the United States but not in other countries).

- **Foreground designs and artwork.** The *foreground* contains the unique text and graphic elements that make up each individual slide. Foreground elements can be either functional or decorative. *Functional artwork* includes photos, technical drawings, charts, and other visual elements containing information that's part of your message. In contrast, *decorative artwork* simply enhances the look of your slides and should be using sparingly, if at all.

- **Typefaces and type styles.** Type is harder to read on screen than on the printed page, so you need to choose fonts and type styles with care. Sans serif fonts (such as Arial and Calibri) are usually easier to read than serif fonts (such as Times New Roman). Use both uppercase and lowercase letters, with generous space between lines of text, and limit the number of fonts to one or two per slide. Choose font sizes that are easy to read from anywhere in the room, usually between 28 and 36 points, and test them in the room if possible. Headings of the same level of importance should use the same font, type size, and colour. Once you have selected your fonts and type styles, test them for readability by viewing sample slides from a distance.

Maintaining design consistency is critical because audiences start to assign meaning to visual elements beginning with the first slide. For instance, if yellow is used to call attention to the first major point in your presentation, viewers will expect the next occurrence of yellow to also signal an important point. The *slide master* feature makes consistency easy to achieve because it applies consistent design choices to every slide in a presentation.

> Design inconsistencies confuse and annoy audiences; don't change colours and other design elements randomly throughout your presentation.

ADDING ANIMATION AND SPECIAL EFFECTS Presentation software offers a wide array of options for livening up your slides, including sound, animation, video clips, transition effects, and hyperlinks. Think about the impact that all these effects will have on your audience and use only those special effects that support your message.[22]

> You can animate just about everything in an electronic presentation; resist the temptation to do so—ensure that the animation has a purpose.

Functional animation involves motion that is directly related to your message, such as a highlight arrow that moves around the screen to emphasize specific points in a technical diagram. Such animation is also a good way to demonstrate sequences and procedures. For a training session on machinery repair, for example, you can show a schematic diagram of the machinery and walk your audience through each step of the troubleshooting process, highlighting each step onscreen as you address it verbally. In contrast, *decorative animation*, such as having a block of text cartwheel in from offscreen, needs to be used with great care. These effects don't add any functional value, and they easily distract audiences.

Slide transitions control how one slide replaces another, such as having the current slide gently fade out before the next slide fades in. Subtle transitions like this can ease your viewers' gaze from one slide to the next, but many of the transition effects are little more than distractions and are best avoided. **Slide builds** control the release of text, graphics, and other elements on individual slides. With builds you can make key points appear one at a time rather than having all of them appear on a slide at once, thereby making it easier for you and the audience to focus on each new message point.

> If you use transitions between slides, make sure they are subtle; they should do nothing more than ease the eye from one slide to the next.

A *hyperlink* instructs your computer to jump to another slide in your presentation, to a website, or to another program entirely. Using hyperlinks is also an effective way to build flexibility into your presentations, so that you can instantly change the flow of your presentation in response to audience feedback.

> Hyperlinks let you build flexibility into your presentations.

Multimedia elements offer the ultimate in active presentations. Using audio and video clips can be a great way to complement your textual message. Just be sure to keep these elements brief and relevant, as supporting points for your presentation, not as replacements for it.

Completing a Presentation

The completion step for presentations involves a wider range of tasks than most printed documents require. Make sure you allow enough time to test your presentation slides, verify equipment operation, practise your speech, and create handout materials. With a first draft of your presentation in hand, revise your slides to make sure they are readable, concise, consistent, and fully operational (including transitions, builds, animation, and multimedia). Complete your production efforts by finalizing your slides, creating handouts, choosing your presentation method, and practising your delivery. The most effective speakers seek early feedback and adjust their presentations several times.

FINALIZING SLIDES

Electronic presentation software can help you throughout the editing and revision process. The *slide sorter view* (different programs have different names for this feature) lets you see some or all of the slides in your presentation on a single screen. Examining thumbnails of slides is the best way to check the overall design of your final product. The slide sorter also makes it easy to review the order and organization of your presentation; you can change the position of any slide simply by clicking and dragging it to a new position.

In addition to the content slides, you can help your audience follow the flow of your presentation by creating slides for your title, agenda and program details, and navigation:

- **Title slide(s).** Make a good first impression on your audience with one or two title slides, the equivalent of a report's cover and title page (see Figures 14–8a and 14–8b). A title slide should contain the title of your presentation (and subtitle, if appropriate), your name, your department affiliation (for internal audiences), your company affiliation (for external audiences), and the date of your presentation.
- **Agenda and program details.** These slides communicate both the agenda for your presentation and any additional information your audience might need (see Figures 14–8c and 14–8d).
- **Navigation slides.** To tell your audience where you're going and where you've been, you can use a series of **navigation slides** based on your outline or agenda. As you complete each section, repeat the agenda slide but indicate which material has been covered and which section you are about to begin (see Figure 14–9a). This sort of slide is sometimes referred to as a *moving blueprint slide* or *blueprint slide*. As an alternative to the repeating agenda slide, you can insert a simple *bumper slide* (see Figure 14–9b) at each major section break, announcing the title of the section you're about to begin.[23]

Navigation slides help your audience keep track of what you've covered already and what you plan to cover next.

CREATING EFFECTIVE HANDOUTS

Use handout materials to support the points made in your presentation and to offer the audience additional information on your topic.

Handouts, any printed materials you give the audience to supplement your talk, should be considered an integral part of your presentation strategy. Handouts can include detailed charts and tables, case studies, research results, magazine articles, and anything else that supports the main idea of your presentation.

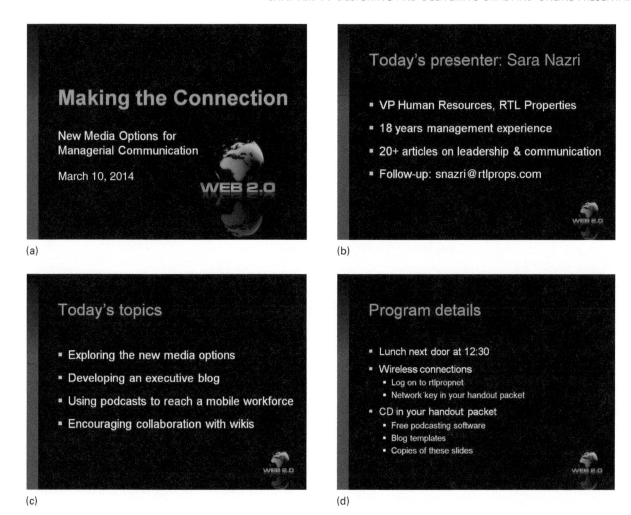

Figure 14–8 Navigation and Support Slides

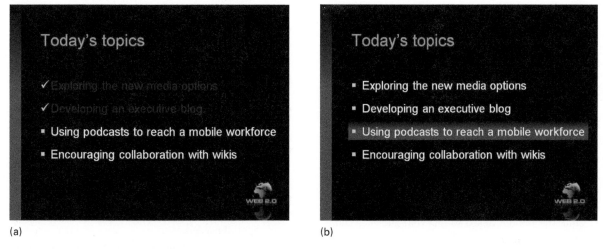

Figure 14–9 Moving Blueprint Slides

Plan your handouts as you develop your presentation so that you use each medium as effectively as possible. Your presentation should paint the big picture, convey and connect major ideas, set the emotional tone, and rouse the audience to action (if that is relevant to your talk). Your handouts can then carry the rest of the information load, providing the supporting details that audience members can consume at their own speed, on their own time. You won't need to worry about stuffing every detail into your slides, because you have the more appropriate medium of printed documents to do that. As Garr Reynolds puts it, "Handouts can set you free."[24]

Finally, think about a backup plan. What will you do if your laptop won't boot up or the projector dies? Can you get by without your slides? For important presentations, consider having backup equipment on standby, loaded with your presentation and ready to go. Having a backup copy of your presentation slides on a CD-ROM or flash drive or saved to the cloud is a good idea. At the very least, have enough printed handouts ready to give to the audience so that, as a last resort, you can give your presentation "on paper."

For a quick review of the key steps in creating effective visuals, see "Checklist: Enhancing Presentations with Visuals."

✓ Checklist   Enhancing Presentations with Visuals

A. Plan your presentation visuals.
- Your visuals should tell a story, but make sure you and your message, not your visuals, remain the focus of your presentation.
- Follow effective design principles, with an emphasis on simplicity and authenticity.

B. Choose structured or free-form slides.
- Structured slides using bullet-point templates are easy to create, require little design time or skill, and can be completed in a hurry. Best uses: routine, internal presentations.
- Free-form slides make it easier to combine textual and visual information, to create a more dynamic and engaging experience, and to maintain a conversational connection with the audience. Best uses: motivational, educational, and persuasive presentations.

C. Design effective slides.
- Avoid the temptation to create slides that are so packed with information that they can be read as standalone documents.
- Use a key visual to organize related ideas in a clear and meaningful way.
- Write text content that will be readable from everywhere in the room.
- Write short, active, parallel phrases that support, not replace, your spoken message.
- Limit the amount of text so that your audience can focus on listening, not reading.
- Replace bullets with flow diagrams, charts, or images to demonstrate key points. Visuals tend to be more dramatic in conveying important comparisons or ideas.
- Use colour to emphasize important ideas, but limit colours to a few compatible choices and use them consistently.

- Make sure your slide background doesn't compete with the foreground. Check the impact of room lighting.
- Use decorative artwork sparingly and only to support your message.
- Emphasize functional artwork—photos, technical drawings, charts, and other visual elements containing information that is part of your message.
- Choose typefaces that are easy to read onscreen; limit the number of typefaces, and use them consistently.
- Use slide masters to maintain consistency throughout your presentation.
- Use functional animation when it can support your message.
- Make sure slide transitions are subtle, if used at all.
- Use builds carefully to control the release of information.
- Use hyperlinks and action buttons to add flexibility to your presentation.
- Incorporate multimedia elements that can help engage your audience and deliver your message.

D. Complete slides and support materials.
- Review every slide carefully to ensure accuracy, consistency, and clarity.
- Make sure that all slides are fully operational.
- Use the slide sorter to verify and adjust the sequence of slides, if needed.
- Have a backup plan in case your electronic presentation plan fails.
- Create navigation and support slides.
- Create handouts to complement and support your presentation message.
- Provide contact information when appropriate.

CHOOSING YOUR PRESENTATION METHOD

Speaking with the help of an outline, note cards, or visuals, is one of the easiest delivery modes for speakers. This approach gives you something to refer to and still allows for plenty of eye contact, a natural speaking flow, interaction with the audience, and improvisation in response to audience feedback. The challenge, however, is to not get "hijacked" by the notes.

Many influential speakers present extemporaneously and use the support of multimedia to reinforce their message. The ability to speak freely without the use of notes or cue cards allows them to move back and forth between the visuals and the audience in a more relaxed fashion, thus connecting easily with listeners and reinforcing their credibility. Outlining the content and practising delivery of the material helps to keep speakers on point and on time.

You can use a variety of navigation and support slides to introduce yourself and your presentation, to let the audience know what your presentation will cover, and to provide essential details.

In contrast, reciting your speech from memory is usually less effective. Even if you can memorize the entire presentation, you will sound stiff and overly formal because you are "delivering lines," rather than talking to your audience. However, memorizing a quotation, an opening statement, or a few concluding remarks can bolster your confidence and strengthen your delivery. Show your enthusiasm for the topic. Your level of energy, demonstrated through tone of voice and body language, will affect how the audience responds to your message.

Reading a speech is necessary in rare instances, such as when delivering legal information, policy statements, or other messages that must be conveyed in an exact manner. However, for all other business presentations, reading is a poor choice because it limits your interaction with the audience and lacks the fresh, dynamic feel of natural talking.

Another important decision at this point is preparing the venue where you will speak. In many instances, you won't have much of a choice, and in some situations, you won't even be able to visit the venue ahead of time. However, if you do have some control over the environment, think carefully about the seating for the audience, your position in the room, and the lighting. For instance, dimming the lights is common practice for many presenters, but dimming the lights too far can hamper the nonverbal communication between you and your audience and therefore limit opportunities for interaction.[25]

Speaking with the help of carefully prepared, brief notes is one of the easiest delivery mode for many speakers.

Matthew Ward/DK Images

Practising your oral presentation with a co-worker or a friend is an effective way to polish your public speaking skills in a relaxed setting. What should your audience look for to help you improve as a speaker?

PRACTISING YOUR DELIVERY

Practising your presentation is essential. Practice helps ensure that you appear polished and confident, reduces anxiety, gives you the chance to smooth out any rough spots, and lets you verify the operation of slides and equipment. A test audience can tell you if your slides are understandable and whether your delivery is effective. A day or two before you're ready to step on stage for an important talk, make sure you and your presentation are ready:

- Can you present your material naturally, without reading your slides?
- Could you still make a compelling and complete presentation if you experience an equipment failure and have to proceed without using your slides at all?

The more you practise, the more confidence you'll have in yourself and your material.

You'll know you've practised enough when you can present the material at a comfortable pace and in a conversational tone, without the need to read your slides or constantly refer to your notes.

- Is the equipment working, and do you know how to work it?
- Is your timing on track? Have you practised the points of transition with other team members, if appropriate?
- Can you easily pronounce all the words you plan to use? Is your choice of words appropriate and meaningful for the audience?
- Have you anticipated likely questions and objections? How will team members handle questions? Is there a way for the audience to contact you, if appropriate?

If you're addressing an audience that doesn't speak your language, consider using an interpreter. Send your interpreter a copy of your speech and visuals as far in advance of your presentation as possible. If your audience is likely to include persons with hearing impairments, be sure to team up with a sign-language interpreter as well.

Delivering a Presentation

OVERCOMING ANXIETY

If you're nervous about facing an audience, you're not alone: even speakers with years of experience feel some anxiety about getting up in front of an audience. Polished speakers know how to use that nervous energy to their advantage. As you practise your speech, think of nervousness as an indication that you care about your audience, your topic, and the occasion. If your palms get wet or your mouth goes dry, don't think of it as nerves—think of it as excitement. Such stimulation can give you the extra energy you need to make your presentation sparkle. Here are some ways to harness your nervous energy to become a more confident speaker:[26]

Dennis MacDonald/PhotoEdit

From time to time, you may have to give an *impromptu*, or unrehearsed, speech when you have virtually no time at all to prepare. When you're asked to speak "off the cuff," take a moment to think through what you'll say and then focus on your key points. How can you prepare for situations where you might need to speak spontaneously?

Practice is the best antidote for anxiety; it gives you confidence that you know your material and that you can recover from any glitches you might encounter.

- **Stop worrying about being perfect.** Successful speakers focus on making an authentic connection with their listeners, rather than on trying to deliver a note-perfect presentation.
- **Know your subject.** The more familiar you are with your material, the less panic you'll feel.
- **Practise, practise, practise.** The more you rehearse, the more confident you will feel.
- **Visualize success.** Visualize mental images of yourself in front of the audience, feeling confident, prepared, and able to handle any situation that might arise.[27] Get into the zone. Bear in mind that your audience wants you to succeed, too.
- **Remember to breathe.** Tension can lead people to breathe in a rapid and shallow fashion, which can create a lightheaded feeling. Breathe slowly and deeply to maintain a sense of calm and confidence.
- **Be ready with your opening line.** Have your first sentence memorized and on the tip of your tongue.
- **Be comfortable.** Dress as comfortably as is appropriate. Drink plenty of water ahead of time to hydrate your voice (bring a bottle of water with you, too).
- **Take a three-second break.** If you sense that you're starting to race—a natural response when you're nervous—pause and arrange your notes or perform some other small task while taking several deep breaths. Then, start again at your normal pace.

- **Concentrate on your message and your audience, not on yourself.** When you're busy thinking about your subject and observing your audience's response, you tend to forget your fears.
- **Maintain eye contact with friendly audience members.** Eye contact not only makes you appear sincere, confident, and trustworthy, but can give you positive feedback as well.
- **Keep going.** Remember, you are the expert on the subject matter. The audience wants to hear what you have to say. Your confidence level will increase as you continue, with each successful minute giving you more and more self-assurance.

HANDLING QUESTIONS RESPONSIVELY

The question-and-answer (Q&A) period is one of the most important parts of an oral presentation. It gives you a chance to obtain important information, to emphasize your main idea and supporting points, and to build enthusiasm for your point of view. When you're speaking to high-ranking executives in your company, the Q&A period will often consume most of the time allotted for your presentation.[28]

Whether or not you can establish ground rules for Q&A depends on the audience and the situation. If you're presenting to upper managers or potential investors, for example, you will probably have no say in the matter: audience members will likely ask questions at any time to get the information they need. On the other hand, if you are presenting to your peers or a large public audience, try to establish some guidelines, such as the number of questions allowed per person and the overall time limit for questions.

Don't assume that you can handle whatever comes up without some preparation.[29] Learn enough about your audience members to get an idea of their concerns and think through answers to potential questions. If possible, be prepared with backup documentation or slides.

When people ask questions, pay attention to the questioner's body language and facial expression to help determine what the person really means. Repeat the question to confirm your understanding and to ensure that the entire audience has heard it. If the question is vague or confusing, ask for clarification; then give a simple, direct answer.

If you are asked a complex or difficult question, answer carefully. Break down the different parts of the question. Offer to meet with the questioner afterward if the issue isn't relevant to the rest of the audience or if giving an adequate answer would take too long. Make a note of the question so that you can follow up. If you don't know the answer, don't pretend that you do. Instead, offer to get a complete answer as soon as possible or ask someone in the audience to volunteer information.

Be on guard for audience members who use questions to make impromptu speeches or to take control of your presentation. Without offending the questioner, find a way to stay in control. You might admit that you and the questioner

Don't leave the question-and-answer period to chance: anticipate potential questions and think through your answers.

Maintaining control during the question-and-answer session can be a challenge, particularly if any audience members outrank you in the corporate hierarchy.

If you don't have a satisfactory answer to an important question from the audience, offer to provide it after the presentation.

The question-and-answer session is often the most valuable part of a presentation. How should you prepare for it? How can the question-and-answer session enhance your reputation before your audience?

Noel Hendrickson/Photodisc/Getty Images

have differing opinions and, before calling on someone else, offer to get back to the questioner after you've done more research.[30]

If a question ever puts you on the hot seat, respond honestly but keep your cool. Look the person in the eye, answer the question as well as you can, and keep your emotions under control. Avoid getting into a heated argument. Defuse hostility by paraphrasing the question and asking the questioner to confirm that you've understood it correctly. Maintain a businesslike tone of voice and a pleasant expression.[31]

When the time allotted for your presentation is up, call a halt to the Q&A session. Prepare the audience for the end by saying something such as "Our time is almost up. Let's have one more question." After you've made your reply, summarize the main idea of the presentation and thank people for their attention. Conclude with the same confident demeanour you've had from the beginning. Indicate how the audience can reach you or where they can obtain additional information if needed.

If you ever face hostile questions, respond honestly and directly while keeping your cool.

EMBRACING THE BACKCHANNEL

7 **LEARNING OBJECTIVE**

Describe the important aspects of delivering a presentation in today's online environment.

Many business presentations these days involve more than just the spoken conversation between the speaker and his or her audience. Using Twitter and other electronic media, audience members often carry on their own parallel communication during a presentation via the **backchannel**, which presentation expert Cliff Atkinson defines as "a line of communication created by people in an audience to connect with others inside or outside the room, with or without the knowledge of the speaker."[32] Chances are you've participated in a backchannel already, such as when texting with your classmates or live-blogging during a lecture.

The backchannel presents both risks and rewards for business presenters. On the negative side, for example, listeners can research your claims the instant you make them and spread the word quickly if they think your information is shaky. The backchannel also gives contrary audience members more leverage, which can lead to presentations spinning out of control. On the plus side, listeners who are excited about your message can build support for it, expand on it, and spread it to a much larger audience in a matter of seconds. You can also get valuable feedback during and after presentations.[33]

By embracing the backchannel, rather than trying to fight or ignore it, presenters can use this powerful force to their advantage. Follow these tips to make the backchannel work for you:[34]

Twitter and other social media are dramatically changing business presentations by making it easy for all audience members to participate in the backchannel.

Resist the urge to ignore or fight the backchannel; instead, learn how to use it to your advantage.

- **Integrate social media into the presentation process.** For example, you can set up a formal backchannel yourself using tools such as TodaysMeet (http://todaysmeet.com), create a website for the presentation so that people can access relevant resources during or after the presentation, create a Twitter hashtag that everyone can use when sending tweets, or display the Twitterstream during Q&A so that everyone can see the questions and comments on the backchannel.
- **Monitor and ask for feedback.** Using a free service such as TweetDeck (http://tweetdeck.com), you can monitor in real time what the people in the audience are writing about. To avoid trying to monitor the backchannel while speaking, you can schedule "Twitter breaks," during which you review comments and respond as needed.
- **Review comments to improve your presentation.** After a presentation is over, review comments on audience members' Twitter accounts and blogs to see how you can improve your content or your presentation habits.
- **Automatically tweet key points from your presentation while you speak.** Add-ons for presentation software can send out prewritten tweets as you

show specific slides during a presentation. By making your key points readily available, you make it easy for listeners to retweet and comment on your presentation.

- **Establish expectations with the audience.** Explain that you welcome audience participation, but to ensure a positive experience for everyone, ask that comments be civil, relevant, and productive.

GIVING PRESENTATIONS ONLINE

The benefits of online presentations are considerable, including the opportunity to communicate with a geographically dispersed audience at a fraction of the cost of travel. However, the challenges for a presenter can be significant, thanks to that layer of technology between you and your audience. Many of those "human moments" that guide and encourage you through an in-person presentation won't travel across the digital divide. For example, it's often difficult to tell whether your audience is bored or confused because your view of them is usually confined to small video images (and sometimes not even that). Understanding your audience is as critical for an online presentation as it is for a face-to-face presentation, perhaps even more so since visual feedback will be difficult to obtain. Practice runs are also important to flesh out possible system issues.

Online presentations let you reach a wide audience but are characterized by lack of direct contact. What should you do to engage your audience when delivering an online presentation?

To ensure successful online presentations, regardless of the system you're using, keep the following advice in mind:

- **Consider sending preview study materials ahead of time.** If your presentation covers complicated or unfamiliar material, consider sending a brief message ahead of time so your audience can familiarize itself with any important background information. If you are sending a lengthy report, point out key aspects that will be reviewed during the presentation.
- **Keep your content—and your presentation of it—as simple as possible.** Break complicated slides into multiple slides if necessary, and keep the direction of your discussion clear so that no one gets lost. Moreover, make sure any streaming video presentations are short; audiences dislike being forced to sit through long speeches online.[35]
- **Ask for feedback frequently.** Many online viewers will be reluctant to call attention to themselves by interrupting you to ask for clarification. So, to ensure that your audience is on track, draw out feedback as you go. Setting up a backchannel via Twitter or as part of your online meeting system gives viewers a chance to ask questions without interrupting.
- **Consider the viewing experience from the audience's side.** Will they be able to see what you think they can see? For example, webcast video is typically displayed in a small window onscreen, so viewers may miss important details.
- **Allow plenty of time for everyone to get connected and familiar with the screen they're viewing.** Build extra time into your schedule to ensure that everyone is connected and ready to start. Depending on the group size, allow time for introductions and outline the flow of the presentation, including the protocol for asking questions.

Finally, don't get lost in the technology. Use these tools whenever they'll help, but remember that the most important aspect of any presentation is getting the audience to receive, understand, and embrace your message.

SUMMARY OF LEARNING OBJECTIVES

1 **Explain the importance of oral presentations in your career success.** Oral presentations give you the opportunity to highlight all of your communication skills, from planning and researching a project to producing and delivering it. Executives will note your ability to deal with audiences, react spontaneously to questions, and present information through effective visuals—all qualities that will show your ability to handle challenging assignments.

2 **Explain how to adapt the planning step of the three-step process to oral presentations.** Both written and oral communication require analyzing the situation, determining your purpose, doing research, and organizing information. For oral messages, you must also consider the presenting medium (such as live, in-person presentations or webcasts). You must also incorporate flexibility into your presentations in order to accommodate audience feedback. Furthermore, you must define your main idea, limit your scope, choose your approach, and prepare your outline. Also, you must adapt your presentation to your audience so that listeners will remember what is said.

3 **Discuss the three functions of an effective introduction, and identify different ways to get your audience's attention.** An effective introduction arouses audience interest, sometimes in imaginative ways, such as by uniting the audience around a common goal, asking a question, telling a story, or stating a startling statistic. An effective introduction also builds the speaker's credibility to gain the audience's trust and previews the message to keep the audience on track.

4 **Identify six ways to keep your audience's attention during your presentation.** Keep your audience's attention by relating your information to their needs. In addition, use concrete and familiar language to keep your audience engaged, explain the relationship between your subject and familiar ideas, limit the number of points,

pause for feedback as needed to promote audience interest, and illustrate your ideas with visuals.

5 **Describe the six major design and writing tasks required to enhance your presentation with effective visuals.** First, decide whether to use conventional structured slides or free-form slides. Second, design slides so that your information is organized around a key visual. Third, write readable content; don't overstuff slides with too much content. Fourth, create charts and tables, which must be simpler for presentations than for written reports. Fifth, select design elements, including colour, background and foreground designs and artwork, and typefaces and type styles. Sixth, consider carefully whether and how you will add animation and multimedia, as these elements can reduce your presentation's impact.

6 **Identify six methods that effective speakers use to handle questions responsively.** Effective speakers predict questions so they can give informed answers. They are also sensitive to the questioner's body language to determine any deeper meanings to the questions. Furthermore, effective speakers answer the question asked, limit the length of their responses, establish time limits or other rules for questions, and respond to hostile questions honestly, directly, and calmly.

7 **Describe the important aspects of delivering a presentation in today's online environment.** First, when delivering a presentation in today's digital age, integrate social media into your presentation. One way is to create a Twitter hashtag to handle comments and questions. Second, keep your presentation simple, to keep online audiences on track. Third, ask for feedback frequently, via Twitter or your online meeting system, as some listeners may be hesitant to initiate questions. Fourth, don't start your presentation until you're sure everyone is connected.

ON THE JOB   PERFORMING COMMUNICATION TASKS AT TELEFILM CANADA

Carolle Brabant speaks to a variety of industry and government audiences. To succeed with each one, she must focus her purpose and tailor her content to reach them successfully. As an intern with Telefilm Canada's head office, you are asked to help plan a speech Brabant will deliver to an audience of directors, producers, and actors as well as journalists at the Toronto International Film Festival. Brabant's topic is Telefilm's recent successes, and she is allocated about 10 minutes for her talk. For the following situations, choose the best solution and explain your answer.

1. How should Brabant begin her speech?

   a. Brabant should immediately list films supported by Telefilm that have been box-office hits.

   b. Brabant should discuss the history of Telefilm.

   c. Brabant should show some brief video clips of successful Telefilm-supported productions.

   d. Brabant should ask the audience what they know about Telefilm.

2. You are considering including statistics in Brabant's speech, such as the number of awards Telefilm-supported films have won, the amount of worldwide distribution, and profits. What is the best way of presenting this quantitative information?

   a. Brabant should use electronic slides to highlight this information.

   b. Brabant should express this information orally.

   c. Brabant should use overhead transparencies.

   d. Statistical information should not be used.

3. How should Brabant end her speech?

   a. Brabant should discuss the need for more funding for Telefilm Canada and ask Canadian audience members to write to the Standing Committee on Canadian Heritage, Telefilm's supervisory body.

   b. Show brief film clips of Telefilm-sponsored movies.

   c. Make positive, unifying remarks; thank the audience; and distribute handouts about Telefilm Canada.

   d. Make positive, unifying remarks and thank the audience, but do not distribute handouts about Telefilm Canada.

TEST YOUR KNOWLEDGE

1. What is an effective way to respond if you feel nervous right before giving a presentation?

2. How does the completion stage of the three-step writing process differ between reports and presentations?

3. Why do you have to limit your scope when planning a presentation?

4. What do you want to achieve with the introduction to your speech? With the close of your speech?

5. If you suspect that your audience doesn't really care about the topic you plan to discuss, how can you generate interest in your presentation?

6. If you're giving a presentation in a subject area that you've researched thoroughly but in which you don't have any hands-on experience, how do you build credibility?

7. What are the key rules for designing effective visuals?

8. As a speaker, what nonverbal signals can you send to appear more confident?

9. What can speakers do to maintain control during the question-and-answer period of a presentation?

10. What must you consider for online presentations?

APPLY YOUR KNOWLEDGE

1. Would you rather (a) deliver an oral presentation to an outside audience, (b) be interviewed for a news story, or (c) make a presentation to a departmental meeting? Why? How do the communication skills differ among those situations? Explain.

2. How might the audience's attitude affect the amount of audience interaction during or after a presentation? Explain your answer.

3. How does embracing the backchannel reflect the "you" attitude?

4. What are the pros and cons of speaking from your notes?

5. **Ethical Choices** Is it ethical to use design elements and special effects to persuade an audience? Why or why not?

RUNNING CASES

> CASE 1 Noreen

The Petro-Go senior management team has decided to move forward with the merger of the "Go Points" department and the credit card sales/service department. They approved Noreen's proposal and report and decided to implement this plan across all national and international centres.

   Noreen is about to deliver a business presentation to the staff in both departments. She needs to introduce herself, explain how the departments have merged, and discuss how job roles will change. She plans to show the new organizational chart during her presentation and mention that all centres will merge the two departments, so all credit card sales/service staff will also market the points program and all "Go Points" staff will now conduct credit card sales and offer service to existing credit card customers. Staff will be provided with product,

systems, and service training as well as new phone scripts and procedures manuals.

QUESTIONS

   a. What features will Noreen's audience have in common?

   b. When creating slides, what principles must Noreen remember?

   c. Is the direct or indirect approach best?

   d. How can Noreen arouse the audience's interest on this topic?

   e. In the event the equipment fails during Noreen's speech, what backup plan should she have?

YOUR TASK

Prepare this presentation. Assume that you are Noreen. Create a speech outline and an electronic slide show. Deliver the presentation to a group.

> CASE 2 Kwong

Kwong has to prepare a presentation for his final course in his CGA program and seeks his manager's permission to use ET Canada as his case study. Kwong will have to gather some company information and get approval to use it for his course project. Kwong's manager would like to see his project before Kwong presents it to his class. Kwong plans to discuss the software systems used at ET Canada and the policies and procedures the company follows to gather information electronically from the national branches into the head office. System screen shots (pictures of data screens) will be used, and charts, graphs, or other reported information may be included in Kwong's presentation.

QUESTIONS

a. What must Kwong consider when sharing company data with the public?

b. How can Kwong arouse the audience's interest on this topic?

c. Should Kwong prepare handouts for the audience? If so, when should he hand them out?

d. How will Kwong ensure that the audience can clearly see the screen shots and other visuals in the slide show?

e. What should Kwong include in the introductory part of the speech?

YOUR TASK

Create a similar presentation. Investigate how your college or university computer labs work. How are they networked? What software is loaded? How can students get access? Where can students get help? How much does it cost? Who maintains the network and software licences/upgrades? Take some screen shots and include them in an electronic slide show. Prepare a speech outline and then present your findings to a group.

PRACTISE YOUR KNOWLEDGE

DOCUMENT 14.A

Examine the slide in Figure 14–10 and point out any problems you notice. How would you correct these problems?

DOCUMENT 14.B

Examine the graph in Figure 14–11 and explain how to modify it for an electronic presentation using the guidelines discussed in this chapter.

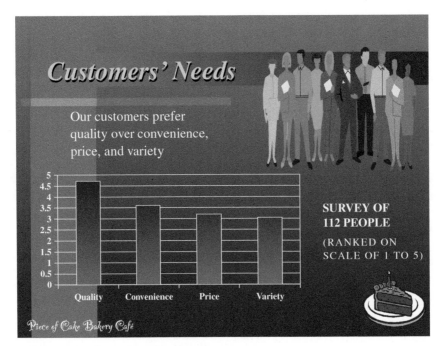

Figure 14–10 Piece of Cake Bakery Electronic Slide #8

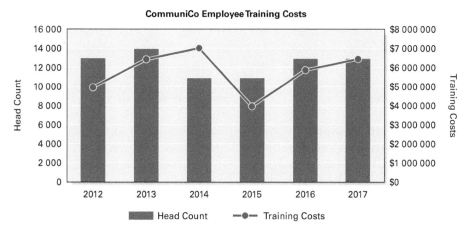

Figure 14–11 CommuniCo Employee Training Costs

EXERCISES

14.1 Mastering Delivery: Analysis

Attend a presentation at your school or in your area, or watch a speech on television. Categorize the speech as one that motivates or entertains, one that informs or analyzes, or one that persuades or urges collaboration. Then, compare the speaker's delivery with this chapter's guidelines for developing a presentation.

Write a two-page report analyzing the speaker's performance and suggesting improvements.

14.2 Mastering Delivery: Nonverbal Signals

Observe and analyze the delivery of a speaker in a school, at work, or in another setting such as the online Ted Talks at www.ted.com/talks. What type of delivery did the speaker use? Was this delivery appropriate for the occasion? What nonverbal signals did the speaker use to emphasize key points? Were these signals effective? Which nonverbal signals

would you suggest to further enhance the delivery of this oral presentation—and why?

14.3 Ethical Choices

Think again about the oral presentation you observed and analyzed in Exercise 14.2. How could the speaker have used nonverbal signals unethically to manipulate the audience's attitudes or actions?

14.4 Completing Oral Presentations: Self-Assessment

How good are you at planning, writing, and delivering oral presentations? Rate yourself on each of the elements of the oral presentation process in the table below. Then, examine your ratings to identify where you are strongest and where you can improve, using the tips in this chapter.

Element of Presentation Process	Always	Frequently	Occasionally	Never
1. I start by defining my purpose.				
2. I analyze my audience before writing an oral presentation.				
3. I match my presentation length to the allotted time.				
4. I begin my oral presentations with an attention-getting introduction.				
5. I look for ways to build credibility as a speaker.				
6. I cover only a few main points in the body of my presentation.				
7. I use transitions to help listeners follow my ideas.				
8. I review main points and describe next steps in the close.				
9. I practise my presentation beforehand.				
10. I prepare in advance for questions and objections.				
11. I conclude oral presentations by summarizing my main idea.				

14.5 Creating Effective Slides: Content

Look through recent issues (print or online) of *Canadian Business*, *BusinessWeek*, *Fortune*, or other business publications for articles discussing challenges that a specific company or industry is facing. Using the guidelines discussed in this chapter, create three to five slides summarizing these issues.

14.6 Planning a Presentation: Research

Select one of the following topics. Then research your topic as needed and prepare a brief presentation (5 to 10 minutes) to be given to your class. What steps will you follow in the development of your presentations? What factors will you need to consider given the allotted time of 5 to 10 minutes?

a. What I expect to learn in this course

b. Past public speaking experiences: the good, the bad, and the ugly

c. I would be good at teaching _____.

d. I am afraid of _____.

e. It's easy for me to _____.

f. I get angry when _____.

g. I am happiest when I _____.

h. People would be surprised if they knew that I _____.

i. My favourite older person

j. My favourite charity

k. My favourite place

l. My favourite sport

m. My favourite store

n. My favourite television show

o. You are speaking to the Humane Society. Support or oppose the use of animals for medical research purposes.

p. You are talking to civic leaders of your community. Try to convince them to build an art gallery.

q. You are talking to civic leaders of your community. Try to convince them to build a community centre to keep young people occupied after school and on weekends.

r. You are speaking to a grade 1 class at an elementary school. Explain why they should brush their teeth after meals.

s. You are speaking to a group of elderly people. Convince them to adopt an exercise program.

t. Energy issues (supply, conservation, alternative sources, national security, global warming, pollution, etc.)

u. Financial issues (banking, investing, family finances, etc.)

v. Interesting new technologies (virtual reality, geographic information systems, nanotechnology, bioengineering, etc.)

w. Politics (political parties, elections, legislative bodies and legislation, etc.)

x. Sports (amateur and professional, baseball, football, golf, hang gliding, hockey, rock climbing, tennis, etc.)

14.7 Delivering a Presentation: Using Twitter

In a team of six students, develop a 10-minute slide presentation on any topic that interests you. Nominate one person to give the presentation; the other five will participate via a Twitter backchannel. Create a webpage that holds at least one downloadable file that will be discussed during the presentation, and set up a backchannel on TodaysMeet (http://todaysmeet.com) or a similar service. Practise using the backchannel, including using a hashtag for the meeting and having the presenter ask for audience feedback during a "Twitter break." Be ready to discuss your experience with the entire class.

14.8 Business Communications 2.0

1. Visit www.SlideShare.net and find two presentations on the same business topic, such as public relations, financial matters, leadership, or even giving presentations. View and compare the two presentations in terms of content. Which presentation is clearer? More credible? More convincing? What specific steps did this presenter take to ensure clarity and confidence?

2. Now compare those two presentations in terms of their visual design. Do their designs help or hinder the communication effort? If you see any weaknesses, what improvements would you suggest?

14.9 Planning and Developing a Presentation: Analyzing a Corporate Speech

Locate the transcript of a speech, either online or through your school library. Good sources include the University of Pennsylvania Library website (http://gethelp.library.upenn.edu/guides/hist/speeches.html) and Vital Speeches of the Day (https://www.vsotd.com/). Many corporate websites also have archives of executives' speeches; look in the "investor relations" section. Examine both the introduction and the close of the speech you've chosen, and then analyze how these two sections work together to emphasize the main idea. What action does the speaker want the audience to take? Next, identify the transitional sentences or phrases that clarify the speech's structure for the listener, especially those that help the speaker shift between supporting points. Using these transitions as clues, list the main message and supporting points; then indicate how each transitional phrase links the current supporting point to the succeeding one. Prepare a two- to three-minute presentation summarizing your analysis for your class.

LEARNING OBJECTIVES   After studying this chapter, you will be able to

1 Explain the importance and features of an employment portfolio

2 Describe the key steps to finding the ideal opportunity in today's job market

3 Discuss how to choose the appropriate résumé organization and length

4 Describe the problem of résumé fraud

5 Outline the major sections of a traditional résumé

6 Describe the completing step for résumés

MyLab Business Communication   Visit MyLab Business Communication to access a variety of online resources directly related to this chapter's content.

ON THE JOB: COMMUNICATING AT TIM HORTONS

Avava/Fotolia

Through effective workforce recruiting, Tim Hortons has achieved a dominant position in the fast-food business. Managed by the TDL Group, the renowned Canadian franchise offers job seekers opportunities in finance, marketing, human resources, property management, and other fields that support the growth of the retail chain.

Recruiting Top Talent

www.timhortons.com

With more than 4500 locations nationally and such programs as the Tim Horton Children's Foundation Camp, Smile Cookie charity donations, and Earn-a-Bike, Tim Hortons is both Canada's most recognized fast-food chain and an influential corporate citizen. Supporting the famous franchise is the TDL Group, the operator that manages the Tim Hortons chain's continuing growth across Canada and the United States. Through such areas as distribution, purchasing, owner training, real estate, and financial planning, this behind-the-scenes company administers the entire Tim Hortons system.

TDL looks for people who like challenges, approach their job with a "can do" attitude, enjoy working on a team, and "appreciate the freedom to develop their skills and move ahead." By searching under "Join Our Team" and then "Corporate Opportunities" on the Tim Hortons website, applicants will find a variety of challenging jobs. These include bilingual customer service agent: liaising between store owners and centralized shipping and operations, the applicant must be fluent in both French and English as well as have high-level computer skills, particularly in warehouse management software. The position of employee relations representative requires up-to-date knowledge of human resources practices and employment law. The work of district supervisor demands extensive experience in the hospitality industry and strong problem-solving skills. All positions require high interpersonal, organizational, and communication competence.

Job seekers are asked to complete an online application by providing a cover letter and résumé and by answering a series of questions about their experience in the food service field, their education, and their salary expectations. They are required to list skills they feel are relevant to the position, noting their proficiency level on a scale from "no knowledge" to "expert," and the number of years they've used that skill. TDL makes contact after reviewing the submission.

Tuition reimbursement, training programs, and opportunities to be involved with the Tim Horton Children's Foundation are some of the benefits of working for TDL. The company prides itself on innovation, excellence, hard work— and respect for its employees. If you were interested in working at TDL, how would you do research for a corporate-level position? How would you plan and prepare your résumé to be noticed by recruiters?[1]

Building a Career with Your Communication Skills

Successful job hunters view the search as a comprehensive process—and put all of their communication skills to work.

Obtaining the job that's right for you takes more than sending out a few résumés and application letters. As you get ready to enter (or re-enter) the workplace, explore the wide range of actions you can take to maximize your perceived value and find the ideal career opportunities. The skills you've learned in research, planning, and writing will help you every step of the way.

UNDERSTANDING THE DYNAMIC WORKPLACE

For many workers, the employment picture is less stable today than it was in years past.

Social, political, and financial events continue to change workplace conditions from year to year, so the job market you read about this year might not be the same market you try to enter a year or two from now. However, you can count on a few forces that are likely to affect your entry into the job market and your career success in years to come:[2]

- **Unpredictability.** Your career probably won't be as stable as careers were in your parents' generation. In today's business world, your career will be affected by globalization, mergers and acquisitions, short-term mentality driven by the demands of stockholders, ethical upheavals, and the relentless quest for lower costs. On the plus side, new opportunities, new companies, and even entire industries can appear almost overnight.
- **Flexibility.** As companies try to become more agile in a globalized economy, many employees—sometimes of their choice and sometimes not— are going solo and setting up shop as independent contractors. Innovations in electronic communication and social media will continue to spur the growth of *virtual organizations* and *virtual teams*, in which independent contractors and companies of various sizes join forces for long- or short-term projects.
- **Economic globalization.** Commerce across borders has been going on for thousands of years, but the volume of international business has roughly tripled in the past 30 years. One significant result is *economic globalization*, the increasing integration and interdependence of national economies around the world. Just as companies now compete across borders, as an employee or independent contractor you also compete globally.
- **Growth of small business.** More than 1 million small businesses operate in Canada, so chances are good that you'll work for a small firm at some point.[3]

Patti McConville/Alamy Stock Photo

Digital communication has fuelled the growth of small business. Would you like to pursue a career in business but have the flexibility to work from home? What special communication skills might be needed to be a successful entrepreneur?

What do all these forces mean to you? First, take charge of your career—and stay in charge of it. Understand your options, have a plan, and don't count on others to watch out for your future. Second, understanding your audience is key to successful communication, starting with understanding how employers view today's job market.

Changes in the job market mean you need to take charge of your career, rather than counting on a single employer to look out for you.

HOW EMPLOYERS VIEW TODAY'S JOB MARKET From the employer's perspective, the employment process is always a question of balance. Maintaining a stable workforce can improve practically every aspect of business performance, yet many employers feel they need the flexibility to shrink and expand payrolls as business conditions change. Employers obviously want to attract the best talent, but the best talent is more expensive and more vulnerable to offers from competitors, so there are always financial trade-offs to consider.

Employers also struggle with the ups and downs of the economy, just as employees do. When unemployment is low, the balance of power shifts to employees, and employers have to compete to attract and keep top talent. When unemployment is high, the power shifts back to employers, who can afford to be more selective and less accommodating. In other words, pay attention to the economy and its impact on different industries whenever you're job-hunting; at times you can be more aggressive, but at other times you should be more accommodating.

The nature of the job market fluctuates with the ups and downs of the economy.

Many employers fill some needs by hiring temporary workers or engaging contractors on a project-by-project basis. Depending on strategic or political interests, Canadian and U.S. employers have moved jobs to cheaper labour markets outside the country and recruited globally to fill local positions. Both trends have stirred controversy, especially in the technology sector, as firms recruit top engineers and scientists from abroad while shifting mid- and low-range jobs to India, China, Russia, and other countries with lower wage structures.[4]

WHAT EMPLOYERS LOOK FOR IN JOB APPLICANTS Given the complex forces in the contemporary workplace and the unrelenting pressure of global competition, what are employers looking for in the candidates they hire? The short answer is: a lot. Like all "buyers," companies want to get as much as they can for the money they spend. The closer you can get to presenting yourself as the ideal candidate, the better your chances of getting the job.

Most employers value employees who are flexible, adaptable, and sensitive to the complex dynamics of today's business world.

TIPS FOR SUCCESS

"Companies look for employees with strong communication skills and monitor and observe employee communication habits with the following considerations in mind:
- How well does the individual interpret information and are those inferences correct?
- How well does the individual interact with colleagues and what role do they take on in group situations?
- How does the individual respond when criticized and does the employee actively listen to feedback?
- Can the individual write well, speak well or even improvise well?"

Tristan Boutros, The Perfect Candidate: 10 Traits of the Ideal Employee. May 19, 2015, Retrieve from : https://www.linkedin.com/pulse/perfect-employee-15-traits-ideal-tristan-boutro

Specific expectations vary by profession and position, of course, but virtually all employers look for the following general skills and attributes:[5]

- **Communication skills.** The reason this item is listed first isn't that you're reading a business communication textbook. Communication is listed first because it is far and away the most commonly mentioned skill set when employers are asked about what they look for in employees. Improving your communication skills will help in every aspect of your professional life.

- **Interpersonal and team skills.** You will have many individual responsibilities on the job, but chances are you won't work alone very often. Learn to work with others—and help them succeed as you succeed.
- **Intercultural and international awareness and sensitivity.** Successful employers tend to be responsive to diverse workforces, markets, and communities, and they look for employees with the same outlook.
- **Data collection, analysis, and decision-making skills.** Employers want people who know how to identify information needs, find the necessary data, convert the data into useful knowledge, and make sound decisions.
- **Computer and electronic media skills.** Today's workers need to know how to use common office software and to communicate using a wide range of electronic media.
- **Time and resource management.** If you've had to juggle multiple priorities during your schooling, consider that great training for the business world. Your ability to plan projects and manage the time and resources available to you will make a big difference on the job.
- **Flexibility and adaptability.** Employees who can adapt to changing business priorities and circumstances will go further (and be happier) than employees who resist change.
- **Professionalism.** Professionalism is the quality of performing at the highest possible level and conducting oneself with confidence, purpose, and pride. True professionals strive to excel, continue to hone their skills and build their knowledge, are dependable and accountable, demonstrate a sense of business etiquette, make ethical decisions, show loyalty and commitment, don't give up when things get tough, and maintain a positive outlook.

ADAPTING TO A CHANGING JOB MARKET

Adapting to the workplace is a lifelong process of seeking the best fit between what you want to do and what employers (or clients, if you work independently) are willing to pay you to do. It's important to know what you want to do, what you have to offer, and how to make yourself more attractive to employers.

WHAT DO YOU WANT TO DO? Economic necessities and the vagaries of the marketplace will influence much of what happens in your career, of course; nevertheless, it's wise to start your employment search by examining your own values and interests. Identify what you want to do first and then see whether you can find a position that satisfies you at a personal level while also meeting your financial needs. Consider these questions:

Have you thought long and hard about what you really want to do in your career? The choices you make now could influence your life for years to come.

- **What would you like to do every day?** Research occupations that interest you. Find out what people really do every day. Ask friends, relatives, or alumni from your school and contacts in your social networks. Read interviews with people in various professions to get a sense of what their careers are like. Attend job fairs and networking events to meet with individuals from different fields of work. Let them know you are interested in hearing about their careers and how they came about. Look for internship opportunities to get a sense of the working environment and job responsibilities. Make an appointment with a representative from your campus career centre to discuss the services they provide and how they can help you develop a career plan.
- **How would you like to work?** Consider how much independence you want on the job, how much variety you like, and whether you prefer to work with products, machines, people, ideas, figures, or some combination thereof.

- **How do your financial goals fit with your other priorities?** For instance, many high-paying jobs involve a lot of stress, sacrifices of time with family and friends, and frequent travel or relocation. If location, lifestyle, intriguing work, or other factors are more important to you, you may well have to sacrifice some level of pay to achieve them.
- **Have you established some general career goals?** For example, do you want to pursue a career specialty such as finance or manufacturing, or do you want to gain experience in multiple areas with an eye toward upper management?
- **What sort of corporate culture are you most comfortable with?** Would you be happy in a formal hierarchy with clear reporting relationships? Or do you prefer less structure? Teamwork or individualism? Do you like a competitive environment?
- **What location would you like?** Would you like to work in a city, a suburb, a small town, or an industrial area? Do you favour a particular part of the country? Another country? (See "Communicating across Cultures: Looking for Work around the World.")

You might need some time in the workforce to figure out what you really want to do or to work your way into the job you really want, but it's never too early to start thinking about where you want to be.

WHAT DO YOU HAVE TO OFFER? Knowing what you *want* to do is one thing. Knowing what a company is willing to pay you to do is another. You may already have a good idea of what you can offer employers. If not, some brainstorming can help you identify your skills, interests, and characteristics. Start by jotting down all of your achievements to date. Think about what specific skills these achievements demanded of you. For example, leadership skills, speaking ability, and artistic talent may have helped you coordinate a successful class project. As you analyze your achievements, you may well begin to recognize a pattern of skills. Which of them might be valuable to potential employers?

> ### TIPS FOR SUCCESS
> "The best way to get started is to brainstorm about your natural talents and abilities. Write down everything you've accomplished, even as far back as childhood. This is a confidence boost and also can help you get everything out on paper that you could possibly include in your résumé."
>
> Hallie Crawford, Professional Coach

Next, look at your educational preparation, work experience, and extracurricular activities. What do your knowledge and experience qualify you to do? What have you learned from volunteer work or class projects that could benefit you on the job? Have you held any offices, won any awards or scholarships, mastered a second language? What skills have you developed in nonbusiness situations that could transfer to a business position?

Take stock of your personal characteristics. Are you aggressive, a born leader? Or would you rather follow? Are you outgoing, articulate, great with people? Or do you prefer working alone? Make a list of what you believe are your four or five most important qualities. Ask a relative or friend to rate your traits as well.

If you're having difficulty figuring out your interests, characteristics, or capabilities, consult your school's career centre. Many campuses administer a variety of tests to help you identify interests, aptitudes, and personality traits. These tests won't reveal your "perfect" job, but they'll help you focus on the types of work best suited to your personality.

No matter what profession you're in, you are a valuable package of skills and capabilities; ensure that you have a clear picture of your own strengths.

Your school's career centre can point you to a variety of tests to gauge your interest and suitability for a variety of career possibilities.

COMMUNICATING ACROSS CULTURES Looking for Work around the World

If your goal is a career with an international focus, check out your school's office of international affairs for work or study abroad opportunities. You will find extensive information on its website and access to advisors and students who have international work experience. You'll be able to sign on with an organization that offers students assistance with foreign work permits and provides housing and job leads.

To help ensure success in your own search for employment abroad, keep these points in mind:

- **Give yourself plenty of time.** Finding a job in another country is a complicated process that requires extensive and time-consuming research.
- **Research thoroughly, both online and off.** In addition to your school's resources, you can find numerous websites that offer advice, job listings, and other information. For a good look at the range of international opportunities, visit www.goabroad.com/intern-abroad, www.goabroad.com/volunteer-abroad, www.goabroad.com/teach-abroad, http://jobs.goabroad.com, and www.myworldabroad.com. However, people with international experience will tell you that you can't limit your research to the Web. Like any job search, networking is crucial, so join cultural societies with international interests, volunteer with exchange student programs, or find other ways to connect with people who have international experience.

- **Consider all the possibilities.** Keep an open mind when you're exploring your options; you'll probably run across situations you hadn't considered at the beginning of your search. For example, you might find that an unpaid internship in your future profession would help your career prospects more than a paying position in some other industry. If your school offers a study abroad option, consider applying to study in a different country for a semester. This is a good way to learn about different cultures while earning credits toward your degree.
- **Be flexible.** If you have to settle for something less than that dream job, focus on the big picture, which for most students is the cultural opportunity.

Finding a job in another country can be a lot of work, but the rewards can be considerable. As many students have found, working in a culture is the best way to get a true sense of it.

CAREER APPLICATIONS

1. How might international work experience help you in a career in Canada, even if you never work abroad again?
2. If your work history involves political activities, either paid or volunteer, explain how you might present this information on a résumé intended for international readers.

Take an active approach to making yourself a more attractive job candidate—and it's never too early to start.

HOW CAN YOU MAKE YOURSELF MORE VALUABLE? While you're figuring out what you want from a job and what you can offer an employer, you can take positive steps toward building your career. First, look for volunteer projects, temporary jobs, freelance work, or internships that will help expand your experience base and skill set.[6] Develop a co-curricular record (CCR)—a complement to your academic record or transcript that shows student involvement in different campus activities, including participation in workshops, volunteering, tutoring, student government positions, awards, etc. Available through most university career and planning centres, a CCR can help you demonstrate leadership and communication skills, teamwork, flexibility, and creativity. The CCR is usually an online template with guidelines for eligible activities and organizations that students can update and self-manage. You can look for freelance projects on Craigslist (www.craigslist.org) and numerous other websites; some of these jobs have only nominal pay, but they do provide an opportunity for you to display your skills. Also consider applying your talents to *crowdsourcing* projects, in which companies and nonprofit organizations invite the public to contribute solutions to various challenges. These opportunities help you gain valuable experience and relevant contacts, provide you with important references and work samples for your *employment portfolio*, and help you establish your focus as a job seeker.

Second, learn more about the industry or industries in which you want to work, and stay on top of new developments. Join networks of professional colleagues and friends who can help you keep up with trends and events. Many professional societies have student chapters or offer students discounted memberships. Your school alumni are also good resources to interview for information about their own job-searching experiences and trends in their current fields. Many career and planning centres provide forums in which you can meet and network with alumni and industry professionals. Take courses and pursue other educational or life experiences that would be difficult while working full time.

BUILDING AN EMPLOYMENT PORTFOLIO

To further prove that you have the skills necessary to succeed on the job, you can create and maintain an *employment portfolio*, which is a collection of projects that demonstrate your skills and knowledge. You can create both a print portfolio and an e-portfolio. A print portfolio gives you something tangible to bring to interviews, and it lets you collect project results that might not be easy to show online, such as a handsomely bound report.

An e-portfolio is a multimedia presentation of your skills and experiences.[7] Think of it as a website that contains your résumé, work samples, letters of recommendation, articles you may have written, and other information about you and your skills. If you have set up a *lifestream* (a real-time aggregation of your content creation, online interests, and social media interactions) that is professionally focused, consider adding that to your e-portfolio. Be creative. For example, a student who was pursuing a degree in meteorology added a video clip of himself delivering a weather forecast.[8] The portfolio can be burned on a CD or DVD for physical distribution or, more commonly, it can be saved to a flash drive or posted online—whether it's on a personal website, your school's site (if student pages are available), a specialized portfolio-hosting site such as Behance (www. behance.net), or a résumé-hosting site such as VisualCV (www.visualcv.com) that offers multimedia résumés.

> ## TIPS FOR SUCCESS
> "Don't worry if you are the youngest person in the room with the least amount of professional experience. If you bring a unique perspective and speak up, you're a valuable asset."
>
> Vivian Giang

By combining your CCR, projects, and samples of work from your courses, you can create a compelling portfolio by the time you're ready to start interviewing. Your portfolio is also a valuable resource for writing your résumé because it reminds you of all the great work you've done over the years. Moreover, you can continue to refine and expand your portfolio throughout your career; many professionals, such as graphic designers, use e-portfolios to advertise their services.

As you assemble your portfolio, collect anything that shows your ability to perform, whether it's in school, on the job, or in other venues. However, you *must* check with an employer before including any items you created while you were an employee and check with clients before including any *work products* (anything you wrote, designed, programmed, and so on) they purchased from you. Many business documents contain confidential information that companies don't want distributed to outside audiences.

To get started, first check with the career centre at your university or college; many schools now offer e-portfolio systems with specific guidelines and suggestions for their students. To see a selection of student e-portfolios, visit MyBCommLab.

For each item you add to your portfolio, write a brief description that helps other people understand the meaning and significance of the project. Include information about the project's background, project objectives, whether you

1 **LEARNING OBJECTIVE**

Explain the importance and features of an employment portfolio.

Employers look for candidates who conduct themselves with confidence and pride. Be sure that all of your resources, including reports, résumés, letters, photos, and blogs, are consistent and reflect the image and personal brand you want to present. This can also apply to your online connections.

worked with others, the team dynamic, time and budget constraints, the result, and what you learned during the course of the project.

Keep in mind that the portfolio itself is a communication project, too, so be sure to apply everything you know about effective communication and good design. Assume that every potential employer will find your e-portfolio site (even if you don't tell them about it), so don't include anything that could come back to haunt you. Also, if you have anything embarrassing on Facebook, Instagram, or any other social networking site, remove it immediately. As well, some employers are beginning to contact people in a candidate's network for background information, even if the candidate doesn't list those people as references.[9]

Finding the Ideal Opportunity in Today's Job Market

2   LEARNING OBJECTIVE

Describe the key steps to finding the ideal opportunity in today's job market.

Finding the ideal job opportunity involves a six-step process that you might repeat a number of times during your career. Figure 15–1 shows the most important tasks in the employment search process, starting with the examination of different opportunities and the preparation of employment messages that communicate your story or personal brand.

The skills you're developing in this course will give you a competitive advantage. This section offers a general job-search strategy with advice that applies to just about any career path you might want to pursue. As you craft your personal strategy, keep these guidelines in mind:

- **Get organized.** Your job search could last many months and involve multiple contacts with dozens of companies. You need to keep all the details straight to make sure you don't miss opportunities or make mistakes, such as losing someone's email address or forgetting an appointment.
- **Start now and stick to it.** Even if you are a year or more away from graduation, now is not too early to get started with some of the essential research, planning, and developing tasks. If you wait until the last minute, you will miss opportunities and you won't be as prepared as the candidates you'll be competing against.

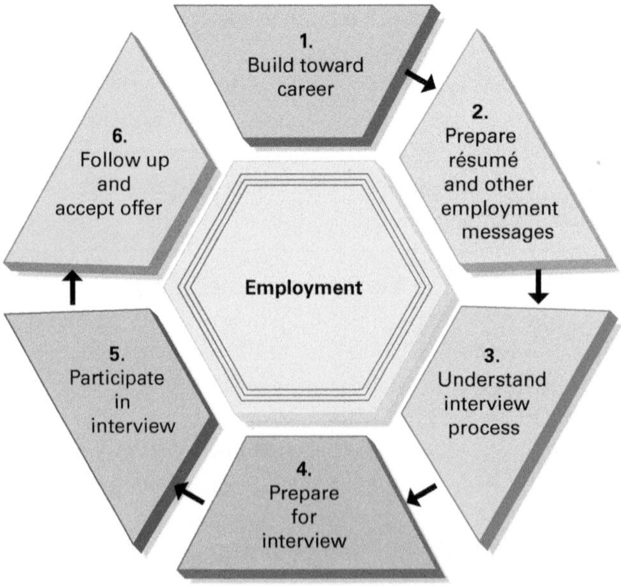

Figure 15–1 The Employment Search

DETERMINE THE STORY OF YOU

As the section on adapting to today's job market explains, take the time now to explore the possibilities, find your passion, and identify appealing career paths. Begin writing the "story of you": the things you are passionate about, the skills you possess, your ability to help an organization reach its goals, the path you've been on so far, and the path you want to follow in the future. Think in terms of an image or a theme you'd like to project. Are you academically gifted? An effective leader? A well-rounded professional with wide-ranging talents? A creative problem solver? A technical wizard? Writing your story is a valuable planning exercise that helps you think about where you want to go and how to present yourself to target employers. In marketing terms, what is your "brand" and how do your want to position yourself? In the previous pages we reviewed the employment portfolio. What message do you want your portfolio to send?

LEARN TO THINK LIKE AN EMPLOYER

Now that you know your side of the hiring equation a little better, switch sides and look at it from an employer's perspective. To begin with, recognize that companies take risks with every hiring decision—the risk that the person hired won't meet expectations and the risk that a better candidate has slipped through their fingers. Many companies judge the success of their recruiting efforts by *quality of hire*, a measure of how closely new employees meet the company's needs.[10] What steps can you take to present yourself as the low-risk, high-reward choice, as someone who can make a meaningful contribution to the organization?

Your perceived ability to perform the job is obviously an essential part of your potential quality as a new hire. However, hiring managers consider more than just your ability to handle the responsibilities you'll be given. They want to know if you'll be reliable and motivated, if you're somebody who "gets it" when it comes to being a professional in today's workplace. A great way to get inside the heads of corporate recruiters is to "eavesdrop" on their professional conversations by reading periodicals such as *Workforce Magazine* (www.workforce.com) and blogs such as *Fistful of Talent* (www.fistfuloftalent.com) and *The HR Capitalist* (www.hrcapitalist.com).

> Employers judge their recruiting success by *quality of hire*, and you can take steps to be—and look like—a high-quality hire.

RESEARCH INDUSTRIES AND COMPANIES OF INTEREST

Learning more about professions, industries, and individual companies is easy with the library and online resources available to you. Table 15–1 lists some of the many websites where you can learn more about companies and find job openings. Start with Service Canada's Job Bank, www.jobbank.gc.ca, where you can search jobs and find links to other job sites. Your school's career centre placement office probably maintains an up-to-date list as well.

To learn more about contemporary business topics, peruse some of these leading business periodicals and newspapers with significant business sections (in some cases, you may need to go through your library's online databases to gain full access):

> Employers expect you to be familiar with important developments in their industries, so stay on top of business news.

- *Globe and Mail:* www.globeandmail.com
- *National Post:* www.nationalpost.com
- *Canadian Business:* www.canadianbusiness.com
- *Wall Street Journal:* http://online.wsj.com
- *New York Times:* www.nytimes.com
- *Bloomberg Businessweek:* www.businessweek.com

- *Fast Company:* www.fastcompany.com
- *Fortune:* www.fortune.com
- *Forbes:* www.forbes.com

Follow leading organizations on LinkedIn or Twitter, and keep up to date on their latest developments. In addition, thousands of bloggers and podcasters offer news and commentary on the business world. To identify those you might find helpful, start with directories such as EatonWeb (http://portal.eatonweb.com/) for blogs or Podcast Alley (www.podcastalley.com; select the "Business" genre) for podcasts. Alltop (http://alltop.com) is another good resource for finding articles about topics that interest you. In addition to learning more about professions and opportunities, this research will help you get comfortable with the jargon and buzzwords currently in use in a particular field—including essential *keywords* to use in your résumé (see the section titled "Compose Your Résumé").

Don't forget a company's own website. Look for the "About Us" or "Company" part of the site to find a company profile, executive biographies, press releases, financial information, and information on employment opportunities. You can download annual reports, descriptive brochures, or newsletters. Any company's website is going to present the firm in the most positive light possible, so look for outside sources as well, such as the periodicals listed above.

TRANSLATE YOUR GENERAL POTENTIAL INTO A SPECIFIC SOLUTION FOR EACH EMPLOYER

An important aspect of the quality-of-hire challenge is trying to determine how well a candidate's attributes and experience will translate to the challenges of a specific position. As Jim Schaper, CEO of software company Infor Global Solutions, puts it, "We try to determine if newly minted graduates can apply knowledge they've already gained."[11] Customizing your résumé to each job opening is an important step in showing employers that you will be a good fit. From your initial contact all the way through the interviewing process, in fact, you will have opportunities to impress recruiters by explaining how your general potential translates to the specific needs of the position.

David de Lossy/Photodisc/Getty Images

Would you like a career that keeps you on your feet and out of an office? Specialized job boards offer unique short- and long-term opportunities in the food industry, building trades, and the environment. Check out www.canadiancareers.com for jobs such as these. How would you sell yourself for this kind of employment?

Table 15–1	**Selected Job-Search Websites**	

Website*	URL	Highlights
Job Bank (Service Canada)	www.jobbank.gc.ca	Comprehensive site for government and private-sector jobs. Create a job account, and save it on the site with a personalized service code. You can create a job profile and receive job alerts by email that match it. French and English.
Monster	www.monster.ca	One of the most popular job sites, with hundreds of thousands of openings, many from hard-to-find smaller companies; extensive collection of advice on the job-search process.
Workopolis	www.workopolis.com	Billed as "Canada's biggest job site," Workopolis contains tips and advice from experts in addition to an extensive job list classified by province and career track.
Indeed.ca	www.indeed.ca	Aggregates postings from many job boards in one location. Information from different company career pages are compiled, allowing job seekers to look at local and global opportunities.
CareerBuilder	www.careerbuilder.ca	Affiliated with more than 100 local newspapers around the country that include career advice.
CareerOwl	www.careerowl.ca	Browse by occupation and read recent articles about the Canadian job scene. Contains numerous job search resources.
Dice.com	www.dice.com	One of the best sites for high-technology jobs in both Canada and the United States.

*This list represents only a fraction of the hundreds of job-posting sites and other resources available online; ensure that you check with your school's career centre for the latest information.

TAKE THE INITIATIVE TO FIND OPPORTUNITIES

When it comes to finding the right opportunities, the easiest ways are not always the most productive ones. The major job boards such as Monster and classified services such as Craigslist might have thousands of openings—but many thousands of job seekers are looking at and applying for these same openings. Moreover, posting job openings on these sites is often a company's last resort, after it has exhausted other possibilities.

Instead of searching through the same job openings as everyone else, take the initiative and go find opportunities. Identify the companies you want to work for and focus your efforts on them. Get in touch with their human resources departments (or individual managers, if possible), describe what you can offer the company, and ask to be considered if any opportunities come up.[12] Your message might appear right when a company is busy looking for someone but hasn't yet advertised the opening to the outside world.

An essential task in your job search is presenting your skills and accomplishments in a way that is relevant to the employer's business challenges.

BUILD A NETWORK

Networking is the process of making informal connections with a broad sphere of mutually beneficial business contacts. Networking takes place wherever and whenever people talk, for example, at industry functions, at social gatherings, and all over the Internet, from LinkedIn and Twitter to Facebook and Google+. In addition to making connections through social media tools, you can get yourself noticed by company recruiters. As more candidates get connected and more companies use these media, the percentage of hires found via LinkedIn and other sites is likely to rise.

Don't hesitate to contact interesting companies even if they haven't advertised job openings to the public yet—they might be looking for somebody just like you.

Networking may be perceived as difficult, but it is an essential activity because the vast majority of job openings are never advertised to the general public. To avoid the time and expense of sifting through thousands of applications and the risk of hiring complete strangers, many companies ask their employees for recommendations first.[13] The more people who know you, the better chance you have of being recommended for one of these hidden job openings. Furthermore, leading-edge companies have identified that "network-oriented" individuals contribute to enterprise success through their ability to "build internal and external trust-based relationships."[14] So whether you are trying to get a job or be successful in your current role, knowing how to network effectively is an important skill.

Start thinking like a networker now; your classmates could turn out to be some of your most important business contacts.

Start building your network now. Your classmates could end up being some of your most valuable contacts, if not right away then possibly later in your career. Then branch out by identifying people with similar interests in your target professions, industries, and companies. Follow industry leaders on Twitter. You can also follow individual executives at your target companies to learn about their interests and concerns.[15] Be on the lookout for career-oriented *Tweetups*, in which people who've connected on Twitter get together for in-person networking events. Connect with people on LinkedIn and Facebook, particularly in groups dedicated to particular career interests. Depending on the system and the settings on individual users' accounts, you may be able to introduce yourself via private messages. Just make sure you are respectful of people and don't take up much of their time.[16]

Participate in student business organizations, especially those with ties to professional organizations such as the Canadian Marketing Association or an affiliate of the Canadian Council of Human Resources Associations. Visit

Job fairs are good places to start your job search. How should you prepare to attend a job fair? What should you bring with you? How should you dress?

trade shows that cater to an industry you're interested in. You will learn plenty about that sector of the workplace and meet people who actually work in the industry.[17] Don't overlook volunteering; you not only meet people but also demonstrate your ability to solve problems, plan projects, and lead others. You can do some good while creating a network for yourself.

It's a good idea to have a strategy when attending a networking event. Here are some things to keep in mind:[18]

Networking is a mutually beneficial activity, so look for opportunities to help others in some way.

1. **Identify your objective and who you want to meet.** Why are you attending or participating in the event? Look at the program or guest list and identify who you want to meet; don't just try to collect names. Look at their LinkedIn profiles or websites to learn about them and what they do. Prepare some questions in advance that you can ask these individuals, but don't barrage the people you meet with a lot of requests.

2. **Know what you want to say.** Decide on what you are going to say about yourself: your "story." What will you offer? Prepare your "elevator speech " or "elevator pitch" and briefly offer solutions or ideas. Be succinct and respectful.

3. **Arrive early.** This gives you an opportunity to explore the layout of the room and get comfortable in the environment. If applicable, you can also thank the host for inviting you and talk about what they hope to achieve through the event. See if you can meet the speakers before they present. Your introduction can provide them with a "friendly audience member," and if there is an opportunity you can follow up with them afterward.

4. **Be memorable in a positive way.** Dress appropriately for the event. Be approachable and offer a warm handshake. Don't stand by a crowded bar or hold up the line at the buffet. Be yourself. Offer compliments if appropriate, but don't fawn over the other party. Be sure your business cards are current. When exchanging business cards, acknowledge the other party by showing interest in the information you have just received; notice the company, location, name, and position, and verify the role of the other party. All of these details provide fodder for taking the conversation further.

5. **Follow up and say "Thank you."** Do this with your host and with the people you meet. This can be done in person or through a brief note with an article attached that builds on your recent discussion. Log your contacts by geography, industry, and purpose. Connect with them on LinkedIn and, if appropriate, follow them on Twitter or follow their organizations on LinkedIn. Every so often, check in with them to continue to build relationships.

6. **Be professional and ask for permission.** Don't give out other people's names or contact information without their permission. Networking is not a competition of how many people you know. It is about building trust, so ask questions that will develop the relationship. Focus on what is important to the other person. Ask about "their story." Don't send out your résumé to just anyone. Make sure your "message" is consistent across all communication channels.

7. **Be tech-wise.** Keep your phone ringer turned off or on vibrate. Use your digital device as a resource, not a crutch. If your attention is on reading emails or texting others, you are sending the signal that you are not interested in making real connections. Certainly, there are apps that can capture business card info, and you will likely want to use your digital calendar to check future meeting dates, but keep your time spent checking your device to a minimum.

8. **Practise.** Whether attending a networking event or standing in line at the library or a local coffee shop, take every opportunity to practise your networking skills. Greet the person at the service counter by looking him or her in the eye and smiling when you say hello before you place your order. Suggest a group lunch for your project team. Put down your digital device and get to know someone new during a

class break. Observe how people interact around you. What seems to work to open communication? What seems to hinder communication? Ask your friends, colleagues, and family members about their impression of your "professional image," including your posture, articulation, business card design, résumé, LinkedIn and Facebook pages, and tweets. What message do they send? Are they consistent?

> ### TIPS FOR SUCCESS
> " People mistakenly believe that networking is the art of selling yourself, and it doesn't work when you think it's about you…Networking is successful when the interaction is about the other person. "
>
> Ken Morse, Chairman of Entrepreneurship Ventures

To become a valued network member, you need to be able to help others in some way; think "learning and giving" versus "talking and taking." You may not have any influential contacts yet, but because you're actively researching a number of industries and trends in your own job search, you probably have valuable information you can share via your social networks, blog, or Twitter account. Or you might simply be able to connect one person with another person who can help. The more you network, the more valuable you become in your network—and the more valuable your network becomes to you.

SEEK CAREER COUNSELLING

College and university career and placement offices offer a wide variety of services, including individual counselling, credential services, job fairs, on-campus interviews, and job listings. Counsellors can give you advice on career planning and provide workshops in job-search techniques, résumé preparation, job readiness training, interview techniques, and more.[19] You can also find job counselling online. Many of the websites listed in Table 15–1 offer articles and online tests to help you choose a career path, identify essential skills, and prepare to enter the job market.

Don't overlook the many resources available through your college's or university's career centre.

BE PROFESSIONAL AND CHECK FOR MISTAKES

While you're making all these positive moves to show employers you will be a quality hire, take care to avoid the simple blunders that can ruin a job search, such as not catching mistakes in your résumé, misspelling the name of a manager you're writing to, showing up late for an interview, tweeting something unprofessional, leaving embarrassing images or messages open to public view on your social media accounts, failing to complete application forms correctly, asking for information that you can easily find yourself on a company's website, or making any other error that could flag you as someone who is careless, clueless, or disrespectful. For example, nearly half of all employers now check out candidates' social networking profiles—and a third have rejected candidates because of what they've found there.[20]

To understand why even a minor mistake can hurt your chances, look at the situation from a recruiter's point of view. At one U.S. bank, for example, a recruiter typically has 25 to 30 open positions at any given time.[21] If a hundred people are applying for each position—and the number can be much higher in a slow job market—a single recruiter could be considering 2500 to 3000 candidates at once. As recruiters work to narrow down the possibilities, even a seemingly inconsequential mistake on your part can give them a reason to bump you out of the candidate pool.

You have worked hard to develop a professional image—a "personal brand" demonstrated through your employment portfolio (résumé, projects, videos, etc.), social media posts and images, LinkedIn and Facebook pages, and business cards. Don't let a silly mistake knock you out of contention for a great job. Check for errors or inconsistencies. Do all of your communications send the same message?

1 Planning →	**2 Writing** →	**3 Completing**
Analyze the Situation Recognize that the purpose of your résumé is to get an interview, not to get a job. Research target industries and companies so you know what they're looking for in new hires; learn about various jobs and what to expect; and learn about the hiring manager, if possible. **Gather Information** Use your employment portfolio as a basis, or start from scratch to gather pertinent personal history. **Select the Right Medium** Start with a traditional paper résumé, and develop scannable, electronic plain-text, PDF, and online versions as needed. Consider using PowerPoint and video for your e-portfolio. **Organize the Information** Choose an organizational model that highlights your strengths and addresses shortcomings. Identify the appropriate structure for the industry and the stage of your career.	**Adapt to Your Audience** Plan your wording carefully so that you can catch a recruiter's eye within seconds; translate your education and experience into attributes that target employers find valuable. **Compose the Message** Write clearly and succinctly, using active, powerful language that is appropriate for the target audience and is accurate; use a professional tone in all communications.	**Revise the Message** Evaluate content and review readability, and then edit and rewrite for conciseness and clarity. **Produce the Message** Use effective design elements and suitable layout for a clean, professional appearance; seamlessly combine text and graphical elements. When printing, use quality paper and a good printer. **Proofread the Message** Review for errors in layout, spelling, and mechanics; mistakes can cost you interview opportunities. Check that your message and style is consistent across all communication platforms you are using (e.g., LinkedIn, Facebook), including your e-portfolio, if you have chosen to use one as part of your job-search strategy. **Distribute the Message** Deliver your résumé, carefully following the specific instructions of each employer or job board website. Keep the résumé current by updating it regularly along with your online presence.

Figure 15–2 Three-Step Writing Process for Résumés

Planning a Résumé

Although you will create many messages during your career search, your résumé will be the most important document in this process. You will be able to use it directly in many instances, adapt it to a variety of uses such as an e-portfolio, and reuse pieces of it in social networking profiles and online application forms.

Writing a résumé is one of those projects that really benefits from multiple planning, writing, and completing sessions spread out over several days or weeks. You are trying to summarize a complex subject (yourself!) and present a compelling story to complete strangers in a brief document. Follow the three-step writing process (see Figure 15–2) and give yourself plenty of time. Remember to pay particular attention to the "you" attitude and presentation quality; your résumé will probably get tossed aside if it doesn't speak to audience needs or if it contains mistakes.

ANALYZE YOUR PURPOSE AND AUDIENCE

Once you view your résumé as a persuasive business message, it's easier to decide what should and shouldn't be in it.

A **résumé** is a structured, written summary of a person's education, employment background, and job qualifications. Before you begin writing a résumé, make sure you understand its true function—as a brief, persuasive business

Table 15–2	**Fallacies and Facts about Résumés**
Fallacy	**Fact**
The purpose of a résumé is to list all your skills and abilities.	The purpose of a résumé is to kindle interest and generate an interview.
A good résumé will get you the job you want.	All a résumé can do is get you in the door.
Your résumé will be read carefully and thoroughly.	In most cases, your résumé needs to make a positive impression within 30 or 45 seconds; only then will someone read it in detail. Moreover, it may be screened by a computer looking for keywords first, and if it doesn't contain the right keywords, a human being may never see it.
The more good information you present about yourself in your résumé, the better.	Recruiters don't need that much information about you at the initial screening stage, and they probably won't read it.
If you want a really good résumé, have it prepared by a résumé service.	You have the skills needed to prepare an effective résumé, so prepare it yourself—unless the position is especially high-level or specialized. Even then, check industry practices and qualify the service before using it.

message intended to stimulate an employer's interest in meeting you and learning more about you (see Table 15–2). In other words, the purpose of a résumé is not to get you a job but rather to get you an interview.[22]

As you conduct your research on various professions, industries, companies, and individual managers, you will have a better perspective on your target readers and their information needs. Learn as much as you can about the individuals who may be reading your résumé. Many professionals and managers are bloggers, Twitter users, and LinkedIn members, for example, so you can learn more about them online even if you've never met them. Any bit of information can help you craft a more effective message.

The term curriculum vitae (CV) *essentially refers to a résumé but, depending on the profession, a CV can contain more details.*

GATHER PERTINENT INFORMATION

Gather your pertinent personal history, including all the specific dates, duties, and accomplishments of any previous jobs you've held. Compile relevant educational experience that adds to your qualifications—formal degrees, skills certificates, academic awards, or scholarships. Also, gather any information about school or volunteer activities that might be relevant to your job search, including offices you may have held in a club or professional organization, or presentations you might have given to a community group. You probably won't use every piece of information you come up with, but you'll want to have it at your fingertips before you begin composing your résumé.

Include the information in your employment portfolio as part of your research.

SELECT THE BEST MEDIUM

You should expect to produce your résumé in several media and formats. "Produce Your Résumé" later in this chapter explores the various options.

ORGANIZE YOUR RÉSUMÉ AROUND YOUR STRENGTHS

Although there are a number of ways to organize a résumé, most are some variation of chronological, functional, or a combination of the two. The right choice depends on your background and your goals, as the following sections explain.

3 LEARNING OBJECTIVE

Discuss how to choose the appropriate résumé organization and length.

THE CHRONOLOGICAL RÉSUMÉ In a **chronological résumé**, the work-experience section dominates and is placed immediately after your contact information and introductory statement. The chronological approach is the most common way to organize a résumé, and many employers prefer this format because it

The chronological résumé is the most common approach, but it might not be right for you at a particular stage in your career.

presents your professional history in a clear, easy-to-follow arrangement.[23] If you're just graduating from college or university with limited professional experience, you can vary this chronological approach by putting your educational qualifications before your experience.

Develop your work experience section by listing your jobs in reverse chronological order, beginning with the most recent one and giving more space to the most recent positions. For each job, start by listing the employer's name and location, your official job title, and the dates you held the position (write "to present" if you are still in your most recent job). Next, in a short block of text, highlight your accomplishments in a way that is relevant to your readers. Doing so may require "translating" the terminology used in a particular industry or profession into terms that are more meaningful to your target readers. If the general responsibilities of the position are not obvious from the job title, provide a little background to help readers understand what you did.

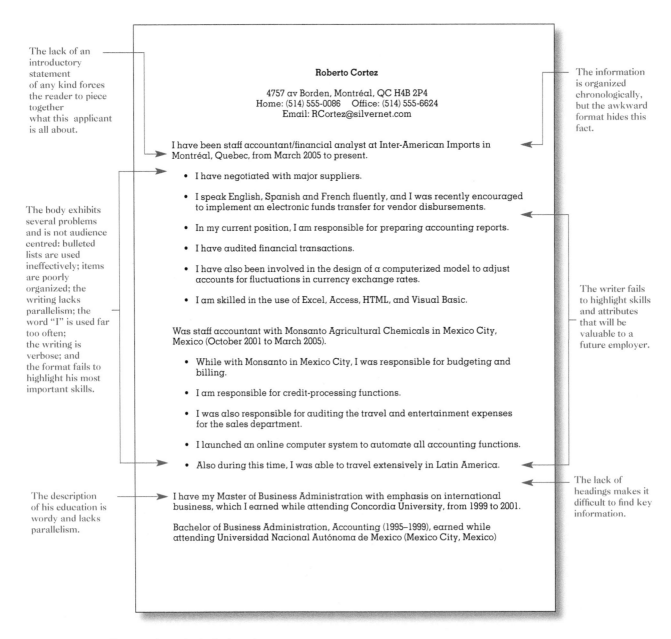

Figure 15–3 Ineffective Chronological Résumé

The chronological approach is especially appropriate if you have a strong employment history and are aiming for a job that builds on your current career path. This is the case for Roberto Cortez. Compare the ineffective and effective versions of Cortez's résumé in Figures 15–3 and 15–4. What impression do you get when reading these resumes? What roles do language, tone, and format play in making this impression? How easy is it to find key information?

THE FUNCTIONAL RÉSUMÉ A **functional résumé**, sometimes called a *skills résumé*, emphasizes your skills and capabilities while identifying employers and academic experience in subordinate sections. This arrangement stresses individual areas of competence rather than job history. The functional approach also has three advantages: (1) Without having to read through job descriptions, employers can see what you can do for them; (2) you can emphasize earlier job experience; and (3) you can de-emphasize any lengthy unemployment or lack of career progress. However, you should be aware that because the functional résumé can obscure your work history, many employment professionals are suspicious of it.[24] If you don't believe the chronological format will work for you, consider the combination résumé instead.

The functional résumé is considered by people with limited or spotty employment history, but many employers are suspicious of this format.

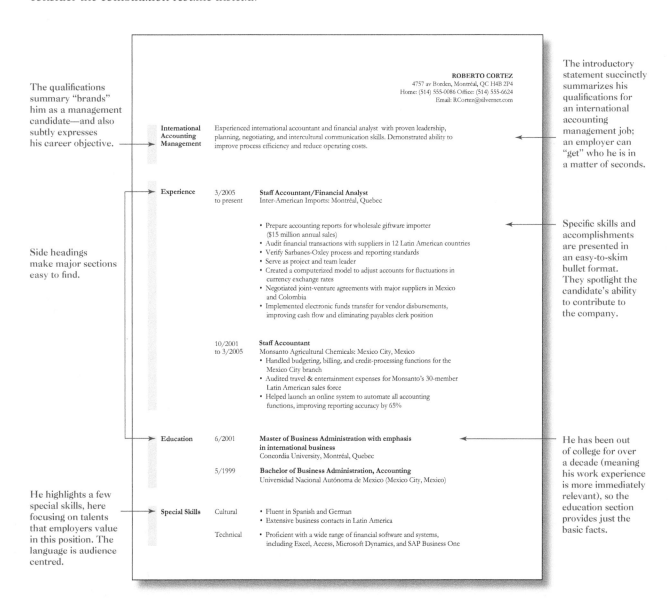

Figure 15–4 Effective Chronological Résumé

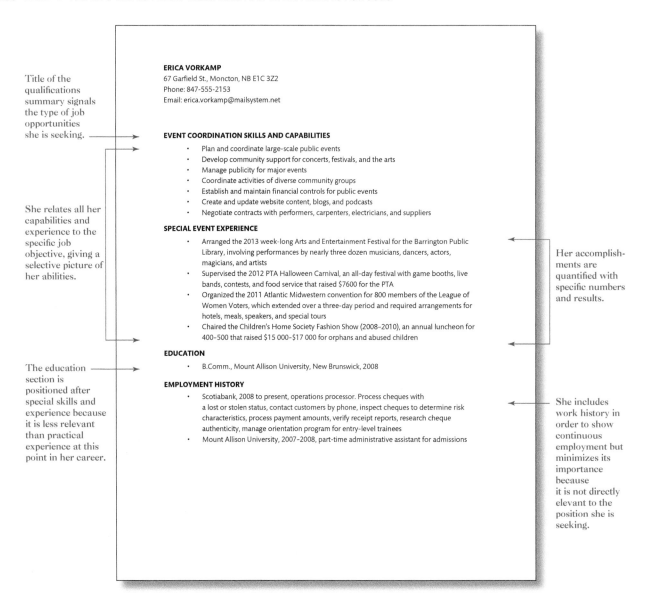

Title of the qualifications summary signals the type of job opportunities she is seeking.

She relates all her capabilities and experience to the specific job objective, giving a selective picture of her abilities.

The education section is positioned after special skills and experience because it is less relevant than practical experience at this point in her career.

ERICA VORKAMP
67 Garfield St., Moncton, NB E1C 3Z2
Phone: 847-555-2153
Email: erica.vorkamp@mailsystem.net

EVENT COORDINATION SKILLS AND CAPABILITIES
- Plan and coordinate large-scale public events
- Develop community support for concerts, festivals, and the arts
- Manage publicity for major events
- Coordinate activities of diverse community groups
- Establish and maintain financial controls for public events
- Create and update website content, blogs, and podcasts
- Negotiate contracts with performers, carpenters, electricians, and suppliers

SPECIAL EVENT EXPERIENCE
- Arranged the 2013 week-long Arts and Entertainment Festival for the Barrington Public Library, involving performances by nearly three dozen musicians, dancers, actors, magicians, and artists
- Supervised the 2012 PTA Halloween Carnival, an all-day festival with game booths, live bands, contests, and food service that raised $7600 for the PTA
- Organized the 2011 Atlantic Midwestern convention for 800 members of the League of Women Voters, which extended over a three-day period and required arrangements for hotels, meals, speakers, and special tours
- Chaired the Children's Home Society Fashion Show (2008–2010), an annual luncheon for 400–500 that raised $15 000–$17 000 for orphans and abused children

EDUCATION
- B.Comm., Mount Allison University, New Brunswick, 2008

EMPLOYMENT HISTORY
- Scotiabank, 2008 to present, operations processor. Process cheques with a lost or stolen status, contact customers by phone, inspect cheques to determine risk characteristics, process payment amounts, verify receipt reports, research cheque authenticity, manage orientation program for entry-level trainees
- Mount Allison University, 2007–2008, part-time administrative assistant for admissions

Her accomplishments are quantified with specific numbers and results.

She includes work history in order to show continuous employment but minimizes its importance because it is not directly elevant to the position she is seeking.

Figure 15–5 Combination Résumé

If you don't have a lot of work history to show, consider a combination résumé to highlight your skills while still providing a chronological history of your employment.

THE COMBINATION RÉSUMÉ A **combination résumé** meshes the skills focus of the functional format with the job history focus of the chronological format. The chief advantage of this format is that it allows you to focus attention on your capabilities when you don't have a long or steady employment history, without raising concerns that you might be hiding something about your past.

With her limited work experience in her field of interest, Erica Vorkamp opted for a combination résumé to highlight her skills (see Figure 15–5). Her employment history is complete and easy to find, but it isn't featured to the same degree as the other elements. Notice how she uses the title of the introductory statement to identify the job opportunities she is looking for.

As you look at a number of sample résumés, you'll probably notice many variations on the three basic formats presented here. Study these other options and choose one that seems like the best fit for your unique situation.

Once you have chosen your résumé format, you will also want to decide on length. Kim Isaacs, résumé expert at Monster.com, recommends a few factors to consider when deciding on résumé length: career objective, industry, work experience and accomplishments, and education and training. For example, if you have less than 10 years' experience, have worked for only two employers, or are planning to make a significant change in occupation, you will most likely use a one-page résumé. If you have 10+ years of experience, are in a higher-level position, or are working in a technical field where your list of achievements could include publications, speaking engagements, or patents, you may need more pages to highlight your experience.[25]

ADDRESS AREAS OF CONCERN

Many people have gaps in their careers or other issues that could be a concern for employers. Here are some common issues and suggestions for handling them in a résumé:[26]

- **Frequent job changes.** If you've had a number of short-term jobs of a similar type, such as independent contracting and temporary assignments, try to group them under a single heading. Also, if past job positions were eliminated as a result of layoffs or mergers, find a subtle way to convey that information (if not in your résumé, then in your cover letter). Reasonable employers understand that many professionals have been forced to job hop by circumstances beyond their control.
- **Gaps in work history.** Mention relevant experience and education you gained during employment gaps, such as volunteer or community work.
- **Inexperience.** Mention related volunteer work and membership in professional groups. List relevant course work and internships.
- **Overqualification.** Tone down your résumé, focusing exclusively on the experience and skills that relate to the position.
- **Long-term employment with one company.** Itemize each position held at the firm to show both professional growth and career growth within the organization and increasing responsibilities along the way.
- **Job termination for cause.** Be honest with interviewers and address their concerns with proof, such as recommendations and examples of completed projects.

Frequent job changes and gaps in your work history are two of the more common issues that employers may perceive as weaknesses.

Writing a Résumé

Your résumé is one of the most important documents you'll ever write. Follow the three-step process and help ensure success by remembering four key points:

- **First, treat your résumé with the respect it deserves.** A single mistake or oversight can cost you interview opportunities.
- **Second, give yourself plenty of time.** Don't put off preparing your résumé until the last second and then try to write it in one sitting.
- **Third, learn from good models.** You can find sample résumés online at job sites such as Monster.ca.
- **Fourth, don't get frustrated by the conflicting advice you'll read about résumés.** Résumés are more art than science. Consider the alternatives and choose the approach that makes the most sense to you, given everything you know about successful business communication.

If you feel uncomfortable writing about yourself, you're not alone. Many people, even accomplished writers, find it difficult to write their own résumés. If you get stuck, find a classmate or friend who is also writing a résumé and swap projects for a while. By working on each other's résumés, you might be able to speed up the process for both of you.

KEEP YOUR RÉSUMÉ HONEST

Résumé fraud has reached epidemic proportions, but employers are fighting back with more rigorous screening techniques.

Estimates vary, but one comprehensive study uncovered lies about work history in more than 40 percent of the résumés tested.[27] And dishonest applicants are getting bolder all the time—going so far as to buy fake diplomas online, pay computer hackers to insert their names into prestigious universities' graduation records, and sign up for services that offer phony employment verification.[28]

Applicants with integrity know they don't need to stoop to lying. If you are tempted to stretch the truth, bear in mind that professional recruiters have seen every trick, and frustrated employers are working aggressively to uncover the truth. Nearly all employers do some form of background checking, from contacting references and verifying employment to checking criminal records and sending résumés through verification services.[29] Employers are also beginning to craft certain interview questions specifically to uncover dishonest résumé entries.[30]

More than 90 percent of companies that find lies on résumés refuse to hire the offending applicants, even if that means withdrawing formal job offers.[31] And if you do sneak past these filters and get hired, you'll probably be exposed on the job when you can't live up to your own résumé. Given the networked nature of today's job market, lying on a résumé could haunt you for years—and could force you to keep lying throughout your career to hide the original misrepresentations on your résumé.[32]

ADAPT YOUR RÉSUMÉ TO YOUR AUDIENCE

Translate your past accomplishments into a compelling picture of what you can do for employers in the future.

The importance of adapting your résumé to your target readers' needs and interests cannot be overstated. In a competitive job market, the more you look like a good fit, the better your chances of securing interviews. Address your readers' business concerns by showing how your capabilities meet the demands and expectations of the position and of the organization as a whole. For example, if you are applying for work in public relations (PR), you would need to know that an internal corporate PR department and an independent PR agency perform many of the same tasks, but the outside agency must also sell its services to multiple clients. Consequently, it needs employees who are skilled at attracting and keeping paying customers, in addition to being skilled at PR.

Adapting to your readers can mean customizing your résumé, sometimes for each job opening. However, the effort can pay off in more interviewing opportunities.

Military service and other specialized experiences may need to be "translated" into terms more readily understandable by your target readers.

Use what you've learned about your target readers to express your experience using the terminology of the hiring organization. For example, military experience can develop a number of skills that are valuable in business, but military terminology can sound like a foreign language to people who aren't familiar with it. Isolate the important general concepts, and present them in common business language. Similarly, educational achievements in other countries might not align with the standard Canadian definitions of high schools, colleges, polytechnics, and universities. If necessary, include a brief statement explaining how your degree or certificate relates to Canadian expectations—or how your Canadian degree relates to expectations in other countries, if you're applying for work abroad.

COMPOSE YOUR RÉSUMÉ

Draft your résumé using short, crisp phrases built around strong verbs and nouns.

Write your résumé using a simple and direct style. Use short, crisp phrases instead of whole sentences, and focus on what your reader needs to know. Avoid using the word *I*, which can sound both self-involved and repetitious by the time you outline all your skills and accomplishments. Instead, start your phrases with strong action verbs such as these:[33]

accomplished	achieved	administered	approved	arranged
assisted	assumed	budgeted	chaired	changed
complied	completed	coordinated	created	demonstrated
developed	directed	established	explored	forecast
generated	identified	implemented	improved	initiated
installed	introduced	investigated	joined	launched
maintained	managed	motivated	operated	organized
oversaw	participated	performed	planned	presented
proposed	raised	recommended	reduced	reorganized
resolved	saved	served	set up	simplified
sparked	streamlined	strengthened	succeeded	supervised
systematized	targeted	trained	transformed	upgraded

For example, you might say, "Created a campus organization for students interested in entrepreneurship" or "Managed a fast-food restaurant and four employees." Whenever you can, quantify the results so that your claims don't come across as empty puffery. Don't just say you're a team player or detail oriented—show who you are by offering concrete proof.[34] Here are some additional examples of how to phrase your accomplishments using active statements that show results:

Avoid Weak Statements	Use Active Statements That Show Results
Responsible for developing a new filing system	Developed a new filing system that reduced paperwork by 50 percent
I was in charge of customer complaints and all ordering problems.	Handled all customer complaints and resolved all product order discrepancies, resulting in a 15 percent increase in customer loyalty
I won a trip to Europe for opening the most new customer accounts in my department.	Generated the highest number of new customer accounts in my department
Member of special campus task force to resolve student problems with existing cafeteria assignments	Assisted in implementing new campus dining program that balances student wishes with cafeteria capacity

Providing specific supporting evidence is vital, but make sure you don't go overboard with small details.[35]

In addition to clear writing with specific examples, the particular words and phrases you use throughout your résumé are critically important. The majority of résumés are now subjected to *keyword searches* in an applicant tracking system (ATS) or other database, in which a recruiter searches for résumés most likely to match the requirements of a particular job. Résumés that don't match the requirements closely may never be seen by a human reader, so it is essential to use the words and phrases that a recruiter is most likely to search for. (Although most experts used to advise including a separate *keyword summary* as a standalone list, the trend nowadays is to incorporate your keywords into your introductory statement and other sections of your résumé.)[36]

Identifying these keywords requires some research, but you can uncover many of them while you are researching various industries and companies.

Include relevant *keywords* in your introductory statement, work history, and education sections.

The trick is to study job descriptions carefully and to understand your target audience's needs. In contrast to the action verbs that catch a human reader's attention, keywords that catch a computer's attention are usually nouns that describe the specific skills, attributes, and experiences an employer is looking for in a candidate. Keywords can include the business and technical terms associated with a specific profession, industry-specific jargon, names or types of products or systems used in a profession, job titles, and university and college degrees.[37] Finally, beware of clichés that are used on so many résumés and social media profiles that they've probably lost most of their impact. For example, LinkedIn issues an annual list of 10 buzzwords and phrases that are overused in attempts to attract recruiters or build a network. In 2010, the list included *extensive experience, innovative, motivated, results-oriented, dynamic, proven track record, team player, fast-paced, problem solver,* and *entrepreneurial.*[38] In 2017, the top 10 overused buzzwords were *specialized, leadership, passionate, strategic, experienced, focused, expert, certified, creative,* and *excellent.*[39] Although some of the words have changed, the approach that will make your profile or résumé stand out remains the same. For example, instead of just saying you are passionate, demonstrate this by providing evidence of what you have to offer. Do this consistently across all of your communication platforms and your target reader will be more inclined to pay attention.

5 **LEARNING OBJECTIVE**

Outline the major sections of a traditional résumé.

Be sure to provide complete and accurate contact information. If you are posting a résumé in an unsecured online location, leave out your physical address for security purposes.

Get a professional-sounding email address for business correspondence (such as firstname.lastname@ something.com), if you don't already have one.

You can choose to open with a career objective, a qualifications summary, or a career summary.

NAME AND CONTACT INFORMATION Your name and contact information constitute the heading of your résumé, so include the following:

- Your name
- Physical address (both permanent and temporary if you're likely to move during the job-search process; however, if you're posting a résumé in an unsecured location online, leave out your physical address for security purposes)
- Email address—make sure it is professional
- Phone number(s)
- The URL of your personal webpage, e-portfolio, or social media résumé (if you have one)

Be sure that everything in your résumé heading is well organized and clearly laid out on the page.

If the only email address you have is through your current employer, get a free personal email address from one of the many services that offer them. It's not fair to your current employer to use company resources for a job search, and it sends a bad signal to potential employers. Also, if your personal email address is anything like precious.princess@something.com or HeyMe@something.com, get a new email address for your business correspondence.

INTRODUCTORY STATEMENT Of all the parts of a résumé, the brief introductory statement that follows your name and contact information probably generates the most disagreement. You have three choices here:[40]

- **Career objective.** A career objective identifies either a specific job you want to land or a general career track you would like to pursue. Some experts advise against including a career objective because it can categorize you so narrowly that you miss out on interesting opportunities, and it is essentially about fulfilling your desires, not about meeting the employer's needs. In the past, most résumés included a career objective, but in recent years more job seekers are using a qualifications summary or a career summary. However, if you have little or no work experience in your target profession, a career objective might be your best option. If you do opt for an objective, word it in a way that relates your qualifications to employer needs:

A software position in a growing company requiring international experience.

Advertising assistant with print media emphasis requiring strong customer-contact skills.

Avoid such self-absorbed statements as "A fulfilling position that provides ample opportunity for career growth and personal satisfaction."

- **Qualifications summary.** A qualifications summary offers a brief view of your key qualifications. The goal is to let a reader know within a few seconds what you can deliver. You can title this section generically as "Qualifications Summary" or "Summary of Qualifications," Consider using a qualifications summary if you have one or more important qualifications but don't yet have a long career history:

Summary of qualifications: Ten years of experience in commission selling, consistently meeting or exceeding sales goals through creative lead generation, effective closing techniques, and solid customer service.

> If you have a reasonably focused skill set but don't yet have a long career history, a qualifications summary is probably the best type of introductory statement for you.

Also, if you haven't been working long but your university or college education has given you a dominant professional "theme," such as multimedia design or statistical analysis, you can craft a qualifications summary that highlights your educational preparedness.

- **Career summary.** A career summary offers a brief recap of your career, with the goal of presenting increasing levels of responsibility and performance. A career summary can be particularly useful for executives who have demonstrated the ability to manage increasingly larger and more complicated business operations—a key consideration when companies look to hire upper-level managers. If you have decided to include this in your résumé, identify which qualifications your targeted employers have ranked as most important, and write about your experience, education, and specials skills that match these.

EDUCATION If you're still in school, education is probably your strongest selling point. Present your educational background in depth, choosing facts that support your "theme." Give this section a heading such as "Education," "Technical Training," or "Academic Preparation," as appropriate. Then, starting with the most recent, list the name and location of each school you attended, the month and year of your graduation (say "anticipated graduation in _____" if you haven't graduated yet), your major and minor fields of study, significant skills and abilities you've developed in your course work, and the degrees or certificates you've earned. If you're still working toward a degree, include in parentheses the expected date of completion. Showcase your qualifications by listing

Remember to check your college or university's career office for help in writing your résumé. Why is it important to speak with a career expert at your school?

If you are early in your career, your education is probably your strongest selling point.

courses that have directly equipped you for the job you are seeking, and indicate any scholarships, awards, or academic honours you've received.

The education section should also include off-campus training sponsored by business or government. Include any relevant seminars or workshops you've attended, as well as the certificates or other documents you've received. Mention high school only if the associated achievements are pertinent to your career goals.

Whether you list your grade-point average (GPA) depends on the job you want and the quality of your grades. If you choose to show a grade-point average, ensure that you mention the scale, especially if a five-point scale is used instead of a four-point scale. If you don't show your GPA on your résumé—and there's no rule saying you have to—be prepared to answer questions about it during the interview process because many employers will assume that your GPA is not spectacular if you didn't show it on your résumé. If your grades are better within your major than in other courses, you can also list your GPA as "Major GPA" and include only those courses within your major.

WORK EXPERIENCE, SKILLS, AND ACCOMPLISHMENTS Like the education section, the work experience should focus on your overall theme in a way that shows how your past can contribute to an employer's future. Use keywords to draw attention to the skills you've developed on the job and to your ability to handle increasing responsibility.

When you describe past job responsibilities, identify the skills and knowledge that you can apply to a future job.

List your jobs in reverse chronological order, starting with the most recent. Include military service and any internships and part-time or temporary jobs related to your career objective. Include the name and location of the employer, and if readers are unlikely to recognize the organization, briefly describe what it does. When you want to keep the name of your current employer confidential, you can identify the firm by industry only ("a large video game developer"). If an organization's name or location has changed since you worked there, state the current name and location and include the old information preceded by "formerly. . . ." Before or after each job listing, state your job title and give the years you worked in the job; use the phrase "to present" to denote current employment. Indicate whether a job was part time.

Devote the most space to jobs that are related to your target position.

Devote the most space to the jobs that are related to your target position. If you were personally responsible for significant achievements, be sure to mention it ("Devised a new collection system that accelerated payment of overdue receivables"). Facts about your skills and accomplishments are the most important information you can give a prospective employer, so quantify them whenever possible:

Whenever you can, quantify your accomplishments in numerical terms: sales increases, customer satisfaction scores, measured productivity, and so on.

Designed a new ad that increased sales by 9 percent.
Raised $2500 in 15 days for cancer research.

One helpful exercise is to write a 30-second "commercial" for each major skill you want to highlight. The commercial should offer proof that you really do possess the skill. For your résumé, distill the commercials down to brief phrases; you can use the more detailed proof statements in cover letters and as answers to interview questions.[41]

If you have had a number of part-time, temporary, or entry-level jobs that don't relate to your career objective, you have to use your best judgment when it comes to including or excluding them. Too many minor and irrelevant work details can clutter your résumé, particularly if you've been in the professional workforce for a few years. However, if you don't have a long employment history, including these jobs shows your ability and willingness to keep working.

You may also include information describing other aspects of your background that pertain to your career objective, such as fluency in another language. If you have an array of special skills, group them together and include them near your education or work-experience section. You might categorize such additional information as "Special Skills," "Work-Related Skills," "Other Experience," "Language Skills," or "Computer Skills." If samples of your work might increase your chances of getting the job, insert a line at the end of your résumé offering to supply them on request, or indicate they're available in your e-portfolio.

ACTIVITIES AND ACHIEVEMENTS Many employers look beyond your formal employment to assess your total character and personality. Your activities and achievements outside work speak volumes about who you are and what you value. Use this section to list volunteer activities that demonstrate important abilities such as leadership, organization, teamwork, and cooperation. Emphasize career-related activities such as "member of the Student Marketing Association." List skills you learned in these activities and explain how these skills are related to your target job. Include speaking, writing, or tutoring experience; participation in athletics or creative projects; fundraising or community-service activities; and offices held in academic or professional organizations.

Note any awards you've received. Again, quantify your achievements whenever possible. Instead of saying that you addressed various student groups, state how many and the approximate audience sizes. If your activities have been extensive, you may want to group them into divisions such as "School Activities," "Community Service," "Professional Associations," "Seminars and Workshops," and "Speaking Activities."

> Include personal accomplishments that indicate special skills or qualities, but ensure that they are relevant to the jobs you're seeking.

PERSONAL DATA AND REFERENCES The question of what personal data to provide is a common source of confusion with résumés. Most experts advise you to skip personal interests unless including them enhances the employer's understanding of why you would be the best candidate for the job.[42] Just make sure that any personal interests and accomplishments relate to the employer's business, culture, or customers. For example, your achievements as an amateur artist could appeal to an advertising agency, even if you're applying for a technical or business position, because it shows an appreciation for the creative process. Similarly, an interest in sports and outdoor activities could show that you'll fit in nicely at a company such as Mountain Equipment Co-op.

Some information is best excluded from your résumé. Human rights legislation prohibits employers from discriminating on the basis of gender, marital or family status, age, race, colour, religion, national origin, and physical or mental disability. So ensure that you exclude any items that could encourage discrimination, even subconsciously. Experts also recommend excluding salary information, reasons for leaving jobs, and personal identification codes; save these items for the interview and then offer them only if the employer specifically requests them. Supply your social insurance number only when you are offered the job and are completing the required Canada Revenue Agency and company benefit forms.

The availability of references is usually assumed, so you don't necessarily need to put "References available upon request" at the end of your résumé. Whether you include this line or not, be sure to have a list of several references available when you begin applying for jobs. You will probably be asked for it at some point in the selection process. Prepare your reference sheet with your name and contact information at the top. For a finished look, use the same design and layout you use at the top of your résumé. Then list three or four people who have agreed to serve as references. (Don't list anyone who hasn't agreed to be listed.) Include each person's name, job title, organization, address, telephone number, and email address (if the reference prefers to be contacted by email).

Completing a Résumé

Completing your résumé involves revising it for optimum quality, producing it in the various forms and media you'll need, and proofreading it for any errors before distributing it or publishing it online. Producing and distributing a résumé used to be fairly straightforward: you printed it on quality paper and mailed or faxed it to employers. However, the advent of **applicant tracking systems** or **ATSs** (databases that let managers sort through incoming applications to find the most promising candidates), social media, and other innovations has dramatically changed the nature of résumé production and distribution. Be prepared to produce several versions of your résumé, in multiple formats and multiple media.

Most of your application efforts will take place online, but starting with a traditional paper résumé is still useful.

Even if most or all of your application efforts take place online, starting with a traditional paper résumé is still useful, for several reasons. First, a traditional printed résumé is a great opportunity to organize your background information and identify your unique strengths. Second, the planning and writing tasks involved in creating a conventional résumé will help you generate blocks of text that you can reuse in multiple ways throughout the job-search process. Third, you'll never know when someone might ask for your résumé during a networking event or other in-person encounter, and you don't want to let that interest fade in the time it might take for the person to get to your information online.

REVISE YOUR RÉSUMÉ

Avoid the common errors that will get your résumé excluded from consideration.

Ask professional recruiters to list the most common mistakes they see on résumés, and you'll hear the same complaints over and over again. Keep your résumé out of the recycling bin by avoiding these flaws:

- **Too long.** The résumé is not concise, relevant, and to the point.
- **Too short or sketchy.** The résumé does not give enough information for a proper evaluation of the applicant.
- **Hard to read.** The résumé lacks enough white space and devices such as indentions and boldfacing to make the reader's job easier, or the print is faint.
- **Inconsistent.** The résumé appears to have been written by someone other than the applicant, which raises the question of whether the qualifications have been exaggerated.
- **Amateurish.** The résumé includes the wrong information or presents it awkwardly, or the paper is cheap and inappropriate, which indicates that the applicant has little understanding of the business world or of a particular industry.
- **Misspelled words and ungrammatical writing throughout.** The document contains mistakes that indicate the candidate lacks the verbal skills that are so important on the job.
- **Boastful.** The overconfident tone makes the reader wonder whether the applicant's self-evaluation is realistic.
- **Gimmicky.** The words, structure, decoration, or material used in the résumé depart so far from the usual as to make the résumé ineffective.

PRODUCE YOUR RÉSUMÉ

Effective résumé designs are simple, clean, and professional—not gaudy, clever, or cute. Keep in mind that complex layouts can confuse applicant tracking sytems and render your information illegible.

No matter how many media and formats you eventually choose for producing your résumé, a clean, professional-looking design is a must. Unless you have some experience in graphic design and you're applying in a field such as advertising or retail merchandising, where visual creativity is viewed as an asset, resist the urge to "get creative" with your résumé layout.[43] Recruiters and hiring managers want to skim your essential information in a matter of seconds, and anything that distracts or delays them will work against you. Moreover, complex layouts can confuse an applicant tracking system, which can result in your information getting garbled.

Fortunately, good résumé design is not difficult to achieve. As you can see in Figures 15–4 and 15–5, good designs feature simplicity, order, plenty of white space, and clear typefaces. If your résumé will be viewed online in any format, use a typeface such as Georgia, which was designed for onscreen display, rather than the traditional Times New Roman, which was designed for printing and doesn't render as sharply on screen.[44] Make subheadings easy to find and easy to read, placing them either above each section or in the left margin. Use lists to itemize your most important qualifications. Colour is not necessary by any means, but if you add colour, make it subtle and sophisticated, such as a thin horizontal line under your name and address. If any part of the design "jumps out at you," tone it down. The most common way to get into trouble with résumé design is going overboard. The résumé in Figure 15–6 tries too hard to be creative and eye-catching, resulting in a document that is difficult to read—and that probably won't get read. Recruiters have seen every conceivable design gimmick, so don't try to stand out from the crowd with unusual design. Instead, provide compelling, employer-focused information that is easy to find.

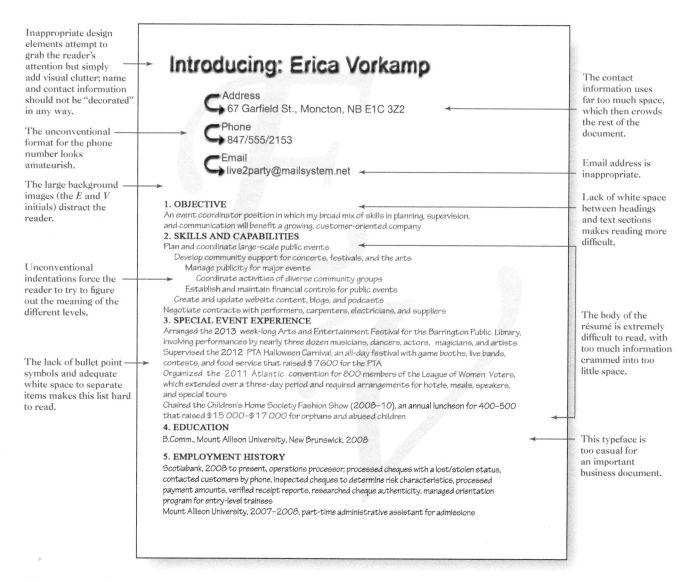

Figure 15–6 Ineffective Résumé Design

Job recruiters can receive hundreds of résumés a month. A well-formatted résumé makes their job easier and helps yours get noticed. How much time have you put into résumé preparation? What techniques can you use to streamline the process?

Steve Gorton/Dorling Kindersley, Ltd.

Be prepared to produce several versions of your résumé in multiple media.

Depending on the companies you apply to, you might want to produce your résumé in as many as six formats (all are explained in the following sections):

- Printed traditional résumé
- Printed scannable résumé
- Electronic plain-text file
- Microsoft Word file
- PDF file
- Online résumé, also called a *multimedia résumé* or *social media résumé*

Most of these versions are easy to create, as you'll see in the following sections.

Unfortunately, there is no single format or medium that works for all the situations you will encounter, and employer expectations continue to change as technology evolves. Find out what each employer or job posting website expects, and provide your résumé in that specific format but keep the following in mind:

Photos: For print or electronic documents that you will be submitting to employers or job websites, the safest advice is to avoid photos. Visual cues of the age, ethnicity, and gender of candidates early in the selection process exposes employers to complaints of discriminatory hiring practices. In fact, some employers won't even look at résumés that include photos, and some applicant tracking systems automatically discard résumés with any kind of extra files.[45] However, photographs are acceptable for social media résumés and other online formats where you are not actually submitting a résumé to an employer.

PowerPoint résumé: In addition to the six main formats, some applicants create PowerPoint presentations, videos, or even infographics to supplement a conventional résumé. Two key advantages of a PowerPoint résumé are the flexibility and multimedia capabilities. For instance, you can present a menu of choices on the opening screen and allow viewers to click through to sections of interest. (Note that most of the things you can accomplish with PowerPoint can be done with an online résumé, which is probably more convenient for most readers.)

Video résumé: Depending on your field of interest, a video résumé can be a compelling supplement. Be aware that some employment law experts advise employers not to view videos, at least not until after candidates have been evaluated solely on their credentials. The reason for this caution is the same as with photographs. In addition, videos are more cumbersome to evaluate than paper or electronic résumés, and some recruiters refuse to watch them.[46] However, if you decide to create one, dress professionally and keep the video to three minutes or less.

Infographic résumé: An infographic résumé attempts to convey a person's career development and skill set graphically through a visual metaphor such as a timeline or subway map or as a poster with an array of individual elements. A well-designed infographic could be an intriguing element of the job-search package for candidates in certain situations and professions because it can definitely stand out from traditional résumés and can show a high level of skill in visual communication, especially if you're applying for work in a graphics or design-related field. However, infographics are likely to be incompatible with most applicant tracking systems and with the screening habits of most recruiters, so you might get tossed out if you try to use an infographic in place of a conventional résumé. In addition, successful infographics require skills in graphical design, and if you lack those skills, you'll need to hire a designer.

If you're applying in other fields, consider whether a visual approach might help you stand out or communicate key strengths in ways that a conventional résumé can't. In virtually every situation, however, an infographic should complement a conventional résumé, not replace it. A quick search online will provide insight into the many interesting ways in which others are using infographics.

PRODUCING A TRADITIONAL PRINTED RÉSUMÉ The traditional paper résumé still has a place in this world of electronic job searches, if only to have a few ready whenever one of your networking contacts asks for a copy. Avoid basic, low-cost white bond paper intended for general office use and gimmicky papers with borders and backgrounds. Choose a heavier, higher-quality paper designed specifically for résumés and other important documents. White or slightly off-white is the best colour choice. This paper is more expensive, but you don't need much, and it's a worthwhile investment.

> Use high-quality paper when printing your résumé.

When you're ready to print your résumé, find a well-maintained, quality printer. Don't tolerate any streaks, stray lines, or poor print quality. You wouldn't walk into an interview looking messy, so make sure your résumé doesn't look that way, either.

PRINTING A SCANNABLE RÉSUMÉ You might encounter a company that prefers *scannable résumés*, a type of printed résumé that is specially formatted to be compatible with optical scanning systems that convert printed documents to electronic text. These systems were quite common just a few years ago, but their use appears to be declining rapidly as more employers prefer email delivery or website application forms.[47] A scannable résumé differs from the traditional format in two major ways: it should always include a keyword summary, and it should be formatted in a simpler fashion that avoids underlining, special characters, and other elements that can confuse the scanning system. If you need to produce a scannable résumé, search online for "formatting a scannable résumé" to get detailed instructions.

> Some employers still prefer résumés in scannable format, but most now want electronic submissions.

CREATING A PLAIN-TEXT FILE OF YOUR RÉSUMÉ A *plain-text file* (sometimes known as an ASCII text file) is an electronic version of your résumé that has no font formatting, no bullet symbols, no colours, and no lines or boxes or other special formatting. The plain-text version can be used in two ways. First, you can include it in the body of an email message, for employers who want email delivery but don't want file attachments. Second, you can copy and paste the sections into the application forms on an employer's website.

> A plain-text version of your résumé is simply a computer file without any of the formatting that you typically apply using a word processor.

A plain-text version is easy to create with your word processor. Start with the file you used to create your résumé, use the "Save As" choice to save it as "plain text" or whichever similarly labelled option your software has, and verify the result by using a basic text editor (such as Microsoft Notepad). If necessary, reformat the page manually, moving text and inserting space as needed. For simplicity's sake, left-justify all your headings rather than trying to centre them manually.

> Make sure you verify the plain-text file that you create with your word processor; it might need a few manual adjustments using a text editor such as Notepad.

CREATING A WORD FILE OF YOUR RÉSUMÉ In some cases, an employer or job-posting website will let you upload a Microsoft Word file or attach it to an email message. (Although there are certainly other word processors on the market, Microsoft Word is the de facto standard used in business today.) This method of transferring information preserves the design and layout of your résumé and saves you the trouble of creating a plain-text version. However, before you submit a Word file to anyone, make sure your computer is free of viruses. Infecting a potential employer's computer will not make a good first impression.

CREATING A PDF VERSION OF YOUR RÉSUMÉ Creating a PDF version of your file is a simple procedure, but you need the right software. Adobe Acrobat (not the free Acrobat Reader) is the best-known program, but many others are available, including some free versions. Many employers prefer PDF files, since the original résumé formatting is retained and the document cannot be changed.

CREATING AN ONLINE RÉSUMÉ A variety of terms are used to describe online résumés, including *personal webpage*, *e-portfolio*, *social media résumé*, and *multimedia résumé*. Whatever the terminology used on a particular site, all these formats provide the opportunity to expand on the information contained in your basic résumé with links to projects, publications, screencasts, online videos, course lists, social networking profiles, and other elements that give employers a more complete picture of who you are and what you can offer (see Figure 15–7).

A good place to start is your school's career centre. Ask whether the career centre (or perhaps the information technology department) hosts online résumés or e-portfolios for students.

A commercial hosting service is another good possibility for an online résumé. For instance, the free service VisualCV (www.visualcv.com) lets you build an online résumé with video clips and other multimedia elements. This site is a good place to see numerous examples, from students just about to enter the workforce full time all the way up to corporate CEOs.[48]

> You have many options for creating an online résumé, from university- or college-hosted e-portfolios to multimedia résumés on commercial websites.

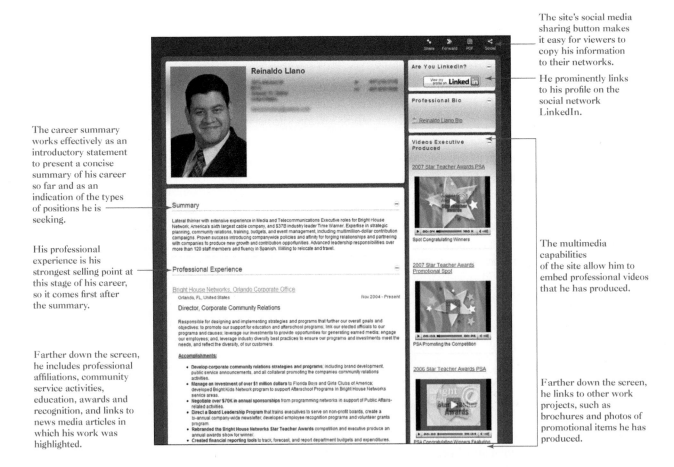

The career summary works effectively as an introductory statement to present a concise summary of his career so far and as an indication of the types of positions he is seeking.

His professional experience is his strongest selling point at this stage of his career, so it comes first after the summary.

Farther down the screen, he includes professional affiliations, community service activities, education, awards and recognition, and links to news media articles in which his work was highlighted.

The site's social media sharing button makes it easy for viewers to copy his information to their networks.

He prominently links to his profile on the social network LinkedIn.

The multimedia capabilities of the site allow him to embed professional videos that he has produced.

Farther down the screen, he links to other work projects, such as brochures and photos of promotional items he has produced.

Figure 15–7 Online Résumé

Courtesy: Reinaldo Llano

Regardless of the approach you take to creating an online résumé, keep these helpful tips in mind:

- **Remember that your online presence is a career-management tool.** The way you are portrayed online can work for you or against you, and it's up to you to create a positive impression. Most employers now conduct online searches to learn more about promising candidates, and 70 percent of those who do so have rejected applicants because of information they dug up online.[49] Check your online "content" for professionalism and what it has to offer the reader. Tell a compelling story. Be visible in a way that demonstrates how you can help a prospective employer or colleague achieve their goals.
- **Take advantage of social networking.** Use whatever tools are available to direct people to your online résumé, such as including the URL of your online résumé on the "Info" tab on your Facebook page.
- **During the application process, don't expect or ask employers to retrieve a résumé from your website.** Submit your résumé using whatever method and medium each employer prefers. If employers then want to know more about you, they will likely do a web search on you and find your site, or you can refer them to your site in your résumé or application materials.

PROOFREAD YOUR RÉSUMÉ

Employers view your résumé, regardless of the medium or format used, as a concrete example of how you will prepare material on the job. It doesn't need to be good or pretty good; it needs to be *perfect*. Although it may not seem fair, just one or two errors in a job application package are enough to doom a candidate's chances.[50]

Your résumé is one of the most important documents you'll ever write, so don't rush or cut corners when it comes to proofreading. Check all headings and lists for clarity and parallelism, and be sure that your grammar, spelling, and punctuation are correct. Double-check all dates, phone numbers, email addresses, and other essential data. Depending on the industry, you may need to include photos. Be sure these are current and professional. If you are asked for a scannable résumé, check that the format lends itself easily to this technology. Work to build a consistent message about you—your brand—across all communication points, so that when a prospective employer wants to learn more about you, your background and skills are presented in the best possible way. Ask at least three other people to review your materials.

Your résumé can't be "pretty good" or "almost perfect"—it needs to be *perfect*, so proofread it thoroughly and ask several other people to verify it, too.

DISTRIBUTE YOUR RÉSUMÉ

How you distribute your résumé depends on the number of employers you target and their preferences for receiving résumés. Employers usually list their preferences on their websites, so verify this information to ensure that your résumé ends up in the right format and in the right channel. Beyond that, here are some general delivery tips:

- **Mailing your traditional and scannable résumés.** Take some care with the packaging. Spend a few extra cents to mail these documents in a flat 9" x 12" envelope, or better yet, use Canada Post's Priority™ service with a sturdy cardboard mailer and faster delivery for just a few dollars more.
- **Emailing your résumé.** Some employers want applicants to include the text of their résumés in the body of an email message; others prefer an attached Microsoft Word file. If you have a reference number or a job ad number, include it in the subject line of your email message.

When distributing your résumé, pay close attention to the specific instructions provided by every employer, job website, or other recipient.

- **Submitting your résumé to an employer's website.** Many employers, including most large companies, now prefer or require applicants to submit their résumés online. In some instances, you will be asked to upload a complete file. In others, you will need to copy and paste sections of your résumé into individual boxes in an online application form.

- **Posting your résumé on job websites.** You can post your résumé (or create one online, on some sites) on general-purpose job websites (see Table 15–1) and on more specialized websites (see www.jobs.ca for a list). You will find numerous job boards online, so spend some time looking for sites that specialize in your target industries, regions, or professions.[51] Before you upload your résumé to any site, however, learn about its confidentiality protection. Some sites allow you to specify levels of confidentiality, such as letting employers search your qualifications without seeing your personal contact information or preventing your current employer from seeing your résumé. Don't post your résumé to any website that doesn't give you the option of restricting the display of your contact information. Only employers that are registered clients of the service should be able to see your contact information.[52]

- **Keep your résumé and online presence up to date and relevant.** You want to be ready when the next exciting job opportunity arises. Keeping your résumé and online image current and professional looking will allow you to submit your application right away, without having to spend time writing updates. On average, a resume should be updated every 6 to 12 months or when a new relevant skill or experience is achieved.[53]

For a quick summary of the steps to take when planning, writing, and completing your résumé, refer to "Checklist: Writing an Effective Résumé."

✓ Checklist   Writing an Effective Résumé

A. Plan your résumé.

- Analyze your purpose and audience carefully to make sure that your message meets employers' needs.
- Research your target companies.
- Gather pertinent information about yourself. Use your CCR or employment portfolio, if you have already developed one, as a base.
- Select the best medium by researching the preferences of each employer.
- Organize your résumé around your strengths, and use the appropriate structure for the industry and stage of your career.

B. Write your résumé.

- Keep your résumé honest.
- Adapt your résumé to your audience to highlight the qualifications each employer is looking for.
- Create a concise and reader-focused qualifications or career summary that spotlights your strengths and makes it easier for employers to identify what you have to offer.
- Use precise language to convey your name and contact information, introductory statement or career

summary, education, work experience, skills, work or school accomplishments, and personal activities and achievements.

C. Complete your résumé.

- Revise your résumé until it is clear, concise, and compelling.
- Produce your résumé in all the formats you might need: printed traditional résumé, printed scannable résumé, electronic plain-text file, Microsoft Word file, PDF file, and online/multimedia/social media résumé. Check for a consistent professional message across all communication channels.
- Proofread your résumé to ensure that it is absolutely perfect.
- Check for consistency across all formats and online reference points, such as LinkedIn, Facebook, or Twitter.
- Distribute your résumé using the means that each employer prefers.
- Keep your résumé current but still concise and relevant. Proofread your documents after each change.

SUMMARY OF LEARNING OBJECTIVES

1 **Explain the importance and features of an employment portfolio.** An employment portfolio, either in hard copy or multimedia format, shows potential employers evidence of your skills and abilities. Containing your résumé, work samples, recommendation letters, school projects, and other information highlighting your skills, this portfolio can be expanded throughout your career as you seek work opportunities.

2 **Describe the key steps to finding the ideal opportunity in today's job market.** Finding the ideal work opportunity begins with organizing potential employer contact information, staying organized, analyzing your own aspirations and skills, and researching industries and companies by reading business periodicals, searching job banks, and learning about firms through their websites. Then, determine how you can translate your skills into employer needs. Look for job opportunities through job boards and classified services; practise your networking skills; and begin building a network of contacts through classmates, student organizations, and volunteering opportunities. Be sure to explore the services offered by your school's career office, such as job fairs and interview techniques.

3 **Discuss how to choose the appropriate résumé organization and length.** If you have a lot of employment experience, choose the chronological approach because it focuses on your work history. The advantages of the chronological résumé are that it helps employers easily locate necessary information, highlights your professional growth and career progress, and emphasizes continuity and stability in your employment background. The functional approach focuses on particular skills and competencies you've developed. The advantages of the functional résumé are that it helps employers easily see what you can do for them, allows you to emphasize earlier job experience, and lets you downplay any lengthy periods of unemployment or a lack of career progress. The combination approach highlights your capabilities when you don't have a continuous employment history, thus allowing

potential employers to focus on your skills rather than gaps in chronology. Once you have created your résumé, make sure to update it every 6 to 12 months or when new skills or experiences are acquired. Adjust the structure of the résumé as needed.

4 **Describe the problem of résumé fraud.** Approximately 40 percent of résumés currently sent to potential employers contain false information. Although it may be tempting to exaggerate qualifications, recruiters will use various methods, including reference and background checks, to confirm a candidate's skills and qualifications. Even if an employee serves an employer for many years, discovery of fraud will lead to severe consequences. An honest résumé truly represents whether a candidate is the right fit for the position.

5 **Outline the major sections of a traditional résumé.** Your résumé must include three sections: (1) your name and contact information, (2) your educational background (with related skills and accomplishments), and (3) your work experience (with related skills and accomplishments). Options include listing your career objective or summary of qualifications, describing related activities and achievements, and perhaps (although not necessarily recommended) explaining relevant personal data.

6 **Describe the completing step for résumés.** After writing your résumé, ensure that you provide enough information about yourself, but in a concise manner. Make sure that it is formatted for accessibility, the information is correct, and grammar and spelling are perfect. Production values, such as paper quality and appearance, must project professionalism. The most common formats for producing a résumé are the printed traditional résumé, printed scannable résumé, electronic plain-text file, Microsoft Word file, PDF file, and online résumé (also called a *multimedia résumé* or *social media résumé*). When preparing your résumé for transmission, be sure to use the appropriate format(s) for your audience's needs. Be sure your online "persona" is professional and consistent.

ON THE JOB | PERFORMING COMMUNICATION TASKS AT TIM HORTONS

You recently joined the recruiting team at the TDL Group, the operators of the Tim Hortons chain. Your responsibilities include analyzing résumés and applications to help the company identify the most promising candidates to be interviewed. Your current task is finding candidates to fill a staff accountant position in the finance department.

1. You've learned to pay close attention to the career objectives on résumés to ensure that you match applicants' interests with appropriate job openings. You've selected four résumés for the accountant position; from them,

which of the following is the most compelling statement of objectives for this position?

a. An entry-level financial position in a large company

b. To invest my accounting and financial talent and business savvy in shepherding Tim Hortons toward explosive growth

c. A position in which my degree in business administration and my experience in cash management will make a valuable contribution

d. To learn all I can about back office operations in an exciting environment with a company whose reputation is as outstanding as Tim Hortons

2. Of the education sections included in the résumés, which of the following is the most effective?

a. University of Calgary, Calgary, AB, 2009–2013. Received a BA degree with a major in Business Administration and a minor in Finance. Graduated with a 3.65 grade-point average. Played varsity football and basketball. Worked 15 hours per week in the library. Coordinated the local student chapter of the Canadian Management Association. Member of Alpha Phi Alpha social fraternity.

b. I attended Mohawk College in Hamilton for two years and then transferred to Ryerson University, Toronto, where I completed my studies. My program of study was economics, but I also took many business management courses, including human resources, small business administration, introduction to marketing, and organizational behaviour. I selected courses based on the professors' reputation for excellence, and I received mostly As and Bs. Unlike many students, I viewed the acquisition of knowledge—rather than career preparation—as my primary goal. I believe I have received a well-rounded education that has prepared me to approach management situations as problem-solving exercises.

c. St. Francis Xavier University, Antigonish, NS. Graduated with a BA degree in 2013. Majored in Physical Education. Minored in Business Administration. Graduated with a 2.85 average.

d. University of Regina, Regina, SK. Received BA and MBA degrees. I majored in business as an undergraduate and concentrated in manufacturing management during my MBA program. Received a special $2500 scholarship offered by Rotary International recognizing academic achievement in business courses. I also won the MEGA award in 2011. Honour student.

3. While you would naturally prefer to hire someone with directly relevant experience in accounting, you recognize that this isn't always possible. When you can't find a candidate with such experience, you look for people who are able to translate their work experience into terms that are relevant to the positions they're applying for. Which of the following candidates does the best job of describing his or her work experience in a way that reflects the "Background and Experience" section of the staff accountant job description?

a. McDonald's, The Pas, MB, 2007–2012. Part-time cook. Worked 15 hours per week while attending high school. Prepared hamburgers, chicken nuggets, and french fries. Received employee-of-the-month award for outstanding work habits.

    University Grill, Saskatoon, SK, 2004–07. Part-time cook. Worked 20 hours per week while attending university. Prepared hot and cold sandwiches. Helped manager purchase ingredients. Trained new kitchen workers. Prepared work schedules for kitchen staff.

b. Although I have never held a full-time job, I have worked part time and during summer vacations throughout my high school and university years. During my first and second years in high school, I bagged groceries at the Loblaws store three afternoons a week. The work was not terribly challenging, but I liked the customers and the other employees. During my third and fourth years, I worked at the YMCA as an after-school counsellor for elementary school children. The kids were really sweet, and I still get letters from some of them. During summer vacations while I was in university, I did construction work for a local homebuilder. The job paid well, and I also learned a lot about carpentry. The guys I worked with were a mixed bag who expanded my vocabulary and knowledge of the world. I also worked part time in university in the student cafeteria, where I scooped food onto plates. This did not require much talent, but it taught me a lot about how people behave when standing in line.

c. The Broadway Department Store, Moncton, NB, Summers 2007–2012. Sales Consultant, Furniture Department. I interacted with a diverse group of customers, including suburban matrons, teenagers, career women, and professional couples. I endeavoured to satisfy their individual needs and make their shopping experience memorable, efficient, and enjoyable. Under the direction of the sales manager, I helped prepare employee schedules and fill out departmental reports. I also helped manage the inventory, worked the cash register, and handled a variety of special orders and customer complaints with courtesy and aplomb. During the 2008 annual storewide sale, I sold more merchandise than any other salesperson in the entire furniture department.

d. Medicine Hat, AB, Civilian Member of Public Safety Committee, January–December 2011.

> Organized and promoted a lecture series on vacation safety and home security for the residents of Medicine Hat; recruited and trained seven committee members to help plan and produce the lectures; persuaded local businesses to finance the program; designed, printed, and distributed flyers; wrote and distributed press releases; attracted an average of 120 people to each of three lectures

> Developed a questionnaire to determine local residents' home security needs; directed the efforts of 10 volunteers working on the survey; prepared written report for city council and delivered oral summary of findings at town meeting; helped persuade city to fund new home security program

> Initiated the Business Security Forum as an annual meeting at which local business leaders could meet to discuss safety and security issues; created promotional flyers for the first forum; convinced 19 business owners to fund a business security survey; arranged press coverage of the first forum

TEST YOUR KNOWLEDGE

1. What is the purpose of maintaining an employment portfolio? How does a portfolio influence employers?

2. What challenges do job seekers face today?

3. What skills do employers seek in today's job applicants?

4. What are key online sources for a career and employment search?

5. What is a résumé? Why is it important to adopt a "you" attitude when preparing one? How is a résumé different from a CV?

6. How does a chronological résumé differ from a functional résumé? When is each appropriate?

7. What elements are commonly included in a résumé?

8. What are different types of introductory statements and when are they used?

9. What are some of the most common problems with résumés?

10. What must you keep in mind when distributing your résumé online or in a scannable format?

11. How can your online presence affect your job search?

12. How often should you update your résumé and why?

APPLY YOUR KNOWLEDGE

1. If you're still a year or two away from graduation, should you worry about your job search? Explain your answer.

2. How can you "think like an employer" if you have no professional business experience?

3. Can you use a qualifications summary if you don't yet have extensive professional experience in your desired career? Why or why not?

4. Some people don't have a clear career path when they enter the job market. If you're in that situation, how would your uncertainty affect the way you write your résumé?

5. **Ethical Choices** Between your second and third years in university, you quit school for a year to earn the money to complete your education. You worked as a loan-processing assistant in a finance company, checking references on loan applications, typing, and filing. Your manager made a lot of the fact that he had never attended university. He seemed to resent you for pursuing your education, but he never criticized your work, so you thought you were doing okay. After you'd been working there for six months, he fired you, saying that you failed to be thorough enough in your credit checks. You were actually glad to leave, and you found another job right away at a bank doing similar duties. Now that you've graduated from university, you're writing your résumé. Will you include the finance company job in your work history? Please explain.

RUNNING CASES

> CASE 1 Noreen

The "Go Points" department and the credit card sales/service department have merged, and Petro-Go plans to combine these two departments in all their international centres. The senior management team is hiring for a new position of Merger Project Manager, and Noreen wants to apply. The project is expected to last two years, and the chosen candidate will travel to 12 countries and 40 call centres to implement the merger.

QUESTIONS

a. What is the purpose of the cover letter and résumé?

b. What skills should Noreen emphasize?

c. How many pages long should her résumé be?

d. What is the best organizational style for Noreen's résumé? Why?

e. What common mistakes with résumé fonts must Noreen be sure not to make?

YOUR TASK

Create a cover letter and résumé for Noreen. Refer to the cases for Noreen at the back of each chapter to read about her skills and background. You may use your imagination to add skills and experience to Noreen's résumé as you see fit. What could Noreen add to her e-portfolio to complement her application?

> CASE 2 Kwong

Kwong has obtained his CGA credentials and opened an accounting firm. His firm, CG Accounting, has been operating for three months and has 20 corporate account customers and 167 personal account customers. His sister is working in his office as the office administrator, and he has one other tax preparer working on the accounts with him. His sister is leaving, and he needs to hire a new administrative assistant who will answer phones, advise customers, prepare forms for signature, email, file, and so on. He has placed a job advertisement in the newspaper and is now reviewing résumés.

QUESTIONS

a. List three main skills for which Kwong will look.

b. Is experience necessary?

c. What skills should the cover letter emphasize?

d. List two questions Kwong might ask an overqualified candidate.

e. List two questions Kwong might ask an underqualified candidate.

f. What could Kwong check for online when he wants to learn more about the candidates?

YOUR TASK

Create a cover letter for this position. Use your résumé and fit it to this position. Work in pairs and exchange your cover letter and résumé with another student. Each of you will give feedback and suggestions for improvement to the other.

PRACTISE YOUR KNOWLEDGE

DOCUMENT 15.A: WRITING A RÉSUMÉ

Read the following résumé information, and then (1) analyze the strengths or weaknesses of the information and (2) create a résumé that follows the guidelines presented in this chapter.

Sylvia Manchester
66 Bernick Drive
Barrie, ON L4M 2V6
(705) 111-5254
smanchester@rcnmail.com

PERSONAL: Single, excellent health, 5'8", 116 lbs.; hobbies include cooking, dancing, and reading.

JOB OBJECTIVE: To obtain a responsible position in marketing or sales with a good company.

EDUCATION: BA degree in biology, Memorial University, 1999. Graduated with a 3.0 average. Member of the varsity cheerleading squad.

WORK EXPERIENCE   *Fisher Scientific Instruments, 2005 to present, field sales representative.* Responsible for calling on customers and explaining the features of Fisher's line of laboratory instruments. Also responsible for writing sales letters, attending trade shows, and preparing weekly sales reports.

Fisher Scientific Instruments, 2001–2004, customer service representative. Was responsible for handling incoming phone calls from customers who had questions about delivery, quality, or operation of Fisher's line of laboratory instruments. Also handled miscellaneous correspondence with customers.

Medical Electronics, Inc., 1998–2001, administrative assistant to the vice president of marketing. In addition to handling typical secretarial chores for the vice president of marketing, I was in charge of compiling the monthly sales reports, using figures provided by members of the field sales force. I also was given responsibility for doing various market research activities.

Visitors Bureau, 1995–1998, summers, tour guide. During the summers of my university years, I led tours of St. John's for tourists visiting the city. My duties included greeting conventioneers and their spouses at hotels, explaining the history and features of the city during an all-day sight-seeing tour, and answering questions about St. John's and its attractions. During my fourth summer with the Bureau, I was asked to help train the new tour guides. I prepared a handbook that provided interesting facts about the various tourist attractions, as well as answers to the most commonly asked tourist questions. The Bureau was so impressed with the handbook they had it printed up so that it could be given as a gift to visitors.

Memorial University, 1996–1999, part-time clerk in admissions office. While I was a student in university, I worked 15 hours a week in the admissions office. My duties included filing, processing applications, and handling correspondence with high school students and administrators.

EXERCISES

15.1 Work-Related Preferences: Self-Assessment

What work-related activities and situations do you prefer? Your campus career and planning centre will most likely have questionnaires to help you assess your preferences. Also, there are a number of career assessment questionnaires available online through Career Professionals of Canada (http://careerprocanada.ca/career-exploration-assessments/).

15.2 Internet: Career Match

Based on the preferences you identified in the self-assessment (Exercise 15.1) and the academic, professional, and personal qualities you have to offer, perform an online search for a career that matches your interests (starting with the websites listed in Table 15–1). Draft a brief report for your instructor, indicating how the career you select and the job openings you find match your strengths and preferences.

15.3 Teamwork: Action Verbs

Working with another student, change the following statements to make them more effective for a résumé by using action verbs.

a. Have some experience with database design.
b. Assigned to a project to analyze the cost accounting methods for a large manufacturer.
c. I was part of a team that developed a new inventory control system.
d. Am responsible for preparing the quarterly department budget.
e. Was a manager of a department with seven employees working for me.
f. Was responsible for developing a spreadsheet to analyze monthly sales by department.
g. Put in place a new program for ordering supplies.

15.4 Résumé Preparation: Work Accomplishments

Use your team's answers to Exercise 15.3 to make the statements stronger by quantifying them (make up any numbers you need).

15.5 Ethical Choices: Describing Teamwork

Assume that you achieved all the tasks shown in Exercise 15.3, not as an individual employee but as part of a work team. In your résumé, must you mention other team members? Explain your answer.

15.6 Completing a Résumé: Electronic Plain-Text Version

Using your revised version of the résumé in Document 15.A: Writing a Résumé, create a plain-text file that Sylvia Manchester could use to include in email messages.

15.7 It's Show Time: Creating a Video to Supplement Your Application

Imagine that you are applying for work in a field that involves speaking in front of an audience, such as sales, consulting, management, or training. Record a two- to three-minute video demonstration of your speaking and presentation skills. Record yourself speaking to an audience, if one can be arranged.

CASES	APPLYING THE THREE-STEP WRITING PROCESS TO CASES

Apply each step to the following cases, as assigned by your instructor.

| Career SKILLS |

1. Taking Stock and Taking Aim: Résumé Tailored for the Right Job

Think about yourself. What are some things that come easily to you? What do you enjoy doing? In what part of the country would you like to live? Do you like to work indoors? Outdoors? A combination of the two? How much do you like to travel? Would you like to spend considerable time on the road? Do you like to work closely with others or more independently? What conditions make a job unpleasant? Do you delegate responsibility easily, or do you like to do things yourself? Are you better with words or numbers? Better at speaking or writing? Do you like to work under fixed deadlines? How important is job security to you? Do you want your supervisor to state clearly what is expected of you, or do you like the freedom to make many of your own decisions?

Your task: After answering these questions, gather information about possible jobs that suit your profile by consulting reference materials (from your college or university library or placement centre) and by searching online. Next, choose a location, a company, and a job that interests you. With guidance from your instructor, decide whether to apply for a job you're qualified for now or one you'll be qualified for with additional education. Then, as directed by your instructor, write a résumé.

| Career SKILLS | | Email SKILLS |

2. Career Planning: Researching Career Opportunities

Knowing the jargon and "hot button" issues in a particular profession or industry can give you a big advantage when it comes to writing your résumé and participating in job interviews. You can fine-tune your résumé for both human readers and applicant tracking systems, sound more confident and informed in interviews, and present yourself as a professional-class individual with an inquiring mind.

Your task: Imagine a specific job category in a company that has an informative, comprehensive website (to facilitate the research you'll need to do). This doesn't have to be a current job opening but a position that you know exists or is likely to exist in this company, such as a business systems analyst at Apple or a brand manager at Unilever.

Explore the company's website and other online sources to find the following: (1) A brief description of what this job entails, with enough detail that you could describe it to a fellow student. (2) Some of the terminology used in the profession or the industry, both formal terms that might serve as keywords on your résumé and informal terms and phrases that insiders are likely to use in publications and conversations. (3) An ongoing online conversation among people in this profession. For example, this might be a LinkedIn group, a popular industry or professional blog that seems to get quite a few comments, or an industry or professional publication that attracts a lot of comments. (4) At least one significant issue that will affect people in this profession or companies in this industry over the next few years. For example, if your chosen profession involves accounting in a publicly traded corporation, upcoming changes in international financial reporting standards would be a significant issue. Similarly, for a company in the consumer electronics industry, the recycling and disposal of *e-waste* is an issue. Write a brief email message summarizing your findings and explaining how you could use this information on your résumé and during job interviews.

| Career SKILLS |

3. "Help Wanted": Application for a Job Listed in the Classified Section

Among the jobs listed in today's *Province* (301 Granville Street, Vancouver, BC, V6C 2N4) are the following:

- **Accounting Assistant:** Established leader in the vacation ownership industry, Nelson Corp., has an immediate opening in its accounting dept. for an Accounting Assistant. Responsibilities include bank reconciliation, preparation of deposits, AP, and cash receipt posting. Join our fast-growing company and enjoy our great benefits package. Flex work hours, medical, dental insurance. Email résumé to Lisa: Lisa@Nelson-Corp.ca.

- **Administrative Assistant:** Fast-paced Burnaby office seeks professional with strong computer skills. Proficient in MS Office applications. Must be detail oriented, able to handle multiple tasks, and possess strong communication skills. Excellent benefits, salary, and work environment. Email résumé to Yuki@HiringforYou.ca.

- **Customer Service:** A nationally known computer software developer has an exciting opportunity in customer service and inside sales support in its fast-paced downtown Vancouver office. You'll help resolve customer problems over the phone, provide information, assist in account management, and administer orders. If you're friendly, self-motivated, energetic, and have 2 years of experience, excellent problem-solving skills, organizational, communication, and PC skills, and communicate well over the phone, mail résumé to J. Haber, 2359 Venables St., Vancouver, BC V5K 1J5.

- **Sales-Account Manager:** MidCity Baking Company is seeking an Account Manager to sell and coordinate our programs to major accounts in the Vancouver market. The candidate should possess strong analytical and selling skills and proficiency in MS Office applications. Previous sales experience with major account level assignment desired. A degree in business or equivalent experience preferred. For confidential consideration, please mail résumé to Steven Crane, Director of Sales, MidCity Baking Company, PO Box 23727, Vancouver, BC, V7C 1X9.

Your task: Write a résumé for one of these potential employers (make up any information you need or adapt your résumé).

| Presentation SKILLS | | Career SKILLS |

4. Message Strategies: Completing a Résumé

Creating presentations and other multimedia supplements can be a great way to expand on the brief overview that a résumé provides.

Your task: Starting with any version of a résumé that you've created for yourself, create a PowerPoint presentation that expands on your résumé information to give potential employers a more complete picture of what you can contribute. Include samples of your work, testimonials from current or past employers and colleagues, videos of speeches you've made, and anything else that tells the story of the professional "you." If you have a specific job or type of job in mind, focus your presentation on that. Otherwise, present a more general picture that shows why you would be a great employee for any company to consider. Be sure to review what you know about creating professional-quality presentations.

16 Applying and Interviewing for Employment

LEARNING OBJECTIVES   After studying this chapter, you will be able to

1 Define the purpose of application letters, and explain how to apply the AIDA organizational approach to them

2 Describe the typical sequence of job interviews

3 Describe briefly what employers look for during an employment interview and pre-employment testing

4 Outline six tasks you need to complete to prepare for a successful job interview

5 Explain the three stages of a successful employment interview

6 Identify the most common employment messages that follow an interview, and explain when you would use each one

MyLab Business Communication   Visit MyLab Business Communication to access a variety of online resources directly related to this chapter's content.

ON THE JOB: COMMUNICATING AT GOOGLE

dpa picture alliance/Alamy Stock Photo

Google aims to hire thousands of the most innovative online business and technical specialists in the world. Its work culture encourages creative approaches to research and development.

Googling the Best Talent on the Web
www.google.com

Are you looking for a company that's fun and stimulating? One that inspires you to stretch your mind? A workplace with a global reach but a small-town, friendly atmosphere? You might try Google, rated by *Fortune* magazine in 2017 as the number one place to work, for the sixth year in a row.

With its strong corporate identity and specific ideas about hiring and management, Google has maintained its lead in search-engine technology and continues to develop new tools that range from digital libraries to geographic information systems such as Google Earth. To keep its prominence, Google pursues exceptionally talented software engineers. Most are either young risk-takers with adventurous outside interests or experienced superstars from top research labs or respected technology firms. Googlers, as employees are informally known, come from every corner of the business world—and beyond. As the company puts it, "Googlers have been Olympic athletes and Jeopardy champions; professional chefs and independent filmmakers."

Interviews are challenging. As Google states, candidates will face in-depth questions "intended to let us get a peek at how you think about complicated things." They are asked to write code and discuss the intricacies of their technical work. The goal is to hire people who will drive the company forward in its mission: "to organize the world's information and make it universally accessible and useful."

But Google is more than engineers. Performing routine business functions and sustaining Google's global profile requires managers, communicators, and marketers. Non-technicians, such as facilities managers, make Google work by maintaining building and mechanical systems, overseeing vendor contracts, and coordinating space planning. Account planners provide sales support by running such events as "Getting to Know Google" and by cultivating client contacts. Along with software engineers, professionals such as these have made Google the primary Internet search engine around the world.

You may never apply to Google, but it's important to gain insights about the companies you want to work for: your research will definitely give you a competitive edge. Google provides a great deal of information on its website about its work life, but not all companies do. You may have to do some extra digging through magazines, newsgroups, employment-related blogs, and other sources. When you start your job search, how will you prepare?[1]

Submitting Your Résumé

Whether you plan to apply to Google or any other company, your résumé in some form will usually be the centrepiece of your job-search package. However, it needs support from several other employment messages before, during, and after the interview process. These messages can include application letters, job-inquiry letters, application forms, and follow-up notes.

1 LEARNING OBJECTIVE

Define the purpose of application letters, and explain how to apply the AIDA organizational approach to them.

WRITING APPLICATION LETTERS

Whenever you mail, email, hand-deliver, or upload your résumé, you should include an **application letter**, also known as a *cover letter*, to let readers know what you're sending, why you're sending it, and how they can benefit from reading it. (Although this message is often not a printed letter anymore, many professionals still refer to it as a letter.) Take the same care with your application letter that you took with your résumé. A poorly written application letter can prompt employers to skip over your résumé, even if you are a good fit for a job.[2] Staffing specialist Abby Kohut calls the application letter "a writing-skills evaluation in disguise" and emphasizes that even a single error can get you bounced from contention.[3]

The best approach for an application letter depends on whether you are sending a **solicited application letter** to apply for an identified job opening or are *prospecting* with an **unsolicited application letter**—taking the initiative to write to companies even though they haven't announced a job opening that is right for you.[4] In many ways, the difference between the two is like the difference between solicited and unsolicited proposals.

Figure 16–1 shows an application message written in response to a posted job opening. The writer highlights his qualifications while mirroring the requirements specified in the posting. Following the AIDA model, he grabs attention immediately by letting the reader know that he is familiar with the company and the global transportation business.

Prospecting is more challenging because you don't have the clear target you have with a solicited message. You will need to do more research to identify the qualities that a company would probably seek for the position you hope to occupy. Using this information in your application letter helps you establish common ground with your reader—and it shows that you are tuned in to what is going on in the industry. Also, search for news items that involve the company, its customers, the profession, or the individual manager to whom you are writing. In Figure 16–2, Glenda Johns uses her experience as a clerk and an assistant manager to craft the opening of her letter.

The AIDA model is a persuasive approach. Messages are organized as follows:
A—Attention: engages the reader
I—Interest: shows relevance
D—Desire: links benefits
A—Action: motivates action

[handwritten annotation: AIDA model]

[handwritten annotation: application letter]

Always accompany your résumé with an application message (letter or email) that motivates the recipient to read the résumé.

[handwritten annotation: solicited vs. unsolicited application letters]

An unsolicited application letter is more challenging because you must identify the qualities the company would likely be looking for in the position you would like to get.

Position			Supply Chain Pricing Analyst		Apply
Position code	T23-6678	Location	Vancouver, BC	Status	Full-time

Sea-Air Global Transport has an immediate opening for a supply chain pricing analyst in our Vancouver, BC, headquarters. This challenging position requires excellent communication skills in a variety of media, a polished customer service presence both in person and over the phone, and proven aptitude in statistical analysis and business mathematics.

The minimum educational requirement for this position is a bachelor's degree or equivalent, preferably in business, statistical methods, or applied mathematics. Experience in customer service is highly desirable, and experience in transportation or logistics is a major plus.

Click here to learn more about Sea-Air or click here to explore the attractive compensation and benefits packages we offer all employees.

Smith's application letter mirrors the language of the job posting.

2141 Michelle Crescent
Kelowna, BC V1Z 2W2
March 13, 2018

Sea-Air Global Transport
2000 Marine Drive
Vancouver, BC
V2P 2U7

Dear Hiring Manager:

Sea-Air Global Transport consistently appeared as a top transportation firm in the research I did for my senior project in global supply chain management, so imagine my delight when I discovered the opening for an export pricing analyst in your Vancouver headquarters (Position Code: T23-6678). With a major in business and a minor in statistical methods, my education has been ideal preparation for the challenges of this position.

In fact, my senior project demonstrates most of the skills listed in your job description, including written communication skills, analytical abilities, and math aptitude. I enjoyed the opportunity to put my math skills to the test as part of the statistical comparison of various freight modes. The e-portfolio at http://DaltonSmith.com/eportfolio shows examples of this work.

As you can see from my résumé, I also have more than three years of part-time experience working with customers in both retail and commercial settings. This experience taught me the importance of customer service, and I want to start my professional career with a company that truly values the customer. In reviewing your website and reading several articles on Lloyd's List and other trade websites, I am impressed by Sea-Air's constant attention to customer service in this highly competitive industry.

My verbal communication skills would be best demonstrated in an interview, of course. I would be happy to meet with a representative of your company at their earliest convenience. I can be reached at dalton.k.smith@gmail.com or by phone at 604-555-3737.

Sincerely,

Dalton Smith

The first sentence grabs Attention by indicating knowledge of the company and its industry.

The reference to his résumé emphasizes his customer service orientation and also shows he has done his homework by researching the company.

The letter doesn't include a handwritten signature because it was uploaded to a website along with his résumé.

The opening paragraph identifies the specific job for which he is applying.

In this discussion of his skills, he builds Interest and Desire by echoing the qualifications stated in the job posting.

In the close, he politely asks for an interview (an Action) in a way that emphasizes yet another job-related skill.

Figure 16–1 Solicited Application Message

For either type of letter, follow these tips to be more effective:[5]

- Resist the temptation to use generic, one-size-fits-all letters or to stand out with gimmicky application letters; impress with knowledge and professionalism instead.
- If the name of an individual manager is at all findable, address your letter to that person, rather than to something generic such as "Dear Hiring Manager." Search LinkedIn, the company's website, industry directories, Twitter, and anything else you can think of to find an appropriate name. Ask the

[handwritten note: ✱search for manager who you can address your letter to]

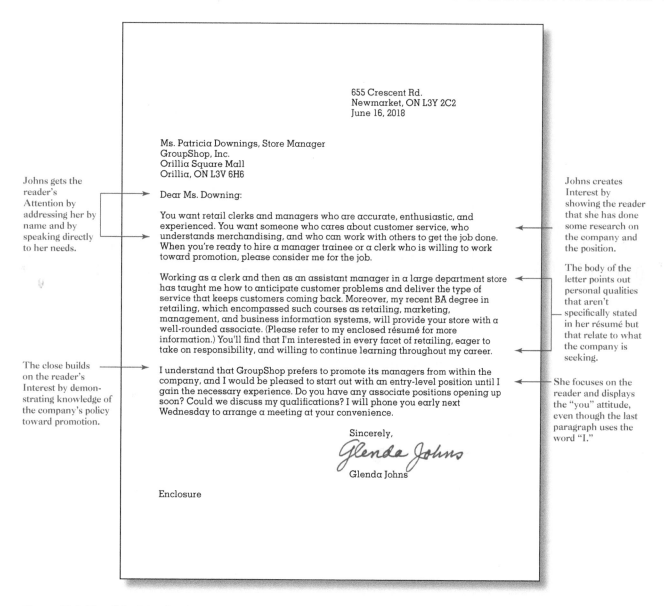

Johns gets the reader's Attention by addressing her by name and by speaking directly to her needs.

Johns creates Interest by showing the reader that she has done some research on the company and the position.

The body of the letter points out personal qualities that aren't specifically stated in her résumé but that relate to what the company is seeking.

The close builds on the reader's Interest by demonstrating knowledge of the company's policy toward promotion.

She focuses on the reader and displays the "you" attitude, even though the last paragraph uses the word "I."

The letter content:

655 Crescent Rd.
Newmarket, ON L3Y 2C2
June 16, 2018

Ms. Patricia Downings, Store Manager
GroupShop, Inc.
Orillia Square Mall
Orillia, ON L3V 6H6

Dear Ms. Downing:

You want retail clerks and managers who are accurate, enthusiastic, and experienced. You want someone who cares about customer service, who understands merchandising, and who can work with others to get the job done. When you're ready to hire a manager trainee or a clerk who is willing to work toward promotion, please consider me for the job.

Working as a clerk and then as an assistant manager in a large department store has taught me how to anticipate customer problems and deliver the type of service that keeps customers coming back. Moreover, my recent BA degree in retailing, which encompassed such courses as retailing, marketing, management, and business information systems, will provide your store with a well-rounded associate. (Please refer to my enclosed résumé for more information.) You'll find that I'm interested in every facet of retailing, eager to take on responsibility, and willing to continue learning throughout my career.

I understand that GroupShop prefers to promote its managers from within the company, and I would be pleased to start out with an entry-level position until I gain the necessary experience. Do you have any associate positions opening up soon? Could we discuss my qualifications? I will phone you early next Wednesday to arrange a meeting at your convenience.

Sincerely,

Glenda Johns

Glenda Johns

Enclosure

Figure 16–2 Unsolicited Application Letter

people in your network if they know a name. If another applicant finds a name and you don't, you're at a disadvantage.

- Clearly identify the opportunity you are applying for or expressing interest in.
- Show that you understand the company and its marketplace.
- Never volunteer salary history or requirements unless an employer has asked for this information.
- Keep it short—no more than three or four paragraphs. Keep in mind that all you are trying to do at this point is move the conversation forward one step.
- Show some personality, while maintaining a business-appropriate tone. The letter gives you the opportunity to balance the facts-only tone of your résumé.
- Project confidence without being arrogant.
- Follow the employer's instructions for submitting your cover letter and résumé.

Because application letters are persuasive messages, the AIDA approach is ideal, as the following sections explain.

The opening paragraph of your application letter needs to convey clearly the reason you're writing and give the recipient a compelling reason to keep reading.

Tips for getting attention (1st paragraph)

GETTING ATTENTION The opening paragraph of your application letter has two important tasks to accomplish: (1) clearly stating your reason for writing and (2) giving the recipient a reason to keep reading. Why would a recruiter want to keep reading your letter instead of the hundred others piling up on his or her desk? Because you show some immediate potential for meeting the company's needs. You've researched the company and the position, and you know something about the industry and its current challenges. Consider this opening:

> With the recent slowdown in corporate purchasing, I can certainly appreciate the challenge of new fleet sales in this business environment. With my high energy level and 16 months of new-car sales experience, I believe I can produce the results you listed as vital in your September 23 ad in the *St. John's Evening Telegram*.

This applicant does a smooth job of mirroring the company's stated needs while highlighting his personal qualifications along with evidence that he understands the broader market. He balances his relative lack of experience with enthusiasm and knowledge of the industry. Table 16–1 highlights some other ways that you can spark interest and grab attention in your opening paragraph. All of these openings demonstrate the "you" attitude, and many indicate how the applicant can serve the employer.

Use the middle section of your application letter to expand on your opening and present a more complete picture of your strengths.

BUILDING INTEREST AND INCREASING DESIRE The middle section of your application letter presents your strongest selling points in terms of their potential benefit to the organization, thereby building interest in you and creating a desire to interview you. As with the opening, the more specific you can be, the better. And back up your assertions with some convincing evidence of your ability to

Table 16–1	**Tips for Getting Attention in Application Letters**

Tip	Example
Unsolicited Application Letters	
Show how your strongest skills will benefit the organization.	If you need a regional sales specialist who consistently meets sales targets while fostering strong customer relationships, please consider my qualifications.
Describe your understanding of the job's requirements, and then show how well your qualifications fit them.	Your annual report stated that improving manufacturing efficiency is one of the company's top priorities for next year. Through my postgraduate research in systems engineering and consulting work for several companies in the industry, I've developed reliable methods for quickly identifying ways to cut production time while reducing resource usage.
Mention the name of a person known to and highly regarded by the reader.	When Janice McHugh of your franchise sales division spoke to our business communication class last week, she said you often need promising new marketing graduates at this time of year.
Refer to publicized company activities, achievements, changes, or new procedures.	Today's issue of the *Winnipeg Free Press* reports that you may need the expertise of computer programmers versed in robotics when your Elmwood tire plant automates this spring.
Use a question to demonstrate your understanding of the organization's needs.	Can your fast-growing market research division use an interviewer with two years of field survey experience, a BA in public relations, and a real desire to succeed? If so, please consider me for the position.
Use a catchphrase opening if the job requires ingenuity and imagination.	*Haut monde*—whether said in French, Italian, or Arabic—still means "high society." As an interior designer for your Yorkville showroom, not only could I serve and sell to your distinguished clientele but I could do it in all these languages. I speak, read, and write them fluently.
Solicited Application Letters	
Identify where you discovered the job opening; describe what you have to offer.	Your ad in the April issue of *Travel & Leisure* for a cruise-line social director caught my eye. My eight years of experience as a social director in the travel industry would allow me to serve your new Caribbean cruise division well.

perform, but don't let the "I"s dominate the content. Remember, you are writing the letter with the interests of the reader in mind.

> **Poor:** I completed three university courses in business communication, earning an A in each course, and have worked for the past year at Imperial Construction.
>
> **Improved:** Using the skills gained from three semesters of university training in business communication, I developed a collection system for Imperial Construction that reduced annual bad-debt losses by 25 percent. By emphasizing a win–win scenario for the company and its clients with incentives for on-time payment, the system was also credited with improving customer satisfaction.

When writing a solicited letter, be sure to discuss each requirement specified in the ad. If you are deficient in any of these requirements, stress other solid selling points to help strengthen your overall presentation.

Don't restrict your message to just core job duties. Also highlight personal characteristics, as long as they apply to the targeted position, such as your diligence or your ability to work hard, learn quickly, handle responsibility, or get along with people:

> While attending university full-time, I trained three hours a day with the varsity track team. In addition, I worked part-time during the school year and up to 60 hours a week each summer to be totally self-supporting. I can offer your organization the same level of effort and perseverance.

Mention your salary requirements at this stage only if the organization has asked you to state them. If you don't know the salary that's appropriate for the position and someone with your qualifications, you can find salary ranges for hundreds of jobs at the Service Canada website, www.workingincanada.gc.ca, or a number of commercial sites, including workopolis.com. If you do state a target salary, tie it to the benefits you would bring to the organization:

> For the past two years, I have been helping a company similar to yours organize its database marketing efforts. I would therefore like to receive a salary in the same range (the mid-40s) for helping your company set up a more efficient customer database.

Toward the end of this section, refer the reader to your résumé by citing a specific fact or general point covered there:

> As you can see in the attached résumé, I've been working part-time with a local publisher since my second year in university. During that time, I've used client interactions as an opportunity to build strong customer-service skills.

MOTIVATING ACTION The final paragraph of your application letter has two important functions: to ask the reader for a specific action (usually an interview) and to facilitate a reply. Offer to come to the employer's office at a convenient time or, if the firm is some distance away, to meet with its nearest representative or arrange a telephone or online interview using a video application such as Skype. Include your email address and phone number, as well as the best time to reach you. Alternatively, you can take the initiative and say that you will follow up with a phone call. Refer again to your strongest selling point and, if desired, your date of availability:

> After you have reviewed my qualifications, could we discuss the possibility of putting my marketing skills to work for your company? Since I will be on spring break the week of March 8, I would like to arrange a time to talk then. I will call in February to schedule a convenient time when we could discuss employment opportunities at your company.

Don't bring up salary in your application letter unless the recipient has asked you to include your salary requirements.

In the final paragraph of your application letter, respectfully ask for specific action and make it easy for the reader to respond.

After editing and proofreading your application letter, give it a final quality check by referring to "Checklist: Writing Application Letters." When submitting your résumé and cover letter, follow the instructions provided by the employer. Make it as easy as possible for them to receive the documentation. For example, if you are asked to upload a PDF of your résumé, convert your cover letter to a PDF format. And if you send the résumé via email, remove tabs and margins that might not align properly and make sure the subject line is clear and identifies the specific job you are seeking.[6]

✓ **Checklist** | **Writing Application Letters**

- Take the same care with your application letter that you took with your résumé.
- If you are prospecting using an unsolicited message, do deep research to identify the qualities the company likely wants and to whom the letter should be addressed.
- For solicited messages in response to a posted job opening, word your message in a way that echoes back the qualifications listed in the posting.
- Open the letter by capturing the reader's attention in a businesslike way.
- Use specific language to clearly state your interests and objectives.

- Build interest and desire in your potential contribution by presenting your key qualifications for the job.
- Link your education, experience, and personal qualities to the job requirements. Refer to your e-portfolio to demonstrate special skills.
- Outline salary requirements only if the organization has requested that you provide them.
- Request an interview at a time and place that is convenient for the reader.
- Make it easy to comply with your request by providing your complete contact information and good times to reach you.
- Adapt your style for cultural variations, if required.

FOLLOWING UP AFTER SUBMITTING A RÉSUMÉ

Think creatively about a follow-up message; show that you've continued to add to your skills or that you've learned more about the company or the industry.

Deciding if, when, and how to follow up after submitting your résumé and application letter is one of the trickiest parts of a job search. First and foremost, keep in mind that employers continue to evaluate your communication efforts and professionalism during this phase, so don't say or do anything to leave a negative impression. Second, adhere to whatever instructions the employer has provided. If a job posting says "no calls," for example, don't call. Third, if the job posting lists a *close date*, don't call or write before then, because the company is still collecting applications and will not have made a decision about inviting people for interviews. Wait a week or so after the close date. If no close date is given and you have no other information to suggest a timeline, you can generally contact the company starting a week or two after submitting your résumé.[7] Keep in mind that a single instance of poor etiquette or clumsy communication can undo all your hard work in a job search, so maintain your professional behaviour every step of the way.

When you follow up by email or telephone, you can share an additional piece of information that links your qualifications to the position (keep an eye out for late-breaking news about the company, too) and ask a question about the hiring process as a way to gather some information about your status. Good questions to ask include the following:[8]

- Has a hiring decision been made yet?
- Can you tell me what to expect next in terms of the hiring process?
- What is the company's time frame for filling this position?

- Could I follow up in another week if you haven't had the chance to contact me yet?
- Can I provide any additional information regarding my qualifications for the position?

Whatever the circumstances, a follow-up message can demonstrate that you're sincerely interested in working for the organization, persistent in pursuing your goals, and committed to upgrading your skills.

If you don't land a job at your dream company on the first attempt, don't give up. You can apply again if a new opening appears, or you can send an updated résumé with a new unsolicited application letter that describes how you have gained additional experience, taken a relevant course, or otherwise improved your skill set. Many leading employers take note of applicants who came close but didn't quite make it and may extend offers when positions open up in the future.[9]

Phovoir/Shutterstock

Understanding the Interviewing Process

An **employment interview** is a formal meeting during which both you and the prospective employer ask questions and exchange information. The organization's objective is to find the best talent to fill available job openings, and your main objective is to find the right match for your goals and capabilities.

Asking questions of your own is as important as answering the interviewer's questions. Not only do you get vital information but you also show initiative and curiosity. How can you prepare your own questions for a job interview?

As you get ready to begin interviewing, keep two vital points in mind. First, recognize that the process takes time. Start your preparation and research early; the best job offers usually go to the best-prepared candidates. Second, don't limit your options by looking at only a few companies. By exploring a wide range of firms and positions, you might uncover great opportunities that you would not have found otherwise. You'll increase the odds of getting more job offers, too.

THE TYPICAL SEQUENCE OF INTERVIEWS

Most employers interview an applicant multiple times before deciding to make a job offer. At the most selective companies, you might have a dozen or more individual interviews across several stages.[10] Depending on the company and the position, the process may stretch out over many weeks, or it may be completed in a matter of days.[11]

Employers start with the *screening stage*, in which they filter out applicants who are unqualified or otherwise not a good fit for the position. Screening can take place on your school's campus, at company offices, via telephone (including Skype or another Internet-based phone service), or through a computer-based screening system. Time is limited in screening interviews, so keep your answers short while providing a few key points that differentiate you from other candidates. If your screening interview will take place by phone, try to schedule it for a time when you can be focused and free from interruptions.[12]

The next stage of interviews, the *selection stage*, helps the organization identify the top candidates from all those who qualify. During these interviews, show keen interest in the job, relate your skills and experience to the organization's needs, listen attentively, and ask insightful questions that show you've done your research.

2 LEARNING OBJECTIVE

Describe the typical sequence of job interviews.

Start preparing early for your interviews—and be sure to consider a wide range of options.

During the screening stage of interviews, use the limited time available to differentiate yourself from other candidates.

During the selection stage, continue to show how your skills and attributes can help the company.

During the final stage, the interviewer may try to sell you on working for the firm.

If the interviewers agree that you're a good candidate, you may receive a job offer on the spot or a few days later by phone, mail, or email. In other instances, you may be invited back for a final evaluation by a higher-ranking executive. The objective of the *final stage* is often to sell you on the advantages of joining the organization.

COMMON TYPES OF INTERVIEWS

Employers can use a variety of interviewing methods throughout the interviewing process, and you need to recognize the different types and be prepared for each one. These methods can be distinguished by the way they are structured, the number of people involved, and the purpose of the interview.

A structured interview follows a set sequence of questions, allowing the interview team to compare answers from all candidates.

STRUCTURED VERSUS UNSTRUCTURED INTERVIEWS In a **structured interview** the interviewer (or a computer program) asks a series of prepared questions in a predetermined order. Structured interviews help employers identify candidates who don't meet basic job criteria, and they make it easier for the interview team to compare answers from multiple candidates.[13]

In an open-ended interview, the interviewer adapts the line of questioning based on your responses and questions.

In contrast, in an **open-ended or unstructured interview** the interviewer adapts his or her line of questioning based on the answers you give and any questions you ask. Even though it may feel like a conversation, remember that it's still an interview, so use your active listening skills to clarify the questions and provide succinct but complete answers.

In a panel interview, you meet with several interviewers at once; in a group interview, you and several other candidates meet with one or more interviewers at once.

PANEL AND GROUP INTERVIEWS Although one-on-one interviews are the most common format, some employers use panel or group interviews as well. In a **panel interview**, you meet with several interviewers at once.[14] Take note of the titles on business cards and try to make a connection with each person on the panel; keep in mind that each person has a different perspective, so tailor your responses accordingly.[15] For example, an upper-level manager is likely to be interested in your overall business sense and strategic perspective, whereas a potential colleague might be more interested in your technical skills and ability to work in a team. In a **group interview**, one or more interviewers meet with several candidates simultaneously. A key purpose of a group interview is to observe how the candidates interact with potential peers.[16]

In a behavioural interview, you are asked to describe how you handled situations from your past.

BEHAVIOURAL, SITUATIONAL, WORKING, AND STRESS INTERVIEWS Perhaps the most common type of interview these days is the **behavioural interview**, in which you are asked to relate specific incidents and experiences from your past.[17] Generic interview questions can often be answered with "canned" responses, but behavioural questions require candidates to use their own experiences and attributes to craft answers. Studies show that behavioural interviewing is a much better predictor of success on the job than traditional interview questions.[18] To prepare for a behavioural interview, review your work or school experiences to recall several instances in which you demonstrated an important job-related attribute or dealt with a challenge such as uncooperative team members or heavy workloads. Get ready with responses that quickly summarize the situation, the actions you took, and the outcome of those actions.[19]

In a situational interview, you're asked to explain how you would handle various hypothetical situations.

A **situational interview** is similar to a behavioural interview except that the questions focus on how you would handle various hypothetical situations on the job. The situations will likely relate to the job you're applying for, so the more you know about the position, the better prepared you'll be.

In a working interview, you actually perform work-related tasks.

A **working interview** is the most realistic type of interview: you actually perform a job-related activity during the interview. You may be asked to lead a brainstorming session, solve a business problem, engage in role playing, or even make a presentation.[20]

The most unnerving type of interview is the **stress interview**, during which you might be asked questions designed to unsettle you, or you might be subjected to long periods of silence, criticism, interruptions, or even hostile reactions by the interviewer. The theory behind this approach is that you'll reveal how well you handle stressful situations, although some experts find the technique of dubious value.[21] If you find yourself in a stress interview, recognize what is happening and collect your thoughts for a few seconds before you respond.

The theory behind stress interviews is to let recruiters see how you handle yourself under pressure.

INTERVIEW MEDIA

Expect to be interviewed through a variety of media. Employers trying to cut travel costs and the demands on staff time now interview candidates via telephone, email, instant messaging (IM), virtual online systems, and videoconferencing, in addition to traditional face-to-face meetings.

Expect to use a variety of media when you interview, from in-person conversations to virtual meetings.

TELEPHONE To succeed at a telephone interview, make sure you treat it as seriously as an in-person interview. Be prepared with a copy of all the materials you have sent the employer, including your résumé and any correspondence. In addition, prepare some note cards with key message points you'd like to make and questions you'd like to ask. If possible, arrange to speak on a landline so you don't have to worry about mobile phone reception problems. And remember that you won't be able to use a pleasant smile, a firm handshake, and other nonverbal signals to create a good impression. A positive, alert tone of voice is therefore vital.[22]

EMAIL AND IM Email and IM are also sometimes used in the screening stage. While you have almost no opportunity to send and receive nonverbal signals with these formats, you do have the major advantage of being able to review and edit each response before you send it. Maintain a professional style in your responses, and be sure to ask questions that demonstrate your knowledge of the company and the position.[23]

Virtual job fairs, such as the Working Worlds event hosted by Luxembourg's GAX Technologies, allow candidates and recruiters to interact without the time and expense of travel. How do you prepare for a virtual job fair? How is it different from preparing for a live, face-to-face job fair?

VIDEO Many employers use video technology for both live and recorded interviews. For example, Zappos, an online shoe and clothing retailer, often uses video interviews on Skype to select the top two or three finalists for each position and then invites those candidates for in-person interviews.[24] With recorded video interviews, an online system asks a set of questions and records the respondent's answers. Recruiters then watch the videos as part of the screening process.[25] Prepare for a video interview as you would for an in-person interview—including dressing and grooming—and take the extra steps needed to become familiar with the equipment and the process. If you're interviewing from home, arrange your space so that the webcam doesn't pick up anything distracting or embarrassing in the background. During a video interview, remember to sit up straight, focus on the camera, and look attentive to the other party.

Treat a telephone interview as seriously as you would an in-person interview.

When interviewing via email or IM, be sure to take a moment to review your responses before sending them.

In a video interview, speak to the camera as though you are addressing the interviewer in person.

ONLINE Online interviews can range from simple structured questionnaires and tests to sophisticated job simulations that are similar to working interviews (see Figure 16–3). Some banks, for example, use computerized simulations to see how well candidates can perform job-related tasks and decision-making scenarios. These simulations help identify good candidates and give applicants an idea of what the job is like.[26]

Computer-based virtual interviews range from simple structured interviews to realistic job simulations to meetings in virtual worlds.

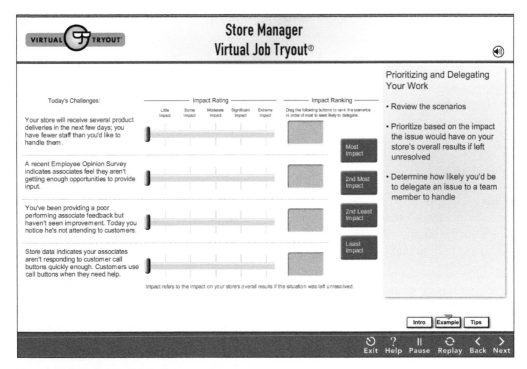

Figure 16–3 Job Task Simulations

Courtesy: Shaker Consulting Group

WHAT EMPLOYERS LOOK FOR IN AN INTERVIEW

3 **LEARNING OBJECTIVE**

Describe briefly what employers look for during an employment interview and pre-employment testing.

Suitability for a specific job is judged on the basis of
• Academic preparation
• Work experience
• Job-related personality traits

Compatibility with the organization is judged on the basis of personal background, attitudes, and style.

Interviews give employers a chance to go beyond the basic data of your résumé to answer two essential questions. The first is whether you can handle the responsibilities of the position. Naturally, the more you know about the demands of the position, and the more you've thought about how your skills match those demands, the better you'll be able to respond.

The second essential question is whether you will be a good fit with the organization and the target position. This line of inquiry includes both a general and a specific aspect. The general aspect concerns your overall personality and approach to work. All good employers want people who are confident, dedicated, positive, curious, courteous, ethical, and willing to commit to something larger than their own individual goals. The specific aspect involves the fit with a particular company and position. Just like people, companies have different "personalities." Some are intense; others are more laid back. Some emphasize teamwork; others expect employees to forge their own way and even compete with one another. Expectations also vary from job to job within a company and from industry to industry. An outgoing personality is essential for sales but less so for research, for instance.

PRE-EMPLOYMENT TESTING AND BACKGROUND CHECKS

In an effort to improve the predictability of the selection process, many employers now conduct a variety of pre-employment evaluations and investigations. Here are types of assessments you are likely to encounter during your job search:[27]

Pre-employment tests attempt to provide objective, quantitative information about a candidate's skills, attitudes, and habits.

• **Integrity tests.** Integrity tests attempt to measure how truthful and trustworthy a candidate is likely to be.
• **Personality tests.** Personality tests are designed to gauge such aspects as attitudes toward work, interests, managerial potential, dependability, commitment, and motivation.

- **Cognitive tests.** Cognitive tests measure a variety of attributes involved in acquiring, processing, analyzing, using, and remembering information. Typical tests involve reading comprehension, mathematics, problem solving, and decision making.
- **Job knowledge and job skills tests.** These assessments measure the knowledge and skills required to succeed in a particular position. An accounting candidate, for example, might be tested on accounting principles and legal matters (knowledge) and asked to create a simple balance sheet or income statement (skills).
- **Background checks.** In addition to testing, most companies conduct some sort of background check, including reviewing your credit record, checking to see whether you have a criminal history, and verifying your education. Moreover, you should assume that every employer will conduct a general online search on you. To help prevent a background check from tripping you up, verify that your school transcripts are current, look for any mistakes or outdated information in your credit record, plug your name into multiple search engines to see whether anything embarrassing shows up, and scour your social network profiles and connections for potential problems.

When recruiters interview potential employees, they look for people who communicate well. How do your interview skills rank? Where are your strengths? What are your areas for improvement?

Monkey Business Images/Shutterstock

If you're concerned about any pre-employment test, ask the employer for more information or ask your campus placement office for advice. You can also get more information from both the federal and your provincial or territorial human rights commissions.

Interviewers expect you to know some basic information about the company and its industry.

Preparing for a Job Interview

Now that you're armed with insights into the interviewing and assessment process, you're ready to begin preparing for your interviews. Preparation will help you feel more confident and perform better under pressure, and preparation starts with learning about the organization.

4 **LEARNING OBJECTIVE**

Outline six tasks you need to complete to prepare for a successful job interview.

I. LEARN ABOUT THE ORGANIZATION AND YOUR INTERVIEWERS

Today's companies expect serious candidates to demonstrate an understanding of the company's operations, its markets, and its strategic and tactical challenges.[28] You've already done some initial research to identify companies of interest, but when you're invited to interview, it's time to dig a little deeper (see Table 16–2). Making this effort demonstrates your interest in the company, and it identifies you as a business professional who knows the importance of investigation and analysis.

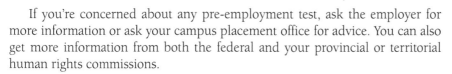

TIPS FOR SUCCESS
"One of the first questions a good interviewer asks is, 'What do you know about our organization?' They want to know that applicants have done their homework."

Paul Munoz, Human Resources Consultant

II. THINK AHEAD ABOUT QUESTIONS

Planning ahead for the interviewer's questions will help you handle them more confidently and successfully. In addition, you will want to prepare insightful questions of your own.

Table 16–2	**Investigating an Organization and a Job Opportunity**

Where to Look and What You Can Learn

- *Company website, blogs, and social media accounts:* Overall information about the company, including key executives, products and services, locations and divisions, employee benefits, job descriptions
- *Competitors' websites, blogs, and social media accounts:* Similar information from competitors, including the strengths these companies claim to have
- *Industry-related websites and blogs:* Objective analysis and criticism of the company, its products, its reputation, and its management
- *Marketing materials (print and online):* The company's marketing strategy and customer communication style
- *Company publications (print and online):* Key events, stories about employees, new products
- *Your social network contacts:* Names and job titles of potential contacts within a company
- *Periodicals (newspapers and trade journals, both print and online):* In-depth stories about the company and its strategies, products, successes, and failures; you may find profiles of top executives
- *Career centre at your school:* Often provides a wide array of information about companies that hire graduates
- *Current and former employees:* Insights into the work environment

Points to Learn about the Organization

- Full name
- Location (headquarters and divisions, branches, subsidiaries, or other units)
- Brief history (origins, culture, values and labour practices, and, if possible, dress code)
- Products and services
- Industry position (whether company is leader or minor player; an innovator or more of a follower; number of employees; and sales)
- Key financial points (such as stock price and trend, if a public company)
- Growth prospects (is the company investing in its future through research and development; is it in a thriving industry?)

Points to Learn about the Position

- Title
- Functions and responsibilities
- Qualifications and expectations
- Possible career paths
- Salary range
- Travel expectations and opportunities
- Relocation expectations and opportunities

You can expect to face a number of common questions in your interviews, so be sure to prepare for them.

PLANNING FOR THE EMPLOYER'S QUESTIONS Many general interview questions are "stock" queries that you can expect to hear again and again during your interviews. Get ready to face these five at the very least:

- **What is the hardest decision you've ever had to make?** Be prepared with a good example (that isn't too personal), explaining why the decision was difficult, how you made the choice you made, and what you learned from the experience.
- **What are your greatest weaknesses?** This question seems to be a favourite of some interviewers, although it probably rarely yields useful information. One good strategy is to mention a skill or attribute you haven't had the opportunity to develop yet but would like to in your next position.[29]
- **Where do you want to be five years from now?** This question tests (1) whether you're merely using this job as a stopover until something better comes along and (2) whether you've given thought to your long-term goals. Whatever you plan to say, your answer should reflect your desire to contribute to the employer's long-term goals, not just your own goals. Whether this question often yields useful information is also a matter of debate, but be prepared to answer it.[30]

- **What didn't you like about previous jobs you've held?** Answer this one carefully: the interviewer is trying to predict whether you'll be an unhappy or difficult employee.[31] Describe something that you didn't like in a way that puts you in a positive light, such as having limited opportunities to apply your skills or education. Avoid making negative comments about former employers or colleagues.
- **Tell me something about yourself.** One good strategy is to *briefly* share the "story of you," quickly summarizing where you have been and where you would like to go—in a way that aligns your interests with the company's. Alternatively, you can focus on a specific skill that you know is valuable to the company, share something business-relevant that you are passionate about, or offer a short summary of what colleagues or customers think about you.[32] Whatever tactic you choose, this is not the time to be shy or indecisive, so be ready with a confident, memorable answer.

Continue your preparation by planning a brief answer to each question in Table 16–3. As you prepare answers, look for ways to frame your responses as brief stories (again, 30 to 90 seconds) rather than simple declarative answers.[33]

The library is an excellent place to learn about employment interviews. How would you organize a search to find relevant material?

Table 16–3	**Twenty-Five Common Interview Questions**

Questions about College and University

1. What courses did you like most? Least? Why?
2. Do you think your extracurricular activities were worth the time you spent on them? Why or why not?
3. When did you choose your program of study? Did you ever change it? If so, why?
4. Do you feel you did the best scholastic work you are capable of?
5. How has your education prepared you for this position?

Questions about Employers and Jobs

6. What jobs have you held? Why did you leave?
7. What percentage of your school expenses did you earn? How?
8. Why did you choose your particular field of work?
9. What are the disadvantages of your chosen field?
10. Have you served in the military? What rank did you achieve? What jobs did you perform?
11. What do you think about how this industry operates today?
12. Why do you think you would like this particular type of job?

Questions about Work Experiences and Expectations

13. Do you prefer to work in any specific geographic location? If so, why?
14. What motivates you? Why?
15. What do you think determines a person's progress in a good organization?
16. Describe an experience in which you learned from one of your mistakes.
17. Why do you want this job?
18. What have you done that shows initiative and willingness to work?
19. Why should I hire you?

Questions about Work Habits and Adaptability

20. Do you prefer working with others or by yourself?
21. What type of boss do you prefer?
22. Have you ever had any difficulty getting along with colleagues or supervisors? With instructors? With other students?
23. Would you prefer to work in a large or a small organization? Why?
24. How do you feel about overtime work?
25. What have you done that shows initiative and willingness to work?

Table 16–4	Twelve Questions to Consider Asking the Interviewer
Question	**Reason for Asking**
1. What are the job's major responsibilities? (unless already outlined in the job posting/description)	A vague answer could mean that the responsibilities have not been clearly defined, which is almost guaranteed to cause frustration if you take the job.
2. What qualities do you want in the person who fills this position?	This will help you go beyond the job description to understand what the company really wants.
3. How do you measure success for someone in this position?	A vague or incomplete answer could mean that the expectations you will face are unrealistic or ill defined.
4. What is the first problem that needs the attention of the person you hire?	Not only will this help you prepare but it can signal whether you're about to jump into a problematic situation.
5. Would relocation be required now or in the future?	If you're not willing to move often or at all, you need to know those expectations now.
6. Why is this job now vacant?	If the previous employee got promoted, that's a good sign. If the person quit, that might not be such a good sign.
7. What makes your organization different from others in the industry?	The answer will help you assess whether the company has a clear strategy to succeed in its industry and whether top managers communicate this to lower-level employees.
8. How would you define your organization's managerial philosophy?	You want to know whether the managerial philosophy is consistent with your own working values.
9. What is a typical workday like for you?	The interviewer's response can give you clues about daily life at the company.
10. What systems and policies are in place to help employees stay up to date in their professions and continue to expand their skills?	If the company doesn't have a strong commitment to employee development, chances are it isn't going to stay competitive for very long.
11. How would you describe this company's culture?	The question targets the corporate philosophy of a company with respect to its employees.
12. Can you tell me the steps that need to be completed before your company can provide an offer of employment?	This provides a timeline for a potential offer and helps you gauge when you should follow up.

Source: http://www.businessinsider.com/questions-to-ask-at-end-of-job-interview-2016-4/#-4.

Look for ways to frame your responses as brief stories rather than as dry facts or statements.

Cohesive stories tend to stick in the listener's mind more effectively than disconnected facts and statements. This is an opportunity to reinforce the "personal brand" message that got you the interview.

PLANNING QUESTIONS OF YOUR OWN Remember that the interview is a two-way conversation: the questions you ask are just as important as the answers you provide. By asking insightful questions, you can demonstrate your understanding of the organization, steer the discussion into those areas that allow you to present your qualifications to best advantage, and verify for yourself whether this a good opportunity. Plus, interviewers expect you to ask questions and tend to look negatively on candidates who don't have any questions to ask. Have two to four purposeful questions prepared in advance. These should not include questions to which you could have easily found answers while researching the company. See Table 16–4 for a place to start.

III. BOLSTER YOUR CONFIDENCE

The best way to build your confidence is to prepare thoroughly and address shortcomings as best you can—in other words, take action.

Interviewing is stressful for everyone, so some nervousness is natural. However, you can take steps to feel more confident. Start by reminding yourself that you have value to offer the employer, and the employer already thinks highly enough of you to invite you to an interview.

If some aspect of appearance or background makes you uneasy, correct it or offset it by emphasizing positive traits such as warmth, wit, intelligence, or charm. Instead of dwelling on your weaknesses, focus on your strengths. Instead of worrying about how you will perform in the interview, focus on how you can help the organization succeed. As with public speaking, the more prepared you are, the more confident you'll be.

IV. POLISH YOUR INTERVIEW STYLE

Competence and confidence are the foundation of your interviewing style, and you can enhance those by giving the interviewer an impression of poise, good manners, and good judgment. You can develop an adept style by staging mock interviews with a friend or using an interview simulator. Record these mock interviews so you can evaluate yourself. Experts advise you to practise your interview skills as much as possible. You can use a friend or classmate as a practice partner, or you might be able to use one of the interview simulators now available. Ask at your career centre, or search online for "practice interviews" or "interview simulators."

Interview simulators, such as this system from Perfect Interview, let you interact with a virtual interviewer and then review and improve your responses. Is this a useful tool to help you relax in job interviews? Why? Why not?

After each practice session, look for opportunities to improve. Have your mock interview partner critique your performance, or critique yourself if you're able to record your practice interviews, using the list of warning signs shown in Table 16–5. Pay close attention to the length of your planned answers as well. Interviewers want you to give complete answers, but they don't want you to take up valuable time or test their patience by chatting about minor or irrelevant details.[34]

In addition to reviewing your answers, evaluate your nonverbal behaviour, including your posture, eye contact, facial expressions, and hand gestures and

Evaluate the length and clarity of your answers, your nonverbal behaviour, and the quality of your voice.

Table 16–5	Warning Signs: Twenty-Five Attributes That Interviewers Don't Like to See

1. Poor personal appearance
2. Overbearing, overly aggressive, or conceited demeanour; a "superiority complex"; a know-it-all attitude
3. Inability to express ideas clearly; poor voice, diction, or grammar
4. Lack of knowledge or experience
5. Poor preparation for the interview
6. Lack of interest in the job
7. Lack of planning for career; lack of purpose or goals
8. Lack of enthusiasm; passive and indifferent demeanour (including showing up late for the interview)
9. Lack of confidence and poise; appearance of being nervous and ill at ease
10. Insufficient evidence of achievement
11. Failure to participate in extracurricular activities
12. Overemphasis on money; interest only in the best dollar offer
13. Poor scholastic record

14. Unwillingness to start at the bottom; expecting too much too soon
15. Tendency to make excuses
16. Evasive answers; hedging on unfavourable factors in record
17. Lack of tact
18. Lack of maturity
19. Lack of courtesy and common sense, including answering mobile phones, texting, or chewing gum during the interview
20. Being critical of past or present employers
21. Lack of social skills (including texting or answering the phone during the interview)
22. Marked dislike for schoolwork
23. Lack of vitality
24. Failure to look interviewer in the eye
25. Limp, weak handshake

Make a positive first impression with careful grooming and attire. Why is it important to look clean, prepared, and professional? How can you evaluate and improve your professional image?

movements. Do you come across as alert and upbeat or passive and withdrawn? Pay close attention to your speaking voice as well. If you tend to speak in a monotone, for instance, practise speaking in a livelier style, with more inflection and emphasis. And watch out for "filler words" such as *uh* and *um*. Many people start sentences with a filler without being conscious of doing so. Train yourself to pause silently for a moment instead as you gather your thoughts and plan what to say.

V. PRESENT A PROFESSIONAL IMAGE

Clothing and grooming are important elements of preparation because they reveal something about your personality, professionalism, and ability to sense the unspoken "rules" of a situation. Inappropriate dress is a common criticism levelled at interviewees, so stand out by looking professional.[35] Your research into various companies, industries, and professions should give you insight into expectations for business attire. If you're not sure what to wear and the company hasn't provided any guidance, ask someone who works in the same industry. And don't be afraid to call the company for advice.

Dress conservatively and be well groomed for every interview; there's plenty of time to be casual after you get the job.

You don't need to spend a fortune on interview clothes, but your clothes must be clean, pressed, and appropriate. The following conservative look will serve you well in most business interview situations:[36]

- Neat, "adult" hairstyle
- Conservative business suit (for women, that means no exposed midriffs, short skirts, or plunging necklines) in a dark solid colour or a subtle pattern such as pinstripes
- Solid colour shirt for men (white in more conservative professions); coordinated blouse for women
- Conservative tie (classic stripes or subtle patterns) for men
- Limited jewellery (men, especially, should wear very little jewellery)
- No visible piercings other than one or two earrings
- No visible tattoos
- Stylish but professional-looking shoes (no extreme high heels or casual shoes)
- Clean hands and nicely trimmed fingernails
- Little or no perfume or cologne (some people are allergic, and many people are put off by strong smells)
- Subtle makeup
- Exemplary personal hygiene

Do a little extra research to find out about the company dress code. Ask human resources; check the corporate website, annual report, or blogs; or contact others in your network.[37] Remember, an interview is a place to send a clear signal that you understand the business world and know how to adapt to it. You won't be taken seriously otherwise.

VI. BE READY WHEN YOU ARRIVE

When you go to your interview, take a small notebook, a pen, a list of the questions you want to ask, two copies of your résumé (protected in a folder), an outline of what you have learned about the organization, and any past correspondence

Blend Images/Alamy Stock Photo

about the position. You may also want to take a small calendar, a transcript of your college or university grades, a list of references, and a portfolio containing samples of your work, performance reviews, and certificates of achievement.[38] Think carefully if you plan to use a tablet computer or any other device for note taking or reference during an interview. You don't want to waste any of the interviewer's time fumbling with it. Also, turn off your mobile phone; in a recent survey of hiring professionals, answering calls and texting while in an interview were identified as the most common mistakes made by job candidates.[39]

Be sure you know when and where the interview will be held. The worst way to start any interview is to be late, and arriving in a stressed-out state isn't much better. Check the route you will take, but don't rely on time estimates from a bus or subway service or from an online mapping service. If you're not familiar with the route, the safest choice is to travel to the location a few days before the interview, if possible, to verify it for yourself. Leave yourself plenty of time for unforeseen problems.

When you arrive, remind yourself that you are fully prepared and confident, and then try to relax. You may have to wait a little while, so bring along something business oriented to read. If company literature is available in the lobby, read it while you wait. At every step, show respect for everyone you encounter. If the opportunity presents itself, ask a few questions about the organization or express enthusiasm for the job. Refrain from smoking before the interview (non-smokers can smell smoke on the clothing of interviewees), and avoid chewing gum or otherwise eating in the waiting area. Anything you do or say while you wait may well get back to the interviewer, so make sure your best qualities show from the moment you enter the premises. That way, you'll be ready for the interview itself once it actually begins. To review the steps for planning a successful interview, see "Checklist: Planning for a Successful Job Interview."

> Be ready to go the minute you arrive at the interviewing site; don't fumble around for your résumé or your list of questions.

✓ Checklist   Planning for a Successful Job Interview

- Learn about the organization, including its operations, markets, and challenges.
- Learn as much as you can about the people who will be interviewing you, if you can find their names.
- Plan for the employer's questions, including questions about tough decisions you've made, your weaknesses, what you didn't like about previous jobs, and your career plans.
- Plan questions of your own to find out whether this is really the job and the organization for you, and to show that you've done your research.
- Bolster your confidence by removing as many sources of apprehension as you can.

- Polish your interview style by staging mock interviews.
- Present a professional appearance with appropriate dress and grooming.
- Be ready when you arrive, and bring along a pen, paper, list of questions, copies of your résumé, an outline of your research on the company, and any correspondence you've had regarding the position.
- Double-check the location and time of the interview and map out the route beforehand.
- Relax and be flexible; the schedule and interview arrangements may change when you arrive.

Interviewing for Success

At this point, you have a good sense of the overall process and know how to prepare for your interviews. The next step is to get familiar with the three stages that occur in some form in all interviews: the warm-up, the question-and-answer stage, and the close.

5 LEARNING OBJECTIVE

Explain the three stages of a successful employment interview.

I. THE WARM-UP

The first minute of the interview is crucial, so stay alert and be on your best business behaviour.

Of the three stages, the warm-up is the most important, even though it may account for only a small fraction of the time you spend in the interview. Studies suggest that many interviewers, particularly those who are poorly trained in interviewing techniques, make up their minds within the first 20 seconds of contact with a candidate.[40] Don't let your guard down if it appears the interviewer wants to engage in what feels like small talk; these exchanges are every bit as important as structured questions.

Body language is important at this point. Stand or sit up straight, maintain regular but natural eye contact, and don't fidget. When the interviewer extends a hand, respond with a firm but not overpowering handshake. Repeat the interviewer's name when you're introduced ("It's a pleasure to meet you, Ms. Litton"). Wait until you're asked to be seated or the interviewer has taken a seat. Let the interviewer start the discussion, and be ready to answer one or two substantial questions right away. The following are some common openers:[41]

Recognize that you could face substantial questions as soon as your interview starts, so make sure you are prepared and ready to go.

- Why do you want to work here?
- What do you know about us?
- Tell me a little about yourself.

II. THE QUESTION-AND-ANSWER STAGE

Questions and answers will usually consume the greatest part of the interview. Depending on the type of interview, the interviewer will likely ask you about your qualifications, discuss some points mentioned in your résumé, and ask about how you have handled particular situations in the past or would handle them in the future. You'll also ask questions of your own. (See "Sharpening Your Career Skills: Don't Talk Yourself Right Out of a Job.")

Listen carefully to questions before you answer.

DEALING WITH QUESTIONS Let the interviewer lead the conversation, and never answer a question before he or she has finished asking it. Not only is this type of interruption rude, but the last few words of the question might alter how you respond. As much as possible, avoid one-word yes-or-no answers. Use the opportunity to expand on a positive response or explain a negative response. If you're asked a difficult question or the offbeat questions that companies such as Google are known to use, pause before responding. Think through the implications of the question. For instance, the recruiter may know that you can't answer a question and only wants to know how you'll respond under pressure.

Whenever you're asked if you have any questions, or whenever doing so naturally fits the flow of the conversation, ask a question from the list you've prepared. Probe for what the company is looking for in its new employees so that you can show how you meet the firm's needs. Also try to zero in on any reservations the interviewer might have about you so that you can dispel them.

Paying attention to both verbal and nonverbal messages can help you turn the question-and-answer stage to your advantage.

LISTENING TO THE INTERVIEWER Paying attention when the interviewer speaks can be as important as giving good answers or asking good questions. The interviewer's facial expressions, eye movements, gestures, and posture may tell you the real meaning of what is being said. Be especially aware of how your comments are received. Does the interviewer nod in agreement or smile to show approval? If so, you're making progress. If not, you might want to introduce another topic or modify your approach.

FIELDING DISCRIMINATORY QUESTIONS Employers cannot legally discriminate against a job candidate on the basis of race, ancestry, place of origin, colour, ethnic origin, citizenship, creed, sex, sexual orientation, age, record of offences, marital status, same-sex partnership status, family status, and handicap. As the

SHARPENING YOUR CAREER SKILLS

Don't Talk Yourself Right Out of a Job

Even well-qualified applicants sometimes talk themselves right out of an opportunity by making avoidable blunders during the job interview. As you develop your interviewing style, avoid these all-too-common mistakes:

- **Being defensive.** An interview isn't an interrogation, and the interviewer isn't out to get you. Treat interviews as business conversations, an exchange of information in which both sides have something of value to share. You'll give (and get) better information that way.

- **Failing to ask questions.** Interviewers expect you to ask questions, both during the interview and at its conclusion when they ask if you have any questions. If you have nothing to ask, you come across as someone who isn't really interested in the job or the company. Prepare a list of questions before every interview.

- **Failing to answer questions—or bluffing your way through difficult questions.** If you simply can't answer a question, don't talk your way around it or fake your way through it. Remember that sometimes interviewers ask strange questions just to see how you'll respond. What kind of fish would you like to be? How would you go about nailing jelly to the ceiling? Why are manhole covers round? Some of these questions are designed to test your grace under pressure, whereas others actually expect you to think through a logical answer (manhole covers are round because that's the only shape that can't fall through an open hole of slightly smaller size, by the way). Don't act like the question is stupid or refuse to answer it. Sit quietly for a few seconds, imagine why the interviewer has asked the question, and then frame an answer that links your strengths to the company's needs.

- **Freezing up.** The human brain seems to have the capacity to just freeze up under stressful situations. An interviewer might have asked you a simple question, or perhaps you were halfway through an intelligent answer, and suddenly all your thoughts disappear and you can't organize words in any logical order. Quickly replay the last few seconds of the conversation in your mind to see if you can recapture the conversational thread. If that fails, you're probably better off explaining to the reviewer that your mind has gone blank and asking him or her to repeat the question. Doing so is embarrassing, but not as embarrassing as chattering on and on with no idea of what you're saying, hoping you'll stumble back onto the topic.

- **Failing to understand your potential to contribute to the organization.** Interviewers care less about your history than about how you can help their organization in the future. Unless you've inventoried your own skills, researched their needs, and found a match between the two, you won't be able to answer these questions quickly and intelligently.

CAREER APPLICATIONS

1. What should you do if you suddenly realize that something you said earlier in the interview is incorrect or incomplete? Explain your answer.

2. How would you answer the following question: "How do you respond to colleagues who make you angry?" Explain your answer.

Ontario Human Rights Code states, "Employment decisions should be based on the applicant's ability to do the job and not on factors that are unrelated to the job." Employers must be familiar with the employment and hiring policies enshrined in their province's or territory's code.

If an interviewer asks personal questions, consider your options carefully before you respond. You can answer the question as it was asked; you can ask tactfully whether the question might be prohibited; you can simply refuse to answer it; or you can try to answer "the question behind the question."[42] For example, if an interviewer inappropriately asks whether you are married or have strong family ties in the area, he or she might be trying to figure out if you're willing to travel or relocate—both of which are acceptable questions. Only you can decide which is the right choice based on the situation.

If you believe an interviewer's questions are unreasonable, unrelated to the job, or an attempt to discriminate, you may complain to your province's or territory's human rights commission. The commission's website will have a link to the complaint-filing process where you will find information to assist you in completing the complaint form.

Think about how you might respond if you are asked a potentially unlawful question.

III. THE CLOSE

Like the warm-up, the end of the interview is more important than its brief duration would indicate. These last few minutes allow you to re-emphasize your value to the organization and to correct any misconceptions the interviewer might have. Many interviewers will ask whether you have any more questions at this point. Take this opportunity to find out more about the job and the company.

Conclude an interview with courtesy and enthusiasm.

CONCLUDING GRACEFULLY You can usually tell when the interviewer is trying to conclude the session. He or she may ask whether you have any more questions, check the time, summarize the discussion, change position, indicate with a gesture that the interview is over, or simply tell you that the allotted time for the interview is up. When you get the signal, be sure to thank the interviewer for the opportunity and express your interest in the organization. The interviewer may also ask you about references, which you could provide at that time or as part of a follow-up letter. If you can do so comfortably, pin down what will happen next, but don't press for an immediate decision. Ask the interviewer for a business card, if you have not already received one. This can help when you want to send a follow-up email or note.

If this is your second or third visit to the organization, the interview may culminate with an offer of employment. If you have other offers or need time to think about this offer, it's perfectly acceptable to thank the interviewer for the offer and ask for some time to consider it. If no job offer is made, the interviewer may not have reached a decision yet, but you may tactfully ask when you can expect to know the decision.

Research salary ranges in your job, industry, and geographic region before you try to negotiate salary.

DISCUSSING SALARY If you receive an offer during the interview, you'll naturally want to discuss salary. However, let the interviewer raise the subject. If asked your salary requirements during the interview or on a job application, you can say that your salary requirements are open or negotiable or that you would expect a competitive compensation package.[43]

Negotiating benefits may be one way to get more value from an employment package.

How far you can negotiate depends on several factors, including market demand for your skills, the strength of the job market, the company's compensation policies, the company's financial health, and whether you have other job offers. Remember that you're negotiating a business deal, not asking for personal favours, so focus on the unique value you can bring to the job. The more information you have, the stronger your position will be.

If salary isn't negotiable, look at the overall compensation and benefits package. You may find flexibility in a signing bonus, profit sharing, retirement benefits, health coverage, vacation time, and other valuable elements.[44]

To review the important tips for successful interviews, see "Checklist: Making a Positive Impression in Job Interviews."

INTERVIEW NOTES

Maintain a notebook or simple database with information about each company, interviewers' answers to your questions, contact information for each interviewer, the status of thank-you notes and other follow-up communication, and upcoming interview appointments. Then quickly evaluate your performance during the interview, listing what you handled well and what you didn't.

Dmitri Ma/Shutterstock

It's good practice to jot down the questions you were asked, and your answers, while the interview is fresh in your mind. Should you keep handwritten notes, or transfer them into a computer file? What are the advantages of maintaining an electronic record of your interviews?

✓ Checklist Making a Positive Impression in Job Interviews

A. Be ready to make a positive impression in the warm-up stage.

- Be alert from the moment you arrive; even initial small talk is part of the interviewing process.
- Greet the interviewer by name, with a smile and direct eye contact.
- Offer a firm (not crushing) handshake if the interviewer extends a hand. Offer your business card.
- Take a seat only after the interviewer invites you to sit or has taken his or her own seat.
- Listen for clues about what the questions reveal about yourself and your qualifications.
- Exhibit positive body language, including standing up straight, walking with purpose, and sitting up straight.

B. Convey your value to the organization during the question-and-answer stage.

- Let the interviewer lead the conversation.
- Never answer a question before the interviewer finishes asking it.
- Listen carefully to the interviewer and watch for nonverbal signals.
- Don't limit yourself to simple yes-or-no answers; expand on the answer to show your knowledge of the company (but don't ramble on).
- If you encounter a potentially discriminatory question, decide how you want to respond before you say anything.
- When you have the opportunity, ask questions from the list you've prepared; remember that interviewers expect you to ask questions.

C. Close on a strong note.

- Watch and listen for signs that the interview is about to end.
- Quickly evaluate how well you've done and correct any misperceptions the interviewer might have.
- If you receive an offer and aren't ready to decide, it's entirely appropriate to ask for time to think about it.
- Don't bring up salary, but be prepared to discuss it if the interviewer raises the subject.
- End with a warm smile and a handshake, and thank the interviewer for meeting with you.

Going over these notes can help you improve your performance in the future.[45] In addition to improving your performance during interviews, your interview notes will help you keep track of any follow-up messages you'll need to send.

Keep a written record of your job interviews, and keep your notes organized so that you can compare companies and opportunities.

Following Up After the Interview

Staying in contact with the prospective employer after the interview, either by phone or in writing, shows that you really want the job and are determined to get it. Doing so also gives you another chance to demonstrate your communication skills and sense of business etiquette. Following up brings your name to the interviewer's attention once again and reminds him or her that you're actively looking and waiting for the decision.

Any time you hear from a company during the application or interview process, be sure to respond quickly. Companies flooded with résumés may move on to another candidate if they don't hear back from you within 24 hours.[46]

6   LEARNING OBJECTIVE

Identify the most common employment messages that follow an interview, and explain when you would use each one.

THANK-YOU MESSAGE

Write a thank-you message within two days after the interview, even if you feel you have little chance of getting the job. In addition to demonstrating good etiquette, a thank-you message gives you the opportunity to reinforce the reasons you are a good choice for the position and lets you respond to any negatives that might have arisen in the interview.[47] Acknowledge the interviewer's time and courtesy, convey your continued interest, reinforce the reasons that you are a

A thank-you message is more than a professional courtesy; it's another chance to promote yourself to an employer.

The second paragraph emphasizes his flexibility and commitment to the job, if hired.

The close maintains a confident but reader-oriented tone and ends with a request for a decision.

Espinosa uses the opening to remind the recipient of their interaction the day before and graciously acknowledges the consideration he was shown.

He then uses this statement about meeting the company's needs as an opportunity to remind the recruiter of his valuable qualifications.

Figure 16–4 Thank-You Message

good fit for the position, and ask politely for a decision. In Figure 16–4, Michael Espinosa accomplishes all of this in three brief paragraphs.

Depending on the company and the relationship you've established with the interviewer, the thank-you message can be handled via letter, email, or handwritten note on personal stationery. Be brief and sound positive without sounding overconfident.

MESSAGE OF INQUIRY

Use the model for a direct request when you write an inquiry about a hiring decision.

If you're not advised of the interviewer's decision by the promised date or within two weeks, you might make an inquiry. A message of inquiry (which can be handled by email if the interviewer has given you his or her email address) is particularly appropriate if you've received a job offer from a second firm and don't want to accept it before you have an answer from the first. The following message illustrates the general plan for a direct request:

Identifies the position and introduces the main idea

> When we talked on April 7 about the fashion coordinator position in your Design Walk showroom, you indicated that a decision would be made by May 1. I am still enthusiastic about the position and eager to know what conclusion you have reached.

Places the reason for the request second

> To complicate matters, another firm has now offered me a position and has asked that I reply within the next two weeks.

Makes a courteous request for specific action last, while clearly stating a preference for this organization

> Because your company seems to offer a greater challenge, I would appreciate knowing about your decision by Thursday, May 10. If you need more information before then, please let me know.

REQUEST FOR A TIME EXTENSION

If you receive a job offer while other interviews are still pending, you'll probably want more time to decide, so write to the offering organization and ask for a time extension. Open with a strong statement of your continued interest in the job, ask for more time to consider the offer, provide specific reasons for the request, and assure the reader that you will respond by a specific date. The letter in Figure 16–5 is a good example.

LETTER OF ACCEPTANCE

When you receive a job offer that you want to accept, reply within five days. Begin by accepting the position and expressing thanks. Identify the job that you're accepting. In the next paragraph, cover any necessary details. Conclude by saying that you look forward to reporting for work. As always, a positive message should convey your enthusiasm and eagerness to cooperate:

Your job search will require dealing with voicemail. When leaving a message, first state your name and phone number, then describe the purpose of your call, and end by restating your name and number. Write down and rehearse what you want to say so your delivery is smooth and clear. Why are voicemail skills important to employers?

The opening starts with a strong statement of interest in the job, setting a positive tone for the entire message.

Emphasizing specific reasons for preferring the first job offer helps reassure the reader of the writer's sincerity.

Dear Mr. Lapuzo:

The e-commerce director position at Lone Star Foods is an exciting challenge and a great opportunity. I'm very pleased that you offered it to me.

Because of another commitment, I would appreciate your giving me until January 25 to make a decision. Before our interview, I scheduled a follow-up interview with another company. I'm interested in your organization because of its commitment to quality and team-based management style, but I do feel obligated to keep my appointment.

If you need my decision immediately, I'll gladly let you know. However, if you can allow me the added time to fulfill the earlier commitment, I'd be grateful. Please let me know at your earliest convenience.

Sincerely,

Chang Li
844 Newport Avenue
Thunder Bay, ON P7A 6K2
807-555-5697

The reasoning offered is general but entirely sufficient and expressed in a professional way.

The close expresses a willingness to yield or compromise while conveying continued interest in the position.

Figure 16–5 Request for a Time Extension

Confirms the specific terms of the offer with a good-news statement at the beginning → I'm delighted to accept the graphic design position in your advertising department at the salary of $3275 a month.

Covers miscellaneous details in the middle → Enclosed are the health insurance forms you asked me to complete and sign. I've already given notice to my current employer and will be able to start work on Monday, January 18.

Closes with another reference to the good news and a look toward the future → The prospect of joining your firm is exciting. Thank you for giving me this opportunity for what I'm sure will be a challenging future.

Use the model for positive messages when you write a letter of acceptance.

Written acceptance of a job offer can be considered a legally binding contract.

Be aware that a job offer and a written acceptance of that offer can constitute a legally binding contract, for both you and the employer. Before you write an acceptance letter, ensure that you want the job.

LETTER DECLINING A JOB OFFER

If you decide to decline a job offer, do so tactfully, using the model for negative messages.

After all your interviews, you may find that you need to write a letter declining a job offer. Use the techniques for negative messages: open warmly; state the reasons for refusing the offer; decline the offer explicitly; and close on a pleasant note, expressing gratitude. By taking the time to write a sincere, tactful letter, you leave the door open for future contact:

Uses a buffer in the opening paragraph → Thank you for your hospitality during my interview at your Montreal facility last month. I'm flattered that you would offer me the computer analyst position that we talked about.

Precedes the bad news with tactfully phrased reasons for the applicant's unfavourable decision and leaves the door open → I was fortunate to receive two job offers during my search. Because my desire to work abroad can more readily be satisfied by the other company, I have accepted that job offer.

Lets the reader down gently with a sincere and cordial ending → I deeply appreciate the time you spent talking with me. Thank you again for your consideration and kindness.

LETTER OF RESIGNATION

Letters of resignation should always be written in a gracious and professional style that avoids criticism of your employer or your colleagues.

If you get a job offer and are currently employed, you can maintain good relations with your current employer by writing a letter of resignation to your immediate supervisor. Follow the approach for negative messages and make the letter sound as positive as possible, regardless of how you feel. Don't take this letter as an opportunity to vent any frustrations you may have. Say something favourable about the organization, the people you work with, or what you've learned on the job. Then state your intention to leave and give the date of your last day on the job. Be sure to give your current employer at least two weeks' notice:

Uses an appreciative opening to serve as a buffer → My sincere thanks to you and to all the other Emblem Corporation employees for helping me learn so much about serving the public these past two years. You have given me untold help and encouragement.

States reasons before the bad news itself, using tactful phrasing to help keep the relationship friendly, should the writer later want letters of recommendation → You may recall that when you first interviewed me, my goal was to become a customer relations supervisor. Because that opportunity has been offered to me by another organization, I am submitting my resignation. I will miss my friends and colleagues at Emblem, but I want to take advantage of this opportunity.

Discusses necessary details in an extra paragraph → I would like to terminate my work here two weeks from today but can arrange to work an additional week if you want me to train a replacement.

Tempers any disappointment with a cordial close → My sincere thanks and best wishes to all of you.

To verify the content and style of your follow-up messages, consult the tips in "Checklist: Writing Follow-Up Messages."

✓ Checklist   Writing Follow-Up Messages

A. Thank-you messages
- Write a brief thank-you letter within two days of the interview.
- Acknowledge the interviewer's time and courtesy.
- Restate the specific job you're applying for.
- Express your enthusiasm about the organization and the job.
- Add any new facts that may help your chances.
- Politely ask for a decision.

B. Messages of inquiry
- If you haven't heard from the interviewer by the promised date, write a brief message of inquiry.
- Use a direct approach: main idea, necessary details, and specific request.

C. Requests for a time extension
- Request an extension if you have pending interviews and need time to decide about an offer.
- Open on a friendly note.
- Explain why you need more time and express continued interest in the company.
- In the close, promise a quick decision if your request is denied and ask for a confirmation if your request is granted.

D. Letters of acceptance
- Send this message within five days of receiving the offer.
- State clearly that you accept the offer, identify the job you're accepting, and confirm vital details such as salary and start date.
- Make sure you want the job; an acceptance letter can be treated as a legally binding contract.

E. Letters declining a job offer
- Use the indirect approach for negative messages.
- Open on a warm and appreciative note and then explain why you are refusing the offer.
- End on a sincere, positive note.

F. Letters of resignation
- Send a letter of resignation to your current employer as soon as possible.
- Begin with an appreciative buffer.
- In the middle section, state your reasons for leaving and actually state that you are resigning.
- Close cordially.

SUMMARY OF LEARNING OBJECTIVES

1 Define the purpose of application letters, and explain how to apply the AIDA organizational approach to them. The purpose of an application letter is to convince readers to look at your résumé. This makes application letters a type of sales letter, so you'll want to use the AIDA organizational approach. Get attention in the opening paragraph by showing how your work skills could benefit the organization, by explaining how your qualifications fit the job, or by demonstrating an understanding of the organization's needs. Build interest and desire by showing how you can meet the job requirements, and ensure that you refer your reader to your résumé near the end of this section. Finally, motivate action by making your request easy to fulfill and by including all necessary contact information.

2 Describe the typical sequence of job interviews. Most companies interview a candidate several times before making the job offer. The first stage in the sequence is the screening stage, when a short list of suitable applicants

is developed. The second is the selection stage: here, you will show your skills and professionalism. In the final stage, your interviewers will persuade you to join the company if they want to hire you.

3 Describe briefly what employers look for during an employment interview and pre-employment testing. Employers want to see whether you will fit with the corporate culture and whether you can handle the responsibilities of the position. They will ask you about your personal interests, previous experience, industry knowledge, and work habits. Pre-employment testing helps the organization determine your work ethic, skills, and ability to think critically and make decisions.

4 Outline six tasks you need to complete to prepare for a successful job interview. To prepare for a successful job interview, (1) learn as much as you can about the company and its needs, so you can demonstrate your fit with the organization; (2) predict questions—both those you'll need to answer and those you'll want to ask; (3) bolster your confidence by focusing on your strengths to overcome any apprehension; (4) refine your interview style by staging mock interviews and paying close attention to nonverbal behaviours; (5) plan to look your best with businesslike clothing and good grooming; and (6) arrive on time feeling confident and ready to begin.

5 **Explain the three stages of a successful employment interview.** All employment interviews have three stages. The warm-up stage is the most important because first impressions greatly influence an interviewer's decision. The question-and-answer stage is the longest: here you will describe your qualifications and demonstrate your suitability for the job. Listening carefully and watching the interviewer's nonverbal clues help you determine how the interview is going. The close is also important because you need to evaluate your performance to see whether the interviewer has any misconceptions that you must correct.

6 **Identify the most common employment messages that follow an interview, and explain when you would use each one.** Thanking the interviewer for the interview and inquiring about the decision are the most common post-interview messages. The thank-you message should be sent, either by letter or email, within two days after your interview to show appreciation, reinforce your suitability for the job, and politely ask for a decision. You should send an inquiry if you haven't received the interviewer's decision by the date promised or within two weeks of the interview—especially if you've received a job offer from another firm. The remaining four employment messages are best sent in letter form, to document any official action. You request a time extension if you receive a job offer while other interviews are pending and you want more time to complete those interviews before making a decision. You send a letter of acceptance within five days of receiving a job offer that you want to take. You send a letter declining a job offer when you want to refuse an offer tactfully and leave the door open for future contact. You send a letter of resignation when you receive a job offer that you want to accept while you are currently employed.

ON THE JOB PERFORMING COMMUNICATION TASKS AT GOOGLE

Google recruiters work year-round arranging career fairs, booking speaking engagements, and responding to inquiries—all to attract the best students for the company. As a member of Google's human resources department at its Toronto location, you are responsible for screening job candidates and arranging for candidates to interview with members of Google's professional staff. Your responsibilities include developing interview questions and participating in evaluation interviews. In each of the following situations, choose the best alternative and be prepared to justify your choice.

1. During the on-campus screening interviews, you ask several candidates, "Why do you want to work for Google?" Of the following responses, which would you rank the highest?

    a. "I'd like to work here because I'm interested in the computer software industry. I've always been fascinated by technology. In addition to studying computer programming, I have taken courses in marketing and finance. I also have some personal experience in building computers. I enjoy helping my friends construct computer systems for their needs."

    b. "I'm an independent person with a lot of internal drive. I do my best work when I'm given a fairly free rein to use my creativity. From what I've read about your corporate culture, I think my working style would fit very well with your management philosophy. I'm also the sort of person who identifies very strongly with my job. For better or worse, I define myself through my affiliation with my employer. I get a great sense of pride from being part of a first-rate operation, and I think Google is first-rate. I've read about your selection as one of North America's best companies to work for. The articles say that Google is a well-managed company. I think I would learn a lot working here, and I think my drive and creativity would be appreciated."

    c. "There are a couple of reasons why I'd like to work for Google. I have friends who work here, and they both say it's terrific. I've also heard good things about your compensation and benefits."

    d. "My ultimate goal is to start my own company, but first I need to learn more about managing a business. I read in *Fortune* that Google is one of North America's best companies to work for. I think I could learn a lot by joining your software development group and observing your operations."

2. You are preparing questions for the professional staff to use when conducting follow-up interviews. You want a question that will reveal something about the candidates' probable loyalty to the organization. Which of the following questions is the best choice?

    a. If you knew you could be one of the world's most successful people in a single occupation, such as music, politics, medicine, or business, what occupation would you choose? If you knew you had only a 10 percent chance of being so successful, would you still choose the same occupation?

    b. We value loyalty among our employees. Tell me something about yourself that demonstrates your loyalty as a member of an organization.

c. What would you do if you discovered that a co-worker routinely made personal, unauthorized long-distance phone calls from work?

d. What other companies are you interviewing with?

3. In concluding an evaluation interview, you ask the candidate, "Do you have any questions?" Which of the following answers would you respond most favourably to?

a. "No. I can't think of anything. You've been very thorough in describing the job and the company. Thank you for taking the time to talk with me."

b. "Yes. I have an interview with one of your competitors, next week. How would you sum up the differences between your two firms?"

c. "Yes. If I were offered a position here, what would my chances be of getting promoted within the next 12 months?"

d. "Yes. Do you think Google will be a better or worse company 15 years from now?"

TEST YOUR KNOWLEDGE

1. What are key tips for writing application letters?

2. How does a structured interview differ from an unstructured interview?

3. What typically occurs during a stress interview?

4. Why do employers conduct pre-employment testing?

5. Why are the questions you ask during an interview as important as the answers you give to the interviewer's questions?

6. What are the three stages of every interview? Which is the most important?

7. How should you respond if an interviewer at a company where you want to work asks you a question that seems too personal or unethical?

8. What should you say in a thank-you message after an interview?

9. What is the purpose of sending a letter of inquiry after an interview?

10. What organizational plan is appropriate for a letter of resignation? Why?

APPLY YOUR KNOWLEDGE

1. How can you distinguish yourself from other candidates in a screening interview and still keep your responses short and to the point? Explain.

2. What can you do to make a favourable impression when you discover that an open-ended interview has turned into a stress interview? Briefly explain your answer.

3. If you want to switch jobs because you can't work with your supervisor, how can you explain this situation to a prospective employer? Give an example.

4. If you lack one important qualification for a job but have made it past the initial screening stage, how should you prepare to handle this issue during the next round of interviews? Explain your answer.

5. **Ethical Choices** Why is it important to distinguish unethical or illegal interview questions from acceptable questions? Explain.

RUNNING CASES

> CASE 1 Noreen

After submitting her cover letter and résumé for the position of Merger Project Manager, Noreen is selected for an interview. Noreen arrives 10 minutes early. She remains in the waiting area until she is asked to enter the meeting room. She walks in and sees six senior management staff sitting around a large table. She is asked to sit down. The managers introduce themselves to Noreen. Noreen knows two of them already.

QUESTIONS

a. What should Noreen wear to the interview?

b. What questions might she be asked?

c. What questions might she have?

d. Since this is an internal interview (she already works for the company), should she assume that this will be an informal or casual interview?

e. List three topics that Noreen should not discuss during the interview.

YOUR TASK

Form a group to role play this interview. First, select one person to be Noreen. Noreen needs to prepare answers and questions for the interview. The group needs to prepare questions and answers for Noreen. Second, in this role play Noreen gets a call after the interview and is offered the position. Noreen then needs to negotiate more money than offered as well as a written guarantee that she may return to her previous position or equivalent upon completion of the merger project.

> CASE 2 Kwong

Kwong is interviewing potential candidates for the administrative assistant position in his firm, CG Accounting. Some are overqualified and some have no work experience at all, which in his opinion makes them underqualified. One job applicant is very impressive and answers Kwong's questions confidently and accurately during the interview. Kwong feels this person has the right education but has no work experience. He decides to hire this job applicant anyway.

QUESTIONS

a. Will the job applicant do well in the job without work experience?
b. What would the "right education" be in this case?
c. Should Kwong discuss salary during the interview?
d. Is Kwong legally allowed to ask the applicant if he or she is able to work overtime?
e. List three ways the applicant can demonstrate his or her interest in the position during the interview.

YOUR TASK

Role play this interview in a group of three students. One student can play Kwong, one can play his sister, and the other can play the job applicant. The job applicant needs to prepare answers for the interviewers, and Kwong and his sister need to prepare questions for the job applicant.

In this role play ask the job applicant if he or she feels over- or underqualified for this position and have the applicant explain his or her answer. Have Kwong ask the applicant why he or she is applying for this position and how long he or she plans to stay in this position. Have Kwong's sister ask if the applicant is married and what religion the applicant practises. Kwong's sister should explain that she is asking because there is overtime work during tax season and the company wants to ensure the availability of employees. These are illegal questions to ask during a job interview in Canada, so have the actors in the role play deal with them.

PRACTISE YOUR KNOWLEDGE

Read the following documents and then (1) analyze the strengths or weaknesses of each document and (2) revise each document so that it follows this chapter's guidelines.

DOCUMENT 16.A: WRITING AN APPLICATION LETTER

I'm writing to let you know about my availability for the brand manager job you advertised. As you can see from my enclosed résumé, my background is perfect for the position. Even though I don't have any real job experience, my grades have been outstanding considering that I went to a top-ranked business school.

I did many things during my undergraduate years to prepare me for this job:

- Earned a 3.4 out of a 4.0 with a 3.8 in my business courses
- Elected to the student governing association
- Selected to receive the Lamar Franklin Award
- Worked to earn a portion of my tuition

I am sending my résumé to all the top firms, but I like yours better than any of the rest. Your reputation is tops in the industry, and I want to be associated with a business that can really say it's the best.

If you wish for me to come in for an interview, I can come on a Friday afternoon or anytime on weekends when I don't have classes. Again, thanks for considering me for your brand manager position.

DOCUMENT 16.B: WRITING APPLICATION FOLLOW-UP MESSAGES

Did you receive my résumé? I sent it to you at least two months ago and haven't heard anything. I know you keep résumés on file, but I just want to ensure that you keep me in mind. I heard you are hiring health care managers and certainly would like to be considered for one of those positions.

Since I last wrote you, I've worked in a variety of positions that have helped prepare me for management. You'll want to know I've become lunch manager at the restaurant where I work, which involved a raise in pay. I now manage a wait staff of 12 girls and take the lunch receipts to the bank every day.

Of course, I'd much rather be working at a real job, and that's why I'm writing again. Is there anything else you would like to know about my background or me? I would really like to know more about your company. Is there any literature you could send me? If so, I would really appreciate it.

I think one reason I haven't been hired yet is that I don't want to leave Winnipeg. So I hope when you think of me, it's for a position that wouldn't require moving. Thanks again for considering my application.

DOCUMENT 16.C: THANK-YOU MESSAGE

Thank you for the really awesome opportunity to meet you and your colleagues at Starret Engine Company. I really enjoyed touring your facilities and talking with all the people there. What an awesome group! Some of the other companies I have visited have been so rigid and uptight that I can't imagine how I would fit in. It's a relief to run into a group of people who seem to enjoy their work as much as all of you do.

I know that you must be looking at many other candidates for this job, and I know that some of them will probably be more experienced than I am. But I do want to emphasize that my hitch in the Royal Canadian Navy involved a good deal of engineering work. I don't think I mentioned all my shipboard responsibilities during the interview.

Please give me a call within the next week to let me know your decision. You can usually find me at my dormitory in the evening after dinner (phone: 902-555-9080).

DOCUMENT 16.D: LETTER OF INQUIRY

I have recently received a very attractive job offer from the Wellington Company. But before I let them know one way or another, I would like to consider any offer that your firm may extend. I was quite impressed with your company during my recent interview, and I am still very interested in a career there.

I don't mean to pressure you, but Wellington has asked for my decision within 10 days. Could you let me know by Tuesday whether you plan to offer me a position? That would give me enough time to compare the two offers.

DOCUMENT 16.E: LETTER DECLINING A JOB OFFER

I'm writing to say that I must decline your job offer. Another company has made me a more generous offer, and I have decided to accept. However, if things don't work out for me there, I will let you know. I sincerely appreciate your interest in me.

EXERCISES

16.1 Career Management: Researching Target Employers

Select a medium or large company (one that you can easily find information on) where you might like to work. Use online sources to gather some preliminary research on the company; don't limit your search to the company's own website.

  a. What did you learn about this organization that would help you during an interview there?
  b. What online sources did you use to obtain this information?
  c. Armed with this information, what aspects of your background do you think might appeal to this company's recruiters?
  d. Based on what you've learned about this company's culture, what aspects of your personality should you try to highlight during an interview?

16.2 Career Management: Interviewing

Divide the class into two groups. Half the class will be recruiters for a large chain of national department stores looking to fill manager trainee positions (there are 16 openings). The other half will be candidates for the job. The company is specifically looking for candidates who demonstrate these three qualities: initiative, dependability, and willingness to assume responsibility.

  a. Have each recruiter select and interview an applicant for 10 minutes.
  b. Have all the recruiters discuss how they assessed the applicant in each of the three desired qualities. What

questions did they ask, or what did they use as an indicator to determine whether the candidate possessed the quality?
  c. Have all the applicants discuss what they said to convince the recruiters that they possessed each quality.

16.3 Career Management: Understanding Qualifications

Write a short email to your instructor discussing what you believe are your greatest strengths and weaknesses from an employment perspective. Next, explain how these strengths and weaknesses would be viewed by interviewers evaluating your qualifications.

16.4 Career Management: Interviewing

Prepare written answers to 10 of the questions listed in Table 16–3, "Twenty-Five Common Interview Questions."

16.5 Ethical Choices: Leaving Your Employer

You have decided to accept a new position with a competitor of your company. Write a letter of resignation to your supervisor announcing your decision.

  a. Will you notify your employer that you are joining a competing firm? Please explain.
  b. Will you use the direct or the indirect approach? Please explain.
  c. Will you send your letter by email, send it by regular mail, or place it on your supervisor's desk?

CASES	PREPARING DIFFERENT TYPES OF EMPLOYMENT MESSAGES

❚Email SKILLS ❚

1. Application Letters: Echoing a Job Description

Use Job Bank (Service Canada) (www.jobbank.gc.ca), Monster (www.monster.ca), Workopolis (www.workopolis.com), CareerBuilder (www.careerbuilder.ca), CareerOwl (www.careerowl.ca), or Dice.com (www.dice.com) to find a job opening in your target profession. If you haven't narrowed down your job search to one career field yet, choose a business job for which you will have at least some qualifications at the time of your graduation.

Your task: Write an email message that would serve as your application letter if you were to apply for this job. Base your message on your actual qualifications for the position, and be sure to "echo" the requirements listed in the job description. Include the job description in your email message when you submit it to your instructor.

❚Email SKILLS ❚

2. Application Letter: A Job with Google Earth

You've applied yourself with vigour and resolve for four years, and you're just about to graduate with your business degree. While cruising the Web to relax one night, you decide to explore Google Earth. You're hooked instantly by the ability to zoom all around the globe and look at detailed satellite photos of places you've been to or dreamed of visiting. You can even type in the address of your apartment and get an aerial view of your neighbourhood. You're amazed at the three-dimensional renderings of major Canadian cities. Plus, the photographs and maps are linked to Google's other search technologies, allowing you to locate everything from ATMs to coffee shops in your neighbourhood.

You've loved maps since you were a kid, and discovering Google Earth is making you wish you had majored in geography instead. Knowing how important it is to follow your heart, you decide to apply to Google anyway, even though you don't have a strong background in geographic information systems. What you do have is a passion for maps and a good head for business.

Your task: Visit www.google.com/earth/index.html and explore the system's capabilities. (You can download a free copy of the software.) In particular, look at the business and government applications of the technology, such as customized aerial photos and maps for real estate sales, land use and environmental impact analysis, and emergency planning. Ensure that you visit the Community pages as well, where you can learn more about the many interesting applications of this technology. Now draft an application email to Google asking to be considered for the Google Earth team. Think about how you could help the company develop the commercial potential of this product line, and ensure that your enthusiasm shines through in the message.

Interviewing with Potential Employers

❚Teamwork SKILLS ❚ **❚Blogging** SKILLS ❚

3. Career Management: Researching Target Employers

Research is a critical element of the job-search process. With information in hand, you increase the chance of finding the right opportunity (and avoiding bad choices), and you impress interviewers in multiple ways by demonstrating initiative, curiosity, research and analysis skills, an appreciation for the complex challenges of running a business, and willingness to work to achieve results.

Your task: With a small team of classmates, use online job listings to identify an intriguing job opening that at least one member of the team would seriously consider pursuing as graduation approaches. (You'll find it helpful if the career is related to at least one team member's major or on-the-job experience so that the team can benefit from some knowledge of the profession in question.) Next, research the company, its competitors, its markets, and this specific position to identify five questions that would (1) help the team member decide if this is a good opportunity and (2) show an interviewer that you've really done your homework. Go beyond the basic and obvious questions to identify current, specific, and complex issues that only deep research can uncover. For example, is the company facing significant technical, financial, legal, or regulatory challenges that threaten its ability to grow or perhaps even survive in the long term? Or is the market evolving in a way that positions this particular company for dramatic growth? In a post for your class blog, list your five questions, identify how you uncovered the issue, and explain why each is significant.

❚Teamwork SKILLS ❚

4. Career Management: Interviewing

Interviewing is clearly an interactive process involving at least two people. The best way to practise for interviews is to work with others.

Your task: You and all other members of your class are to write letters of application for an entry-level or management-trainee position requiring a pleasant personality and intelligence but a minimum of specialized education or experience. Sign your letter with a fictitious name that conceals your identity. Next, polish (or create) a résumé that accurately identifies you and your educational and professional accomplishments.

Now, three members of the class who volunteer as interviewers divide up all the anonymously written application letters. Then, each interviewer selects a candidate who seems the most pleasant and convincing in his or her letter. At this time the selected candidates identify themselves and give the interviewers their résumés.

Each interviewer then interviews his or her chosen candidate in front of the class, seeking to understand how the items on the résumé qualify the candidate for the job. At the end of the interviews, the class may decide who gets the job and discuss why this candidate was successful. Afterward, retrieve your letter, sign it with the right name, and submit it to the instructor for credit.

❙Teamwork SKILLS **❙**

5. Career Management: Interviewing

Select a company in an industry in which you might like to work, and then identify an interesting position within the company. Study the company, industry, products or services using business resources such as www.annualreports.com, www.cbr.ca, www.frasers.com, www.hoovers.com, www.lc.gc.ca and www.companyspotlight.com. Collect the information that you will need to prepare for an interview with that company.

Your task: Working with a classmate, take turns interviewing each other for your chosen positions. Interviewers should take notes during the interview. Once the interview is complete, critique each other's performance. (Interviewers should critique how well candidates prepared for the interview and answered the questions; interviewees should critique the quality of the questions asked.) Write a follow-up letter thanking your interviewer, and submit the letter to your instructor.

Following Up after the Interview

❙Letter Writing SKILLS **❙**

6. Message Strategies: Request for a Time Extension

Because of a mix-up in your job application scheduling, you accidentally applied for your third-choice job before going after what you really wanted. What you want to do is work in retail marketing with the upscale department store Holt Renfrew in Victoria; what you have been offered is a similar job with Sears in Regina.

You review your notes. Your Regina interview was three weeks ago with human resources manager R. P. Bronson, a congenial person who has just written to offer you the position. The store's address is P.O. Box 79801, Regina, SK, S4N 0A0.

Mr. Bronson notes that he can hold the position open for 10 days. You have an interview scheduled with Holt Renfrew next week, but it is unlikely that you will know the store's decision within this 10-day period.

Your task: Write to R. P. Bronson, requesting a reasonable delay in your consideration of his job offer.

❙Letter Writing SKILLS **❙**

7. Message Strategies: A Set of Employment-Related Letters to a Single Company

Where would you like to work? Choose one of your favourite products, find out which company either manufactures it or sells it in Canada (if it's manufactured in another country). Assume that a month ago you sent your résumé and application letter. Not long afterward, you were invited to come for an interview, which seemed to go very well.

Your task: Use your imagination to write the following: (a) a thank-you letter for the interview, (b) a note of inquiry, (c) a request for more time to decide, (d) a letter of acceptance, and (e) a letter declining the job offer.

Format and Layout of Business Documents

The format and layout of business documents vary from country to country. In addition, many organizations develop their own variations of standard styles, adapting documents to the types of messages they send and the kinds of audiences they communicate with. The formats described here are the most common approaches used in Canadian and U.S. business correspondence, but be sure to follow whatever practices are expected at your company.

First Impressions

Your documents tell readers a lot about you and about your company's professionalism. All your documents must look neat, present a professional image, and be easy to read. Your audience's first impression of a document comes from the quality of its paper, the way it is customized, and its general appearance.

PAPER

To give a quality impression, businesspeople consider carefully the paper they use. Several aspects of paper contribute to the overall impression:

- **Weight.** Paper quality is judged by the weight of four reams (each a 500-sheet package) of letter-size paper. The weight most commonly used by Canadian and U.S. businesses is 20-pound paper, but 16- and 24-pound versions are also used.
- **Cotton content.** Paper quality is also judged by the percentage of cotton in the paper. Cotton doesn't yellow over time the way wood pulp does, plus it's both strong and soft. For letters and outside reports, use paper with a 25 percent cotton content. For memos and other internal documents, you can use a lighter-weight paper with lower cotton content. Airmail-weight paper may save money for international correspondence, but ensure that it isn't too flimsy.[1]
- **Size.** In Canada and the United States, the standard paper size for business documents is 8½ by 11 inches. Standard legal documents are 8½ by 14 inches. Executives sometimes have heavier 7-by-10-inch paper on hand (with matching envelopes) for personal messages such as congratulations and recommendations.[2] They may also have a box of notecards imprinted with their initials and a box of plain folded notes for condolences or for acknowledging formal invitations.
- **Colour.** White is the standard colour for business purposes, although neutral colours such as grey and ivory are sometimes used. Memos can be produced on pastel-coloured paper to distinguish them from external correspondence. In addition, memos are sometimes produced on various colours of paper for routing to separate departments. Light-coloured papers are appropriate, since bright or dark colours make reading difficult and may appear too frivolous.

CUSTOMIZATION

For letters to outsiders, Canadian and U.S. businesses commonly use letterhead stationery, which may be either professionally printed or designed in-house using word-processing templates and graphics. Letterhead typically contains the company name, logo, address, telephone and fax numbers, general email address, website URL, and possibly one or more social media URLs.

In Canada and the United States, businesses always use letterhead for the first page of a letter. Successive pages are usually plain sheets of paper that match the letterhead in colour and quality. Some companies use a specially printed second-page letterhead that bears only the company's name.

APPEARANCE

Nearly all business documents are produced using an inkjet or laser printer; make sure to use a clean, high-quality printer. Certain documents, however, should be handwritten (such as a short informal memo or a note of condolence). Be sure to handwrite, print, or type the envelope to match the document. However, even a letter on the best-quality paper with the best-designed letterhead may look unprofessional if it's poorly produced. So pay close attention to all the factors affecting appearance, including the following:

- **Margins.** Business letters typically use 1-inch margins at the top, bottom, and sides of the page, although these parameters are sometimes adjusted to accommodate letterhead elements.
- **Line length.** Lines are rarely justified, because the resulting text looks too much like a form letter and can be hard to read. Varying line length makes the document look more personal and interesting.
- **Character spacing.** Use proper spacing between characters and after punctuation. For example, Canadian conventions include leaving one space after commas, semicolons, colons, and sentence-ending periods.

Each letter in a person's initials is followed by a period and a single space. However, abbreviations such as U.S.A. or MBA may or may not have periods, but they never have internal spaces.

- **Special symbols.** Take advantage of the many special symbols available with your computer's selection of fonts. In addition, see if your company has a style guide for documents, which may include other symbols you are expected to use.
- **Corrections.** Messy corrections are unacceptable in business documents. If you notice an error after printing a document with your word processor, correct the mistake and reprint. (With informal memos to members of your own team or department, the occasional small correction in pen or pencil is acceptable, but never in formal documents.)

Letters

All business letters have certain elements in common. Several of these elements appear in every letter; others appear only when desirable or appropriate. In addition, these letter parts are usually arranged in one of three basic formats.

STANDARD LETTER PARTS

The letter in Figure A–1 shows the placement of standard letter parts. The writer of this business letter had no letterhead available but correctly included a heading. All business letters typically include these seven elements.

HEADING The elements of the letterhead make up the heading of a letter in most cases. If letterhead stationery

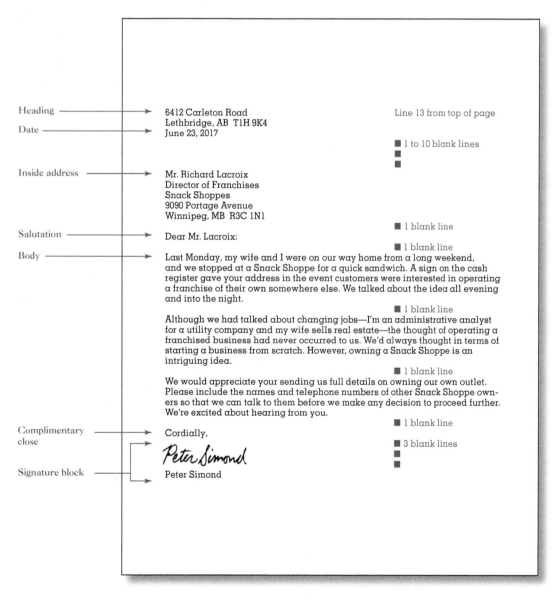

Figure A–1 Standard Letter Parts

Table A–1	**Common Date Forms**		
Convention	**Description**	**Date—Mixed**	**Date—All Numerals**
Canadian standard	Month (spelled out) day, year	July 16, 2017	7/16/17
Canadian government and some Canadian industries	Day (in numerals) month (spelled out) year	16 July 2017	16/7/17
European	Replace Canadian solidus (diagonal line) with periods	16 July 2017	16.7.2017
International standard (ISO)	Year month day	2017 July 16	2017-07-16

is not available, the heading includes a return address (but no name) and starts 13 lines from the top of the page, which leaves a 2-inch top margin.

DATE If you're using letterhead, place the date at least one blank line beneath the lowest part of the letterhead. Without letterhead, place the date immediately below the return address. The standard method of writing the date in Canada uses the full name of the month (no abbreviations), followed by the day (in numerals, without *st*, *nd*, *rd*, or *th*), a comma, and then the year: July 16, 2017. Some organizations follow other conventions (see Table A–1). To maintain the utmost clarity in international correspondence, always spell out the name of the month in dates.[3]

INSIDE ADDRESS The inside address identifies the recipient of the letter. For Canadian correspondence, begin the inside address at least one line below the date. Precede the addressee's name with a courtesy title, such as *Dr.*, *Mr.*, or *Ms.* The accepted courtesy title for women in business is *Ms.*, although a woman known to prefer the title *Miss* or *Mrs.* is always accommodated. If you don't know whether a person is a man or a woman (and you have no way of finding out), omit the courtesy title. For example, *Terry Smith* could be either a man or a woman. The first line of the inside address would be just *Terry Smith*, and the salutation would be *Dear Terry Smith*. The same is true if you know only a person's initials, as in *S. J. Adams*.

Spell out and capitalize titles that precede a person's name, such as *Professor* or *General* (see Table A–2 for the proper forms of address). The person's organizational title, such as *Director*, may be included on this first line (if it is short) or on the line below; the name of a department may follow. In addresses and signature lines, don't forget to capitalize any professional title that follows a person's name:

Mr. Ray Johnson, Dean
Ms. Patricia T. Higgins
Assistant Vice President

Table A–2	**Forms of Address**	
Person	**In Address**	**In Salutation**
Personal Titles		
Man	Mr. [first & last name]	Dear Mr. [last name]:
Woman*	Ms. [first & last name]	Dear Ms. [last name]:
Two men (*or more*)	Mr. [first & last name] and Mr. [first & last name]	Dear Mr. [last name] and Mr. [last name] *or* Messrs. [last name] and [last name]:
Two women (*or more*)	Ms. [first & last name] and Ms. [first & last name] *or* Mrs. [first & last name] and Mrs. [first & last name] Miss [first & last name] Mrs. [first & last name]	Dear Ms. [last name] and Ms. [last name] *or* Mses. [last name] and [last name]: Dear Mrs. [last name] and Mrs. [last name]: *or* Dear Mesdames [last name] and [last name] *or* Mesdames: Dear Miss [last name] and Mrs. [last name]:
One woman and one man	Ms. [first & last name] and Mr. [first & last name]	Dear Ms. [last name] and Mr. [last name]:
Couple (married)	Mr. [husband's first name] and Mrs. [wife's first name] [couple's last name]	Dear Mr. and Mrs. [last name]:

Table A–2	Forms of Address *(continued)*	
Person	**In Address**	**In Salutation**
Couple (married with different last names)	Mr. [first & last name of husband] Ms. [first & last name of wife]	Dear Mr. [husband's last name] and Ms. [wife's last name]:
Couple (married professionals with same title and same last name)	[title in plural form] [husband's first name] and [wife's first name] [couple's last name]	Dear [title in plural form] [last name]:
Couple (married professionals with different titles and same last name)	[title] [first & last name of husband] and [title] [first & last name of wife]	Dear [title] and [title] [last name]:
Professional Titles		
President of a college or university (doctor)	Dr. [first & last name], President	Dear Dr. [last name]:
Dean of a school, college, or faculty	Dean [first & last name] *or* Dr., Mr., Ms., Mrs., *or* Miss [first & last name] Dean of [title]	Dear Dean [last name]: *or* Dear Dr., Mr., Ms., Mrs., *or* Miss [last name]:
Professor	Professor [first & last name]	Dear Professor [last name]:
Physician	[first & last name], M.D.	Dear Dr. [last name]:
Lawyer	Mr., Ms., Mrs., *or* Miss [first & last name]	Dear Mr., Ms., Mrs., *or* Miss [last name]:
Armed forces personnel	[full rank, first & last name, abbreviation of service designation] (add *Retired* if applicable)	Dear [rank] [last name]:
Company or corporation	[name of organization]	Ladies and Gentlemen: *or* Gentlemen and Ladies:
Governmental Titles		
Prime Minister of Canada	The Right Honourable [first & last name]	Dear Prime Minister:
Federal Minister	The Honourable [first & last name], MP	Dear Mr. *or* Ms. [last name] *or* Dear Minister:
Member of Parliament	Mr. *or* Ms. [first & last name], MP	Dear Mr. *or* Ms. [last name]:
Judge	The Honourable [first & last name]	Dear Mr. *or* Madam Justice [last name]:
Mayor	Mayor [first & last name]	Dear Mr. *or* Madam Mayor:
Councillor	Councillor [first & last name]	Dear Mr. *or* Ms. [last name]:

*Use *Mrs.* or *Miss* only if the recipient has specifically requested that you use one of these titles; otherwise *always* use *Ms.* in business correspondence. Also, never refer to a woman by her husband's name (e.g., Mrs. Robert Washington) unless she specifically requests that you do so.

However, professional titles not appearing in an address or signature line are capitalized only when they directly precede the name.

President Kenneth Johanson will deliver the speech.

Maria Morales, president of ABC Enterprises, will deliver the speech.

The Honourable Laurie Hawn, member of Parliament for Edmonton Centre, Alberta, will deliver the speech.

If the name of a specific person is unavailable, you may address the letter to the department or to a specific position within the department. Also, ensure that you spell out company names in full, unless the company itself uses abbreviations in its official name.

Other address information includes the treatment of buildings, house numbers, and compass directions (see Table A–3). The following example shows all the information that may be included in the inside address and its proper order for Canadian correspondence:

Dr. H. C. Armstrong
Research and Development
Commonwealth Mining Consortium
The Chelton Building, Suite 301
585 Second St. SW
Calgary, Alberta T2P 2P5

U.S. addresses are similar:

Ms. Linda Coolidge, Vice President
Corporate Planning Department
Midwest Airlines
Kowalski Building, Suite 21-A
7279 Bristol Ave.
Toledo, Ohio 43617

Table A–3	Inside Address Information	
Description		**Example**
Capitalize building names.		Royal Bank Plaza
Capitalize locations within buildings (apartments, suites, and rooms).		Suite 1073
Use numerals for all house or building numbers, except the number one.		One Trinity Lane 637 Adams Ave., Apt. 7
Spell out compass directions that fall within a street address.		1074 West Connover St.
Abbreviate compass directions that follow the street address.		27–783 Main St., N.E.

The order and layout of address information vary from country to country. So when addressing correspondence for other countries, carefully follow the format and information that appear in the company's letterhead. However, when you're sending mail from Canada, ensure that the name of the destination country appears on the last line of the address in capital letters. Use the English version of the country name so that your mail is routed from Canada to the right country. Then, to ensure that your mail is routed correctly *within* the destination country, also include the foreign spelling of the city name (using the characters and diacritical marks, signs indicating phonetical differences, that would be commonly used in the region). For example, the following address uses *Köln* instead of *Cologne*:

H. R. Veith, Director	Addressee
Eisfieren Glaswerk	Company name
Blaubachstrasse 13	Street address
Postfach 10 80 07	Post office box
d-5000 Köln I	District, city
GERMANY	Country

Be sure to use organizational titles correctly when addressing international correspondence. Job designations vary around the world. In England, for example, a managing director is often what a Canadian company would call its chief executive officer or president, and a British deputy is the equivalent of a vice president. In France, responsibilities are assigned to individuals without regard to title or organizational structure, and in China the title *project manager* has meaning, but the title *sales manager* may not.

To complicate matters further, businesspeople in some countries sign correspondence without their names typed below. In Germany, for example, the belief is that employees represent the company, so it's inappropriate to emphasize personal names. Use the examples in Table A–4 as guidelines when addressing correspondence to countries outside Canada.[4]

SALUTATION In the salutation of your letter, follow the style of the first line of the inside address. If the first line is a person's name, the salutation is *Dear Mr.* or *Ms. Name*. The formality of the salutation depends on your relationship with the addressee. If in conversation you would say "Mary," your letter's salutation should be *Dear Mary*, followed by a comma. Otherwise, include the courtesy title and last name, followed by a colon. Presuming to write *Dear Lewis* instead of *Dear Professor Chang* demonstrates a disrespectful familiarity that the recipient will probably resent.

If the first line of the inside address is a position title such as *Director of Personnel*, then use *Dear Director*. If the addressee is unknown, use a polite description, such as *Dear Alumnus*, *Dear SPCA Supporter*, or *Dear Voter*. If the first line is plural (a department or company), then use *Ladies and Gentlemen* (look again at Table A–2). When you do not know whether you're writing to an individual or a group (for example, when writing a reference or a letter of recommendation), use *To whom it may concern*.

In Canada some letter writers use a "salutopening" on the salutation line. A salutopening omits *Dear* but includes the first few words of the opening paragraph along with the recipient's name.

After this line, the sentence continues a double space below as part of the body of the letter, as in these examples:

Thank you, Mr. Brown,	Salutopening
for your prompt payment of your bill.	Body
Congratulations, Ms. Lake!	Salutopening
Your promotion is well deserved.	Body

Whether your salutation is informal or formal, be especially careful that names are spelled correctly. A misspelled name is glaring evidence of carelessness, and it belies the personal interest you're trying to express.

BODY The body of the letter is your message. Almost all letters are single-spaced, with one blank line before

Table A–4	**International Addresses and Salutations**		
Country	**Postal Address**	**Address Elements**	**Salutations**
Argentina	Sr. Juan Pérez Editorial Internacional S.A. Av. Sarmiento 1337, 8° P.C. C1035AAB BUENOS AIRES–CF ARGENTINA	S.A. = Sociedad Anónima (corporation) Av. Sarmiento (name of street) 1337 (building number) 8° = 8th. P = Piso (floor) C (room or suite) C1035AAB (postcode + city) CF = Capital Federal (federal capital)	Sr. = Señor (Mr.) Sra. = Señora (Mrs.) Srta. = Señorita (Miss) Don't use given names except with people you know well.
Australia	Mr. Roger Lewis International Publishing Pty. Ltd. 166 Kent Street, Level 9 GPO Box 3542 SYDNEY NSW 2001 AUSTRALIA	Pty. Ltd. = Proprietary Limited (corp.) 166 (building number) Kent Street (name of street) Level (floor) GPO Box (post office box) City + state (abbrev.) + postcode	Mr. and Mrs. used on first contact. Ms. not common (avoid use). Business is informal—use given name freely.
Austria	Herrn Dipl.-Ing.J.Gerdenitsch International Verlag Ges.m.b.H. Glockengasse 159 1010 WIEN AUSTRIA	Herrn = To Mr. (separate line) Dipl.-Ing. (engineering degree) Ges.m.b.H. (a corporation) Glockengasse (street name) 159 (building number) 1010 (postcode + city) WIEN (Vienna)	Herr (Mr.) Frau (Mrs.) Fräulein (Miss) obsolete in business, so do not use. Given names are almost never used in business.
Brazil	Ilmo. Sr. Gilberto Rabello Ribeiro Editores Internacionais S.A. Rua da Ajuda, 228-6° Andar Caixa Postal 2574 20040-000 RIO DE JANEIRO–RJ BRAZIL	Ilmo. = Ilustrissimo (honorific) Ilma. = Ilustrissima (hon. female) S.A. = Sociedade Anônima (corporation) Rua = street, da Ajuda (street name) 228 (building number) 6° = 6th. Andar (floor) Caixa Postal (P.O. box) 20040-000 (postcode + city) –RJ (state abbrev.)	Sr. = Senhor (Mr.) Sra. = Senhora (Mrs.) Srta. = Senhorita (Miss) Family name at end, e.g., Senhor Ribeiro (Rabello is mother's family name—as in Portugal) Given names readily used in business.
China	Xia Zhiyi International Publishing Ltd. 14 Jianguolu Chaoyangqu BEIJING 100025 CHINA	Ltd. (limited liability corporation) 14 (building number) Jianguolu (street name), lu (street) Chaoyangqu (district name) (city + postcode)	Family name (single syllable) first. Given name (2 syllables) second, sometimes reversed. Use Mr. or Ms. at all times (Mr. Xia).
France	Monsieur LEFÈVRE Alain Éditions Internationales S.A. Siège Social Immeuble Le Bonaparte 64–68, av. Galliéni B.P. 154 75942 PARIS CEDEX 19 FRANCE	S.A. = Société Anonyme Siège Social (head office) Immeuble (building + name) 64–68 (building occupies 64, 66, 68) av. = avenue (no initial capital) B.P. = Boîte Postale (P.O. box) 75942 (postcode + city) CEDEX (postcode for P.O. box)	Monsieur (Mr.) Madame (Mrs.) Mademoiselle (Miss) Best not to abbreviate. Family name is sometimes in all caps with given name following.
Germany	Herrn Gerhardt Schneider International Verlag GmbH Schillerstraβe 159 44147 DORTMUND GERMANY	Herrn = To Herr (on a separate line) GmbH (inc.—incorporated) -straβe (street—"β" often written "ss") 159 (building number) 44147 (postcode + city)	Herr (Mr.) Frau (Mrs.) Fräulein (Miss) obsolete in business, so do not use. Business is formal: (1) do not use given names unless invited, and (2) use academic titles precisely.

(continued)

Table A–4	International Addresses and Salutations *(continued)*		
Country	**Postal Address**	**Address Elements**	**Salutations**
India	Sr. Shyam Lal Gupta International Publishing (Pvt.) Ltd. 1820 Rehaja Centre 214, Darussalam Road Andheri East MUMBAI–400049 INDIA	(Pvt.) (privately owned) Ltd. (limited liability corporation) 1820 (possibly office #20 on 18th floor) Rehaja Centre (building name) 214 (building number) Andheri East (suburb name) (city + hyphen + postcode)	Shri (Mr.), Shrimati (Mrs.) but English is common business language, so use Mr., Mrs., Miss. Given names are used only by family and close friends.
Italy	Egr. Sig. Giacomo Mariotti Edizioni Internazionali S.p.A. Via Terenzio, 21 20138 MILANO ITALY	Egr. = Egregio (honorific) Sig. = Signor (not nec. a separate line) S.p.A. = Società per Azioni (corp.) Via (street) 21 (building number) 20138 (postcode + city)	Sig. = Signore (Mr.) Sig.ra = Signora (Mrs.) Sig.a = (Ms.) Women in business are addressed as Signora. Use given name only when invited.
Japan	Mr. Taro Tanaka Kokusai Shuppan K.K. 10–23, 5-chome, Minamiazabu Minato-ku TOKYO 106 JAPAN	K.K. = Kabushiki Kaisha (corporation) 10 (lot number) 23 (building number) 5-chome (area #5) Minamiazabu (neighbourhood name) Minato-ku (city district) (city + postcode)	Given names are not used in business. Use family name + job title. Or use family name + "-san" (Tanaka-san) or more used respect- fully, add "-sama" or "-dono."
Korea	Mr. KIM Chang-ik International Publishers Ltd. Room 206, Korea Building 33-4 Nonhyon-dong Kangnam-ku SEOUL 135-010 KOREA	English company names common Ltd. (a corporation) 206 (office number inside the building) 33-4 (area 4 of subdivision 33) -dong (city neighbourhood name) -ku (subdivision of city) (city + postcode)	Family name is normally first but sometimes placed after given name. A two-part name is the given name. Use Mr. or Mrs. in letters, but use job title in speech.
Mexico	Sr. Francisco Pérez Martínez Editores Internacionales S.A. Independencia No.322 Col. Juárez 06050 MEXICO D.F.	S.A. = Sociedad Anónima (corporation) Independencia (street name) No. = Número (number) 322 (building number) Col. = Colonia (city district) Juárez (locality name) 06050 (postcode + city) D.F. = Distrito Federal (federal capital)	Sr. Señor (Mr.) Sra. = Señora (Mrs.) Srta. = Señorita (Miss) Family name in middle: e.g., Sr. Pérez (Martínez is mother's family name). Given names are used in business.
South Africa	Mr. Mandla Ntuli International Publishing (Pty.) Ltd. Private Bag X2581 JOHANNESBURG 2000 SOUTH AFRICA	Pty. = Proprietary (privately owned) Ltd. (a corporation) Private Bag (P.O. box) (city + postcode) or (postcode + city)	Mnr = Meneer (Mr.) Mev. = Mevrou (Mrs.) Mejuffrou (Miss) is not used in business. Business is becoming less formal, so the use of given names is possible.
United Kingdom	Mr. N. J. Lancaster International Publishing Ltd. Kingsbury House 12 Kingsbury Road EDGWARE Middlesex HA8 9XG ENGLAND	N. J. (initials of given names) Ltd. (limited liability corporation) Kingsbury House (building name) 12 (building number) Kingsbury Road (name of street/road) EDGWARE (town or city—all caps) Middlesex (county—not all caps) HA8 9XG (postcode—on a separate line)	Mr. and Ms. used mostly. Mrs. and Miss sometimes used in North and by older women. Given names are used in business after some time. Wait to be invited.
United States	Ellen Krueger Murphy International Publishing Inc. 16850 S. Union St., Suite 2250 HOUSTON TX 77002	Inc. = Incorporated (a corporation) 16850 (building number) S. = South section Union St. (name of street) Suite (shared office in large building) 2250 (suite number) HOUSTON (city name) TX (standard 2-letter state abbreviation) 77002 (ZIP code)	Mr. and Ms. used in correspon- dence. (Mrs. and Miss rarely used in business.) Mr. and Ms. used on first contact, but change to given names quickly.

and after the salutation or salutopening, between paragraphs, and before the complimentary close. The body may include indented lists, entire paragraphs indented for emphasis, and even subheadings. If it does, all similar elements should be treated in the same way. Your department or company may select a format to use for all letters.

COMPLIMENTARY CLOSE The complimentary close begins on the second line below the body of the letter. Alternatives for wording are available, but currently the trend seems to be toward using one-word closes, such as *Sincerely*, *Cordially*, *Respectfully*, or *Best*. In any case, the complimentary close reflects the relationship between you and the person you're writing to. Avoid cute closes, such as *Yours for bigger profits*. If your audience doesn't know you well, your sense of humour may be misunderstood.

SIGNATURE BLOCK Leave three blank lines for a written signature below the complimentary close and then include the sender's name (unless it appears in the letterhead). The person's title may appear on the same line as the name or on the line below:

Cordially,

Raymond Brodsky
Director of Personnel

Your letterhead indicates that you're representing your company. However, if your letter is on plain paper or runs to a second page, you may want to emphasize that you're speaking legally for the company. The accepted way of doing that is to place the company's name in capital letters a double space below the complimentary close and then include the sender's name and title four lines below that:

Sincerely,

WENTWORTH INDUSTRIES

(Mrs.) Helen B. Yamaguchi
President

If your name could be taken for either a man's or a woman's, a courtesy title indicating gender should be included, with or without parentheses. Also, women who prefer a particular courtesy title should include it:

Mrs. Nancy Winters

(Miss) Juana Flores

Ms. Pat Li

(Mr.) Jamie Saunders

ADDITIONAL LETTER PARTS

Letters vary greatly in subject matter and thus in the identifying information they need and the format they adopt. The letter in Figure A–2 shows how these additional parts should be arranged. The following elements may be used in any combination, depending on the requirements of the particular letter:

- **Addressee notation.** Letters that have a restricted readership or that must be handled in a special way should include such addressee notations as *PERSONAL*, *CONFIDENTIAL*, or *PLEASE FORWARD*. This sort of notation appears a double space above the inside address, in all-capital letters.
- **Attention line.** Although not frequently used today, an attention line can be used if you know only the last name of the person you're writing to. It can also direct a letter to a position title or department. Place the attention line on the first line of the inside address and put the company name on the second.[5] Match the address on the envelope with the style of the inside address. An attention line may take any of the following forms or variants of them:

Attention Dr. McHenry

Attention Director of Marketing

Attention Marketing Department

- **Subject line.** The subject line tells recipients at a glance what the letter is about (and indicates where to file the letter for future reference). It usually appears below the salutation, either against the left margin, indented (as a paragraph in the body), or centred. It can be placed above the salutation or at the very top of the page, and it can be highlighted in boldface or underscored. Some businesses omit the word *Subject*, and some organizations replace it with *Re:* or *In re:* (meaning "concerning" or "in the matter of"). The subject line may take a variety of forms, including the following:

Subject: RainMaster Sprinklers

About your February 4, 2017, order

FALL 2017 SALES MEETING

Reference Order No. 27920

- **Second-page heading.** Use a second-page heading whenever an additional page is required. Some companies have second-page letterhead (with the company name and address on one line and in a smaller typeface). The heading bears the name (person or organization) from the first line of the inside address, the page number, the date, and perhaps a

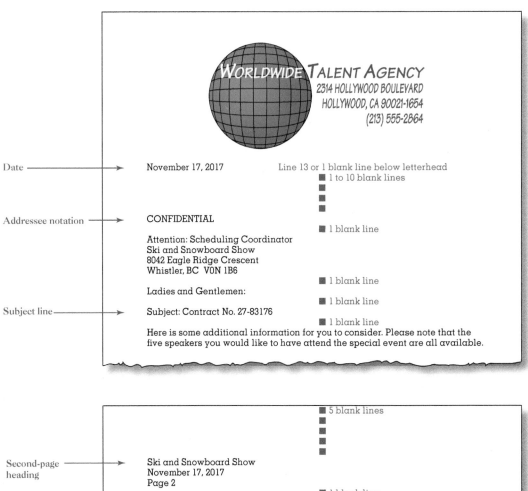

Date

Addressee notation

Subject line

WORLDWIDE TALENT AGENCY
2314 HOLLYWOOD BOULEVARD
HOLLYWOOD, CA 90021-1654
(213) 555-2864

November 17, 2017   Line 13 or 1 blank line below letterhead
■ 1 to 10 blank lines
■
■
■

CONFIDENTIAL
■ 1 blank line

Attention: Scheduling Coordinator
Ski and Snowboard Show
8042 Eagle Ridge Crescent
Whistler, BC V0N 1B6
■ 1 blank line

Ladies and Gentlemen:
■ 1 blank line

Subject: Contract No. 27-83176
■ 1 blank line

Here is some additional information for you to consider. Please note that the
five speakers you would like to have attend the special event are all available.

■ 5 blank lines
■
■
■
■

Second-page heading

Company name

Reference initials

Enclosure notation

Copy notation

Mailing notation

Postscript

Ski and Snowboard Show
November 17, 2017
Page 2
■ 1 blank line

This information should clarify our commitment to you. I look forward to good
news from you in the near future.
■ 1 blank line

Sincerely,
■ 1 blank line

WORLDWIDE TALENT AGENCY
■ 3 blank lines
■
■

J. Elizabeth Spencer
President
■ 1 blank line

nt
■ 1 blank line

Enclosures: Talent Roster
            Commission Schedule
■ 1 blank line

Copy to Everett Cunningham, Chairperson of the Board, InterHosts, Inc.
■ 1 blank line

Special Delivery
■ 1 blank line

PS: The lunch you treated me to the other day was a fine display of Canadian
hospitality. Thanks again.

Figure A–2 Additional Letter Parts

reference number. Leave two blank lines before the body. Make sure that at least two lines of a continued paragraph appear on the first and second pages. Never allow the closing lines to appear alone on a continued

page. Precede the complimentary close or signature lines with at least two lines of the body. Also, don't hyphenate the last word on a page. All the following are acceptable forms for second-page headings:

Ms. Melissa Baker

May 9, 2017

Page 2

Ms. Melissa Baker, May 9, 2017, Page 2

Ms. Melissa Baker -2- May 9, 2017

- **Company name.** If you include the company name in the signature block, put it all in capital letters a double space below the complimentary close. You usually include the company name in the signature block only when the writer is serving as the company's official spokesperson or when letterhead has not been used.
- **Reference initials.** When businesspeople keyboard their own letters, reference initials are unnecessary, so they are becoming rare. When one person dictates a letter and another person produces it, reference initials show who helped prepare it. Place initials at the left margin, a double space below the signature block. When the signature block includes the writer's name, use only the preparer's initials. If the signature block includes only the department, use both sets of initials, usually in one of the following forms: *RSR/sm*, *RSR:sm*, or *RSR:SM* (writer/preparer). When the writer and the signer are different people, at least the file copy should bear both their initials as well as the typist's: *JFS/RSR/sm* (signer/writer/preparer).
- **Enclosure notation.** Enclosure notations appear at the bottom of a letter, one or two lines below the reference initials. Some common forms include the following:

Enclosure

Enclosures (2)

Enclosures: Résumé

   Photograph

   Attachment

- **Copy notation.** Copy notations may follow reference initials or enclosure notations. They indicate who's receiving a *courtesy copy* (*cc*). Some companies indicate copies made on a photocopier (*pc*), or they simply use *copy* (*c*). Recipients are listed in order of rank or (rank being equal) in alphabetical order. Among the forms used are the following:

cc: David Wentworth, Vice President
Copy to Peter Simond
6412 Carleton Rd.
Lethbridge, AB T1H 9K4

- **Mailing notation.** You may place a mailing notation (such as *Special Delivery* or *Registered Mail*) at the bottom of the letter, after reference initials or enclosure notations (whichever is last) and before copy notations. Or you may place it at the top of the letter, either above the inside address on the left side or just below the date on the right side. For greater visibility, mailing notations may appear in capital letters.
- **Postscript.** A postscript is an afterthought to the letter, a message that requires emphasis, or a personal note. It is usually the last element on any letter and may be preceded by *P.S.*, *PS.*, *PS:*, or nothing at all. A second afterthought would be designated *P.P.S.* (post postscript).

LETTER FORMATS

A letter format is the way of arranging all the basic letter parts. Sometimes a company adopts a certain format as its policy; sometimes the individual letter writer or preparer is allowed to choose the most appropriate format. In Canada, three major letter formats are commonly used:

1. **Block format.** Each letter part begins at the left margin. The main advantage is quick and efficient preparation (see Figure A–3).
2. **Modified block format.** Same as block format, except that the date, complimentary close, and signature block start near the centre of the page (see Figure A–4). The modified block format does permit indentions as an option. This format mixes preparation speed with traditional placement of some letter parts. It also looks more balanced on the page than the block format does. (Note: The address and contact information in the left margin of this letter are part of this company's particular stationery design; other designs put this information at the top or bottom of the page.)
3. **Simplified format.** Instead of using a salutation, this format often weaves the reader's name into the first line or two of the body and often includes a subject line in capital letters (see Figure A–5). This format does not include a complimentary close, so your signature appears after the body text. Because certain letter parts are eliminated, some line spacing is changed.

These three formats differ in the way paragraphs are indented, in the way letter parts are placed, and in some punctuation. However, the elements are always separated by at least one blank line, and the printed name is always separated from the line above by at least three blank lines to allow space for a signature. If paragraphs are indented, the indention is normally five spaces. The most common formats for intercultural business letters are the block style and the modified block style.

Delauny Music
19 Main Street • Saint John, NB E3R 2F3
506-555-1001 • delaunymusic.net

June 21, 2017

Line 13 or one line below letterhead
■ 1 to 10 blank lines
■

Ms. Claudia Banks
3542 Fundy Drive
Saint John, NB E2M 5L4

■ 1 blank line
Dear Ms. Banks: ■ 1 blank line

Thank you for your recent purchase. We wish you many years of satisfaction with your new Yamaha CG1 grand piano. The CG1 carries more than a century of Yamaha's heritage in design and production of world-class musical instruments and will give you many years of playing and listening pleasure.

■ 1 blank line

Our commitment to your satisfaction doesn't stop with your purchase, however. As a vital first step, please remember to call us sometime within three to eight months after your piano was delivered to take advantage of the Yamaha Servicebond[SM] Assurance Program. This free service program includes a thorough evaluation and adjustment of the instrument after you've had some time to play your piano and your piano has had time to adapt to its environment.

■ 1 blank line

In addition to this important service appointment, a regular program of tuning is essential to ensure your piano's impeccable performance. Our piano specialists recommend four tunings during the first year and two tunings every year thereafter. As your local Yamaha dealer, we are ideally positioned to provide you with optimum service for both regular tuning and any maintenance or repair needs you may have.   ■ 1 blank line

Sincerely,   ■ 3 blank lines
■
■

Madeline Delauny
Owner

■ 1 blank line

tjr

■ 1 blank line

Figure A–3 Block Letter Format

In addition to these three letter formats, letters may also be classified according to their style of punctuation. *Standard*, or *mixed*, *punctuation* uses a colon after the salutation (a comma if the letter is social or personal) and a comma after the complimentary close. *Open punctuation* uses no colon or comma after the salutation or the complimentary close. Although the most popular style in business communication is mixed punctuation, either style of punctuation may be used with block or modified block letter formats. Because the simplified letter format has no salutation or complimentary close, the style of punctuation is irrelevant.

Envelopes

For a first impression, the quality of the envelope is just as important as the quality of the stationery. Letterhead and envelopes should be of the same paper stock, have the same colour ink, and be imprinted with the same address and logo. Most envelopes used by Canadian businesses are No. 10 envelopes (9½ inches long), which are sized for an 8½-by-11-inch piece of paper folded in thirds. Some occasions call for a smaller, No. 6¾, envelope or for envelopes proportioned to fit

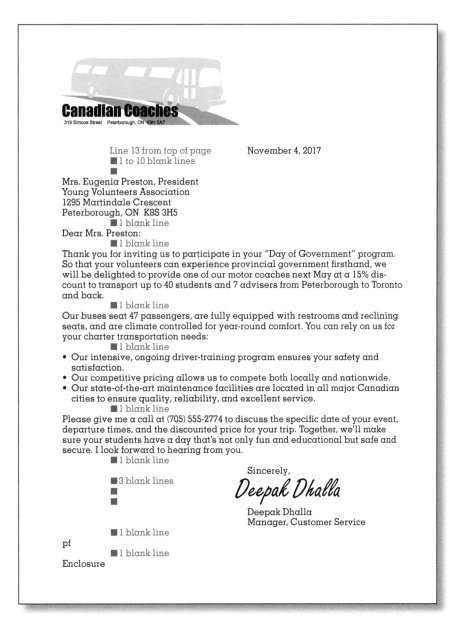

Canadian Coaches
319 Simcoe Street   Peterborough, ON K9H 5A7

Line 13 from top of page   November 4, 2017
■1 to 10 blank lines
■
Mrs. Eugenia Preston, President
Young Volunteers Association
1295 Martindale Crescent
Peterborough, ON K8S 3H5
■1 blank line
Dear Mrs. Preston:
■1 blank line
Thank you for inviting us to participate in your "Day of Government" program.
So that your volunteers can experience provincial government firsthand, we
will be delighted to provide one of our motor coaches next May at a 15% discount to transport up to 40 students and 7 advisers from Peterborough to Toronto
and back.
■1 blank line
Our buses seat 47 passengers, are fully equipped with restrooms and reclining
seats, and are climate controlled for year-round comfort. You can rely on us for
your charter transportation needs:
■1 blank line
• Our intensive, ongoing driver-training program ensures your safety and
  satisfaction.
• Our competitive pricing allows us to compete both locally and nationwide.
• Our state-of-the-art maintenance facilities are located in all major Canadian
  cities to ensure quality, reliability, and excellent service.
■1 blank line
Please give me a call at (705) 555-2774 to discuss the specific date of your event,
departure times, and the discounted price for your trip. Together, we'll make
sure your students have a day that's not only fun and educational but safe and
secure. I look forward to hearing from you.
■1 blank line
                                        Sincerely,
■3 blank lines
■
■   *Deepak Dhalla*

                                        Deepak Dhalla
                                        Manager, Customer Service
■1 blank line
pf
■1 blank line
Enclosure

Figure A–4 Modified Block Letter Format

special stationery. Figure A–6 shows the two most common sizes.

ADDRESSING THE ENVELOPE

No matter what size the envelope, the address is always single-spaced with all lines aligned on the left. The address on the envelope is in the same style as the inside address and presents the same information. The order to follow is from the smallest division to the largest:

1. Name and title of recipient

2. Name of department or subgroup

3. Name of organization

4. Name of building

5. Street address and suite number, or post office box number

6. City, province or state, and postal or ZIP code

7. Name of country (if the letter is being sent abroad)

PERFORMANCETOOLS **INTERNATIONAL**
9553 Tecumseh Road, Windsor, ON N8R 3Z9

May 5, 2017

Line 13 from top of page
■ 1 to 10 blank lines
■
■

Mr. Michael Ferraro
Pacific Coast Appliances
595 Briceland Street
Kingston, ON K7K 9L3

■ 1 blank line

NEW PRODUCT INFORMATION

■ 1 blank line

Thank you, Mr. Ferraro, for your recent inquiry about our product line. We appreciate your enthusiasm for our products, and we are confident that your customers will enjoy the improved performance of the new product line.

■ 1 blank line

I have enclosed a package of information for your review, including product specifications, dealer prices, and an order form. The package also contains reprints of PerformanceTools reviews and a comparison sheet showing how our products measure up against competing brands.

■ 1 blank line

Please call with any questions you may have about shipping or payment arrangements.

■ 3 blank lines
■
■

Joanna Davis

Joanna Davis
Product Specialist

■ 1 blank line

ek

■ 1 blank line

Enclosures

Figure A–5 Simplified Letter Format

Canada Post's optical scanning equipment can read both handwritten and typed addresses, and their addressing guidelines accommodate the requirements of French and English and the preferences of their customers. Businesses can use upper and lower case letters and accents when addressing envelopes and spell out and punctuate all address elements if they want. However, Canada Post does encourage customers to follow specific formats because their mail will be handled more efficiently. Following are examples:

- When a civic number suffix is present in the address, do not insert a space when it is a letter (123A), but insert one space when it is a fraction (123 ½). (A civic number is the official number a municipality assigns to an address.)
- Use common abbreviations for street types (for example, ST and AVE). The only street types that may be translated are ST (RUE), AVE (AV), and BLVD (BOUL).

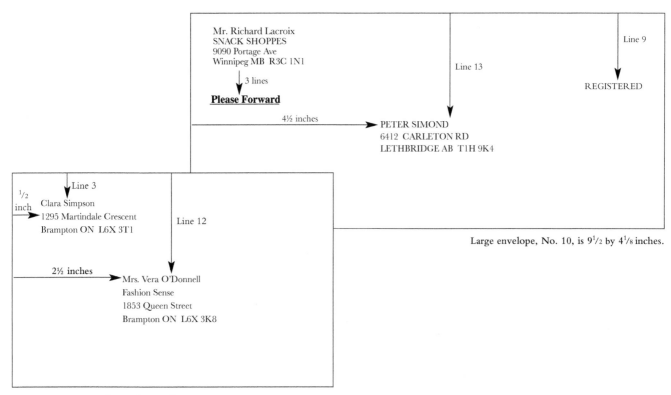

Mr. Richard Lacroix
SNACK SHOPPES
9090 Portage Ave
Winnipeg MB R3C 1N1

↓ 3 lines

Please Forward

Line 9

Line 13

REGISTERED

4½ inches

PETER SIMOND
6412 CARLETON RD
LETHBRIDGE AB T1H 9K4

Large envelope, No. 10, is 9½ by 4⅛ inches.

Line 3

½ inch

Clara Simpson
1295 Martindale Crescent
Brampton ON L6X 3T1

Line 12

2½ inches

Mrs. Vera O'Donnell
Fashion Sense
1853 Queen Street
Brampton ON L6X 3K8

Small envelope, No. 6¾, is 6½ by 3⅝ inches.

Figure A–6 Prescribed Envelope Format

- Always place a French street type before the street name, unless it is an ordinal number (1er, 2e) (PREMIÈRE, DEUXIÈME).
- Do not translate the French street name: it is the official name recognized by each municipality and should remain in the original form (for example, "Main" is not "Principale").

Canada Post also prefers customers to use the recognized two-letter province abbreviation (see Table A–5). In addition, write the postal code in upper case and

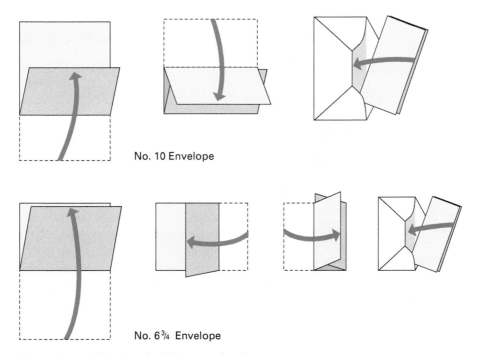

No. 10 Envelope

No. 6¾ Envelope

Figure A–7 Folding Standard-Size Letterhead

Table A–5		Two-Letter Mailing Abbreviations for Canada and the United States			
Province/Territory/State	**Abbreviation**	**Province/Territory/State**	**Abbreviation**	**Province/Territory/State**	**Abbreviation**
Canada		District of Columbia	DC	New York	NY
Alberta	AB	Florida	FL	North Carolina	NC
British Columbia	BC	Georgia	GA	North Dakota	ND
Manitoba	MB	Guam	GU	Northern Mariana	MP
New Brunswick	NB	Hawaii	HI	Ohio	OH
Newfoundland and Labrador	NL	Idaho	ID	Oklahoma	OK
Northwest Territories	NT	Illinois	IL	Oregon	OR
Nova Scotia	NS	Indiana	IN	Pennsylvania	PA
Nunavut	NU	Iowa	IA	Puerto Rico	PR
Ontario	ON	Kansas	KS	Rhode Island	RI
Prince Edward Island	PE	Kentucky	KY	South Carolina	SC
Quebec	QC	Louisiana	LA	South Dakota	SD
Saskatchewan	SK	Maine	ME	Tennessee	TN
Yukon Territory	YT	Maryland	MD	Texas	TX
		Massachusetts	MA	Trust Territories	TT
United States		Michigan	MI	Utah	UT
Alabama	AL	Minnesota	MN	Vermont	VT
Alaska	AK	Mississippi	MS	Virgin Islands	VI
American Samoa	AS	Missouri	MO	Virginia	VA
Arizona	AZ	Montana	MT	Washington	WA
Arkansas	AR	Nebraska	NE	West Virginia	WV
California	CA	Nevada	NV	Wisconsin	WI
Colorado	CO	New Hampshire	NH	Wyoming	WY
Connecticut	CT	New Jersey	NJ		
Delaware	DE	New Mexico	NM		

place it two spaces to the right of the province, with one space between the first three and the last three characters. Review the Canada Post Addressing Guidelines PDF document, available at the Canada Post website (www.canadapost.ca), for the details governing address format.

Follow U.S. Postal Service guidelines when addressing envelopes to customers in the United States. As with Canada Post, the U.S. Postal Service prefers the two-letter state abbreviation over the full state name. The ZIP code must be separated from the state short form by two spaces. The ZIP code may be five or nine digits. A hyphen separates the fifth and sixth digits. For example:

MR. DAMON SMITH
1277 MORRIS AVE APT 7-B
BRONX NY 10451-4598

FOLDING TO FIT

The way a letter is folded also contributes to the recipient's overall impression of your organization's professionalism. When sending a standard-size piece of paper in a No. 10 envelope, fold it in thirds, with the bottom folded up first and the top folded down over it (see Figure A–7); the open end should be at the top of the envelope and facing out. Fit smaller stationery neatly into the appropriate envelope simply by folding it in half or in thirds. When sending a standard-size letterhead in a No. 6¾ envelope, fold it in half from top to bottom and then in thirds from side to side.

INTERNATIONAL MAIL

Postal service differs from country to country. It's usually a good idea to investigate the quality and availability of various services before sending messages and packages internationally. Also, remember to check the postage; rates for sending mail to most other countries differ from the rates for sending mail within your own country.

Canada Post offers different methods for sending mail internationally (see https://www.canadapost.ca/web/en/home.page and scroll over *Sending*). Compare these to services offered by delivery companies such as UPS and FedEx to find the best rates and options for each destination and type of shipment. No matter which service you choose, remember that international mail requires more planning than domestic mail. For example, for anything beyond simple letters, you generally need to prepare *customs forms* and possibly other documents, depending on the country of destination and the type of shipment.

You are responsible for abiding by Canadian law and the law of any countries to which you send mail and packages.

Therefore, when preparing material for international destinations, it would be prudent to follow Canada Post instructions (e.g., see the International Destination Listing at https://www.canadapost.ca/tools/pg/manual/PGintdest-e.asp) regarding restricted destinations and types of shipments as well as to observe customs requirements. You can access Canada Border Services Agency at www.cbsa-asfc.gc.ca for more information

Memos

Electronic media have replaced most internal printed memos in many companies, but you may have occasion to send printed memos from time to time. These can be simple announcements or messages, or they can be short reports using the memo format (see Figure A–8).

On your document, include a title such as *MEMO* or *INTEROFFICE CORRESPONDENCE* (all in capitals) centred at the top of the page or aligned with the left margin. Also at the top, include the words *Date*, *To*, *From*, and *Subject*—followed by the appropriate information—with a blank line between, as shown here:

MEMO

DATE:

TO:

FROM:

SUBJECT:

Sometimes the heading is organized like this:

MEMO

TO: DATE:

FROM: SUBJECT:

The following guidelines will help you effectively format specific memo elements:

- **Addressees.** When sending a memo to a long list of people, include the notation *See distribution list* or *See below* in the *To* position at the top; then list the names at the end of the memo. Arrange this list alphabetically, except when high-ranking officials deserve more prominent placement. You can also address memos to groups of people—*All Sales Representatives*, *Production Group*, *New Product Team*.
- **Courtesy titles.** You need not use courtesy titles anywhere in a memo; first initials and last names, first names, or even initials alone are often sufficient. However, use a courtesy title if you would use one in a face-to-face encounter with the person.
- **Subject line.** The subject line of a memo helps busy colleagues quickly find out what your memo is about, so take care to make it concise and informative.
- **Body.** Start the body of the memo on the second or third line below the heading. Like the body of a letter, it's usually single-spaced with blank lines between paragraphs. Indenting paragraphs is optional. Handle lists, important passages, and subheadings as you do in letters.
- **Second page.** If the memo carries over to a second page, head the second page just as you head the second page of a letter.
- **Writer's initials.** Unlike a letter, a memo doesn't require a complimentary close or a signature, because your name is already prominent at the top. However, you may initial the memo—either beside the name appearing at the top of the memo or at the bottom of the memo.
- **Other elements.** Treat elements such as reference initials, enclosure notations, and copy notations just as you would in a letter. One difference between letters and memos is that while letters use the term *enclosure* to refer to other pieces included with the letter, memos usually use the word *attachment*.

Memos may be delivered by hand, by the post office (when the recipient works at a different location), or through interoffice mail. Interoffice mail may require the use of special reusable envelopes that have spaces for the recipient's name and department or room number; the name of the previous recipient is simply crossed out. If a regular envelope is used, the words *Interoffice Mail* appear where the stamp normally goes, so it won't accidentally be stamped and mailed with the rest of the office correspondence.

Informal, routine, or brief reports for distribution within a company are often presented in memo form.

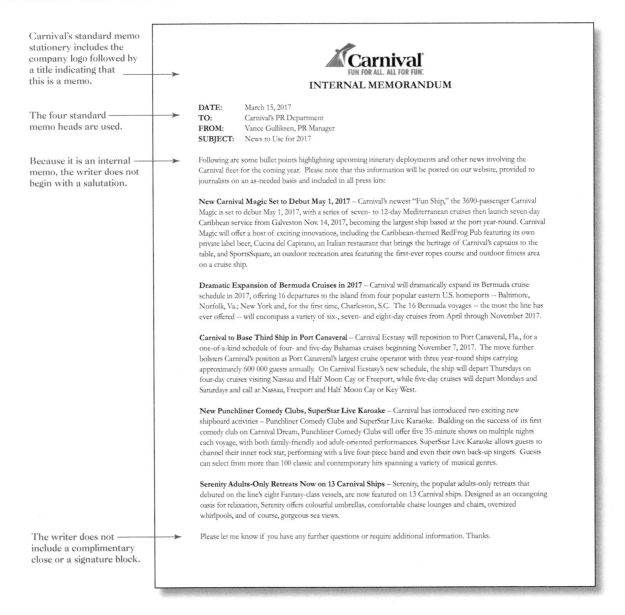

Carnival's standard memo stationery includes the company logo followed by a title indicating that this is a memo.

The four standard memo heads are used.

Because it is an internal memo, the writer does not begin with a salutation.

The writer does not include a complimentary close or a signature block.

Carnival
FUN FOR ALL. ALL FOR FUN.

INTERNAL MEMORANDUM

DATE: March 15, 2017
TO: Carnival's PR Department
FROM: Vance Gulliksen, PR Manager
SUBJECT: News to Use for 2017

Following are some bullet points highlighting upcoming itinerary deployments and other news involving the Carnival fleet for the coming year. Please note that this information will be posted on our website, provided to journalists on an as-needed basis and included in all press kits:

New Carnival Magic Set to Debut May 1, 2017 – Carnival's newest "Fun Ship," the 3690-passenger Carnival Magic is set to debut May 1, 2017, with a series of seven- to 12-day Mediterranean cruises then launch seven-day Caribbean service from Galveston Nov. 14, 2017, becoming the largest ship based at the port year-round. Carnival Magic will offer a host of exciting innovations, including the Caribbean-themed RedFrog Pub featuring its own private label beer, Cucina del Capitano, an Italian restaurant that brings the heritage of Carnival's captains to the table, and SportsSquare, an outdoor recreation area featuring the first-ever ropes course and outdoor fitness area on a cruise ship.

Dramatic Expansion of Bermuda Cruises in 2017 – Carnival will dramatically expand its Bermuda cruise schedule in 2017, offering 16 departures to the island from four popular eastern U.S. homeports -- Baltimore, Norfolk, Va.; New York and, for the first time, Charleston, S.C. The 16 Bermuda voyages -- the most the line has ever offered -- will encompass a variety of six-, seven- and eight-day cruises from April through November 2017.

Carnival to Base Third Ship in Port Canaveral – Carnival Ecstasy will reposition to Port Canaveral, Fla., for a one-of-a-kind schedule of four- and five-day Bahamas cruises beginning November 7, 2017. The move further bolsters Carnival's position as Port Canaveral's largest cruise operator with three year-round ships carrying approximately 600 000 guests annually. On Carnival Ecstasy's new schedule, the ship will depart Thursdays on four-day cruises visiting Nassau and Half Moon Cay or Freeport, while five-day cruises will depart Mondays and Saturdays and call at Nassau, Freeport and Half Moon Cay or Key West.

New Punchliner Comedy Clubs, SuperStar Live Karoake – Carnival has introduced two exciting new shipboard activities – Punchliner Comedy Clubs and SuperStar Live Karaoke. Building on the success of its first comedy club on Carnival Dream, Punchliner Comedy Clubs will offer five 35-minute shows on multiple nights each voyage, with both family-friendly and adult-oriented performances. SuperStar Live Karaoke allows guests to channel their inner rock star, performing with a live four-piece band and even their own back-up singers. Guests can select from more than 100 classic and contemporary hits spanning a variety of musical genres.

Serenity Adults-Only Retreats Now on 13 Carnival Ships – Serenity, the popular adults-only retreats that debuted on the line's eight Fantasy-class vessels, are now featured on 13 Carnival ships. Designed as an oceangoing oasis for relaxation, Serenity offers colourful umbrellas, comfortable chaise lounges and chairs, oversized whirlpools, and of course, gorgeous sea views.

Please let me know if you have any further questions or require additional information. Thanks.

Figure A–8 Short Report Using the Memo Format

Courtesy: Carnival Corporation.

Don't include report parts, such as a table of contents and appendices, but write the body of the memo report just as carefully as you'd write a formal report.

Reports

Enhance the effectiveness of your reports by paying careful attention to their appearance and layout. Follow whatever guidelines your organization prefers, always being neat and consistent throughout. If it's up to you to decide formatting questions, the following conventions may help you decide how to handle margins, headings, spacing and indention, and page numbers.

MARGINS

All margins on a report page are at least 1 inch wide. The top, left, and right margins are usually the same, but the bottom margins can be 1½ times deeper. Some special pages also have deeper top margins. Set top margins as deep as 2 inches for pages that contain major titles: prefatory parts (such as the table of contents or the executive summary), supplementary parts (such as the reference notes or bibliography), and textual parts (such as the first page of the text or the first page of each chapter).

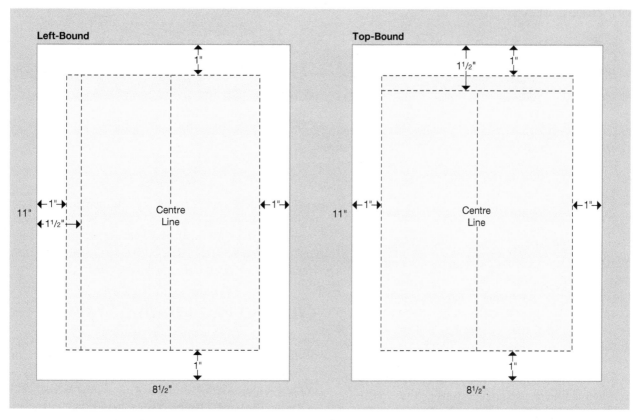

Figure A–9 Margins for Formal Reports

If you're going to bind your report at the left or at the top, use a 1½-inch margin on the bound edge (see Figure A–9). The space taken by the binding on left-bound reports shifts the centre point of the text ¼ inch to the right of the centre of the paper. Ensure that you centre headings between the margins, not between the edges of the paper.

HEADINGS

If you don't have a template supplied by your employer, choose a design for headings and subheadings that clearly distinguishes the various levels in the hierarchy. The first-level headings should be the most prominent, on down to the lowest-level subheading.

PAGE NUMBERS

Every page in the report is counted; however, not all pages show numbers. The first page of the report, normally the title page, is unnumbered. All other pages in the prefatory section are numbered with a lowercase roman numeral, beginning with *ii* and continuing with *iii*, *iv*, *v*, and so on. Then use Arabic numerals (1, 2, 3, etc.) when numbering the pages of the body of the report.

You have many options for placing and formatting the page numbers, although these choices are usually made for you in a template. If you're not using a standard company template, position the page number where it is easy to see as the reader flips through the report. If the report will be stapled or otherwise bound along the left side, for instance, the best place for the page number is the upper right or lower right corner.

By providing information about your sources, you improve your own credibility as well as the credibility of the facts and opinions you present. Documentation gives readers the means for checking your findings and pursuing the subject further. Also, documenting your report is the accepted way to give credit to the people whose work you have drawn from.

What style should you use to document your report? Experts recommend various documentation forms, depending on your field or discipline. Moreover, your employer or client may use a form different from those the experts suggest. Don't let this discrepancy confuse you. If your employer specifies a form, use it; the standardized form is easier for colleagues to understand. However, if the choice of form is left to you, adopt one of the styles described here. Whatever style you choose, be consistent within any given report, using the same order, punctuation, and format from one reference citation or bibliography entry to the next.

A wide variety of style manuals provide detailed information on documentation. The three main resources are as follows:

- American Psychological Association, *Publication Manual of the American Psychological Association*, 6th ed. (Washington, DC: American Psychological Association, 2010). Details the author-date system, which is preferred in the social sciences and often in the natural sciences as well.
- *The Chicago Manual of Style*, 16th ed. (Chicago: University of Chicago Press, 2010). Often referred to only as "*Chicago*" and widely used in the publishing industry; provides detailed treatment of source documentation and many other aspects of document preparation.
- Joseph Gibaldi, *MLA Handbook for Writers of Research Papers*, 8th ed. (New York: Modern Language Association, 2016). Serves as the basis for the note and bibliography style used in much academic writing and is recommended in many university and college textbooks on writing term papers; provides many examples in the humanities.

Although many systems have been proposed for organizing the information in source notes, all of them break the information into parts:

1. Information about the author (name)

2. Information about the work (title, edition, volume number)

3. Information about the publication (place, publisher)

4. Information about the date

5. Information on relevant page ranges

In the following sections, we summarize the major conventions for documenting sources in *The Chicago Manual of Style* (*Chicago*), the *Publication Manual of the American Psychological Association* (APA), and the *MLA Handbook for Writers of Research Papers* (MLA).

Chicago Humanities Style

The Chicago Manual of Style recommends two types of documentation systems. The *documentary-note*, or *humanities*, style gives bibliographic citations in notes—either footnotes (when printed at the bottom of a page) or endnotes (when printed at the end of the report). The humanities system is often used in literature, history, and the arts. The other system strongly recommended by *Chicago* is the *author-date* system, which cites the author's last name and the date of publication in the text, usually in parentheses, reserving full documentation for the reference list (or bibliography). For the purpose of comparing styles, we will concentrate on the humanities system, which is described in detail in *Chicago*.

IN-TEXT CITATION—*CHICAGO* HUMANITIES STYLE

To document report sources in text, the humanities system relies on superscripts—Arabic numerals placed just above the line of type at the end of the reference:

> Toward the end of his speech, Myers sounded a note of caution, saying that even though the economy is expected to grow, it could easily slow a bit.[10]

The superscript lets the reader know how to look for source information in either a footnote or an endnote (see Figure B–1). Some readers prefer footnotes so that they can simply glance at the bottom of the page for information. Others prefer endnotes so that they can read the text without a clutter of notes on the page. Also, endnotes relieve the writer from worrying about how long each note will be and how much space it will take away from the page. Both footnotes and endnotes are handled automatically by today's word-processing software.

NOTES

Journal article with volume and issue numbers

1. Jonathan Clifton, "Beyond Taxonomies of Influence," *Journal of Business Communication* 46, no. 1 (2009): 57–79.

Brochure

2. BestTemp Staffing Services, *An Employer's Guide to Staffing Services*, 2nd ed. (Denver: BestTemp Information Center, 2011), 31.

Newspaper article, no author

3. "Toyota Sets Sights on Sales Record," *Globe and Mail Report on Business*, September 1, 2007, B10.

Annual report

4. Suncor, *2013 Annual Report* (Calgary, AB: Suncor, 2014), 5.

Magazine article

5. Denis Sequin, "A Hollywood Ending?" *Canadian Business*, August 13, 2007, 11.

Television broadcast

6. Wendy Mesley, "How Not to Get Nailed," *Marketplace* (Toronto: CBC TV, August 17, 2007).

Internet, World Wide Web

7. "Intel—Company Capsule," Hoover's Online, accessed June 19, 2011, http://www.hoovers.com/intel/-ID_13787-/free-co-factsheet.xhtml.

Book, component parts

8. Julia C. Gluesing, Tara C. Alcordo, and Margaret A. Neale, "The Development of Global Virtual Teams," in *Virtual Teams that Work: Creating Conditions for Virtual Team Effectiveness*, ed. Cristina B. Gibson and Susan G. Cohen (San Francisco: Jossey-Bass, 2003), 356.

Unpublished dissertation or thesis

9. Changhui Zhou, "Transnational Flow of Knowledge in Multinational Corporations: R&D Co-Practice as an Integrating Force" (PhD diss, University of Western Ontario, 2002), 34–43.

Paper presented at a meeting

10. Jeanette S. Martin and Lillian H. Chaney, "Integrating Global Conversational Customs into Business Courses" (paper presented at the Association for Business Communication 70th Annual Convention, Irvine, CA, October, 2005), 2–3.

Online magazine article

11. Michael E. Porter and Mark R. Kramer, "The Competitive Advantage of Corporate Philanthropy," *Harvard Business Review* 80, no. 12 (December 2002): 59, http://hbr.org/2002/12/the-competitive-advantage-of-corporate-philanthropy/ar/pr.

Article from an electronic database

12. Steven V. Davis and Andrew Gilman, "Communication Coordination," *Risk Management* 49, no.8 (August 2002): 38–40, ProQuest (148778291).

CD-ROM encyclopedia article, one author

13. *The Concise Columbia Encyclopedia,* s.v. "Eastman, George" (by Robert Parkings), CD-ROM (New York: Columbia University Press, 1998).

Interview

14. Georgia Stainer, general manager, Day Cable and Communications, interview by author, March 2, 2011, Topeka, KS.

Newspaper article, one author

15. Nathan VanderKlippe, "B.C. Salmon Industry in Rough Water," *Financial Post*, September 1, 2007, FP3.

Book, two authors

16. Paul A. Argenti and Janis Forman, *The Power of Corporate Communication: Crafting the Voice and Image of Your Business* (New York: McGraw Hill, 2006), 102–3.

Government publication

17. Office of Consumer Affairs, Industry Canada, *Canadian Consumer Handbook* (Ottawa, ON: Office of Consumer Affairs, 2009), 17.

Figure B–1 Sample Endnotes—*Chicago* Humanities Style

For the reader's convenience, you can use footnotes for **content notes** (which may supplement your main text with asides about a particular issue or event, provide a cross-reference to another section of your report, or direct the reader to a related source). Then, you can use endnotes for **source notes** (which document direct quotations, paraphrased passages, and visual aids). Consider which type of note is most common in your report and then choose whether to present these notes all as endnotes or all as footnotes. Regardless of the method you choose for referencing textual information in your report, notes for visual aids (both content notes and source notes) are placed on the same page as the visual.

BIBLIOGRAPHY—*CHICAGO* HUMANITIES STYLE

The humanities system may or may not be accompanied by a bibliography (because the notes give all the necessary bibliographic information). However, endnotes are arranged in order of appearance in the text, so an alphabetical bibliography can be valuable to your readers. The bibliography may be titled *Bibliography, Reference List, Sources, Works Cited* (if you include only those sources you actually cited in your report), or *Works Consulted* (if you include uncited sources as well). This list of sources may also serve

BIBLIOGRAPHY

Book, two authors

Argenti, Paul A., and Janis Forman. *The Power of Corporate Communication: Crafting the Voice and Image of Your Business.* New York: McGraw Hill, 2006.

Brochure

BestTemp Staffing Services. *An Employer's Guide to Staffing Services.* 2nd ed. Denver: BestTemp Information Center, 2011.

Journal article with volume and issue numbers

Clifton, Jonathan. "Beyond Taxonomies of Influence." *Journal of Business Communication* 46, no. 1 (2009): 57–79.

CD-ROM encyclopedia article, one author

The Concise Columbia Encyclopedia. s.v. "Eastman, George" (by Robert Parkings). CD-ROM, 1998.

Article from an electronic database

Davis, Steven V., and Andrew Gilman. "Communication Coordination." *Risk Management* 49, no. 8 (August 2002): 38–43. Proquest, Document ID 148778291 (accessed 27 October 2008).

Book, component parts

Gluesing, Julia C., Tara C. Alcordo, and Margaret A. Neale. "The Development of Global Virtual Teams." In *Virtual Teams that Work: Creating Conditions for Virtual Team Effectiveness,* edited by Cristina B. Gibson and Susan G. Cohen. San Francisco: Jossey-Bass, 2003.

Internet, World Wide Web

"Intel—Company Capsule." Hoover's Online. Accessed June 19, 2011. http://www.hoovers.com/intel/-ID_13787-/free-co-factsheet.xhtml.

Paper presented at a meeting

Martin, Jeanette S., and Lillian H. Chaney. "Integrating Global Conversational Customs into Business Courses." Paper presented at the Association for Business Communication 70th Annual Convention, Irvine, CA, October 2005.

Television broadcast

Mesley, Wendy. "How Not to Get Nailed." *Marketplace.* Toronto: CBC TV, August 17, 2007.

Government publication

Office of Consumer Affairs. Industry Canada. *Canadian Consumer Handbook.* Ottawa: Office of Consumer Affairs, 2009.

Online magazine article

Porter, Michael E., and Mark R. Kramer. "The Competitive Advantage of Corporate Philanthropy," Harvard Business Review 80, no. 12 (December 2002): 56–68. http://hbr.org/2002/12/the-competitive-advantage-of-corporate-philanthropy/ar/pr.

Magazine article

Sequin, Denis. "A Hollywood Ending?" *Canadian Business,* August 13, 2007, 11–12.

Interview

Stainer, Georgia, general manager, Day Cable and Communications. Interview by author. Topeka, KS, March 2, 2011.

Annual report

Suncor. *2013 Annual Report.* Calgary, AB: Suncor, 2014.

Newspaper article, no author

"Toyota Sets Sights on Sales Record." *Globe and Mail Report on Business,* September 1, 2007, B10.

Newspaper article, one author

VanderKlippe, Nathan. "B.C. Salmon Industry in Rough Water." *Financial Post,* September 1, 2007, FP3.

Unpublished dissertation or thesis

Zhou, Changhui. "Transnational Flow of Knowledge in Multinational Corporations: R&D Co-Practice as an Integrating Force." PhD diss., University of Western Ontario, 2002.

Figure B–2 Sample Bibliography—*Chicago* Humanities Style

as a reading list for those who want to pursue the subject of your report further, so consider annotating each entry—that is, comment on the subject matter and viewpoint of the source, as well as on its usefulness to readers. Annotations may be written in either complete or incomplete sentences. (See the annotated list of style manuals early in this appendix.) A bibliography may also be more manageable if you subdivide it into categories (a classified bibliography), either by type of reference (for example, books, articles, and unpublished material) or by subject matter (for example, government regulations or market forces). The major conventions for developing a bibliography

according to *Chicago* style (see Figure B–2) are as follows:

- Exclude any page numbers that may be cited in source notes, except for journals, periodicals, and newspapers.
- Alphabetize entries by the last name of the lead author (listing last name first). The names of second and succeeding authors are listed in normal order. Entries without an author name are alphabetized by the first important word in the title.
- Format entries as hanging indents (indent second and succeeding lines 3 to 5 spaces).
- Arrange entries in the following general order:

1. Author name
2. Title information
3. Publication information
4. Date
5. Periodical page range

- Use quotation marks around the titles of articles from magazines, newspapers, and journals. Capitalize the first and last words, as well as all other important words (except prepositions, articles, and coordinating conjunctions).
- Use italics to set off the names of books, newspapers, journals, and other complete publications—capitalizing the first and last words, as well as all other important words.
- Include the volume number and the issue number (if necessary) for journal articles. Include the year of publication inside parentheses and follow with a colon and the page range of the article: *Canadian Journal of Communication* 38, no. 2 (2013): 16–24. (In this source, the volume is 38, the number is 2, and the page range is 16 to 24.)
- Explain how electronic references can be reached: http://www.spaceless.com/WWWVL.
- Use brackets to identify all electronic references: [Online database] or [CD-ROM].
- For online references, give the publication date: last modified August 23, 2013. If no such date is available, give the access date: accessed February 14, 2014.

APA Style

The American Psychological Association (APA) recommends the author-date system of documentation, which is popular in the physical, natural, and social sciences. When using this system, you simply insert the author's last name and the year of publication within parentheses following the text discussion of the material cited. Include a page number if you use a direct quote. This approach briefly identifies the source so readers can locate complete information in the alphabetical reference list at the end of the report. The author-date system is both brief and clear, saving readers time and effort.

IN-TEXT CITATION—APA STYLE

To document report sources in text using APA style, insert the author's surname and the date of publication at the end of a statement. Enclose this information in parentheses. If the author's name is referred to in the text itself, then the name can be omitted from parenthetical material.

Some experts recommend that corporations partner with charities and educational institutions to benefit society and raise their company profiles (Porter & Kramer, 2002).

Porter and Kramer (2002) make a strong case for corporations partnering with charities and educational institutions to benefit society and raise their company profiles.

Personal communications and interviews conducted by the author would not be listed in the reference list at all. Such citations would appear in the text only.

Increasing the role of cable companies is high on the list of Georgia Stainer, general manager at Day Cable and Communications (personal communication, March 2, 2011).

LIST OF REFERENCES—APA STYLE

For APA style, list only those works actually cited in the text (so you would not include works for background or for further reading). Report writers must choose their references judiciously. The major conventions for developing a reference list according to APA style (see Figure B–3) are as follows:

- Format entries as hanging indents.
- List all author names in reversed order (last name first), and use only initials for the first and middle names.
- Arrange entries in the following general order:

  1. Author name
  2. Date
  3. Title information
  4. Publication information
  5. Periodical page range

- Follow the author name with the date of publication in parentheses.
- List titles of articles from magazines, newspapers, and journals without underlines or quotation marks. Capitalize only the first word of the title, any proper nouns, and the first word to follow an internal colon.
- Italicize titles of books, capitalizing only the first word, any proper nouns, and the first word to follow a colon.
- Italicize names of magazines, newspapers, journals, and other complete publications. Capitalize all the important words.
- For journal articles, include the volume number (in italics) and, if necessary, the issue number (in parentheses). Finally, include the page range of the article: *Canadian Journal of Communication, 38*(2), 16–24.

REFERENCES

Book, two authors — Argenti, P. A., & Forman, J. (2006). *The power of corporate communication: Crafting the voice and image of your business*. New York, NY: McGraw Hill.

Brochure — BestTemp Staffing Services. (2011). *An employer's guide to staffing services* (2nd ed.) [Brochure]. Denver, CO: BestTemp Information Center.

Journal article with volume and issue numbers — Clifton, J. (2009). Beyond Taxonomies of Influence. Journal of Business Communication 46(1), 57.

Article from an electronic database — Davis, S. V., & Gilman, A. (2002, August). Communication coordination. *Risk Management* 49(8), 38–43. Retrieved from ProQuest database.

Book, component parts — Gluesing, J. C., Alcordo, T. C., & Neale, M. A. (2003). The development of global virtual teams. In C. B. Gibson & S. G. Cohen (Eds.), *Virtual teams that work: Creating conditions for virtual team effectiveness* (pp. 353–380). San Francisco, CA: Jossey-Bass.

Internet, World Wide Web — Hoover's Online. (2011). *Intel—Company capsule*. Retrieved from http://www.hoovers.com/intel/-ID_13787-/free-co-factsheet.xhtml

Paper presented at a meeting — Martin, J. S., & Chaney, L. H. (2005, October). *Integrating global conversational customs into business courses*. Paper presented at the Association for Business Communication 70th Annual Convention, Irvine, CA.

Television broadcast — Mesley, W. (Writer). (2007, August 17). How not to get nailed. [Television series episode]. In J. Fowler (Producer), *Marketplace*. Toronto, ON: CBC TV.

Government publication — Office of Consumer Affairs. Industry Canada. (2009). *Canadian consumer handbook*. Ottawa, ON: Office of Consumer Affairs.

CD-ROM encyclopedia article, one author — Parkings, R. (1998). George Eastman. *The concise Columbia encyclopaedia* [CD-ROM]. New York, NY: Columbia University Press.

Online magazine article — Porter, M. E., & Kramer, M. R. (2002, December). The competitive advantage of corporate philanthropy. *Harvard Business Review*, *80*(12), 56–68. Retrieved from http://hbr.org/2002/12/the-competitive-advantage-of-corporate-philanthropy/ar/pr

Magazine article — Sequin, D. (2007, August 13). A Hollywood ending? *Canadian Business*, 11–12.

Annual report — Suncor. (2014). *2013 Annual report*. Calgary, AB: Author.

Newspaper article, no author — Toyota sets sights on sales record. (2007, September 1). *Globe and Mail Report on Business*, p. B10.

Newspaper article, one author — VanderKlippe, N. (2007, September 1). B.C. salmon industry in rough water. *Financial Post*, p. FP3.

Unpublished dissertation or thesis — Zhou, C. (2002). Transnational flow of knowledge in multinational corporations: R&D co-practice as an integrating force. Unpublished doctoral dissertation, University of Western Ontario, London, Ontario, Canada.

Interview — [cited in text only, not in the list of references]

Figure B–3 Sample References—APA Style

(In this example, the volume is 38, the number is 2, and the page range is 16 to 24.)

- Include personal communications (for example, letters, memos, email, and conversations) only in text, not in reference lists.
- Electronic references include author, date of publication, title of article, name of publication (if one), volume, and the URL.
- For webpages with extremely long URLs, use your best judgment to determine which URL from the site to use. For example, rather than giving the URL of a specific news release with a long URL, you can provide the URL of the "Media relations" webpage.
- APA citation guidelines for social media are still evolving. For the latest information, visit the APA Style Blog at http://blog.apastyle.org.
- For online journals or periodicals that assign a digital object identifier (DOI), include that instead of a conventional URL (for example, doi:13.2057/12345678). If no DOI is available, include the URL of the publication's home page (such as http://www.theglobeandmail.com).

MLA Style

The style recommended by the Modern Language Association of America is used widely in the humanities, especially in the study of language and literature. Like APA style, MLA style uses brief parenthetical citations in the text. However, instead of including author name and year, MLA citations include author name and page reference.

IN-TEXT CITATION—MLA STYLE

To document report sources in text using MLA style, insert the author's last name and a page reference inside parentheses following the cited material: (Porter and Kramer 63). If the author's name is mentioned in the text reference, the name can be omitted from the parenthetical citation: (63). The citation indicates that the reference came from page 63 of an article by Michael Porter and Mark Kramer. With the author's name, readers can find complete publication information in the alphabetically arranged list of works cited that comes at the end of the report.

> Some experts recommend that corporations partner with charities and educational institutions to benefit society and raise their company profiles (Porter and Kramer 63).
>
> Porter and Kramer (63) make a strong case for corporations partnering with charities and educational institutions to benefit society and raise their company profiles.

LIST OF WORKS CITED—MLA STYLE

The *MLA Handbook for Writers of Research Papers* recommends preparing the list of works cited first, so you will know what information to give in the parenthetical citation (for example, whether to add a short title if you're citing more than one work by the same author, or whether to give an initial or first name if you're citing two authors who have the same last name). The list of works cited appears at the end of your report, contains all the works that you cite in your text, and lists them in alphabetical order. The major conventions for developing a reference list according to MLA style, eighth edition (see Figure B–4), are as follows:

- Double-space the list
- Either use a hanging indent for the second line of an entry or use 5 spaces
- The eighth edition of the *MLA Handbook* introduces a new model for entries in the works-cited list, which reflects today's nature of published works (e.g.,

book, DVD, webpage, etc.) that are often combined. Therefore, when citing a book, DVD, or webpage, the researcher or writer should arrange entries using the following MLA core elements:

1. Author
2. Title of source
3. Title of container
4. Other contributors
5. Version
6. Number
7. Publisher
8. Publication date
9. Location

- List the lead author's name in reverse order (last name first), using either full first names or initials. List second author names in normal order. When a source has three or more authors, include only the last name, first name, and initial (if appropriate) of the first author; follow this by a comma and then "et al." Abbreviations such as "ed." for "editor" and "trans." for "translated by" should be spelled out fully.
- Use quotation marks around the titles of articles from magazines, newspapers, and journals. Capitalize all important words.
- Italicize the names of books, newspapers, journals, reports, websites, broadcasts, films, plays, CDs, and other complete publications, capitalizing all main words in the title.
- Page numbers in the works-cited list should be preceded by *p.* or *pp.* This does not apply to in-text citations.
- For journal articles, include the abbreviation "vol." and the "no." of the issue (if necessary). Include the month or season (if available) along with the year and follow that with a comma and the page range of the article: *Canadian Journal of Communication*, vol. 4, no. 6, July 2017, pp. 1–3.
- The city of publication and medium of publication (e.g., Print, Web) are no longer required.
- Including the date when an online work was accessed by the researcher is optional, and placeholders for unknown information such as *n.d.* (for "no date") are no longer used.
- The URL for electronic sources must be as accurate and complete as possible. If the URL is extremely long, use the URL of the website's home page or the URL of the site's search page if you used the site's search function to find the article. Remove the http:// or https:// from the URLs/web addresses.

WORKS CITED

Book, two authors	Argenti, Paul A., and Janis Forman. *The Power of Corporate Communication: Crafting the Voice and Image of Your Business*, McGraw Hill, 2006.
Brochure	BestTemp Staffing Services. *An Employer's Guide to Staffing Services*. 2nd ed., BestTemp Information Center, 2011.
Government publication	Canada. Industry Canada. Office of Consumer Affairs. *Canadian Consumer Handbook*, Office of Consumer Affairs, 2009.
Journal article with volume and issue numbers	Clifton, Jonathan. "Beyond Taxonomies of Influence." *Journal of Business Communication*, vol. 46, no. 1, 2009, pp. 57–79, *ProQuest* 148778291. Accessed 27 Oct. 2008.
Article from an electronic database	Davis, Steven V., and Andrew Gilman. "Communication Coordination." *Risk Management*, vol. 49, no. 8, August 2002, pp. 38–43.
Book, component parts	Gluesing, Julia C., "The Development of Global Virtual Teams." *Virtual Teams that Work: Creating Conditions for Virtual Team Effectiveness*. Edited by Cristina B. Gibson and Susan G. Cohen, Jossey-Bass, 2003, pp. 353–380.
Internet, World Wide Web	Hoover's Online. *Intel—Company Capsule*. www.hoovers.com/intel-corp./--ID_13787--/free-co-factsheet.xhtml
Television broadcast	"How Not to Get Nailed." *Marketplace*, Produced by Jennifer Fowler, Hosted by Wendy Mesley, season 34, episode 1, CBC TV, 17 Aug. 2007
Social media post (Twitter)	jk_rowling. "God, I hate this stuff. I've winged it my whole life. I've messed up regularly. There are no rules. Do you think." *Twitter*, 12 June 2016, 10:03 a.m., twitter.com/jk_rowling/status/742039536688107520.
Paper presented at a meeting	Martin, Jeanette S., and Lillian H. Chaney. "Integrating Global Conversational Customs into Business Courses." Association for Business Communication 70th Annual Convention, 20–25 Oct. 2005.
CD-ROM encyclopedia article, one author	Parkings, Robert. "George Eastman." *The Concise Columbia Encyclopedia*. Columbia UP, 1998.
Online magazine article	Porter, Michael E., and Mark R. Kramer. "The Competitive Advantage of Corporate Philanthropy." *Harvard Business Review*, Dec. 2002, hbr.org/2002/12/the-competitive-advantage-of-corporate-philanthropy
Magazine article	Sequin, Denis. "A Hollywood Ending?" *Canadian Business*, 13 Aug. 2007, pp. 11–12.
Interview	Stainer, Georgia, Day Cable and Communications, 2 Mar. 2011.
Annual report	Suncor, *2013 Annual Report*, 2014.
Newspaper article, no author	"Toyota Sets Sights on Sales Record." *Globe and Mail Report on Business*, 1 Sept. 2007, p. 10.
Newspaper article, one author	VanderKlippe, Nathan. "B.C. Salmon Industry in Rough Water." *Financial Post*, 1 Sept. 2007, p. 3.
Unpublished dissertation or thesis	Zhou, Changhui. "Transitional Flow of Knowledge in Multinational Corporations: R&D Co-Practice as an Integrating Force." Diss. U of Western Ontario, 2002.

Figure B–4 Sample Works Cited—MLA 8 Style
Note: This example of Works Cited is shown as single-spaced without leaving an extra space between sources. In practice, it should be double-spaced without leaving an extra space between sources.

- For social media posts, use the following style: Author. "Full text of post." *Name of Social Media Website*, Date, Time, URL. When the author's name begins with "@", disregard it and alphabetize the work in the works-cited list using the character that comes right after the "@".
- A period always follows the last element of the citation.

Refer to https://www.mla.org/MLA-Style/What-s-New-in-the-Eighth-Edition for additional information on what has changed in the MLA guide and links to practice templates. Your school's library webpage will also most likely provide guidelines for the different documentation forms.

Endnotes

Chapter 1

1. Wave Accounting website, http://www.waveapp.com; Deloitte Technology Fast 50 Winners, https://www2.deloitte.com/content/dam/Deloitte/ca/Documents/technology-media-telecommunications/ca-EN_Fast50_winners_AODA.PDF; and Sara Angeles, "Wave Review: Best Free Accounting Software for Businesses," *Business News Daily*, March 24, 2017, http://www.businessnewsdaily.com/7545-best-free-accounting-software.html.

2. Richard L. Daft, *Management*, 6th ed. (Cincinnati: Thomson South-Western, 2003), 580.

3. Canadian Centre for Ethics & Corporate Policy website, http://www.ethicscentre.ca/EN/resources/.

4. Philip C. Kolin, *Successful Writing at Work,* 6th ed. (Boston: Houghton Mifflin, 2001), 17–23.

5. J. David Johnson, William A. Donohoe, Charles K. Atkin, and Sally Johnson, "Differences between Formal and Informal Communication Channels," *Journal of Business Communication* 31, no. 2 (1994): 111–122.

6. Lorenzo Sierra, "Tell It to the Grapevine," *Communication World* 19, no. 4 (2002): 28.

7. Tim Laseter and Rob Cross, "The Craft of Connection," *Strategy + Business*, Autumn 2006, 26–32.

8. Citizenship and Immigration Canada, "Preliminary Tables—Permanent and Temporary Residents, 2011: Canada—Permanent Residents by Category, 2007–2011," http://www.cic.gc.ca/english/resources/statistics/facts2011-preliminary/01.asp.

9. "Canada's Multiculturalism Aids Trade Efforts, Pettigrew Says," *Canada Newswire*, May 25, 2000.

10. "Five Case Studies on Successful Teams," *HR Focus*, April 2002, 181.

11. Stephanie Vozza, "Eight Career Skills You Need to Be Competitive in 2016," Fast Company, January 13, 2016, https://www.fastcompany.com/3055352/the-future-of-work/eight-career-skills-you-need-to-becompetitive-in-2016.

12. Government of Canada, "Canadians Have Your Say on Cyber Security," http://news.gc.ca/web/article-en.do?nid=1111999.

13. Angela Stelmakowich, "Cyber Security Must Be Viewed as a Business Issue, Not a Technology-Only Issue: PwC Canada," *Canadian Underwriter*, January 14, 2016, http://www.canadianunderwriter.ca/insurance/cyber-security-must-be-viewed-as-a-business-issue-not-a-technology-only-issue-pwc-1003978981/; and Canadian Underwriter, "One-Quarter of Canadian Small and Medium Businesses with Revenue over $10M Victims of Cyberattack: Study," *Canadian Underwriter*, October 12, 2016, http://www.canadianunderwriter.ca/commercial-lines/one-quarter-canadian-small-medium-businesses-revenue-10m-victims-cyberattack-study-1004101356/.

14. Lucian Constantin, "WannaCry Attacks Are Only the Beginning, Experts Warn," *PCWorld*, May 15, 2017, http://www.pcworld.com/article/3196927/security/wannacry-attacks-are-only-the-beginning.html.

15. Government of Canada, "Canadians Have Your Say on Cyber Security."

16. Pete Cashmore, "10 Web Trends to Watch in 2010," *CNN Tech*, December 3, 2009, http://www.cnn.com.

17. Jeff Davidson, "Fighting Information Overload," *Canadian Manager*, Spring 2005, 161.

18. Chuck Williams, *Management*, 2nd ed. (Cincinnati: Thomson/SouthWestern, 2002), 690.

19. Don Hellriegel, Susan E. Jackson, and John W. Slocum Jr., *Management: A Competency-Based Approach* (Cincinnati: Thomson/South-Western, 2002), 447.

20. Gillian Flynn, "Pillsbury's Recipe Is Candid Talk," *Workforce* (February 1998): 556–571.

21. Charles E. Pettijohn, Nancy K. Keith, and Melissa S. Burnett, "Managerial and Peer Influence on Ethical Behavioral Intentions in Personal Selling Context," *Journal of Promotion Management* 17 (2011): 144; Bruce W. Speck, "Writing Professional Codes of Ethics to Introduce Ethics in Business Writing," *Bulletin of the Association for Business Communication* 53, no. 3 (1990): 21–26; H. W. Love, "Communication, Accountability and Professional Discourse: The Interaction of Language Values and Ethical Values," *Journal of Business Ethics* 11 (1992): 883–892; and Kathryn C. Rentz and Mary Beth Debs, "Language and Corporate Values: Teaching Ethics in Business Writing Courses," *Journal of Business Communication* 24, no. 3 (1987): 37–48.

22. Tamar Lewin, "Study Finds Widespread Neglect of Writing Skills," *Desert Sun* April 26, 2003, A12.

23. Hellriegel et al., *Management: A Competency-Based Approach*, 451.

24. Paul Martin Lester, *Visual Communication: Images with Messages* (Belmont, CA: Thomson South-Western, 2006), 6–8.

25. Michael R. Solomon, *Consumer Behavior: Buying, Having, and Being*, 6th ed. (Upper Saddle River, NJ: Pearson Prentice Hall, 2004), 65.

26. Anne Field, "What You Say, What They Hear," *Harvard Management Communication Letter* (Winter 2005): 3–5.

27. Charles G. Morris and Albert A. Maisto, *Psychology: An Introduction*, 12th ed. (Upper Saddle River, NJ: Pearson Prentice Hall, 2005), 226–239; Saundra K. Ciccarelli and Glenn E. Meyer, *Psychology* (Upper Saddle River, NJ: Prentice Hall, 2006), 210–229; and Mark H. Ashcraft, *Cognition*, 4th ed. (Upper Saddle River, NJ: Prentice Hall, 2006), 44–54.

28. John Owens, "Good Communication in Workplace Is Basic to Getting Any Job Done," *Knight Ridder Tribune Business News*, July 9, 2003, 1.

29. Williams, *Management*, 706–707.

30. Niall Harbison, "Seven Important Social Media Trends for the Next Year," *TNW Social Media*, September 2010, 12, http://thenextweb.com.

31. Jacques Bughin and Michael Chu, "The Rise of the Networked Enterprise: Web 2.0 Finds Its Payday," *McKinsey Quarterly*, December 2010, http://www.mckinseyquarterly.com.

32. "Capitalizing on Complexity: Insights from the Global Chief Executive Study," IBM Corporation, May 2010, http://www.ibm.com.

33. Tara Craig, "How to Avoid Information Overload," *Personnel Today*, June 10, 2008, 31; and Jeff Davidson, "Fighting Information Overload," *Canadian Manager*, Spring 2005, 161.

34. "The Top Ten Ways Workers Waste Time Online," *24/7 Wall St.*, September 30, 2010, http://247wallst.com.

35. Eric J. Sinrod, "Perspective: It's My Internet—I Can Do What I Want," *News.com*, March 29, 2006, http://www.news.com.

36. Eric J. Sinrod, "Time to Crack Down on Tech at Work?" *News.com*, June 14, 2006, http://www.news.com.

37. Thomas A. Young, "Ethics in Business: Business of Ethics," *Vital Speeches* 15 (September 1992): 725–730.

38. Kolin, *Successful Writing at Work*, 24–30.

39. Nancy K. Kubasek, Bartley A. Brennan, and M. Neil Browne, *The Legal Environment of Business*, 3rd ed. (Upper Saddle River, NJ: Prentice Hall, 2003), 172.

40. Michael Oliveira, "Netflix Apologizes for Using Actors to Meet Press at Canadian Launch," *Globe and Mail*, September 22, 2010, http://www.theglobeandmail.com.

41. "WOM 101," Word of Mouth Marketing Association, http://womma.org; Nate Anderson, Arstechnica.com; "Undercover Marketing Uncovered," *CBSnews.com*, July 25, 2004, http://www.cbsnews.com; and Stephanie Dunnewind, "Teen Recruits Create Word-of-Mouth 'Buzz' to Hook Peers on Products," *Seattle Times*, November 20, 2004, http://www.seattletimes.com.

42. Linda Pophal, "Tweet Ethics: Trust and Transparency in a Web 2.0 World." *CW Bulletin*, September 2009, http://www.iabc.com.

43. Daft, *Management*, 155.

44. Bell Canada Enterprises, *Bell Canada Enterprises Code of Business Conduct* (Bell Canada, 2011), 2.

45. Based in part on Robert Kreitner, *Management*, 9th ed. (Boston: Houghton Mifflin, 2004), 163.

46. Henry R. Cheeseman, *Contemporary Business and E-Commerce Law*, 4th ed. (Upper Saddle River, NJ: Prentice Hall, 2003), 201.

47. Cheeseman, *Contemporary Business and E-Commerce Law*, 325.

48. Kubasek et al., *The Legal Environment of Business*, 306.

49. Robert Plummer, "Will Fake Business Blogs Crash and Burn?" *BBC News*, May 22, 2008, http://news.bbc.co.uk.

50. Tim Arango, "Soon, Bloggers Must Give Full Disclosure," *New York Times*, October 5, 2009, http://www.nytimes.com.

Chapter 2

1. Adapted from Royal Bank Financial Group website and *Royal Bank Annual Report 2011*; *Royal Bank of Canada 2011 Corporate Responsibility Report and Public Accountability Statement*; *RBC at a Glance, Spring 2012*; Royal Bank of Canada, "RBC One of the Best Workplaces in Canada," news release, April 18, 2012; Royal Bank of Canada, "From War to Work: RBC Ex-Military Recruitment Program," news release, December 21, 2011; Charles Coffey, "Investing in People: Work/Life Solutions" (speech, Robert Half International Breakfast Session, Toronto, ON, January 15, 2003); http://www.rbc.com/newsroom/news5-2002-2005.html#2003; Kristi Nelson, "Royal Bank of Canada Optimizes Work Force," *Bank Systems + Technology* 39, no. 6 (2002): 42; Jay Sanford, "A Royal Return," *Canadian Business* 79, no. 10 (Summer 2006), ProQuest Document ID: 105051531; *Employer Review: RBC/Royal Bank of Canada*, http://www.eluta.ca/top-employer-rbc; and "RBC Recognized as One of the 'Best Workplaces in Canada,'" http://www.rbc.com/aboutus/2016-04-22-best-workplace.html.

2. Courtland L. Bovée and John V. Thill, *Business in Action*, 5th ed. (Upper Saddle River, NJ: Pearson Prentice Hall, 2011), 172.

3. Glenn Parker, "Leading a Team of Strangers: Most Teams Now Are Diverse or Virtual," *T&D* 57, no. 2 (2003): 21; and Rajesh Sethi, Daniel C. Smith, and C. Whan Park, "Cross-functional Product Development Teams and the Innovativeness of New Consumer Products," *Marketing Science Institute*, 2001, http://www.msi.org/reports/cross-functional-product-development-teams-and-the-innovativeness-of-new-co/.

4. Ellen Neuborne, "Companies Save, But Workers Pay," *USA Today*, February 25, 1997, B2; Richard L. Daft, *Management*, 4th ed. (Fort Worth: Dryden, 1997), 338; and Richard Moderow, "Teamwork Is the Key to Cutting Costs," *Modern Healthcare* 29 (April 1996): 138.

5. Keith Ferrazzi, "Getting Virtual Teams Right," *Harvard Business Review*, December 2014, https://hbr.org/2014/12/getting-virtual-teams-right#.

6. Stephen R. Robbins, *Essentials of Organizational Behavior*, 6th ed. (Upper Saddle River, NJ: Prentice Hall, 2000), 98.

7. Max Landsberg and Madeline Pfau, "Developing Diversity: Lessons from Top Teams," *Strategy + Business*, Winter 2005, 10–12.

8. "Groups Best at Complex Problems," *Industrial Engineer*, June 2006, 14.

9. Nicola A. Nelson, "Leading Teams," *Defense AT&L*, July–August 2006: 26–29; Larry Cole and Michael Cole, "Why Is the Teamwork Buzz Word Not Working?" *Communication World*, February–March 1999: 29; Patricia Buhler, "Managing in the 90s: Creating Flexibility in Today's Workplace," *Supervision*, January 1997: 24+; and Allison W. Amason, Allen C. Hochwarter, Wayne A. Thompson, and Kenneth R. Harrison, "Conflict: An Important Dimension in Successful Management Teams," *Organizational Dynamics*, Autumn 1995: 201.

10. Geoffrey Colvin, "Why Dream Teams Fail," *Fortune*, June 12, 2006, 87–92.

11. Alex "Sandy" Pentland, "The New Science of Building Great Teams," *Harvard Business Review*, April 2012, https://hbr.org/2012/04/the-new-science-of-building-great-teams.

12. Colvin, "Why Dream Teams Fail," 87–92.

13. Tiziana Casciaro and Miguel Sousa Lobo, "Competent Jerks, Lovable Fools, and the Formation of Social Networks," *Harvard Business Review*, June 2005: 92–99.

14. Stephen P. Robbins and David A. DeCenzo, *Fundamentals of Management*, 4th ed. (Upper Saddle River, NJ: Prentice Hall, 2004), 266–267; and Jerald Greenberg and Robert A. Baron, *Behavior in Organizations*, 8th ed. (Upper Saddle River, NJ: Prentice Hall, 2003), 279–280.

15. "Team Building: Managing the Norms of Informal Groups in the Workplace," *Accel-Team.com*, accessed August 16, 2006, http://www.accelteam.com.

16. B. Aubrey Fisher, *Small Group Decision Making: Communication and the Group Process*, 2nd ed. (New York: McGraw-Hill, 1980), 145–149; Steven P. Robbins and David A. DeCenzo, *Fundamentals of Management*, 3rd. ed. (Upper Saddle River, NJ: Prentice Hall, 2001), 334–335; and Daft, *Management*, 602–603.

17. Michael Laff, "Effective Team Building: More Than Just Fun at Work," *Training + Development*, August 2006, 24–35.

18. Claire Sookman, "Building Your Virtual Team," *Network World*, June 21, 2004, 91.

19. Lawrence Magid, "Groupthink Can Be Fatal," *Information Week*, April 14, 1997, 114.

20. Jared Sandberg, "Brainstorming Works Best If People Scramble for Ideas on Their Own," *Wall Street Journal*, June 13, 2006, B1.

21. Mark K. Smith, "Bruce W. Tuckman—Forming, Storming, Norming, and Performing in Groups," *Infed.org*, 2005, http://www.infed.org.

22. Robbins and DeCenzo, *Fundamentals of Management*, 258–259.

23. Daft, *Management*, 609–612.

24. Andy Boynton and Bill Fischer, *Virtuoso Teams: Lessons from Teams That Changed Their Worlds* (Harrow, England: FT Prentice Hall, 2005), 10.

25. Thomas K. Capozzoli, "Conflict Resolution—A Key Ingredient in Successful Teams," *Supervision*, November 1999: 14–16.

26. Jesse S. Nirenberg, *Getting through to People* (Paramus, NJ: Prentice Hall, 1973), 134–142.

27. Nirenberg, *Getting through to People*.

28. Nirenberg, *Getting through to People*.

29. Jon Hanke, "Presenting as a Team, *Presentations*, January 1998, 74–82.

30. William P. Galle Jr., Beverly H. Nelson, Donna W. Luse, and Maurice F. Villere, *Business Communication: A Technology-Based Approach* (Chicago: Irwin, 1996), 260.

31. Claire Sookman, "Building Your Virtual Team," *Network World*, June 21, 2004, 91.

32. Mark Choate, "What Makes an Enterprise Wiki?" *CMS Watch*, April 28, 2006, http://www.cmswatch.com.

33. Choate, "What Makes an Enterprise Wiki?"

34. Rob Koplowitz, "Building a Collaboration Strategy," *KM World*, November/December 2009, 14–15.

35. Christopher Carfi and Leif Chastaine, "Social Networking for Businesses & Organizations" (white paper, accessed August 13, 2008, http://www.cerado.com).

36. Richard McDermott and Douglas Archibald, "Harnessing Your Staff's Informal Networks," *Harvard Business Review*, March 2010, 82–89.

37. Tony Hsieh, "Why I Sold Zappos," *Inc.*, June 1, 2010, http://www.inc.com.

38. Ron Ashkenas, "Why We Secretly Love Meetings," *Harvard Business Review* blogs, October 5, 2010, http://blogs.hbr.org.

39. Douglas Kimberly, "Ten Pitfalls of Pitiful Meetings," *Payroll Manager's Report*, January 2010, 1, 11; and "Making the Most of Meetings," *Journal of Accountancy*, March 2009: 22.

40. "Better Meetings Benefit Everyone: How to Make Yours More Productive," *Working Communicator Bonus Report*, July 1998, 1.

41. Roger O. Crockett, "The 21st Century Meeting," *BusinessWeek*, February 26, 2007, 72–79.

42. Steve Lohr, "As Travel Costs Rise, More Meetings Go Virtual," *New York Times*, July 22, 2008, http://www.nytimes.com.

43. "Unlock the Full Power of the Web Conferencing," *CEOworld.biz*, November 20, 2007, http://www.ceoworld.biz.

44. IBM Jam Events website, accessed June 10, 2010, http://www.collaborationjam.com; and "Big Blue Brainstorm," *BusinessWeek*, August 7, 2006, http://www.businessweek.com.

45. "17 Tips for More Productive Conference Calls," *Accu-Conference*, accessed January 30, 2008, http://www.accuconference.com.

46. Augusta M. Simon, "Effective Listening: Barriers to Listening in a Diverse Business Environment," *Bulletin of the Association for Business Communication* 54, no. 3 (September 1991): 73–74.

47. Judi Brownell, *Listening*, 2nd ed. (Boston: Allyn & Bacon, 2002), 9, 10.

48. Laura Fowlie, "Gauging Success by One's Attributes, Not Resume: More Companies Are Using the Competency Profile as a Benchmark in Assessing an Employee's Performance," *Financial Post*, October 17, 1998, R8.

49. Bob Lamons, "Good Listeners Are Better Communicators," *Marketing News*, September 11, 1995, 131; and Phillip Morgan and H. Kent Baker, "Building a Professional Image: Improving Listening Behavior," *Supervisory Management*, November 1985: 35–36.

50. Robyn D. Clarke, "Do You Hear What I Hear?" *Black Enterprise*, May 1998: 129; and Dot Yandle, "Listening to Understand," *Pryor Report Management Newsletter Supplement* 15, no. 8 (Aug. 1998): 13.

51. Brownell, *Listening*, 14; Dennis M. Kratz and Abby Robinson Kratz, *Effective Listening Skills* (New York: McGraw-Hill, 1995), 8–9; Sherwyn P. Morreale and Courtland L. Bovée, *Excellence in Public Speaking* (Orlando, FL: Harcourt Brace, 1998), 72–76; and Lyman K. Steil, Larry L. Barker, and Kittie W. Watson, *Effective Listening: Key to Your Success* (Reading, MA: Addison Wesley, 1983), 21–22.

52. Kratz and Kratz, *Effective Listening Skills*, 45-53, 78-79; J. Michael Sproule, *Communication Today* (Glenview, IL: Scott, Foresman, 1981), 69; Ronald B. Adler and George Rodman, *Understanding Human Communication*, 8th ed. (New York: Oxford University Press, 2003), 126 -130; and Brownell, *Listening*, 230–231.

53. Patrick J. Collins, *Say It with Power and Confidence* (Upper Saddle River, NJ: Prentice Hall, 1997), 40–45.

54. Morreale and Bovée, *Excellence in Public Speaking*, 296.

55. Dale G. Leathers, *Successful Nonverbal Communication: Principles and Applications* (New York: Macmillan, 1986), 19.

56. Gerald H. Graham, Jeanne Unrue, and Paul Jennings, "The Impact of Nonverbal Communication in Organizations: A Survey of Perceptions," *Journal of Business Communication* 28, no. 1 (Winter 1991): 45–62.

57. Virginia P. Richmond and James C. McCroskey, *Nonverbal Behavior in Interpersonal Relations* (Boston: Allyn and Bacon, 2000), 153–157.

58. Richmond and McCroskey, *Nonverbal Behavior in Interpersonal Relations*, 2–3.

59. Joe Navarro, "Body Language Myths," *Psychology Today*, October 25, 2009, http://www.psychologytoday.com; and Richmond and McCroskey, *Nonverbal Behavior in Interpersonal Relations*, 2–3.

Chapter 3

1. IBM website, http://www.ibm.com; IBM, "Corporate Service Corps," http://www.ibm.com/ibm/responsibility/corporateservicecorps/programdetails.html; Carol Hymowitz, "Managing: In the Lead: IBM Combines Volunteer Service, Teamwork to Cultivate Emerging Markets," *Wall Street Journal*, August 4, 2008, B6; Sylvia Ann Hewlett, "Volunteer to Juice Your Career," *Forbes*, January 2, 2012, http://www.forbes.com; Deirdre White, "The Job Corps Movement," *Corporate Responsibility Magazine*, October 2011, http://www.thecro.com; "Big-Hearted Blue," *Economist*, October 30, 2010; IBM, "Corporate Service Corps Progress Report: Making a Difference through Citizen Diplomacy," August 2016, https://www.ibm.com/ibm/responsibility/corporateservicecorps/pdf/IBM-Corporate-Service-Corps-2016-Progress-Report.pdf.

2. Export Development Canada, *White Paper: Foreign Footprints*, 2016, http://www.edc.ca/EN/Knowledge-Centre/Economic-Analysis-and-Research/Documents/foreign-footprints.pdf.

3. Nancy R. Lockwood, "Workplace Diversity: Leveraging the Power of Difference for Competitive Advantage," *HR Magazine*, June 2005, Special Section, 1–10.

4. Gordon Nixon, "Canada's Diversity Imperative: 2010 and Beyond" (speech delivered to the Vancouver Board of Trade, May 10, 2006), http://www.rbc.com/newsroom/20060510nixon.html.

5. Citizenship and Immigration Canada, "Government of Canada Announces 2011 Immigration Plan," news release, November 1, 2010, http://www.cic.gc.ca/english/department/media/releases/2010/2010-11-01a.asp.

6. Government of Canada, "Key Highlights 2017 Immigration Levels Plan," October 31, 2016, http://news.gc.ca/web/article-en.do?nid=1145319.

7. Renée Huang, "The Fine Art of Canadian Conversation," *Globe and Mail*, March 17, 2003; and Dalton Pharma Services, "Benefits," http://www.dalton.com/benefits.aspx.

8. Government of Canada, "Key Highlights 2017 Immigration Levels Plan," October 31, 2016, http://news.gc.ca/web/article-en.do?nid=1145319.

9. RBC, "What Is Diversity & Inclusion?", http://www.rbc.com/diversity/what-is-diversity.html.

10. Tracy Novinger, *Intercultural Communication, A Practical Guide* (Austin, TX: University of Texas Press, 2001), 15.

11. Arthur Chin, "Understanding Cultural Competency," *New Zealand Business*, December 2010/January 2011, 34–35; Sanjeeta R. Gupta, "Achieve Cultural Competency," *Training*, February 2009, 16–17; and Diane Shannon, "Cultural Competency in Health Care Organizations: Why and How," *Physician Executive*, September–October 2010, 15–22.

12. Linda Beamer and Iris Varner, *Intercultural Communication in the Workplace*, 2nd ed. (New York: McGraw-Hill Irwin, 2001), 3.

13. Philip R. Harris and Robert T. Moran, *Managing Cultural Differences*, 3rd ed. (Houston: Gulf, 1991), 394–397, 429–430.

14. Lillian H. Chaney and Jeanette S. Martin, *Intercultural Business Communication*, 2nd ed. (Upper Saddle River, NJ: Prentice Hall, 2000), 6.

15. Beamer and Varner, *Intercultural Communication in the Workplace*, 4.

16. Chaney and Martin, *Intercultural Business Communication*, 9.

17. Richard L. Daft, *Management*, 6th ed. (Cincinnati: Thomson South-Western, 2003), 455.

18. Project Implicit website, https:/implicit.harvard.edu/implicit.

19. Linda Beamer, "Teaching English Business Writing to Chinese-Speaking Business Students," *Bulletin of the Association for Business Communication* 57, no. 1 (1994): 12–18.

20. Edward T. Hall, "Context and Meaning," in *Intercultural Communication: A Reader*, 6th ed., ed. Larry A. Samovar and Richard E. Porter (Belmont, CA: Wadsworth, 1991), 46–55.

21. Richard L. Daft, *Management*, 4th ed. (Fort Worth, TX: Dryden, 1997), 459.

22. Charley H. Dodd, *Dynamics of Intercultural Communication*, 3rd ed. (Dubuque, Iowa, IA: Brown, 1991), 69–70.

23. Daft, *Management*, 4th ed., 459.
24. Hannah Seligson, "For American Workers in China, a Culture Clash," *New York Times*, December 23, 2009, http://www.nytimes.com.
25. Beamer and Varner, *Intercultural Communication in the Workplace*, 230–233.
26. Gus Lubin, "These 8 Scales Reveal Everything You Should Know about Different Cultures," *Business Insider*, January 20, 2015, http://www.businessinsider.com/the-culture-map-8-scales-for-work-2015-1; Carol Kinsey Goman, "How Culture Controls Communication," Forbes, November 28, 2011, https://www.forbes.com/sites/carolkinseygoman/2011/11/28/how-culture-controls-communication/print/.
27. James Wilfong and Toni Seger, *Taking Your Business Global* (Franklin Lakes, NJ: Career Press, 1997), 277–278.
28. Guo-Ming Chen and William J. Starosta, *Foundations of Intercultural Communication* (Boston: Allyn & Bacon, 1998), 288–289.
29. Robert O. Joy, "Cultural and Procedural Differences That Influence Business Strategies and Operations in the People's Republic of China," *SAM Advanced Management Journal*, Summer 1989: 29–33.
30. Laraine Kaminsky, "Preparing for Life, and Business, in China," *Canadian HR Reporter* 26 (September 2005): 8–9.
31. Chaney and Martin, *Intercultural Business Communication*, 122–123.
32. Peter Coy, "Old. Smart. Productive." *BusinessWeek*, June 27, 2005, http://www.businessweek.com; and Beamer and Varner, *Intercultural Communication in the Workplace*, 107–108.
33. Beamer and Varner, *Intercultural Communication in the Workplace*, 107–108.
34. Steff Gelston, "Gen Y, Gen X and the Baby Boomers: Workplace Generation Wars," *CIO*, January 30, 2008, http://www.cio.com.
35. Tonya Vinas, "A Place at the Table," *IndustryWeek*, July 1, 2003, 22.
36. P. Christopher Earley and Elaine Mosakowsi, "Cultural Intelligence," *Harvard Business Review*, October 2004: 139–146.
37. Wendy A. Conklin, "An Inside Look at Two Diversity Intranet Sites: IBM and Merck," *The Diversity Factor*, Summer 2005.
38. Bob Nelson, "Motivating Workers Worldwide," *Global Workforce*, November 1998: 25–27.
39. Mona Casady and Lynn Wasson, "Written Communication Skills of International Business Persons," *Bulletin of the Association for Business Communication* 57, no. 4 (1994): 36–40.
40. Lynn Gaertner-Johnston, "Found in Translation," *Business Writing Blog*, November 25, 2005, http://www.businesswritingblog.com.
41. Myron W. Lustig and Jolene Koester, *Intercultural Competence*, 4th ed. (Boston: Allyn & Bacon, 2003), 196.
42. Wilfong and Seger, *Taking Your Business Global*, 232.
43. Sheridan Prasso, ed., "It's All Greek to These Sites," *BusinessWeek*, July 22, 2002, 18.

Chapter 4

1. MaRS website, http://www.marsdd.com; MaRS, "MaRS at a Glance," August 2011 (brochure); and MaRS Job Board, "MaRS Communication Manager," July 21, 2011 (job posting).
2. Sanford Kaye, "Writing under Pressure," *Soundview Executive Book Summaries* 10, no. 12, (December 1988): 1–8.
3. Peter Bracher, "Process, Pedagogy, and Business Writing," *Journal of Business Communication* 24, no. 1 (Winter 1987): 43–50.
4. Linda Duyle, "Get Out of Your Office," *HR Magazine*, July 2006, 99–101.
5. Frank Martin Hein, "Making the Best Use of Electronic Media," *Communication World*, November–December 2006, 20–23.
6. "About Skype," Skype website, http://about.skype.com.
7. Caroline McCarthy, "The Future of Web Apps Will See the Death of Email," *Webware Blog*, February 29, 2008, http://news.cnet.com; and Kris Maher, "The Jungle," *Wall Street Journal*, October 5,

2004, B10; and Kevin Maney, "Surge in Text Messaging Makes Cell Operators :-)," *USA Today*, July 28, 2005, B1–B2.
8. Laurey Berk and Phillip G. Clampitt, "Finding the Right Path in the Communication Maze," *IABC Communication World*, October 1991, 28–32.
9. Samantha R. Murray and Joseph Peyrefitte, "Knowledge Type and Communication Media Choice in the Knowledge Transfer Process," *Journal of Managerial Issues* (Spring 2007): 111–133.
10. Raymond M. Olderman, *10 Minute Guide to Business Communication* (New York: Alpha Books, 1997), 19–20.
11. Mohan R. Limaye and David A. Victor, "Cross-Cultural Business Communication Research: State of the Art and Hypotheses for the 1990s," *Journal of Business Communication* 28, no. 3 (Summer 1991): 277–299.
12. Holly Weeks, "The Best Memo You'll Ever Write," *Harvard Management Communication Letter*, Spring 2005, 3–5.

Chapter 5

1. Creative Commons website, http://creativecommons.org; Ariana Eunjung Cha, "Creative Commons Is Rewriting Rules of Copyright," *Washington Post*, March 15, 2005, http://www.washingtonpost.com; Steven Levy, "Lawrence Lessig's Supreme Showdown," *Wired*, October, 2002, http://www.wired.com; and "Happy Birthday: We'll Sue,"*Snopes.com*, http://www.snopes.com.
2. Elizabeth Blackburn and Kelly Belanger, "You-Attitude and Positive Emphasis: Testing Received Wisdom in Business Communication," *Bulletin of the Association for Business Communication* 56, no. 2 (June 1993): 1–9.
3. Annette N. Shelby and N. Lamar Reinsch Jr., "Positive Emphasis and You Attitude: An Empirical Study," *Journal of Business Communication* 32, no. 4 (1995): 303–322.
4. Sherryl Kleinman, "Why Sexist Language Matters," *Qualitative Sociology* 25, no. 2 (Summer 2002): 299–304.
5. Judy E. Pickens, "Terms of Equality: A Guide to Bias-Free Language," *Personnel Journal* (August 1985): 24.
6. Lisa Taylor, "Communicating about People with Disabilities: Does the Language We Use Make a Difference?" *Bulletin of the Association for Business Communication* 53, no. 3 (September 1990): 65–67.
7. Susan Benjamin, *Words at Work* (Reading, MA: Addison-Wesley, 1997), 136–137.
8. Mary A. DeVries, *Internationally Yours* (Boston: Houghton Mifflin, 1994), 61.
9. Stuart Crainer and Des Dearlove, "Making Yourself Understood," *Across the Board*, May–June 2004, 23–27.
10. Plain English Campaign website, http://www.plainenglish.co.uk.
11. Susan Jaderstrom and Joanne Miller, "Active Writing," *Office Pro*, November/December 2003, 29.
12. Creative Commons website, http://creativecommons.org.
13. Peter Crow, "Plain English: What Counts Besides Readability?" *Journal of Business Communication* 25, no. 1 (Winter 1988): 87–95.
14. Susan Jaderstrom and Joanne Miller, "Active Writing," *Office Pro*, November/December 2003: 29.
15. Portions of this section are adapted from Courtland L. Bovée, *Techniques of Writing Business Letters, Memos, and Reports* (Sherman Oaks, CA: Banner Books International, 1978), 13–90.
16. Janice Obuchowski, "Communicate to Inform, Not Impress," *Harvard Management Communication Letter* (Winter 2006): 3–4; and Robert Hartwell Fiske, *The Dimwit's Dictionary* (Oak Park, IL: Marion Street Press, 2002), 1620.
17. See Note 1.
18. Food Allergy Initiative website, http://www.foodallergyinitiative.org; Diana Keough, "Snacks That Can Kill; Schools Take Steps to Protect Kids Who Have Severe Allergies to Nuts," *Plain Dealer*, July 15, 2003, E1; "Dawdling Over Food Labels," *New York Times*, June 2, 2003, A16; Sheila McNulty, "A Matter of Life and Death," *Financial Times*, September 10, 2003, 14; and "Food Allergies and

Intolerances," Health Canada website, http://www.hc-sc.gc.ca/fn-an/securit/allerg/index-eng.php.

19. Apple iTunes website, accessed September 23, 2006, http://www.apple.com/itunes.

Chapter 6

1. Free The Children website, http://www.freethechildren.com; Free The Children, *2011 Annual Report*; and Free the Children Media Kit.

2. William Zinsser, *On Writing Well*, 5th ed. (New York: HarperCollins, 1994), 9.

3. Zinsser, *On Writing Well*, 7, 17.

4. Mary A. DeVries, *Internationally Yours* (Boston: Houghton Mifflin, 1994), 160.

5. Zinsser, *On Writing Well*, 126.

6. Deborah Gunn, "Looking Good on Paper," *Office Pro*, March 2004, 10–11.

7. Jennifer Saranow, "Memo to Web Sites: Grow Up!" *Wall Street Journal*, November 15, 2004, R14–R15.

8. The writing sample in this exercise was adapted from material on the Marsh Risk Consulting website (accessed October 2, 2006), http://www.marshrikconsulting.com.

Chapter 7

1. PumpTalk blog, http://www.pumptalk.ca; Petro-Canada website, http://www.petro-canada.ca; Suncor website, http://www.suncor.ca; Petro-Canada, "About the PumpTalk blog: About Our Contributors," http://www.pumptalk.ca/about-pumptalk.html#contributors; Petro-Canada, Blogue et vidéos Pleins gaz, http://retail.petro-canada.ca/fr/fuelsavings/pumptalk.aspx.

2. The Radicati Group, *Email Statistics Report*, 2016-2020, March 2016, http://www.radicati.com/wp/wp-content/uploads/2016/01/Email_Statistics_Report_2016-2020_Executive_Summary.pdf.

3. "Ten Ways to Use Texting for Business," *Inc.*, accessed July 21, 2010, http://www.inc.com/ss/ten-ways-use-texting-business; Kate Maddox, "Warrillow Finds 39% of Small-Business Owners Use Text Messaging," *BtoB*, August 1, 2008, http://www.btobonline.com; and Dave Carpenter, "Companies Discover Marketing Power of Text Messaging," *Seattle Times*, September 25, 2006, http://www.seattletimes.com.

4. "Burson-Marsteller Fortune Global 10 Social Media Study," *The Burson-Marsteller* (blog), February 23, 2010, http://www.burson-marsteller.com.

5. "The New Messages," *Facebook.com*, accessed January 30, 2011, http://www.facebook.com.

6. Richard Edelman, "Teaching Social Media: What Skills Do Communicators Need?" in *Engaging the New Influencers: Third Annual Social Media Academic Summit* (white paper, Georgetown University, 2009), http://www.newmediaacademicsummit.com.

7. Catherine Toole, "My 7 Deadly Sins of Writing for Social Media—Am I Right?" *Econsultancy* (blog), June 19, 2007, http://www.econsultancy.com; Muhammad Saleem, "How to Write a Social Media Press Release," *Copyblogger*, August 31, 2007, http://www.copyblogger.com; and Melanie McBride, "5 Tips for (Better) Social Media Writing," *Melanie McBride Online*, June 11, 2008, http://melaniemcbride.net.

8. "Facebook Analytics: Full-on Facebook Tracking and Measurement," *Webtrends*, accessed July 10, 2010, http://www.webtrends.com; "Facebook Statistics Page," *Facebook.com*, accessed July 10, 2010, http://www.facebook.com; and Facebook pages of Adidas, Red Bull, and Starbucks, accessed July 11, 2010, http://www.facebook.com.

9. Todd Henneman, "At Lockheed Martin, Social Networking Fills Key Workforce Needs While Improving Efficiency and Lowering Costs," *Workforce Management*, March 2010, http://www.workforce.com.

10. Sheryl Kingstone and Zeus Kerravala, "Social Media Means Serious Business," (white paper, Yankee Group, June 2010), http://www.siemens-enterprise.com; and Sharon Gaudin, "Companies Not Using Social Nets at Risk, Report Says," *Computerworld*, July 15, 2010, http://www.computerworld.com.

11. Alex Wright, "Mining the Web for Feelings, Not Facts," *New York Times*, August 23, 2009, http://www.nytimes.com.

12. Erica Swallow, "How to Use Social Media for Lead Generation," *Mashable*, June 24, 2010, http://mashable.com.

13. Susan Fournier and Lara Lee, "Getting Brand Communities Right," *Harvard Business Review* (April 2009): 105–111.

14. Patrick Hanlon and Josh Hawkins, "Expand Your Brand Community Online," *Advertising Age*, January 7, 2008, 14–15; Ryan Holmes, "How Companies Will Use Social Media in 2017," Fast Company, January 1, 2016, https://www.fastcompany.com/3066100/how-companies-will-use-social-media-in-2017; and BrightLocal, "Local Consumer Review Survey 2016," https://www.brightlocal.com/learn/local-consumer-review-survey/.

15. Josh Bernoff, "Social Strategy for Exciting (and Not So Exciting) Brands," *Marketing News*, May 15, 2009, 18; Larry Weber, *Marketing to the Social Web* (Hoboken, NJ: Wiley, 2007), 12–14; David Meerman Scott, *The New Rules of Marketing and PR* (Hoboken, NJ: Wiley, 2007), 62; Paul Gillin, *The New Influencers* (Sanger, CA: Quill Driver Books, 2007), 34–35; and Jeremy Wright, *Blog Marketing: The Revolutionary Way to Increase Sales, Build Your Brand, and Get Exceptional Results* (New York: McGraw-Hill, 2006), 263–365.

16. Matt Rhodes, "Build Your Own Community or Go Where People Are? Do Both," *FreshNetworks* (blog), May 12, 2009, http://www.freshnetworks.com.

17. Ryan Erskine, "5 Ways to Strengthen Your Online Reputation," *Entrepreneur*, October 14, 2016, https://www.entrepreneur.com/article/283560.

18. Brian Solis, *Engage!* (Hoboken, NJ: Wiley, 2010), 13.

19. Zachary Sniderman, "5 Ways to Clean Up Your Social Media Identity," *Mashable*, July 7, 2010, http://mashable.com.

20. HP company profiles on LinkedIn and Facebook, accessed July 21, 2010, http://www.facebook.com/hp and http://www.linkedin.com/hp.

21. Ben Hanna, "2009 Business Social Media Benchmarking Study," *Business.com*, November 2, 2009, 22; and Writtent, "25 Experts Share Top 3 Content Marketing Trends for 2017," http://writtent.com/blog/content-marketing-trends/.

22. Vanessa Pappas, "5 Ways to Build a Loyal Audience on YouTube," *Mashable*, June 15, 2010, http://www.mashable.com.

23. Tamar Weinberg, *The New Community Rules: Marketing on the Social Web* (Sebastopol, CA: O'Reilly Media, 2009), 288; and Writtent, "25 Experts Share Top 3 Content Marketing Trends for 2017."

24. "About Us," *Yelp*, accessed January 30, 2011, http://www.yelp.com; and Lisa Barone, "Keynote Conversation with Yelp Chief Operating Officer Geoff Donaker," *Outspoken Media*, October 5, 2010, http://outspokenmedia.com.

25. Reid Goldborough, "More Trends for 2009: What to Expect with Personal Technology," *Public Relations Tactics*, February 2009, 9.

26. Jessica E. Vascellaro, "Why Email No Longer Rules . . ." *Wall Street Journal*, October 12, 2008, http://online.wsj.com.

27. Matt Cain, "Managing Email Hygiene," *ZDNet Tech Update*, February 5, 2004, http://www.techupdate.zdnet.com.

28. Hilary Potkewitz and Rachel Brown, "Spread of Email Has Altered Communication Habits at Work," *Los Angeles Business Journal*, April 18, 2005, http://www.findarticles.com; and Nancy Flynn, *Instant Messaging Rules* (New York: AMACOM, 2004), 47–54.

29. Phillip Vassallo, "Egad! Another Email: Using Email Sensibly" (book review), *ETC: A Review of General Semantics* 59, no. 4 (2002): 448–453.

30. Mary Munter, Priscilla S. Rogers, and Jone Rymer, "Business Email: Guidelines for Users," *Business Communication Quarterly*, March 2003, 261; and Renee B. Horowitz and Marian G. Barchilon, "Stylistic Guidelines for Email," *IEEE Transactions on Professional Communication* 37, no. 4 (December 1994): 207–212.

31. Steve Rubel, "Tip: Tweetify the Lead of Your Emails," *The Steve Rubel Stream* (blog), July 20, 2010, http://www.steverubel.com.

32. Jack Powers, Electric Pages, "Writing for the Web, Part I," accessed June 28, 2000, http://www.electric-pages.com/articles/wftwl.htm.

33. Jack Aronson, "Use Text Messaging in Your Business," *ClickZ*, June 12, 2009, http://www.clickz.com; Paul Mah, "Using Text Messaging in Business," *Mobile Enterprise* (blog), February 4, 2008, http://blogs.techrepublic.com.com/wireless; Paul Kedrosky, "Why We Don't Get the (Text) Message," *Business 2.0*, October 2, 2006, http://www.business2.com; and Carpenter, "Companies Discover Marketing Power of Text Messaging."

34. "About StarStar Numbers," *Zoove*, accessed July 7, 2011, http://www.zoove.com.

35. Mark Gibbs, "Racing to Instant Messaging," *NetworkWorld*, February 17, 2003, 74.

36. "Email Is So Five Minutes Ago,"*BusinessWeek*, November 28, 2005, http://www.businessweek.com.

37. Clint Boulton, "IDC: IM Use Is Booming in Business," *InstantMessagingPlanet.com*, October 5, 2005, http://www.instantmessaging-planet.com; Jenny Goodbody, "Critical Success Factors for Global Virtual Teams," *Strategic Communication Management*, February/March 2005, 18–21; Ann Majchrzak, Arvind Malhotra, Jeffrey Stamps, and Jessica Lipnack, "Can Absence Make a Team Grow Stronger?" *Harvard Business Review* (May 2004): 131–137; Christine Y. Chen, "The IM Invasion," *Fortune*, May 26, 2003, 135–138; Yudhijit Bhattacharjee, "A Swarm of Little Notes," *Time*, September 2002, A3–A8; Mark Bruno, "Taming the Wild Frontiers of Instant Messaging," *Bank Technology News*, December 2002, 30–31; Richard Grigonis, "Enterprise-Strength Instant Messaging," *Convergence.com*, accessed March 2003, http://www.convergence.com; and John Pallato, "Instant Messaging Unites Work Groups and Inspires Collaboration," *Internet World*, December 1, 2002, 141.

38. Valeria Maltoni, "Corporate Blogs: How's Your Elevator Pitch These Days?" *Conversation Agent* (blog), July 6, 2010, http://www.conversationagent.com.

39. Amy Porterfield, "10 Top Business Blogs and Why They Are Successful," *Social Media Examiner*, January 25, 2011, http://www.socialmediaexaminer.com.

40. Dr. Laundry (blog), http://www.drlaundryblog.com.

41. Debbie Weil, "Why Your Blog Is the Hub of Social Media Marketing," *Social Media Insights* (blog), January 12, 2010, http://debbieweil.com; Ross Dawson, "A List of Business Applications for Blogging in the Enterprise," *Trends in the Living Network* (blog), July 7, 2009, http://rossdawsonblog.com; Fredrik Wackå, "Six Types of Blogs—A Classification," *CorporateBlogging.Info*, August 10, 2004, http://www.corporateblogging.info; Stephen Baker, "The Inside Story on Company Blogs," *BusinessWeek*, February 14, 2006, http://www.businessweek.com; Jeremy Wright, *Blog Marketing* (New York: McGraw-Hill, 2006), 45–56; and Paul Chaney, "Blogs: Beyond the Hype!" *Radiant Marketing Group*, May 26, 2005, http://radiantmarketinggroup.com.

42. Evolve24 website, accessed January 31, 2011, http://www.evolve24.com.

43. Solis, *Engage!* 86.

44. Weinberg, *The New Community Rules: Marketing on the Social Web*, 89.

45. Stephen Baker and Heather Green, "Blogs Will Change Your Business," *BusinessWeek*, May 2, 2005, 57–67; and Rand Fishkin, "21 Tactics to Increase Blog Traffic (Updated 2014)," Moz, January 17, 2012, https://moz.com/blog/21-tactics-to-increase-blog-traffic-2012.

46. Joel Falconer, "Six Rules for Writing Great Web Content," *Blog News Watch*, November 9, 2007, http://www.blognewswatch.com.

47. Brian Honigman, "8 Ways to Use Your Analytics to Improve Traffic Quality," Jumplead, January 10, 2017, https://blog.jumplead.com/2017/01/10/8-ways-to-use-your-analytics-to-improve-quality-traffic/.

48. Dion Hinchcliffe, "Twitter on Your Intranet: 17 Microblogging Tools for Business," *ZDNet*, June 1, 2009, http://www.zdnet.com.

49. Hinchcliffe, "Twitter on Your Intranet: 17 Microblogging Tools for Business."

50. "Warner Brothers Television Group Social Media Contacts," *Warner Brothers*, accessed August 9, 2010, http://mediatogo.thewb.com/uncategorized/2013/06/wbsdcc2013socialmediacontacts/.

51. "Social Media Policies Reduce Discovery Risks: Are You Prepared?" *Armstrong Teasdale*, November 3, 2010, http://www.jdsupra.com; "The Library of Congress Is Archiving Your Tweets," *NPR*, July 19, 2010, http://www.npr.org; Simon Quance, "The Guide to Social Media Etiquette for Businesses," *MyCustomer.com*, August 16, 2010, http://www.mycustomer.com; Tony Schwartz, "Digital Incivility: The Unseemly Rise of Rudeness," *Harvard Business Review* (blogs), September 14, 2010, http://blogs.hbr.org; and Gillian Shaw, "Twitter Can Be a Legal Minefield: Watch What You Say," *Vancouver Sun*, October 17, 2009, http://www.vancouversun.com.

52. "Turn Your Feed into a Podcast," *Lifehacker* (blog), January 12, 2006, http://www.lifehacker.com.

53. "Set Up Your Podcast for Success," *FeedForAll*, accessed October 4, 2006, http://www.feedforall.com.

54. Shel Holtz, "Ten Guidelines for B2B Podcasts," *Webpronews.com*, October 12, 2005, http://www.webpronews.com.

55. Adapted from "Side Impact Protection Explained," *Britax*, accessed September 18, 2008, http://www.britaxusa.com.

56. Everipedia, "Logan (magazine)," https://www.everipedia.com/Logan_%28magazine%29/.

57. ABILITY Magazine website, https://abilitymagazine.com; and ABILITY Magazine, "About Us," https://abilitymagazine.com/home/about-us/.

58. Adapted from Crutchfield website, accessed February 3, 2011, http://www.crutchfield.com.

59. Adapted from Comic-Con website, accessed July 19, 2010, http://www.comic-con.org; Tom Spurgeon, "Welcome to Nerd Vegas: A Guide to Visiting and Enjoying Comic-Con International in San Diego, 2006!" *The Comics Reporter.com*, July 11, 2006, http://www.comicsreporter.com; and Rebecca Winters Keegan, "Boys Who Like Toys," *Time*, April 19, 2007, http://www.time.com.

60. JetBlue Twitter page, accessed February 3, 2011, http://twitter.com/JetBlue; and "JetBlue Lands on eBay," *JetBlue*, accessed September 18, 2008, http://jetblue.com/ebay.

Chapter 8

1. Based on "Our Company," Indigo Books and Music website, http://www.chapters.indigo.ca; Josh O'Kane, "Indigo Gives Its Customers a Soapbox," *Globe and Mail*, February 28, 2013; Hollie Shaw, "Indigo CEO Reisman Grapples with Future Growth of E-Books," *Globe and Mail*, June 27, 2012; John Lorinc, "The Indigo Way: Stylish and Savvy, Canada's #2 Chain Marches to Its Own Beat," *Quill & Quire*, 66.2 (2000): 22–23; Katherine Macklem, "The Book Lady," *Macleans*, February 26, 2001, 40–45; Hollie Braun, "Indigo Pens Next Chapter," *National Post*, June 22, 2007, FP3; Holly Braun, "Winning on the Web," *National Post*, June 26, 2007, FP3; and Thomas Watson, "Live and Learn: Heather Reisman," *Canadian Business*, September 29, 2008, 114.

2. Adapted from Stuart Rudner, "Reference Letters Not So Risky," *Canadian Employment Law Today*, July 29, 2009, 3, 5; Brian Smeek, "Bad References Can Be Bad News for Employers," *Canadian Employment Law Today*, December 5, 2007, 5–6; "No Obligation to Provide Glowing Reference Letter," *Canadian Employment Law Today*, September 28, 2005, 3493; Diane Cadrain, "HR Professionals Stymied by Vanishing Job References," *HR Magazine*, November 2004, 31–40; and "Five (or More) Ways You Can Be Sued for Writing (or Not Writing) Recommendation Letters," *Fair Employment Practice Guidelines*, July 2006.

3. "Review Offer Letters Carefully to Avoid Binding Promises," *Fair Employment Practices Guidelines*, May 15, 2001, 5–6.

4. Fraser P. Seitel, *The Practice of Public Relations*, 9th ed. (Upper Saddle River, NJ: Pearson Prentice-Hall, 2004), 402–411; and

Techniques for Communicators (Chicago: Lawrence Ragan Communication, 1995), 34, 36.

5. David Meerman Scott, *The New Rules of Marketing and PR* (Hoboken, NJ: Wiley, 2007), 62.

6. Shel Holz, "Next-Generation Press Releases," *CW Bulletin*, September 2009, http://www.iabc.com; and Steph Gray, "Baby Steps in Social Media News Releases," *Helpful Technology* (blog), May 15, 2009, http://blog.helpfultechnology.com.

7. Adapted from Floorgraphics website, http://www.floorgraphics.com; John Grossman, "It's an Ad, Ad, Ad, Ad World," *Inc.*, March 2000, 23–26; David Wellman, "Floor 'Toons'" *Supermarket Business*, November 15, 1999, 47; and "Floorshow," *Dallas Morning News*, September 4, 1998, 11D.

8. Adapted from Tom Abate, "Need to Preserve Cash Generates Wave of Layoffs in Biotech Industry," *San Francisco Chronicle*, February 10, 2003, http://www.sfgate.com.

9. Adapted from CES website, http://www.cesweb.org.

10. Adapted from Lisa DiCarlo, "IBM Gets the Message—Instantly," *Forbes.com*, July 7, 2002, http://www.forbes.com; "IBM Introduces Breakthrough Messaging Technology for Customers and Business Partners," *M2 Presswire*, February 19, 2003, http://www.proquest.com; and "IBM and America Online Team for Instant Messaging Pilot," *M2 Presswire*, February 4, 2003, http://www.proquest.com.

11. Adapted from Jane Costello, "Check Your Insurance Before Renting an SUV," *Wall Street Journal*, June 13, 2001, http://interactive.wsj.com/articles/SB991402678854239871.htm.

12. Adapted from Burt Helm, "Wal-Mart, Please Don't Leave Me," *BusinessWeek*, October 9, 2006, 84–89.

13. Public Relations Society of America website, http://www.prsa.org.

14. Based on ABC Canada Literacy Foundation website, http://abclifeliteracy.ca/.

15. Sal D. Rinalla and Robert J. Kopecky, "Recruitment: Burger King Hooks Employees with Educational Incentives," *Personnel Journal*, (October 1989): 90–99.

16. Mary Mitchell, "The Circle of Life—Condolence Letters," *LiveandLearn.com*, accessed July 18, 2005, http://www.liveandlearn.com; and Donna Larcen, "Authors Share the Words of Condolence," *Los Angeles Times*, December 20, 1991, E11.

Chapter 9

1. Based on Maple Leaf Foods Action website, http://www.mapleleafaction.com; Maple Leaf Foods, "Health Hazard Alert Sure Slice Brand Roast Beef and Corned Beef May Contain *Listeria Monocytogenes*," news release, August 17, 2008, http://www.mapleleaf.com; Maple Leaf Foods, "Maple Leaf Broadens Product Recall from Toronto Plant as a Precautionary Measure," news release, August 20, 2008, http://www.mapleleaf.com; Maple Leaf Foods, "Maple Leaf CEO Michael H. McCain Responds to Determination of Link to Plant," news release, August 23, 2008, http://www.mapleleaf.com; Kristine Owram, "Maple Leaf Foods CEO Michael McCain Named Business Newsmaker of the Year," *Canadian Press*, January 1, 2009; Gordon Pitts, "The Testing of Michael McCain," *Report on Business Magazine*, November 2008, 601, ProQuest; and Misty Harris, "Maple Leaf Winning the Battle to Bring Customers Back," *CanWest News*, January 22, 2009.

2. Ian McDonald, "Marsh Can Do $600 Million, But Apologize?" *Wall Street Journal*, January 14, 2005, C1, C3; Adrienne Carter and Amy Borrus, "What If Companies Fessed Up?" *BusinessWeek*, January 24, 2005, 59–60; and Patrick J. Kiger, "The Art of the Apology," *Workforce* (October 2004): 57–62.

3. Ameeta Patel and Lamar Reinsch, "Companies Can Apologize: Corporate Apologies and Legal Liability," *Business Communication Quarterly*, March 2003, http://www.elibrary.com.

4. "Advice from the Pros on the Best Way to Deliver Bad News," *Report on Customer Relationship Management*, February 1, 2003, http://www.elibrary.com.

5. Ben Levisohn, "Getting More Workers to Whistle," *BusinessWeek*, January 28, 2008, 18.

6. Grant Thornton, "Less Than Half of Privately Held Businesses Support Whistleblowing," news release, accessed October 13, 2008, http://www.gti.org/Press-room/Less-than-half-of-private-businesses-support-whistleblowing.asp.

7. See Parliament of Canada, Bill S-6 Public Service Whistleblowing Act, October 8, 2002, http://www.parl.gc.ca; Julius Melnitzer, "Canada Ramps up Whistleblowing Enforcement," *Law Times*, August 15, 2011; and Steve Karnowski, "New Food Safety Law Protects Whistleblowers," *Bloomberg Businessweek*, February 11, 2011, http://www.businessweek.com.

8. Sue Shellenbarger, "How to Keep Your Cool in Angry Times," *Wall Street Journal*, September 22, 2010, http://online.wsj.com.

9. Courtand L. Bovée, John V. Thill, George P. Dovel, and Marian Burk Wood, *Advertising Excellence* (New York: McGraw-Hill, 1995), 508–509; and John Holusha, "Exxon's Public-Relations Problem," *New York Times*, April 12, 1989: D1.

10. "Throw Out the Old Handbook in Favor of Today's Crisis Drills," *PR News*, January 27, 2003, 1.

11. "Protecting Your Firm," *Canadian HR Reporter*, March 24, 2003, 5.

12. See Brian Smeek, "Bad References Can Be Bad News for Employers," *Canadian Employment Law Today*, December 5, 2009, 1, 6; "Case Notes," *Focus on Canadian Employment & Equality Rights* 5, no. 24 (1999): 188; Stacey Ball, "Employers Should Exercise Care When Writing References for Former Employees," *Financial Post* (National Post), June 1–3, 1996, 21; and Howard Levitt, "If You Can't Say Something Good, Say Something Bad," *Financial Post* (National Post), November 27, 1998, C17.

13. Omowale Casselle, "Really, You Want ME to Write YOU a LinkedIn Recommendation," *RecruitingBlogs*, April 22, 2010, http://www.recruitingblogs.com.

14. "LinkedIn Profiles to Career Introductions: When You Can't Recommend Your Friend," *Seattle Post-Intelligencer Personal Finance* (blog), November 16, 2010, http://blog.seattlepi.com.

15. Neal Schaffer, "How Should I Deal with a LinkedIn Recommendation Request I Don't Want to Give?" *Social Web School*, January 20, 2010, http://humancapitalleague.com.

16. Dawn Wolf, "Job Applicant Rejection Letter Dos and Donts—Writing an Appropriate 'Dear John' Letter to an Unsuccessful Applicant," *Employment Blawg.com*, May 31, 2009, http://www.employmentblawg.com; Susan M. Heathfield, "Candidate Rejection Letter," *About.com*, accessed July 14, 2010, http://humanresources.about.com; and "Rejection Letters under Scrutiny: 7 Do's & Don'ts," *Business Management Daily*, April 1, 2009, http://www.businessmanagementdaily.com.

17. Judi Brownell, "The Performance Appraisal Interviews: A Multipurpose Communication Assignment," *Bulletin of the Association for Business Communication* 57, no. 2 (1994): 11–21.

18. Gary Dessler, *A Framework for Human Resource Management*, 3rd ed. (Upper Saddle River, NJ: Pearson Prentice Hall, 2004), 198.

19. Kelly Spors, "Why Performance Reviews Don't Work—And What You Can Do About It," *Independent Street* (blog), *Wall Street Journal*, October 21, 2008, http://blogs.wsj.com.

20. Carrie Brodzinski, "Avoiding Wrongful Termination Suits," *National Underwriter Property & Casualty—Risk & Benefits Management*, October 13, 2003, http://www.elibrary.com.

21. Rita Pyrillis, "Is Your Performance Review Underperforming?" *Workforce Management*, May 2011, 20–22, 24–25.

22. Susan Friedfel, "Protecting Yourself in the Performance Review Process," *Workforce Management*, April 2009, http://www.workforce.com.

23. Friedfel, "Protecting Yourself in the Performance Review Process."

24. E. Michelle Bohreer and Todd J. Zucker, "Five Mistakes Managers Make When Terminating Employees," *Texas Lawyer*, May 2, 2006, http://www.law.com; Deborah Muller, "The Right Things to Do to Avoid Wrongful Termination Claims," *Workforce Management*,

October 2008, http://www.workforce.com; and Maria Greco Danaher, "Termination: Telling an Employee," *Workforce Management*, May 1, 2000, http://www.workforce.com.

25. Based on Michelle Higgins, "The Ballet Shoe Gets a Makeover, But Few Yet See the Pointe," *Wall Street Journal*, August 8, 1998, A1, A6.

26. Adapted from "Bathtub Curve," *Engineering Statistics Handbook*, National Institute of Standards and Technology website, accessed April 16, 2005, http://www.nist.gov; Robert Berner, "The Warranty Windfall," *BusinessWeek*, December 20, 2004, 84–86; and Larry Armstrong, "When Service Contracts Make Sense," *BusinessWeek*, December 20, 2004, 86.

27. Adapted from Pui-Wing Tam, Erin White, Nick Wingfield, and Kris Maher, "Snooping E-mail by Software Is Now a Workplace Norm," *Wall Street Journal*, March 9, 2005, B11.

28. Adapted from Stanton website, http://www.stanton.com.

29. Based on "No Cell Calls on Nfld. Roads," *Gazette* (Montreal), August 24, 2003, A4; and Ellen van Wangeningen, "Fatal Driver Pleads Guilty," *Windsor Star*, February 25, 2003, A5.

30. Adapted from Twitter/JetBlue website, http://twitter.com/JetBlue.

31. Adapted from Sean Doherty, "Dynamic Communications," *Network Computing*, March 31, 2003, 26, http://www.networkcomputing.com/unified-communications-voip/dynamic-communications/229624368; Todd Wasserman, "Post-Merger HP Invents New Image to Challenge Tech Foes IBM and Dell," *Brandweek*, November 18, 2002, 9, search.epnet.com/direct.asp?an58887152&db5bsh&tg5AN; and R. P. Srikanth, "IM Tools Are Latest Tech Toys for Corporate Users," *Express Computer*, July 1, 2002, http://www.expresscomputeronline.com/20020701/indtrend1.shtml.

Chapter 10

1. Based on the Canadian Youth Business Foundation website; Canadian Youth Business Federation, *2012 Annual Report*, http://www.cybf.ca; Daryl-Lynn Carlson, "Advice Helps Snap Up Funding," *Financial Post*, December 15, 2008, http://www.financialpost.com; Daryl-Lynn Carlson, "Finance: Be Resourceful in Hard Times," *Financial Post*, January 26, 2009, http://www.financialpost.com; Daryl-Lynn Carlson, "Good Applications Get Stamp of Approval" *Financial Post*, February 9, 2009, http://www.financialpost.com; and Daryl-Lynn Carlson, "Recessions Breed New Generation of Entrepreneurs," *Financial Post*, March 20, 2009, http://www.financialpost.com.

2. Jay A. Conger, "The Necessary Art of Persuasion," *Harvard Business Review* (May–June 1998): 84–95; Jeanette W. Gilsdorf, "Write Me Your Best Case for . . .," *Bulletin of the Association for Business Communication* 54, no. 1 (March 1991): 7–12.

3. Mary Cross, "Aristotle and Business Writing: Why We Need to Teach Persuasion," *Bulletin of the Association for Business Communication* 54, no. 1 (March 1991): 3–6.

4. Tom Chandler, "The Copywriter's Best Friend," *The Copywriter Underground* blog, December 20, 2006, http://copywriterunderground.com.

5. Raymond M. Olderman, *10-Minute Guide to Business Communication* (New York: Macmillan Spectrum/Alpha Books, 1997), 57–61.

6. John D. Ramage and John C. Bean, *Writing Arguments: A Rhetoric with Readings*, 3rd ed. (Boston: Allyn & Bacon, 1995), 430–442.

7. Philip Vassallo, "Persuading Powerfully: Tips for Writing Persuasive Documents," *et Cetera* (Spring 2002): 65–71.

8. Dianna Booher, *Communicate with Confidence* (New York: McGraw-Hill, 1994), 102.

9. "Social Factors in Developing a Web Accessibility Business Case for Your Organization," *World Wide Web Consortium (W3C)*, accessed July 17, 2010, http://www.w3.org.

10. iPod main product page, Apple website, accessed April 14, 2013, http://www.apple.ca/ipod.

11. Bell Canada website, http://bundles.bell.ca//en.

12. Biokleen home page, accessed July 17, 2010, http://biokleenhome.com.

13. Bell Canada, Bell TV product page, Bell Canada website, accessed April 14, 2013, http://www.bell.ca.

14. Mint.com website, http://www.mint.com.

15. FlightWise Carry-on Backpack product page, Lands End website, accessed July 17, 2010, http://www.landsend.com.

16. Apple, iPod Touch product page, Apple website, accessed April 14, 2013, http://www.apple.com/ipodtouch/what-is/gaming-device.html.

17. "More Than Virtual: Marketing the Total Brand 'Experience,'" *Knowledge@Wharton*, June 7, 2011, http://knowledge.wharton.upenn.edu.

18. Larry Weber, *Marketing to the Social Web* (Hoboken, NJ: Wiley, 2007), 12–14; David Meerman Scott, *The New Rules of Marketing and PR* (Hoboken, NJ: Wiley, 2007), 62; Paul Gillin, *The New Influencers* (Sanger, CA: Quill Driver Books, 2007), 34–35; and Jeremy Wright, *Blog Marketing: The Revolutionary Way to Increase Sales, Build Your Brand, and Get Exceptional Results* (New York: McGraw-Hill, 2006), 263–365.

19. "Content Marketing 101: How to Build Your Business with Content," *Copyblogger*, accessed February 19, 2011, http://www.copyblogger.com.

20. Michael Zeisser, "Unlocking the Elusive Potential of Social Networks," *McKinsey Quarterly*, June 2010, http://www.mckinseyquarterly.com.

21. Gilsdorf, "Write Me Your Best Case for . . ."

22. "Law and Litigation: About the Acts," Competition Bureau Canada website, accessed July 15, 2007, http://www.competitionbureau.gc.ca/internet/index.cfm?itemID=148&lg=e#packaging.

23. "Competition Bureau Participates in Worldwide Blitz on Hidden Traps Online," news release, March 3, 2006, Competition Bureau Canada, News and Resources website, http://www.competitionbureau.gc.ca/internet/index.cfm?itemID=2031&lg=e.

24. Adapted from Samsung website, http://www.samsung.com.

25. Adapted from Canadian Blood Services website, http://www.bloodservices.ca; American National Red Cross website, http://www.redcrossblood.org; and American Red Cross San Diego Chapter website, accessed July 19, 2010, http://www.sdarc.org.

26. Adapted from Cathy Werblin, "Korean Business Owners Want Signs to Mark Area," *Los Angeles Times*, March 29, 1997, B3.

27. Adapted from Courtland L. Bovée and John V. Thill, *Business in Action*, 3rd ed. (Upper Saddle River, NJ: Pearson Prentice Hall, 2005), 236–237; The Telework Coalition website, http://www.telcoa.org; Jason Roberson, "Rush-Hour Rebellion," *Dallas Business Journal*, June 22, 2001: 31; Carole Hawkins, "Ready, Set, Go Home," *Black Enterprise*, August 2001, 118–124; and Wayne Tompkins, "Telecommuting in Transition," *Courier-Journal* (Louisville, KY), July 9, 2001, C10.

28. Adapted from Andrew Ferguson, "Supermarket of the Vanities," *Fortune*, June 10, 1996, 30, 32.

29. Adapted from advertisement, *The Atlantic Monthly*, January 2000, 19; and Endless Pools, Inc. website, http://www.endlesspools.com.

30. Adapted from Juice website, http://juicereceiver.sourceforge.net.

31. Adapted from Hangers Cleaners (Kansas City) website, http://www.hangerskc.com; Charles Fishman, "The Greener Cleaners," *Fast Company*, accessed 11 July 2000, http://fastcompany.com; Micell Technologies website, http://www.micell.com; and Cool Clean Technologies, Inc., website, http://www.coolclean.com.

32. Adapted from IBM website, http://www.ibm.com/ibm/ibmgives; IBM website, "DAS Faces an Assured Future with IBM," accessed January 16, 2004, http://www.306.ibm.com/software/success/cssdb.nsf/CS/DNSD-5S6KTF; and IBM website, "Sametime," accessed January 16, 2004, http://www.lotus.com/products/lotussametime.nsf/wdocs/homepage.

33. Adapted from "Web Accessibility Initiative," *World Wide Web Consortium (WC3)*, accessed November 7, 2008, http://www.w3.org.

Chapter 11

1. Dell Inc., *Annual Report 2012*, http://www.dell.com; Ben Worthen and Ian Sherr, "Dell Still Struggling Amid Shift in Computer Market," *Wall Street Journal*, November 16, 2012, B5; "Dell Completes Acquisition of Credant Technologies," *Mergers & Acquisitions Week*, January 2, 2013, 35; and "Sources: Dell Talking Buyout," *Calgary Herald*, January 15, 2013, D2.

2. Courtland L. Bovée, Michael J. Houston, and John V. Thill, *Marketing*, 2nd ed. (New York: McGraw-Hill, 1995), 194–196.

3. Legal-Definitions.com, accessed December 17, 2003, http://www.legal-definitions.com.

4. Tom Krazit, "FAQ: The HP 'Pretexting' Scandal," *ZDNet.com*, September 6, 2006, http://www.zdnet.com.

5. Lynn Quitman Troyka, *Simon & Schuster Handbook for Writers*, 6th ed. (Upper Saddle River, NJ: Simon & Schuster, 2002), 481.

6. "How to Paraphrase Effectively: 6 Steps to Follow," *ResearchPaper.com*, accessed October 26, 1998, http://www.researchpaper.com/writing_center/30.html.

7. "Mahalo," *CrunchBase*, accessed July 2010, http://www.crunchbase.com.

8. AllTheWeb.com advanced search page, accessed August 27, 2005, http://www.alltheweb.com; Google advanced search page, accessed August 27, 2005, http://www.google.com; and Yahoo! advanced search page, accessed August 27, 2005, http://www.yahoo.com.

9. Christina Warren, "Yolink Helps Web Researchers Search Behind Links," *Mashable*, July 24, 2010, http://mashable.com.

10. University of Ottawa, Canadian Internet Policy and Public Interest Clinic, "Copyright Law," accessed April 14, 2009, http://www.cippic.ca/copyright-law; and Copyright Board of Canada, "Copyright Act," accessed April 14, 2009, http://www.cb-cda.gc.ca/info/act-e.html.

11. Henry R. Cheeseman, *Contemporary Business and E-Commerce Law*, 4th ed. (Upper Saddle River, NJ: Prentice Hall, 2003), 325.

12. Eric Badartscher and Kathy Reese, "Taking the Confusion Out of Copyright in an Internet Age," *Information Outlook* 12, no. 6 (June 2008): 62–67; and "The Apple Case Isn't Just A Blow to Bloggers: Why Should Bloggers Be Denied Rights Given a Pamphleteer in the Past?" (editorial) *BusinessWeek*, March 28, 2005, 128.

13. A. B. Blankenship and George Edward Breen, *State of the Art Marketing Research* (Lincolnwood, IL: NTC Business Books, 1992), 136.

14. Naresh K. Malhotra, *Basic Marketing Research* (Upper Saddle River, NJ: Prentice-Hall, 2002), 314–317; and "How to Design and Conduct A Study," *Credit Union Magazine*, October 1983, 36–46.

15. Product features page, SurveyMonkey.com, accessed October 29, 2006, http://www.surveymonkey.com.

16. Sherwyn P. Morreale and Courtland L. Bovée, *Excellence in Public Speaking* (Fort Worth, TX: Harcourt Brace College Publishers, 1998), 177.

17. Morreale and Bovée, *Excellence in Public Speaking*, 182.

18. Blankenship and Breen, *State of the Art Marketing Research*, 225.

19. Jakob Nielsen, "How Users Read on the Web," accessed November 11, 2004, http://www.useit.com/alertbox/9710a.html.

20. Reid Goldsborough, "Words for the Wise," *Link-Up*, September–October 1999, 25–26.

21. Julie Rohovit, "Computer Eye Strain: The Dilbert Syndrome," Virtual Hospital website, May 2004, http://www.vh.org.

22. Shel Holtz, "Writing for the Wired World," *International Association of Business Communicators*, 1999, 6–9.

23. Adapted from SXSW website, accessed July 27, 2010, http://sxsw.com; and Catherine Holahan and Spencer E. Ante, "SXSW: Where Tech Mingles with Music," *BusinessWeek*, March 7, 2008, http://www.businessweek.com.

Chapter 12

1. Federal Express website, http://www.fedex.com, http://www.fedex.ca; "A Budding Network," *Forbes*, May 7, 2007, 64; FedEx Corp. "Company Overview," *Hoover's Online*, October 27, 1997; "All Strung Up," *Economist*, April 17, 1993, 70; Gary M. Stern, "Improving Verbal Communications," *Internal Auditor*, August 1993, 49–54; Gary Hoover, Alta Campbell, and Patrick J. Spain, *Hoover's Handbook of American Business 1994* (Austin, TX: Reference Press, 1993), 488–489; "Pass the Parcel," *Economist*, March 21, 1992, 73–74; and "Federal Express," *Personnel Journal* (January 1992): 52.

2. A. S. C. Ehrenberg, "Report Writing—Six Simple Rules for Better Business Documents," *Admap*, June 1992, 39–42.

3. Michael Netzley and Craig Snow, *Guide to Report Writing* (Upper Saddle River, NJ: Prentice Hall, 2001), 15.

4. "Message to our Shareholders," *FEDEX 2012 Annual Report*, http://www.fedex.com.

5. Claudia Mon Pere McIsaac, "Improving Student Summaries Through Sequencing," *Bulletin of the Association for Business Communication*, September 1987, 17–20.

6. David A. Hayes, "Helping Students GRASP the Knack of Writing Summaries," *Journal of Reading* (November 1989): 96–101.

7. Philip C. Kolin, *Successful Writing at Work*, 6th ed. (Boston: Houghton Mifflin, 2001), 552–555.

8. Martin James, "PDF Virus Spreads without Exploiting any Flaw," *IT Pro*, April 8, 2010, http://www.itpro.co.uk.

9. Sant Corporation website, http://www.santcorp.com.

10. "Web Writing: How to Avoid Pitfalls," *Investor Relations Business*, November 1, 1999, 15.

11. "Codex: Guidelines," WordPress website, http://wordpress.org; Michael Shanks, "Wiki Guidelines," Traumwerk website, accessed August 18, 2006, http://metamedia.stanford.edu/projects/traumwerk/home; Joe Moxley, M. C. Morgan, Matt Barton, and Donna Hanak, "For Teachers New to Wikis," *Writing Wiki*, accessed August 18, 2006, http://writingwiki.org; and "Wiki Guidelines," *Psi*, accessed August 18, 2006, http://psi-im.org.

12. Rachael King, "No Rest for the Wiki," *BusinessWeek*, March 12, 2007, www.businessweek.com.

13. "Codex: Guidelines," *WordPress*, accessed February 14, 2008, http://wordpress.org.

14. Alexis Gerard and Bob Goldstein, *Going Visual* (Hoboken, NJ: Wiley, 2005), 18.

15. Joshua David McClurg-Genevese, "The Principles of Design," *Digital Web Magazine*, June 13, 2005, http://www.digital-web.com.

16. Gerard and Goldstein, *Going Visual*, 103–106.

17. Edward R. Tufte, *Visual Explanations: Images and Quantities, Evidence and Narrative* (Cheshire, CT: Graphics Press, 1997), 82.

18. McClurg-Genevese, "The Principles of Design."

19. Charles Kostelnick and Michael Hassett, *Shaping Information: The Rhetoric of Visual Conventions* (Carbondale, IL: Southern Illinois University Press, 2003), 17.

20. Kostelnick and Hassett, *Shaping Information: The Rhetoric of Visual Conventions*, 216.

21. Edward R. Tufte, *The Visual Display of Quantitative Information* (Cheshire, CT: Graphic Press, 1983), 113.

22. Tufte, *Visual Explanations: Images and Quantities, Evidence and Narrative*, 73.

23. Based in part on Tufte, *Visual Explanations: Images and Quantities, Evidence and Narrative*, 29–37, 53; and Paul Martin Lester, *Visual Communication: Images with Messages*, 4th ed. (Belmont, CA: Thomson Wadsworth, 2006), 95–105, 194–196.

24. Maria Popova, "Data Visualization: Stories for the Information Age," *BusinessWeek*, August 12, 2009, http://www.businessweek.com.

25. R. Craig Endicott, "Leaders Back Brands with $51.2 Billion in Ads" (100 Leading National Advertisers Supplement), *Advertising Age*, September 29, 1997, S63.

26. Adapted from Air-Trak website, http://public.air-trak.com.

Chapter 13

1. Gates Foundation website, http://www.gatesfoundation.org; Richard Klausner and Pedro Alonso, "An Attack on All Fronts," *Nature,* August 19, 2004, 930–931; "Richard Klausner Spends to Save Lives," *Fast Company,* November 2002, 128; and Kent Allen, "The Gatekeeper," *U.S. News & World Report,* December 8, 2003, 64–66.
2. John Morkes and Jakob Nielsen, "Concise, Scannable, and Objective: How to Write for the Web," *UseIt.com,* January 1, 1997, http://www.useit.com.
3. Michael Netzley and Craig Snow, *Guide to Report Writing* (Upper Saddle River, NJ: Prentice Hall, 2001), 57.
4. Oswald M. T. Ratteray, "Hit the Mark with Better Summaries," *Supervisory Management* (September 1989): 43–45.
5. Netzley and Snow, *Guide to Report Writing,* 43.
6. Alice Reid, "A Practical Guide for Writing Proposals," accessed May 31, 2001, http://members.dca.net/areid/proposal.htm.
7. Liz Hughes, "Enhancing Communication Skills," *WIB,* September/October 2003, 21.
8. See Note 1.
9. Adapted from "Home Depot Says E-Learning Is Paying for Itself," *Workforce Management,* February 25, 2004, http://www.workforce.com; Robert Celaschi, "The Insider: Training," *Workforce Management,* August 2004, 67–69; Joe Mullich, "A Second Act for E-Learning," *Workforce Management,* February 2004, 51–55, Gail Johnson, "Brewing the Perfect Blend," *Training,* December 2003, 30+; Tammy Galvin, "2003 Industry Report," *Training,* October 2003, 21+; William C. Symonds, "Giving It the Old Online Try," *BusinessWeek,* December 3, 2001, 76–80; Karen Frankola, "Why Online Learners Drop Out," *Workforce Management,* October 2001, 52–60; and Mary Lord, "They're Online and on the Job: Managers and Hamburger Flippers Are Being E-trained at Work," *U.S. News & World Report,* October 15, 2001, 72–77.

Chapter 14

1. Based on Telefilm Canada website, http://www.telefilm.ca; Carolle Brabant, untitled speech, Telefilm Canada Public Assembly, Toronto, Ontario, November 15, 2012; Carolle Brabant, untitled speech, The Academy of Canadian Cinema & Television, Toronto, Ontario, June 22, 2010; Carolle Brabant, "The Canadian Audiovisual Industry: We Mean Business," Quebec MBA Association, Montreal, Quebec, April 25, 2012; and Telefilm Canada, *Annual Report 2010–2011,* 2011, http://www.telefilm.gc.ca; and Canadian Media Producers Association, *Profile 2015: Economic Report on the Screen-based Media Production Industry in Canada,* http://www.cmpa.ca/sites/default/files/Profile%202015%20%28English%29.pdf.
2. Nancy Duarte, *Slide:ology: The Art and Science of Creating Great Presentations* (Sebastopol, CA: O'Reilly Media, 2008), 13.
3. Amber Naslund, "Twebinar: GE's Tweetsquad," August 4, 2009, http://www.radian6.com/blog.
4. Carmine Gallo, "How to Deliver a Presentation Under Pressure," *BusinessWeek,* September 18, 2008, http://www.businessweek.com.
5. Sarah Lary and Karen Pruente, "Powerless Point: Common PowerPoint Mistakes to Avoid," *Public Relations Tactics,* February 2004, 28.
6. Garr Reynolds, *Presentation Zen: Simple Ideas on Presentation Design and Delivery* (Berkeley, CA: New Riders, 2008), 39–42.
7. Cliff Atkinson, *Beyond Bullet Points: Using Microsoft PowerPoint to Create Presentations That Inform, Motivate, and Inspire* (Redmond, WA: Microsoft Press, 2005), 29, 55, 65.
8. Sherwyn P. Morreale and Courtland L. Bovée, *Excellence in Public Speaking* (Fort Worth, TX: Harcourt Brace, 1998), 234–237.
9. John Windsor, "Presenting Smart: Keeping the Goal in Sight," *Presentations,* March 6, 2008, http://www.presentations.com.
10. Morreale and Bovée, *Excellence in Public Speaking,* 241–243.
11. "Choose and Use Your Words Deliberately," *Soundview Executive Book Summaries* 20, no. 6, pt. 2 (June 1998): 3.

12. Adapted from Eric J. Adams, "Management Focus: User-Friendly Presentation Software," *World Trade,* March 1995, 92.
13. Carmine Gallo, "Grab Your Audience Fast," *BusinessWeek,* September 13, 2006, 19.
14. Walter Kiechel III, "How to Give a Speech," *Fortune,* June 8, 1987, 180.
15. Carmine Gallo, *Talk Like TED: The 9 Public Speaking Secrets of the World's Top Minds,* 1st ed. (New York, NY: St. Martin's Press, 2014), 183-186.
16. *Communication and Leadership Program* (Santa Ana, CA: Toastmasters International, 1980), 44, 45.
17. Gwen Moran, "The 7 Habits of the Best Public Speakers," *Fast Company,* February 26, 2016, https://www.fastcompany.com/3057007/how-to-be-a-success-at-everything/7-habits-of-the-best-public-speakers; and Chip Heath and Dan Heath, *Made to Stick: Why Some Ideas Survive and Others Die,* 1st ed. (New York, NY: Random House, 2007), 130–164.
18. Reynolds, *Presentation Zen: Simple Ideas on Presentation Design and Delivery,* 10.
19. Margo Halverson, "Choosing the Right Colors for Your Next Presentation," *3M Meeting Network,* accessed 8 June 2001, http://www.mmm.com/meetingnetwork/readingroom/meetingguide_right_color.html.
20. Carol Klinger and Joel G. Siegel, "Computer Multimedia Presentations," *CPA Journal* (June 1996): 46.
21. Jon Hanke, "Five Tips for Better Visuals," *3M Meeting Network,* accessed June 8, 2001, http://www.mmm.com/meetingnetwork/presentations/pmag_better_visuals.html.
22. Sarah Lary and Karen Pruente, "Powerless Point: Common PowerPoint Mistakes to Avoid," *Public Relations Tactics,* February 2004, 28.
23. Jerry Weissman, *Presenting to Win: The Art of Telling Your Story* (Upper Saddle River, NJ: Pearson Prentice-Hall, 2006), 162.
24. Reynolds, *Presentation Zen: Simple Ideas on Presentation Design and Delivery,* 66.
25. Reynolds, *Presentation Zen: Simple Ideas on Presentation Design and Delivery,* 208.
26. Richard Zeoli, "The Seven Things You Must Know about Public Speaking," *Forbes,* June 3, 2009, http://www.forbes.com; and Morreale and Bovée, *Excellence in Public Speaking,* 24–25.
27. Jennifer Rotondo and Mike Rotondo Jr., *Presentation Skills for Managers* (New York: McGraw-Hill, 2002), 9.
28. Rick Gilbert, "Presentation Advice for Boardroom Success," *Financial Executive,* September 2005, 12.
29. Rotondo and Rotondo, *Presentation Skills for Managers,* 151.
30. Teresa Brady, "Fielding Abrasive Questions During Presentations," *Supervisory Management,* February 1993, 6.
31. Robert L. Montgomery, "Listening on Your Feet," *The Toastmaster,* July 1987, 14–15.
32. Cliff Atkinson, *The Backchannel* (Berkeley, CA: New Riders, 2010), 17.
33. Atkinson, *The Backchannel,* 51, 68–73.
34. Olivia Mitchell, "10 Tools for Presenting with Twitter," *Speaking about Presenting* (blog), November 3, 2009, http://www.speakingaboutpresenting.com; and Atkinson, *The Backchannel,* 51, 68–73, 99.
35. Jeff Yocom, "TechRepublic Survey Yields Advice on Streaming Video," *TechRepublic website,* accessed February 16, 2004, http://ww.techrepublic.com.

Chapter 15

1. Based on Tim Hortons website, http://www.timhortons.com.
2. Kathryn Blaze Carlson, "Today's Graduates: Too Few Jobs, Not Enough Pay," *National Post,* November 28, 2013, http://www.nationalpost.com; Denise Deveau, "Canada Must Streamline Education to Turn Degrees into Jobs," *National Post,* February 19,

2013, http://www.nationalpost.com; Adam Carter, "5 Tips for Recent Grads Looking for Work," *CBC News.ca*, September 7, 2012; Denise Deveau, "When Does a University Degree Really Pay Off?" *National Post*, January 29, 2013, http://www.nationalpost.com; Claire Penhorwood, "Canada's Youth Face Job Crunch," *CBC News.ca*, March 26, 2012; Jeanne C. Meister and Karie Willyerd, "Leading Virtual Teams to Real Results," *Harvard Business Review* (blogs), June 30, 2010, http://blogs.hbr.org; Malik Singleton, "Same Markets, New Marketplaces," *Black Enterprise*, September 2004, 34; Edmund L. Andrews, "Where Do the Jobs Come From?" *New York Times*, September 21, 2004, E1, E11; Maureen Jenkins, "Yours for the Taking," *Boeing Frontiers Online*, June 2004, http://www.boeing.com; "Firm Predicts Top 10 Workforce/Workplace Trends for 2004," *Enterprise*, December 8–14, 2003, 1–2; and Ricky W. Griffin and Michael W. Pustay, *International Business*, 6th ed. (Upper Saddle River, NJ: Pearson Prentice Hall, 2010), 21.

3. Daryl-Lynn Carlson, "The New Generation of Entrepreneurs: A Paradigm Shift Is Underway That Has Business Startups Rising on the Heels of Corporate Layoffs," *National Post*, March 23, 2009, FP5; and "Canada's Small Business World," *Canadian Business*, October 24, 2011, ProQuest.

4. Vivian Yeo, "India Still Top Choice for Offshoring," *BusinessWeek*, June 27, 2008, http://www.businessweek.com; and Jim Puzzanghera, "Coalition of High-Tech Firms to Urge Officials to Help Keep U.S. Competitive," *San Jose Mercury News*, January 8, 2004, http://www.ebscohost.com.

5. Courtland L. Bovée and John V. Thill, *Business in Action*, 5th ed. (Upper Saddle River, NJ: Pearson Prentice Hall, 2010), 18–21; and Randall S. Hansen and Katharine Hansen, "What Do Employers Really Want? Top Skills and Values Employers Seek from Job-Seekers," *QuintCareers.com*, accessed 17 August 2010, http://www.quintcareers.com.

6. Nancy M. Somerick, "Managing a Communication Internship Program," *Bulletin of the Association for Business Communication 56*, no. 3 (1993): 10–20.

7. Jeffrey R. Young, "'E-Portfolios' Could Give Students a New Sense of Their Accomplishments," *Chronicle of Higher Education*, March 8, 2002, A31.

8. Brian Carcione, e-portfolio, accessed December 20, 2006, http://eportfolio.psu.edu.

9. Eve Tahmincioglu, "Employers Digging Deep on Prospective Workers," *MSNBC.com*, October 26, 2009, http://www.msnbc.com.

10. Bovée and Thill, *Business in Action*, 5th ed., 241–242.

11. Jim Schaper, "Finding Your Future Talent Stars," *BusinessWeek*, July 2, 2010, http://www.businessweek.com.

12. Eve Tahmincioglu, "Revamping Your Job-Search Strategy," *MSNBC.com*, February 28, 2010, http://www.msnbc.com.

13. Jessica Dickler, "The Hidden Job Market," *CNNMoney.com*, June 10, 2009, http://money.cnn.com.

14. Lynne Waymon, André Alphonso, and Will Kitchen, "Internal Networking: Time-Waster or Value Creator?" *TD Magazine*, October 8, 2013, https://www.td.org/Publications/Magazines/TD/TD-Archive/2013/10/Internal-Networking.

15. Tara Weiss, "Twitter to Find a Job," *Forbes*, April 7, 2009, http://www.forbes.com.

16. Miriam Saltpeter, "Using Facebook Groups for Job Hunting," *Keppie Careers* (blog), November 13, 2008, http://www.keppiecareers.com.

17. Anne Fisher, "Greener Pastures in a New Field," *Fortune*, January 26, 2004, 48.

18. Judith Humphrey, "How to Approach a VIP at a Crowded Networking Event," *Fast Company*, November 8, 2016, https://www.fastcompany.com/3065381/how-to-approach-a-vip-at-a-crowded-networking-event; Vivian Giang, "The Secrets to Successful Networking from the Most Connected Women," *Fast Company*, November 20, 2014, https://www.fastcompany.com/3038750/the-secrets-to-successful-networking-from-the-most-connected-women; Josephine Fairley, "Networking: 9 Tips to Help You Work the Room Like a Pro," *The Telegraph*, August 18, 2014, http://www.telegraph.co.uk/women/womens-business/11037202/Networking-for-work-and-business-9-tips-to-help-you-workthe-room-like-a-pro.html; Stephanie Speisman, "10 Tips for Successful Business Networking," Business Know-How, http://www.businessknowhow.com/tips/networking.htm; and Jonathan Moules, "When Networking, Think Quality, Not Quantity," *Financial Times*, September 2, 2010, http://www.ft.com/content/d4579732-aae7-11df-9e6b-00144feabdc0.

19. Career and Employment Services, Danville Area Community College website, accessed March 23, 2008, http://www.dacc.edu/career; Career Counseling, Sarah Lawrence College website, accessed March 23, 2008, http://www.slc.edu/occ/index.php; and Cheryl L. Noll, "Collaborating with the Career Planning and Placement Center in the Job-Search Project," *Business Communication Quarterly 58*, no. 3 (1995): 53–55.

20. Erica Swallow, "How to: Spruce Up a Boring Résumé," *Mashable*, accessed July 21, 2011, http://mashable.com.

21. Fay Hansen, "Recruiters Bear a Bigger Load as Hiring Takes Off," *Workforce Management*, May 2010, http://www.workforce.com.

22. Randall S. Hansen and Katharine Hansen, "What Résumé Format Is Best for You?" *QuintCareers.com*, accessed August 7, 2010, http://www.quintcareers.com.

23. Hansen and Hansen, "What Résumé Format Is Best for You?"

24. Katharine Hansen, "Should You Consider a Functional Format for Your Resume?" *QuintCareers.com*, accessed August 7, 2010, http://www.quintcareers.com.

25. Kim Isaacs, "How Long Should My Resume Be?" *Monster.com*, https://www.monster.com/career-advice/article/how-to-decide-on-resume-length; "Résumé Length: What It Should Be and Why It Matters to Recruiters," *HR Focus*, June 2007, 9.

26. Kim Isaacs, "Resume Dilemma: Criminal Record," *Monster.com*, accessed May 23, 2006, http://www.monster.com; Kim Isaacs, "Resume Dilemma: Employment Gaps and Job-Hopping," *Monster.com*, accessed May 23, 2006, http://www.monster.com; and Susan Vaughn, "Answer the Hard Questions Before Asked," *Los Angeles Times*, July 29, 2001, W1–W2.

27. "How to Ferret Out Instances of Résumé Padding and Fraud," *Compensation & Benefits for Law Offices*, June 2006, 11.

28. Anupama Chandrasekaran, "Resumé Fraud Gets Slicker and Easier," *CNN.com*, accessed March 11, 2004, http://www.cnn.com.

29. Cari Tuna and Keith J. Winstein, "Economy Promises to Fuel Résumé Fraud," *Wall Street Journal*, November 17, 2008, http://online.wsj.com; Lisa Takeuchi Cullen, "Getting Wise to Lies," *Time*, May 1, 2006, 59; Anupama Chandrasekaran, "Resumé Fraud Gets Slicker and Easier"; and Employment Research Services website, accessed March 18, 2004, http://www.erscheck.com.

30. "How to Ferret Out Instances of Résumé Padding and Fraud."

31. Jacqueline Durett, "Redoing Your Résumé? Leave Off the Lies," *Training*, December 2006, 9; and "Employers Turn Their Fire on Untruthful CVs," *Supply Management*, June 23, 2005, 13.

32. Cynthia E. Conn, "Integrating Writing Skills and Ethics Training in Business Communication Pedagogy: A Résumé Case Study Exemplar," *Business Communication Quarterly*, June 2008, 138–151; and Marilyn Moats Kennedy, "Don't Get Burned by Résumé Inflation," *Marketing News*, April 15, 2007, 37–38.

33. Rockport Institute, "How to Write a Masterpiece of a Résumé," https://rockportinstitute.com/resources/how-to-write-a-masterpiece-of-a-resume/.

34. Lora Morsch, "25 Words That Hurt Your Resume," *CNN.com*, January 20, 2006, http://www.cnn.com.

35. Liz Ryan, "The Reengineered Résumé," *BusinessWeek*, December 3, 2007, SC12.

36. Katharine Hansen, "Tapping the Power of Keywords to Enhance Your Resume's Effectiveness," *QuintCareers.com*, accessed August 7, 2010, http://www.quintcareers.com.

37. Hansen, "Tapping the Power of Keywords to Enhance Your Resume's Effectiveness."

38. Jolie O'Dell, "LinkedIn Reveals the 10 Most Overused Job-Hunter Buzzwords," *Mashable*, December 14, 2010, http://mashable.com.

39. Brenda Bernstein, "LinkedIn's Overused Buzzwords for 2017: Do You Really Need to Avoid Them?" *The Essay Expert*, January 30, 2017, https://theessayexpert.com/linkedins-overused-buzzwords-2017-really-need-avoid/.

40. Dave Johnson, "10 Resume Errors That Will Land You in the Trash," *BNET*, February 22, 2010, http://www.bnet.com; Anthony Balderrama, "Resume Blunders That Will Keep You from Getting Hired," *CNN.com*, March 19, 2008, http://www.cnn.com; Michelle Dumas, "5 Resume Writing Myths," *Distinctive Documents* (blog), July 17, 2007, http://blog.distinctiveweb.com; and Kim Isaacs, "Resume Dilemma: Recent Graduate," *Monster.com*, accessed March 26, 2008, http://career-advice.monster.com.

41. Karl L. Smart, "Articulating Skills in the Job Search," *Business Communication Quarterly* 67, no. 2 (June 2004): 198–205.

42. Rockport Institute, "How to Write a Masterpiece of a Résumé."

43. Rachel Zupek, "Seven Exceptions to Job Search Rules," *CNN.com*, September 3, 2008, http://www.cnn.com.

44. Swallow, "How to: Spruce Up a Boring Résumé."

45. John Hazard, "Resume Tips: No Pictures, Please and No PDFs," *Career-Line.com*, May 26, 2009, http://www.career-line.com; and "25 Things You Should Never Include on a Resume," *HR World*, December 18, 2007, http://www.hrworld.com.

46. John Sullivan, "Résumés: Paper, Please," *Workforce Management*, October 22, 2007, 50; and "Video Résumés Offer Both Pros and Cons During Recruiting," *HR Focus*, July 2007, 8.

47. Nancy M. Schullery, Linda Ickes, and Stephen E. Schullery, "Employer Preferences for Résumés and Cover Letters," *Business Communication Quarterly*, June 2009, 163–176.

48. VisualCV website, accessed August 10, 2010, http://www.visualcv.com.

49. Elizabeth Garone, "Five Mistakes Online Job Hunters Make," *Wall Street Journal*, July 28, 2010, http://online.wsj.com.

50. "10 Reasons Why You Are Not Getting Any Interviews," *Miami Times*, November 7–13, 2007, 6D.

51. Deborah Silver, "Niche Sites Gain Monster-Sized Following," *Workforce Management*, March 2011, 10–11.

52. "Protect Yourself From Identity Theft When Hunting for a Job Online," *Office Pro*, May 2007, 6.

53. "5 Steps for Updating Your Resume," *Monster.com*, https://www.monster.com/career-advice/article/five-steps-for-updating-your-resume-hot-jobs.

Chapter 16

1. "What's It Like to Work at Google?" *Google.com*, accessed May 19, 2013, http://www.google.com; "The 100 Best Companies to Work for," *Fortune*, April 2, 2013, ProQuest; Fred Vogelstein, "Can Google Grow Up?" *Fortune*, December 8, 2003, 102; Quentin Hardy, "All Eyes on Google," *Forbes*, May 26, 2003, 100; Keith H. Hammonds, "Growth Search," *Fast Company*, April 2003, 74–81; Stanley Bing, "How Not to Succeed in Business," *Fortune*, December 30, 2002, 210; Pierre Mornell, "Zero Defect Hiring," *Inc.*, March 1998, 74; Adam Lashinsky, "Search and Enjoy," *Fortune*, January 22, 2007, 70; "100 Best Companies to Work For," *Fortune*, February 4, 2008, http://www.cnnmoney.com; and "100 Best Companies to Work For," *Fortune*, 2017, http://fortune.com/best-companies, http://fortune.com/best-companies/google/.

2. Matthew Rothenberg, "Manuscript vs. Machine," *The Ladders*, December 15, 2009, http://www.theladders.com; and Joann Lublin, "Cover Letters Get You in the Door, So Be Sure Not to Dash Them Off," *Wall Street Journal*, April 6, 2004, B1.

3. Lisa Vaas, "How to Write a Great Cover Letter," *The Ladders*, August 11, 2014, https://www.theladders.com/p/809/how-to-write-cover-letter.

4. Alison Doyle, "Introduction to Cover Letters," *About.com*, accessed August 13, 2010, http://jobsearch.about.com.

5. Doyle, "Introduction to Cover Letters"; Vaas, "How to Write a Great Cover Letter"; and Toni Logan, "The Perfect Cover Story," *Kinko's Impress* 2 (2000): 32, 34.

6. Larry Buhl, "8 Tips for Better Email Cover Letters," *Monster.com*, https://www.monster.com/career-advice/article/tips-for-better-email-cover-letters-hot-jobs.

7. Lisa Vaas, "How to Follow Up a Résumé Submission," *The Ladders*, August 9, 2010, http://www.theladders.com.

8. Alison Doyle, "How to Follow Up After Submitting a Resume," About.com, accessed 13 August 2010, http://jobsearch.about.com; and Vaas, "How to Follow Up a Résumé Submission."

9. Anne Fisher, "How to Get Hired by a 'Best' Company," *Fortune*, February 4, 2008, 96.

10. Fisher, "How to Get Hired by a 'Best' Company."

11. Sarah E. Needleman, "Speed Interviewing Grows as Skills Shortage Looms; Strategy May Help Lock in Top Picks; Some Drawbacks," *Wall Street Journal*, November 6, 2007, B15.

12. Scott Beagrie, "How to Handle a Telephone Job Interview," *Personnel Today*, June 26, 2007, 29.

13. John Olmstead, "Predict Future Success with Structured Interviews," *Nursing Management*, March 2007, 52–53.

14. Fisher, "How to Get Hired by a 'Best' Company."

15. Erinn R. Johnson, "Pressure Sessions," *Black Enterprise*, October 2007, 72.

16. "What's a Group Interview?" *About.com Tech Careers*, accessed April 5, 2008, http://jobsearchtech.about.com.

17. Fisher, "How to Get Hired by a 'Best' Company."

18. Katherine Hansen, "Behavioral Job Interviewing Strategies for Job-Seekers," *QuintCareers.com*, accessed August 13, 2010, http://www.quintcareers.com.

19. Hansen, "Behavioral Job Interviewing Strategies for Job-Seekers."

20. Chris Pentilla, "Testing the Waters," *Entrepreneur*, January 2004, http://www.entrepreneur.com; Terry McKenna, "Behavior-Based Interviewing," *National Petroleum News*, January 2004, 16; and Nancy K. Austin, "Goodbye Gimmicks," *Incentive*, May 1996, 241.

21. William Poundstone, "Beware the Interview Inquisition," *Harvard Business Review* (May 2003): 18+.

22. Peter Vogt, "Mastering the Phone Interview," *Monster.com*, accessed December 13, 2006, http://www.monster.com; and Nina Segal, "The Global Interview: Tips for Successful, Unconventional Interview Techniques," *Monster.com*, accessed December 13, 2006, http://www.monster.com.

23. Segal, "The Global Interview: Tips for Successful, Unconventional Interview Techniques."

24. Barbara Kiviat, "How Skype Is Changing the Job Interview," *Time*, October 20, 2009, accessed August 13, 2010, http://www.time.com.

25. HireVue website, http://www.hirevue.com; in2View website, http://www.in2view.biz; and Victoria Reitz, "Interview without Leaving Home," *Machine Design*, April 1, 2004, 66.

26. Gina Ruiz, "Job Candidate Assessment Tests Go Virtual," *Workforce Management*, January 2008, http://wwwworkforce.com; and Connie Winkler, "Job Tryouts Go Virtual," *HR Magazine*, September 2006, 131–134.

27. Jonathan Katz, "Rethinking Drug Testing," *Industry Week*, March 2010, 16–18; Ashley Shadday, "Assessments 101: An Introduction to Candidate Testing," *Workforce Management*, January 2010, http://www.workforce.com; Dino di Mattia, "Testing Methods and Effectiveness of Tests," *Supervision*, August 2005, 4–5; David W. Arnold and John W. Jones, "Who the Devil's Applying Now?" *Security Management*, March 2002, 85–88; and Matthew J. Heller, "Digging Deeper," *Workforce Management*, March 3, 2008, 35–39.

28. Austin, "Goodbye Gimmicks."

29. Rachel Zupek, "How to Answer 10 Tough Interview Questions," *CNN.com*, March 4, 2009, http://www.cnn.com; and Barbara Safani, "How to Answer Tough Interview Questions Authentically," *The Ladders*, December 5, 2009, http://www.theladders.com.

30. Nick Corcodilos, "How to Answer a Misguided Interview Question," *Seattle Times*, March 30, 2008, http://www.seattletimes.com.

31. Katherine Spencer Lee, "Tackling Tough Interview Questions," *Certification Magazine*, May 2005, 35.

32. Scott Ginsberg, "10 Good Ways to 'Tell Me About Yourself,'" *The Ladders*, June 26, 2010, http://www.theladders.com.

33. Joe Turner, "An Interview Strategy: Telling Stories," *Yahoo! HotJobs*, accessed April 5, 2008, http://hotjobs.yahoo.com.

34. "A Word of Caution for Chatty Job Candidates," *Public Relations Tactics*, January 2008, 4.

35. "Employers Reveal Outrageous and Common Mistakes Candidates Made in Job Interviews, According to New CareerBuilder Survey," *CareerBuilder.com*, January 12, 2011, http://www.careerbuilder .com.

36. Randall S. Hansen, "When Job-Hunting: Dress for Success," *QuintCareers.com*, accessed April 5, 2008, http://www.quintcareers .com.

37. Phil Rosenberg, "What to Wear? Acing the Interview," *Fast Company*, September 23, 2008, https://www.fastcompany.com/1015464/ what-wear-acing-interview; and Pat Boer, "Business Casual: The New Dress Code," *Monster.com*, https://www.monster.ca/career-advice/article/business-casual-the-new-dress-code-canada.

38. William S. Frank, "Job Interview: Pre-Flight Checklist," *The Career Advisor*, accessed September 28, 2005, http://careerplanning. about.com.

39. "Employers Reveal Outrageous and Common Mistakes Candidates Made in Job Interviews, According to New CareerBuilder Survey."

40. T. Shawn Taylor, "Most Managers Have No Idea How to Hire the Right Person for the Job," *Chicago Tribune*, July 23, 2002, http:// www.ebsco.com.

41. "10 Minutes to Impress," *Journal of Accountancy* (July 2007): 13.

42. Todd Anten, "How to Handle Illegal Interview Questions," *Yahoo! HotJobs*, accessed August 7, 2009, http://hotjobs.com.

43. "Negotiating Salary: An Introduction," *InformationWeek*, accessed February 22, 2004, http://www.informationweek.com.

44. "Negotiating Salary: An Introduction."

45. Harold H. Hellwig, "Job Interviewing: Process and Practice," *Bulletin of the Association for Business Communication* 55, no. 2 (1992): 8–14.

46. Lisa Vaas, "Resume, Meet Technology: Making Your Resume Format Machine-Friendly," *The Ladders*, accessed August 13, 2010, http://www.theladders.com.

47. Joan S. Lublin, "Notes to Interviewers Should Go Beyond a Simple Thank You," *Wall Street Journal*, February 5, 2008, B1.

Appendix A

1. Mary A. De Vries, *Internationally Yours* (Boston: Houghton Mifflin, 1994), 9.

2. Patricia A. Dreyfus, "Paper That's Letter Perfect," *Money*, May 1985, 184.

3. Linda Driskill, *Business and Managerial Communication: New Perspectives* (Orlando, FL: Harcourt Brace Jovanovich, 1992), 470.

4. Sercomtel website, http://pessoal.sercomtel.com.br/assis/English/ Glossaries%20&%20Resources/Miscellanea/Virtual%20Desk/ address.html#WEBSTER.

5. De Vries, *Internationally Yours*, 8.

Name Index

Note: An *f* following a page reference indicates a figure or a photo; a *t* following a page reference indicates a table; and an *n* following a page reference indicates a source note.

Subject Index

Note: An *f* following a page reference indicates a figure or a photo; a *t* following a page reference indicates a table; and an *n* following a page reference indicates a source note.

A

Aboriginal peoples, 88*f*, 120
abstract, 436
abstract word, 129
academic journals, 335
acceptance letter, 433, 551–552
access control, 43
accessibility, 97
Accessibility for Ontarians with Disabilities Act (AODA), 163
accessible language, 124*t*
accomplishments, 466, 503, 509, 512–513
accuracy, 89, 372, 404
achievement, need for, 287*t*
achievements, 493, 508, 513
action (AIDA model), 294, 306, 529, 530*f*, 533–534
action, requests for. *See* requests for action
action verbs, 509
active listening, 41, 51
active statements, 509
active voice, 125–126, 126*t*
activities, 513
adapt to your audience, 84
    audience needs, sensitivity to, 114–120
    building strong relationships, 120–127
    negative messages, 248–249
    presentations, 465, 468
    proposals, 368–369
    reports, 368–369
    résumé, 508
    style and tone, 123–127
    website content, 384
adaptability, 492
address, 73–74
addressee notation, 567
adjourning, 39
adjustments, requests for. *See* requests for adjustments
adventure, need for, 287*t*
advice, 118
aesthetic appreciation, 287*t*
affiliation, need for, 287*t*
age bias, 119*t*, 120
age differences, 68, 69
agenda, 45, 46*f*, 467, 476
AIDA model, 292–294, 293*f*, 298, 298*f*, 301, 302, 303–306, 303*f*, 307, 308, 327, 377, 529, 530*f*, 531
alliance, 40
almanacs, 335
ambiguous questions, 341
American Psychological Association (APA). *See* APA style
analogy, 295, 296
analysis of situation, 83, 85–87, 286–287, 322–324, 457–459
analytical reports, 322, 324, 351–357
    categories of, 351
    conclusions, 352, 352*f*
    direct *vs.* indirect approach, 375
    logical arguments, 353–357

recommendations, 352–353
statement of purpose, 323
structure of, 353*t*
three-step writing process, 328
    2 + 2 = 4 approach, 353–354, 354–355*f*
    yardstick approach, 354–357, 356*f*
animation, 401, 475–476
announcements, 179, 258
anticipation of objections, 296–297
anxiety, 457, 479–480
APA style, 439, 578, 581–582
    in-text citation, 581
    list of references, 581–582, 582*f*
appearance, 560–561
appearance, personal, 54, 543*t*, 544
appendix, 438
applicant tracking systems, 514
application letters, 529–534, 532*t*
appreciation, 230
area chart, 393–394
arguments, 7, 41, 292–294
assumptions, 65
attacking an opponent, 295
attention, 152, 292, 304, 529–531, 530*f*, 531*f*, 532, 532*t*
attention line, 567
attractiveness, 377
audience
    adapting to. *See* adapt to your audience
    blogs, 193, 195
    compatibility, design for, 17
    composition, 86
    decoding the message, 4, 17–18
    ease of use, 17
    empathy, 17
    expectations, 17, 87
    familiarity, 17
    feedback, 4
    forecasting probable reaction, 87
    know your audience, 18–19
    level of understanding, 86
    media requirements of, 326
    mindsets, 459*f*
    needs, 88, 114–120, 121, 300, 467
    persuasive messages, 286–287, 289–290
    preferences, 87, 96
    presentations, 457–459, 458*t*, 459*f*, 465–466
    primary audience, 86
    receiving the message, 4, 17
    required information, 88
    response to message, 4, 18
    for résumé, 502–503
    secondary audience, 86
audience analysis worksheet, 87*f*
audience-centred approach, 17–19, 19*f*
audience-focused document, 90*f*, 91*f*
audience profile, 86–87, 87*f*
augmented reality, 94
authenticity, 307–308, 470
authorization, 373
authorization letter, 433

autocompletion, 136
autocorrection, 136
avatars, 49, 96*f*
awkward references, 154*t*, 155

B

Baby Boomers, 69
backchannel, 459, 482–483
background, 373, 378
background checks, 538–539
background designs and artwork, 474
backgrounders, 345
back-translation, 76
bad news about transactions, 260–262
balance, 161, 373, 388
bar chart, 391, 394, 394–396*f*
bar graph, 394
behavioural interview, 536
being real, 307–308
belonging, need for, 287*t*
benefits, 301–302, 301*t*
bias, 331
bias-free language, 119–120, 119*t*
bibliography, 438–439
blind courtesy copy (bcc), 188
block format, 569, 570*f*
blog, 191
blog search engines and directories, 338*t*
bloggers, 28
blogging, 176, 191–198
    business applications of, 193–195
    checklist, 198
    elements of business blogging, 193
    three-step writing process, 195–197
    tips for business blogging, 192*t*
blueprint slide, 476
body
    formal reports, 437
    letters, 564–567
    presentations, 467–468
    proposals, 371–372, 378–380, 440–441
    reports, 371–372, 375
boilerplate, 136, 383
book search engines, 338*t*
bookmark, 332
Boolean search, 339
bragging, 124
brainstorming, 39, 49, 100, 194
brand communities, 182
branded channel, 177, 184, 401
broadcasting mindset, 22
buffer, 252, 253*t*
bulleted lists, 150–152, 165
bumper slide, 476, 477*f*
business books, 335
business communication, 11–21
    see also communication
    audience-centred approach, 17–19, 19*f*
    business language, 123–125, 124*t*
    challenges of, 11–15
    effective, 16 –21
    electronic media for, 176–180